NIALL FERGUSON

Kissinger

1923–1968: *The Idealist*

PENGUIN BOOKS

PENGUIN BOOKS

UK | USA | Canada | Ireland | Australia
India | New Zealand | South Africa

Penguin Books is part of the Penguin Random House group of companies
whose addresses can be found at global.penguinrandomhouse.com.

First published in the United States of America by Penguin Press,
an imprint of Penguin Random House LLC 2015
First published in Great Britain by Allen Lane 2015
Published in Penguin Books 2016

001

Text copyright © Niall Ferguson, 2015

Photograph credits appear on page 946

The moral right of the author has been asserted

Set in 10.1/13.55 pt Bembo Std
Printed in Great Britain by Clays Ltd, St Ives plc

A CIP catalogue record for this book is available from the British Library

ISBN: 978–0–141–02200–0

Contents

Preface

Indeed I cannot conceive a more perfect mode of writing
any man's life, than not only relating all the most important
events of it in their order, but interweaving what he
privately wrote, and said, and thought; by which mankind
are enabled as it were to see him live, and to "live o'er each
scene" with him, as he actually advanced through the
several stages of his life. . . . I will venture to say that he
will be seen in this work more completely than any man
who has ever yet lived. And he will be seen as he really was;
for I profess to write, not his panegyrick, which must be all
praise, but his Life. . . . [I]n every picture there should be
shade as well as light.

—BOSWELL, *Life of Johnson*[1]

The task of the biographer, as James Boswell understood, is to enable
the reader to see, in her mind's eye, his subject live. To achieve this, the
biographer must know his subject. That means reading all that he
wrote as well as much that was written about him. It also means, if the
subject is living, not merely interviewing him but getting to know
him, as Boswell got to know Johnson: conversing with him, supping
with him, even traveling with him. The challenge is, of course, to do
so without falling so much under the subject's influence that the reader
ceases to believe the disclaimer that the work is a life, not a panegyric.
Boswell, who grew to love Johnson, achieved this feat in two ways: by
making explicit Johnson's boorish manners and slovenly appearance,
but also (as Jorge Luis Borges noted) by making himself a figure of
fun—a straight man to Johnson's wit, an overexcitable Scot to Johnson's dry Englishman.[2] My approach has been different.

In addition to the help of all those thanked in the acknowledgments, this author has had one noteworthy advantage over his predecessors: I have had access to Henry Kissinger's private papers, not only the papers from his time in government, housed at the Library of Congress, but also the private papers donated to Yale University in 2011, which include more than a hundred boxes of personal writings, letters, and diaries dating back to the 1940s. I have also been able to interview the subject of the work on multiple occasions and at considerable length. Not only has this book been written with Henry Kissinger's cooperation; it was written at his suggestion.

For this reason, I can predict with certainty that hostile reviewers will allege that I have in some way been influenced or induced to paint a falsely flattering picture. This is not the case. Although I was granted access to the Kissinger papers and was given some assistance with the arrangement of interviews with family members and former colleagues, my sole commitment was to make my "best efforts to record [his] life 'as it actually was' on the basis of an informed study of the documentary and other evidence available." This commitment was part of a legal agreement between us, drawn up in 2004, which ended with the following clause:

> While the authority of the Work will be enhanced by the extent of the Grantor's [i.e., Kissinger's] assistance . . . it will be enhanced still more by the fact of the Author's independence; thus, it is understood and agreed that . . . the Author shall have full editorial control over the final manuscript of the Work, and the Grantor shall have no right to vet, edit, amend or prevent the publication of the finished manuscript of the Work.

The sole exception was that, at Dr. Kissinger's request, I would not use quotations from his private papers that contained sensitive personal information. I am glad to say that he exercised this right on only a handful of occasions and always in connection with purely personal—and indeed intimate familial—matters.

This book has been just over ten years in the making. Throughout this long endeavor, I believe I have been true to my resolve to write the life of Henry Kissinger "as it actually was"—*wie es eigentlich gewesen,* in Ranke's famous phrase (which is perhaps better translated "as it essentially was"). Ranke believed that the historian's vocation was to infer historical truth from documents—not a dozen documents (the total number cited in one widely read book about Kissinger) but many thousands. I certainly cannot count how many documents I and my research assistant Jason Rockett have looked at in the course of our work. I can count only those that we thought worthy of inclusion in our digital database. The current total of documents is 8,380—a total of 37,645 pages. But these documents are drawn not just from Kissinger's private and public papers. In all, we have drawn material from 111 archives all around the world, ranging from the major presidential libraries to obscure private collections. (A full list of those consulted for this volume is provided in the sources.) There are of course archives that remain closed and documents that remain classified. However, compared with most periods before and since, the 1970s stand out for the abundance of primary sources. This was the age of the Xerox machine and the audio tape recorder. The former made it easy for institutions to make multiple copies of important documents, increasing the probability that one of them would become accessible to a future historian. Nixon's and Kissinger's fondness for the latter, combined with the expansion of freedom of information that followed Watergate, ensured that many conversations that might never have found their way into the historical record are now freely available for all to read.

My motivation in casting the widest and deepest possible net in my trawl for material was straightforward. I was determined to see Kissinger's life not just from his vantage point but from multiple vantage points, and not just from the American perspective but from the perspectives of friends, foes, and the nonaligned. Henry Kissinger was a man who, at the height of his power, could justly be said to bestride the world. Such a man's life requires a global biography.

I always intended to write two volumes. The question was where to break the story. In the end, I decided to conclude the first volume just after Richard Nixon announced to the world that Kissinger was to be his national security adviser, but before Kissinger had moved into his office in the West Wing basement and actually started work. There were two reasons for this choice. First, at the end of 1968 Henry Kissinger was forty-five years old. As I write, he is ninety-one. So this volume covers more or less exactly the first half of his life. Second, I wanted to draw a clear line between Kissinger the thinker and Kissinger the actor. It is true that Kissinger was more than just a scholar before 1969. As an adviser to presidents and presidential candidates, he was directly involved in the formulation of foreign policy throughout the 1960s. By 1967, if not before, he had become an active participant in the diplomatic effort to begin negotiations with the North Vietnamese government in the hope of ending the Vietnam War. Yet he had no experience of executive office. He was more a consultant than a true adviser, much less a decision maker. Indeed, that was former president Dwight Eisenhower's reason for objecting to his appointment. "But Kissinger is a professor," he exclaimed when he heard of Nixon's choice. "You ask professors to study things, but you never put them in charge of anything. . . . I'm going to call Dick about that."[3] Kissinger was indeed a professor before he was a practitioner. It therefore makes sense to consider him first as what I believe he was before 1969: one of the most important theorists about foreign policy ever to be produced by the United States of America. Had Kissinger never entered government, this volume would still have been worth writing, just as Robert Skidelsky would still have had good reason to write his superb life of John Maynard Keynes even if Keynes had never left the courtyards of Cambridge for the corridors of power in His Majesty's Treasury.

It was in London, in a bookshop, that Boswell first met Johnson. My first meeting with Kissinger was also in London, at a party given by Conrad Black. I was an Oxford don who dabbled in journalism, and I was naturally flattered when the elder statesman expressed his admiration for a book I had written about the First World War. (I was also impressed by the speed with which I was dropped when the model Elle Macpherson entered the room.) But I was more intimidated than pleased when, some months later, Kissinger suggested to me that I might write his biography. I knew enough to be aware that another British historian had been offered and had accepted this commission, only to get cold feet. At the time, I could see only the arguments against stepping into his evidently chilly shoes. I was under contract to write other books (including another biography). I was not an expert on postwar U.S. foreign policy. I would need to immerse myself in a sea of documents. I would inevitably be savaged by Christopher Hitchens and others. And so in early March 2004, after several meetings, telephone calls, and letters, I said no. This was to be my introduction to the diplomacy of Henry Kissinger:

> What a pity! I received your letter just as I was hunting for your telephone number to tell you of the discovery of files I thought had been lost: 145 boxes which had been placed in a repository in Connecticut by a groundkeeper who has since died. These contain all my files—writings, letters, sporadic diaries, at least to 1955 and probably to 1950, together with some twenty boxes of private correspondence from my government service. . . .
>
> Be that as it may, our conversations had given me the confidence—after admittedly some hesitation—that you would have done a definitive—if not necessarily positive—evaluation.
>
> For that I am grateful even as it magnifies my regret.[4]

A few weeks later I was in Kent, Connecticut, turning pages.

Yet it was the documents, more than their author, that persuaded me. I remember vividly the ones I read. A letter to his parents dated July 28, 1948: "To me there is not only right or wrong but many shades in between. . . . The real tragedies in life are not in choices between right and wrong. Only the most callous of persons choose what they *know* to be wrong." A letter from McGeorge Bundy dated February 17, 1956: "I have often thought that Harvard gives her sons—her undergraduates— the opportunity to be shaped by what they love. This, as a Harvard man, you have had. For her faculty, she reserves the opportunity— dangerous, perhaps fatal—to be shaped by what they hate." A letter from Fritz Kraemer, dated February 12, 1957: "[U]ntil now things were easier. You had to resist only the wholly ordinary temptations of the ambitious, like avarice, and the academic intrigue industry. *Now* the trap is in your own character. You are being tempted . . . with your own deepest principles." A diary of the 1964 Republican National Convention:

"As we left . . . some Goldwaterite was checking off names on a list. I was not on it. But he knew me and said, 'Kissinger—don't think we'll forget your name.'" Another diary of a visit to Vietnam in the fall of 1965: "[Clark] Clifford then asked me what I thought of the position of the President. I said I had great sympathy for the difficulties of the President, but what was at stake here was the future world position of the United States. . . . Clifford asked me whether I thought the Vietnamese were worth saving. I said that that was no longer the issue." The more I read, the more I realized that I had no choice. I had to write this book. I had not been so excited by a collection of documents since my first day at the Rothschild Archive in London more than ten years before.

This book, then, is the product of a decade of painstaking archival research. In writing it, I have faithfully adhered to the three propositions of the great philosopher of history R. G. Collingwood.

1. All history is the history of thought.
2. Historical knowledge is the re-enactment in the historian's mind of the thought whose history he is studying.
3. Historical knowledge is the re-enactment of a past thought incapsulated in a context of present thoughts which, by contradicting it, confine it to a plane different from theirs.[5]

In trying to reconstitute the past thoughts of Kissinger and his contemporaries, I have nearly always given preference to the documents or audio recordings of the time over testimony from interviews conducted many years later, not because documents are always accurate records of what their authors thought, but because memories generally play bigger tricks than letters, diaries, and memoranda.

Yet there are limitations to the traditional historian's methods, no matter how critical a reader he has trained himself to be, particularly when one of the defining traits of his subject is (or is said to be) secretiveness. Let me illustrate the point. A few weeks after finishing chapter 20—which deals with Kissinger's ultimately abortive attempt to open negotiations with the North Vietnamese through their representative in

Paris, Mai Van Bo—I went to dinner with the Kissingers. The chapter had been by far the hardest to write of the entire book, but I felt that I had succeeded where others had failed in making sense of the secret peace initiative that the Johnson administration had code-named PENNSYLVANIA. I had shown, I thought, that the novice diplomat had allowed himself (despite his earlier academic strictures on the subject) to become the captive of his own negotiation, prolonging it far beyond what was justified and falling into Hanoi's trap, which was to flirt with the idea of talks without actually committing to them, in the hope of reducing if not halting the American air attacks on their major cities.

Mrs. Kissinger, who did not intend to join us for dinner, surprised me by sitting down. She had a question. There was a pause. "Why do you suppose," she asked me, "that Henry was *really* making all those trips to Paris?"

I had completely missed—because it was nowhere documented— that Kissinger's prime motive for being in Paris in 1967 was the fact that she was studying at the Sorbonne that year.

The history of Kissinger's relationship with his second wife may serve as a warning to all biographers, but particularly to biographers of Henry Kissinger. Walter Isaacson correctly established that Kissinger had first met Nancy Maginnes in 1964 at the Republican National Convention in San Francisco.[6] But in chronicling Kissinger's career as a less than secret "swinger" during his time as Nixon's national security adviser, Isaacson assumed that she was no more than Kissinger's "most regular date." In his chapter on Kissinger's "Celebrity," he listed no fewer than a dozen other women whom Kissinger went out with in the early 1970s.[7]

Isaacson was right that his fellow journalists had missed the story. Nancy Maginnes went wholly unmentioned by *The New York Times* until May 28, 1973—nine years after their first meeting—when the newspaper reported that she (characterized as "a frequent companion of Dr. Kissinger") had arranged for his fiftieth birthday dinner to be held at the Colony Club, of which she was a member.[8] Four months later, when she was Kissinger's guest at a dinner for the UN diplomatic corps at the Metropolitan Museum of Art, the *Times* was informed by a spokesman for the secretary of state, "She's just another guest, not a hostess."[9] On December 21, 1973, another Kissinger spokesman "flatly denied" that he was going to marry Nancy Maginnes.[10] On January 3, 1974, Kissinger himself declined to "make any comment on my personal plans."[11] The next day they were spotted dining together with none other than the proprietor of *The Washington Post;* the newspaper promptly published Kissinger's denial that they intended to wed.[12] Despite being subsequently sighted at an ice hockey game and at a cocktail party with Vice President Gerald Ford, the couple succeeded in completely surprising the media with their wedding on March 30. Indeed, Kissinger went straight to the ceremony from a press conference at which he made no reference whatsoever to his private life.[13] The announcement was not made until half an hour after they had taken off for their honeymoon in Acapulco. As the *Post* reported in aggrieved tones,

> So eager were the couple for privacy that the one reporter who saw them leaving the [State] Department was forcefully restrained by a uniformed guard so that she could not approach them. Her building pass was then taken and information copied down before it was returned. An aide to Kissinger had drawn his car up so as to prevent anyone from following the couple from the basement parking area.[14]

This at a time when *The Washington Post* was leading the campaign to expose the far bigger secret of Richard Nixon's complicity in the Watergate scandal!

Yet the secrecy surrounding Kissinger's second marriage cannot be explained solely by "the aversion to publicity expected of a well-bred lady."[15] For it was Kissinger, too, who ensured that their relationship remained a purely private matter for close to ten years. To understand why that was, the biographer needs a kind of knowledge that cannot always be found in documents: knowledge of the inner and largely unwritten life that a man lives in his roles as a son, a brother, a lover, a husband, a father, a divorcé. In addition, to understand *how* the Kissingers preserved their privacy for so long, the biographer must understand the complicity that then still existed between the news media and the political elite. For the reality was that press barons and

Beltway reporters alike knew full well about Kissinger and Maginnes; knew that for years they were together either in New York or in Washington roughly one weekend in every two. It was just that they tacitly agreed not to print what they knew.

No biographer finds out everything, because not everything can be known—not even to the subject himself. No doubt there are important events I have missed, relationships I have misunderstood or underestimated, thoughts that simply were not written down and are now forgotten even by their thinker. But if so, this has not been for want of effort. I leave it to the reader to decide how far I have succeeded in being, in some sense, Kissinger's Boswell—and how far I have avoided precisely that trap.

Cambridge, Massachusetts
April 2015

Introduction

After all, didn't what happened to me actually happen by chance? Good God, I was a completely unknown professor. How could I have said to myself: "Now I'm going to maneuver things so as to become internationally famous?" It would have been pure folly. . . . One might then say it happened because it had to happen. That's what they always say when things have happened. They never say that about things that don't happen—the history of things that didn't happen has never been written.

—HENRY KISSINGER to Oriana Fallaci, Nov. 4, 1972[1]

I

Surely no statesman in modern times, and certainly no American secretary of state, has been as revered and then as reviled as Henry Kissinger.

When Oriana Fallaci interviewed him in November 1972, Kissinger had not yet attained the zenith of his fame. Looking back on their encounter a few years later, Fallaci sardonically parodied the magazine covers of the time:

This too famous, too important, too lucky man, whom they call Superman, Superstar, Superkraut, and who stitches together paradoxical alliances, reaches impossible agreements, keeps the world holding its breath as though the world were his students at Harvard. This incredible, inexplicable, unbearable personage, who meets Mao Tse-tung when he likes, enters the Kremlin when he feels like it, wakens the president of the

United States and goes into his bedroom when he thinks it appropriate. This absurd character with horn-rimmed glasses, beside whom James Bond becomes a flavorless creation. He does not shoot, nor use his fists, nor leap from speeding automobiles like James Bond, but he advises on wars, ends wars, pretends to change our destiny, and does change it.[2]

Clad as Superman, tights, cape, and all, Kissinger did in fact appear as a cartoon "Super K" on the cover of *Newsweek* in June 1974. Successive *Newsweek* covers had depicted him as "The Man in the White House Basement," as "Nixon's Secret Agent," and as an American Gulliver, swarmed over by Lilliputian figures representing "A World of Woes." *Time* magazine was even more captivated. While in office, Kissinger appeared on its cover no fewer than fifteen times. He was, according to one *Time* profile, "the world's indispensable man."[3]

Of course, there was an element of humor in all this. The joke was already doing the rounds by late 1972: "Just think what would happen if Kissinger died. Richard Nixon would become president of the United States!"[4] The compound word "Nixinger" was briefly in vogue to imply Kissinger's parity with the president. On the cover of Charles Ashman's *Kissinger: The Adventures of Super-Kraut,* published in 1972, the eponymous superhero appeared disheveled, with telltale lipstick on his cheek.

Yet Kissinger's popularity was real. That same year he came in fourth in Gallup's "Most Admired Man Index"; in 1973 he was number one. In May of that year, 78 percent of Americans were able to identify Kissinger, a proportion otherwise achieved only by presidents, presidential candidates, and the biggest stars of sport and screen.[5] By the middle of 1974 his approval rating, according to the regular Harris survey, was an astounding 85 percent.

All secretaries of state, sooner or later, are interviewed by Charlie Rose. Only Henry Kissinger appeared on Rose's show nearly forty times, to say nothing of his cameos in the soap opera *Dynasty*[6] and *The Colbert Report.* All secretaries of state are caricatured in the newspapers. Only Kissinger became an animated cartoon character in three television series (in *Freakazoid*,[7] *The Simpsons*,[8] and *Family Guy*).[9]

Yet as Kissinger was all too well aware even in 1972, this kind of celebrity can easily flip into notoriety. "The consequences of what I do, I mean the public's judgment[s]," he assured Oriana Fallaci, "have never bothered me.

> I don't ask for popularity, I'm not looking for popularity. On the contrary, if you really want to know, I care nothing about popularity. I'm not at all afraid of losing my public; I can allow myself to say what I think. . . . If I were to let myself be disturbed by the reactions of the public, if I were to act solely on the basis of a calculated technique, I would accomplish nothing. . . . I don't say that all this has to go on forever. In fact, it may evaporate as quickly as it came.[10]

He was right.

Fame is double-edged; to be famous is also to be mocked. In 1971 Woody Allen parodied Kissinger in a half-hour "mockumentary" made for PBS and entitled *Men of Crisis: The Harvey Wallinger Story*. Hurriedly written and filmed after Allen had finished "*Everything You Always Wanted to Know About Sex* *But Were Afraid to Ask*," the film was due to air in February 1972 but was almost certainly pulled for political reasons.[11] (PBS claimed it could not show the film in an election year without giving other candidates equal coverage, but the reality was that the government-funded broadcaster could not persuade Allen to drop his sharpest digs at, among others, Pat Nixon and feared arousing the ire of the White House.)[12] Typical of the film is the scene in which Wallinger—played by Allen—is heard on the phone demanding "an injunction against the *Times*. It's a New York, Jewish, Communist, left-wing newspaper, and that's just the sports section." In another scene, Wallinger is asked to comment on President Nixon's (authentic) statement that "we shall end the war [in Vietnam] and win the peace." "What Mr. Nixon means," Allen mumbles, "is that, uh, it's important to win the war and also win the peace; or, at the very least, lose the war and lose the peace; or, uh, win at least part of the peace, or win two peaces, perhaps, or lose a few peaces but win a piece of the war. The other alternative would be to win a piece of the war, or lose a piece of Mr. Nixon."

INTERVIEWER: There's a lot of talk around Washington
that you have an extremely active social life.
WALLINGER: Well that's greatly exaggerated I think, I . . .
I . . . like attractive women, I like sex, but, um, but it
must be American sex. I don't like un-American sex.
INTERVIEWER: Well how would you distinguish American sex?
WALLINGER: If you're ashamed of it, it's American sex.
You know, uh, that's important, if you feel guilt . . .
and shame, otherwise I think sex without guilt is bad
because it almost becomes pleasurable.[13]

Responding to the objection by the PBS top brass that the film was in
bad taste, Allen quipped, "It's hard to say anything about that administration that wouldn't be in bad taste."[14]

Wisecracks about the Nixon administration were standard fare for
Manhattan comedians long before the president's downfall. For Kissinger, being second only to Nixon in the government meant being
second only to him as a target—in every available medium. The satirical songwriter Tom Lehrer's ditties are now mostly forgotten, but the
same cannot be said for his remark that "political satire became obsolete when Henry Kissinger was awarded the Nobel peace prize."[15] Earlier, the French singer-songwriter Henri Salvador had composed the
irritatingly catchy "Kissinger, Le Duc Tho" to mock the lack of progress in the negotiations between the United States and North Vietnam.
The cartoonist David Levine produced perhaps the most savage of all
pictorial attacks on Kissinger—more than a dozen in all, including two
that even the left-liberal *New York Review of Books* found too egregious
to publish: one of a naked Kissinger, his back covered in macabre tat-
toos, the other of Kissinger under a stars-and-stripes bedcover, gleefully ravishing a naked female whose head is the globe. (Despite protests
from his staff, Victor Navasky published the latter caricature in *The
Nation*.)[16]

It is as if Henry Kissinger's personality—his very name—hit some
neuralgic spot in the collective brain of a generation. In Joseph Heller's
1979 novel *Good as Gold,* the protagonist, a middle-aged professor of

English literature named Bruce Gold, is working on a book about none
other than:

> Kissinger.
> How he loved and hated that hissing name.
> Even apart from his jealousy, which was formidable, Gold
> had hated Henry Kissinger from the moment of his emergence
> as a public figure and hated him still.[17]

Inane though it is, Eric Idle's song for Monty Python shows that the
neuralgia was transatlantic:

> *Henry Kissinger,*
> *How I'm missing yer,*
> *You're the Doctor of my dreams.*
> *With your crinkly hair,*
> *And your glassy stare,*
> *And your Machiavellian schemes.*[18]

An entire era is distilled in the moment at Madison Square Garden
when Idle and Ronnie Wood of the Rolling Stones made "silly faces"
behind Kissinger's back after they had all seen Muhammad Ali fight.
As soon as Kissinger had gone, the two English entertainers "collapsed
howling in a heap on the floor."[19]

II

Some laughed at Kissinger. Others froze. "An eel icier than ice" was
how Fallaci put it. "God, what an icy man!"

> During the whole interview he never changed that expression-
> less countenance, that hard or ironic look, and never altered
> the tone of that sad, monotonous, unchanging voice. The nee-
> dle on the tape recorder shifts when a word is pronounced in a
> higher or lower key. With him it remained still, and more than

once I had to check to make sure that the machine was working. Do you know that obsessive, hammering sound of rain
falling on a roof? His voice is like that. And basically his
thoughts as well.

To enter the realm of journalism about Henry Kissinger is to
encounter much in this hysterical vein. He was, Fallaci went on, "the
most guilty representative of the kind of power of which Bertrand
Russell speaks: If they say 'Die,' we shall die. If they say 'live,' we shall
live." He based "his actions on secrecy, absolutism, and the ignorance
of people not yet awakened to the discovery of their rights."[20]

Sometimes the hysteria tips over into outright lunacy. Wild allegations against Kissinger can be found on a host of websites purporting
to expose the nefarious activities of the Bilderberg Group, the Council
on Foreign Relations, and the Trilateral Commission, organizations
allegedly established by the "Illuminati" to realize their evil scheme for
"world government."[21] Such claims come in at least four flavors: Anglophobe, paranoid anti-Communist, deranged-fantasist, and leftist-
populist.

The Anglophobe version derives from the work of the Georgetown
University historian Carroll Quigley, who traced a British plot against
America back to Cecil Rhodes and Alfred Milner and identified J. P.
Morgan, the Council on Foreign Relations, and *The New Republic* mag-
azine as key conspirators.[22] According to the former Trotskyite Lyndon
LaRouche, "Sir" Henry Kissinger was all along a "British Agent of
Influence" (the evidence: his honorary knighthood and a 1982 Chatham
House speech).[23] LaRouche's associates have also alleged that William
Yandell Elliott, Kissinger's Harvard mentor, belonged to "a network of
unreconstructed Confederates who continued Britain's Civil War
against the United States through cultural and other means." Their aim
was "to establish . . . a new 'dark age' of globally extended medieval
feudalism, built on the ruined remains of the United States and any
nation which strove to establish itself on any approximation of American principles." This network bound together the Ku Klux Klan, the
Tennessee Templars, the Round Table, the Royal Institute of Interna-

tional Affairs (Chatham House), and the Harvard International Seminar run by Kissinger.[24]

A much graver though equally unfounded allegation is that Kissinger was a Soviet spy. According to Gary Allen—a member of the John Birch Society and speechwriter for the segregationist George Wallace—Kissinger was not only "an agent of the mightiest combine of power, finance, and influence in American politics: The House of Rockefeller"; he was also a Communist with the KGB code name "Bor." Having inveigled his way into the White House, his "conspiratorial campaign" was "to effect the clandestine unilateral strategic disarmament of the United States *by means of the prolongation of the Vietnam War.*"[25] Similar charges were leveled in a rambling tome entitled *Kissinger on the Couch* (1975) by the ultraconservative antifeminist Phyllis Schlafly and retired admiral Chester Ward, who accused Kissinger of making "the entire population of the United States hostages to the Kremlin."[26] The bizarre claim that the Soviets had recruited Kissinger in postwar Germany can be traced back to a 1976 article by Alan Stang in the far-right magazine *American Opinion,* which cited testimony from the Polish defector Michael Goleniewski that Kissinger had worked for a Soviet counterintelligence network code-named ODRA. Goleniewski's evidence was good enough to expose at least six Soviet moles operating inside Western intelligence agencies, including the British traitor George Blake, who had been "turned" when captured during the Korean War and whose activities cost the lives of at least forty MI6 agents. However, the allegations against "Bor" were never substantiated, and Goleniewski's later claim to be the Tsarevich Alexei Nikolaevich—the son of Nicholas II and heir to the Russian throne—irreparably damaged his credibility in sane minds.

The out-and-out fantasists do not even pretend to have documentary evidence. The Texan journalist Jim Marrs's best-selling *Rule by Secrecy* identifies Kissinger as part of a wholly imagined conspiracy involving the Council on Foreign Relations, the Trilateral Commission, and the Freemasons.[27] In a similar vein, Wesman Todd Shaw calls Kissinger the "master architect of the New World Order . . . one of the single most evil individuals still living, or to have ever lived."[28] Len Horowitz asserts that Kissinger is part of a global conspiracy of pharmaceutical companies that are intentionally spreading the HIV-AIDS virus, a claim that appears to rest on an alphanumerical breakdown of Kissinger's name (which, we are told, "deciphers to 666").[29] According to Alan Watt, Kissinger's motive for his "AIDS project" was to address the problem of overpopulation; he also blames him for the rise of Islamic fundamentalism.[30] A plainly unhinged woman writing as "Brice Taylor" insists that, when she was a child, Kissinger turned her into a "mind-controlled slave," repeatedly making her eat her alphabet cereal in reverse order and taking her on the "It's a Small World" ride at Disneyland.[31] Maddest of all is David Icke, whose "List of Famous Satanists" includes not only Kissinger but also the Astors, Bushes, Clintons, DuPonts, Habsburgs, Kennedys, Rockefellers, Rothschilds, and the entire British royal family—not to mention Tony Blair, Winston Churchill, Adolf Hitler, Mikhail Gorbachev, and Joseph Stalin. (The comedian Bob Hope also makes the list.) According to Icke, Kissinger is "one of the Illuminati's foremost master minds of the agenda." Not only is he a "Satanist, mind controller, child torturer, creator of wars of mass murder and destruction"; he is also a "shape-shifter" with a "reptilian bloodline." "By 'Satanists,' of course," Icke helpfully explains, "I mean those involved in human sacrifice."[32]

No rational people take such nonsense seriously. But the same cannot be said for the allegations made by conspiracy theorists of the left, who are a great deal more influential. In his *People's History of the United States,* Howard Zinn argues that Kissinger's policies in Chile were intended at least in part to serve the economic interests of International Telephone and Telegraph.[33] In place of evidence, such diatribes tend to offer gratuitous insult. According to Zinn, Kissinger "surrendered himself with ease to the princes of war and destruction."[34] In their *Untold History of the United States,* the film director Oliver Stone and Peter Kuznick refer to Kissinger as a "psychopath" (admittedly quoting Nixon).[35] The doyen of "gonzo" journalism, Hunter S. Thompson, called him "a slippery little devil, a world-class hustler with a thick German accent and a very keen eye for weak spots at the top of the power structure"—adding, for good measure, "pervert."[36] One left-of-center website recently accused Kissinger of having been somehow involved in the anthrax attacks of September 2001, when anthrax spores were mailed to various media and

Senate offices, killing five people.[37] In terms of scholarship, the conspiracy theorists make as valuable a contribution to historical knowledge as the creators of the cartoon series *The Venture Bros.,* which features "a mysterious figure dressed in a black uniform and accompanied by a medical bag that he affectionately calls his 'Magic Murder Bag' . . . Dr. Henry Killinger."

III

All this vitriol is at first sight puzzling. From January 20, 1969, until November 3, 1975, Henry Kissinger served as assistant to the president for national security affairs, first under Richard Nixon, then under Gerald Ford. From September 22, 1973, until January 20, 1977, he was secretary of state—the first foreign-born citizen to hold that office, the highest-ranking post in the executive branch after the presidency and vice presidency. Nor was his influence over U.S. foreign policy confined to those years. Before 1969, he played important roles as a consultant and an unofficial envoy for John F. Kennedy and Lyndon B. Johnson. Under Ronald Reagan, he chaired the National Bipartisan Commission on Central America, which met between 1983 and 1985. From 1984 until 1990, he served as a member of the President's Foreign Intelligence Advisory Board. He was also a member of the Commission on Integrated Long-Term Strategy (1986–88) and the Defense Policy Board (from 2001 to the present). In 1973 the Norwegian Nobel Committee jointly awarded Kissinger and Le Duc Tho the Nobel Peace Prize, citing their perseverance in the negotiations that produced the Paris Peace Accords. Four years later Kissinger received the Presidential Medal of Freedom and, in 1986, the Medal of Liberty. In 1995 he was made an Honorary Knight Commander of the Order of St. Michael and St. George.

Nor can it easily be argued that these offices and honors were wholly undeserved. He was responsible—to name only his most obvious achievements—for negotiating the first Strategic Arms Limitation Treaty (SALT I) and the Anti-Ballistic Missile Treaty with the Soviet Union. While he held office, the United States ratified the nuclear arms Non-Proliferation Treaty, the international convention banning biological weapons, and the Helsinki Final Act, Article 10 of which (little though Kissinger liked it) committed signatories on both sides of the iron curtain to "respect human rights and fundamental freedoms, including the freedom of thought, conscience, religion or belief, for all without distinction as to race, sex, language or religion." It was Kissinger who, with Zhou Enlai, opened diplomatic communications between the United States and the People's Republic of China, arguably one of the turning points in the Cold War. It was Kissinger who negotiated the end of the Yom Kippur War between the Arab states and Israel and whose shuttle diplomacy paved the way for the Camp David Accords.

How, then, are we to explain the visceral hostility that the name Henry Kissinger arouses? In *The Trial of Henry Kissinger,* the British journalist Christopher Hitchens went so far as to accuse Kissinger of "war crimes and crimes against humanity in Indochina, Chile, Argentina, Cyprus, East Timor, and several other places" (in fact, the only other place discussed in his book is Bangladesh), alleging that Kissinger "ordered and sanctioned the destruction of civilian populations, the assassination of inconvenient politicians, the kidnapping and disappearance of soldiers and journalists and clerics who got in his way."[38] Genocide, mass killing, assassination, and murder all feature in the indictment.

Hitchens was a gifted polemicist; his abilities as a historian are more open to question. Nevertheless, for each of the cases he cited, more thoroughly researched studies exist that come to comparable if less bombastically stated verdicts: William Shawcross's study of the "catastrophe" and "crime" in Cambodia;[39] Gary Bass on the bloodbath in Bangladesh;[40] José Ramos-Horta on East Timor;[41] Jonathan Haslam and Peter Kornbluh on Chile;[42] not forgetting Noam Chomsky on the missed opportunity for peace in the Middle East in 1970–71.[43] Moreover, the charges of criminality have gained credibility from the attempts in 2001 and 2002 by various judges and lawyers in Argentina, Chile, France, and Spain to compel Kissinger at least to give evidence in cases relating to Operation Condor, the clandestine campaign by six South American governments to "disappear" left-wing activists. In the light of all this, it is not surprising that so many journalists now freely bandy about terms like "mass murderer," "killer," and "monster" when Henry Kissinger's name comes up.

This volume covers the first half of Kissinger's life, ending in 1969, at the moment he entered the White House to serve as Richard Nixon's national security adviser. It therefore does not deal with the issues listed above. But it does deal with the foreign policies of Nixon's four predecessors. As will become clear, each one of these administrations could just as easily be accused of war crimes and crimes against humanity. There is no doubt whatever, to take just a single example, that the Central Intelligence Agency had a direct hand in the coup that overthrew the elected government of Jacobo Árbenz Guzmán in Guatemala in 1954. It also played an active role in the subsequent campaign of violence against the Guatemalan left. Nearly a hundred times as many people (around 200,000) died in this campaign than were "disappeared" in Chile after 1973 (2,279). Yet you will search the libraries in vain for *The Trial of John Foster Dulles*. According to a study by the Brookings Institution, the United States used military action or threats of military action three times more often in the Kennedy years than in the Kissinger years.[44] Interventions ranged from an abortive invasion of Cuba to a bloody coup d'état in South Vietnam. And yet no great polemicist has troubled to indict Dean Rusk as a war criminal.

A similar argument might be made about American administrations after 1976. Twenty-five years after publishing *Sideshow,* William Shawcross argued that "after 9/11 the US had no choice but to overthrow Saddam [Hussein], who had defied the world for years and was the only national leader to praise that merciless attack."[45] In an article in *The New York Times,* coauthored with Kissinger's friend and colleague Peter Rodman, Shawcross argued that "American defeat in Iraq would embolden the extremists in the Muslim world, demoralize and perhaps destabilize many moderate friendly governments, and accelerate the radicalization of every conflict in the Middle East. Our conduct in Iraq is a crucial test of our credibility."[46] Replace *Iraq* with *Vietnam* and *Muslim* with *Communist,* and you have precisely the argument that Kissinger made in 1969 against abandoning South Vietnam to its fate. Hitchens, too, discovered late in life that there were many worse things in the world than American power, going so far as to argue in 2005 that "prison conditions at Abu Ghraib [had] improved markedly and dramatically since the arrival of Coalition troops in Baghdad."[47]

The interesting question, then, is why the double standard? One possible, if facile, answer is that no amount of self-deprecating humor would ever have sufficed to parry the envy of Kissinger's contemporaries. On one occasion, at a big dinner in Washington, a man approached him and said, "Dr. Kissinger, I want to thank you for saving the world." Without missing a beat, Kissinger replied, "You're welcome."[48] Asked by journalists how they should now address him, following his swearing-in as secretary of state, Kissinger replied, "I do not stand on protocol. If you just call me Excellency, it will be okay."[49] The many lists of Henry Kissinger quotations all include the following one-liners:

> People are generally amazed that I would take an interest in any forum that would require me to stop talking for three hours.

> The longer I am out of office, the more infallible I appear to myself.

> The nice thing about being a celebrity is that, if you bore people, they think it's their fault.

> There cannot be a crisis next week. My schedule is already full.

Each of these employs the same rhetorical device, the reductio ad absurdum. Reputed to be arrogant, Kissinger sought to disarm his critics by saying things so arrogant as to be patent self-mockery. Those who had been raised on the Marx Brothers doubtless recognized the influence of Groucho. But it was a characteristic feature of the "counterculture" generation of the 1960s and 1970s that it did not find the Marx Brothers funny. "The illegal we do immediately; the unconstitutional takes a little longer" are among Kissinger's most frequently cited words. Rarely are they acknowledged to be a joke, prefaced by "Before the Freedom of Information Act, I used to say at meetings . . ."

and followed in the official "memcon" by "[laughter]." If Kissinger had genuinely been "afraid to say things like that" since the Freedom of Information Act, presumably he would not have said them.[50]

In dictionaries of quotations, Kissinger has more wisecracks to his name than most professional comedians. "Ninety percent of the politicians give the other ten percent a bad reputation." "If eighty percent of your sales come from twenty percent of all of your items, just carry those twenty percent." And a line worthy of Woody Allen himself: "Nobody will ever win the Battle of the Sexes. There's just too much fraternizing with the enemy." His finest aphorisms, too, deserve to endure: "To be absolutely certain about something, one must know everything or nothing about it," "Each success only buys an admission ticket to a more difficult problem," and perhaps the most famous of all, "Power is the ultimate aphrodisiac." Yet the sharpness of Kissinger's wit seems ultimately to have been in inverse proportion to his popularity. Perhaps the boasting about sex was simply a mistake. Kissinger's line about the aphrodisiac quality of power was, once again, intended to be self-deprecating. Of the women he dated, he once said, "They are . . . attracted only to my power. But what happens when my power is gone? They're not going to sit around and play chess with me."[51] This is not the language of Don Juan. Once again Kissinger was too candid with Oriana Fallaci:

> When I speak to Le Duc Tho, I know what I have to do with Le Duc Tho, and when I'm with girls, I know what I must do with girls. Besides, Le Duc Tho doesn't at all agree to negotiate with me because I represent an example of moral rectitude. . . . [T]his frivolous reputation . . . it's partly exaggerated, of course. . . . What counts is to what degree women are part of my life, a central preoccupation. Well, they aren't that at all. For me women are only a diversion, a hobby. Nobody spends too much time with his hobbies.[52]

This was true. The glamorous women with whom Kissinger very publicly dined in the years before his second marriage were generally left to their own devices after dessert as Kissinger returned to the White House or State Department. We know now (see the preface) that none of these relationships was more than a friendship: Kissinger loved Nancy Maginnes, and she put up with the smoke screen in the gossip columns as the price of her privacy. Yet the starlets, combined with the attendant publicity, could only fuel the jealousy of others. Nor could Kissinger resist another one-liner: "I am," he announced at a party given for the feminist Gloria Steinem by the television talk show host Barbara Howar, "a secret swinger."[53] There was of course nothing secret about it. A two-page spread in *Life* magazine in January 1972 pictured Kissinger not only with Steinem and Howar but also with "movie starlet" Judy Brown, "film star" Samantha Eggar, "movie actress" Jill St. John, "TV star" Marlo Thomas, "starlet" Angel Tomkins, and "bosomy pinup girl" June Wilkinson.[54] Nor were all Kissinger's dates from the second tier of acting talent. The Norwegian actress Liv Ullmann had been nominated for an Oscar two years before she caused Kissinger to miss the announcement of his own nomination as secretary of state. Candice Bergen was a rising star when, over dinner, Kissinger gave her "the sense of shared secrets—probably the same set he gave every antiwar actress." For the press, the story was irresistible: the dowdy Harvard professor reborn in Hollywood as "Cary Grant with a German accent."[55] When Marlon Brando pulled out of the New York premiere of *The Godfather,* its executive producer Robert Evans unhesitatingly called Kissinger—and Kissinger obligingly flew up, despite blizzard conditions and a schedule the next day that began with an early-morning meeting with the Joint Chiefs of Staff to discuss the mining of Haiphong harbor and ended with a secret flight to Moscow:

> REPORTER: Dr. Kissinger, why are you here tonight?
> KISSINGER: I was forced.
> R: By who?
> K: By Bobby [Evans].
> R: Did he make you an offer you couldn't refuse?
> K: Yes.[56]

As they fought their way through the throng, Evans had Kissinger on one arm and Ali MacGraw on the other.

The obvious retort to all this is that hostility to Kissinger had much more to do with actions like the mining of Haiphong harbor than with appearances at movie premieres. Still, less irenic motives for animosity cannot be dismissed out of hand. As early as January 1971, the columnist Joseph Kraft could report that Kissinger's "closest friends and associates" had come to see him as "a suspect figure, personifying the treason of the intellectuals," because he was working "to reinforce and legitimize the President's hard-line instincts on most major international business."[37] The previous May, thirteen of his Harvard colleagues—among them Francis Bator, William Capron, Paul Doty, George Kistiakowsky, Richard Neustadt, Thomas Schelling, and Adam Yarmolinsky—had traveled to Washington to meet with him. Kissinger had expected to host a private lunch for them. Instead, according to one well-known account of the meeting, Schelling began by saying he should explain who they were. Kissinger was perplexed.

"I know who you are," he said, "you're all good friends from Harvard."

"No," said Schelling, "we're a group of people who have completely lost confidence in the ability of the White House to conduct our foreign policy, and we have come to tell you so. We are no longer at your disposal as personal advisers." Each of them then proceeded to berate him, taking five minutes apiece.[38]

The group's stated reason for breaking with Kissinger was the invasion of Cambodia. (As their spokesman Schelling put it, "There are two possibilities. Either, one, the President didn't understand . . . that he was invading another country; or, two, he did understand. We just don't know which one is scarier.")[39] No doubt Schelling and his colleagues had cogent reasons to criticize Nixon's decision. Still, there was something suspiciously staged about their showdown with Kissinger. Each one of those named above had experience in government, and at high levels. Bator, for example, had served as deputy national security adviser to Nixon's predecessor, Lyndon Johnson, and had therefore enjoyed a ringside seat for the escalation of the war against North Vietnam. As Bator confessed to *The Harvard Crimson,* "Some of us here at Harvard have been working on the inside for a long time." Neustadt, too, admitted that he had "regarded the executive branch as . . . home for twenty or thirty years. . . . This is the first time in years that I've come to Washington and stayed at the Hay-Adams and had to pay the bill out of my own pocket."

For these men, publicly breaking with Kissinger—with journalists briefed in advance about the breach—was a form of self-exculpation, not to say an insurance policy as student radicals back on the Harvard campus ran riot. When Neustadt told the *Crimson,* "I think it's safe to say we're afraid," he did not specify of what. Others were more candid. As Schelling put it, "If Cambodia succeeds, it will be a disaster not just because my Harvard office may be burned down when I get home, but it will even be a disaster in [the administration's] own terms." The historian Ernest May, who had rushed down from an emergency faculty meeting called to address student demands about examinations, told Kissinger, "You're tearing the country apart domestically." The country he meant was not Cambodia. After their meeting with Kissinger, as if to underline their contrition for past misdeeds, Neustadt and two of the others joined a much larger "Peace Action Strike" of Harvard students and faculty led by the antiwar firebrand Everett Mendelsohn. But the campus radicals were not propitiated. That same day the Center for International Affairs, where both Bator and Schelling had their offices, was invaded and "trashed" by demonstrators.[60]

IV

Even if they have not always objected to his policies, critics have long taken exception to Henry Kissinger's mode of operation. Driven by "excessive ambition," he was "a consummate network-builder, operating on a nearly worldwide scale."[61] He was "the media's best friend."[62] "A distinguished journalist once complained that it took him three days after every conversation with Henry Kissinger to recover his critical sense; unfortunately, in the meantime he had written his column."[63] Kissinger, we are told, loved secrecy almost as much as the diabolical Richard Nixon, with whom (in the eyes of Harvard, at least) he had made his Faustian pact.[64] He wiretapped even members of his own staff, notably Morton Halperin.[65] He was a sycophant, willing to put up with Nixon's obnoxious anti-Semitism.[66] But he was also deeply insecure, needing to be reassured by Nixon's chief of staff H. R. Haldeman "almost every day, certainly at least every week . . . that the President really did love him and appreciate him and couldn't get along without him."[67] One of Kissinger's most relentless critics, Anthony Lewis of *The New York Times,* posed the question: "How [could] . . . Kissinger involve himself in their horrors[?] . . . How could he humiliate himself, use locker-room language, engage in such things as wiretapping?" The answer, Lewis argued, was "not in doubt: he did what had to be done to acquire and keep power—and to exercise it in secret."[68] In all these accounts, Kissinger is like an American equivalent of Kenneth Widmerpool in Anthony Powell's *Dance to the Music of Time* novels—at once hateful and unstoppable.

The other possibility is that a great deal of what has been said against Kissinger stems from those with grudges against him. When, for example, George Ball described Kissinger as "self-centered and conspiratorial," he was expressing the view of a State Department insider who resented the way he undermined Nixon's now-all-but-forgotten secretary of state William P. Rogers.[69] Raymond Garthoff was another official with an ax to grind: while negotiating the terms of SALT with the Soviets, he had been kept in the dark about Kissinger's "back channel" to the Soviet ambassador.[70] Hans Morgenthau once memorably described Kissinger as, like Odysseus, "*polytropos,* that is, 'many-sided' or 'of many appearances.'"

> From that quality stems the fascination with which friends and foes, colleagues and strangers behold him. That quality encloses the secret of his success. Kissinger is like a good actor who does not *play* the role of Hamlet today, of Caesar tomorrow, but who *is* Hamlet today and Caesar tomorrow.[71]

The Israeli press later boiled this down to a charge of "two faced diplomacy."[72] But was Morgenthau entirely disinterested in his criticism? Older than Kissinger by nearly ten years and, like Kissinger, of German-Jewish origin, he is regarded to this day as the founder of the "realist" school of U.S. foreign policy. Yet his Washington career—as a consultant to the Pentagon under Johnson—had ended when he refused to the toe the line on Vietnam. If anyone flinched to hear Kissinger hailed as the archrealist, it was Morgenthau.

A favorite theme of Kissinger's critics was that he was fundamentally hostile, or at least indifferent, to democracy. "A policy commitment to stability and identifying instability with communism," Morgenthau wrote, "is compelled by the logic of its interpretation of reality to suppress in the name of anticommunism all manifestations of popular discontent. . . . Thus, in an essentially unstable world, tyranny becomes the last resort of a policy committed to stability as its ultimate standard."[73] Similar sentiments can be found in multiple polemics. According to Richard Falk, Kissinger's effectiveness stemmed from "his capacity to avoid unpleasant criticisms about . . . domestic indecencies"—a "Machiavellian posture" that was a welcome relief to the world's dictators.[74] Why a man who had fled the Third Reich and found success in the United States should be averse to democracy is not immediately obvious. But writer after writer has resolved the paradox by arguing that, in the words of David Landau, Kissinger was "a child of Weimar," haunted by "the dread specter of revolution and political anarchy, the demise of all recognizable authority."[75] "Witnessing these events firsthand," writes Jeremi Suri, "Henry Kissinger could only conclude that democracies were weak and ineffective at combating destructive enemies. . . . The solution was . . . to build space for charismatic, forward-looking undemocratic decisionmaking in government."[76] Thus he "often acted against what he saw as dangerous domestic opinion. To do otherwise, in his eyes, would repeat the mistakes of the democratic purists in the 1930s and bow to the weaknesses and extremes of mass politics . . . to the people protesting in the streets."[77] As we shall see, the defect of this argument is that Henry Kissinger was not yet ten years old when the Weimar Republic died, an age at which even quite precocious children are unlikely to have formed strong political opinions. His earliest political memories were of the regime that came next. Did growing up under Hitler somehow prejudice Kissinger against democracy? Bruce Mazlish offered the psychoanalytical interpretation that Kissinger's "identification with the aggressor" was his way of "dealing with the Nazi experience."[78] As we shall see, however, a much more straightforward reading is possible.

In this context, it is a strange irony of the Kissinger literature that so many of the critiques of Kissinger's mode of operation have a subtle undertone of anti-Semitism. The more books I have read about Kissinger, the more I have been reminded of the dreadful books I had to read twenty years ago when writing the history of the Rothschild family. When other nineteenth-century banks made loans to conservative regimes or to countries at war, no one seemed to notice. But when the Rothschilds did it, the pamphleteers could scarcely control their indignation. Indeed, it would take a great many shelves to contain all the shrill anti-Rothschild polemics produced by Victorian antecedents of today's conspiracy theorists (who, as we have seen, still like to drag in the Rothschilds). This prompts the question: might the ferocity of the criticism that Kissinger has attracted perhaps have something to do with the fact that he, like the Rothschilds, is Jewish?

This is not to imply that his critics are anti-Semites. Some of the Rothschilds' fiercest critics were themselves Jews. So are some of Kissinger's. Bruce Gold, Heller's Kissinger-hating professor, advances the "covert and remarkable hypothesis that Henry Kissinger was not a Jew"—a hypothesis based partly on his father's insight that "no cowboy was ever a Jew."

> In Gold's conservative opinion, Kissinger would not be recalled in history as a Bismarck, Metternich, or Castlereagh, but as an odious *shlump* who made war gladly and did not often exude much of that legendary sympathy for weakness and suffering with which Jews regularly were credited. It was not a *shayna Yid* who would go down on his knees on a carpet to pray to Yahweh with that *shmendrick* Nixon, or a *haimisha mentsh* who would act with such cruelty against the free population of Chile. . . . Such a *pisk* on the *pisher* to speak with such *chutzpah*![79]

To say that American Jews have been ambivalent toward the man who is arguably their community's most distinguished son would be an understatement. Even sympathetic biographers like Mazlish and Suri use questionable phrases like "court Jew" or "policy Jew" to characterize Kissinger's relationship with Nixon.[80]

V

The crux of the matter, nevertheless, is how we judge Kissinger's foreign policy—both its theory and its practice. For the vast majority of commentators, the theory is clear-cut. Kissinger is a realist, and that implies, in Anthony Lewis's crude definition of the "Kissinger Doctrine," "an obsession with order and power at the expense of humanity."[81] According to Marvin and Bernard Kalb, Nixon and Kissinger "shared a global *realpolitik* that placed a higher priority on pragmatism than on morality."[82] In the 1960s, Stanley Hoffmann had been more than a colleague to Kissinger; he had been a friend and admirer, who had welcomed his appointment by Nixon. Yet by the time Kissinger published the first volume of his memoirs, he, too, had joined this club. Kissinger had, he wrote in a venomous review, "an almost devilish psychological intuition, an instinct for grasping the hidden springs of character, of knowing what drives or what dooms another person." He also had "the gift for the manipulation of power—exploiting the weaknesses and strengths of character of his counterparts." But

> [i]f there was a vision beyond the geopolitical game, if the complex manipulation of rewards and punishments needed to create equilibrium and to restrain the troublemakers was aimed at a certain ideal of world order, we are left free to guess what it might have been. . . . [His] is a world in which power is all: equilibrium is not just the prerequisite to order, the precondition for justice, it *is* order, it amounts to justice.[83]

Like so many other less learned authors, Hoffmann concluded that both Nixon and Kissinger (the former "instinctively," the latter "intellectually") were "Machiavellians—men who believed that the preservation of the state (inseparable in Machiavelli from that of the Prince) requires both ruthlessness and deceit at the expense of foreign and internal adversaries."[84] This kind of judgment recurs again and again. According to Walter Isaacson, "power-oriented *realpolitik* and secretive diplomatic maneuvering . . . were the basis of [Kissinger's] policies."[85] John Gaddis calls the Nixon-Kissinger combination "the triumph of geopolitics over ideology," with their conception of American national interests always paramount.[86] Kissinger, says Suri, was "hardened against idealistic rhetoric that neglected the 'realistic' importance of extensive armed force and preparations to use it."[87] He invariably placed the "demands of the state above other ethical scruples."[88]

So deeply rooted is this view of Kissinger as an amoral realist—a "hard-boiled master of *realpolitik* who will not sacrifice one iota of American interest"—that the overwhelming majority of writers have simply assumed that Kissinger modeled himself on his "heroes" Metternich and Bismarck.[89] Kissinger did indeed write about both men in, respectively, the 1950s and the 1960s. But only someone who has not read (or who has willfully misread) what he actually wrote could possibly think that he set out in the 1970s to replicate their approaches to foreign policy. One of the quirks of the "Killinger" literature is that, by comparison, so little is made of Kissinger's book *Nuclear Weapons and Foreign Policy*. With its cold, calculated argument for the graduated use of nuclear weapons, this might very easily be presented as evidence that Dr. Kissinger was indeed the inspiration for Stanley Kubrick's Dr. Strangelove. Yet Kissinger's critics prefer different battlegrounds to those of Central Europe, the core conflict zone of the First and Second World Wars, which even a limited nuclear war would have laid waste.

VI

The Cold War, which was the defining event of Henry Kissinger's two careers as a scholar and as a policy maker, took many forms. It was a nuclear arms race that on more than one occasion came close to turning into a devastating thermonuclear war. It was also, in some respects, a contest between two great empires, an American and a Russian, which sent their legions all around the world, though they seldom met face-to-face. It was a competition between two economic systems, capitalist and socialist, symbolized by Nixon's "kitchen debate" with Khrushchev in Moscow in 1959. It was a great if deadly game between intelligence agencies, glamorized in the novels of Ian Fleming, more accurately rendered in those of John le Carré. It was a cultural battle, in which chattering professors, touring jazz bands, and defecting ballet dancers all played their parts. Yet at its root, the Cold War was a struggle between two rival ideologies: the theories of the Enlightenment as encapsulated in the American Constitution, and the theories of Marx and Lenin as articulated by successive Soviet leaders. Only one of these ideologies was intent, as a matter of theoretical principle, on struggle. And only one of these states was wholly unconstrained by the rule of law.

The mass murderers of the Cold War were not to be found in Washington, much less in the capitals of U.S. allies in Western Europe. According to the estimates in the *Black Book of Communism,* the "grand total of victims of Communism was between 85 and 100 million" for the twentieth century as a whole.[90] Mao alone, as Frank Dikötter has shown, accounted for tens of millions: 2 million between 1949 and 1951, another 3 million by the end of the 1950s, a staggering 45 million in the man-made famine known as the "Great Leap Forward," yet more in the mayhem of the Cultural Revolution.[91] According to the lowest estimate, the total number of Soviet citizens who lost their lives as a direct result of Stalin's policies was more than 20 million, a quarter of them in the years after World War II.[92] Even the less bloodthirsty regimes of Eastern Europe killed and imprisoned their citizens on a shocking scale.[93] In the Soviet Union, 2.75 million people were in the Gulag at Stalin's death. The numbers were greatly reduced thereafter, but until the very end of the Soviet system its inhabitants lived in the knowledge that there was nothing but their own guile to protect them from an arbitrary and corrupt state. These stark and incontrovertible facts make a mockery of the efforts of the so-called revisionist historians, beginning with William Appleman Williams, to assert a moral equivalence between the Soviet Union and the United States during the Cold War.[94]

All Communist regimes everywhere, without exception, were merciless in their treatment of "class enemies," from the North Korea of the Kims to the Vietnam of Ho Chi Minh, from the Ethiopia of Mengistu Haile Mariam to the Angola of Agostinho Neto. Pol Pot was the worst of them all, but even Castro's Cuba was no workers' paradise. And Communist regimes were aggressive, too, overtly invading country after country during the Cold War. Through which foreign cities did American tanks drive in 1956, when Soviet tanks crushed resistance in Budapest? In 1968, when Soviet armor rolled into Prague, U.S. tanks were in Saigon and Hue, their commanders little suspecting that within less than six months they would be defending those cities against a massive North Vietnamese offensive. Did South Korea invade North Korea? Did South Vietnam invade North Vietnam?

Moreover, we now know from the secret documents brought to the West by Vasili Mitrokhin just how extensive and ruthless the KGB's system of international espionage and subversion was.[95] In the global Cold War, inextricably entangled as it was with the fall of the European empires, the Soviet Union nearly always made the first move, leaving the United States to retaliate where it could.[96] That retaliation took many ugly forms, no doubt. Graham Greene had it right when he mocked *The Quiet American,* whose talk of a "third force" sounded just like imperialism to everyone else. But in terms of both economic growth and political freedom, it was always better for ordinary people and their children if the United States won. The burden of proof is therefore on the critics of U.S. policy to show that a policy of nonintervention—of the sort that had been adopted by the Western powers when the Soviet Union, Nazi Germany, and fascist Italy took sides in the Spanish Civil War, and again when the Germans demanded the breakup of Czechoslovakia—would have produced better results. As Kissinger pointed out to Oriana Fallaci, "the history of things that didn't happen" needs to be considered before we may pass any judgment on the history of things that did happen. We need to consider not only the consequences of what American governments did during the Cold War, but also the probable consequences of the different foreign policies that might have been adopted.

What if the United States had never adopted George Kennan's policy of containment but had opted again for isolationism after 1945? What, conversely, if the United States had adopted a more aggressive strategy aimed at "rolling back" Soviet gains, at the risk of precipitating a nuclear war? Both alternatives had their advocates at the time, just as there were advocates of both less and more forceful policies during Kissinger's time in office. Anyone who presumes to condemn what decision makers did in this or that location must be able to argue plausibly that their preferred alternative policy would have had fewer American and non-American casualties and no large negative second-order effects in other parts of the world. In particular, arguments that focus on loss of life in strategically marginal countries—and there is no other way of describing Argentina, Bangladesh, Cambodia, Chile, Cyprus, and East Timor—must be tested against this question: how, in each case, would an alternative decision have affected U.S. relations with strategically important countries like the Soviet Union, China, and the major Western European powers? For, as Kissinger himself once observed, the statesman is not like a judge, who can treat each individual case on its merits. The maker of grand strategy in the Cold War had to consider all cases simultaneously in the context of a prolonged struggle against a hostile and heavily armed rival.

From this standpoint, the real puzzle of the Cold War is why it took so long for the United States to win it. Far wealthier than the Soviet Union by any measure (according to the best available estimates, the Soviet economy was on average less than two-fifths the size of the American throughout), technologically nearly always in front, and with a markedly more attractive political system and popular culture, the United States on the eve of Henry Kissinger's appointment as national security adviser was already a mighty empire—but an "empire by invitation" rather than imposition.[97] American service personnel were stationed in sixty-four countries.[98] The United States had treaties of alliance with no fewer than forty-eight of them.[99] Not only were American forces generally better armed than anyone else; the United States was not afraid to use them. Between 1946 and 1965, according to one estimate, there had been 168 separate instances of American armed intervention overseas.[100] U.S. forces were permanently based in key countries, including the two major aggressors of World War II, Germany and Japan. Yet the Cold War was set to endure for another twenty years. Moreover, throughout the era of superpower rivalry, the United States tended to have a harder time than its rival when it came to imposing its will outside its own borders. According to one assessment of seven Cold War interventions by the United States, only four were successful in the sense of establishing stable democratic systems: West Germany and

Japan after World War II, and Grenada and Panama in the 1980s. Even if the list is expanded to include the striking success of South Korea, the colossal failure of Vietnam hangs like a cloud of acrid smoke over the American record.[101]

In the summer of 1947, George Kennan published his anonymous essay in *Foreign Affairs,* "The Sources of Soviet Conduct," one of the foundational texts of the strategy he called "containment." In a startling passage, Kennan likened the seeming power of the Soviet Union to that of the grand merchant family in Thomas Mann's novel *Buddenbrooks.*

> Observing that human institutions often show the greatest outward brilliance at a moment when inner decay is in reality farthest advanced, [Mann] compared the Buddenbrook family, in the days of its greatest glamour, to one of those stars whose light shines most brightly on this world when in reality it has long since ceased to exist. And who can say with assurance that the strong light still cast by the Kremlin on the dissatisfied peoples of the western world is not the powerful afterglow of a constellation which is in actuality on the wane? . . . [T]he possibility remains . . . that Soviet power . . . bears within it the seeds of its own decay, and that the sprouting of these seeds is well advanced.[102]

Kennan was forty-three when he wrote those words. He was eighty-seven when the Soviet Union was finally dissolved in December 1991. Why was this? Why was the Cold War so interminable and so intractable? A large part of the interest of this book lies in the fact that, by rejecting both historical materialism and economic determinism from an early stage of his career, Henry Kissinger was able to offer a compelling answer to that question. The Cold War was not about economics. It was not even about nuclear stockpiles, much less tank divisions. It was primarily about ideals.

VII

Was Kissinger, as nearly all his critics assume, *really* a realist? The answer matters a good deal. For if he was not in fact a latter-day Metternich or Bismarck, then his conduct as a policy maker ought not to be judged by the standard realist criterion: were American interests best served, regardless of the means employed? "Realism," Robert Kaplan has written, "is about the ultimate moral ambition in foreign policy: the avoidance of war through a favorable balance of power. . . . [A]s a European-style realist, Kissinger has thought more about morality and ethics than most self-styled moralists."[103] Like Mazlish's skeptical allusion to Kissinger's "higher moral purposes,"[104] this is closer to the target than the wild accusations of amorality and immorality favored by the conspiracy theorists, though it is still wide of the bull's-eye.

Asked in 1976 to assess his own achievement as a statesman, Kissinger replied, "I have tried—with what success historians will have to judge—to have an overriding concept." There is no question, as we shall see, that Kissinger entered the White House in 1969 with such a concept. He had indeed spent most of the preceding twenty years devising and defining it.[105] As he famously observed, "High office teaches decision making, not substance. It consumes intellectual capital; it does not create it. Most high officials leave office with the perceptions and insights with which they entered; they learn how to make decisions but not what decisions to make."[106] But to an extent that says much about modern standards of scholarship, remarkably few of those who have taken it upon themselves to pass judgment on Henry Kissinger have done more than skim his published work, which prior to 1969 included four weighty books, more than a dozen substantial articles for magazines such as *Foreign Affairs,* and a fair amount of journalism. The first task of a biographer who undertakes to write the life of a scholar—even if that scholar goes on to attain high office—ought surely to be to read his writings. Doing so reveals that Kissinger's intellectual capital had a dual foundation: the study of history and the philosophy of idealism.

Kissinger's wartime mentor, Fritz Kraemer, once described his protégé as being "musically attuned to history. This is not something you can learn, no matter how intelligent you are. It is a gift from God."[107] His Harvard contemporary John Stoessinger recalled an early meeting with Kissinger when they were both first-year graduate students: "He argued forcefully for the abiding importance of history. Quoting Thucydides, he asserted that the present, while never repeating the past exactly, must inevitably resemble it. Hence, so must the future. . . . More than ever . . . one should study history in order to see why nations and men succeeded and why they failed."[108] This was to be a lifelong leitmotif. The single thing that differentiated Kissinger from most other students of international relations in his generation was that he revered history above theory—or rather, Kissinger's theory of foreign policy was defined by the insight that states and statesmen act on the basis of their own historical self-understanding and cannot be comprehended in any other way.

Yet there was something that preceded Kissinger the historian, and that was Kissinger the philosopher of history. It is here that the most fundamental misunderstanding has occurred. Like nearly all Kissinger scholars, Oriana Fallaci took it for granted that Kissinger was "much influenced" by Machiavelli and was therefore an admirer of Metternich. Kissinger gave her a frank and illuminating answer:

> There is really very little of Machiavelli that can be accepted or used in the modern world. The only thing I find interesting in Machiavelli is his way of considering the will of the prince. Interesting, but not to the point of influencing me. If you want to know who has influenced me the most, I'll answer with the names of two philosophers: Spinoza and Kant. So it's curious that you choose to associate me with Machiavelli. People rather associate me with the name of Metternich. Which is actually childish. On Metternich I've written only one book, which was to be the beginning of a long series of books on the construction and disintegration of the international order of the nineteenth century. It was a series that was to end with the First World War. That's all. There can be nothing in common between me and Metternich.[109]

To my knowledge only one previous writer has fully understood the significance of that candid response.* Far from being a Machiavellian realist, Henry Kissinger was in fact from the outset of his career an idealist, having immersed himself as an undergraduate in the philosophy of the great Prussian philosopher Immanuel Kant. Indeed, as the historian Peter Dickson pointed out as early as 1978, Kissinger considered himself "more Kantian than Kant."[110] His unpublished senior thesis, "The Meaning of History," is at root an overambitious but deeply sincere critique of Kant's philosophy of history. More than a quarter of a century after its completion, Kissinger was still citing Kant to explain why he discerned "a clear conflict between two moral imperatives" in foreign policy: the obligation to defend freedom and the necessity for coexistence with adversaries.[111] Though habitually categorized as a realist, Dickson argued, in reality Kissinger owed much more to idealism than to the likes of Morgenthau.[112] I believe this is correct. Indeed, it is compellingly borne out by Kissinger's *World Order,* published in his ninety-first year, which quotes Kant at length.[113] I also believe that the failure of writer after writer to understand Kissinger's idealism has vitiated severely, if not fatally, the historical judgments they have passed on him.

To be clear, I am not suggesting that the young Kissinger was an idealist in the sense in which the word is often used to characterize the tradition in U.S. foreign policy that emphasized the subordination of "might" to supranational laws and courts.[114] Rather, I am using the term "idealism" in its philosophical sense, meaning the strand of Western philosophy, extending back to Anaxagoras and Plato, that holds that (in Kant's formulation) "we can never be certain whether all of our putative outer experience is not mere imagining" because "the reality of external objects does not admit of strict proof." Not all idealists are Kantian, it need hardly be said. Plato regarded matter as real and existing independently of perception. Bishop Berkeley insisted that reality was all in the mind; experience itself was an illusion. In Kant's "transcendental"

---

* This is, admittedly, in part because Kissinger himself has tended to avoid the subject. In 2004 the historian Jeremi Suri asked him, "What are your core moral principles—the principles you would not violate?" Kissinger replied, "I am not prepared to share that yet."

idealism, by contrast, "the whole material world" was "nothing but a phenomenal appearance in the sensibility of ourselves as a subject," but there were such things as noumena, or "things in themselves," which the mind shaped into phenomena on the basis of experience rather than "pure reason." As we shall see, Kissinger's reading of Kant had a profound and enduring influence on his own thought, not least because it made him skeptical of the various materialist theories of capitalist superiority that U.S. social scientists devised as antidotes to Marxism-Leninism. He showed no interest whatever in the version of idealism developed by Georg Wilhelm Friedrich Hegel as a comprehensive theory of history, in which the dialectical fusion of theses and antitheses propelled the world inexorably onward. For Kissinger, the burning historical question was how far Kant's view of the human predicament—as one in which the individual freely faced meaningful moral dilemmas—could be reconciled with the philosopher's vision of a world ultimately destined for "perpetual peace." It was no facile allusion when Kissinger referred to Kant's essay in his address to the United Nations General Assembly on September 24, 1973, just two days after he had been confirmed as secretary of state:

> Two centuries ago, the philosopher Kant predicted that perpetual peace would come eventually—either as the creation of man's moral aspirations or as the consequence of physical necessity. What seemed utopian then looms as tomorrow's reality; soon there will be no alternative. Our only choice is whether the world envisaged in the [United Nations] charter will come about as the result of our vision or of a catastrophe invited by our shortsightedness.[115]

As we know, the Cold War did not end in catastrophe. In its aftermath, though still a long way from perpetual peace, the world has become a markedly more peaceful place, with striking declines in the levels of organized violence in all regions of the world except the Middle East and North Africa.[116] How far that outcome owed anything to Henry Kissinger's vision is, to say the least, a question that has not hitherto received an adequate answer. Suffice for now to say that, having escalated alarmingly during the 1960s, global violence, as measured by total deaths due to warfare, fell sharply between 1971 and 1976.

Presciently, Peter Dickson foresaw what Kissinger's predicament would be if the Cold War did indeed end, as it did, with a more or less bloodless American victory:

> [Kissinger's] notion that discord can surreptitiously lead to cooperation, the concept of self-limitation, and his character-ization of foreign policy as a hierarchy of imperatives were all designed to inject a sense of purpose . . . [in]to American political culture as a whole . . . to restore meaning to history when Americans began to question seriously their nation's role in the world. . . . Kissinger's political philosophy constitute[d] a major break with the rationale of all postwar policy, which rested on the notion of America as a redeemer nation, as the guarantor of freedom and democracy. . . . [I]f at some future time the United States succeeds in fulfilling the role of redeemer, then Kissinger will be seen as a defeatist leader, as an historical pessimist who underestimated the appeal and rele-vance of democratic ideals and principles.[117]

It is surely no accident that the most bitter denunciations of Kissinger came after the Soviet threat had—as if by magic—disappeared.

VIII

I have spent a substantial proportion of the last twenty years trying to understand better the nature of power and the causes of war and peace. Though I initially focused on the German Reich and the British Empire, my focus since moving across the Atlantic has been, perhaps inevitably, on that strange empire that dare not speak its name, the United States of America. My critique has been, if nothing else, nonpartisan. In 2001 I summed up Bill Clinton's foreign policy as a case of "understretch," in that the administration was too preoccupied with domestic scandal and too averse to casualties to make proper use of America's vast capabilities.[118] Three years later, in the early phase of the Bush administration's occupation of Iraq, I published a meditation on the American predicament: the heir to a British tradition of liberal imperialism, convinced of the benefits of free trade and representative government, yet constrained—perhaps fatally—by three deficits: a fiscal deficit (in the sense that spiraling welfare entitlements and debt must inevitably squeeze the resources available for national security), a manpower deficit (in the sense that not many Americans want to spend very long sorting out hot, poor countries), and above all, an attention deficit (in the sense that any major foreign intervention is likely to lose popularity within a four-year election cycle).[119] I foresaw the direction we would take under Bush's successor—"an imminent retreat from the principles of preemption and the practice of unilateralism"—well before his identity was known. I also anticipated some of the consequences of the coming American retreat.[120]

Yet in researching the life and times of Henry Kissinger, I have come to realize that my approach was unsubtle. In particular, I had missed the crucial importance in American foreign policy of the *history deficit:* the fact that key decision makers know almost nothing not just of other countries' pasts but also of their own. Worse, they often do not see what is wrong with their ignorance. Worst of all, they know just enough history to have confidence but not enough to have understanding. Like the official who assured me in early 2003 that the future of a post-Saddam Iraq would closely resemble that of post-Communist Poland, too many highly accomplished Americans simply do not appreciate the value, but also the danger, of historical analogy.

This is the biography of an intellectual, but it is more than just an intellectual biography because, in the evolution of Kissinger's thought, the interplay of study and experience was singularly close. For that reason, I have come to see this volume as what is known in Germany as a bildungsroman—the story of an education that was both philosophical and sentimental. The story is subdivided into five books. The first takes Kissinger from his childhood in interwar Germany through forced emigration to the United States and back to Germany in a U.S. Army uniform. The second is about his early Harvard career, as an undergraduate, a doctoral student, and a junior professor, but it is also about his emergence as a public intellectual as a result of his work on nuclear strategy for the Council on Foreign Relations. The third describes his first experiences as an adviser, first to a candidate for the presidency—Nelson Rockefeller—and then to a president—John F. Kennedy. The fourth leads him down the twisted road to Vietnam and to the realization that the war there could not be won by the United States. The fifth and final book details the events leading up to his wholly unexpected appointment as national security adviser by Nixon.

Kissinger was a voracious reader, and so a part of his education self-evidently came from writers, from Immanuel Kant to Herman Kahn. Yet in many ways the biggest influences on him were not books but mentors, beginning with Fritz Kraemer—Mephistopheles to Kissinger's Faust. And the most important lessons he learned came as much from his own experience as from their instruction. I have concluded that four precepts in particular should be considered as the essential assets in the intellectual capital that Kissinger brought with him as he entered the White House in January 1969: his sense that most strategic choices are between lesser and greater evils; his belief in history as the mother lode of both analogies and insights into the self-understanding of other actors; his realization that any decision is essentially conjectural and that the political payoffs to some courses of action may be lower than the payoffs of inaction and retaliation, even though the ultimate costs of the latter course may be higher; and finally, his awareness that realism in foreign policy, as exemplified by Bismarck, is fraught with perils, not least the alienation of the public and the slippage of the statesman into regarding power as an end in itself.

In aspiring to loftier ends, I believe, the young Kissinger was indeed an idealist.

Book I

Heimat

Fürth ist mir ziemlich egal. (Fürth is a matter of indifference
to me.)

—HENRY KISSINGER, 2004[1]

I

Where exactly is a biographer to begin when his subject flatly denies
the significance of his childhood for his later life?

It has often been suggested that growing up in the Germany of the
1930s "cast a traumatic shadow over [Kissinger's] . . . adolescence." For
example: "The feeling of constantly being liable to unpredictable violence obviously laid deep in Kissinger's psyche a kind of groundwork on
which his later attitudes (even to nuclear war) could be built."[2] Another
author has speculated that in the 1970s Kissinger "feared a return to the
violence, chaos and collapse of Weimar Germany." His attitudes to both
the Vietnam War and the Watergate scandal, so the argument runs, are
intelligible only in the light of his youthful experiences in Germany.
Indeed, his entire philosophical and political outlook is said to have
deep German roots. "The experience of Weimar Germany's collapse . . .
convinced . . . [him] that democracy had a very dark side." That same
experience supposedly made him a lifelong cultural pessimist.[3]

Kissinger himself has repeatedly dismissed such theories. "My life
in Fürth," he declared in 1958, during a visit to his Bavarian birthplace,
"seems to have passed without [leaving] any deeper impressions; I cannot recall any interesting or amusing incident."[4] Interviewed by Al
Ellenberg of the *New York Post* in March 1974, he laconically conceded
that he had "often . . . been chased through the streets, and beaten up"

as a boy growing up in Nazi Germany. But he was quick to add, "That part of my childhood was not a key to anything. I was not consciously unhappy, I was not acutely aware of what was going on. For children, these things are not that serious. . . . It is fashionable now to explain everything psychoanalytically. But let me tell you, the political persecutions of my childhood are not what control my life."[5]

In his memoirs of his career in government, Kissinger alludes only once to his German boyhood.[6] His birthplace, he remarked in 2004, meant little to him.[7] Those who seek the key to his career in his German-Jewish origins are therefore wasting their time.

> I experienced the impact of Nazism and it was very unpleasant, but it did not interfere in my friendship with Jewish people of my age so that I did not find it traumatic. . . . I have resisted the psychiatric explanations [which] argue that I developed a passion for order over justice and that I translated it into profound interpretations of the international system. I wasn't concerned with the international system. I was concerned with the standing of the football team of the town in which I lived.[8]

Kissinger's readiness in later life to revisit Fürth has served to reinforce the impression that his youth was not a time of trauma. He paid a visit during a trip to Germany in December 1958, when his return— as the associate director of the Center for International Affairs at Harvard University—rated two paragraphs in the local paper.[9] The media attention was far greater seventeen years later when, as U.S. secretary of state, he traveled to Fürth to receive a "citizen's gold medal," accompanied by his parents and younger brother, as well as his wife.[10] The event was a carefully choreographed celebration of (in Kissinger's words) "the extraordinary renewal of the friendship between the American and German peoples." Before an audience of Bavarian worthies, he and the German foreign minister, Hans-Dietrich Genscher, exchanged what today might seem like diplomatic platitudes.

> In the shadow of a nuclear catastrophe [declared Kissinger] . . . we must not bow to the supposed inevitability of historical

tragedy. . . . Our shared task is to collaborate in building a system of international relations which ensures the stability of continents and the security of peoples, which binds the peoples of the world together through their common interests, and which demands restraint and moderation in international affairs. Our goal is a peace for which all of us work—small as well as big states—a peace that is enduring because all wish to uphold it—strong as well as weak states.[11]

Yet the more memorable speech was the unscheduled one given by Kissinger's father, Louis, making his first visit to Germany since 1938. Though noting that he had been "forced to leave" Germany in that year, he generously referred to Fürth's earlier tradition of religious tolerance. ("While, in past centuries, intolerance and prejudice were predominant in many German cities, in Fürth the various faiths lived together in harmony.") His son was being honored in his birthplace not just because of his worldly success but because, like Trygaeus, the hero in Aristophanes's comedy *Peace,* he

has seen it as his life's work to dedicate his time and energy to furthering and maintaining peace in the world. Working together with the President of the United States, he has the great idea of ushering in an era of understanding and peaceful collaboration between nations. . . . It is a gratifying feeling for us parents that today the name Kissinger is seen around the world as interchangeable with the term "peace"; that the name Kissinger has become a synonym for peace.[12]

It was December 1975. Angola was sliding into civil war, less than a month after the end of Portuguese colonial rule. A matter of days before the Kissingers' trip to Fürth, the Pathet Lao, supported by Vietnam and the Soviet Union, had overthrown the king of Laos, and the Indonesian military had invaded the briefly independent state of East Timor. Just eight days after the medal ceremony, the CIA's head of station in Athens was shot dead. The newspapers that month were full of terrorist outrages: by the Irish Republican Army in London, by the Palestine

Liberation Organization in Vienna, by South Moluccan separatists in the Netherlands. There was even a fatal bomb explosion at New York's La Guardia airport. To some young German Social Democrats, it seemed incongruous to honor the American secretary of state at such a time.[13] Perhaps only the older Germans present understood the significance of Kissinger's call for "a world, in which it is reconciliation and not power that fills peoples with pride; an era, in which convictions are a source of moral strength and not of intolerance and of hate."[14] These were no empty phrases. For the Kissinger family, what was "especially moving" about this "homecoming" was the fact that the country they had once fled now feted them.[15]

May 1923 was the month Heinz Alfred Kissinger was born in Fürth. That, too, was a year of turmoil in the world. In January the town of Rosewood, Florida, had been razed to the ground in a race riot that left six people dead. In June the Bulgarian prime minister, Aleksandar Stamboliyski, was overthrown (and subsequently killed) in a coup. In September General Miguel Primo de Rivera seized power in Spain, while Japan was devastated by the Great Kanto Earthquake. In October another military strongman, Mustafa Kemal, proclaimed the Republic of Turkey amid the ruins of the Ottoman Empire. The world was still reeling from the political aftershocks of the First World War. In many countries, from Ireland to Russia, bloody civil wars were only now coming to an end. The revolution in the latter had been a human catastrophe, claiming the lives of millions—including its leader, Lenin, who that same month was forced to retire to his estate at Gorki, his health never having recovered from an assassination attempt in 1918.

Nowhere, however, was the upheaval of 1923 greater than in Germany. In January French and Belgian troops had occupied the coal-rich Ruhr area in retaliation for Germany's failure to fulfill its obligations under the Treaty of Versailles. The German government called for a general strike. The crisis was the coup de grâce for the German currency, which nose-dived into worthlessness. The country threatened to fall apart, with separatist movements in the Rhineland, Bavaria, Saxony, and even Hamburg, where the Communists attempted to seize power. In Munich on November 8 Adolf Hitler launched a putsch from the huge beer hall known as the Bürgerbräukeller. He would not have been the first uniformed demagogue to seize power with such a stunt; Benito Mussolini's March on Rome had succeeded just over a year before. It took a concerted effort by the head of the Reichswehr, Hans von Seeckt; the leader of the German People's Party, Gustav von Stresemann; and the banker Hjalmar Schacht to restore the authority of the central government and begin the process of currency reform and stabilization.

It was into this chaos, in the Middle Franconian town of Fürth, that Heinz Kissinger was born.

II

Stifling in its narrow dreariness, our ungardened city, city of soot, of a thousand chimneys, of clanging machinery and hammers, of beer-shops, of sullen, sordid greed in business or craft, of petty and mean people crowded together, with poverty and lovelessness. . . . In the environs, a barren, sandy plain, dirty factory streams, the slow, murky river, the uniformly straight canal, gaunt woods, melancholy villages, hideous quarries, dust, clay, broom.[16]

Fürth lacked charm. The author Jakob Wassermann, who was born there in 1873, recalled its "peculiar formlessness, a certain aridity and meagreness."[17] The contrast with its ancient neighbor, Nuremberg, was especially striking. One of the three most important cities of the Holy Roman Empire, Nuremberg was all "ancient houses, courtyards, streets, cathedrals, bridges, fountains and walls."[18] Separated by just five miles— a short train ride away—the two cities were, in Wassermann's words, an incongruous "union of antiquity and recentness, art and industry, romance and manufacturing, design and dissolution, form and deformity."[19] Even more sharp was the contrast between grimy industrial Fürth and the pretty, hilly countryside around Ansbach to the south, a landscape of "flower gardens, orchards, fish ponds, deserted castles, ruins full of legends, village fairs, simple people."[20]

First referred to in the eleventh century, Fürth alternately prospered then suffered from the fragmentation of political authority in medieval and early modern Germany. For a time, sovereignty over the town was shared between the bishop of Bamberg and the margrave of Ansbach. But such loose arrangements exposed the town to devastation during the Thirty Years' War that ravaged Germany during the first half of the seventeenth century. (Not far southwest of Fürth is the Alte Veste, where Albrecht von Wallenstein defeated the Swedish king Gustavus Adolphus in 1632.) A Bavarian possession from 1806, Fürth was a beneficiary of two concurrent nineteenth-century processes: the industrialization of continental Europe and the unification of Germany. It was no accident that the first railway in Germany, the Ludwigsbahn, was built in 1835 to link Nuremberg to Fürth.[21] The little town on the banks of the Rednitz sprang into life as one of the hubs of South German manufacturing. Fürth became famous for the mirrors made by companies like S. Bendit & Söhne, as well as for spectacles and other optical instruments. Bronze goods, wooden furniture, gold leaf decoration, toys, and pens: Fürth made them all, often for export to the United States. Its breweries, too, were renowned throughout South Germany. This was scarcely mass production. Most firms were small, with 84 percent of them employing fewer than five people at the turn of the century. The technology was relatively primitive and working conditions—especially in the mercury-intensive mirror industry—often hazardous. Still, there was no mistaking the dynamism of the place. Its population quintupled between 1819 and 1910, from 12,769 to 66,553.

Travelers in search of picturesque Bavarian vistas found Fürth an eyesore. On their way to Nuremberg, the British artist Arthur George Bell and his wife approached Fürth by rail in the early 1900s. They, too, were struck by the contrast between town and country:

> The fields and pastures, the vineyards and hops plantations, undivided by hedges, are enlivened with groups of peasants. Men, women, and children, all equally hard at work, are to be seen toiling in primitive fashion with clumsy agricultural instruments, such as the hand-sickle, long since abandoned elsewhere, and it is no unusual thing for a threshing machine,

drawn by a pair of cows or oxen, to creep slowly along whilst the driver trudges, half asleep, beside it. . . .

As the train nears Fürth[, however], the premonition of the approaching destruction of all that is primitive and rural becomes ever more accentuated, and it is through a heavy pall of smoke, between rows of unsightly houses, that the final stage of the journey is performed.[22]

Fürth, in short, was an ugly, smoggy agglomeration of sweatshops, a modern excrescence in an otherwise picturesque kingdom.

Yet even Fürth retained some vestiges of the medieval past. At the end of September each year the townsfolk celebrated (as they still do) the St. Michael's Festival (Michaeliskirchweih or "Kärwa" in local dialect), a twelve-day carnival dating back to the construction of the St. Michael's church around 1100. The town also had its own mystery play derived from the legend of Saint George, in which the mayor's daughter was rescued from the local dragon by a plucky peasant lad named Udo.[23] Despite such quaint customs, Fürth was in fact a staunchly Protestant town, like most of Franconia. More than two-thirds of the population were Lutheran, and like most nineteenth-century Protestant towns on both sides of the Atlantic, the Fürthers had a rich secular associational life. At the turn of the century the town had around 280 associations, ranging from the singing groups to stamp collectors.[24] In 1902 a new town theater had opened its doors, funded entirely by 382 private subscriptions. As a cultural center, Fürth was no match for Nuremberg, but it could at least hire its own Meistersinger: their inaugural performance was of Beethoven's *Fidelio*.[25] However, opera was not the Fürthers' favorite pastime. That was without doubt soccer. The Spielvereinigung Fürth was founded in 1906 and won its first national title just eight years later under an English coach named William Townley. Here, too, Fürth had to contend with its bigger and grander neighbor. In 1920 the two teams met in the championship final (Fürth lost). Four years later the German national side was made up exclusively of Fürth and Nuremberg players, though the rivalry between the two clubs was so intense that the players traveled in separate rail coaches.

Soccer was and remains a working-class sport, and its popularity in

Fürth from the early 1900s showed how industry was changing the town. The same was true in politics. Already at the time of the 1848 Revolutions, Fürth had acquired a reputation as a "nest of Democrats" (a term then connoting political radicalism). Fürthers were also active in the formation of the new Bavarian Progressive Party (Fortschrittspartei), founded in 1863. Five years later the Fürth socialist Gabriel Löwenstein established the workers' association "Future" (Zukunft), which soon became part of the nationwide German Social Democratic Party (SPD). In the 1870s the SPD could win the Erlangen-Fürth district only by joining forces with the left-liberal People's Party.[26] But by the 1890s the Social Democrats commanded a plurality of votes in Reichstag elections; only a united front of "bourgeois parties" in the second round of voting kept the SPD candidate out, so that it was not until 1912 that "Red Fürth" sent a Social Democrat deputy to the Reichstag.[27]

The town acquired its red reputation for two distinct reasons. The first and more obvious was the large concentration of skilled and usually unionized workers in the town's manufacturing industry. The second, however, was the large proportion of Jews in the population. To be sure, not all of Fürth's Jews were men of the left like Löwenstein. But enough were to make the elision of socialism and Judaism a plausible rhetorical trope with the increasingly numerous demagogues of the German right.

III

There had been a Jewish community in Fürth since 1528. Thirty years before, Nuremberg had followed the example of many other European cities and states by expelling Jews from its territory. But Fürth offered a refuge. Indeed, by the late sixteenth century Jews were being encouraged to settle there as a way of diverting trade away from Nuremberg.[28] Already by the early 1600s Fürth had its own rabbi, a Talmudic academy, and its first synagogue, built in 1616–17 and modeled on the Pinkas synagogue in Prague. Rabbi Schabbatai Scheftel Horowitz, who lived there between 1628 and 1632, praised "the sacred community of Fürth, a small city but one which appeared to me to be as great as Antioch because here erudite people were gathered together for daily study."[29] The Thirty Years' War was a perilous time for Jews in Germany, but the Fürth community got off lightly, apart from some damage to the synagogue when it was used by a Croatian cavalry regiment as stables.[30] Two new synagogues were built in the 1690s: the Klaus and the Mannheimer. By the early nineteenth century the town had seven in all, four of which were grouped around the Schulhof, along with the congregational offices, ritual bathhouse, and kosher butcher. The Jewish population by this time accounted for just under a fifth of the population of Fürth, though that proportion would subsequently decline (to just 4 percent by 1910) as the town expanded. At its numerical peak in 1880, the Jewish community numbered 3,300, making it the third largest in Bavaria, after Munich and Nuremberg, and the eleventh largest in Germany.[31]

In many ways, the Jews of Fürth were tightly knit. In the 1920s, for example, more than two-thirds of them were concentrated in just fifteen of the town's sixty-five voting districts. A Jewish home could be distinguished by the *mezuzah* on the door—a small metal case containing a parchment and bearing the Hebrew letter "shin" (ש), short for *Shaddai,* a name for God. To be sure, it was an overwhelmingly middle-class population of businessmen, professionals, and civil servants, who were economically highly integrated into the gentile society that surrounded them. But they remained socially and culturally distinct, with their own network of associations: the Bikkur Cholim (health insurance union), the three Chewra Kaddischa (burial societies), the Hachnassat Kalla (dowry association), the Hachnassat Orchim (association for innkeepers), and the Bar Kochba (sports club).[32] With good reason the nineteenth-century satirist Moritz Gottlieb Saphir could call Fürth "the Bavarian Jerusalem."

Yet in one crucial respect the Jewish community of Fürth was divided: between a Reform or liberal minority and an Orthodox majority. Proponents of Reform, like Isaak Loewi, who became chief rabbi in 1831, wished (among other things) that Jewish worship should conform more to the style of Christian worship. Under his influence, the main synagogue was given a more churchlike layout, with standing desks replaced by pews and the addition of an organ in 1873; worshippers no longer wore the *tallit*.[33] These changes were part of a wave of assimilation among German Jews, who sought to efface the outward differences between themselves and German Christians in the hope of thereby achieving full equality before the law. A few Jews went even further, either converting to Christianity or embracing the radical skepticism of the political left. But the majority of Fürth Jews reacted against the Reform movement. Thus, while the liberal congregation controlled the main synagogue, the other smaller synagogues around the Schulhof were the domain of Orthodoxy. The division extended into the realm of education. The children of Reform Jews attended the public Gymnasium or the Girls' Lyceum, along with their gentile contemporaries, while the children of Orthodox families were sent to the Jewish High School (*Realschule*) at 31 Blumenstrasse, where there were no Saturday lessons.[34]

To an extent that is often forgotten, Jewish assimilation succeeded in pre-1914 Germany. Formally, to be sure, there remained restrictions. The Bavarian *Judenedikt* of 1813 had granted Jews Bavarian citizenship but had set a limit on their numbers in any one place—which explains the stagnation of the Fürth community in the mid-nineteenth century and its absolute decline after 1880. That statute remained in force until 1920, despite a brief period of relaxation after the 1848 Revolutions.[35] Yet in practice the Jews of Fürth had ceased to be second-class citizens by 1900 at the latest. Not only could they vote in local, state, and national elections; they could also serve as magistrates. They played leading roles in the local legal, medical, and teaching professions. As one Fürth Jew recalled, his hometown produced "the first Jewish attorney, the first Jewish deputy to the Bavarian diet, the first Jewish judge in Bavaria, the first Jewish headmaster."[36] Among the distinguished products of the community were the publisher Leopold Ullstein, born in Fürth in 1826, who by the time of his death in 1899 was one of Germany's leading newspaper proprietors. In 1906 another luminary, the pencil manufacturer Heinrich Berolzheimer, bequeathed to the town the Berolzheimerianum as a "home for popular education" to "serve the whole population . . . regardless of social class, religion or political opinions." This building, with its large public library and auditorium, symbolized the apogee of South German–Jewish integration.

Yet there was always a seed of doubt. The author Jakob Wassermann was born in Fürth in 1873, the son of an unsuccessful businessman. Looking back on his unhappy childhood in a memoir published in 1921, Wassermann recalled how the mid-nineteenth-century restrictions "like those on numbers, on freedom of movement and on occupation . . . [had] provided constant nourishment for sinister religious fanaticism, for ghetto obstinacy and ghetto fear."[37] Admittedly, those restrictions had ceased to operate by the time of his youth, so much so that his father would exclaim contentedly, "We live in an age of tolerance!"

> As far as clothing, language and mode of life were concerned, adaptation was complete. I attended a public government school. We lived among Christians, associated with Christians. The progressive Jews, of whom my father was one, felt that the Jewish community existed only in the sense of religious worship and tradition. Religious worship, fleeing the seductive power of modern life, became concentrated more and more in secret, unworldly groups of zealots. Tradition became a legend, and finally degenerated into mere phrases, an empty shell.[38]

Wassermann's recollections need to be read with caution. He was doubly an outsider, an autodidact atheist who despised his father's mechanical observance, and a lover of German literature who felt the tiniest hint of racial prejudice as a personal affront. Yet his account of the religious and social life of the Fürth Jews is unmatched and illuminating. "Religion was a study," he recalled "and not a pleasant one. A lesson taught soullessly by a soulless old man. Even today I sometimes see his evil, conceited old face in my dreams. . . . [He] thrashed formulas into us, antiquated Hebrew prayers that we translated mechanically, without any actual knowledge of the language; what he taught was paltry, dead, mummified."

> Religious services were even worse. A purely business-like affair, an unsanctified assembly, the noisy performance of ceremonies become habitual, devoid of symbolism, mere drill. . . . The conservative and orthodox Jews conducted their services in

the so-called shuls, tiny places of worship, often only little rooms in obscure, out-of-the-way alleys. There one could still see heads and figures such as Rembrandt drew, fanatic faces, ascetic eyes burning with the memory of unforgotten persecutions.[39]

When the young Wassermann expressed interest in the works of Spinoza, he was warned, "in a tone of sibylline gloom, that whoever read these books must become insane."[40]

Wassermann rightly saw through the facade of assimilation. One night the family's Christian housemaid took him in her arms and said, "You could be a good Christian, you have a Christian heart." Her words frightened the boy "because they contained a tacit condemnation of being Jewish."[41] He sensed the same ambivalence in the families of his gentile playmates: "In childhood my brothers and sisters and I were so closely bound up with the daily life of our Christian neighbors of the working and middle classes that we had our playmates there, our protectors. . . . But watchfulness and a feeling of strangeness persisted. I was only a guest."[42]

To live as a Jew in Fürth was to grow accustomed to things Wassermann found intolerable: "A sneering appellation in the street, a venomous glance, a scornfully appraising look, a certain recurrent contempt—all this was the usual thing."[43] What was worse was to discover that such attitudes were not peculiar to Fürth. As a conscript in the Bavarian army, Wassermann also encountered

that dull, rigid, almost mute hatred that has penetrated the national organism. The word *anti-Semitism* does not serve to describe it. . . . It contains elements of superstition and voluntary delusion, of fanatic terror and priest-inspired callousness, of ignorance and rancor of him who is wronged and betrayed, of unscrupulousness and falsehood as well as of an excusable weapon of self-defense, of apish malice as well as of religious bigotry. Greed and curiosity are involved here, bloodthirstiness and the fear of being lured or seduced, love of mystery and scanty self-esteem. In its constituents and background it is a peculiarly German phenomenon. It is a German hatred.[44]

Wassermann was once asked by a foreigner, "What is the reason for the German hatred of the Jews? . . . What do the Germans want?" His reply was striking.

> I should have answered: Hate. . . .
>
> I should have answered: They want a scapegoat. . . .
>
> But what I did say was: A non-German cannot possibly imagine the heartbreaking position of the German Jew. German Jew—you must place full emphasis on both words. You must understand them as the final product of a lengthy evolutionary process. His twofold love and his struggle on two fronts drive him close to the brink of despair. The German and the Jew: I once dreamt an allegorical dream. . . . I placed the surfaces of two mirrors together; and I felt as if the human images contained and preserved in the two mirrors would have to fight one another tooth and nail.[45]

These words were published in 1921, just two years before the birth of Henry Kissinger. Idiosyncratic Wassermann may have been—an exemplar, some would say, of Jewish "self-hatred"—but his anatomy of German-Jewish melancholy was darkly prophetic.[46]

IV

The Kissingers descended from Meyer Löb (1767–1838), a Jewish teacher from Kleineibstadt who in 1817 took his surname from his adopted home of Bad Kissingen (complying with an 1813 Bavarian edict that required Jews to have surnames).[47] By his first wife he had two children, Isak and Löb, but she died giving birth to the latter in May 1812. Meyer Löb then married her sister, Schoenlein. Of their ten children, only one—Abraham Kissinger (1818–99)—had issue. The descendants of Isak and Löb Kissinger were tailors; the descendants of Abraham were teachers.[48] Abraham himself was a successful weaver and merchant. He and his wife, Fanny Stern, had nine children in all, including four sons, Joseph, Maier, Simon, and David (1860–1947), all of whom became rabbis. David Kissinger taught religion to the Jewish community of Ermershausen, a village on the Bavarian-Thuringian border. On August 3, 1884, he married Karoline (Lina) Zeilberger (1863–1906), the daughter of a prosperous farmer, who provided her with a ten-thousand-mark dowry.[49] They had eight children: Jenny (who died aged six in 1901), Louis (born on February 2, 1887), Ida (born in 1888), Fanny (1892), Karl (1898), Arno (1901), Selma and Simon.[50]

Louis Kissinger's youth was an advertisement for what an intelligent, hardworking Jewish boy could achieve in imperial Germany. At the age of eighteen—without even a diploma, much less a university degree—he embarked on a teaching career. His first job was in Fürth, at the private Heckmannschule for (mainly Jewish) boys, where he was paid 1,000 marks per annum, plus 255 per month for health and old age insurance, to teach German, arithmetic, and science for four hours a day. He remained at the post for fourteen years.[51] Despite formally becoming a citizen of Fürth in 1917,[52] he seems to have contemplated moving, applying for posts in northern Bavaria and Upper Silesia, but he declined these jobs when offered them. Instead, at the age of thirty, he opted belatedly to sit his school-leaving examination—the *Reifeprüfung*—at the Fürth Realgymnasium, the town's senior boys' school. Equipped with his diploma, he was able to attend courses at Erlangen University. More important, he was able to apply for a more prestigious post at one of Fürth's public schools: the senior girls' school known today as the Helene-Lange-Gymnasium. With his appointment as *Hauptlehrer* (literally "chief teacher") in 1921, Louis Kissinger became in effect a senior civil servant. Though he continued to teach arithmetic and science—and appears also to have given occasional instruction at the town's business school (*Handelsschule*)[53]—his preferred subject was German literature. "Kissus," as the girls nicknamed him, was not a strict teacher. He enjoyed introducing his pupils to classics of German poetry like Goethe's "Der Adler und die Taube" ("The Eagle and the Dove") and Heinrich Heine's "Jetzt wohin?" ("Now where?"). The latter would later acquire a painful personal significance. In the poem, written in the wake of the 1848 Revolutions, the exile Heine wonders where he should go if he faces a death sentence in his German homeland.

Where to now? My foolish feet
To Germany would gladly go
But my wiser head is shaking
And seems to tell me "No":

The war may well be over,
But martial law is still in force. . . .

I sometimes get to thinking
To America I should sail,
To the stable yard of freedom
Whence egalitarians hail.

But I'm fearful of a country
Where the people chew tobacco
Where they bowl without a monarch
Where they spit without spittoons.

Louis Kissinger surely shared Heine's preference for the land of his birth. Like Heine, he felt as much a German as a Jew.

That Louis Kissinger was a German patriot is not in doubt. He was a member of the national association expressly set up to represent "German citizens of the Jewish faith" (the Centralverein deutscher Staatsbürger jüdischen Glaubens).[54] Unlike the majority of German men of his generation, he did not fight in the First World War, but this was for health reasons.[55] Other members of the Kissinger family are known to have served in the Bavarian army, which was notably friendlier toward Jews than its larger Prussian counterpart, Jakob Wassermann's experiences notwithstanding. Louis's brother Karl saw active service; his future father-in-law, as we shall see, was also called up. Two of his cousins lost their lives in the war.[56] To many German Jews of that era, there was no better proof of their commitment to the Reich than this sacrifice. The claim that Jews were underrepresented on the front lines and in the casualty lists was angrily rebutted by patriotic organizations like the one to which Louis Kissinger belonged. Unlike some of his contemporaries, however, Louis felt under no pressure to dilute his religious faith as proof of his patriotism. He adhered firmly to the Orthodox part of the Fürth community, attending the Neuschul synagogue presided over by Rabbi Yehuda Leib (Leo) Breslauer, rather than the rival Reform congregation of Rabbi Siegfried Behrens. Like Breslauer (and unlike his brother Karl), Louis was uneasy about the Zionist movement, which called on the Jews to establish their own nation-state in Palestine—an idea that was proving especially attractive to Bavarian Jews.[57] As his wife later recalled, "He [Louis] knew about [the Zionist leader Theodor] Herzl and everything. He knew but he was never [convinced]. . . . He was deeply religious but like a child, he believed everything . . . and he studied Zionism but he couldn't accept it. He felt so German."[58]

Paula Kissinger—the woman who spoke those words—was born thirty-five miles to the west of Fürth in the village of Leutershausen, on February 24, 1901. Her father, Falk Stern, was a prosperous farmer and cattle dealer and a pillar of the local Jewish community, serving as its chairman (Vorsitzender) for fifteen years. Three years after his daughter's birth, Falk and his brother David pooled their resources to buy the imposing house that still stands at number 8 Am Markt. Paula was brought up in an Orthodox household, learning to read Hebrew fluently and always eating at home in order to keep kosher. As in Fürth, however, religious separation did not imply social segregation. Paula's closest childhood friend was a Protestant girl named Babette "Babby" Hammerder. "You never saw or felt any anti-Semitism 'til Hitler came," Paula later recalled. "In fact, they sought you out, they looked for you, they wanted you."[59] Paula was just twelve when her mother, Peppi, died. A bright girl, she was sent by her grieving father to the girls' school in Fürth, where she lived with her aunt, Berta Fleischmann, whose husband ran the kosher butcher's in the Hirschenstrasse.

Despite being a widower in his mid-forties, Falk Stern was drafted in June 1915 and served in the infantry in Belgium until his discharge eleven months later. On his return from the front, Paula was summoned back to Leutershausen to keep house for her father and uncle. "I was eighteen," she later remembered, "and . . . terribly lonesome in that small town, which had no intellectual [life] . . . nothing to keep your mind busy. I had to go to the next town to get books from the library."

She already dreamed of going to "faraway places" like Capri, but instead she was confined to the kitchen. "My aunt . . . taught me how to cook and I hated it. I wanted to read, and when she came I was sitting there and reading instead of doing my work."[60] Escape came when her father married Fanny Walter in April 1918. Not long after that, Paula took a job as an au pair in Halberstadt in North Germany, where she looked after the four children of a wealthy Jewish metal manufacturer. It was not quite Capri, but the family's summer villa in the Harz Mountains was an improvement over the kitchen in Leutershausen. It was on a visit to her relatives in Fürth that Paula was introduced to the new teacher at her old school. Though Louis Kissinger was fourteen years her elder, they fell in love. In December 1921 they became engaged. Eight months later, on July 28, 1922, they were married.

Louis and Paula Kissinger married amid a revolution no less violent than the one that had driven his favorite poet Heine into exile ninety years before. Even before the formal armistice ended the First World War, the imperial regime had been toppled by the revolutionary wave that swept through Germany. On November 9, 1918, Fürth came briefly under the control of a Workers' and Soldiers' Council; the red flag flew high above the town hall. In April 1919 the revolutionaries sought to align themselves with the Munich "revolutionary central council," set up in imitation of the Soviets in Russia. But as elsewhere in Germany, the Fürth Social Democrats repudiated the Bolshevik model and within just four days the city authorities (the Magistrat and the Kollegium der Gemeindebevollmächtigten) were restored to power.[61] The revolution did not end there, however. In every year between 1919 and 1923, there was at least one attempt from either the left or the right to overthrow the new Weimar Republic (named after the Thuringian town where its constitution was drafted). Political violence was accompanied by economic insecurity. Intent on proving the unsustainability of the reparations debt imposed on Germany under the Versailles Treaty, Weimar's ministers pursued a conscious policy of deficit finance and money printing. The short-term benefit was to boost investment, employment, and exports. The long-term cost was a disastrous hyper-inflation that inflicted permanent damage on the financial system, the social order, and the political legitimacy of the republic. On the eve of the First World War, the exchange rate of the German mark had been fixed, under the gold standard, at 4.20 marks to the dollar. By Sunday, May 27, 1923—the day of Heinz Kissinger's birth[62]—a dollar bought nearly 59,000 paper marks. The annual inflation rate was approaching 10,000 percent. By the end of the year the rate was 182 billion percent. A paper mark was worth precisely one trillionth of a prewar mark.

Needless to say, the Kissingers' newborn baby was oblivious to all this, but he was not unaffected by it. For no social group was harder hit by the inflation than higher civil servants like Louis Kissinger. Workers were able at least partly to protect themselves against spiraling prices by striking for higher wages. A respectable schoolmaster could do no such thing. In the postwar years, unskilled workers' wages initially held up in real terms, finally falling by around 30 percent in the collapse of 1922–23. By contrast, when adjusted for inflation, a civil servant's salary fell by between 60 and 70 percent. At the same time, the cash savings of middle-class families like the Kissingers were wiped out. In the great leveling produced by the Weimar hyperinflation, men like Louis Kissinger were among the biggest losers. It was not until January 1925 that he could afford to move his growing family from their cramped first-floor apartment at 23 Mathildenstrasse to nearby 5 Marienstrasse, where Heinz's brother, Walter, was born.

V

Henry Kissinger once joked that if it hadn't been for Hitler, he might have spent his life "quietly as a *Studienrat* in Nuremberg." In fact, as a boy he did not seem very likely to follow in his studious father's footsteps. When they were first sent to kindergarten, their mother later recalled, he and his brother "hated it and . . . were terribly naughty and hard to handle. . . . They would run away and I had to find them."[63] Later, the two attended the old Heckmann private school, where his father had first taught: a photograph from 1931 shows Heinz with his teacher, a man named Merz, and eight other students (five of whom are identified as Jewish).[64] Contemporaries later differed about Heinz Kissinger's academic ability as a boy. Menahem (formerly Heinz) Lion, who ended up living in Israel, later admitted to having been "envious of his essays. . . . They were remarkable for their form, their style, and their ideas, and they were often read out to the class."[65] But others remembered him as an "average" pupil at school.[66] Shimon Eldad, who taught him English and French when he attended the Jewish High School, recalled a "good but not outstanding student. . . . He was a spirited and scintillating youth, but I didn't notice anything special in him. His English didn't exactly excite me, and it seems that way still today."[67]

It seems clear that the Kissinger brothers were brought up in a fairly strict Orthodox household. Menahem Lion remembered going "together to synagogue every morning before school. On Saturdays Lion's father taught them both the Torah. They attended an Orthodox youth club, Ezra, together."[68] Tzipora Jochsberger had similar memories.[69] A cousin, John Heiman, who came to live with the family when Kissinger was seven, later described

> one Saturday when he and Henry took a stroll beyond the *eruv,* a sort of understood boundary encircling [the Jewish community]. Outside the *eruv,* under the teachings of their religion, Orthodox Jews were not permitted to carry anything in their hands or in their pockets. . . . [W]hen he and Kissinger crossed the boundary, Henry stopped and reminded him that "carrying" was forbidden. They took their handkerchiefs from their pockets and tied them to their wrists.[70]

Yet as he grew into a teenager, Heinz Kissinger increasingly rebelled against his parents' way of life. Their idea of entertainment was to hear *Fidelio* at the Fürth Theater. For pleasure, Louis Kissinger read the great works of Friedrich Schiller and Theodor Mommsen and even researched and wrote local history. Heinz's passion, by contrast, was for soccer.[71]

The Spielvereinigung in those days was a team worth following. They were German champions in 1926 and 1929—beating Hertha BSC Berlin in the final on both occasions—and got as far as the semifinals in 1923 and 1931. In the same period, they also won the South German Cup four times. The Fürth-Nuremberg rivalry had the intense quality of other neighborly feuds in European soccer, such as Rangers-Celtic in

Glasgow. Heinz Kissinger was soon an ardent Fürth fan. As he later recollected,

> Fürth was to soccer as Green Bay was to [American] football.
> It was a small town . . . that in a ten-year period won three
> German championships. . . . I started playing when I was about
> six. My grandfather had a farm [at Leutershausen] near Fürth,
> and they had a big courtyard and we played pickup games
> there. I played goalie for a brief period, then I broke my hand.
> After that, I played inside-right and then mid-field. I played
> until I was fifteen. I really wasn't very good though I took the
> game very seriously.

Though no great athlete, Heinz Kissinger was already a shrewd tactician, devising for his team "a system that, as it turned out, is the way the Italians play soccer. . . . The system was to drive the other team nuts by not letting them score, by keeping so many people back as defenders. . . . It's very hard to score when ten players are lined up in front of the goal."[72] So ardent did his soccer mania become that for a time his parents banned him from attending Fürth fixtures.

Soccer was not the only passion that brought Heinz Kissinger into conflict with his parents. As his boyhood friend remembered,

> Heinz Kissinger spent many hours in my home. They lived
> near us and Heinz would ride over on his bike. He liked being
> with us. It seems to me he had a problem with his father. If
> I'm not mistaken, he was afraid of him because he was a very
> pedantic man. . . . His father was always checking Heinz's
> homework, and kept a close watch on him. Heinz told me
> more than once he couldn't discuss anything with his father,
> especially not girls.

As Lion later related, "the only time that Kissinger brought home a less than satisfactory report card was when he started paying attention to girls—or girls started paying attention to him. He was only twelve at the time and the girls were already chasing after him, but he didn't pay any attention to them. His first love was a charming blonde." According to Lion, the two boys used to take girlfriends for walks in the local park on Friday evenings. When Lion returned late from one of these walks, his parents blamed Kissinger's influence and forbade their son to see "the Kissinger boy" for a whole week. Later they sent Lion off to a summer camp for six weeks "to get him away from Heinz Kissinger, who had earned a reputation as a skirt chaser."[73] Memory plays tricks, and this story had probably improved in the telling over thirty years. Still, even Kissinger's mother noted her elder son's penchant for "keeping everything locked up inside—never discussing your innermost thoughts!"[74] Corporal punishment was not unknown in the Kissinger household, as in most households of the time.[75] It paid to keep mischief quiet.

VI

Ball games, bicycles, girlfriends, and summer vacations at Granddad's house;[76] at first glance, Heinz Kissinger's childhood was not much different from what he might have experienced growing up in the United States. And yet the bright and rebellious boy can scarcely have been oblivious to the dramatic changes going on around him as Germany lurched from depression to dictatorship—especially as the principal scapegoat for the country's misfortunes was the religious minority to which he belonged.

Why was it that the assimilation of the German Jews, which appeared to have been so successful prior to 1914, was so dramatically reversed thereafter, culminating in their near annihilation? There are few more difficult questions in history. One argument—which was Jakob Wassermann's—is that assimilation was never complete and that there always remained a strain of exceptionally aggressive anti-Semitism in German culture. Another is that we should understand the surge of support for anti-Semitic policies as a backlash against assimilation, precipitated in large measure by economic crisis. It is surely no coincidence that the high points of electoral support for anti-Semitic parties came immediately after the hyperinflation of 1922–23 and the depression of 1929–32. Jews were in relative terms the most successful ethnic group in Germany: they were less than 1 percent of the population but had significantly more than 1 percent of the wealth. Moreover, territorial and political changes to the east of Germany led to an influx of so-called *Ostjuden,* who attracted public disapprobation precisely because they were not assimilated.[77] The virulently anti-Semitic magazine *Der Stürmer* began weekly publication in Nuremberg in April 1923, the month before Heinz Kissinger's birth. The front-page masthead for each issue read simply "The Jews Are Our Misfortune." Even before the Nazis came to power, steps were already being taken in Bavaria to restrict the rights of Jews, notably the 1929 vote by the Bavarian *Landtag* to ban ritual slaughter by Jewish butchers.[78]

To some extent, the Jews of Fürth could comfort themselves that their gentile neighbors were ideologically hostile to National Socialism. When the various far-right organizations held a special "German Day" in Nuremberg on September 1–2, 1923, those attending were given short shrift if they passed through Fürth, where people wearing swastika insignia found themselves being asked to remove them or risk having them torn off. As they arrived at Fürth railway station, one group of brownshirts from Munich were assailed by a hundred-strong crowd chanting "Down with Reaction!," "Kill them!," and "Down with Hitler!" When the SA (Sturmabteilung) men started to sing the *Erhardtlied,* an early Nazi favorite, the crowd retorted with the *Internationale* and shouts of "Heil Moskau!"[79] When a branch of the National Socialist German Workers' Party (NSDAP) was established in Fürth shortly after the "German Day," only 170 people joined.[80] And when the party tried to hold a meeting in Fürth on February 3, 1924, the event ended in chaos when the speaker was forced to flee by Communist hecklers. True, the far-right Völkische Bloc did well in the May 1924 national elections, winning over 25 percent of the Fürth vote, compared with just 6.5 percent at the national level. But it did much less well when elections were held again seven months later, slumping to just 8 percent of votes cast. As in Germany as a whole, it was splinter parties like the Economic Party that flourished in the relatively stable economic conditions of the mid-1920s. When the Nazis held a rally in Fürth in September 1925, they fielded a star-studded cast of speakers, including Hitler himself and Julius Streicher, the editor of *Der Stürmer.* They hoped to fill the Geismann Hall, one of the town's biggest venues, but less than a third of the expected fifteen thousand people turned up. The local party leader Albert Forster—later the gauleiter of Danzig—ruefully welcomed Hitler to the "citadel of the Jews" (*Hochburg der Juden*). Hitler responded with a speech lamenting the fact that Germans had become "slaves of Jewry" ("*Sklaven . . . für das Judentum*").[81] Nazi Party membership in Fürth was down to 200 by 1927. Visits by Hitler in March 1928 and Streicher a year later did nothing to stop the rot. The party's share of the local vote sank to just 6.6 percent in the elections of May 1928.

In Fürth, as in the rest of Germany, it was the Depression that saved Hitler's movement. The entire period from 1914 to 1933 was an economic disaster for Fürth because the town's economy was so heavily reliant on exports. Even in the period of relative prosperity between 1924 and 1928, unemployment remained very high—above 6,000 at the beginning of 1927, though things improved in the course of the year as the prospects of the brewing and building industries seemed to brighten. But then conditions began to deteriorate again. At the end of June 1929 there were 3,286 workers receiving one of three forms of welfare available to the unemployed. By February 1930 that number had soared above 8,000. By the end of January 1932 it reached a peak of 14,558. In effect, half of all the workers in Fürth were out of a job. Employment in the once buoyant mirror industry had slumped from around 5,000 to just 1,000. Toy exports had collapsed.[82] It was not only workers who were affected but small businessmen, too. By October 1932, 185 formerly independent craftsmen were reliant on public welfare. But welfare payments were so modest that many people were reduced to begging and to petty crime.[83]

The causes of the Great Depression continue to be hotly debated. Certainly, a large part of the explanation lies in the policy errors made in the United States during the period. The Federal Reserve first allowed a stock market bubble to inflate by keeping monetary conditions too loose, then allowed the banking system to implode by keeping monetary conditions too tight. Congress increased already high protectionist tariffs. Not until 1933 did the federal government respond to the crisis with anything resembling fiscal stimulus. There was also a complete breakdown in international policy coordination. The large public debts incurred during and after the First World War might have been rationally restructured; instead there were moratoriums and defaults after austerity policies had failed. The Germans made matters worse for themselves by creating a welfare state they could not afford, allowing the trade unions to drive real wages up, and tolerating anti-competitive practices in their industries. But forces were at work beyond the influence of any policy maker. Despite the war, there was an oversupply of young men. Because of the war, there was overcapacity in agriculture, iron, and steel and shipbuilding.

None of this was remotely intelligible to the unemployed and impoverished people living in a provincial Franconian industrial town. The challenge is to explain why, of all the explanations offered to them for the crisis, Adolf Hitler's was the one they ended up embracing. The big breakthrough for the Nazis came in the Reichstag election of September 14, 1930, which saw their share of the national vote rise from 2.6 to 18.3 percent. In Fürth they won 23.6 percent of votes cast, up fourfold from 1928. This was the beginning of a sustained ascent. Hitler won 34 percent of the Fürth vote in the first round of the 1932 presidential election. In the Bavarian *Landtag* elections, the Nazis' share of the vote rose to 37.7, exceeding the Social Democrats' for the first time. In the Reichstag election of July 31, 1932, the Nazis won 38.7 percent of the vote. They lost ground in the election of November 6, 1932, but then surged to 44.8 percent of the Fürth vote in the election of March 5, 1933. In that election, more than 22,000 Fürthers voted Nazi (see table).

THE NAZI VOTE IN FÜRTH AND GERMANY[84]

	NAZI VOTES	SHARE OF FÜRTH TOTAL	NAZI SHARE OF REICH TOTAL
May 4, 1924	9,612	25.6	6.5
December 7, 1924	3,045	8.2	3.0
May 20, 1928	2,725	6.6	2.6
September 14, 1930	10,872	23.6	18.3
July 31, 1932	17,853	38.7	37.3
November 6, 1932	16,469	35.6	33.1
March 5, 1933	22,458	44.8	43.9

As at the national level, the Nazis won votes disproportionately from the old "bourgeois parties": the National People's Party, the People's Party, and the Democratic Party. Defections from the Social Democrats, Communists, and Catholic Center Party were more rare. This transfer of allegiance was in many ways led or mediated by economic splinter groups like the German Nationalist Clerical Workers' Association and conservative organizations like the monarchist Royal Bavarian Homeland League, the "Faithful to Fürth" society, and veterans' associations like the Kyffhäuser League.[85] Typical of the proto-Nazi associations that flourished in South Germany in the Weimar period was Young Bavaria, which proudly proclaimed its rejection of "the exclusive rule of pure reason, a legacy of the French Revolution."[86] An equally important factor was the strongly "German national" tone of some Protestant clergy, which echoed the often explicitly religious language of some Nazi propaganda.[87] For the historian Walter Frank, born in Fürth in 1905 and already an ardent German nationalist in his teens, the transition from his father's German Nationalist milieu to the National Socialists was easy. He was among many academic overachievers who gravitated toward the Nazis at this time; Ludwig Erhard, another talented Fürther of the same generation, was unusual in being immune to their charm without being a socialist.[88]

The remarkable thing is that all these socially respectable groups ended up giving their votes to a movement that systematically used violence as an electoral tactic and explicitly advocated it as a governmental strategy. Part of the explanation is simply that the Nazis ran more effective campaigns than their rivals. First, NSDAP membership in Fürth rose from 185 in March 1930 to 1,500 in August 1932. The new recruits worked hard for their party. After police restrictions were lifted in early 1932, the party held almost weekly events in Fürth, organizing no fewer than twenty-six meetings in the two weeks before the first election of that year.[89] In the run-up to the second election of 1932, the Nazis held eight major election meetings and almost nightly "evening discussions" (*Sprechabende*). But violence also played a crucial role.

That the streets of Fürth became increasingly dangerous was not entirely the Nazis' fault. On the left, the Communist Party (KPD) and socialist organizations like the Reichsbanner also liked to stage rowdy demonstrations and to disrupt the meetings of their political opponents. As in the 1920s, the Nazis found much of Fürth to be hostile territory. On April 9, 1932, fifteen SA men were set upon by Iron Front members as they left the pro-Nazi Yellow Lion pub. Two months later Nazi supporter Fritz Reingruber was beaten up for being a "Swastikist"; the same fate befell another Nazi caught selling the NSDAP newspaper, the *Völkische Beobachter*.[90] The police watched helplessly on the evening of July 30 as a mob threw potatoes and stones at a Nazi motorcade going from Fürth airport to the Nuremberg stadium; the car carrying Hitler himself was among the vehicles hit.[91] There was more muted hostility in January 1933 when Sturmabteilung, Schutzstaffel (SS), and Hitler Youth members participated in the town's annual *Fasching* (Mardi Gras) parade. A public meeting in the Geismann Hall ended in yet more violence when KPD members refused to stand for the national anthem.[92]

Fürth was not Chicago. Firearms played no role in the gang warfare between Communists and Nazis. Yet the effect of all this unruly behavior was insidious. At one and the same time, it made people yearn for the old German ideal of "tranquillity and order" (*Ruhe und Ordnung*) and accept that further violence might be necessary as a means to that end. With Hitler's appointment as Reich chancellor on January 31, 1933, the Nazis seized their moment, staging a large torch-lit parade through the town center, from the Kurgartenstrasse through the Nürnbergstrasse and the Königstrasse to Dreikönigsplatz. Now they took the offensive. On the night of February 3, between sixty and seventy SA men attacked the Communist pub Am Gänsberg. After the Reichstag fire at the end of the same month had provided the perfect pretext for emergency legislation "For the Protection of the People and the State," the election of March 1933 could be conducted in a new atmosphere of official intimidation. On March 3 there was another large-scale torch-lit parade through Fürth. On the evening of March 9 a crowd of between ten and twelve thousand people gathered outside the Rathaus to watch the raising of the red Nazi flag together with the reassuring old imperial black, white, and red flag above its tower, and to hear the *Landtag* deputy and Streicher sidekick, Karl Holz, proclaim the "German Revolution." "Today," Holz declared, "marks the beginning of the great clean-up in Bavaria. Out with the black Mamelukes [*sic*].

Even Fürth, which was once red and totally jewified [*verjudet*], will once again be made into a clean and honest German town."[93]

Those words foretold a far graver threat to the Jews of Fürth—including the loyal patriot Louis Kissinger and his family—than even the most pessimistic among them yet understood.

Escape

> If we could go back 13 years over the hatred and the
> intolerance, I would find that it had been a long hard road.
> It had been covered with humiliation, with disappointment.
> —HENRY KISSINGER to his parents, 1945[1]

I

It was late September 1934. On the eve of the annual St. Michael's Festival in Fürth, the town preacher Paul Fronmüller spoke for many when he gave thanks to God "for sending us Adolf Hitler, our rescuer from the alien onslaught of the godless horde, and the builder of the new Reich, in which the Christian religion will be the foundation of our life as a people."[2]

For the majority of Fürth's Christian population, life had already improved after barely eighteen months of Nazi rule, and it continued to get better with scarcely a pause until the summer of 1938. In January 1933 the number of welfare claimants was more than 8,700. By June 1938 it would be down below 1,300.[3] The Nazi economic recovery was real, and Fürth felt it.

The town looked different, too. The Rathaus was bedecked with bright red National Socialist flags; swastikas and portraits of the Führer were becoming ubiquitous. Some street names had also changed. Königswarterstrasse was now "Adolf-Hitler-Strasse"; the main square was renamed Schlageterplatz, after the proto-Nazi "martyr" Albert Leo Schlageter, who—on the eve of Heinz Kissinger's birth—had been executed by the French for sabotaging trains in the occupied Ruhr. True, Fürth had nothing to match the annual Nuremberg rallies, weeklong festivals that attracted up to a million members of the party and affiliated organizations from all over Germany. But there were still at least fourteen official holidays and festivals, like the May 1 "Festival of the People" (appropriated from the Social Democrats' May Day) and the April 20 celebration of Hitler's birthday.[4] And for those who preferred a night at the opera to a street parade, the new director of the reopened and refurbished city theater, Bruno F. Mackay, offered a wholesomely Germanic diet including Goethe's *Egmont,* Schiller's *Kabale und Liebe,* and Lessing's *Minna von Barnhelm.* When Hitler himself paid a visit to Fürth on February 11, 1935, he was treated to a performance of *Wenn Liebe befiehlt* ("When Love Commands"), an innocuous operetta. The echo of the Nazi slogan *Führer befiehl, wir folgen!* ("Führer Command, We'll Follow!") was apt.

Yet behind the good cheer of National Socialist propaganda lay a reality of coercion and terror. What the Nazis euphemistically called "synchronization" (*Gleichschaltung*) began on March 10, 1933, with the arrest of between fifteen and twenty Communist Party, Communist trade union, and Social Democratic officials and the occupation of the Social Democratic trade union headquarters. The left-liberal Lord Mayor (*Oberbürgermeister*) Robert Wild was sent on indefinite leave; his deputy resigned on grounds of age. A week later the purge of left-leaning officials continued with the forced retirement of the chief of police, the director of the city hospital, the chief medical officer, and the head of the health insurance fund. More arrests of Communist activists followed on March 28 and April 25: most were detained in "protective custody" (*Schutzhaft*), another Nazi euphemism, signifying that they had been sent to the newly created penal camp at Dachau, a hundred miles to the south.

Synchronization proceeded relentlessly; each week brought further restrictions on the Nazis' political opponents. The press ceased to be free on April 1, with the announcement that henceforth the *Fürther Anzeiger* would be the "official organ of the NSDAP in the Fürth district." The local council was reconstituted so that a majority of its members were now Nazis, including the new Lord Mayor, Franz Jakob (previously a Nazi deputy in the Bavarian parliament), and his two deputies. The local libraries were also purged with a ceremonial burning of "subversive" books on the night of May 10–11.[5] The next day the Fürth branch of the Social Democratic Party dissolved itself, in advance of the nationwide ban on its activities on June 22. On June 30 the party's leaders in Fürth were arrested and sent to join their Communist counterparts in Dachau. All the old middle-class parties, who had lost so many of their supporters to the Nazis, were either dissolved or merged with the NSDAP. Young Bavaria was absorbed into the Hitler Youth. Similar fates befell all Fürth's independent economic organizations and sporting associations—even the singing and gardening clubs.[6]

From the earliest phase of the National Socialist regime, however, it was the Jews who were targeted for the most relentless persecution. After their leaders had been arrested, the ordinary rank-and-file Communist and Social Democratic voters had the chance to conform and consent. This chance was not given to anyone whom the Nazis defined as Jewish by race, which included converts to Christianity and even the issue of mixed marriages. To understand what it was like to grow up as a Jew in Nazi Germany, it is necessary to grasp the way the regime systematically sliced away the rights of Jews, week after week, month after month. With every passing year between 1933 and 1938, the level of insecurity went up. The experience was especially harrowing in a town like Fürth. Not only had it earned the Nazis' contempt as a "jew-ified" town. It was also next door to Nuremberg, one of the "capitals of the movement" and home of the odious Julius Streicher, editor of *Der Stürmer* and now gauleiter of Middle Franconia. Moreover, Fürth was in Bavaria, where the SA leader Ernst Röhm was state commissar and the *Reichsführer-SS* Heinrich Himmler was in charge of the Political Police. All this meant that anti-Semitic measures and "spontaneous" actions tended to come sooner to Fürth than elsewhere and to be implemented with more zeal.[7]

Readers who have no experience of life in a totalitarian state must struggle to imagine what it is like, in the space of five years, to lose the right to practice one's profession or trade, to use public facilities from swimming pools to schools, and to speak freely; more important, to lose the protection of the law from arbitrary arrest, abuse, assault, and expropriation. This was the fate of the Jews of Germany between 1933 and

1938. In Fürth it began on March 21, 1933, with the suspension and temporary arrest of the director of the town hospital, Dr. Jakob Frank. Two other Jewish doctors and a nurse were also fired. A week later all nine Jewish doctors in Fürth lost their posts.[8] The Nazis then turned their attention to Fürth's large Jewish business community. On March 25 the well-known general store Bauernfreund-Pachmayr was forced to close amid allegations that mouse droppings and animal hair had been found in its food.[9] Six days later a NSDAP demonstration heralded the next day's nationwide boycott of Jewish business, ostensibly in retaliation for the anti-German boycott proposed by some American Jewish organizations. On the morning of April 1, SA men began putting up posters throughout the town center that urged citizens to "Boycott the Jews! Boycott their cronies [*Handlangern*]" and listed all 720 of Fürth's Jewish-owned businesses, which represented at least 50 percent of wholesalers, 24 percent of manufacturers, and 15 percent of retailers— remarkable market shares for less than 4 percent of the population.[10] One especially prominent target of the boycott was the Jewish-owned Fortuna cinema.[11] Next it was the turn of Jewish civil servants— including teachers in public schools like Louis Kissinger—who were ejected from their posts under the April 1933 "Law for the Restoration of the Career Civil Service." Another major legislative milestone were the so-called Nuremberg Laws, drafted at the party's annual gathering in 1935, the first of which—the "Law for the Protection of German Blood and Honor"—prohibited mixed marriages as well as interracial sex and banned Jews from employing non-Jews as domestic servants. The second "Reich Citizenship Law" deprived Jews of full citizenship.

Discrimination against Jews was mandated centrally but enforced and sometimes also extended locally. The segregation of Jews—their exclusion from public spaces—proceeded at different paces from region to region. In Fürth, for example, it was at the height of the summer heat, in August 1933, that Jews were banned from using the public bathing area in the River Rednitz. In April 1934 a ceiling of 1.5 percent was imposed on the proportion of Jewish pupils that could study at public schools. By 1936, however, all the major Fürth schools—the Girls' Lyceum, the Humanistic Gymnasium, the Oberrealschule, and the Commercial School—could proudly proclaim themselves "Jew-free" (*judenrein*). Henceforth all Jewish children had to attend either the Jewish Realschule or the Jewish Volksschule.[12]

As rights were stripped away, so too was dignity. The *Fürther Anzeiger* published a steady stream of anti-Semitic articles in the sneering style of Streicher. The author of one typical story described hearing Jewish schoolchildren singing the German national anthem. "Oh you comical Jew folk," he gloated. "How you must fear the Germany that is now being built."[13] On May 27, 1934, Streicher himself was made an honorary citizen of Fürth. In his acceptance speech, he did not mince his words: "We are heading toward serious times. If another war comes, all the Jews in Franconia will be shot, [because] the Jews were responsible for the [last] war."[14] The annual *Fasching* parade the following year featured a number of grotesquely anti-Semitic floats, with clowns dressed as caricature Jews in various humiliating postures.[15] But anti-Semitism in Bavaria was much more than playacting. Already in 1933 there was more than a hint of physical menace in the way the SA conducted the boycott campaign. Where this might lead became clear on the night of March 25, 1934, when the village of Gunzenhausen, around thirty miles southwest of Fürth, erupted in a pogrom that left two of the local Jewish community dead: one from hanging, the other from stab wounds.[16]

By this time the "national revolution" was threatening to run out of control, to the extent that—in Fürth as elsewhere—the army had to step in to restrain the SA.[17] But even after the so-called Night of the Long Knives (the purge of the SA leadership, including Ernst Röhm, between June 30 and July 2, 1934), the persecution continued, though now with legalistic trappings. Theodor Bergmann, a leading member of the Fürth Jewish community, was arrested for insulting an "Aryan" woman; he committed suicide while in a concentration camp. On March 10, 1935, Dr. Rudolf Benario was arrested and dragged from his sickbed, despite suffering from a high fever. He and Ernst Goldmann were sent to Dachau, where they were both shot—in yet another infamous euphemism—"while trying to escape."[18] A year later three Jewish youths, also from Fürth, were sentenced to twelve, ten, and five months, respectively, for having the audacity to tell "horror stories" (*Greuelnach-*

richten) about the treatment of Jews in Germany.[19] Such grim ironies abounded in Fürth. On November 26, 1937, a seventy-two-year-old Jew from the town was sentenced to eight months in prison for daring to suggest that Jews in Germany were being persecuted. A year later three Fürth Jews were arrested and charged under the Nuremberg Laws with "racial defilement." They received jail sentences of between five and ten years.[20]

II

For Louis Kissinger, the stripping away of his hard-won respectability as a senior staff member at a public high school was a bewildering nightmare. On May 2, 1933, along with *Studienrätin* Hermine Bassfreund, the other Jewish teacher at the Fürth Girls' School, he was "sent on mandatory leave" and then, a few months later, "permanently retired."[21] He was not yet fifty. His son Walter remembered how he "withdrew into his study" after his dismissal.[22] But it was not just the premature termination of his career that shocked Louis. As his wife later recalled, "the colleagues of my husband, the former colleagues, ignored him completely as if he would never have [existed]." To keep himself active, he founded "a school that Jewish children who couldn't go to public schools any more could [attend]. . . . He taught them commercial sciences, which he had taught before."[23] Curiously, he did not move to teach at the Jewish Realschule, where both his sons began studying in the summer of 1933. It is not entirely clear from the existing records why they went there so early—before the Jewish quotas had been imposed on the public schools.[24] According to Kissinger, his parents intended that he should go to the Gymnasium after four years at the Realschule (which would not have been unusual for a boy from an Orthodox family).[25] By that time, however, the quota was in place.

The Realschule, which was just around the corner from the Kissingers' home, was by no means a bad institution. Its director, Fritz Prager, had recruited at least one able teacher, Hermann Mandelbaum, who taught arithmetic, geography, and writing as well as economics and shorthand. Mandelbaum liked to make his pupils squirm with difficult questions. His catchphrase in class was "Who's chattering?" (*Wer schwätzt?*)[26] But Kissinger's mother recalled that "the teachers [at the Realschule] were not of the first grade, and Henry, who was very gifted, was bored. Both [boys] were not happy in school. . . . [T]he children were frustrated, really, and they didn't do their best."[27] Such evidence as survives confirms that Kissinger did not shine there.[28] A further cause of frustration was the way Nazi legislation was excluding the boys from all their favorite extracurricular activities. Barred from public swimming pools, from playing soccer with gentiles, and from watching their beloved Spielvereinigung, the boys had to join the Zionist Bar-Kochba sport association and to use the facilities of the new Jewish Sports Club, founded in October 1936 with its playing fields in the Karolinenstrasse.[29] As Kissinger later remembered,

> Jews were segregated from 1933 on . . . but there was a Jewish team and I played in the junior team. We could only play against the other Jewish teams. . . . During that period . . . watching and participating in sports provided me with relief from the environment. I used to sneak out to catch the local soccer team play, even though, as a Jew, you ran the risk of getting beaten up if you were there and they recognized you.[30]

Not all of Kissinger's contemporaries had memories of street violence. Jules Wallerstein, who attended the same school as the Kissingers, recalled that until 1938, "My friends were Jewish and non-Jewish. We played soldiers, went to each other's homes and made fun of some of the Nazi leaders. My non-Jewish friends never called me foul names or called me a dirty Jew."[31] But others—notably Frank Harris (Franz Hess) and Raphael Hallemann, the son of the director of the Jewish orphanage—confirm Kissinger's account.[32] It was no longer safe for a Jewish boy to walk through the streets of Fürth.

Yet there were other forms of recreation than sport. It was at some point during the Nazi period that the young Heinz Kissinger joined the Orthodox organization Agudath (Union), the political arm of Ashkenazi Torah Judaism, a creation of the First World War that for a time called itself Shlumei Emunei Yisroel (the Union of Faithful Jewry).

Agudath's aim was to strengthen Orthodox institutions in Europe independently of the Zionist movement and ultimately to unite Western European and Eastern European Orthodoxy—a fact of which Kissinger was reminded forty years later by the Orthodox rabbi Morris Sherer, who joked that he had "under lock and key a paper you wrote back then" for Agudath.[33] This long-forgotten "paper" is the earliest of Henry Kissinger's writings to survive. It consists of the minutes of a meeting of the Esra Orthodox youth group run by Leo Höchster, a slightly older Jewish boy.[34] At the time of the meeting, on July 3, 1937, Heinz Kissinger was just fourteen years old; Höchster was eighteen. Five other "members" attended the meeting: Alfred Bechhöfer, Raphael Hallemann, Manfred Koschland, Hans Wangersheimer, and Kissinger's friend Heinz Lion. The original is in Kissinger's own hand in a combination of Sütterlin (the old German script) and Hebrew. It is worth quoting in full for the light it sheds on his early religious and political outlook.

> We met in our room punctually at 3:45 [p.m.]. First we discussed *dinim* [religious laws]. We set out the *dinim* about *Shabbat* [*rules of the Sabbath*]. We talked about *muktseh* [excluded things, i.e., things that may not be carried on the Sabbath].
>
> One distinguishes between four forms of *muktseh*:
>
> *muktseh mahamat isur*—[excluded] because of a specific prohibition [e.g., a pen, which is used for writing, a prohibited activity on *Shabbat*]
>
> *muktseh mahamat mitsva*—[excluded] to prevent one carrying out a *Mitzvah* [commandment inappropriate on *Shabbat*] (e.g. [wearing] *Tefillin*) [a reference to the small black leather boxes containing verses from the Torah that observant Jews wear during weekday morning prayers but not on *Shabbat*]
>
> *muktseh mahamat avera*—[excluded] so that one doesn't commit an *avera* [sin; for example, an object like an altar for worshipping idols, a sinful act]
>
> *muktseh mahamat mius*—[excluded] because it is hateful [*hässlich*], therefore is inappropriate for *Shabbat* [for example, something dirty].

Then there is also a 5th form of *muktseh,* for example when
one says before *Shabbat* that one will not take something if it is
muktseh for the relevant *Shabbat.*

Then it was time to see who was the best in the group at
[remembering] this. The decision was reached that Heinz Lion
and I each received half a point.

For the most part this was simply a Torah study group, drilling the
younger boys in the finer points of Hilchatic law. But the tone changes
completely in the final sentences:

Then we discussed the impending partition of Palestine. A partition would be the greatest sacrilege [*hilul ha-Shem*] in the history of the world. A Jewish state governed not by the *Torah* but
by a general law code is unthinkable. That was the end [of the
meeting].

Heinz K.[35]

Events in distant Palestine were having their impact even in Franconia.
Since April 1936 an Arab revolt had been raging against British Mandatory rule in Palestine. In large measure a response to increasing Jewish
immigration, the revolt—which had begun as a general strike but
quickly escalated into violence against both Jewish settlers and British
forces—had forced the British to review the governance of the former
Ottoman province. Heinz Kissinger and his friends were meeting just
four days before the publication of the keenly anticipated report of the
Royal Commission chaired by Earl Peel, which would recommend
partition of Palestine into a small Jewish state along the coastal plain but
also including Galilee, a residual Mandatory corridor from Jerusalem to
the coast (including Haifa), and a larger Arab territory to the south and
east, which would be joined to the neighboring Emirate of Transjor-
dan. (That the report would recommend partition along these lines had
already been anticipated in the British press since early April, so it is not
so strange that an obscure Orthodox youth group in Fürth already
knew its contents.) Though they wanted much more territory, the Zi-

onist leaders Chaim Weizmann and David Ben-Gurion were willing to accept the Peel Commission's report as the basis for negotiation, not least because it envisaged large-scale population transfers that would have resettled up to 225,000 Arabs outside the planned Jewish state. But the report was rejected by both the Arabs and non-Zionist Jewish groups like Agudath, and ultimately the idea of partition was shelved by the British themselves.[36] It is remarkable that Henry Kissinger was already at the age of just fourteen an ardent opponent of Palestinian partition. Even if the view that it would be the "greatest sacrilege in the history of the world" was not his own but that of the group of which he was a member, he certainly did not dissent from it when recording the minutes of their meeting. Nor did he dissent from their repudiation of the idea of a secular Jewish state, based (as Israel would be) on a law code other than the Torah. At least one of the boys in the Höchster group would later end up a refugee in Palestine and in due course a citizen of Israel. But this was never likely to be the fate of Heinz Kissinger, who seemed to have embraced wholeheartedly his father's anti-Zionism.

III

It was time, nevertheless, to leave Germany. Two of Louis Kissinger's brothers had already done so. In June 1933 Karl Kissinger, who helped manage his father-in-law's shoe store business, had been arrested and sent to Dachau, where he was subjected to beatings and death threats. After his wife secured his release more than a year later, in December 1934, they resolved to emigrate and in 1937 moved to Palestine with their three children, Herbert, Erwin, and Margot. Another of Louis's brothers, Arno, moved to Stockholm in the mid-1930s, where he was later joined by their father, David, in early 1939. A Leutershausen friend, Karl Hezner, urged Louis to follow his brothers' example. But Louis was more than ten years older than Karl and Arno. As his wife later put it, "It wasn't so easy to give up everything and go away with two children to an uncertain future."[37] His father, David, and brother Simon urged them not to give up on Germany. And there was a further obstacle to emigration. Paula Kissinger's father had been diagnosed with cancer.

Yet Paula had to put her children first. What kind of future did they have in Germany, where the "Hitler State" showed every sign of enduring and where the position of Jews seemed much more likely to deteriorate than to improve? After graduating from the Jewish Realschule, Heinz had enrolled for three months in a Jewish teacher-training college in Würzburg, for want of any better option.[38] As his mother later told Walter Isaacson, "It was my decision and I did it because of the children. I knew there was not a life to be made for them if we stayed."[39]

It was, to say the least, fortunate for the Kissingers that one of Paula's mother's elder sisters had already emigrated to the United States, years before Hitler was even heard of. Her daughter—and therefore Paula's cousin—Sarah Ascher had been born in Brooklyn but now lived in Larchmont, Westchester County. When Paula suggested sending Heinz and Walter across the Atlantic to safety, her American cousin urged the whole family to come. On October 28, 1937, she signed the crucial "affidavit of support" that pledged to give the Kissingers financial support if they came. (Quotas on immigration to the United States dating back to the 1920s meant that without such a pledge even refugees from Nazism could not be admitted.)* Though her income was just $4,000 a year, Sarah Ascher had stocks worth $8,000 and other savings worth $15,000, so her pledge was credible.[40] (The Kissingers in fact had wealthier U.S. relatives, the descendants of Louis Baehr in Pittsburgh, but their assistance was not required.) On April 21, 1938, Louis and Paula Kissinger—officially identified as "German nationals, Jews by race and belief"—notified the Emigration Advisory Bureau in Munich of their intention to emigrate.[41] The request had to clear multiple hurdles, but it was processed and approved in less than three weeks. First, Louis Kissinger applied to the Fürth police for passports.[42] The Gestapo then had to check that none of the family had a criminal

---

* Under the quotas imposed in 1924, the number of German immigrants could not exceed 2 percent of the existing German population in the United States, and no more than 10 percent of the annual quota could come in a given month. As a result, by the 1930s the German annual quota was 27,370, with a monthly maximum of 2,737. The events of 1938 led to a surge in applications: 139,163 by June 30, 1939; 240,748 by the end of the year. But the only way in was to get a quota visa from a U.S. consulate, which required proof that the applicant would not be a burden on the community—hence the need for affidavits from existing U.S. citizens.

record. The mayor of Fürth gave his approval on April 29, followed by the Gestapo on May 5,[43] the municipal finance office on May 6,[44] and German customs on May 9.[45] After receiving payment of 12 marks and 70 pfennigs, plus 5 marks 28 for a character reference, the police issued the four passports on May 10.[46]

It was not until August 10 that the Kissingers officially told the Fürth police of their intention to depart, however. There were painful farewells to make, not least to Paula's ailing father—the first occasion in their lives when Heinz and Walter had seen their father moved to tears.[47] "When my family was about to leave the country of my birth," Kissinger recalled many years later, "I called on my grandfather, to whom I was very attached, in the little village where he lived, to say good-bye. He was suffering from cancer, and I knew I would never see him again. My grandfather took the finality out of the encounter by telling me that we were not really parting, because he would pay me a final visit at my parents' home a few weeks hence. Though I did not really believe it, the prospect proved remarkably consoling."[48] They also had to bid farewell to most of their possessions; Nazi regulations ensured that Jews who quit the Reich left behind not only most of their savings but also most of their furniture (worth, in the Kissingers' case, an estimated 23,000 marks, including the piano).[49] There was a regulation-sized crate that Jews leaving the Third Reich were allowed to fill; Kissinger recalled his mother making the doleful selection of what could come with them.[50] On August 20 the family set sail from one of the Belgian Channel ports, bound for England. They spent just over a week in London, at the Golders Green home of Paula's aunt Berta and her husband, Sigmund Fleischmann—formerly the kosher butcher in Fürth—with whom Paula had lodged as a schoolgirl. Then, on August 30, 1938, they took the train to Southampton and boarded the *Île de France*, bound for New York. Heinz Kissinger was fifteen years old. His best friend, Heinz Lion, had already left for Palestine in March.

The Kissingers were just 4 among 1,578 Bavarian Jews who emigrated in 1938.[51] They did not leave Germany a moment too soon.

IV

On the same day the Kissingers informed the Fürth police of their departure, the principal Nuremberg synagogue was destroyed. The main synagogue in Munich had suffered a similar fate the previous June. The more radically anti-Semitic elements within the Nazi Party—not least Hitler himself—were growing impatient with mere segregation. With good reason, the Jewish community in Fürth began preparing for trouble. The most valuable scrolls and silver ornaments were removed from the synagogues for safekeeping.[52] A further warning of the impending storm came on October 16, 1938, when a mob attacked the Leutershausen synagogue and broke the windows of Jewish homes, including Falk and Fanny Stern's farmhouse. In the wake of the pogrom, Stern was forced to sell the house he had bought with his brother thirty-four years before. He and Fanny moved to his sister Minna Fleischmann's house in Fürth, where he would succumb to cancer on May 26, 1939. By that time Fürth, too, had ceased to be a safe place for Jews.

Kristallnacht—the "Night of Broken Glass"—was a moment of truth in the history of the Third Reich. Whatever facade had been erected to give a semblance of legality to the regime's racial policy was torn away by a nationwide orgy of violence and vandalism. The pretext for the worst pogrom in German history since the Middle Ages was the murder in the German embassy in Paris of the diplomat Ernst vom Rath by a seventeen-year-old Jewish exile from Hanover named Herschel Grynszpan, who had been incensed by the deportation from Germany of his parents, who were Polish nationals. He shot vom Rath at point-blank range on November 7, 1938. Two days later the diplomat was dead. This was Hitler's cue. With Goebbels's excited encouragement, he unleashed an ostensibly "spontaneous" assault on the Jewish population.

There was a farcical quality to the way these orders were carried out in Fürth. November 9 was the anniversary of the abortive "beer hall putsch" of 1923, a day when the Nazis commemorated their martyrs. As a result, the local party bigwigs were celebrating bibulously in the Café Fink when the order came through to attack the Jews and, in particular, to destroy the town's synagogues. The mayor was red-faced and brim-ming over with beer. He had no objection at all to organizing a pogrom. But he was concerned about the consequences of burning down so many synagogues, most of them located in the densely built town cen-ter. With that curious mixture of callousness and punctiliousness so characteristic of the Nazis, he summoned the chief of the town's fire brigade, Johannes Rachfahl, and ordered him to prepare to protect all buildings in the vicinity of the synagogues that were about to be incin-erated. Rachfahl was flabbergasted: "The Herr Oberbürgermeister likes his little joke" was his immediate reaction. He patiently explained to the mayor the impossibility of controlling the kind of fire there would be if all the synagogues around the Schulplatz were set ablaze. Reluctantly the mayor compromised. Only the main synagogue would be burned down.[53]

At around one a.m. in the small hours of November 10, a force of 150 SA men broke down the iron gates of Schulhof and then smashed in the oak doors of the main synagogue. Once inside they broke pews and ornaments, then piled up whatever Torah scrolls they could find, doused them with petrol, and set them ablaze. Dragged from his bed, Dr. Albert Neuburger, a leading member of the Jewish community, was left semi-conscious and bloody after his head was used as a battering ram to break down the door of the community's welfare office. At 3:15 a.m., with the main synagogue now burning fiercely, the fire brigade was summoned to the scene, but the SA prevented their hoses from being used on the synagogue. Indeed, the *Oberbürgermeister* ordered them to let the fire spread to the caretaker's house and the adjoining prayer hall (*Betsaal*). Also destroyed that night was the ritual bathhouse and the synagogue at 30 Mohrenstrasse. The Jewish cemetery was also vandalized, as were the Jewish hospital, the Realschule, the orphanage, and many Jewish-owned shops, including the café in the Moststrasse. Anti-Semitic slo-gans were painted on the walls of the orphanage—"We will not let a Jew murder a German"—and the Realschule—"Croak Judas! Revenge for Paris!"

Nor was that all. The entire Jewish community, including the chil-dren from the orphanage, were now herded into the Schlageterplatz (today known as Fürther Freiheit) and left standing there in the

November cold for five hours. Entertainment was provided by an assault on the Kissingers' rabbi, Leo Breslauer, culminating in the forcible shaving off of his beard. Watching with horror was the young Edgar Rosenberg, whose recollections capture not only the fear but also the horrible dissension among the helpless victims.

> At about 5:30 . . . the Jews were ordered to execute a smart about-face in the direction of the Schulhof: the sky had turned crimson; the synagogues burned. And at that moment the time-honored religious schisms among us, which seem not to desert us even in days of wrath, burst eerily into the open. For now the orthodox Jews—the members of the Neuschul, the Mannheimer Shul, the Klaus Shul—set up a heart-rending wail to see their *bet knesset* aflame; but these seemed above all to intimidate, even terrify, the reformed Jews, who took it for granted that these pious howls could only inflame the troopers and turn it into a bloodbath. In this they over-reacted.[54]

There would be no bloodbath; not here, not yet. At nine a.m. all the women and children were sent home, while the men were marched to the former Berolzheimerianum (it too had been renamed), where the verbal and physical abuse continued. Rosenberg remembered "my nosy townsmen . . . crowd[ing] into the streets, spitting, yodeling, screaming, 'Well, high time!' and 'None too soon!' and bursting into a chorus of 'Jew Sow' and 'Croak Judas!' . . . [then] break[ing] the ranks of the Brownshirts to get a good close-up of the Jew Kahn [*sic*], the religious whose beard has been ripped off."[55] In total, 132 men were subsequently sent to Nuremberg and then on to Dachau, including the Kissinger brothers' teacher Hermann Mandelbaum, who was held there for forty-seven days, and Rosenberg's father, who subsequently escaped to Switzerland.[56]

The pillage was not over. Back in Fürth, the Jewish community's leaders were forced to sign a document selling the two Jewish cemeteries, hospital, and much other community property to the municipality for the risible sum of one hundred marks. They were also threatened with death if they refused to reveal the whereabouts of a nonexistent, supposedly hidden synagogue. (Their assailants had in mind a school for sick children called the Waldschule, which had been established by a Jewish philanthropist in 1907.) In the succeeding days, a number of Jewish firms were also compelled to sell their real estate for similar negligible sums—a prelude to the law of November 12, 1938, which formally excluded Jews from German economic life and paved the way for the formal "Aryanization" of all Jewish-owned firms.[57] Later on the morning of November 10, the SA men returned to march through the still smoldering Schulhof in triumph. They had blood as well as ashes on their hands. One man had died of the injuries inflicted on him during the night; another had committed suicide. Rabbi Breslauer survived, but he was so badly brutalized that, even years later, "he could not speak loudly because of the tortures to which the Nazis had subjected him on Kristallnacht."[58]

To the victims of the pogrom, it seemed incredible. As one incredulous eyewitness put it, "When I was a young man we took dance classes, Jews and Christians together, intermingling without any problems. There was virtually no anti-Semitism . . . until the time of Hitler. We Jews never believed that there could be such anti-Semitism in Fürth."[59]

And yet there was. It took thirteen years to bring those responsible for the events of November 10, 1938, in Fürth to justice. Of five ringleaders who survived to face prosecution in 1951, just one was found guilty. He was sentenced to two and a half years in prison. A year later, a second case came to trial in Karlsruhe; two more defendants were convicted and sentenced to, respectively, two years and four months. By that time, however, many far worse crimes had been committed against the Jews of Fürth.

V

Fürth is but a dull town and a measure of its unimportance beneath the stars came home to me . . . in 1945. [While] Nuremberg lay in dust and ashes, a heap of broken icons and crumbled idols, a tribute to its Babylonian wickedness, Fürth was still there, all of a piece, squatting pacifically in the sun. . . .

Of course, the missing synagogue left a certain hole in the jigsaw puzzle. . . .

Nuremberg . . . has . . . its golden tradition and its trumpeted trials; the reader is easily oriented: ah, says he, Nuremberg, I know that: Albrecht Dürer, the Nazi Congress, the Tower, Justice Jackson, the hangings, the bratwursts; but whenever I whisper "Fürth," the echo replies: spell it.[60]

Edgar Rosenberg was one of those Fürth-born Jews who survived World War II, having escaped to the United States, via Haiti, after *Kristallnacht*. He was ironically surprised to find so much of his hometown still intact when he returned in an American uniform at the end of the war.

Not that Fürth was unscathed. The war that Hitler launched in September 1939 pitted Germany against seemingly weaker opposition than the war he himself had fought in twenty-five years before. By the summer of 1940, Germany bestrode the European continent, triumphant after defeating France and driving the British Expeditionary Force back across the Channel from Dunkirk. Yet the resources of the British Empire remained enormous. As early as August 1940 and again the following October, Royal Air Force planes dropped bombs on Fürth and Nuremberg, an industrial conurbation high on the British list of targets for strategic bombing. This was but a foretaste of what lay ahead. There were sporadic raids in 1941 and 1942, but in 1943—by which time Germany was also at war with both the Soviet Union and the United States—the scale of aerial bombardment soared. On the night of August 10–11, 1943, the entire district of Wohrd in Nuremberg was destroyed. In 1944 there were twelve major Allied air raids on Middle and Upper Franconia, which killed over a thousand people. Three times that number were killed by devastating strikes on January 2 and February 21–22, 1945. By the end of the war, 6 percent of prewar buildings in Fürth had been totally destroyed, 30 percent moderately to badly damaged, and 54 percent slightly damaged.[61] According to reports of a small raid on Nuremberg-Fürth in March 1945, "the majority of the bombs fell on fields of ruins."[62]

The last film to be screened in Fürth before the final collapse of the

Third Reich was a light comedy with a cruelly fitting title: *It Began So Harmlessly (Es fing so harmlos an)*.[63] Perhaps that was how Hitler's accession to power appeared in retrospect to those who had voted Nazi in 1932 and 1933. But there had never been anything harmless about Hitler from the vantage point of German Jews. In January 1939, even before the outbreak of war, he had made a chilling prophecy: "If the international Jewish financiers in and outside Europe should succeed in plunging the nations once more into a world war, then the result will not be the Bolshevization of the earth, and thus the victory of Jewry, but the annihilation of the Jewish race in Europe!"[64]

With the outbreak of war, the Nazis felt emboldened to fulfill that threat. Of 1,990 Jews who had lived in Fürth in 1933, fewer than 40 were left by the end. Of those who had not emigrated by the war's outbreak, most—511 in all—were deported by train to German-occupied territory in Eastern Europe, where they were either shot, gassed, or worked to death.[65] The first deportation was to Riga on November 29, 1941. This was followed on March 22–24, 1942, by a large-scale deportation to Izbica. From there the deportees were sent to the death camps at Sobibór or Bełżec or to the forced labor camp at Trawniki. A month later another contingent of Fürth Jews was dispatched to Kraśniczyn. Those remaining were sent to either Theresienstadt (September 10, 1942) or Auschwitz (June 18, 1943). The Nazis concluded the liquidation of Fürth's Jewish community by deporting a small group of converts and *Mischlinge* ("half-breeds") on January 17, 1944. Among the victims were all 33 pupils at the Jewish orphanage, who were sent to Izbica, along with the director of the orphanage, Dr. Isaak Hallemann, and his family.[66] (His proposal to move the orphanage to Palestine had been rejected by the Jewish community on the ground that the benefactors of the orphanage had specified Fürth as its location.)[67] By 1945 all that remained of the "Bavarian Jerusalem" was a handful of survivors and a few repurposed buildings. The old Jewish cemetery had been totally destroyed, the gravestones used as stone for building air defenses, the burial ground flooded to create a makeshift reservoir for the fire brigade.[68]

If the Kissingers had not left Germany when they did, there can be little doubt what their fate would have been. It is unlikely that Heinz Kissinger would have lived to see his twentieth birthday. Of his close family, according to his own estimate, thirteen relatives were killed in the Holocaust, including his father's three sisters, Selma, Ida, and Fanny; their husbands, Max Blattner, Siegbert Friedmann, and Jakob Rau; his great-uncle Simon, along with his sons Ferdinand and Julius; and Paula Kissinger's stepmother, Fanny Stern.[69] Although she was not a blood relative, Kissinger had regarded Fanny as his grandmother. "For [her]," he later recalled, "I was a genuine grandchild and for me, I didn't know she was my stepgrandmother, so that was a very warm, caring relationship." Deceptively, the family continued to receive pro forma postcards from her even after her deportation. They subsequently learned that she had been sent to the death camp at Bełżec, only to perish on a forced march westward after the camp was dismantled.[70] Falk Stern's sister Minna died at Theresienstadt and her husband, Max, at Auschwitz. Also among the victims were Kissinger's cousins Louise Blattner, Lilli Friedmann, and Norbert Rau.[71]

In fact, the figure of thirteen understates the number of Henry Kissinger's relatives who perished at the hands of the Nazis. According to "The Kissingers," a manuscript family history compiled by either Charles Stanton or Martin Kissinger, the correct figure is twenty-three. Even that figure may be too low. Of all the known descendants of Meyer Löb Kissinger, no fewer than fifty-seven died in the years of the Holocaust. This total may of course include people who died outside German-occupied territory of natural causes, but it may also exclude victims of the Holocaust whose deaths were not documented. Suffice to say that the figure of twenty-three is a minimum; the total number of Kissinger's relatives killed was probably closer to thirty.

What was the impact of this calamity on Henry Kissinger? Thirty years after the end of the war, now secretary of state, he was invited to return to his birthplace to receive a medal of honorary citizenship.[72] For his parents' sake, he accepted and they accompanied him. His father was publicly forgiving, his mother privately implacable. ("I was offended in my heart that day, but said nothing," she later said. "In my heart, I knew they would have burned us with the others if we had stayed.")[73] Kissinger himself has always been at pains to deny that the Holocaust was crucial to his development. "My first political experiences were as a member of a persecuted Jewish minority," he said in an interview in 2007.

> And . . . many members of my family, and about 70 per cent of the people I went to school with, died in concentration camps. So that is something one cannot forget. . . . [Nor is it] possible to have lived in Nazi Germany and to . . . be emotionally indifferent to the fate of Israel. . . . [But] I do not agree with [the view] that analyzes everything in terms of my alleged Jewish origin. I have not thought of myself in those terms.[74]

Kissinger was still a devoutly Orthodox Jew when he left Germany in August 1938. But at some point between then and 1945, something happened to change that. As a result, for most of his adult life, he characterized himself as Jewish by ethnicity rather than by faith: "I'm not a religious man in the sense of practicing a particular religion. Of course I'm Jewish and always affirm that, but I am religious in the sense that I do believe—in the sense of Spinoza—that there probably is a fitness in the universe which we can no more understand than an ant could understand an interpretation of our universe."[75]

And yet it was not the horror of the Shoah, despite its calamitous impact on his family, that brought Kissinger to this realization of the limits of human understanding. It was the searing experience of waging war against the Nazis.

CHAPTER 3

Fürth on the Hudson

Almost a year has passed since I left Germany. You will
certainly have often recalled my promise to write as soon as
possible. Yet it was not just laziness that prevented me from
writing. Rather it was the fact that in these eight months so
much has changed within me and around me that I have
neither the desire nor the peace to write letters.

—HENRY KISSINGER, July 1939[1]

New York was not merely the vital metropolis, brimming
with politics and contention, that has since become a
sentimental legend; it was also the brutal, ugly, frightening,
the foul smelling jungle . . . the embodiment of that alien
world which every boy raised in a Jewish immigrant home
has been taught . . . to look upon with suspicion.

—IRVING HOWE[2]

I

It is tempting to draw a stark contrast between the country the Kissingers left behind in the summer of 1938 and the one they settled in. The
German Reich, now firmly in Hitler's ruthless grip, stood on the brink
of an abyss of lawlessness and violence. The United States was the land
of "Happy Days Are Here Again," the song Franklin Roosevelt had
chosen as the theme tune of his 1932 presidential election campaign.
The Kissingers had narrowly avoided burning synagogues in Fürth. The
Manhattan skyline that greeted them as the *Île de France* sailed in past
Brooklyn—on a day of welcoming sunshine—was dominated by the

dazzling Empire State Building, the highest skyscraper in the world. Germany was the land of oppression. America was the land of the free.

There were, of course, profound differences between the family's old and new homes. And yet it would be a mistake to understate the problems of the United States in 1938—problems that very quickly had a direct bearing on the Kissingers' lives. They, like most refugees to the United States, probably arrived with somewhat unrealistic expectations of their newly adopted homeland.[3] If so, they were soon disabused of them.

Unlike in Germany, in the United States the Depression was not yet over in 1938. On the contrary, after four years of recovery, the economy had slumped back into recession in the second half of 1937. In October 1937 the stock market had capitulated. "We are headed right into another Depression," Treasury Secretary Henry Morgenthau warned. From peak to trough, stocks fell by a third. Industrial production slumped 40 percent. A total of two million workers had been laid off by the end of the winter of 1937–38, driving the unemployment rate back up to 19 percent. Roosevelt and his sidekicks complained of a "capitalist strike"; the capitalists retorted that the New Deal had created too much uncertainty for business to invest with confidence. The New Dealers within the administration blamed monetary and fiscal tightening for the "Roosevelt Recession." The most influential American Keynesian, Harvard's Alvin H. Hansen, argued in his 1938 tract, *Full Recovery or Stagnation,* that only massive government deficits could maintain full employment—and certainly, it took the approach of war and unprecedented public borrowing to generate recovery. From the vantage point of Republicans, however, deficits were one of the things eroding business confidence.[4] Meanwhile, the still-large agricultural sector of the economy languished. Dorothea Lange and Paul Taylor captured the agony of the economic migration from the Dust Bowl in *An American Exodus: A Record of Human Erosion,* published in 1938.[5]

It was not only Nazi Germany that could be described as a "racial state." In the United States, racial segregation extended far beyond the South. Signs like "We Cater to White Trade Only" could be seen in shops all over America. Lynchings claimed more than one hundred lives between 1930 and 1938. It was in 1938 that Gunnar Myrdal began the research that would produce *An American Dilemma: The Negro Problem and Modern Democracy.*[6] Thirty states still retained constitutional or legal bans on interracial marriage, and many of these had recently extended or tightened their rules. It was not only African Americans and American Indians who were affected; some states also discriminated against Chinese, Japanese, Koreans, "Malays" (Filipinos), and "Hindus" (Indians). Moreover, the influence of eugenics in the United States had added a new tier of discriminatory legislation that was not only similar to that introduced in Germany in the 1930s but also the inspiration for some Nazi legislation. No fewer than forty-one states used eugenic categories to restrict marriages of the mentally ill, while twenty-seven states passed laws mandating sterilization for certain categories of people. In 1933 alone California forcibly sterilized 1,278 people. Hitler openly acknowledged his debt to American eugenicists.[7]

Meanwhile, the political power of the segregationists in Congress was waxing, not waning. They successfully stymied an Anti-Lynching Bill in 1938. They also prevented Roosevelt from enacting minimum wage legislation; South Carolina's senator Ellison Smith ("Cotton Ed") boasted that in his state a man—meaning a black man—could live on fifty cents a day.[8] The year 1938 marked the effective end of the New Deal in the face of such congressional opposition. In the midterm elections held that year, the Republicans won thirteen governorships, doubled their representation in the House, and gained seven new Senate seats. Roosevelt's attempt to replace at least some southern Democrats with New Dealers abjectly failed.[9]

The American right was fighting back in more ways than one. In June 1938 Texas congressman Martin Dies chaired the first hearings before the House Committee to Investigate Un-American Activities. Fear of Communism was stoked by dissension within the U.S. labor movement, with AFL representatives openly accusing their CIO rivals of running "a seminary of Communist sedition."[10] Labor market friction was especially severe in New York. In September 1938 the city was hit by an unofficial truck drivers' strike.[11] Another labor dispute led to the bombings of seven fur shops on West 29th Street.[12]

In Germany the government itself had been taken over by criminals. In the United States the criminals wielded power in different ways. The 1930s were the heyday of gangsters like Meyer Lansky (born Meyer Suchowljansky), Bugsy Siegel (born Benjamin Siegelbaum), and Charles "Lucky" Luciano (Salvatore Lucania), who had successfully switched from bootlegging to gambling and other rackets after the end of Prohibition in 1933. It was Luciano who, emerging as the dominant figure in the New York Mafia underworld, established "The Commission" in order to impose some kind of central governance not just on the Five Families of New York but on organized crime throughout America. Luciano's reign had effectively ended in 1936, when he was arrested and successfully prosecuted by special prosecutor (later governor) Thomas E. Dewey for running a prostitution racket. But his place was soon taken by Frank Costello (born Francesco Castiglia).[13] And the links from such men to the political machines that ran urban America were real. For every Dewey there was at least one corrupt ward boss in the pay of the Mob.

And yet, amid all this turmoil, the United States remained an astonishingly dynamic and creative society. The year Henry Kissinger arrived in New York was the year when Errol Flynn starred in *The Adventures of Robin Hood* (one of four films he appeared in that year), Jimmy Cagney in *Angels with Dirty Faces,* Cary Grant and Katharine Hepburn in *Bringing Up Baby,* and Fred Astaire and Ginger Rogers in *Carefree.* Ronald Reagan was kept busy in ten B movies, including *Accidents Will Happen, Going Places,* and *Girls on Probation.* In truth, the best film in American cinemas in 1938 was French: Jean Renoir's antiwar masterpiece *La Grande Illusion,* while the most commercially successful was Disney's full-length cartoon *Snow White and the Seven Dwarfs* (which had opened in December the year before). But the Oscar for Best Picture went to Frank Capra's adaptation of the Broadway screwball comedy *You Can't Take It with You,* in which Jimmy Stewart, playing a banker's son, becomes romantically entangled with a member of an eccentric immigrant household. Set in Manhattan, the movie made light of the social cleavages of the time (though it is best remembered today for its timeless exchange about income tax). Also appearing regularly in American cinemas in the year of the Kissingers' arrival were Lucille Ball, Humphrey Bogart, Bing Crosby, Bette Davis, W. C.

Fields, Henry Fonda, Judy Garland, Betty Grable, Bob Hope, Edward G. Robinson, Mickey Rooney, Spencer Tracy, and John Wayne—not forgetting Shirley Temple, Stan Laurel and Oliver Hardy, and the Marx Brothers. If Hollywood ever had a true golden age, then this was it.

As ubiquitous as the movies in American life was the radio. In 1938 most American households were served by NBC's two principal networks, which offered everything from *Amos 'n' Andy* to Arturo Toscanini's NBC Symphony Orchestra. The songs most likely to be heard on air in 1938 included the originally Yiddish hit "Bei Mir Bistu Shein," recorded by the Andrews Sisters, "A-Tisket A-Tasket" by Ella Fitzgerald, "I Can't Get Started" by Bunny Berigan, "Jeepers Creepers" by Al Donahue, and the Gershwins' "Nice Work if You Can Get It," sung by Fred Astaire. But it was Bing Crosby who was America's preeminent crooner, counting among his 1938 hits "You Must Have Been a Beautiful Baby" and "Alexander's Ragtime Band." For all the economic difficulties of the time, this was also the golden age of the big band: Count Basie, Tommy Dorsey, Duke Ellington, Benny Goodman, Artie Shaw—all these bandleaders were at the peak of their powers, touring the nation with their big brass and reed orchestras. Yet the radio sensation of 1938 was not musical; it was Orson Welles's dramatization of H. G. Wells's science fiction novel *The War of the Worlds,* which caused panic across the nation when broadcast on October 30.

Among the year's best-selling books was *The Yearling,* a tale of hardship in rural Florida, which won its author, Marjorie Kinnan Rawlings, a Pulitzer Prize. British authors were strongly represented in the bookstores that year, among them A. J. Cronin, Howard Spring, and Daphne du Maurier, whose *Rebecca* was a bestseller in the United States. A further intimation of the deepening political crisis on the other side of the Atlantic was provided by *The Mortal Storm,* an anti-Nazi love story by another English writer, Phyllis Bottome. Broadway offered less challenging fare in the form of the musical *Hellzapoppin,* which began a run of more than a thousand performances in the month the Kissingers arrived in New York.

The Depression was also a remarkable time in the history of American sport. On June 22, 1938, in a richly symbolic fight, the African American heavyweight boxer Joe Louis knocked out the German Max

Schmeling in front of seventy thousand people at Yankee Stadium, the second of their two encounters in the ring. The Yankees themselves won four successive World Series titles between 1936 and 1939, a period that saw the ailing Lou Gehrig retire and the young Joe DiMaggio shoot to fame as the "Yankee Clipper." New York seemed to dominate American sports. In December, the Giants defeated the Green Bay Packers to win the National Football League title. It was the kind of performance that inspired improvised games of street football in neighborhoods like Washington Heights and Harlem.[14] Here, perhaps, was the most striking contrast between Germany and America, at least for a teenage boy: soccer was nowhere to be seen. For fifteen-year-old Heinz Kissinger, it was time to study batting averages.

II

In one crucial respect, New York was not such unfamiliar territory for a family like the Kissingers. It was among the most Jewish cities in the world. There had been a Jewish community in the city since the early 1700s, but it was from the late nineteenth century that the Jewish population of the city exploded as a result of immigration from Central and Eastern Europe. In 1870 there had been around 60,000 Jews in New York. By 1910 there were more than one and a quarter million, around a quarter of the total population. Jews were arriving in New York at the rate of 50,000 a year between 1915 and 1924, until legal restrictions on immigration (enacted in 1921 and 1924) drove the annual influx down below 20,000. At their peak share in 1920, the Jews accounted for just over 29 percent of the population of New York City. At that time, the city's Jewish population was larger than that of any European city including Warsaw. By 1940, to be sure, the Jewish share had fallen below 24 percent.[15] Nevertheless, the city retained a distinctively Jewish character. Or, to be more precise, parts of it did.

Jews had been leaving Manhattan in droves since the early 1920s. In particular, the Lower East Side's Jewish population had collapsed from 314,000 to 74,000. Yorkville, Morningside Heights, and East Harlem had also seen steep declines.[16] By the time of the Kissingers' arrival, there were more Jews in Brooklyn (857,000) and the Bronx (538,000) than in Manhattan (270,000). One exception to this rule was the area of Manhattan known as Washington Heights, in the far north of the island, where there was still a very high concentration of Jewish settlement. Those who had expected the newcomers' children to be absorbed or assimilated into the wider population were proved wrong. By the end of the 1920s, 72 percent of Jewish New Yorkers lived in neighborhoods with at least 40 percent Jewish populations.[17] Ethnic segregation actually increased in the 1920s, as Jewish property developers built smart new streets like the Grand Concourse in the Bronx, and stayed high through the 1930s. Washington Heights was an example of the "new kind of ghetto, a closed community of middle-class Jews whose social life was carried on exclusively with Jews of appropriate status."[18] This segregation was not wholly voluntary. There were subtle "restrictions" on Jewish residents in certain apartment buildings in Jackson Heights Queens, and in the Fieldston section of Riverdale.[19] But mostly Jews lived in close proximity to one another because they preferred, for a variety of reasons, to do so. In the words of Nathaniel Zalowitz,

> There [are] Ghettos for foreign born Jews and Ghettos for native born Jews. Ghettos for poor Jews and ghettos for middle class and for rich Jews, for Russian Jews and for German Jews. The East Side is one kind of Ghetto, Washington Heights another kind, West Bronx a third, Riverside Drive a fourth . . . and Brooklyn has a dozen different kinds and styles of Ghettos of its own. . . . [As a result] four-fifths of all Jews . . . practically have no social contact with the Gentiles.[20]

The German-Jewish exiles were therefore latecomers to a long-running process. Most, as we have seen, came after the summer of 1938: the total number of German refugees from January 1933 to June 1938 was just 27,000.[21] In the period 1938–40, however, 157,000 came to the United States, of whom just under half were Jewish.[22] Most settled in New York, despite the efforts of organizations like the interdenominational organization "Selfhelp" to get them to move inland.[23] Jews were socially rather than geographically mobile. After fifteen to twenty-five years, half of Jewish immigrants achieved white-collar status.[24] By the 1930s, Jews owned two-thirds of the 24,000 factories in New York City, the same proportion of the more than 100,000 wholesale and retail firms, and two-thirds of the 11,000 restaurants.[25] But they moved en masse to more affluent neighborhoods within New York's five boroughs, sticking together in the same streets and apartment buildings.

Jews were not in fact the largest religious minority in New York. By the 1930s, that position was occupied by Roman Catholics, mostly of Irish or Italian origin.[26] Indirectly, this helped the Jews preserve their own religious and cultural identity, since Catholics were not only more numerous but also highly resistant to becoming assimilated into the Protestant "native" population—still a decided majority of the U.S. population as a whole—through intermarriage or education. On the other hand, there was no love lost between New York's different religious and ethnic groups. For ethnic conflict was not unique to Europe in the 1930s and 1940s. It occurred—albeit on a much less violent scale—in the United States, too. Jews knew to avoid the established German areas like Yorkville on the Upper East Side. But anti-Semitism was by no means uniquely German. For New York's Irish-Americans, who had borne the brunt of nativist antagonism in the second half of the nineteenth century, the arrival of poor southern Italians and Eastern European Jews provided an opportunity to turn the tables. So Jewish refugees also had to steer clear of Irish neighborhoods like Bainbridge and Kingsbridge in the Bronx. Interethnic competition over jobs and housing was commonplace. The Depression intensified such conflicts as the proportion of the population in employment slumped from 46 percent in 1930 to 38 percent in 1940. During the "Roosevelt Recession," unskilled workers had the highest unemployment rates; this affected the Irish and Italians more than Jews, because the latter had been much quicker than other immigrant groups to move into more skilled sectors of the economy.[27]

Jewish upward mobility extended to the realm of politics. In the course of the 1920s, the formerly Republican New York Jews had been brought into the fold of the Democratic Party's "ethnic coalition," along with other immigrant groups. Governor Alfred E. Smith and his successor, Franklin Roosevelt, could count on Democratic bosses like Brownsville's Hymie Schorenstein. Another Jew, Herbert H. Lehman, was elected to succeed Roosevelt as governor of New York in 1932; he held the post for four successive terms. And another, Irwin Steingut, became speaker of the New York State Assembly in 1935. Two years before, the election of the Republican–City Fusion candidate Fiorello La Guardia as mayor of New York City had ended Tammany Hall's stranglehold on public sector jobs.[28] La Guardia's victory was hailed as an Italian victory, but it was equally a Jewish victory as his mother, Irene Coen, was a Jew from Fiume (Rijeka). (Significantly, the wholly Jewish Nathan Straus had decided not to run for the post as it seemed to him "extremely doubtful . . . that it would be advisable for there to be a Jewish Governor and a Jewish Mayor.")[29] La Guardia soon signaled his allegiance, becoming the vice chairman of the American League for the Defense of Jewish Rights, one of the organizations set up to boycott German goods in retaliation for the Nazis' anti-Jewish boycott in Germany.[30] The Jewish vote was in fact quite evenly split between La Guardia and his opponents in 1933, which explains why all candidates worked so hard to attract Jewish voters. Under La Guardia's mayoralty, however, Jews began to get more and more elected and unelected posts in the city government. In 1937 more than two-thirds of all Jews voted for La Guardia, and in 1941 very nearly three-quarters. In presidential elections, New York Jews overwhelmingly endorsed Roosevelt in 1932, 1936, and 1940 (when FDR won no less than 88 percent of their votes).[31]

The sharp increase under La Guardia in the number of Jews getting city government and teaching jobs angered the long-dominant Irish-Americans. The mainly Irish "Christian Front" was openly hostile to the "Jew Deal." Anti-Semitism manifested itself in vandalism and anti-Jewish specifications in help-wanted advertisements.[32] Even the former governor Al Smith (a political progressive) could say,

> All my life I've been hearing about the plight of the poor Jews some place in the world. . . . As I look around the room tonight, I see the Governor here, Herby Lehman. He's Jewish. Take the Mayor, he's half Jewish. The President of the Board of Aldermen, my old job, Bernie Deutsch, he's Jewish and so is Sam Levy, the Borough President of Manhattan. I'm begin-

ning to wonder if someone shouldn't do something for the
poor Irish here in New York.[33]

Under the strain of the Depression, the Democratic ethnic coalition
threatened to fall apart.

It did not help that key members of the New York Communist Party
were Jews.[34] Post–First World War socialism had also found its strongest
support among New York's Jews.[35] And Jews accounted for between 20
and 40 percent of the New York vote for the American Labor Party
between 1936 and 1941.[36] As in Europe, so in America, it was not so hard
for demagogues to equate "Reds" with "Jews." In reality, the real bias
in Jewish politics was toward liberalism, broadly defined.[37]

Events in Europe only widened all these domestic cleavages. To be
sure, a Gallup poll on December 9, 1938 (a month after the *Kristallnacht*
pogrom), showed that the American public overwhelmingly condemned
Hitler's persecution of the Jews.[38] But few Americans were willing to
increase immigration quotas to accommodate refugees, while more
than two-thirds agreed that "with conditions as they are we should try
to keep them out." Roosevelt himself was sympathetic but gently pushed
aside Governor Lehman's argument (after Hitler's annexation of Austria)
that the immigration quota should be increased. Asked after *Kristallnacht*
by a reporter, "Would you recommend a relaxation of our immigration
restrictions so that the Jewish refugees could be received in this country?" Roosevelt replied bluntly, "That is not in contemplation. We have
the quota system." After Senator Robert Wagner of New York and
Representative Edith Nourse Rogers of Massachusetts introduced a bill
to allow twenty thousand German children under fourteen years of age
to enter outside the quota limits, two-thirds of those polled in January
1939 said they opposed the bill. In mid-1939, a *Fortune* poll asked, "If you
were a member of Congress, would you vote yes or no on a bill to open
the doors . . . to a larger number of European refugees?" Eighty-five
percent of Protestants, 84 percent of Catholics, and nearly 26 percent of
Jews answered no.[39] More than two-fifths of Americans surveyed in
1940 were opposed to mixed marriages between gentiles and Jews. Just
under a fifth of Americans considered Jews a "menace to America," and

nearly a third expected "a widespread campaign against Jews in this country," which more than 10 percent said they would support. Just under half of Americans polled in 1942 thought that Jews had "too much power in the United States."[40]

The parallel world of a Nazi America imagined in Philip Roth's novel *The Plot Against America* is not without its credibility. In October 1938, just weeks after their arrival, the Kissingers could have read a report of a meeting of the New York branch of the Daughters of the American Revolution at which one speaker called for curbs on "the alien menace," including an end to the admission of refugees to the United States, as well as an investigation of "alien, atheistic, communistic and radical professors" at New York University and Hunter College.[41] Other organizations were explicitly anti-Semitic, notably the Defenders of the Christian Faith, founded in 1925 by the Kansas preacher and Nazi sympathizer Gerald B. Winrod, and the Silver Shirt legions, which flourished in 1930s South Carolina under the leadership of William Dudley Pelley, a Methodist preacher's son who dreamed of being the "American Hitler."

Especially influential in New York was the National Union for Social Justice (NUSJ), founded by the Detroit-based priest Charles E. Coughlin, whose radio broadcasts against the "Jewish Communist threat" had up to 3.5 million listeners, mostly lower-class Catholics. Coughlin went so far as to defend the *Kristallnacht* pogrom in one of his tirades on the radio station WMCA and to publish the bogus "Protocols of the Elders of Zion" in his periodical *Social Justice*. The NUSJ had its own branch at West 59th Street, where a substantial number of policemen were said to be members.[42] Coughlin was also the inspiration for the Christian Front, formed by anti-Semitic Irish Catholics like John Cassidy in Brooklyn in 1938. An even more radical group were the Christian Mobilizers, who refused to drop their pro-Hitler stance even after the Nazi-Soviet Pact of 1939. The climax of this process of radicalization was the arrest of Christian Front members by the FBI in January 1940. They were charged with planning a coup against the government, which would have been accompanied by terrorist bombings of Jewish neighborhoods and assassinations of Jewish congressmen.[43]

The most overtly pro-Nazi organization in New York, however, was the Freunde des Neuen Deutschland—known from 1936 as the

German-American Bund (Amerikadeutscher Volksbund). Its New York *Gau* (centered on Yorkville) was the hub of the Nazi movement in the United States. By the late 1930s, according to the Justice Department, this organization had between 8,000 and 10,000 members (the American Legion put the figure higher at 25,000), most of them recent immigrants or nonnaturalized Germans, as well as its own German-language newspaper, the *Deutsche Weckruf und Beobachter* ("The German Alarm Call and Observer"). To some, it was a mere pawn of Berlin, but probably only a small minority of its members were genuine fifth columnists.[44] The Bund did not confine itself to organizing parades of brown-shirted activists.[45] It also sought to put pressure on the long-established German-language newspaper the *New Yorker Staats-Zeitung,* as well as on German-American clubs like the Steuben Society of America and the Roland Society, to support the Hitler regime. It was only the increasing strength of anti-Nazi feeling in the United States—especially after *Kristallnacht*—that deterred more German-Americans from backing the Bund.[46]

The approach of war only worsened interethnic relations in New York. "New York is a veritable powder keg," wrote one advocate of U.S. neutrality, "and our entry into the war might touch it off." Predictably, Coughlinites strongly backed the anti-interventionist America First Committee, which also had the support of Henry Ford and Charles Lindbergh. Few Irish-Americans had an appetite for fighting another war on the same side as the British Empire. By contrast, New York's Jewish organizations agreed with the administration's view that "the choice [was] between Hitler and civilization."[47]

III

Like most New York neighborhoods, Washington Heights—the area of Manhattan where the Kissingers made their home—is not a precise geographical location. If you had asked where it was in 1938, you might well have been told "the area around 159th Street near the intersection of Broadway and Fort Washington Avenue" or "the area to the north and west of Harlem." Looking back, a near contemporary of Kissinger's defined it somewhat differently:

For me, the early boundaries of the neighborhood were 173rd
Street to the south, 177th Street to the north, South Pinehurst
Avenue to the west and Broadway to the east. The only exceptions were if I was in Jay Hood Wright Park, I could go to the
extreme rear, which was at Haven Avenue, one block west of
South Pinehurst. If I was on Broadway, I could go to 181st
Street to the movies; or if on Ft. Washington Avenue, I could
go to 178th Street to the "Y." . . . On the corner of 181st Street
and Broadway was . . . the Harlem Savings Bank and, opposite
it, the RKO Coliseum.[48]

Hilly and surrounded on three sides by rivers, Washington Heights was
the last part of Manhattan to be urbanized, a process that was still not
quite complete in the 1930s. The developers favored five- and six-story
brick apartment buildings, but parks like Fort Tryon and Inwood Hill
made this one of Manhattan's most verdant districts. That may explain its
appeal to the mostly middle-class exiles from Hitler's Germany.

By the outbreak of World War II, Washington Heights had such a
large population of German-Jewish refugees that it was jokingly known
as the "Fourth Reich."[49] Other nicknames were "Cincinnati," a pun on
the German question *"Sind Sie net' die Frau soundso?"* ("Aren't you Mrs.
So-and-so?") and *"Kanton Englisch,"* another pun meaning "Not a word
[*Kein Ton*] of English."[50] Altogether, between 20,000 and 25,000 German-
Jewish refugees settled there, close to a quarter of the nearly 100,000
Jewish refugees from Hitler's Germany to the United States.[51] But Jews
were never more than three-eighths of the Washington Heights population, and by the time of the war that proportion had fallen.[52] The fact that
the refugees were relatively elderly (22 percent were over forty) and
favored small families meant that they were never likely to compete with
the Irish and Greek populations.[53] Partly for that reason, Washington
Heights was less outwardly Jewish than, say, Brownsville in Brooklyn.

Washington Heights was, by almost any definition, a middle-class
neighborhood. Median family income in 1930 had been just over $4,000,
three times what it was in the Lower East Side, but half what it was in
the Upper West Side, home of the wealthy "alrightniks."[54] The refugees, however, arrived with little cash. Often, like the Kissingers, they

had only a crateful of furniture. What made Washington Heights so attractive was that it was both *bürgerlich* and affordable. Rents were relatively low, and because most apartments had between six and eight bedrooms (some of which had originally been intended for servants), it was possible to sublet for cash.[55] As in other parts of New York, the different ethnic groups engaged in residential self-segregation by street and even apartment building, so that in some streets all-Jewish buildings could be found not far from all-Irish ones.[56]

The degree of separateness of the Jewish community came as a surprise to many of the newcomers. Writing in 1951, the Frankfurt-born Ernest Stock—who had arrived in New York in 1940—recalled, "It came as a shock to discover how much [the United States] is a series of rather tight ethnic enclaves. . . . German Jewish professionals frequented the homes of other German professionals, whereas, in New York, Jewish doctors and lawyers tend to visit the homes of other Jewish doctors and lawyers."[57] For such professionals, it was far from easy to find work. Physicians had to pass state medical examinations; German-trained lawyers had almost no chance of practicing again. The best option was to set up a small business catering mainly to one's fellow Jews. Already by 1940 there were eight kosher butchers in Washington Heights. Jewish bakeries also sprang up, specializing in poppyseed-covered *barches*.[58] A few Washington Heights firms succeeded in finding a wider market, notably the Odenwald Bird Company and the Barton candy store. But most stayed small. For many men, the choice was between idleness and door-to-door sales; for many women, between their own housework and that of others.[59]

Even to their fellow Jews in New York, the refugees were to some extent alien. According to one refugee, American Jews regarded the newcomers as "conceited": "they 'stick together and won't mix with the rest of us,' they are 'arrogant,' they are 'schemers,' they are 'mercenary'—a long list of accusations sounding not too much unlike the ideas about Jews generally harbored by anti-Semites."[60] For nearly everyone in Washington Heights, life in pre-Hitler Germany had been better than their new exile existence. A popular joke had one dachshund saying to another, "In Germany I ate white bread every day." The second replies, "That's nothing, in Germany I was a Saint Bernard."[61]

For those refugees who could not at first find work—and Louis Kissinger was one of them—life in Washington Heights revolved around "agreeable socializing with coffee and cake."[62] Lublo's Palm Garden offered "Viennese cuisine" (though the proprietor was in fact from Stuttgart). Other German-Jewish restaurants in the neighborhood included Orner's, the College Inn, and Restaurant Derrick. There one might pass the time reading *Aufbau,* the weekly newspaper published by the Deutsch-jüdischer Club (later the German-Jewish Club, later the New World Club) or its smaller local rival *Jewish Way,* published in German by Max and Alice Oppenheimer from 1940 to 1965.[63] Alternatively, there was the Prospect Unity Club, with its headquarters at 558 West 158th Street. Other associations included the Immigrant Jewish War Veterans and Agudath Israel of Washington Heights. For younger people there was the Maccabi Athletic Club, which had its clubhouse on 150th Street, or ALTEO (All Loyal To Each Other), another youth organization.[64]

Such clubs, however, were less important in the life of the refugee Jewish community than the numerous religious and charitable organizations (*chevras*) they founded. Jewish immigrants to New York tended to begin by creating small synagogues for themselves and their *landslayt* (countrymen), usually meeting in rented rooms. In the second generation, Jews in places like Brooklyn and Flatbush built more formal "synagogue centers" ("a pool with a school and a shul"), which mixed the religious and the secular (from physical fitness to Zionism). Secularization was hard to resist. By the 1930s, the typical New York Jew did not regularly attend religious services; he would turn out for Rosh Hashanah and Yom Kippur, when temporary "mushroom" synagogues had to be set up.[65]

The Jews of Washington Heights were different. This was partly because of circumstances that predated the arrival of the German-Jewish refugees. In the mid-1920s a group of wealthy Orthodox Jews had financed the foundation of Yeshiva College, which was (and is) located on Amsterdam Avenue and West 185th Street. Under the leadership of Bernard Revel, the college grew out of the Rabbi Isaac Elchanan Theological Seminary, but it was intended to be much more than a seminary. Revel was motivated partly by the restriction of Jewish admission to the Ivy League universities in the years after the First

World War. His aim was to take Orthodox Judaism "out of the ghettos" by combining study of the Talmud with a broad liberal arts program.[66] Washington Heights was therefore already a center for Jewish scholarship ten years before the Kissingers arrived there. It was also home to several Jewish congregations, including the Hebrew Tabernacle, the Fort Tryon Jewish Center, and Washington Heights Congregation. Yet the newcomers proved reluctant to become involved with any of these institutions.

To other Jews in New York, the German Jews were *Yekkes,* characterized by their "exaggerated discipline in daily life, love of order taken to grotesque lengths [and] overvaluing of humanistic education." Compared with Jews who had come to America from Eastern Europe, certainly, the German Jews seemed much more buttoned-up in their worship. People arrived early, services began punctually, they sat on fixed pews in rows facing the same way, they had formal choirs led by cantors, and there was none of the swaying or chanting in prayer to be seen in the synagogues of the Lower East Side or Brooklyn.[67] Though strict in their observance of religious law—they were more likely to keep kosher than other New York Jews[68]—Orthodox German Jews did not dress like Hasidim.[69] Men wore hats (or less commonly, yarmulkes) at all times, but they shaved—in Washington Heights, beards were for rabbis only. Women dressed plainly but not anachronistically: "One black dress, one blue dress, and one brown dress are considered an entirely adequate wardrobe."[70]

Predominantly Orthodox, predominantly South German, the refugees brought with them cleavages that meant little in the United States.[71] In Germany, where all Jews were required to belong to single local communities (*Gemeinde*), there had been a rift between followers of communal or unitary Orthodoxy, led by Seligman Baer Bamberger, and those of separatist Orthodoxy, led by Samson Raphael Hirsch. Confusingly, the former were more conservative in their mode of observance but favored coexistence with proponents of Reform and even of Zionism; the latter, while somewhat closer to Reform in their mode of worship, strongly rejected both Reform and Zionism. The persistence of such differences explains why the Orthodox German-Jewish refugees founded so many new congregations.[72] By 1944 there were twenty-two "refugee communities" in New York.[73] Of the twelve founded in Washington Heights, four were unitary and four separatist.[74] The first to be established was Kultusgemeinde Gates of Hope in 1935, followed three years later by the Synagogengemeinde Washington Heights, Tikwoh Chadoshoh (New Hope), and K'hal Adath Jeshurun (also known as "Breuer's," after its rabbi, Joseph Breuer). The only new Liberal congregation was Beth Hillel, founded in 1940 by exiles from Munich and Nuremberg.[75]

It is doubly significant that the Kissingers opted to join K'hal Adath Jeshurun. Breuer, who had been born in Hungary but from 1926 until 1938 had been head of the Samson Raphael Hirsch School in Frankfurt, was a strict separatist, whose ideal was the all-embracing, exclusively Orthodox community (*kehilla*).[76] For Breuer, the synagogue was merely the center of a complex of institutions and services, which included a separate school (*yeshiva*), ritual bath, *kashruth* supervision (of kosher food producers), and even a monthly newsletter. In an early edition, the German-language *Mitteilungen* ("Notices") warned newcomers to the United States:

> Here in this country . . . there is no organized community. Whatever there is of organization is voluntary and subject to the changes inherent to voluntary organizations. The authority over Jewish questions, including Kashruth, is not established. Rabbis whose knowledge of the law qualifies them to be authorities may not be recognized by the community as such. Others lacking the knowledge may have forced themselves into authoritative positions from where they unscrupulously give their pronouncements.[77]

Accordingly, the *Mitteilungen* listed retailers and products that could be relied upon to be kosher. Moreover, like their rabbi in Fürth, Leo Breslauer, Breuer was strongly anti-Zionist. In September 1940, he published a revealing summation of recent Jewish history.

> Emancipation led to Assimilation, whose proponents were the men of the so-called Reform Judaism [movement]. Complete

alienation and mass baptism were the inevitable consequences. Assimilation led to the revival of anti-Semitism, which is always what happens according to G*d's eternal truths. Anti-Semitism precipitated the Zionist movement, which just continued the madness of Assimilation under a different flag, and directed it down no less disastrous, because wholly un-Jewish, paths. The result of it all is the catastrophe of the present time, with all its horrible manifestations.[78]

It was the Zionist sympathies of the Yeshiva Rabbi Moses Soloveitchik that persuaded Breuer to set up his own Yeshiva Rabbi Samson Raphael Hirsch.[79] The only puzzle is why the Kissingers stuck with Breuer when their former rabbi, Leo Breslauer, arrived in New York and set up his own synagogue, Kehillath Yaakov.[80] Kissinger suspected it was because Breuer was the more charismatic figure. He soon grew accustomed to hearing his fiery sermons once a week.[81]

The great counterbalance to the influence of men like Breuer was public school. Young refugees like Heinz and Walter Kissinger swiftly found themselves existing in two worlds: the backward-looking Orthodox world of their religious community and the self-consciously progressive world of the secular high school. At first sight, this seems strange. American public schools remained broadly Christian, in the sense that they observed Christian holidays. The priorities of interwar educationalists were also explicitly secular and integrative. Extracurricular activities—from athletics to journalism—were intended to train "efficient citizens." Yet the belief of Orthodox parents that their children could enjoy the benefits of secular education without losing their religious faith had profound consequences. While Irish-American and Italian-American families often eschewed the public system in favor of Catholic schools, Jews enthusiastically adopted the public schools in their neighborhoods. Jewish pupils were soon overrepresented in the new extracurricular activities.[82] Increasingly, they were taught by Jewish teachers: by 1940, more than half of all new teachers in New York public schools were Jewish.[83] This symbiosis manifested itself in the board of education's recognition of Hebrew as a foreign language worthy of study.

George Washington High School, which would give the future Harvard professor his introduction to American education, was not the most Jewish high school in New York City. That honor belonged to Seward Park in the Lower East Side, where 74 percent of the pupils were Jewish, followed by New Utrecht (in Bensonhurst) and Evander Childs (in Pelham Parkway). Nevertheless, between 1931 and 1947, around 40 percent of pupils at George Washington were Jewish, compared with around 20 percent who were white Protestant, 5 percent who were African American, and 4 percent who were Italian or Irish. In this period, Jewish boys were conspicuously overrepresented in academic clubs and the honor society Arista, and underrepresented in all sports except basketball. However, they were also underrepresented as presidents and as editors of the school newspaper, among the most prestigious positions a student could hold. Here the native-born students were still dominant.[84]

For an intelligent Jewish boy, George Washington High offered not just formal education but socialization. Born in the United States rather than in Germany, the future chairman of the Federal Reserve Alan Greenspan recalled more clearly the pleasures than the pains of his years at George Washington: watching the Giants at the Polo Grounds, following the Yankees on the radio, going to see Hopalong Cassidy at the cinema, and listening to the Glenn Miller band at the Hotel Pennsylvania.[85]

Yet there was another, less appealing side to teenage life in Washington Heights. As many had feared, the outbreak of war exacerbated already serious ethnic friction. Gangs like the Amsterdams and the Shamrocks attacked Jewish boys with cries of "Kill the Jews!"[86] Anti-Semitic groups like the Christian Front and the Christian Mobilizers carried out attacks on synagogues and Jewish cemeteries in Washington Heights.[87] Coughlin's NUSJ explicitly protested against the Jewish community, mobilizing the local Irish population against supposedly job-destroying Jewish innovations like self-service stores.[88] To German-Jewish refugees, the failure of the authorities to clamp down effectively on such violence and intimidation was a sobering reminder that they could not be complacent about their new home. As one journalist complained, "We are tired of approaching a police captain, hat in hand, saying 'Please Captain McCarthy (or O'Brien) . . . My boy was hit because he is a Jew. Will you send a cop?' And we are damned sick and tired of watching the sickly Hitler-like grin and hearing the usual answer: 'Ah, the boys are just playing.'"[89] It was not until 1944 that any gang members were prosecuted and the Catholic hierarchy openly disavowed their behavior.

Until the end of their lives, many of the refugees of Washington Heights felt—and were made to feel—more "American Jewish" or "German Jewish" than "American."[90] As the character of their neighbors changed—as African Americans and Puerto Ricans moved into the area south of 158th Street—the Jewish population of Washington Heights felt even more beleaguered—one reason for their political switch to the Republican Party in the early 1950s.[91]

IV

What impression did New York make on the fifteen-year-old Heinz Kissinger? Many years later, in his memoirs, he stressed the contrast between Germany and America.

> Until I emigrated to America, my family and I endured progressive ostracism and discrimination. . . . Every walk in the street turned into an adventure, for my German contemporaries were free to beat up Jewish children without interference by the police. Through this period America acquired a wondrous quality for me. When I was a boy it was a dream, an incredible place where tolerance was natural and personal freedom unchallenged. . . . I always remembered the thrill when I first walked the streets of New York City. Seeing a group of boys, I began to cross to the other side to avoid being beaten up. And then I remembered where I was.[92]

As we have seen, however, the risk of being beaten up also existed for a Jew in Washington Heights. Another writer has speculated that the young Kissinger found assimilation relatively easy ("as a German Jew [he] was prepared by his own culture to take on, in large part, the trappings and spirit of another culture while retaining his inner integrity").[93]

An alternative hypothesis is that his parents' membership in an Ortho-dox community in fact prevented assimilation and, in particular, "rein-forced Henry Kissinger's now deeply rooted discomfort with mass democracy."[94] Such assessments are surely wide of the mark.

From the moment the Kissingers' ship docked at the terminal on Manhattan's West Side ("Hell's Kitchen"), the family was preoccupied with practicalities. Although they had sufficient means to have their papers processed on board, sparing them the indignities of Ellis Island, the Kissingers had painfully little to live on. There had been five bed-rooms in their apartment in Fürth. Now they were reduced to two. After a brief stay with their aunt, they moved to Washington Heights, first at 736 West 181st Street and then in a cramped apartment at 615 Fort Washington Avenue (well to the west of Broadway, in a solidly Jewish neighborhood). The fact that they got an apartment at all was no mean feat; in the rush of immigration that followed *Kristallnacht,* many new arrivals initially found themselves in communal accommodations like the Congress House on West 68th Street run by Rabbi Stephen Wise and his wife.[95] Kissinger later recalled the hardships of the time.

> My brother and I . . . slept in the living room. We had no pri-vacy. Today I can't imagine how I did it, [but] in those days I didn't think . . . I didn't feel sorry for myself. I didn't think I was suffering. . . . Today when I visited my mother in that apartment, where she stayed until she died, I couldn't believe I lived there and slept in the living room on the double couch. [I] did my school work in the kitchen. But all these books say that I suffered as a refugee. . . . [I]t's not true . . . it's nonsense.[96]

The family's single biggest problem was that Louis Kissinger could not find work. Handicapped by his imperfect English,* ill at ease in his new surroundings, he confided in his wife, "I am the loneliest man in this big city." As she later recalled, "I didn't know how to get started, he didn't know how to get started." At first, they lived on money from

---

*To speed up the process of learning, the family spoke only English at home and listened regularly to the radio in the apartment kitchen.

another relative in Pittsburgh.[97] Although Louis finally succeeded in getting a bookkeeping job in the firm of a friend, he was plagued by ill health and depression; henceforth Paula was the family's breadwinner, after the Council of Jewish Women helped train her as a servant and caterer.[98] Younger and more adaptable than her husband, she mastered English quickly and lost no time in building a small catering business—a typical refugee story.[99] The pressure was therefore on her sons—and especially the elder of them—to begin earning money. As soon as they were able to, the Kissinger boys enrolled at George Washington High School. It was a big school, with around three thousand students[100] and an ethos of "sink or swim." Surviving examples of Kissinger's schoolwork suggest that he adapted swiftly to his new milieu.[101] In January 1940, however, he switched to evening classes in order to take a full-time job, paying $11 a week, in the shaving brush factory owned by his mother's cousin's husband. The factory was located downtown, at 22 West 15th Street, and the work was far from pleasant. Kissinger toiled from eight a.m. until five p.m., squeezing acid out of the badger bristles from which the brushes were made, until he was promoted into the shipping department, which meant delivering brushes all over Manhattan. After the forty-minute subway ride back to Washington Heights and a hasty dinner, he then had to get through three hours of night school. Yet the sixteen-year-old's performance did not suffer. That semester he achieved scores of 95 for Grade 3 French, 95 for Grade 2 American History, 90 for Grade 1 American History, 90 for Grade 6 English, 85 for Grade 7 English, and 75 for Advanced Algebra.[102] For all its flaws, the Jewish Realschule in Fürth had put Kissinger ahead of his classmates in math, history, and geography.[103] He was ahead in other ways, too, already reading Dostoevsky for pleasure.

The single biggest obstacle to overcome was of course linguistic. As Kissinger later recalled, "In those days nobody said, 'These poor refugees, let's teach them in German.' They threw us into a school and we had to do it in English and . . . I had to learn English very fast. I didn't know any when I came here."[104] That was not strictly true, as he had studied English in Germany and had a rudimentary ability to read it. But there is a world of difference between studying a foreign language and studying *in* a foreign language. It was one thing to exchange

"Heinz" for "Henry." It was another to *sound* American. According to one account,

> The school record noted that the new student had a "foreign
> language handicap." It was a "handicap" that contributed to
> the shyness of his George Washington days as well as to his
> sense of being a loner. His command and use of the new lan-
> guage would later win the respect of diplomats throughout the
> world, but his accent—once described by a German-born
> friend of his as "ridiculously Bavarian rather than Prussian"—
> would stay with him until adulthood. "I was terribly self-
> conscious of it," he would say years later.[105]

Much has been written about Kissinger's distinctively Central European accent, the persistence of which seems strange, given that his younger brother largely lost his, in common with most refugees young enough to attend a U.S. high school.[106] It was the older refugees who clung to German. As late as April 1941, the Kissingers' synagogue was still debating whether to switch its services and newsletter from German into English.[107] As one contemporary noted, "The importance of this can hardly be overestimated: often the German accent makes the difference between complete integration in American life and perma-nent status as an 'outsider.'"[108] It is indeed remarkable that someone so intelligent and ambitious retained his German accent for so long, at a time when speaking accentless English was seen as the prerequisite for social mobility.[109] However, it was from his arithmetical rather than his linguistic skills that the young Kissinger hoped to make a living. After graduating from George Washington, he applied to City College of New York to study accountancy.[110]

The old world was losing its power over the young man. His father and mother devoutly attended the K'hal Adath Jeshurun synagogue. Leo Hexter, another refugee from Fürth to Washington Heights, recalled Kissinger's "thirst for religious knowledge."[111] But in a first sign of rebellion against his parents' Orthodoxy, he joined a youth group organized by the Reform synagogue Beth Hillel.[112] Like many of the newcomers from Germany, Kissinger found his faith changing under the new influences he encountered in New York. He was, he recalled, "certainly not Orthodox" any longer, as he was regularly working on Jewish holidays, as was his brother.[113] As one contemporary put it, writing not long after the war, "A great many of [the German-Jewish refugees] never come to *shul* except on High Holidays. . . . In the United States . . . religious observance has been gradually abandoned. . . . The fight for a living in the new country, they claimed, was too exhausting. . . . There was also the argument that in a world where one's relatives are burnt to death, there could be no God."[114]

Of course, few people in the United States could anticipate at this stage the magnitude of the horrors that would later become known as the Holocaust. But none were better acquainted with the Nazi regime's potential for violence than the refugees newly arrived in New York. Among the very few pieces of Kissinger's writing to survive from this period is a sketch for a newspaper entitled "Voice of the Union: *Eine Zeitung im Aufbau*! [Newspaper under construction]," dated May 1, 1939, and marked "World-wide edition—Publication in Germany prohibited." It is emphatically secular in tone, foreseeing the need to lend assistance to future waves of refugees from Nazism:

> Members of the Union,
>
> Six years have passed since a massive event—bigger in scale than any natural disaster—intervened deeply in our fate. Its effects are greater than anyone could ever remotely have anticipated. National Socialism is relentless in its will to annihilate and it acknowledges no restrictions!
>
> At first, the Jewish people were hit the hardest, but the spirit of Hitler is spreading its poison further, over lands and seas; it destroys families, house and home, and penetrates into the smallest parts of our lives. Only a few people were able to grasp the full extent of this misfortune soon enough. Too many believed that there was still a way out and that the civilization of the twentieth century would protect us from the worst. Today

we know that this hope was a great illusion. As the pressure became ever greater, there began the great problem of emigration. I need not say any more. We all know the sad road of emigration, made the rockier by the fact that many countries closed their doors to us. One country remained our hope: the USA. We who have had the good fortune to come here to the classical land of freedom wish to prove our gratitude by playing a part in the great system of assistance for those who will come in the future through the foundation of "the Reunion of Comrades."[115]

Kissinger's thinking on Zionism was also evolving. In 1937 he had described the idea of a secular Jewish state in Palestine as "unthinkable." Before leaving Germany, however, he had written to a friend, "My future lies in America, but my hope lies in Palestine . . . the land of our mutual yearning." But by the summer of 1939 his attitude had changed: "Look at what has become of this illusion. 'Our' Palestine is a toy of great power politics, torn apart by civil war and handed over to the Arabs."[116] Some of those members of Agudath Israel with whom Kissinger had associated in Fürth had become even more strident in their anti-Zionism since moving to the United States. Indeed Rabbi Breslauer came close to supporting the anti-Zionist Neturei Karta.[117] But Leo Hexter later denied that Kissinger followed this lead.[118]

The reality was that the teenage Kissinger found himself in the midst of a real-life "reunion of comrades"—one that was forcing him not only to question his earlier beliefs but also to lose faith in his former friends. Writing to one of them in July 1939, he candidly revealed his ambivalence about this new home, "New-York":

My personal impression of America is very two-sided: in some regards I admire it, in others I despise the approach to life here. I admire American technology, the American tempo of work, American freedom. It is powerful what America has achieved in its short history. This is only possible in nations that live in such security and that have never experienced serious crises. You need to have been to the skyscraper area of New York to understand what modern technology can create. You need to have driven on an American highway into the countryside to be able to understand the exaggerated patriotism of Americans. But the greater the light, the greater the shadow sides are. Alongside the most beautiful houses in the world you see here the most wretched, alongside excessive wealth, unspeakable poverty. And then this individualism! You stand completely on your own, no one cares about you, you have to make your own way upwards.[119]

Much of this was in fact quite typical of German-Jewish refugees, who were at once dazzled by the scale of the American achievement as embodied in New York and dismayed by its more rough-hewn aspects.[120] But Kissinger had a further, and deeper complaint: "The American trait I dislike the most is their casual approach to life. No one thinks ahead further than the next minute, no one has the courage to look life squarely in the eye, difficult [things] are always avoided. No youth of my age has any kind of spiritual problem that he seriously concerns himself with." American superficiality had direct social consequences for the earnest young German: as he admitted, this was "one of the main reasons why I have had difficulty making friends with any American."

Yet it was not the lack of new friends that was the real problem. It was the presence of old ones—three "former schoolmates" who, like Kissinger, had ended up in New York.[121] One of these was Walter Oppenheim, whose family had made the same journey as the Kissingers, from Fürth to Washington Heights. The others were Hans (later John) Sachs and Kurt Reichold. On the surface, the young refugees were learning to work hard and play hard like true New Yorkers. They didn't just slave by day and study by night. They went to baseball* and football games, following both the Yankees and the Giants. They played tennis.[122] They went to dancing classes. They learned to drive.

---

*Kissinger later told Andrew Schlesinger that he had been introduced to the game by "Italian friends."

And they dated girls, among them Kissinger's future wife Anneliese Fleischer.[123]

But it was another young women, named Edith, whose arrival from Fürth turned the reunion of friends into a maelstrom of romantic rivalry. In March 1940, Kissinger—already taking pride in his command of written English—had mailed Edith two of his school book reports. She had never replied. After simmering for two weeks, the young man penned a third missive, in which he laid bare his adolescent soul:

> Since you do not seem to be in the habit of answering letters, even if one goes through considerable trouble in securing you one's bookreports [*sic*], I am forced however reluctantly to write you a third and final time. I am indeed mystified over that silence of yours, the least thing you could have done was to confirm the receipt of the documents. But now as to the purpose of my letter: I would be very grateful to you, if you were to return to me as soon as possible the 2 bookreports and the essay, because I am collecting them. If you do not want to write to me, you can give them to Hans or Oppus [Oppenheim's nickname] when you see them again.
>
> "Here perhaps I ought to stop. But a solicitude for your welfare . . . urges me to give you some advice . . . which can be offered all the more freely, as you can see in it only the disinterested warning of a parting friend." (Quotation from Washington's farewell address). While I wanted for a long time to clarify my position and, as far as possible, the one of the rest of us too, towards you orally, I realize now, that this is the only way left to me. I write you this letter, because I feel that it would be unfair towards you, to make you believe, that there exists something like an amity among us five where this amity was only artificially construed in order to give some of us an opportunity to see you. In short, what you see of us is only our best side, and hardly ever will you see any of us as he really is. It is therefore, that I want to caution you against a too rash involvement into a friendship with any one of us.

Kissinger was sixteen. He had been in New York less than two years. He was in the grip of an intense teenage crush and a violent jealousy of his rivals:

> You are the first girl of our class, to come here, and a rather attractive one at that, so that it is only natural that there should be a general desire to win your friendship. The two chief exponents, that try or tried to gain your friendship, are, excluding me, Oppus and Kurt. I think it is necessary, to write you some of their disadvantages, since the only thing you see are their advantages. I want to caution you against Kurt because of his wickedness, his utter disregard of any moral standards, while he is pursuing his ambitions, and against a friendship with Oppus, because of his desire to dominate you ideologically and monopolize you physically. This does not mean that a friendship with Oppus is impossible, I would only advise you, not to become to [sic] fascinated by him lest you become too dependent upon him.
>
> To substantiate this, it is necessary, that I explain to you, what has happened among ourselves since your arrival in this country. Oppus was the first one to learn of it and he therefore considered it as his prerogative to contol [sic] access to you by withholding your address. This was especially directed against Kurt, partly because of an old feud, dating back to your days in Fuerth, and partly because Oppus felt, that Kurt's crooked ways should not always succeed. In this scheme, he wanted me to try to gain your friendship. However, I refused to see you, a fact which I will explain later on.—After some time Kurt learned of your arrival in this country. A quarrel with Oppus was only averted because Kurt did not want to spoil his chances of getting your adress [sic]. Long discussions followed, culminating in a meeting of all five of us and the decision to invite you to a meeting at Kurt's.
>
> Now as to my first refusal to see you. This was motivated by one of three reasons. Firstly I did not want to quarell [sic] with my friends in return for a doubtful friendship with you.

Secondly, I did not want to make a fool out of myself. I knew that if I saw you, I would again be captivated by you and make a fool out of myself, which I subsequently did. Thirdly, I had the feeling, that you considered me more of a clown than anything else. However, I later revised all these three points of view, because I realized, that I was only running away from myself.

While concluding, may I reiterate again, that I would regret it very much if you were to ascribe purely selfish motives to my writing this letter. I wrote it, because I got sick and tired of pretending to be somebody, which I am not and in order to be of some help to you, if possible, as far as your relations with the other members of our former class are concerned.

In the hope, that within these limits set, the letter succeeded, I sign,

very truly yours,

Kissus.[124]

Many an intelligent young man, on having his advances rebuffed, has written with equal vehemence to the object of his affections. But what makes this letter stand out—aside from its still Teutonic punctuation and occasional minor misspellings—is its analytical precision and psychological penetration. Amid the Sturm und Drang of being sixteen, Kissinger had anatomized the relationships between the friends and how the reunion had changed them, reviving the old rivalry between Oppenheim and Reichold and intensifying the feelings of insecurity that had made Kissinger seem aloof ("I had the feeling, that you considered me . . . a clown"). In the end, "Kissus" had enough sense not to mail his solipsistic screed, instead preserving it as a testament to the dark intensity of his life as a young immigrant.

In an earlier letter to another girl, this time writing less awkwardly in German, Kissinger had given an account of his life since coming to New York "in 2 phases: My spiritual and my general life." What he had to say about the former was revealing:

As I already mentioned at the beginning [of this letter] a great deal has changed within me. The 8 months here have turned me from an idealist into a skeptic. That does not mean I no longer have any ideals. It means that, since 95% of my previous ideals have suffered shipwreck, I no longer have any clearly delineated goals, but I have broader ideas that are not yet clear to me. I am not so much pursuing a durable ideal as trying to find one.[125]

Coming to America had changed nearly everything for the young man. He had been emotionally as well as geographically displaced. He little knew in July 1939, on the eve of the most destructive war in all history, that the "durable ideal" he sought would find him first—in the unlikely setting of a U.S. Army training camp, preparing for a perilous journey that would take him all the way back to Germany.

CHAPTER 4

An Unexpected Private

Having set ourselves the task of seeing Mephisto as a
distinct individual, we must see him as more than just
Faust's other (less important) ego. . . . We also need to
draw Mephisto out from the shadow that Faust casts right
over him and to stand him next to his opponent or
partner. . . . Only through ever more purposeful
development of the ego can we ultimately reach the path to
the *Übermensch*.

    —Fritz Kraemer, "The Pact Between Mephistopheles
and Faust," 1926[1]

In politics, as in any other field of human activity, character,
values and faith are at least as important as those other
factors which may be described, roughly, as "economic." I
revenge myself by thinking that it is far more fantastic to
believe that the world of realities consists almost exclusively
of "wages," "raw materials" and "industrial production."

    —Fritz Kraemer, 1940[2]

I

On September 11, 1941, in a speech in Des Moines, Iowa, the aviator-turned-demagogue Charles Lindbergh accused "Jewish groups in this country" of "agitating for war."

Lindbergh had been a national celebrity since his solo, nonstop Atlantic crossing from New York to Paris in 1927. By 1941, as the leading spokesman for the America First Committee, he was the most influential of all the voices urging the United States to stay out of the Second World War. "Instead of agitating for war," Lindbergh declared, the Jewish groups in this country should be opposing it in every possible way for they will be among the first to feel its consequences.

Tolerance is a virtue that depends upon peace and strength. History shows that it cannot survive war and devastations. A few far-sighted Jewish people realize this and stand opposed to intervention. But the majority still do not.

Their greatest danger to this country lies in their large ownership and influence in our motion pictures, our press, our radio and our government.

The leaders of the Jewish people, Lindbergh concluded, "for reasons which are as understandable from their viewpoint as they are inadvisable from ours, for reasons which are not American, wish to involve us in the war. . . . We cannot allow the natural passions and prejudices of other peoples to lead our country to destruction."[3]

Less than three months later, on December 7, 1941, Japan attacked Pearl Harbor, nullifying at a stroke this and other arguments for American neutrality.

The young Henry Kissinger could certainly not have been accused of "agitating for war." When the news of Pearl Harbor reached New York, he "was at a football game . . . watching the New York Giants play the Brooklyn Dodgers, who at that time had a football team. It was the first professional game I'd seen . . . and when I came out, they had a Sunday paper . . . with a headline about an attack on Pearl Harbor. I didn't know where Pearl Harbor was."[4] Kissinger was now a student at City College of New York, an institution long popular with academically ambitious immigrants, which was just a twenty-minute subway ride from his parents' apartment. He was doing well, obtaining As in nearly every course (ironically, his only B was for history). In his free time, he liked to watch football or baseball, or to play tennis at the courts under the George Washington Bridge.[5] A career in accountancy seemed to beckon.[6]

Yet the studious young man was hardly blind to the approach of war. The German-Jewish refugee community in Washington Heights had been watching developments in Europe with growing anxiety, not least because so many families—including the Kissingers—had relatives still living in Germany. Contrary to Lindbergh's claims, few people in Washington Heights had been "agitating for war." Yet war, when it came, was a kind of relief for the refugees, if only because it rendered obsolete the accusation that their interests as Jews were different from America's national interest. The monthly magazine published by the Kissingers' synagogue quoted Jeremiah 29:7: "And seek the welfare of the city whither I have banished you and pray in its behalf unto the Lord: for in its welfare shall ye fare well." As Rabbi Breuer put it, "In this grave hour, not only the feeling of deepest gratitude drives us to do our duty. . . . With the welfare and the future of this country the future and welfare of our people is [*sic*] closely connected."[7]

It was by no means inevitable, however, that Henry Kissinger—along with around 9,500 other German-Jewish refugees—would end up donning an American uniform to fight against the land of his birth. In June 1940 Congress had passed the Alien Registration Act, which imposed a number of restrictions on residents of the United States who had been born in Germany and had not yet been naturalized. Among these was exclusion from the military. This created an anomaly, since the Selective Training and Service Act had introduced the draft for all men resident in the United States between the ages of twenty-one and thirty-six. It was not until March 1942 that the Second War Powers Act introduced a system of accelerated naturalization, which allowed "enemy aliens" who had served honorably in the armed forces for at least three months to become citizens.[8] Only with the reduction of the draft age to eighteen the following November did Kissinger become eligible for conscription. Even then, there remained restrictions on the jobs that could be assigned to a "selectee" of German origin. Indeed, Kissinger's brother, Walter, was pulled out of the 26th Infantry Division and sent to the Pacific Theater on account of his German origins.[9] It took time for the head of the Office of Strategic Services (OSS), William J. ("Wild Bill") Donovan, to convince the army that men of German origin had "specialized qualifications" that were "urgent[ly] need[ed]" in combat units.[10]

In all, around 500,000 Jews served in the American army, of whom 35,000 lost their lives.[11] The participation rate for Jewish refugees was somewhat higher than the national average.[12] Now that America was in the war, such men had a unique combination of incentives to fight. As one refugee soldier put it, "I, who have been robbed of all I possessed and driven out of my homeland, have so much more reason for wanting to get a whack at Hitler than has the average American citizen who has not yet suffered from him."[13] Such men were "not following blindly a leader, fighting a battle they don't know what for. All are not only fighting for America but fighting for the eternal rights of their Jewish people. . . . Among them is the right of freedom of religion, giving each soldier the right to worship and practice his religion the way he wants."[14] As we shall see, however, the realities of army life sometimes seemed calculated to make a mockery of such fine sentiments.

II

Henry Kissinger's draft notice arrived not long after his nineteenth birthday. The angst-ridden teenage refugee was now a studious young New Yorker, going steady with Anneliese [Anne] Fleischer—an unassuming local girl of whom his parents approved—seemingly destined for a life of blameless obscurity as an accountant in Washington Heights.[15] Once again history had intervened. In mid-February 1943, after a farewell family dinner at the Iceland Restaurant near Times Square, Kissinger found himself on a train bound for Camp Croft, five miles south of Spartanburg, South Carolina, a sprawling complex of barracks and shooting ranges capable of accommodating, and inflicting basic training on, up to twenty thousand men at a time. On arrival, as Kissinger described it to his brother, he was unceremoniously "pushed around and inoculated, counted, and stood at attention."[16] For the next seventeen weeks, he was at the mercy of his lieutenant, whom he grew to hate "beyond description and probably for no real reason."[17] On June 19, having survived three months of basic training, Kissinger was entitled to become a naturalized U.S. citizen. Raising his right hand, he swore the following oath:

> I hereby declare . . . that I absolutely and entirely renounce and
> abjure all allegiance and fidelity to any foreign prince, poten-
> tate, state, or sovereignty, and particularly to Germany, of
> whom (which) I have heretofore been subject (or citizen); that

I will support and defend the Constitution and laws of the United States of America against all enemies, foreign and domestic; that I will bear true faith and allegiance to the same; and that I take this obligation freely without any mental reservation or purpose of evasion: So help me God.[18]

He was now an American soldier.

Camp Croft was as different as could be imagined from the insular, homogeneous refugee community of Washington Heights. In theory, soldiers enjoyed freedom of religion; in practice, there was scant regard for the rules and rites that an Orthodox Jew was supposed to observe. By design, the draft put men from every walk of life, from every section of society, into uniform. Only the continued segregation of African Americans prevented the army from being a truly integrative institution.[19] But it was not only drill and target practice that the new recruits were being introduced to; there was also gambling, drinking, and whoring, the favorite recreations of the average GI. Kissinger's candid advice to his younger brother about how to survive basic training speaks for itself.

[Keep] your eyes and ears open and your mouth closed. . . .

Always stand in the middle because details are always picked from the end. Always remain inconspicuous because as long as they don't know you, they can't pick on you. So please repress your natural tendencies and don't push to the forefront. . . .

Don't become too friendly with the scum you invariably meet there. Don't gamble! There are always a few professional crooks in the crowd and they skin you alive. Don't lend out money. It will be no good to you. You will have a hard time getting your money back and you will lose your friends into the bargain. Don't go to a whore-house. I like a woman, as you do. But I wouldn't think of touching those filthy, syphilis-infected camp followers. . . .

You and I sometimes didn't get along so well, but I guess you knew, as I did, that in the "clutch" we could count on each other. We are in the clutch now.[20]

Some Jewish GIs did their best to abide by the rules of their religion, even at boot camp.[21] For others, however, "eating ham for Uncle Sam" was less difficult than they might have expected. There was, of course, no shortage of abusive anti-Semitic language at a place like Camp Croft. But as another Jewish conscript observed—the novelist Norman Mailer—in such a heterogeneous army, there was a term of racial or ethnic abuse available for almost everyone: Jew, Italian, Irishman, Mexican, Pole.[22] Officially, moreover, the army outlawed anti-Semitism, promoting the idea that the United States was fighting for "Judeo-Christian values."[23] In any case, for northern recruits who had never previously visited the South, camps like Camp Croft provided an introduction to a whole new world of prejudice. One foreign-born Jewish GI from New York was astonished when some southerners called him a "damn Yankee."[24] As another soldier recalled,

> There were Catholics, Protestants and Jews. Some were functionally illiterate southern dirt farmers. Others—the schoolboys—were much more educated. Some had nearly finished college. . . . The Army homogenized them all—even . . . the talkative high-school egghead. It made no difference what anyone thought was home. This was a new world, with new standards. . . . You were judged by one chief measure—whether you could be relied upon when the chips were down.[25]

In one important respect, Jews stood out, even if they were not observant. They accounted for a disproportionate number of the "eggheads," generally doing much better than average in the Army General Classification Test taken by every new recruit. This mattered because any soldier scoring above 110 became eligible for what appeared to be one of the army's most attractive opportunities: the Army Specialized Training Program (ASTP). The rationale behind the ASTP was threefold: to increase the supply of potential officers; to increase the number of technical specialists in the army; and to prevent colleges being financially eviscerated by the draft. Announced in December 1942, the program sent academically able soldiers to colleges all over the country for accelerated courses in engineering, foreign language, medical, dental, and veterinary studies—subjects considered valuable by the army. In three twelve-week terms, separated by just a week, ASTPers were supposed to cover the equivalent of the first year and a half of college. By December 1943 there were around 300,000 of these so-called "quiz kids" in four hundred different universities and colleges, of whom 74,000 were studying basic engineering and 15,000 advanced engineering.[26] Henry Kissinger was one of them; so was his brother.

For those selected, the ASTP was a heavenly release from the discomforts of basic training and the prospect of immediate consignment to the war as infantry replacements. The "quiz kids" were free from noon Saturday until one a.m. Monday morning, allowing those allocated to colleges near their homes to visit family and friends. Compared with the likes of Camp Croft, college accommodation was "one step short of paradise—food served on stainless steel trays, with as much cold milk as you could drink, and clean bedding in the dorm."[27] True, the work was demanding—courses were highly compressed—and about one in five of those admitted to the program dropped out in the first two terms. But intensive engineering was certainly far better than the available alternative—hence the song (to the tune of "My Bonnie Lies over the Ocean"):

> *Oh, take down your service flag, Mother,*
> *Your son's in the A.S.T.P.*
> *He won't get hurt by his slide rule,*
> *So the gold star never need be.*

> *He's just a Joe College in khaki,*
> *More boy scout than soldier is he,*
> *So take down your service flag, Mother,*
> *Your son's in the A.S.T.P.*

> *The Air Corps may take all the glory.*
> *The Infantry takes all the guts.*
> *But wait till we tell you our story*
> *How we sat out this war on our butts.*

Six months ago, we were all soldiers,
We thought we'd fight Japs overseas,
Now the Army's a dim recollection
Since we got in the A.S.T.P.

Oh, after this war game is over
And grandchildren sit on our knee,
We'll blush when we have to tell them
That we fought in the A.S.T.P.[28]

Even the insignia of the program—a lamp with a burning light—was nicknamed the "flaming pisspot."[29]

Kissinger was not complaining. After further vetting at Clemson College in South Carolina, he had the good luck to be sent to study engineering at Lafayette College, a liberal arts college in Easton, Pennsylvania. Since its elegant nineteenth-century campus is located just over eighty miles from New York, he could spend weekends at home with his family and girlfriend. His roommate and fellow "quiz kid," Charles J. Coyle, vividly remembered life with the young Kissinger. "He took the 'normal' course of study in stride," Coyle later recalled, "and then spent his enthusiasm . . . in piecing together new bits of reasoning. He seemed not so much concerned with what the instructors were saying as he was intent on what they were planning to mean." Even by the standards of the ASTP, Kissinger was exceptionally bookish. But what Coyle was most impressed by was Kissinger's unusually aggressive reading style.

> [I] spent half my time tripping over books that he ate up and the other half in awe of his trap-like brain. . . . He didn't read books, he ate them with his eyes, his fingers, his squirming in the chair or bed, and with his mumbling criticism. He'd be slouching over a book and suddenly explode with an indignant, German-accented "BULL-SHIT!" blasting the author's reasoning. Then he'd tear it apart, explosive words prevailing, and make sense of it. . . . Like everything else he did right, he

was precise in picking up vocabulary and pronunciation and to my Brooklyn ears it was a new experience to hear a man in a temper taking the time to put in "-ing" on his four-letter words. . . . The guy was so damned bright and so damn intellectual it was strange to most of us—and we were the ones who'd been selected for our intelligence. He'd come into the living room of our suite. Three or four of us would be talking, probably about sex. He'd flop on the couch and start reading a book like Stendhal's *The Red and the Black*—for fun![30]

Another sign of Kissinger's intellectual seriousness was his unmilitary appearance.

No one dressed sloppier than he did. It was, to use his word, "ridiculous." Army clothes never fit anybody unless they were altered or tailored but those were two words Henry never thought of. For him, dressing was a farce. He could dress faster with each piece of clothing facing the wrong direction, and do it differently each time, than it took me to slip into fatigues. At inspection time, everybody who passed Henry could find a different piece of clothing that needed adjusting.[31]

But Kissinger was not at Lafayette to grace a guard of honor. Between October 1943, when he was formally enrolled, and April 1944, he took twelve courses, including chemistry, English, history, geography, mathematics, physics, and military science. His scores ranged between 80 and 95 percent, apart from a perfect 100 in chemistry and a disappointing 72 percent in math.[32] "Mr. Kissinger is without doubt one of the finest students I have in all my classes," wrote his physics instructor. "He has a keen mind, shows an active interest in all his work, comes to class thoroughly prepared daily, does all assigned work and frequently goes beyond the requirements set for the remainder of the class. . . . I can certainly recommend Mr. Kissinger most highly for any type of work requiring an individual having an alert, keen, thorough, analytical, and inquiring mind."[33] Unfortunately, that was not the type of work the army now had in mind for him.

In truth, the ASTP was always vulnerable to any increase in the armed services' demand for combat manpower, and by the end of 1943—when Congress set the army's size at 7.7 million—that demand was surging. The commanding general of the Army Ground Forces, Lesley J. McNair, had always doubted (wrongly) that a college education significantly enhanced a soldier's combat quality. The problem as he saw it was not a lack of skills but a lack of raw numbers, not least because of Congress's overgenerous deferment rules, which exempted 5 million men from the draft for occupational reasons as well as deferring it for fathers. Ultimately, Secretary of War Henry L. Stimson yielded to pressure from the generals. On February 18, 1944, it was announced that ASTP would be wound up.[34] Eight out of ten "quiz kids" were summarily ordered back into the infantry.

This was the kind of illogical snafu for which the U.S. Army has long been famed.[35] More than a hundred thousand men had been handpicked for their brains. They had spent months acquiring new and valuable knowledge. During those months, they had missed out on the opportunity for promotion. And now they were to be sent back to square one, without any regard whatever for their innate intelligence or new skills. "Throw your slide rule into the sea," the quiz kids now sang bitterly, "and march on to the POE [point of embarkation]." The initials of the program's basic training center at Camp Hood (ASTPBTC) were now said to stand for "All Shot to Pieces by the Congress." Chinese speakers were sent to Europe; Italian and German speakers (among them Walter Kissinger) to Asia. Worse, the returning "quiz kids" were liable to be abused as "boy scouts" or, worse, "youse dumb college fucks." Because so many ASTPers were assigned as riflemen, one critic halfseriously wondered whether "the disbanding of the ASTP was a plot to place the best brainpower in the country in the most vulnerable positions, where the largest number were likely to be killed." One victim of the new policy later asked, "Why did we cull out the most intelligent people in the military service and then throw them into the meat grinder where they would sustain the highest casualties?"[36] When the news reached Lafayette that "we were all to be shipped to the Infantry as privates," Charles Coyle recalled, "we all screamed and moaned, and Henry '–ing'ed in his fashion."[37] The only way to avoid the meat grinder was to switch to medical school, since the army still acknowledged the need for more doctors. Kissinger took the test, but the only available place went to Leonard Weiss, who Kissinger later acknowledged had "saved me from being a doctor."[38]

III

Camp Claiborne, Louisiana, was the antithesis of Lafayette College, with its quaint quadrangles and wood-paneled libraries. Situated in the flat, hot countryside just north of the town of Forest Hill, the camp consisted of rows of "tar paper shacks," each containing twenty-four double-deck bunk beds. In summer the heat was sweltering; the tiny windows in each shack provided next to no relief.[39] From November 1943, this was home to the 84th Infantry Division, to which Henry Kissinger, along with 2,800 former ASTP men, had been assigned. The division's nickname—"the Railsplitters"—did not imply a great need for intellectuals. Kissinger and his fellow former quiz kids had a long train ride in which to contemplate the reversal of their fortunes.[40] Donald Edwards, another ASTPer, recalled arriving at Claiborne to the accompaniment of a military band. As one of the newcomers muttered, "Better if they played a funeral march as far as I am concerned."[41] They had gone from being academic highfliers back to being mere cogs in the vast American military machine.

The 84th Division was one of forty-five U.S. Army divisions that were assigned to the European theater of war. Each division at full strength consisted of around 14,000 men, subdivided into three regiments, each of 3,000 men, plus the division artillery. Each regiment in turn was made up of three battalions, comprising approximately 850 men apiece, each battalion of five companies, each company of four platoons, and each platoon of three twelve-man squads.[42] After six weeks of accelerated basic training, Private Henry Kissinger, serial no. 32816775, was assigned to G Company in the 2nd Battalion of the 335th Infantry Regiment. He was now just another GI, a doughboy, a dogface.[43]

Life at Camp Claiborne was as hard as life at Lafayette had been cushy. Some days were spent on forced marches "where we had to go nine miles in a little over an hour," others on "twenty-five-mile hike[s] with full pack." There were "water ration" days, when men were confined to one canteen of water for the whole day. Then there were "field problems," which entailed sleeping in pup tents in snake-infested swamps. There was swimming practice ahead of amphibious operations, as well as training in parachute use. Tedious hours were spent wiping the oily brown Cosmoline off new rifles and stenciling serial numbers onto duffel bags, helmets, and boots.[44] Recreational facilities were available in the nearest large town, Alexandria, in the form of bars, where GIs fought, and whorehouses, where they contracted VD.[45] Closer to the camp was "Boomtown . . . that damn collection of shacks."[46]

"My infantry division was mainly Wisconsin and Illinois and Indiana boys, real middle Americans," Kissinger later recalled. "I found that I liked these people very much. The significant thing about the army is that it made me feel like an American."[47] In fact, some soldiers nicknamed him "Ja" precisely because of his German accent.[48] But his work as company education officer, briefing soldiers once a week about the "current orientation of the war," earned him popularity.[49] As Charles Coyle recalled, "He was able to take the daily and weekly sources of news, contradictory, confusing and puzzling as they were, and present his interpretation of them to the extent that each of us . . . felt just a little bit more in control of what the next day would bring. . . . We claimed that Henry was the only man that could out-opinion *Time* magazine . . . but constructively."[50] Already the bookworm had learned the value of humor as a defense, as Coyle recalled. "He was too smart to get into a fight. Henry would just be patient with the kids from the hills, and they ended up liking him. Sometimes he would ridicule the army, sometimes he would ridicule himself, and there were times when he would ridicule some of us. But he did it with a smile. It was typical New York humor."[51]

Sometimes, however, Kissinger had to listen. Most army lectures were soporific affairs in terms of both content and delivery. But one day there came the exception that proved the rule. His name was Fritz Kraemer. Like Kissinger, he had been born and raised in Germany. Like Kissinger, he was a mere private. But he was, in the words of his immediate superior, "a most unexpected sort of a 'private.'"

IV

Henry Kissinger later called Fritz Kraemer "the greatest single influence on my formative years."[52] It is tempting to call him the Mephistopheles to Kissinger's Faust; certainly, Kraemer knew Goethe's play intimately, having written an insightful essay about it at the age of seventeen.[53] Born in industrial Essen in 1908, Fritz Gustav Anton Krämer (he later dropped the umlaut) was the son of an ambitious lawyer who had married the daughter of a wealthy chemicals manufacturer. A sickly child, young Fritz spent four of his school years studying at home with private tutors.[54] He was also the product of a broken home, something of a rarity in those days. While his father rose through the legal ranks to become the public prosecutor (*Erster Staatsanwalt*) in Hagen and later Koblenz, his mother established a boarding school for "difficult children" in a village in the hills outside Frankfurt.[55]

Fifteen years older than Kissinger, Kraemer spent his formative years during those of the First World War, the November Revolution, and the Weimar Republic. He came to believe that the war "had destroyed all foundations—lives, institutions, values, and faiths. He vividly remembered battles, blockade, hunger, the Bolshevik Revolution, the coup against the Kaiser, the Versailles Treaty, the French occupation of the Rhineland, the loss of his family's fortune to inflation, and revolution in Germany's streets." For many middle-class Germans of Kraemer's generation, precisely these experiences made Hitler an attractive national "redeemer." But Kraemer was unusual. He studied abroad, first in Geneva, then at the London School of Economics, finally in Rome. He married a Swede. Repelled as much by fascism as by socialism, he embraced a conservatism that at times verged on self-parody. From the age of seventeen, he wore a monocle ("in his strong eye . . . so the weak eye would be forced to work harder") and habitually wore jodhpurs and knee-length riding boots.[56] But his was an unusual conservatism, very different from that of the German National People's Party, which historians tend to see as the heir of the Wilhelmine Conservative Party, but which was easily swallowed up by the Nazis.

Peter Drucker, the future management "guru," first encountered Kraemer in 1929, when they were both students in Frankfurt. Walking by the River Main one cold April day, he was startled to see a kayak containing "a cadaverous man, naked except for the scantiest of black bathing trunks and a monocle on a wide black ribbon . . . furiously paddling upstream," with "the black, white and red pennant of the defunct German Imperial Navy" fluttering as he rowed.[57] With his "big, triangular, sharp nose that jutted out of his face like a sail[,] high cheekbones[,] . . . sharp chin[,] and piercing slate-gray eyes," Kraemer made Drucker think of "a cross between a greyhound and a timber-wolf." Known to his fellow students as "the young Fritz" because of his resemblance to and admiration for Frederick the Great, "Kraemer considered himself a genuine Conservative, a Prussian monarchist of the old pre-Bismarck, Lutheran and Spartan persuasion . . . opposed alike to the ugliness and barbarism that was coming up so fast behind the Nazi swastika, and to the well-meaning and decent but weak and gutless liberalism of the 'good German.'"[58] Not yet twenty-one, Kraemer told Drucker that he had "only two ambitions in life: he wanted to be the political adviser to the Chief of the General Staff of the Army; and he wanted to be the political mentor of a great Foreign Secretary." Drucker asked why Kraemer himself did not aspire to be the "great Foreign Secretary." Kraemer replied, "I am a thinker and not a doer. . . . I don't belong in the limelight and don't make speeches."[59]

Always an elitist—better, a moral aristocrat—Kraemer had a Nietzschean contempt for the vulgarities of populist politics but an equal aversion to what he called "cleverling" intellectuals. Neither this nor his sartorial idiosyncrasies should deceive us. In later life, he would come to be seen as the éminence grise of neoconservatism, a kind of cross between Leo Strauss and Dr. Strangelove. But Kraemer was nothing of the sort. His academic training was in fact in international law, a highly unlikely focus for an orthodox Prussian conservative. At Geneva he studied with Eugène Borel, an authority on international law, and William E. Rappard, the academic and diplomat who had helped persuade Woodrow Wilson that the League of Nations should be based in Geneva, and who served as director of the League's Mandate Department.[60] In London Kraemer's professors included Philip

Noel Baker, who had acted as assistant to the League's first secretary-general, and Arnold McNair, founder (with Hersch Lauterpacht) of the *Annual Digest of International Law,* who went on to become Whewell Professor of International Law at Cambridge.[61] Finally, in Frankfurt, Kraemer became a pupil of Karl Strupp, one of the leading German experts on international law.[62] It was under Strupp's supervision that Kraemer wrote his doctoral dissertation on "The Relationship Between the French Treaties of Alliance, the League of Nations Covenant, and the Locarno Pact." Published in 1932, it provides invaluable insights into Kraemer's intellectual development.

Kraemer's core argument was that the League of Nations and Locarno Pact (as well as the Kellogg-Briand Pact) were contradicted by France's postwar defensive alliances with Belgium, Czechoslovakia, Poland, Romania, and Yugoslavia. In particular, the French alliances were incompatible with Article 10 of the League Covenant, which had committed signatories "to respect and preserve as against external aggression the territorial integrity and existing political independence of all Members of the League." Not only should that article have made bilateral defensive alliances redundant, Kraemer argued, but the French "alliance system" also placed a "permanent" and "*general* political pressure" on Germany (not to mention Hungary), which significantly and unacceptably restricted its freedom of movement.[63] It therefore constituted an inadmissible "league within the League."[64] Three things stand out about this argument. The first is its historical character: nearly half the dissertation is an analysis of the pre-1914 European alliance system. The second is its clear distinction between power and law—*Macht* and *Recht*—as exemplified by Kraemer's bald assertion that it "is self-evident that England entered the war [in 1914] not because of Belgium but because it was France's ally."[65] Like his mentor Strupp, Kraemer reasoned that whatever might formally be stated in a treaty of mutual defense, in practice such a relationship has meaning only if it implies combined action against a common enemy. As such, its very existence increases the risk of war. In a crucial passage, Kraemer warns against forgetting that "the absolute *security of one* state, since it is predicated on the exclusion of the free play of opposing political forces and the suspension of the balance of power, must necessarily become the hegemony of the power that enjoys that security, and thus [implies] insecurity for all others."

Like the overwhelming majority of Germans, then, Kraemer rejected the international order established by the post-1918 treaty system: not just the Treaty of Versailles, with its objectionable assertion of German "war guilt," but the entire complex of treaties of which France was a signatory. Nevertheless (and this is the third striking point about the dissertation) he did so in a way that implicitly accepted the legitimacy of the League of Nations as an institution. Like that of Strupp and his contemporary Albrecht Mendelssohn-Bartholdy, Kraemer's position was that Wilson's idealistic vision of collective security was being subverted by the cynical behavior of France and England. By the standards of 1920s Germany, this was a liberal, not a conservative standpoint. Not entirely coincidentally, both Strupp and Mendelssohn-Bartholdy were Jews. Both lost their academic posts within a short time of the Nazi seizure of power in 1933. Such was the intellectual pedigree of the man who would become Henry Kissinger's Mephistopheles.

Despite his taste in teachers, Kraemer was outwardly a Prussian monarchist—almost a caricature of a German conservative—and nearly all contemporaries took him at face value. The reality was rather different. His father, Georg Krämer, had in fact been born a Jew, though he had converted to Christianity at the age of nineteen; his mother, whose maiden name was Goldschmidt, was also a convert. A Protestant, a Ph.D., and a reserve officer, Georg Krämer had striven to become a model Prussian. Though his Jewish origins, his divorce, and then the war had slowed his progress, by 1921 he had worked his way to the coveted post of public prosecutor. With his veteran status and "wholly conservative" outlook, the elder Krämer was able to ride out the initial Nazi purge of those they defined as Jews, but in 1935 he was forced into retirement under the terms of the Reich Citizenship Law, which rendered all "non-Aryans" second-class citizens.[66] In January 1941 he was arrested for failing to wear the yellow star, by then mandatory for Jews. In May 1942 he was forced to give up his home to an "Aryan" family. Two months later he was deported to Theresienstadt concentration camp. He died there of malnutrition on November 1, 1942.[67]

Unlike his father—about whom he never spoke—Fritz Kraemer had the good sense to leave Germany as soon as Hitler came to power, immediately giving up his position as clerk to a municipal court judge and moving to Italy. After securing Italian validation of his German Ph.D. at the University of Rome, he accepted a post at the International Institute for the Unification of Private Law in Rome (UNIDROIT), which had been set up in 1926 as an auxiliary organ of the League of Nations.[68] As a student of international law, Kraemer practiced what he preached. When a German naval attaché sought to prevent him from flying the imperial flag on his kayak, Kraemer went to court, arguing that under international law he was free to fly whichever flag he chose.[69] But Mussolini's Italy was hardly the best place to thumb one's nose at the Third Reich, especially as the two dictators drew closer to each other. In 1937, fearing that he was no longer safe in Italy, Kraemer sent his wife and son back to Germany, to stay with his mother. With Drucker's help, he was able to get a visa to travel to the United States.[70] Unable to find a university post, Kraemer initially worked on a Maine potato farm, before finding a job at the Library of Congress, where he began work on "a historico-juridical reference book on 'The Parliaments of Continental Europe from 1815 to 1914.'"[71] At the same time, he attempted to help his mentor Strupp and his wife, who had left Germany but got no farther west than Paris before Strupp's death.[72]

One important lesson Kraemer learned from his experiences in the 1930s—and one that he would instill in his pupil Henry Kissinger—was the primacy of the moral over the material. "I find," he wrote in a letter in November 1940,

> that even good friends denounce as romantic and rather fantastic my conviction that in politics, as in any other field of human activity, character, values and faith are at least as important as those other factors which may be described, roughly, as "economic." I revenge myself by thinking that it is far more fantastic to believe that the world of realities consists almost exclusively of "wages," "raw materials" and "industrial production," or of other measurable entities the value of which can be expressed in exact figures. I am, indeed, entirely unable to understand how

anybody with even a rudimentary knowledge of history can fail to perceive that a man's love for his wife, children or country, his feeling of honour, his sense of duty, his willingness to sacrifice himself for some idea or ideal, or perhaps the repercussions produced in his soul by a beautiful sunset are quite as likely to influence the shaping of our political reality as—let us say—a piece of labour legislation. Thousands of the most modern tanks will be of no use for the defense of a country, if the men in these tanks are unwilling to fight for their country to the end. The best laws, the most progressive legislation, are not worth the paper on which they are written, if the moral qualities of the judges who have to apply them are doubtful.

To this credo Kraemer remained faithful all his life. But he recognized that the spirit of the age was materialistic, both in Europe, where varieties of socialism vied with one another, and in America, where the disciplines of economics and political science were ascendant. It was at around this time—presumably as a result of encounters with the American intelligentsia—that Kraemer's hostility to intellectuals hardened. "Those who with pride and more often with arrogance call themselves the intellectuals must learn," he wrote darkly, "that a 'brilliant' brain, the mere technical perfection of the methods of thinking and analyzing, are not the only and not even the highest values in this world. If without profound convictions, without faith, and without self-discipline they continue to play with their brains, our civilization, very probably, will be doomed."[73]

In May 1943 Kraemer was given the opportunity to turn words into deeds when he was drafted. Much more than Kissinger, Kraemer had to be viewed with suspicion by the U.S. military. True, he had the kind of knowledge that the army needed as it came to grips with fighting the Germans. Not only was he fluent in German and English, he spoke no fewer than ten other languages. But there was much else that was fishy. In order to protect his wife and son, who were both still in Germany (and remained there until the end of the war), Kraemer had explicitly stated on a pre-induction form that he would prefer not to fight against the country of his birth. In reality, he had no objection whatever to fighting against the Nazis, but "as a lawyer I had carefully worded the statement in such a manner that on the one hand I would be accepted for service and that on the other there would be, technically, no 'high treason' with ensuing German reprisals against my family, should the nonclassified questionnaire fall into the wrong hands."[74] Nor was that all. Kraemer's FBI file reveals that from early 1942 he was repeatedly investigated by the bureau, first at the instigation of Paul F. Douglass, the devoutly Methodist president of the American University, in whose Washington home Kraemer had lodged while he was working at the Library of Congress. (Douglass's suspicions were aroused by the picture of Kaiser Wilhelm II on Kraemer's dresser, his "distinctly Jewish" features, and his idiosyncratic habit of entering upstairs rooms by climbing up the outside wall and through the windows.) Another informant was perplexed by the fact that Kraemer was "probably 100 per cent pro-German but also definitely anti-Hitler." A "first-class exhibition dancer" who wore riding breeches and boots because he had no other clothes, a Prussian monarchist who also spent time at the distinctly liberal World Fellowship Center in Albany, New Hampshire, a married man who (according to another informant) "had been intimate with scores of girls," Kraemer was suspect in multiple ways.[75] This explains why, although he was sent directly (without basic training) to the special Military Intelligence Training Center at Camp Ritchie, Maryland—which specialized in turning out interrogators—he was passed over by OSS and ended up instead with the 84th Infantry Division. Kraemer wondered if the OSS decision had to do with his "marked skepticism regarding the Eastern [Russian] dictatorship."[76] But his anti-Soviet sentiments were the last thing the U.S. authorities were worried about.

Fortunately for Kraemer, the disquiet of J. Edgar Hoover was not shared by General Alexander R. Bolling, who took over command of the 84th Division in June, the month of the D-Day landings in Normandy. A decorated veteran of the First World War and, before that, of the unsuccessful expedition to capture the Mexican revolutionary general Pancho Villa, Bolling understood better than most generals that morale can be built through explanation. Legend has it that he heard Kraemer barking commands in German during an exercise. "What are you doing, soldier?" the general asked. "Making German battle noises,

Sir," Kraemer replied—upon which he was assigned to headquarters.[77] In reality, Kraemer had already been transferred to the division's G-2 section—with responsibility for lecturing "on enemy order of battle, general indoctrination, and current events"—before Bolling's appointment. But Bolling recognized Kraemer's talent; more important, he saw that the rationale for fighting Germany could scarcely be more convincingly conveyed than by a caricature German apparently supplied by central casting. As Kraemer himself put it, "I knew better perhaps than most other men what dictatorship meant and why this war was being fought."[78] Significantly, Kraemer remained a private. But as one officer put it, "His bareness of rank is . . . a condition upon which depends, to a great extent, the success of his mission."[79]

V

It was the summer of 1944, and the men of G Company were resting after a ten-mile hike through the Louisiana heat. Suddenly they found themselves being addressed by a monocle-wearing private carrying a riding crop. "Who's in command here?" he barked. A startled lieutenant admitted that he was. "Sir," said Kraemer, "I've been sent by the general, and I'm going to speak to your company about why we are in this war."[80]

The G Company men were impressed by what they heard, and none more so than Private Kissinger. As he later recalled, "The subject was the moral and political stakes of the war. . . . Kraemer spoke with such passion, erudition, and overwhelming force, as if he were addressing each member of the regiment individually. For the first time in my life and perhaps the only one . . . I wrote to a speaker to say how much he had moved me."

The letter Kissinger wrote was almost naïvely direct: "Dear Pvt. Kraemer. I heard you speak yesterday. This is how it should be done. Can I help you in any way? Pvt. Kissinger."[81] But Kraemer appreciated the lack of flannel. "His letter had no frills," he later recalled. "None of that 'exhilarating,' 'wonderful,' et cetera, stuff I dislike. 'This—' I said—'This is a man of discipline and initiative.'" A few days later he invited the younger man to dinner at the enlisted men's club, "at which he questioned me about my views and spoke to me about his values," Kissinger recalled. "Out of this encounter grew a relationship that changed my life."[82]

It seems unnecessary to engage in psychological speculation about Kissinger's need for a surrogate father at this stage in his life.[83] Kraemer was an impressive figure: older, far better read, with strong opinions formed and tested in some of the great intellectual centers of the interwar period. He was unabashed about speaking in German about German ideas.[84] The more remarkable thing was Kraemer's apparently near instantaneous recognition of Kissinger's intellectual potential. According to Kraemer's account, within just twenty minutes he realized that "this little nineteen-year-old [*sic*] Jewish refugee, whose people knew nothing really of the great currents of history that were overcoming them," was a kindred spirit. He had "the urgent desire not to understand the superficial thing but the underlying causes. He wanted to grasp things."[85] Kissinger was "musically attuned to history. This is not something you can learn, no matter how intelligent you are. It is a gift from God." Kraemer later hotly denied that he had been Kissinger's "discoverer," arguing that he had merely "evoke[d] him to himself." "Henry," he told his protégé, "you are something absolutely unique, you are unbelievably gifted."[86] Later, when they were working together in Europe, Kissinger recalled how Kraemer "sort of taught me history. He was very interested in history and we would walk at night and talk at night and that generated my systematic interest in history. Kraemer . . . was focused on statesmanship and on the relationship between values and conduct. And on the impact of society on the individual, illustrated by historic examples."[87]

At the time of their meeting, of course, both men were acutely aware of how far their own fates as individuals were about to be determined by vast historical forces—or rather, by the statesmanship of others.

VI

On or around September 21, 1944, Winston Churchill sailed past Henry Kissinger, entirely oblivious of his existence. The prime minister was on board the luxurious *Queen Mary* and was speeding back to

London from Quebec, where he and Britain's most senior military chiefs had spent five arduous days conferring with President Roosevelt and the top brass of the U.S. Army and Navy. Private Kissinger, by contrast, was on an overcrowded troopship, bound for the front line in Western Europe.

The second Quebec conference came at a crucial juncture in the Second World War. Operation Overlord, launched on June 6, 1944, had been a success. Allied troops had established a bridgehead in Normandy. Operation Dragoon (August 15) saw an equally successful amphibious assault on southern France. Paris and Brussels had been liberated. By September the Allies had fought their way as far as the Dutch–German border. The vast economic and manpower advantage that the Allies had enjoyed since the German attack on the Soviet Union and the entry of the United States into the war now made the final outcome inevitable. In the East, in the wake of the Red Army's Operation Bagration, Romania and Finland sought peace with Stalin; the German Army Group North found itself cut off on the Courland peninsula in Latvia. But the Axis armies were far from beaten, and the mood at Quebec was less than self-congratulatory; indeed, at times it was acrimonious. Field Marshal Sir Alan Brooke had confided to his diary on the way to Canada that Churchill "knows no details, has only got half the picture in his mind, talks absurdities and makes my blood boil to listen to his nonsense." Churchill made a point of reminding Roosevelt that "if Britain had not fought as she did at the start, while others were getting under way, America would have had to fight for her existence." The British proposed marching on Vienna to preempt Stalin's ambitions in Central Europe, but an increasingly frail Roosevelt seemed unmoved by Churchill's warnings about "the rapid encroachment of the Russians into the Balkans and the consequent dangerous spread of Russian influence in the area." The British also pressed to be given a bigger naval role in the war against Japan; Churchill was adamant that Singapore should be recovered "in battle." Admiral Ernest J. King, the American chief of naval operations, left no one in any doubt that he preferred to beat Japan without the Royal Navy (which he called a "liability"), prompting "blunt speeches and some frayed tempers." There was yet more dissension when Churchill and Roosevelt initialed the plan drawn up by U.S. Treasury secretary Morgenthau to return Germany to being "a country primarily agricultural and pastoral in character," a plan vehemently and presciently opposed by Brooke on the ground that Germany would be needed as an ally against "the Russian threat of twenty-five years hence."[88]

First, however, Germany had to be defeated. With Hitler's armies falling back behind the borders of the pre-1939 Reich, the end appeared to be in sight. Some even dared to hope the war might "be over by Christmas," as if forgetting how wrong those words had been thirty years before. Roosevelt was right to warn that "the Germans could not be counted out and one more big battle would have to be fought."[89] By the time of the Quebec conference, the Allied advance in Western Europe was losing momentum. As supreme commander of the Allied forces in Europe, the cool, cautious cardplayer Dwight D. Eisenhower struggled to rein in the egotistical Bernard Montgomery and the bloodthirsty George Patton, both of whom chafed at Ike's strategy of steady advance along a broad front. Even as the Quebec conference drew to a close, Montgomery's bold attempt to use airborne forces to go around the northern end of the Siegfried Line was foundering at Arnhem. Worse, continuing supply problems arising from the Allies' failure to secure the Scheldt estuary were slowing down progress along the entire western front.[90] Meanwhile, German resistance was hardening rather than crumbling, thanks to the Nazi regime's formidable combination of bureaucracy, propaganda, and terror, as well as to the growing awareness of ordinary Germans that defeat would bring harsh retribution before it brought peace.[91]

The ordinary Americans of the 84th Division knew little, if anything, of all this. As they bade farewell to Camp Claiborne on the night of September 6–7, 1944, to the jaunty strains of "Over There" played by the camp band, the mood was optimistic.[92] One private, Donald Edwards, noted in his diary, "Everyone was hoping that the breakthrough which was occurring in France would continue so that the 84th Division would be nothing more than a peace keeping outfit."[93] Indeed, Edwards bet another soldier that the war would be "finished in three months."[94] Rumors swept up and down the train: "We were headed for China, India, Burma, Italy, Greece, France, or England."

But it was a long enough journey—more than two full days rolling through Memphis, Atlanta, Richmond, Washington, and Baltimore—just to get to Camp Kilmer, New Jersey. There the "big talk at the camp PX [post exchanges, the camp general store] was that the old 84th . . . was to have a good deal. 'Yeah,' said a permanent Kilmer cadreman, 'you guys got a good deal—Army of Occupation.'"[95]

With its two-story wooden buildings painted in multiple colors, Camp Kilmer was a smarter place than Camp Claiborne, but after ten days of drill and calisthenics—punctuated by cheerful lectures on how to abandon a sinking ship, on what to do if taken prisoner, and on "straightening your personal affairs"—it was time to leave. Grumbling under the weight of their thirty-pound backpacks and duffel bags, the men were conveyed by trains and ferry to Manhattan's Pier 57, where they boarded the *Stirling Castle,* a converted Castle Line passenger ship. Whatever excitement Kissinger and his comrades may have felt was short-lived. G Company was given the job of cleaning the ship prior to general embarkation as well as being designated KP ("Kitchen Police"), which meant assisting the ship's cooks for the entire voyage. Not only were conditions on the converted liner unpleasantly cramped, but the ship's kitchens also proved to be vermin-infested and the cooks to be foul-mouthed limeys. "The trouble was that it was English food prepared by English cooks and eaten by Yanks who were accustomed to American chow. . . . It was either raw or overdone or it had too little seasoning." The coffee tasted "like mud," the peas were "like pebbles," the potatoes "as tough as rocks," and the meat "tougher than boulders." Worse was to come. No sooner had the *Stirling Castle* set sail on September 21 than it ran into thick fog just off New York. After just five hours at sea, the ship collided with a tanker and was forced to spend the night at anchor with its lights on and foghorn blaring before returning to harbor the next morning. The man who had bet they would see the Statue of Liberty again before Christmas collected his winnings much sooner than he had expected.[96] Fully a week elapsed before the repaired ship could sail again.

An Atlantic crossing in September 1944 was not without its hazards, the biggest of which was still posed by German submarines. (In that month alone, thirteen Allied ships were sunk by U-boats.) However, the convoy in which the *Stirling Castle* sailed was able to reach Liverpool without incident after eleven tedious days. Even the weather was unre-markable.[97] The men of the 84th were welcomed ashore by a British military band and marched through the city to the main railway station, the majority marveling at the preponderance of old stone housing, small vehicles driving on the wrong side of the road, and narrow-gauge loco-motives. Their destination was Crawley Court, a country estate between Winchester and Stockbridge.[98] For some GIs, this was their introduc-tion to the British class system. As one private complained to another after acting as KP for the officers' mess, "This reminds me of an old southern plantation before the Civil War. All the slaves standing around to serve their master with every detail. I sometimes think I'll drop some soup on someone's head."[99] Kissinger had the advantage of having rela-tives in London, the Fleischmanns, whom he was able to visit on a two-day leave.[100] Other GIs saw a very different side of British life when they visited London. Even in the "dim-out" (the partial blackout that was in force now that German air raids had diminished), the "open flesh mar-ket" at Piccadilly Circus was a breathtaking spectacle.[101] There was a strong temptation to make the most of any such opportunity. As Octo-ber drew to a close, the news from the continent was not encouraging. And as one badly wounded man told the rookies of the 84th, "Those fucking Germans are the best soldiers in the world. They never seem to give up unless it's hopeless. They're real tough."[102]

Private Henry Kissinger would soon discover the truth of these words.

CHAPTER 5

The Living and the Dead

> So I am back where I wanted to be. I think of the cruelty
> and barbarism those people out there in the ruins showed
> when they were on top. And then I feel proud and happy to
> be able to enter here as a free American soldier.
>
> —HENRY KISSINGER to his parents, November 1944[1]

> That is humanity in the 20th century. People reach such a
> stupor of suffering that life and death, animation or
> immobility can't be differentiated any more. And then, who
> is dead and who is alive, the man whose agonized face stares
> at me from the cot or [the man] who stands with bowed
> head and emaciated body? Who was lucky, the man who
> draws circles in the sand and mumbles "I am free" or the
> bones that are interred in the hillside?
>
> —HENRY KISSINGER, April or May 1945[2]

I

The 84th Infantry Division crossed the English Channel from
Southampton on November 1–2, 1944, landing at Omaha Beach.
Aboard the HMS *Duke of Wellington,* GIs of voting age got to cast their
absentee ballots in the presidential election, the fourth in a row to be
won by Franklin Roosevelt. Though old enough, Henry Kissinger
did not vote—a surprising omission considering how often he and
his comrades had been told they were fighting for political as well
as religious freedom.[3] As they clambered from the landing craft that
took them ashore, the young Americans looked with fascination at
the relics of D-Day that still littered the beach and its immediate

surroundings. After a ten-mile march with full packs, however, they had grown indifferent to the sight of burnt-out German tanks. In heavy rain, the men were loaded in groups of twenty aboard two-and-a-half-ton trucks. As their convoy passed through Saint-Lô, there was something new to marvel at: the spectacle of a town reduced to rubble. They had only the briefest glimpse of Paris before heading north through Belgium and on to the Dutch-German border.[4]

On November 25, just over six years since his family had fled Nazi persecution, Henry Kissinger found himself once again on German soil. Ahead of him lay the Siegfried Line—the formidable wall of for-tifications, tank traps, and pillboxes that the Nazis had built along Ger-many's western frontier. It felt like a moment of triumph. Late that night, Kissinger wrote a hasty but exultant note to his parents.

> It is very late and I haven't much time, but I must write a letter, just so that I can affix to it the legend "Somewhere in Ger-many." So I have made it. Out in the darkness that envelopes [*sic*] this town, rows and rows of shattered buildings line the roads. People wander through the ruins. War has come to Germany.
>
> So I am back where I wanted to be. I think of the cruelty and barbarism those people out there in the ruins showed when they were on top. And then I feel proud and happy to be able to enter here as a free American soldier.[5]

In truth, the Allies had been more or less stuck in front of the Sieg-fried Line (or "West Wall") since Aachen had fallen on October 21, more than a month after the first troops had crossed the German bor-der. Allied supply lines were now as overstretched as German supply lines were compressed. The loss of momentum since the summer had given the Germans the chance to reorganize. There were now around fifty new infantry divisions and a dozen panzer divisions ready to resist further Allied advances. The 84th was to be in the vanguard of just such an advance as part of XIII Corps, which in turn was part of the Ninth Army under Lieutenant General William H. Simpson.[6] The enemy welcomed the newcomers with a volley from their feared 88mm guns (originally antiaircraft artillery that by 1944 had been adapted for use against tanks). The men of G Company were bivouacked on a wooded hillside near Herzogenrath, to the northwest of Aachen.[7] As one of them remembered, "We were all scared stiff and hit the ground whenever anything came within hearing distance."[8]

Even before the German 88s opened up, the Americans had encountered a second enemy: the mud. The weather was "cold, wet and grey," and as the 84th's official historian recalled, "The roads were muddy and the fields [sugar beet] were swamps. . . . After weeks of bombing and big guns, of trucks and tanks that dug into the roads, always sinking deeper and deeper, and the complete absence of a living thing not in uniform, it was grim":

> Now and then we fought the enemy, for a few hours or a few days. The mud we fought always, every miserable minute. The mud was Germany. It is amazing what a little mud in the wrong place can do. It will make your rifle a worthless piece of junk. It will jam it just when you need it most. It will ooze through your shoes and through your socks and eat away your feet. It will make your foxhole a slimy, slippery, smelly jail. It will creep into your hair, your food, your teeth, your clothes and sometimes your mind. The enemy's best ally in the Siegfried Line was trench foot.[9]

In some cases, the ravages of trench foot and frostbite were so bad that amputation was necessary.[10] Hunger, too, was a problem. In his first letter home from "somewhere in Germany," Kissinger begged his parents to send him not only a replacement scarf but also "CANNED MEAT COOKIES CANDY PS As you see, I am starved."[11]

Before Kissinger's arrival, on the night of November 10, the 335th Infantry Regiment had been sent to the line near Aachen as part of a temporary assignment to the 30th Infantry Division.[12] C Company had its first contact with the enemy that night when a German patrol approached their foxholes.[13] This, however, was not the main event. On November 12, Field Order 3 had sent the 84th into action north of Aachen as part of an attempt to break through the Siegfried Line and clear the Geilenkirchen salient of enemy forces (Operation Clipper). This was no easy task. The Germans had clear fields of fire across the flat, open fields between the Rivers Würm and Roer. Impediments to the Allied advance included large and well-concealed pillboxes with six-foot walls and surrounding trenches; minefields that had to be cleared using heavy chains as "flails"; and the antitank obstacles known as "dragon's teeth," which consisted of three or four rows of triangular reinforced-concrete obstacles.[14] True, the Allies had the advantage of air superiority over the now terminally weakened Luftwaffe. But this advantage was negated when the weather was murky or when—as often happened—radio communication from the front line to the rear broke down. As they advanced laboriously across beet fields from one village to the next—Alsdorf to Ofden, Hongen to Gereonsweiler, and so on toward Prummern—the riflemen of the 84th were exposed not only to machine gun and sniper fire, but also to German howitzers, mortars, and tanks.

The "Amis" fought well. At dawn on November 19, the 3rd Battalion of the 334th Regiment successfully repulsed a counterattack by the 10th Panzer Grenadier Regiment, proceeding to mop up what was left of the small salient at Geilenkirchen.[15] But the going was tough. When G Company came under artillery fire outside Gereonsweiler on November 22, "each man in the section expected to find everyone else dead in the morning." It was indeed there that the company suffered its first two fatalities.[16] There were further casualties when a frontal assault on the Würm-Lindern-Beeck triangle of villages failed. Only by approaching them one by one was the 84th able to get to Leiffarth, which brought the Americans within striking distance of the River Roer.[17] The 2nd Battalion lost half its front-line troops in one of these attacks.[18]

At one point, G Company found itself pinned down by enemy machine guns, which made a sound "like a curtain tearing" as they spat out twenty-five rounds a second.[19] With several soldiers wounded and one NCO killed, the company dug in, but it was menaced from all sides. On the night of the twenty-ninth, "a German tank went around our right flank and came up behind us. Several soldiers got out of the tank and yelled for us to surrender. No one answered." Second Lieutenant Charles McCaskey was killed by a sniper.[20] "Water was so scarce that the men used to drink out of mud holes and tank tracks. Soon they would be eating snow."[21] On the night of December 2, after four days of uninterrupted fighting, the company was pulled out of the line and sent to Palenberg for some rest. There was hardly a man who did not attend a religious service on the Sunday after the first attack. Just a few days later, however, they were back in the firing line.[22] Soon the Americans came to appreciate a new hazard of this kind of warfare: uncoordinated or even fake surrenders by individual Germans, which could be fatal for would-be captors. With every passing week, the list of those who had "gone for a beer" (been wounded) or "gone to the bar" (been killed) grew longer.[23] As one weary infantryman muttered, "There are only two ways to leave here. Either back to the hospital or you're dead."[24]

The casualties among American infantrymen were certainly high. In all, nearly 110,000 Americans lost their lives in northwestern Europe, more than 356,000 were wounded, and over 56,000 were taken prisoner. On average, U.S. infantry divisions suffered losses of 17 percent killed and 61 percent wounded.[25] For Kissinger's battalion, the 2nd of the 335th Regiment, around 9 percent of enlisted men were killed in action or died of wounds.[26] But his company, G Company, suffered disproportionately high casualties. Of the original 182 men, 21 were killed in action, 40 wounded, and 1 taken prisoner—losses of more than a third.[27] So Private Henry Kissinger was indeed fortunate that, at some point after his arrival in Europe, he was transferred from G Company to the G-2 section of divisional headquarters.[28] According to Kissinger's war record, from then until the end of the war, he was a "Special Agent in charge of Reg[imenta]l CIC [Counter Intelligence Corps] team charged with the security of tactical troops, the prevention of sabotage, and security of lines of supply."[29]

Now Kissinger had the chance to take stock. On the night of November 29, he wrote once again to his parents, still marveling at where he was.

> Night has fallen. A pale moon illuminates this German town. The muddy streets are deserted. In the distance one hears artillery. . . .
>
> So here I am in Germany. Those who have sown the wind have indeed reaped the whirlwind. Nary a house is whole or undamaged in the town. Store fronts are ripped open, goods

strewn all over the street. Roofs are caved in and rubble senseless and insensate is thrown all over. People live in houses with
cardboard in place of windows, with quagmires instead of
streets. Incongruously such personal things as arm-chairs,
sofas, pictures, books are on street corners, in gardens, in door-
ways. Our headquarters is in an abandoned railway-station.
Amidst the twisted wreckage of control-towers, the shattered
remnants of rails one sometimes finds such incongruities as a
sign stating "Local to . . . ," "express to. . . ."

Kissinger's new job was to "evacuate[e] . . . [German] civilians considered unreliable" as well as to comb through captured German mail for
intelligence. Especially striking are his first reflections on the vanquished
Germans he was encountering. Kissinger could feel compassion, even for
the "unreliable civilians" (meaning committed Nazis) he was helping to
weed out: "Germany now knows what it means to wander and to be
forced to leave places dear to one's heart. I had to assist in the evacuation
of civilians considered unreliable. It is tragic no matter how [much] you
hate the Germans. A suit-case in one hand, a handkerchief in the other,
people part. Yet they don't go far and will be able to come back soon.
They are not mistreated. We are no Gestapo." He felt the same flicker of
empathy when he read a letter from a German girl, which

in its universal pathos, is characteristic of this war. In big,
childish hand-writing it stares at me. A young girl writes to the
buddy of her fiancé who has been killed. ". . . You know him
and appreciate what I have lost. I can not believe that I will not
see him again, that is impossible.—Believe me, it is a terrible
pain, I can not think it out, always I must go back to the
thought, it is all a bad dream and lies, yes lies. And in this
insanity, yes it is insanity, I know I am a fool, I wait for my
Hans. And one day he just must come back."

But Kissinger's bottom line was unequivocal: "Well, they started it."
And now they had lost it.

Like many Americans in late 1944, Kissinger made the mistake of thinking the war was nearly over. "Germany is licked," he told his parents. "One look at the prisoners convinces one of that. None of them thinks they can win. . . . Their arrogance is gone and so is their cockiness. Dazed and dishevelled they shuffle in." He drew the same inference from the captured letters he saw.

> Each one is penetrated with a sense of doom and hopelessness
> that is inescapable. Here is one excerpt: "Cologne is in ruins.
> No gas, no water, no electricity, no newspapers for 2 weeks.
> How will it all end?" Here is another: "Bonn has been levelled
> by a big terror-attack in 12 minutes. We are still alive. How
> long?" Another: "Why don't you surrender to the Americans?
> It is still the best way out." And so they go, advices to play sick,
> longing for relatives, defeatism, that is the point to which Hit-
> lerism has brought Germany.[30]

Kissinger was clearly enjoying his new role. "I have to work long hours," he wrote home, "up at 7 and hardly to bed before 1 A.M. I have forgotten what a day off is, but who minds? I enjoy my work and that's all that matters." It would be a mistake, however, to imagine that his new job was entirely cushy. True, it got him out of the freezing foxholes where his former G Company comrades were spending the most uncomfortable and dangerous winter of their lives. But because of the highly fluid nature of the fighting at this juncture of the war, as one rifleman remembered, "no real front could ever be described, since it ebbed and flowed."[31] When the Germans launched their Füh-rer's last desperate bid to regain the initiative on the western front, Special Agent Kissinger soon found himself in an exceptionally exposed situation—one that might easily have cost him his life.

II

Operation Autumn Mist began on December 16, 1944. The increas-ingly delusional Hitler imagined that German armor might be able to repeat the triumph of May 1940, slicing through enemy defenses in the

Ardennes and racing all the way to the Channel coast. But this was blitzkrieg on empty. Each of the eighteen hundred tanks that spearheaded the offensive had just a single load of gasoline; only if they succeeded in capturing Allied fuel dumps would they stand any chance of reaching Antwerp as planned. This time, however, the Germans encountered far stiffer resistance than four years previously. Of the two German thrusts, the one led by Sepp Dietrich's Sixth Panzer Army toward Malmédy and Liège was the first to grind to a halt. Farther south, General Hasso von Manteuffel's Fifth Panzer Army fared better. It was the hard task of the 84th Division to try to arrest his progress before the German panzers reached the River Meuse.

The German offensive was not confined to the Ardennes; there were also smaller attacks to the north, in the Aachen area.[32] As early as December 19, however, the 84th was preparing to rush seventy-five miles south.[33] The Allied position around the ancient Walloon town of Bastogne was precarious. The nearby towns of Laroche and St. Vith were on the point of being captured. If the Allies could not hold Marche-en-Famenne, between Namur and Bastogne, "it seemed very likely that the Germans would roll on to the Meuse."[34] General Bolling liked to lead from the front. At nine a.m. on December 20, he and his senior staff left Palenburg in two cars, bound for the Ardennes.[35] The fog of war was thick at this point; by the time they reached Marche, it was dark and the roads were choked with fleeing civilians. German tanks on the outskirts of the town were close enough to shell the center. The 334th Regiment had to be hastily rerouted to avoid enemy-controlled sectors. Such was the confusion that at one point Bolling himself had to direct the traffic.

Bearing down on Marche were the 2nd Panzer Division and the 116th Panzer Division. As the 84th Division's historian put it, "With nothing on our left flank, above Hotton, and nothing on our right flank, below Marche . . . the 84th was an island of resistance, holding back what was . . . threatening to become a tidal wave of German Panzers," among them Tigers equipped with 88s. Their orders were to hold the line from Marche to Hotton "at all costs."[36] It was at this time that the Germans dropped demands for surrender on the besieged Allied troops in Bastogne. "The fortune of war is changing," declared the leaflets. "This time the U.S.A. forces . . . have been encircled by strong German armored units."[37] (General Anthony McAuliffe of the 101st Airborne Division famously replied, "Nuts.") At Marche the American line of defense was so thinly stretched that there were gaps of more than a mile between companies.[38] It took guts to defy the German Panzers. In one early encounter, "an E company man knocked out the lead German tank with a bazooka, stopping the attack."[39] The experience of Kissinger's former company was not atypical. Shivering in their foxholes, they contemplated "Jerry armor extending as far their eyes could see. . . . We just didn't dare take our shoes off since being unready for even a moment might mean a German patrol and death."[40] The fighting was especially bitter at Rochefort, which the 3rd Battalion had to abandon after sustaining heavy losses.[41] The after action report provides graphic detail.

> So aggressive was the initial attack, supported by tanks and artillery, that the enemy had to be driven out of the streets with grenades and other weapons of close combat. Dead enemy littered the streets. . . . All day long, [our] dwindling forces continued to beat off attack after attack while attempting to disengage itself. At 1500, the B[attalio]n Commander gave the order to get out, but was informed by Co[mpany] I that its vehicles had been knocked out by enemy fire. At this time, the Bn commander sent messages to Regiment that his escape route was out, all roads blocked, and the supply route impossible. (A four tank convoy couldn't get through.) The enemy fire was terrific, streets a living inferno and enemy personnel were in buildings surrounding the battalion C[ommand] P[ost].[42]

Even where the Americans were successful in holding the line, mopping-up operations were messy: "It was necessary to enter every room of every house and barn."[43]

To read such accounts is to understand why Kissinger made light of his own experiences. Compared with the ordinary rifleman he might have been, his new job was indeed relatively safe. As he told his brother in a letter dated just over a month after the defense of Marche:

I not only *say* that I am not in danger where I am, I actually am not. Or, as a witty comrade of mine put it in a letter to his wife the other day: "I am in much less danger over here than I will care to admit after the war." . . .

I am . . . connected with Divisional Headquarters, and it is in the nature of things that only under very special circumstances, the members of Div. Hqrs. are exposed to danger. This, at least, is true of any front, where the enemy air force and long range artillery are virtually non-existent. Now, there can be little doubt that at this late date the opposing forces are totally deficient in both these branches of their Armed Forces. It is to be expected, therefore, that your absent-minded and slightly myoptic [sic] brother will be run over by a street car one day rather than killed in action.*[44]

This was the style of self-deprecating humor that Kissinger had been honing since coming to America (not least because it was without question the best way for a highly intelligent German-Jewish immigrant to win friends). In reality, his very presence in Marche was hazardous in the extreme. True, the United States had P-47 Thunderbolt fighters in the air, as well as the 84th's own highly effective mobile artillery on the ground.[45] But that did not stop German shells—88s, mortar shells, and even a V-1 rocket on one occasion—from pulverizing the narrow streets of the town center where the divisional HQ was based.[46]

Kissinger had no illusions about the danger he was in, having seen, before the division even reached Marche, "a military report stating in an entirely matter of fact way, that the town in question, the place we were to go to, had fallen into enemy hands. . . . [W]e were driving straight into the lion's mouth . . . on roads that seemed dangerously empty."[47]

---

*Though dated February 1945, this long letter was in fact coauthored by himself and Fritz Kraemer much later—in January 1947—and was intended for publication. "Don't let the names fool you," he explained to his family. "I have merely chosen, for sentimental reasons, names of typical exponents of each category. The story is fictitious in the sense that none of the events happened all to one character & is true in the sense that most occurrences mentioned did happen" (Feb. 16, 1947). In other words, what the letter describes is an amalgam of the two men's experiences, though these cannot have been too different under the circumstances.

Indeed, the American position in Marche was so precarious that, as late as January 10, the daily situation map in the *Stars and Stripes* newspaper still showed it as being in German hands.[48] As a former German citizen in American uniform—and, of course, as a Jew—Kissinger would very likely have faced execution if he had been captured. Another former refugee in a similar situation recalled, "There is no doubt about it that you were thinking that you might be captured. . . . A former citizen of the Jewish faith—Goodbye Charlie!" After all, a soldier's religion was indicated by a single letter on the lower-right-hand corner of his dog tag; for Jews it was either *J* or *H* (Hebrew). Early in 1945, an entire team of U.S. interrogators (IPWs) of German-Jewish origin were captured by the Germans; they were shot on the spot. When the historian Werner Angress was captured on D-Day plus 9, he was thankful he had taken the precaution of changing the *H* on his dog tag to a *P* (Protestant).[49]

Kissinger not only spoke German, he also had some basic French, though Kraemer's was fluent. It therefore fell to him to reassure the many terrified Belgian civilians they encountered that "no one would break through to this particular place." As he told his brother,

> Women with black scarfs around their shoulders would immediately pass my word on to the quickly assembling crowds. The latin capacity for being dramatic under almost any circumstances showed itself in such splendid remarks as "Il dit qu'ils ne passeront jamais" (He says that they shall never pass). This neat phrase, as you may remember, was successfully used by a French General in the First World War with regard to the flaming fortress of Verdun. French Generals of World War II, in pathetic proclamations to under-equipped, ill-led troops, used the very same words, but Verdun, nonetheless, disappeared like a tumbling stone in the avalanche of the gray-clad armies. Obviously, the magic of words has its limits. In spite of my own reassuring remarks and in spite also of what I might almost call my knowledge of the limitation of German power, I felt uneasy. . . . The obvious despair of the people and their apparent lack of faith in our capacity for protecting them was not without effect.[50]

The GIs tried to cheer themselves and the Belgians up by throwing candy to the children they passed and propositioning every young woman in sight.

> The convoy halted. I jumped off the truck, stopped a girl with a bicycle, and asked how large the town was and how nice. As usual one of the men asked me in English to find out whether she would sleep with him. I was just starting on my standard reply to similar demands: "Gentlemen, the art of seduction is a highly personal art, you will kindly seduce your girls yourselves," when she remarked, distinctly unembarrassed, that she understood perfectly, although otherwise she knew no English.[51]

Such light relief was a badly needed salve for frayed nerves. Rumors abounded of "German soldiers in American uniforms and parachutists that had been seen drifting from the skies." Kissinger was sent to find a locksmith to open the door of the town courthouse. The task was not made easier by American sentries with "itchy fingers."

> Stumbling through the darkness toward the school house assigned to us for quarters I was halted three times in as many minutes and asked the password by guards whose voices sounded decidedly impolite. [Kissinger's accent can hardly have been reassuring.] I would have been somewhat less amused and thrilled had I known then what I learned weeks later, namely, that we did not have any contact with friendly units either to the right or to the left. In other words, we hang [*sic*] there in the dark loosely connected with the rear by long roads easily cut by an enemy, whose whereabouts were highly uncertain, and our flanks were completely unprotected. We and our town were hardly part of a front line but a mere strong point established at a road centre to defend it and deny its use to the enemy. . . . During the following days the situation grew, almost audibly, more dangerous.[52]

Kissinger's most memorable experience in Marche had an almost surreal quality. It vividly illustrates the kind of welcome American soldiers grew accustomed to in liberated countries, but it also underlines how perilous his situation was. One pitch-black night he got out of bed in the school building where he was billeted and noticed a light in the cellar: "Up floated the sounds of an old gramophone and the shuffling of dancing feet. Several men shouted my name like exited [*sic*] school boys meeting a friend unexpectedly at a bar, where they had already been drinking for a while. Actually nobody had any alcohol but the mere presence of the girls made them slightly drunk . . . with emotion."

The soldiers, mostly journalists with the army newspaper, were being entertained by a Belgian family: "a very broad mother, all smiles and friendliness, a grinning father (the concierge of the school) and assorted daughters, daughters-in-law and their girl friends." It did not take long before the young men and women were dancing.

> A kitchen stove gave more heat than was necessary and dancing we bumped into other couples continuously, while sweat began to flow from our foreheads. One of the girls was a "foreigner" from a big town, very soft and [an] extremely good dancer, she had merely visited friends and was now caught in the town. . . . My rifle, helmet, and bayonet I had thrown into a corner, when everybody had dragged me into the circle while the girls gave little shrieks of delight finding out that I could even make jokes in French and tell them silly stories. In a pleasantly exuberant mood I did some Russian dancing,* which caused the enthusiasm to rise further. My comrades began to hold hands with the girls, while a French-speaking captain sat on the sofa in the corner engaged in a more serious conversation with some more mature women. A girl in black told us that her husband had been shot by the Germans, because he had worked for the underground. She fetches [*sic*] his picture from somewhere, showed it to us, and was very sad for a little while. Father and Mother described with many gestures the sufferings of the populations

---

*This passage was almost certainly written by Kraemer rather than Kissinger. The earlier exchange about "the art of seduction" also seems more likely to have come from Kraemer.

during the occupation, which of course, led to the eternal question: Do you think they will be back again? We lied some more, although by that time we knew that fighting was going on 6 km S and SW of the town.[53]

The following evening the group reassembled, and the dancing grew more intimate.

Again we danced in the kitchen that was too hot. We played games (always liked by those who don't believe in the art of conversation as a subtle opening for less subtle sequences): games which inevitably led to some boy fervidly kissing a girl, while the others were held dancing half walking around in a circle. I made the best of it and chose as my partner the soft and nice-looking girl from the big town.[54]

And then the shelling started. Windows were shattered. The soldiers who had been guarding the building came clattering down the stairs to seek shelter. The shells were so close now that they seemed to be landing in the courtyard behind the school. "God damn it," someone muttered, "this one was close, can't be more than 20 yards away." The brothers of the dancers began to fret that they would be taken as slave laborers if the Germans captured Marche. The other civilians resumed their questioning of the French-speaking Americans: "Wasn't it time to leave? Tomorrow morning at the earliest?" Kissinger came close to blurting out, "Get out of this trap as soon as you can, particularly the young men," but managed to restrain himself. Meanwhile, with literary panache, "the man who had written [a] book in prewar days asked the soft girl from the big town what she wanted most in a man. Very pale she said 'La tendresse.'" Still the shells kept falling.

Every 30 seconds or so, the cellar shook in agony. Nobody shrieked in that crowd of civilians, not even the small children. The women prayed. The soldiers talked in half whispers to each other, exchanging their ideas on the caliber of the firing

guns, their possible distance from us, and the type of shells.
The air very soon grew stiff. The place seemed a submarine
that had been under water too long.[55]

It was at this point that Kissinger (and Kraemer) did something very
foolish indeed.

Feeling "helpless and uncomfortable," unnerved by "flashing
visions of a shell hitting into the midst of these people who were leaning, very pale and suddenly tired, against the brick wall," Kissinger
found himself thinking "with dismay . . . of the simple and naked danger of being wiped out in this barrage, how stupid it would be, after all
these years of struggle and tenacity, to be killed in a cellar passively and
rather useless not even knowing where the attack came from."
Unwilling—perhaps even unable—to remain "in this hole that seemed
like a prearranged coffin," he asked if anyone would come up with him
"to see what was going on." It was said with a smile of mock bravado;
in fact, as Kissinger admitted to his brother, he was actuated more by
claustrophobia than by bravery. Another intellectual in uniform—a
mathematician "whose mind, in some respects, is as abstract as mine"—
volunteered to join him. This act was psychologically effective: both
men "were thrilled by our own adventurousness" and climbed up the
stairs and out into the street "with tense nerves, but greatly lessened
fear." This was, of course, the height of irrationality. The school cellar
had not been perfectly safe, to be sure. But to walk out in the open in
the midst of a barrage of shells was significantly to increase the chance
of death or severe injury. Kissinger and his companion could think of
nothing else to do but to walk to their workplace in the courthouse.
They found to their surprise "officers, more or less well dressed . . .
working without the slightest sign of being disturbed" and "men
typ[ing] orders as usual." The barrage appeared to have stopped, though
Kissinger in his anxious state could not recall if shells had continued to
fall after he emerged from the shelter. At a loss for something to do, he
returned to his bedroom on the third floor of the school. Despite
momentary "visions once more of being blown into the street by an 88
mm shell hitting the third floor squarely," which he allayed by moving

so as not to sleep directly under one of the huge beams in the ceiling, he was soon asleep "and woke only infrequently, when the Art[iller]y (ours or theirs?) (God knows) became particularly noisy."[56]

Roughly three-quarters of Allied soldiers killed in the Second World War were the victims of artillery shells, mortars, grenades, or bombs dropped by planes. If Private Henry Kissinger had been unlucky that night, he would have been added to a long list of American soldiers who fell victim to their own recklessness under fire. Three things are striking about the episode (even after allowance is made for Kraemer's influence on the letter's self-consciously literary composition). The first is that the protagonist felt unable passively to await his fate in a crowded cellar "after all these years of struggle and tenacity." The second is his readiness to take a risk. The third is his ability to conceal his fear with nonchalance. These traits would reappear more than once in Kissinger's postwar life.

III

The story goes that Kissinger was one of those who remained behind when a large part of the 84th Division left Marche.[57] This is fiction. The very day after exposing himself to enemy artillery, he was withdrawn from the town as divisional HQ was moved to a château a few miles away from the front line. Kissinger was not sorry to leave; he "had the impression that the grey green uniforms were very near" and certainly did not envy his former comrades—"half heroic and half forsaken and sacrificed"—who were left behind in the now eerily empty town. They expected to have a "bitter fight."[58] It never came. As the official historian of the 84th puts it, the fight for Marche had been "Manteuffel's last gasp. The German drive to the Meuse was finished."[59]

Just a few weeks later, ordered by his colonel to buy some "good Belgian pipes," Kissinger was able to revisit Marche and, his mission accomplished, to pay a couple of social calls: first to "a house where I had once spent a harmless evening with the parents of an unusually charming daughter," where he "kissed the hands of the slightly amazed daughter" and entertained her father by sketching a map of the Russian advance to the East, and then to the old schoolhouse, where he found only the mother and previously invisible grandfather. As one of the successful defenders of Marche, Kissinger was warmly received: "They smothered us with coffee, excellent bread, real butter and home made prune-marmelade [*sic*], urging us to take second, third, and fourth helpings."[60] By now the town was in the hands of the British 53rd (Welsh) Division, who patronizingly told the Americans they were relieving, "We came here to help you."[61]

The tide was now turning in what became known as the Battle of the Bulge. On January 3, the Allies launched a three-pronged attack on the enormous German salient that the Ardennes offensive had created. Patton's Third Army struck northward from Bastogne, while Montgomery's XXX Corps struck southward from Marche along with— under Monty's command—the U.S. First Army, including the 84th Infantry Division. The Allied offensive was supposed to be primarily an armored attack, but the generals had not reckoned with the weather. There was exceptionally heavy snow, and the temperature plummeted to as low as 13 degrees (Celsius) below zero (8 degrees Fahrenheit). So thick was the ice on the roads that tanks simply skidded off. It therefore fell to the infantry to take the lead.

The mud around Aachen had been bad; the ice of the Ardennes—"the Belgian Siberia"—was worse. "We always thought [Hell] was a hot, fiery place," recalled the veterans who wrote G Company's history, "but in the Ardennes we learned it was a cold, frozen one. . . . The depression among the troops was terrible. . . . The men's overcoats were frozen stiff, breath turned into ice on the garments. . . . It was so bad that the men just had to keep digging to stay warm; they didn't dare try to sleep or they'd freeze to death."[62]

Nor were they battling only the cold. Though now retreating, and with little realistic hope of ever again advancing, the Germans had by no means lost their fighting spirit.[63] Tanks and artillery were able to inflict heavy casualties on the slowly advancing Americans.[64] An especially lethal hazard of the Battle of the Bulge were the "tree bursts" caused by shells fired into wooded areas, which peppered troops with both shrapnel and splinters of wood.[65] Determined to prevent an orderly German withdrawal to the Siegfried Line, Allied commanders gave their men little respite.[66]

Kissinger was no longer a rifleman, but he and other men attached to divisional headquarters were not far behind the sharp end of the American offensive. They were certainly less exposed than the men of G Company to enemy small-arms fire, but they were not much less vulnerable to the cold, the shells, and the exhaustion. Kissinger has never sought to represent himself as a war hero; quite the reverse. But the reminiscences of his comrade in arms David C. Laing in 1986 confirm that he was still sharing many of the risks and hardships of the ordinary infantryman when the 84th reached Gouvy after the closing of the Bulge.[67] From divisional and company histories, we can therefore trace the long, hard route he took: from Dochamps to Samrée, from Bérismenil to Ollomont, from the château de Biron to Laroche and finally to Houffalize, the fall of which was regarded as marking the end of the battle.[68] This was war at its most punishing. The 84th Division had suffered heavy casualties by the time it was granted a proper rest at Xhoris.[69]

The Battle of the Bulge was over; the war was not. Indeed, there was an unpleasant feeling of going back to square one when, on February 7, the men of the 84th found themselves back in front of the Siegfried Line—more or less exactly where they had been on the eve of the Germans' Ardennes offensive. Divisional HQ was now in Lindern, and it was from there that the plans were carefully worked out for Operation Grenade: the crossing of the River Roer, an operation made all the more difficult by the German destruction of dams, which flooded much of the surrounding countryside. On February 23, after a formidable artillery barrage, the 1st Battalion led the way across the river, advancing swiftly on to Körrenzig, Rurich, and Baal, where the Germans attempted a counterattack. Within two days the 84th had taken Houverath, Hetzerath, and Granterath. Cold, clear weather and more open country meant that the Allies could now capitalize on their superiority in the air. Despite the first sightings of the new German jet planes, G Company had less to fear from the Luftwaffe than from snipers.[70] They also now encountered for the first time the irregular militia known as the Volkssturm: the barely trained, poorly armed groups of teenagers and old men who were the clearest indication that the Third Reich was running out of effective military manpower.[71] It was at this point—the last week of February 1945—that the Americans began to take much larger numbers of Wehrmacht prisoners, a sure sign that German resistance was crumbling.[72]

Better weather and weaker opposition meant that the American advance could finally accelerate, as the tanks belatedly took over the lead. The men of the 84th now found themselves fighting a very different kind of war as part of Task Force Church. After the agonizing foot-slog of the Ardennes, the advance through Germany was "a wild ride from one town to the other," with Bolling once again leading from the front and the infantry mopping up in the wake of the motorized spear-head.[73] Houverath, Harbeck, Golkrath, Hoven, Genhof, and Genieken: the place-names soon became a blur to the average GI. From Süchteln the Americans swept northward, encountering only a few serious pockets of resistance, not least because the Germans had expected them to head due east, into the country's heavy industrial heartland, the Ruhr. It was only after Boisheim that the Americans swung eastward, toward Krefeld.[74] On March 4 the first members of the division reached the Rhine after "a wild night and a wild shooting party"—"like mob fighting mob"—in the village of Mörs.[75] Krefeld, by contrast, yielded with minimal resistance. Although plans had been hatched in Berlin to make Krefeld the "Stalingrad of the West," or to leave only scorched earth behind if the city had to be abandoned,[76] the commander charged with its defense saw no sense in making a last stand with inadequately armed forces and incomplete defenses. In any case, the Germans needed every available man to try to stop the Americans from capturing the bridge across the Rhine at Uerdingen.

The Americans had been welcomed as deliverers by the Belgians. Their reception by German civilians was very different. Matzerath was the first German town to be overrun by the 84th Division with its civilian population still intact. The Americans were surprised to find ordinary Germans filled with apprehension. "Apparently they were told we could kill them all," according to the divisional historian.[77] By contrast, in Krefeld "the general atmosphere was submissive and, on the part of many civilians, even cooperative." Some waved white handkerchiefs and sheets as the Americans entered the city.[78] But these were signs of surrender, not of welcome. In the course of very nearly a month of rest and recuperation in Krefeld, the Americans came to realize that "we were definitely not wanted. The Germans were more unfriendly than any other place we had been."[79]

Legend has it that Kissinger was now appointed "the administrator of Krefeld . . . decree[ing] that the people in charge of each municipal function—gas, water, power, transportation, garbage—report to him. . . . Within eight days he built a civilian government," having "weeded out the obvious Nazis."[80] It was certainly not unknown for soldiers of German origin to be given considerable authority in the early phase of the Allied occupation of Germany.[81] There is, however, no documentary evidence to support the story that Henry Kissinger played this kind of role, aside from a letter of recommendation written by Kraemer in 1949.[82] Indeed, Kissinger's name is conspicuously absent from all the scholarly literature on Krefeld under American occupation, though he was certainly there for three weeks.

One of the industrial centers selected by the Royal Air Force for strategic bombing, Krefeld by March 1945 was in ruins, having been the target of major air raids in June 1943 and January–February 1945. Around 60 percent of prewar housing had been damaged and 27 percent was completely destroyed.[83] The population had been reduced to 110,000 by the time the Americans arrived, compared with 172,000 in 1939.[84] For those who remained, life had effectively moved underground into massive concrete bomb shelters. When Alan Moorehead of the *Daily Express* and Christopher Buckley of the *Telegraph* reached Krefeld, they found tens of thousands of German civilians living in a vast bunker under the main railway station.[85] Conditions were squalid. For people there, "the war [had] ended in the ruin of nearly every normal thing in life."[86] A similar seven-story bunker in Uerdingen was entirely without water and electricity when the Americans discovered it.[87] On the other hand, the Nazis had made it a priority to keep the Ruhr economy going to the bitter end. Although the major public utilities—post, telephone, transport, electricity, gas, and water—were subject to disruption, they still continued to function. Supplies of food and coal had been maintained. What was lacking when the Americans occupied Krefeld was local government. Nearly all officials, including the *Oberbürgermeister,* the chief of police, and the party *Kreisleiter,* had fled across the Rhine by March 1, along with nearly all the regular armed forces. There was no one authorized to surrender the town.[88]

This vacuum of power took the U.S. Army by surprise; they had been expecting resistance by a fanatical underground, not ordinary Germans desperate to return to the surface. As a precaution, it was decided to keep people in their shelters for all but one hour a day and to enforce the "nonfraternization" policy that had been ordered by Eisenhower. The result was anarchy. Battle-hardened GIs, suddenly relieved from combat, ran riot. For G Company, "Krefeld turned out to be a soft deal. There were terrific quarters and plenty of wine, cognac, and schnapps."[89] No army on earth knew better how to throw a party than the Americans. Within a few days, "there were 15 motion picture units in bars, stores, and courthouses. There were U.S.O. shows, including Lily Pons, division band shows, Red Cross girls, and doughnuts." There was even ice cream.[90] But these officially sanctioned pleasures were much less popular than the illicit delights of fraternization.[91] For the doughboys of the 84th Division, there had been nothing like it since Piccadilly Circus.

From the point of view of the German civilians, however, liberation from the Nazis meant house searches, looting of valuables, and at least three cases of rape. People whose houses were still intact found themselves summarily expelled to make way for American officers because the rules against fraternization—selectively enforced—prohibited Germans and Americans from sharing accommodation.[92] Curfew rules varied from one part of town to another, depending on whether it was controlled by the 84th Division or the 102nd. There were numerous arrests, many of them unwarranted in the eyes of the locals. Worst of all, vengeful Eastern European slave workers (soon to be known as DPs—"displaced persons") ran amok, plundering the food stores at Vorster Strasse and ransacking nearby farms. According to one account, as many as twenty-four Germans were murdered in the violence.[93]

For one elderly man in the suburb of Linn, a veteran of the First World War and an anti-Nazi, American occupation meant chaos.[94] His diary entry for April 9 summed up his disillusionment: "Robbery and theft day and night are the order of the day. . . . It reminds one of the Thirty Years War."[95] Another diarist lamented that the decision to confine Germans to their bomb shelters was preventing nothing but the restoration of normality.[96] A third complained that a group of soldiers not only plundered but also vandalized his house, tearing pages out of books "like wild men" (*wie die Wilden*).[97] When he protested that the Americans were essentially turning a blind eye to murder by their "allies," the DPs,[98] an American translator told him bluntly, "We did not come to Germany to free your country from the Russians; you brought them here yourselves. The Americans have come to free Holland, Belgium, and France from the Germans."[99] This kind of attitude was widespread in the U.S. Army; indeed, it was positively encouraged by anti-German films and literature designed to justify the nonfraternization policy. Despite the legend of Kissinger in Krefeld, it was only after the distinctly more magnanimous British took over the city on April 23 that anything like orderly administration was reestablished in the town.

IV

What, then, was Henry Kissinger's real role in Krefeld? His 1947 Harvard application makes it clear: "By February 1945 I was placed in charge of a Regimental Counter-Intelligence Corps [CIC] team. Our principle [*sic*] tasks were the prevention of espionage and sabotage, such as the large-scale German penetration efforts during the Battle of the Bulge."[100] The CIC's secondary role was to dissolve the Nazi Party, to arrest members of specified groups such as senior military officers for interrogation, and to exclude Nazis from the civil service.[101] The restoration of civilian administration, in other words, was not the Americans' top priority. Kissinger certainly had a hand in trying to restore essential public services, but this was to serve the needs of the U.S. troops, not German civilians. Of much more importance was the process of denazification to which Washington was firmly committed.

The United States was not wrong to regard Germany in 1945 as a hotbed of fanaticism. Although the war-weary majority of the population were ready to submit to whatever regime was imposed on them by the victorious Allies, there remained a core of ideologically convinced supporters of the Hitler regime who were prepared not only to fight until the bitter end but also to make that end as bitter as possible for both internal and external foes.[102] The Americans may have exaggerated the scale of fanaticism in Germany in 1945, but they did not imagine it. The leader of the Office of Strategic Services' Psychological Warfare Division, Saul K. Padover, was among the first American experts on Germany to reach Krefeld. His first impressions were contradictory. The old man in whose house he slept on the first night was craven in the extreme, to the point of lunacy. But the cocky Hitler Youth who showed him around the ruins of Krefeld the next day appeared to have been thoroughly brainwashed by Goebbels's propaganda. Even the former members of the Social Democratic and Catholic Center Parties who had managed to lie low for the past dozen years seemed strangely cut off from reality.[103] The meetings Padover had were part of an effort by the Americans to work out which Germans, if any, they could work with. They were naturally suspicious of those who put themselves forward. One official, Richard Lorentzen, had been authorized by the departing Nazi *Oberbürgermeister* Alois Heuyng to form a "residual authority."[104] Amid the chaos of the first week of March, Lorentzen presented himself to the Americans, explained his position, and recommended the appointment of the former mayor of Kleve, an anti-Nazi lawyer named Dr. Johannes Stepkes, as *Bürgermeister*.[105] But could either Lorentzen or Stepkes be trusted? Suddenly the army needed men who could quickly and accurately carry out background checks on potential German collaborators to weed out the committed Nazis. It was a task to which Henry Kissinger was ideally suited.

"Administration . . . is not the only problem facing the occupation forces," begins the first surviving report coauthored by Henry Kissinger in his capacity as a CIC agent, which dates from March 17, 1945, little more than two weeks after the Americans had taken Krefeld. "There is also a political problem. For twelve years the Nazis have had a stranglehold on those in public office. Officialdom and Nazism have, as a result, become almost synonymous in the public mind. It becomes the duty therefore of the occupying authorities to clean the city administration of these cliques of Nazi ideologists." The document is based on the testimony of eight informants, among them priests and members of the pre-1933 socialist or liberal parties—groups the Americans regarded as reliably anti-Nazi. Lorentzen, Stepkes, and his secretary, Heinrick Kesting, were all certified as non-Nazis. But the same could not be said of ten other officials, including the city auditor, the inspector of schools, the head of the license bureau, and even the man in charge of the Krefeld abattoir, who were classified either as "ardent Nazis" or as "opportunists."[106] News of their summary dismissals soon spread. The Linn diarist noted with satisfaction on March 28 that "a number of Nazi hacks" (*Nazibonzen*) had been removed from office by the Americans.[107] Kissinger's new career as a Nazi catcher had begun. He was almost certainly the coauthor of an impressively detailed CIC report on the Krefeld Gestapo, dated April 18, 1945;[108] its methodology and style closely resemble those of a later report on the Darmstadt Gestapo, which does bear his signature.[109]

The process of denazification was by its very nature an exercise in historical research but also in psychology. The task of distinguishing ardent Nazis from fellow travelers was far from easy, and the kind of evidence to be gleaned from interrogating suspects was unlikely to make it easier. The biggest difficulty, we now appreciate, was the extent to which the repressive force of the Hitler state had been directed at Jews and other ideologically stigmatized minorities like Communists and Jehovah's Witnesses. In 1933 fewer than 1 percent of Krefeld's population had been Jews, yet they and other suspect groups had accounted for over half of the 3,500 investigations undertaken by the town's dozen Gestapo officers. There was, in other words, a sharp distinction between "ordinary Germans" and targeted enemies of the regime. The former were not harassed and were treated comparatively leniently when they transgressed. The latter the Gestapo systematically persecuted: spying on them, harassing them, beating them, torturing them, driving some of them abroad, and with increasing frequency after 1939, deporting them to their deaths. By the summer of 1942, nearly all Krefeld's Jews had been sent to the death camps. Only those in mixed marriages remained, and the Gestapo thirsted to get rid of them, too. By the end of the war, 90 percent of the 832 Krefeld Jews who had not emigrated from Germany in the 1930s were dead, only 83 of them through natural causes.[110] By the time Kissinger arrived there, just four Jews remained in Krefeld, and they were in hiding. By contrast, just one in ten of the ordinary Germans investigated by the Gestapo ended up in a concentration camp or protective custody. Ordinary Germans were in fact just as likely to denounce other people to the Gestapo as to be investigated by them. More than two-fifths of cases brought against Krefeld Jews before the war were initiated by denunciations, double the proportion started by the Gestapo and its spies.[111] It was not difficult to identify the worst offenders, like August Schiffer or Ludwig Jung, the Gestapo chief from 1940 to 1945.[112] The difficulty was to know where to draw the line between the active perpetrators and the much larger number of Germans who had paved the way to the death camps with mere malice or indifference. Few of the victims had survived to testify; few of the accessories to murder had an interest in telling the truth.

It was his ability to overcome such difficulties that earned Henry Kissinger both promotion and decoration. Once again, however, myths have sprung up around these events. According to one recent account, for example, "Kissinger famously crossed enemy lines, posing as a German civilian, to interrogate Nazi soldiers in April 1945. He received a Bronze Star for his courage and acumen."[113] It was in fact his mentor Kraemer who ended up behind enemy lines (at Geilenkirchen), and he was captured. Only by persuading his captors to lay down their arms was he able to extricate himself, a feat for which Kraemer was awarded a Bronze Star and a battlefield commission.[114] He and Kissinger were now firm friends. On their nights off, Kissinger recalled, they would "walk the streets of battle-scarred towns . . . during total blackouts, while Kraemer spoke of history and post-war challenges in his stentorian voice—sometimes in German, tempting nervous sentries."[115] It was not in Krefeld that Kissinger earned his Bronze Star, much less behind enemy lines. It was on the other side of the River Rhine, which he and his comrades in the 84th Division crossed at Wesel on April 1, 1945.

V

The final phase of the war in Europe was in many ways exhilarating for the men of the U.S. Army. Compared with the hard slog that had followed D-Day, they swept from the Rhine to the Elbe in an American version of blitzkrieg. The challenges were increasingly logistical: how to keep this highly motorized force supplied with gasoline and tires, how to keep the best-fed army in history provided with "chow." Often, as at Krefeld, they encountered next to no resistance. (Civilians in areas that had been heavily bombed were, perhaps paradoxically, more likely to wave white flags and welcome Allied troops than those farther removed from the industrial centers.) Demoralized Volkssturm units—which included boys as young as eleven—were also quite likely just to give up. Positively enthusiastic about their liberation, though difficult to restrain from acts of vengeance or plunder, were the DPs.

Periodically, however, the Americans would run into stiff resistance from Wehrmacht and especially SS units that were determined to fight to the last bullet, if not the last man. This was the 84th Division's experience as it crossed the River Weser, when it was hit by German "screaming mimis"[116] and again at Buckeburg on the other side.[117] It remains hard to understand why young men, sometimes equipped with nothing more than an antitank *Panzerfaust* or machine gun, were willing to risk and usually lose their lives against overwhelmingly superior forces, especially with the war so obviously lost. The extent to which they were being terrorized into doing so, with an exponentially growing number of summary hangings for "defeatism" and similar offenses, was not immediately obvious to those they were shooting at. The more obvious explanation was that many young Germans were indeed fanatical Nazis, inspired by education or propaganda or both to give the Third Reich an ending worthy of Wagner's *Götterdämmerung*. This diagnosis gave a heightened importance to the work of CIC agents like Kissinger. If the Nazis were indeed planning to wage a partisan or terrorist campaign against the occupying forces, it was vital to disrupt it before it could gather momentum. With the benefit of hindsight, we know that, in the end, the zones of Germany occupied by the Western powers reemerged as an economically dynamic and democratic Federal Republic. But that happy outcome did not seem at all likely in 1945. Indeed, in the smoldering ruins of the Third Reich, an anti-Allied insurgency seemed a far more likely scenario. It should not be forgotten that between 3,000 and 5,000 people were in fact killed by members of Werwolf and Freikorps "Adolf Hitler" groups before and after the German surrender.[118]

By April 9—eight days after Goebbels's Werwolf Radio had begun broadcasting its bloodthirsty incitements to partisan warfare—the 84th Division had reached the outskirts of Hanover, the riflemen happily riding atop Sherman tanks.[119] The next day's attack was launched in dense fog, allowing the Americans to take the defenders by surprise. After a short skirmish, it was all over. As in Krefeld, the GIs were soon making the most of a "tremendous supply of wine, food, and schnapps."[120] The newly promoted Sergeant Kissinger found the locals "docile. As a matter of fact when we entered our jeep was mobbed and we were cheered so that for a minute I thought I was in Belgium. More deponent sayeth not," suggesting that fraternization was again the order of the day.[121]

Now the hard work for CIC began. On April 13 Kissinger and his fellow agent Robert Taylor arrested and interrogated Willi Hooge, a member of the Hanover Gestapo. Hooge admitted that six of his Gestapo colleagues had been left behind in the Hanover area to form the backbone of an underground resistance organization. Early the next morning Kissinger and Taylor led armed raids on the six suspects' homes. All but one of the men, Hermann Wittig, were absent, but their wives were arrested. The interrogation of Wittig produced two more names; they in turn were arrested. Adolf Rinne was tracked down to a cottage on the edge of the Deister Forest; Erich Binder to a nearby farm, where he was working under a fake identity. Binder was the most senior Gestapo officer involved, and it was his interrogation that definitively confirmed Hooge's original story.[122] The statements of the arrested men are notable not only for their admissions of involvement in a planned campaign of sabotage against American forces in occupied Germany, but also for the evidence they provided of earlier acts of violence in various parts of German-occupied Europe.[123]

It was primarily for breaking up this Gestapo sleeper cell that

Kissinger was awarded the Bronze Star on April 27, though the official citation referred more broadly to "meritorious service in connection with military operations against the enemy in Germany, 28 February to 18 April 1945."[124] What happened in Hanover was, wrote his superior officer, an "outstanding accomplishment," reflecting Kissinger's "unusual ability."[125] By the time Kissinger was promoted to staff sergeant four months later, according to the official letter of recommendation, "his exceptional knowledge of the German people and his linguistic ability [had] enabled him to capture many high ranking Nazi Officials including at least a dozen Gestapo agents. . . . This young man takes his work very seriously."[126]

That Kissinger was serious about his role as a CIC agent is scarcely surprising. With every passing day of the Allied occupation, horrifying new evidence of the crimes of the Nazi regime was coming to light. Even before he left New York, Kissinger and his family had been aware of what would come to be called the Holocaust. As early as December 1942, Rabbi Breuer was referring publicly to "the news of unimaginable mass murders, carried out against hundreds of thousands of our unfortunate brothers and sisters."[127] Later he described the "victims claimed by a bestial criminality" as "countless."[128] But it was another thing altogether to see the consequences of genocide for oneself.

On April 10, just days before the roundup of the Gestapo sleeper cell, Kissinger stared the Holocaust in the face when he and other members of the 84th Division stumbled upon the concentration camp at Ahlem. For many years, this was an event Kissinger did not talk about. Indeed, his presence only came to light because one of his fellow GIs, a radio operator named Vernon Tott, decided to publish the photographs he had taken on that day. Seeing Ahlem, Kissinger later acknowledged, was "one of the most horrifying experiences of my life."[129]

The camp at Ahlem, which was located five miles west of Hanover, was one of sixty-five satellites of the major Hamburg concentration camp at Neuengamme. It consisted of little more than five stables that had been converted into barracks and surrounded by two barbed-wire fences, one of them electrified, with an elevated guard post at each of the four corners. Formally, it was a labor camp, not a death camp, though the distinction had little meaning by 1945. The prisoners were forced to work at the neighboring quarry, which was being enlarged to house an underground factory complex code-named Doebel I and II, part of the empire of enslavement and annihilation operated by the SS Main Economic and Administrative Office (Wirtschafts-Verwaltungshauptamt).[130] Conditions in the quarry were atrocious, while the food and shelter provided at the camp were woefully insufficient. By January 1945, nearly a quarter—204—of the 850 Jewish prisoners originally sent to Ahlem had died. Four days before the arrival of the Americans, the camp commandant ordered the able-bodied prisoners to be marched to Bergen-Belsen, one of the many "death marches" that marked the last phase of the Nazi racial state. According to one account, between 220 and 250 prisoners were too ill to move and were left (though another source gives much lower numbers). The intention had been to kill this remnant and burn down the camp buildings in the hope of effacing the evidence of the criminal acts that had been committed there. The only reason this did not happen was the unanticipated speed of the American advance.

It was therefore the dying as well as the dead that the Americans found at Ahlem. As Tott put it, the camp was "Hell on Earth." Outside there were piles of emaciated bodies, some in trash cans, some in pits. There were also numerous corpses inside the barracks and around 750 bodies buried in a nearby mass grave. Tott counted only thirty-five survivors—men and boys "full of lice and disease."[131] "In one . . . bunk," he later recalled, "there was a boy, about fifteen years old, who was lying in his own vomit, urine and stool. When he looked at me, I could see he was crying for help. . . . Our troop had just come through six months of bloody battle but what we were seeing here made us sick to our stomachs and some even cried."[132] Donald Edwards was a messenger who had seen his share of death and destruction since the 84th Division had landed in Normandy. "What I've just seen," he told his best friend, "I don't think I'll ever forget. The war will probably fade from memory, but those were the most pathetic human beings I have ever seen or hope to see in my whole life."[133] Wherever they turned, the incredulous soldiers encountered new horrors. The stench inside the barracks was "beyond description." As Edwards observed, "When they show on Movietone news how the concentration camps looked, they'll never be able to convey the stench."[134] The barracks themselves were so cramped, the Americans could scarcely walk between the two rows of wooden bunks: "On the floor were piles of human excretion. Vomited food was also present on the floor. Dirt had been allowed to accumulate on the wood floor until it was no longer possible to clean it. Every tick [straw mat on the bunks] stenched with urine. Inside the hut, we noted several huge bull whips as well as some cat-o-nine tails. We knew their use."[135] The Americans also suspected that one of the buildings was a gas chamber.

Yet perhaps the most shocking thing was what the survivors told them. "What's been the worst thing that happened to you?" Edwards asked a Polish Jew who spoke English. "The beatings by the SS guards," he replied. "Whenever they wanted to, they just hit you. It might be with a butt, a whip or their hands. They seemed to like to hit us."[136] The welts all over his body confirmed his account. Benjamin Sieradzki was originally from Zgierz, a suburb of Łódź, and was just eighteen years old. He had watched as his parents were physically dragged away from the Łódź ghetto for "resettlement" (they were in fact taken to Chełmno and gassed). After the liquidation of the ghetto, he and his sister had been sent to Auschwitz, but he was then selected for work and ended up being moved to Ahlem on November 30, 1944. When the Americans found him, he weighed just eighty pounds and was suffering from tuberculosis and typhoid as well as malnutrition.[137] Henry Pius was also from Łódź. As the Americans had approached Ahlem, a fearful German civilian had asked him, "What are you going to do with us?" "Look at me," he replied, "am I physically in any shape to fight or hurt anyone?"[138]

For ordinary American GIs like Vernon Tott and Don Edwards, the monstrous scenes at Ahlem were unforgettable. But it was worse still for their Jewish—and especially German-Jewish—comrades. Edwards remembered how his fellow messenger Bernie Cohn "began to sob quietly" after they left the camp.[139] How did Henry Kissinger react? Sixty years later, his memories remained fresh: the "shocking incongruities" like "the SS people who . . . [had] stayed because they thought they'd be needed to administer a continuing enterprise"; the "barely recognizable human" state of the prisoners, who were so weak that "it took four or five of them to get hold of one SS man and he was brushing them off"; the "immediate instinct . . . to feed them and . . . to save lives," which in fact killed some prisoners who were no longer able to digest solid food.[140] His kindness was also remembered. One survivor, Moshe Miedzinski, remembered that it was Kissinger who told him, "You are free."[141]

Yet these accounts date from many decades after the liberation of Ahlem. Altogether more powerful, because written very shortly after the event, was the two-page manuscript that Kissinger entitled "The Eternal Jew"—an ironical reference to the Nazis' anti-Semitic propaganda film *Der ewige Jude*. This document is of such importance—recording as it does Kissinger's immediate, anguished reactions to the worst crime ever committed by a supposedly civilized society—that it deserves to be reproduced without abridgement or comment:

THE ETERNAL JEW.

The concentration camp of Ahlem was built on a hillside overlooking Hannover. Barbed wire surrounded it. And as our jeep travelled down the street skeletons in striped suits lined the road. There was a tunnel in the side of the hill where the inmates worked 20 hours a day in semi-darkness.

I stopped the jeep. Cloth seemed to fall from the bodies, the head was held up by a stick that once might have been a throat. Poles hang from the sides where arms should be, poles are the legs. "What's your name?" And the man's eyes cloud and he takes off his hat in anticipation of a blow. "Folek . . . Folek Sama." "Don't take off your hat, you are free now."

And as I say it, I look over the camp. I see the huts, I observe the empty faces, the dead eyes. You are free now. I, with my pressed uniform, I haven't lived in filth and squalor, I haven't been beaten and kicked. What kind of freedom can I offer? I see my friend enter one of the huts and come out with tears in his eyes: "Don't go in there. We had to kick them to tell the dead from the living."

That is humanity in the 20th century. People reach such a stupor of suffering that life and death, animation or immobility can't be differentiated any more. And then, who is dead and who is alive, the man whose agonized face stares at me from the cot or Folek Sama, who stands with bowed head and emaciated body? Who was lucky, the man who draws circles in the sand and mumbles "I am free" or the bones that are interred in the hillside?

Folek Sama, your foot has been crushed so that you can't run away, your face is 40, your body is ageless, yet all your birth certificate reads is 16. And I stand there with my clean clothes and make a speech to you and your comrades.

Folek Sama, humanity stands accused in you. I, Joe Smith, human dignity, everybody has failed you. You should be preserved in cement up here on the hillside for future generation[s] to look upon and take stock. Human dignity, objective values have stopped at this barbed wire. What differentiates you and your comrades from animals[?] Why do we in the 20th century countenance you?

Yet, Folek, you are still human. You stand before me and tears run down your cheek. Hysterical sobbing follows. Go ahead and cry, Folek Sama, because your tears testify to your humanity, because they will be absorbed in this cursed soil, dedicating it.

As long as conscience exists as a conception in this world you will personify it. Nothing done for you will ever restore you.

You are eternal in this respect.[142]

CHAPTER 6

In the Ruins of the Reich

After totally defeating our enemies, we brought them back
to the community of nations. Only Americans could have
done that.

— HARRY TRUMAN to Henry Kissinger, 1961[1]

To me there is not only right or wrong but many shades in
between. . . . The real tragedies in life are not in choices
between right and wrong. Only the most callous of persons
choose what they *know* to be wrong. . . . Real dilemmas are
difficulties of the soul, provoking agonies, which you in
your world of black and white can't even begin to
comprehend.

— HENRY KISSINGER to his parents, July 1948[2]

I

It would take a Hieronymus Bosch to do justice to Germany in the
aftermath of World War II. It was a country of ruins and cadavers. By the
end, the war had cost the lives of at least 5.2 million German servicemen—
nearly three in every ten men mobilized—and more than 2.4 million
German civilians. Total mortality approached 10 percent of Germany's
prewar population. To a remarkable extent, these casualties were inflicted
in the final year of the war. More German soldiers lost their lives in the
last twelve months of fighting than in the whole of the rest of the war.
Civilian casualties also soared. In total, between 300,000 and 400,000
German soldiers and civilians lost their lives every month between
D-Day (June 6, 1944) and Germany's unconditional surrender on May 8,
1945. The Germans had launched a war that propelled the Wehrmacht as

far afield as the Caucasus and the Channel Islands, from Norway to North Africa. But retribution was meted out to them largely on German soil. The death toll of the final year was inflated still further by the Nazi regime's own murderous character, which grew more pronounced even as its end drew nigh. Of just over 714,000 concentration camp inmates who still remained in January 1945, around 250,000 perished in death marches, including 15,000 of the 60,000 evacuated from Auschwitz. For most of its existence, the Hitler state had targeted minorities, in particular Jews. In its death throes, however, the "national revolution" devoured its own offspring. Between 1942 and 1944 German courts passed more than 14,000 death sentences, nearly ten times the number during the first three years of the war. But these figures do not include the numerous extrajudicial executions carried out by the SS. The pathology of Nazism was a bloodlust that seemed to grow with the feeding.

In the end, the killers killed themselves. It was not only the top Nazi leaders who, like Hitler, Goebbels, and Himmler, opted for suicide rather than face the victors' justice. Many ordinary Germans chose death over defeat. In April 1945 there were 3,881 recorded suicides in Berlin, nearly twenty times the figure for March. It is tempting to see this wave of self-immolation as a final triumph of Hitler's Wagnerian vision. But some of those who took their own lives were responding to authentically intolerable aspects of their country's conquest. One Red Army officer remarked that the first-echelon troops stole the watches, the second wave raped the women, and the third echelon made off with the household goods.[3] The two main Berlin hospitals estimated the number of rape victims in the capital at between 95,000 and 130,000. Altogether it seems likely that Soviet soldiers raped over two million German women, part of a systematic campaign of violent vengeance encouraged by Stalin's propaganda.[4] Also vengeful, as we have seen, were the six or seven million slave laborers whom the Nazis had imported to the Reich to work in their industrial war machine, as well as those concentration camp survivors who had the strength left to avenge themselves.

Into this charnel house poured the expelled: ethnic Germans driven from their traditional homes to the east of the Rivers Oder and Neisse. This was in part a consequence of Stalin's decision, more or less sanctioned at the Tehran Conference (November 27–December 1, 1943), to move the Polish border westward, so that East Prussia, West Prussia, Pomerania, Posen, and Silesia all ceased to be German territory. But the stream of refugees also included Germans from Czechoslovakia, Hungary, Romania, and Yugoslavia. In the final year of the war around 5.6 million *Volksdeutsche* had fled westward to elude the Red Army or Slav neighbors bent on retaliation for the Germans' earlier ethnic cleansing. They were followed after the German surrender by around seven million more. The number of people who died in this great upheaval may have been as high as two million.[5] The survivors merely added to the number of mouths to feed in the rump Germany. This was no small challenge. At the end of 1945 the economy was "practically at a standstill."[6] Production was down to perhaps a third of its 1936 level. Not until the last quarter of 1948 did western German industrial output recover to 75 percent of its prewar level.[7] There were chronic shortages of food, fuel, and shelter.

Yet perhaps the most pernicious legacies of the Third Reich were not material but spiritual. A substantial proportion of the population continued to adhere to at least parts of Hitler's racialist Weltanschauung, blaming their harsh treatment at the hands of the Allies on the all-powerful Jews who supposedly ran Moscow and Washington. Nazism had corrupted German society in other ways, too. Bribery, black marketeering, and peculation were rampant; in this, Hitler's Germany was like all one-party states with planned economies. Like its totalitarian rival, the Soviet Union, the Third Reich had fostered mendacity and mistrust. The habits of denunciation that the Gestapo and the SS had encouraged were hard to break.

For the men who had been fighting Germany—in some cases for close to six years—it was no easy thing to shift from waging total war against a formidably ruthless military machine to occupying and governing a devastated and demoralized country. It did not help that the occupation of Germany was itself a multinational enterprise. At the Yalta Conference in February 1945, the Big Three had agreed vaguely to divide Germany into zones of occupation, and this duly happened. The area from the River Elbe to the new Polish frontier along the Oder and Neisse Rivers—what had once been central Germany—became the Soviet zone of occupation. Western Germany was carved up between

Britain, the United States, and France, while Berlin became a four-power island in the Soviet zone. Austria, too, was carved up; the Vienna of Graham Greene's Harry Lime was another four-power condominium, like Berlin. In the words of an American intelligence officer, "The Russians got the agriculture (Prussia); the British, the industry and coal (the Ruhr); and the Americans, the scenery (Bavaria and the Alps)."[8]

There was no glory in occupying even the scenic part of Germany. In the words of the man who took over the American zone from Eisenhower, General Lucius D. Clay, managing "a defeated area while the war was still going on in the Pacific was about as dead-looking an end for a soldier as you could find."[9] The professional warriors itched to be off to fight the Japanese; most conscripts just longed to get home. For that reason, Clay struggled to retain good-quality officers in Germany.[10] As he later recalled, "It was hard work, and it was not fun. . . . If we had not had our army officers to call on originally, and then to persuade them to stay as civilians, I do not think that we could ever have staffed the occupation."[11] Among those who stayed in Germany was Sergeant Henry A. Kissinger.

For Kissinger, the U.S. Army had proved an unexpectedly congenial environment. He had enjoyed the "camaraderie" of the 84th Division. His unit had been, he later recalled, "the classic American group, and it was a very significant unit experience. They were the only group I've ever been with in America that didn't ask me about my German origin, to a point where I'd even forgotten, where I thought I had lost my accent, unbelievable as it seems today."[12] "Henry forgot about the past," recalled one of his comrades, himself of Syrian descent. "He was fighting for America. He was fighting as a soldier against the Nazis not because the Nazis did something bad for the Jews, but because the Nazis were the enemy of America. He was more American than I have ever seen any American."[13] The contrast between this experience of assimilation and what he saw on his return to Germany could scarcely have been starker. The revelation of the concentration camps shocked the most battle-hardened Americans; even Patton was physically sickened by what he saw at the Buchenwald subcamp at Ohrdruf. For many GIs, the exposure of the crimes of the Nazis provided a vindication of the war itself, reconciling them with the sufferings they had endured in combat.[14] But for a German Jew like Kissinger, the impact of the Holocaust was another thing entirely.

The mass graves at Ahlem had been but a foretaste of the personal loss that lay ahead. After the war's end, Kissinger recalled, "I started looking for members of my family . . . and didn't find any."[15] As we have seen, his grandmother and at least a dozen other members of the Kissinger family were among the victims. Fanny Stern had been sent to Bełzec but appears to have died in a death march during the final days of the conflict. How did her grandson make sense of such horror? "It crossed my mind it might have been the fate of my parents and to some extent . . . my own fate," he once admitted. But "I must say I was so shocked by the human tragedy that I did not put it immediately into direct relationship to myself. . . . . When I came back [to Germany] of course I experienced aspects of the Holocaust in a way that were unimaginable when I was a child, but those were then from the point of view of a member of the army of occupation and so I insisted . . . on allowing me to develop my own thinking, rather than presenting [myself] as some traumatized victim."[16]

This distancing of himself from the counterfactual of his own fate had his parents not escaped to America—like the temporary use of *Henry* as a surname when dealing with Germans—was an essential defensive measure. Any other approach might have been debilitating. But distancing did not preclude understanding. As is abundantly clear from a letter Kissinger wrote to the aunt of a concentration camp survivor—possibly Harold Reissner, one of the few survivors of the Fürth Jewish community, who had been liberated from Buchenwald—"Mr. Henry" was able to empathize very well indeed with the victims of the "Final Solution," offering insights that in some ways anticipated the later writings of Primo Levi. "A completely erroneous picture exists in the [United] States of the former inmates of the concentration camps," wrote Kissinger, because of people "who out of inner goodness surround everything with an idealistic hue, who in their eagerness to do good, report conditions as they would like them to be, not as they are."

The popular conception of a former concentration camp inmate in the States is that of a man broken in body and spirit, who carries his cross of misery, bravely but nonetheless futilely, who can never forget what has been and whose memories bar positive action in the future. This man is to be treated with infinite compassion and understanding, as befits one who has returned from the dead. This man supposedly yearns for love, for sympathy. . . .

[But] concentration camps were not only mills of death. They were also testing grounds. Here men persisted, and in a sense fought for survival, with the stake always nothing less than one's life, with the slightest slip, a fatal error. Such was the filth, the compulsion, the debasement that a person had to be possessed of extraordinary powers, both of physique and of will to even want to survive. The intellectuals, the idealists, the men of high morals had no chance. . . . But having once made up one's mind to survive, it was a necessity to follow through with a singleness of purpose, inconceivable to you sheltered people in the States. Such singleness of purpose broached no stopping in front of accepted sets of values, it had to disregard ordinary standards of morality. One would only survive through lies, tricks, and by somehow acquiring food to fill one's belly. The weak, the old had no chance.

And so liberation came. The survivors were not within the ordinary pale of human events anymore. They had learned that looking back meant sorrow, that sorrow was weakness, and weakness synonymous with death. They knew that having survived the camp, surviving the liberation was no problem.

So they applied themselves to the peace with the same singleness of purpose and sometimes the same disregard of accepted standards as they had learned in camp. Above all they wanted no pity. Pity made them uncomfortable, jumpy. . . .

All these people want is a chance for the future, a chance they will follow with a strict consequentness [sic]. They will resent pity, they will be suspicious of oversolicitousness. They have seen man from his most evil side, who can blame them for being suspicious? They will resent having somebody plan every little detail for them. And in all fairness, who can blame them for that? Have they not lived in the land of the dead and so what can be so terrifying about the land of the living?[17]

The man who wrote these words was just twenty-two years old.

Many another man in Kissinger's position might have been driven to a lifelong hatred of all Germans. For a time he was certainly "very hostile" toward them. His own parents were, he recalled, "on the vengeful side. But they had no concrete idea what that meant."[18] As a counterintelligence agent with responsibilities for denazification, he found himself "in the position one dreamt about when one was persecuted, that I had almost unlimited power to take revenge. In the sense that I could arrest I had unlimited power to arrest anybody and just section them off to a camp. There were no procedures that existed for the first weeks." But Kissinger did not act vengefully, for reasons he explained to his parents:

> You, dear father, say: be tough to the Germans. Like all generalities, that is a platitude. I am tough, even ruthless, with the persons whose participation in the party is responsible for all this misery. But somewhere this negativism must end, somewhere we must produce something positive or we'll have to remain here, as guardians over chaos, forever. We must also prove to the Germans by the firmness of our actions, by the justness of our decisions, by the speed of their executions that democracy is indeed a workable [sic] solution. That is also our duty. I say be tough, yes. But show them also why you are tough. Prove to them that you are here in Germany because you are better, not that you are better because you are here. Be fair in your decision, be ruthless in your execution. Lose no opportunity to prove by word and deed the virility of our ideals. These instructions I have given to every member of my team.[19]

Not long after the end of the war, he visited his paternal grandfather, David, who had moved to Sweden in the late 1930s. His grandfather's advice was clear: "Since we Jews . . . resented it when they treated us racially and said all Jews [were] as bad, we have no right to treat the Germans as if they're all evil. . . . I should be careful. . . . He said go after the ones that had committed crimes, but don't feel hatred towards all of the Germans."[20] Kissinger agreed

> that it was important, having been myself persecuted, that I would show a distinction between the former victims and their persecutors. So that I would not turn all the Germans into a persecuted people. . . . And not [act] on the basis of personal revenge. I carried that to the point that when I was head of intelligence in [the Bergstrasse district] . . . I changed my name, so that it didn't look like Jews taking revenge. They undoubtedly saw through that but I was very young. . . . I . . . had no patience then and [have] no patience now with SS Nazi leaders, but I had maybe a greater tolerance for opportunists.[21]

It was, in any case, "very depressing to arrest people and have weeping wives no matter what they [had done]."[22]

On a trip to his native Fürth, Kissinger was shocked to find that of the town's old Jewish population, only thirty-seven people remained. They were outnumbered by more than two hundred DPs. Among the survivors was Harold Reissner, whom Kissinger, along with his former school friend Frank Harris, sought to help (in Reissner's words) "to get back in touch with my aunt, to [get] whatever I needed to look after my health and wellbeing."[23] Yet for all the pathos of such encounters, Kissinger was still capable of taking the Germans as he found them. Attending a soccer match for the first time since Nazi regulations had excluded him from the Spielvereinigung stadium, Kissinger was bleakly amused by one home fan's behavior: "Fürth lost and the referee got beaten up, which was standard practice. The German police couldn't rescue him, so the American military police came and rescued the referee, and one guy sitting down next to me got up and yelled: 'So that's the democracy you guys are bringing us!'"[24] For all Kissinger knew, just a few months before, this same man might have been among the Wehrmacht and Volkssturm formations that had fought in Fürth until the bitter end.[25]

Kissinger returned to Fürth in February 1946. This time he opted for high culture, buying tickets for Verdi's *Un ballo in maschera.* "How times [have] changed," he wrote to his parents. "I was conducted to the honor loge, you know right at the left of the stage. I am usually not smug or self-satisfied but in Fuerth yes." Nor did he neglect to visit his grandfather's grave, which he made sure was "the best kept in the cemetery."[26]

II

For Henry Kissinger, World War II ended on the banks of the River Elbe "in the supreme, miserable, uplifting and depressing days when East and West approached across the body of a prostrate nation, with masses of humanity clamoring to cross over to fancied safety and finally we met and with one blow the drama was over, the river was quiet & so was Germany." On May 2, 1945, units of the 333rd Infantry made contact with members of the 89th Soviet Army Corps at Bälow.[27] "My contacts with the Russians were many and varied," Kissinger wrote home. "I met them first when I was strafed by a Russian plane who mistook my vehicle for a German. I saw them again a few days later when a cloud of dust on the other side of the Elbe showed us that the Russians had arrived. After that I saw many Russians: at official receptions, at parades (and I don't think I'll ever see anything more imposing than the parade of a Cossack division) and at many an official party. Discipline in the Red Army seems good, although the average soldier is somewhat more coarse than a Western European. Some of the Cossacks particularly were a rather terrifying crew." The highlight of the victory festivities was provided by his mentor Fritz (now Lieutenant) Kraemer, who "outperformed the Russian champions in Cossack dance."[28]

By contrast, on May 8—the day designated as VE Day—Kraemer was ordered by General Bolling to use a sound truck to deliver "a brief talk . . . to the townspeople [in our sector] on the significance of the German surrender and the consequences which any further resistance might entail for the German people." As the divisional historian recorded, "Most listened quietly, almost rigidly. Some women sobbed."[29] Like the forced visits to concentration camps, such lectures were the first tentative moves in what became an ambitious attempt to denazify

German society. But who exactly was to undertake this daunting task? The answer was the agency to which Kissinger now belonged: the Counter Intelligence Corps.

An army counterespionage agency, originally called the Corps of Intelligence Police, the CIC dated back to the First World War but had all but vanished by 1939. Prior to Pearl Harbor, it had focused on domestic counterespionage.[30] Indeed, in June 1940 the total staff of CIC had numbered just fifteen. After Pearl Harbor, however, it expanded rapidly under the leadership of Major W. S. Holbrook. In addition to the core Domestic Intelligence Section, it soon built up a network of agents in the nine U.S. corps areas, as well as in Iceland and the Caribbean. Since there were in fact not many German spies in any of these locations, the CIC initially had to focus on "Counter Subversive" efforts at home, which meant vetting around two million civilian workers, looking for suspect elements.[31] (One notable coup was the surveillance of Eleanor Roosevelt and her alleged lover and future biographer Joseph P. Lash.)[32] At this point, the CIC was evolving into a kind of military FBI—a somewhat superfluous entity given the extent of J. Edgar Hoover's ambitions for the FBI itself. But this changed with the occupation of Germany.[33] To begin with, as we have seen, the Americans had expected to be confronted with a partisan resistance movement of fanatical "Werwolves." When that failed to materialize, the CIC was tasked with registering all ex-Wehrmacht personnel and rounding up leading Nazis.[34] Here, surely, was the ultimate criminal racket: National Socialism. For the "G-Men in Khaki," Nazi hunting promised to trump the gangster busting that had made heroes of their civilian counterparts.[35]

The five thousand or so men who, like Kissinger, became CIC agents were drawn from all walks of American life. Not all had prior experience of detective work; not all had foreign languages. They were, however, among the smartest men the War Department had drafted. In the London office alone there were eight Ph.D.s[36] Not only did a future secretary of state serve as a CIC agent in Germany, so did the future author of *The Catcher in the Rye,* J. D. Salinger, whose experiences closely paralleled Kissinger's.[37] Unlike the elite Office of Strategic Services (OSS), the CIC was composed mostly of noncommissioned officers. In a hierarchical military, this might have been a handicap, but for the fact that CIC agents did not wear any badges of rank. They wore either civilian clothes or Class "A" officer's uniforms with a brass "U.S." insignia on each lapel, and they carried a gold badge inscribed "War Department Military Intelligence."[38] As CIC agent Ib Melchior recollected,

> Because our duties were such that we might easily find ourselves in a situation requiring the immediate and unquestioned assistance of available troops, we were empowered to request such assistance—if need be, *order* it—from any officer up to and including a full colonel. Only general officers were entitled to know our true rank. To all others our standard reply to the inevitable question, "What is your rank?" was simply a firm, "My rank is confidential, but at this moment I am not outranked."[39]

There were times when CIC agents in Germany did indeed engage in thrilling cloak-and-dagger operations, a notable example being the operation to arrest Artur Axmann and other former Hitler Youth leaders.[40] But a large part of the job involved pen pushing. As one of the agents involved in the Axmann case recalled,

> Automatic arrests [people arrested because of their position in the Nazi Party, the SS, or other organizations] were being ferreted out in large numbers daily, interrogated and shipped on to detention quarters according to their importance. Germans were denouncing each other to CIC and MG [Military Government], producing long-winded documents listing the crime or political beliefs their victims were supposed to have committed or believed in.[41]

The great challenge of denazification was where to draw the line. In theory, there was a clear distinction between convinced Nazis and "opportunists," between leaders and followers, between perpetrators and the passive. In practice, such distinctions blurred. After four early stabs at the problem, a directive of July 7, 1945, alighted on the notion of "guilt-by-office holding," creating 136 mandatory removal categories. Eisenhower's order on "Removal of Nazis and Militarists," dated August 15, 1945, extended the CIC's remit to include "Nazis and militarists" in business and the professions, not just in public service. Such people were not only to lose their jobs; their assets could also be confiscated.[42] Supplementary to this was Clay's Law No. 8 of September 26, which decreed that former Nazis in the 136 mandatory removal categories could be reemployed only in menial jobs. Comparably ambitious were the plans envisaged in JCS 1067 to establish "a coordinated system of control over German education and an affirmative program of reorientation . . . designed completely to eliminate Nazi and militaristic doctrines."[43] It is against this background that we should understand Kissinger's activity as a CIC agent in Bensheim, the biggest town in the pretty wine-growing district of Hesse known as Bergstrasse.

Kissinger's subsequent fame awakened local memories of the young man who had turned up in the summer of 1945 calling himself "Mr. Henry." Elizabeth Heid, who worked as his secretary, remembered his saying to her, "We have not come here for revenge." On the other hand, she recalled, he was "a master of keeping his distance."[44] One author alludes to "stories of his affairs with German women and his lavish dinner parties."[45] According to local lore—surely fanciful—"Mr. Henry" had a relationship with a Bensheim woman twenty years older than him, the daughter of a banker of Jewish origin, whose husband had perished in a concentration camp and whose son had been killed flying in the RAF.[46] Even without a mistress, Kissinger certainly lived more comfortably than most of the inhabitants. He changed his residence several times, moving from a modest building (Gärtnerweg 20) to the more imposing Weiherstrasse 10, then to nearby Zwingenberg, to a villa belonging to the pharmaceutical manufacturer Arthur Sauer, and finally to another villa (Ernst-Ludwig-Promenade 24) at the foot of the Melibokus mountain. In the last of these residences, he enjoyed the services of a cook, chambermaid, cleaning lady, housekeeper, and guard, as well as guard dogs.[47] "I live rather comfortably at present," he told his parents. "Another comrade and myself & [illegible] live in a 6-room house. We also took over the butler so that now we get our shoes shined . . . clothes pressed, baths drawn & whatever else a butler does."[48] He played the part of "Mr. Henry" to the extent of giving instructions to the domestic staff in English and even attending an American-German service of reconciliation in the main Protestant church. How far he was identified as a German-born Jew is not clear.[49] Nor is it clear how much we can rely on such local recollections. (To give just one example, the car Kissinger rented from a local man was in fact an Opel Kapitän, not the white Mercedes of folk memory.)[50] Perhaps it was inevitable, given the investigative work he was doing, that Kissinger took a dislike to the Bensheimers: "a false, crawling, double-timing, gossiping people."[51]

The situation in Bensheim in the immediate aftermath of World War II was chaotic to an extent that the present-day visitor to this picturesque place can scarcely imagine. The town had been bombed twice, in February and March 1945, leaving the town hall and the principal church in ruins. Around 140 families had lost their homes in the bombing, and another 135 now had to make way for the occupying Americans. There were around 2,000 displaced persons in makeshift camps. The shortage of housing was chronic and grew worse with the arrival of thousands of refugees from the Sudetenland, now reclaimed by Czechoslovakia. (Not surprisingly, when granted leave, Kissinger often spent it outside shattered Germany, in London,[52] Salzburg,[53] Copenhagen,[54] and Paris.)[55]

For CIC agent Kissinger, the task of identifying malefactors was a daunting one. The headquarters of the regional Gestapo had been moved to Bensheim after bomb damage to the Hessian capital, Darmstadt. Its officers—under the leadership of SS *Sturmbahnführer* Richard Fritz Girke and his deputy, Heinz Hellenbroich—had not been idle in the dying days of the war. On March 24, three days before the arrival of the U.S. Army, fourteen of the seventeen prisoners in the Gestapo's cells had been marched to a field and shot by an eight-man *Sonderkommando* acting on Girke's instructions.[56] That same night, at the orders of Hellenbroich, the Gestapo also murdered two American prisoners of war whose plane had been shot down nearby.[57] Kissinger's first task in Bensheim was to draw up a comprehensive list of all known Gestapo employees in the Bergstrasse region, including secretarial staff, and begin rounding them up. By the end of July, twelve men had been apprehended and a further nine of the secretarial staff placed under house arrest "pending further interrogation."[58] Girke, Hellenbroich, and two other Gestapo men were subsequently caught and put on trial before an American military court in March 1947. They were sentenced to death and hanged in October 1948.[59]

The scope of Kissinger's work for the CIC sometimes extended beyond the Bergstrasse district. One wanted man—the former Darmstadt Gestapo officer Gerhard Benkwitz, who was suspected of organizing a "sabotage group"—had to be arrested in the British zone near Düsseldorf, where he was lying low.[60] But the principal concern of the unit Kissinger headed—Counter Intelligence team 970/59—was "static intelligence in an area of 180,000 [people]." Determined though he was not to seek revenge, "Mr. Henry" was nevertheless exceptionally thorough in his approach to denazification. "It requires a lot of tact," as he explained to his parents, "since many old C.I.C. agents are working under me. It also requires a feeling of responsibility, an understanding of psychology and a sense of proportion."[61] His team of sixteen men undertook a comprehensive survey "of every stratum of civilian life, such as industry, professions, trade and commerce and the civil service . . . [using] the information thus obtained . . . as a nucleus in determining de-nazification criteria."[62] When the commander of the Seventh Army issued the orders for Operation Lifebuoy—which aimed to purge the civil service of Nazis—Kissinger already "had the complete plans for a de-Nazification program in Kreis Bergstrasse in full swing." Over and above the remit of Operation Lifebuoy, Kissinger also "conducted surveys to de-Nazi further all strata of German social groups, namely, industrialists, professionals (doctors, lawyers, etc.), clergy, commerce and trade." In the words of a superior officer,

> He has made full use of the civilian police and the Landrat [senior German civil servant] in the accomplishment of this mission. He sees the police chief daily, the Landrat at least once a week, and he speaks to all of the burgermeisters at their monthly meetings. By doing this and making full use of his informatisystem [*sic*] which covers all strat[a] of civilians he has maintained complete control of Kreis Bergstrasse.[63]

Even before the arrival in Bergstrasse of the refugees from the Sudetenland, Kissinger set up "concentration centers" for "preliminary screening" of the newcomers, designed to identify "politically tainted elements [that] might imperil the state of order existing in the area."[64]

In effect, this was police work, involving a mixture of detection, interrogation, and detention. It was work Kissinger excelled at. In recommending him for promotion to the rank of staff sergeant in August 1945, his commanding officer described him as "the most valuable man in the Bensheim office," adding, "This young man . . . commands the respect of the other men to the extent that they enjoy working under his guidance."[65] That same month, he was commended by General Bolling "for work done in Denazification of Kreis Bergstrasse," and by Colonel Charles Sixel, deputy chief of staff, Seventh Army, who also commented upon his "outstanding performance of duties," as well as the exceptional thoroughness of his work in screening the Bergstrasse population for evidence of participation in the Nazi regime."[66] Two months later he was placed in charge of the entire Bergstrasse Subsection of Region No. 2 (a substantial part of the total area occupied by the Seventh Army).[67] In April 1946 he was nominated by the regional chief of Region No. 2 of the U.S. zone for the position of "chief investigator for the CIC in the European Theatre"—a remarkable accolade.[68] Even when his responsibilities were extended to include administration and the handling of supplies, Kissinger "continued to turn in superior caliber work." In the words of one enthusiastic superior officer, he had, despite his relative youth, "a knack of keeping one eye on the present and the other on plans for future operations."[69] This positive verdict was later echoed by Fritz Kraemer, who praised "not only . . . his impartiality, understanding of intangibles, self-discipline and idealism, but also . . . his methods of work and . . . the practical results he obtained."[70]

Yet such zeal was quickly out of fashion. Virtually all the senior administrative personnel of the previous regime had been Nazis in one way or another. To purge them all was a recipe for chaos. As early as the winter of 1945–46, the disruption caused by the removal of so many officials convinced Clay of the need to change tack. As he put it in March 1946, "With 10,000 people I couldn't do the job of de-Nazification. It's got to be done by the Germans."[71] What this meant was an inundation of questionnaires, designed to get the Germans to rank themselves on a precisely calibrated scale of malfeasance: major offenders, offenders, lesser offenders, followers, fellow travelers, and (as the Germans joked) the "Persil white." Predictably, not everyone gave a completely truthful answer to the question "Have you ever been a member of the NSDAP?"—one of 131 posed on the standard form. By mid-1946 it had become apparent to Clay and his colleagues that the kind of denazification attempted in Operation Lifebuoy—which had led to the dismissal of a third of all the officials in the American zone[72]—was simply incompatible with a smooth transition to German self-government. Clay later called denazification his "biggest mistake," a "hopelessly ambiguous procedure" that had created a "pathetic 'community of fate' between small and big Nazis."[73]

It was time to rein in the G-men. In May 1946 Kissinger recommended that Joachim George Boeckh—a specialist in Baroque-era German literature—be dismissed from the faculty of Heidelberg University because of his strongly pro-Nazi conduct in the 1930s and 1940s. His recommendation was not heeded; Boeckh remained at Heidelberg until 1949, when he moved to the Soviet zone, spending the remainder of his career in East Berlin.[74] He was one of many thousands of committed Nazis who went unpunished as the initial drive for denazification gave way to a more pragmatic policy.

III

Denazification began as righteous retribution; it ended in murky local politics. In November 1945 allegations surfaced in the London *Daily Mail* that Nazi Party meetings were continuing to be held in Bensheim. A U.S. Army private even claimed—on the basis of testimony from the *Bürgermeister* and *Landrat* of nearby Birkenau—that elements of the Military Government were subverting the CIC's efforts because of "an affair between . . . one of the members of the Military Government Detachment in Bensheim" and "the interpreter chosen . . . as intermediary between the Detachment and the German people," who was "none other than the Ringfuehrerin of the B.D.M. (Female Hitler Youth), a Fraeulein Wilms . . . an exceptionally personable blonde, very attractive."[75] Kissinger duly investigated these allegations but concluded that it was a "grudge case" linked to the dismissal of the *Landrat* for foot-dragging over denazification. The woman in question had indeed been employed as an interpreter but had been dismissed after her Nazi past was exposed by the CIC. As for the alleged affair, there was no evidence of any social contacts whatever between her and U.S. personnel.[76]

As we have seen, the occupying Americans had anticipated organized Nazi resistance to their presence, if not an outright insurgency. Any signs of nostalgia for the Hitler regime were therefore of the utmost interest to the CIC. The case against Fräulein Wilms had not stood up, but that was no reason to drop one's guard. In September 1945 Kissinger had demanded that the newly installed mayor of Bensheim provide him with a comprehensive report on local popular sentiment, including attitudes toward the Nazis, the Military Government, the Allies, Allied propaganda, the former Wehrmacht, the restoration of political parties, separatist tendencies, and the future of Germany in general.[77] The resulting report was highly negative, warning about increasing hostility toward the occupying forces, especially among "disgruntled" young men, and led to ten arrests.[78] Subsequent CIC reports on public opinion, such as this one from October 1945, provide vivid insights into the fraught postwar months.

> New disturbances occurred with the Hitler-Youth in Viernheim. Tactical troops complained of groups of young men on street corners displaying an arrogant and provocative attitude. A swastika was painted on an American vehicle. One young man was overhead bragging about his knowledge of hidden weapons. Agents from this office arrested 15 former Hitler-Youth leaders in Viernheim. They will be detained pending detailed interrogation.[79]

As time passed, however, evidence of residual Hitlerism petered out, to be replaced by reports of public "jumpiness" about the denazification policy itself.[80] One consequence of Operation Lifebuoy was to sow discord among authentic anti-Nazi elements, to whom the

Americans had turned for reliable local leadership, fellow travelers, ardent Nazis, and—in some ways the most problematic group—former Nazis who now sought to ingratiate themselves with the Americans by denouncing their former *Volksgenossen* (literally "folk comrades"). Some Germans (including a number of priests) condemned denunciations as "un-Christian." Others complained about "the arbitrary dividing line separating mandatory from discretionary removals and the inelasticity inherent in such measures."[81] The CIC aim "to make de-Nazification not only an American-directed policy, but [to] reduce much of it to the level of an internal German problem" was only partly achieved.[82] When the Americans adopted more lax criteria, there were fresh complaints.[83]

With the approach of winter, the public mood darkened. "The population is becoming ever more pessimistic regarding Germany's future," reported Kissinger's CIC team. "The approach of a coalless winter, the realization of Germany's complete isolation, the absence of any prospects for relief have created an atmosphere of rampant pessimism."[84] There would be no warm welcome for the refugees from the East, since they would only worsen the food, fuel, and housing shortages. As for the efforts of the occupying forces to "Americanize" the Germans with jazz and movies, these, too, seemed to backfire.

> Many well-meaning Germans question the wisdom of stressing American music for German listeners. Without any explanation of its background, the music frequently sounds degenerate and unmelodious to German ears and is allegedly hardly a good representative of American culture. . . . American films are not too well received. Since the majority of the pictures shown so far have been typical entertainment pictures, picturing a life of glitter, opulence, sweetness and light, they are not very well received by a threadbare, cold and hungry population.[85]

But the most bitter—and wounding—complaint was that the CIC was simply the "Gestapo of the Americans." To a population all too familiar with the pattern of denunciation, interrogation, and conviction, the idea that the U.S. forces were attempting some kind of benign "reeducation" was almost entirely foreign. "We Americans have come here to make a decent man out of you," Kissinger told a former leader of the Hitler Youth. When the German answered that his parents had already taken care of that, Kissinger replied stonily, "OK—you may leave."[86]

In one respect, CIC was indeed the successor to the Gestapo: in its reliance on informers. This proved to be the Achilles' heel of denazification. On his arrival in Bensheim, Kissinger had lost little time in recruiting several of these, among them Erwin Kiesewetter, a forty-nine-year-old former police instructor, who claimed to have been dismissed from his post in 1944 for being a Social Democrat. On July 10, apparently as a result of CIC pressure, Kiesewetter was appointed director of police for Bensheim, replacing a former Wehrmacht NCO named Richard Graf. The man who at least nominally appointed Kiesewetter to this post was Willy Klapproth, whom the Americans had installed as mayor after their first nominee, a Social Democrat named Gottfried Kräge, had stepped down for health reasons. Klapproth was also a Social Democrat; like Kiesewetter, he had been a police officer in the Weimar years. The two men soon clashed, however. In early August, Kiesewetter sought to use his power as police chief to intervene in one of the many disputes about housing that were raging in Bensheim.[87] Three weeks later Klapproth sought to impose his authority on Kiesewetter, requesting twice-weekly briefings on all arrests,[88] then abruptly imposing a salary reduction on him.[89] After a heated telephone conversation on September 1, Kiesewetter resigned.[90]

This was distinctly unwelcome news for CIC agent "Mr. Henry," who prized Kiesewetter for his "record of anti-Nazi activity" and "value as an informant."[91] The result was a bitter bureaucratic battle, the details of which Klapproth was careful to record with Germanic precision, though not necessarily truthfulness. On the night of Kiesewetter's resignation, at eleven-thirty p.m., Kissinger summoned a local councilor named Muschard to his office, defended Kiesewetter, and threatened to break off relations with the Bensheim local government, saying, "If we did not stop the business with Kiesewetter, we would find out just how strong CIC could be." Two days later Kissinger went to Klapproth's office and, without coming through the door, shouted in "a more than harsh tone" that he should come to the CIC office the next morning at eleven. When Klapproth presented himself, Kissinger brusquely told him that he would no longer deal directly with either him or Muschard; that they should name new representatives to deal with him; that he required a desk from them; and that the son of a former Nazi official named Nolde could no longer serve as an auxiliary policeman. As requested, Klapproth sent another councilor, the Communist Hans Lehmann-Lauprecht, to see Kissinger. This time Kissinger was ready with no fewer than seven demands, among them:

a) that Lehmann-Lauprecht must appear at the CIC every Tuesday and Friday at eleven a.m.;

b) that he must understand that the CIC and the Military Government were "two quite distinct institutions, which were wholly independent of one another";

c) that Klapproth should come up with suggestions for propaganda leaflets regarding the forced labor being imposed on over a hundred convicted Nazis (*Nazi-Arbeitseinsatz*) to ensure that the names of those concerned be published;

d) that the "political shenanigans" should cease; and

e) that Nazi posters with the slogans "This We Owe to the Führer" and "Give Me Ten Years' Time and You Will No Longer Recognize Germany" should be prominently displayed in Bensheim.

Nor was "Mr. Henry" finished. That same day Klapproth was summoned to Kissinger's office and told in no uncertain terms not "to play the military government and the CIC off against one another" because "viewed in the long run the CIC was stronger than the military government."

Even allowing for the fact that this was Klapproth's version of events, Kissinger's conduct was strikingly confrontational. Even if he was merely being thorough rather than vengeful, "Mr. Henry" was clearly not yet as ready as his superiors to hand local power back to the likes of

Klapproth. But the younger man was underestimating his opponent (a man who went on to be Frankfurt's chief of police, until his career was cut short when he perjured himself in a corruption case). With the advantage of thirty years' more pen-pushing experience, Klapproth the German bureaucrat got the better of Kissinger the would-be G-man. Writing indignantly to the head of the Military Government in Bergstrasse,[92] he begged him to intercede with "Herr Henry" so that relations between the mayor and the CIC could be more "harmonious," pointedly emphasizing his own democratic credentials ("You know that I have waited 12 years for the Americans and for liberation").[93] Kiesewetter was not reinstated; instead, he took a job in the private sector, while continuing to work as a CIC informant.[94] When Kissinger requested that Kiesewetter be allowed to retain a room in the police station, Klapproth flatly refused.[95] The mayor was duly vindicated when he found witnesses willing to swear that Kiesewetter had in fact been an early Nazi (an *alter Kämpfer,* literally "old fighter").[96] It emerged that he had been a member of the SA, as well as a notorious fraudster.[97] On January 16, 1946, Kissinger's man was arrested. The following month he was sentenced to six months in prison and a fine of 10,000 Reichsmarks for "theft of patents and giving false information to the American authorities."[98]

The Kiesewetter case illustrates the extreme difficulty of CIC's task in postwar Germany. The Americans were heavily reliant on Germans for intelligence, but which Germans could they trust? Often, like Kiesewetter, those most eager to collaborate with the occupiers were precisely the people who had something to hide. On the other hand, a reliable source of intelligence about the Nazi past might well be the target of a false denunciation by those fearful of being incriminated. Another doubtful informant employed by Kissinger during his time in Bensheim was Alfred Lungspeer. Born in New York, Lungspeer had moved to Germany after his parents died. During the Third Reich he had established a reputation for himself as a graphologist—publishing several books on handwriting analysis under the name "Noeck Sylvus"—and worked for a number of industrial concerns in that capacity. Lungspeer was not a Nazi Party member; he was, however, a self-seeking opportunist, who lost no time in offering his services as a handwriting analyst and an agent for undercover missions.[99] It is in itself intriguing that Kissinger at this time regarded graphology as a legitimate science, though in this he was far from unusual in his generation.[100] There is also, however, clear evidence that Lungspeer sought to exploit his position as a CIC informant to intimidate former Nazi Party members in yet another housing dispute.[101] Once again Klapproth was able to bemoan the unreliability of "Mr. Henry"'s protégés.[102] In the first bureaucratic battle of his career, Henry Kissinger was roundly defeated.

Klapproth's days as *Bürgermeister* were numbered, however, for democracy was returning to Germany, even if denazification was being quietly dropped. As early as October 1945, the U.S. Military Government had created a Council of Minister Presidents (the *Länderrat*) in Stuttgart, to which Clay delegated an increasing number of administrative responsibilities. By the end of 1945, all the new or reconstituted states (*Länder*) throughout the U.S. zone had German governments and "pre-parliaments." And in the first half of the following year, local governments were formed and elections held. In Bensheim, as in much of southwestern Germany, victory went to the new Christian Democratic Union (CDU), an indirect descendant of the old Catholic Center Party. Joseph Treffert succeeded Klapproth on April 1, 1946.[103] It was not long, however, before the new mayor was complaining about the "persistent tension between the Military Government and the CIC" and the tendency for "the one authority to order what the other has forbidden."[104]

Perhaps because he was weary of such friction, perhaps simply because he was now eligible for his discharge from the army, as early as November 1945 Kissinger applied for a civilian job, seeking employment in "political research, survey type of investigation, [or] civil administration."[105] He made a point of emphasizing the range of his educational achievements: "I can speak, read, and write German as well as French fluently. My education consists of two years at the College of the City of New York where I specialized in Business Administration. I also studied [in] the Army Foreign Area and Language program, specializing in European History, sociology, and economics."[106]

Interestingly, among the first jobs he was offered was to become one of the "investigators and interrogators in connection with War

Crimes activities for the European and Mediterranean theaters of oper-ation." Kissinger was certainly interested in the Nuremberg trials; at some point in 1946 he attended the cross-examination of Ernst Kalten-brunner, head of the Reich Main Security Office and the highest-ranking SS officer to stand trial. Another option was a job as a "political Intelligence and News Control Officer" with the Military Govern-ment.[107] But either of these positions would have meant remaining in the army, albeit with the rank of second lieutenant.[108] Kissinger had clearly had enough of both interrogations and uniforms, not to men-tion the "moribund & bureaucratic" aspects of military life. Instead, he accepted his first-ever teaching post, as instructor in the Occupational Orientation Department of the U.S. Forces European Theater Intelli-gence School in Oberammergau, Bavaria.[109]

The tensions Kissinger left behind him in Bensheim were inherent in the dual American objectives of denazification and democratiza-tion. His successor, a CIC agent named Samuels, lost no time in im-pressing on *Bürgermeister* Treffert that he was "not weaker than [Mr.] Henry." The mayor should not make the mistake of thinking that "another policy would be pursued because Mr. Henry was no longer in charge." Like Kissinger, Samuels—whose name suggests that he, too, was Jewish—was more interested in rooting out Nazism than in return-ing Germany to democracy. Both men evidently suspected that the CDU included more than a few unreconstructed elements from the previous regime. As Samuels put it, the initials *CDU* seemed to many Americans to stand for "Centrale Deutsche Untergrundbewegung"—an allusion to the Nazi underground that the CIC had expected to encounter in Germany.[110] Such suspicions—which were, in any case, far from groundless—persisted long after the handover of power to German politicians. For most of his career, despite repeated protesta-tions of admiration for the Federal Republic that emerged from the ruins of the Reich, Kissinger harbored doubts about the strength of the Germans' new commitment to democracy.

Yet the fact remains that Kissinger chose to stay in Germany when he could just as easily have sought employment in the United States, and when his family were pressing him to come home. Why did he stay? Kissinger's answer was passionate.

You'll never understand it & I would never explain it except in blood & misery & hope. Sometimes when I look down our table and see the empty spaces of our good and capable men, the men that should be here to nail down what we fought for, I think of Osterberg [?] & the night Hitler's death was announced. That night Bob Taylor & I agreed that no matter what happened, no matter who weakened, we would stay to do in our little way what we could to make all previous sacrifices meaningful. We would stay just long enough to do that.

And so Taylor is to-day in [illegible] although he could have gone last October & I am here. And so, I'll stay a little while longer. I won't stay a year, I'll come home in 1946, but I want to do a few things first.

In short, Kissinger had sworn to play his part in the political reeducation of Germany. His only hesitation in accepting the Oberammergau post was "because actually I want to *do* something directly not teach."[111]

IV

By early 1946, however, a new enemy was looming larger in American minds than crypto-Nazis, an enemy that encouraged the transition from a policy of aggressive denazification to one of forgetfulness, if not forgiveness, of past sins. Few among the leaders of the Western Allies had been as swift as Alan Brooke to foresee that no sooner had Germany been defeated than the Soviet Union would be transformed from friend into foe. Roosevelt and a number of his advisers—not least Harry Dexter White, the coauthor of the Bretton Woods financial system and, it later emerged, a reliable source of intelligence to the Soviet Union—wholly failed to anticipate how ruthlessly Stalin would adopt attack, in the form of the political subversion of European democracy, as the best form of defense.

The most celebrated call for a more realistic policy was, of course, the career diplomat George F. Kennan's top secret five-thousand-word Long Telegram—cable number 511—sent to Washington from Moscow on February 22, 1946. Kennan's telegram was strong meat; at one point he likened international Communism to a "malignant parasite which feeds only on diseased tissue."[112] Yet this was only one of a number of striking metaphors of the time. Just two weeks later, speaking at Westminster College in Fulton, Missouri, Churchill famously warned that an "iron curtain" had descended on the European continent. Behind that curtain was a "Soviet sphere," encompassing Warsaw, Berlin, Prague, Vienna, Budapest, Belgrade, Bucharest, and Sofia. On March 10, five days after Churchill's lecture, George Orwell wrote in the *Observer* that "[a]fter the Moscow conference last December, Russia began to make a 'cold war' on Britain and the British Empire."

It had been the last vain hope of the Nazis that the Western Allies would recognize the Soviet threat in time to make common cause with them against Stalin. The ground having been prepared by Goebbels's propaganda, ordinary Germans were therefore even quicker to anticipate such a conflict. As early as Christmas 1945, rumors in Bergstrasse included "the alleged arming of German soldiers for a war against Russia" and "a war this winter between Russia and the Western Powers."[113] But the Cold War was to take very different forms from World War II. As we have seen, the Americans had not scrupled to appoint members of the German Communist Party (KPD) to positions of responsibility in their zone of occupation. Any "anti-Nazi" was considered eligible. Only slowly did it become clear that the KPD might be acting as a Soviet fifth column. "The best organized party in Kreis Bergstrasse are [the] Communists," according to a CIC report of October 1945, which added darkly, "Their organization is closely modeled on that of the Nazis."[114] The Communists themselves changed their tactics in early 1946—not least because of their failure to win local elections—thereafter adopting a policy of extraparliamentary opposition.[115] As Kissinger later recalled, "From December 1945 to June 1946 our mission [in Bergstrasse] gradually changed, concentrating . . . on foreign penetration efforts."[116] Even before then, the CIC was trying (vainly) to block the appointment of the Communist Wilhelm Hammann as *Landrat* for the district of Gross-Gerau, on the ground that "Subject misused his office to further one political party."[117] This was the beginning of a sustained American campaign against Hammann that culminated in his arrest.

(Despite the evidence that Hammann had saved the lives of more than a hundred Jewish children while a prisoner in Buchenwald, he was accused by the U.S. authorities of crimes against humanity. After an international outcry, the charges were dropped.)

At first sight, Oberammergau seemed a highly unlikely Cold War battleground. Nestling on the banks of the River Ammer, in the foothills of the Bavarian Alps, the little town was (and remains) best known for its Passion Play, a homespun dramatization of the New Testament story. Every ten years since 1634 the villagers of Oberammergau had staged the play, having pledged to do so in a bid to secure divine protection from an outbreak of plague.[118] But by the Victorian era, it had become a tourist attraction. The 1860 revision by the priest Joseph Alois Daisenberger had purged the text of medieval vulgarities and baroque mannerisms, ensuring that it could be enjoyed by prudish Protestants.[119] Visitors were delighted in equal measure by the quaintly rustic ensemble and the pleasing Alpine backdrop of the Kofel, the bare-topped mountain that towers above the town. Above all, they admired the literal quality of the production.[120] Along with the Ettal monastery up the Kienberg Hill, which had revived as a Lourdes-style shrine following its dissolution in 1900, and the ancient Wieskirche, the Oberammergau Passion Play offered travelers both literal and metaphorical uplift.[121] By the 1920s, it was one of Thomas Cook's top European destinations, attracting tens of thousands of British and American tourists.

But inextricably linked to the Passion Play was anti-Semitism. Traditionally, such plays were associated with violence against Jews, which was one reason the Bavarian authorities had banned them in 1770, a ban from which Oberammergau obtained an exemption only with difficulty.[122] In Daisenberger's revised text, however, the Jews had become the play's main villains.[123] Toward the end, they proclaimed their collective guilt for Christ's death, crying, "His blood upon us and upon our children!"[124]

Seventy years later, after seeing the 1930 production, an American rabbi named Philip Bernstein wondered about "its probable effects on the attitude" of Christians toward Jews, who were represented as "completely responsible" for the death of Jesus.[125] Staged in 1934, on its three hundredth anniversary, the play was endorsed with a visit from Hitler, which was enthusiastically, not to say "hysterically," celebrated by the villagers.[126] Of the 714 members of the cast in the 1934 production, 152 had joined the Nazi Party before May 1937 (the date used by the Allies to define "pure Nazis"), including Alois Lang, who played Jesus, Anni Rutz, the Virgin Mary, and eight of the twelve apostles.[127]

True, important elements of the Oberammergau population remained loyal to the Catholic Bavarian People's Party and to the Roman Catholic Church.[128] The local clergy strove to warn their flock against "false prophets" and successfully resisted any overt nazification of the Passion Play text.[129] Compared with some, the people of Oberammergau were protective of Jews and "half-Jews" in their midst, and produced at least one anti-Nazi resistance group.[130] In the end, however, Mayor Raimund Lang embraced the Nazis' anti-Semitism with few qualms, proudly describing the Passion Play as "the most anti-Semitic play that we have."[131] Anton Preisinger, the man who would go on to play Christ in the 1950 and 1960 productions, took part in a *Kristallnacht* attack on Max Peter Meyer, a Jewish-born composer who had converted to Christianity and moved to Oberammergau in the hope of avoiding persecution.[132]

Oberammergau was doubly complicit in the Third Reich's crimes. For it was here, in a complex partly built into the nearby mountains, that the Augsburg-based Messerschmitt moved its design branch ("Upper Bavarian Research Institute") responsible for the new jet-propelled planes, the Me-262 and P1101-VI, as well as the Ezian rocket.[133] The Prussian physicist Wernher von Braun—the designer of the V-2 rocket and the prototype "American" intercontinental missile—was relocated to Oberammergau in early April 1945, along with four hundred other scientists. Braun and his colleagues had their own reasons for wanting to distance themselves from the Dora concentration camp that had supplied the slave labor for their rocket production line at Mittelwerk. As Luftwaffe personnel, however, they found themselves under orders from SS *Obergruppenführer* Hans Kammler, the engineer who had built the death camp at Auschwitz, to take the "Vengeance Express" train four hundred miles south to Oberammergau. This may have been part of the semiserious scheme for the Nazi leadership to retreat into an "Alpine redoubt"; or perhaps Kammler hoped that the rocket scientists could be a bargaining chip in negotiations with the victorious Allies. In any case, Kammler simply disappeared, while Braun persuaded the SS to spread the rocket scientists out (ostensibly to reduce the risk of their being hit by the U.S. P-47 Thunderbolts that regularly strafed the area, but more likely to reduce the risk that the SS would kill them all rather than let them fall into Allied hands). In the confusion of the German collapse, many were able to escape to Tyrol.[134]

Units of the American Seventh Army reached Oberammergau on April 29, 1945. Von Braun, his brother Magnus, and a few key collaborators, notably Walter Dornberger, who had been the military commander of the rocket program, lost no time in handing themselves over.[135] They and their colleagues were duly interrogated, and 118 of the most technically skilled were then absorbed by the U.S. military as part of Operation Overcast (renamed Paperclip in 1946), along with V-2 components and the cache of documents that had been buried in a mine in the Harz Mountains. Though von Braun's past membership in both the Nazi Party and the SS quickly became public knowledge, it did not prevent his becoming the key figure in the subsequent development of U.S. intermediate-range nuclear missiles and, later, the NASA space program.[136]

As in Bensheim, so in Oberammergau: the immediate postwar period was marked by a chaos that denazification tended to exacerbate. The Americans arrested the town's leading Nazis, beginning with Mayor Lang and Georg Lang, the director of the 1930 and 1934 plays.[137] When Rabbi Philip Bernstein returned to Bavaria after the war as an adviser to the Military Government, he told a UN commission, "If the United States Army were to withdraw tomorrow, there would be pogroms the following day." A 1946 survey showed that 59 percent of Bavarians fell into the categories of "racist," "anti-Semite," or "intense anti-Semite."[138] As elsewhere, however, deteriorating economic and social conditions militated against a comprehensive purge of local elites. Oberammergau saw a wave of rapes and crimes against property, unruly behavior by DPs and near-feral children, and chronic food shortages, malnutrition, and disease. The Americans were somewhat scandalized to find that the supposedly pious Oberammergauers were energetic black marketeers, readily exchanging their famous wooden carvings for gin and cigarettes.[139]

Denazification ended with the imposition of fines in near-worthless Reichsmarks and the swift rehabilitation of the Langs and others.[140] Whereas an attempted revival of the Passion Play in 1946 had been abandoned because key cast members were still in captivity,[141] by 1947 American officials were giving the village a $350,000 grant to support a new production.[142] The following year Raimund Lang was elected mayor with the strong support of ex-Nazis and expelled Sudeten Germans. By 1949 it was business as usual, with Georg Lang declaring, "We have a clear conscience." When the Passion Committee's cast list was released, somebody was heard to ask, "Have the Nazis won?"[143] Although the revived play was strongly supported by the Western powers, with more than thirty thousand seats reserved for GIs and the opening performance attended by both the U.S. and U.K. high commissioners, old attitudes were soon on display.[144] It was said that Anni Rutz was demoted from the Virgin Mary to Mary Magdalene after she was spotted dancing with an American soldier.[145]

The idea of establishing a military academy in this somewhat surreal setting was none other than Fritz Kraemer's. The European Theater Intelligence School (ETIS 7707), later the European Command Intelligence School, was intended "to give training to intelligence personnel who had not been adequately trained to meet the problems of occupation."[146] That meant, in the first instance, teaching them the German language, German history, and German culture. It was no easy task. It was hard to impose classroom discipline on men who had so recently been waging total war. Soldiers smoked and put their feet on the desks; their enthusiastic fraternization with the locals led to an epidemic of venereal disease. Kraemer turned to the renowned German feminist and politician Marie-Elisabeth Lüders—the first German woman to receive a doctorate—to introduce some Prussian discipline to the school.[147] She also helped to train Kraemer's inexperienced team of instructors. This now included Kraemer's favorite, Henry Kissinger.

From Kissinger's point of view, the job was highly attractive. The salary of $3,640 a year (plus a 25 percent "overseas differential" of $910 and earned overtime above forty hours per week) was more than double the median U.S. income, which was just $1,811 in 1945.[148] He was required to teach two courses: "German History & Mental[ity]" and "Intelligence Investigation." The latter was mainly based on his experiences as a CIC agent in Bergstrasse, though with emphasis on (in Kraemer's words) "the often neglected psychological aspects of Intelligence work."[149] The former, as is clear from the surviving, detailed notes for a lecture on "The German Mentality," was altogether more ambitious. The talk began with "Importance of realization of psychological difference between Germans and Americans" and proceeded through four German characteristics ("Selfishness," "Lack of inner assurance," "Submissiveness," and "Lack of sense of proportions"). It then covered "Prussianism (10 minutes)," "Nationalism (10 minutes)," and "Militarism (8 minutes)," concluding with two recommendations: "Re-education by [the] creation of free institutions" and "Reform of [the] school system." Especially striking is the young lecturer's treatment of the Prussian state's "ascendancy . . . over the individual," its "Philosophical foundations (Luther, Kant, Fichte, Hegel)," and—here the debt to Kraemer is clear—its self-appraisal "in terms of external success rather than of internal merits."[150] There was little here to which a more experienced historian of the period would have objected; indeed, there may even have been a debt to A.J.P. Taylor's popular *Course of German History*. So successful was Kissinger as an instructor that he was soon asked to add a course on "Eastern Europe . . . presenting background and current developments of Poland, Czechoslovakia, Hungary, Romania, Bulgaria, Greece, and Turkey."[151]

This last topic was a revealing choice. According to Jane Brister, an adjutant at the school, it reflected a top-level decision taken "to drop [denazification] and go into anti-Sovietization." Kissinger's role was therefore twofold: "training both counter-intelligence and intelligence officers in denazification procedures and starting to get them indoctrinated on what the Soviet threat was."[152] This new responsibility appears to have been one that Kissinger relished. While others may have questioned the Kennan-Churchill-Orwell view that a Cold War was under way with the Soviets, he most certainly did not. In a remarkable report for the school's commanding officer, Kissinger strongly criticized internal security at Oberammergau. "Very little respect is shown to U.S. principles or directives," he warned.

This is expressed in a series of snide remarks or anti-occupation
statements [by German employees] . . . [which] are indicative
of an attitude that makes more difficult the enforcement of
orders or the control of the civilian personnel. . . . The only
manner by which long-range penetration can be avoided is to
continually watch key employees. . . . Surveillance further
includes knowing as much as possible about the towns in
the vicinity, specifically Oberammergau. It will be of prime
importance, for example, to know who the Communists are,
and which of them are particularly friendly with or maybe
even related to any employees on this post. . . . [E]ven personnel [who are] basically indifferent may occasionally give information to outside powers.[153]

Kissinger's recommendations to combat Communist subversion
were draconian. There should be "continuous . . . surveillance of civilian personnel," including the use of "informants" and the "checking" of
the mail and telephone conversations. "Transient personnel" in the area
should also "continuously be watched," especially "members of the
Communist party." "As a general rule," he wrote, "Communists should
not be employed on this post and persons known to be friendly to Communists should be closely observed." The aim should be to "intimidat[e]
the weaklings, the cowards and the indifferent" and thereby to "restrict
security leakage to a small group of fanatics that is more easily watched."[154]

As at Bensheim, Kissinger was not chained to his desk in Oberammergau. He was sent to lecture in Berlin, Bad Nauheim, and Baden-
Baden (in the French zone),[155] as well as in Wiesbaden. These trips
allowed him and his fellow instructors to "acquaint themselves with
problems faced by CIC offices in the field." On their way back from
Baden-Baden, they found evidence of "a major Communist attack on
American authority," including a Communist "mass meeting" in Bensheim, at which members of the Military Government were "labeled
as idiots" and various CIC informants were "named and their non-
Communistic party affiliations stressed."[156] Likewise, on his way back
from Wiesbaden in October 1946, Kissinger stopped off in Darmstadt
to find out more about "current Russian penetration methods and

American attempts to counteract these tendencies." His report makes it clear why denazification so quickly gave way to the search for "Reds under the bed."

> While up to June 1946 the principal objective of CIC was the security control of civilian population, the most latent danger at present seems [to be] the attempt by Russian dominated groups, particularly the Communists, to negate our policies, as well as outright espionage. Two principal methods are used. An attempt is made to gain control of key positions and administer them in such a fashion as to discredit U.S. policies and to enforce laws in such a manner as to show the lack of ability of U.S. policy makers. A case in point is the use made of . . . the tribunals for liberation from Nazism. In most areas visited, the Communists, through a variety of reasons, have gained control of these tribunals. . . . Other methods consist of infiltrating Communists in key positions particularly the German police to serve as cover for espionage activities. In Reg[ion] III an espionage ring was discovered, which, utilizing German police channels, supplied information to the Russians.[157]

As Kissinger noted, the problems of the CIC had changed "from technical problems capable of being carried out by a forceful personality, where raids, arrests and physical interrogation of suspects were the main weapons, to the more subtle objective of observing subversive groups, of analyzing their modes of operation, of understanding how certain seemingly meaningless acts take on meaning if projected against the requirements of a foreign power." The school at Oberammergau needed to devote more attention to "forces shaping politics of foreign powers in Germany," to "trends in their intelligence activities," and to "the background, history and objectives of subversive groups."[158]

V

Oberammergau introduced Kissinger to more than just the specter of Communist subversion. It was also his introduction to the kind of academic milieu where he would spend so much of the next twenty years of his life. Kraemer had an eye for talent, and the faculty of ETIS included three other brilliant young men who would become Kissinger's lifelong friends and colleagues: Helmut "Hal" Sonnenfeldt, another German-Jewish refugee, later one of the State Department's leading experts on the Soviet Union; George Springer, a Jewish refugee from Czechoslovakia and a gifted mathematician; and Henry Rosovsky, born in Danzig to Russian-Jewish parents, who would later specialize in the Japanese economy.[159] Despite the challenges of their early years, each would go on to distinguished careers in academic and public life.

In 1946, however, they were still young men, only recently released from the constraints of military life. Social life in Oberammergau revolved around the Pension "Friedenshöhe" in the König-Ludwig-Strasse, which had been a popular haunt of Thomas Mann's family in the 1920s and was still run by the Schmid family after the war. Kraemer lived there with his wife and son, while Kissinger rented a room in the Schmid family home in Passionswiese 1. That he and his friends knew how to enjoy themselves is confirmed by an incident in October 1946 when Kissinger, along with George Springer; his wife, Marjorie; and a German civilian instructor named Leonie Harbert, were arrested and charged with speeding and driving under the influence of alcohol. Two things about their altercation with the military police are noteworthy. First, Kissinger reacted intemperately to the behavior of the police. "Please cease using such tactics," he told the man who had arrested them, "they can get you into more trouble than you realize." The desk sergeant interpreted this as a threat and took the opportunity to lock Kissinger up in a tiny basement cell for an hour,[160] though the charge of drunk driving was subsequently dropped.[161] Second, one of those arrested along with Kissinger—Leonie Harbert—was in fact Kissinger's girlfriend. That same October, on a trip to Paris, Kissinger bought a pet dog, a two-month-old yellow and white cocker spaniel.[162] When he returned to the United States, it was Harbert who arranged for the dog to be shipped there by air.[163] Claims have previously been made that Kissinger had a German girlfriend during his time at Oberammergau— even that he got in a fistfight over her.[164] The fistfight is fiction; the relationship was real.[165]

Clearly Kissinger's relationship with Leonie Harbert was not all that serious. J. D. Salinger, by contrast, married his German sweetheart and brought her back home, with unhappy results. But Kissinger remained in touch with Harbert for many years after his return to the United States—indeed, for the rest of her life. And it was also serious in the sense that a romance with a German gentile was hardly likely to be welcomed by Kissinger's parents, who hoped to see their son marry a Jewish girl, preferably from their own Orthodox community. Kissinger tenaciously resisted. "I don't know how I'll feel when I return," he told them in February 1947. "I certainly am not in a marrying or engaging mood. Anything but."[166] When his mother warned him against making a "hasty decision," he grew impatient: "There is absolutely no danger of that. Don't forget I am not 19 anymore. . . . Whatever my decisions might be they won't be hasty. There is no chance of my committing myself for quite some time."[167]

The marriage issue, which is crucial to any family committed to Orthodox Judaism, revealed an important change that military service had brought about. Kissinger had lost his religious faith. "In the army," as he later recalled, "there was not much opportunity to practice any particular orthodox view. . . . [Y]ou cannot be part of a society that has suffered what the Jewish people have suffered for millennia without a strong sense of identification with it and sense of obligation to it [the Jewish faith]. But that doesn't include necessarily the practice of any particular aspect of it."[168] When his parents later learned of this, they were evidently unhappy enough to prompt Kissinger to write a startlingly frank letter in his own defense.

> To me there is not only right or wrong but many shades in
> between. . . . The real tragedies in life are not in choices between

right and wrong. Only the most callous of persons choose what they *know* to be wrong. Real tragedy comes [illegible] in a dilemma of evaluating what is right. . . . Real dilemmas are difficulties of the soul, provoking agonies, which you in your world of black and white can't even begin to comprehend.

Nor did Kissinger stop there. "I am not like other children," he told his parents, "but this is neither my fault nor yours. It is the fault of the world I was born in." It was parental disapproval of his conduct over a prolonged period that had "forced me into the attitude I have today, of aloofness, of slight irony, an attitude designed to prevent rejection before it occurs."[169]

This extraordinary *apologia pro vita sua* tells us much about how the experiences of emigration and army life had changed Kissinger. Like so many of the millions of young men who fought in World War II, he would return home to find the United States little altered. But he knew that he himself was quite different. "Very soon now 3 years of hope & work will lie behind me," he wrote in early April 1947. "Very soon I shall return to a future that may be uncertain but which I face with supreme confidence. . . . Now I know exactly what I want & I shall go after it." His plan was to go to college "because whatever I shall do I will need a college degree for." But which one?

I would prefer not to study in N.Y., since I hate N.Y. but I want to be close enough to come home on week-ends. I have sent several letters to leading Eastern universities including Columbia & shall make my decision after I hear from them.

Another thing. One thing the past 12 years should have taught us is that one can't plan the future with minutest details. One must to a great extent live in the present. I have no masterplan for my future nor am I ever likely to have one. I shall finish college, I shall write, I may lecture later on . . . I have extreme confidence. . . .

Also, don't worry so much about re-adjustment. After all, not everybody came out of this war a psycho-neurotic.[170]

By now, Kissinger knew very well that every letter he sent from Germany was disquieting his parents further. It was all so unnerving, from the regular requests for "CIGARETTES," to the vagueness about the timing of his return, to the revelation that he was planning to use up his leave allowance with a two-week trip to Paris, London, Nice, Rome, Florence, Venice, and Trieste—in the company of a friend's wife. ("Don't be shocked it is with her husband's knowledge & purely platonic.")[171] He had no interest in his old friends. ("I was not aware of any difference on any plane, ideological or otherwise, with John Sachs. . . . I don't believe that any of these so-called friends will still appeal to me when I return.")[172] He was cavalier about money. ("What is money to-day? And what is life if not an ability to enjoy what is beautiful and fine while one can? . . . One can't go through life always drudging.") And he refused point-blank to consider any college that was not "smart" or "well known" (which precluded a return to City College).[173] Each letter was more inflammatory than the one before.

At last, in June 1947, he was ready to return. Like many a young man returning from war, he knew that the homecoming would not be easy.

> I have only one hope [he wrote to his parents] & that is that I may not disappoint your high expectations. The last years have left their mark on me. In certain ways I have become very set, maybe egotistical. A lot of mutual adjustments lie ahead. Please don't forget that what you call a "normal family life" has been a concept very remote from me for several years. We have learned to live from one day to the next. I have known high hopes & sad disappointments. But all that does not mean that I'll be bubbling over with either. It is much more likely that you'll consider me overly retiring. I have lived my own life for so long that I may not be able to share it spontaneously. Certain ties bound in convention mean little to me. I have come to judge men on their merits. I have lived in a cooperative group so long, that I don't know how the competitive civilian life will strike me. I have known great things & I have done great things. How will a petty day-to-day existence appear? All

these problems are there. I can promise you no more than the best intentions. I can ask no more than patience.

And so my last letter from Europe ends. Appropriately it is a dismal day outside. Low hang the clouds on the mountain. 2 years ago when the Bergstrasse was blooming, when our men were still young, & the war unforgotten we each day discovered bits of the past & forged links to the future. We thought we had moved worlds and given our youth to something greater than ourselves. To-day the war is truly over & a return from the war in 1947 anti-climactic.[174]

The returning warrior had learned much. He had yet to learn that unflinching candor is seldom the way to preempt a conflict, least of all with one's parents.

Book II

The Idealist

The thinkers in their youth are almost always very lonely
creatures. . . . The university most worthy of rational
admiration is that one in which your lonely thinker can feel
himself least lonely, most positively furthered and most
richly fed.

—WILLIAM JAMES[1]

Only when you have worked alone—when you have felt
around you a black gulf of solitude more isolating than that
which surrounds the dying man, and in hope and despair
have trusted to your own unshaken will—then only will
you have achieved. Thus only can you gain the secret
isolated joy of the thinker, who knows that, a hundred years
after he is dead and forgotten, men who never heard of him
will be moving to the measure of his thought.

—OLIVER WENDELL HOLMES[2]

Harvard was a new world to me then, its mysteries hidden
behind studied informality. I did not know what to make of
the experiences I had had or what relevance Harvard's
values would have to my life. It never occurred to me that I
would never really leave Harvard again.

—HENRY KISSINGER[3]

I

Henry Kissinger was one of more than two million American
servicemen who took advantage of the GI Bill to go to college. The
Servicemen's Readjustment Act of 1944, which paid the tuition of

homecoming veterans who wished to study, was the federal government's single most important contribution to social mobility in the postwar era. Without it, Kissinger would have had little option but to get a job. Without it, Harvard would have remained an unattainable dream.

Kissinger's application was nothing if not self-confident. "I . . . wish to enroll at your university for the fall-term under the 'GI Bill of Rights,'" he wrote on April 2, 1947. "I would appreciate any information you could give me as to whether any credit is allowed for experience while with the Armed Forces, and the earliest possible time of my enrollment. . . . I would like to major in English and Political Science." That was in fact an impossibility at Harvard, where only a single "concentration" was permitted and where "Government" was studied, not political science. Moreover, April was a very late stage in the academic year to send in such an application; the other colleges to which Kissinger wrote (Columbia, Cornell, New York University, the University of Pennsylvania, and Princeton) rejected him out of hand. His chances, he acknowledged, were "none too bright. All I can do is hope."[4] Nervously, he urged his parents to send Harvard "my complete records (grades, subjects, report cards) of both George Washington H.S. & Lafayette College, but not from City College since (1) Harvard gives no credit for night school and (2) attendance at City College undermines my chances rather than helps them. . . . *Speed is of the greatest essence*."[5] His fears were groundless. So impressive was his application that Kissinger was not only accepted by Harvard; he was also awarded one of the two Harvard National Scholarships given to New Yorkers that year.[6] He returned to the United States from Germany that July, paid his first visit to Cambridge later that same month,[7] and began his studies in September, in effect as a sophomore, as Harvard (after all) gave him credit for his prewar studies at City College.[8]

Kissinger's early academic career benefited from the enthusiastic support of his army mentor, Fritz Kraemer. Kraemer, too, had returned to the United States, but to Washington, where he served first as political and economic adviser to the assistant secretary of the army and then as senior research assistant to the chief historian of the United Nations Relief and Rehabilitation Administration.[9] "I do not hesitate to state that I consider Kissinger's qualifications exceptional," Kraemer wrote in one of his characteristically trenchant letters of reference. He had that "capacity for patient and diligent study and research without which even the most intelligent are doomed to remain brilliant amateurs." He was "the rare type of undergraduate who studies to gain a deeper understanding of phenomena rather than to obtain a degree." He would not develop "into that frequent type of intellectual who turns to shoulder[-]shrugging cynicism, nihilistic relativism or political radicalism." He was "surprisingly selfless and free of that ambitiousness and glaring smartness found in many of the so-called bright boys." Perhaps Kissinger's only weakness, Kraemer concluded, was "his somewhat unyouthful, though friendly, seriousness which is coupled with the absence of an active sense of humor."[10] What Kraemer omitted to mention was that this earnest young man, so industrious and apparently so humorless, was not coming to Harvard alone. With him came Smoky.

Purchased on a whim in Paris, Smoky the cocker spaniel had not been left behind in Oberammergau (unlike Kissinger's girlfriend, whose melancholy duty it had been to arrange Smoky's flight to New York). "I am aware of the difficulties," he told his parents, "but my decision to bring him home is unchangeable. If you loved dogs you would know that one just doesn't leave one's dog behind."[11] When he realized that the dog was going to arrive before him, Kissinger bombarded his parents with six and a half pages of detailed instructions on canine care. "Smoky means very much to me," he explained. "You may say it is only a dog. But on the other hand he has been a good pal to me over here & would be a wonderful link between a life that was & one that will be. So please take good care of him. . . . To know Smoky is to love him. . . . *Don't ever beat him.*"[12] Happily, his mother took to the dog. A year after his return, Kissinger replied to a letter from home in the style of "Your loving grandson, Smoky." "Of course, ordinarily I would answer myself," the dog supposedly wrote. "Yet I feel confident that you who know me, will realize that . . . I am at present occupied in studying the atomic structure of fossil (bone to the ignorant)."[13]

"As charming as dogs may ever hope to be," in Kraemer's ironical phrase, Smoky posed, and still poses, a problem.[14] The young Kissinger is sometimes represented as a dour conformist.[15] But a man who not only writes letters on his dog's behalf but also brings the dog to college hardly matches that description, not least because pets were expressly prohibited in the university's residential houses. Though his room-mates grew to tolerate Smoky's tendency to jump and drool on visitors' laps, the "biddies" (maids) reported his presence, forcing Kissinger to "borrow a car every morning, deposit Smoky in a Cambridge kennel and smuggle him back to the dorm later, when the maids had gone."[16]

The truth was that Smoky was a comfort in an unfamiliar and intimidating place. "I was completely unsure of myself," Kissinger later recalled. "I had gotten out of the Army and I felt like an immigrant again. When I went into the Army I was a refugee, and when I got out I was an immigrant."[17] In the end, Smoky's presence was tolerated, but not because (as his owner later joked) the Harvard authorities "thought they had a shell-shock case on their hands."[18] He was tolerated because Kissinger was one member of a unique generation whose arrival would change Harvard forever. Many members of the Class of 1950 came to college as veterans—as men who had experienced the hardships and horrors of war. Most of them would never have had a chance of attending America's most prestigious university had it not been for the war. After years in uniform, it was not easy for them to adjust to being "Harvard men," with all that that phrase implied. Harvard had to adjust to them. So well did it adjust to Kissinger that he would spend the next twenty-one years of his life there.

II

Harvard today can claim to be the world's greatest university. It was not always so. When the Oxford historian of political thought Isaiah Berlin visited Harvard in 1940, he was unimpressed. The students, he complained, were "silly & sophisticated at the same time, & I am glad I don't have to teach them. They are sceptical about opinions & naïve about facts which they swallow uncritically, which is the wrong way around. After Oxford, Harvard is a desert."[19] His colleague Hugh Trevor-Roper was equally disdainful nine years later, by which time Henry Kissinger was in his junior year. "Their standard of education is really

very saddening!" he wrote to his friend the art historian Bernard Berenson (himself a Harvard alumnus). "Harvard depressed me a great deal."[20]

From the exalted vantage points of All Souls and Christ Church,
two of Oxford's grandest colleges, Harvard may indeed have seemed
an intellectual wasteland. When those institutions were founded in,
respectively, 1438 and 1546, Harvard had not existed. Established by the
fledgling British colony of Massachusetts in 1636, its early years were
modest, not to say precarious. Its location—among cattle yards on the
muddy banks of the Charles River—was not at first salubrious. Its initial buildings were primitive (none built before 1720 survives). It relied
heavily on the colonial government for its funding and was regularly
buffeted by the colonists' religious enthusiasms.[21]

Yet Harvard survived, flourished, and ultimately surpassed the
ancient English universities—indeed was already surpassing them in the
1940s, as Berlin and Trevor-Roper might have seen if they had looked
more closely. How? First, it was successfully steered away from becoming a mere sectarian seminary by successive presidents, who upheld the
objective of educating gentlemen, not clergymen. In the words of the
resident fellows in 1721, "[T]he great End for which the College was
founded, was a Learned, and pious Education of Youth, their Instruction in Languages, Arts, and Sciences, and having their minds and manners form'd aright." John Leverett (president between 1708 and 1724)
boasted that Harvard produced not only ministers but also scholars,
judges, physicians, soldiers, merchants, and simple farmers "whom academic culture serves but to soften and polish rustic manners." He and
his successors (notably Edward Holyoke) withstood countless attacks on
"godless Harvard" from Congregationalists and others, establishing a
tradition of academic freedom that was to prove vital. Second, from
1717 Harvard's governance diverged from that of the Oxbridge colleges
in that the resident tutors were excluded from the governing corporation, the fellows of which became more like external trustees—often
wealthy Boston "Brahmins" whose bequests gradually grew into a substantial endowment, ending the need for state support in 1823. With the
nineteenth-century transformation of the board of overseers into a body
of elected graduates, rather than representatives of "church and state,"

Harvard's independence from government was established.[22] Third, Harvard backed the winning side in the War of Independence. Samuel and John Adams were among the eight Harvard signatories of the Declaration of Independence; only 16 percent of graduates were Loyalists. Fourth, in imitation of the Scottish universities, Harvard was not slow to establish professional schools: the Medical School (1782), Law School (1817), and Theological School (1819) put it far ahead of Oxford and Cambridge, where the entrenched power of the "dons," simultaneously fellows and tutors, acted as a brake on most innovation. Fifth, and for the same reason, Harvard was much more open than its English counterparts to the benign influence of the German universities in their nineteenth-century heyday. As president, the chemist Charles William Eliot imported the German ideal of *Lernfreiheit*—academic freedom—so that students were steadily freed from requirements and allowed to choose between "elective" courses. The first German-style Ph.D. was awarded in 1873.

As a consequence of these and other reforms, nineteenth-century Harvard was in reality far from an intellectual backwater. Ralph Waldo Emerson gave his famous address "The American Scholar" to the Harvard chapter of Phi Beta Kappa in 1837. He and the other members of the Saturday Club—Nathaniel Hawthorne, Henry Longfellow, Richard Henry Dana, Jr., James Russell Lowell, and Charles Eliot Norton—were among the greatest American thinkers of the era. Perhaps even more impressive were their successors, the legal scholar and later Supreme Court justice Oliver Wendell Holmes, the philosopher William James, and the polymath Charles Sanders Peirce, whose short-lived Metaphysical Club was the birthplace of American pragmatism.

A term borrowed from Immanuel Kant's *Critique of Pure Reason*, pragmatism has been portrayed by Louis Menand as an intellectual reaction to the bloody polarization of the American Civil War. For Holmes, who had fought in the war, pragmatism meant recognizing that "some of us don't know that we know anything." For Peirce, it implied a collective, cumulative view of knowledge: "The opinion which is fated to be ultimately agreed to by all who investigate is what we mean by the truth." For James, "Truth *happens* to an idea. It *becomes* true, *is* made true by events. Its verity is in fact an event, a process." Or as he put it elsewhere, "Beliefs . . . are really rules for action. . . . The true is the name of whatever proves itself to be good in the way of belief. . . . If the hypothesis of God works satisfactorily . . . it is true." The pragmatic generation, in Menand's words, "wished to avoid the violence they saw hidden in abstractions."[23]

The influence of pragmatism extended far beyond Harvard. It encouraged James to see the universe (and the United States) as "pluralistic." In the booming but strife-torn Chicago of the 1890s, it inspired John Dewey to turn against laissez-faire capitalism and Social Darwinism. At Oxford, it made the Rhodes scholars Horace Kallen and Alain Locke—one Jewish, the other African American—consider the possibility of "cultural pluralism" in a multiracial America. Among James's pupils was W.E.B. Du Bois, the first black man to receive a Harvard doctorate (for his dissertation on "The Suppression of the African Slave Trade"). Harvard on the eve of the First World War was itself increasingly pluralistic. The journalists Walter Lippmann and John Reed cut their political teeth as members of Harvard's Socialist Club. As Reed recalled,

> [The club's] members wrote articles in the college papers challenging undergraduate ideals, and muckraked the University for not paying its servants living wages. . . . Out of the agitation sprang the Harvard Men's League for Women's Suffrage . . . [and] an Anarchist group. The faculty was petitioned for a course in socialism. . . . All over the place radicals sprang up, in music, painting, poetry, the theatre. The more serious college papers took a socialistic, or at least a progressive tinge.[24]

Small wonder the young English socialist Harold Laski, a standard-bearer for the new pluralism, preferred Harvard to his politically somnolent alma mater Oxford.

Admittedly, Lippmann and Reed were hardly typical Harvard students. As a college for would-be gentlemen, Harvard had an undergraduate culture not so different from that of Oxford in the same era. The "idle Fops" Benjamin Franklin had complained about, with their drunken pranks and secret clubs—beginning in the 1790s with the creation of the

Porcellian for "The Bloods of Harvard" and the frivolous Hasty Pudding—had been succeeded by "the clubmen and athletes": muscular New Englanders disproportionately drawn from private preparatory schools like the august academies Phillips (Andover) and Phillips Exeter and from the newer Browne & Nichols, Groton, Milton, and St. Paul's.[25] Their passions were football, a mutilated form of rugby pioneered at Harvard in which forward passes and tackling off the ball were permitted, and more orthodox Oxbridge-style rowing and sculling. Their rooms were in plush halls like Beck, Felton, and Claverly, which clustered on Mount Auburn Street's "Gold Coast," a short walk—but a far cry—from the Spartan quarters of Harvard Yard.[26] And their social life revolved around a pyramid of clubs. At the base was the Institute of 1770, which selected a hundred men from each new class, the top eighty of whom became members of the DKE ("Dickey" or "Deeks"), who in turn hoped for election to "waiting clubs," S.K. and Iroquois, from whose ranks a lucky few were chosen by the "final clubs," the Porcellian, A.D., Fly, Spee, Delphic, Owl, Fox, and D.U. (in descending order of prestige).[27] These, Harvard's equivalent of fraternities, admitted no more than 12 percent of students, with the crème de la crème belonging to four or more clubs. Even the satirical magazine the *Lampoon* evolved into a kind of club. Snobbery was rife, with membership of the social elite signaled by the distinctive Harvard accent, in which the letter *a* was pronounced English fashion, "as in father."[28] For those at the apex of the pyramid, Father was generally a member of the Country Club in Brookline.

Eliot's successor as president, Abbott Lawrence Lowell, is sometimes portrayed as an upholder of this hierarchical social order. It is certainly true that he sought to make Harvard more like Oxford and less like Heidelberg. It is also true, as we shall see, that he held at least some of the racial prejudices of his era. Yet in many respects Lowell was a formidable modernizer, whose reforms ended the oligarchical reign of the Gold Coast. He is best remembered for creating the first seven residential houses—Dunster, Lowell, Eliot, Winthrop, Kirkland, Leverett, and Adams—so that the three upper classes could enjoy a version of Oxbridge collegiate life, complete with resident tutors, dining halls, and common rooms. But equally important was Lowell's insistence that all freshmen must reside in the dormitories of the Yard. These innovations were consciously designed to increase Harvard's "intellectual and social cohesion."[29] Lowell's presidency also saw five additional foundations: of the Business School (1908), the School of Architecture (1914), the Graduate School of Education (1920), the School of City Planning (1929), and the Society of Fellows (1933). Lowell it was who gave the Harvard campus its understated look, resisting the contemporary architectural temptations of "collegiate Gothic" and "imperial Elizabethan." And it was he who introduced concentrations and distributions, designed to impose some intellectual discipline on the free-for-all of Eliot's elective system by requiring "every student to make a choice of electives that will secure a systematic education, based on the principle of knowing a little of everything and something well."[30] This was pragmatism as an educational strategy.

In seeking to increase Harvard's social cohesion, however, Lowell was concerned not only to eliminate the class divisions exemplified by the Gold Coast. He was equally uneasy about the dramatic increase in the numbers of Jewish students at Harvard. Although Hebrew had been studied at Harvard in its earliest years, Jews had played a minimal role there before the late nineteenth century. Indeed, prior to 1886, no more than a dozen Jews had graduated from the college. By 1906, the surge of Jewish immigration from Central Europe, combined with the disproportionate literacy and numeracy of the immigrants, had changed that. There were soon "enough Russian Jewish lads from the Boston public schools" to found a Menorah Society for "the study and advancement of Hebraic culture and ideals."[31] Between 1900 and 1922 the proportion of Jewish students at Harvard surged from 7 percent to 22 percent, more than double the share at Yale.[32] All this had perfectly accorded with President Eliot's ambition to make Harvard cosmopolitan and "undenominational"; it was precisely why he had pushed through the abolition of compulsory chapel attendance in 1886, forty years ahead of Yale.[33] Eliot's view had been that "a great university exert[ed] a unifying social influence" precisely by opening its doors to all young men with appropriate academic aptitude.[34] But Lowell saw little sign of Harvard's "unifying" Jewish and gentile students. Only a tiny percentage of the Jews were elected to the social clubs. Instead they founded their own fraternities. Jews were more likely to be "commuters" from the Boston area, poorer students who had to "eat their bag lunches in the basement of Philips Brooks House or on the steps of Widener."[35] They were less likely to be involved in athletics and other extracurricular activities, with the sole exceptions of debating and music. On the other hand, they were clearly overrepresented among the students in the first two rank lists for academic attainment, and they won a rising share of the merit scholarships Eliot had created. Convinced that all these trends were increasing "race antagonism," Lowell proposed "limit[ing] any group of men who do not mingle indistinguishably with the general stream."[36]

As vice president of the Immigration Restriction League, Lowell did not confine his prejudices to Jews: "orientals," "colored men," and indeed French-Canadians struck him as dangerously alien. From 1922, Lowell specified that the proportion of scholarships going to Jews should not exceed their share of the freshman class and made it clear that, by limiting transfers from other colleges, he intended to reduce the share of Jews in the student body from 22 to 15 percent.[37] There ensued a fierce battle between Lowell and the faculty over the issue of admissions criteria ("principles and methods of sifting candidates"). Even before the report of the committee set up to review these principles and methods, a new application form was introduced with questions like "What change, if any, has been made since birth in your own name or that of your father? (Explain fully.)"[38] True, Lowell's idea of quotas was defeated, and the simultaneous relaxation of admissions academic criteria—which was supposed to end Harvard's regional bias toward New England and New York—only increased the share of Jews admitted, to a peak of 27 percent in 1925. From 1926, however, Harvard followed a lead already taken by Columbia, NYU, Yale, and Princeton, capping the total freshman class at one thousand and basing admissions decisions partly on nonacademic criteria such as "character." The data are not quite reliable, but the result appears to have been a drop in the share of Jewish freshmen back to 16 percent in 1928.[39]

The position of Jews at Harvard in the 1940s was so controversial that at least two senior theses were devoted to the subject. Bruce Stedman's anthropological study of Jewish upperclassmen in the classes of

1942 and 1943 was methodologically flawed, not least because he identified Jews partly on the basis of "the presence . . . of Jewish physical
characteristics."[40] But his thesis is still useful in two ways. First, it confirms that there was anti-Semitism at Harvard.[41] In October 1941 he
recorded the following exchange with another student:

> I told A-9 that D-9 had told me that Jews outnumbered non-
> Jews on a certain Student Council Committee (for which
> members are picked purely on a basis of academic achievement)
> two to one.
>
> A-9 said, "That's too many Jews."
>
> I said, "Jews surely are bright, though. I've never known a
> stupid Jew, I don't think."
>
> A-9 replied, "They aren't so bright as they are clever. A lot
> of them seem able to fill a prescribed form, or perform a habit-
> ual function, but when it comes to creative work they fall
> down."[42]

Second, Stedman showed how the Jews in his house responded to such
prejudices "by cultivating non-Jewish friends or by disavowing knowledge of the Hebrew religion etc. Another effort toward the same end
may be seen in the adoption of non-Jewish nick-names."[43]

By comparison, Marvin Kraus's thesis on the Jews in the classes of
1951, 1953, and 1954 was a good deal more rigorous, but his conclusion
was essentially the same. Harvard Jews were scrambling to assimilate
themselves. They were less religious than their parents; more than half
attended a religious service only once a year; 29 percent did not observe
Rosh Hashanah; 49 percent did not fast on Yom Kippur; hardly any (5
percent) observed the Jewish dietary laws or refrained from work on
the Sabbath; and a remarkable proportion (79 percent) dated non-Jews.
Yet they remained to a significant degree segregated, with nearly half
having only Jewish roommates, half participating in Hillel, and a third
identifying their "social crowd" as predominantly Jewish.[44]

When Theodore White, the son of an impecunious immigrant to
Boston from Pinsk, went to Harvard in 1934, he classified himself as
one of the "meatballs," at the bottom of the social heap. At the top

were the "white men, with names like Morgan, Rockefeller and Roosevelt and Kennedy, who had automobiles . . . went to Boston deb parties, football games [and] the June crew race against Yale"; then came
the "grey men . . . public-high-school boys, sturdy sons of America's
middle class," who "went out for football and baseball, manned the
Crimson and the Lampoon [and] ran for class committees." The "meatballs," by contrast, had come to Harvard "not to enjoy the games, the
girls, the burlesque shows of the Old Howard, the companionship, the
elms, the turning leaves of fall, the grassy banks of the Charles. We had
come to get the Harvard badge, which says 'Veritas' but really means a
job . . . in some bureaucracy, in some institution, in some school, labo-
ratory, university or law firm. . . . We were on the make." Though
there were Irish and Italians among the meatballs, the most driven
were the Jews like White.[45]

With Lowell's departure from the presidency in 1933 and the
appointment of James Bryant Conant, the Jewish question began to
lose its salience. A chemist by training, Conant was said to have turned
Harvard into "a meritocracy in which students and professors vied for
honors with little mercy or kindness."[46] Though not notably more
philo-Semitic than Lowell, Conant's priority was academic ability and
achievement. It was he who introduced the "up or out" rule that faculty members who did not secure tenure had their employment terminated. This and other meritocratic policies had the effect of favoring
Jewish scholars. A 1939 report entitled "Some Problems of Personnel in
the Faculty of Arts and Sciences" acknowledged the role of "anti-
Semitic feeling" in hindering the promotion of Jewish academics,[47] but
such prejudices were fast losing their legitimacy, partly because of the
growing revulsion against the conduct of the National Socialist regime
in Germany, and partly because of the ensuing exodus of undeniably
brilliant Jewish academics from Central Europe.

A third force was at work. In the ferment of the 1930s and 1940s,
ideology was becoming a more salient source of conflict than racial
prejudice. Arthur Schlesinger, Jr., grew up in a Harvard household, the
grandson of an East Prussian Jew who had settled in Ohio and converted to Protestantism, and the son of a distinguished historian of the
United States. The Schlesingers were New Deal liberals, whose circle

of friends included the future Supreme Court justice Felix Frankfurter and the leftist novelist John Dos Passos.[48] As an undergraduate, the younger Schlesinger joined the Communist-controlled American Student Union and was acquainted with the card-carrying historian Richard Schlatter and the fellow traveler Francis Matthiessen. But after the war, returning to Harvard as an associate professor, Schlesinger broke with the Communists. His memoir vividly recalls the rift in liberal Harvard between the Communists (CPUSA members) and fellow travelers, on the one side, and, on the other, the anti-Communist left, which Schlesinger thought of as "the vital center."[49] Over time such political differences gradually took precedence over ethnic differences, insofar as they did not coincide with them.

III

The Class of 1950 was the biggest in Harvard's history up until that point, with 1,588 graduates. Henry Kissinger was not the only member of the class who was destined for public service. James Schlesinger would go on to become CIA director, defense secretary, and energy secretary. Herbert J. Spiro later served on the Policy Planning Staff at the State Department and as U.S. ambassador to Cameroon and Equatorial Guinea. Another diplomat was William Harrop, who became ambassador to Israel. John T. Bennett was deputy director of the USAID mission in Saigon—from whence he was evacuated in 1975—and also served in Seoul and Guatemala. The 1950 graduates also included two Republican congressmen, Sedgwick William Green and Amory Houghton, the eminent New York lawyer and Democratic Party activist George Dwight, and George Cabot Lodge, son of the Massachusetts senator, ambassador, and vice-presidential candidate Henry Cabot Lodge, Jr., who himself ran for the Senate in 1962. The class also produced journalists—Jonathan Spivak of *The Wall Street Journal* and William Graves of *National Geographic*—as well as the author Lawrence Osgood and the artist Edward Gorey. There were some bankers and businessmen, as might be expected. But the majority were destined for the professions, or, like Kissinger, to become professors.[50]

Most young men who go to university make their firmest friendships there. That was not Henry Kissinger's experience. Journalists who sought out his Harvard contemporaries were struck by this absence of friendship, bordering in at least one case on hostility ("He had no charm").[51] Yet there were good reasons for it. We may be tempted to imagine Harvard in the late 1940s in romantic terms, as a point of transition between the intense Harvard of George Weller's *Not to Eat, Not for Love* (1933) and the schmaltzy Harvard of Erich Segal's *Love Story* (1970). Nothing could be more misleading. Harvard in the fall of 1947 was an unwelcoming shambles. To begin with, there was a chronic shortage of housing. As the troops returned, a university that before the war had been accustomed to a total student body of around 8,000 struggled to cope with a figure closer to 12,500. The pressure on the facilities of the undergraduate college was especially severe. Having been admitted at the last minute, Kissinger was probably bound to fare badly in the allocation of housing.[52] Along with around 180 other unlucky freshmen, he spent his first few weeks at Harvard as a resident of the Indoor Athletic Building (now the Malkin Athletic Center), the basketball hall of which had been turned into a makeshift barracks.[53]

Nor did the indignity end there. When a room was finally found for him, it was in the unloved Claverly Hall—"once the vault of Gold Coast opulence," as the *Crimson* put it, now "the dungeon of scholastic indolence." Built in 1893, Claverly was a monument to Gilded Age taste, its rooms much larger than those in the Yard or the Houses, but its ornate mantelpieces and marble washbasins showed their age. More important, the lack of dining facilities and hence of any real "fraternization" between the various floors (known as "entries") had made Claverly deeply unpopular by the 1940s—so much so that it was referred to as "a Mount Auburn St. Siberia." There was, in short, a stigma attached to it.[54] The nature of that stigma may be guessed from the fact that Kissinger's two roommates in Room 39 were both Jews: Edward Hendel and Arthur Gillman—as was Kissinger's friend from Oberammergau Henry Rosovsky, who later became one of the tutors at Claverly. The era of residential segregation of Jews was ending, but slowly.[55]

Even if Kissinger had wanted to be sociable, then, Harvard did not make it easy for him. Like so many Jewish students at that time, he had no desire to emphasize his Jewish identity by attending the Hillel Club, much less the Temple Beth-El synagogue. As a freshman, he ate his meals at the Harvard Union (now the Barker Humanities Center), a club that had been set up for the clubless and was notorious for its lack of ambience.[56] But Kissinger clearly did not want to be sociable. He had come to Harvard to study, and study he did, with an intensity that intimidated his roommates. As Hendel recalled, "He worked harder, studied more. He'd read until 1 or 2 a.m. He had tremendous drive and discipline. He spent a lot of time thinking. He was absorbing everything." Another remembered the young Kissinger as "very serious. . . . He sat in that overstuffed chair . . . studying from morning till night and biting his nails to the quick, till there was blood."[57] He did not chase the Radcliffe girls. He did not bother about his clothes. He largely ignored (and certainly did not play) college sports. Even when he was admitted to the Adams House—next door to Claverly, but several steps up in social terms[58]—he did not become more outgoing. Having been formed by merging three Gold Coast halls, Adams House was renowned for its swimming pool in "B" entry, its squash courts, its Saturday night dances, and its lively political life.[59] On December 1, 1949, for example, Kissinger could have attended a Common Room debate between former Adams man Arthur Schlesinger, Jr., and the radical historian H. Stuart Hughes.[60] But if the young Kissinger played a part in the life of the House, no trace of it has survived. He seemed to be "something of a recluse"—"the invisible man."[61]

What the younger students did not appreciate was that Kissinger had not just one but two lives outside the Harvard community. The first was his life as a veteran. College friendship is one thing; for those who fought in World War II, the brotherhood of arms was altogether more important. As an undergraduate, Kissinger continued to serve as a reserve CIC officer, which consumed a considerable amount of his vacation time.[62] He remained in regular contact with the friends he had made in the army, not least his mentor Kraemer, whom he visited in Washington.[63] It was still to Kraemer that Kissinger confided his innermost thoughts, like the one he proffered in a letter of November 1949: "Perhaps man's striving for value, the certainty of greater truths can never be approached with the pedantic method of philosophy, but needs the poet who sees the totality of life and not just its manifestations."[64] (Kraemer's characteristic response was "Omit the first word in the above statement.") A year after beginning his studies at Harvard, and shortly before returning for his second year, Kissinger wrote a poignant letter from a Maryland army camp to a friend he had made in Germany:

> I think often and happily about those so extraordinary and uplifting days of 1945–46, when everything seemed possible and unstable.
>
> Since my return my life has changed a great deal. For eight months of the year I am once again a student, which is interesting but sometimes somewhat constraining. During the summer, as can be seen from my address here, I find myself once again engaged in a field of activity that is much closer to my earlier one [in Germany] than student life is.[65]

His Harvard roommates may have seen a humorless bookworm. His former comrades in arms knew a very different Kissinger, as is clear from a downright zany letter sent to Kissinger at around the same time by his fellow CIC officer Victor Guala, who clearly intended to mock the bureaucratic language of CIC communications in the style of the Marx Brothers:

> 1. Request information as to the future whereabouts of HENRY KISSINGER, aka Mr. Henry, aka Herr CIC Ahghent, aka Herr Henry, aka Der Bensheimer Kerl der fuer Herrn L. arbeitet. It is desired to know specifically whether this individual will be in the vicinity of NYC during the coming week-end, or any coming week-end, or, if this goes thru channels, was he here at all during 1948?
>
> 2. Check of our files indicates no correspondence of note in the past between these two agencies; your attention is directed to AR (Acquired Reflex) #0001.01, Para. 1, Line 3, Word 76493a, which states, in effect, that it is

normally to be expected that these two agencies will
maintain inadequate liason (pronounced: lyuhsun) (spelled:
liaison), thereby adding materially to the snafu of the
service. In view of the above, if you belive [*sic*] in the
above, the Commandeering Gent has expressed his
intention of presenting the below and without on the
telephone, whereas, the party of the second part,
hereinafter to be referred to as the party of the first part,
and the party of the first part, hereinafter to be referred to
as Subject, aka THE Party, aka the first-part party, aka the
4th party, as distinguished from the 3rd, Dem and Rep
parties and all other parties hereinafter and here to fore
mentioned or ignored is entirely coincidental and
unintentional.[66]

It is not known if Kissinger accepted this particular invitation to
New York, but he certainly visited his home city on a regular basis
while at Harvard. Like all New Yorkers who attend the university on
the banks of the Charles, he doubtless found Cambridge a little dull at
weekends. In any case, Kissinger's other life—his private life—was in
New York, not Massachusetts. The reason he showed no interest in the
"Radcliffe girls" was simple: at some point in late 1948—after a night
at the theater to see the whimsical musical *Finian's Rainbow*—he had
become engaged to Anne Fleischer.

The Fleischers came from precisely the same world of German-
Jewish Orthodoxy as the Kissingers. Like them, they had made a new
but not wholly different life in Washington Heights. Anne had lived a
little, to be sure. She had spent a year in Colorado Springs, where she
worked at a hotel and audited some courses. She had studied bookkeeping with her brother-in-law Gerald Reich and worked for a time at an
interior decorating firm.[67] But her marriage to Henry Kissinger in February 1949 represented an unambiguous victory for his parents. While
in Germany, their elder son had shocked them by having an affair with
a gentile and a German one at that. He had, as we have seen, vigorously
resisted their pressure on him to get engaged to Anne. His return to the
United States brought him back into the fold. The marriage service was

even performed in the Kissingers' apartment by Rabbi Leo Breslauer, the ultra-Orthodox rabbi who had survived the 1938 pogrom in Fürth and had joined other survivors from his congregation in New York.

Why had Kissinger changed his mind? It was certainly not because he had refound his lost religious faith. Even on the wedding day there was renewed friction on that score when he objected to Breslauer's insistence that Anne take the ritual bath, the *mikvah,* before the cere-mony.[68] One plausible answer is that Kissinger was trying to mollify his parents, not least because his younger brother was doing the very opposite (and would ultimately defy them by eloping with a Christian girl). Another explanation is that a year of undergraduate life at Har-vard had made married life seem suddenly more attractive. As his brother, Walter,* recalled, "He had difficulty adapting to the frivolity of college life. Both of us had a hell of a time adjusting to living in a dorm with a bunch of kids just out of prep school. Marrying Ann [she dropped the "e" after her marriage] allowed him to be serious."[69] In particular, Ann could extricate Kissinger from Adams House and allow him to live as an adult without his having to give up his studies. Tra-ditional though their wedding was, their marriage was modern in at least one key respect: Ann was a breadwinner. It was she who went apartment-hunting for them;[70] she who found their first home at 49 Florence Street, Arlington, and their second one at 495 Lowell Avenue, in Newton, around eight miles to the west of the Harvard campus; she who worked as a bookkeeper for a Malden furniture store. Her savings ($700) and earnings ($1,100 a year) were a crucial supplement to his wartime savings and the support he received under the GI Bill.[71] More-over, like the wives of so many 1950s academics, Ann provided Kis-singer with free secretarial support, typing out the senior thesis that he composed in longhand, as well as doing all the housework and putting

---

*Walter had returned home from the war even later than his brother. Having served with the 24th Army Corps at Okinawa and risen to the rank of sergeant, he accepted a job with the postwar government in Korea, where he was responsible for reopening the country's coal mines. On returning to the United States, he studied at Princeton and later Harvard Business School—motivated, according to his mother, by "sibling rivalry." In fact, it was Walter who first stated his intention to pursue a career in the diplomatic service, though he later opted for business.

food on the table. What remains harder to ascertain is how far the marriage brought Kissinger happiness. If it did, it was not for long.

Marriage may have meant a measure of financial support for a mature student. But it also had obvious implications about his future gainful employment. The question was as yet unanswered: What exactly had Kissinger come to Harvard to learn? And where would that learning lead him? It was far from obvious at first that the answer would be to an academic career in Harvard's government department.

IV

As President Eliot had intended, the Harvard undergraduate program gave students choice—the chance to experiment. Henry Kissinger took advantage of that chance. In his first term, he had taken introductory courses in French, government, history, and mathematics, obtaining an A in each, as well as chemistry as a fifth course for no credit.[72] For a time he toyed with the idea of pursuing chemistry further. His professor, George Kistiakowsky, was an impressive figure who had worked on the Manhattan Project at Los Alamos during the war. But when Kissinger asked his advice, Kistiakowsky replied, "If you have to ask, you shouldn't."*[73] Kissinger also attended lectures by the great physicist Percy W. Bridgman, whose work on high pressure won him the 1946 Nobel Prize. That same year Kissinger tried his hand at philosophy, studying with the diminutive and depressive Henry M. Sheffer, best known for introducing to formal logic the vertical line known as the "Sheffer stroke." To Kissinger's dismay (and to the delight of at least one rival), he got a B in Sheffer's course, the only letter grade below A- he ever received.[74] (It may have been in answer to this that he inserted an abstruse and barely relevant philosophical appendix at the

---

*Kistiakowsky later served on the Ballistic Missiles Advisory Committee set up in 1953 and the President's Science Advisory Committee created after the *Sputnik* crisis. From 1959 until 1960 he served as Eisenhower's special assistant for science and technology. Kissinger later joked that if Kistiakowsky had only advised him to stick to science, "he could have kept me out of years of trouble by allowing me to become a mediocre chemist."

end of his senior thesis.) His overall performance was excellent but not the very best. Although his grades were good enough to secure him a senior faculty member as his adviser, his election to the academic elite—the Harvard chapter of Phi Beta Kappa—did not come until his senior year.

Two puzzles present themselves about Kissinger's undergraduate career. First, why did he become a government concentrator rather than majoring in history? In view of his lifelong interest in historical subjects, he might have been expected to follow in the footsteps of Arthur Schlesinger, Jr., whose own father was one of a group of distinguished historians then teaching at Harvard. Paul Buck had won the Pulitzer Prize for his *Road to Reunion, 1865–1900*, and was one of the country's leading historians of the American South. Crane Brinton, a specialist in the French Revolution and a major influence on Samuel Huntington, was the widely read author of *The Anatomy of Revolution*. Edwin O. Reischauer was the leading U.S. historian of Japan and had formed a strong teaching partnership with John King Fairbank, Harvard's first specialist in Chinese history.[75] A man who later wrote a senior thesis entitled "The Meaning of History" and whose doctoral thesis focused on the period of the Congress of Vienna should surely have been first in line for Brinton's popular breakfast course on revolutionary France. A man who would go on to transform relations between the United States and China ought at least to have considered taking Fairbank's and Reischauer's survey course on East Asia (affectionately known to students as "rice paddies"). Instead, probably on Kraemer's advice, he chose to major in political science, or (in Harvard parlance) to "concentrate in Government."[76]

The second question is why, once Kissinger made that choice, he became a pupil of William Yandell Elliott, when Carl Friedrich would have been the more obvious adviser. A student of Max Weber's brother Alfred, Friedrich had come to Harvard from Heidelberg in 1926 and established himself as a leading authority on modern Germany and in particular on democratic constitutions. In 1949 he had just returned from advising the Office of Military Government in Germany. His reputation as a "good German" was at its zenith. Friedrich's most influential book of the 1940s had been *The New Belief in the Common Man* (1942), which he reissued in an enlarged edition in 1950 as *The New Image of the Common Man*.[77] Trenchantly antitotalitarian, Friedrich's book takes swings at José Ortega y Gasset's "revolt of the masses" and Vilfredo Pareto's theory of elites. It seeks to find a middle way between pluralism and "state idolatry" by elevating the quintessentially American ideal of the "common man" as the fount of democratic wisdom. Generally, Friedrich argues, the common man is right, but

> [t]here is . . . one extremely important field of governmental activity in which most of what we have said concerning the judgment of the common man does not necessarily hold. That is the field of foreign affairs. The decisions in this field are of a nature that removes them from the average man's grasp. Nor do they bear any striking relationship to his folkways, traditions, and beliefs. . . . Since the common man . . . shuns foreign policy, such policy in democratic national government oscillates, as American democracy has oscillated, between isolationism and internationalism.[78]

This can hardly have been an uncongenial argument to the young Kissinger, even if Friedrich's concluding call for "Pan-Humanism" was not altogether convincing.[79] Moreover, Friedrich was no dry academic who expected his pupils to spend their entire lives in libraries and lecture halls. Among his students in the 1950s was Zbigniew Brzezinski—also born in Europe, also an immigrant of the 1938 vintage—who would again follow Kissinger by becoming national security adviser in 1977.

But Friedrich and Kissinger were never kindred spirits. One theory is that, after Kraemer, Kissinger had no need of another German *Meister*. Another is that Friedrich was less impressed by Kissinger's intellect than was his colleague.[80] According to Friedrich himself, Kissinger told him bluntly, "I am interested in the practical politics of international relations, and you are interested in philosophy and scholarship."[81] A more likely explanation is the humdrum one. Had he been a graduate student, Friedrich and Elliott might well have vied for his allegiance. As a mere undergraduate, however, Kissinger was assigned to Elliott by the government department for purely bureaucratic reasons.

The son of a Tennessee lawyer who died when he was just three, William Yandell Elliott III was raised by his mother in Nashville, where she became the librarian of the Vanderbilt Law School. He himself had a successful undergraduate career at Vanderbilt, where he became part of the informal group of young southern poets known as the Fugitives,* who saw themselves as "rescuing . . . the ideals of friendship, personal loyalty and sectional pride . . . from the creeping anonymity of the twentieth century."[82] Elliott served as a first lieutenant with the 114th Field Artillery in 1917–18 and then spent several months studying at the Sorbonne before returning to Vanderbilt, gaining his M.A. in 1920, and beginning his academic career as an instructor in English literature. That same year a Rhodes scholarship took him to Oxford. During his time at Balliol College, Elliott mingled in literary circles with Robert Graves and W. B. Yeats. He almost certainly came under the influence of the "Round Table Group" founded by the British politician and colonial administrator Alfred Milner, to which a number of Balliol fellows belonged.[83] But the principal influence on Elliott was the Scottish philosopher A. D. ("Sandy") Lindsay, an authority on Plato and Henri Bergson and a man of the moderate left. After a brief period as a junior professor at Berkeley, Elliott was appointed lecturer and tutor at Harvard's department of government. He ascended the academic ladder steadily and by 1942 had a named chair, the highest academic position at Harvard short of a university professorship.

The book that made Elliott's reputation was *The Pragmatic Revolt in Politics: Syndicalism, Fascism, and the Constitutional State* (1928). Dedicated to Lindsay, it makes for strange reading today. Verbose, bombastic, and repetitive, the book makes connections from the American philosophical school of pragmatism to contemporary movements in European politics that can only be described as tendentious. Elliott's starting point is "the attack now taking formidable shape in practice as well as theory, over a great part of Europe, against the constitutional and democratic state." In all its forms—ranging from syndicalism to fascism—this attack

---

*The other members of the group were John Crowe Ransom, Allen Tate, Donald Davidson, and Robert Penn Warren. Although Elliott never adopted the mantle of Agrarianism, as Ransom did in *I'll Take My Stand*, he remained sympathetic to the Anglophile conservatism of his southern friends.

is presented by Elliott as "part of a deeply rooted anti-intellectualism" associated with pragmatism.[84]

Where Elliott was right was that a great many intellectuals on both sides of the Atlantic were reluctant to face the scale of the threat posed to interwar democracy—not to mention the threat to the system of collective security centered on the League of Nations—by illiberal ideologies. More questionable was his claim that there were any meaningful links from William James to Mussolini. On close inspection, *The Pragmatic Revolt* was a hodgepodge of reviews—of Georges Sorel, Harold Laski, G.D.H. Cole, John Dewey, and Léon Duguit—held together by the flimsiest of threads. (By 1928 it was already clear that Mussolini believed much more earnestly in the power of the state than its corporative constituents.) Not surprisingly, no one today remembers Elliott's theory of the "co-organic state," which was supposed to rescue "the legal sovereignty of the democratically organized Nation-State" from the supposed subversions of the pragmatists. But Elliott's timing was good, as Americans began slowly to grasp the seriousness of what was going on in Italy and as the heirs of James slithered from pragmatism to a pluralism that seemed to challenge the legitimacy of the democratic state itself. As a reassertion of the pre-Jamesian verities, a defense of Woodrow Wilson's postwar vision, and an intimation of what the United States would end up fighting for under Franklin Roosevelt, *The Pragmatic Revolt* served its purpose. Elliott made no secret of his sympathy with "the rationalistic efforts of democratic liberalism to create a political vehicle such as parliamentary government, which strives to provide for social evolution under law and to extend that machinery gradually from constitutional nationalism to a World League." Like Friedrich, he came back to Kant and the "belief that government under law is the expression of a shared moral purpose toward an ideal of the good life."[85]

Elliott has been presented as a conservative, fighting a vain rearguard action against the "paradigm shift" that would establish pluralism as the dominant theory of the state in American political science.[86] He was certainly no match for the proponents of pluralism like the Cornell-based Englishman George Catlin, author of *The Science and Method of Politics,* who did so much to move American political science away from both political theory and history.[87] But Elliott's historical significance lies elsewhere. First, as we shall see, he (along with Friedrich) championed a somewhat vulgarized but nevertheless potent idealism. At a time when Harvard philosophy was still under the sway of A. N. Whitehead,* who had died just a few months after Kissinger's arrival in Cambridge, Elliott urged his students to go back to Kant. In a way, as his pupil Louis Hartz put it, he was the last of the Oxford idealists, "the conscience of political study at Harvard, forcing it always back to the ethical assumptions which it involves."[88] From Lindsay he had picked up traces of T. H. Green and F. H. Bradley, and he brought some residue of their thought back with him to Harvard.[89] The "pragmatic revolt" was not wholly an imaginary construct; Elliott was leading a revolt against pragmatism at Harvard.

Second, Elliott more than fulfilled his obligations to the Rhodes Trust by becoming a very early proponent of the Atlantic alliance. After *The Pragmatic Revolt,* his next two major works, *The New British Empire* (1932) and *The Need for Constitutional Reform* (1935), amounted to a manifesto for Anglo-American convergence, the former urging the transformation of the empire into "a workable league of nations within the world League, on a purely consultative and cooperative basis, divesting itself of a mercantilist philosophy of exploitation," the latter proposing to Anglicize the U.S. political system by establishing a permanent civil service, giving the president more prime ministerial powers, and creating new "regional commonwealths" modeled on the Canadian provinces. In short, Elliott believed that the British Empire and the United States should become more like one another, an argument bearing the indelible stamp of his time at Balliol.[90] Unlike some of Milner's Round Table heirs, however, Elliott was (like Sandy Lindsay) an active opponent of the policy of appeasement, "several times thwart[ing] [the Cliveden Set's] machinations when they were trying to turn the policy of *The Christian-Science Monitor* [in America] in this direction and in other maneuvers."[91] Before America's involvement in World War II even began,

---

*The coauthor with Bertrand Russell of the *Principia Mathematica* and author of the dauntingly abstruse *Process and Reality,* Whitehead had driven philosophy toward mathematics and physics and far away from politics.

Elliott was already cooperating with the Mazzini Society, a group of Italian émigré antifascists including Gaetano Salvemini and Count Carlo Sforza.[92] He was in many respects an authentically Churchillian figure.[93]

Third and perhaps most important for Henry Kissinger, Elliott set out to show that a professor could also be a political actor. Conservative as he certainly came to be compared with the average Harvard professor, he nevertheless had no qualms about joining Roosevelt's Committee on Administrative Management and played minor parts in the design of the Reorganization Act of 1939 and the creation of the Executive Office of the President. In 1937 he was appointed to the Business Advisory Council created by Secretary of Commerce Daniel C. Roper to give industry a louder voice in Washington, serving under its chairman, the banker (later diplomat and politician) W. Averell Harriman, for five years. It was at this time that Elliott became preoccupied with the issue of strategic commodities. As one of the coauthors of *International Control in the Non-Ferrous Metals* (1938), he argued for an Anglo-American condominium to control the world's supply of nonferrous metals and other war matériel.

Elliott had real political courage. A vocal opponent of American neutrality, who urged repeal of the Neutrality Act following the German invasion of Poland, as well as financial support for Finland and military preparation to resist German, Italian, and Japanese aggression, he made himself deeply unpopular with the noninterventionist elements at Harvard. When, in late 1940, Roosevelt sent Churchill fifty aging American destroyers in return for the use of British naval bases, protesters at Harvard demonstrated with placards reading, "Send Fifty Over-Aged Professors to Britain."[94] Looking back on the 1930s in July 1942, Elliott lamented "the reluctance [of Britain and the United States] to apply sanctions at a time when there could have been small danger in applying sanctions in the incipient stages of fascism and Japanese militarism from 1931 to 1938. Only blindness can explain that—the blindness of public apathy and the pressures of certain interests for profits which proved to be more powerful than any concern for public interest during these crucial pre-war years."[95]

Events vindicated the "over-aged professor," who was duly rewarded in 1940 with a place on the National Defense Advisory Commission and a job as deputy chief of the Commodity, Stockpile and Shipping Imports Branch of the Office of Production Management. Pressing his advantage, he proposed to Secretary of State Cordell Hull that loans to the British Commonwealth be granted on the condition that the recipients' raw materials be pooled, to "set up for the first time in history a really sensible international control of the world's major raw materials, with a view to their proper development from the point of view of long-run conservation and planned production."[96] Elliott was prescient once again when, in September 1941, he warned that "this country must also be concerned, and almost equally, with the Battle of the Pacific" and that the weakly defended British naval base at Singapore was the "Achilles' heel" of the U.S. defense program.[97] After Pearl Harbor and the fall of Singapore proved him right once again, Elliott looked forward with relish to the creation of a future "world system" under the leadership of an America that was finally "committed to a destiny of world leadership."[98] He continued to be productive as a scholar in the war years, coauthoring *The British Commonwealth at War* (1943) with the Balliol historian H. Duncan Hall, and *Anglo-American Postwar Economic Problems* (1945) with the Princeton economist Frank D. Graham. But his main energies were now expended in Washington, not in Cambridge, and for the rest of his Harvard career he shuttled back and forth between the two, sometimes on a weekly basis.

Like most professors, Elliott was readily caricatured by students. "Tall, robust, with bushy eyebrows, outsized features, and booming voice," he and his southern background and Anglophile tendencies made him an easy target for mockery. To some he was "Wild Bill," to others "the Senator for Tennessee." Stories circulated, surely fictitious, about cockfights in the basement of his home in Concord. No book that he wrote has endured; nor did he attain the high executive office some thought he craved. It is not surprising to find traces of racial prejudice in his correspondence. "He is a Jew," he wrote of one job applicant in 1952, "but he is in every respect a healthy and fine type, with no feeling of being a Jew."[99] "There are some parts of the desegregation business that I cannot stomach," he confessed in 1956.[100] Yet Elliott deserves better than the condescension of posterity. At a time when most American professors preferred to lecture than to converse with students, Elliott imported to Harvard the Oxford tutorial method. Despite his frequent excursions to Washington and the heavy lecturing load imposed by the introductory course Government 1, which he taught for thirty years, he still found time to meet with individual students. Those who caught his eye were asked, Oxford fashion, to wade through a long list of books, write an essay, read it aloud, and then verbally spar with him. It was this readiness to pay attention to undergraduates that drew to Elliott students of the caliber of John F. Kennedy, Dean Rusk, and McGeorge Bundy, not to mention Pierre Trudeau. Elliott's academic protégés included Louis Hartz, author of *The Liberal Tradition in America* (1955), the influential systems theorist David Easton, and Samuel Huntington, who made his name with *The Soldier and the State* (1957).[101]

When Kissinger first met Elliott, as the then supplicant recalled many years later, he was

> shuffling papers with a weary air, sitting at a desk which at any moment threatened to topple under the weight of the documents covering it. I had penetrated into his study because his secretary was out of the office. My purpose was to ask what I now recognize as a sacrilegious question: whether, in view of my Army experience, it was necessary for me to take Government 1. The question seemed to magnify Bill's melancholy.[102]

Elliott wearily advised Kissinger to take another course: Government 1a, also taught by him. Kissinger was more impressed by the form than the content of the lectures. "Obviously, Bill Elliott cared. Political theory to him was not an abstract subject to be studied historically or to be used as a demonstration of dialectic brilliance. It was an adventure where good and evil were in a constant struggle to give meaning to existence, and where epics seemed to be prescriptions for action." For this reason, Kissinger was by no means sorry to be assigned Elliott as his tutor. But

> [w]hen I reported this fact to [Elliott] he intimated that his duties were growing excessive. He said I should return after reading Kant's *Critique of Pure Reason*. This was not a simple

assignment for someone with little training in philosophy. As a result, it took me until the term was half over to finish my paper. Bill made me read it to him, and somewhere in the middle of it his seeming indifference disappeared. He suggested that I work on political theory, not as an historian but as a creative philosopher. This idea had never occurred to me.[103]

This is a story that has been told more than once. In other versions, the near-impossible assignment is a comparison of *The Critique of Pure Reason* and *The Critique of Practical Reason*. So impressed was Elliott by the paper (which has not survived) that he pronounced Kissinger to be "a combination of Kant and Spinoza."[104]

Like Kraemer before him, Elliott had spotted talent. His response was to plunge Kissinger into the classics not just of Western philosophy but also of literature: the reading assignments ranged from Homer to Dostoevsky, by way of Hegel and much else. By the time Kissinger entered his senior year, Elliott was asking him to comment on his own manuscripts. Writing a letter of recommendation to Phi Beta Kappa in October 1949, Elliott described his pupil as "more like a mature colleague than a student. . . . I would say that I have not had any students in the past five years, even among Summa cum Laude group, who have had the depth and philosophical insight shown by Mr. Kissinger."[105] Elliott had his reservations, to be sure, but his criticisms were more revealing of his own prejudices than his pupil's defects. Kissinger's mind, he wrote, "lacks grace and is Teutonic in its systematic thoroughness. He has a certain emotional bent, perhaps from a refugee origin, that occasionally comes out. . . . He needs to develop his range in the arts and in some aspects of the humanities, particularly on the aesthetic side."[106] It is worth adding that this reference was written before Kissinger delivered the senior thesis that was to be the crowning achievement of his undergraduate career and an enduring proof of William Yandell Elliott's influence on him.

V

"The Meaning of History" has gone down in history—as the longest-ever thesis written by a Harvard senior and the origin of the current limit on length (35,000 words, or around 140 pages, still known to some as "the Kissinger rule").[107] The thesis was 388 pages long—and this was after chapters on Hegel and Schweitzer had been cut. According to one account, Friedrich refused to read past page 150.[108] But its size was not the most remarkable thing about it. In a dazzling distillation of three years' worth of reading, Kissinger gives us not just Spengler, Toynbee, and Kant but also Collingwood, Dante, Darwin, Descartes, Dostoevsky, Goethe, Hegel, Hobbes, Holmes, Homer, Hume, Locke, Milton, Plato, Sartre, Schweitzer, Spinoza, Tolstoy, Vico, Virgil, and Whitehead—as well as Bradley, Huntington, Joseph, Poincaré, Reichenbach, Royce, Russell, Sheffer, Stebbing, and Veblen in the appendix on the logic of meaning. It is unmistakably a young man's book: an exercise in academic exhibitionism, marred by jejune slips like misspelling Sartre as "Satre" and treating *data* and *phenomena* as singular and *polis* as plural (reminders that Kissinger had been denied a classical education in Germany).[109] Much of the dissertation is taken up with detailed exposition of the three key authors' arguments, but—partly because Kissinger omitted phrases like "As Spengler says" in order to save space—it is sometimes hard to tell where the authors' views end and Kissinger's commentary begins. As a result, more than one reader has wrongly attributed Spengler's cultural pessimism to Kissinger himself.[110] Yet the thesis, for all its flaws, deserved its Summa grade. It also provides valuable insights into Elliott's influence on Kissinger, which extended far beyond the old-fashioned substitution of "ever" for "always," an idiosyncrasy picked up from Elliott's orotund prose.

Oswald Spengler, Arnold J. Toynbee, and Immanuel Kant were strange bedfellows, to say the least. Whereas Kant, then as now, was revered as one of the towering figures of Western philosophy, Spengler was a maverick polemicist whose obscure prophecies in *Der Untergang des*

Abendlandes—published in two volumes between 1918 and 1923—had been tainted by association with the German right (he was the bête noire of the founder of the Harvard sociology department, Pitirim Sorokin), while Toynbee's twelve-volume history of the rise and fall of civilizations was only half finished at the time of Kissinger's writing. The selection of Toynbee—another Balliol man—probably owed something to Elliott. But it may also have reflected the remarkable popular success of the first six volumes of *A Study of History,* which had been published in an abridged single volume in the United States in 1947 and sold over 300,000 copies there, doubtless helped by a *Time* magazine cover story in March of that year. "Our Civilization Is Not Inevitably Doomed" was the *Time* headline—always a welcome message for Americans, as was Toynbee's affirmation of the vital importance of Christianity to the West. Since Toynbee was being hailed by the press as the anti-Spengler, Kissinger's choice of authors was in fact highly topical. And given that an enthusiasm for Kant's "Perpetual Peace" was virtually all that his senior academic advisers had in common, it made good strategic sense for an ambitious young scholar to show how superior Kant was as a thinker to both Spengler and Toynbee.

Surprisingly, Kissinger elected not to discuss the obvious question, namely how the three authors thought differently about causation in history.[111] Instead, he chose to focus on a deeper and more difficult question: their treatment of the fundamental tension in the human condition between any theory of historical determinism and our sense as individuals of free will. As is clear from his introduction, this was a question in which he had an intensely personal interest.

> In the life of every person there comes a point when he realizes that out of all the seemingly limitless possibilities of his youth he has in fact become one actuality. No longer is life a broad plain with forests and mountains beckoning all-around, but it becomes apparent that one's journey across the meadows has indeed followed a regular path. . . . We have come up against the problem of Necessity and Freedom, of the irrevocability of our actions, of the directedness of our life. . . . The desire to

reconcile our experience of freedom with a determined environment is the lament of poetry and the dilemma of philosophy. . . . What is the meaning of a causality that accomplishes itself under the mode of freedom?"[112]

As Kissinger showed, each of his chosen authorities offered a different answer to this question. Spengler was the strictest determinist of the three. For him, history "represent[ed] the growth and decline of organic cultures, their essence a mystery, their moving force longing and their manifestation power."[113] There is no need here to dwell on Kissinger's somewhat protracted exegesis. All that matters is that Spengler's insistence on a universal cycle from biology to culture to civilization and back to biology left Kissinger unconvinced: "The opposition between waking-consciousness and becoming, between Time and Space, History and Causality[,] expresses, but does not resolve, the dilemma of the experience of freedom in a determined environment."[114]

Toynbee also fell short—indeed, a good deal shorter. True, he appeared to offer a role for purposiveness in history, as against Spengler's fatalism. Civilizations can choose to respond to an environmental challenge, can choose to continue clawing their way up the metaphorical cliff face of history. Yet if the ultimate meaning of history is a working out of God's will, then as Kissinger wrote, "[w]e have not really transcended Spengler" at all. "History is not a book designed to illustrate the New Testament," he declared, dismissing Toynbee's magnum opus as mere "superimposition of an empirical method on a theological foundation."[115]

As he had been taught by Elliott to do, Kissinger showed how Kant had established a realm for freedom by drawing a distinction between the phenomenal world, which is both perceived by reason and deterministic, and the noumenal world of things-in-themselves, perceptible only by inward experience. "The experience of freedom in a determined environment is [thus] seen to be potentially meaningful after all. . . . Purposiveness is not revealed by phenomenal reality but constitutes the resolve of a soul. Freedom does have a place in a determined universe."[116] Kissinger also praised Kant's idea of the categorical imperative.* Aside from its significance in the realm of ethics, the categorical imperative provided "the frame-work for Kant's philosophy of history," for "[i]f the transcendental experience of freedom represents the condition for the apprehension of the greater [noumenal] truth at the core of all phenomenal appearances, then its maxims must [also] constitute norms in the political field. Peace is therefore the noblest goal of human endeavor, the affirmation of the ultimacy of man's moral personality."[117]

In other words, the pursuit of peace is the noblest of all acts of free will. But here Kissinger believed he had caught Kant out. In the essay on "Perpetual Peace," Kissinger argued, "the duty to work for peace appears first as an emanation of the categorical imperative, only to stand revealed as the objective principle governing historical events."[118] To Kissinger, this represented just another attempt, like Toynbee's, "to expand the philosophy of history into a guarantee for the attainability of the moral law."[119] "In order to establish the validity of his categorical imperative as foundation of eternal peace, Kant was forced to demonstrate the possibility of its application. But his proof of feasibility became a dictum of necessity and seems to negate the moral basis of the categorical imperative."[120]

In that sense, "Kant too [had] considered and failed to solve completely the dilemma inherent in all philosophy of history . . . the connection between the necessary and the possible."[121] Though Kant scholars may quibble that Kissinger was conflating the two kingdoms of Nature and of Ends, which Kant insisted were separate, there is no denying that in "Perpetual Peace" (as well as in his "Idea for Universal History from a Cosmopolitan Point of View") Kant did introduce a teleological version of history, acknowledging the existence of a "higher cause which determines the course of nature and directs it to the objective final end of the human race," namely perpetual peace.[122]

---

*Kant provided three distinct formulations of the categorical (as opposed to hypothetical) imperative in his *Grounding for the Metaphysics of Morals* (1785): "Act only according to that maxim whereby you can at the same time will that it should become a universal law without contradiction"; "Act in such a way that you treat humanity, whether in your own person or in the person of any other, never merely as a means to an end, but always at the same time as an end"; and "Act as if you are through your maxim always a legislating member in the universal kingdom of ends."

So where does Kissinger himself stand in the end? The answer is with freedom over necessity, with choice understood as an inward experience. "Freedom," he writes in a key passage, "is not a definitional quality, but an inner experience of life as a process of deciding meaningful alternatives.

> This . . . does not mean unlimited choice. Everybody is a product of an age, a nation, and environment. But, beyond that, he constitutes what is essentially unapproachable by analysis . . . the creative essence of history, the moral personality. *However we may explain actions in retrospect, their accomplishment occurred with the inner conviction of choice. . . .* Man can find the sanction for his actions only within himself.[123]

And again: "Freedom is . . . an inner state which seeks its own stimulus. . . . Freedom depends less on the existence, than on the recognition of alternatives, not on a set of conditions, but [on] an inward experience."[124]

In sum, "The realm of freedom and necessity can not be reconciled except by inward experience."[125] This emphasis on inwardness makes it clear that Kissinger's penultimate page, with its allusions to the events of the 1930s and 1940s, is in fact optimistic:

> The generation of Buchenwalde [*sic*] and the Siberian labor-camps can not talk with the same optimism as its fathers. The bliss of Dante has been lost in our civilization. But this describes merely a fact of decline and not its necessity. . . . To be sure[,] these may be tired times. But . . . the experience of freedom enables us to rise beyond the suffering of the past and the frustrations of history. In this spirituality resides humanity's essence, the unique which each man imparts to the necessity of his life, the self-transcendence which gives peace.[126]

It has been argued that there is no "hidden connection between [Kissinger's] philosophical perspective on history and his role in formulating and executing foreign policy" after 1968.[127] According to this account,

Auschwitz made it impossible for Kissinger to believe in the universal moral principles and eternal values that formed the basis for Kant's faith in human progress. . . . For Kissinger, God died at Auschwitz. . . . The glaring contrast between Kissinger's Realpolitik and Kantian Idealism suggests that the lengthy undergraduate thesis was an intellectual exercise that reflected no long-term aspect of his personality and value system.[128]

This is at least debatable. Certainly the Kissinger who wrote "The Meaning of History" was not a "lapsed Kantian." Nor had he come down on the side of Spinoza's bleak skepticism, with its essentially Hobbesian view of power.[129] Spinoza was scarcely mentioned in "The Meaning of History." And wholly absent from the senior thesis was Machiavelli, whose influence on Kissinger has so often been wrongly alleged.

The correct reading of "The Meaning of History" is as an authentically idealist tract. Under Elliott's influence, Kissinger had done his homework—had read "Perpetual Peace"—but detected a flaw in Kant's reasoning. Peace might indeed be the ultimate goal of history. From the point of view of the individual, however—inwardly confronting his options and thus genuinely experiencing freedom—any such deterministic schema was simply irrelevant: *"Whatever one's conception about the necessity of events, at the moment of their performance their inevitability could offer no guide to action."*[130]

That fundamental insight had important consequences for the world of 1950. First, as Kissinger made clear in his conclusion, his reflections on the meaning of history had left him deeply skeptical about the claims of economics—increasingly seen as the concentration of choice for an ambitious Harvard man:

As . . . the cold materialistic intellect replaces the sentimentality of the romantic, life emerges as but a technical problem. The frantic search for social solutions, for economic panaceas, testifies to the emptiness of a soul to which necessity is an objective state . . . and which ever believes that just a little

more knowledge, just one more formula will solve the increasing bafflement of a materialistic surrounding.[131]

Second (though Kissinger thought it prudent to consign this reference to contemporary politics to a footnote), the limits of materialism
implied that it was dangerous to allow "an argument about democracy
[to] become a discussion of the efficiency of economic systems, which is
on the plane of objective necessity and therefore debatable." By contrast,
"[t]he inward intuition of freedom . . . would reject totalitarianism even
if it were economically more efficient." Third and most important,
"arguments that international conferences with Russia can magically
resolve all differences seem fallacious. . . . *Permanent understanding on the
basis of inward reconciliation seems to require more than conferences, since the
differences are more than just misunderstandings.*"[132]

With those words, we come at last to the historical event that implicitly informed every word about individual freedom Kissinger wrote in
his senior thesis, the event that was to be the setting for his rise to academic preeminence and then to political power, the event that, in 1950,
made Kant's perpetual peace seem—even to a committed idealist—as
remote as Toynbee's moment of Christian salvation: the Cold War.

CHAPTER 8

Psychological Warfare

Our aim in the "cold war" is not conquering of territory
or subjugation by force. Our aim is more subtle, more
pervasive, more complete. We are trying to get the world,
by peaceful means, to believe the truth. That truth is that
Americans want a world at peace, a world in which all
people shall have opportunity for maximum individual
development. The means we shall employ to spread this
truth are often called "psychological." Don't be afraid of
that term just because it's a five-dollar, five-syllable word.
"Psychological warfare" is the struggle for the minds and
wills of men.

—Dwight D. Eisenhower, 1952[1]

It is true that ours is an attempt to exhibit Western values,
but less by what we *say* than by what we *do*.

—Henry Kissinger, 1954[2]

I

As a species, we seem to have an innate love of ritual. The modern
age has been hard on traditional rites of passage, however, so that many
people today experience only the most perfunctory rituals in the course
of their lives, marrying each other in drab state registries and parting
from the dead in antiseptic crematoria. Graduation from university
therefore acquires a special importance. Quite apart from publicly confirming that someone has fulfilled the academic requirements to be
given a degree—a qualification for more cerebral and better paid
employment than is generally available—a graduation ceremony is a

rare chance to participate in a festival of anachronism. Few universities can match Harvard in this regard.

It is one of Harvard University's many idiosyncrasies that the final, culminating event of a student's academic career—graduation—is referred to as "Commencement." But that name is the least of the day-long ritual's oddities. In some of the undergraduate houses, the day begins with a bagpiper summoning the seniors to breakfast with faculty members. Representing the forces of law and order (the latter of which was far from assured in earlier times), the sheriffs of Middlesex and Suffolk Counties enter Harvard Yard on horseback. Candidates for degrees and alumni then assemble to watch the president's procession, participants in which wear the most elaborate academic dress—complete with gowns, hoods, mortarboards, and other antique headgear—to which they are entitled. At the head of the procession are the local sheriffs, clad in morning coats and armed with swords and scabbards, followed by the university marshal, the president of Harvard, former presidents, the fellows of Harvard College, the board of overseers, the governor of Massachusetts, and the candidates for honorary degrees. In their wake march the deans, professors, and other faculty members in order of rank.

The morning "Exercises" take place in the middle of Harvard Yard, in an open space now known as the Tercentenary Theater. (Graduands can only pray for clement weather.) With the president installed in the ancient and notoriously uncomfortable Holyoke Chair, the university marshal summons the Middlesex sheriff to call the meeting to order, after which three students deliver addresses, one of them a "dissertation" in Latin. Degrees are then conferred en masse, school by school. The recipients of bachelor's degrees are welcomed to "the fellowship of educated men and women," after which the honorary degrees are awarded. All then sing the Harvard Hymn, the only other part of the ritual that is in Latin. The ceremony having been concluded, the president's procession departs, the Harvard band strikes up, and the Memorial Church bell peals. Lunch is then served in the various schools and houses; it is at this stage that individuals are summoned by name and handed their diplomas. The crowning event of the day, however, is the afternoon gathering of the Harvard Alumni Association. It is here that the president and the Commencement Day speaker give their addresses.

Even in the rain, Commencement is a joyous occasion. These days, however, it can also seem frivolous. It was different in Henry Kissinger's day. In the academic year before he arrived at Harvard, the Commencement address had been given by the U.S. secretary of state, General George C. Marshall. It was in this speech—delivered in Marshall's signature deadpan monotone on June 5, 1947—that the United States committed itself to the massive program of economic aid to Europe that history remembers as the Marshall Plan. Kissinger and his Harvard contemporaries therefore expected anything but frivolity when the announcement was made that their Commencement speaker would be Marshall's successor, Dean Acheson.

Despite his very strong academic record—and mammoth senior thesis—Henry Kissinger played no starring role in the Commencement rites of June 1950, the 299th in the university's long history. He was not a member of the five-man Permanent Class Committee; nor did he deliver one of the student addresses. He was just one of the three thousand graduating foot soldiers in the great university march-past. Though one of the lucky few entitled to attend the annual literary exercises of the Harvard chapter of Phi Beta Kappa—at which Robert Lowell read a new poem—he almost certainly absented himself from the other pre-Commencement events: the Lowell House "Senior Spread and dance," the moonlight cruise in Boston Harbor, the Reserve Office Training Corps commissioning ceremony—not to mention the Harvard-Yale baseball game and the Harvard Band and Glee Club concert. These were the kinds of juvenile occasions that the studious and married war veteran generally eschewed. Commencement itself was another matter, however. For all the antique pomp and youthful high spirits, Acheson's speech would give the occasion real gravitas.

Thursday, June 22, 1950, was one of those sun-drenched early summer days that make Commencement especially uplifting. There were also clouds over Harvard Yard, however—and no ordinary clouds. It was not without significance that one of the honorary doctorates that day was conferred on John von Neumann.* Fiercely hostile to both fascism and Communism (not to mention Keynesianism), he had played a key role in the design of the first atomic bomb and would go on to be one of the inventors of the hydrogen bomb, the intercontinental ballistic missile, as well as the digital computer. Although Acheson was to give the main Commencement address, he was preceded by General Carlos Romulo, the Filipino president of the UN General Assembly and chairman of the UN Security Council. Although he was the foreign minister of the Philippines for a total of nearly twenty years, Romulo's name is largely forgotten today. But his words were to prove a great deal more prescient than Acheson's. "To see Asia through Asian eyes—that is the prime requisite for Western policy towards Asia," Romulo declared. "You cannot prepare a policy mold for Europe and . . . assume that it will do for Asia as well."

> The tendency to brand any nationalist movements whatever in Asia as Communistic rests on another of those assumptions which need to be re-examined. . . . There are unquestionably nationalist movements in Asia which are Communist-led or which are abetted by Communists. But the fact does not necessarily invalidate the intrinsic quality of the genuine nationalist movements in the region. . . . These movements, though originally sprung from a people's natural aspirations to freedom, are subsequently taken away by the politically sly and ruthless Communists from the hands of the timid and confused liberals lacking prompt and effective support from their friends in the West.[3]

These were words Acheson—and his successors at the State Department—would have done well to ponder.

---

*A Hungarian-born mathematician and physicist of prodigious intellect and Jewish origin, Neumann had already made pioneering contributions to set theory, geometry, and quantum mechanics before being invited in 1930 to Princeton, where he proceeded to revolutionize mathematics with a stream of papers on ergodic theory, operator theory, lattice theory, and quantum logic, as well as transforming economics with the introduction of game theory.

The Connecticut-born, Yale-educated son of an English-born clergyman and a Canadian heiress, Acheson was suspect in Massachusetts. (*The Boston Herald* noted dubiously that he "look[ed] like a British aristocrat.") He was, however, a graduate of Harvard Law School and a lifelong Democrat. He was guaranteed a sympathetic hearing at Harvard not least because of the sustained war on his reputation then being waged by the fiercely anti-Communist and deeply unscrupulous Republican senator from Wisconsin, Joseph McCarthy, who just four months before had publicly alleged that the State Department was "infested with Communists." In fact, Acheson was in the process of radically hardening his own line toward the Soviet Union. Having favored some kind of accommodation with Stalin in the immediate postwar period, by 1950 he had become one of the administration's most decided hawks—so much so that his visit to Cambridge prompted hostile demonstrations by a so-called peace group, the Massachusetts Action Committee for Peace, led by the Rev. Robert H. Muir, an Episcopalian clergyman from Roxbury. (Later that day Muir was arrested for addressing Boston University students on the Charles River Esplanade without the necessary permit.)[4] One of the demonstrators' placards read "Acheson, Peace Not Bombs." Another urged him to "End War Talks."

Acheson's more hawkish stance was a response more to Stalin's conduct than to McCarthy's pressure. Indeed, his Commencement address consisted largely of a recitation of hostile Soviet moves since 1945. According to Acheson, the Soviet Union had "renewed intimidating pressures" on Iran and Turkey, imposed "governments of its own choosing" on Bulgaria, Romania, and Poland, assisted "Communist-dominated guerillas in Greece," "Sovietize[d] the Eastern zone of Germany," "consummated [its] control of Hungary," and attempted "to block the political and economic recovery of France and Italy by strikes and other disruptive activities." It was this behavior that had persuaded the Truman administration to send aid to Greece and Turkey and then to Western Europe in 1947. The subsequent Communist takeover of Czechoslovakia had persuaded the United States to go still further by signing the treaty of mutual defense that established the North Atlantic Treaty Organization, which Acheson proudly likened to the Magna Carta or the American Declaration of Independence. His peroration was unequivocal: "Until the Soviet leaders do genuinely accept a 'live and let live' philosophy, then no approach from the free world, however imaginative, and no Trojan dove from the Communist movement, will help to resolve our mutual problems." Yet—perhaps because the mixed metaphor was so clumsy—it was not the "Trojan dove" phrase that attracted the most press attention.[5] For Acheson also added, perhaps as a sop to the pacifist demonstrators outside, "War is not inevitable."[6]

Less than three days later, as dawn broke on Sunday, June 25, 1950, North Korean forces crossed the 38th parallel. The Korean War had begun.

II

As the Cold War recedes from memory into history, the most important thing to remember about it is that it *was* a war. It was not a Hot Peace. The second most important thing to remember about it was that it was never the war that its many prophets foresaw from the moment the phrase *Cold War* was first borrowed from Orwell by the journalist Herbert Bayard Swope and popularized by Walter Lippmann. Through the distorting rearview mirror of hindsight, we see either a classical tale of two rival empires or a Manichean struggle between two incompatible ideologies—or rather, we see both. On closer inspection, what happened was rather peculiar. Most of those who predicted a U.S.-Soviet conflict in the later 1940s assumed that it would at some point manifest itself as a full-scale "Third World War"—nuclear and/ or conventional—with Europe as the principal battleground. That, indeed, is the war that the generals on both sides prepared for right down to the 1980s. But that was precisely the war that did not happen. Instead, the Cold War was fought as a series of localized conflicts almost everywhere *except* Europe, with Asia as the main war zone. American and Soviet forces never directly fought one another, but at least one of the sides in every war fought between 1950 and 1990 was— or was believed to be—a superpower proxy.

The Cold War, John Gaddis has argued, was the most unexpected of inevitabilities.[7] To begin with, the rapid breakdown of the wartime coalition between the United States and the Soviet Union was not as unavoidable as it now seems.[8] Stalin seemed flexible in preparing for the postwar period. Socialism, he remarked, could be achieved in other ways, under other "political systems—for example by a democracy, a parliamentary republic and even by a constitutional monarchy."[9] In June 1944 he told the Lublin Poles that their country would "need alliances with the Western states, with Great Britain, France, and friendly relations with America."[10] Truman, too, had good reasons to continue the wartime coalition. "I like Stalin," he wrote his wife after his first meeting with the great tyrant. "He is straightforward. Knows what he wants and will compromise when he can't get it."[11]

Why, then, did the division of the spoils between Germany's conquerors not remain amicable? The "percentage agreement" Churchill and Stalin had sketched in Moscow in October 1944 seemed not unreasonable, carving up the Balkans more or less equally. Roosevelt's tacit sacrifice of the Poles at Yalta was ignoble, but it too might have formed the basis for peaceful coexistence. There was nothing in what Stalin said to Milovan Djilas—"Whoever occupies a territory also imposes his own social system"—that made superpower conflict inevitable, provided the respective spheres of influence were recognized and respected. The problem was the nagging suspicion, first articulated on the American side by Secretary of the Navy James Forrestal, that Stalin would not rest content with any agreed percentage of Europe or any other region. As early as October 27, 1945, Truman was telling himself (in a note), "Unless Russia is faced with an iron fist and strong language another war is in the making."[12] This sentiment was given strategic substance four months later, when George Kennan sent the State Department his Long Telegram, perhaps the most famous communication in the history of American foreign policy.[13]

The son of a Scottish Presbyterian from Wisconsin, Kennan had seen Stalinism at close quarters during a spell at the U.S. embassy in Moscow at the height of the purges. He had become so disillusioned with the failure of both Roosevelt and his successor Harry Truman to discern Stalin's true intentions that in August 1945 he had offered his resignation, citing "a deep sense of frustration over our squandering of the political assets won at such cost by our recent war effort [and] over our failure to follow up our victories politically."[14] Toward the end of his second posting to Russia, however, he was asked by the State Department to comment on recent Soviet actions. His reply was to lay the foundation for an entire generation of American strategists, not least Henry Kissinger. Read today, with due allowance for the telegraphic style, the Long Telegram is a surprisingly subtle document. "USSR still lives in antagonistic 'capitalist encirclement,'" Kennan argued, "with which in the long run there can be no permanent peaceful coexistence. . . . At bottom of Kremlin's neurotic view of world affairs is traditional . . . sense of insecurity." (As Kennan arrestingly put it in a dispatch in March 1946, "Nothing short of complete disarmament, delivery of our air and naval forces to Russia and resigning of powers of government to American Communists" would allay Stalin's "baleful misgivings.")[15] For both ideological and historical reasons, Soviet policy could therefore be summed up as follows:

> Everything must be done to advance relative strength of USSR as factor in international society. Conversely, no opportunity must be missed to reduce strength and influence . . . of capitalist powers. . . . We have here a political force committed fanatically to the belief that with US there can be no permanent *modus vivendi*[;] that it is desirable and necessary that the internal harmony of our society be disrupted, our traditional way of life be destroyed, the international authority of our state be broken, if Soviet power is to be secure.[16]

Kennan was quite clear that the Soviets intended to extend their influence not just in Europe but all over the world. In the Long Telegram, he named as potential targets northern Iran, Turkey, the Middle East, and even Argentina. Economic blandishments would achieve nothing, because "in international economic matters, Soviet policy will really be dominated by pursuit of autarchy." There was only one thing to which Moscow would respond: force. "Impervious to logic of reason [but] highly sensitive to logic of force . . . it can easily withdraw—and usually does when strong resistance is encountered."

Any successful intervention in strategic debate succeeds because it crystallizes what others are already thinking. Kennan's argument dove-tailed perfectly with Churchill's clarion warning at Fulton, Missouri, of an "iron curtain" descending across Europe. Two other American experts, Clark Clifford and George Elsey, were even more alarmist in arguing, just a few months later, that "the Soviet Union . . . was bent on world domination."[17] In Truman's mind, what lent credibility to such analyses was not Stalin's drive to install pro-Soviet governments in Eastern Europe so much as his demand in August 1946 that Turkey grant him territory and even naval bases in the Dardanelles. When Truman sent the Sixth Fleet into the eastern Mediterranean, Stalin backed down—precisely as Kennan had foreseen.[18] The president was now convinced. When Commerce Secretary Henry Wallace spoke up against "getting tough," he was forced to resign. In Kennan's phrase, there would be no more "fatuous gestures of appeasement."[19]

Yet Kennan was no warmonger. In his address to the Council on Foreign Relations in New York on January 7, 1947, he argued that it would be possible for the United States and its allies to "contain" Soviet power—"if it were done courteously and in a non-provocative way"—for long enough to allow internal changes to come about in Russia.[20] Later that year Kennan elaborated on what he meant by "containment" in a *Foreign Affairs* article entitled "The Sources of Soviet Conduct," published under the sensational byline "X." "Soviet power," he argued, ". . . bears within it the seeds of its own decay, and . . . the sprouting of these seeds is well advanced." Any "mystical, messianic movement" would "adjust[] itself in one way or another," either by breaking up or "mellowing," if it was effectively "frustrated." U.S. policy should therefore be "a long-term, patient but firm and vigilant containment of Russian expansive tendencies . . . by the adroit and vigilant application of counterforce at a series of constantly shifting geographical and political points, corresponding to the shifts and maneuvers of Soviet policy."[21] As a diplomat, Kennan conceived of containment as a primarily diplomatic rather than military strategy; its firmness would be conveyed in telegrams, rather than in armored divisions or missiles. In the context of 1947, however, it was not difficult to read at least one of his definitions of the new strategy—"to confront the Russians with unalterable counterforce at every point where they show signs of encroaching upon the interests of a peaceful and stable world"—as a mandate for the worldwide use of force even in response to mere "signs" of Soviet encroachment.[22]

At first, as it turned out, containment would be economic. When the financially overstretched British government announced the cancellation of aid to Greece and Turkey, the "Truman doctrine" was devised to persuade Congress that the United States should step into the breach. All that was really wanted was money, but—encouraged by Marshall, Acheson, and Assistant Secretary of State Will Clayton—Truman couched the request as part of a worldwide struggle between two "alternative ways of life," in which the United States should "support free peoples who are resisting attempted subjugation by armed minorities or by outside pressures." (Kennan in fact disapproved of the messianic rhetoric of Truman's speech, but even to an astute commentator like Lippmann, it was functionally indistinguishable from containment as Kennan had defined it.)[23] The next phase of containment was also economic: the Marshall Plan. Again, all the United States needed to send Europe was money—a sum equivalent to 1.1 percent of GDP each year from 1946 to 1952. But this time there was a twist of Kennan's devising: the Soviets and their Eastern European puppets were invited to participate in the "European Recovery Program" on the carefully calculated assumption that Stalin would refuse—which he duly did. A further twist was Marshall's insistence on not just the economic recovery but also the political reorganization of the western zones of Germany. Stalin—who, on reflection, preferred the idea of a united but demilitarized Germany—was outmaneuvered again. When he sought to turn the tables by blockading access to West Berlin by road or rail, he suffered a third reverse in the form of the airlift of supplies, a triumph of American logistics.

It is not difficult to imagine different outcomes from the threefold partition—of Europe, Germany, and Berlin—that was more or less complete by May 1949, when the Federal Republic of Germany was established. Kennan himself hankered after a united, neutral Germany ("Program A") and the Soviets repeatedly proposed such a solution.[24] Indeed, this was probably the "Trojan dove" Acheson referred to in his Commencement address. There was nothing preordained about Communist rule in Eastern Europe: that had to be imposed by brutal methods and in some cases (East Berlin 1953, Budapest 1956, Prague 1968,

Gdańsk 1981) reimposed. Nor was it inevitable that the Communists of Western Europe would all fail in their bids for power: in France and Italy, where they could count on up to a fifth of the popular vote, the Americans had to act to ensure their exclusion, though their methods were far more subtle than the Soviets'. Perhaps the surprising thing is that so few European countries ended up in the "gray areas" occupied by Finland (capitalist, democratic, but neutral if not actually pro-Soviet) or Yugoslavia (Communist, undemocratic, but outside the Soviet bloc).

What made the process of polarization so far-reaching was the fact that, in the course of 1948, containment began to evolve—to Kennan's growing dismay—into a military rather than just a diplomatic or economic strategy. The brazenness of the Soviet coup in Prague was one reason this happened. Another was the initiative of the Western Europeans themselves: the precursor to NATO was the Brussels Treaty, a fifty-year defensive military alliance between Britain, France, Belgium, the Netherlands, and Luxembourg. But the principal reason was the American realization that the unexpectedly swift crumbling of the European colonial empires was presenting the Soviets with even richer pickings than Eastern Europe. Stalin's injunction to the Politburo in March 1948 to "energetically support the revolutionary struggle of the oppressed peoples of the dependent and colonial countries against the imperialism of America, England, and France" was inspired. In the Middle East, to be sure, it was difficult to disrupt the transition from British and French rule to American hegemony, though the Soviets did their best to align themselves with Arab nationalism. In Asia, however, the Communist advance seemed unstoppable.

It is not easy to overstate how dramatically the strategic balance seemed to swing back in Stalin's favor between the summer of 1949 and the summer of 1950. Shanghai fell to Mao Zedong's Communist forces in May 1949; on October 1, Mao proclaimed the People's Republic of China (PRC); on December 10, Chiang Kai-shek fled to the island of Formosa (later Taiwan). Mao had already signaled that he intended to align China with the Soviet Union; in December 1949 he set off for Moscow to pledge his allegiance to Stalin, returning—after much gratuitous humiliation—with a treaty of mutual defense. For Truman, unexpectedly reelected in 1948 and triumphant in Berlin in 1949, the first half of 1950 was a disaster. No sooner had China been "lost" than the conviction of Alger Hiss for perjury and the exposure of Klaus Fuchs as a Soviet spy set the scene for McCarthy to launch his anti-Communist witch hunt. Embarrassed by his friendship with Hiss and genuinely alarmed by the Soviet threat, Acheson scrambled to turn containment into a military strategy, proclaiming a "defensive perimeter" plan to defend Japan, Okinawa, and the Philippines. (Taiwan and South Korea were conspicuously absent from the list.) The too-subtle Kennan was replaced as chief of Policy Planning by Paul H. Nitze, the former vice chairman of the U.S. Strategic Bombing Survey. For Nitze, as we shall see, the principal justification for the massive military buildup proposed in NSC-68—the National Security Council document entitled "United States Objectives and Programs for National Security"—was not the loss of China but the still more devastating news that the Soviets had acquired, through espionage and their own efforts, the ability to make an atomic bomb and perhaps also a version of the vastly more destructive thermonuclear bomb the Americans were working on. However, NSC-68 was a call to conventional as well as nuclear arms.

NSC-68—a document that would be declassified many years later, when Kissinger himself was secretary of state—proposed "A Rapid Build-Up of Political, Economic, and Military Strength in the Free World."[25] Its premise was that the Soviets had a "design . . . for the complete subversion or forcible destruction of the machinery of government and structure of society in the countries of the non-Soviet world and their replacement by an apparatus and structure subservient to and controlled from the Kremlin." As the main obstacle to that design, the United States was "the principal enemy whose integrity and vitality must be subverted or destroyed by one means or another."[26] Moreover, the Soviets were increasing their military expenditures in relative and even, in some respects, in absolute terms above the level of the United States and its allies. In the face of the "widening . . . gap between its [the Soviet Union's] preparedness for war and the unpreparedness of the free world for war," the United States must therefore increase significantly the percentage of its gross national product being spent on defense, which Nitze estimated at between 6 and 7 percent. NSC-68 spelled the end not just of Kennan's vision of diplomatic containment but of Truman's "Fair Deal" of domestic programs financed by defense cuts. It was hardly surprising that there was resistance to it within the administration—from the new defense secretary, Louis Johnson, as well as from Kennan himself and the other State Department experts on the USSR. But all this was before the Soviet-backed invasion of South Korea.

The Harvard Commencement of 1950 was thus a beginning—not only of three thousand postgraduation careers but also of a new and dangerous era. For Henry Kissinger and his contemporaries, their lives would henceforth be lived, for very nearly forty years, under the shadow of a Third World War. We know now that the Cold War did not escalate to the point of outright war between the United States and the Soviet Union. To the Class of 1950, however, the probability of a "Long Peace" lasting until the late 1980s and ending with the kind of Soviet collapse Kennan had predicted in the Long Telegram seemed very low indeed. To the generation that had fought the Germans and the Japanese, the Korean War looked very much like the prelude to the next global conflagration. The return to the fray of Douglas MacArthur, outflanking the North Korean army at Inchon and driving them back across the 38th parallel, was a moment of sublime nostalgia, followed within months by abject panic as the Chinese launched their offensive across the Yalu River and almost routed MacArthur's forces. True, by May 1951 Truman had sacked MacArthur for insubordination, and his replacement, General Matthew B. Ridgway, had halted Mao's advance, while the Soviets had put out the first peace feelers in New York. Still, the atmosphere between the superpowers remained poisonous throughout the early 1950s, exemplified in October 1952 by the ignominious expulsion of Kennan from Russia after the briefest of tenures as U.S. ambassador. True, it was an uncharacteristic gaffe for Kennan to tell reporters in Berlin that "his isolation in the Soviet capital today is worse than he experienced as an interned U.S. diplomat in Germany after . . . the Nazis declared war on the United States." But he was certainly not alone in regarding this new phase of the Cold War as the all-too-familiar process whereby a regional war begets a world war.

III

Today many academics find it difficult to understand, much less to condone, the commitment of America's preeminent university to the national security strategy of the United States during the Cold War. A tone of indignation pervades many accounts of the relationships between academia and the various federal agencies responsible for countering the Soviet threat, as if there were something fundamentally wrong about professors contributing to the defense of their country.[27] To repeat: the Cold War *was* a war. The Soviet Union never invaded the United States, of course, but it pointed nuclear missiles at it, deployed spies against it, and hurled abuse at it. The Kremlin also showed itself adept at exporting its profoundly illiberal ideology and system of government to other countries, including some, like Cuba, geographically close to the United States. To imply that Harvard should somehow have declined to assist the Department of Defense or the CIA is to underestimate both the magnitude of the threat posed by Soviet Communism and the value of the assistance that the university could offer.

To the newly minted bachelor of arts Henry Kissinger, as to the honorary doctor of science John von Neumann, it was a matter of course that they, as scholars forced to leave Europe by the menace of totalitarianism, should offer their services to the government that, of all governments in the world, made the most explicit commitment to uphold individual liberty. Nor was it necessary to be a refugee to take that view. President Conant used his own Commencement address to denounce "the rapid spread of a philosophy which denies the premises which all scholars once took for granted. I am referring, of course, to the attitude of all who subscribe to the Soviet interpretation of the philosophy known as 'dialectical materialism' . . . an authoritarian doctrine interpreted by the central committee of the Communist Party."[28] As a member of the General Advisory Committee of the Atomic Energy Commission as well as the Joint Research and Development Board, Conant was second only to J. Robert Oppenheimer as an adviser to the government on military as well as civilian applications of the nuclear technology developed during the war. Unlike Oppenheimer, however, Conant was above suspicion on the question of Communism: as early as September 1948, he had called for a ban on hiring teachers who were Communists.[29]

It was Yale rather than Harvard that did the most Cold War dirty work, in the sense of working for or with the CIA. With their Whiffen-poof Song and YWAT ("Yale Way of Thinking"), the men from New Haven played a markedly larger role in the wartime Office of Strategic Services and in the early years of the CIA.[30] It was said of the Yale historian Sherman Kent that he knew "how to throw [a] knife better than the Sicilians."* Other Yale academics who were active in the CIA were Walter Notestein and Norman Holmes Pearson.[31] Princeton, too, was an important "P-Source" (CIA code for academic intelligence), hosting the "Princeton Consultants," a panel of senior academic advisers that convened four times a year under the chairmanship of Allen Dulles (Class of 1914) in the university's Nassau Club.[32] But it would be a mistake to understate Harvard's role in early Cold War intelligence. William L. Langer, the Coolidge Professor of History, was the director of Research and Analysis at OSS, which went on to become, still under his leadership, the CIA's Office of National Estimates. Though he was educated at Yale, it was at Harvard that McGeorge Bundy† became a tenured professor and, in 1953, dean of the Faculty of Arts and Sciences. Bundy was proud of the fact that the postwar area studies programs at Harvard were "manned, directed, or stimulated by graduates of the OSS—a remarkable institution, half cops and robbers, half faculty meeting." It was entirely desirable, he told an audience at Johns Hopkins, that there should be "a big measure of interpenetration between universities with area programs and the information-gathering agencies of the United States."[33]

---

*Kent's Law of Coups was "that those coups that are known about in advance don't take place"; his Law of Intelligence was that "of the things our state must know about other states some 90 percent may be discovered through overt means."

†Before coming to Harvard in the fall of 1949, Bundy had coauthored the memoirs of Henry Stimson, Roosevelt's wartime secretary of war. Like Kissinger, Bundy found an invaluable patron in Bill Elliott, who was willing to hire the thirty-one-year-old scholar, despite his never having taken a course in political science.

It is not difficult retrospectively to depict this interpenetration in a sinister light, with Harvard reduced to a mere "extension of government" and the young, ambitious, yet insecure Kissinger eagerly aligning himself with the national security state for his own self-advancement.[34] But this misreads the evidence. Kissinger was a student of government. The two professors with whom he had most to do were keenly interested in the formulation of U.S. strategy toward the Soviet Union. It was hardly surprising that he followed their lead. Carl Friedrich had in fact foreseen as early as November 1941 that

> the [postwar] world would be divided between the Anglo-American and the Soviet Russian sphere of influence—unless England, too, had gone communist (which is conceivable, though not too likely). . . . A considerable number of peoples, in the Americas and Western Europe, probably will be clustered around the United States, while a good part of Asia and Eastern Europe will be grouped around Moscow. . . . The polarity of outlook between Moscow and Washington will be reflected in internal tensions everywhere, giving rise to civil war situations in marginal territories.[35]

In his *New Image of the Common Man,* Friedrich had noted the "entirely unprecedented" nature of the Cold War.

> History knows balanced systems of several states. History knows universal empires. . . . [H]istory does not know the polarity of two giant continental powers with peculiar opportunities for defense and autonomy. But what is more unusual yet is that each of these two powers rests upon a creed. Each resembles a church and shares with churches the wish to convert everyone to their creed: They are missionary, and cannot help being missionary.[36]

One of the tasks he gave Kissinger as a graduate student was to help him edit a handbook on East Germany intended for use by the U.S. military.

It was William Yandell Elliott, nevertheless, who remained much the bigger influence on Kissinger. Elliott itched to do his bit for American security. As early as 1946, he was proposing to counter the Soviet "power system" by increasing the powers of the United Nations.[37] He was among those who argued for putting nuclear weapons under international control to avoid an "armament race."[38] The UN's Universal Declaration of Human Rights struck him as offering a basis for Kant's "perpetual peace," were it not for the Soviet Union's refusal to vote for it.[39] By the late 1940s, Elliott was acting as an "occasional consultant" to Frank Wisner, the CIA's deputy director for plans, who had been a highly effective OSS agent in Istanbul and the Balkans.[40] However, despite his lobbying of William Jackson, the agency's deputy director, he could ascend no higher.[41] In 1951 Elliott had to accept "inactive status" at the CIA, with all future consulting work to be done "gratis." Yet no rebuff was strong enough to keep him away from the nation's capital. He became an adviser to the House Special Committee on Postwar Economic Policy and Planning, chaired by Mississippi Democrat William M. Colmer. He also served as staff director for the House Committee on Foreign Affairs and the House Select Committee on Foreign Aid, headed by Christian A. Herter of Massachusetts (later briefly secretary of state), writing most of the Herter Committee's report on postwar conditions in Europe, a crucial source of support for the Marshall Plan. It was on this committee that Elliott first encountered a freshman representative from California named Richard Nixon, a shy and untrusting Quaker who had a knack for stirring up an audience and who came to national attention with his implacable pursuit of Alger Hiss.[42] The Herter Committee also brought Nixon into contact for the first time with Frank Lindsay, then with the CIA, a friendship that was to bear important fruit nearly two decades later.[43]

Elliott was indefatigable. He wrote an article about U.S. aid to developing countries;[44] he served as assistant director of the Office of Defense Mobilization during the Korean War; he chaired the foreign policy study group of the Woodrow Wilson Foundation and the Committee on American Education and Communism, which advanced a program to teach the youth of the country the "cold, basic, hard facts about international Communism"; he also served (along with Bundy, Kennan, and

Arthur Schlesinger) on another Woodrow Wilson study group charged with investigating "how the structure and practices of our government might be improved to permit the full and effective discharge of American responsibilities and obligations." Significantly, the answer the group provided was to increase presidential power relative to both Congress and the bureaucracy of the various executive departments.[45] Elliott was prepared to go even further than his colleagues in this direction, praising the British practice of placing "strict limits [on] parliamentary inquiries into matters affecting foreign policy."[46] He also argued for "giv[ing] the President the constitutional power to call one election during his term on an issue of his own choosing—an election in which both he and Congressmen would stand"—in other words, giving the president the prime ministerial power to "go to the country" at will.[47]

At times, Elliott's enthusiasm for all things British verged on self-parody, as in his radio lecture on "The British Commonwealth Spirit."[48] He lobbied vainly for more than a decade to establish an American version of the "Round Table" he had encountered as a Rhodes scholar at Balliol.[49] He lamented the American decision not to back the United Kingdom during the Suez Crisis, arguing that Nasser had been the aggressor in nationalizing the canal company.[50] Even in the late 1950s, Elliott was still hostile to Arab, Asian, and African nationalism, assuring Nixon that colonial peoples were not yet ready for "the responsibilities of modern statehood."[51] Yet Elliott's arguments for increasing presidential power in the field of foreign policy were to prove more influential than is generally recognized. Toward the end of Truman's presidency, as his successor pondered how to improve the process of strategic decision making, Elliott identified the urgent need "to coordinate the work of the various White House Executive Office Agencies . . . the Bureau of the Budget, the National Security Council, the National Security Resources Board, the Council of Economic Advisors, and now the Office of the Director for Mutual Security, as well as the Office of Defense Mobilization." Elliott's initial recommendation was to "lift . . . the Director of the Bureau of Budget to a super level, as a sort of Chief of Staff or Chief Presidential Secretary."[52] But he later revised this proposal, suggesting instead that Eisenhower use the National Security Council as a "staff agency" rather than a "secretariat."

It is impossible for the President to devolve on any other official in the Government sufficient authority to force a settlement where there is a strong divergence of views among his principal Cabinet officials. He cannot set up an Assistant President who will have the power of decision. [But] he can and, in my judgment, should set up an Executive Director or a Staff Director of the National Security Council who will be more than a Secretary. If a man of the right caliber is found who possesses sufficient diplomatic skill and capacity to use a staff, agreement between agencies can be facilitated and a fair assessment of the real alternatives of policy can be presented to the President. . . . [The] Executive Director of the Council [should] . . . see that policy directives made by the President on the basis of the advice of the Council do not remain mere exhortations. . . . [T]he President's backing of an Executive Director, or Staff Director, of the Council is essential but it is equally essential that the Staff Director be able to operate always in the name of the President.[53]

Sixteen years later, as we shall see, Elliott's pupil Henry Kissinger would find himself playing exactly this role. It is not without significance that Elliott's memo also considered the possibility that the vice president would play a more important role in decision making, perhaps as a member of the NSC. This can hardly have failed to interest Richard Nixon, whom Eisenhower had chosen as his youthful running mate in the 1952 election.[54]

Elliott was a fount of ideas. In 1955 he chaired yet another Woodrow Wilson Study Group, the report of which (*The Political Economy of American Foreign Policy*) proposed that America and Canada be associated in some way with the nascent European Economic Community.[55] Six years later both countries became members of the Paris-based Organization for Economic Co-operation and Development. The quintessential Atlanticist, Elliott was a founding member of the Foreign Policy Research Institute at the University of Pennsylvania. But he was also quick to realize that the third world was to be "the area of decisive combat in the political struggle which is now the main battleground with the Soviets."⁵⁶ Like so many American armchair strategists in the late 1950s, he urged that the United States engage in "the kind of training of security forces, and perhaps even military forces, capable of a 'back up' of the newly emerging regimes in some of these countries."⁵⁷ Yet his strong preference was for what came to be known as "psychological warfare." As early as 1950, in a report to the Senate drawn up for the Office of Production Management, he was urging "peacetime psychological warfare" as an alternative to military intervention.⁵⁸

What exactly was psychological warfare? As Elliott's own multifarious activities make clear, it was more than one thing. As a founding trustee of the American Committee for Liberation in 1951, Elliott was involved with the launch of Radio Liberty (originally Radio Liberation), a U.S. broadcaster targeting the Soviet Union. He was also a firm believer in "cultural exchange" programs that would bring foreign students to the United States from countries that were "beginning to serve us with resources."⁵⁹ As he put it in a 1960 lecture at the National War College, "We must help find and train people to run a country before they can develop a country, before they can do anything really." But psychological warfare also involved winning hearts and minds at home. In April 1953, Elliott wrote a memorandum to Charles Douglas Jackson, shortly before Jackson's appointment as adviser to the president, on the "Organization of Psychological Defense Measures at Home." Elliott's argument was that there could be no reliance on "the survival of ideas in a free market and in open competition."⁶⁰ The State Department needed to be more active in setting up "consultative groups" where intellectuals could be "educated and often converted to the Department's point of view."⁶¹

The origins of "psy-war," or "PW," can be traced back to the wartime OSS, which had a separate division dedicated to what were initially known as "Morale Operations."⁶² The idea was revived in 1947 when the very first NSC directive, NSC-1/1, authorized covert action in the Italian elections to counter the Communists and bolster the Christian Democrats.* Initially, under NSC-4-A, it was the CIA that was given

---

*Kennan was so fearful of the Communist threat that in his ill-conceived "short telegram" from Manila on March 15, 1948, he suggested canceling the Italian elections and outlawing the Communist Party, even at the risk of civil war and an American reoccupation of military bases on the peninsula.

the mandate to conduct "covert psychological operations designed to counteract Soviet and Soviet-inspired activities."[63] But almost immediately a new Office of Special Projects (later the Office of Policy Coordination, or OPC) was set up under Frank Wisner. Though housed within the CIA, it was also supposed to receive input from the State Department's Policy Planning Staff. The OPC specialized in setting up front organizations: the National Committee for a Free Europe, which ran Radio Free Europe, the Free Trade Union Committee, Americans for Intellectual Freedom, and the Congress for Cultural Freedom, to name just four. Wisner likened OPC to a "Mighty Wurlitzer" organ,[64] but almost from the outset the music it played was discordant. This was partly because psy-war was too fashionable to be monopolized by one agency; everyone wanted to play the Wurlitzer. But it was also because the kinds of people who were ready to support organizations like the Congress for Cultural Freedom were themselves inordinately fond of quarreling. Liberal and even socialist anti-Communists had little in common with converts from Communism or McCarthyites, beyond a detestation of the Soviet Union. In 1951 a new Psychological Strategy Board (PSB) was set up to try to restore harmony.[65] However, the discord continued. While some elements within the PSB, notably its executive secretary, Palmer Putnam, wanted to bring about the "collapse of the World Communist Movement" and the breakup of the Soviet bloc ("liberation"), more cautious voices in Policy Planning (and the CIA) recommended "coexistence." "Look, you just forget about policy," an exasperated Nitze told the director of the PSB, Gordon Gray. "We'll make the policy and then you put it on your damn radios."[66] Yet the State Department's and CIA's own efforts—which included "clandestine support of 'friendly' foreign elements, 'black' psychological warfare, and even encouragement of underground resistance in hostile states" (Kennan's words)—were not notably successful.[67]

IV

That Henry Kissinger was fascinated by all of this—from the major issues of grand strategy down to the operational challenges of psychological warfare—is scarcely surprising. This was the new "great game," and the best and the brightest from the Ivy League colleges thirsted to play it. It was one thing to talk to one's fellow students about the Soviet threat in the Middle East, or the riskiness of Truman's decision to recognize the State of Israel.[68] The question was how to become a participant, as opposed to a mere spectator. It cannot be said that Kissinger chose the obvious route to power, which would have been either a Ph.D. in one of the social sciences or a law degree.

Kissinger's initial thought was to follow in Elliott's footsteps by applying to Oxford to do "graduate work in Political Science."[69] Elliott himself was discouraging. Kissinger, he wrote, did not have "quite the obvious personal qualities for [a] Knox [Fellowship]." The fact that he was married also counted against him.[70] But this was not the reason the Oxford plan was abandoned. As Kissinger explained to the senior tutor at Balliol College, "Unfortunately the international situation prevents my leaving the United States. I hold a reserve commission in the United States Army and expect to remain on extended active duty."[71] This was the reality for a substantial proportion of the Class of 1950: no sooner had they graduated than they faced a return to army life. It might be thought that Kissinger would have dreaded this fate, but this would be to understate the satisfaction he derived from his military activities and to overstate his commitment to an academic career. The reserved, aloof bibliophile that Harvard saw had an ebullient alter ego known only to his fellow veterans. Fritz Kraemer knew this Henry Kissinger better than anybody. "Should you ever," wrote Kraemer in September 1950, "in a sudden outburst of provocative exuberance throw stones at my window after midnight to read me your latest poem or tell me about the beautiful eyes of your mistress—I know you are married and frown on mistresses, but just suppose—I would come to the door unhesitatingly, pour you a drink and another one for myself, and enjoy myself profoundly."[72] The two men remained firm friends, Kraemer recommending Kissinger for an intelligence job—"he might well be used *alternately* for more or less 'theoretical' desk work in headquarters and for practical missions in the field"[73]—Kissinger reciprocating by trying to get Kraemer's son, Sven, a scholarship to attend a private school.[74] In March 1950—in other words, before the outbreak of the Korean War—Kissinger had volunteered for a "90-day tour of active duty training"[75] at the CIC School located at Camp (later Fort) Holabird just outside Baltimore, where courses included "the detection of treason, sedition and subversive activities, as well as the prevention and detection of sabotage and espionage."[76] He continued to impress his superior officers within CIC. "Kissinger has a most unusual sense of living, objective ethical values," wrote one of them in July 1950, in an unusually thoughtful assessment. "His personality is of a rare type insomuch as his own standards do not make him intolerant or without understanding for lives, individual, or collective, led according to standards far different from his own."

> Kissinger has given his allegiance to this country after making successfully very conscious effort to understand its true nature and its true objectives. He has done this without falling into the obvious trap of condoning wholesale all of our policies or all of our methods. For his insight is allied to an intellectual courage which has often prompted him to make a clinical criticism of our errors. . . . [But] I have yet to hear him make a sterile criticism, or suggest a solution to a problem which would in any way run counter to either the letter or the finer spirit of our highest national ethics.[77]

Kissinger's route into Cold War intelligence, including psychological warfare, thus ran through the army, not Harvard. Early in 1951 he became a consultant to the army's Operations Research Office (ORO), a hybrid institution that was formally part of the Johns Hopkins University but was based at Fort McNair in Washington.[78] The army defined operations research as "[t]he analytical study of military problems undertaken to provide responsible commanders and staff agencies with a scientific basis for decision on action to improve military operations."[79] Most of the work done by ORO was in fact on weapons, and more than half its personnel were trained in sciences. But C. Darwin Stolzenbach— a former air force program analyst who had joined ORO as a senior operations research analyst after stints at the Bureau of the Budget and the Commerce Department—was looking for a different kind of expertise. Project Legate—one of seventeen ORO projects then under way at Fort McNair—was "directed toward conclusions concerning the conduct of military government in occupied areas." In particular, the army wanted someone to conduct field research on the "psychological impact" of American military occupation on the Korean people.[80] Despite Kissinger's complete ignorance of East Asia, and despite the fact that there were surely numerous veterans of the Pacific War better qualified to go to Korea (his own brother, for one), he got the job.[81] Such is army life.

There was a Japanese prelude to Kissinger's Korean mission. Because of the itinerary of the military plane, he had to travel via Tokyo, where he held meetings with a variety of academics, journalists, and Diet members. The Japanese detour was interesting in itself: one of his interlocutors in Tokyo told him "with emphasis: We want US to separate China from Soviet [Union]." But if he hoped that such contacts in Japan might be helpful in Korea, he was underestimating the anti-Japanese sentiment in a country that had been a Japanese colony from 1910 until the Japanese defeat in 1945. The most that could be achieved was to compare the Japanese and South Korean experiences of American occupation. Arriving in Korea in the late summer of 1951, Kissinger set to work with his customary thoroughness, interviewing American and Korean personnel on everything from the rationing of food for refugees from the combat zone to the lack of capable interpreters and the extent of corruption among Korean officials.[82] The final forty-nine-page report recommended a variety of specific changes to the way the occupation was being managed, notably with respect to the treatment of displaced civilians.[83] But it concluded in more general terms by emphasizing "the inseparability of military command and civil affairs responsibilities, and the importance of . . . a single focus of responsibility within the Army for all civil affairs functions," the need for "officers qualified in civil affairs functions, including officers skilled in the language of the area," and the need "to alert commanders and other military personnel to the importance of civil affairs in attaining military and political objectives."

The significance of this report is twofold. First, it is clear that the army's interest was not in Korea per se but in the problems of occupation generally, suggesting that at least someone in the Pentagon expected the United States to be conducting more such military interventions in the foreseeable future, most likely in Indochina, where the French were manifestly struggling to reimpose their prewar authority. Second, Kissinger revealed himself to be a highly effective army pen pusher when it came to negotiating the final draft with Stolzenbach:

> I know you feel reluctant to make recommendations that our data cannot support. With this I am in complete accord. Nevertheless it is methodologically impossible to make a recommendation *completely* supported by data; in that case you would have a description. In other words recommendations always involve an element of interpretation—you are always somewhat out on a limb. Now I believe that the recommendations we are making really are a minimum. If we water it down any further it will be unassailable but also meaningless. As our study develops we may amend some conclusions. There is nothing wrong with this. If one waits until one can say everything before saying anything, one will wind up saying nothing. . . . If we write a report that every last colonel in the Pentagon understands we must accept the fact that every last colonel will feel he could have written it equally well.

Kissinger's impatience was revealing of more than just his combative personality: "If we start major substantive revisions," he told Stolzenbach, "we will still be arguing while the army is fighting in Indo-China."[84]

One thing led to another. Emboldened by the success of his Korean report, Kissinger wrote to Colonel William Kintner,* the author of *The Front Is Everywhere* (1950), offering to draft a "memorandum outlining a possible program for Japan" as part of a "major psychological effort in the Far East."[85] Meanwhile, at the instigation of Averell Harriman, Kissinger's old mentor Kraemer had been drafted into the Psychological Strategy Board to work on Germany as part of what later became Panel "F" of the National Psychological Strategy Plan.[86] It was not long before Kissinger followed him in the role of consultant. Here was an opportunity for more travel, this time to a country he knew better than any other. The resulting memorandum, based on "several weeks in Germany," explored the "pervasive distrust of the U.S." in the newly established Federal Republic.

Psychological warfare, as Kissinger understood it, meant seeing through the veil of stated grievances to discern the essence of a people's state of mind. Ostensibly, West Germans were disgruntled about the prospect of their country's becoming permanently divided, about the treatment of war criminals, and about the implications of their country's rearmament. Yet, Kissinger argued, "it would be a mistake to overemphasize the specific complaints except as symptoms of a more fundamental resentment" and an even bigger mistake to make concessions on specific issues.

> They would be taken as one more indication that the U.S. never understands what really moves the German people; that it is talking about legal instruments while the Germans describe a historical experience.
>
> This gives a tragic and almost inextricable quality to American-German relations. The Germans have experienced three upheavals in the past thirty years: the collapse of the Empire, of the Weimar Republic, of Nazi Germany. The older generation is of a cynicism that knows only one impetus: to be, by all means, on the winning side next time. The younger generation is confused and groping. American invocations of a Communist peril seem to them all too reminiscent of the

---

*Kissinger had been introduced to Kintner by Fritz Kraemer.

propaganda of Goebbels and all too shallow in terms of their own experience with the Soviet Union. . . . The sudden shift of American policy in 1950 [on the question of German rearmament] is considered by most Germans not as magnanimity but as utter cynicism. Above all, the Germans are weary and almost neurotic and any exhortation is apt to be resented because of its very existence. The fear of a new war, new bombings, and new occupations is pervasive.

Kissinger cited surveys that showed, counterintuitively, that Germans in the western zones of Germany regarded the Americans as worse—more brutal, more arrogant—than the Russians. "This exaltation of Soviet strength," he noted, "is the reverse of a disdain for the U.S. There has grown up a stereotype of the American as arrogant, brutal, inconsiderate, without sensibilities and animated by a shallow cynicism." What was to be done about this? His answer exemplified his approach to "psy-war." There was "practically no danger" of Germany "go[ing] Communist," he argued. The real threat was that "a nationalist reaction fed on a dogmatic anti-Americanism may bring to power a government which will lean on the USSR to achieve its independence from the West whatever its ideological differences. This reverse Titoism is by no means impossible." The United States had "attempted to create a framework of legal relationships," but it had "neglected the psychological climate which would make these relationships effective." At the same time, it had made German rearmament seem entirely a matter of American convenience. The Soviet Union, by contrast, had "pursued its minimum objective, the neutralization of Germany, by emphasizing the German interests involved": "By advocating German unity, by playing on German fears of rearmament, by emphasizing the devastation of Korea, they are creating the conditions of a neutralism which seems achievable only by opposition to the U.S."

Kissinger's conclusion was clear. The United States would not be able to "remedy its position [in Germany] until it emphasizes the psychological component of its political strategy." But this could not be done through "official sources nor [through] official personnel." The key was to work "on an unofficial basis on all levels." That meant sending a few, highly selected individuals to Germany, to give them a "cover" which will permit them to travel widely and to establish contacts. A university, large foundation, newspaper and similar organization would seem most suitable. . . . Above all, it is important to engage Germans and Americans on cooperative projects so that by working together a community of interests might be created. This could take the form of study groups, cultural congresses, exchange professorships and intern programs, wherever possible under non-governmental auspices.[87]

In short, psychological warfare was—as Eisenhower later acknowledged—a rather sinister way of describing a process of cultural exchange that, at least on the face of it, was not sinister in the least.

Returning to Germany revived Kissinger's ambivalence about the land of his birth. In the five years since he had left Oberammergau, the country's economic recovery had been astounding. "Whatever you may think of Germany, their recovery has been fantastic," he told his parents. Yet the Germans themselves remained strangely unchanged, as if the horrors of the Nazi years had not happened. "The Bavarians drink as in the days of old, while the Hessians are as disgusting as ever." As for the German industrialists he met in Düsseldorf on a visit to the Krupp munitions plant, he mused, "Who would have thought" that they would ever hold a dinner in honor of Henry Kissinger?[88]

Even more gratifying was the offer of a permanent position at the ORO in succession to Stolzenbach, who was being sent to run the organization's Tokyo office. It was tempting to accept. Far from missing academia, Kissinger had thoroughly enjoyed his return to military intelligence work. It had been exhilarating to be back near "the combat zone" in Korea. It had also been a relief to be back in a work environment where tough talk and risqué humor were both appreciated. (Kissinger could not even file an expenses claim without flirting with Stolzenbach's secretary: "I know how empty your life is without ticket stubs and how empty mine is without money.")[89] There was something appealingly manly about military life. "I always experience . . . [a] feeling of exhilaration . . . when among men who do things rather than talk about them," he confessed to a friend. Returning to Harvard, by contrast, meant returning to "the home of the conditional phrase and the contingent statement. . . . The Harvard atmosphere still seems a little unreal, particularly the serious discussion of such profound subjects as what certain grounds exist for action. I feel that more can be learned on the issue north of the Uijeongbu* than in a seminar at Cambridge."[90]

Such comparisons recur in his correspondence in the early 1950s. "I wish some of our academic communities would learn something of the loyalty that animates most parts of the Army with which I have had anything to do," he wrote in October 1952.[91] "Whatever feelings they [the staff at Fort Holabird] may have," he complained two years later, "they are more human than many associates here [at Harvard]."[92]

Why, then, did Kissinger turn down Stolzenbach's job offer,[93] choosing the "unreality" of the academy over the nitty-gritty of the intelligence community? Why, by the end of 1952, had he "cut [his] Washington activities to a minimum," giving up even the role of consultant at ORO?[94]

V

A married man does not have complete freedom. Yet it is hard to believe that his wife was the decisive factor in Henry Kissinger's decision to stay on at Harvard. Ann appears to have expected him to apply to law school.[95] That would have been the safe option preferred by Washington Heights. Instead, Kissinger turned to the professor who had been his most generous patron with the idea of becoming a doctor of philosophy under his direction. There is no reason to doubt that Kissinger was being sincere when he expressed his gratitude to Elliott for his role in his undergraduate years:

> I came to Harvard in a somewhat discouraged frame of mind
> for it seemed to me that a quest for technical solutions had
> replaced the perhaps somewhat naive or youthful moral fervor

---

*The area north of Seoul where many U.S. troops were (and still are) based.

of the period immediately following the war years. I felt that all the hope of the world was being dissipated in the superficiality of economic promises and that an undercurrent of nihilism might throw the youth into the arms of a dictatorship, acceptable only because it filled a spiritual void.

I consider it my good fortune that at this point I came, for the second time in my life, under the influence of a person who taught by example, not by dogma; who represented values instead of demonstrating them. Much of such inward growth as I experienced during the past three years has been due to your guidance which was all the more powerful because it never relied on the fact of academic position but persuaded by indicating the tendencies of possible development, the attainment of which, as in all truly worthwhile endeavors[,] remained a personal task.[96]

Yet it is impossible to believe that Kissinger opted to be Elliott's dissertation advisee and academic protégé because he sincerely coveted his intellectual guidance. The strictly academic relationship between Elliott and Kissinger was bizarrely dysfunctional, to judge by a transcript of a seminar at which the graduate student was supposed to present a paper on "The Relationship Between Metaphysics, Epistemology and Empirical Knowledge," with his adviser in the chair. Despite repeated attempts, Kissinger manages to read no more than a few opening sentences of the paper. Again and again Elliott interrupts him, often in ways that seem frivolous or beside the point:

> KISSINGER: This paper will deal with the relationship between metaphysics, epistemology and empirical knowledge. It is not to be taken as an attempt to validate a metaphysical conception of truth—nor is it an attack on empiricism. It is concerned solely with the . . .
> ELLIOTT: Now, Henry . . . let me ask you this question and put it to the members of the Seminar. Do all of you have a fairly good idea of the difference between logical positivism and positivism as the nineteenth century

type of Comte, for instance? Both are alike in assuming
that no metaphysics is necessary for knowledge, but
there are some differences, and do you deal with this
later in your paper, Henry?

KISSINGER: I'll deal with it to the extent that it's implied in
the differences between Bridgman and Reichenbach.

Elliott then presses Kissinger to answer his question, which he does.
But before he has finished his answer, Elliott interrupts again:

KISSINGER: For example, if you had the feeling of awe
with regard to divinity, this in logical positivistic terms
is meaningless . . .

ELLIOTT: No, that isn't quite right. Excuse me . . . the
logical positivist is really trying to do something quite
necessary within this framework. He's trying to answer
Hume, as much as Kant was, but he's trying to do it to
save Science—I think—to save Science and naturalism.
Isn't he?

KISSINGER: As I'll point out later on, he really approxi-
mates an idealist's construction, because what it depends
on is whether you can imagine some kind of . . .

ELLIOTT: Well, now, I'm sorry to interrupt you, but I do
believe this kind of framework is necessary as a common
denominator to the Seminar.

At one point Elliott starts to give a very rough account of Heisen-
berg's Uncertainty Principle, forcing Kissinger politely to correct him.
But more often it is Elliott who is interrupting to put Kissinger right.
On nearly every occasion, Kissinger responds with a curt "Exactly"
before plowing on. As far as can be made out from the transcript, only
a few fragments of the paper were actually presented. The general
impression the reader is left with is that Elliott was a somewhat overbearing windbag whom Kissinger had no alternative but to humor.[97]

Why, then, did Kissinger put up with this kind of fruitless interaction? The answer is that both he and Elliott had other fish to fry. What

Kissinger had learned from his trip to Germany was, as we have seen, that "psychological warfare" was best waged through unofficial cultural exchanges. Where better to conduct such exchanges than on the campus of Harvard University? This was the simple but highly effective idea behind the Harvard International Seminar, set up by Elliott in 1951 as an offshoot of the Harvard Summer School. The stated aim was to "improve the understanding and the attitude of cultural leaders from a good many parts of the world where we badly need friends" by inviting thirty or forty of what would now be called "young leaders" to spend a part of the summer recess on the Harvard campus. There can be little doubt that the impetus for the International Seminar came from Kissinger; Elliott merely provided the professorial imprimatur. It was Kissinger who spelled out the key objectives of the venture in an "Informal Memorandum for Professor Elliott": "to swing the spiritual balance in favor of the U.S." by dispelling the European prejudice, fed by Soviet propaganda, that Americans were "bloated, materialistic, and culturally barbarian," and by "creat[ing] nuclei of understanding of the true values of a democracy and of spiritual resistance to Communism." It was Kissinger who initially targeted Europe (with the exception of Britain, Scandinavia, and Switzerland on the ground that they all possessed "a firm democratic tradition"). And it was Kissinger who managed the rigorous selection process, including the sifting of hundreds of applications by a screening committee in Cambridge, as well as dozens of interviews in Europe, which he himself conducted.[98] The Canadian-born historian John J. Conway* was in no doubt that the enterprise was Kissinger's plan for "getting at the cult of neutralism that is now popular in Europe."[99] Elliott certainly liked the idea, enthusing that it would be "far more effective than any amount of propaganda."[100] But he made no secret of the fact that Kissinger was "the guiding genius of the Seminar."[101] "My own part in it," he conceded, "was merely to get the conception lined up, to raise some of the initial funds, and

---

*Conway, who had lost a hand when serving with the Canadian infantry in Italy in 1944, was master of Leverett House from 1957 to 1963 and a dedicated undergraduate teacher. He published a number of books on Canadian history.

devote some time to participation in meetings and seeing that the students were entertained."[102]

As anyone who has organized an international conference will attest, the work of bringing successful young people from around the world to a single place even for a few days is far from easy. But Kissinger was aiming at something more: a two-month program that was both academic and social in character and would be held on an annual basis. Moreover, his intention from the outset was to increase the scope of the seminar. In its second year, 1952, half the forty participants were from Asia. On arriving in Cambridge, they were divided into three groups, one dealing with politics, another with economics and sociology, and the third with the humanities. Each group was presided over by an American professor and also included an American participant-observer. The groups met three times a week, on Mondays, Tuesdays, and Thursdays, for an hour and a half in the morning, with participants taking turns presenting papers. In the afternoon there were guest lecturers, with Kissinger invariably in the chair.

Part of the challenge was, of course, to find suitable lecturers at a time of year when most faculty members were out of town. Among the first guest speakers Kissinger was able to attract was Leonid Strakhovsky, a specialist in Russian history from the University of Toronto. But he was careful not to make the content of the seminar too narrowly academic. In 1954, for example, the lineup included not only Bundy, Friedrich, and Schlesinger but also the cartoonist Al Capp, creator of *Li'l Abner*. Others who spoke more than once at the seminar included Eleanor Roosevelt,* the trade union leader Walther Reuther, the author Thornton Wilder, and the journalist James Reston. On Wednesday evenings there was a public forum at which two of the participants would present papers on questions relating to their own countries; this was followed by a "punch party," which generally lasted until after eleven o'clock.[103] As Kissinger himself put it in 1953, he paid "great attention . . . to conducting the academic program in the form of a

---

*It was during an International Seminar visit to her at Hyde Park, New York, that Kissinger's beloved Smoky died of heat exhaustion, having been inadvertently locked in a sealed car.

dialogue . . . [as] substantial people, aware of their quality . . . wish to contribute and not only to receive."[104] On top of all that, the participants were also taken on excursions: to a car factory assembly plant, to the Boston Museum of Fine Arts, or to a public housing development to meet with "the ordinary Americans that are so often cut off from our foreign visitors"—including members of the local black community.[105]

The experience of the International Seminar cannot have been an especially comfortable one. No matter what eminence the participants might already have achieved in their home countries, they were expected to swelter in Harvard's undergraduate dormitories and to eat their meals in the hangarlike Harvard Union.[106] But often they would be invited to dine with the Kissingers in their home, where "the talk would go on for many hours, politics being the principal subject." In the words of Stephen Graubard, who was recruited to help Kissinger run the seminar, "From the day they arrived, Seminar participants . . . knew that they owed their summer in Cambridge to Kissinger."[107] One of the 1954 participants, the Indian literary scholar P. S. Sundaram, went on All-India Radio to pay tribute to "Mr. Kissinger, the Executive Director, an unusual combination of efficiency and great personal charm."[108] As his participation suggests, the International Seminar swiftly became less European and more authentically international. A German participant, Marianne Feuersenger, remembered Kissinger's engagement with the students regardless of sex or race: "He was not interested in gender, only in what you had to say. I remember he did two things with gusto—he ate, and he discussed things."[109] Another German participant admired the showmanship of Kissinger's lecturing.[110]

Since 1967, when *The New York Times* ran a story with the headline "Harvard Programs Received C.I.A. Help," historians have lined up to express their shock that the International Seminar—among other Harvard-based institutions—was "subsidized" by the Central Intelligence Agency.[111] There is certainly no doubt that Elliott encouraged Kissinger to approach his contacts in the CIA for financial support for the seminar. Indeed, he went further than that: he sought to get Kissinger onto the CIA's books. As early as November 1950, Elliott recommended his pupil to H. Gates Lloyd, Jr., the Princeton-educated banker who had just been appointed the CIA's deputy director for administration.[112] The following year Elliott wrote to Frank Wisner, requesting that Kissinger be given "an inactive consultant status similar to my own, but one that could be changed at need."[113] By that time Kissinger had already met Lloyd and had even furnished him with a "number of phase lines for our project"—the seminar—including the most pressing expense, which was the budget for the participant selection process. The total sum requested was $28,500.[114] In a later letter, Kissinger was at pains to stress his belief in "the need for United States efforts in the psychological realm."[115] Funding subsequently followed from sources—notably the Ford Foundation and the Farfield Foundation—that are often represented as mere conduits for CIA money.

There are two problems with this story. The first is that the Ford Foundation's own internal discussions of the International Seminar stressed that "a major asset of this program is the fact that it is sponsored and conducted entirely independent of government. Indeed, the high quality of the participants is probably largely due to this factor, since the position of many of them is such that they could not have accepted even partial sponsorship by the U.S. Government."[116] Kissinger agreed that mere "cover" was not enough. As he explained to Allen Dulles himself in October 1952, "Many of our key people, including a number invaluable for intelligence projects, have told me flatly that they would have refused to come under governmental auspices."[117]

Second, if this was disingenuous, why did it prove so difficult to raise funds for the seminar from the likes of Ford? To begin with, the Ford Foundation in fact declined to back the International Seminar, so that its first year was financed (laboriously) with a series of small donations. By end of summer 1952, it is true, Elliott had secured $66,000 from Ford, but this was half the amount he had requested for a two-year period.[118] Elliott complained that he was reduced to "dunning friends" to cover costs.[119] By late 1953, with the budget fixed at $64,780,[120] Kissinger and Elliott were having to battle to keep the money coming in. Elliott approached the Carnegie Endowment;[121] other targets included the Sloane, Whitney, Mellon, and Paley Foundations. By the end of 1953, Elliott had "become quite weary of begging friar," as he complained to Bundy, and was contemplating "throw[ing] in the sponge."[122] Kissinger, too, was discouraged, complaining bitterly to Kraemer:

[I]t is almost certain now that there will not be a Seminar. There is a complete lack of understanding about the value of intangibles and I have obtained no support in raising money. Elliott has wasted three months chasing after phantoms with a degree of abstractedness which is akin to irresponsibility and in doing so has prevented me from making any efforts until very recently. All the so-called "big" people do not comprehend what we are after and console themselves with the fact that we can simply start this up again whenever it suits their fancy.[123]

Rebuffed on all sides, Kissinger returned to Ford,[124] this time with backing from McGeorge Bundy, recently elevated to the deanship of the Harvard Faculty of Arts and Sciences ("which has not apparently lowered his self esteem").[125] In October 1954 Ford came through with $80,000 over two years,[126] but when the Rockefeller Foundation declined to match this, there was no alternative but to make economies. By 1954 the International Seminar's annual budget had stabilized at $55,000.[127] The following year additional funding to the tune of $45,000 was pledged by the Asia Society.[128] Seeking financial assistance from the Ford Foundation made Kissinger feel, he lamented, "like a Kafka character who has sat in front of the door for so long that he has forgotten what is on the other side and remembers only that he wants to get it."[129] In September 1956 Ford cut off funding altogether, to encourage the seminar to "continue to broaden its support," reducing Kissinger to scattergun tactics. That November he wrote letters to nearly thirty different foundations, corporations, and wealthy individuals; they all turned him down. This is scarcely the story of a well-oiled appendage of the national security state. CIA money certainly went to foundations such as Ford. But the International Seminar had to compete for Ford funding, just as scientists today compete for research money that originates with the federal government.

Kissinger made life difficult for himself by overreaching. Not content with running the seminar, he also embarked on a wildly ambitious plan to publish a quarterly journal, *Confluence*. This was essentially a different means to the same end: "to give European and American intellectuals an opportunity to discuss contemporary problems on as high a level as we can reach," as Elliott put it. As with the seminar, he and Kissinger went out of their way to represent a broad spectrum of (anti-Communist) opinion. "It seems to me," Elliott explained to Milton Katz of the Ford Foundation, "the best possible propaganda is not to propagandise . . . Therefore, we are purposely inviting characteristic statements by people who do not share our own views." Austerely academic in appearance, *Confluence* was intended, again in Elliott's words, to help "painfully and even slowly, in spite of every wish for speed, [to] build up the moral consensus without which common policies are really impossible."[130] But he and Kissinger met with more or less the same response. The Rockefeller Foundation was unforthcoming.[131] Shepard Stone at the Ford Foundation was more sympathetic[132] and arranged funding through Intercultural Publications, Inc., a Ford Foundation operation. But as with the seminar, the Ford people were reluctant to be the initiative's sole financiers.[133]

The men running the Ford Foundation were not amateurs. One of the key decision makers, Frank Lindsay, had been an OSS hero in wartime Yugoslavia.[134] He had also been (briefly) a strong proponent of "rolling back" the Soviets from Eastern Europe while at the CIA.[135] He and his colleagues were doing more than run a slush fund. When they looked at the early volumes of *Confluence,* they were somewhat underwhelmed, recommending that Elliott and Kissinger bring in an "editorial consultant" to "up their standard a bit."[136] Only the publisher James Laughlin (a friend of Ezra Pound and founder of *New Directions*) was convinced by Kissinger, who struck him "as a thoroughly sincere person (terribly earnest Germanic type) who is trying his hardest to do an idealistic job."[137] In 1954, when Ford decided to stop funding publications, Kissinger's "first reaction was to let CONFLUENCE die, since I am a little tired of playing the Grand Inquisitor." Only with difficulty was he persuaded to keep it going.[138] The magazine limped on until the summer of 1958, then quietly died.

All of this sheds revealing light on what has come to be called the "cultural Cold War." Compared with other initiatives, notably the CIA's funding of the National Student Association, the amount of government money that went to the Harvard International Seminar was trivial. Compared with journals like *Encounter* and *Partisan Review,* Kissinger's *Confluence* was a sideshow, suspected of being a "boondoggle" by the CIA itself. Not only did it lack backers, it lacked readers, too. The first two issues were sent free to around two thousand people on mailing lists that Kissinger himself had painstakingly assembled. He never got close to his aim of increasing circulation by a factor of ten and charging readers a subscription.[139] Psychological warfare was waged on a very broad front in the 1950s, with CIA funds going not only to academic organizations and magazines but also to trade unions, women's groups, Catholic organizations, exhibitions of modern art, and even animated films.[140] In this context, Kissinger's activities at Harvard were among the most staid operations of the cultural Cold War. In modern terminology, it was soft power at its softest.

As for the oft-repeated charge that Kissinger was actuated by self-interest, inviting participants to the seminar and contributors to *Confluence* who would be useful to him in later life, this seems unfair. Of the six hundred foreign students who participated in the International Seminar between 1951 and its final year in 1968, some did indeed go on to become leaders of their countries: the Japanese prime minister Yasuhiro Nakasone, who attended the seminar in 1953, the French president Valéry Giscard d'Estaing (1954), the Turkish prime minister Mustafa Bülent Ecevit (1958), the Belgian prime minister Leo Tindemans (1962), and the Malaysian prime minister Mahathir bin Mohamad (1968).[141] But most seminar participants went on to lead lives of obscurity. To claim that Kissinger succeeded in creating "a self-contained group of Cold War elites who forged a collective identity as intellectual practitioners and protectors of civilization in a threatening world" is to believe that the International Seminar achieved all the aims it advertised to potential donors.[142] To argue that Kissinger was "incorrigibly attracted to powerful, charismatic, and wealthy people" is to glamorize the distinctly drab activities of organizing a conference and editing a journal.[143] The most that can be said is that running the International Seminar and *Confluence* in the early years of their existence gave Kissinger access to people who might not, in the normal course of events, have paid much attention to a mere graduate student. But when he traveled to Europe in early 1953, it was to see not power brokers but intellectuals: the likes of Raymond Aron, Albert Camus, André Malraux, and Jean-Paul Sartre in Paris; Max Beloff, Isaiah Berlin, Alan Bullock, and William Deakin in Oxford.[144] Then again, taking on these onerous responsibilities did not make Kissinger's life as a graduate student any easier. A more plausible conclusion is that Kissinger sincerely saw the two parallel ventures as the most effective contributions he could make to a psychological war against Soviet Communism to which he was sincerely committed.

It is dangerous indeed to judge the early 1950s from the vantage point of the late 1960s, much less from where we stand today. Senator Joseph McCarthy was not some lone renegade. In July 1946 more than a third of Americans polled said that domestic Communists should be either killed or imprisoned.[145] J. Edgar Hoover, director of the FBI, told the House Un-American Activities Committee that Communists needed to be "identified and exposed, because the public will take the first step of quarantining them so they can do no harm."[146] That process of identification and exposure was in full swing by 1950; indeed, it was almost out of control. And among the favorite targets of the "Red hunters" was Harvard University.

Beginning in March 1950, the *Chicago Tribune* ran a series of articles by the journalists Eugene Griffith and William Fulton, the gist of which was that Harvard was a hotbed of Communism. "Happy Hunting for Red Front at Harvard U. Leftist Profs Push Ideas There" was the *Tribune* headline on April 7, 1951, above a story that called Harvard "a happy hunting ground for Communists, doctrinaire pinks, and radicals of all hues" and implied that the university was allowing "the fomenting of subversive alien theories" as well as leaking atomic secrets. The article was as tendentious as it was scurrilous. (It was hardly a clinching fact that Alger Hiss "went thru Harvard Law School.") *The Harvard Crimson* replied with a spoof headline of its own: "Chicago Trib Writer Returns for 4th Annual Red Hunt."[147] But the report the *Tribune* cited by the National Council for American Education was not to be dismissed so lightly. "Red-ucators at Harvard University" was a list of Harvard faculty members' questionable political associations, a list that could easily be compared with the "Guide to Subversive Organizations and Publications" produced in March 1951 by the Un-American Activities Committee. The organizations in question ranged from the "Committee of One Thousand," which had raised funds for the Hollywood figures who had refused to answer questions before McCarthy's committee, to the American Friends of Spanish Democracy, a relic of the 1930s. The *Tribune* alleged that no fewer than sixty-eight Harvard faculty members were members of such "Red façade groups," but it singled out for special attention Carl Friedrich, the architect Walter Gropius (then teaching at the Graduate School of Design), and three historians: Crane Brinton, Samuel Eliot Morison, and the younger Arthur Schlesinger. According to the "Red-ucators" report, Schlesinger had at least ten suspect affiliations.[148]

Schlesinger was of course anything but a Communist; he was a liberal with progressive leanings, who supported the civil rights movement for much the same reasons that he had supported the Spanish Republic before the war. Yet in the febrile atmosphere of the Korean War, the McCarthyites were doing their best to represent not only liberalism but even "internationalism" as un-American. The *Tribune*'s assault on Harvard coincided with an attempt to get a bill through the Massachusetts legislature that would have banned the Communist Party in the state. When Albert Sprague Coolidge, the eminent chemist, opposed this measure in the name of "civil liberties," he was added to the *Tribune*'s roster of suspect professors.[149] Fulton even accused President Conant of being "a globalist and red hot interventionist" for supporting universal military training. Another target of *Tribune* ire was John King Fairbank, Harvard's China specialist; somehow the McCarthyites were able to combine isolationism with caring about "who lost China." It is in this context that we need to see Kissinger's response to an incident in July 1953, when identical envelopes appeared in the mail addressed to all the participants in the International Seminar. When Kissinger opened one, he was dismayed to find that it contained "ban the bomb" flyers attacking U.S. foreign policy. His immediate reaction was to contact the FBI.[150] Later writers have condemned this as illegal and unethical. But it was certainly not imprudent in the midst of the "Red scare." (That same year, Kennan judged it wise to seek J. Edgar Hoover's permission before subscribing to *Pravda*.)[151]

An important indicator of Kissinger's political outlook at this time comes in a letter to Arthur Schlesinger, Jr., who had sent him a draft article about McCarthyism. "I have found," wrote Kissinger,

> practically no European with the possible exception of Raymond Aron who knew that there had been in fact a problem of Communist penetration in the United States, particularly in the Army Information Services and in certain other key spots. Similarly, the real meaning of the Alger Hiss case as indeed of the Rosenberg case was completely lost. . . . A grievous error is to suppose that just because McCarthy and [his ally Senator Pat] McCarran are attacking a problem in a reprehensible manner . . . no problem exists at all.[152]

On the other hand, Kissinger recognized all too well what McCarthy represented—as only someone who had personally experienced totalitarian rule could. Inviting Camus to write a piece on "the ethics of loyalty," Kissinger sought to define the problem that McCarthyism presented:

> The issue . . . is how to rescue the individual from the claims of the group, and the conflict between the morality of the group and the moral precepts of the individual. I think that our European contributors have a great deal to tell us about their own experience with a problem which is not fully understood in the United States. It seems to me that Europe has had its own profound experience of the conflict of loyalties brought on either by foreign occupations or by totalitarian dictatorships or both. . . . Should, in such a situation, the individual concerned about his values go immediately into open opposition; or can the opposition become most effective by operating within the apparatus? It is clear that very often the knave and the hero are distinguished less by their action than by their

motivation, and this may contribute to the erosion of all moral restraints during totalitarian periods.[153]

In March 1954 Kissinger wrote to Schlesinger again on the subject of McCarthyism:

> There can be no doubt that at the moment we are living at a critical juncture. We are witnessing, it seems to me, something that far transcends McCarthy, the emergence of totalitarian democracy. It is the essence of a democratic system that the loser can accept his defeat with relative grace. It is the essence of a totalitarian system that the victor assumes the right to proscribe his opponents. . . . When the risks of electoral defeat are so fearful, campaigns will be fought with a bitterness which must erode the democratic process. When the issue becomes juridical instead of political, political contests will take on the characteristics of a civil war . . . even if physical conflict is temporarily delayed. That most people, and particularly the conservative element, believe this cannot happen here is a sign of internal strength but at the same time an asset to the totalitarian movement. It took some of the best elements in Germany six years after Hitler came to power to realize that a criminal was running their country which they had been so proud of considering a moral state[,] so much that they were unable to comprehend what had in fact happened. . . .
>
> The real problem it seems to me right now is . . . to convince the conservative element that true conservatism at the moment requires at least opposition to McCarthy.[154]

As we shall see, Kissinger sought to have a broad range of political views represented in the pages of *Confluence*. One of the few articles he rejected outright was a defense of McCarthy by the archconservative William F. Buckley, Jr.[155] (It was a rejection Buckley forgave.)

VI

Though *Confluence* was a failure, it was by no means a bad magazine. Kissinger assembled an impressive advisory board to help him drum up support: in addition to Bundy and Schlesinger, it comprised Arthur Sutherland of the Law School, the lawyer Huntington Cairns, the Freudian political psychologist Harold Lasswell, and the president of Brooklyn College, Harry D. Gideonse.[156] As an editor, Kissinger was relentless in soliciting articles from some of the Western world's leading writers. Not every big fish took the bait: Camus never contributed, nor did Graham Greene, and E. M. Forster firmly declined. But it was no small feat for a graduate student to get original copy out of the likes of Hannah Arendt, Raymond Aron, and Reinhold Niebuhr—to say nothing of Seymour Martin Lipset, Hans Morgenthau, Paul Nitze, and Walt Rostow. Kissinger not only succeeded in persuading some of the most talented public intellectuals of the time to write for him; he also succeeded in getting interesting pieces out of them. He was an energetic editor, often requiring contributors to rewrite their copy—even Arthur Schlesinger was asked to rework an article on American conservatism that was found wanting.[157] True, the criticism of one English reader was not wholly without substance: "The articles are often highly generalized, merely opinionative, wordy and even cobwebby." The same reader also had a point about "the anti-Communist clichés which creep into some of your articles."[158] There were structural problems, too. Certain names, august though they were, appeared a little too frequently; East Asia was scarcely represented at all. Because of the perennial difficulty of getting articles delivered on time, themes that were intended to be discussed in a single issue ended up spilling over into the next one or even two. Yet despite all these defects, to read *Confluence* is still to be transported back to a heroic age of public discourse.

"Are there any really common values that underlie the civilization of the West?" was the question posed by Elliott at the start of volume 1, number 1, to which Niebuhr certainly gave the most profound answer.[159] "Is the democratic method adequate for the solution of present-day problems?" was the question Kissinger assigned to contributors to the second issue.[160] Such examination-style questions soon gave way to less confining topics like "The Diffusion of Ideologies." On this subject, Aron expressed Gallic skepticism about the American ambition "to cure the revolutionary virus by the active improvement of living conditions."[161] Rostow disagreed; people just had to be helped to see how much better off they would be by adopting the American model.[162] Arendt warned against trying to counter Communism by "try[ing] to inspire public-political life once more with 'religious passion.'"[163] Schlesinger expressed his (rewritten) qualms about "The New Conservatism in America."[164]

Kissinger probably did not intend *Confluence* to be dominated by political subjects. He commissioned articles on a succession of relatively unpolitical themes: "The Social Role of Art and Philosophy," "The Media of Mass Communication," "The Role of Science," "The Problems of Religion," "Education Today," and "The City in Society." But his own preoccupations, combined with the underlying goal of the whole exercise, made it inevitable that political topics came to the fore: "The Problem of Minorities" (about which Lillian Smith, author of the seminal civil rights text *Strange Fruit,* contributed an essay), "The Problems of the Nuclear Period" (which featured the young Labour Party hawk Denis Healey), not to mention "The Problems of Liberalism," "The International Situation," and in the final issues of 1958, "The Prospects for Socialist Parties and Labor Movements." It was the essays Kissinger commissioned on "The Ethics of Loyalty," however, that had the greatest impact—though in a way he cannot have intended.

A central problem of the Cold War was that, from the very outset, anti-Communism was a very broad church, encompassing ex-Communists, Social Democrats, classical liberals, progressives, Christian Democrats, conservatives, reactionaries, and downright fascists. A magazine aiming at a balanced representation of this spectrum could not easily ignore the latter categories, any more than a policy of containing the Soviet Union could dispense with them. As a German-born Jew and refugee from Nazism, Kissinger perhaps felt in a stronger position than most to offer page space to intellectuals on the German right. He did not reckon with the response of his readers to the appearance in *Confluence* of the names Ernst Jünger and Ernst von Salomon.

A decorated hero of the First World War, Jünger had shot to fame in Germany with the publication of his novel *In Stahlgewittern* (*Storm of Steel*) in 1920. Unyielding in his rejection of Nazism, and dismissed from the army because of his associations with the aristocratic conspirators who tried to kill Hitler in 1944, Jünger was nevertheless viewed with considerable suspicion in the postwar period because of his earlier celebration of the transfiguring effects of war on the individual and his trenchant antimodernism. His article "The Retreat into the Forest" predicted that the "*elites* are about to begin the struggle for a new freedom which will require great sacrifice . . . compared to [which] . . . the storming of the Bastille—an event which still provides nourishment for the current notion of freedom—appears like a Sunday stroll into the suburbs." Jünger identified himself with the "wanderers in the forest (*Waldgänger*)" who were "prepared to oppose the automatism" of the modern world. He concluded with the hope that "among the faceless millions one perfect human may arise."[165] This was strong stuff to publish in an American journal less than ten years after the end of World War II.

By comparison, Salomon's defense of the German resistance to Hitler seems tame.[166] But the identity of the author was outrageous in its own right. A convicted murderer, Salomon had been sentenced to five years in prison for his part in the assassination of the German foreign minister Walther Rathenau, whose identity as a Jew, an industrialist, and a proponent of "fulfillment" of the Versailles Treaty had made him the bête noire of the extreme right. In 1927 Salomon had been jailed again for an attempted political murder, and though he declined to join the Nazi Party, he was never reconciled with democracy. Indeed, he wrote the script for the pro-colonial propaganda film *Carl Peters* (1941), and his postwar book *Der Fragebogen* (*The Questionnaire*) offered brazenly ironical answers to the official form that was the basis for denazification. The appearance of Salomon's article prompted indignant letters from, among others, Shepard Stone of the Ford Foundation—a letter Kissinger cannot have relished reading, much less publishing—and the historian Adam Ulam.[167]

In a letter to Kraemer, the beleaguered editor feigned insouciance. "I forgot to mention to you," he wrote, "that, as in most other things, I have now joined you as a cardinal villain in liberal demonology. It appears that my publishing of Salomon and Jünger is a symptom of my totalitarian and even Nazi sympathies and has caused some of the guardians of our democratic values here to protest to some of the foundations supporting us."[168] But this was serious. Ulam was a specialist in the history of socialism and Communism, who would go on to become one of his generation's leading authorities on the Soviet Union; he was also, like Kissinger, an immigrant of Jewish origin. Moreover, he had just been given tenure by Kissinger's own department. Renowned for what his colleague Samuel Beer would later call his "dark integrity," he was the worst kind of enemy for a young graduate student to make. Up until this point, Kissinger had deliberately played the invisible editor, offering no commentary, no *Confluence* "line." As he put it, at a time when sincerity in public debate was "measured in decibels" and "real dialogue" was at a discount, he had "attempted to represent as many different significant points of view as possible" and had "therefore . . . refrained both from writing editorials or expressing my own opinion in the form of an article." The Salomon crisis forced him to take a public stand. The result, in the form of a reply to Ulam, was heartfelt—and revealing.

Kissinger did not seek to defend Salomon. He had been a murderer; he was now a publicist whose writings "exhibited a tendency I personally deplore, a cynical nihilism. . . . None of this qualifies him as one of the more elevated representatives of our ethical norms." Yet Salomon also exemplified an important phenomenon: the response of a generation of Germans "whose values collapsed in the first World War." While some had chosen "the road of opportunism," others, like Salomon, had concluded from their disillusionment that "all belief is meaningless, all faith hypocrisy." Kissinger himself might not care for such "nihilists . . . even when they are on the side of the angels," but they undeniably offered an insight into the problem of loyalty: "That has been their life and indeed its dilemma, [so much so] that they have lost the capacity to think in terms of duty which presupposes a moral standard and can see relationships only in personal terms of loyalty." In short, a discussion of "The Ethics of Loyalty" without someone like Salomon would have been incomplete.

Having made the case for publishing Salomon as a way of "illumi-nat[ing] an aspect of [the] total problem" of loyalty, Kissinger now turned to Ulam. He began with a surprising concession. "You may feel," he wrote, ". . . that I have gone too far. I will even grant you that I may err occasionally on the side of too great tolerance." Ulam had objected par-ticularly to the fact that Salomon had never expressed contrition. But

> I would reply that there are some things it is impossible to be contrite about. The sentimental self-justifications of so many of our intellectuals, moving from Communism, to Freudian-ism, to religion, always precisely attuned to popular currents, is not necessarily morally superior. To me Salomon is a damned soul driven by the furies. As a political and moral phenomenon I dislike him, but I do not delude myself that what he repre-sents is a personal accident and not a symptom of certain ten-dencies of our age. I will oppose what he stands for, but not in the strident fashion of so many of our apostles of hate, who are so consumed by their passions that they resemble their enemies more and more.[169]

That had also been George Kennan's most prescient warning in his Long Telegram: "The greatest danger that can befall us in coping with . . . Soviet communism, is that we shall allow ourselves to become like those with whom we are coping." Kissinger's ambition as director of the Harvard International Seminar and editor of *Confluence* had been precisely to avoid that—"to exhibit Western values, but less by what we *say* than by what we *do*." Ulam's attack had flushed him out of his stud-ied position of editorial neutrality. Kissinger had found his own voice. What would he say with it next? And what would he do?

Those who represent Henry Kissinger as ruthlessly bent on ascend-ing the greasy pole of the "Cold War university" cannot easily explain why, in that case, he chose to make his first major scholarly contribu-tion not on "psychological warfare"—nor on any of the highly topical subjects featured in the pages of *Confluence*—but on the obscure, not to say downright dusty, subject of early nineteenth-century European diplomacy.

CHAPTER 9

Doctor Kissinger

I think an analysis of the thought of most great statesmen
will show a more substantial consistency than psychologists
would admit.

—HENRY KISSINGER[1]

I asked my colleagues, "Do we want a political scientist
who knows something about Metternich?" And they said,
"Hell, no."

—CHARLES KINDLEBERGER[2]

I

"Peace, Legitimacy, and the Equilibrium (A Study of the Statesmanship of Castlereagh and Metternich)," Henry Kissinger's 1954 doctoral
dissertation, not only sufficed to earn him the title of *philosophiae doctor;*
it also won the Senator Charles Sumner Prize, awarded each year by the
Harvard department of government for the best dissertation "from the
legal, political, historical, economic, social, or ethnic approach, dealing
with any means or measures tending toward the prevention of war and
the establishment of universal peace."[3] Published three years later—
almost unaltered—as *A World Restored: Metternich, Castlereagh and the
Problems of Peace, 1812–1822*, the book has long been read as a kind of
overture to Kissinger's own career as a statesman. Francis Fukuyama has
called it one of "the classic statement[s] of political realism," suggesting
that in the book Kissinger "lays out the general principles of the
balance-of-power diplomacy that would characterize his own policies
as national security adviser and secretary." It was here, according to
Fukuyama, that the future secretary of state first "argued his case that

international peace was best guaranteed not through law or international organizations but through a distribution of power that moderated the ambitions of the strong.'⁴ Robert Kaplan has seen it as "evidence of how the Holocaust, along with the larger record of modern European history, made Kissinger a 'realist,'" in the sense of an anti-appeaser, resolved to think "impersonally and inhumanly" about power, and to defend "vital interest[s] . . . violently . . . if necessary.'⁵ Successive biographers have likewise detected in the text all kinds of anticipations of its author's future conduct.⁶ According to one account, "Kissinger showed how conservative statesmen, who sought to preserve world order, learned to deal with a revolutionary nation through artfully tending to balances of power. In doing so, he laid the foundation for his philosophy of realpolitik and the conservative outlook that endured throughout his career."⁷ "For Kissinger," writes another, "diplomatic history was useful as an instrument for contemporary policymaking."⁸

Yet the reality was quite different. Kissinger's decision to write what was essentially a work of history—albeit one based solely on published rather than archival sources—was hardly calculated to advance his career in either the academy or public service. At a time when most graduate students in the government department were intently focused on contemporary questions,* it was close to an act of self-immolation to spend a full four years studying the diplomatic history of Europe in the decade after Napoleon's retreat from Moscow. The choice of subject was entirely Kissinger's own. It bore no relation whatever to the interests of William Yandell Elliott, his strongest backer at Harvard, though the published version was dedicated to Elliott. The choice was made without any consultation (of the sort that would be expected today) with the leading authorities in the field, such as the Oxford historian A.J.P. Taylor, whose masterpiece *The Struggle for Mastery in Europe, 1848–1918*, was published in 1954. (Admittedly, Taylor's book came out some months after Kis-

---

*Of the other thirteen Harvard political science doctorates awarded in 1954, six were on contemporary international themes: on labor policy in occupied Japan, on Iranian nationalism, on the British National Health Service (two dissertations), on United Nations peacekeeping and international refugees. The only other student of the nineteenth century was Gordon Lewis, who had written about the Christian Socialists of 1848.

singer's dissertation was completed, but it had been public knowledge that he was working on such a book since 1942.) Harvard's expert on European diplomatic history, William Langer, was apparently never consulted. The evidence strongly suggests that Kissinger's friend Stephen Graubard was right when he said, "His purpose in writing was principally to instruct himself."[9] So arcane did the subject matter seem that, even after his next book made him a minor celebrity, he still could not find an American university press that was willing to publish *A World Restored*. The book was snapped up by the ambitious London publisher George Weidenfeld, another refugee from Nazism, who was quick to spot Kissinger's talent (and to Anglicize his spelling).[10]

Judged in its own terms, the dissertation is a remarkable piece of work, especially considering how much else Kissinger had on his plate between the summer of 1950 and the beginning of 1954, when the manuscript was more or less complete. True, it covers a shorter time frame than Kissinger had originally intended, which had been the entire "period of peace lasting almost one hundred years" from the Congress of Vienna to the beginning of World War I.[11] By the end of 1953, Kissinger had not even begun the section he had planned to write on Bismarck.[12] Yet there is no disputing the depth of his knowledge of both published documents and secondary historical works. The most pedantic academic reviewers could find no more than two omissions from the bibliography.[13] Even more impressive is Kissinger's brilliance as a prose stylist. Each of the key characters in the narrative is introduced with a memorable flourish. Prince Metternich, the Austrian foreign minister, "was a Rococo figure, complex, finely carved, all surface, like an intricately cut prism. His face was delicate but without depth, his conversation brilliant but without ultimate seriousness."[14] "Misunderstood at home," the British foreign secretary Lord Castlereagh "conducted himself with . . . methodical reserve, cumbersomely persuasive, motivated by an instinct always surer than his capacity for expression."[15] The life of the Russian tsar Alexander I was one "whose fulfilments were found only in anticipation."[16] The French diplomat Talleyrand "failed of ultimate stature because his actions were always too precisely attuned to the dominant mood, because nothing ever engaged him so completely that he would bring it the sacrifice of personal advancement. This may have been due to a sincere attempt to remain in a position to moderate events; outsiders may be forgiven if they considered it opportunism."[17]

Like A.J.P. Taylor, Kissinger could not help being infected by the epigrammatic style favored by many nineteenth-century diplomats. "It is the essence of mediocrity that it prefers the tangible advantage to the intangible gain in position."[18] "A series of paradoxes may be intriguing for the philosopher but they are a nightmare for the statesman, for the latter must not only contemplate but resolve them."[19] "Infinity achieved by finite stages loses its terrors and its temptations."[20] "Luck, in politics as in other activities, is but the residue of design."[21] "To the uninspired all problems are equally difficult—and equally easy."[22] These and other obiter dicta are part of the enduring appeal of *A World Restored,* though they surely were a little out of place in a doctoral dissertation.

The most striking formulations relate to the art of diplomacy and are worth listing because of the light they shed on Kissinger's early— and at this point entirely theoretical—view of the subject. "[P]erfect flexibility in diplomacy is the illusion of amateurs," wrote the then amateur. "To plan policy on the assumption of the equal possibility of all contingencies is to confuse statesmanship with mathematics. Since it is impossible to be prepared for all eventualities, the assumption of the opponent's perfect flexibility leads to paralysis of action."[23] This notion of self-paralysis was one Kissinger returned to more than once. "[C]alculations of absolute power," he wrote, "lead to a paralysis of action . . . strength depends on the *relative* position of states."[24] He was already keenly aware of the danger of having too much time to calculate, and the paradoxical advantages of being in a crisis: "[T]o divine the direction on a calm sea may prove more difficult than to chart a course through tempestuous waters, where the violence of the elements imparts inspiration through the need for survival."[25] And he paid tribute to the importance of remaining dispassionate—a lesson learned from Metternich above all: "[E]nthusiasm can be dangerous when negotiating . . . for it deprives the negotiator of the pretence of freedom of choice which is his most effective bargaining weapon."[26]

A central theme of the book is the role of force in diplomacy. It was not only Metternich's genius that restored Europe to some kind of equilibrium: it was also Napoleon's lack of genius off the battlefield. "A man who has been used to command," writes Kissinger, "finds it almost impossible to learn to negotiate, because negotiation is an admission of finite power."[27] This difficulty of switching between the two modes of policy—from war to peace—prompts the reflection:

> [W]ar has its own legitimacy and it is victory, not peace. To talk of conditions of peace during total wars appears almost as blasphemy, as petty calculation. When power reigns supreme, any conditions seem restrictive and a threat to the exhilaration of common action. . . . Moderation in an hour of triumph is appreciated only by posterity, rarely by contemporaries to whom it tends to appear as a needless surrender.[28]

Having served as a soldier, Kissinger always retained a skepticism about the warrior's ability to achieve political goals. "[I]t is the characteristic of a policy which bases itself on purely military considerations," he notes, "to be immoderate in triumph and panicky in adversity."[29] He dutifully acknowledges that "in any negotiation it is understood that force is the ultimate recourse," but adds,

> [I]t is the art of diplomacy to keep this threat potential, to keep its extent indeterminate and to commit it only as a last resort. For once power has been made actual, negotiations in the proper sense cease. A threat to use force which proves unavailing does not return the negotiation to the point before the threat was made. It destroys the bargaining position altogether, for it is a confession not of finite power but of impotence.[30]

Moreover, a weak state unable to make that threat can still achieve its objective of "preserv[ing] the status quo without exhausting its resources" by "the creation of a moral consensus."[31] Psychological factors, in other words, are ultimately more important than stark military capabilities—a key preoccupation of Kissinger's at this time, as we have seen.

It is therefore wrong to think of *A World Restored* as some kind of anticipatory guide to statecraft by a future practitioner. The real significance of the book is as a contrarian tract for the times. Kissinger's first target is political science itself. "A scholarship of social determinism," he writes, "has reduced the statesman to a lever on a machine called 'history,' to the agent of a fate which he may dimly discern but which he accomplishes regardless of his will." As he had made clear in his exchanges with Darwin Stolzenbach over their 1952 report on Korea, Kissinger was deeply hostile to the claims of all the social sciences insofar as they elevated materialism—or to be more precise, empirical data—over thought. "To say that policy does not create its own substance," he writes in *A World Restored,* "is not the same as saying that the substance is self-implementing." In the case of the early nineteenth century—but also as a general rule—"[t]he choice between . . . policies did not reside in the 'facts,' but in their interpretation. *It involved what was essentially a moral act:* an estimate which depended for its validity on a conception of goals as much as on an understanding of the available material, which was based on knowledge but not identical with it."[32]

A key illustration of Kissinger's antimaterialist philosophy is his treatment of national identity and, in particular, the role of history in shaping a people's understanding of their own self-interest:

> The memory of states is the test of truth of their policy. The more elementary the experience, the more profound its impact on a nation's interpretation of the present in the light of the past. It is even possible for a nation to undergo an experience so shattering that it becomes the prisoner of its past. . . . Who is to quarrel with a people's interpretation of its past? It is its only means of facing the future, and what "really" happened is often less important than what is thought to have happened.[33]

To "the outsider" (or to the American political scientist) "states may appear . . . as factors in a security arrangement." But in fact all states "consider themselves as expressions of historical forces. It is not the equilibrium as an end that concerns them . . . but as a means towards realizing their historical aspirations in relative safety."[34]

Among the most important themes in Kissinger's doctoral dissertation is the nature of conservatism. At this time, it is important to emphasize, Kissinger explicitly thought of himself as a conservative. It was in that role that he debated issues in contemporary American politics with the overtly liberal Arthur Schlesinger. At a time when the majority of Jewish immigrants tended to gravitate toward the Democratic Party—not least because significant elements of the Republican Party remained more or less openly anti-Semitic—Kissinger's conservatism requires some explanation. *A World Restored* provides it. At its core is the challenge posed by revolution—not only the heir of the French Revolution, Napoleon, but also the revolutionary figure of Tsar Alexander I. Kissinger is never wholly explicit about what he has against revolution, but the strong implication is that it is associated with disorder or "chaos." In a crucial passage, Kissinger draws a clear distinction between two definitions of freedom: "freedom as the absence of restraint or freedom as the voluntary acceptance of authority. The former position considers freedom to reside outside of the sphere of authority; the latter conceives freedom as a *quality* of authority."[35] The reader is left in no doubt that it is the second definition that the author prefers. Kissinger then adds a second distinction, between motivations. In a revolutionary period—that is, one in which freedom is understood as the absence of restraint—the key motivation is "a concept of *loyalty,* where the act of submitting the will acquires a symbolic and even ritualistic significance, because alternatives seem ever present." The conservative motivation, by contrast, is "a concept of *duty* . . . where alternative courses of action are not rejected but inconceivable."

> "Right or wrong my country"—this is the language of loyalty.
> "So act that your actions could become by your will universal
> laws of nature"—this is the language of duty. Duty expresses
> the aspect of universality, loyalty that of contingency.

The echo here of Kissinger's Kant-inspired senior thesis is unmistakable.

There is, however, a paradox. The modern conservative's "fundamental position" is "a denial of the validity of the questions regarding the nature of authority." Yet as soon as he answers such questions, he can be represented as implicitly conceding their validity. "It is the dilemma of conservatism," writes Kissinger, "that it must fight revolution anonymously, by what it is, not by what it says."[36] In a separate essay, he defined that dilemma as threefold: "[T]hat it is the task of the conservative not to defeat but to forestall revolutions, that a society which cannot prevent a revolution, the disintegration of whose values has been demonstrated by the fact of revolution, will not be able to defeat it by conservative means, [and] that order once shattered can be restored only by the experience of chaos."[37] Whether, like Burke, one resists the revolution in the name of historical forces or, like Metternich, in the name of reason, conservatism must be primarily a matter of deeds not words, because too many of the words at issue have been coined by the revolutionaries. Significantly, Kissinger seems to lean in the direction of Burke, noting Metternich's "rigidity" and repeatedly reverting to a Burkean conception of nations and peoples as historically constituted. As we shall see, this version of conservatism was far from indigenous to the United States. Kissinger's relationship to the more common forms of American conservatism would never be an easy one.

A third contrarian theme of *A World Restored* is its distinctly old-fashioned view of history as an essentially tragic discipline. "Not for nothing," Kissinger writes, "is history associated with the figure of Nemesis, which defeats man by fulfilling his wishes in a different form or by answering his prayers too completely." Had he completed his projected trilogy on the century from 1815 to 1914, it is very clear what the overarching narrative would have been: that the very success of the statesmen at the Congress of Vienna in establishing a sustainable European balance of power made the catastrophe of 1914 inevitable. The heart of the matter—and of the July 1914 crisis—was Austria. "[A]s in Greek tragedy," Kissinger writes, "the success of Clemens von Metternich made inevitable the ultimate collapse of the state he had fought so long to preserve."[38]

> An ancient Empire, barely recovering from two disastrous wars, cannot be reformed while it is about to struggle for survival. The statesman cannot choose his policies as if all courses were equally open. As a multi-national state, Austria could not fight a national war; as a financially exhausted state, it could not

fight a long war. The "spirit of the age" was against the continuation of a polyglot Empire, but it is too much to ask its statesman to elevate national suicide into a principle of policy.[39]

The fairer yardstick for judging Metternich's policy, Kissinger concludes, should not be its ultimate failure, but rather "the length of time it staved off inevitable disaster."[40] Generalizing from the specific case of Metternich, he notes that statesmen generally have a "tragic quality," because they are condemned to struggle with "factors which are not amenable to will and which cannot be changed in one lifetime."[41] The key problem, as Kissinger argues (and as he would never forget), is that foreign policy needs to be conducted "with a premonition of catastrophe."[42] This comes most naturally to a power that has suffered disaster in the recent past, because the memory is still fresh. "[T]he impetus of domestic policy is a direct social experience; but that of foreign policy is not actual, but potential experience—the threat of war—which statesmanship attempts to avoid being made explicit." As a general rule, however, "[i]t is in the nature of successful policies that posterity forgets how easily things might have been otherwise."[43] This was a chronic problem for a power with relatively few memories of disaster.

The counterfactual—what might be and might have been—is always alive in the mind of Kissinger's statesman. The peace he achieves is always by definition a disaster that has been averted. "The statesman is therefore like one of the heroes in classical drama who has had a vision of the future but who cannot transmit it directly to his fellow-men and who cannot validate its 'truth.' Nations learn only by experience; they 'know' only when it is too late to act. But statesmen must act *as if* their intuition were already experience, as if their aspiration were truth." Worse, there will often be times when the statesman cannot reveal his intentions because "to show one's purpose is to court disaster." For example, in periods when a foe has to be conciliated because a state lacks the power to resist, it may be necessary to feign collaboration. But—and here Kissinger reverted to a theme he had first addressed in *Confluence*—"[i]n such periods the knave and the hero, the traitor and the statesman are distinguished, not by their acts, but by their motives."[44] In other words, it may well be necessary for the statesman to stoop in order to conquer. By the same token, in revolutionary periods much diplomatic activity may have the character of a charade. A conference with a revolutionary power has only a psychological value: "[I]t attempts to establish a motive for action and is directed primarily to those not yet committed. . . . [T]he chief difficulty of a revolutionary period [is] to convince the uncommitted that the revolutionary is, in fact, a revolutionary, that his objectives are unlimited."[45]

The fourth and perhaps most important argument of *A World Restored* is that the world of the Cold War was not in fact unprecedented and that, by analogy, useful insights could be gleaned from the study of nineteenth-century Europe. Preempting his contemporaries' most obvious objections to this historical approach, Kissinger was quick to acknowledge that "Napoleon is not exactly equivalent to Hitler or Castlereagh to Churchill." The analogies he drew did not imply "a precise correspondence" but a "similarity of the problems" being confronted.

> [H]istory teaches by analogy, not identity. This means that the lessons of history are never automatic, that they can be apprehended only by a standard which admits the significance of a range of experience, that the answers we obtain will never be better than the questions we pose. . . . No significant conclusions are possible in the study of foreign affairs—the study of states acting as units—without an awareness of the historical context.

Thus history was doubly important: as a source of analogies for the statesman, but also as the defining factor in national identity. True, "positivist scholars" might insist that "at any given moment a state is but a collection of individuals." But in reality a people defines its identity "through the consciousness of a common history. . . . History is the memory of states."

In *A World Restored,* then, Kissinger set out simultaneously an idealist methodology, a conservative ideology, a philosophy of history, and a tragic sensibility. The challenge to the modern reader is to appreciate the full richness of his argument by analogy because so much of it is left implicit.

The explicit parts are straightforward. The success of the Congress system in creating a "legitimate order" after 1815 stands in stark contrast to the failure of the Paris peace treaties to do the same after 1919. Revolutionary leaders—Hitler and Stalin—rise to pose their existential challenges to the legitimate order, just as Napoleon and then, unexpectedly, the Russian tsar himself posed challenges to the old order of the pre-1789 era. The United Kingdom in the nineteenth century resembles the United States in its offshore location and insular mentality.[46] As we shall see, Kissinger's historically informed instinct was that the United States should as far as possible play the same role as Britain after 1815— that of the offshore balancing power. Yet in practice the United States was playing a part much more like that of Metternich's Austria, an active participant in the continental struggle, with the much more difficult challenge of maintaining an alliance against the revolutionary power. This is a vital point to grasp because it clarifies the ambivalence toward Metternich that characterizes Kissinger's account—an ambivalence that has frequently been overlooked.

Did Kissinger identify with Metternich? He clearly admired him. "[A] man who came to dominate every coalition in which he participated, who was considered by two foreign monarchs as more trustworthy than their own ministers, who for three years was in effect Prime Minister of Europe, such a man could not be of mean consequence."[47] But a passage like this should not be misconstrued:

> The kind of game Metternich decided to play was . . . not one of the bold manœuvre, which risked everything on a quick checkmate. Rather it was deliberate and cunning, a game where the advantage lay in a gradual transformation of the position, in which the opponent's moves were utilized first to paralyse and then to destroy him, while the player marshalled his resources. It was a game whose daring resided in the loneliness in which it had to be played, in the face of non-comprehension and abuse by both friend and foe; whose courage lay in its imperturbability

when one wrong move might mean disaster and loss of confidence might spell isolation; whose greatness derived from the skill of its moves and not from the inspiration of its conception.[48]

While Kissinger would come to be associated with such tactics by journalists attracted to the idea of the diplomat as master ducker and weaver, the crucial point here comes at the end. For the lack of inspiration underlying Metternich's strategic conception is, for Kissinger, a fatal defect. "The successes [Metternich] liked to ascribe to the moral superiority of his maxims," writes Kissinger in another critical passage, "were more often due to the extraordinary skill of his diplomacy. His genius was instrumental, not creative; he excelled at manipulation, not construction."[49] Metternich was

> doctrinaire . . . [and yet] devious, because the very certainty of his convictions made him extremely flexible in his choice of means; matter-of-fact and aloof; coldly pursuing the art of statecraft. His characteristic quality was tact, the sensibility to nuance. . . . A mediocre strategist but a great tactician, he was a master of the set battle in periods when the framework was given or the objectives imposed from the outside.[50]

His strength lay "not in creativity but in the ability . . . to achieve seemingly at random the best adaptation to circumstance."[51] What is significant in *A World Restored* is in fact Kissinger's emphasis on "the limits of Metternich's abilities": "For statesmen must be judged not only by their actions but also by their conception of alternatives. Those statesmen who have achieved final greatness did not do so through resignation, however well founded."[52] His concluding verdict is in fact quite damning:

> Metternich's smug self-satisfaction with an essentially technical virtuosity . . . prevented him from achieving the tragic stature he might have. . . . Lacking in Metternich is the attribute which has enabled the spirit to transcend an impasse at so many crises of history: the ability to contemplate an abyss, not

with the detachment of a scientist, but as a challenge to overcome—or to perish in the process.[53]

The true hero of *A World Restored* is not Metternich but Castlereagh, who did indeed perish in the quest for equipoise. Aloof, awkward, and unloved, the aristocratic Tory foreign secretary nevertheless understood that "the repose of Europe was paramount" and that "doctrines of government had to be subordinated to international tranquillity."[54] Unlike Metternich, Castlereagh was an authentically tragic statesman precisely because he could not hope to persuade his insular countrymen that a permanent European alliance could "cement the peace." His "vision of the unity of Europe achieved by good faith . . . was a mirage which doomed its advocate to destruction."[55] This was not primarily a matter of personality, however. Some of the most incisive passages in *A World Restored* contrast the situations of the two protagonists. As a student of geopolitics, Kissinger made clear the fundamental difference of location between Castlereagh's British Isles and Metternich's Central European empire. But he was equally alive to the difference between the two political systems:

> Every statesman must attempt to reconcile what is considered just with what is considered possible. What is considered just depends on the domestic structure of his state; what is possible depends on its resources, geographic position and determination, and on the resources, determination and domestic structure of other states. Thus Castlereagh, secure in the knowledge of England's insular safety, tended to oppose only overt aggression. But Metternich, the statesman of a power situated in the centre of the Continent, sought above all to forestall upheavals. Convinced of the unassailability of its domestic institutions, the insular power developed a doctrine of "non-interference" in the domestic affairs of other states. Oppressed by the vulnerability of its domestic structure in an age of nationalism, the polyglot Austro-Hungarian empire insisted on a generalized right of interference to defeat social unrest wherever it occurred.[56]

II

Kissinger well understood that *A World Restored* would strike many readers as out of date. He begins his introduction to the book, "It is not surprising that an age faced with the threat of thermonuclear extinction should look nostalgically to periods when diplomacy carried with it less drastic penalties, when wars were limited and catastrophe almost inconceivable." True, the period from 1815 to 1914 was not perfect, but it was "sane" and "balanced": "It may not have fulfilled all the hopes of an idealistic generation, but it gave this generation something perhaps more precious: a period of stability which permitted their hopes to be realized without a major war or a permanent revolution."[57] How had this come about? For Kissinger, the answer lay in a paradox: "Those ages which in retrospect seem most peaceful were least in search of peace. Those whose quest for it seems unending appear least able to achieve tranquillity." For Kissinger, the practical significance of the era of Castlereagh and Metternich lies here: they pursued achievable *stability* rather than perpetual peace. Perhaps the most memorable lines in the entire book are these: "Whenever peace—conceived as the avoidance of war—has been the primary objective of a power or a group of powers, the international system has been at the mercy of the most ruthless member of the international community. Whenever the international order has acknowledged that certain principles could not be compromised even for the sake of peace, stability based on an equilibrium of forces was at least conceivable." The allusion is to the failure of appeasement in the 1930s; the inference is that the 1950s must be different. But how exactly?

The argument of *A World Restored* most directly relevant to the early Cold War is about how a revolutionary period can be ended and stability reestablished. The key to stability is that it comes from "a generally accepted legitimacy . . . [which] implies the acceptance of the framework of the international order by all major powers, at least to the extent that no state is so dissatisfied that . . . it expresses its dissatisfaction in a revolutionary foreign policy."[58] The century of stability after

1815 was proof in itself that a legitimate order had been established.[59] This could not be said of the time of Kissinger's writing. In 1954 the Soviet Union still seemed to be a revolutionary state, though not for the same reasons that Germany had been after 1919. As Kissinger notes, "the motivation of the revolutionary power may well be defensive [and] it may well be sincere in its protestations of feeling threatened." But

> the distinguishing feature of a revolutionary power is not that it feels threatened—such feeling is inherent in the nature of international relations based on sovereign states—but that nothing can reassure it. Only absolute security—the neutralization of the opponent—is considered a sufficient guarantee, and thus the desire of one power for absolute security means absolute insecurity for all the others. . . . Diplomacy, the art of restraining the exercise of power, cannot function in such an environment. . . . [And] because in revolutionary situations the contending systems are less concerned with the adjustment of differences than with the subversion of loyalties, diplomacy is replaced either by war or by an armaments race.[60]

Here, albeit in cryptic form, was a critique of the policies not just of the 1930s but also of the 1950s. In particular, Kissinger was pouring cold water on those who insisted that dialogue with the Soviet Union would yield anything other than (as he put it) "sterile repetitions of basic positions and accusations of bad faith, or allegations of 'unreasonableness' and 'subversion.'" So long as there was a revolutionary power at large, conferences could be nothing more than "elaborate stage plays which attempt to attach as yet uncommitted powers to one of the opposing systems." In particular, he poured scorn on those who favored "treating the revolutionary power as if its protestations were merely tactical; as if it really accepted the existing legitimacy but overstated its case for bargaining purposes; as if it were motivated by specific grievances to be assuaged by limited concessions."[61] As he put it in a 1956 article that made the parallel with contemporary superpower talks quite explicit, "the negotiators at Vienna did not confuse the atmosphere of the conference table with the elements of stability of the international system."[62]

Yet there was nothing here to distinguish Kissinger from the proponents of containment, whether in its original Kennanite form or in its later, more militarized, Nitzean form. It is only by reading carefully Kissinger's narrative of events from 1812 to 1822 that one can discern what was truly original about his contribution.

The first half of the narrative of *A World Restored* is provided by Metternich's transitions from collaboration with France, when the Austrian position was at its weakest, to alliance, to mediation, to neutrality, to outright antagonism. Metternich's goal—a reconstructed legitimate order in which liberalism itself was illegitimate—differed fundamentally from Castlereagh's, which was essentially a scheme for five-power balance in which Britain played the part of "balancer."[63] Unlike the Austrians, the British were fighting "a war for security not for doctrine, against universal conquest not against revolution."[64] The challenge for both parties was to persuade other actors that these goals were in their interests, too—to ensure that "what might have been considered a declaration of . . . self-interest came to be seen as the expression of simple justice."[65] The only way for Metternich to achieve this was by means of "a tortuous and deliberate diplomacy" to establish "the moral framework of the alliance." Much more than Castlereagh, Metternich was concerned with "the essentially moral question of how to legitimize the settlement."[66]

Kissinger marvels at Metternich's "dexterous . . . juggling."[67] But a crucial reason for his success was Napoleon's failure to recognize his own limits;[68] in particular, his failure to contemplate the possibility that the Austrian emperor, whose daughter he had married, would be willing to go to war with his own son-in-law (chapter 5). Complicating Metternich's policy was the emergence of the tsar as a potential revolutionary, aspiring to be the "arbiter of Europe" following Napoleon's defeat in Russia. These two factors—Napoleon's self-destruction and Alexander's ambition—meant that Metternich and Castlereagh had to work very hard indeed to impose a moderate peace on France. Here Kissinger drew an explicit contrast between Vienna in 1814 and Versailles in 1919, which had important implications for his view of Europe after Potsdam in 1945. The logic of total war implies a punitive peace.[69] The choice is between a retrospective and vindictive peace or a prospective and magnanimous peace. The former—as at Versailles—"seeks to crush the enemy so that he is unable to fight again; its opposite will deal with the enemy so that he does not wish to attack again." A retrospective peace inadvertently creates a new revolutionary situation "because the defeated nation, unless completely dismembered, will not accept its humiliation." A prospective peace, by contrast, recognizes that "the task of statesmanship is not to punish, but to integrate": only a settlement accepted by the vanquished power can hope to be the basis for a legitimate international order.[70] In such an order, no one—neither the winners nor the losers of the war—can have "absolute security," which is a chimera:

> The foundation of a stable order is the relative security—and therefore the relative insecurity—of its members. Its stability reflects, not the absence of unsatisfied claims, but the absence of a grievance of such magnitude that redress will be sought in overturning the settlement rather than through an adjustment within its framework. An order whose structure is accepted by all major powers is "legitimate."

A legitimate international order is based on neither a mechanical nor mathematical balance; nor is it based on some shared aspiration to harmony. Rather it requires an almost constant process of adjustment between multiple actors—each actuated by its own historical vision of itself—who agree only on the broad rules of the game.[71]

This is why Castlereagh, more than Metternich, is the hero of *A World Restored*.[72] It was Castlereagh, Kissinger argues, who achieved the compromises over Poland and Saxony that made the settlement possible. It was Castlereagh who violated his own instructions from London and dissolved the victorious wartime coalition (chapter 9). It was Castlereagh who, after Napoleon's return from Elba, pressed for moderation when others were demanding the dismemberment of France (chapter 10). Metternich, by contrast, grew ever more dogmatic, aspiring to an illusory restoration of the old order (chapter 11).[73] Ultimately, Britain could not commit itself to uphold a counterrevolutionary European order of the sort Metternich aspired to create, and which he encouraged the tsar to believe was his own idea. Political crises in Spain,

Naples, and later Piedmont were, in Metternich's eyes, life-threatening menaces to the new order; to the British they seemed like little local difficulties, intervention in which might unbalance that same order.[74] At Troppau—the high point of Metternich's diplomatic skill—he was able to represent his doomed "battle against nationalism and liberalism" as a European rather than an Austrian enterprise (chapter 14).[75] Castlereagh saw only too clearly that Russia would be equally willing to intervene on the side of nationalism if, as in the Balkans, it was directed against the Ottoman Empire (chapter 16). But on August 12, 1822, Castlereagh, exhausted and despairing, cut his own throat with a penknife, his tragedy complete. All that remained after the Congress of Verona was "the legitimizing principle"—at once counterrevolutionary and anti-French—as the basis for the "Holy Alliance" between Austria, Prussia, and Russia.[76]

To a significant extent, *A World Restored* is indeed a retrospective critique of the peace treaties that followed the First World War.[77] "Collective security" as embodied by the League of Nations (and, by implication, its successor, the United Nations) is one of many aspects of the interwar order that Kissinger excoriates. But the book is also an oblique critique of post-1945 American policy. It should now be apparent what lesson Kissinger wished to draw from the Congress of Vienna: that the aim of U.S. policy should be the creation of an "international order [in which] no power [was] so dissatisfied that it did not prefer to seek its remedy within the framework of the . . . settlement rather than in overturning it . . . [a] political order [that] did not contain a 'revolutionary' power, its relations . . . increasingly spontaneous, based on the growing certainty that a catastrophic upheaval was unlikely."[78] But that could be achieved only with Metternich's skill and Castlereagh's wisdom. The mistake had already been made of imposing unconditional surrender on the Third Reich and partitioning Germany. The danger therefore existed of a revanchist Germany emerging once again as the revolutionary power, intent on overturning the international order. Simply because we now know that did not happen does not mean it was a danger Kissinger and his contemporaries could disregard—and it was clearly Kissinger's intention to devote much of his next historical volume to "the

German Question" and Bismarck's answer to it (foreshadowed in chapter 13). More important, it was inconceivable that the same kind of victory could ever be won over the Soviet Union at a cost acceptable to Americans. The only way of establishing international order must therefore be by transforming the Soviet Union from a revolutionary power—which it certainly was under Stalin—into a status quo power. Here was the seed of the policy that would come to be known as détente. What made that seed flourish in Kissinger's mind was the mounting evidence, even before Stalin's death, that the leaders of the Soviet Union were no longer true revolutionaries and were certainly not those "prophets" whom Kissinger considered the statesman's mortal enemies.[79]

III

Kissinger concludes *A World Restored* with an essay on the difference between the statesman, on the one hand, and the two kinds of revolutionary, on the other: the Conqueror and the Prophet. As he had done in his senior thesis, he appends a heartfelt personal credo to an academic treatise. "[T]he claims of the prophet," he writes, "are a counsel of perfection, and perfection implies uniformity. [But] utopias are not achieved except by a process of leveling and dislocation which must erode all patterns of obligation . . . [while] to rely entirely on the moral purity of an individual is to abandon the possibility of restraint." Against the prophet, Kissinger sides with the statesman, who "must remain forever suspicious of these efforts, not because he enjoys the pettiness of manipulation, but because he must be prepared for the worst contingency." Part of the statesman's tragedy is that he will always be in the minority, for "it is not balance which inspires men but universality, not security but immortality."[80] People yearn for transcendence; that makes them susceptible to prophets. Moreover, people feel a strong attachment to their own national definition of "justice." Here Kissinger very clearly had Americans in mind and their tendency to judge the world by their own supposedly universal but in reality idiosyncratic yardsticks.

> If a society legitimizes itself by a principle which claims both
> universality and exclusiveness, if its concept of "justice," in
> short, does not include the existence of different principles of
> legitimacy, relations between it and other societies will come
> to be based on force. . . . Not for nothing do so many nations
> exhibit a powerful if subconscious, rebellion against foreign
> policy. . . . It is for this reason that statesmen often share the
> fate of prophets, that they are without honour in their own
> country. A statesman who too far outruns the experience of his
> people will fail in achieving a domestic consensus, however
> wise his policies.[81]

Yet the statesman's tragedy has another aspect: his policy must also
be sold to his government's bureaucracy. Here was the first manifestation of another leitmotif that was to run through Kissinger's career: the
tension between the statesman-virtuoso and the pen pushers he relies
on to execute policy.

> The spirit of policy and that of bureaucracy are diametrically
> opposed. The essence of policy is its contingency; its success
> depends on the correctness of an estimate which is in part con-
> jectural. The essence of bureaucracy is its quest for safety; its
> success is calculability. . . . The attempt to conduct policy
> bureaucratically leads to a quest for calculability which tends to
> become a prisoner of events.[82]

Kissinger's ideal, then, is an American Castlereagh: a conservative statesman who must struggle at one and the same time to educate a parochi-
ally idealistic public and to galvanize an inert and risk-averse bureaucracy,
in pursuit of a legitimate, self-reinforcing international order based on
the balance of power between domestically heterogeneous states.[83]

Today, with the benefit of hindsight, we may choose to read *A
World Restored* as a prologue to Kissinger's future career as a statesman.[84]
Of course, that was not how the book was received by contemporaries,
who mostly read it as a pure work of history. The British historian Sir
Charles Webster (the leading authority on Castlereagh) was damning.

The book struck him as "rather pretentious," not least because Metternich's "vain" claims to have "foreseen everything and pulled all the strings" were "accepted by Dr. Kissinger at face value.

> So strongly is he under Metternich's influence that in some cases he is led into biassed accounts and un-convincing explanations. He even imitates Metternich's obscure style and often uses the same kind of jargon in his analysis, devoting pages to the statement of propositions that could be better described in a few sentences.[85]

The German historian Ernst Birke was more respectful but (like Webster) could not resist pointing out an omission in Kissinger's bibliography.[86] Only a few Americans appreciated Kissinger's true purpose. The reviewer for *World Affairs* found it "truly stimulating" and its last chapter on statesmanship "of outstanding importance."[87] Writing in *The New York Times,* the historian Hans Kohn was also positive.[88] The most insightful review was by Quincy Wright of the University of Chicago in the *American Historical Review.* Correctly identifying the analogies Kissinger wished to draw between the era of Metternich and the early Cold War, Wright recommended the book warmly to "both students and practitioners of international politics."[89]

That review was surely welcome to the novice author. But of far more importance for Kissinger's academic career was the reception of the original dissertation at Harvard. The fact that it won the Sumner Prize makes it clear that at least some senior members of the government department approved of it. Among its readers was McGeorge Bundy, now the powerful dean of the Faculty of Arts and Sciences. His comments have not been preserved, but Kissinger's response to them suggests that Bundy shared Charles Webster's view that the author was too much in thrall to Metternich, not to mention his prose style. "It is extremely difficult to do anything with Metternich," Kissinger countered, "because in him an essentially sterile conception of statesmanship was coupled with a most extraordinary diplomatic skill." He was not, he insisted, bedazzled. Metternich's achievement was "no more than a tour de force, and as fragile as a house of cards.

But in order to show its fragility, I have first to demonstrate its successes. The trouble with Metternich's statesmanship was, as I see it, not its short term sterility but its long term lack of conception. It would be easy enough to show that he failed because he failed to recognize the trend of the times, but this makes it much too simple. He recognized it, but did his best to arrest it.

Bundy had also objected to the assumption—evident in Kissinger's treatment of both Castlereagh and Metternich—that a statesman has a unitary character.

I . . . agree with you as an abstract proposition [Kissinger replied] that no statesman is all "one." Nevertheless, in any given instance, this may not apply. I think an analysis of the thought of most great statesmen will show a more substantial consistency than psychologists would admit. . . . The difference between a man like Acheson and the statesmen I am considering is not that they were wiser, but that they had a longer tenure of office and fewer domestic pressures, and were therefore able to implement their maxims more consistently.[90]

IV

How exactly, then, did the study of early nineteenth-century Europe inform Kissinger's thinking about men like Dean Acheson? We can answer that question with considerable precision thanks to the survival of a number of letters and unpublished memoranda written by Kissinger during the period when he was writing his doctoral dissertation. The first was addressed to his adviser, Bill Elliott, in the immediate aftermath of the outbreak of the Korean War.

Here was a bizarre state of affairs. North Korea, with Soviet approval, had invaded South Korea. Truman, inspired as much by the memory of the 1930s as by the logic of containment, had secured UN approval to intervene. But the initial U.S. military effort failed to halt the North Korean advance. Kissinger—writing in July 1950, before he had even begun his doctoral researches—began with a swing at bureaucracy. There had been, he noted, a "rather severe intelligence breakdown" on the U.S. side, in particular "the wide gulf between a rather vague prediction of [Soviet] potentialities and the specific forecast of a definite threat," which had been wholly absent:

> Anybody familiar with the operations of a bureaucracy will know that in a situation of obviously limited alternatives, the safe course involves the prediction of as many contingencies as possible, for which however no special information is required and which are consequently largely discounted. Security consciousness tends to become the subterfuge of mediocrity and imagination is submerged in superficiality.

The more important point about the Korean crisis, however, was "the complete moral fiasco of our method of achieving alliances." Kissinger based this view "not . . . on the appearance of the present battle-line which I assume will be reversed, but on the fact that the status quo ante will be achieved by the almost exclusive committal of major U.S. forces." The South Koreans had simply collapsed under the North Korean assault.

> This underlines a concept of foreign policy too frequently overlooked: the various recipient[s] of U.S. aid need us more than we need them and the attempt to win "friends" by constant concessions is no substitute for a certain inward firmness and consciousness of basic objectives. . . . Dollars will not supply the moral hold without which no government can long exist. I hope that we will not mistake the nature of whatever successes we may gain in Korea. Military victory should not be considered the sole goal but the condition for a reevaluation of our previous approach. There is little point in continually giving in to governments which will collapse under their impotence as soon as exposed to the slightest strain. I am very much afraid that the resistance of West Germany and Western Europe will not greatly surpass the Korean effort.[91]

For a man who had only just received his bachelor's degree, this was forthright indeed. Economic aid, Kissinger was arguing, had next to no strategic value if the recipients proved incapable of defending themselves.

Five months later, in December 1950—by which time MacArthur had routed the North Koreans at Inchon and Seoul, crossed the 38th parallel, and taken Pyongyang, only to be thrown back by a Chinese army he had disastrously underestimated—Kissinger returned to the subject with an even more far-reaching critique of the policy of containment. "The fundamental failure of our foreign policy," he began with a young man's sweeping self-assurance, "results from an inadequate appraisal of Russian intentions and tactics and a state of mind which mistakes clever formulae for accomplished solutions.

> All the statements about "settlements," "conferences" and "negotiations" imply that the present crisis reflects a misunderstanding, or perhaps a grievance of a specific nature, to be resolved by reasonable men in a spirit of compromise. The stark fact of the situation is, however, that Soviet expansionism is directed against our existence, not against our policies. Any concession therefore would become merely a springboard for new sallies.

Kissinger conceded that containment had "contained the germs of a profound idea." But its application had "exposed such a fundamental timidity and at times superficiality of conception, that it became in effect an instrument of Soviet policy:

> Containment to be effective implied the checking of Russian moves by the threat of a major war with the U.S. It did not mean (in terms of the U.S. manpower situation could not mean) that the United States would physically counter every Soviet threat wherever it occurred around the Soviet periphery. *By treating Soviet moves as military problems, we have enabled the USSR to select points of involvement for maximum United States discomfort, leading to a fragmentation of our forces and their committal in strategi-*

cally unproductive areas. The very tentativeness of our reactions, the exhortations of world opinion as a means of defining United States policy, limiting all measures to the lowest common denominator—all served to convince Soviet leaders that any adventure should be localized at their discretion and that a major war with the United States (the only real deterring threat) would not come about through United States initiative in forcing a showdown on fundamental issues. . . . Since we committed ourselves to treat Soviet moves as isolated thrusts, not as aspects of a pattern, and to react to them on an ad hoc basis, rather than to force a total resolution, *we have in effect allowed the Soviet General Staff in a strategic sense to deploy our resources and in a tactical sense to lure our armies into endless adventures.*

Here Kissinger was echoing the critique of containment that Walter Lippmann and others had already made. More original was the "total reappraisal of Russian strategy" he now proposed. War with the Soviet Union, he argued, was "inevitable, not because of United States policies but because of the existence of the United States as a symbol of capitalist democracy." The Soviets were committed by their Marxist-Leninist ideology not to "work for an illusory peace" but "to get into the war under the best possible circumstances." The United States must therefore adopt the same approach, seeking to fight the war on its terms, by exploiting its superior mobility "due to command of the seas, technological superiority and exterior lines of communication," and avoiding any conflict that would allow the Soviets to exploit their "massed manpower" and "sheer ruthlessness." If the Soviets wanted to lure the United States into a contest between large land armies, the United States should counter in the following way:

A. A line should be clearly defined, any transgression of which would mean a major war, though not necessarily at the point where the Soviet move occurs. . . .

B. In case of war, the United States should attempt (at least until Europe is in a position to carry the brunt of the initial battles) to force Russia into battles where terrain makes the employment of large armies unprofitable and where technological know-how is at a premium (for example, the Middle East). If crippling losses are avoided in the early stages of the conflict (or through fragmentation of United States forces in a period of semi-war designed by Russia to make American dispositions determinate), it should be possible (1) to achieve local superiorities around the Soviet periphery (particularly through interdiction of their communications systems), (2) to reduce Soviet morale by a series of hit-and-run actions, and (3) to disperse their armies so that the eventual major land battles can be fought against a weakened foe.[92]

This was an astonishing recommendation for December 1950: in effect to draw a red line, the crossing of which by Moscow would trigger a full-scale war between the superpowers, preferably fought in theaters like the Middle East, where the United States would enjoy an advantage. It illustrates that at this stage Kissinger shared the widespread view that the Soviet Union was an uncompromisingly revolutionary power with whom no kind of peaceful equilibrium could be attained. It also illustrates how pessimistic Kissinger was. Like many of his generation, he saw events in Korea as merely a prelude to a world war that would have to be fought directly against the Soviets. Revealingly, he confessed to Elliott that he had "felt like a Cassandra since last August."[93]

Kissinger revisited and refined these arguments in a March 1951 letter to Elliott prompted by a comment by Secretary of the Air Force Thomas K. Finletter on the problem of so-called "gray areas"—regions of the world geographically far from the United States and without the presence of U.S. ground forces. Once again Kissinger characterized containment (in its post-NSC-68 variant) as "the physical containment of the Soviet Union by the assembly of superior force at every point around the Soviet periphery." Once again he argued that limited wars on the periphery did not constitute an effective deterrent; that only "the threat of a major war with the United States" would effectively discourage Soviet aggression. Once again he made the point that "by attempting to achieve situations of strength at each point around the Soviet periphery as a condition for our policy, we in effect allow the Soviet General Staff to deploy our forces and to lure our Armed Forces into endless adventures." Once again he stressed that the United States was being sucked into localized conflicts on the Soviet periphery in which Moscow had a natural advantage because of its interior lines of communication, adding that any one of these conflicts had the potential to escalate into a world war. Once again he urged the drawing of a "clearly defined" line, "any transgression of which would involve a major war." And once again he urged the United States to use the Middle East, along with Turkey, as the base for a "compact, highly mobile U.S. strategic reserve, within striking distance of Soviet vital centers." The new argument that Kissinger now introduced was that, after witnessing the devastation of Korea, few other "gray areas" would care to become testing grounds for superpower military strength. An unintended consequence of Acheson's version of containment was that it "compound[ed] the psychological strain on the threatened countries and encourage[d] attempts to purchase neutrality in order to divert Soviet moves to other areas." It would be better instead to encourage American allies, especially in Europe, "to sustain a vastly expanded defensive effort," which in turn would "reflect a psychological condition, a will-to-fight, to be bolstered by limited U.S. ground support, the certainty of a consistent, self-reliant U.S. foreign policy and other psychological measures."[94]

In most of this armchair strategizing, the historical context was implicit. The striking exception is the letter Kissinger wrote to Colonel William Kintner, one of the CIA's leading theorists of psychological warfare, in November 1951, by which time the Korean War had settled into a stalemate that was more World War I than World War II. Here, far more than he dared in his dissertation, he was able to set out the similarities—but just as important, the differences—between 1951 and 1815. "A balance of power," he wrote, "depends . . . on the following factors:

> (a) A geographically determinate area, (b) An equilibrium of strength within that area, (c) An outside balancer with a profound conception of national strategy and unencumbered by ideological considerations, (d) A large measure of agreement

on basic values within that "concert of powers." . . . [B]efore
you can have a balance of power there must be power to be balanced. The balancer must not himself be part of the equilibrium,
except to tip the scale. Above all, policy must be conceived as a
continuing process, with war as merely an instrument for the
achievement of determinate objectives. The balance of power is
incompatible with the assertion of absolute values.[95]

But, as Kissinger put it emphatically, "the present situation meets
none of these conditions." Not only was a global balance—as opposed
to a purely European one—almost impossibly difficult, but the United
States was not in a position to play the traditionally British balancing role:

> Maybe Europe will recover its morale and provide an indepen-
> dent force. Possibly the emergent East will provide another
> center of power. If so, the United States should play in relation
> to Eurasia the traditional role of an island power towards a
> land-mass—to prevent the consolidation of that continent
> under a single rule. [But] at the moment the United States is
> not a balancer but a direct contestant on a world-wide scale;
> and, moreover, not by choice.

This was a crucial difference in Kissinger's eyes. The United States was
already too much entangled with its military alliances in Europe and
Asia to have the option of behaving like nineteenth-century Britain.
Moreover, it existed in too polarized a world for such a "British" strategy to be viable.

> It would be strain enough on U.S. wisdom to be suddenly pro-
> jected into Britain's traditional role. But a more awful respon-
> sibility awaits us. The injection of an ideological element into
> policy makes self-limitation an almost unattainable Ideal. Pol-
> icy begins to be conceived as the means of an absolute attitude,
> not as the definition of continuing relation. In the inevitable
> atmosphere of distrust each side tends to play for absolute

LEFT: Heinz Kissinger (right) with his younger brother, Walter, and their grandparents' pet cat in the back garden of the grandparental home in Leutershausen.

BELOW: "Yes to the Führer": Nazi banners on a school in Schwabacher Strasse, Fürth, Germany, August 19, 1934. Germans voted overwhelmingly to unite the powers of the Reich chancellor and president in Hitler's hands.

ABOVE: Fourteen-year-old Heinz Kissinger (bottom left) and other students at the Jewish Realschule in Fürth, 1938.

RIGHT: Nazi Party members march through Fürth on their way back from the 1938 Nuremberg party rally. The sign reads "Fürth City Limits: Jews Are Our Misfortune." The building on the right was a factory that had formerly belonged to the "Aryanized" (i.e., formerly Jewish-owned) firm J. W. Spear.

LEFT: Second from right, with his family in London, en route to the United States, August 28, 1938. Also pictured (in the center of the photograph) are Paula Kissinger's aunt Berta and her husband, Sigmund Fleischmann, with whom the Kissingers stayed in Golders Green.

BELOW: The men of G Company, 2nd Battalion, 335th Infantry Regiment, 84th Infantry Division ("Railsplitters"), before being sent to Europe in 1944. Henry Kissinger is sixth from the left in the fourth row.

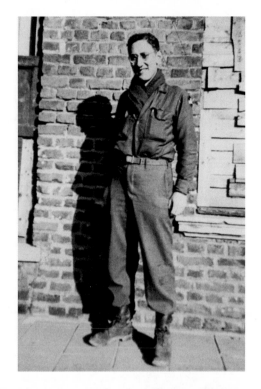

RIGHT: On the eve of battle in Eygelshoven, Netherlands, in early November 1944. Within days Kissinger would be at the front line facing the Siegfried Line at Aachen. His return to Germany came just over six years after his family had been driven into exile by the Nazis.

BELOW: American troops moving through a devastated Bensheim, March 27, 1945. Kissinger's role as a Counter Intelligence Corps officer was to root out the most committed Nazis in the Bensheim area.

ABOVE: The concentration camp at Ahlem, west of Hanover, which members of the 84th Division, among them Henry Kissinger, liberated on April 10, 1945. In the words of Vernon Tott, who took this photograph, it was "Hell on Earth." One survivor, Moshe Miedzinski, remembered that it was Kissinger who told him, "You are free."

LEFT: One of the prisoners at Ahlem shortly after the liberation of the camp, possibly Folek Sama, to whom Kissinger addressed his short essay "The Eternal Jew": "Humanity stands accused in you. I, Joe Smith, human dignity, everybody has failed you. . . . Human dignity, objective values have stopped at this barbed wire."

ABOVE: Mephistopheles to Kissinger's Faust: Fritz Kraemer (right), who successfully presented himself to Americans as an anti-Nazi Prussian officer but was, in fact, a Jewish-born specialist in international law. The flamboyant pose is characteristic. Kissinger later called him "the greatest single influence on my formative years."

RIGHT: A scene from the 1950 Passion Play at Oberammergau, Bavaria, the home of the Occupational Orientation Department of the U.S. Forces European Theater Intelligence School. It was an unlikely place for a lapsed Jew to begin his teaching career.

LEFT: William Yandell Elliott, Kissinger's mentor in Harvard's Government Department: in his lectures, political theory was "an adventure where good and evil were in a constant struggle to give meaning to existence." An ardent Anglophile (and an Atlanticist) who had discovered philosophical idealism while a Rhodes Scholar at Balliol College, Bill Elliott personified for the young Kissinger the active academic, forever shuttling from one end of "Boswash" to the other. He is pictured here with his wife and pet raccoon.

BELOW: The idealistic generation: Kissinger in conversation with students at the Student Conference on U.S. Affairs, West Point, 1956.

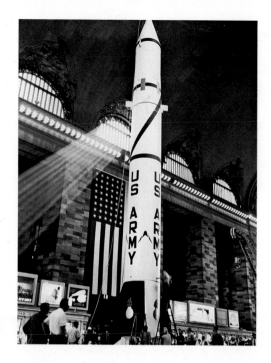

LEFT: A PGM-11 Redstone missile—the first to carry a nuclear warhead—on display in Grand Central Station, New York City, July 7, 1957.

BELOW: *Pravda* announces the successful launch of *Sputnik*, October 6, 1957.

ABOVE: The Soviet "peace offensive" goes to Hollywood: Nikita Khrushchev and his wife, Nina, with Shirley MacLaine and Frank Sinatra on the set of *Can-Can*, 1959.

RIGHT: Khrushchev hugs the leader of the Cuban Revolution, Fidel Castro, at the United Nations, New York City, 1960.

ABOVE: "The great challenge," February 19, 1961. Kissinger debates "The World Strategy of the United States as a Great Power" with the economist Paul A. Samuelson, then president of the American Economic Association; Lewis L. Strauss, former chairman of the Atomic Energy Commission; Adlai Stevenson, then U.S. ambassador to the United Nations; and the historian Arnold Toynbee. No record appears to survive of this discussion, which was televised by CBS.

LEFT: U.S. M48 tanks face off against Soviet T-54s and T-55s at Checkpoint Charlie, Berlin, October 1961. Kissinger was dismayed by the Kennedy administration's decision to acquiesce in the construction of the Berlin Wall. "I am filled with a sense of imminent national disaster," he wrote.

The remains of the American U-2 spy plane shot down
during the Cuban Missile Crisis, 1962.

President Kennedy meets with members of the executive committee at the
White House during the Cuban Missile Crisis, October 29, 1962.

"This hurts me more than it hurts you!" Ed Valtman's cartoon in *The Hartford Times* mocks Khrushchev's decision to remove the Soviet missiles from Cuba. The American public was unaware of the deal the Kennedy brothers had made to trade American missiles in Turkey for the Soviet missiles in Cuba.

Making the best of a bad job: a Soviet cartoon satirizing American plans to bring Cuba to heel, *Krokodil*, May 20, 1963.

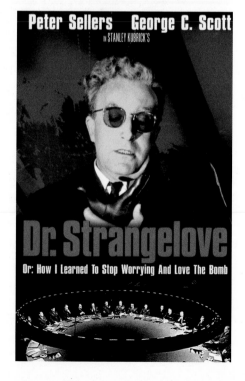

Dr. Strangelove, the crazed nuclear strategist played by Peter Sellers in Stanley Kubrick's film, was more Herman Kahn than Henry Kissinger.

Vice President Lyndon B. Johnson, President Kennedy, Mrs. Kennedy, and others watch the flight of astronaut Alan Shepard on television at the White House, May 5, 1961.

Vice President Johnson, President Kennedy, and Defense Secretary Robert McNamara at NASA Launch Complex 39, built to fulfill Kennedy's dream of a lunar landing.

TOP LEFT: Overweight and unhappily married in 1962.

TOP RIGHT: Being interviewed by Radio Free Europe in Berlin, November 1962. The U.S.-funded radio station transmitted to listeners in Bulgaria, Czechoslovakia, Hungary, Poland, and Romania.

LEFT: Slimmed down for the Sixties. After his divorce in 1964, Kissinger shed pounds. He lightened up socially, too.

security, which means absolute insecurity (i.e., neutralization) of its opponent. This would be true even if only one side were to introduce the ideological element.

Kissinger ended his letter to Kintner with a surprising reflection on what lay ahead for the United States.

I know there is a tendency to point to the religious toleration following the wars of the Reformation as a possible substitute for ideological conflict. But surely the significant point is that this balance was achieved only after a Thirty-Years' War. . . . I do not think this period will follow the pattern of the 17th century. I think we will find ourselves in the role of Rome after the Carthaginian wars, and this is why I used the adjective "awful" to describe our future.[96]

In other words, Kissinger confidently expected the American Rome to triumph over the Soviet Carthage. It was what came next that worried him, when "within a generation [we may] find ourselves in a world in which we must supply our challenges from within ourselves. This is a real issue for long-range thinking, and its solution requires a profound doctrine."[97] Here was an unusual thing to worry about in 1951: the onset of imperial decadence in the aftermath of an American victory over the Soviets.

Unlike George Kennan, whose published writings he certainly read, Kissinger was no expert on the Soviet Union. His argument in a December 1951 memorandum entitled "Soviet Strategy—Possible U.S. Countermeasures" was highly conventional. The Russians, for historical and ideological reasons, were inclined to see war as inevitable and therefore to seek to expand the Soviet security belt for reasons they conceived of as defensive. For the time being, they could be deterred by the threat of all-out war, but that would change. As they built up their strategic air force and atomic capability, they would aim for a showdown in Western Europe. In this, the Korean crisis had been like an early feint in a strategy designed to get the United States to disperse its land forces around the globe. Hence the need for Washington urgently to switch from a "physical containment" (as practiced by Acheson) to "a total military strategy" based on "psychological" considerations, including the creation of Kissinger's Middle Eastern mobile strategic reserve.[98]

V

Nearly two years passed before Kissinger wrote anything more in this vein. By the time he returned to the field of contemporary strategy, much had changed. Harry Truman had left the White House, to be replaced by Dwight Eisenhower, the only general to serve as president in the twentieth century. Unlike most other twentieth-century presidents, "Ike" had not craved the highest office. He might legitimately have retired altogether in 1952, after serving as NATO supreme commander, his reputation secure as one of the key architects of the Allied victory in World War II. But the hostility toward NATO—indeed the downright isolationism—of the front-runner for the Republican nomination, Senator Robert Taft of Ohio, had persuaded him to run. While projecting a genial grandfatherly image, playing golf, watching Westerns, and dabbling in painting, Eisenhower was as steely a strategist as ever. He refused any further escalation of the Korean War, but intimated to the Soviets and the Chinese that he might use nuclear weapons to end the stalemate. The result was a negotiated settlement that cut Korea in two. He was equally decisive at home. When Joseph McCarthy had the temerity to make the U.S. Army the next target of his anti-Communist witch hunt, Eisenhower had his vice president condemn McCarthy's "reckless talk and questionable methods."

The Soviet Union, too, was different. In the early hours of March 1, 1953, Stalin suffered a stroke. Four days later he was dead. Almost immediately the triumvirate who succeeded him—Lavrentiy Beria, Georgy Malenkov, and Vyacheslav Molotov—moved to reduce international tensions. "At the present time," Malenkov told the Supreme Soviet just nine days after Stalin's death had been announced, "there is no disputed or unresolved question that cannot be settled peacefully by mutual agreement of the interested countries. This applies to our relations with all states, including the United States of America."[99] The tone of Soviet propaganda had also changed, with the advent of the so-called peace offensive. Here was a new threat: not actual war but the psychological variety, taking the form of proposals for German reunification—like the one Stalin himself had made in March 1952—that were as attractive to ordinary Germans as they were disingenuous to American policy makers. The Americans who had pressed for German rearmament had underestimated the need to establish the right "psychological climate" for it. They had underestimated the danger of what Kissinger called "reverse Titoism—nationalist governments who to prove their independence of the U.S. will lean increasingly on the U.S.S.R." For this reason, he regarded "a conciliatory attitude on the part of the Soviet Union" as "more dangerous than a continuation of the cold war."

The good news was that, with Stalin gone, the Cold War was losing some of its ideological intensity and reverting to the more familiar patterns of geopolitics. As a result, in an important shift, Kissinger saw the analogy he had repudiated in 1951 as having a potential applicability:

> In relation to the Eurasian continent, the U.S. is in the position of Great Britain to the Continent in the 19th century. It is an island power with inferior resources, at present only in manpower but in time even in industrial capacity.* Therefore, the U.S. cannot permit the consolidation of the Eurasian continent under the domination or control of one power whatever its form of government. . . . [Rather], in order to conserve its own resources, U.S. strategy should attempt to create a balance of force on the Eurasian continent. This means that the Soviet sphere can under no circumstances be permitted to expand—in fact, it should be reduced, for the consolidation of a Chinese-Soviet-East European satellite bloc must in time present mortal dangers to the security of the U.S.

---

*For most of the Cold War, the overwhelming majority of American experts, including Kissinger, consistently overrated the Soviet system's economic capacity and potential. In 1953 the Soviet economy was one-third the size of the U.S. economy.

This was an important shift of emphasis: now the United States could hope to act as a British-style balancing power. But how exactly was this to be done? A forcible reduction of the core of the Soviet bloc was clearly out of the question precisely because it implied war. However, "a split between the U.S.S.R. and its satellites including China" was a distinct "possibility." Here was the seed of another strategic concept that would come to fruition fully two decades later.

On the basis of this analysis, Kissinger had a specific proposal to make. The death of Stalin, he argued, had presented a "great opportunity" for U.S. diplomacy "boldly [to] capture the peace offensive" by calling a four-power meeting to discuss European problems, in particular the divided Germany. At this meeting, the United States should propose "the conclusion of a treaty of peace and all-German elections"—in other words German reunification. Such a scenario was, Kissinger argued, "less to be feared by us than by the U.S.S.R.," though clearly there would have to be guarantees of Germany's borders along the lines of the 1925 Treaty of Locarno. True, the move would postpone, if not wholly derail, the plan under discussion for a European Defense Community (EDC), but Kissinger correctly reasoned that the EDC had "little prospect of ratification in any case." By contrast, there would be real benefits in Asia if the American move were successful: "The effect on China of such a Four-Power meeting sacrificing a Soviet satellite might be profound, particularly if a subsequent Asian conference should prove unproductive. . . . This distrust may be reinforced by putting on the agenda a mutual guarantee of each other's borders by the Four Powers, but excluding China." Kissinger admitted it was unlikely that the Soviets would agree to such a meeting. But "should the conference fail, as is likely, EDC and the cold war could be resumed in a much healthier political climate."[100]

Kissinger's memorandum on "The Soviet Peace Offensive" was widely circulated and almost as widely admired. Bundy was enthused, telling Kissinger, "You made so much sense in such a short space," and forwarding it to his friend Robert Bowie at Policy Planning.[101] But one former colleague, George Pettee of ORO, was not wholly convinced. He made a telling criticism: "[I]n the process of making excellent use of the past and its knowledge, there are places where you tend to attribute characteristics to the future which were true of the past but may not be true of the future. The suggestion that a Locarno type pact might be important is the kind of thing I mean."[102]

Kissinger defended himself, insisting that he did not mean to repeat the mistakes of the 1920s; the idea for a treaty was only there because of the "profound psychological effect" it would have. As he put it, "All my proposals are, in any case, designed to recapture the initiative. It stands to reason that if the Soviet governmental bureaucracy is anything like ours—there is no reason to suppose that bureaucracy differs radically in spirit—the more ideas we can throw into the hopper the less time they will have for original thought and the less flexibility they will tend to have."[103] Pettee had nevertheless articulated a thought that others undoubtedly shared: Kissinger was too fond of his historical parallels, too reluctant to acknowledge that in certain respects the present was not like the past.

By the summer of 1953 Kissinger was beginning to feel the frustration that sooner or later all amateur strategists feel: he was brimming over with ideas, but no one was listening. Bowie may have seen his paper on German unity; he may indeed have read it. Certainly, it had been made timely by events in East Berlin, where a wave of strikes beginning on June 16, 1953, had been forcibly suppressed by Soviet forces. No one, however, summoned Kissinger to Washington. He was driven back to private correspondence with kindred spirits like Schlesinger, a man of the left but, more important, a historian. Kissinger was unimpressed by what is often seen as the greatest success of U.S. psychological warfare in the early Cold War. As in 1948, the Christian Democrats had won the Italian election of 1953—with significant help from the CIA. But Kissinger saw the result as just "one other proof of the futility of conducting foreign policy by gimmick." "Foreign policy, unfortunately, is different from pleading a case at the bar where, after the jury's verdict is in, the lies you have told can't come back to hound you."[104] On the other hand, the Democratic contender for the presidency, Adlai Stevenson, seemed no better than Eisenhower:

While I agree with Stevenson that we must not bomb Moscow if Italy goes Communist, I think it equally senseless to announce beforehand that we would not bomb Moscow under any circumstances. Nor do I think it wise to fight any more Koreas.

I also wish the candidates would finally quit talking about a "peace to be won" as if on a certain date "peace will break out" and tensions will magically disappear. I know of no period in which this was true in all history except under the Roman Empire. I can conceive no settlement with Russia which will permit us to say that there will be no longer any tensions, and this would be true even if the Kremlin were ruled by arch-angels. For in a world of two superpowers under conditions of sovereignty, tensions are inevitable.[105]

This was not so very different from an argument that had been made by Carl Friedrich ten years before. But did Kissinger really need to bring in the Roman Empire to make his point?

VI

It was not unknown at the Harvard of 1954 for a successful doctoral student to be given an assistant professorship not long after completing his dissertation. Despite some lobbying by Elliott, no such offer was made to Henry Kissinger. Nor was he successful in his application to the Harvard Society of Fellows, an elite institution similar to Oxford's All Souls College.[106] A variety of explanations have been given for this reverse: some faculty members saw him as too worldly; some felt he had put more energy into the International Seminar and *Confluence* than into his duties as a teaching fellow for Sam Beer's Social Science 2 course.[107] We know he had declined to help Bundy with his course, Government 180, in the spring semester of 1953.[108] Probably not too much credence should be given to the latter, obviously spiteful reminiscences of former colleagues who had become political enemies in the 1970s, though it is possible that some near-contemporaries—Adam Ulam especially—had already taken against Kissinger.[109] But there is another and more plausible explanation. According to Charles Kindleberger, the brilliant financial historian at MIT, Elliott had "asked if we could give Kissinger a job because there were no openings at Harvard. So I asked my colleagues, 'Do we want a political scientist who knows something about Metternich?' And they said, 'Hell, no.'"[110] Like many another new Ph.D., Kissinger was forced to eke out his existence on a postdoctoral grant: in his case $4,000 from the Rockefeller Foundation "to enable Mr. Henry A. Kissinger to study the decline in the observance of the political maxims of the 19th century during the period from 1870 to 1914."[111] The award was funded under the Rockefeller Foundation's new program in legal and political philosophy. It sufficed for Harvard to appoint Kissinger as a research fellow in political science.[112]

There can be no doubt that Kissinger was disappointed. On June 8, 1954, he took the extraordinary step of addressing a heartfelt letter to McGeorge Bundy on "one of the chief problems facing higher education and Harvard in particular: the state of mind of the graduate student and junior faculty member." Though couched in general terms, the letter was unmistakably a personal lament. Kissinger began, arrestingly and revealingly, by defining the graduate student's state of mind as

> a strange mixture of insecurity and self-righteousness, of gentility and the most devious kind of manipulation, of strained application and indolent drifting. It is without humor and without joy. Despite its appearance of pedantry, it is always on the verge of hysteria. Despite its claims of universality, it is characterized by almost total isolation. While occasionally substantial works are produced[,] they testify to the strength of an individual to transcend his environment, not to an impetus derived from it. Nothing makes for creativity, for spontaneity, for inspiration. All the pressures make for conformity, a high level of mediocrity and safety.

Such was the lack of "joy" in academic life, he went on, that "I, too, have seriously thought about giving up the academic career and going to Law School." This was not for financial reasons but because "the academic profession will remain unattractive whatever its salary scale until a beginning is made to reform some of its present attitudes."

> In no other profession is one so dependent on the approbation of one's colleagues and yet in no profession must one so much create the substance out of oneself. In no other field is the disparity between the creative act and its reception so marked. The academic profession requires a special degree of dedication, therefore. More than any other activity it must be done for its own sake. To an unusual extent it depends on an atmosphere which does not inhibit inspiration. Its crucial problem is to maintain its standards against the forces that tend to dissolve them. But just because there exist no "objective" standards or because true creativity constantly transcends existing norms the danger of atrophy or mediocrity always lurks beneath the surface. It is not that quality will be consciously suppressed; it is rather that the *sense for quality* may be lost.

Kissinger bitterly condemned Harvard's "increasingly narrow and even sterile" atmosphere and its debilitating "spirit of atomism": "No one cares about anyone else's work and even less about his human development." A rare exception to this rule was his old mentor Elliott, "the person most responsible for my development, [who] did not do so primarily because of his learning but above all because of his humanity, by giving me the feeling that someone I could respect was concerned with my growth." But he conspicuously did not exempt Elliott from his next complaint, that graduate life revolved around the "eagles" (senior faculty) in the government department. Since Harvard graduate students all aspired to become tenured Harvard professors, they were bound to become slavish conformists. Kissinger concluded his tirade with three concrete recommendations: the creation at Harvard of something like Princeton's Institute for Advanced Study, to encourage high-level interdisciplinary work; the transfer of decisions about appointments from departments to the dean (i.e., to Bundy); and earlier awards of tenure.[113]

To say the least, this was a remarkable letter for a brand-new Ph.D. to write to the dean of the Faculty of Arts and Sciences, in many respects the second most powerful Harvard official after the president. Even allowing for his relatively close acquaintance with Bundy, not least thanks to *Confluence,* it was risky—even reckless—for Kissinger to unburden himself in this way. He cannot seriously have expected his proposals to be acted upon, given their obviously self-interested character. Nevertheless, with his dissertation finally complete, he could not resist giving vent to his frustrations. No copy of Bundy's reply can be found in the Harvard archives; perhaps he conveyed his views verbally. Relations between the two men remained cordial, with Bundy continuing to accept Kissinger's invitations to address the summer school participants, and Kissinger continuing to be invited to lunch with distinguished visitors (for example, Harold Stassen, the former governor of Minnesota and quadrennial contender for the Republican presidential nomination). Yet if Kissinger hoped that his letter would improve his prospects of a professorship, he was disappointed. In the fall of 1954, Bundy appears to have offered Kissinger some kind of position— probably that of an "instructor," the lowest rung on the academic ladder—but Kissinger's lukewarm reaction makes it clear that it fell short of his expectations.[114] Even when armed with an offer of a professorship from the University of Chicago, Kissinger could not secure a matching offer from his alma mater. By the end of 1954 it seemed as if his Harvard career were drawing to an anticlimactic close.

VII

Nearly twenty years later, Kissinger had occasion to reflect again on the pathologies of academic life. It was March 1972, and he was sitting in the Oval Office with President Richard Nixon. "What the Christ is the matter with them?" asked Nixon, meaning American academics, so many of whom were critical of his foreign policy. The exchange that followed revealed how little the intervening years—and worldly success—had changed Kissinger's view:

KISSINGER: But academic life is a depressing period, so they all . . .

NIXON: Why is it depressing? Don't they have visible accomplishments?

KISSINGER: Well, first of all, because you're spending your life with a group of teenagers, Mr. President. And it is, after all, instead of helping the teenagers grow up they become almost as irresponsible as the people for whom, with whom they meet with day in and day out. Secondly it's an insecure making profession. Not for the top people . . .

NIXON: Yeah.

KISSINGER: . . . who got a national reputation, uh, like Arthur Schlesinger [Jr.] or myself. But for the—even the average Harvard professor has a terrible time because he goes through ten years of maddening insecurity before he ever gets tenured. And if he doesn't make it in a good place, there is—it isn't like in a law school, where in your second year you know whether you're good or not.

NIXON: Yeah.

KISSINGER: And you can't fake it.

NIXON: Yeah.

KISSINGER: And you can—you can pretty well predict where you're gonna be in terms of the availability of law firms.

NIXON: Yeah.

KISSINGER: In academic life you are entirely dependent on the personal recommendation of some egomaniac. Nobody knows how good you are. Hell, I at Harvard—in '54 at Harvard, I was always an oddball, I was always in that sense an outsider. I had one hell of a time. . . . My first book . . . was about 19th Century diplomacy and the average person wasn't that interested in it. . . . It was a very thoughtful book. It was about how peace was made in 1815, and . . .

NIXON: Right, oh yeah.

KISSINGER: That was, that was a thoughtful book. But it is a very insecure making profession. Then they are very influenced by Socialist Theory. And . . .

NIXON: Now why? That's the point I make. Why? They always have been, but . . .

KISSINGER: They believe in manipulation, Mr. President. And therefore, it grates on them. In this society, intellectuals are not as a class highly respected; that gets them.[115]

Disgust with academic politics is surprisingly common among academics. The philosopher George Santayana, who studied at Harvard and taught philosophy there between 1890 and 1912, said he "never had a real friend who was a professor" and asked himself, "Is it jealousy, as among women, and a secret unwillingness to be wholly pleased? Or is it the consciousness that a professor or a woman has to be partly a sham; whence a mixture of contempt and pity for such a poor victim of necessity?"[116] Nor is this sentiment unique to Harvard professors. It was not in fact Henry Kissinger who coined the saying that "the reason academic politics are so bitter is that so little is at stake"; it was Wallace Stanley Sayre, a professor of public administration at Columbia and author of *Governing New York City* (where the stakes were manifestly higher). But Kissinger was certainly fond of repeating Sayre's "Law" that "in any dispute the intensity of feeling is inversely proportional to the value of the issues at stake" and citing Harvard politics as the classic illustration.

Yet the stakes cannot have seemed so low to Kissinger one summer day in 1954, as he walked despondently across Harvard Yard, contemplating the stalling of his once brilliant academic career. As he greeted his friend Arthur Schlesinger, enviably ensconced as a tenured professor in the history department, already a Pulitzer Prize winner, Kissinger had no inkling that the conversation he was about to have would change the course of his life. The "political scientist who knew something about Metternich" was about to go nuclear.

CHAPTER 10

Strangelove?

Mr. Kissinger believes that (1) we must be [as] prepared to
meet an all-out attack as limited aggression; (2) an all-out
attack must be met with an all-out counter-attack; (3) a
limited aggression must be repelled by limited warfare. In
each case we should use the most appropriate weapon for
the task. The most appropriate weapon is usually a nuclear
weapon.

—EDWARD TELLER, 1957[1]

Of course Kissinger is right in conceiving the problems of
policy planning and strategy in terms of national power, in
rough analogy to the national struggles of the 19th century;
yet I have the impression that there are deep things abroad
in the world, which in time are going to turn the flank of
all struggles so conceived. This will not happen today, nor
easily as long as Soviet power continues great and unaltered;
but nevertheless I think in time the transnational communities
in our culture will begin to play a prominent part in the
political structure of the world, and even affect the exercise
of power by states.

—J. ROBERT OPPENHEIMER, 1957[2]

I

In the summer of 1954 Henry Kissinger had a Ph.D. in early
nineteenth-century history but not much else. Harvard had declined
to give him the junior professorship he thought was his due. He had an
offer of a position at the University of Chicago but had no desire to go
there; the University of Pennsylvania offered "more money but little

prestige."[3] He was eking out an existence on a small grant from the Rockefeller Foundation, wasting his time trying to publish chapters from his doctoral dissertation as more or less obscure scholarly articles in academic journals. Yet just three years later, Kissinger would be one of the foremost American experts on nuclear strategy, a best-selling author, a star guest on television talk shows, the subject of debate in Washington, and the object of denunciation in Moscow. By 1964 he was being mentioned as the inspiration for the sinister characters of Professor Groeteschele, the cold-blooded political scientist played by Walter Matthau in Sidney Lumet's *Fail Safe,* and (less plausibly) Dr. Strangelove, the downright mad nuclear strategist played by Peter Sellers in Stanley Kubrick's eponymous comedy.* How was all this possible? The answer begins ten years before *Dr. Strangelove,* with a chance meeting in Harvard Yard.

Though politically far from aligned, Arthur Schlesinger, Jr., and Henry Kissinger were friends. Kissinger would always attend the Commencement cocktail party thrown each year by the Schlesingers and their neighbors the Galbraiths, where cocktails[†] were the only drink on offer and cigarettes were freely available in bowls. In return, as Marian Schlesinger recalled, she and her husband would dine chez Kissinger, where "the prefect Herr Professor" and his wife offered "heavy food [and] heavy thought. . . . Everything was white. The dishes, even the food."[4] After Fritz Kraemer, Schlesinger was the man to whom Kissinger was most ready to share his uppermost (if not his innermost) thoughts. Schlesinger was happy to introduce his clever friend to the liberal grandees in his circle, among them Eleanor Roosevelt, Adlai Stevenson, and the Kennedy brothers.[5] It was after a brief, impromptu exchange in Harvard Yard that Kissinger (as he put it) "got drawn by Arthur Schlesinger, Jr., into a three-cornered discussion between him,

---

*The primary inspiration for Strangelove was in reality Herman Kahn, a number of whose ideas are directly referenced in Kubrick's script. Like Kissinger, however, Kahn was of Jewish origin, and unlike Kissinger, he had been born in the United States. Strangelove, by contrast, is clearly a former Nazi and in that respect bears a resemblance to Wernher von Braun, the rocket scientist.

[†]It should be remembered that, while Kissinger himself was never a drinker, practically everyone else in 1950s America was consuming quantities of spirits that would now be considered excessive. See for details DeVoto, *Hour.*

the Alsop brothers [Joseph and Stewart]* and Paul Nitze," the author of NSC-68.[6] The starting point was the letter from former air force secretary Thomas Finletter that Schlesinger happened to have in his pocket, which, on the spur of the moment, he suggested Kissinger read.[7] Disagreeing with Finletter's defense of the administration's reliance on the threat of massive retaliation, Kissinger dashed off an essay entitled "The Impasse of American Policy and Preventive War." It was this essay that launched his career in the emerging field of strategic studies.[†]

The essay's starting point was that, after a year and a half in office, the foreign policy of the Eisenhower administration was failing:

> The collapse of South-East Asia [a reference to the French
> defeat in Indochina, which had culminated at Dien Bien Phu
> just four months before], the hesitations of our Western Allies,
> the rumblings in Japan, the changing weapons balance, all
> point to a crisis nonetheless serious for being denied in official
> pronouncements from Washington. Within the past fifteen
> months, the USSR has managed to capture the peace offensive
> so that all over the world the U.S. increasingly appears as the
> obstacle to peace; it has made great strides in the development
> of its nuclear weapons and thus confronted Western Europe at
> least with imminent neutralization; it holds the diplomatic ini-
> tiative in every corner of the globe with the U.S. vacillating
> between bombast and pliability but in any case reduced to rela-
> tive ineffectiveness.

As for the European Defense Community, it had become "a mortgage on American prestige," while mooted the Southeast Asia Treaty Orga-

---

*From 1945 until 1958, Joseph and Stewart Alsop wrote the thrice-weekly "Matter of Fact" column for the *New York Herald Tribune*. Harvard men of impeccable WASP heritage, they described themselves as "Republicans by inheritance and registration, and . . . conservatives by political conviction."

†"Well, Arthur," Kissinger told Schlesinger many years later, "you are the one who promoted me into the public arena, you have only yourself to blame for the damage you cause to the country." Kissinger remained grateful to Schlesinger for the rest of his life, as the latter's son Andrew records in more than one entry in his as-yet-unpublished diary, and as Kissinger himself made clear in his eulogy for Schlesinger in 2007.

nization (SEATO) would merely "add weakness to weakness." Kissinger identified three reasons for this litany of failure. First, the United States, "righteously fixated on the Soviet threat," had underestimated the appetite of the rest of the world for peace and its "reluctance . . . to believe in unbridgeable schism." In terms of psychological warfare, the United States had been wrong-footed by the Soviet "peace offensive" that had followed the death of Stalin. Second, American policy makers were attaching a naïve importance to their alliances with other states. This was a chance to recycle a favorite line: "If in practice [an alliance] leads to a conception of unity as an end in itself, it becomes self-defeating. For if an alliance is equated with the consensus of its members, its policy is shaped by its weakest components." The United States was a hegemon; it had to *lead* its allies.

These were arguments Kissinger had made before; they surely struck Schlesinger as familiar. But the third one was new: it was an argument about actual war, not the psychological variety: "Confronted with possible neutralization, [we may see] war . . . as the preferable alternative and preventive war the means to force a showdown before the cards become hopelessly stacked against us. But war is too serious a matter to be undertaken in a fit of frustration." The problem was that the administration's self-styled "New Look" defense policy could not decide "whether it is a strategy for fighting the cold war or a means of winning a shooting war." If the former, it was misconceived. And if the latter? Kissinger was not explicit, but his readers got the point.[8] As he put it in a letter to one of them, "I am, in effect, saying a local war is possible."[9] This was doubly provocative. The Eisenhower position was that Korea starkly exposed the perils of a local war. It was cheaper as well as more effective to deter Soviet aggression with the threat of general—meaning nuclear—war. Kissinger seemed to be implying that the United States could have the best of both strategies: a local war that was also nuclear.

The liberal optimist Schlesinger was much more ready to believe in a new and more "flexible" disposition in Moscow than Kissinger.[10] Nevertheless he was more than usually excited by Kissinger's draft, calling it "the most interesting and useful discussion of the current foreign policy impasse I have read anywhere"[11] and offering to circulate it to such luminaries as Adlai Stevenson, whom Eisenhower had defeated for the presidency two years before, as well as Thomas Finletter, whose letter to Schlesinger had prompted the paper.* Kissinger's old friend at ORO, George Pettee, offered a conservative cynic's view.

> The trouble with the piece is that it has no sugar coating for anybody. Everybody wants either Acheson or Dulles to be cracked up as hot stuff [i.e., for partisan reasons]. Each was a technician [who] would have looked good any time last century and you rightly treat both as missing the point [about nuclear weapons]. Your paper is a good test, in a way, because it has no attraction whatever for either of the party variants on the pharisaical position of rationalist-legalist-idealist diplomacy. If anybody likes your paper, therefore, that fact will be worth knowing about that person.[12]

But it was Finletter's response that had the biggest impact, in that it explicitly challenged the military element in Kissinger's analysis, defending the idea that the threat of "general war" was the best way of deterring further Soviet expansion. "I confess," Kissinger replied, with an uncharacteristic allusion to the role of economics, "it simply does not make sense to me to think of the unlimited potentialities militarily of a country [the USSR] that has a steel production of less than five million tons."[13] Regardless of the true extent of Soviet power, however, Kissinger still questioned Finletter's reasoning: "The willingness to engage in a general war by itself is not enough to deter aggression for unless the Soviet bloc knows the extent of U.S. determination it may engage in a probing action which may then result in an avoidable general war, avoidable because the probing action might not have been undertaken had our intentions been fully understood." The real problem, Kissinger argued, was one of credibility:

---

*Prior to succeeding Stuart Symington as secretary of the air force, Finletter had been chairman of Truman's Air Policy Commission.

Assuming that essential areas are defined and that the U.S. has left no doubt about its willingness to defend them, what then? One of two consequences seems almost inevitable: either the Soviet bloc believes us which would involve the corollary that all areas not defined as essential by the U.S. could be absorbed against at most local resistance. Or else the Soviet bloc would consider our announcement a bluff—a not unlikely eventuality after two years of "massive retaliation"—and then we will be right back at Dienbienphu.[14]

Kissinger was no expert on military matters; he was a student of diplomatic history. Nor was he by any means the first to advance such arguments. Yet his critique of the Eisenhower administration's doctrine of deterrence was welcomed by influential military men. At the Army War College, according to General Richard G. Stilwell, it had "captured the fancy of all faculty members who have had the opportunity to peruse it."[15] Air force general James McCormack, then deputy commander of the Air Research and Development Command, also approved.[16] Encouraged by this response, Kissinger began to wonder if he had hit on an important insight: that waging a limited war *with* nuclear weapons was a viable alternative to the threat of an all-out war. Dismissive of all the many schemes for disarmament then in vogue,* he told Schlesinger that it was wrong

to think that local wars and the tactical employment of nuclear weapons will necessarily lead to all-out atomic war, because the Russians will not be able to make fine distinctions. This seems to me to confuse a logical inference with strategical reality. All the pressures will be on the Russians to make precisely this distinction. I think they could be trusted to know the

---

*"I am not overly sympathetic to disarmament proposals except for their psychological impact. In history disarmament has usually followed, not preceded, a detente. If nations could agree on disarmament they could agree on other things, and then in turn the need for the armaments would disappear."

difference between the destruction of Moscow and an atomic bomb exploding over a battlefield.

Warming to his new theme, Kissinger argued that "the destructiveness of present [i.e., strategic] nuclear weapons" was so great that they would only ever be used "due to bureaucratic inertia.

> The major use of S.A.C. [Strategic Air Command] as I see it is to permit us to fight local wars on our terms; or let us put it another way—the destructiveness of nuclear weapons is such that the only thing they deter is their use by the other side. Thus, the side which has an alternative weapon system can keep the ultimate weapons as a deterrent against the other, to keep it from starting a general war. Thus, if we have a weapon system which permits the tactical employment of nuclear weapons and enables us to fight local wars, and if we integrate this into a diplomacy which makes clear that we are interested only in local transformation and not in unconditional surrender, S.A.C. may deter the Russians from a major war.[17]

Here was the essence of the distinctly counterintuitive argument that would make Kissinger's name.

The emergence of Henry Kissinger as a public intellectual in the nascent field of strategic studies can be dated from April 1955, which saw the appearance in *Foreign Affairs* of his article "Military Policy and the Defense of the 'Grey Areas.'"[18] Published since 1922 by the Council on Foreign Relations, *Foreign Affairs* was (as it still is) sufficiently journalistic to be readable and sufficiently academic to be respectable. Kissinger did not take long to master the house style. What had begun as a hasty memorandum for Schlesinger[19] had by now evolved into a bold and stylish critique of American strategic thinking—though it was still no more than a first installment of the magnum opus that was to follow two years later.

"It is surprising," Kissinger began coolly, "how little affected American strategic thinking has been by the fact that within just a few years the U.S.S.R. will have the capacity to deliver a powerful attack with nuclear weapons on the United States." Leaving aside the notion of some kind of preventive first strike ("a program so contrary to the sense of the country and the constitutional limits within which American foreign policy must be conducted"),[20] the Eisenhower administration had nothing more plausible to offer than John Foster Dulles's grim threat of "massive retaliation," which meant "major reliance . . . on the development of our Strategic Air Force and on increasing the power of our nuclear arsenal." This was the theory behind the so-called "New Look." In practice, however, the administration wished to avoid being drawn into attritional wars in what Finletter (in his book *Power and Policy*) had called the world's "gray areas," meaning non-NATO territories on the Eurasian periphery.[21]

Kissinger's response was in five parts. First, the rapid growth of the Soviet Union's nuclear capability was increasing by leaps and bounds the potential costs to the United States of a general war. Second, a limited war of the sort that had been fought in Korea, while hardly pleasant, might be "a better model for our future strategy than an all-out atomic conflict," which the United States was less and less likely to risk—save in the case of a direct attack on U.S. territory—as Soviet nuclear capability grew.[22] Third, the Soviets had no interest in a general war either; they could achieve "their ultimate goal, the neutralization of the United States, at much less risk by gradually eroding the peripheral areas, which will imperceptibly shift the balance of power against us without ever presenting us with a clear-cut challenge."[23]

> If we refused to fight in Indo-China when the Soviet nuclear capability was relatively small because of the danger that a limited war might become general, we shall hardly be readier to risk nuclear bombing for the sake of Burma or Iran or even Jugoslavia.[24]

Fourth, relying exclusively on the threat of massive retaliation was bound to undermine the system of American alliances, as "either our Allies will feel that any military effort on their part is unnecessary, or they may be led to the conviction that peace is preferable to war almost at any price."[25] Finally, there was the paradoxical risk that the deterrent would not deter.

[I]f the other side becomes convinced that . . . our threats of instant retaliation are bluff . . . [it] may then decide, as its nuclear arsenal grows, to absorb the "grey areas" and confront us with the choice between relinquishing them or risking the destruction of American cities. And because the Sino-Soviet leaders may well be mistaken in their assessment of our reaction when faced with such an alternative, our present military policy may bring about the total war which it seeks to prevent.[26]

As Kissinger saw it, then, the Eisenhower administration was running a small risk of Armageddon but a big risk of isolation. Here he took the opportunity to offer the readers of *Foreign Affairs* a new version of his favorite historical analogy:

[I]n relation to Eurasia the United States is an island Power with inferior resources at present only in manpower, but later on even in industrial capacity. Thus we are confronted by the traditional problem of an "island" Power—of Carthage with respect to Italy, of Britain with respect to the Continent—that its survival depends on preventing the opposite land-mass from falling under the control of a single Power, above all one avowedly hostile. If Eurasia were to fall under the control of a single Power or group of Powers, and if this hostile Power were given sufficient time to exploit its resources, we should confront an overpowering threat. At best we would be forced into a military effort not consistent with what is now considered the "American way of life." If the United States ever became confined to "Fortress America," or even if Soviet expansion in the "grey areas" went far enough to sap our allies' will to resist, Americans would be confronted by three-quarters of the human race and not much less of its resources[,] and their continued existence would be precarious.[27]

What, then, was the alternative? The answer was twofold. First, the United States should be ready to fight and win decisively the next Korean-style limited war. Korea itself had been winnable, after all: "Had we committed even four more divisions, indeed even if we had put a time limit on the truce negotiations, we might have achieved a substantial military victory [in Korea]."[28] Moreover, Korea had been "an advantageous location for the Chinese," which was not true of Southeast Asia. "In Indo-China," Kissinger reasoned, "an all-out American effort may still save at least Laos and Cambodia."[29] The crucial thing was to have "indigenous governments of sufficient stability so that the Soviets can take over only by open aggression, and indigenous military forces capable of fighting a delaying action." If these conditions could be met, the United States need only maintain a "strategic reserve (say in the Philippines, Malaya or Pakistan) capable of redressing the balance and . . . a weapons system capable of translating our technological advantage into local superiority." One clear benefit of being able to fight such local wars was that it would put the Sino-Soviet bloc under pressure. Even at this early stage of the Cold War, there were American strategists hoping that traditional antagonism between the Chinese and the Russians would cause their alliance to break down of its own accord; in a prescient aside Kissinger argued that such a rift would "not come by itself.

> Too much is to be gained by unity, too many prizes are still to be won, the memory of Tito is still too fresh in the Kremlin, for us to be able to count on Soviet mistakes. A split between the U.S.S.R. and its satellites, and even more a split with China, can come about only through outside pressure, through the creation of contingencies which may force a divergence of views into the open.[30]

Here was another lesson of the Korean War: "Had we defeated the Chinese army in Korea in 1951 we would have confronted the U.S.S.R. with the dilemma whether to risk everything for the sake of increasing the power of China; and had we followed our victory with a conciliatory political proposal to Peking we could have caused it to reflect whether American goodwill might not represent a better protection than blindly following the Soviet line." Moreover, "the Indo-Chinese problem would hardly have assumed its present dimensions had China suffered a decisive reversal in her first military encounter with the

United States."[31] A final lesson of Korea was not to be too hidebound by allies: "In local wars we do not need them and should not insist on their assistance if they have no direct interest at stake."[32]

This was bold and original in itself; apart from anything else, it illustrates just how early in his career Kissinger began to reflect on how the Sino-Soviet alliance might be broken, as well as on what to do about a post-French Indochina. But it was Kissinger's second point that was calculated to cause a stir. It was one thing to advocate some third middle option between nuclear apocalypse and surrender. By itself, recommending "an improvement in our capacity for local war" was not especially controversial; Sir Basil Liddell Hart, among others, had been making such arguments since 1946 on the basis that "an unlimited war waged with atomic power . . . would be mutually suicidal."[33] Robert E. Osgood was already hard at work on a book with the title *Limited War*.[34] But Kissinger was arguing that the capacity in question should include "tactical nuclear weapons." This was altogether stronger stuff. True, the idea that smaller atomic bombs could be used against purely military targets—that is, not major conurbations—had been publicly aired elsewhere.[35] Bernard Brodie had already published two (somewhat vague) articles on the subject.[36] As we shall see, it had also been debated within the Eisenhower administration, but thus far it had been rejected by the president. It was therefore somewhat startling to find the case for tactical nuclear weapons being made by a Harvard-trained student of diplomatic history in the pages of *Foreign Affairs*.

Almost as remarkable was the piece Kissinger published a month later in that bastion of American liberal thought, *The New Republic*. "The Limitations of Diplomacy" looked ahead with ambivalence toward the four-power summit that was to be held in Geneva in July 1955.* For a scholar who had dedicated so many years to the study of diplomatic

---

*This was the first such "summit" meeting of U.S. and Soviet leaders since Potsdam ten years before, at which the British prime minister, Clement Attlee, had also been present. At Geneva, Eisenhower, Premier Nikolai Bulganin, and Prime Minister Anthony Eden were to be joined by the French prime minister, Edgar Faure. Four-power meetings were already an anachronism. From 1959 onward, the key summits of the Cold War would be bilateral. In all there would be more than twenty "superpower" summits, involving only the U.S. and Soviet leaders.

history, Kissinger was brusquely dismissive of what was likely to be achieved. The "picture of an international conference reducing or even eliminating tensions behind closed doors" might be "alluring." But diplomacy in the world of 1955 was doubly circumscribed by the "inherent element of rigidity . . . in a two-power world" (even if the British and French leaders would also be present), and by the fact that a revolutionary power was on the other side of the conference table, challenging the very framework of the international system. "We should have no illusions that [negotiations with the Sino-Soviet bloc] will bring about a drastic amelioration of the situation directly," Kissinger concluded. The most that could be achieved was to "clarify conditions in their impact on our allies and the uncommitted in Asia," in that rejecting proposals for conferences might "delay our immediate aims to bring about mutual assistance arrangements" and refusing to negotiate altogether would ultimately "disintegrate our system of alliances."[37] This argument—that peace talks with the Soviets were little better than kabuki theater—was the obverse of Kissinger's assertion in *Foreign Affairs* that limited nuclear war had to be an option open to U.S. policy makers.

Kissinger's debut as a public intellectual was a success. He confessed to his younger colleague Samuel Huntington to being "a little frightened of the reaction."

> It [the piece in *Foreign Affairs*] has become required reading matter at the Air War College, at the Army War College, and the National War College; General [John H.] Michaelis has distributed it to the Major Press Association, and General [James M.] Gavin, the Deputy Chief of Staff, has made it required reading at the Pentagon. . . . I am too well aware of its genesis not to be a little concerned about how reputations are made in this country.[38]

Even more remarkably, some of his Harvard colleagues, Huntington among them, liked it, too.[39] More important, Bundy was impressed. The centerpiece of his popular lecture course "Government 180: The U.S. in World Affairs" was a condemnation of the policy of appeasement in the Munich crisis; prudent use of force, Bundy argued, would have been far more effective.[40] Kissinger's argument was therefore congenial to him. It also gave him an opportunity to help Kissinger out of career limbo. Before coming to Harvard, Bundy had worked briefly at the Council on Foreign Relations. When Kissinger—his confidence boosted by seeing his name in the pages of *Foreign Affairs*—expressed interest in a job at the council, Bundy gave him strong backing. Though the editor of *Foreign Affairs,* Hamilton Fish Armstrong,* decided against hiring Kissinger as his deputy, he was able to offer him the post of staff director of a study group working on the implications of nuclear weapons for U.S. foreign policy.[41]

II

When Henry Kissinger moved from Cambridge to New York, it was to grapple with a conundrum. Why had the United States secured so little benefit from its temporary nuclear monopoly under Truman? Between the destruction of Hiroshima and Nagasaki and the first Soviet atomic test in August 1949, there had been only one nuclear power. Until August 1953, the United States monopolized the hydrogen bomb and until 1955 was the only power with bombs in the megaton range. Even as the Soviets caught up in terms of technology, they still lagged behind in terms of quantity. In April 1947 as shrewd an observer as George Kennan could argue that "ten good hits with atomic bombs" would be enough to wipe out Soviet industry. "I think we and our friends have a preponderance of strength in the world right now," he concluded.[42] That preponderance turned out to count for little. Throughout this period the Soviets achieved a series of indisputable geopolitical victories, bringing nearly all of Eastern Europe under their control (with the notable exception of Yugoslavia), backing the Communist takeover of China, and fighting a protracted war by proxy against U.S. forces in Korea. Far from feeling confident, Washington

---

*Kissinger later said of Armstrong, "He thinks that God on the seventh day created *Foreign Affairs*."

grew increasingly fearful. As early as NSC-68, Nitze and others were imagining a Soviet stockpile of fission bombs so large that by 1955 Moscow might "be tempted to strike swiftly and with stealth."[43]

The arms race was not an inevitability. A plan for international control of atomic energy had been hatched by Robert Oppenheimer and David E. Lilienthal, but Bernard Baruch's version of it had been rejected by the Soviets.[44] By July 1949, Truman had given up on the idea. "We'll never obtain international control," he said. "Since we can't obtain international control we must be strongest in atomic weapons."[45] This view was essentially endorsed by the gloomy report of the panel chaired by Oppenheimer, which recommended withdrawing from the UN Disarmament Committee on the ground that its efforts were "futile."[46] With the benefit of hindsight, we can say that the Cold War evolved into a "self-regulating system . . . which nobody designed or even thought could last for very long, which was based not upon the dictates of morality and justice but rather upon an arbitrary and strikingly artificial division of the world into spheres of influence, and which incorporated within it some of the most bitter and persistent antagonisms short of war in modern history" but which nevertheless "survived twice as long as the far more carefully designed World War I settlement."[47] After the fact, we can speculate why that was: the inherent simplicity of a bipolar system; the essential separation of the superpowers from each other; the domestic constraints on both of them; the coexistence of "paranoia and prudence" that was at the heart of mutual deterrence; the modicum of transparency made possible by reconnaissance (not to mention rampant espionage); the rejection by each side of the goal of unconditional surrender by the other; and the evolution of a variety of conflict-minimizing "rules of the game." Because the world avoided nuclear Armageddon, historians are tempted to conclude that the "balance of terror" worked as a system of mutual deterrence.[48]

At the time, however, almost no one expected such a benign outcome, and most informed observers saw the superpower rivalry as highly unstable. Already during World War II, Eisenhower anticipated with dread a postwar world where "communism and anarchy [would] . . . spread rapidly, while crime and disorder, loss of personal liberties, and abject poverty [would] curse the areas that witness any amount of fight-ing.'[49] As president, he was very clear what the consequences of all-out war would be. "[L]et me tell you that if war comes, it will be horrible," he told the South Korean president Syngman Rhee in 1954. "Atomic war will destroy civilization. . . . There will be millions of people dead. . . . [T]he results are too horrible to contemplate. I can't even imagine them." A top-secret assessment a year and a half later persuaded him that in the wake of a full-blown war, "something on the order of 65 percent of the [U.S.] population would require some kind of medical care, and in most instances, no opportunity whatsoever to get it. . . . It would literally be a business of digging ourselves out of the ashes, start-ing again."[50]

Partly under Nitze's influence, Truman had ended up pursuing an "all of the above strategy," not only building up the nuclear stockpile but also investing heavily in conventional forces and even waging a war in Korea. Eisenhower regarded this approach as fundamentally unsus-tainable, not least because of the fiscal overstretch—a quadrupling of the defense budget—it necessarily implied. "Spiritual force, multiplied by economic force, multiplied by military force, is roughly equal to security," he wrote in his diary.[51] If the cost of the arms race eroded the American way of life and the country's economic health, it would be self-defeating. What was more, the Soviets understood this and were deliberately seeking "by their military threat . . . to force upon Amer-ica and the free world an unbearable security burden leading to eco-nomic disaster."[52] In any case, Eisenhower had seen total war at first hand. He was deeply skeptical about the idea that a limited war—conventional or nuclear—could be fought against the Soviets; any such conflict was bound to escalate.[53] This helps explain his consistent emphasis on a strategy of massive retaliation: not only did he want to deter the enemy, by persuading "*all* adversaries that *any* such conflict *might* escalate to a level at which *none* could hope to prevail"; he also wanted to deter his own advisers.[54] Superficially, as articulated in the adversarial style of John Foster Dulles, the New Look was indeed a crude combination of the threat of massive retaliation and "brinkman-ship." In reality, Eisenhower's strategy was subtle and nuanced. The seven pillars of Eisenhower's strategy—thrashed out at the meetings of a revamped National Security Council,* nearly all of which he chaired—were the imperative of preventing a nuclear holocaust; the feasibility of deterrence; the necessity of a secure "second strike" capability; the abandonment of forcible "rollback" of the Soviet empire as a U.S. goal; the recognition of the long-term character of the Cold War; the strengthening of U.S. alliances in Europe and Asia; and the pursuit of realistic forms of arms control.[55] Moreover, the means to those ends extended far beyond the Strategic Air Command, embracing diplomacy, psychological warfare, and covert operations.

All this represented a refinement of containment. At the same time, Eisenhower did his best to counter the post-Stalin Soviet "peace offensive." His "Chance for Peace" speech of April 16, 1953, sincerely lamented the expense of the arms race. ("The cost of one modern heavy bomber is this: a modern brick school in more than 30 cities.")[56] The British wanted to get in on the act; hence Churchill's plea for a four-power meeting.[57] But what exactly was peace to be based on? In his speech, Eisenhower blamed the Soviets squarely for "eight years of fear and force" and proposed "the initiation of political discussions leading to the holding of free elections in a united Korea" as well as "an end to the direct and indirect attacks upon the security of Indochina and Malaya." There was little chance of the Soviets agreeing to any of that. True, the new leadership in Moscow was willing to make concessions, relinquishing its territorial claims on Turkey, for example. But the pivotal question of the postwar era—the German Question—remained as far as ever from resolution. Neither the Americans nor the Russians could view German reunification with unalloyed enthusiasm; on the contrary, Washington was intently focused on integrating a rearmed West Germany into both NATO and a new European Defense Community.

In truth, the mood in Washington was far from dovish.[58] Secretary of State Dulles sounded much less emollient than the president in his speech to the Society of Newspaper Editors two days after Eisenhower's "Chance for Peace." When the president formed three task forces to consider his strategic options, the mildest scenario was essentially to

---

*A crucial role in this regard was played by General Andrew J. Goodpaster, Eisenhower's staff secretary.

maintain the status quo: the others were to complete a defense perimeter encircling the Sino-Soviet bloc or (most radical of all) to roll it back, reducing its territorial extent. The final report of "Project Solarium," which became NSC-162/2, enshrined the "capability to inflict massive retaliatory damage by offensive strategic striking power" as the keystone of Eisenhower's strategy, though other U.S. and allied forces would remain available to counter Soviet aggression in vital areas. The key question, as we have seen, was whether these other forces would include nuclear bombs.[59] What no one outside the highest levels of government could know was that Eisenhower had not wholly ruled out that they would. Indeed, one of his administration's earliest acts was secretly to deploy tactical nuclear weapons to Western Europe. At a meeting of the NSC on October 7, 1953, the final text of NSC-162/2 was agreed. It included the line: "In the event of hostilities, the United States will consider nuclear weapons to be as available for use as other munitions."[60] Six days later the president himself confirmed what this meant. In response to a question from Admiral Arthur Radford, the chairman of the Joint Chiefs of Staff (JCS), Eisenhower said that "we should use the bomb in Korea if the aggression is renewed" by the Chinese.[61] (The JCS took that to include targets in China, too.) That December, Eisenhower himself sought to persuade Anthony Eden that

> the American public no longer distinguished between atomic and other nuclear weapons . . . nor is there any logical distinction. . . . Why should they confine themselves to high explosives requiring thousands of aircraft in attacking China's bases when they can do it more cheaply and easily with atoms? The development of smaller atomic weapons and the use of atomic artillery makes [*sic*] the distinction impossible to sustain.[62]

Similar arguments were made by Vice President Nixon the following year: he was even prepared to use atomic weapons to shore up the French position in Indochina.[63] "The United States cannot afford to preclude itself from using nuclear weapons even in a local situation," Eisenhower stated in early 1955, "if such use will bring the aggression to a swift and positive cessation, and if, on a balance of political and military consideration, such use will best advance U.S. security interests."[64] Eisenhower continued to insist that any limited war would likely escalate into a full-scale nuclear conflict. ("[W]hen you resort to force as the arbiter of human difficulty, you don't know where you are going. . . . [I]f you get deeper and deeper, there is just no limit except what is imposed by the limitations of force itself.")[65] Yet he repeatedly told the U.S. military that "planning should go ahead on the basis of the use of tactical atomic weapons against military targets in any small war in which the United States might be involved."[66]

The puzzle about the Eisenhower administration—and it is a puzzle with which historians still grapple—is that its public statements were so often at odds with such private deliberations. In the same month that Eisenhower was selling atomic strikes on the Chinese to Eden, he was telling the UN General Assembly—and the world*—that the United States and other nuclear-armed governments should "begin now and continue to make joint contributions from their stockpiles of normal uranium and fissionable materials to an International Atomic Energy Agency" under the UN's aegis.[67] "Atoms for Peace"—as Eisenhower's speech came to be known[68]—was not quite the oxymoron it seemed. The United States followed through on the president's pledge to make fissile material available for the construction of nuclear reactors abroad. But the speech coincided with the adoption of a three-year defense program that not only increased the SAC's budget but also invested in a variety of defense systems, including Arctic radar early warning networks, designed to detect and intercept a Soviet nuclear attack, and the Lockheed U-2 spy plane, capable of flying at altitudes of seventy thousand feet.[69] A month later Dulles gave a speech at the Council on Foreign Relations that appalled even Nitze in its stark formulation of the doctrine of massive retaliation.[70] When the Soviets retorted to "Atoms for Peace" with a call for "the unconditional banning of atomic and hydrogen weapons," the administration was caught off guard.[71] No sooner had Dulles been persuaded of the advantages to the United States

---

*The "Atoms for Peace" speech was among the most publicized in history. There was saturation coverage in U.S. newspapers, radio, television, and newsreel. Voice of America carried the speech live in over thirty languages. There was even a commemorative stamp.

of a ban on nuclear tests—an idea that also appealed to Eisenhower—than he changed his mind.[72]

The real problem was that by 1955 strategy was the product of a process that was not just bureaucratically complex but also intellectually congested. Once nuclear weapons had been the province of the physicists who devised them. They still played a significant role: witness the influence of the Technological Capabilities Panel, chaired by James Killian, the president of MIT, later Eisenhower's first special assistant for science.[73] But the scientists were increasingly divided. A victim of McCarthy's witch hunt, Oppenheimer was being stripped of his high-level government clearance as a result of allegations that he was "an agent of the Soviet Union."[74] At the other extreme, the physicist Edward Teller dismissed all talk of arms reductions or test bans as wrongheaded and weak-kneed. Meanwhile, the soldiers, sailors, and airmen had acquired views of their own; not surprisingly, the army and navy resented the substantial shift in resources to the air force, and particularly the Strategic Air Command, implicit in massive retaliation. For professional politicians like Harold Stassen the terrain was increasingly treacherous: his role as Eisenhower's special assistant for disarmament ("Secretary for Peace") posed too obvious a challenge to Dulles.[75] Disarmament was hard to oppose in public, but there was no expert consensus as to how the arms race might be stopped. By the spring of 1955, as the president uneasily prepared for the Geneva summit, a deadlock had developed. At the United Nations, the Soviets were making ever more reasonable-sounding proposals for disarmament. Was there any U.S. response that was, at one and the same time, scientifically possible, militarily feasible, and politically viable? This was an opportunity for a fourth group of professional experts to insert themselves into the policy-making process. The birth of strategic studies as a distinct academic field would surely have been delayed had the scientists, soldiers, and statesmen of the Eisenhower administration been able to agree.

III

The battles over nuclear strategy that went on in Washington were not easily followed from Harvard. The speeches one could read, of course; but the deliberations of the NSC were almost entirely unknown to the public, professors included. The era of leaks and "freedom of information" was still a decade away. The best Kissinger could do was to invite key players in the drama to address his and Elliott's International Seminar. The vice president declined to be the opening speaker in July 1955, the first of many nonmeetings between Nixon and Kissinger,[76] but Stassen came. Kissinger thought his speech "a great success, the air-conditioning at the Hotel Continental excepted."[77] Bundy found Stassen "a most puzzling and interesting man."[78] The Harvard men could hardly have been more out of the loop.

It was Bundy who gave Kissinger his break. Not only did the job at the Council on Foreign Relations extricate him from Harvard, it also plunged him into a world he had hitherto been confined to reading about in the newspapers. Originally established in 1918 as a businessmen's club, the CFR had been reconstituted by former members of Woodrow Wilson's postwar planning "Inquiry" in 1921 and was essentially an American answer to the Royal Institute of International Affairs housed in London at (and often known as) Chatham House.[79] The council's War and Peace Studies made an important contribution to American thinking about the new international order. Its members were all male, often Ivy League, and—when they were not directly involved in making U.S. foreign policy in Washington or abroad*—felt themselves very much at home in their elegant clubhouse on Park Avenue and 68th Street.[80] The CFR was influential—though not as all-powerful, and certainly not as sinister, as has sometimes been claimed.[81]

---

*A survey of 502 government officials who held high positions from 1945 to 1972 found that more than half of them were members of the Council on Foreign Relations. At any given time in the period, the proportion of the membership accounted for by government employees was close to a fifth. As a New York–based entity, the CFR's members were mostly in finance, the media, or academia.

The members of the nuclear weapons study group who met there on May 5, 1955, were nearly all "insiders" with considerable firsthand experience of either government or the military. In the chair was Gordon Dean, the former head of the Atomic Energy Commission. Having served as director of Policy Planning, Paul Nitze was now based at the Johns Hopkins School of Advanced International Studies (SAIS), which he had cofounded in Washington, awaiting the return of a Democrat to the White House. Frank Pace had served Truman as secretary of the army, while Frank C. Nash had been assistant secretary of defense for international security affairs in the same administration. In addition, there were three distinguished military men. General James M. Gavin had led the 82nd Airborne Division in Operation Market Garden. As army chief of research and development, he was a pioneer of the idea of transporting armor and artillery as well as troops by air, a concept that (as we shall see) he successfully sold to Kissinger.* During the war, General Richard C. Lindsay had been chief of the Combined Joint Staff Division of the Army Air Forces Headquarters; he would later serve as commander of NATO air forces in southern Europe. Colonel William Kintner had already published a book on psychological warfare; in 1953 he had published *Atomic Weapons in Land Combat.* Finally, the academics included Caryl P. Haskins, the biologist and founder of Haskins Laboratories, and Shields Warren, an authority on the physiological effects of radiation. Though not a scientist, Carroll L. Wilson had been the first general manager of the Atomic Energy Commission. On the international relations side were the Sterling Professor of International Relations at Yale, Arnold Wolfers, and Don K. Price, later the founding dean of Harvard's Kennedy School.†

---

*Gavin—whose fondness of parachute jumps had earned him the soubriquet "Jumpin' Jim"—would resign from the army in 1958 in the belief that the United States was lagging behind in the arms race.
†Also present that day were Frank Altschul of the General American Investors Company, Hanson W. Baldwin of *The New York Times,* Ben T. Moore, Charles P. Noyes II, and Henry L. Roberts. The remaining members of the study group, who were absent, were Hamilton Fish Armstrong, editor of *Foreign Affairs;* William A. M. Burden, president of the Museum of Modern Art; Thomas K. Finletter, the former air force secretary; the lawyer Roswell Gilpatric, who had been undersecretary of the air force under Truman; Joseph E. Johnson, president of the Carnegie Endowment for

What exactly would Kissinger's role be? As George S. Franklin, the executive director of the CFR, explained to Oppenheimer, whom he asked to brief the new hire, it was "to spend 15 months thinking through some of the problems raised in the group" and then to "write a book which I hope will be an interesting and important contribution." He and his colleagues knew full well that they were inviting an amateur. "Mr. Kissinger has not had as much experience in this field as certain people we might have gotten," conceded Franklin, "but after meeting him I believe you will feel that his ability and objectivity more than make up for this."[82] Kissinger himself was not slow to acknowledge his lack of expertise. "Although I am usually distrustful of people who, after taking a job, announce their humility before it," he confessed to Oppenheimer, "I find myself somewhat overawed by the enormity of the subject."[83] With just a hint of irony, Bundy offered a consoling reflection. "The subject is one which steadily reminds any student that he is a mortal, and its heights compel respect. So this is a field in which very important things can be done without the presumption that every-thing has been attended to. There is a good case to be made for believ-ing in all assignments with such built-in inducements to humility."[84] It is doubtful, however, that humility was Henry Kissinger's predominant emotion after his first encounter with the CFR study group. Rarely can a gathering of luminaries have amounted to so much less than the sum of its parts.

It was already the group's sixth meeting; it therefore took chutzpah to offer, as Kissinger did, an opening summary of the "the trend of the meetings" so far, based on his reading of minutes and conversations with participants. He offered three observations and a question. First, the U.S. armed services were becoming increasingly dependent upon nuclear weapons. Second, the use of tactical atomic weapons in a lim-ited war was coming to be seen as impossible because of the difficulty of drawing a clean line between tactical and strategic uses and the

---

International Peace; the physicist Isidor Isaac Rabi, who had succeeded Oppenheimer as chairman of the Atomic Energy Commission; Walter Bedell Smith, who had been Eisenhower's chief of staff, then director of central intelligence and undersecretary of state; and Henry DeWolf Smyth, who had been a member of the AEC but had resigned after Oppenheimer lost his security clearance.

likelihood that a losing belligerent would not go down without unleashing all his destructive capabilities. Third, there was "a very real danger that Soviet fear of the American nuclear potential [might] lead the Kremlin to try to strike the first blow." Finally, Kissinger asked how the U.S. government should "order the political scheme before commencing any necessary limited military operation so as to make it evident that this country's goals are limited."[85] What followed was as near to a free-for-all as the Council on Foreign Relations can ever have witnessed.

Nitze was dismissive of most of Kissinger's observations. He "did not agree that the consensus of the group is that the armed services are becoming unable to fight a conventional war." He was also skeptical (as were others) about the idea that rules of limited war could be agreed to in advance with an opponent as untrustworthy as the USSR. Arnold Wolfers then sketched a scenario in which a limited war in Europe nevertheless rapidly escalated to the point when strategic weapons ended up being used. Hanson Baldwin of *The New York Times* agreed that limited war would be exceedingly difficult to keep limited in Europe because of the continent's high population density.

The military men took different views. General Lindsay argued that the war of the future would likely be prolonged and would involve the use of "all sorts of devices for either offensive or defensive purposes." General Gavin went further:

> In his opinion, the United States could whip the Soviet Union without using any atomic devices, by virtue of its superior fire power. Therefore, he concluded that as long as the US is willing to expend its conventional forces, it might be in its own interests not to introduce the atom as a weapon. . . . [Gavin] suggested an analogy to the role of police within a community. The patrolman may have a tommy gun back at the station house as his ultimate weapon, but he uses his night stick to subdue the criminal without punching holes in the general populace. By the same token, the United States has got to demonstrate that it has the power and the discretion to win local scraps without destroying European civilization.

The same argument applied in the less populous Middle East, Gavin argued. But General Lindsay "disagreed that the job could be done conventionally." Moreover, he argued, there would be a better chance of limiting an atomic war in the Middle East than in Europe. Gavin conceded that the army had "a comprehensive atomic arsenal which it would like to be free to use so long as such an action did not trigger a nuclear war" and that "local forces would be considerably stiffened through the use of small yield atomic weapons . . . against military targets." However, he did not feel that the United States should publicize its intentions of defending allied areas with atomic weapons.

At least two of the "lay" members of the study group saw such tactical nuclear weapons as indispensable, at least for the defense of the Middle East against Soviet aggression. One (Charles Noyes) "noted that if the United States decides that it cannot use tactical A-bombs against open aggression moving into Iran through a sparsely settled area, against Caucasians, and in the interests and perhaps at the request of the natives—thus eliminating many of the political objections to using atomic devices—it would never be able to use them." The conclusion of the discussion was sobering. Nitze observed that "in the final analysis the political leaders must ask the military what would happen if the United States is forced to attack the Soviet Union, and if the answer is that the U.S. as we know it would be destroyed, then the politicians must be prepared to accept the humiliation of retreat." This surely was a counsel of defeat. If, at the beginning of this discussion, Kissinger had been open to Nitze's view of the matter ("that once a war becomes nuclear it is much harder to set any effective limits"), by the end he was listening closely to the military men. There had to be some alternative to massive retaliation—especially if in practice it was an empty threat behind which lurked the prospect of massive humiliation.

Kissinger's presence at such discussions, as he drily put it in a letter to Arthur Schlesinger, was "a process that can only be called research by osmosis. It seems to be the belief of the Council that the proximity to great men, or at least to great names, by itself produces superior efforts."[86] As if to put this proposition to a further test, Kissinger was about to come into still closer proximity to a man widely regarded as bearing one of the greatest names in all America: Rockefeller.

IV

It would be difficult to imagine two men with more different backgrounds than Henry Kissinger and Nelson Rockefeller. Kissinger, a teenage refugee whose first job in America was in a Chelsea sweatshop, had slogged his way to Park Avenue by way of a U.S. Army boot camp and a GI Bill scholarship. Aside from brains, guts, and loving parents, he had been born with nothing. By comparison, Nelson Rockefeller had inherited the earth. The grandson of the oil tycoon John D. Rockefeller (and on his mother's side, of Senator Nelson Aldrich, one of the architects of the Federal Reserve System), he grew up amid power and privilege. After Phillips Exeter Academy and Dartmouth, he was immediately handed a job in the family business empire, working for the Chase National Bank; Rockefeller Center, Inc.; and Creole Petroleum, the Venezuelan subsidiary of Standard Oil. In fact, Rockefeller's vocation was politics, followed by philanthropy; business came a distant third. But that did not matter. As a Rockefeller, he was welcome in Washington, too. Roosevelt made him coordinator of inter-American affairs and then assistant secretary of state for American republic affairs (the beginning of a lifelong interest in Latin America). Truman named him chairman of the International Development Advisory Board. And then Eisenhower gave him the job of chairing his Advisory Committee on Government Organization. When that committee proposed the creation of a new Department of Health, Education, and Welfare, Rockefeller briefly became its undersecretary. In 1954, however, Eisenhower persuaded Rockefeller to come to the White House to be a special presidential assistant, entrusted with building "increased understanding and co-operation among all peoples," as well as his representative on the Operations Coordinating Board (which had replaced the Psychological Strategy Board in 1953).[87] Whereas his predecessor, C. D. Jackson, had been Eisenhower's adviser on psychological warfare, Rockefeller's mandate was broader. In effect, he was supposed to be the answer to the problem posed by the Soviet "peace offensive." As such, he immediately found himself at loggerheads with some of the biggest beasts in the administration, in particular Secretary of State Dulles, who viewed the interloping plutocrat with understandable suspicion.

Privileged as he was, Rockefeller knew his limitations. His mother had encouraged him to seek out his intellectual "superiors" for counsel; this suited a man who maintained that the best way to read a book was to meet its author. In order to make the maximum impact in his new role, Rockefeller summoned an unusual mixture of thinkers to the Marine Corps Officer Candidates School at Quantico, Virginia: economists and sociologists as well as defense specialists and intelligence operatives. After five days of deliberation, the group came up with, among other things, the idea of "Open Skies," the proposal for reciprocal aerial surveillance of military installations, which—despite Dulles's disapproval and his own reservations—Eisenhower put forward at the Geneva summit, the effect heightened by a well-timed thunderstorm.[88] (A characteristic feature of Rockefeller's approach was the connection from Quantico to the private sector. Among those present was ex-CIA agent Frank Lindsay, who would later become chief executive of Itek, the Rockefeller-backed company that would manufacture the cameras for U.S. spy satellites.)[89]

"Open Skies" was expected to be a trump card. World opinion would welcome American transparency and would condemn the Soviets when they turned the idea down, as they were certain to do. The feeling that the Soviets had nevertheless won the psychological battle at Geneva, significantly improving their image in the eyes of Western voters, prompted a new initiative: a study panel on "Psychological Aspects of a Future U.S. Strategy."[90] It was this second group—sometimes misleadingly called Quantico II—that Henry Kissinger was invited to join. His Harvard mentor Bill Elliott later claimed the credit for having "put the idea in his mind and given Nelson the tip to use Henry Kissinger."[91] But his name was in fact first suggested by William Kintner, who had gotten to know Kissinger four years earlier.[92] From inside the Pentagon, Fritz Kraemer may also have recommended him.[93]

Though the intended recipient of its report was clearly the president and other officials, the panel itself was funded by the Rockefeller Brothers Fund, which Nelson Rockefeller and his three siblings had established in 1940. Like the CFR study group, then, this was an unofficial entity, but once again it brought Kissinger into direct contact with some eminent policy insiders, this time in Washington itself.[94] Its chairman was retired air force general Frederick Anderson, a veteran of the wartime bombing of Germany; the other members included C. D. Jackson, Rockefeller's "psy-war" predecessor, who in 1955 had returned to TimeLife, and Colonel George A. Lincoln, who had prepared Roosevelt and Marshall for the Yalta Conference and was now head of West Point's Department of Social Sciences. Through his work with the Operations Research Office, Kissinger already knew Ellis A. Johnson, Paul Linebarger, and George Pettee; he had certainly encountered the economists Max F. Millikan and Walt Rostow at MIT and the Sovietologist Philip E. Mosely at CFR; but this was probably his first encounter with the Austrian-born strategic thinker Stefan Possony.* When the panel first met in Washington in late August 1955, they were addressed by the chairman of Joint Chiefs of Staff and the deputy director of the CIA.[95] Though not strictly speaking government work, Kissinger's role on Rockefeller's panel was another step closer to the corridors of power.

Kissinger's first impression of Rockefeller was unfavorable. He "entered the room slapping the backs of the assembled academics, grinning and calling each by the closest approximation of his first name that he could remember" (or "fellah" if no name came to mind).[96] Moreover, the work he was being asked to do was in many ways less challenging than the work for the council on nuclear weapons. As we have seen, Kissinger had already been a student of psychological warfare for the better part of a decade. As he told Rostow after the first meeting of the Rockefeller panel, he had been "insisting for the past several years that the most important component of our foreign policy is the psychological one."[97] Inevitably, the subject of nuclear weapons was central to the panel's deliberations. It doubtless contributed to Kissinger's evolving view of the subject that one of the military presentations they heard explicitly acknowledged that "nuclear weapons will be used in situa-

---

*Johnson was a physicist by training; Linebarger an Asia specialist who (as "Cordwainer Smith") wrote science fiction on the side; Possony would go on to devise the Strategic Defense Initiative for Ronald Reagan; Millikan and Rostow (who was not formally a member of the panel but seems to have been involved anyway) became ardent proponents of economic aid as a Cold War lever.

tions other than all-out war. . . . Agreement was expressed that it might make the world happier if tactical A-weapons were used in a small war that didn't expand into a large war."[98] But the two papers Kissinger was assigned to write dealt with other, more familiar matters: "The Problem of German Unity" and "Psychological and Pressure Aspects of Negotiations with the USSR."

The German Question was the central problem of the Cold War, with Berlin as its fulcrum. The division of Germany was a substitute for a peace treaty at the end of World War II—a de facto partition that reflected and then perpetuated the military realities at the moment of the Third Reich's collapse. In practice, the arrangement suited both the United States and the Soviet Union quite well, but it was unpopular with most Germans, especially with Social Democratic voters in the Federal Republic. Soviet propaganda had targeted the integration of West Germany into NATO as evidence that the American imperialists and the crypto-Nazi warmongers were in cahoots; Moscow could risk proposing German reunification and neutralization in the knowledge that its puppets in East Berlin would do as they were told. What made matters worse, from an American perspective, was the fundamentally indefensible nature of West Berlin, a western enclave entirely surrounded by East German territory and Soviet troops.[99] Yet politically West Berlin was a threat to the legitimacy of the Soviet puppet regime, an advertisement for freedom more potent than any CIA-funded exhibit. By itself, the division of Germany might have proved stable; the division of Berlin clearly was not. It had been the 1953 workers' revolt in East Berlin that had given Nikita Khrushchev—the rising power broker on the Soviet Communist Party Central Committee—his opportunity to overthrow Beria, who had earlier argued for a reunited but neutral Germany. The next Berlin crisis might have international as well as domestic political ramifications.

In Kissinger's analysis, the United States had to regain the initiative before too many West Germans saw "a direct deal with the USSR" as an attractive alternative to "a [U.S.-USSR] detente bought at the expense of Germany's primary goal: reunification"—a phantom that would haunt him for many years to come, as we shall see. Washington should therefore propose reunification on the basis of "all-German elections and . . . some kind of security arrangement based on bilateral force reduction." If (as they were bound to) the Soviets rejected this, then the United States should counter with a proposal for "economic unity, beginning with an Economic Parliament for all of Germany" to be located in a neutralized Berlin. If that too were rejected, the third option should be to propose free movement between West and East Germany. The point of these proposals was not, of course, that Moscow was likely to accept any of them; it was that Soviet rejection would bolster the standing of the United States in Germany and thereby strengthen the domestic position of Chancellor Konrad Adenauer.[100] This was diplomacy as psychological warfare, in marked contrast to George Kennan's 1957 proposal for reunification on the basis of demilitarization (see next chapter), which he fondly imagined might be acceptable in Moscow.

Kissinger's second paper was much broader in scope and began with a characteristically bold comparison between the world of 1955 and the world, so dear to his heart, of 1815. "Confronted by a power which for over a generation has claimed for its nation both exclusiveness and universality of social justice; which has based its domestic control apparatus on the myth of a permanently hostile outside world; and which is building a nuclear capacity to inflict catastrophic blows on [us]," the United States simply could not rely on traditional diplomacy. The issue was "no longer the adjustment of local disputes between protagonists agreed on a basic framework, but the basic framework itself." For Kissinger, the "predominant aspect" of what he called the "new diplomacy" was its "psychological dimension." It was just conceivable that the Soviet "peace offensive" was sincere; but it was more likely that Moscow was "simply playing for time" until its nuclear capacity was "more nearly commensurable with that of the U.S. and until the constellation of forces in the non-Communist world" improved. In that case, "a too rapid surrender to Soviet blandishments" would be disastrous. The problem was that the Soviet tactic of "talking about peace, in general," while focusing on the specific issue of West German rearmament, had effectively gained the moral high ground by representing the United States as the aggressive superpower. The solution was for the president to propose that "the Soviet leaders associate themselves with him in a declaration that the Big Four oppose the settlement of disputes by force" and come to "a conference to discuss concrete measures to lift the Iron Curtain, perhaps beginning with a proposal for free travel within Germany." The key was to learn from the example of Yugoslav leader Josip Tito, who had "replied to every Soviet blandishment with a demand for deeds and not words, until Khrushchev appeared in Belgrade." But Kissinger could not resist ending with a reflection on the implications of his recommended diplomatic strategy for the nuclear arms race:

> It may be argued that a continued high level of defense expenditure coupled with a refusal to negotiate unless the USSR makes concessions may lure the Soviets into an anticipatory strike. But it is more than doubtful that the USSR will launch a "preventive war" unless it considers its chances better than even, a situation which our force levels should always be adequate to prevent. . . .
>
> The real significance of thermonuclear weapons may well be that they place a premium on a strategy which shifts the risk of their use to the other side. . . . If we stake everything on an all-or-nothing military policy one of two consequences becomes inevitable: either our allies will feel that peace is preferable to war almost at any price; or they reduce their military expenditures on the assumption that events cannot be affected by their action.[101]

Kissinger's contributions were just two of twenty papers that Rockefeller presented to Eisenhower in November 1955 under the heading "Psychological Aspects of United States Strategy," the bottom line of which was that defense expenditure must go up. For Kissinger, it had been—or so he told Rockefeller—"one of the most satisfying, if exhausting, experiences that I have had over the last few years."[102] It had been moderately lucrative, too: his fee as a consultant was $1,530 (around $60,000 in 2013 dollars).[103] Yet it cannot be said that the panel's "hectic" efforts had much impact. The position of special assistant lacked an institutional power base. Rockefeller had already run into resistance from the State Department and Treasury. Following the creation of a new Planning Coordination Group under Rockefeller's chairmanship, Allen Dulles joined his brother in what amounted to a campaign of passive resistance. It worked. Eisenhower, recovering from a stroke, made it clear that he would not adopt the Quantico II recommendations. In December, Kissinger was "saddened" to hear that Rockefeller had resigned.[104] Privately, he was frustrated that his efforts had come to nothing. "Stassen gave a talk the other day in which he listed as Republican accomplishments the Indo-China truce, the Korean armistice and the fact that for the first time since 1912 the world has known a year without war," he grumbled to Arthur Schlesinger.

> It seems to me that this kind of talk can seem plausible only in an environment where all standards of rational discussion have disintegrated. I think that what is required is a speech which, area by area, explains how we have failed and how our policy could be improved. Also, quite frankly, I have an aversion to such phrases as that "we are working toward peace" because it gives the impression that on some magical day, peace will suddenly break out.[105]

Conservative he may have been, but at this juncture in his career Kissinger was in revolt against Republican foreign policy: "the insincerity of the security program, the incommensurability between the campaign promises in foreign affairs and reality." Eisenhower had been put on a pedestal by "the advertising agencies," he complained to Schlesinger, but an effective critique could expose the president as "sanctimonious and pretentious."[106]

Yet Kissinger was still trying to work out a coherent alternative to Eisenhower's policy. His draft memorandum "Soviet Strategy— Possible U.S. Countermeasures" began with a restatement of Kennan's old containment thesis and reiterated arguments Kissinger had been making for some time. Containment under Truman had drawn the United States into "peripheral actions" in Asia and elsewhere that allowed the Soviet leaders to exploit their advantages. The Eisenhower alternative—an excessive reliance on the threat of all-out war—only increased the danger of "the world sliding into war." "A line should be clearly defined," Kissinger argued, "any transgression of which would involve a major war, though not necessarily at the point of aggression." He once again sketched his plan for a "highly mobile U.S. strategic reserve, within striking distance of Soviet vital centers, in areas where the terrain maximizes U.S. technological superiority"—in particular the Middle East. Perhaps, he mused, the British and (bizarrely) the South Africans could contribute troops to this force, which could be based in Jordan or Cyrenea (Libya). To free up resources for this initiative, Japan could be rearmed.[107]

This was still work in progress.

V

Psychological warfare against a foreign foe is not easily waged during an election year. Repeatedly in 1956 Kissinger was dismayed by the things politicians would say in their quest for votes. "I thought [John Foster] Dulles' performance in *Life** quite appalling," he complained to Schlesinger,

> but I also feel that [Adlai] Stevenson [the Democratic challenger] and [Hubert] Humphrey [who sought the vice presidential nomination] hardly distinguished themselves. It is one thing to say that Quemoy and Matsu [islands controlled by Taiwan, which had been shelled by the People's Republic of China in 1954] are not worth a nuclear war; it is quite another to assert that we can never threaten war at all. The slogan "there is no alternative to peace" [used by Eisenhower at the time of Geneva] amounts to giving the Soviets a blank check, at least for this election year.[108]

---

*This was the interview in which Dulles described "the ability to get to the verge without getting into the war" as "the necessary art": "If you cannot master it, you inevitably get into a war. If you try to run away from it, if you are scared to go to the brink, you are lost." Henceforth his name would always be associated with "brinkmanship."

Kissinger's response was two articles in *Foreign Affairs* in the space of six months: "Force and Diplomacy in the Nuclear Age" and "Reflections on American Diplomacy." The first opened with a blunt attack on the rhetoric of the campaign: phrases like "massive retaliation" and "there is no alternative to peace" were dangerous, the former because it posed "risks for us out of proportion to the objectives to be achieved," the latter because it removed "a powerful brake on Soviet probing actions and any incentive for the Soviet Union to make concessions."[109] Now, however, Kissinger went on to outline his rapidly crystallizing view on the viability of limited nuclear war. For the first time, he was explicit: "[N]uclear weapons, particularly of the low-yield type, seem to offer the best opportunity to compensate for our inferiority in manpower and to use our superiority in technology to best advantage."[110] The Soviets were furiously trying to delegitimize this claim by insisting that limited nuclear war was an impossibility and pressing for comprehensive disarmament ("Ban the Bomb"). But this was merely a ploy to prevent the United States from seizing the opportunity presented by tactical nuclear weapons. Whereas the Soviets were configured for a prolonged war of attrition with high concentrations of troops, "on a nuclear battlefield, dispersion [would be] the key to survival and mobility the prerequisite of success"—to say nothing of "leadership of a high order, personal initiative and mechanical aptitude, all qualities in which our military organization probably excels that of the U.S.S.R."[111]

The key to preventing a limited nuclear war from escalating was for "our diplomacy to convey to the Soviet bloc that we are capable of courses other than all-out war or inaction, and that we intend to use this capability," though not in pursuit of unconditional surrender.[112] That message had to be conveyed not just to the Soviets but also to American allies, as well as to the nonaligned countries. The former had to be reassured that war did not mean "inevitabl[e] . . . national catastrophe"; the latter had to be "show[n] the flag . . . to impress [them] with our capacity for action." Kissinger concluded with a restatement of his case for:

> a weapons system that can deal with the tensions most likely to
> arise in the uncommitted areas—tensions which do not lend
> themselves to the massive employment of thermonuclear

weapons: civil war, peripheral attacks or a war among the uncommitted. To be sure, this is an ungrateful and indeed an unpopular course. But we will not be able to avoid unpopularity. In the short run, all we can hope for is respect.[113]

At a time when Eisenhower was restating the case for massive retaliation as "the key to survival," Kissinger offered an alternative.[114]

"Reflections on American Diplomacy" was even more self-confident in its tone. U.S. foreign policy, Kissinger stated bluntly, had reached "an impasse because of our penchant for happy endings." Not only were Americans too eager to fall for Soviet peace propaganda. They had a "penchant for ad hoc solutions," based on a naïve belief that foreign policy could be conducted as a science, when it was in fact "the art of weighing probabilities . . . [of] grasping the nuances of possibilities."[115] Moreover, despite Eisenhower's remodeling of the NSC, U.S. policy making was bedeviled by bureaucracy: multiple committees, subordinate officials overwhelming their superiors with piles of trivia, feuding departments negotiating policy, decisions so hard to reach that they become impossible to reappraise. Worse still, Americans were too optimistic; they lacked "tragic experience."

> [T]o many of our most responsible men, particularly in the
> business community, the warnings of impending peril or of
> imminent disaster sound like the Cassandra cries of abstracted
> "egg-heads." . . . [Defense Secretary Charles Wilson and Trea-
> sury Secretary George Humphrey] simply cannot believe that
> in the nuclear age the penalty for miscalculation may be
> national catastrophe. They may know in their heads, but they
> cannot accept in their hearts, that the society they helped to
> build could disappear as did Rome or Carthage or Byzantium,
> which probably seemed as eternal to their citizens. . . . The
> irrevocable error is not yet part of the American experience.[116]

For all these reasons, Kissinger argued, Americans were psychologically ill suited to making foreign policy in what he regarded as a revolutionary period. They failed to understand that "in a revolutionary order the protagonists at the conference table address not so much one another as the world at large."[117] Paradoxically, "we, the empiricists, appear to the world as rigid, unimaginative and even somewhat cynical, while the dogmatic Bolsheviks exhibit flexibility, daring and subtlety."[118] The net result was "a crisis in our system of alliances and . . . substantial Soviet gains among the uncommitted peoples of the world." The Cold War had become a "contest for the allegiance of humanity" and the United States was losing it.

In this article (which, it should be noted, did an injustice to Eisenhower's exceedingly well-run NSC),[119] Kissinger's remedies were diplomatic rather than military. Allies had to be persuaded that "their best chance of avoiding thermonuclear war resides in our ability to make local aggression too costly," which meant securing an effective contribution from the allies themselves. As for the "uncommitted areas," America should seek not popularity but respect. "In its relations with the uncommitted," Kissinger concluded somewhat pompously, "the United States must develop not only a greater compassion but also a greater majesty." "We have wanted to be liked for our own sakes and we have wished to succeed because of the persuasiveness of our principles rather than through our strength."[120]

Kissinger had come a long way since his undergraduate enthusiasm for Kant. Detectable in his 1956 writing was a first trace of Machiavelli's influence. In chapter 17 of *The Prince,* Machiavelli asks "whether it be better to be loved than feared or feared than loved?" He answers that "one should wish to be both, but, because it is difficult to unite them in one person, it is much safer to be feared than loved, when, of the two, either must be dispensed with." If ever a book was written to inspire fear rather than love of the United States, it was *Nuclear Weapons and Foreign Policy.*

VI

Kissinger sweated over the book through the fall of 1956, neglecting his duties elsewhere (which included the editing of *Confluence* and fund-raising for the International Seminar and a new project for Rockefeller) because, as he explained to Bundy, "when I write I neglect all other things."[121] "It has proved . . . difficult," he went on, "because, while the subject is very important, so little is known about it that almost anything one writes approaches pure conjecture; and there is additional psychological pressure because everyone at the Council, in their kindness, expects a masterpiece, while I have no idea what a masterpiece on the subject would look like."[122] There had been no such pressure when he was writing *A World Restored*. By mid-November he was complaining to Graubard of being "sick" of the book, and this was with five chapters still unwritten.[123] By the end of the year it was "a close race between my sanity and the end of it."[124] His wife saw little of him. She put trays of food through his study door and retreated.[125]

One reason Kissinger found *Nuclear Weapons and Foreign Policy* so hard to write was that the ideas in it were not all his own. It was not just that he had been asked to synthesize the disparate and indeed contradictory views of a study group. He had also made every effort to consult other experts in the field, ranging from Oppenheimer to his old mentor Fritz Kraemer. "Its contents will hardly be a surprise to you," he told Kraemer—"in fact, in many passages we will have a hard time remembering who thought which points first."[126] As Kissinger explained to Edward Teller, his relationship with the study group had been deliberately semi-detached: "The point is that there never was an attempt to reach a consensus. It was always understood that I would be solely responsible for the book and that the group would be largely advisory. The whole second half of the book was never discussed in the study group and none of the manuscript was ever submitted to it."[127]

Moreover, substantial parts of the book had been published before, in *Foreign Affairs* and elsewhere; there were even passages rehashed from *A World Restored*. One of the most remarkable things about *Nuclear*

Weapons is that, despite all this, the book is coherent. Knowing that its length—482 pages—might put off all but the specialist reader, Kissinger was at pains to summarize its argument. Unusually, he did so fully two months before its publication. On April 15, 1957, he gave a speech before the Economic Club of Detroit on "How the Revolution in Weapons Will Affect Our Strategy and Foreign Policy."[128] This was essentially a synopsis. Simultaneously, he published yet another essay in *Foreign Affairs:* "Strategy and Organization."[129] As John Eisenhower put it in a handwritten note to his father, the article was "a brief of the brief of the brief of the book."[130]

Any summary is of course selective. It is therefore revealing that in "Strategy and Organization" Kissinger chose to focus much less on the limited nuclear war that was at the heart of his argument and much more on the policy making that would precede it and the diplomacy that would go on during it. His first point was that the United States lacked a "strategic doctrine" for the nuclear age. Instead it had, at best, "the attainable consensus among sovereign departments." The interdepartmental and interservice haggling "only defers the doctrinal dilemma until some crisis or the budgetary process forces a reconsideration under the pressure of events."[131] Because of "the predominance of fiscal considerations in our defense planning . . . doctrine is tailored and if necessary invented to fit budgetary requests. . . . The quest for numbers is a symptom of the abdication of doctrine."[132] As a consequence, there had been a failure to grasp the full implications of thermonuclear war, namely that there could be no winner in an all-out conflict "because even the weaker side may be able to inflict a degree of destruction which no society can support."[133] Kissinger's doctrine of limited nuclear war could be stated simply:

> Against the ominous background of thermonuclear devastation, the goal of war can no longer be military victory as we have known it. Rather it should be the attainment of certain specific political conditions which are fully understood by the opponent. The purpose of limited war is to inflict losses or to pose risks for the enemy out of proportion to the objectives under dispute. The more moderate the objective, the less violent the war is likely to be.[134]

This had several practical implications. First, the United States needed to have "an understanding of the psychology by which the opponent calculates his risks and the ability to present him at every point with an opportunity for a settlement that appears more favorable than would result if the war were continued."[135] There would need to be "pauses for calculation" between bouts of fighting and negotiation between two sides even as the war was going on. Second, the enemy's retaliatory (second-strike) nuclear forces had to be ruled out as targets; otherwise any war would be bound to escalate. Third, U.S. military forces would need to be reorganized. While the army, navy, and air force would continue as administrative and training units, they would be subordinated to two overarching organizations: the Strategic Force and the Tactical Force. Fourth, the defense budget cycle would be extended from one to two years.[136]

Conspicuous by its absence from this précis was any serious discussion of what a limited nuclear war might actually be like. Kissinger's one explicit remark on the subject—"battles will approach the stylized contests of the feudal period which were as much a test of will as a trial in strength"—even seemed to imply that future war would be *less* destructive than the conventional conflicts of the prenuclear period.[137] There was a reason for this uncharacteristic imprecision, as we shall see. For rhetorical purposes, the crucial point was to emphasize the horrific implications of all-out nuclear war. As Kissinger argued in another "trailer" for his book—a short article in *The Reporter**—the defects of "prevailing strategic doctrines" made a catastrophic all-out war much more likely than people appreciated:

> As things now stand, the major powers could conceivably be
> drawn into a war entirely against their wishes. The conflict
> over the Suez Canal was hardly foreseen by the western powers
> and perhaps not even by the Soviet Union. And the Hungarian
> revolution came as a rude shock to the Kremlin. Both upheavals

---

The Reporter had been founded in 1949 by Max Ascoli, a refugee from fascist Italy, and the journalist James Reston, and was highly influential as an outlet for broadly hawkish anti-Communist commentary. It was absorbed by *Harper's Magazine* in 1968.

resulted in military action that prevailing strategic doctrines
might easily have spread to an all-out war. Similar Soviet moves
in East Germany or Poland would be fraught with even more
danger.

For Kissinger, however, Armageddon was not the nightmare. Rather, it
was what the fear of Armageddon might do. "The absence of any generally understood limits to war," he warned, "undermines the psychological framework of resistance to Communist moves. Where war is
considered tantamount to national suicide, surrender may appear the
lesser of two evils."[138]

Nuclear Weapons and Foreign Policy was published on June 26, 1957.
Despite McGeorge Bundy's objection to its "tone and . . . attitude of
critical superiority," most readers were impressed by the book's authoritative critique of Eisenhower's national security strategy.[139] In particular, there was an appealing toughness to the argument. The "challenge
of the nuclear age," Kissinger argued, was that "the enormity of modern weapons makes the thought of war repugnant, but the refusal to
run any risks would amount to giving the Soviet rulers a blank check."[140]
The thermonuclear deterrent, he ventured to argue, was analogous to
the French Maginot Line in the 1930s. Just seventeen years after that
line's abject failure to keep out the Wehrmacht, this was a comparison
that still had the power to shock. But, as Kissinger argued, the American defense establishment was stuck in the era of World War II in more
ways than one. There was still an assumption that, as at Pearl Harbor,
the next war would begin with a surprise attack, to which the U.S. Air
Force would react with devastating aerial bombardment of enemy cities. The only difference would be that this time all the bombs would
be nuclear. Meanwhile, the navy would sail and the army would march,
each with nuclear weapons of its own. Yet these assumptions were
wholly anachronistic in the nuclear age and left the United States
exposed to a quite different Soviet strategy (as in Korea) of attacking
peripheral countries, keeping the stakes low enough that massive retaliation was never the appropriate response. What was needed was "a
strategy of intermediate objectives."[141]

Other authors had already tried to describe what a nuclear war would be like, but Kissinger's account in chapters 3 and 4 of *Nuclear Weapons* was pioneering, appearing as it did two years before Nevil Shute's best-selling novel *On the Beach* and three years before the publication of Herman Kahn's *On Thermonuclear War*. Beginning by estimating the destructive effects of a ten-megaton bomb dropped on New York, Kissinger extrapolates that an all-out Soviet attack on the fifty largest U.S. cities would kill between 15 and 20 million people and injure between 20 and 25 million; a further 5 to 10 million would die from the effects of radioactive fallout, while perhaps another 7 to 10 million would become sick. Those who survived would face "social disintegration."[142] Even then the United States would still be able to inflict comparable devastation on the Soviet Union: "Henceforth the only outcome of an all-out war will be that *both* contenders must lose."[143] Unlike many later writers, however, Kissinger's aim was not to argue for nuclear disarmament. Indeed, he was quite explicit that "the horrors of nuclear war [were] not likely to be avoided by a reduction of nuclear armaments" or, for that matter, by systems of weapons inspection.[144] If "all-out war [had] therefore ceased to be a meaningful instrument of policy," Kissinger asked, was it nevertheless "possible to imagine applications of power less catastrophic than all-out thermonuclear war?"[145] His answer, as we have seen, was yes: a limited nuclear war was indeed possible.

The fact that a limited nuclear war did not happen during the Cold War is not compelling evidence that Kissinger's thesis was wrong. On the contrary, the book was clearly right in the sense that, subsequent to its publication, both superpowers set about acquiring a substantial tactical nuclear capability and were still enhancing that capability in the early 1980s. That it was never used is irrelevant; what matters is that such weapons were considered usable by both sides. The flaws in *Nuclear Weapons and Foreign Policy* are subtler and reflect the reality that—despite Kissinger's sole authorship—the book remained, at root, the work of a committee.

Much of Kissinger's critique of the Eisenhower administration's strategy is by now familiar. We have already encountered the argument that reliance on the threat of massive retaliation must tend to undermine the U.S. system of regional alliances, especially in Europe; also familiar is Kissinger's analysis of Soviet and Chinese strategic thinking, which adumbrates his earlier ideas about the way revolutionary powers behave, his analysis of the Soviet "peace offensive," and his recommendation to merge the armed services and create new and strictly separate strategic and tactical forces. The novel chapters concern the nature of a limited nuclear war itself. It is here that Kissinger was most reliant on the military men of the CFR study group—and it is here, as a result, that his argument is at its weakest.

The first weak link in the "argument in favor of the possibility of limited war" is Kissinger's claim that "both sides have a common and overwhelming interest in preventing it from spreading" above "the threshold which would unleash an all-out war."[146] Indeed, he suggests, their Marxist ideology made the Soviet and Chinese leaders highly unlikely to "risk everything to prevent changes adverse to them, so long as their national survival is not directly affected."[147] However, Kissinger adds a number of qualifications to this argument. There would need to be "sanctuary areas immune to attack, because any threat to the opponent's strategic striking force [would] invite a thermonuclear holocaust." For example, strategic air force bases and towns above a certain size must be off limits.[148] There would also need to be identifiably different "delivery mechanisms that cannot be mistaken for strategic forces."[149] Kissinger even proposes rules on the sizes of weapons that could be deployed, suggesting at one point a 500-kiloton maximum. If such rules make limited war sound more like a game than a violent struggle, so too does Kissinger's notion of diplomatic pauses:

> Every campaign should be conceived in a series of self-contained phases, each of which implies a political objective and with a sufficient interval between them to permit the application of political and psychological pressures. . . . [I]t will be necessary to give up the notion that diplomatic contact ceases during military operations. Rather, direct contact will be more than ever necessary to ensure that both sides possess the correct information about the consequences of expanding a war and to be able to present formulas for a political settlement.[150]

The modern reader cannot help but wonder how effective such limiting devices would have been in practice, had such a limited nuclear war broken out. The experience of the world wars did not give much support to the notion that diplomatic channels of communication would remain open after hostilities had begun. Indeed, at the time of the publication of *Nuclear Weapons,* Thomas Schelling had already begun work on an economic theory of bargaining that would raise serious questions about how easily escalation could be avoided in any two-player game based partly on threats.[151]

The second and related problem has to do with the precise character of limited nuclear war itself. Kissinger argues that such a war would be waged by "units of high mobility and considerable firepower which can be quickly moved to trouble spots and which can bring their power to bear with discrimination."[152] In chapter 6, he draws an analogy to traditional naval warfare, "in which self-contained units with great firepower gradually gain the upper hand by destroying their enemy counterparts without physically occupying territory or establishing a front-line." Forces in this future war would be moved around the battlefield in "troop-carrying helicopters"; indeed, "even the individual soldier in some units [would be] given a rudimentary ability to transport himself through the air by means of the 'flying platform.'" Targets would not be cities, airfield, or industrial capacity but simply the enemy's mobile units.[153] Some of this has the quality of historical fiction; some of it is pure science fiction.

A third difficulty is the argument that the United States would have innate advantages in such a conflict, because of its "superior industrial potential, the broader range of our technology and the adaptability of our social institutions . . . [as well as] leadership of a high order, personal initiative and mechanical aptitude, qualities more prevalent in our society than in the regimented system of the U.S.S.R."[154] It is not at all clear why, if that were true, the Soviet Union would have any incentive to accept the rules of engagement of a limited war. Indeed, as Kissinger acknowledges in chapter 11, the Russians had already devoted a considerable amount of propaganda to the argument that a limited nuclear war was an impossibility.

In short, the core of *Nuclear Weapons and Foreign Policy*—its vision of tactical nuclear weapons being deployed in battle by helicopter-borne army units—fails to convince. Why, then, was the book so successful, both critically and commercially? Part of the answer is the effectiveness of its critique of Eisenhower and Dulles. Another part is its underlying pessimism: as we shall see, the book was perfectly timed to coincide with a wave of public anxiety about the Soviets' catching up in the arms race. But there is a third explanation. The philosophical underpinning of *Nuclear Weapons* is that an apparently abhorrent thing like a limited nuclear war may be the lesser evil if the alternatives are impotence or annihilation. In his final chapter, Kissinger spells out a general theory of lesser evils that may be seen as a kind of credo for his career as a whole:

> [U]nless we maintain at least an equilibrium of power . . . we will have no chance to undertake any positive measures. And maintaining this equilibrium may require some very difficult choices. We are certain to be confronted with situations of extraordinary ambiguity, such as civil wars or domestic coups. . . . There can be no doubt that we should seek to forestall such occurrences. But once they have occurred, we must find the will to act and to run risks in a situation which permits only a choice among evils. While we should never give up our principles, we must also realize that we cannot maintain our principles unless we survive. . . . It would be comforting if we could confine our actions to situations in which our moral, legal and military positions are completely in harmony and where legitimacy is most in accord with the requirements of survival. But, as the strongest power in the world, we will probably never again be afforded the simple moral choices on which we could insist in our more secure past. . . . To deal with problems of such ambiguity presupposes above all a moral act: a willingness to run risks on partial knowledge and for a less than perfect application of one's principles. The insistence on absolutes . . . is a prescription for inaction.[155]

This was Kissinger in his more familiar Kantian vein: it was an inherently moral act to make a choice between lesser and greater evils.

VII

"I could not live with myself, were I to do anything less than the very best that I am capable of for the Council," Kissinger had written a year before the publication of *Nuclear Weapons and Foreign Policy*. "It is not simply a question of finishing *a* book, but of finishing a really first-rate book."[156] Few authors know for certain if their work is first-rate; most wait on tenterhooks for the verdicts of others, beginning with those solicited by their publishers. It is not difficult to imagine the relief Henry Kissinger felt to read the following blurb:

> Dr. Kissinger's history-making book is extraordinarily well informed, and in this respect quite unprecedented in the field of nuclear armament. It is scrupulous in its regard for fact, and at once passionate and tough in argument. His thesis is that war, far from having become "unthinkable," is indeed thinkable, and needs the most clear-headed, sober, original thought if it is either to be prevented, limited, directed to serve the interests of our country, or planned to avert unimaginable catastrophy [*sic*]. I hope that all who feel themselves responsibly involved with the future of our country will read it.[157]

The fact that those words were written by Robert Oppenheimer, the father of the atomic bomb, was reassurance that Kissinger's lack of scientific expertise had not proved fatal to his enterprise. Privately, Oppenheimer was enthusiastic, too: the book was "a masterful and potentially very important beginning . . . far and away the best thing I have seen in public, and enormously better than anything that existed in the official papers during the years when I had to look at them." As for his caveat, quoted in the epigraph to this chapter, it could easily be dismissed as utopian: in 1957 there was little sign of transnational communities displacing nation-states in the realm of power politics. There were other prepublication endorsements—from Caryl Haskins and Clare Boothe Luce*—but it was Oppenheimer's that mattered.[158]

The first reviews were, as Kissinger put it, "fairly good."[159] Chalmers Roberts of *The Washington Post* called it "the most important book of 1957 . . . a probing, intelligent and challenging discussion . . . [that] should be read by every top civilian and military leader in the Nation."[160] Writing in the *Chicago Tribune,* Robert E. Osgood praised the author's "acute penetration, fertile imagination, and impressive analytical skill."[161] The *New York Herald Tribune*'s reviewer found the book "deeply thoughtful [and] hard-headedly candid,"[162] while *The Christian Science Monitor* called Kissinger a "master logician," adding the rider that the book was "difficult reading to the degree that intensely rational thought in a relatively new area is bound to be difficult."[163] Edward Teller agreed that it was "not only fairly long, [but] also somewhat difficult to read," but his review in *The New York Times*—often the arbiter of a book's success in the United States—was otherwise positive.[164] Another important endorsement ("great brilliance, wide knowledge, and good judgment") came from Hans Morgenthau, whose *Politics Among Nations* (1948) had already established him as the doyen of American foreign policy realism.[165] From London, *The Economist* found the book "prolix and at times rather obtuse, but nevertheless most ingenious and thought-provoking."[166] The first note of skepticism came in an article in the *Herald Tribune,* where Ralph E. Lapp, the director of the Nuclear Science Service, expressed his doubts about the possibility of a limited nuclear war.[167]

The real resistance began in *The New Republic.* James E. King, Jr., began by challenging Kissinger's seemingly amoral approach to the question of nuclear war. The book's "point of departure," he suggested, was "realistic." Nowhere in it would "the reader discover any disposition to rest conclusions on moral premises."[168] Yet two key points in the argument were not realistic at all: the first that a limited nuclear war

---

*The witty and glamorous wife of the publisher of *Time,* Luce had just returned from serving as the U.S. ambassador in Rome. It was she who coined the phrase "No good deed goes unpunished."

would not quickly escalate into a total war, and the second that a limited nuclear war would be waged like a sea battle in the age of sail. Even more scathing was Paul Nitze's review in *The Reporter,* which found the book's argument "oversimplified and overdrawn"—especially when it came to criticizing decisions under Truman in which Nitze had been directly involved. There were "several hundred passages in which either the facts or the logic seem doubtful, or at least unclear." Kissinger had understated the damage caused by nuclear bombs by asserting that the blast and heat effects of weapons increase only by the cube root of their stepped-up explosive power, whereas in fact it was by the *square* of the cube root:

> A megaton weapon has a blast effect ten thousand times that of a one-ton TNT weapon, not one hundred times, which is what it would be if Kissinger's cube-root rule were in fact valid. This may possibly explain why Kissinger thinks that five-hundred-kiloton weapons are appropriate for inclusion in an arsenal for a limited nuclear strategy designed to spare from annihilation the inhabitants of the geographic area in which the campaign is to be fought. Errors in fact of an order of magnitude of one hundred to one can have significant implications for doctrine.*

Would Kissinger's "open cities" (cities declared to be free of nuclear weapons) be spared all military action or just nuclear action? If the former, Nitze reasoned, there would be an incentive to build up conventional forces in those cities ahead of any conflict; if the latter, "then the war may become largely a conventional war for control of the areas excluded from nuclear attack." In general, in Nitze's view, Kissinger was understating the likelihood that most, if not all, future wars would in fact be conventional. "In the nuclear age," he concluded,

> everyone must be for the limitation of war, if war itself cannot be eliminated. But if the limitations are really to stand up under

---

*It is surprising that Oppenheimer had overlooked this error.

the immense pressures of even a "little" war, it would seem
something more is required than a Rube Goldberg chart of
arbitrary limitations, weightless weapons, flying platforms with
no fuel requirements, and tactics based on no targets for attack
and no logistic or communication vulnerabilities to defend.[169]

It was an extraordinary broadside from a man who had served on the
study group Kissinger was in some sense representing, and it left the
author reeling. (According to Nitze, Kissinger later joked that he "got
to page 147 of [a] rebuttal and decided that if the rebuttal took that
many pages, there must be something wrong with my position.")[170]

As is often the case with books by academics that attract much
attention and sell many copies, *Nuclear Weapons and Foreign Policy* was
savaged by the reviewers in more scholarly journals. It was perhaps
inevitable that men who had spent much more time than Kissinger
thinking about the problem of nuclear war should resent his ambition.
Nitze, for one, had been beaten to the punch; in truth, his own argument about how a limited nuclear war might be fought—published in
Foreign Affairs in January 1956—had contained at least as many holes as
he found in Kissinger's book.[171] But matters were perhaps made worse
by the fact that the book was published by the Council on Foreign
Relations, the most venerable of American institutions dedicated to the
study of international affairs and therefore the perfect target for new
think tanks eager to make their mark. The RAND Corporation (short
for "Research and Development") had been established by the Douglas
Aircraft Company in 1946 but became an independent entity two years
later. Other new entrants were the Center for Research on World
Political Institutions (CRWPI), founded at Princeton in 1950, and the
Center for International Studies founded a year later, also at Princeton.
Of even more recent origin was the Foreign Policy Research Institute
founded at the University of Pennsylvania in 1955. Writers affiliated
with these institutions went even further than King and Nitze in seeking to demolish Kissinger's reasoning. Richard W. Van Wagenen, the
director of the Princeton CRWPI, dismissed the distinction between
limited and all-out nuclear war as "ingenious but dubious" (a verdict
echoed in Hans Morgenthau's otherwise friendly review).[172] Bernard

Brodie of RAND made it clear that he felt insufficiently acknowledged as the pioneer of the debate on limited war.[173] Stefan Possony, who was shortly to join Stanford's Hoover Institution, sniped at Kissinger's "academic 'Blimpism,'" arguing that the book simply did not grasp "the intricacies of modern strategy" and overlooked the reality that the United States was already devoting about 60 percent of its defense budget "precisely for the cause Dr. Kissinger is pleading," namely nonstrategic capabilities usable in a limited war.[174]

Much the most hostile review, however, came from Brodie's RAND colleague William W. Kaufmann. Kissinger, he argued, had skimmed over the crucial questions of how much damage tactical nuclear weapons actually did, how much it would actually cost to adopt a strategy of limited nuclear war, and how alarmed America's allies would be by its doing so. For Kaufmann, *Nuclear Weapons* underestimated all three of these things:

> Kissinger describes the 500-kiloton bomb as the largest that can be used without danger of significant fallout, and therefore the maximum size that should be permitted in a limited war. Leaving aside the problem of how this ceiling would be imposed and enforced, one wonders where he obtained the notion that such a bomb, even if used in rather small numbers, would not create significant amounts of radioactivity. One also wonders how he can talk about using such weapons in a discriminating fashion when a free air-burst 500-kiloton bomb will cause serious blast damage to objects such as reinforced concrete buildings over an area of about fifteen square miles, and produce very severe thermal effects over an even larger area.

At the same time, Kissinger's more or less benign vision of limited nuclear war was based on a wholly unrealistic view of current and future military technology:

> [A] reasonable familiarity with military technology would suggest that the vertical-takeoff-and-landing aircraft is unlikely to become an operationally useful weapon before the mid-1960's,

that we are nowhere near a substitute for the internal combustion engine, that nuclear trucks do not look like very promising vehicles for the next decade or so, and that the Army has not yet come close to freeing itself from logistic bases and lines of communication . . . [T]o read Kissinger's chapters on limited warfare is to believe that the military equivalent of the stringless yo-yo is at hand.[175]

VIII

Why, when the verdict of experts like William Kaufmann proved to be so negative, was *Nuclear Weapons and Foreign Policy* still such a success, with an initial print run of seventy thousand hardback copies and selection by Book-of-the-Month Club? Part of the answer is that relatively few people read journals like *World Politics*. But a better answer is that Kissinger's book furnished critics of the doctrine of massive retaliation inside and outside the Eisenhower administration with what seemed like useful ammunition. Even more important, within a few months of the book's appearance, events outside—and above—the United States lent an unlooked-for credibility to Kissinger's argument that American strategy was in crisis.

It was inevitable that the official line would be dismissive. Defense Secretary Charles E. Wilson put it bluntly: "There isn't going to be any little war with the Russians." This was also the view of Admiral Arthur W. Radford, chairman of the Joint Chiefs of Staff.[176] Colonel Ephraim M. Hampton, deputy for evaluation at the Air War College, called the distinction between limited and total war an "escapist device—a case of candy coating the bitter truth."[177] But the Washington establishment did not speak with one voice. As the member of the CFR study group to whom Kissinger had paid the most heed, General James M. Gavin was hardly likely to disown what he called "a splendid book . . . one of the most, if not the most significant books of our time."[178] Gavin's boss, Secretary of the Army Wilber M. Brucker, also came out in support of the idea of limited war.[179] As *The Washington Post* reported, Kissinger's book had caused "a lot of soul-searching at the Pentagon, at State and at the Capitol."[180] The newspaper might have added the White House to that list. Vice President Nixon found the book "most stimulating and constructive."[181] Henry Cabot Lodge, Jr., the former senator for Massachusetts whom Eisenhower had made his representative to the United Nations, recommended *Nuclear Weapons* to the president as "clear-headed, profound and constructive."[182] A detailed summary was duly prepared by General Andrew Goodpaster, Eisenhower's trusted staff secretary.[183] In turn, Eisenhower was sufficiently impressed by the summary to recommend the book to Dulles.

> I do not mean that you will agree with everything the man says. I think there are flaws in his arguments and, at the very least, if we were to organize and maintain military forces along the lines he suggests, we would have what George Humphrey [who had just stepped down as Treasury secretary] always calls "both the old and the new." This would undoubtedly be a more expensive operation than we are carrying on at this time.
>
> However, the author directs his arguments to some general or popular conceptions and misconceptions, and . . . I think you will find interesting and worth reading at least this much of the book.[184]

On August 11, *The New York Times* ran a front-page report that "officials at the highest government levels" were reading Kissinger.[185] There was no denying it.

The summer of 1957 was a time of change in Eisenhower's administration. Not only was Humphrey out; Wilson left the Pentagon shortly after the publication of Kissinger's book, to be replaced by Neil McElroy from Procter & Gamble, while Radford was replaced as chairman of the Joint Chiefs by General Nathan F. Twining. Detecting more than just a reshuffle, the *Manchester Guardian*'s influential correspondent in Washington, Alistair Cooke, compared Kissinger's impact with that of Kennan at the genesis of the strategy of containment.[186] *Time* carried a similar report.[187]

These changes came after a series of foreign policy crises that had made the time ripe for a critique such as Kissinger's. On October 29,

1956, without consulting the United States, Britain, France, and Israel had launched an invasion of Egypt designed not merely to reverse President Gamal Abdel Nasser's nationalization of the Suez Canal but also to overthrow Nasser himself. Within less than a week, on November 4, the Red Army had invaded Hungary in order to crush the reformist regime of Imre Nagy. Eisenhower had been working hard to woo Arab leaders, fearing that they might be drawn into the Soviet orbit. Like many on the left in Britain, he felt unable simultaneously to condemn the invasion of Hungary and to endorse the invasion of Egypt. It was not difficult for a well-informed outsider to heap scorn on the administration, and Kissinger did. "What I object to most with recent events," he thundered in a letter to Stephen Graubard,

> is not so much the folly of our policy, which in my view approaches the treasonable, but above all the pedantry and the lack of style of our behavior. The petty bureaucrats in Washington were more outraged with Britain and France than with the Soviets because the British upset their plans more completely. And they were even a little bit irritated with the Hungarians because they forced them into making decisions it would have been simpler never to have had to face. If Christ had had a Policy Planning Staff he surely would never have mounted the Cross.

This was the cue for one of Kissinger's increasingly frequent attacks on the administration's legalistic approach to foreign policy.

> The pedantic denial of the tragic element of life which is our outstanding characteristic may well spell our doom. The clever lawyers who run our government seem to have an answer to everything except inward commitment. But the West would still be an insignificant appendage to a barbaric Eurasia had it always been animated by an absence of a sense of mission and a quest for minimum risk which is our most outstanding characteristic. In our situation, the insistence on pure morality is in itself the most immoral of postures. And the Hungarians have

shown us the insignificance of our moral stature. The Europeans are not blameless because they have been preaching pacifism for so long that they have paralyzed both us and themselves, but I think that their reaction is healthier than ours.[188]

In early February, long after Britain and France had submitted to UN resolutions and withdrawn their forces from Egypt, Kissinger still railed against the "pedantry and self-righteousness" of the U.S. response to the crisis. "We may have proved that aggression does not pay," he told Bundy, "but we have done so to people least likely to disturb the peace and at a price to their national pride, which will not become fully apparent for some time. . . . I would feel happier about professions of high moral principles if they did not so frequently coincide with a policy of minimum risk."[189]

It is doubtful that many Americans shared Kissinger's indignation about events in distant Hungary and Egypt. In early 1957, most still felt a certain nonchalance about the nuclear threat, a mood nicely captured by the Five Stars' doo-wop song "Atom Bomb Baby."* There was, however, broad congressional support for Eisenhower's vaguely worded resolution of January 1957, which pledged the United States to defend "the Middle East" against "overt armed aggression from any nation controlled by International Communism."[190] Support was unquestionably growing for the proposition that the threat of massive retaliation was insufficient to prevent a creeping Soviet expansion. But it was the night of October 4, 1957, that ensured Kissinger's celebrity. The successful launch of *Sputnik 1*, the first artificial satellite, into an elliptical orbit around the earth crystallized the growing American anxiety that the Soviets were catching up not only in military terms but technologically and economically, too. Twice the size of a basketball, *Sputnik* (short for "elementary satellite") could complete its orbit in ninety-six minutes and was both visible in the night sky and audible, beeping short-wave radio signals down to Earth. In itself, it was harmless, but the fact that the Soviets had been able to launch it indicated that they

---

*"Atom bomb baby, boy she can start / One of those chain reactions in my heart / A big explosion, big and loud / Mushrooms me right up on a cloud."

might also be capable of producing long-range missiles that could reach targets in the United States.* The result was a wave of media-fueled public panic.[191] "Russian science [had] whipped American science," declared *The Boston Globe*. With the U.S. satellite program lagging far behind, the CIA desperately tried to devise stunts that could quickly match the Soviet feat. (One suggestion was to use a hydrogen bomb to halt a typhoon.)[192] Significantly, Eisenhower's considered response to the crisis—he had initially dismissed it as a "gimmick"—emphasized American advantages in weaponry that would have made little sense without the possibility of a limited nuclear war.[193]

Sputnik launched Kissinger into a new orbit. Suddenly he was visible and audible everywhere: a "Man to Watch," in the words of the *New York Herald Tribune*.[194] Ten days after the launch of the Soviet satellite, the *Herald Tribune* ran a special "emergency" editorial under the headline "Kissinger Speaks," based on an interview that was probably the first of Kissinger's career. He did not pull his punches. "The Soviets have outstripped us," he was quoted as saying. "We're really in trouble now. We've been pushed back gradually, position by position. . . . The basic trend is against us." In particular, *Sputnik* had revealed "how the Russians conduct their military programs. They can cut down their lead-time in a way which we are unable to do."

> The Soviets are on a technological curve. Each invention implies that there are other inventions waiting to be revealed. It's hard to stop their progress. . . . The worrisome thing about the satellite is what it shows us about the state of their rocket engines, and the state of our own intelligence. . . . Their economy is only half as big as ours and their pool of trained manpower is smaller, although increasing. This indicates superior organization and superior doctrine.

---

*This was in fact correct: the R7 that had placed *Sputnik* in orbit was the first intercontinental ballistic missile, and it had been designed specifically to deliver hydrogen bombs to U.S. targets. The American equivalent, the Atlas D, was not successfully tested until July 1959, nearly two years after *Sputnik*. In this respect, there was a missile gap in the late 1950s.

By contrast, "the Department of Defense is not organized to fight a war. It is organized for internal management." Nor did Kissinger stop there. "If things continue as they are," he declared, "our expulsion from Eurasia is a mathematical certainty. . . . Eight years ago it would have seemed fantastic that the Soviets would become a major power in the Middle East. We like to smile now at Baldwin and Chamberlain in 1938, but they thought of themselves as tough realists."[195] Kissinger evidently had second thoughts about some of this when he saw it in print. But his rather pedantic follow-up ("the fitting of a rather extended conversation into limited space has conveyed a tone of dogmatism which does not correspond to my views in the full") could not efface the alarmism of the original piece. Prior to *Sputnik* he had been invited to just a single book event; after October 4 the invitations streamed in, from the Research Institute of America,[196] from the Association of the United States Army,[197] and—ensuring a huge nationwide audience— from CBS's Sunday talk show *Face the Nation*, which had begun its extraordinary sixty-year run in 1954.

Kissinger's television debut on November 10, 1957, pitted him against three journalists: John Madigan of the *Chicago American*, Richard C. Hottelet of CBS News, and Chalmers Roberts of *The Washington Post*. As so often on *Face the Nation*, the pace was frenetic and the subject changed regularly and abruptly. For a television novice, Kissinger coped well. He delivered his critique of Eisenhower's policy: "We believed for too long that we were relatively invulnerable. . . . We have been more concerned with peace, while our opponent has been more concerned with victory, which has created a psychological inequality." He set out the thesis of his book: "I think it is possible to fight a limited war with nuclear weapons." And he gave a concrete example: that United States should be ready to fight a limited war to check Soviet aggression in the Middle East. "I believe," he declared, "that it will take a somewhat firmer attitude and a willingness, a somewhat greater willingness, to run risks." Again he illustrated the point: the United States should have "made the Russians pay the maximum price for crushing Hungary," airlifting supplies to the anti-Soviet forces "even if the Russians had shot down the planes." Asked if he was a

Democrat or a Republican, he replied tersely (and prudently), "I am an Independent."[198]

Perhaps the ultimate accolade for any American Cold War intellectual was to be denounced by the other side. As the CIA's Foreign Broadcast Information Service noted, Kissinger was not mentioned by name, but it was no accident that there was a "spate of routine propaganda attacking the U.S. thesis of 'small' nuclear wars . . . in broadcasts both for foreign and domestic consumption, shortly after the publication" of *Nuclear Weapons and Foreign Policy*.[199] The key question, however, was how far U.S. policy would actually be changed by Kissinger's arguments. Superficially, it was. In January 1958 Eisenhower set aside earlier arguments against deploying 280mm nuclear cannons and 762mm "Honest John" rockets in South Korea. A year later the air force added a squadron of nuclear-tipped Matador cruise missiles capable of hitting targets not only in North Korea but also in the Soviet Union and China.[200] As we have seen, however, this was not a new departure; Eisenhower had always quietly retained the option of using tactical nuclear weapons, even as he insisted publicly that any conflict would be bound to escalate into all-out war. In this and other respects, we see the limits of the public intellectual's role. Through the Council on Foreign Relations and Nelson Rockefeller, Kissinger had come closer than he had ever been to the commanding heights of the U.S. government. Yet he remained on the outside, with only the most limited access to classified documents. It was on the basis of newspaper reports read in distant Cambridge that he slammed the Washington bureaucracy. Even as he basked in the arc lights of the CBS studio, he could not know that, just a few days before his *Face the Nation* debut, a far more comprehensive—but top secret—critique of the administration's strategy had been presented to the president. The title of the report was "Deterrence and Survival in the Nuclear Age," though it came to be known as the Gaither Report after the committee's chairman, H. Rowan Gaither. And its analysis was far more alarming—and its recommendations far more daunting—than anything in *Nuclear Weapons and Foreign Policy*.

Henry Kissinger deserved the fame that *Nuclear Weapons* brought him. Even if the future the book envisaged—of tactical weapons being used in the field of battle in a limited nuclear war—never happened, that does not detract from the effectiveness of the book's critique of the Eisenhower administration's strategy. It was not so much that the launch of *Sputnik* vindicated Kissinger, though the timing could scarcely have been better. It was more that, in the intellectual arms race to formulate a coherent critique of American strategy, Kissinger had achieved the first strike.

Boswash

Your own extraordinary gifts of intellect and character are
such that you will be a famous and influential man. . . .
I have often thought that Harvard gives her sons—her
undergraduates—the opportunity to be shaped by what
they love. This, as a Harvard man, you have had. For her
faculty, she reserves the opportunity—dangerous, perhaps
fatal—to be shaped by what they hate.

—JOHN CONWAY, 1956[1]

[I]n some respects the intellectual has never been more in
demand; that he makes such a relatively small contribution
is not because he is rejected but because his function
is misunderstood. He is sought after enthusiastically
but for the wrong reasons and in pursuit of the wrong
purposes. . . . [A]ll too often what the policymaker wants
from the intellectual is not ideas but endorsement.

—HENRY KISSINGER, 1959[2]

I

Henry Kissinger's time at the Council on Foreign Relations was
drawing to a close. Now what? Harvard had spurned him and, though
former colleagues like John Conway and Sam Huntington commiser-
ated,[3] a new and "very advantageous" offer from the University of Chicago was not to be sniffed at.[4] Established in 1890—with Rockefeller
money—it had an international reputation in political science as well as
in economics. But despite "Mac" Bundy's advice to accept the offer, Kissinger remained deeply reluctant to go there. "Aside from the aesthetic

objection to Chicago," he told Bundy, the "incommensurability between what [academic life] could be and what it is" seemed "particularly poignant" at that particular university.[5] By "the aesthetic objection to Chicago," Kissinger may have been alluding to the deterioration of the Hyde Park neighborhood, which already in the mid-1950s was acquiring a reputation for crime. But his real objection to the job was different. The academic standing of Chicago was high, no doubt. But professors there played a far smaller role in American public life—and particularly in government—than their counterparts at Harvard. For Henry Kissinger, as for many other academics of his generation, the road to Washington, D.C., led through Cambridge—to be precise, through Harvard Yard. It was not until 1965 that Herman Kahn and Anthony Wiener coined the name *Boswash* to describe the nascent megalopolis stretching from New England to Virginia. But Kissinger was already a citizen of Boswash in 1956. He would spend much of the rest of his life shuttling back and forth—by plane, by train, and when necessary by car—along the narrow corridor that connected Boston to New York to Washington, linking brains to money to power.

Even as he was writing *Nuclear Weapons and Foreign Policy,* scribbling away in his New York apartment, Kissinger was clinging to the East Coast by his fingernails. Salvation of a sort came from Nelson Rockefeller. So impressed had he been by Kissinger's work that in May 1956 he invited him to the Quantico reunion[6] and then offered him a full-time job at the Rockefeller Brothers Fund, to play a leading role in his new Special Studies Project, a bold attempt to identify and address the strategic challenges facing the United States in the second half of the twentieth century.[7] This was more than Kissinger wanted; he remained committed to the academic path, suspecting—rightly—that to succumb entirely to the Rockefeller embrace would be to lose all intellectual and political freedom. But Rockefeller was ingenious. When Kissinger pleaded other commitments—not only the still unfinished book for the Council on Foreign Relations, but also his offer from Chicago—he was astounded to find that Rockefeller had already taken care of all that. "Really incredible pressure was put on me," he complained to Stephen Graubard.

[E]ither he or his brothers, without my knowledge, went to the Council and to the University of Chicago, asking them to release me for a three months period. The Chancellor of the University of Chicago then wrote me a letter urging me to work with Rockefeller. I could hardly insist on a commitment to the University of Chicago when the University itself released me from it for a period of three months.[8]

The result was a compromise. Kissinger accepted the post of director of Special Studies at the Rockefeller Brothers Fund until March 1957, after which—if all else failed—he would go to Chicago.[9]

Kissinger's rationalization of this fudged decision was revealing. "I quite honestly do not feel that I owe anything in particular to academic life," he told Graubard. "The disparity between my reputation outside academic life and inside academic life is so great as to be ludicrous. . . . I don't see any particular challenge ahead except to have every generous motivation interpreted in the lowest possible manner." Nevertheless,

I will go to Chicago in April and give academic life one more chance. . . . I ask only one of two things of it. Either that it gives me a challenge directly, or that it permits me to create my own challenges. I do not consider fighting my way up an academic ladder at an undignified salary, surrounded by individuals whom I find unattractive, a particular challenge, but this may be different at Chicago, and I shall, for this reason, go out there in April.

By contrast, it was impossible not to be attracted to working for Rockefeller, "who, whatever his limitations, is putting a great deal of his resources and much of his prestige into an effort from which he personally has nothing to gain." Kissinger and Graubard had "often spoken of the absence of an aristocracy in this country."

I feel that one owes to a person of Rockefeller's motivation at least not to discourage him too much. . . . The Rockefeller project is an extremely interesting one, not only substantively, but from a sociological point of view. The power of these people is unbelievable, and their method of operation extremely fascinating. On the other hand, they seem to me to come fairly close to performing the function of a good aristocracy—a lot more so than some of the French people that Sombart* was describing so eloquently.[10]

Kissinger's hedging strategy worked. In the nick of time, before he had to drag himself "out there" to Chicago, Bundy threw him a lifeline from Harvard, inviting him to return to "help launch" the university's new Center for International Affairs (CFIA).[11] Bundy found Kissinger "just a little uncertain as to whether he wanted to come back to a department which had not been unanimously friendly to him a year ago," but he "tried to cheer him up on that point." The government department voted unanimously to make Kissinger a lecturer for "three or four years" (the same kind of post, auspiciously, that Bundy had been given on his return to Harvard); at the same time, he was appointed associate director of the new center.[12] It may be that Bundy hinted to Kissinger that he would not have to wait long for promotion to a tenured professorship. However, Kissinger was taking no chances. Not content with a job from Rockefeller and a post at Harvard, he proceeded to add to his portfolio a $4,000-a-year relationship with the newly established Foreign Policy Research Institute (FPRI) at the University of Pennsylvania.[13] He also did a deal to work two days a month as a consultant to the Carnegie Corporation after he had finished his work for Rockefeller.[14] As if that were not enough, it was reported in at least one newspaper that he was working as a consultant to the Joint Chiefs of Staff, too.[15] The only commitment Kissinger gave up, in 1959, was his reserve officer commission, pleading "pressure of other obligations and the conviction that I can be of greater service in a higher rank in case an emergency necessitates this step."[16]

Young academics who, after years of toiling in obscurity, suddenly

---

*The allusion is to Nicolaus Sombart, the libertine son of the more famous historical sociologist Werner Sombart, who had written his doctoral thesis on Henri, comte de Saint-Simon, the aristocratic prophet of a partly socialist, partly meritocratic industrial utopia.

find themselves in demand very often overcommit themselves. Such was the case here. So packed was Kissinger's schedule that he had to decline to take undergraduate tutees in the fall 1957 semester.[17] Graubard recalled "the increasingly disorganized character of his life" at this time; "he seemed always to be running, always late, and constantly harassed."[18] His frequent absences from Harvard were likely the initial cause of the friction between him and the CFIA director Robert Bowie. Worse, his failure to do any work whatever for the FPRI led to an exchange with Stefan Possony so acrimonious that Fritz Kraemer had to intervene. Kraemer took Kissinger's side in the argument, but in a handwritten note in German, he privately warned his former protégé, "Something is not right with you. As your friend and as someone who understands your situation probably even at the subconscious level, I have to tell you that you are forgetting things that as a human being you ought not forget." Not only was Kissinger alienating colleagues like Possony; according to Kraemer, he was also neglecting his own parents. "You are beginning to behave in a way that is no longer human [*menschlich*] and people who admire you are starting to regard you as cool, perhaps even cold. . . . You are in danger of allowing your heart and soul to burn out in your incessant work. You see too many 'important' and not enough 'real' people."[19] It was not the last time that Kraemer would sermonize in this way, nor the last time that he would cast Kissinger as Doctor Faustus, the brilliant academic who had sold his soul to the devil for the sake of worldly power. Yet Kraemer could hardly complain. Was it not thanks partly to Kissinger's support that he had just been appointed to the faculty of the National War College? Was he, too, not receiving Rockefeller largesse as a contributor to the Special Studies series that Kissinger was now directing?[20]

II

The Rockefeller Brothers Fund Special Studies Project, of which Henry Kissinger was the director, grew out of the belief, as Kissinger phrased it, that "many of our difficulties, both domestic and foreign, are due not so much to an absence of good ideas but to our inability to find concepts and attitudes to deal with a situation changing more rapidly and in directions different from what our national experiences led us to expect."²¹ The challenges facing the United States in 1957—the year when much of the writing was done—were certainly novel. In the nuclear arms race, the Soviet Union appeared to be catching up with the United States, perhaps even overtaking it. As Europe's colonial empires in Asia, Africa, and the Middle East crumbled, few of the "new nations" seemed keen to align themselves with the capitalist West. At home, too, there was ferment. The governor of Arkansas called out the National Guard to prevent black students from enrolling in Little Rock's Central High School, prompting Eisenhower to send federal troops to give the "Little Rock Nine" safe passage to the school. Elvis Presley appeared on *The Ed Sullivan Show,* but only from the waist up. *Jailhouse Rock* hit cinemas. *West Side Story* opened on Broadway. Jack Kerouac's *On the Road* went on sale. Allen Ginsberg's *Howl* was banned.

It must be admitted that the Special Studies Project had little to say about civil rights and less to say about rock 'n' roll.²² Rockefeller and Kissinger convened six panels and a coordinating "Overall Panel." Their assigned topics and ranking make it clear that foreign policy was their primary concern:

> I: U.S. International Objectives and Strategy
>
> II: U.S. International Security Objectives and Strategy
>
> III: Foreign Economic Policy for the Twentieth Century
>
> IV: U.S. Economic and Social Policy
>
> V: U.S. Utilization of Human Resources
>
> VI: U.S. Democratic Process—Its Challenge and
> Opportunity

A seventh panel, proposed by economist Robert Heilbroner, was supposed to address the moral dimensions of the national purpose, but that was stillborn. The organizational challenge was itself daunting. All told, Kissinger had to manage the contributions (and the egos) of 108 panelists and 102 consultants and authors.²³ (The only venue large enough for the initial meeting in May 1955 was the Radio City rehearsal hall.)²⁴ The twenty-six members of the Overall Panel included Robert

B. Anderson, who was appointed Treasury secretary during its deliberations; Christian Herter, the governor of Massachusetts, who would
succeed Dulles at the State Department; James R. Killian, the president
of MIT, who became Eisenhower's scientific adviser; Henry Luce,
editor-in-chief of Time Inc.; and Dean Rusk, the president of the
Rockefeller Foundation.[25] To give these grandees raw material to chew
on, Kissinger first turned to his old mentors: not only Kraemer for
draft papers on Germany but also Elliott, who was invited to write on
"Integration of Presidential Control of Foreign Policy in the Federal
Government"[26] and the "United States Democratic Process."[27] At first,
Kissinger did much of the writing himself, but in the course of 1957 his
role became editorial and ultimately managerial.[28]

The six reports were published as they became ready. Perhaps it was
inevitable, given Kissinger's simultaneous work on *Nuclear Weapons and
Foreign Policy,* that the second report—now titled "International Security: The Military Aspect"—was finished first. The fact that Edward
Teller was a member of Panel II also helped. Teller did not suffer people
of average intelligence gladly, much less fools; he and Kissinger hit it
off, finding themselves "in almost complete agreement" on the issue of
limited nuclear war.[29] (On one occasion Teller threw his watch at the
New Deal veteran Adolf Berle.)[30] They were reinforced by Itek director
Theodore Walkowicz, whose deeply pessimistic paper on "Survival in
an Age of Technological Contest" also impressed Kissinger.[31] Panel
members who dared to differ stood little chance. Yet external forces
also served to propel the military report into pole position. First, as we
have seen, there was the public panic over *Sputnik.* Then came the news
of a "Secret Report" that, according to *The Washington Post,* portrayed
the United States as being "in the gravest danger in its history."

> It finds America's long-term prospect one of cataclysmic peril
> in the face of rocketing Soviet-military might and of a power-
> ful, growing Soviet economy and technology which will
> bring . . . assaults on freedom all around the globe. . . . [T]he
> report strips away the complacency and lays bare the highly
> unpleasant truth.[32]

The Gaither Report was indeed alarming—more so, in fact, than Kissinger's *Nuclear Weapons* book. It argued that the United States could soon become vulnerable to a Soviet surprise nuclear attack if it did not accelerate the production of intercontinental and submarine-launched ballistic missiles, improve the protection of its own retaliatory "second strike force" by dispersing it more widely and "hardening" launch sites, and build more shelters to protect the American people from radioactive fallout in the wake of an attack.[33] Even the fiscal implications of this analysis were alarming, since the cost of implementing Gaither's recommendations would have been between $19 and $44 billion on top of the existing defense budget of $33 billion.[34] Eisenhower regarded such an increase in spending as not only inflationary but also likely to turn the United States into a "garrison state," but he could not ignore the report entirely; nor could he deny its existence, though he flatly refused to make it public. The stage could scarcely have been better set for the Rockefeller Special Studies report. Under intense pressure from Rockefeller, who scented a public relations coup, Kissinger scrambled to get the report finished, working every waking hour of December 1957, oblivious to the holiday season.[35]

The report chimed perfectly with the public mood. Mankind faced "two somber threats . . . the Communist threat to achieve world domination . . . and the new weapons technology capable of obliterating civilization." The United States was falling behind not only in terms of military spending but also in "major fields of technology. In certain areas assigned high priority by the Kremlin, the Soviet Union has surpassed us qualitatively as well as quantitatively."[36] The defense budget would have to be increased (though by just $3 billion, far less than the hike proposed by Gaither). The Defense Department would need to be wholly reorganized to increase the power of the secretary and reduce interservice rivalry.[37] The panel proposed the creation of a large "instantly ready retaliatory force," equipped with nuclear weapons. "Willingness to engage in nuclear war, when necessary," the report argued, was "part of the price of our freedom." Kissinger even went so far as to claim that "very powerful nuclear weapons" could be used "in such a manner that they have negligible effects on civilian populations."[38]

Released on January 6, 1958, the "Rockefeller Report" more than fulfilled its creator's hopes. Books written by committees seldom become bestsellers. This one did. When Rockefeller appeared on NBC's *Today* show, the host mentioned that viewers wanting to read the report could simply send in their names to NBC. "You'll have to give away a Ford V-8 with every copy," one of the producers joked. He could not have been more wrong. After more than a quarter of a million applications had been received, the publisher had to terminate the offer.[39] In total, the six reports sold over six hundred thousand copies in less than three years.[40] This success was partly due to Kissinger's effectiveness as a writer and editor. Arthur Schlesinger had complained of "blandness" in some of the early drafts he saw,[41] but he admired the "trenchancy" of the published version.[42] As with *Nuclear Weapons and Foreign Policy,* however, timing was crucial. "Unlike the Gaither Report, which . . . has not been made public," opined *The Philadelphia Inquirer,* "the Rockefeller report has been released. But both groups, composed of eminently qualified men . . . conclude broadly that the U.S. is in grave danger of falling behind Russia . . . [and] this is a matter for grave concern on the part of all Americans."[43] Just four days after the publication of the Panel II report, Rockefeller was called before the Senate Preparedness Subcommittee. On February 3, Prescott Bush, the Republican senator for Connecticut, endorsed the report's recommendations for a unified military command.[44]

The other reports, by comparison, were less sensational in their impact. The report of Panel IV, which appeared in April 1958, added little beyond noting the "Key Importance of Growth [preferably at 5 percent a year] to Achieve National Goals" (though its deliberations were notable for the objection raised by Anna Rosenberg, one of the few women to serve as a panelist, to the negative economic implications of the higher defense spending recommended by Panel II).[45] Two months later Panel III, chaired by Milton Katz, the former director of the Marshall Plan, recommended a combination of free trade and private (rather than public) international capital flows.[46] The report of Panel V on "Education and the Future of America" also appeared in June 1958. But it was not until December of the following year that Panel I's report on U.S. foreign policy finally saw the light of day, while the sixth report—"The Power of the Democratic Idea"—appeared only in September 1960.[47] Although Rockefeller called it "the most exciting and intellectually stimulating experience I have ever had," not everyone agreed.[48] Instinctively wary of anything bearing the Rockefeller name, William F. Buckley, Jr.'s *National Review* dismissed the reports as an amalgam of "existing Liberal blueprints."[49] Perhaps, but there was no gainsaying their influence. Clearly in response to the report of Panel II, Eisenhower announced a reevaluation of Defense Department organization, though the Joint Chiefs of Staff did their best to emasculate the enterprise. Rockefeller's pet phrase "national purpose" was soon ubiquitous, inspiring books by Oscar Handlin and Hans Morgenthau as well as a series of articles in *Time*.[50] It has been suggested that the primary goal of the reports was to "ke[ep] Nelson in the news as a serious student of government."[51] Certainly, by publishing them over a two-and-a-half-year period and then rounding the process off with the single-volume digest *Prospect for America,* Rockefeller ensured that he remained a figure on the national stage throughout. Yet there was an irony to come, as we shall see, for the Special Studies would have their biggest impact on the administration of a Democratic president.[52]

For Kissinger, the experience of managing the Special Studies Project was transformative. For the first time—unless one counts his running of the International Seminar at Harvard—he had been entrusted with significant administrative responsibility; for the first time he had to manage people, as opposed to books and articles. Like many academics, accustomed to working in isolation—intellectually self-confident but socially unpolished—he found it hard to begin with. Universities do not have strongly hierarchical structures; deans are not quite bosses. Now in Rockefeller, Kissinger had a boss, and one who was accustomed to having his orders followed. Rockefeller's biographers offer contrasting accounts of the relationship between the two men. One writes of "a romance of foreign-policy soul mates";[53] another suggests a more ambivalent and occasionally explosive affinity.[54] According to this latter version, Kissinger was "downright fawning in Rockefeller's presence" but "mocking . . . belittling . . . [and] deprecating" behind his back. This does not ring true. Theirs was a turbulent friendship. On one occasion, Kissinger "walked out" on Rockefeller after it emerged at a dinner that copies of Kissinger's drafts had been sent to various aides for comments and amendments, ignoring the injunction "*Nobody* edits my copy." "The next time you buy a painting," Kissinger angrily asked the great art collector, "will you have an expert for hands and an expert for feet?" When Kissinger returned to the office the next day to clear his desk, he found Rockefeller waiting. "You're a strong man and I'm a strong man," he said. "Now, we have two choices. We can try to destroy each other, or we can try to work together."[55] Rockefeller admired Kissinger's intellect enough to put up with his occasional tantrums. "I think Henry Kissinger is one of the real comers in this country," he told the former Democratic senator William Benton in August 1957.[56]

Although he had declined to work full time for Rockefeller, Kissinger was being paid for his labors. In 1958, for example, he received $3,000 for his services. But this did little more than replace the income he forfeited from Harvard by taking time off to work for Rockefeller.[57] It was not money that was his motivation; if anything, he felt somewhat underpaid considering the "incredibly hectic" work involved, which did not even leave him with time to get his hair cut. There was something gratifying about being on increasingly intimate terms with the most dynamic of the grandsons of America's most celebrated tycoon. "If nothing else," he wrote to Graubard in November 1956, "it is a fascinating sociological study."[58] Three weeks later he went further. "My respect for the Rockefeller family continues to mount. . . . They seem to me to perform the most useful function of an upper class—to encourage excellence—and they do not have the approach of a bureaucrat who pretends to judge the substance of every work."[59]

The job had exotic perks. As a Christmas gift, Rockefeller gave Kissinger a lithograph by the post-Impressionist French artist Jean-Édouard Vuillard; Kissinger reciprocated with Truman Capote's new book *The Muses Are Heard,* a humorous account of a cultural mission by an American opera company to the Soviet Union.[60] By 1957 Rockefeller was offering Kissinger the use of one of the houses at Pocantico Hills, the three-thousand-acre Rockefeller estate in Westchester County.[61] A year later Rockefeller's palatial Manhattan apartment, with its dazzling art collection, was at his disposal. No doubt the association with the voracious collector also helped smooth Kissinger's election to the Century

Association, the all-male club favored by artists and writers.[62] All this was surely gratifying to a man whose parents still lived modestly in a cluttered apartment in Washington Heights. But it was also exhausting. "The benevolent maniac, NAR, had to keep me occupied with his article which turned into more work than one of my own," Kissinger complained to his mother in March 1958. "I spent three days in New York staying at Nelson's apartment. He and his wife were very sweet. But right now I wish he would just leave me alone for a while."[63]

Henry Kissinger is surely not the first man in history to have coped with a demanding boss by being even more demanding to his own subordinates. It was in the offices of the Rockefeller Special Studies Project that a new facet of his personality emerged, a facet that would become familiar to all who later worked under him in government. He learned to rant and rage. The woman who saw—and heard—the most of this in the 1950s was Nancy Hanks, the executive secretary of Special Studies as well as a member of the project's planning committee. Born in Miami Beach and educated at Duke University, Hanks had first worked for Rockefeller when he was chairman of Eisenhower's Advisory Committee on Government Organization and had gone on to become his personal assistant when he briefly ran the Department of Health. Her letters to her parents are full of complaints about "fight[ing] HAK."[64] "HAK has for my money let me and everyone else down," she wrote after one especially bitter row. "He's just close to being a psychological case. . . . Really has been like a child and dropped all responsibility as far as directing the Project is concerned. Puts all the blame on NAR [Rockefeller] and Oscar [Ruebhausen]*—for silly things such as not keeping in touch with him, etc. . . . Oscar and NAR just plumb fed up of him."[65] In 1961, with the publication of the final volume, Nancy Hanks looked back on "many 'happy experiences,' which at the time would probably better have been classified as 'knock-down-drag-out fights.'"[66] Ruebhausen would later recall how Kissinger "suffered a great deal by taking things personally, simple things, like whether or not a car met him at the airport and whether it was a Cadillac or not. He would

---

*Ruebhausen had been Rockefeller's roommate at Dartmouth. Kissinger thought him a lightweight and could not stand him. The animosity was reciprocated.

weep on one's shoulders at some slight . . . it was candor and Machiavellian scheming at the same time."[67]

Yet office politics at the Special Studies Project was more complex than it appeared. Intelligent and attractive, Nancy Hanks personified the challenges facing any woman who wished to have a professional career in the 1950s. She had become Rockefeller's lover at a time when he was living apart from his wife and five children; Hanks had reason to hope that he would seek a divorce.[68] As it gradually became apparent that her hopes were to be disappointed,* Kissinger proved that there was sensitivity behind his bluster. "Henry isn't half as obnoxious as he used to be," Hanks confided in her parents in 1960. "He is about the only person Nelson is talking to or listening to. As long as I can keep encouraging Henry along the right track we are all right. . . . It has only been through his efforts that we have a 'team' to play with. Things had gotten really terrible. Our friend [Rockefeller] had just stopped listening to everyone."[69] The correspondence between Kissinger and Hanks reveals that they grew closer as Rockefeller drifted away from her. Apologetically, he asked her to reassure the Special Studies staff that "my unpleasant manners are a reflection of my character and not on their ability."[70] He was sorry, too, that he had been like a "hair shirt" to Francis Jamieson, Rockefeller's head of PR.[71] By 1960 Kissinger was signing his telegrams to Hanks "LOVE Henry."[72] She reciprocated, even when "angry" with him.[73] In March 1960 he sent her flowers—a "magnificent rose."[74] By this time the relationship was downright flirtatious: "I was really so tickled and have completely ruined your reputation by telling everyone about MY rose. The whole world is going to be under the impression that you are kind and thoughtful! It will take years to undo the 'damage' you have done. And oh what damage you have done to me! . . . I wanted to preserve YOUR FLOWER for all time."[75]

---

*Rockefeller broke off the relationship with Hanks when he became governor of New York. However, he soon began another adulterous relationship with Margaretta "Happy" Murphy, a family friend who had worked on his campaign and joined his staff in Albany. Unlike Hanks, she was married. In 1962 Rockefeller's wife sued for divorce. The following year Murphy and her husband were also divorced. A month later she and Rockefeller were married. During this period Hanks had been diagnosed with cancer and endured a mastectomy and a hysterectomy.

But this was surely no more than flirtation, tinged with sympathy for what Hanks was going through. The tone of their letters remained more screwball comedy than romance. "I knew you could forge one of the Rockefellers' signatures," he wrote when she sent him a copy of the final Special Studies volume, signed by Nelson and Laurance, "but to forge both is a real feat."[76] In June 1960 he teased her about "reports" he had heard that "you were most charming." "You must be getting soft . . . we can't have that in Special Studies or *I'll* come back."[77]

For by now Kissinger had returned to Harvard, apparently happily married and now, at the age of thirty-five, a father. At first he and Ann had been content to live with their pet dog (Smoky's replacement was another cocker spaniel named Herby) in a modest semidetached house in Frost Street, next door to the historian Klaus Epstein* and his wife, Elizabeth. As his position at the university became more secure, however, he felt able to move up in the world. As pictured in the *Boston Traveler,* the Kissinger residence at 104 Fletcher Road, Belmont, was the quintessential Harvard professor's home, its walls book-lined, its dining room large enough to entertain colleagues, students, and visiting academics. According to the article, Ann was happy to "take care of all [his] personal correspondence," to maintain "scrapbooks on [her] husband's job," and to prepare chicken and rice for their dinner parties.[78] Their first child, Elizabeth, was born in March 1959; a son, David, arrived two years later. Though neither Kissinger nor his wife was any longer a practicing Jew, David was circumcised at a bris, a family occasion that prompted Kissinger to look back "with pride over many difficult years" and to reflect that he "owe[d] almost everything to the spirit of our family, which has kept us together in good days as in bad."[79] Yet even as he wrote those lines, the family spirit was flickering and dying at 104 Fletcher Road. Ann had come back to Cambridge intending to put down roots. For Kissinger, however, Harvard was a staging post on the way to greater things in the other parts of Boswash. Working for Rockefeller had given him a glimpse of more glamorous worlds:

---

*Another refugee from Nazi Germany, Epstein had just published his definitive biography of the Weimar politician Matthias Erzberger.

the wealth of Manhattan, the might of Washington, D.C. As he strove to gain admission to those worlds, Ann would be left behind.

The fame Kissinger had won with *Nuclear Weapons and Foreign Policy* had made him more self-assured. "Five feet nine inches tall, stocky and wearing horn-rimmed glasses," according to one early newspaper profile, "Dr. Kissinger describes himself as a 'fair' tennis player and a 'pretty good' chess player."[80] In his brother's eyes, he now "dominated" Ann in an unhealthy way. Walter Kissinger had taken a different American path, in two respects. He was winning a reputation for himself as a businessman who could turn ailing companies around. First at General Tire in Akron, Ohio, then at Sperry Rand, the company that made UNIVAC—the second commercial computer produced in the United States—Walter was honing his skills as a corporate executive. He, too, was growing more confident. In 1958 he stunned his parents by eloping with Eugenie Van Drooge, a twenty-six-year-old Radcliffe graduate he had met when she was an intern at the semiconductor company he was running. She was an Episcopalian. It was soon clear that the couple had no intention of bringing up their children in the Jewish tradition.[81]

III

"Honesty forces me to report," wrote Henry Kissinger to Nelson Rockefeller in January 1960, "that [the junior faculty] are not much more interesting than the senior faculty."[82] There are at least two different versions of Kissinger's return to Harvard. The first emphasizes his tendency to be "anti-Harvard," simultaneously estranged from the residual WASP ascendancy and disdainful of the faculty's less worldly intellects.[83] The other portrays him as the archetypal "Cold War public intellectual," taking full advantage of the opportunities on offer at the preeminent "Cold War university."[84] Certainly, the place was changing fast. During the presidency of Nathan Pusey, and with Wilbur Bender in charge of admissions, Harvard became more academically rigorous in its admissions policy (though not as rigorous as scientists like George Kistiakowsky would have liked); more international and more eclectic in its curriculum; and more reliant on federal grants for its research, especially in chemistry, engineering, and medicine.[85] Between 1953 and 1963 the amount of federal funds going to Harvard to support research rose fivefold from $8 million to $30 million a year.[86] Before the war, the majority of all instructors had had Harvard degrees, but that proportion was rapidly shrinking to just a third as professors were recruited or promoted "because an *ad hoc* committee [chaired by the president himself] had judged them preeminent in their field."[87] Though himself a scholar of English literature and ancient history, Pusey presided over a utilitarian era. "Centers" with this or that regional or disciplinary focus proliferated, notably the Russian Research Center, founded in 1948 under the anthropologist Clyde Kluckhohn, and the East Asian Research Center, established seven years later under John K. Fairbank. In the early 1950s Kissinger and his patron, Bill Elliott, had been forced to beg and scrape to finance their International Seminar and its associated magazine, *Confluence*. With the creation of the Center for International Affairs, such indignities could be consigned to the past. The International Seminar lived on as a "labor of love," in Elliott's phrase, but *Confluence* was quietly left to die, as much for lack of time as for lack of funding.[88] In 1959 it was decided to switch over to annual publication, but no further issues ever appeared.[89]

The decision to establish a center for international studies dated back to 1954, when a committee had been convened as part of a Ford Foundation initiative to review the behavioral sciences at the university. Although there were thirteen courses then offered on aspects of international politics, the field tended to be dismissed as merely "a branch of current events" or "commentaries on yesterday's *Times*."[90] Bundy's first choice for a director was Robert R. Bowie, who was then director of Policy Planning at the State Department and assistant secretary of state. Bowie was a lawyer by training; prior to his appointment at State in December 1955, he had been a specialist in antitrust law at the Law School. However, having previously served as assistant to General Lucius Clay in the U.S. zone of occupation in postwar Germany and as general counsel to the U.S. high commissioner for Germany, John J. McCloy, Bowie also had accumulated considerable expertise on Western Europe. Though he was tempted to decline the Harvard offer and remain in government, Bundy was persuasive. Not only did he lure Bowie back to Harvard with the offer of the CFIA directorship and a half-time chair in the government department, he also persuaded him that Kissinger would be a helpful associate director.

Although the relationship between Bowie and Kissinger rapidly soured,[91] the two men at first spoke with one voice. Judging by its language, the program of the new center, published in 1958, was at least partly coauthored:

> Today no region is isolated, none can be ignored; actions and events in remote places may have immediate world-wide impact. . . . At the same time, vast forces are reshaping the world with headlong speed. Under the impact of wars, nationalism, technology and communism, the old order has been shattered; nations once dominant are forced to adapt to shrunken influence. New nations have emerged and are struggling to survive. . . . And over all broods the atom, with its promise and its threat.[92]

There would be five areas of research: European relations, economic and political development, the role of force and arms control, international organization, and the Far East. The center would not teach undergraduates or graduates—Bowie and Kissinger would perform those duties elsewhere as government department professors.[93] Rather, it would "combine basic research in foreign affairs with advanced study by experienced individuals . . . free from the pressures of day-to-day concerns."[94]

Always alive to the potential for institutional turf wars, Kissinger worried that the center might end up being little more than "an adjunct of existing departments," particularly of "a Political Science [i.e., Government] Department accustomed to treating International Relations as a subdivision of Government," if not actually "deny[ing] the validity of International Relations as a subject." The center, he warned Bowie, would have to be "ruthless in [its] insistence on independence of conception and execution." It was not "simply a problem of developing a program"; it was also "necessary to bring about an attitude and an intellectual discipline. Such a goal is anathema to many trends at Harvard. It is, however, the only real road to achievement."[95] He and Bowie agreed at the outset that "there was little point in doing once more what every other research organization and center of international affairs is attempting also . . . [because] the supply of talent is too thin [and] the subjects to be discussed [are] . . . so limited." Their only real disagreement was about Bowie's proposal for midcareer "Fellows . . . drawn from government, academic life, business, the professions and the press," who would spend between six months and two years at the center. Kissinger preferred the exclusively academic structure of Princeton's Institute for Advanced Studies.[96]

The swift degeneration of the Bowie-Kissinger relationship into a somewhat absurd microcosm of the Cold War they both studied has obscured the early success of their partnership. Initially located at 6 Divinity Avenue, the former home of the Harvard Semitic Museum, the CFIA was quick to flourish. It helped that the next two senior hires were of high quality: the development economist Edward Mason, who moved over from being dean of the Graduate School of Public Administration, and the game theorist Thomas Schelling, who had been at Yale since leaving the Truman administration in 1953. Kissinger's relationship with Schelling would also end in acrimony and estrangement, but for many years they exchanged ideas on European affairs and nuclear strategy on the basis of mutual intellectual respect. With ample financial support from the Ford Foundation ($100,000), the Rockefeller Foundation ($120,000), the Rockefeller Brothers Fund ($105,000), the Dillon family, Standard Oil, and IBM—as well as the university itself—Bowie and Kissinger did not have to devote much time to fund-raising. Contrary to Kissinger's expectations, the Fellows program was a success, not least because the regular seminars helped to reduce the barriers between disciplines and build an esprit de corps.[97] The cafeteria, with its long tables chosen by Bowie to encourage "intellectual cross-pollination" over lunch, was seldom empty.[98] Above all, the center succeeded in attracting first-class scholars, notably Zbigniew Brzezinski, Morton Halperin, Samuel Huntington, and Joseph Nye. Nor did it take long for the center to establish itself as a significant participant in the debate on U.S. foreign policy. As early as 1960, it produced two weighty reports—one on *Ideology and Foreign Affairs* for the Senate Committee on Foreign Relations, the other on *The North Atlantic Nations* for Secretary of State Herter.[99]

So what went wrong? It does not seem plausible that subtle differences of opinion played a part. True, Kissinger was never persuaded by Bowie's argument for a multilateral nuclear force (MLF), which would have established a seaborne (mostly submarine) nuclear force under NATO control, with multinational crews.[100] But this was a matter for academic debate, not a personal feud. Nor can the Bowie-Kissinger rift be blamed on politics; both were relatively conservative figures at a university where to be on the right was to be (as Bill Elliott once observed) "one against many."[101] One hypothesis is that Bowie was precisely the kind of "legalistic oriented government servant" that Kissinger would repeatedly deride in his writing in the late 1950s and early 1960s; another is that he was "the foxy Yankee, the quintessential WASP" (in fact he came from an old Chesapeake family) and as such fundamentally hostile to his junior (and Jewish) colleague.[102] In reality, the problem was a structural one. After several years in a senior government post, Bowie expected the CFIA to be run as a hierarchical institution; he saw Kissinger as his *assistant* director.[103] Kissinger took a different view. He was the one who had written the bestseller; he was the one whose counsel Nelson Rockefeller valued; he was the one being interviewed on television. He was a busy man. His office in Cambridge was one of two: the other was at the Rockefeller Brothers Fund in New York.[104] The Special Studies Project continued to eat up time until the publication of the final volume in 1961. On top of his New York commitments, Kissinger now had a succession of speaking engagements all over the country. All this had somehow to be scheduled around his twice- or thrice-weekly Harvard lectures. His new Harvard assistant noted that she had no "complaints—except the unavoidable one of not seeing him enough."[105] That soon became one of Bowie's many grievances. He accused Kissinger of "writ[ing] in order to get into the newspapers," of being "published largely because of [his] reputation," and of doing work that was "below acceptable standards.[106] The breakdown in relations began with blazing rows. "I got into an insane rassle with the malicious maniac, Bowie, which took all my energies for a while,"

Kissinger told his mother in March 1958, explaining why he had failed to visit her on her birthday. It ended with frosty silence. Schelling recalled how the two men—whose offices were adjoining—would "sometimes check with their secretaries before coming out to make sure the other was not there," though this was poetic exaggeration.[107]

Bundy, however, honored his side of the deal. In July 1959 he used a Ford Foundation grant to endow two half-chairs in the government department, one of which he earmarked for Kissinger, the other for the French scholar Stanley Hoffmann.[108] As both posts had the rank of associate professor with tenure, there needed to be departmental votes (by existing tenured faculty) as well as ad hoc committees. But despite the reservations of some—notably the Soviet specialist Adam Ulam, who regarded Kissinger's *Nuclear Weapons* book as unscholarly—both appointments were confirmed.[109] Kissinger now had the ultimate job security. As a tenured Harvard professor, he was effectively unsackable. Indeed, he had a job for life if he so chose.

What exactly did the job entail? As a teacher, Kissinger had a preference for graduate seminars, where more mature students would hear papers from visiting experts, followed by a Kissinger-led discussion. Along with Hoffmann and the Francophile Quaker Larry Wylie, Kissinger ran one on Western Europe. He also ran the Defense Policy Seminar, which was part of the Defense Studies Program, endeavoring to reduce the preponderance of ex-military students from Harvard Business School and to increase the quality of the outside speakers (among them a Republican congressman from Grand Rapids named Gerald Ford and the hawkish young senator from Washington, Henry M. "Scoop" Jackson).[110] An unusually high-level seminar, attended only by faculty, was the Harvard–MIT Joint Arms Control Seminar, founded in 1960 in the wake of two influential studies on the subject funded by the American Academy of Arts and Sciences. A joint venture between the CFIA and the MIT Center for International Studies, the Arms Control Seminar met regularly every two or three weeks to discuss precirculated papers by one or more participants.[111] These were evening affairs, usually held in one of the dingy upstairs rooms at the Harvard Faculty Club on Quincy Street. The old world surroundings, not to mention the tweed jackets and pipes favored by some participants, belied the innovative character of the discussions. Kissinger and Schelling were regular attendees, along with experts on science and technology like the biochemist Paul Doty, Richard Leghorn of Itek, and Carl Overhage of MIT's Lincoln Lab.[112] The young Morton Halperin acted as rapporteur (as well as teaching assistant for Kissinger's Defense Policy Seminar). The level of the discussion was high, the participants all experts in the burgeoning field. Typical was the December 1960 meeting at which those who had attended the sixth Pugwash conference* in Moscow gave their impressions of the event.[113]

But Kissinger also taught undergraduates. His "Principles of International Politics" (Government 180) was popular, regularly attracting more than a hundred students despite its daunting four-page reading list. Covering (as the syllabus put it) "the principal concepts and issues of international politics with emphasis on the basic problems of power including the nature, strategies and controls of 'power politics,'" the first iteration of the course had ten "required" texts, including Thucydides's *Peloponnesian War*, Machiavelli's *The Prince*, Burke's *Reflections on the Revolution in France*, Churchill's *Gathering Storm*, Morgenthau's *Politics Among Nations*—and Kissinger's own *Nuclear Weapons and Foreign Policy*. (Later, Thucydides and Machiavelli were replaced by more recent—and mostly British—historians like Alan Bullock and Michael Howard, though by 1963 they in turn had been supplanted by U.S.-based international relations theorists like John Herz and Kenneth Waltz.) The "suggested" readings were a mixture of books on past and contemporary international relations, with a pronounced bias toward nineteenth- and twentieth-century European history. The 1963 edition of the students' Confidential Guide to Courses captured Kissinger's lecturing style: "[He] is quite a sight as he struts back and forth across the lecture platform alternately praising Metternich, castigating Kennedy, and tossing laurel wreaths to Kissinger for Kissinger's solutions to the evils that beset our mismanaged foreign policy."[114] *The Harvard Crimson*

---

*The conferences were set up in response to the 1955 manifesto issued by Bertrand Russell and Albert Einstein calling for scientists to meet together to assess and counter the dangers posed by "weapons of mass destruction."

affectionately summed up Kissinger and his colleague Hoffmann in a parody dialogue:

> Q: While we're on the subject of individuals, let me ask
>   you about Henry Kissinger?
> A: Studying the complexities.
> Q: Of what?
> A: Of the situation.
> Q: I see. And Professor Hoffmann?
> A: Making the difficult distinctions.[115]

Like his own undergraduate mentor, Bill Elliott, Kissinger was too often "out of town" to be available on demand for every student in his class. He had seen how Elliott managed his schedule and took more than one leaf out of his book. But that is not to say he was unpopular with students. On the contrary, those who enrolled for Government 180 generally enjoyed Kissinger's readiness to answer their questions on current affairs and relished the mordant wit of his replies. For the majority, as is still often the case at Harvard, there was a small thrill in attending the lectures of a professor sufficiently well known to appear on *Face the Nation*. It was left to a few earnest types to express their doubts about Boswash Man. Charles Maier was a senior in the college when he published "The Professors' Role as Government Adviser" in the *Crimson,* an article conspicuously illustrated with a photograph of Kissinger. "The growth of the new class of professor-advisers entails dangers as well as promise," he warned. The principal danger was that this "new professorial class" might become so "arrogant in pomposity and so enchanted with its newfound recognition" as to be "complacent and intellectually blunted." The strong implication was that the professor-adviser risked "chang[ing] his traditional role of critic to that of spokesman for the regime."[116] It was June 1960. Three years later the *Crimson* carried an article in which Kissinger and Schelling were repre-sented as unaccountable "civilian militarists," incapable of seeing "how reason can be used to prevent conflict." All they did in their CFIA offices was to "accumulate data and feed them into a computer and then determine that such and such date would be the most propitious time for dropping the bomb on the Soviet Union."[117] Before the decade was out, such doubts about the relationship between Harvard faculty members and the "national security state" would be transformed into violent acts of protest.

IV

While the "professor-adviser" struck some students as being too close to government, in one respect he was altogether too far away from it. The Cold War was not the game theorists' epic duel waged in public. Much that was public was false, like the propaganda that conjured up imaginary missile gaps, and much that was true was covert, like the secret war between intelligence agencies. Even the best-informed outsider could have only an inkling of the Cold War's lies and mysteries. Only when Henry Kissinger entered the inner circle of government—only when he was privy to "top secret" documents—did he appreciate that his commentary on foreign policy in the 1950s had in many ways been naïve; that he had significantly underestimated the guile of Eisenhower's administration.

This was especially true of the global Cold War: the conflict between the superpowers for predominance in the third world, which might equally well be called the Third World's War.[118] If the threat of mutually assured destruction ultimately sufficed to produce a "long peace" for the United States, the Soviet Union, and a divided Europe, the same was not true for much of Africa, Asia, Latin America, and the Middle East. There the war between the superpowers, often waged through proxies, had a shockingly high cost in human life. We now know much more about that war than anyone outside official circles knew at the time. True, it was no secret that, as the European empires fell apart or dismantled themselves in the great postwar scramble to "decolonize," the Soviet Union had an advantage. "Almost any one of the new-born states of the world," grumbled Eisenhower, "would far rather embrace Communism or any other form of dictatorship than to acknowledge the political domination of another government." The "new countries" reminded him of a row of dominoes waiting to topple one after another.* At times this process seemed to be happening even more rapidly than the "sweep of the dictators" in the 1930s.[119] "The Korean invasion, the Huk activities in the Philippines, the determined effort to overrun all Viet Nam, the attempted subversion of Laos, Cambodia and Burma, the well-nigh successful attempt to take over Iran, the exploitation of the trouble spot of Trieste, and the penetration attempted in Guatemala" were all examples "of Soviet pressure designed to accelerate Communist conquest of every country where the Soviet government could make its influence felt."[120] Eisenhower and Dulles might have come into office talking about "liberation," as if the Soviet empire could somehow be rolled back; they very quickly realized that (as Kennan noted with the sharp schadenfreude of a man ousted from the classified world) they were "saddled" with containment.[121] Although Cuba and, arguably, North Vietnam were the only countries lost to Communism on Eisenhower's watch, that was not for want of trying on the part of Moscow. In January 1961 Khrushchev explicitly pledged Soviet support for "national wars of liberation." The idea was to ride the wave of decolonization by representing Moscow as the ally of all revolutionaries and branding the United States as the new imperialist. It is all too easy to forget just how successful this strategy was. Short of fighting multiple Korean-style wars, it was only through a huge campaign of "grey" and "black" propaganda and covert operations that the United States was able to slow the spread of Soviet influence.[122] Ideas about psychological warfare that had developed during World War II were now deployed in any country thought to be vulnerable.

The geographical range of the global Cold War was vast. South Vietnam was flooded with USIA†-produced anti-Communist literature; North Vietnam was penetrated by CIA-trained saboteurs and provocateurs;[123] Indonesia, Laos, and Thailand were swamped with

---

*Eisenhower's first reference to the domino theory was at a press conference following the French defeat at Dien Bien Phu: "You have a row of dominos set up. You knock over the first one. . . . What will happen to the last one is the certainty that it will go over very quickly." This was odd, as he had done next to nothing to prevent the French domino from falling.
†The United States Information Agency, also known as USIS (United States Information Service) when operating abroad.

propaganda. There was also a huge American effort to lock Pakistan into a "northern tier" of pro-Western states (along with Turkey, Iran, and Iraq) and to combat neutralism in India.[124] James Eichelberger, who was installed in Egypt as Nasser's public relations adviser, was in fact a CIA agent.[125] This was a multimedia campaign that involved not only economic and military aid but also trade fairs, exchange programs, cultural tours, libraries, mobile cinemas, and radio broadcasts.[126] In this regard, psychological warfare was of a piece with contemporary trends in commercial advertising: the assumption was that "hidden persuaders" could be as effective in foreign policy as in sales. But the results of all this were undoubtedly mixed. The American struggle to exert influence abroad without replicating European colonialism was readily mocked in books like Graham Greene's *The Quiet American* (1955) and William Lederer and Eugene Burdick's *The Ugly American* (1957). "Despite our massive economic aid and military assistance . . . our anti-colonial record, our recognized good intentions, our free and diverse society," complained a report by the President's Committee on Information Activities Abroad, "we seem to be becoming more identified with the negative aspects of the past and the status quo, particularly among younger people."[127] It was by definition difficult to make independent states comply with American wishes. Radio Cairo pocketed American cash and proceeded to denounce America's principal European ally. To make matters worse, when third world leaders— such as Thava Raja, a Malayan citizen and secretary of the Johore Postal Workers' Union—visited the United States on exchange programs, they often found themselves the victims of racial discrimination.[128]

When persuasion failed, the alternative was of course subversion. To Allen Dulles and his contemporaries, who had learned their craft during World War II and had then watched with dismay as the Soviets ruthlessly changed regimes in Eastern Europe, there was no obvious reason why the United States should play by different rules. Thus, under Dulles, the CIA "organized the overthrow of two foreign governments . . . attempted unsuccessfully to overthrow two others . . . and at least considered—if it did not participate in—assassination plots against several foreign leaders."[129] The overthrow of Mohammed Mossadeq had in fact been a British initiative following his nationalization of the British-controlled

Anglo-Iranian Oil Company, but the CIA soon got involved, greatly increasing the resources available to fund the coup.[130] In Guatemala the initiative came from an American business interest, the United Fruit Company, which had been nationalized by Jacobo Árbenz after his election in 1951. It was the CIA that organized the military coup that overthrew Árbenz, painstakingly fabricating and spreading the story that he was a Kremlin stooge.[131] This kind of operation was confirmed as legitimate by NSC-5412, approved by Eisenhower on March 15, 1954, which entrusted responsibility for planning covert operations to Allen Dulles but ensured that the White House, the State Department, and the Defense Department had the right of approval through the so-called "Special Group."[132] When Fidel Castro seized power in Cuba in January 1959, it was only natural that the CIA should begin work on an operation to get rid of him, too. As deputy director for plans, the ebullient Richard Bissell was quite ready to contemplate assassinations, not only against Castro but also against Rafael Trujillo of the Dominican Republic and Patrice Lumumba, the Congolese prime minister. Though the assassins who killed Trujillo and Lumumba in 1961 were not themselves CIA agents, the weapons they used were supplied by the agency.[133] Little thought was given to the potential "blowback" there might be when—as was surely inevitable in a society with a free press—these and other covert operations were exposed to public gaze. The fact that the KGB was fighting just as dirty a Cold War would not suffice as a justification, especially when so many of the regimes targeted by the United States were nationalist as much as they were Communist.

V

The Henry Kissinger of the late 1950s knew little of the Third World's War. He surely underestimated the extent of his own ignorance of what the Eisenhower administration was in fact doing, by foul means as well as fair, to combat the spread of Communism. Yet he was not oblivious to this increasingly important facet of the Cold War. In a remarkable half-hour interview with ABC's Mike Wallace in July 1958, Kissinger was drawn by his interlocutor away from the previous year's debates on the relative merits of massive retaliation and limited war. The exchange reveals much about how success had changed Kissinger. He was far more assured than in his first TV appearance, occasionally allowing himself a sly smile as Wallace's questions became more searching, but generally delivering his more hair-raising lines in the deadpan style that Walter Matthau would perfect in the role of Professor Groeteschele in *Fail Safe*.[134]

> WALLACE: In order to better understand your proposal for limited war, perhaps it would be well for you to define what you understand to be our current United States military policy. What is our military policy?
>
> KISSINGER: Our current military policy is based on the doctrine of massive retaliation, that we threaten an all-out attack on the Soviet Union in case the Soviet Union engages in aggression anywhere. This means that we base our policy on a threat that will involve the destruction of all mankind. This is too risky and I think too expensive.
>
> WALLACE: You obviously think it's wrong—dangerous to our security. I wonder if you would expand on that. Just because of what you call the risk and just because of the expense, it is not worthwhile?
>
> KISSINGER: No. What it will mean is that in every crisis an American President will have to make the choice whether a given objective is worth the destruction of American cities. The American President will have to decide whether Beirut or whatever the issue may be is worth thirty million American lives. In practice I am afraid the American President will have to decide that it is not worth it and it will therefore encourage the piecemeal taking over of the world by Soviet aggression.
>
> WALLACE: Because you believe the Soviets understand our unwillingness or inability—certainly our unwillingness—to wage an all-out war?

KISSINGER: The Soviets will understand our increasing unwillingness to engage in this kind of war and therefore their task will be to present us with a challenge which does not ever seem worth taking the final jump, but the accumulation of which is going to lead to the destruction of the free world. . . . I do not advise that we initiate war. The question of war will arise only if the Soviet Union attacks. Then if the Soviet Union attacks and in fact we are very much more afraid of total war than they are—they will gradually blackmail the free world into surrender. Everything that I say is based on the assumption that we are as willing to run risks as the Soviet Union. If this is not the case, we are lost, and I think we ought to face that fact. . . .

WALLACE: Then you think American strategy should be re-evaluated to restore war as a usable instrument of policy?

KISSINGER: American strategy has to face the fact that it may be confronted with war and that if Soviet aggression confronts us with war and we are unwilling to resist, it will mean the end of our freedom. It boils down then to a value choice. In these terms, yes, I think war must be made a usable instrument of policy.[135]

The conversation broke new ground, however, when Wallace pressed Kissinger to provide examples of how his preferred alternative of limited war might actually work. Without missing a beat, Kissinger offered a topical scenario, the "case of a Soviet attack, say, on Iraq." Speaking just twenty-four hours before a coup d'état by Pan-Arab army officers would overthrow the Hashemite monarchy in Baghdad, Kissinger argued that Iraq was just the kind of place the United States lacked the conventional military forces to defend. "If we had more divisions and if we had air transport, then . . . we could airlift a few divisions into the area and, together with local forces, attempt a defense."[136] When Wallace accused him of offering only "war policies" and no "positive peace policies," Kissinger rounded on him, rejecting the dichotomy as a false one.

> KISSINGER: Defense policies are essential to maintain the peace. They are not, however, going to solve the political problems of the world. They are only going to give us a shield behind which we can engage in constructive measures. What is essential right now is that we identify ourselves with the tremendous revolution that is sweeping across the world, that we have some image for the construction of the free world which is based on other motives than simply defending the world against communism. We must make clear what we are for rather than what we are against. If we were clearer about the kind of world we want to bring about, if we could project this concern to other people, then we wouldn't always seem so intransigently militant, then we would be identified with positive measures rather than simply with military alliances.[137]

Again, Wallace pressed for specifics, raising another country in the news: the French colony of Algeria, now in the fourth year of an insurgency that would ultimately achieve independence after another four years of bloodshed. Kissinger's response was again revealing:

> KISSINGER: In general, we should oppose colonial regimes. On the other hand, we should come up with ideas . . . an independent Algeria cannot survive as a purely independent state. The great paradox of this period is that, on the one hand, you have a drive towards more and more sovereign states and, on the other hand, there is no such thing as a purely independent state any more. The thing that has always attracted me, therefore, is that we could advocate a North African federation which could be tied together economically and for other development projects and that Algeria would find

its place as part of that rather than as a purely independent state.[138]

Would Nasser's newly created United Arab Republic, which had combined Egypt and Syria earlier that year, be invited to join? Kissinger
thought not, adding that U.S. policy toward Nasser had been "not
friendly enough to make him a friend and not hostile enough to put
him down. . . . I would say, however, that Ibn Saud does not represent
the force with which we should be identified in the Middle East"[139]—
an allusion to the Saudi monarch, whose preference for Sharia law over
secular Pan-Arabism had led him to order an abortive attempt on
Nasser's life.

In much of this, the influence of Rockefeller on Kissinger was
obvious—both the uncompromising hostility to colonial regimes and
the enthusiasm for federal solutions. But there is no question that Kissinger was also expressing his own distinctly idealistic views. Asked by
Wallace if he thought the United States could exist "in a completely
socialist revolutionary world," Kissinger gave a heartfelt reply:

> KISSINGER: Well, you know, you could argue that the iden-
> tification of socialist and revolutionary is not a very good
> identification. You could well argue that a capitalist soci-
> ety or, what is more interesting to me, a free society is
> a more revolutionary phenomenon than nineteenth-
> century socialism, and this illustrates precisely one of our
> problems. I think we should go on the spiritual offensive
> in the world. We should identify ourselves with the rev-
> olution. We should say that freedom, if it is liberated, can
> achieve many of these things. . . . Even when we have
> engaged in constructive steps . . . we have always justi-
> fied them on the basis of a Communist threat, very rarely
> on the basis of things we wanted to do because of our
> intrinsic dynamism. I believe, for instance, that we
> reacted very wrongly to the riots in Latin America [an
> allusion to the protests sparked by Vice President Nixon's
> visits to Peru and Venezuela the previous May]. Rather

than saying, "These are Communist-inspired and we must keep Latin America from going Communist," we should have said, "This recalls us to our duty. These are things we want to do because of the values we stand for, not because we want to beat the Communists."[140]

This was scarcely the language of realism. Indeed, Kissinger went out of his way to lambaste Secretary Dulles for "being so infatuated with the mechanics of foreign policy and with the negotiation aspect of foreign policy that he has not succeeded in projecting the deeper things we stand for and often has created great distrust abroad."[141]

There was only one moment in the interview when Kissinger faltered, and that was at the end, when the discussion turned to domestic politics. Wallace quoted a statement Kissinger had made to another ABC reporter that "[w]e have an administration of old men, happy with the life they have led." Smiling, Kissinger stood his ground.

> KISSINGER: I made this statement. I think that the groups I was referring to are very well-meaning, very sincere, very patriotic people. The difficulty they have is that they think that the world in which they grew up is the normal world. Their tendency is, when a crisis arises, to try to smooth it over and then to wait . . . to expect that the normal forces would reassert themselves. Therefore, they conduct policy a little bit like, oh maybe, small-town bankers who think one can always draw interest on a good situation.

But when Wallace asked him to identify himself with a politician in the next generation, Kissinger became evasive, saying only that he did not discern "any great moral dynamism" on either side of the party political divide. Wallace tried again:

> WALLACE: Who, if any, are the men in public life whom you admire and look to for leadership in the United States, Dr. Kissinger?

KISSINGER: Well, I must say, first of all, that I am here as a non-partisan, that I am an independent. I don't stand for either party in this. It depends. I have respected Mr. Stevenson in many of his utterances, respected Mr. Acheson in many of his utterances, although I have disagreed with him very much on other things. Er . . . It is very difficult for a party out of power to prove what it can do.

WALLACE: But there is no Republican who comes readily to your mind, in whom you have the confidence that that man has the understanding that we need to lead us at this time.

KISSINGER: I hate to engage in personalities. I think that Mr. Nixon in his public utterances recently has shown an awareness of the situation. But I'd rather not deal in personalities if you ask me.

This was a strange response indeed from a man who was already so closely associated with Nelson Rockefeller in the public mind. The political education of Henry Kissinger was only just beginning—and had a very long way to go.

BOOK III

Book III

CHAPTER 12

The Intellectual and
the Policy Maker

When you go to Spain and you buy a Picasso and you bring
it back and hang it in the Governor's Mansion, you don't
hire a housepainter to touch it up.

—HENRY KISSINGER to Nelson Rockefeller[1]

For some time I have thought that the best role for me in
this matter was not to operate through Henry Kissinger. I
find that intermediary a doubtful channel.

—WILLIAM ELLIOTT to Richard Nixon[2]

I

By 1958 Henry Kissinger was more than just a "professor-adviser";
he was an intellectual-celebrity. Rival candidates for the presidency
dropped his name in their speeches.* When the U.S. Junior Chamber of
Commerce named him as one of the "Ten Outstanding Young Men" of
1958, he found himself ranked alongside the pop singer Pat Boone.[3]
Much as he relished his sudden fame, Kissinger was only too well aware
of the difficulties of oscillating between one end of Boswash and the
other. In a long and distinctly introspective essay entitled "The Policymaker and the Intellectual," published in *The Reporter* in 1959, Kissinger
sought to identify these difficulties—and to suggest a solution to them.

---

*See for example John F. Kennedy's speech in the Senate on August 14, 1958: "We have
developed what Henry Kissinger has called a Maginot-line mentality." Kennedy felt no
need to explain who Kissinger was.

In theory, to be sure, the intellectual who was willing to step outside the cloister could counter the undesirable tendency of "an increasingly specialized, bureaucratized society" to produce leaders constrained by committees, dedicated to the "avoidance of risk rather than boldness of conception." Precisely for that reason, however, organizations were scrambling to employ intellectuals like himself. But there were two problems. First, the intellectuals "soon find themselves so burdened that their pace of life hardly differs from that of the executives whom they advise. They cannot supply perspective because they are as harassed as the policymakers." The result: the loss of that very creativity that was supposed to be the intellectual's trump card. Second, "individuals who challenge the presuppositions of the bureaucracy, governmental or private, rarely can keep their positions as advisers"—in contrast to those willing "to elaborate on familiar themes rather than risk new departures." The intellectual whose consulting contract got renewed was the one who offered "not ideas but endorsement."[4]

Not that the alternative of reverting to scholarly aloofness was preferable. Kissinger could already see all around him at Harvard where that led.

> The search for universality, which has produced so much of the greatest intellectual effort, may lead to something close to dogmatism in national affairs. The result can be a tendency to recoil before the act of choosing among alternatives which is inseparable from policymaking, and to ignore the tragic aspect of policymaking which lies precisely in its unavoidable component of conjecture. . . . The technicians who act as if the cold war were its own purpose are confronted by others who sometimes talk as if the cold war could be ended by redefining the term.[5]

The only solution lay, he concluded, in a combination of engagement and independence. The intellectual must not shy away from the policy making process, with all its snakes and ladders. But he must retain his "freedom to deal with the policymaker from a position of independence, and to reserve the right to assess the policymaker's demands in terms of his own standards."[6]

It is illuminating, in light of this article, to follow the trajectory of Kissinger's role as an adviser to Nelson Rockefeller, the man who so often in the years from 1958 until 1968 seemed tantalizingly close to a successful run for the presidency of the United States.

II

The stakes were already high in July 1958, when Rockefeller asked Kissinger to "get together on two or three short key speeches."[7] At this point Rockefeller was seeking the Republican nomination for the governorship of New York, which he duly secured that August.[8] But it was obvious to all concerned that this might well serve as a launch pad for a presidential bid. Why else give speeches on a new and more positive style of foreign policy, when foreign policy was hardly within the competence of a state governor?[9]

Rockefeller's political entourage was almost as fissiparous as his private life. Some, like old hands Frank Jamieson and George Hinman, urged Rockefeller to bide his time and consolidate his position in Albany. Others, like his loyal gatekeeper Bill Ronan and his flamboyant speechwriter Emmet J. Hughes, egged him on. Kissinger lost no time in asserting his dominance in the foreign policy speechwriting process, protesting against Rockefeller's preference for a protracted and collective process of revision ("it shouldn't go through 25 different hands")[10] and urging him to "lift the [foreign policy] discussion above that of pure tactics."[11] The results were, however, mixed. At least one Kissinger-drafted speech was an unmitigated flop, its contents far too academic for an audience that had been to "at least two cocktail parties" beforehand.[12] Arthur Schlesinger was probably being sarcastic when he asked if Rockefeller was going to name Kissinger as his secretary of state if he won the governorship.* (The job was one for which he was entirely unqualified.)[13]

Rockefeller's biggest challenge was that he was up against an incum-

---

*The secretary of state of New York is responsible for regulating a variety of professions and businesses in the state.

bent vice president with a solid base of support in the Republican Party *apparat*. Richard Nixon was not loved by the party's conservative wing, but Rockefeller was positively loathed by them. Moreover, in the period running up to the 1960 presidential election, Nixon was being allowed to play an increasingly prominent role in U.S. foreign policy, even confronting Khrushchev face-to-face in the famous televised "kitchen debate" at the American National Exhibition in Moscow in July 1959. At the same time, relations between the superpowers showed signs of improving, which tended to undercut the alarmism showcased in the Rockefeller Special Studies.

Two issues came to dominate the foreign policy debate in the twilight years of the Eisenhower presidency. The first was the campaign for a ban on nuclear testing, which had been gathering momentum as public awareness grew of the dangers posed by fallout. With the backing of prominent scientists as well as politicians (notably Averell Harriman, who had lost the New York governorship to Rockefeller after serving one term), the "test ban" was a difficult thing to oppose once the Soviets formally proposed it in the immediate aftermath of the *Sputnik* launch and even more so after they announced a unilateral test ban in March 1958. The second, equally contentious issue was Germany: variously its demilitarization, denuclearization, neutralization, and reunification. "Disengagement" in Central Europe also had prominent supporters, not least the architect of containment, George Kennan, in his 1957 BBC Reith Lectures.[14] This, too, was hard to oppose after the Soviets began to argue for it, backing their words with actions in January 1958 by reducing the Red Army by 300,000.[15] Who, so soon after the horrors of World War II, could seriously blame Khrushchev for opposing German rearmament?

Kissinger's positions on both these issues were uncompromising. "At a time when there is fatuous talk of 'summit conferences,' 'disengagement' and 'neutrality' [and] when Mr. Kennan delivers lectures whose reasonable tone only obscures their explosive and potentially disastrous quality," there could be no softening. A test ban was a bad idea. Any kind of concession on Germany was even worse. In "Missiles and the Western Alliance" (1958), he urged readers of *Foreign Affairs* to dismiss such notions, revisiting his earlier argument for limited nuclear war with a scheme for a NATO "missile system which can be moved by motor, a major part of which is constantly shifting position," with the aim "not primarily to destroy the Soviet homeland but to pose risks out of proportion to any gains Soviet forces might make in Europe."[16] The Rapacki Plan for the denuclearization of Central Europe—put forward by the Polish foreign minister Adam Rapacki in 1957—would effectively have removed U.S. nuclear forces from Europe, while leaving their Soviet counterparts just six hundred miles from Western European targets. A much better scheme, Kissinger argued, would be to induce a system of inspection rather than disarmament.[17] The headline in the *Herald Tribune* cut through the author's sometimes-dense prose: "Kissinger Urges Europe to Accept Missile Bases."[18] Privately, Kissinger was scathing about Kennan's "hysterical" and "self-righteous" proposals.[19] The challenge, as he put it to Arthur Schlesinger, was to devise alternatives to Eisenhower's approach that were both different and credible.[20] The trouble was that both issues—the test ban and Germany—were inherently complicated and certainly not the stuff of a successful political campaign.

To the public, a ban on nuclear testing was an attractive idea. The Atomic Energy Commission, now chaired by John McCone, was against it. The scientists were divided: while Isidor Rabi favored a test ban, Edward Teller and Lewis Strauss vehemently opposed it.[21] On August 22, 1958, Eisenhower, bowing to "world opinion," announced a one-year suspension of U.S. nuclear testing, beginning on October 31, as the prelude to negotiations with the Soviets.[22] Absurdly, both superpowers had by that time gone on a veritable testing binge in anticipation of a ban: there were eighty-one nuclear detonations around the world in the first ten months of 1958.[23] Matters were further complicated by scientific evidence on the difficulty of distinguishing underground nuclear tests from natural seismic activity.[24] Kissinger tried his best to strike a balance. "I have always believed it essential that there be a dispassionate, careful study of the problems of disarmament," he told *The Harvard Crimson* in October 1958, after an article had portrayed him as opposed to arms control. The United States should "always be ready to negotiate on this subject."[25] The problem was the extreme difficulty of securing binding commitments from the other side in the absence of some supranational authority with extensive powers of inspection and enforcement. "If our only alternatives were war or world government," Kissinger warned, "we were likely to have war before we have world government."[26] His article on the test ban issue, published the same month in *Foreign Affairs,* argued that a test ban would make sense only as part of "a general disarmament agreement which includes conventional weapons." On its own, a test ban would simply erode U.S. technological capability, while the Soviets would seek to cheat. In any case, was it really likely that an agreement would be honored by "the men who arrested the leaders of the [1956] Hungarian revolution while negotiating an armistice with them and who executed them despite a promise of safe conduct"? Kissinger therefore offered a proposal of his own. The United States should invite the Soviet Union to join a UN committee. This would set a maximum dosage of permissible fallout from testing well below the recent level. The UN committee would then "assign a quota to the United States and its allies and another to the Soviet bloc on a 50–50 basis." For two years both sides would agree to register with the UN all tests that involved fallout and both sides would agree not to exceed their quota. During those two years the quota would be progressively reduced, ultimately to zero. Afterward, the only permissible tests would be surface tests of "clean" weapons, underground tests, and tests in outer space. "Technical experts from both sides would agree on an adequate inspection mechanism," Kissinger concluded, "which could be relatively simple."[27]

This elegant scheme won the warm approval of Edward Teller, to whom the idea of a test ban was anathema—perhaps because he was confident that the compulsively secretive Soviets would reject the last part about inspection.[28] Yet in its complexity Kissinger's proposal offered markedly fewer political benefits than the earlier "Open Skies" suggestion. In the event, the Eisenhower administration shifted its position, proposing a limited agreement that banned all tests in the atmosphere and those above a certain threshold underground. When the Soviets balked at the number of inspection stations that would have been necessary to police the agreement, the United States yielded. By now Eisenhower's view was that any agreement was "better than no agreement at all."[29]

This was precisely the kind of agreement for agreement's sake that Kissinger most despised. In an interview ahead of a speech in Omaha, Nebraska, he lashed out against the administration: "Most Americans are like spectators at a play that does not concern them. . . . We're losing the Cold War and people all over the world are turning to Communism." Korea, he argued, had been when the rot set in. As an observer in Korea in 1951, he had found it "absolutely heartbreaking" to see the U.S.-led forces fail to win a decisive victory. "It started with Korea. We simply lost our nerve. Since then we've been timid and unimaginative."[30] Writing to Rockefeller in February 1959, he expressed his conviction that "we are heading for a desperate situation not dissimilar to that of Britain after Dunkirk."[31] Rockefeller, in turn, thanked Kissinger for improving his "understanding of the breadth and interrelation of so many of the forces which not only affect the future of our lives, but which create a current of deep concern to the people of our country."[32]

III

Kissinger's reputation was growing overseas as well as in the United States. In June 1959 he traveled to Britain as a delegate to the "Atlantic Congress" that marked NATO's tenth anniversary, where he was able to meet David Ormsby-Gore, then minister of state at the Foreign Office, as well as three leading lights of the Labour Opposition: its leader, Hugh Gaitskell, the deputy leader Aneurin Bevan, and his ally Richard Crossman.[33] But it was in Germany, the country of his birth, that Kissinger had the biggest impact. In late 1958 Kissinger flew to Germany at the invitation of the government of the Federal Republic on a lecture tour that included Munich, Bonn, and Hamburg, as well as his birthplace Fürth.[34] In Munich he addressed the Gesellschaft für Auslandskunde (Society for Statecraft), the West German equivalent of the Council on Foreign Relations, which had been founded in 1948,[35] and it was also there that he first met the then deputy editor of *Die Zeit,*

Marion Countess Dönhoff.* They got on well "(I think) despite my views on Kennan"—and despite, Kissinger might have added, the vast difference in their social origins.[36]

His timing was good. A crisis over Berlin was brewing. The Cold War, Eisenhower was warned, was entering "a period in which risk of world war will rise to a very high point, perhaps higher than any so far."[37] That November, Khrushchev demanded that Western troops leave Berlin and that the control of access to the city be handed over to the East German authorities. Neither Eisenhower nor his ambassador in Bonn, David Bruce, liked the status of West Berlin as a Western "island . . . surrounded by hostile territory." If there had been a way of neutralizing Berlin as a Free City without appearing to surrender to Soviet pressure, they might well have done it, just as they might well have agreed to German reunification if the Soviets had not so blatantly intended to subvert the western part's fledgling democracy. Because Berlin clearly could not be defended by conventional forces, there was therefore no alternative but to threaten, once again, all-out war. (As the poker-playing president put it, "In order to avoid beginning with the white chips and working up to the blue, we should place them on notice that our whole stack is in play.")[38] It was the special vulnerability of West Berlin, as well as the uniquely sensitive nature of the German Question, that made it the ultimate Cold War flashpoint.[39] The West German government was well pleased to have Kissinger— born in Germany but now a professor at Harvard—explain why any kind of Western military "disengagement" would increase rather than reduce the risks of war.[40] His arguments were publicly endorsed by the bellicose Bavarian defense minister, Franz Josef Strauss.[41]

Yet there was a fundamental weakness with the U.S. position, as became clear when Kissinger gave a lengthy interview to Rudolf Augstein and Konrad Ahlers of *Der Spiegel,* which had already established itself as the hardest-hitting political weekly in Central Europe. Kissinger argued that if the Soviets blockaded West Berlin, then the United

---

*They formed an enduring friendship, though it was not until her seventy-fifth birthday—by which time they had known each other for thirty years—that she suggested they start using the familiar *Du* instead of *Sie.*

States should send a convoy through East German territory to West Berlin. If the Soviets attacked the convoy, then NATO would defend it. And if the Soviets drove NATO forces out of East German territory and took West Berlin? In that case, Kissinger replied, "I should be in favor of giving the Soviets an ultimatum and, if necessary, of conducting a total war." *Spiegel:* "Total war for Berlin and Germany?" Kissinger: "Yes, if there is no other way to defend the freedom of [West] Berlin." What was more, if other Western European allies were reluctant to fight such a war, then the United States and the Federal Republic would fight it alone.[42] That answer gave the *Spiegel* editors their headline. Predictably, the East German media jumped on it as an example of reckless American warmongering.[43] Of course, Kissinger was doing no more than spelling out the implications of U.S. policy. It nevertheless illustrated the difficulty with his own thesis in *Nuclear Weapons and Foreign Policy*. For even he found it impossible to argue that a *limited* nuclear war could be waged over West Berlin.

Kissinger returned to the United States filled with foreboding. Speaking at an event in Harvard, he and his junior colleague Zbigniew Brzezinski, a talented Polish émigré who was then an assistant professor in the government department, debated Berlin. For Brzezinski, building his reputation as an expert on Soviet politics, Moscow was bluffing. "The Russians have no intent of war," he argued. Their demands were "a facade to hide their real motive of trying to stop the exit of refugees from East Germany." Kissinger was more pessimistic. He expected "continued trouble from the Soviets," adding that Eisenhower's handling of the issue had left him "displeased and unhappy."[44] Preparations were getting under way for yet another four-power conference. Such meetings had previously happened in London and Moscow (1945 and 1947), New York (1946), Paris (1946, 1948, and 1949), Berlin (1954), Vienna and Geneva (1955—the year of "Open Skies"). On each occasion it had proved impossible to reach an agreement on Germany. But Kissinger worried that this time—as over the test ban—Eisenhower would yield to the popular pressure for a bad deal rather than no deal.[45] Written during the conference, his next *Foreign Affairs* article, "The Search for Stability," was a detailed evisceration of the latest Soviet proposal for German unification on the basis of neutralization.[46]

"The Search for Stability" is noteworthy not only as a contribution to the debate on Berlin. It also illustrates how far Kissinger at this time still saw himself as a critic of foreign policy realism. "An excess of 'realism' about accepting the division of Germany," he argued, "will enable the Soviet Union to shift the responsibility for thwarting unification on us." On this issue, without question, Kissinger saw himself as an idealist, willing to take a mighty gamble on the German Question by advocating reunification:

> The West . . . must advocate German unification despite the experiences of two world wars and despite the understandable fear of a revival of German truculence. The West may have to acquiesce in the division of Germany but it cannot condone it. Any other course will in the end bring on what we should fear most: a militant, dissatisfied power in the center of the Continent. To strive for German unification is not a bargaining device but the condition for European stability.[47]

German reunification was a matter of principle: the principle of self-determination, as enunciated forty years previously by Woodrow Wilson, the arch-idealist among presidents. "Are we to deny in Europe what we have defended in Asia and Africa?" asked Kissinger. "During Suez we insisted that we would uphold our principles even against our allies. Are we to leave the impression now that we will uphold them only against our allies?" As the quid pro quo for reunification, Kissinger was prepared to contemplate the possibility of withdrawing NATO and Warsaw Pact* forces from some kind of "neutral belt." He even suggested five different schemes to that end,† which read like

---

*The Warsaw Pact was the 1955 collective defense treaty binding the Soviet Union to Albania, Bulgaria, Czechoslovakia, East Germany, Hungary, Poland, and Romania. It was a direct response to the Western decision to make West Germany a member of NATO. The original intention had been for the Federal Republic to join a European Defense Community, but the 1952 treaty creating the EDC failed to secure ratification by the French National Assembly.

†"[1] United States, British and French forces could withdraw to the line of the Weser while Soviet forces could retire to the Vistula. The German forces between the Weser and the Oder would be restricted to defensive armaments, as would the Polish forces

variations on a theme by Kennan. Yet on close inspection Kissinger's proposals were carefully crafted to be certain of rejection by the Russians. A neutral belt, Kissinger wrote, was "conceivable only . . . if it is made part of a satisfactory plan for German unification on the basis of free elections [and] if a careful study shows that substantial United States and British forces can be stationed in the Low Countries and France."[48]

As Kissinger put it, the Soviets were "likely to reject any proposal compatible with our values and interests. In that case it is essential that we be prepared to admit failure and make neither agreement nor negotiation an end in itself."[49] This assertion of the need to base American policy on "strong convictions," regardless of the consequences of diplomatic failure, was the antithesis of realism.

How are we to understand the idealism of Kissinger's answer to the German Question? One answer is that his visits to West Germany (he went there again in 1960) had moved him more deeply than he acknowledged in print. The West German leaders—not only Adenauer but also the mayor of Berlin, Willy Brandt—had impressed him as men of "stature." Adenauer's guiding principle had been to "tie Germany so closely to the West during his lifetime that even the most mediocre successor will not be able to break it away." Both Adenauer and Brandt were determined to resist any concession to the Soviets. To some in Washington, they seemed to aspire to wielding "a veto over the summit." Yet Kissinger could "not for the world see why the Germans cannot have a veto over the fate of a German city."[50] Predictably, he was dismissive of what was agreed by the four powers: a five-year "interim agreement" on Berlin, which included a commitment by the Western

---

between the Oder and the Vistula. [2] . . . A ceiling could be placed on NATO forces between the Rhine and the Eastern frontiers of the Federal Republic and on Warsaw Pact forces in the East German satellite so that the two military establishments would be substantially equal in number. [3] Or else NATO and Soviet forces could withdraw, say 100 miles, from the Elbe. A control system could be established between the Rhine and the Oder. [4] . . . the neutralization of Germany [could be coupled] with that of Poland, Czechoslovakia and Hungary. [Or] [5] we should strive for a demarcation line on the Oder, with Warsaw Pact and NATO forces withdrawn an equal distance, leaving a buffer zone manned by balanced German and Polish-Czechoslovak defensive forces under a system of inspection."

powers not to engage in "subversive" activities in the city. In Kissinger's view, this was "a travesty" that implicitly conceded to the Soviets a right to interfere in the politics of West Berlin.[51]

There was, however, another reason for taking such an absolutist position on Germany. Quite simply, if Kissinger's candidate for the presidency were to stand any chance of wresting the Republican nomination from Richard Nixon's hands, he would have to outflank him on national security.

IV

Rockefeller believed that Nixon was beatable. He also believed that Henry Kissinger could help him do it. As Eisenhower put it, "Rocky" was "a gadfly," a man whose inherited wealth had accustomed him "to hiring brains instead of using his own."[52] Henry Kissinger certainly knew more than Rockefeller about nuclear weapons. He may have known more than anyone in the United States about Germany. The problem was that he knew more about Germany than about the United States. Even in the late 1980s, the average American had visited only half of the fifty of the states of the union. Of those states, thirty-nine had been visited by fewer than half of Americans.[53] In 1959 Kissinger had probably visited fewer than ten.

A man who had spent most of his adult life in either New York or Massachusetts was bound to have an exaggerated idea of Nelson Rockefeller's popular appeal relative to his principal Republican rival. Rockefeller had won the New York governorship handsomely in 1958, in a recession year when most Republican candidates had fared badly, tarring Nixon (as the vice president later noted) "with the brush of partisan defeat."[54] By comparison, Nixon was already an established hate figure in the eyes of New York liberals. To the owner of the *New York Post,* Dorothy Schiff, "Nixonism [had] replaced McCarthyism as the greatest threat to the prestige of our nation today."[55] The momentum appeared to be with Rocky. But the next two years were to teach Kissinger that popularity in New York was very far from a guarantee of victory in a nationwide contest. Perhaps sensing the risks of putting all his chips on Rockefeller—at least until he formally declared his intention to run against Nixon—Kissinger declined the invitation to become his full-time adviser. It was, he told Rockefeller in May 1959, "one of the most difficult decisions of my life," but he had to prioritize "establish[ing] myself at Harvard. . . . The greatest tasks seem to me still ahead, and . . . I will be ready to drop everything here at an appropriate moment"—presumably if and when Rockefeller won the GOP nomination.[56]

Rockefeller was not a man who took no for an answer, however. At first, he had to rest content with draft speeches from the professor-adviser.[57] In July 1959, for example, Kissinger offered him some "fairly sharp" paragraphs about the Soviet threat "to counteract the current euphoria."[58] A month later Rockefeller tried again, inviting Kissinger to "handle the farming out and coordination of the foreign policy papers as well as those in the defense area." What he needed was "current facts in order to be useful and effective in influencing national policy, whether it be in the form of private conversation . . . or, as an outside possibility, assertion of positions as a national candidate if he should ever become one."[59] This time Kissinger agreed to "help out."[60] In effect, the Special Studies Project—renamed "the National Studies Program"—was to be revived as the policy wing of the Rockefeller campaign. As he insisted on retaining his Harvard position, Kissinger would share the running of the program with the lawyer Roswell "Rod" Perkins; Stacy May would handle economic policy.[61]

The summer of 1959 looked promising for the strategy of outflanking Nixon on national security. Nixon's trip to the Soviet Union in July 1959—the occasion of the famous "kitchen debate" with Khrushchev—had aroused suspicion in some Republican quarters that the administration was "hobnobbing" with the Soviets when it should be taking a hard line. These suspicions were only heightened by Khrushchev's visit to the United States in September. Kissinger was exceedingly dubious about this visit. "[It] will not change matters," he told Rockefeller in September 1959.

> I cannot conceive what form a success would take. . . . The exchange of visits is very likely to weaken Allied ties over the

long pull. . . . I am not impressed by the ovations for the President. The same was true after Munich. . . . Moreover, I am convinced that by this time next year we will be in the middle of a major crisis on Berlin. . . . At some point . . . Mr. Khrushchev will announce that since negotiations have failed he will have no choice but to sign a peace treaty with East Germany. . . . Those who now are so much trying to capitalize on immediate trends will cut no better figures than the leaders of France and Britain in 1940.[62]

The draft statement he suggested Rockefeller make after his own meeting with Khrushchev was not quite so inflammatory, to be sure.[63] Kissinger recommended that he condescend to rather than confront the Soviet leader, *de haut en bas*. The first secretary of the Soviet Communist Party might outrank the governor of New York. But "for an arriviste and a Bolshevik like Khrushchev to meet with a Rockefeller has a significance similar to that which made Napoleon so eager to be accepted by the established sovereigns. Besides . . . you may be President some day."[64] Kissinger preferred to do the confrontation himself, in print. His *New York Times* article on the "dangers and hopes" surrounding the Khrushchev visit was intended to pour cold water on it. The Cold War was not "the result of a misunderstanding between our leaders and those of the Soviet Union." It was a result of Soviet policies: the suppression of freedom in Eastern Europe, the refusal to compromise on arms control, "pressure on all peripheral areas," and the "unprovoked threat to Berlin." Without in any way compromising on these issues, Khrushchev had been rewarded with "meetings with the President from which our allies are excluded." This was "the culmination of a trend which has seen the Western alliance dangerously close to being split."[65]

Khrushchev and his wife spent several days traveling across America, making stops in New York (where he presented the UN General Assembly with a bold plan for general disarmament), California, Iowa, and Pennsylvania. As with the kitchen debate, the visit was not without its comic moments. Khrushchev became infuriated after being denied a visit to Disneyland, ostensibly for security reasons. But from a Soviet point of view, the trip as a whole was a clear success, culminating with a two-day meeting with Eisenhower at Camp David, the presidential retreat in Maryland's Catoctin Mountains. In return for agreeing not to set a time limit for negotiations on Berlin, Eisenhower agreed to attend yet another four-power summit the following year and to visit Russia after that.[66] At a forum in Cambridge, Kissinger was scornful. "If Khrushchev were to compare his position today with that of a year ago, he must conclude that the best way to deal with the West is to frighten [us]," he was quoted as saying, referring to Berlin. "We have been playing charades with ourselves."[67]

The problem was that he now began to sound like a killjoy at a time when others were enthusing about "the spirit of Camp David." "I do not oppose summit meetings as such," he testily informed the editor of the *Crimson*.[68] "I am not opposed to compromise." Rockefeller himself had to issue a denial that he had opposed the invitation to Khrushchev.[69] He got into similar difficulties in November when he appeared to argue that the United States should unilaterally resume underground testing.[70] It did not help that, by pressing for higher defense expenditure, Rockefeller was antagonizing Eisenhower, who had not failed to notice his "big government" tendency to tax and spend in New York. The strategy was not working, and Rockefeller knew it. In December 1959 he decided, if not to withdraw, then at least not to contest the first primaries. Distraught, Kissinger admitted to a "feeling almost of despair when I learned of your withdrawal—

> despair not for you but for the country and the cause of free-
> dom in the world. Four years is a long time in our age and
> many opportunities which exist now will have disappeared.
> Much suffering which could have been avoided must now be
> experienced. We are heading, I am convinced, for dark, per-
> haps desperate times, and to make matters worse, all seems calm
> now—the calmness, I fear[,] of the eye of the hurricane.[71]

He had perhaps been wise not to commit himself wholly to Rocky.

V

The election of 1960 was destined to be a close one. But for the term limit introduced nine years before by the 22nd Amendment (ironically, a Republican-backed measure), Eisenhower might have been persuaded to run again and would likely have won. That made his endorsement valuable, but he had such grave doubts about both Rockefeller and Nixon that he repeatedly declined to give it. The Democratic front-runner, the photogenic young senator from Massachusetts, John F. Kennedy, was inclined to prefer Nixon as a rival. But he, too, had a race on his hands for his party's nomination. His Texan rival Lyndon Johnson was in some ways a stronger candidate: a Protestant and a southerner at a time when the fissures between northeastern liberals and southern "Dixiecrats" were beginning to widen dangerously, not least over civil rights. Also in contention was the Missouri senator Stuart Symington, who had served under Truman and had the former president's backing.

Under the circumstances, Kissinger was perhaps prudent to insist—even while writing speeches for Rockefeller—that he was a political independent. When he heard that Bundy had told a Harvard student that "Kissinger [was] leaning towards Republicanism," he hastened to dispel the idea:

> I did not think that you thought this ill of me. My feeling towards the parties is, as someone said of the 1945 World Series, that neither party deserves to win, though the Democrats probably a little more than their opponents. Among the candidates (coy or otherwise), I have a preference for Rockefeller though this has not kept me from being on good terms with several of the hopefuls in the other camp. And a good case could be made for the proposition that Rockefeller is the best available alternative to Republicanism.
>
> This is only half serious, but I *have* guarded my independence rather fiercely.[72]

One option, if Rockefeller was not going to run, was simply to change horses. As we have seen, Kissinger had unexpectedly mentioned Nixon, not Rockefeller, when Mike Wallace had asked him to name a Republican with "the understanding that we need to lead us at this time." He had repeatedly and vainly invited Nixon to address the International Seminar at Harvard.[73] In truth, the two men had more in common than Kissinger had with the playboy-plutocrat would-be president Rockefeller. Given that they would ultimately form one of the most extraordinary partnerships in the history of American foreign policy, it is worth asking why that partnership had to wait until 1968 to begin.

Like Kissinger—and unlike Rockefeller—Richard Milhous Nixon was born with no silver spoon in his mouth. His father ran a grocery and gas station in Whittier, to the southeast of Los Angeles; two of his three brothers died before he graduated from college. Like Kissinger, Nixon was raised in a religiously conservative family. As a college senior, he recalled how biblical literalism had been "ground into me" by his "fundamental Quaker" parents, who had "warned [me] against science."[74] Like Kissinger, he was highly intelligent, an academic performer; indeed, he would also have gone to Harvard had his father not needed him to help with the family store, confining him to Whittier College. Like Kissinger, too, he was a worker, "push[ing] himself very hard, on principle . . . think[ing], erroneously, that he performs best out on the borderline of fatigue, when he has worried a thing to its bitter end."[75] And like Kissinger, he had suffered a crisis of religious faith as a young man. Exposure at Whittier to Hume, Mill, and other philosophers led him to exclaim, at the age of twenty, "I am no longer a 'seven-dayer'! . . . I am no longer a fundamentalist. I have not resisted the heresies of college professors."[76]

Even more striking is the fact that, as a young man, Nixon also considered himself an idealist, even quoting Kant as offering the best way of reconciling philosophical knowledge with the existence of God. He was filled with admiration for Woodrow Wilson, despite the fact that—like most Americans in the early 1930s—he regarded the U.S. entry into World War I as "a ghastly mistake" that had "only started the wheels of industry rolling toward another greater war." In his soul-searching senior-year essay "What Can I Believe," Nixon urged the application of Christ's teaching in the international field:

> [R]epeal the obnoxious features of the Versailles Treaty. . . . Disarm all the nations of the world as fast as is humanly possible. Reestablish the League of Nations—for all nations—and add a World Court for economic disputes to our present Court. Put the machinery in motion for a huge program of educational, scientific propaganda whose purpose it will be to draw the peoples of the earth closer together. Work for the eventual abolishment of tariffs and immigration restrictions. . . . I believe that all the problems of the world can be solved by courts of investigation which would consider the individual conflicts and render advisory decisions. . . . I [en]vision a world in which there are no walls between nations, no racial hatreds, no armaments; I see a world in which each nation produces the best it can in the field of economics art, music, etc.; I see a world where men and women of all nationalities, travel together, eat together, even live together. I see a world which cooperates, which strives upward to the final, highest values of life.[77]

This was only one of a number of startlingly liberal positions the young Nixon took. He also favored "democratic control" of the economy to reduce inequality, a relaxation of restrictions on immigration, and even racial intermarriage—something then prohibited in the majority of American states. Yet Nixon remained a conservative, not least on foreign policy. Consistently and militantly anti-Communist, as we have seen, he had made his name in Congress as the scourge of Alger Hiss. It was precisely his ability to take liberal positions on some of the key issues of the 1960s—notably African American civil rights—while at the same time mollifying conservatives with his foreign policy hawkishness that made Nixon such a formidable Republican candidate. In this, too, Nixon had much in common with Kissinger. They even shared certain character traits. Both were hypersensitive to slights, especially from those they considered establishment insiders. Both were capable of savage ill temper toward subordinates when under pressure.[78]

Both were loners at heart, even if Kissinger was already learning how to use his quick wit to good effect at parties. Both were regarded as, and felt themselves to be, perennial outsiders.[79] Neither really knew how to relax.

So Kissinger was more than merely flattered when Nixon wrote to tell him how much he had liked his *New York Times* article on the Khrushchev visit ("superb"), to the point of quoting it in a speech. "In major respects," Nixon assured him, "my views coincide exactly with those you expressed."[80] To be sure, such blandishments had to be taken with a pinch of salt; it was entirely characteristic of Nixon to write in such honeyed tones to his rival's principal adviser. On the other hand, the two men clearly did have views in common. Moreover, there was an obvious channel of communication from Harvard to the Republican front-runner. Even as Kissinger had been cultivating Rockefeller, so his old mentor Bill Elliott—who continued to dream of preferment in Washington—had been assiduously cultivating Nixon, bombarding him not only with invitations to Harvard but with a variety of policy papers on subjects calculated to appeal to the vice president.[81] By 1958 Nixon was referring to Elliott as "my good friend."[82] In particular, Elliott played on Nixon's conviction that he was being persecuted by the liberal media, regularly writing to console him after attacks by *The Nation* and *The New York Times*. He also played a key part in persuading Nixon that there needed to be an overhaul of the executive branch to increase the power of the presidency relative to the bureaucracy and the legislature. With the appointment of Christian Herter as secretary of state, Elliott gained a new nook in the corridors of power: an office at State. Even as Kissinger was bemoaning the iniquities of summit diplomacy, Elliott was flying with Nixon to meet Khrushchev in Moscow. "I would be honored," he wrote in March 1960, "if it were true that I am one of Dick Nixon's principal advisers. I do what I can to be of use to him."[83]

The stars, it seemed, were aligned. Kissinger's mentor at Harvard was advising Nixon; he was even urging him to extend an olive branch to Nelson Rockefeller and to consider enlisting some Harvard brains in his own campaign. Yet this was not to be the moment when Henry met Dick. This was partly because Elliott did not wish it. But it was mainly because Kissinger absolutely refused it.

To Elliott, Kissinger was fast becoming the sorcerer's apprentice; ten years later it would be the pupil, not the master, whom Richard Nixon would appoint as his trusted foreign policy adviser. What made this all the more galling was that the job of national security adviser as Nixon and Kissinger later defined it bore an uncanny resemblance to the kind of "assistant President" that Elliott had for years urged Eisenhower to create—and which the president seriously considered adopting in early 1959, when his brother Milton proposed the creation of two "superadvisers," one for foreign policy, the other for domestic. (However much Nixon liked the idea in theory, he was adamantly opposed to it as long as he himself was vice president, fearing that the new posts might undermine his already weak position in the administration.)[84] Elliott already sensed that his Harvard protégé had become too big for his boots. In January 1960 he suggested that Nixon should try to "work out the kind of understandings with Nelson that will get the maximum help from him without too much compromising your own freedom of future action." But he went out of his way to exclude Kissinger from such overtures:

> I am not sure that I would be the best intermediary to Nelson from you, although as you know, I helped him set up his "Special Project." . . . For some time I have thought that the best role for me in this matter was not to operate through Henry Kissinger. I find that intermediary a doubtful channel, and now one disappointed in [his] ambitions by Nelson's very wise decision.

In the list of Harvard faculty members Elliott urged Nixon to enlist for his campaign, his former student was conspicuous by his absence.[85] Unfortunately for Elliott, his efforts to assist Nixon fizzled out in the spring of 1960, when Nixon's campaign managers effectively sidelined him.[86] Stabbing Kissinger in the back was his last act in the drama of

---

*Cleverly, Nixon argued that appointing two superadvisers would reinforce the public perception that "this President could not work as hard as others." That was enough to kill the idea.

the 1960 election. (So bitter was Elliott about the way Nixon had treated him that he declined to advise him when he embarked on a lecture tour in 1961.)[87]

Yet even Elliott's betrayal did not matter. For Kissinger had in any case set his mind against working with Nixon and would repeatedly reaffirm his disdain for him for years to come. It is worth pondering why. The best explanation is that Nixon's bad reputation preceded him into Kissinger's milieu. A large part of "Middle America" saw and identified with "Nick" Nixon the outsider, the self-made man, the hard worker, the regular guy whose idea of relaxation was drinking beer on a boat with two other regular guys like Bebe Rebozo and Bob Abplanalp: both sons of immigrants, both self-made men.[88] Cambridge and New York saw only "Tricky Dicky." Part of the problem was certainly Nixon's extraordinary social awkwardness. "An introvert in an extrovert's business," as he himself admitted, a pathologically shy man who was most at peace when he was sitting alone, scrawling on a yellow legal pad, Nixon never learned to put people at their ease.[89] First encounters with him were invariably off-putting.[90] Regular people never had this experience because they simply never met Nixon. They "met" him only when they saw him on television or at a podium, where all his relentless preparation and memorization paid off in carefully crafted and targeted political performances. Only the denizens of Boswash had to make small talk with the offstage Nixon at those innumerable social events and fund-raisers that a candidate for high office is bound to attend. The main reason the East Coast liberal bastions distrusted Nixon was, however, his deviousness: the denials during the Hiss case that he had spent time at the key witness Whittaker Chambers's farm;[91] the 1952 funding scandal that nearly cost him his place on the Republican presidential ticket; the apparent relish with which he engaged in negative campaigning and all the other dark political arts; the ineffable quality (as Eisenhower's personal secretary Ann Whitman put it) of "acting like a nice man rather than being one."[92] As a young man, Nixon had dabbled in amateur theatricals. He never could rid himself of that quality of a second-rate actor playing a Shakespearean villain[93]—a "smiling, damned villain": Claudius, if not Iago, the dark and vengeful sower of discord who proclaims in the very first scene of

Othello, "I am not what I am."* Never having met him and unaware of all they had in common, Kissinger simply wanted "nothing to do with" the man one biographer has called "Nixon the hater; Nixon the profane; Nixon the furious; Nixon the unscrupulous player of hardball"[94]— in short, the odious Nixon drawn again and again by *The Washington Post*'s cartoonist Herb Block.

Perhaps the most compelling proof of Kissinger's rejection of Nixon was that he preferred to work with his Democratic rival. As he had hinted to Bundy, he had already been approached by the main Democratic contenders, including Kennedy, in 1959. After Rockefeller's apparent withdrawal, they contacted him again. Indeed, in February 1960 Lyndon Johnson made a point of reading into the Senate record a letter that Kissinger had written to *The New York Times,* which more or less dismissed Eisenhower as over the hill ("expertise acquired in the period up to and through World War II is almost completely irrelevant to the contemporary strategic problem" and even "dangerous . . . in the era of missiles and nuclear weapons").[95] Punctiliously, Kissinger informed Oscar Ruebhausen and Rod Perkins. When the Democrats had originally approached him, prior to his resuming his work for Rockefeller, he had replied, he told Ruebhausen and Perkins, that he would

> answer specific questions but do no writing nor volunteer any advice. I followed this until June. Since then I was in contact with none of them until Nelson's withdrawal. After this I was approached once again by Kennedy and Symington and evaded the issue.
>
> My view is as follows: among our leading public figures the only one in whom I really believe is Nelson. For him I have been prepared to give up my independent position, which I value highly. As for the others, I think I will make my major contribution by not committing myself to anyone and staying out of partisan politics. If Nelson does not run, I propose to sit

---

*Mark Feeney has memorably suggested that Nixon was a composite of Iago, Malvolio, and Richard III, but these other personae were less visible in 1960. The challenge is to remember the prelapsarian Nixon, before Watergate and resignation forever destroyed his reputation.

out the campaign; indeed I propose to be away during part of
the summer, at least in part to be unapproachable.

As long as I am working with Nelson, you can be certain
that I will keep you informed of any conversations I may have
with other leading figures before the event. You should not
credit any newspaper stories you might see if they do not coincide with what I have already told you. I am rather obsessive on
the question of loyalties and there need be no concern.[96]

Kissinger was nevertheless keeping his options open. He urged
Rockefeller not to consider reentering the lists in 1960, even if "lighten-
ing [*sic*] were to strike." Staying above the political fray for now would
make him "the almost inevitable choice for 1964."[97] By March 1960, he
was signaling his intention to resign from the Special Studies Project,
now nearing its conclusion.[98] The problem was that Rockefeller was also
keeping his options open, hoping that either a surge of popular support
or an endorsement from Eisenhower would propel him back into the
race for the Republican nomination. Kissinger was stuck. So long as
Rocky lived in hope, he could not gracefully give up on him. Two years
after the fact, he summed up his position to Arthur Schlesinger:

Had Rockefeller run in 1960, I would have supported him.
Had he been elected, I would no doubt have served on his staff.
Until the campaign of 1960, I was his principal foreign policy
advisor. (I withdrew during the campaign because I wished to
have nothing to do with the Nixon candidacy. Indeed, you
will remember that I did my best to be of help to Kennedy,
both through you and through Walt Rostow.) . . . My support
of Rockefeller in 1960 had nothing to do with party affiliation
in the first place. His being in the Republican Party was, in my
estimate, a drawback. I have never dealt with or supported any
other Republican. I supported Rockefeller because I shared his
convictions and believed in his objectives.[99]

For all its studied precision, there was a complexity to this position that was not readily compatible with the rough-and-tumble of

American political life. Was he with Nelson Rockefeller or not? The professor's answer was, in essence, that it depended.

VI

Eisenhower was serious about disarmament. When in 1960 the Pentagon produced SIOP-62—the first integrated strategic plan, bringing together the three different services—more than 2,500 Soviet targets were identified. The final National Strategic Target List specified 1,050 Designated Ground Zeros (DGZs) for nuclear weapons, including 151 urban-industrial assets. Even the minimal version of the plan envisioned 650 DGZs being hit by over 1,400 weapons with a total yield of 2,100 megatons. In the words of George Kistiakowsky, Eisenhower's new scientific adviser (and Kissinger's former chemistry professor), this was "unnecessary and undesirable overkill." The president confessed that Kistiakowsky's presentation on the subject "'frighten[ed] the devil out of me.'"[100] It seemed as if the three armed services had no more sophisticated strategy than to unload as many as possible of their weapons on the Soviet Union. This only reinforced Eisenhower's suspicion that the defense budget had become bloated with superfluous weaponry.

The goal that seemed within reach, as the Paris four-power conference approached, was a test ban agreement. The Soviets accepted the American proposal for a moratorium on atmospheric tests and larger underground tests. All that remained to be agreed was the duration of the freeze and the number of on-site inspections.[101] But the Paris conference was wrecked when the Soviets downed Gary Powers's U-2 spy plane, which the CIA had sent into Soviet airspace from Pakistan on May 1 (a public holiday when almost nothing else was in the air).[102] As Eisenhower rightly said, it was a "stupid mess."[103] Kissinger was kept busy explaining the technicalities of the test ban issue,[104] while ensuring that Rockefeller was also kept abreast of the still-simmering Berlin crisis.[105] The collapse of the Paris conference presented a fresh opportunity to make the case against Eisenhower's policy. "Inferiority in missiles," Kissinger told Rockefeller, implicitly endorsing the "missile gap" theory, "is not as worrisome as the vulnerability of the entire retaliatory force," which was insufficiently dispersed and defended to deter a Soviet surprise attack. Even if the gap were closed, there would be an unstable equilibrium based on "mutual invulnerability." In earlier critiques, Kissinger had drawn parallels with the 1930s; now he went back further, to the origins of World War I:

> If it becomes apparent over a period of years that our situation of threat and counterthreat will always be resolved by someone's backing down, this very sense of security may produce a showdown. After all, the crisis which led to World War I seemed at first no different from innumerable others which had been resolved by the threat of going to the brink of war. And when war finally came, it was fought as a total war over a relatively trivial issue because no other alternative had been considered.[106]

The remedies were the familiar ones: to maximize the range of military options "between surrender and Armageddon" and to deepen the ties between the United States and the rest of NATO by placing part of the United States and British retaliatory forces under NATO control.[107] By June 1960, Kissinger was no longer debating that "the 'missile gap' will materialize in the period 1960–64"; the only question was whether it would lead to a Soviet surprise attack or merely to "the piecemeal erosion of the free world . . . of which the crisis over Berlin is but an augury."[108]

Now Kissinger's timing was better. With the failure of the Paris summit, the public mood reverted to its post-*Sputnik* funk. Now both Rockefeller and Kennedy were telling audiences and journalists that defense spending needed to be cranked up in order to close the missile gap and to create options other than massive retaliation. Nixon was being squeezed from both sides by what he called the "sitting duck" charge, but he could not concede that the critics had a point without implicitly condemning Eisenhower.[109] Rockefeller had a bigger problem: he needed Eisenhower's endorsement if he was going to leapfrog ahead of Nixon before the Republican convention, but how could he hope to get it while he was castigating the president on the very issue

Ike believed he knew best? To his annoyance, Kissinger was forced to cancel a well-paid lecture tour to Germany in June 1960 in order to be available to brief Rockefeller.[110] He was now being used "for final consultation on foreign policy issues," working with Perkins to manage a team of researchers and to review the position papers they churned out.[111] Among the ideas Kissinger encouraged Rockefeller to consider was one for a North Atlantic Confederation that had been suggested to him by Edward Teller.[112] On June 8 Rockefeller dropped his bombshell: a bombastic "buckshot indictment" of Nixon's candidacy, mostly drafted by Emmet Hughes but with some recognizably Kissingerian lines ("our position in the world is dramatically weaker today than fifteen years ago, at the end of World War II"), which could not have been better calculated to infuriate Eisenhower.[113] When Rockefeller compounded the insult by asking Eisenhower if he should run, the latter let him stew for two days and then bluntly told him that "he did not believe it was right to alarm people unnecessarily" over national security. He advised him not to re-enter the race; he would be ridiculed as "off again, on again, gone again, Finnegan."[114]

Through this comedy of errors, Kissinger was at pains to preserve his public independence. When he appeared on Eleanor Roosevelt's WNEW-TV show *Prospects of Mankind*[115] or when he was interviewed by *The New York Times*,[116] it was not as Rockefeller's adviser but in his own right. A new *Foreign Affairs* essay, "Arms Control, Inspection and Surprise Attack," appeared in July 1960, the critical month of the Republican convention in Chicago. It made no reference to the rivals for the nomination. Indeed, a striking feature of Kissinger's writing at this time is its determinedly apolitical character. The *Foreign Affairs* piece was an argument against disarmament and for enhancing deterrence "not through numbers but through mobility or hardening of our retaliatory force." The goal of "responsible arms-control measures," Kissinger argued, "must be to determine, free of sentimentality, not how to eliminate retaliatory forces but how to maintain an equilibrium between them." The reduction of numbers of nuclear weapons was not the infallible remedy it appeared to be to the disarmament campaigners. There were even limits to what could be achieved by systems of inspection or surveillance: any such system had to be "sufficiently reliable to prevent evasions which can upset the strategic balance, yet not so pervasive as to destroy the security of the retaliatory force." Finally, even Kissinger's own preferred remedy—"stability in numbers of offensive weapons" (in other words, mutual deterrence)—would fail if one side made a technological breakthrough in missile defense.[117] A politician who had tried to base a stump speech on this densely argued and deeply pessimistic article would soon have found himself addressing an empty hall.

The reality was that Kissinger had been in earnest about retaining his independence as an academic thinker. Oblivious to the race for the White House, the editorial board of *Daedalus,* the journal for the American Academy of Arts and Sciences, had asked twenty leading authorities—the majority of them members of the Harvard-MIT Arms Control Seminar—to contribute to a special issue on nuclear weapons and arms control.[118] Kissinger was among them, and he took the opportunity to perform that least political of maneuvers: a U-turn. "Several developments," he wrote, had caused "a shift in my view about the relative emphasis to be given conventional forces as against nuclear forces." Among these was "the disagreement within our military establishment and within the alliance about the nature of limited nuclear war," which had raised "doubts as to whether we would know how to limit nuclear war."

> Since no country has had any experience with the tactical use of nuclear weapons, the possibility of miscalculation is considerable. The temptation to use the same target system as for conventional war and thereby produce vast casualties will be overwhelming. The pace of operations may out strip the possibilities of negotiation. Both sides would be operating in the dark with no precedents to guide them.[119]

This was a remarkable shift in Kissinger's position, as it amounted to a repudiation of the central thesis of his best-selling book on the subject, published just three years earlier. It was in fact a not unreasonable adjustment to the new reality created by the advent of long-range missiles and the rapid growth of the Soviet arsenal. Kissinger had also clearly been listening to the arguments of West German politicians. "If a Soviet attack on Western Germany should lead to the desolation of the Federal Republic," he acknowledged, "the Soviet Union would score a major gain even if it offered at some point to withdraw to its starting point." In the German case, it might well be "to the Communist advantage to settle for the status quo ante in a war that obliterates the disputed area."[120] In any case, the public aversion to the idea of using nuclear weapons was growing, not abating. Under the circumstances, the only rational course of action was to increase the West's conventional arms capability. Once again Kissinger proposed a new command structure: but now, in place of his earlier separation of tactical and strategic forces, he proposed a separation of conventional and nuclear commands. The nuclear option now became a last resort rather than an option available from the outset of a limited war.

Sometimes a volte-face is a proof of academic integrity. As the economist John Maynard Keynes is supposed to have said, "When my information changes, I alter my conclusions. What do you do, sir?" The facts of the nuclear arms race had indeed changed since 1957. Yet for a man who was at least a part-time political adviser, such inconsistency had its disadvantages—not the least of which was the obviously greater expense of the increased conventional forces Kissinger now wished to see. The singular advantage was that this argument dovetailed with those of not just one but two candidates for the presidency; it would probably have been acceptable to Nixon, too, if he had not been constrained by loyalty to Eisenhower.

Kissinger had labored long and hard for Nelson Rockefeller since his return to Harvard. He had drafted speeches, commissioned and edited position papers by others, and made himself available as and when required. But by mid-1960 Rockefeller's chances of becoming the Republican candidate were dwindling by the day. Was all this effort to be for naught? A few academics—some perfectionists, others cowards—habitually leave manuscripts unpublished. As we shall see, Henry Kissinger would later opt to leave the typescript of an entire book to gather dust in a drawer. But in 1960 he was disinclined to consign all the articles and position papers of the preceding three years to oblivion. *The Necessity for Choice* was an appropriate title for the resulting book in more ways than one. Superficially a compendium of his recent writings on various aspects of U.S. foreign policy, the book was at once a subtle statement about the relationship between the historical process and policy formulation, and an implicit exhortation to the next president to choose between alternative courses of action. By making his recommendations independently of any one candidate, of course, Kissinger himself was able to avoid choosing. Indeed, by insisting on publishing "under the auspices" of the Center for International Affairs, rather than directly with it—which would have meant a less commercially attractive contract with Harvard University Press—Kissinger took his insistence on independence so far as to infuriate Robert Bowie.[121]

Any book that turns past articles into chapters runs the risk of incoherence, and any author whose previous book was a bestseller knows what to expect from reviewers. Writing in *The New York Times,* Walter Millis found Kissinger "a bit too prone to flog dead horses by accusing us of fatuities which are no longer ruling." Describing the book as "one long demonstration that . . . the United States cannot define 'for ourselves' a peace both consistent with our values and adequate for our security," Millis concluded, "He stresses the 'necessity of choice' but offers us nothing to choose."[122] "A sound if sometimes turgid account of recent strategic debate" was the verdict of L. W. Martin in the *Political Science Quarterly.* "He needs men at whom to tilt and his sparse acknowledgements are chiefly to those whom he is about to squash."[123] "Sparks fly in many directions," wrote Esmond Wright for Chatham House, "and they illuminate as they pass. Yet there is no clear blueprint here, either for the scholar or the statesman. And despite the plea for sharp analysis and for dexterity in manoeuvre, the standpoint is fixed and rigid, that of Machiavelli offering his Prince thoughts and arguments with which to defend the Republic against the ungiving enemy." The book might be "shrewd [and] incisive," but it was also "quite cheerless."[124]

These judgments now seem wide of the mark. To be sure, *The Necessity for Choice* is a product of the "missile gap" era. Its starting point is the alarming claim that both Truman and Eisenhower had failed to uphold America's postwar position and that "fifteen years more of [such] a deterioration of our position in the world . . . would find us reduced to Fortress America in a world in which we had become largely irrelevant."[125] The United States lacked a strategic doctrine and a coherent military policy; its arms control initiatives contradicted its nuclear strategy; its alliances were fragmenting; and its aid programs in developing countries were not working. As a result, its "margin of survival" had "narrowed dangerously"; indeed, there was a real risk of "tragedy"—of "national disaster." The United States was in "mortal danger" of a Soviet surprise attack. The Western world was "in deep trouble."[126] All this now seems overdone, especially in light of the more recent historical scholarship on Eisenhower. In fact, General Twining, the chairman of the Joint Chiefs, had told the Senate Foreign Relations Committee in closed session (but with Kennedy present) that there was no missile gap as early as February 1959—a judgment based on aerial photographs taken by U-2 spy planes. By 1961 the CIA's Corona spy satellite had established with near certainty that the Soviets had hardly any ICBMs and still lagged some way behind the United States in the nuclear arms race. We also know that, while the Soviets were more than happy to exploit opportunities for brinkmanship in the third world, from Cuba to the Congo, Khrushchev had no serious intention of fighting an all-out war for the sake of such backwaters.[127] But as we shall see, Kissinger was by no means exaggerating the danger that two increasingly well-armed superpowers might end up going to war over Berlin as a result of diplomatic miscalculations, much as the great powers had gone to war over Bosnia and Belgium in 1914. And he was quite right to ridicule the many Western commentators who pinned unrealistic hopes on an imminent liberalization of the Soviet system, or who naïvely approached negotiations with the Soviets as if it helped to arrive with fallback positions or to signal a readiness to find compromises somewhere between initial positions.

Kissinger's concrete policy recommendations are even more impressive, with the benefit of hindsight, because nearly all of them were adopted during the 1960s (though it should be added that they were not uniquely his ideas). He argued once again that, in order to address the risk of a Soviet surprise attack using missiles, the U.S. second-strike capability needed to be made less vulnerable through "dispersal, hardening and, above all, mobility."[128] This was done. Again repudiating his earlier argument for limited nuclear war, Kissinger argued that the United States should build up its conventional forces, so that nonnuclear forces might be available to combat localized "blackmail" by the Soviets. For better or worse, this was also done. He argued that the West should press for German reunification on the basis of a settled Oder-Neisse eastern border,* with equivalent force reductions on either side of that line. This, too, became the goal of U.S. policy, though it was not attained until 1990. He argued for an international nuclear nonproliferation agreement, binding on both nuclear and nonnuclear powers and enforced by a worldwide inspection system under the auspices of the International Atomic Energy Authority, empowered to account for all fissionable materials. Exactly this was first signed in 1968. And he urged the superpowers to "negotiate a cut-off on nuclear production and a reduction of their stockpiles—provided that suitable controls can be devised," precisely the route that would lead to the later Strategic Arms Limitation Talks. The only proposal that went nowhere was to "increase [NATO's] political cohesion so that it begins to approach a federal system" and then place a stockpile of nuclear weapons under its sole control.[129] Ironically, this was the argument Kissinger sought to push hardest in the wake of the book's publication (probably because it was a favorite of Rockefeller's).[130]

Yet the best parts of *The Necessity for Choice* were more philosophical than policy focused. In an inspired chapter entitled "Of Political Evolution: The West, Communism and the New Nations"—which had started life as an exchange with the scientist Caryl Haskins after an argument with the economists J. K. Galbraith and Arthur Lewis[131]—Kissinger set out a new version of his philosophy of history in response to the economists' hypothesis that the Soviet system would evolve in a liberal direction as a result of economic development. He agreed that Communist societies were bound to change:

---

*As things stood, the East German–Polish frontier roughly followed the Oder and Neisse Rivers. That meant the loss of large tracts of historic Prussia. To many Germans—and not only to former Nazis and the highly influential "League of Expellees"—this was unacceptable.

But the nature of the transformation is by no means foreordained. It can move towards liberalization; but it can also produce the gray nightmare of *1984*. It can lead to the enhancement of freedom; it may also refine the tools of slavery. Moreover, the mere fact of a transformation is not the only concern of our generation. Equally important is the time scale by which it occurs. It was, after all, no consolation for Carthage that 150 years after its destruction Rome was transformed into a peaceful status quo power.[132]

As Kissinger wisely observed, "The process of evolution does not operate so smoothly or in so clear a direction as it appears to posterity. The pluralism of the West was the result of hundreds of choices, each of which, if taken otherwise, could have led to an entirely different result." The Reformation's emphasis on the individual conscience was certainly not intended to encourage pluralism. Indeed, the ultimate emergence of democracy in Europe was the result of a multiplicity of such peculiarities: the Greco-Roman heritage, the Christian separation of Church and State, a multiplicity of states, and "a stalemate in religious wars imposing toleration as a practical necessity." In Kissinger's words:

Industrialization was by no means the most significant of these factors. Had any of the others been missing, the course of Western political evolution could have been radically different. . . . [I]t is only to posterity that evolution appears inevitable. The historian . . . deals only with successful elements, and the blatantly successful ones at that. He has no way of knowing what was most significant to the participants: the element of choice which determined success or failure.

For Kissinger, the historical process was fundamentally different from natural history:

[E]volution proceeds not in a straight line but through a series of complicated variations. At every step of the road there are turns and forks, which have to be taken for better or worse. The conditions governing the decision may be of the most delicate shading. The choice may appear in retrospect to be nearly random or else to be the only option possible under the prevailing circumstances. In either case, it is the result of the interaction of the whole sum of previous turnings—reflecting history or tradition or values—plus the immediate pressures of the need for survival.[133]

Kissinger was also alive to the possibility that evolution could also lead to the "rigidity" and "petrification" that were the first symptoms of decline. "The collapse of nations," he argued, was due to "internal rigidity coupled with a decline in the ability, both moral and physical, to shape surrounding circumstances. . . . What would have been Western history if the knights who defeated the Arabs at Tours had surrendered because they believed in the historic inevitability of the triumph of Christianity? Central Europe would today be Moslem."[134]

The serious historical thinker must believe, like Kissinger, in "the necessity of choice" and therefore in the plausibility of the counterfactual. Those who prefer the teleology of historical determinism suffer from either a surfeit of ideology or a poverty of imagination. Yet the most remarkable thing about this chapter is not its insistence on the role of contingency in historical evolution; it is the inference Kissinger drew for U.S. policy in the third world. "Unless we are able to make the concepts of freedom and respect for human dignity meaningful to the new nations," he wrote, "the much-vaunted economic competition between us and Communism in the uncommitted areas will be without meaning." Like many contemporaries, of course, Kissinger exaggerated the capacity of the Soviet Union to win a contest defined in terms of output growth. But he was quite right to argue that the Western claim to superiority needed to be based on human dignity, not on productivity. What made democracy work in the West were certain peculiar limitations on governmental power, ranging from the rule of law to the ordinary man's "conviction that politics does not matter." These limitations were not naturally occurring in the "new countries." Therefore "unless we address ourselves to the problem of encouraging institutions which protect human dignity, the future of freedom is dim indeed." Once again Kissinger was writing not as a realist but as an idealist. The aim of Cold War competition in the third world was not to win a contest between rival models of economic development but above all to "fill . . . a spiritual void," for "even Communism has made many more converts through the theological quality of Marxism than through the materialistic aspect on which it prides itself."[135]

VII

As so often, it all came down to fiscal policy. Rockefeller and Kennedy alike were pressing for a bigger defense budget as well as more spending on foreign aid, often using arguments like the ones presented in *The Necessity for Choice*. Nixon itched to make the same argument but could not without further alienating Eisenhower. Imagine Kissinger's bemusement, under the circumstances, to receive a leaked document from General Robert E. Cushman, Nixon's assistant for national security affairs: a copy of instructions issued by the White House for the fiscal year 1961 defense budget. In its commitment to hold down defense spending, Cushman complained, it read "as if the Summit fiasco never occurred." He had sent it to Kissinger "because I fundamentally believe that you are able to influence the man, whatever his faults, with the greatest share of the qualities which can lead us out of the state we are in. If he responds to attack with a smashing counterattack using material such as this, he will make himself President, and perhaps even on the Democratic ticket."[136] The document was not classified but was stamped "For Official Use Only" and could be traced back to the vice president's staff, which meant that Kissinger could quote it but must not show it to anyone.

It cannot have been clear to Kissinger whether this was a trap set for him and Rockefeller or a genuine overture. It proved to be the latter. As early as May, Nixon had come to the conclusion that walking his way through uncontested primaries to the Republican nomination was actually hurting him; Kennedy's hard-fought wins over Hubert Humphrey were getting much more press coverage. Rockefeller's attempt belatedly to reenter the race for the nomination never posed a serious threat to Nixon. It was pure fantasy that he might be the beneficiary of one of those waves of support that had turned nomination contests at party conventions in the past (most recently when Adlai Stevenson had been "drafted" as the Democratic candidate in 1952). But it now occurred to Nixon that having Rockefeller as his running mate would bolster his position in the liberal Northeast of the country; at the very least getting Rocky on board ahead of the convention would signal Nixon's ability to tack to the center ahead of the final showdown with Kennedy. On July 22, two days before the start of the Republican convention in Chicago, the vice president secretly flew to New York and dined with his rival at the latter's Fifth Avenue apartment. Frankly acknowledging his own electoral calculation, he offered Rockefeller the vice-presidential slot on the ticket, promising that he would increase the post's importance in the event that he won. As Rockefeller later told Kissinger, Nixon offered him "(a) dictation of the platform, (b) complete control over foreign policy, (c) New York state patronage if he would run on the ticket."[137] Rockefeller said no, just as his guest had anticipated, and then produced a statement of "principles" that would have to be in the party platform if Nixon wanted Rockefeller's support. Emmet Hughes dialed in from Chicago to assist the dyslexic Rockefeller with the small print.

Determined to get Rockefeller's endorsement if nothing else, Nixon agreed to everything, even the proposal for the Atlantic Confederation. The sticking point was the defense budget, which Rockefeller wanted to see increased by $3.5 billion or 9 percent. Nixon knew Eisenhower would never swallow that. Rather than specify a figure, they therefore agreed on the following wording: "The United States can afford and must provide the increased expenditures to implement fully this necessary program for strengthening our defense posture. There must be no price ceiling on America's security." The final fourteen points of "the Treaty of Fifth Avenue" were agreed with the platform committee chairman Charles Percy at three-thirty a.m. It was a big story when it broke, but this backroom deal did neither man much good. Eisenhower accused Rockefeller of "personal treachery" and Nixon of "repudiating" the administration's record. Appalled to see a liberal plank on civil rights inserted in the platform, the conservative firebrand Barry Goldwater denounced "the Munich of the Republican Party." Nixon yielded to Ike but not to Goldwater. The civil rights plank stayed in, but the language on defense was further toned down. "The United States can and must provide whatever is necessary to insure its own security," the final version read, "to provide any necessary increased expenditures to meet new situations. . . . To provide more would be wasteful. To provide less would be catastrophic."[138] Now it was Rockefeller who had to yield. His hopes of being drafted crushed, he gave the convention a halfhearted endorsement of "Richard E. [*sic*] Nixon."

Kissinger cannot have been surprised by this outcome. Wisely, he had kept clear of the Chicago convention. In August, however, he paid a visit to the Rockefeller summer retreat at Seal Harbor, Maine, "to explain to him [as he told Arthur Schlesinger] why he couldn't help him in the fall campaign." As Schlesinger recorded in his diary, the reason was clear: "Henry says he will do nothing which might aid Nixon." Rockefeller shared Kissinger's aversion to Nixon: "As Henry says, pronouncing the word in two syllables, 'He lo-athes Nixon.'" But the die was cast. Condemned to campaign on behalf of the man he loathed but had endorsed, Rockefeller "appeared low and sunk . . . quite disappointed at the lack of response in Chicago."[139] Kissinger felt under no such obligation. When approached for advice on national security issues by both the Republican National Committee and the Nixon campaign,[140] he informed them that he was leaving for Japan the next day and was therefore unavailable.[141] Such was his aversion to Richard Nixon in 1960.

Kissinger was loyal to Rockefeller. He continued to regard himself as preeminent among his advisers. ("I cannot remember any foreign policy issue on which the Governor did not first contact me," he told Rod Perkins in November 1960.)[142] He kept up his work on the issue of regional confederation, though his doubts were growing about the practicality of having confederations for both the North Atlantic and the western hemisphere.[143] And he repeatedly urged Rockefeller to begin laying the foundations for a more successful nomination bid in 1964, even suggesting the names of "a few individuals who wish you well," among them the New York senator Jacob K. Javits and the midwestern newspaper publisher John Cowles.[144] Indeed, it is possible to date Kissinger's interest in the oily mechanics of American domestic politics from this period. By December 1960, he was attending weekly meetings with Rockefeller's senior staff in Albany "to define a strategy over the next four years."[145] As early as January 1961, he was advising Rockefeller to preempt the likely Democratic challenge to his position as governor by "think[ing] through the various moves that Kennedy might make, the groups he might try to contact, the manner in which he might try to utilize his family, the influence of old man Kennedy with the financial world, and so forth."[146]

In late February 1961, Kissinger wrote Rockefeller a long letter on how best to prepare for a presidential bid in 1964: "It may be that you will not choose to contest the Presidency at that time, either because Kennedy is carrying out policies with which you essentially agree or because any Republican candidate might simply be a sacrificial lamb. . . . My strong guess[, however,] is that we may well be in the middle of a crisis in which your contribution will be desperately needed." This time around, Rockefeller must learn from the mistakes of 1959–60, when he had been criticized for neglecting his duties in New York but had in reality spent insufficient time on building a nationwide organization.[147] The remarkable thing about this letter is that it was written exactly nineteen days after the news had broken that Kissinger was considering an appointment in the administration of John F. Kennedy—the very man he was urging Rockefeller to run against in three years' time, but also the man who by a hairbreadth had defeated his bête noire Richard Nixon the previous November.

For Kissinger, Rockefeller had seemed to personify the aristocratic ethos, in so far as it could exist in a democracy. As he had put it to Caryl Haskins (in a passage notably toned down for publication in *The Necessity for Choice*):

> [I]t seems to me that the democratic societies that have been
> most successful have been essentially aristocratic (a case could
> be made for the proposition that we lived a long time on the
> moral capital of the Founding Fathers and we have had a writ-
> ten constitution, itself a conservative force). An aristocratic

society—or better a society whose values are shaped by aristocratic concepts—encourages self-restraint, not because aristocrats have superior morality or less selfishness than other
groups. Rather their structure and ethos force them to oppose
individual preeminence and thus absolutist rule. And they
legitimize themselves by a notion of *quality* which runs counter
to the despotism of egalitarian democracy.[148]

Like his old mentor Fritz Kraemer, Kissinger was repelled by much
that he saw in Washington—in particular the sclerotic tendencies of
government bureaucracy. When in 1956 Kraemer had written almost
hysterically about his frustration at having to sit in the Pentagon, writing "searching analytical studies, profound policy reviews and ever so
clever articles," while young Hungarians were fighting Communism
in the streets of Budapest, he had surely struck a chord:

[W]e do know so very well that history is not really made by
pen or printer's ink. Oh yes, we can rationalize what we are
doing, most beautifully. Are not our memoranda and think
pieces very important weapons in the struggle for the minds of
other men? Yet, we are mercifully aware of the fact that, in
truth, men will adopt the bold and imaginative policies we
want them to adopt, not because their brains are convinced by
conclusive arguments, but because their hearts are moved. And
here we sit, overtrained political scientists, not risking our precious existence to propagate a new faith, but arguing in the
manner of lawyers and college professors. Studiously, we cling
to a dehydrated style, eliminating from our outpouring every
last vestige of emotionalism.[149]

The idealist Kissinger, too, craved heroic leadership, even when in
the grip of stylistic dehydration. As he told Schlesinger, "We need
someone who will bring about a big jump—not just an improvement
of existing tendencies, but a shift into a new atmosphere, a new world."[150]
Yet Kraemer, more than Kissinger, worried about the compromises
his protégé had already made for the sake of playing the part of adviser

to the aristocrat to whom Kraemer referred as "N. R." In December 1957, he had written a long and heartfelt letter to Kissinger urging him to remember his "altruistic—in no way egotistical—duty to remain who you are.

> N. R. . . . cannot understand what you represent in . . . the middle of the 20th Century. He collects rare pictures; it would never occur to him to burn them; such barbarism would be quite alien to him. [But] human beings do not have labels stuck on them by experts to declare their value and that is why the danger is so great, in this age when value is measured in facts and figures, that irreplaceable people are burned up, quite simply used as fuel, especially those who have already been ignited by Nature and so are already standing in the flames anyway. The bourgeois is less in danger as he is so much harder to set alight; but the others—the Few, the Rare—how splendidly they burn!

Kraemer knew only too well that what he was about to write would pain Kissinger. Perhaps, he mused, it would have been better if they had never met all those years before at Camp Claiborne. "I am proud of your success," he wrote. "Not only I, but astonishingly many others, are counting on you. You already represent considerably more than yourself."

> But your success must not ruin you inwardly and physically. . . . The valuable man must not let himself be destroyed by "the others," no matter how "nice," how amiable, and how almost above-average they may be, no matter if their "admiration" and well-meaning incomprehension are the prime motives for the destruction. . . .
>
> [A]s I already told you in Claiborne and Palenberg, the secret of independence lies in acting independently; one may not even *aim* for success. You may not, you may never count on things turning out "well" . . . into the bargain. Only if you really do not "calculate" will you have the freedom which

distinguishes you from the little people and makes you as
swindle-proof as anyone. That up until now you have always
held to this is one of the things that make my faith in you so
strong. But until now things were easier. You had to resist only
the wholly ordinary temptations of the ambitious, like avarice,
and the academic intrigue industry. *Now* the trap is in your
own character. You are being tempted, so to speak, with your
own deepest principles: to commit yourself with dedication
and duty. *But* other and more decisive tasks lie ahead.[151]

In the early months of 1961, as Henry Kissinger prepared to answer
the long-awaited summons to the corridors of power, he may well have
recollected and pondered the implications of Kraemer's admonition.

CHAPTER 13

Flexible Responses

I hope the Iron Curtain is not between the pragmatists and
the dogmatists, and I hope also that if the Iron Curtain is
between the pragmatists and the dogmatists, the pragmatists
will not win an unconditional victory. . . . We should ask
ourselves not what we are doing but what we ought to do,
and not where we are but where we are trying to be; and
that it may well turn out that those things which are not so
easily demonstrable of proof are what finally guide the
practice of national security policy; while the very clever
analyses in which we all engage on day-to-day problems are
in a way as illusory as some of the shadows in Plato's caves.
—HENRY KISSINGER, July 1963[1]

My contribution to Berlin planning is that of a kibitzer
shouting random comments from the side-lines.
—HENRY KISSINGER to Arthur Schlesinger,
September 1961[2]

I

John F. Kennedy occupies a unique position in American collective
memory. In a Gallup poll conducted in November 2013, 74 percent of
Americans rated him as an outstanding or above-average president, compared with 61 percent for Ronald Reagan, 49 for Dwight Eisenhower, 30
for Lyndon Johnson, and 15 for Richard Nixon—the lowest score for any
postwar president.[3] In a 2011 poll, 11 percent of Americans named Kennedy as the greatest of all U.S. presidents, compared with just 1 percent
for Eisenhower and less than 0.5 for Johnson and Nixon.[4] Kennedy's reputation is not wholly a consequence of his assassination, greatly though

that event continues to fascinate the public. It is an article of faith for a majority of Americans that Kennedy's administration was idealistic, while Richard M. Nixon's was realistic to the point of being unprincipled. "Let every nation know," declared Kennedy in his inaugural address, "that we shall pay any price, bear any burden, meet any hardship, support any friend, oppose any foe, in order to assure the survival and the success of liberty." Kennedy's soaring rhetoric is still quoted today; no one remembers the comparably noble pledge Nixon made at his first inauguration to "lead the world at last out of the valley of turmoil and onto that high ground of peace that man has dreamed of since the dawn of civilization." As political rivals whose fates could scarcely have been more different—shattering assassination, humiliating resignation—Kennedy and Nixon have come to personify opposite poles of American politics. One complicating fact is that one man—Henry Kissinger—served both presidents. Another is that, in his own eyes at least, it was not Kennedy who was the idealist but Kissinger himself.

Henry Kissinger was just one of a remarkable number of Harvard academics who went to Washington to work for Kennedy. Where he was exceptional was in remaining at heart a Rockefeller loyalist. This had two distinct consequences. First, Kissinger was not wholly trusted by other members of the administration, including his immediate boss, McGeorge Bundy. Second, he had distinctly different views from most of them on key foreign policy issues, especially those relating to Europe. The remarkable thing is that it was Kissinger who criticized—at first privately and later publicly—the *realism* of the Kennedy administration, and it was Kissinger who urged Nelson Rockefeller to adopt a more idealistic stance on the two most flammable foreign policy issues of the Kennedy presidency: Germany and Cuba.

It would be hard to imagine two cities more different than Berlin and Havana in 1961: one a chilly Prussian industrial metropolis, still deeply scarred by the total war that had ended just sixteen years before, the other a tropical colonial capital, with only a few new Soviet-style high-rises and antiaircraft guns to indicate the revolutionary character of its government. And yet it would be in these disparate locations that John F. Kennedy's commitment to the fine, uplifting words of his inaugural address would be put to the ultimate test.

II

"The best and the brightest," David Halberstam called them, unwittingly quoting Shelley.[5] At the time, the press preferred "whiz kids" or "brain trust."[6] To Vice President Lyndon Johnson, with his degree from Southwest Texas State Teachers College, they were simply "the Harvards."[7] The university lost more than fifty instructors to the new administration, including not only Bundy and Kissinger but also Archibald Cox, J. K. Galbraith, Carl Kaysen, Henry Rowen, and Arthur Schlesinger. Small wonder the president's alma mater was seen by some as "the fourth branch of government."[8] Had Bowie and Schelling also accepted their invitations to come to Washington, the Center for International Affairs would have been denuded of nearly all its senior faculty. But even those who remained in Cambridge felt empowered. As Bundy put it, "People from Harvard . . . are in fact closer to the processes of government than many others who are right here [in Washington, D.C.]"[9] In his farewell address to the nation, Eisenhower had warned about the rise of the "military-industrial complex."[*][10] Under Kennedy, it was the academic-intellectual complex that ruled.[11]

Despite his well-known association with Rockefeller, Henry Kissinger had in fact been approached by the Kennedy campaign as early as December 1958. It had been Kennedy's speechwriter, the Nebraska lawyer Ted Sorensen, who had invited him—as Kennedy himself put it in a follow-up letter—"to give some thought now as to what long-range problems and positions ought to be worked out during the next several months . . . particularly this question of weapons reevaluation, the de[-]emphasis on intermediate range ballistic missiles and overseas bases, etc."[12] Kissinger replied that he would be "pleased to contribute to the development of public policy" but requested a meeting "for an exchange of ideas" to help in "defining the issues."[13] On February 15, 1959, the

---

*He had originally intended to refer to "the military-industrial-congressional complex," reflecting his own frustration at the insistence of certain congressmen—including his own successor as president—that there was a missile gap that at all costs needed to be closed. At the last minute, he struck out "congressional."

two men met for lunch at the Harvard Club of Boston, for "some discussion on questions of defense and foreign policy."[14] Kennedy then
asked for Kissinger's opinion of a paper on "the missile program,"[15]
which argued that building thirty Polaris nuclear-armed and -powered
submarines would close the missile gap with the Soviet Union. (Kissinger was skeptical.)[16] Kennedy then asked Kissinger for his views on
Germany, noting presciently that he "[felt] the German problem to be
of enormous importance."[17]

Sooner or later this courtship was bound to become public. On
December 11, 1959, a year after it had begun, *The Boston Globe* broke
the story, mentioning Kissinger as one of fifteen* Harvard, MIT, and
Amherst academics whom Kennedy was recruiting to form "a campus
braintrust."[18] As Abram Chayes of Harvard Law School later recalled,
the newspaper erred only in exaggerating the group's degree of organization and cohesion.[19] As we have seen, Kissinger hastened to reassure his friends in Albany that he was not about to desert Rockefeller;[20]
he might have added that two other Republican professors were also
involved. But, as he admitted to Sally Coxe Taylor (who had married
into the family that owned the *Globe*),

> [w]hat [the paper] reported was basically true . . . I had met
> twice with a group last year in which Kennedy asked a number
> of us to state what we thought the major issues to be.
>
> My objection was directed not against the story but against
> what I took to be an effort by Kennedy to identify me with
> him. I have made clear to him and his staff innumerable times
> that if Nelson didn't run I would support no one and I have
> refused several offers to join his staff.[21]

---

*The other Harvard faculty named were Sam Beer (government), Abram Chayes (law),
Archibald Cox (law), J. K. Galbraith (economics), Fred Holburn (government), Mark
DeWolfe Howe, Jr. (law), W. Barton Leach (law), and Arthur Schlesinger, Jr. (history).
The piece also mentioned five MIT faculty members—David Frisch, Martin Myerton,
Lucian Pye, Walt Rostow, and Robert C. Wood—as well as Earl Latham from
Amherst, who was then visiting at Harvard. The *Globe* omitted Arthur E. Sutherland,
Jr., another Harvard Law School professor whom Kennedy consulted.

A new decade was dawning. For Kissinger, as for everyone in his generation, it was impossible to ignore the first stirrings of what proved to be a vast social and cultural upheaval. In his *Necessity for Choice,* he had put it succinctly: "Our generation will live in the midst of change. Our norm is the fact of upheaval. The success of our actions is not measured by short-term tranquility. . . . The decade of the 1960's will require heroic effort."[22] The difference between Kissinger and those who were already beginning to found the new "counterculture" was that for him the coming upheaval was likely to be geopolitical.

In early 1960 Robert Zimmerman was about to drop out of the University of Minnesota, rename himself "Bob Dylan," and head for Greenwich Village. At roughly the same time, Henry Kissinger was warning that the new decade was "likely to be a time of grave danger." Dylan would soon be articulating his generation's gnawing fear of nuclear fallout in the song "Hard Rain." Kissinger favored the stark language of security studies, warning that a widening missile gap could lead to a Soviet surprise attack. The juxtaposition may seem incongruous, but were not their fears at root the same? In "Blowin' in the Wind," also written in 1962, Dylan would phrase the central question of the era very simply: "How many years can some people exist / Before they're allowed to be free?" It was a song as readily sung by the opponents of colonialism as by the proponents of African American civil rights. But Kissinger was capable of articulating the same basic idea, even if he did so in prose rather than poetry: "We are not only interested in material advancement either for ourselves or for other peoples. We have a concern that the democratic principles in which we believe are applied. We respect a government not primarily because it is efficient but because it secures the freedom and dignity of its people."[23] Discussing the approaching election with Kennedy's most loyal supporter at Harvard, Arthur Schlesinger, Kissinger expressed his hope that a Kennedy victory would signify "a big jump . . . a new atmosphere, a new world. If all Kennedy does is to argue that he can manipulate the status quo better than Nixon, he is lost."[24]

In terms of the popular vote, the 1960 election was the closest of the twentieth century. When, with just two weeks of the campaign remaining, Kissinger said that a Kennedy victory was "certain," he was too confident.[25] True, Kennedy had the better of the televised debates against Nixon, the former glowing after an afternoon of copulation, the latter all stubble and perspiration. But on substance the candidates were neck and neck. Kennedy's accusation that Nixon was part of an administration that had "lost Cuba" was hard to reconcile with his insistence that the same administration should yield Quemoy and Matsu to Beijing. Nixon meanwhile heaped scorn on the idea of an invasion of Cuba, despite the fact that he had been urging Eisenhower to approve one. On foreign policy, there was no clear winner; of more importance was Nixon's hesitant response to the imprisonment in Atlanta of the black civil rights leader Martin Luther King, Jr., which cost him a substantial share of the African American vote. (Few were persuaded by his running mate Henry Cabot Lodge's pledge that there would be one nonwhite cabinet member.) Even so, Nixon won more states than Kennedy and lost the popular vote by a margin of fewer than 113,000 votes—less than two-tenths of a percentage point. The scale of fraud and error in the key states of Illinois and Texas was enough to justify protracted legal challenges and even some criminal convictions. But Nixon, for all his famed political ruthlessness, chose not to contest the result—just as he had refused to play the religion card during the campaign—and so by the narrowest of margins, Kennedy became the country's first Roman Catholic president.

Within a matter of days, Kennedy's transition team was in touch with Kissinger, asking him to suggest candidates for the post of secretary of state. Again he found himself in a quandary. Was this a continuation of the earlier courtship, or one of multiple letters sent to canvass opinion around the country? Did Kennedy really have no one in mind for the most important job in his administration? In a draft reply, Kissinger began a lengthy preamble by warning that Kennedy's administration might face "some of the most serious foreign policy crises in the history of the Republic."

> There will be a crisis over Berlin. Countries like Iran could
> collapse any day. The emergence of new nations in Africa will
> not be completed without new upheavals. . . . Castroism may
> spread in Latin America. . . . In contrast to most of my

colleagues at Harvard, I believe [the new administration's task] to be infinitely more complex than to apply the maxims of the New Deal on a world scale. . . . [I]n major parts of the world economic and social dislocations are coupled with the absence of *any* political framework. At issue is not only the problem of economic progress but also the nature of political legitimacy.

He concluded by recommending Adlai Stevenson, who had vainly sought a third Democratic nomination to run for president. On reflection, however, Kissinger decided not to send this document.[26] Instead he wrote a shorter letter, suggesting Chester Bowles, already established as one of Kennedy's foreign policy advisers.[27] In the event, Bowles was made undersecretary of state, the number-two position; Kennedy opted to give Dean Rusk the top job at Foggy Bottom.*

Rusk had served Truman as assistant secretary of state for Far Eastern affairs, but he had spent the Eisenhower era running the Rockefeller Foundation. In putting him in charge at State, along with Douglas Dillon at Treasury and Robert McNamara at Defense, Kennedy was sending a signal: his would be an administration that was both experienced and bipartisan. (Both Dillon and McNamara were Republicans with private-sector experience.) This made intellectual as well as political sense. After all, Kennedy and Rockefeller had criticized Eisenhower in very similar ways, not least for his overreliance on the threat of "all-out" nuclear war, but also for various domestic sins of omission. Indeed, almost as important as the Harvard connection was the link from the new administration to the Rockefeller Special Studies Project, where so much of that critique had first been formulated. No fewer than 26 of the 210 panelists, consultants, and authors responsible for the Rockefeller reports joined the Kennedy administration: among them were not only Rusk and Bowles but also Roswell Gilpatric, who became the deputy secretary of defense; Harlan Cleveland, assistant secretary of state; and Walt Rostow, the deputy national security adviser.[28] It was therefore in no way surprising that the man who had directed the Special Studies

---

*The area of Washington where the State Department is located, in a building originally intended for the War Department.

Project should also be invited to Washington. It did not hurt that the day after Kennedy's inaugural, with the administration still under construction, *The New Yorker* published a glowing review of *The Necessity for Choice,* in which Richard Rovere—who wrote the magazine's weekly "Letter from Washington"—described Kissinger as "probably our most influential critic of military and foreign policy" and the book as a "basic text" for policy makers.[29] Kennedy himself did not get around to reading the book until 1963, but he certainly saw this review.[30] Kissinger, for his part, was impressed by Kennedy's inaugural. "I thought [it] excellent," he told Arthur Schlesinger. "For selfish reasons, I hope the rumors that you are going to Washington are not true, though if they are you may turn me into a registered Democrat."[31]

If Kissinger felt a twinge of envy on hearing that Schlesinger had been offered a White House job, he did not have long to wait for his own summons to Camelot. The irony cannot have been lost on him that he received it while residing in a Rockefeller palace: Caneel Bay, in the Virgin Islands, a luxury resort originally developed by Laurance Rockefeller. The letter was dated January 28, 1961, and it came from Kissinger's Harvard boss, the dean of the Faculty of Arts and Sciences, Mac Bundy.

> The President has asked me to talk with you at your early con-
> venience about the possibility of your joining up down here[,
> Bundy wrote]. The only complication in the situation, from
> his point of view, is that more than one part of the government
> may want to get you. He does not want to seem to interfere
> with any particular department's needs, but he does want you
> to know that if you should be interested, he himself would like
> to explore the notion of your joining the small group which
> Walt Rostow and I will be putting together for his direct use.[32]

The news broke on February 5. "Dr. Kissinger saw the President Friday and stayed in town overnight," the *Globe* reported breathlessly. His "important assignment" would be "in the field of international politics and strategy."[33]

As Bundy had intimated, there was indeed something of a fight for his services inside the new Beltway.* Rusk also offered him a job at the State Department, but—with Bundy's offer of a White House consulting role already on the table—Kissinger promptly declined it, swayed by "the prospect of working in a pretty direct relation to you," as Bundy put it to Kennedy.[34] Yet—for reasons that will become clear—Kissinger appeared to hesitate. As he told Bundy on February 8, "the assignment you and the President have in mind is challenging as well as delicate." The issue was "less the fact than the mode" of his participation.[35] Though he felt "honored . . . to be invited to join an Administration whose tone, appointments and actions have impressed me profoundly" and though he was "convinced that in the field which concerns me most—that of foreign and national security policy—the next four years will be decisive for the future of the country and perhaps of the democratic idea," he nevertheless pleaded that his Harvard commitments "would make any abrupt departure impossible." He therefore requested a part-time appointment. This would also allow him time to "give some thought in general to the context in which I can make the most effective contribution."[36]

Just over a week later, Kissinger returned to Washington to thrash out the details with Bundy.[37] They finally agreed on "a Consultant's appointment . . . in the general area of weapons and policy and in the special field of thinking about all aspects of the problem of Germany." Bundy suggested the role might be like that of a member of the President's Science Advisory Committee, "the members of which are on call for advice on special problems in a fashion which is determined by the problems and not by any a priori plan."[38] It was agreed that Kissinger would to come to Washington around a week every month during the semester and most of the summer from mid-May to the end of August, aside from June, when he was already committed to visiting Europe.[39] If the part-time arrangement did not work, they would "reconsider the question of a full-time assignment."[40] On February 27 the appointment was announced.[41] Rockefeller's right-hand man, it seemed, had defected to the Democrats.

---

*Interstate 495, the highway known as the Beltway around Washington, D.C., was opened in December 1961.

Given the subsequent deterioration of the relationship between Kissinger and Bundy, it is worth asking why Bundy acted as he did. In accepting the post of special assistant to the president for national security affairs—or national security adviser for short—Bundy had every expectation that he would play a dominant role in the formulation of foreign policy.* Why then bring on board a man who would have played that same role if Rockefeller had become president and who unquestionably had a deeper understanding of at least one of the key issues of the day? The explanation is that it was Kennedy, not Bundy, who wanted Kissinger, and in a full-time role.[42] It was in fact Bundy who persuaded Kissinger to request only a part-time role.[43]

Still, Kissinger had his own reason for declining the full-time position. His close relationship with Rockefeller clearly could not survive a wholehearted commitment to the man whom he fully expected Rockefeller to challenge for the presidency in 1964. Given the press coverage, Kissinger had no option but to make a clean breast of his negotiations with Kennedy. He was as startled as he was impressed when Rockefeller chided him for hesitating. (As he later told Schlesinger, "he urged me to accept any position where I could be of real service. He said also that, though my leaving him would be a blow to him personally, he wanted Kennedy to succeed because this would be a success for all of us, and that he refused to speculate on national disaster.")[44] The part-time job therefore suited Kissinger as much as Bundy. Writing to Rockefeller in the midst of the haggling, Kissinger thanked him warmly for his "understanding . . . with respect to the decisions I have had to make in the last few weeks."[45] Now he could experience at first hand the challenges of working at the highest level of government, with the prospect of being consulted by the president himself, while remaining available to advise the man widely expected to challenge Kennedy at the next election. Throughout his time as a White House consultant, Kissinger continued to advise Rockefeller on an ad hoc basis.[46]

---

*This was not guaranteed, to be sure. Paul Nitze had turned the job down before it was offered to Bundy, in the erroneous belief that a senior position at one of the major departments would be more influential.

To be sure, these were lean times for the female researchers nick-named the "Brownies" in Rockefeller's New York City research office. To the frustration of June Goldthwait and her colleagues, the governor paid next to no attention to their work for most of 1961.[47] She and Kissinger continued to play around with the idea of some kind of Atlantic confederacy, which remained a Rocky hobbyhorse.[48] But by April 1961 Rockefeller had decided to "hold . . . further operations in abeyance."[49] It appeared that he had enough to contend with in governing New York State. Nevertheless, Rockefeller's research staff continued to track Kennedy's performance on a broad range of issues.[50] Indeed, new "Brownies" were recruited, including Nancy Maginnes, then in the early stages of her Berkeley Ph.D. (on the Catholic Church in Vichy France), who came in during the summer months.[51] Although his new position meant he was now seldom in New York, Kissinger continued to oversee the work on foreign policy, directing Goldthwait and her researchers as they prepared "bi-monthly summaries . . . on . . . Defense, Berlin, Latin America, Civil defense, NATO, Iran, Foreign aid, Arms control and South Viet-Nam."[52]

The extent of Kissinger's continued emotional commitment to Rockefeller becomes clear from the notes that have survived of a brainstorming meeting at Rockefeller's Tarrytown residence on April 30, 1961, when he, Kissinger, and Hugh Morrow, Rockefeller's speechwriter and special assistant, sought to thrash out his foreign policy stance in the broadest possible terms. Though it was Morrow who took the notes, there is little doubt that Kissinger did most of the talking.[53] Three clear themes emerge: first, the return of limited nuclear war as an option; second, the need to stand up to Soviet encroachments anywhere and everywhere; and third and most important, the need for idealism in American foreign policy. So striking is this document as an illustration of Kissinger's insistence on the need for a moral foundation for foreign policy that it deserves to be quoted at length.

By the standards of the nascent peace movement—or of Kubrick's *Dr. Strangelove*—the argument that being prepared to use nuclear weapons was a moral act was of course bizarre. But that ignored the fundamental premise that not being prepared to use them might make a Soviet victory in the Cold War inevitable:

Nuclear weapons only balance. Talk of nuclear holocaust hamstrings us. We must be prepared to use nuclear weapons, but build up conventional forces. . . .

If it hadn't been for nuclear weapons, democratic Judeo-christian forces would not exist today. Nuclear weapons, rather than [being] the threat, have preserved civilization.

Resume testing of nuclear weapons—make them clean and for tactical use.

To argue against testing the neutron bomb* was, according to Morrow's notes, based on "completely artificial concepts of morality." As Kissinger put it in a letter to Rockefeller a month later, "the great problem of the West is a peace which preserves our values. We can also have peace by surrendering, of course. In order to preserve our values, however, we may have to face a seeming paradox. We must do everything we honorably can to avoid war. At the same time, we must not stigmatize nuclear weapons to the point where we create the conditions for Communist nuclear blackmail."[54]

In the same way, the second Tarrytown argument—for treating "Cuba, Laos, South Viet-Nam, Berlin [and] Iran [as] testing points of national purpose"—was hardly likely to resonate with the writers of protest songs. Yet the notes make clear that, to Kissinger, losing such places to Communist governments would be a greater evil than fighting back:

We cannot permit further shrinking of the areas of freedom. Here we must stand. We are coming to the point of no return— like a man half way down the ski run and near the jump who is going too fast to stop. . . .

---

*The neutron bomb had first been conceived in 1958 as an "enhanced radiation" weapon. The release of fusion-produced neutrons would be lethal to humans in the vicinity of a neutron bomb's detonation; the relatively smaller thermal and blast effects would mean that buildings and infrastructure would suffer less destruction than from a hydrogen bomb.

If we don't stand in Cuba, Laos and Berlin, we have so undermined the confidence of the free world group that no one will stand with us. . . .

We must organize and train for democratic leadership all over the world. . . .

In the absence of a hemisphere police force, we in the US must exercise police authority until such a force exists. . . .

We can't demand perfection before action. We can't make everyone democratic first. . . . Let's face up to the question of who we support; let's defend the bastards and reform them later. . . .

Nine thousand casualties in Viet-Nam last year alone— 13,000 guerillas in from North Viet-Nam. . . .

Internal subversive action against government is more dangerous than overt military threat. Communists create power base from inside and then say if you come in, we'll come in— meanwhile feeding in guerillas and supplies. Terrorization of civil government. Khrushchev told us he was going to do this. Why don't we pay attention? . . .

We have not incorporated this whole technique (Communist infiltration and subversion) in our domestic political considerations or foreign policy. Since overt military action is not involved, it is not our moral concept to act against it, yet it should be.

Here, unvarnished as they are, Morrow's notes make clear that playing the part of global policeman was bound to involve distasteful alliances with "bastards," not least the ones then governing South Vietnam. But these compromises would be a lesser evil than Communist victories. And here was the crux of the matter. If Communist rule meant—as it certainly had meant in Russia, Central and Eastern Europe, and China—tens of millions of deaths, then wars with death tolls in the tens of thousands *were* morally justifiable:

It is time we stopped kidding ourselves morally. Elimination of a cancerous growth is no more violating moral principles than police moving in on a gang or a doctor operating to remove a malignant growth.

Let's stop kidding the American people. . . . Our military action is not an issue of war and peace—but preserving law, order and justice. . . .

Dignidad and *humanidad*—we haven't got a sense of dignity and humanity; we'll double-cross anyone and then put out a moral statement. This super-righteous morality leads us to be a petty, in-drawn, neurotic society. . . .

Paint the picture of how the world looks at us: we are not moral. We are doing everything the Russians are doing and trying to excuse ourselves morally on the ground that we are not doing it effectively. . . .

Much of the world looks on us as psalm-singing hypocrites and with considerable reason. . . . We think it is moral to go in with 1000 men and fail—but immoral to go in with 10,000 and win. . . . We often put ourselves in the position where what is required for our security and freedom is considered immoral. . . .

"Faith, hope and love and the greatest of these is love."

We need a deeper moral purpose and a willingness to run risks.

Values, propositions, concepts supporting policy—and supporting mechanisms and tools . . . Foreign policy is not an end in itself. . . . We must make policy—not be negotiators.

This was a kind of credo, albeit one sketched out hastily by a speechwriter for a would-be president. Even as he accepted his consultant's fees from Jack Kennedy, Kissinger urged Rockefeller to "serve as the conscience of the nation," pledging to "do whatever is necessary to help you. . . . [A] democratic country cannot survive if its leaders are not willing to confront the people with the tasks that have to be performed."[55] These were not unorthodox ideas in the era of the Cold War, to be sure. Khrushchev himself had quite explicitly argued, two weeks before Kennedy's inaugural, that wars of national liberation in the third world would prove the best means of spreading Communism around the world.[56] Speaking in Salt Lake City in 1963, Kennedy himself identified as one of his central objectives "to support the independence of nations so that one bloc cannot gain sufficient power to finally overcome us."[57] That had, indeed, been the main thrust of his inaugural.* Walt Rostow, too, repudiated "in principle an asymmetry which allows Communist probes into the free community without possibility of riposte."[58] Yet Kissinger strongly suspected that, in practice, the Kennedy administration would find it difficult to live up to its own rhetoric. In many ways, as we shall see, he underrated Kennedy as a president.[59] Yet his fundamental insight that pragmatism would tend to dominate dogma proved to be correct.

III

Outwardly, John F. Kennedy's administration was leaner and more flexible than its predecessor, empowering the president to shape policy and take decisions. Influenced by the Columbia academic Richard Neustadt's recently published book *Presidential Power,* as well as by the interim reports of Senator Henry "Scoop" Jackson's subcommittee on national policy machinery, Kennedy blithely dismantled Eisenhower's complex bureaucratic structure.[60] The Planning Board and the Operation Coordinating Board were both abolished, doing away with the military distinction between planning and operations. As national security adviser, Bundy was supposed to work closely with the president, relying on his small staff of no more than a dozen whiz kids.[61] They, in turn, were divided into geographic subgroups, mirroring State Department organization and producing crisply analytical National Security Action Memorandums (NSAMs) as and when required.[62] The president himself preferred not to meet with the full NSC, instead

---

*"To those new States whom we welcome to the ranks of the free, we pledge our word that one form of colonial control shall not have passed away merely to be replaced by a far more iron tyranny. . . . Let all our neighbors know that we shall join with them to oppose aggression or subversion anywhere in the Americas. . . . Finally, to those nations who would make themselves our adversary, we offer not a pledge but a request: that both sides begin anew the quest for peace. . . . We dare not tempt them with weakness. For only when our arms are sufficient beyond doubt can we be certain beyond doubt that they will never be employed."

favoring regular meetings with Bundy, the secretaries of defense and state, the head of the CIA, and the vice president.[63] Interagency "task forces" were set up to deal with specific issues, often sidelining the State Department.[64] In a crisis, as over Cuba in 1962, a handpicked executive committee of the NSC became Kennedy's kitchen cabinet. Imagining that, in Eisenhower's time, a cumbersome bureaucracy had presented a senescent president with consensus positions to be endorsed, Bundy set out to give Kennedy meaningful choices.[65]

The reality of how the White House functioned under Kennedy was rather different from the grand redesigns of Neustadt and Jackson. The new system effectively gave the national security adviser, by dint of his proximity to the president, an advantage over the secretary of state, especially as Rusk insisted that the "secretary's job was to act on the president's view," which Bundy was much better placed to divine.[66] Inexperienced as he and the other whiz kids were, however, they at first struggled to establish their predominance over the CIA and military. The White House itself was a scene of frantic activity, not all of it productive. Press Secretary Pierre Salinger left a vivid account of how he and his staff, crammed into cubicles "not much larger than a double garage," were forced to put the four wire service teletypes "between the plumbing in the bathroom." The twice-daily press conferences resembled "a New York subway at the height of the evening rush," while the White House correspondents' room, directly across the lobby, was "a disgrace," the desks "a litter of old newspapers, playing cards, and medicine bottles," the floor like "Broadway after a ticker-tape parade." This squalid scene was just seventy-five feet away from the president's office.[67] Yet, despite their proximity to the Oval Office, the press corps turned a blind eye to the extraordinary sexual antics of their commander in chief.

Outwardly, John F. Kennedy's marriage was a fairy tale. Married in 1953, he and his attractive wife, Jackie, were a magazine editor's dream; with their two children, a boy and a girl, they appeared the perfect postwar nuclear family. The reality was very different. Kennedy had numerous extramarital relationships: with Mary Pinchot Meyer, the ex-wife of CIA operative Cord Meyer and sister-in-law of Ben Bradlee (then the Washington bureau chief of *Newsweek*); with Mimi Alford, a nineteen-year-old White House intern; possibly with the film stars Marlene Dietrich and Marilyn Monroe; and very definitely with Judith Campbell, whose other lovers included the Chicago organized crime boss Sam Giancana and his sidekick Johnny Roselli.[68] These and many other "happening babes" were regarded as the president's hobby. "We're a bunch of virgins," grumbled Fred Dutton, secretary of the cabinet, "and he's like God, fucking anybody he wants to, anytime he feels like it." All of this was known to the FBI director J. Edgar Hoover, as well as to Kennedy's inner circle (notably his secretary, Evelyn Lincoln).* It went entirely unreported in the press.[69]

It was, of course, the Sixties, and they were just beginning to swing. Having slumped to a postwar low of just 2.1 per thousand, the divorce rate was embarking on a two-decade surge that would take it to 5.3 per thousand in 1979. It had been hard for those working closely with Nelson Rockefeller in the 1950s to ignore his affairs. Henry Kissinger certainly knew about his relationship with Happy Murphy by March 1962, shortly after Rockefeller's divorce from his first wife, Mary. What Kissinger had not expected was that, a year later, Murphy would also divorce her husband, nor that she and Rockefeller would get married just a month after her first marriage was annulled. Gloomily, he assured Arthur Schlesinger that Murphy "would be disappointed and unhappy if she ever married Nelson; that he was a lonely man, remote and indifferent, for all his surface amiability, and that she would find herself excluded from his life as the first Mrs. Rockefeller did."[70]

Kissinger's judgment cannot have been uninfluenced by his own more or less simultaneous experience of marital breakdown. Despite the fact that their second child, David, was born in September 1961, the Kissingers had been growing apart for years. Ann had been prone to fits of jealousy throughout the marriage; her husband's many absences in Washington and farther afield only fueled her insecurity. Convinced he was being unfaithful, she searched his pockets for incriminating evidence—in vain, for Kissinger was no Jack Kennedy. In an attempt

---

*Of Mrs. Lincoln, the president once said that "if he called to inform her that he had just cut off Jackie's head and wanted to get rid of it, the devoted secretary would appear immediately with a hatbox of appropriate size."

to reduce the friction between them, Kissinger had built "a study over my garage which is away from everything."[71] By November 1962, he was absent from Cambridge so frequently that his father joked he was "in the German military language D.U. . . . 'dauernd untauglich' (unfit for service)." When the children went to New York with their mother to visit their grandparents' home for the first time, their father did not come.[72] One night in fall 1963, in the middle of yet another row over his supposed infidelity, Kissinger snapped. Without any real premeditation, he walked out of the family home, never to return. Soon afterward the couple resolved to separate, Ann remaining in Cambridge with the children, Kissinger moving to a bachelor apartment on Beacon Hill, Boston's most picturesque neighborhood.[73]

Unlike his younger brother, Kissinger had sought to fulfill his expectations of a conventional family life by marrying a "girl next door" from the Washington Heights German–Jewish Orthodox community. He had done this against all the resolutions he had made before returning to the United States from occupied Germany. He had done it out of love and respect for his parents, even though he had lost his own religious faith. It was a compromise that had failed—as such compromises usually do.

IV

Given the indiscipline that pervaded the White House in the first year of John F. Kennedy's presidency, it was perhaps inevitable that he would stumble. The stumbling block proved to be the island of Cuba, ninety miles off the Florida coast. At the beginning of 1959, Fidel Castro's guerrillas had seized power in Cuba, informally an American dependency since the time of Theodore Roosevelt. A charismatic nationalist, Castro had been feted by the media when he visited the United States that spring, not least at Harvard University, where he had addressed—at great length—a crowd of ten thousand at Soldiers Field. (Bundy, who had introduced the speaker on behalf of the Law School forum and the university, could scarcely conceal his distaste for the Caribbean firebrand and his bearded retinue.)[74] However, mounting evidence that Castro was prepare to align himself with the Soviets, combined with increasingly effective lobbying by exiled supporters of the previous Cuban regime, convinced Allen Dulles and Richard Bissell at the CIA that Castro had to go. Confident in his skills when it came to covert operations, Bissell drew up a plan for regime change, involving the creation of a political opposition force, a sustained propaganda campaign, and an invasion of the island by a paramilitary force, ideally supported by an anti-Castro uprising within Cuba.[75] For most American voters, Cuba was not a crucial issue in the 1960 election,[76] but it became a bone of contention in October when Kennedy was reported to favor "U.S. Intervention in Cuba," a position Nixon hypocritically denounced as "probably the most dangerously irresponsible recommendation that he's made during the course of this campaign."[77] Publicly, Kennedy hastened to disavow the use of "naked force." Soon after his election victory, however, he was briefed about Bissell's Operation Pluto and, whatever his doubts, certainly did not move to cancel it.[78]

Four things guaranteed the failure of the operation, renamed Zapata when it was decided to land at the Bay of Pigs rather than the Cuban port of Trinidad. First, there was the inability of the CIA and the Joint Chiefs to agree on a viable invasion plan. (The former favored using a guerrilla force; the latter wanted to deploy regular forces.) Second, what was supposed to be a "covert" operation was so widely anticipated both by Castro's regime and by the U.S. press that any element of surprise was lost. Third, those within the administration who harbored doubts about the plan—notably Arthur Schlesinger and Chet Bowles—failed to make their case, outranked as they were by Rusk, McNamara, and Lyman Lemnitzer (chairman of the JCS), who backed Bissell.[79] At Kennedy's request, Schlesinger even had to draft a white paper justifying intervention.[80] Fourth, and crucially, the president himself ignored the considerable evidence that failure had a high probability, trusting in the experts he had inherited from Eisenhower as well as in his own hitherto prodigious luck.[81] The "doubting Thomases" had done just enough to ensure that the operation went off halfcocked, with nowhere near the military firepower to be assured of success. It was Kennedy himself who ruled out the direct participation of U.S. forces in the invasion, canceled the second air strike against

Castro's air force, and denied air support when the operation began to founder.[82] Four U.S. airmen lost their lives in the operation. More than a hundred Cuban exiles were killed in the three days of fierce fighting; twelve hundred were captured, of whom many were executed in the months after the invasion's failure, along with local opponents of Castro who had risen in support of the coup. "Force is a naked, brutal thing in this world," former president Eisenhower told *Newsday,* disclaiming all responsibility for the fiasco. "If you are going to use it, you have got to be prepared to go all the way."[83]

The best and brightest had produced a dismal disaster. "We really blew this one," fumed Kennedy. "How could that crowd at CIA and the Pentagon be this wrong?"[84] The administration had been "revealed as if no more than a continuation of the Eisenhower-Dulles Past," lamented Schlesinger in his journal. "We not only look like imperialists, we look like ineffectual imperialists, which is worse; and we look like stupid, ineffectual imperialists, which is worst of all."[85] Though Kennedy took responsibility for the debacle in public, heads rolled behind the scenes. Following the damning report of General Maxwell Taylor's study group,[86] Dulles and Bissell were ousted and John McCone, chairman of the Atomic Energy Commission, was made director of central intelligence.[87] In October 1962 Taylor succeeded Lemnitzer as chairman of the Joint Chiefs.[88] The undeserving winner was Bundy, who had in fact failed as badly as anyone to make the key point that the risks of failure far exceeded the costs of outright cancellation.[89] It was Bundy who had insisted on dismantling the Eisenhower "paper mill"; Bundy who had insisted that fewer than a dozen whiz kids could be a substitute for the old NSC, not to mention the State Department.[90] Yet Bundy emerged with his power enhanced. The NSC was relocated to the basement of the West Wing, ensuring that henceforth Bundy would have unrivaled access to the president.[91] The transformation of the basement's bowling alley into the Situation Room (in fact two rooms) next to the NSC offices was intended to give a new focus to the decision-making process, creating "a funnel for all classified information coming from all national security agencies."[92]

It was into this maelstrom that Henry Kissinger walked in his new capacity as a part-time White House consultant, almost wholly ignorant of Cuba and located most of the time in distant Cambridge, to which top secret material was occasionally sent by CIA couriers and stored in a specially purchased safe in his Divinity Avenue office.[93] His first assignment from Bundy plunged him into the midst of the general overhaul of U.S. defense policy for which he had so long argued and Kennedy had campaigned. Invited down to the capital "for a day or two," Kissinger was startled to be asked for his view on the supplementary military budget. This was being thrown in at the deep end, as he later recalled:

> When I arrived . . . I was handed a big volume containing about fifty different recommendations, together with an explanatory text. It represented the work of two task forces, each of which had spent six weeks on its assignment. I was given the report for something like two hours in stretches of half an hour at a time. I was asked to prepare a memorandum of comments and to meet with Mac for a preliminary review after having the volume for less than an hour. I had no opportunity to discuss the report with the authors to find out what they had in mind nor did I know what aspect of it concerned the President. Finally, I stayed up until four in the morning writing a memorandum on a report which had been taken away from me.[94]

Writing under such circumstances, Kissinger had to resort to academic niceties. The Pentagon acknowledged the old Clausewitzian distinction between general war and limited war; very well. But it appeared not to grasp the distinction between finite deterrence, which asserted that "some or all forms of aggression . . . can be deterred by threatening the Soviet Union with unacceptable damage" so that "victory in the traditional sense is eschewed for a capacity for punishment"; and counterforce, meaning either "a retaliatory force strong enough to accept the first blow and still win," which Kissinger thought "senseless," or "a retaliatory force capable of winning by striking first."[95]

If anyone in Washington read this missive from the Harvard–MIT Arms Control Seminar, they did not acknowledge it. Instead there came a second assignment: to comment on Ted Sorensen's memorandum on the concept of "flexible response" as the basis for Kennedy's new defense strategy. Here again Kissinger took a tough line: why was the president proposing to renounce "preventive war, preemptive war or any other massive first strike"?[96] Why rule out these options in return for nothing?

Seeking to take the initiative, Kissinger drafted a long and intricate memorandum for Kennedy on "Major Defense Options," setting out the case against a second-strike counterforce strategy, the cases for and against a first-strike strategy, and the cases for and against finite deterrence. The crux of his argument was, as usual, that overreliance on nuclear deterrence was dangerous because few issues short of a devastating Soviet first strike would seem worthy of all-out war. There needed to be "a substantial step-up of the limited war forces of the free world" precisely so that the United States and its allies retained the option to "intervene locally." But here he made the point in a new way. True, there were risks inseparable from an increased emphasis on conventional forces. It might "panic our allies or tempt the Soviets into rash acts. . . . [W]e must take care not to give the impression that we would prefer to be defeated by conventional forces rather than resort to nuclear arms." But not building up conventional forces carried an even bigger risk: that in a conflict the president might "lose control over the decision to employ nuclear weapons" to a trigger-happy military. Here Kissinger drew a parallel with the outbreak of World War I, which illustrated "the danger of permitting the military to develop plans on the basis of 'purely' strategic considerations. . . . World War I became inevitable . . . partly because no one knew how to back off a mobilization posture."[97] There is no evidence that Kennedy ever read this document. If he had, however, he would probably have found himself in agreement. Although Barbara Tuchman's *The Guns of August* had not yet been published, the Bay of Pigs fiasco had given Kennedy a taste of what it was to be at the mercy of military planners. By the time of the next crisis over Cuba, he would be intensely preoccupied with the fear of what A.J.P. Taylor would later call "war by timetable."

The greatest defect of the academic strategists of the 1960s was their love of abstraction, taken to its logical extreme in game theory. Kissinger, by contrast, thirsted to make the dilemmas of the nuclear age more concrete. "Much of our planning," he complained, "has concerned itself mostly with the forces required for D-day and for a single crisis. If the above analysis is correct, more consideration should be given to the process by which local crises develop over time, particularly to the situation obtaining on D+15, D+30, D+45, etc."[98] For Kissinger, however, Cuba and Laos, another country suspected of slipping into the Soviet orbit, were terra incognita. To his eyes, it was self-evident that the key theater of superpower conflict was Europe and, specifically, Germany.[99] It was on this issue that he felt uniquely well qualified to give advice.[100] For who else among the whiz kids had a better understanding of the German Question?

V

The Berlin Crisis of 1961 is less well remembered than the Cuban Crisis of the following year. Yet in many respects it was the more dangerous of the two. For the U.S. position was significantly weaker in the German case. Precisely for that reason the Kennedy administration was far more willing to threaten nuclear war over Berlin than it was over Cuba. Khrushchev, for his part, doubted the American willingness to go all the way to the brink for what seemed to him a minor change to the status of the former German capital.[101] In June 1961, just as he had in November 1958, Khrushchev issued an ultimatum, giving the three Western powers six months to withdraw their forces from Berlin. His intention was to sign a separate peace treaty with the East German regime, which would henceforth control access to the city. The Soviet leader had two main concerns: first, to halt the flow of migrants from East Berlin to West Berlin, which was threatening the viability of the German Democratic Republic as a state; second, to counter the military revival of West Germany, which he feared would end with its becoming a nuclear power in its own right. It is not entirely clear that testing American resolve was uppermost in his mind.

Kennedy was made aware shortly after his election that the Russians were under "heavy pressures to get the Berlin question settled and to stop the movement of refugees to the West from behind the Iron Curtain."[102] But the American position was complicated by the intransigence of some (though not all) of the country's European allies. Whereas the British were ready to countenance Berlin as a free city, the French would have none of it. "*Any* retreat from Berlin," de Gaulle told Kennedy in Paris, "*any* change of status, *any* withdrawal of troops, *any* new obstacles to transportation and communication, would mean defeat."[103] The problem was, as the Supreme Allied Commander Europe (SACEUR), General Lauris Norstad, put it, that any "war over Berlin was going to be a nuclear war—or an immediate and ignominious defeat."[104] The reason seemed obvious: in a conventional war over Berlin, the West would stand no chance, given the vastly greater size of the Red Army's forces in the vicinity.

The Berlin Crisis was handled quite differently from the Bay of Pigs. Officials from State, Defense, and the JCS collaborated in a large Berlin Task Force, the work of which was coordinated by Assistant Secretary of State Foy Kohler and Assistant Secretary of Defense Paul Nitze, along with the Joint Chiefs' representative, Major General David Gray.[105] But the situation in Berlin itself was anomalous. The U.S. commandant in Berlin reported to the ambassador in Bonn in his political capacity, but in his military capacity he reported to a four-star general in Heidelberg and through him to General Norstad in Paris.[106] In addition to being SACEUR, Norstad was the commander of Live Oak, the secret military organization for the defense of Berlin that had been set up by the three Western powers in November 1958. To complicate matters further, in August 1961 Kennedy sent General Lucius Clay—the former governor of the postwar U.S. zone of occupation— to Berlin as his personal representative. Kennedy was well served by his ambassador in Moscow, Llewellyn Thompson, who was quick to see that the East Germans were likely "to seal off sector boundary in order to stop what they must consider intolerable continuation refugee flow through Berlin."[107] In Washington, however, he was soon under pressure not to yield even on this issue. Among those urging a tough stance was Henry Kissinger.

On Friday, March 10, Kissinger sat in on the National Security Council; the following Monday and Tuesday he spent being briefed on

Berlin by the State Department experts—George McGhee, Henry Morgan, Charles Bohlen, and Martin Hillebrand—as well as by interested parties in the CIA and the Pentagon.[108] At Bundy's suggestion, former secretary of state Dean Acheson was brought in to direct the review group. Acheson's conclusion—which Kissinger heard in its preliminary form at a meeting of the interdepartmental coordinating group on Berlin contingency planning—was stark. The issue over Berlin was a "conflict of wills" that could not be resolved by negotiation. The Soviets had ceased to believe in "U.S. willingness to go to nuclear war" over Berlin. They had to be made to see that Washington was "really prepared to use nuclear weapons for the protection of Berlin on which we had staked our entire prestige." Acheson recommended a buildup of both nuclear and conventional forces, in anticipation of a showdown as soon as there was any attempt to impede Western movement into Berlin. He also urged the preparation of a program of sanctions and covert operations directed against the entire Soviet bloc. But he made clear that "nothing could be more dangerous than to embark upon a course of action of the sort described in this paper in the absence of a decision to accept nuclear war rather than accede to the demands which Khrushchev is now making."[109] Kissinger's view was more or less the same. "We might . . . go so far as to say that neither side should press demands which can be achieved only by war," he told Rostow on April 4. "The reverse side of this is, of course, the implication that we would take drastic action if the Berlin issue were pressed."[110] "The best approach," he argued, "is firmness with respect to military planning and the expression of a clear determination to maintain the position of Berlin."[111]

For the West German government, the position was agonizing. It was not only the fate of their former capital that was at stake, but also the survival of their divided country. Yet the key decisions were being taken in Washington, London, and Paris—not to mention Moscow—rather than in Bonn. On the specific question of Berlin, the West German chancellor, Konrad Adenauer, was in fact deeply ambivalent. Raised in the Roman Catholic Rhineland, he was old enough (at eighty-five) to remember how the Bismarckian regime had discriminated against non-Protestants. Indeed, he half-joked that he preferred to draw the curtains of his compartment when the train to Berlin crossed the river

Elbe, so as to avoid looking at Prussia's "Asian steppe." Privately, too, he had no deep objection to the division of Germany; it was far preferable to a reunification that might put socialists, if not Communists, in power. He was in fact willing to contemplate a swap, giving the East Germans all of Berlin in return for parts of Saxony and Mecklenburg.[112] Adenauer's primary goal, however, was to ensure that the Western—and especially the American—commitment to the defense of West Germany did not waver.

Ahead of the chancellor's visit to Washington, Kissinger tried to explain his complex motivations. "To talk to Adenauer about the wisdom of flexibility in the abstract," he argued, "is like telling a member of Alcoholics Anonymous that one Martini before dinner will not hurt him. Adenauer would rather err on the side of excessive loyalty to his allies than the policy of taking advantage of Germany's central position to play its neighbors off against each other." The West German leader's great fear was that the new administration's emphasis on a buildup of conventional forces "foreshadows the abandonment of Europe by the United States," to be followed by "the withdrawal of American nuclear arms, leaving the German army at the mercy of the Soviet tactical nuclear arsenal."[113] His key insight was that the core assumption of deterrence—that the United States was willing to risk all-out war with the Soviet Union for the sake of West Germans' freedoms—was not really credible. Any change to the U.S. military posture in Europe was therefore bound to be interpreted by Adenauer as a prelude to disengagement and withdrawal. (He had, after all, been mayor of Cologne in the 1920s, when the Western powers had last walked away from Germany.)

It must not be thought that, in his advice on the subject, Kissinger was actuated by some lingering affection for the country of his birth. Constitutionally, of course, the Federal Republic was a true democracy, and the leading Christian Democrats and Social Democrats had unblemished records of opposition to Hitler. But the same could not be said of a significant number of the second tier of men running West Germany's government and industry. Privately, Kissinger could be scathing even about "good Germans" like the industrialist Kurt Birrenbach.* In addition, he was no longer comfortable speaking in German in formal settings. "Strange as it may seem," he confessed to Bundy, "my vocabulary in German is not good enough to speak extemporaneously on a complicated subject. Because my secondary and higher education was in English, all my thinking on international and military affairs has been in English also. (I have a superb German vocabulary for soccer, if that should interest any audiences.)"†114 For their part, the West Germans were bound to regard Kissinger with suspicion; might not his true sentiment toward the people who had killed so many of his relatives be one of antipathy? One of Adenauer's aides confided that the two Americans who worried "the old man" the most were Henry Kissinger and Adlai Stevenson.115 He and his colleagues could not make up their minds which fate Kissinger secretly had in mind for Germany: that it should be reduced to ashes by the waging of a limited nuclear war, or left at the mercy of the Soviets by the removal of the threat of all-out nuclear war.

In reality, as he made clear in a memorandum on the subject on May 5, Kissinger's primary concern was the credibility of American foreign policy. "The fate of Berlin is the touchstone for the future of the North Atlantic Community," he argued, echoing Acheson. "A defeat over Berlin, that is a deterioration of Berlin's possibility to live in freedom, would inevitably demoralize the Federal Republic. . . . All other NATO nations would be bound to draw the indicated conclusions from such a demonstration of the West's impotence. For other parts of the world, the irresistible nature of the Communist movement would be underlined."

But that implied a "showdown" if the Soviets persisted in their

----

*Kissinger described Birrenbach as "belong[ing] to the finger-pointing, lapel clutching variety of German" but "nevertheless a man of some influence. He is in charge of the Thyssen Enterprises. Though old man Thyssen bankrolled Hitler, Birrenbach himself spent the Nazi Period in exile. He is a friend of the Chancellor and is used by the latter to sound out opinion in English-speaking countries, under the mistaken impression that Birrenbach has a special way with Americans" (to Schlesinger, May 25, 1962).

†Kissinger once congratulated Marion Dönhoff on "the fortitude with which you sat through a speech I made in German."

efforts to alter the status quo in Berlin, whether that took the form of breaking the supply lines to the Allied garrison or interrupting civilian traffic. And a showdown had to include the possibility of a nuclear war:

> (a) The Soviets will be able to arrest and probably defeat almost any scale conventional attack we may be able to mount in the direction of Berlin with present forces available to NATO.
>
> (b) An all-out nuclear strike probably could not destroy the Soviet retaliatory force.
>
> (c) If the Soviets are prepared to press matters, we will [therefore] be confronted with the necessity of resorting to nuclear weapons either locally or in a controlled war of retaliation.
>
> It follows that we should undertake no local actions of any sort without having first determined the answer to this question: Are we prepared to accept a defeat by conventional forces or should we employ nuclear weapons if necessary?[116]

Kissinger knew full well that this was not a congenial train of thought for the full-time members of the NSC.[117] McNamara was simultaneously arguing for "the use of substantial conventional force before considering resort to nuclear weapons," including covert operations to spark an uprising in East Germany.[118] Kissinger had also begun to detect Bundy's ambivalence, signified by his reluctance to define what exactly he expected from Kissinger even when given three options to choose from, ranging from "an analysis of our existing war plans, from the point of view of their political impact," to advice on "almost any subject in the NATO area."[119] Yet as the Harvard semester drew to a close in late April 1961, Kissinger had two advantages. First, Bundy and his team were reeling from the fiasco of the Bay of Pigs. Separately from his typed memoranda, Kissinger sent Bundy a handwritten note, deploring an "unfair" attack on him by *The New York Times*. Bundy was appreciative. "When one feels that he has contributed to a blunder," he replied, "it is not easy to keep a straight course and simple friendship helps."[120]

Second, Kissinger was already committed to visiting Bonn and was by now sufficiently well known there—not least for his work on nuclear strategy—to be able to secure meetings with both Adenauer and his pugnacious defense minister, Franz Josef Strauss. There was an almost comic quality to Kissinger's encounter with the latter. Flanked by three German generals, Strauss berated his American visitor, taking the line that the U.S. buildup of conventional forces was in fact bad for German security. Was Kissinger aware that German ground troops were in fact superior to American? Did he know that Social Democrats like "Helmuth [sic] Schmidt" were "quot[ing] Kissinger's book completely out of context to prove that President Kennedy's adviser supported the SPD line on national defense" (i.e., opposition to basing the defense of Western Europe on the threat of massive retaliation)? Over dinner at the American embassy the same evening, "Strauss was much more boisterous than in the afternoon and much less flexible. Perhaps the quantity of drinks consumed was partly to blame."

> He said that on Berlin, United States relations with the Soviets are like his relations with his dog. If he tells his dog to go under the stove and the dog goes instead under the table, he immediately adds: "Or else you can go under the table," in order to maintain the illusion of being in control of events. . . . [Finally] he became out of control and implied that Berlin would be lost no matter what anyone said, particularly from the German side. . . . Somehow the discussion reached the subject of a possible East German uprising. Strauss said that as long as he was Defense Minister, the German army would not move even if Germans were shot down in the street right in front of them on the other side of the line. [Richard] Balken [of the German Foreign Office] then said that if he were a division commander, he would move no matter what Strauss said. Strauss shouted, "Then I would arrest you. In fact, maybe I should arrest you right now." Though he said it jokingly, he is a man who might mean it.[121]

Kissinger's meeting with Adenauer just over a week later shed further light on German thinking. Despite Kissinger's reassurances ("Berlin, I said, was not a German city, but a test of freedom everywhere. . . . Germany could no longer be considered a foreign country"), the chancellor was full of suspicions. The United States had "failed" to lead NATO in the direction of an integrated nuclear strategy. Now, faced not just with a missile gap but with what Adenauer now understood to be a Soviet lead in all nuclear weapons,[122] Eisenhower had secretly promised to "surrender Berlin" to Khrushchev. Macmillan was ready to acquiesce in such "extreme weakness." De Gaulle alone could be relied upon, and this was only because he had an independent nuclear capability.

> Adenauer said that the United States must try to understand European fears. They worry about the situation where an American President is killed during an attack and we do not have the leadership to retaliate. Also, what of American election years? He asked if I could honestly say that Eisenhower would have used the H Bomb to retaliate a month before the election? I said, "As a matter of fact, yes." He asked, "Can Europe really be so dependent on the decisions of one man?"[123]

The significance of this allusion to France's newly achieved nuclear status* was not lost on Kissinger. He had just been fully briefed by the French diplomat François de Rose, who had made it clear that France would consider integrating its *force de frappe* into the NATO command structure only in return for American technical assistance.[124] American policy makers were beginning to grasp a new challenge of the nuclear age: how to prevent the proliferation of nuclear weapons, which even in the hands of allies were bound to increase the probability of an unintended Armageddon—unless some form of American veto could be imposed on their use. Kissinger's meetings with Strauss, Adenauer, and de Rose made him appreciate more than before the

---

*France had successfully detonated a nuclear bomb in southern Algeria on February 13, 1960.

urgent need to strengthen NATO, if only to resist de Gaulle's impulse—and perhaps also Strauss's—to go it alone.[125] If the French and the Germans sincerely believed that "our emphasis on conventional forces was really a device to disengage ourselves from Europe," they could scarcely be blamed for wanting their own nuclear deterrents.[126] A further argument, seldom made explicit by the Europeans, was that it was politically easier to go down this route than to increase their conventional forces.

Kissinger's German trip significantly raised his profile in Washington and the wider world. Both he and Strauss aired their differences publicly; not only the German press but also *The New York Times* and the London *Observer* took note.[127] "The President's recent speech in Congress asking for a rapid buildup in 'conventional' armaments sounded as if it could have been written by Kissinger," enthused the *New York Post* in early June. "And the American promise to fight for Berlin if necessary is a prime Kissinger thesis." Kissinger could not resist giving the *Post* a less-than-diplomatic one-liner: "The difficulty with [John Foster] Dulles' policy was not that he was wrong about communism, but that he was right about so little else."[128] Interesting as Kissinger's "memcons"* may have been, it is hard to believe that Bundy read all this with pleasure. More important, his views were beginning to diverge from those of his outspoken protégé.

For Kissinger, as for Acheson, the issue was clear-cut. He was in no way surprised by Khrushchev's aggressive behavior when he and Kennedy met in Vienna in early June; this was exactly what Kissinger (unlike the more optimistic president) had expected.[129] In Kissinger's mind, a showdown over Berlin was inevitable for the simple reason that the Soviets wanted it. The key thing was to have worked out in detail the phases of the American response—not least to ensure that the president remained in control of the process of escalation. The alternative strategy was quietly to make a concession to the Russians: specifically, to drop the American insistence on free civilian movement within

---

*A "memcon" is a memorandum of a face-to-face conversation. These are the earliest surviving memcons written by Kissinger. Their vivid style contrasts markedly with the staid official reports sent when U.S. diplomats were also present.

Berlin to the extent of tolerating a closure of the border between East and West Berlin, as well as the border between West Berlin and the surrounding German Democratic Republic. This was the move that Llewellyn Thompson correctly predicted from Moscow—the move that had already been decided by the Soviets and the East Germans by early July.[130] As yet, no one in Washington was explicitly discussing such an outcome. But the divergence between hard-liners and soft-liners was already clear.[131] Ahead of the key NSC meeting of July 19, Bundy drew a clear distinction between "a hard wing of the Kohler group, led by Acheson and Nitze," and a softer wing—including, by implication, himself—who favored "now mak[ing] clear that neither the peace treaty nor the substitution of East Germans for Russians along the Autobahn is a fighting matter" and "extend[ing] serious feelers to the Soviets with respect to the elements of an eventual settlement of the crisis."[132]

Arthur Schlesinger had emphatically urged the president himself that "Henry Kissinger should be brought into the center of Berlin planning."[133] It did not happen. At first, Kissinger could not understand Bundy's elusiveness, his reluctance to give him a clear brief. "I am convinced that in order to make a real contribution," he wrote, "I must be able to follow a given problem or a set of problems over a period of time." Instead, Bundy was treating him as "an idea man," handing him this or that document and giving him just an afternoon to formulate his view: "My uneasiness about certain features of our foreign policy, therefore, is bound to express itself in comments which must seem peripheral and irritating to those who have been participating in generating the policy papers. It is like being asked in the middle of a chess game to suggest a move without having been in a position to study the development of the game."[134]

Despite Kissinger's German expertise, the key jobs on Berlin had been assigned to Henry Owen and Carl Kaysen. Frustrated, Kissinger rescinded his offer to work full time for Bundy throughout the summer, proposing to revert to the status of an "*ad hoc* consultant."[135] Bundy initially accepted this with feigned bemusement.[136] There was desultory talk of a "special study of civilian control in NATO . . . as an ad hoc problem"[137] and a further chance to fulminate about the administration's draft position on disarmament. (In Kissinger's words, "it would be better to scrap the whole thing and start from scratch.")[138] But it was only after weeks of inconclusive letters, phone calls, and meetings that the truth came out: "He said that my views on Berlin were too fixed, that my identification with the 'hard' line would embarrass the President with people like [Walter] Lippmann and [Senator William] Fulbright." To avoid that embarrassment, Bundy now suggested that Kissinger work "as a personal consultant to the President on Berlin while someone else, probably a junior staff member, would be given formal responsibility."[139] Kissinger reluctantly agreed to this, but confided his enduring doubts to Rostow.

> Mac agreed that I should attend all meetings dealing with Ber-
> lin. In what capacity? It will be unavoidable that I contact the
> departments. In what role? . . . Frankly, if I felt less desperate
> about the international situation I would withdraw. . . . I made
> an infinitely greater contribution to military policy and NATO
> strategy as a private citizen than I am now as a White House
> consultant. If the same process should now start with respect to
> the Berlin problem, I would feel that I had better return to
> being a professor.[140]

The professor was being given a lesson in Beltway politics that he would never forget, and the lesson was far from over.

By now the shine had come off the best and the brightest. *Time* magazine now heaped scorn on Kennedy's "squad of White House professors and kibitzers," among them "Special Presidential Consultant Henry Kissinger." By the "crucial test of reality," the magazine declared, "John Kennedy's system is not working. In the field of foreign policy, the record is sorry. When trouble has struck, the Kennedy solution has seemed to be activity instead of action."[141] This was unduly harsh. Berlin was an extraordinarily complex problem. Moreover, Kennedy was being bombarded by often-contradictory intelligence and analysis. Perhaps most perplexing—though Kissinger was not aware of it—was the realization, mainly on the basis of the Corona satellite program, that there was in fact no missile gap, or rather that the gap was in favor of the United States.[142] This made Khrushchev's apparent determination to force a confrontation over Berlin—signaled by a one-third increase in defense spending announced in July—all the more puzzling. At the same time, Kennedy was absorbing a new paper by Thomas Schelling that seemed comprehensively to reject the notion of a limited nuclear war using "tactical" missiles.[143] Rightly sensing that Acheson's approach might have been too narrow, Kennedy asked Schlesinger to prepare "an unsigned memorandum about the unexplored issues in the Berlin problem." Schlesinger in turn called in Kissinger and Abe Chayes. The result—hastily drafted on July 6, in the space of just two hours, before the presidential helicopter left for Hyannis Port, Kennedy's Cape Cod retreat—sought to widen the scope of the administration's Berlin strategy by posing a series of worrisome questions.

Was there "any political objective other than present access procedures for which we are prepared to incinerate the world[?]" What was Kennedy's "real intention" with regard to German unification? What if the Soviets did something other than interrupt military access to Berlin, the scenario Acheson had focused on? What "concretely" would nuclear war mean? What role would America's allies play in the scenario of confrontation?[144] It was Kissinger who pressed hardest on the nuclear issue. His nightmare remained that the military would force the president's hand in a crisis before Kennedy himself knew "what is meant by nuclear war" in practice.[145] Suddenly it seemed that Kissinger had what he had been pressing Bundy to give him for months: a role alongside Rowen and Kaysen in devising a plan for a graduated military response to the Soviet challenge—not ruling out the threat of nuclear weapons but calibrating it carefully to avoid World War III.[146] True, it was still Bundy who had access to the president. But at least he was delivering a message that bore Kissinger's stamp. Indeed, Bundy now re-sent Kennedy the "powerful" memorandum on Berlin that Kissinger had written back in May.[147] Kissinger at long last found himself with something worthwhile to do in his office (room 399) in the Executive Office Building, even if he was still spending only two or three days a week in Washington.[148]

"I do not like adjectives like 'hard,' 'soft' or 'firm' as applied to policy," Kissinger said more than once during the crisis. In the case of Berlin, these distinctions were especially meaningless. At the NSC meeting on July 13, Acheson, supported by Vice President Lyndon Johnson, urged the proclamation of a national emergency, the calling up of reserves, an increase in defense spending, and other economic measures. Kissinger, by contrast, proposed a diplomatic initiative, if only to avoid giving the appearance of American intransigence.[149] He opposed declaring an emergency. Indeed, he was prepared to contemplate even de facto recognition of the East German regime if the alternative was nuclear war.[150] Convinced that the president was not being given clearly delineated options by the military, he remained preoccupied with "the military consequences of a failure of negotiations."[151] These arguments did not go unheeded. Addressing the nation on television on the night of July 25, Kennedy called Berlin "the great testing place of Western courage and will"; Rostow referenced *High Noon*.[152] But when the president set out the U.S. position—to Acheson's dismay—he stopped short of declaring an emergency, opting to match Khrushchev's latest increase in defense spending so as to give the army six additional divisions, while at the same time hinting that the United States was now interested only in retaining access to and a presence in *West* Berlin.[153]

Khrushchev got the message. In conversation with John J. McCloy at his dacha near Sochi, he rattled his saber, saying he would "sign peace treaty no matter what; occupation rights thereupon cease, access cut off, and necessary then to make a deal with GDR; if you attempt force way through we will oppose by force; war bound to be thermonuclear and though you and we may survive all your European allies will be completely destroyed."[154] Yet he also "re-affirmed willingness guarantee freedom and independence West Berlin . . . and went so far as to say he thought any Western proposal for such guarantees would be accepted."[155]

In boosting his conventional forces while leaving a door open to negotiation, Kennedy was in some respects following Kissinger's advice. But he was receiving that advice indirectly, from Bundy. Kissinger vented to Schlesinger his "great feeling of being excluded by Mac," complaining that (as Schlesinger recorded)

> though the President had asked him to come down full time,
> Mac had strongly urged him not to do so; that Mac had never

once asked his advice on anything and had not even responded
in any way to the very intelligent series of memoranda Henry
has been writing about Berlin; that when the President had
expressed a desire to see him, Mac had never made clear to him
what he wanted to see him about, and that Henry was in consequence both so ill-prepared and so tense that he could not do
himself justice; and that the whole experience had been humiliating for him.[156]

Shut out as he was from the president's inner circle, Kissinger could
not know that the crucial—and supremely pragmatic—decision had
already been taken to acquiesce if the Soviets decided to close the Berlin
border, as Senator J. William Fulbright publicly predicted they would.[157]
Kennedy himself told Rostow that Khrushchev would "have to do
something to stop the flow of refugees. Perhaps a wall. And we won't
be able to prevent it."[158] In Moscow, Llewellyn Thompson all but spelled
out to Khrushchev that some form of restriction of the outflow from
East Germany would be acceptable to the United States.[159] By August 9
the rest of the Warsaw Pact had agreed to the plan, and the East German
regime had surreptitiously acquired the concrete pillars, barbed wire,
timber, and other materials that would be necessary to ring-fence West
Berlin. Two days later Reuters reported that the East German People's
Chamber had passed an "'enigmatic resolution,' saying that its members
approved whatever measures the East German government wished to
undertake to address the 'revanchist' situation in Berlin."[160] At one a.m.
on the night of August 13, 1961, the East German leader Walter Ulbricht's
helots began building the Berlin Wall.[161] The U.S. commandant in Berlin watched but did nothing. When he heard the news, Kennedy coolly
told Rusk to go to a baseball game and returned to his yacht off Cape
Cod.[162] The most he was prepared to do was to send Lucius Clay to
Berlin, along with Vice President Johnson, and to authorize reinforce-
ment of the American garrison in West Berlin.

From one vantage point, the events that culminated in the building
of the Berlin Wall were a calamity, the result of "inconsistency, indecision, and policy failure."[163] From the pragmatic viewpoint favored by
John F. Kennedy, however, the outcome was optimal.[164] First and most

important, nuclear war had been avoided. ("Goddamit . . . use your head," Kennedy snapped at Roswell Gilpatric, the deputy secretary of defense, at one point during the crisis. "What we are talking about is seventy million dead Americans.")[165] Second, a conventional clash had also been avoided, which would have ended in either nuclear war or humiliation for the West. As Kennedy put it, "A wall is a hell of a lot better than a war."[166] Third, the Soviets and their East German lackeys had been exposed for what they were: stony-faced enemies of freedom. Yet Kennedy was wrong to think that "this was the end of the Berlin crisis."

Perhaps surprisingly, considering how much he was thinking about possible military scenarios, Kissinger had not foreseen the abandonment of the East Berliners to their fate. True, the building of the Berlin Wall merely closed the last chink in the iron curtain. Technically, the wall enclosed West Berlin, not East Berlin. But when East German border guards killed civilians who tried to cross from east to west—the first victim, Günter Litfin, was shot on August 24—it was shockingly clear who exactly had been incarcerated. To Kissinger, this was doubly outrageous. First, the Wall represented an abandonment of any pretense that Germany might be unified in the foreseeable future. Second, it looked like yet another American concession to the Soviets. Here again Kissinger was the idealist, Kennedy the realist.

What Kissinger wanted was an American assertion that the universal principle of national "self-determination"—as enunciated by none other than Woodrow Wilson four decades earlier—should apply to Germany and, indeed, to all of Berlin. U.S. policy should be formulated so that the Soviets would have to "assume the onus for keeping Germany divided." This meant taking literally the West German government's refusal to recognize the legitimacy of the German Democratic Republic (even if Adenauer privately remained content with Germany's de facto division). "I know it will be said that Adenauer should not be able to veto U.S. policy," Kissinger noted in one of many documents he wrote on the subject that summer. "However, it is not clear to me why allies should not have a major voice in decisions affecting the future of their own country."[167] In another, he explicitly rejected the view that "realism should impel us to confirm what we are incapable of changing" and that therefore the United States should "accept the division of Germany as final." On the contrary, he argued, the West "must stand for the unity of Germany despite the experiences of two world wars." Kissinger's argument for reunification was not ingenuous, to be sure. He was convinced that, if the West were seen to accept the division of Germany, then the West Germans might be tempted into a "Rapallo policy"* of "attempt[ing] separate dealings with the East." As he put it, "if the West understands its interests correctly," it would continue to argue for German reunification on the basis of initial confederation, then free elections, combined with demilitarization and the recognition of the Oder-Neisse border with Poland as immutable—not because this would be acceptable in Moscow but precisely because it would be rejected.[168]

Kissinger was right that Washington had underestimated the West German public's revulsion at the building of the Berlin Wall, articulated most passionately by the mayor of Berlin, Willy Brandt.[169] But he was wrong if he thought "Mr. Bundy"—as he now addressed him[170]—would heed his arguments for a principled stand on German unity. In a private letter to Maxwell Taylor, Kissinger made clear his own disgust:

> De Gaulle is right.
>
> The Soviets have made us look like monkeys, weak monkeys and we can't wait to demonstrate our masochism by crawling back and begging them please to negotiate, so that we can give up something else to them.
>
> Instead of whimpering in our notes how illegal the split of Berlin is, we should announce as a prerequisite of negotiation that the concrete walls be torn down and the split ended. . . .
>
> If the Soviets didn't respond, and they probably wouldn't, negotiations would be indefinitely postponed. We would thereupon inform them that we will go to war before we

---

*The allusion was to the Treaty of Rapallo (1922), signed by the Weimar Republic with the Soviet Union, one of many attempts by interwar German governments to extricate themselves from the constraints of the Versailles Treaty by dealing with Moscow. Kissinger would later make similar arguments against Willy Brandt's *Ostpolitik*.

forego [*sic*] our rights in and access to Berlin, calmly carry on with our military buildup, and let them sweat for a change.

The French would be with us 100%, and I believe we could easily get Der Alte [Adenauer] to join the party. This would isolate the British all right but the Kohlers and the Owens don't seem terribly upset by the current isolation of France. As for India, Dahomey, Upper Volta, and the rest of the "uncommitted," we'll worry about them in due time; this Berlin business of 1961 is our problem, right now, and we must stop acting as if it were a popularity contest.[171]

As the vehement tone of this letter suggests, Kissinger was now on the warpath. As far as he was concerned, the Berlin Crisis was far from over; after all, the Soviets might follow the building of the wall with some other action that directly infringed on U.S. rights in the city. Angrily, he warned Taylor that "the State [Department] boys" would soon "have some craven negotiating position all buttoned up as THE U.S. position in quadripartite councils, perhaps initially in the Ambassadorial forum . . . without the President's having had the opportunity of indicating his decision on the general lines our negotiating position should establish." It was crucial that Kennedy be offered tougher options both for the U.S. diplomatic response to the wall and for possible military countermeasures: "He must stand before the ruddy bar of history and choose from among carefully and sharply presented alternatives."[172] If the Soviets sought in any way to restrict air traffic into Tempelhof airport, the United States should not comply. Indeed, "it would be better for many reasons if the Communists were forced to shoot one down."[173] By early September, Kissinger was predicting "a prolonged crisis."[174] Apparently unaware of the new intelligence on the missile gap, he warned that Soviets had resumed nuclear testing precisely because "they are equal and probably ahead of us"; if they expected that superiority to be temporary, then "we must expect a showdown within the year."[175]

Kissinger was in the mood for showdowns. On September 8 he sent Schlesinger an extraordinary eleven-page tirade against Bundy. "It has become apparent to me," he wrote, "that I can no longer make a useful contribution. At first I had intended to submit a formal resignation. But then I decided that it would be best to avoid a public break"—because, as he put it, "a formal resignation at this time is likely to be interpreted abroad as a defeat for the 'firm' line." He had therefore resolved "simply [to] stop coming to Washington. If the past four weeks are any criterion, there will be no request for my services. . . . If I saw the slightest chance of being effective, my misgivings about the trend of events would be a spur to effort rather than a reason for leaving. But my contribution is so negligible, indeed so misleading, that I have no choice except to withdraw." As we have seen, Kissinger's role as a part-time consultant had never been well defined. Perhaps because Bundy saw his Harvard colleague as a threat, perhaps because his views were too "dogmatic," he had kept him at a distance, excluding him from the meetings in the White House that really mattered.

For Kissinger, the experience had been "Kafka-like." After much tergiversation, Bundy had finally asked him to work on Berlin, albeit not as the official "White House 'Berlin man'"; he had even been known to cite Kissinger in presentations to the Berlin Steering Group; yet Kissinger himself had attended no NSC meetings since the spring; he had not been asked to join any of the ten subgroups of the Berlin Working Group; his various memoranda had been ignored; key roles had been "assigned in a fashion to exclude me—sometimes in a particularly humiliating fashion"; and his efforts (at Rostow's suggestion) to contribute to "the problem of intelligence activities in Eastern Germany" had ended in another humiliation. In the week after the building of the wall, he had "spent most of my time reading incoming cables from all over the world" because Bundy had given him nothing to do. ("I must be one of the better-informed people on the White House staff by now," he added wryly, "—though my English is, I fear, permanently ruined.") Excluded from the Situation Room and scarcely even contacted by Bundy, he felt like "a kibitzer shouting random comments from the side-lines." But that was not the most striking image Kissinger conjured up. Turning to the substance of U.S. policy—and in particular to the way the Berlin Crisis was being handled—he likened himself to "a man riding next to a driver heading for a precipice who is being asked to make sure that the gas tank is full and the oil pressure adequate."[176]

It is tempting to read this letter as merely the anguished cri de coeur of a Washington novice whose White House debut had flopped. Schlesinger dutifully showed part of the letter to Kennedy, who in turn prevailed upon Bundy to assuage Kissinger's hurt feelings. In a meeting that cannot have been comfortable for either of them, Bundy assured Kissinger that "many actions were taken on the basis of" his summer work. After effusively complimenting Kissinger on "abilities, dedication, prolificness, etc., etc.," Bundy gave an example: "Well, you know, we were just looking at the problem of calling up the reserves [which Kissinger had opposed], and do you know, Henry, you were responsible for keeping 50,000 men from the front. . . . We may not have said anything, because of course so busy, but you can be sure everything you fired off was carefully considered."

He hoped that he would still be able to call on Kissinger's expertise in the future, as and when required. "MB made a great attempt to grovel," Kissinger noted bitterly after the meeting, "and since he covered almost every point in the letter to AS [Arthur Schlesinger], it seems obvious that he was schooled to make these points." But all he could bring himself to say to Bundy was that he "might run for election on [the] slogan of keeping 50,000 boys from the front." Bundy patronizingly ignored the irony. "And many of them were from Massachusetts, too, Henry," he said as he escorted Kissinger out the door, leaving it wholly unclear if Kissinger had in fact quit.[177]

According to Schlesinger's son Stephen, Kissinger recalled how "Bundy . . . had elbowed him aside in the Kennedy Administration despite promises made to him by JFK." Schlesinger asked why. "Apparently he felt threatened by me," Kissinger replied. "But by barring me from the job with Kennedy, which I would have taken, he put me on the path to a post with Nixon. For if I had become a member of the Kennedy administration, Nixon would never have hired me."[178] Yet there was substance as well as wounded pride in Kissinger's lamentations. As he put it to Schlesinger père at the time,

[M]y concern is not related to such slogans as "soft" and "hard." Rather, I am worried about the lack of an over-all strategy which makes us prisoners of events. I am distressed by an attitude on the part of and towards the bureaucracy which produces too many warmed-over versions of the policies of the previous Administration. The result has been an overconcern with tactics and a lack of a guiding concept which have been responsible for most of our difficulties. . . . [W]hat I have seen of our planning seems to me largely irrelevant to the perils ahead of us. We are heading for a major crisis, perhaps a disaster, while the bureaucracy continues to treat orderly procedure as the chief purpose of government and the President is given plans which do not define his options properly and which in the event will prove hollow.

Kissinger's critique was of both the process and the product. The old bureaucratic habits of the Eisenhower era had stealthily crept back, so that the president was once again being "confronted with faits accomplis by the bureaucracy which he can ratify or modify but which preclude a real consideration of alternatives." As a result, military policy "lack[ed] the flexibility the President desires." The administration's disarmament plan was essentially a retread of Eisenhower's. The U.S. negotiating position on Germany had "yet to be formulated." Above all, the Berlin issue had been incorrectly defined.

The problem is not simply free access to Berlin—as is so often maintained—but the hopes and expectations of the peoples of Berlin, the Federal Republic, and Western Europe. If they lose confidence in us, the current crisis will turn into a major defeat even should we obtain some kind of guarantee of access for Berlin. If present trends continue, the outcome will be a decaying, demoralized city with some access guarantees, a Germany in which neutralism will develop, and a substantially weakened NATO. [Meanwhile] . . . Soviet intransigence has been encouraged until the President may well face what he has sought to avoid: the choice between humiliation and general nuclear war.[179]

Just how far Kissinger's idealism went is illustrated by a subsequent exchange between him and Schlesinger. As a historian of the United

States, the latter felt "a little uneasy about making a fetish of self-determination in the centennial year of our own national decision to suppress that principle"—meaning the Civil War, which had begun at Fort Sumter in April 1861. Kissinger, the historian of Europe, was quick to challenge the implied (and very bad) analogy between the Confederacy and the German Democratic Republic. As he put it, "The situation would be analogous if the French had established a government in Richmond against the will of the Southern states and if the North had been pressured by Great Britain to accept this fact. What do you think this would have done for future United States–Great Britain relations for a generation?" And he repeated his earlier argument: his "nightmare" remained "a resurgence of nationalism in Germany and to Soviet-German deals on a national basis, wrecking the achievements of fifteen years of European integration." While he was "willing to be flexible on security questions, on access procedures and similar matters," he was adamant that "to give up the principle of self-determination as it applies to Germany will have catastrophic consequences."[180]

Kissinger's spat with Bundy was about more than sour grapes. For the Berlin Crisis was not over. Indeed, it would reach a dangerous climax within weeks of their inconclusive showdown—and for more or less the reasons that Kissinger had feared.

VI

Opportunities for contacts between U.S. and Soviet citizens during the Cold War were few. The vast majority of Americans never so much as glimpsed a Russian in the flesh, and vice versa. The exception to the rule was in the interaction between scientists. Every year since 1955, as we have seen, academics concerned with the issue of nuclear disarmament had met at the Pugwash conference. In 1961 the location of the gathering was the village of Stowe, in the Green Mountains of Vermont. Doubtless relieved to escape the humidity as well as the humiliations of Washington, Henry Kissinger was among the participants. What he learned there from the Soviet delegates confirmed his belief that the German Question was still very far from being resolved.

In the course of the plenary session, one of the American delegates, the Russian-born physicist Eugene Rabinowitch, a Manhattan Project veteran and founder of the *Bulletin of the Atomic Scientists,* had complained that "the American government was conducting nineteenth century politics over Berlin at a moment when such measures were completely insane. As a result . . . such phrases as 'if we are pushed around too much over Berlin we will fight' were sheer bluff and were not taken seriously by any American." Kissinger, accompanied by his Harvard colleague-cum-foe Robert Bowie, hastened to assure the Soviet delegates that "I had seen something of the operation of our government [and] I could assure them that our threats over Berlin were meant utterly seriously. A Soviet policy based on the assumption that we were bluffing could only lead to disaster." The Russian historian Vladimir Khvostov replied that this "proved the correctness of the Soviet policy of resuming nuclear testing," to which Kissinger retorted that "if the Soviets were prepared unilaterally to interrupt our access to Berlin they were indeed correct in resuming testing, because any interruption of our access would lead to war." At the initiative of the Russians, this exchange was followed by a longer meeting the following evening, attended by Kissinger, Khvostov, the biochemist Norair Sissakyan, and General Nikolai Talensky of the Red Army's General Staff. After an exchange of now-familiar positions on Berlin, enlivened by Kissinger's usual mordant sense of humor, the conversation turned to the broader question of Germany's eastern border. Prompted by Kissinger, Talensky asked "whether I thought it possible that we would make an agreement with the Soviet Union in which they would guarantee access to Berlin in return for our guarantee of Germany's Eastern frontiers [the Oder-Neisse line that was still rejected by many West German conservatives]. The access guarantees to Berlin could then be made part of a peace treaty which the Soviet Union would sign separately with the GDR." Emphasizing that he was speaking as a private citizen—though the Soviets doubtless discounted that disclaimer—Kissinger said he thought so, subsequently adding a fourth point, that the East Germans would take over the handling of access to West Berlin as agents of the Soviet Union, but insisting that the initiative for such a deal would need to come from Moscow, not Washington.

The next day passed without further exchanges, but on the last day of the conference, as the Soviet delegates were about to board their bus to the airport, Kissinger was once again approached, this time by Khvostov and the physicist Igor Tamm, who bombarded him with new questions. Was he adamant that there could be no Soviet troops in West Berlin? Would a UN guarantee of American rights in West Berlin be acceptable? Kissinger replied that the United States "would not agree to a status which could be changed every year by a majority in the General Assembly. Tamm asked how about a guarantee for five years. I said that was too short. He then asked how about ten years. I replied that if this kept up I would suggest one hundred and fifty years and perhaps we could meet in the middle. He laughed and said we understood each other. I said, 'I am not sure we do.'" Finally, Tamm came to the point: In what form would a Soviet initiative on Germany be acceptable? Would a letter by a scientist to *Pravda* suffice? Kissinger demurred; it would need to come from a Soviet government spokesman. "Khvostov, who had been silent throughout this discussion, said at this point that as a fellow historian he wanted to tell me that I had learned my lessons well."[181]

This was the first of many "back channel" exchanges through which Henry Kissinger would communicate with representatives of the Soviet Union. Such conversations were important in the Cold War precisely because both parties could claim not to be representing official positions, even when each assumed the other was doing just that. (Their unofficial character also created opportunities for Kissingerian wit, which *homo sovieticus,* with his fondness for black humor, tended to enjoy.) Tamm, like his pupil Andrei Sakharov, was himself somewhat skeptical about the value of the Pugwash conferences precisely because the Soviet participants could not speak freely. Yet the signal he had just sent to Washington via Kissinger was an important one.[182] In his speech to the United Nations on September 25, Kennedy was so conciliatory on the subject of Berlin that even the East German official newspaper *Neues Deutschland* praised his "remarkable . . . willingness to negotiate."[183] The Soviet minister for foreign affairs, Andrei Gromyko, by contrast, was unyielding. Echoing Acheson, Kissinger fretted that the Soviets continued to doubt American resolve. Clearly, only some concrete military action would convince them that they could go no further in Berlin.[184] This was not unreasonable. There was, after all, no guarantee that the Soviets, having built their wall, would not now impose restrictions on Western access to their part of the city. The problem was that there still were very few military steps that could be taken in Berlin that would not swiftly escalate into a full-blown nuclear war. Indeed, Kissinger suspected General Norstad of regarding any conventional action as "almost entirely a trigger for [the use of] nuclear weapons."[185]

Throughout the Berlin Crisis, Kissinger was repeatedly accused of being too hawkish. He was incensed when *The Harvard Crimson* ran a story with the headline "Kissinger Cautions Disarmament Might Lead to U.S.S.R. Victory."[186] In truth, as he kept insisting, his position on Berlin was too nuanced to be categorized simply as "hard" or "firm." As we have seen, he favored an uncompromising stance on the issue of German self-determination.[187] He firmly believed that the United States needed to convey to Moscow its resolve not to make further concessions on access to West Berlin, and that military measures— including a resumption of nuclear testing in the atmosphere—might be necessary to achieve that. But as his exchanges at Stowe made clear, Kissinger was willing to negotiate on a wide range of issues, from the status of West Berlin to the eastern German border. And he was sincerely terrified that Norstad's military plan ran "undue risks either of general war or of some form of humiliation."[188] On October 16 Kissinger wrote a harsh memorandum, tearing apart Norstad's recent testimony to the president, the Joint Chiefs, Rusk, and McNamara, accusing Norstad of "arrogat[ing] to himself decisions which are properly the President's" by "asking for a carte blanche to do what seems appropriate to him at the time of crisis, without specifying the contingencies or the next move." Live Oak essentially consisted of "probes" along the autobahn to West Berlin, to be followed at the first sign of Soviet or East German resistance by rapid escalation, presumably— though it was not quite clear when—involving nuclear weapons. Interestingly, when confronted with the scenario of a military showdown over Berlin, Kissinger now reverted to his earlier argument in *Nuclear Weapons and Foreign Policy* that a limited nuclear war could conceivably be waged with tactical missiles. Yet in his eyes this could not be characterized as a "hard" policy if the alternative implied by Live Oak was an unstoppable escalation to an all-out war involving the strategic forces of both superpowers.[189] It was no use. Kissinger's memoranda went unheeded. He was reduced to reading the newspapers for information about the conventional forces buildup.[190]

Kissinger had tried and failed to quit as a consultant before. On October 19 he tried again.[191] Schlesinger, as usual, was sympathetic. ("I regard the whole thing as a terrible shame and miscarriage.")[192] Bundy, as usual, tried to talk him into staying. Kissinger, as usual, left the door open to future "request[s] for advice."[193] This time, however, he resolved to go through with formal resignation, writing directly to Kennedy and asking Schlesinger to deliver the letter, presumably lest Bundy once again demonstrate "his extraordinary skill in moving me from one position of disadvantage to another."[194] Even then Bundy had the last word. "Since on our side there is no change whatever in our desire to have the advantage of your counsel," he wrote, "there seems no particular point in announcing your resignation."[195]

It was checkmate. Kissinger was beside himself. Bundy's only motive, he raged to Schlesinger, had been "to give the President the impression of my participation while continuing to exclude me from even the most trivial responsibilities." He was "outrage[d] that in these critical times personal competitiveness should take such a brutal form."[196] But he had already proposed "not . . . to discuss publicly or privately either the fact or the reasons for my separation." When *Newsweek* called for confirmation that there had been "a sharp disagreement between me and the White House on Berlin policy" and this was "likely to lead to my resignation and a public break," Kissinger had to give a mealymouthed denial:

> I said that the best answer to his question was the fact of my going to Washington next week to sit in on some of the German talks. While inevitably there were different points of view on a subject as complex as Berlin, I would not be going down if I did not wish to support the main lines of our policy. As for the degree of my collaboration with the White House, this was largely a technical matter having to do with my obligations at

Harvard and the kind of responsibilities I could assume in Washington.[197]

Kissinger's debut at the White House had, it seemed, ended with a whimper. His access to classified material was terminated; the CIA safe in his Cambridge office was removed.[198] He was as far as ever from the White House Situation Room—to be precise, giving a lecture at Duke University—when the Berlin Crisis finally reached its climax. Yet in the absence of any public statement, the world continued to regard him as a "JFK aide" and "special consultant to the President."[199]

The crescendo came on Friday, October 27, 1961. Just as Kissinger had foreseen, the Russians had authorized East German border police to demand that Allied civilians present their papers before driving into the Soviet occupation zone. Seizing the initiative, Clay resolved to resist this break with established procedures by providing armed escorts for diplomats crossing into East Berlin. Both sides now deployed tanks in central Berlin. By the night of the twenty-seventh, ten American M48 tanks faced ten T55 Soviet tanks on either side of the shabby sentry post in Friedrichstrasse known as Checkpoint Charlie. Both sides had live ammunition. They were just 160 yards apart. At midnight, with Kennedy on the line from Washington, Clay reported that another twenty Soviet tanks were on their way. The total number of U.S. tanks in the whole city was just thirty. It was one of the decisive moments of the Cold War—and one of the most surreal, as Berliners emerging from the Friedrichstrasse underground station found themselves at the epicenter of what could have been Armageddon.

Clay—remembering his own experience at the time of the Berlin Airlift—was sure the Russians were bluffing. From all we now know about Khrushchev, he was almost certainly correct. Yet Kennedy and his advisers once again pulled back. Secretly, the president sent his brother, the attorney general, Robert Kennedy, to tell the genial Soviet spy Georgi Bolshakov that "if the Russian tanks drove away, the Americans would follow suit within twenty minutes."[200] At the same time, Dean Rusk instructed Clay that entry into Berlin was "not a vital interest which would warrant determined recourse to force to protect and sustain." At ten-thirty the next morning, the Soviet tanks withdrew; half an hour later the American tanks did the same. Speaking at the 22nd Party Congress, Khrushchev duly announced that he was lifting his Berlin Ultimatum.[201] Tacitly it was agreed that American, British, and French officials would continue to enjoy access to the Soviet zone of the city.

The crisis was over—and an important precedent was set. Rather than risk nuclear war, Kennedy was prepared to make concessions through a back channel, so long as he was not publicly seen to have blinked. This was realism in action.

VII

In the wake of the Berlin Crisis, Kennedy reshaped his foreign policy team in what became known as the Thanksgiving Day Massacre. Chester Bowles was replaced as Rusk's deputy by George Ball; Rostow was moved to head up Policy Planning; Carl Kaysen became Bundy's deputy on the NSC; and Michael Forrestal and Robert Komer were brought on board with responsibility for, respectively, Vietnam and the Middle East.[202] The question arises: why exactly did Bundy make so little effective use of the one Harvard colleague who was a genuine expert on Germany, even when the very survival of the United States seemed to hinge on Berlin? Was it really, as Kissinger complained to Schlesinger, just a matter of "personal competitiveness"? The answer is that there was another reason why, from the outset, Bundy had been determined to keep Kissinger at a safe distance from the president. Arthur Schlesinger let it slip at the time of Kissinger's resignation.[203] It was the fact that he was still regarded as a Rockefeller man—and Nelson Rockefeller still seemed the man most likely to challenge Kennedy for the presidency in 1964.

Kissinger was at pains to deny that there was a conflict of loyalties. He pressed Schlesinger to reassure Kennedy that "though he has been an adviser to Governor Rockefeller in the past, he has not consulted with Rockefeller during the White House period and does not propose to do so now. He feels that foreign policy will be in much better hands under a Democratic than a Republican Administration."[204] When Rod Perkins asked him to draft a speech for Rockefeller "reviewing and criticizing the foreign policy of the Kennedy Administration," Kissinger refused on the ground that "it would not be proper for me to contribute to an attack on an Administration . . . as long as I retain a relationship—however tenuous—as a White House consultant." Yet his explanation to Rockefeller made abundantly clear the extent of his disillusionment with Kennedy:

> I am filled with a sense of imminent national disaster. Our German policy has undermined Adenauer and will produce either nationalism or neutralism there within a very few years. The fruits of fifteen years of Atlantic cooperation have been hazarded. Our moral capital has been squandered to the point where a North Atlantic Community will soon be an idle dream. Our indecision and lack of purpose has tempted Soviet intransigence. Our disarmament position is pretentious sham. Much of the bureaucracy is demoralized by chaotic and brutal Administrative methods. Our changed tone in the underdeveloped world cannot overcome the image of indecisiveness and national decline. If present trends continue, I expect not simply a foreign policy setback, but a debacle. Our friends everywhere are becoming demoralized. In South East Asia, in the Congo, in Iran, in Latin America, our margin is so delicate that a collapse could start all the way down the line.

Moreover, Kissinger made it clear that he was on the brink of "cut[ting] my few remaining ties" to the administration "once the current Berlin decisions have become irrevocable, and if they are what I suspect." Although he could not write a speech directly attacking Kennedy, he was prepared to help Rockefeller in almost any other way.

> I will be happy to meet with you at any time to give you my views on current issues. I will be glad to check the work of your research unit for factual accuracy. I would be delighted to look over the Godkin Lectures [which Rockefeller had agreed to give at Harvard, on his pet subject of federalism].[205] I can do anything in which my judgment is requested by one of our

leading citizens and a man for whom I feel deep friendship. . . .
It was a tragedy that the Republican Party did not nominate
you. I believe in you and before too long I expect to be able to
cooperate with you again without any reservation.[206]

The next day he promised to send Rockefeller "by the middle of
November . . . the two memoranda we discussed dealing with the
problem of the political structure of the free world and measures to
make the concept of freedom meaningful."[207]

Having formally resigned in his letter to Kennedy of November 3,
Kissinger could resume his work for Rockefeller with a clear conscience.
A month later he drafted a paper for him on nuclear testing.[208] Later that
same month he wrote a paper on "the nature of freedom"—probably a
draft for the Godkin lectures.[209] By early 1962 he was back to advising
Rockefeller on the full range of foreign policy issues. In his absence,
morale in the New York research office had plummeted. June Goldthwait complained that it was not at all clear whether she was working
"(1) merely [to] serve to provide NAR with political ammunition to defeat JFK and win the '64 election; or (2) to do this, but in addition, to
assist in educating NAR re. some of the issues which he would have to
deal with if elected, and, to some extent, to help develop positive programs and proposals." ("Quite frankly," she added, "I am most skeptical
as to whether or not it is possible to do number (2).")[210] To try to improve
matters, Perkins and Kissinger decided to appoint a new director of the
research unit, offering the job first to Jay Iselin, a former managing editor of *The Harvard Crimson*,[211] and then to John Deardourff, a legislative
assistant to New York congresswoman Jessica Weis.[212] Dismayed at
being passed over for promotion, both Goldthwait and Mary Boland
resigned. The net result was that Kissinger's workload for Rockefeller
went up. By March 1962 he was having regular "conversations with the
Governor . . . on the level of overall national policy."[213]

But there was a complication. Within a year of Kissinger's return to
the Rockefeller camp, a request came from Bundy and Kaysen to revive
his earlier role as a channel of communication between Washington
and Bonn.[214] Kissinger now had to write yet another letter clarifying
where his loyalties lay, this time to Perkins. Bundy, he explained, had

wanted him to undertake "a specific mission having to do with our NATO planning:

> [But] except for that one mission, which took about a week, I have had no relationship with the government since the end of October.
>
> In performing the mission I mentioned above, I was put on the rolls as a consultant again. It would be too complicated to explain the methods b[y] which this was achieved. They form a rather interesting commentary on the political techniques of the New Frontier [a slogan from Kennedy's acceptance speech at the 1960 Democratic Convention].
>
> I go into this at some length because I want you to be perfectly clear that although it has occurred only this one time, I may feel obliged to respond to specific questions put to me by the White House at other times. And when this occurs, I will not be able to participate in the drafting of a position for the Governor when it touches upon the same specific issues.
>
> This is no immediate problem because, as I have said, my connection has been very tenuous and I plan for it to remain so. But precisely because there is no problem now, it is important to leave no doubt that I will be unable to work for the Governor on any matter where I have had access to government information within a reasonable time afterwards. I will of course keep this in mind in judging whether I should undertake any particular assignment for the White House.
>
> The main point I wish to make is to express my conviction that we are in a deep national crisis which obliges me to respond to the Government's request for advice when I feel I can be useful. I need hardly add that Nelson will always have a special claim on me because of my friendship and devotion for him.[215]

"Flexible response" had been one of the signature ideas of the Kennedy administration. The phrase also nicely applies to the way Henry Kissinger had sought to play a part in Kennedy's administration, while at the same time maintaining his association with the man who was among his most prominent political rivals. The shortcomings of flexible response as a military strategy had been exposed by the Berlin Crisis; in the end Kennedy simply had not been convinced that a limited war could be fought that would not rapidly escalate into all-out nuclear war. Lacking a credible military option, he had cut a deal with Khrushchev not once but twice—deals that left Berlin divided by a hideous wall, with a "death strip" (*Todesstreifen*) that would claim the lives of somewhere between 122 and 238 people in the twenty-eight years of its existence.[216]

The crisis had also revealed that flexible response was a poor basis for a career in the executive branch of the U.S. federal government. Here the distinction between realism and idealism—or pragmatism and dogmatism, as Kissinger preferred to say at this time—is relevant once again. On the central issue of Germany, as we have seen, he had been the idealist, insisting on the applicability of the Wilsonian principle of self-determination. Kennedy had been the pragmatist, making concessions on the building of the Berlin Wall and the East German control of access that Kissinger deplored. With the benefit of hindsight, we may thank our lucky stars that pragmatism rather than idealism prevailed in the Situation Room. There is little doubt that Kissinger was more willing than Kennedy to contemplate a war over Berlin in preference to a wall through it.

Yet Kissinger had his own version of pragmatism. Like his mentor Bill Elliott before him, he yearned for admission to the corridors of power. But trying to enter them at the invitation of a Democratic president, while carrying in his pocket a rain check for a Republican administration, was too pragmatic a strategy to work. Bundy had given Henry Kissinger a painful lesson in the dark arts practiced inside the Washington Beltway. Not unreasonably, it might be said, he had sought to minimize his hawkish protégé's role. In doing so, Bundy had taught him that access to the president was not the most important thing in American politics; it was the only thing—and that without it even the best and the brightest of Harvard whiz kids was doomed to impotence. Unfortunately, the next lesson Kissinger had to learn—that there are few things more deceptively dangerous in politics than a journalist's question—would be almost as agonizing.

CHAPTER 14

Facts of Life

When I say that I speak here as a private citizen I realize
I am somewhat in the position of a member of the
Prohibition League who was caught drinking and
somebody said to him, "Now how can you reconcile
yourself as a member of the Prohibition League?" and he
said, I am drinking in my private capacity. (laughter).
—HENRY KISSINGER, 1962[1]

Failing a change in American attitudes, we will all go to
hell, and that is the only thing we will do jointly.
—FRANÇOIS DE ROSE, 1962[2]

I

It was a recurrent theme of Henry Kissinger's mature work that
domestic politics and foreign policy are fundamentally different activities. This was not something that the Kennedy brothers readily discerned. They learned their Realpolitik at home. Growing up a Kennedy
was itself an advanced-level course. Their father a bootlegger, a wom-
anizer, and an appeaser, John and Robert Kennedy lost their eldest
sister to a lobotomy in 1941,* their eldest brother to the war in 1944,
and their second sister to a plane crash in 1948. Jack Kennedy was a war
hero but also a consummate cheat. His compulsive infidelity to his
wife was only one of many deceptions. Throughout his political career,
he concealed the severity of his medical problems (he suffered from

---

*She survived the procedure but suffered permanent mental damage and was
institutionalized for the rest of her long life.

acute back pain, hypothyroidism, and Addison's disease, a condition that causes the adrenal glands to produce insufficient steroid hormones and for which he needed continual cortisone treatments). He deliberately missed the Senate vote censuring Joe McCarthy, who had more than once been a Kennedy houseguest. He lied to his own brother about his decision to make Lyndon Johnson his running mate in 1960. His campaign may have called on Mafia assistance to defeat Richard Nixon that year. Intervening on behalf of the jailed Martin Luther King, Jr., had also helped Kennedy win the 1960 election, but that did not stop Bobby Kennedy as attorney general from authorizing wiretaps on King's phone three years later.[3]

John F. Kennedy had won the presidency of the United States by fighting dirty, state by state. Whatever he said in his lofty inaugural address, he assumed that the Cold War had to be fought in the same way, fighting dirty, state by state. It was not just Cuba and Germany that were in play. As Kissinger noted in 1961, the Soviets and their confederates were also exerting pressure "in South East Asia, in the Congo, in Iran, in Latin America."[4] If flexible response was to have any meaning as a strategic concept, it must enable the United States to take military action in one or more of these locations without blowing the world to kingdom come. If limited war turned out to be too risky—as had certainly been the case over Berlin—then there were other methods available. Even before Kennedy's inauguration, on January 17, 1961, Patrice Lumumba, the first democratically elected prime minister of the Republic of Congo, was shot dead by a firing squad; though not directly responsible, the CIA had been plotting to have him killed. Four months later the military dictator of the Dominican Republic, Rafael Trujillo, was gunned down with MI carbines supplied with CIA approval. These two cases were inherited by Kennedy from his predecessor, but his administration was equally if not more enthusiastic about assassination as an instrument of policy. Next on the list were Fidel Castro and, as we shall see, the South Vietnamese leader Ngo Dinh Diem. Finally, where a hit man was not the solution, there were always deals to be cut.

This approach to "the Third World's War" had two disadvantages. First, there was a tendency to exaggerate the power of the opposing party. Democrats and Republicans were generally quite evenly matched in presidential elections, with comparable resources in terms of support; landslides were not the norm. The contest between the United States and the Soviet Union was not like this. From the outset the U.S. economy was much stronger: in terms of gross domestic product, the Soviet Union was roughly a third of the size. Throughout the 1950s and well into the 1960s the U.S. nuclear arsenal was far larger.* Yet throughout the Cold War, Washington tended to exaggerate Soviet might, both economic and military. This was the major reason Kennedy was inclined to cut deals with Khrushchev when he might legitimately have called his bluff. The other difficulty with treating foreign policy as essentially the same game as domestic politics was the peril of incomprehension. Cuba was not Colorado, Vietnam was not Virginia. These were foreign countries, and they did things differently there. A realism that overlooked that simple truth was not realistic at all.

Nothing illustrates the problem better than the case of Henry Kissinger. He had never in his life been to Southeast Asia, much less to the Congo, Iran, or Latin America. The only Caribbean island he had ever visited was St. John, when he had stayed at the Rockefeller resort of Caneel Bay. Indeed, aside from trips to Japan and Korea in 1951 and Japan in 1960, Kissinger had never traveled outside Europe and the United States. This was, of course, a handicap that could be overcome. Yet paying visits to unfamiliar countries was not without its risks—especially for a man whom the world continued to regard as an adviser to the president of the United States.

II

Henry Kissinger's complex and controversial relationship with Latin America began in May 1962 when, at the suggestion of the State Depart-

---

*To be precise, in 1962 the Soviet Union had 20 intercontinental ballistic missiles; the United States had at least 180. The Soviets had 200 long-range bombers; the Americans had 630. The Soviets had only six submarines with the ability to launch up to three ballistic missiles from the sea; the Americans had twelve Polaris submarines, each carrying twelve nuclear missiles. These figures make it clear how absurd the "missile gap" panic of the late 1950s was, at least in terms of long-range missiles.

ment, he visited Brazil to give a lecture at the National Defense University. The country was then under a left-leaning government that was far from stable. Jânio Quadros had been elected president as leader of the center-right National Democratic Union, but his decisions to establish diplomatic relations with the Soviet Union and China, and to nationalize the iron ore mines of Minas Gerais, had led to his resignation after just seven months. By the time Kissinger arrived, Vice President João Goulart had taken over, but only after a protracted crisis that had ended with the establishment of a parliamentary system designed to limit the powers of the presidency. Thanks to Rockefeller's contacts and the good offices of the U.S. ambassador, Lincoln Gordon, Kissinger was able to meet an assortment of influential Brazilians,[5] including the eminent anthropologist Gilberto Freyre.[6] His first impression was bemused. "Many Brazilians had been telling him to expect a major political crisis—perhaps even a violent upheaval—within a short time," he noted. "But they were not able to explain just what the trouble was."[7] The view at the U.S. embassy was clear: Goulart, like Quadros before him, intended a lurch to the left. On closer inspection, "the short-term prospects in Brazil [were] rather discouraging,"[8] Kissinger concluded, especially after the appointment of the socialist Hermes Lima as prime minister. Kissinger had met Lima. "The New York Times, with its usual perspicacity, described [Lima] as a 'moderate Socialist,'" he told Kraemer. "If he is then I would like to see what a Communist looks like."[9]

The experience of Cuba inclined many Americans to see every Latin American country as being on the verge of "collapse" into Communism.[10] Such was the power of Eisenhower's "domino effect" as an idea. The problem was that there seemed only one reliable antidote, and that was military rule. During his visit, Kissinger had a meeting with General Nelson de Melo, commander of the Second Army, and Antonio Sylvio da Cunha Bueno, a member of parliament from São Paulo. Asked whether Jânio Quadros might win the São Paulo governorship and stage a political comeback, Cunha Bueno replied

> that Janio would never be allowed to take office if elected. The
> military would intervene, preferring a safe dictatorship to
> the imponderable result of Quadros' return to a prominent

political position. General de Mello [*sic*] neither confirmed nor contradicted this, though he overheard the statement clearly. Deputy Cunha Bueno told Dr. Kissinger that the Army generals, with one or two well known exceptions, had democratic convictions and were friendly to the United States.[11]

At the end of March 1964, Goulart would indeed be overthrown by the armed forces in a backlash against his "Basic Reforms," which had included nationalization of the country's oil refineries and the imposition of rent controls. For the next two decades, Brazil was a military dictatorship.

The fact that so many American observers feared Communist subversion in Latin America is not evidence by itself that it was happening; nor, however, is it evidence that it was *not* happening. The KGB was certainly active in Brazil, as it was in most major Latin American countries, in the early 1960s.[12] Yet it is probably fair to say that U.S. policy makers greatly exaggerated its influence, while at the same time underestimating the indigenous sources of grievance against political orders characterized by inequality, corruption, and repression. To a man fighting the Cold War, every radical looks like a Soviet tool, every revolution like a KGB coup. In the same way, when a revolution overthrew the imam of North Yemen in September 1962, Kissinger was not slow to see the beginning of a wider "Middle Eastern Crisis."

> The revolutionary government in Yemen has begun pressing on the British-controlled areas of Aden and the sheikdoms. The Egyptian troops also constitute a threat to Saudi Arabia.
>
> Coupled with the upheavals in Iraq, it is highly likely that within the next few years there will be uprisings in Saudi Arabia and, particularly, in Jordan. If the King of Jordan is killed, the kingdom is unlikely to survive. In that case, if the succeeding government were to join with one of Jordan's larger neighbors, there is certain to be another Arab-Israeli war.[13]

This analysis was at best half-right. The new republican regime in Yemen undoubtedly posed a threat to Britain's colonial outpost of

Aden, and Nasser's regime in Egypt hoped to use it as a bridgehead in the region. The Gulf monarchies, not least the Saudis, recognized the danger and worked with the British government and Secret Intelligence Service to counter it. Kissinger was also right to foresee another Arab-Israeli war, though it did not come until 1967. Yet neither Saudi Arabia nor Jordan followed Iraq and Yemen down the road of revolution; rather it was in Syria and Iraq that Ba'athist regimes seized power in 1963. Here is a perfect illustration of the dangers that arise when academics who are experts about one part of the world believe they can apply their insights indiscriminately in completely different contexts.

It was not to the Middle East that Kissinger traveled at the end of 1961, however, but to South Asia. His foray into Washington had, it seemed, ended badly. His marriage was on the rocks. Invitations to visit both India and Pakistan seemed to offer an attractive respite from these trials, especially as he could expect collegial hospitality from his Harvard colleague J. K. Galbraith, now installed as U.S. ambassador in Delhi. Without question, Kissinger learned a great deal from his tour. But if he set off expecting rest and recuperation, he was soon disappointed.

Kissinger arrived in Delhi less than two weeks after the Indian army had overrun the colonial enclave of Goa, which had been in Portuguese hands for four and a half centuries. This unilateral action was condemned by the Kennedy administration, but the Indian defense minister, the mercurial V. K. Krishna Menon, retorted that Western complaints were mere "vestige(s) of Western imperialism." The incident was significant not least because there were a number of other European colonial relics in Asia, including the Portuguese colony of East Timor and the Dutch colony of Western New Guinea, both of which were claimed by Indonesia. Kissinger was in India as part of the USIS cultural exchange program; he was to give lectures on U.S. foreign policy at the Indian Institute of Public Administration and elsewhere. But he also took advantage of his status as a presidential adviser to meet with senior Indian officials and politicians, who were keen to pick his brains on the issue of nuclear disarmament. His first encounter was with R. K. Nehru, the permanent head of the Indian Foreign Office.[14] He also met with the foreign secretary, M. J. Desai, who suggested referring the Western New Guinea question to the UN General Assembly.[15] On January 8 and 10, Kissinger had two encounters with Krishna Menon, then regarded as second only to Prime Minister Jawaharlal Nehru. These were his first tastes of what might be called the histrionic style in South Asian politics.

> All his assistants seemed to be in a state of terror. I was shown in, bowing and scraping, to his office. He greeted me at the door, took me by the hand, and led me to an easy chair. The Chief of Staff of the Indian Air Force was in the room. Krishna Menon turned to him and bellowed some instructions. The impression was unavoidable that the whole scene had been staged for effect. . . .
>
> Throughout, Krishna Menon made a great effort to be charming, and to prove that he was reasonable. However, he seemed to be a man fighting for self-control and as he began each point, he would start in low, measured tones, and talk himself literally into a frenzy.

American objections to the Indian seizure of Goa, he told Kissinger, "showed the influence of the great English families on American policy." Unspecified foreigners were encouraging India to go to war with China over "absolutely worthless" land on the North East Frontier. Their motive was to undermine "the progressive elements in India" because the opponents of "any advanced social policy . . . could lump it under the label of Communism." But these efforts were "doomed to failure. . . . One could not fight in the Himalayas, and this was well known." (In fact, war broke out in October that year as China decisively reversed the Indian "Forward Policy" of establishing outposts on the Chinese side of the border.) Kissinger was not disconcerted by Menon's "method of presenting an enormous mass of detail, all of which is slightly distorted, to create a picture of American inequity, Indian forbearance, and Communist wisdom." It was, he added in a memorandum of the meeting sent to the State Department, "a frightening thought that Nehru receives a great deal of his information on foreign policy and about the United States from this man."[16]

By contrast, his meeting with Nehru was sedate, though it culminated in a revealing exchange: "I . . . asked him whether India would sign a disarmament agreement to which Communist China was not a party. He said that it seemed to him impossible for India to do this. I asked him whether this applied even to nuclear disarmament. He replied evasively, but indicated that it might."[17] The Indians were increasingly concerned about China's nuclear arms program, which dated back to 1958 but had been slowed by the cancellation of Soviet technical assistance in 1960. Most of Kissinger's subsequent meetings in Delhi—notably with the head of the Indian Atomic Energy Commission—were implicitly concerned with how India should respond and whether American technical assistance might be forthcoming.[18]

All of this was illuminating, no doubt. Unfortunately for Kissinger, a part of the process of cultural exchange involved taking questions from journalists. This was an ordeal he had already experienced a few times in the United States; indeed, he had enjoyed the cut and thrust of American press conferences. But he underestimated the difference between D.C. and Delhi. He also fell into a trap all too familiar to Harvard professors before and since: the trap of thinking that, if a journalist asks one a question about a subject, it must be because he believes one knows something about that subject, and therefore one *must* know something about it.

It was in fact a question from an Israeli journalist about Egypt that started the trouble. According to an Associated Press report, which was picked up by *The Washington Post,* Kissinger—identified as "private adviser to Kennedy on foreign policy"—replied that "recent moves by President Gamal Abdel Nasser and Soviet-UAR* arms deals have provoked crisis in the Middle East." This was enough to spark an official protest from Cairo. In fact, according to other journalists present, what Kissinger had said was that Egyptian arms imports from the Soviet Union were "a factor of tension" and "gave rise for concern"; he had also repeatedly stressed that he was speaking in a private capacity. Nev-

---

*The United Arab Republic had been set up in 1958 as a union between Egypt and Syria. In 1961 Syria had seceded, but Egypt continued to refer to itself as the UAR until 1971.

ertheless, the Egyptian government demanded a public disavowal of Kissinger's remarks.

Worse, Kissinger had also been asked to comment on the long-running territorial dispute between India and Pakistan over Kashmir. His reply was that the U.S. attitude would be based on the merits of the case; Washington would not "spite India because of Goa." Asked to comment on Goa, he was dismissive of the Portuguese claim to the territory, going so far as to dismiss Portuguese membership of NATO as a product of American "pactitis," a neologism intended to mock the Truman administration's enthusiasm for international alliances. These remarks prompted an official protest from the Pakistani Foreign Office, which denounced Kissinger as a "peripatetic pseudo diplomat."[19] Beijing also got in on the act, taking umbrage at an allusion Kissinger had made to the possibility of a Chinese invasion of Indian territory. Despite all Kissinger's efforts to clarify or qualify what he had said, this storm in a teacup raged on for days. In Pakistan, *Dawn* gleefully dubbed him "brick-dropper."[20] The Syrian government requested clarification of remarks by "a senior American advisor to Pres. Kennedy with a name like Kissinger" who had "lately visited Israel to discuss Israeli defenses." It did not help matters that Kissinger was forced to confirm that he was still formally a consultant to the NSC.[21]

Kissinger sought to laugh off the furor when he arrived in Peshawar, where he was the guest of the Government of Pakistan's Public Information Department. He began his speech at the Pakistan Air Force headquarters with self-deprecation: "I would like to make clear first of all that I speak to you not in any official capacity but as an irresponsible Harvard professor. In fact, there is a school of thought in the United States which holds the view that once you have identified yourself as a Harvard professor the adjective, irresponsible, is quite unnecessary (laughter from audience)."[22]

Yet it once again proved difficult to keep the conversation on his chosen topic, which was "American Strategic Thinking." On January 29, Kissinger had met with the Pakistani president, Ayub Khan, as well as with his foreign minister, S. K. Dehlavi, both of whom believed they had secured U.S. support for the Pakistani position on Kashmir, and both of whom threatened that Pakistan would have to reconsider its position if Washington now sided with India, as Kissinger seemed to have implied that it did. Indeed, Ayub hinted at the possibility of neutralism, if not alignment with Russia and China. A Sandhurst-educated army officer who had seized power in 1958, Ayub seemed in some respects like a model ally for the United States: his English perfect, his regime secular albeit undemocratic, his commitment to the alliance demonstrated by his willingness to let American U-2s fly from Pakistani air bases. Kissinger was "impressed," he admitted, by Ayub's "forthrightness and sincerity."[23] Yet Kissinger's comments at the Delhi press conference had been interpreted as casting aspersions on the U.S.-Pakistan alliance. Asked about his use of the word *pactitis,* Kissinger once again responded lightheartedly:

> I read the papers on the sub-continent with never ceasing interest because I find that even the activities in which I am engaged are new to me when I read them in the press (laughter). . . . The statement I made, which due to limitation of space in both the Pakistan and Indian press, was not fully reported, was as follows: I said that any country which believes that the instrument of the alliance is in itself a form of security is suffering from a disease called "pactitis"; that an alliance to be effective requires the will to defend oneself, a readiness to make the efforts to defend oneself, and governments which are supported by their people. When those conditions are met, then an alliance can be effective and is effective; when those conditions are not met, then an alliance becomes merely an exercise in substituting a written document for a real defense, and insofar as an alliance is only a written document without meeting these other requirements one is indeed suffering from what I said was pactitis. This is what I said in India, this is what I am saying here, and I am saying nothing in Pakistan that I didn't say in India or vice versa.[24]

This was not enough for his audience. Kissinger soon found himself having to justify U.S. aid to India and to answer hypothetical questions about what the United States would do if India attacked Pakistan. Nor did his tribulations end in the lecture hall. On his return to the hotel, Kissinger was again besieged by reporters "who refused to be put off when he attempted to avoid answering any of their questions," as his State Department escort reported with thinly veiled schadenfreude:

> Finally, he graciously consented to reply to a few, but the ques-
> tions were so loaded that the reporting officer . . . felt obliged
> to intervene several times. The question asked most insistently
> was whether Dr. Kissinger had seen any evidences of the
> "Pushtunistan stunt" when he visited the Khyber Pass, an allu-
> sion to Afghan activity in the area. After pointing out that he
> had been there only for an hour and that this was his first visit,
> Dr. Kissinger reluctantly said that he had not seen anything
> such as was mentioned.

The next day *Dawn* carried the headline "No Sign of Pro-Kabul Agita-
tion . . . Dr. Kissinger Visits Tribal Area."[25] By the time Kissinger got to Lahore, where he was scheduled to speak at the University of Punjab, the trip had degenerated into farce. He began his final question-and-answer session with "what is for a Harvard professor a historic confession to the effect that I do not know everything about everything."[26]

What he later referred to as "the hysteria in Pakistan" had opened Kissinger's eyes to the ease with which a casual answer to a loaded question could trigger a diplomatic fracas.[27] His difficulties did not go unnoticed in Washington. Irritated by what he called a "great deal of fuss," Bundy stipulated that in future "only full-time officers of this Government should be advertised [by USIS] as having a significant connection with the Administration."[28]

III

The content of Kissinger's Peshawar lecture on "American Strategic Thinking" may not have attracted much attention compared with his less considered comments to the press. Yet it repays reading because, eschewing the more technical language he might have used before an

American audience, Kissinger very clearly framed the central problem of flexible response. First, he acknowledged that deterrence remained fundamental to U.S. strategy. And because "deterrence is trying to prevent the opponent from taking certain steps . . . it is tested . . . by things which do not happen." That meant that "a threat which is intended as a bluff but taken seriously" was more useful than "a threat which is meant seriously but interpreted as a bluff." The U.S. position was that any Soviet attack on Berlin would mean general war. Thus far, this had worked in causing the Soviets to back down. But

> the requirement imposed upon one's foreign policy by relying only on general war is too great because the only way one can communicate one's determination, I think, is by conducting a policy in which one indicates a high capacity for irrationality. What one has to do is prove that in certain situations one is likely to go out of control, and that regardless of what sober calculation would show one is simply so nervous that the gun is going to go off. A madman who is holding a hand grenade in his hand has a very great bargaining advantage.

Unfortunately, "given the public opinion of Western democracy, this is not a policy that can be conducted"—whereas for Khrushchev, banging his shoe on his desk at the UN (as he had in 1960), it clearly was an option. For this reason, the United States was adding to its strategic repertoire, "develop[ing] forces capable of assisting our friends in defending their own territories" with conventional arms and "increas[ing] its tactical nuclear forces." Above all, Washington was seeking to transform its alliances "from what were in effect unilateral American guarantees" into "efforts of real cooperation to prevent threats to countries from being overrun.

> Anyone, therefore, who has analyzed the strategic problem of the U.S. must come to the conclusion that from the military point of view we and our allies have an obligation to assess the situation in terms of a greater effort to assure the defense of threatened areas. This does not mean, I want to stress, that the

U.S. is not going to engage in general war if that is necessary. . . . But there are very many stages between a full-scale
commitment and other things, and it's for this that these forces
are required and that the more flexible response is important.[29]

Such arguments were uncontroversial in Pakistan in 1962, because
the rival powers of South and East Asia had not yet acquired nuclear
weapons. In Western Europe, by contrast, they were viewed with deep
suspicion. As we have seen, despite his growing suspicions of Kissinger
as either a threat or some kind of Rockefeller mole, Bundy continued
to regard him as an asset when it came to selling flexible response to the
Europeans and in particular to the Germans. That was the sole reason
Bundy had fudged the issue of Kissinger's resignation in October 1961.
Indeed, he had specifically asked Kissinger to be present in Washington
during Chancellor Adenauer's visit the following month—one of only
three occasions when Kissinger actually saw Kennedy while he was
president—and asked him to continue working "on the subject of East-
West negotiations" thereafter. While Kissinger was in India, Bundy
wrote again asking if he would be "willing to go to Germany to reassure Adenauer about Administration policy . . . as soon as possible after
my return." Although exhausted from his return flight and admittedly
"out of touch with our German policy since September," Kissinger
agreed. After a day of briefing in Washington, where Bundy had him
sign a new contract as a consultant, Kissinger flew to Europe.[30] The
crucial classified information Bundy had shared with him was the startling new evidence, based on intelligence from U-2 planes and the
Corona satellite program, that, far from having established a missile
gap, the Russians were the true laggards in the nuclear arms race.[31]

Before Bonn, Kissinger stopped off in Paris. He was already beginning to discern the central problem of European politics. In an ideal
world, the United States would have liked a more or less united Western Europe under British leadership, with all European nuclear weapons pooled and subject to some kind of American veto on their use,
and all European armies enlarged. In the real world, the French were
the ones with the veto—on British membership of the European Economic Community. The French and the British also had a veto on any

pooling of nuclear capabilities, since each liked owning an independent deterrent and neither wanted Germany to have even a share in a nuclear capability. Economically, the British bargaining position was weakening fast; within a few years it would be obvious to everyone that the U.K. was the proverbial "sick man of Europe." But even those in charge of the more rapidly growing German and French economies had no desire to increase defense spending; were Britain's balance-of-payments problems not partly a consequence of its vestigial but expensive imperial obligations?

Just how wide the Atlantic was on the core issue of defense against the Soviet Union became glaringly apparent when Kissinger lunched with General Paul Stehlin, chief of the French air force, on February 5. Stehlin, whom Kissinger regarded as "by far the most balanced of French senior officers, the least xenophobic, and by all odds the most pro-American,"* was despondent. De Gaulle's belief was that "an immediate correlation existed between a country's nuclear weapons stockpile and its international influence." His main motive in extricating France from Algeria was to free up resources for the force de frappe. He "spoke scathingly to his general officers about NATO, which he described as an appendage of American policy," and intended to "resist any further effort at integration" of French forces into the alliance's command structure. Stehlin was doubtful that France could in fact develop an effective nuclear force by herself, but he shared de Gaulle's view of NATO.[32] These views were confirmed later the same day by two French generals (Puget and Martin) and the diplomats François de Rose, Jean Laloy, and Jean-Daniel Jurgensen. Over dinner, de Rose was brutally frank.

> The United States had to realize that France was not a little country to be pushed around. Why threaten her with German nuclear arms? France had embarked on its policy after considering the consequences and the constant American harping on the peril of German nuclear arms was either childish or disloyal. The United States had to get through its head that France

---

*After his retirement, be became a consultant for the U.S. defense company Northrop.

was not interested in a NATO force without assistance to its
national force. If the United States continued to sabotage a
French national force, France would sit on her hands with
respect to a NATO nuclear force. . . . Franco-American relations were at an all-time low. He would say they were as low
as it was possible for them to get, had not experience taught
him that the depths of folly were unplumbable.

When Kissinger asked "where all this left us," de Rose replied,
"Failing a change in American attitudes, we will all go to hell, and that
is the only thing we will do jointly." Kissinger was "stunned by the
bitterness of his language." But when they were alone, de Rose became
more fatalistic than bitter. "For years he had fought for Atlantic solidarity," he complained. But his efforts had been in vain. "The obstinacy
of an old man [de Gaulle] and the lack of psychological comprehension
of America would frustrate all effort."[33] Laloy even came to Kissinger's
hotel the next morning to underscore "the impasse in Franco-American
relations."[34]

Ten days later Kissinger was in Germany, armed with a bulging
folder of briefing documents and a packed schedule of meetings with
the country's political leaders, as well as with a group of industrialists.[35]
Mindful of his unhappy experience in South Asia, Kissinger told the
Bonn embassy that he did not "want any press conferences, briefings,
and wishe[d] to keep [the] visit quiet."[36] Two things immediately
became apparent. First, there was intense opposition to any definitive
settlement of East Germany's border with Poland unless it was part of
an acceptable agreement on German reunification. Few German politicians were prepared to relinquish their claims to the "lost territories"
merely in return for a deal with the Soviets on access to West Berlin—a
position spelled out to Kissinger by the veteran diplomat Hans von
Herwarth, then working for the German president, Heinrich Lübke.*

---

*Hans Heinrich Herwarth von Bittenfeld was an aristocratic German diplomat who
served his country more or less uninterruptedly from 1927 until his retirement in 1977.
Lübke had worked for Albert Speer during the war and was certainly aware of the use
of slave labor at the Peenemünde air base; revelations of his role in the Third Reich led
to his resignation in 1969.

He heard much the same story from the Free Democrat leaders Knut von Kühlmann-Stumm, Erich Mende, and Ernst Achenbach (whom Kissinger identified as "one of the most unscrupulous opportunists, and one of the most unpleasant types, in German political life today")* as well as from the industrialists. Yet this was not an exclusively right-wing position. On February 17 Kissinger saw Fritz Erler, the deputy chairman of the Social Democratic Party, who told him that "the younger generation in Germany would not accept indefinitely the argument that they had to pay for the crimes committed by their fathers" and "vehemently rejected my suggestion that the Oder-Neisse line be accepted in return for access guarantees. He said this was paying rent for Berlin and would merely lead to new demands."[37]

The second thing that emerged from Kissinger's meetings in Bonn was the depth of Adenauer's distrust of the Kennedy administration's strategy.[†] Adenauer frankly disbelieved the American claim that, even in the event of a Soviet first strike, the United States would have more weapons and delivery vehicles remaining than the Soviets. In his view, American planning "involved making United States and Soviet Union a sanctuary and causing [the] burden of [a] conflict to fall on western Europe and satellites." He returned to his old fear "about what would happen if the President were assassinated or if there were some other interruption in communication." And he disagreed with U.S. intelligence estimates of Soviet conventional strength in Eastern Europe:

> His own estimate was that rather than 26 divisions, Soviet Union had closer to 80 divisions in this area, including Russian border regions. He therefore thought that conventional action was bound to lead to disaster or to humiliation or to nuclear war. This is why he had proposed a [naval] blockade, an

---

*Kissinger was correct. Unlike Kühlmann-Stumm and Erich Mende, Achenbach had been a Nazi Party member from 1937. As head of the political department of the German embassy in Paris during the war, Achenbach had been directly involved in the deportation of Jews from France to the death camps.

†Kissinger later remembered being asked by Adenauer, "How much time do you spend working for the government?" Kissinger replied that he spent around a quarter of his time. "Then," said Adenauer, "I can assume you are telling me the truth three-quarters of the time."

important stage along way to ultimate confrontation. He added that American conventional forces were far less well equipped than Soviet conventional forces. This made a conventional action particularly foolhardy.

Finally, Adenauer could not resist adding that "he was deeply worried by the decline of prestige of United States. It was noticeable in Europe, in Latin America, and in Asia. In many parts of world, America seemed to lack an ideology in the name of which to fight Communism."

It is a crucial aspect of the art of diplomacy to know how to win over a combative interlocutor. Kissinger was a part-time consultant who had good reason to feel disenchanted with his superiors in Washington and had serious reservations about their European strategy. Yet as the U.S. ambassador recorded with something close to amazement, the amateur diplomat countered all *der Alte*'s points with an extraordinarily effective mixture of patience, empathy, and argument. He set out the evidence that the United States could withstand a first strike. He showed that U.S. strategy did not imply leaving Europe to its fate. Nor was Washington's opposition to the "multiplication of national [nuclear] forces . . . designed to keep Europe in a second class status.

> Rather it reflected conviction that national forces were bound to be ineffective compared to the kind of forces Kissinger has just described. Solution was not a fragmentation of NATO but welding together of Atlantic Community following [the] course Chancellor has so wisely chosen in relations of European nations among each other. . . . United States was in principle prepared to proceed with creation of a multilaterally controlled, multinational NATO force if it seemed to our NATO partners to be desirable.

The chancellor's fears about U.S. conventional forces were also unwarranted.

Thus far, Kissinger had been conciliatory, even obsequious in his responses. But he now took the risk of being combative. In response to Adenauer's argument for a naval blockade as a possible response to any

Soviet challenge, "Kissinger replied he wanted to be quite frank and perhaps somewhat undiplomatic. It was possible to construe this proposal of Chancellor's as an attempt by Federal Republic to shift burden and risk of any countermeasures to other members of the Alliance. It might indicate that Federal Republic was unprepared to fight for Berlin if ground action or a nuclear war might result." This gambit, carefully calculated to sting Adenauer's national pride, worked. At first, the chancellor "denied . . . vehemently" Kissinger's charge. But in his next sentence he was quoting Kissinger back at himself ("one should not engage in a conventional action without being prepared for a nuclear war") and praising the "historic accomplishment of United States in helping its defeated enemies to regain self-respect." Kissinger concluded this tour de force of diplomatic chess with a clinching move:

> [C]hoice before us was very similar to that faced by the Chancellor himself in 1949. We had chance of affirming a general theoretical goal or else we could take specific steps together with our European friends to create a framework for common action whenever this was possible. It was Kissinger's opinion that wiser course was one charted by Chancellor himself with respect to European integration, namely, to work on specific measures for common action rather than to use up energies in theoretical dispute. This was spirit which animated our proposals within NATO.

So successful was Kissinger in winning Adenauer over with Adenauer's own arguments that the chancellor made the Americans late for lunch. As Ambassador Walter C. Dowling recorded,

> On two occasions when Kissinger and I sought to leave he asked us to stay in order to give him another opportunity to express his gratitude for what had been said and his strong concurrence with it. He said he was relieved to see that strength existed to defend freedom and that main task was to see to it that there would be no human failings. Upon leaving, Kissinger said that he wanted the Chancellor to understand that when we spoke of

our power and our dedication to Atlantic Community these were not simply idle phrases. Chancellor replied, "Thank God for this!" On this note the meeting broke up.[38]

Kissinger had been inept in Asia. In Germany he was inspired. Back in Washington, the president himself was perplexed. "The Chancellor had expressed certain concern about matters which we thought had previously been completely clarified," he grumbled to the German ambassador, Wilhelm Grewe. "We had been trying to make the points stressed by Kissinger since last June." Why the "constant need to reassure the Germans"? Why was it "necessary to reiterate repeatedly clarifications of US policy and of our strategic position which we thought had been fully explained during the November visit of the Chancellor"? Secretary Rusk was equally mystified. "Dr. Kissinger had gone to Germany without any special instructions," he noted. "He had covered matters which we took for granted, and yet the Chancellor had found his remarks reassuring as if they contained new information." The reality, as Grewe made clear, was that Kissinger had succeeded where the full-time diplomats had failed.[39] The chancellor himself spelled out to Dowling the difference between what he had heard in Washington in November and what he had heard from Kissinger. The former had been "in general terms, whereas Kissinger had been much more specific, had dealt with concrete facts, and was thus much more informative and reassuring."[40] Small wonder that the newly arrived Russian ambassador to the United States, Anatoly Dobrynin,* named Kissinger as one of four members of the administration he would like to establish some rapport with—the others being Bundy, Schlesinger, and Sorensen.[41]

Kissinger also understood better than his masters in the White House that everything in Europe now hinged on the Franco-German relationship. Few personal relationships in postwar Europe were more

---

*The son of a locksmith, Dobrynin had joined the diplomatic service in 1946 and had briefly served as deputy secretary general at the United Nations in 1957. He was to remain ambassador to the United States until 1986, serving under six U.S. presidents and becoming perhaps Kissinger's single most important foreign interlocutor.

crucial, and few more volatile, than the one between Adenauer and de Gaulle. At times—for example, their famous meeting at de Gaulle's country retreat, Colombey-les-Deux-Églises, in 1958—they seemed to personify Franco-German reconciliation. More often they were at odds, Adenauer convinced that only NATO could preserve West Germany from the Soviet threat and that only European integration could ensure him against American egotism, de Gaulle still yearning for French national parity with the United States and the United Kingdom, itching to limit French involvement in both NATO and the EEC. On February 15—the day before his meeting with Kissinger—Adenauer had met with de Gaulle and their respective foreign ministers in Baden-Baden. In addition to discussing the project for a European political union, the two leaders had exchanged views on security issues and in particular on the need to reduce European reliance on the United States.[42] The day after his meeting with Adenauer, Kissinger flew to Paris for another meeting with Stehlin, who told him that de Gaulle was coming around to the view that France had to add a European track to its defense policy. Kissinger's interpretation, relayed directly to Rusk, was that "the Germans will take up the French option only if we drive them to it."[43] The problem was that "the parties in Germany who are essentially pro–Western alliance are opposed to negotiations, while those who favor negotiations [i.e., the Social Democrats] are essentially nationalist. As long as this attitude persists, the French have a certain leverage." It was therefore crucial to "bring the Germans along and make them assume responsibility in the negotiations over Berlin."[44] At the same time, the United States had to work hard to persuade the French that "the defense of the NATO area cannot be effected except by treating it as a unit."[45]

Kissinger was giving the State Department a lesson in the art of diplomacy. But he also wanted to give the NSC a lesson in strategic thought. In April 1962 he drafted a shrewd critique of the American scheme to create a submarine-based European "Multilateral Force" (MLF) that would give the Europeans a bigger stake in their continent's nuclear defenses. The military justification for this was not obvious, Kissinger argued, because all the targets that might be hit by the

MLF were already covered by the U.S. Strategic Air Command.* The political argument was, ostensibly, "to reduce European fears that we might be reluctant to use nuclear weapons in their behalf, by giving the European nations a share in the planning, control, and targeting of a NATO force"; in reality, "to isolate France and in time atrophy the French nuclear effort." But it was not clear to Kissinger how a "militarily useless force" could be "politically desirable." From the point of view of German hawks like Strauss, the creation of such a force would simply be an invitation to devise a real military use for it.

> As for a voice in our decisions, two possibilities exist: (a) that we retain a veto over the NATO nuclear force or (b) that we construct a NATO nuclear force without a veto.
>
> If we retain a veto, then we have not really given the European allies a voice in our decision. What we will have done is to create two forces: a very large one, under SAC, which we can use at our discretion, and a small, much less effective, one, which in addition to our veto, has a number of other vetoes built into it. . . . [A] NATO nuclear force with an American veto would multiply safety catches but not triggering devices.
>
> If, however, we are prepared to give up the veto, a serious constitutional question will be raised. We will then be part of a force which can compel the United States to go to war without the approval of Congress or of the Commander-in-Chief. While this is not too different from the factual situation, I believe it would raise a constitutional debate in this country, vitiating any possible benefits from this arrangement.

Kissinger's conclusion was a radical one. The United States should support an independent European atomic force, though that would

---

*Here Kissinger surely erred. The advent of nuclear submarines from 1959 onward was crucial in the transition from a potentially explosive Cold War to the equilibrium that Donald Brennan of the Hudson Institute later satirically christened "Mutual Assured Destruction." The key point was that submarines with nuclear missiles were virtually impossible to detect and destroy. Any first strike would therefore inevitably be countered by a devastating counterstrike from beneath the waves.

mean ending the anomalous position in which the United Kingdom's independent national nuclear force was supported by the United States, but the French equivalent was opposed.[46] This was a penetrating analysis of what was wrong with the MLF, even if it was not as witty as Tom Lehrer's anti-German "MLF Lullaby."*

But answer came there none.

IV

Henry Kissinger had had enough. "I have made more 'final' pronouncements in the past year than in all my previous life," he told Arthur Schlesinger in yet another lengthy tirade against Bundy. "Even so, I am forced to go through essentially the same plot endlessly, as if the reel of a Grade B movie had somehow become stuck." After recounting in excruciating detail the sequence of events since his last attempt to leave the Kennedy administration, Kissinger came to the point. Despite his adroit handling of Adenauer, despite his insights into the MLF issue, he was being ignored:

> Since . . . about February 15th I have had to all practical purposes no contact with the White House. No one bothered to acknowledge my European trip (which I undertook solely at the urging of Mac and at great inconvenience to me). I have sent Mac at least ten memoranda about my European visit and my trip to Asia. Not a single one has been acknowledged, much less commented upon—keeping up a record dating to last May. On several occasions when I have been in Washington on other business, I have notified Mac's office a few days ahead of time. None of these calls have been returned.

The explanation was clear. Bundy had once again "maneuvered me into precisely the position he suggested when I first resigned last

---

*"Sleep, baby, sleep, in peace may you slumber, / No danger lurks, your sleep to encumber, / We've got the missiles, peace to determine, / And one of the fingers on the button will be German."

October and which I rejected then": that is, "remaining technically a consultant while giving up any symbol of continuing responsibilities, such as my office. I have been manipulated into an essentially fraudulent posture: I am being used, if at all, for window dressing and to sell policies in the formulation of which I have had no part and the substance of which sometimes makes me highly uneasy."

It was an intolerable situation, born of "manipulativeness and lack of humanity" as well as "the overconcern with tactics which I consider the greatest single weakness of the Administration." Kissinger felt it would be "ridiculous" to submit another formal resignation; in any case, he had no desire to "initiate another series of maneuvers" or indeed to communicate with Bundy any further. Rather, he would "simply let the present arrangement lapse whenever it expires." He would henceforth "respond to requests for advice whenever I can do so responsibly" and would "feel free to take any public stand or engage in any other activity my convictions dictate."[47] As for Bundy's charge that "my relations with the White House have been dominated by an effort to retain freedom of action for 1964"—in other words, his desire to remain available to Nelson Rockefeller, should he opt to challenge Kennedy for the presidency—Kissinger was indignant enough to write Schlesinger a separate, but equally long, refutation. "I began with a consulting relationship," he declared, "not to preserve myself for 1964, but in order to get to know the President's thinking and for him to be able to judge my usefulness."

> Mac's argument reveals an attitude about the nature of ambition and a view of propriety which is perhaps the deepest cause of the trouble. Would it really have been proper for me to attack associates in 1964 because I was "only" a consultant—particularly if my participation in policy-making had been as close as I consistently sought to make it? Can anyone seriously believe that, whatever my formal status, I would have turned in 1964 on colleagues with whom I would then have worked for four years and many of whom had been personal friends for a decade? I do not believe honor depends on such legalistic

distinctions. . . . I started my relationship with the White House with the intention of helping the Administration to succeed—not with the *arrière pensée* of preserving myself for its failure. . . . [M]y sole purpose has been to be of service in a time of crisis. My dedication and energy have been at the disposal of the White House. The outcome I would have liked best would be one that permitted me to devote myself eventually full-time to national service.

Kissinger concluded by noting darkly that "a change in Administration in 1964 [could] come about only as the result of an overwhelming crisis which would discredit many people whom I respect and many values which I want to see realized." He had tried in good faith to avert such a crisis but had been repeatedly rebuffed. Henceforth he would have to stand for his beliefs "as a private and independent citizen."[48]

Kissinger was not about to leave the public sphere altogether, of course. A week after his two letters to Schlesinger, he sent Rockefeller a draft position paper on Berlin.[49] He also recommended as policy options either the creation of a centralized NATO nuclear force or the creation of a European nuclear command within NATO, as well as the creation of a new Council of Ministers within NATO with the power to make decisions binding on the alliance.[50] Now, however, it was Rockefeller's turn to ignore Kissinger. He declined his invitation to speak at the American Council on Germany on the anniversary of the 1953 East Berlin rising.[51] When Kissinger sent him his latest *Foreign Affairs* piece, he received a standardized reply of the sort that Rockefeller's office sent out en masse each day.[52] Kissinger drily asked Nancy Hanks to tell the governor's assistant that "the next time I send him an article . . . the reply should be that it will be turned over to Mr. Kissinger, who handles foreign policy matters." Not until the two men met at Rockefeller's new home in July 1962 did their old friendship-cum-partnership resume.[53]

In that sense, Kissinger's article "The Unsolved Problems of European Defense" truly was the work of a private and independent citizen. Influenced not only by his recent visits to France and Germany but also by correspondence with Basil Liddell Hart, Kissinger set out to reassess flexible response. He traced the origins of the U.S. conventional presence in Western Europe and the relationship between the twenty-two NATO divisions on the ground and the U.S.-controlled nuclear forces of the SAC that would carry out any "counterforce" strategy against the Soviet Union. As things stood at the end of the Eisenhower era, the conventional forces were essentially a symbolic presence; a much smaller force would have sufficed to establish that "something more than a border incursion was taking place" and to signal the need for SAC to launch its missiles and bombers. This in turn incentivized European nations to acquire their own nuclear retaliatory forces, since the American doctrine clearly "defined these as the ultimately decisive weapons." Flexible response had been designed to build up conventional forces to "enable us to meet a Soviet challenge at whatever level of violence it might be presented." But the administration's goal of a thirty-division NATO force risked being "too little for a real local defense, and too much for a counterforce strategy to remain credible" (as any U.S. contingent in Europe would likely be wiped out in the event of a full-blown nuclear war). If NATO was serious about countering a Soviet invasion with purely conventional forces, then "the goal of 30 divisions will have to be substantially increased." If that was politically impossible, then NATO would need to go back to the argument in *Nuclear Weapons and Foreign Policy,* using tactical nuclear weapons "in the battle area . . . as soon as it was clear that a massive Soviet attack was under way."[54] True, as had often been objected (including by Deputy Secretary of Defense Gilpatric), a tactical nuclear exchange might escalate into all-out war. But the pure counterforce strategy made that escalation not a risk but a certainty.

Kissinger's revival of the idea of limited nuclear war was not, however, the most controversial argument in the article. He also proposed that "the atomic arsenal on the Continent should be grouped into a separate command" and even defended the French pursuit of a national nuclear capability as "not as senseless as is often made out." The administration seemed to want the Europeans "to integrate their conventional forces in a joint command and to place increased reliance on a conventional defense, while one partner reserves for itself a monopoly on the means of responding to the Soviet nuclear threat and freedom

of action in employing nuclear weapons." This was "against all reason." Repeating his earlier point that the MLF envisaged by the administration "would multiply safety catches but not triggering devices" (in
other words, would increase only the number of obstacles to the use of
the weapons), he came out strongly in favor of "a European Atomic
Force merging the [existing] British and French nuclear forces" without a U.S. veto, and concluded that support for the French force de
frappe might be the best way of bringing that about.[55]

The author of this densely argued article could have had few illusions about the stir it would cause. It had been, he told Schlesinger
almost apologetically, "the hardest thing I have ever had to write,
and . . . I did so only after all other means of presenting my views had
proved futile."[56] *The Washington Post*'s Chalmers Roberts immediately
spotted the story: "Kennedy Aide Proposes French A-Force Support."[57]
This prompted the inevitable questions to the White House press secretary about Kissinger's status. Awkwardly, Pierre Salinger denied that he
was a "part-time adviser" to the president (as the *Post* had reported) but
had to confirm that Kissinger was still a consultant to the NSC. However, "[h]e has not seen the President this year. He has undertaken one
mission of a classified nature for the National Security Council during
this year. That mission had nothing to do with the subject matter of the
article for *Foreign Affairs*. He has made no recommendations to the
National Security Council on that subject [the French atomic force]."[58]

Within the administration there was consternation. An official critique of Kissinger's article argued that the target of thirty divisions
made sense for the eventuality of a conventional war over Berlin and
that anticipating a limited nuclear war confined to Europe was politically dangerous, as the Europeans would see it as an attempt by the
United States to "disengage from the threat of nuclear attack, while
leaving its partners to bear the brunt." In any case, such a war, if did not
escalate to all-out war, would require vastly more nuclear forces than
were currently available in Europe.[59]

The issue was of more than academic interest. In April 1962 an
American proposal to internationalize the issue of access to Berlin—
ending the postwar four-power arrangements—had been leaked in the
West German press. Such was the revulsion against the idea of an

International Access Authority, in which East Germany would have had equal status with the Federal Republic, that the scheme was dead on arrival. On July 5, Khrushchev wrote to Kennedy demanding that half the Western contingent in West Berlin be replaced by troops from Warsaw Pact and neutral countries. Three weeks later, when Llewellyn Thompson met Khrushchev for the last time in his role as U.S. ambassador in Moscow, he was told that further delay on the issue "was not acceptable to Moscow. . . . It was a matter of Soviet prestige . . . that the Berlin situation be resolved very quickly, and the appropriate peace treaties be signed."[60] In the White House there was more consternation. Why, the president demanded to know, was there so much "disagreement between the US and our Allies on the use of tactical nuclear weapons"? Kennedy could "agree with the Europeans that if the Russians started a mass attack against Europe, we almost would be forced to use nuclear weapons against the first Russian who came across the line." But surely that would not apply in the case of a smaller fight over Berlin. As a compromise, Kennedy suggested telling the Europeans that "we would agree to the early use of tactical nuclear weapons if they would build up 30 divisions." But McNamara begged to differ. If the United States "agreed to the early use of nuclear weapons, our Allies would say this obviated the necessity for going to 30 divisions, just as Kissinger's article had done in the July issue of Foreign Affairs." He and Rusk agreed with Kissinger that "the Allied reluctance to build up conventional forces sprang from two basic factors: they believed that nuclear strategy offered the best hope of insuring deterrence, and also they did not want to spend the money."[61] Kissinger might have been out of sight in the White House, as Bundy had always intended, but he was not out of mind.

In Germany, too, Kissinger was making waves. Defense Minister Strauss wrote personally to tell him that his proposals were not "practicable" ("he is still on the same old tack," Kissinger noted).[62] Attending a conference of the Institute for Strategic Studies in Bad Godesberg, Kissinger met with Karl-Theodor zu Guttenberg, the foreign affairs spokesman for the CDU/CSU bloc in the Bundestag, who flatly rejected the idea of increasing the Bundeswehr by 75,000 men as "politically impossible" and echoed Strauss's concern that the United States was "downgrading" its tactical nuclear weapons.[63] A crisis was brewing in Germany, though in the end it proved to be a domestic political crisis rather than a geopolitical one. The Social Democrat parliamentarian Herbert Wehner was filled with foreboding. "Berlin was lost," he told Kissinger. "The end result of the policies of the last few years meant that sooner or later Berlin was finished." The root of the problem, he explained, was that U.S. interest in Berlin "was bound to be . . . purely juridical," whereas the German interest was a moral one. "We will never accept the wall," he almost shouted. "We will never accept the concentration camp in the East." He foresaw "over the next two or three years a growth of nationalist sentiment in Germany.

> A lot of people who now claimed to be pro-American would turn against us. This, too, he said, was an inevitable consequence of the bankruptcy of Adenauer. The only hope he could see was a coalition between the CDU and the SPD. He said that the dilemma was that the CDU might be ruined by a coalition and the SPD by continued opposition. In any case, a continued split between the two parties would be the end of the democratic forces in Germany. He thought the reaction to the leaked United States proposals in Germany indicated a revival of nationalism. He said that the Right must not again capture all national feelings.

As for East Germany, Wehner felt the Federal Republic had a duty toward it. "If he had his way," he told Kissinger, "he would make an appeal to all East Germans to quit the territory of the Soviet Zone regardless of the consequences. I asked him whether this would not mean that the Polish frontier would be moved to the Elbe. He said the human problem was more important." As we have seen, Kissinger himself constantly worried about such a shift in German domestic politics, so he was bound to be receptive to Wehner's fears. The important insight, however, was that a "grand coalition" between the CDU and the SPD was in the offing. Before the year was out—as a direct consequence of a story about Strauss's defense policy in *Der Spiegel**—Wehner would be attempting to negotiate such a coalition with none other than zu Guttenberg.

Kissinger's intelligence, in short, was high quality. It was no longer, however, going to Bundy. The Bonn embassy was puzzled. "Although Professor Kissinger called on the Embassy for cars, secretaries etc.—and saw many German VIP's," Bundy's point man for Germany grumbled, "he never passed on any information about his activities to the Embassy."[64] In fact, Kissinger did make his memcons of the meetings with zu Guttenberg and Wehner available to the State Department via Helmut ("Hal") Sonnenfeldt,[†] who was also at the ISS conference.[65] But in all other respects he was now an ex-adviser. Just nine months before, he had been lunching with the president. Now he was reduced to asking Schlesinger for a Rose Garden audience with Kennedy for his International Seminar participants.[66] On August 19, 1962, Schlesinger himself came to address the International Seminar. Ruefully, he told the participants that the U.S. president had less power than in the past because there were now four branches of government: legislature, judiciary, presidency, and "executive (bureaucracy)." The new branch—the bureaucracy—had "an infinite capacity to dilute, delay, obstruct, resist and sabotage presidential purposes." Already Schlesinger was nostalgic for the early days of Kennedy's Camelot, to the point of indiscretion. Nineteen sixty-one "was the freewheeling year . . . when we all felt free to act and intervene when we thought we had an idea or when we thought we saw something wrong. But the ice is beginning to form over government again; the press, the Congress and (tacitly) the bureaucracy have begun to pick the New Frontiersmen off as if

---

*On October 8, 1962, the magazine reported that the Bundeswehr was barely ready for the eventuality of a Soviet invasion, which prompted Strauss to order the arrest of the magazine's publisher, its editors-in-chief, and the journalist who wrote the story. When it became clear that Strauss had acted illegally, the FDP threatened to bring down Adenauer's government. Strauss was forced to resign; the grand coalition did not become a reality for another four years.

†Hal Sonnenfeldt, like Kissinger, had been born into a Jewish family in Germany (in 1926), had left the country in 1938, and had served in the U.S. Army. He had joined the State Department in 1952. In 1963 he was appointed head of the Soviet section of the department's Bureau of Intelligence and Research.

from ambush; and the old continuities, the Eisenhower-Dulles continuities, are beginning to reassert themselves."[67]

As if to illustrate the point, a month later Kissinger received a carefully crafted letter from none other than Bundy, proposing a "friendly parting": "My impression of your own position is that holding a continuing appointment as a Consultant places you in a somewhat ambiguous posture, and while I know how much effort you have given to walking a careful line, it is also true for us here that occasionally we are asked if your publicly stated opinions somehow reflect those of the White House." He would not have been Bundy, however, if he had not left "the White House doors . . . open to you whenever you have a particular point that you would like to register privately." Moreover, Bundy added, "we would like to be able to ask for your informal opinion from time to time."[68]

Kissinger's reply was pointed. He had "long been concerned that my public statements about certain aspects of our policy might be misconstrued as White House 'trial balloons.'" This was precisely why he had repeatedly attempted to resign the previous year. "At that time, you were of a different view, and at your urging I agreed to undertake two assignments, one of which never materialized. Since the distinction you then tried to make between my role as a consultant and as a participant in our public debates is obviously not working, I am relieved that you now concur with me."[69] Bundy's last word was a masterpiece of bureaucratic euphemism: their parting, he wrote, was "a necessary recognition of the facts of life as they have developed in a particular situation."[70] To read this exchange today, one would never guess that, between Bundy's first letter and his second, the Kennedy administration had brought the United States closer to the brink of a nuclear catastrophe than at any time in the Cold War.

CHAPTER 15

Crisis

> The American Presidency is . . . formidable because it
> represents the point of ultimate decision in the American
> political system. It is exposed because decision cannot take
> place in a vacuum: the Presidency is the center of the play of
> pressure, interest, and idea in the nation; and the presidential
> office is the vortex into which all the elements of national
> decision are irresistibly drawn. And it is mysterious because
> the essence of ultimate decision remains impenetrable to the
> observer—often, indeed, to the decider himself. . . . There
> will always be the dark and tangled stretches in the
> decision-making process—mysterious even to those who
> may be most intimately involved.
>
> —JOHN F. KENNEDY, 1963[1]

> I was working for Kennedy in those days, and [Truman]
> said what I had learned from Kennedy, and I said, "I've
> learned that the president can't do everything he wants
> because the bureaucracy is the fourth branch of government."
> And he said, "Bullshit." [chuckling] . . . He said, "The
> trouble with Kennedy is he has too many opinions. A
> president has to know what he wants to do."
>
> —HENRY KISSINGER, 1992[2]

I

We know now that the worst did not happen in the Cold War. No
collision between the superpowers escalated to the point of even a limited nuclear war, much less a full-scale conflict. Nor did any of the mis-
haps and false alarms of the period have catastrophic consequences. But

that is not to say that the probability of thermonuclear war was zero throughout the period, or that the logic of mutually assured destruction guaranteed the world a long peace. On the contrary, humanity came perilously close to the verge of Armageddon on more than one occasion during the Cold War. The "doomsday clock," adjusted twice a year by the Science and Security Board of the *Bulletin of the Atomic Scientists,* implied that the risk of "technology-induced catastrophe" reached its peak in the years 1953–59, when the clock showed two minutes before midnight. Perhaps reflecting their political biases, the scientists turned the clock back to 23:48 during the presidency of John F. Kennedy. In reality, it was in the autumn of 1962 that the knell of a nuclear "midnight for . . . civilization" came closest to sounding.[3] Kennedy himself put the odds of disaster—meaning a thermonuclear war that could have claimed the lives of 100 million Americans, more than 100 million Russians, and comparable millions of Europeans—at "between one out of three and even."[4] Arthur Schlesinger later called it simply "the most dangerous moment in human history."[5]

The Cuban Missile Crisis was just the kind of "deep crisis" that Henry Kissinger had warned about during the Berlin Crisis the previous year. What made it so deep was that it was not just about Cuba. The Soviet decision to send missiles to the Caribbean island plainly posed a quite different threat from the decision to challenge the status quo in Berlin, not least because of the proximity of Cuba to the United States. Yet it was also fundamentally the same threat. It was a challenge to which the United States appeared able to respond in only one of two ways: either by capitulating or by taking military action that not everyone believed could be prevented from spiraling out of control. Moreover, Khrushchev had the opportunity, by posing more than one such challenge at a time, to make decision making even harder for Kennedy in that the likelihood of a geographically limited war was from the outset small. The crises over Havana and Berlin interacted with one another, because if one escalated, the other was almost bound to escalate, too.

The crisis also illustrated the danger that the two players in the game would not necessarily arrive at the optimal cooperative solution postulated by game theory. Neither the U.S. government nor the Soviet Politburo was by any stretch of the imagination a strictly rational actor.

Both arrived at decisions in ways that reflected idiosyncrasies of their organizational structures, with bureaucracies on both sides pushing for decisions that "satisficed" in terms of their own short-term interests without necessarily being in the long-run national interest. In each case, too, the man at the top was subject to internal political pressures, not so much from public opinion, which was largely excluded from the decision-making process, as from the competing interest groups and rival individuals represented on the key decision-making committee.[6]

II

Henry Kissinger did not foresee the Cuban Missile Crisis, though he followed the efforts of the Kennedy administration to squeeze the Castro regime, beginning with the import embargo imposed on February 7, 1962 (and still in place at the time of writing).[7] Unbeknownst to him, in November the previous year Kennedy had authorized covert operations to undermine and ultimately overthrow the Castro regime. Operation Mongoose was an interagency operation run out of Robert Kennedy's office under the direction of General Edward Lansdale. While Bundy was opposed to outright U.S. intervention because "overt actions would involve serious consequences all over the world," by August 1962 CIA chief John McCone had persuaded Kennedy to adopt a more aggressive strategy of "deliberately seek[ing] to provoke a full-scale revolt against Castro that might require U.S. intervention to succeed."[8] Early intelligence reports suggested that the Soviets were sending surface-to-air missiles and unassembled Il-28 bombers to Cuba. By September the issue was out in the open: the Senate passed a resolution by Republican senators Kenneth Keating (New York) and Homer Capehart (Indiana) authorizing the use of force against Cuba "to prevent the creation . . . of an externally supported offensive military capability endangering the security of the U.S."[9] When Richard Nixon signaled his return to political life by urging that Cuba be "quarantined," Rockefeller sought Kissinger's advice. Stay out of the Cuban debate, Kissinger told him;[10] indeed, "stay out of the foreign field until November."[11] Nevertheless, he drew up a position paper for

Rockefeller that condemned "the transformation of Cuba into a Communist state maintained by Soviet arms" as a violation of the Monroe Doctrine, as well as of Article 6 of the Inter-American Treaty of Reciprocal Assistance signed at Rio de Janeiro in 1947.

As Kissinger shrewdly noted, it would once have been straightforward for the United States to intervene in a Caribbean or Central American country. As recently as 1954, "a Communist-dominated government in Guatemala could be overthrown without anyone suggesting Soviet reprisals elsewhere or without serious repercussions in the Western Hemisphere. Today—according to the President—this is no longer the case." This marked a troubling "deterioration" of the U.S. position. Hence the "peril" posed by Cuba was "not only Communism in a relatively small island in the Caribbean but chaos in the Western Hemisphere."[12] Yet Kissinger was unequivocal. As in Berlin, military action—whether a naval blockade or an armed attack—could have only two outcomes: "either 1) calling the Soviet bluff or 2) an armed conflict. If the decision is made to use these measures, we must be ready to accept the consequence of possible escalation into a major war and we must commit ourselves militarily to seeing the measures through. We cannot make another half-hearted attempt."[13]

Khrushchev's motivation was not just to defend Cuba's experiment with Marxism, though Castro was more than happy to interpret it in that way.[14] Nor was the Soviet leader merely trying to win a psychological victory. His strategic calculation was twofold. First, by turning Cuba into a launchpad for intermediate-range missiles directed at American targets, he could narrow the gap in nuclear capability between the Soviet Union and the United States, the true nature of which the Soviets knew full well. The plan was to send forty ballistic missiles to Cuba: twenty-four medium-range R-12s (with a range of 1,050 miles, long enough to hit Washington, D.C.) and sixteen intermediate-range R-14s, which had twice that range. Both types carried one-megaton warheads. This would double the number of Soviet missiles capable of reaching the United States, and it would do it far more cheaply than the construction of new intercontinental missiles.

To justify this action, Khrushchev had only to look out from his Georgian holiday house at Pitsunda toward Turkey, where fifteen U.S.

PGM-19 Jupiter missiles had been deployed in 1961 as part of the post-*Sputnik* response to the imaginary missile gap. "What do you see?" he would ask visitors, handing them binoculars. "I see U.S. missiles in Turkey, aimed at my dacha."[15] (The Jupiters were in fact stationed near Izmir, on the Aegean coast.) Soviet missiles on Cuba would simply give the Americans "a little of their own medicine."[16] But it is clear that Khrushchev was thinking less of Turkey than of Germany. His second objective was to checkmate the Americans in Berlin. Kennedy did not initially grasp this, but then the penny dropped: "whatever we do in regard to Cuba, it gives him the chance to do the same with regard to Berlin."[17] A U.S. blockade of Cuba would risk a Soviet blockade of West Berlin. A U.S. attack on Cuba would risk a Soviet attack on West Berlin.

Operation Anadyr was in one respect a triumph of Soviet strategy. In addition to the missiles, the Soviets sent four motorized regiments, two tank battalions, a MiG-21 fighter wing, some antiaircraft gun batteries, twelve SA-2 surface-to-air missile detachments with 144 missile launchers, and forty-two Il-28 medium jet bombers equipped with nuclear bombs. They also sent nuclear warheads for the Sopka coastal defense cruise missiles that had previously been supplied to the Cubans. Ultimately, more than fifty thousand Soviet troops ended up in Cuba. This was a huge operation. Yet between September 8, when the first nuclear ballistic missile reached Cuba, and October 15, when U.S. intelligence identified the missile sites, the U.S. government was oblivious to the fact that the arms being supplied to Cuba were nuclear. Indeed, the period of ignorance might have lasted even longer—perhaps until Khrushchev's planned visit to the United States, when he intended to reveal his masterstroke—if the Soviet troops on Cuba had thought to camouflage the launch sites, or to shoot down the U-2s that spotted them.

Being caught in the act, however, was not the biggest Soviet blunder. "I think we will win this operation," Khrushchev had told his colleagues on the Presidium of the Supreme Soviet as they signed off on the plan on June 8.[18] But a Soviet "win" could occur only if the United States acquiesced, which was never likely, or confined itself to empty threats of retaliation. It was a sign of how unimpressed Khrushchev had been by Kennedy's threats over Berlin that he embarked on such a risky course. It was as if the Soviet leader had himself come to believe in John Foster Dulles's concept of brinkmanship, even as the United States tried to leave it behind. Yet both Khrushchev's own ambassador and his own foreign minister understood that, from the vantage point of U.S. domestic politics, there could be no equivalence whatsoever between Cuba and Berlin. One was four thousand miles away. The other was in America's backyard.

Part of Kissinger's critique of the Kennedy administration was that it had failed to make flexible response credible. There was some truth to this. When the national security team met on September 4, just four days before the first Soviet ballistic missile reached Cuba, Bobby Kennedy urged his brother to announce that the United States would not tolerate Soviet offensive weapons in Cuba. After an inconclusive meeting between the younger Kennedy and an impassive Dobrynin, the president did just that.[19] Three days later the White House requested authority to call up 150,000 reservists. At this stage, the idea of Soviet nuclear missiles on Cuba was still regarded as a hypothetical contingency in Washington. What the Soviets did not know for sure but strongly suspected was that the Americans were already contemplating an attack on Cuba, even before the scale of the Soviet operation was clear.[20] Both air strikes and a naval blockade were already under discussion in September. Indeed, on October 1—two weeks before the U-2s photographed the Soviet missile sites—McNamara ordered the commander in chief of the Atlantic Fleet, Admiral Robert Lee Dennison, to prepare for a blockade. That evening Dennison ordered his fleet commanders to prepare for air strikes by October 20. A full-scale invasion was also being considered.[21]

Khrushchev clearly regarded such American countermoves as quite unlikely. He did not, however, rule them out altogether. What the Americans did not know was that on September 7, he had told his ministry of defense to give the Soviet motorized brigades in Cuba a dozen of the tactical nuclear missiles known as Lunas, each with a range of less than forty miles but an explosive power of between five and twelve kilotons: enough to blow a hole 130 feet wide and deep and to kill everything within a radius of a thousand yards. He intended that these should be used if the U.S. attempted an invasion. Dissuaded by his more prudent military advisers from flying them to Cuba, Khrushchev agreed to ship them, along with the warheads for the intermediate-range missiles. He also ordered nuclear-armed Foxtrot submarines to escort the ships transporting the nuclear arms. On September 11 the Soviet news agency TASS issued an official warning that any attack on Cuba or on the ships en route there would be interpreted as an attack on the Soviet Union itself.[22]

Although Senator Keating asserted as early as October 10 that missiles "capable of striking targets 'in the American heartland' had been installed in Cuba,"[23] it was not until six days later that the president was informed that a U-2 spy plane had spotted missiles near Havana. Kennedy and his key advisers (assembled on what became known as the Executive Committee of the National Security Council, or "ExComm")* were thrown into confusion by the audacity of the Soviet move. Already, the CIA reported, up to eight medium-range missiles could be fired at the United States from Cuba. Within six to eight weeks, the two intermediate-range missile sites would be ready too. Once all the missiles were installed, only 15 percent of U.S. strategic forces would survive a Soviet attack. "[It's] just as if we suddenly began to put a major number of medium range ballistic missiles in Turkey," fumed Kennedy. "Well, we did, Mr. President," someone reminded him.[24] The options Kennedy was initially presented with ranged from air strikes to a naval blockade to a diplomatic appeal to Castro. But the Joint Chiefs, eager though they were to bomb Cuba, could not guarantee that all the missiles would be destroyed in such a raid, leaving the possibility open of Russian nuclear retaliation. Nor did anyone apart from Curtis LeMay, the invariably belligerent air force chief of staff, deny the risk that an attack on Cuba might trigger a Soviet attack on Berlin,[25] to which—as they had all learned the previous year—the only possible responses

---

*The ExComm's core members were: President Kennedy, Vice President Johnson, Secretary of State Rusk, Treasury Secretary Douglas Dillon, Defense Secretary McNamara, Attorney General Kennedy, Director of Central Intelligence McCone, Chairman of the Joint Chiefs Maxwell Taylor, Ambassador-at-Large Llewellyn Thompson, and Special Assistant Bundy. But more than twenty other officials participated in ExComm meetings as and when required.

would be capitulation or all-out nuclear war. Instead, ignoring LeMay's tactless allusions to Munich, Kennedy decided on a twin-track approach. Following McNamara's lead, he decided to impose a partial naval blockade ("defensive quarantine") to halt further Soviet shipments of military hardware to Cuba. But he rejected McNamara's proposal simultaneously to negotiate with the Soviets. Instead, in a television address at seven p.m. on October 22, he issued an ultimatum demanding that the Soviets withdraw their missiles, which he denounced as a "clandestine, reckless and provocative threat to world peace." In case this ultimatum was rejected, Kennedy ordered the preparation of a large invasion force.[26] TASS responded by accusing the United States of "violating international law, initiating piratical operations, and provoking nuclear war."[27]

Compared with earlier in Kennedy's presidency, the decision-making process in October 1962 was much improved. The twelve-man ExComm was small enough to be manageable without being so small that it succumbed to "groupthink." Bundy did his best to give Kennedy meaningful choices, even keeping the air strike option "alive" after the majority of ExComm members had rejected it (at the risk of appearing indecisive himself).[28] Yet in the end it was by going behind the backs of the majority of ExComm members that Kennedy, once again using his brother as a back channel of communication to the Soviets, arrived at a resolution of the crisis. Much as had happened over Berlin, the Kennedy brothers cut a deal with the other side.

Fortunately, Khrushchev was willing to compromise. First, responding to a proposal from UN secretary general U Thant, he ordered the Soviet ships en route to Cuba not to cross the U.S. quarantine line, five hundred miles off the island's coast. Second, after initially seeming to be unimpressed by Kennedy's televised ultimatum, he offered two possible deals, one in the form of a long letter to Kennedy, the other broadcast on Radio Moscow. The first of these, which reached the State Department at nine p.m. on Friday, October 26, simply envisaged a withdrawal of the missiles in return for an American guarantee not to invade Cuba. The second, which reached the White House as the ExComm convened thirteen hours later, offered a withdrawal of the

Cuban missiles in return for the withdrawal of the Jupiter missiles ("analogous weapons") in Turkey ("right next to us"). The fact that the former was secret and the latter public greatly complicated the situation. While exchanging Cuban missiles for Turkish missiles might strike "any . . . rational man" as "a very fair trade," in the president's words, the implications of such a trade for NATO were repugnant to most of the ExComm's members.

That day—Saturday, October 27, 1962—was probably the day the world came closest to destruction. At 10:22 a.m. an American U-2 was shot down over Cuba by a Soviet SA-2 rocket, fired by the local Soviet commander without authorization from Moscow. The pilot was killed. Cuban antiaircraft batteries subsequently fired at other low-flying American reconnaissance planes. Meanwhile another U-2 had unintentionally strayed into Soviet airspace near the Bering Strait. When Soviet MiGs took off to intercept it, Alaskan-based F-102As were scrambled. Elsewhere, mere accidents came close to triggering the apocalypse. A wandering bear at Duluth Air Force Base led to the mobilizing of nuclear-armed F-106s in Minnesota. A routine test at Cape Canaveral was interpreted as a Soviet missile by a radar unit in New Jersey. By the time they met that afternoon, the members of the ExComm were in a state of high anxiety. At four p.m. came the news of the downed U-2. We know from the tape recordings Kennedy secretly made of the ExComm meeting that afternoon how he reacted to this bombshell: "How do we explain the effect?" he asked, barely coherent. "This Khrushchev message of last night and their decision . . . How do we—I mean that's a . . ." The phrase on the tip of his tongue was presumably something like "a provocation we can't ignore." That evening, before the ExComm reconvened, Vice President Lyndon Johnson took advantage of the Kennedy brothers' absence from the cabinet room to inveigh against "backing down," to urge a military response to the downing of the U-2, and—with great vehemence—to oppose any kind of deal that effectively swapped missiles in Cuba for missiles in Turkey. "Why then your whole foreign policy is gone," Johnson told the president when he returned to the table. "You take everything out of Turkey. Twenty thousand men, all your technicians, and all your planes and all your missiles. And *crumble*."[29] Later that night McNamara talked as if the ExComm had already decided for war:

> McNAMARA: You got any doubts?
>
> ROBERT KENNEDY: Well, no. I think that we're doing the only thing we can do, and well, you know. . . .
>
> McNAMARA: I think the one thing, Bobby, we ought to seriously do before we act is be damned sure they understand the consequences. In other words, we need to really show them where we are now, because we need to have two things ready . . . a government for Cuba, because we're going to need one—we go in with bombing aircraft; and, secondly, plans for how to respond to the Soviet Union in Europe, because sure as hell they're going to do something there.
>
> DILLON: You have to pick out the things they might—
>
> McNAMARA: Well, I think, that's right. . . . I would suggest that it will be an eye for an eye.
>
> DILLON: That's the mission.
>
> ROBERT KENNEDY: I'd take Cuba back.
>
> UNIDENTIFIED: I'd take Cuba away from Castro.
>
> UNIDENTIFIED: Suppose we make Bobby mayor of Havana[?][30]

This was humor at its blackest. It seemed like the eve of destruction. Eating chicken with the president upstairs in the family quarters, his special assistant, Dave Powers, thought it was his last meal. McNamara remembered stepping outside the White House to savor the livid sunset. "To look and to smell it," he recalled, "because I thought it was the last Saturday I would ever see." In Moscow at precisely that moment, Fyodor Burlatsky, a senior Kremlin adviser, telephoned his wife. He told her to "drop everything and get out of Moscow."[31]

If Johnson had been president, World War III might well have happened (that was certainly Bobby Kennedy's view). Unbeknownst to Johnson, however, the president had secretly authorized his brother to agree to the Cuban-Turkish missile swap with Dobrynin (in what later came to be called the "Trollope ploy").* Sitting in his office at the Justice Department, manifestly exhausted, the younger Kennedy blustered but then delicately did the deal:

> We had to have a commitment by at least tomorrow that those bases would be moved. This was not an ultimatum, I said, but just a statement of fact. He should understand that if they did not remove those bases, then we would remove them. His country might take retaliatory action, but he should understand that before this was over, while there might be dead Americans, there would also be dead Russians. He then asked me about Khrushchev's other proposal dealing with removal of the missiles from Turkey. I replied that there could be no quid pro quo—no deal of this kind could be made. . . . If some time elapsed—and . . . I mentioned four or five months—I said I was sure that these matters could be resolved satisfactorily.[32]

The crucial point was that the president could not say "anything public in this regard about Turkey." Bobby did not have to spell out his brother's and the Democratic Party's vulnerability on the issue. As we have seen, there had been repeated Republican accusations that the administration was backsliding over Cuba, and congressional elections were due the following month. Only with difficulty, Kennedy hinted to Dobrynin, was his brother holding back the hawks in his cabinet.

Yet domestic politics was not decisive.[33] More important was the question of America's allies. Key ExComm members (and not only the vice president) had in fact rejected this deal on the ground that it would weaken NATO. As Bundy put it, "it would already be clear that we were trying to sell our allies for our interests. That would be the view in all of NATO. Now, it's irrational and it's crazy, but it's a *terribly* powerful fact."[34] Even though they were aware that the Jupiters were

---

*The allusion is to Anthony Trollope's novels *The American Senator* and *John Caldigate,* in which a casual gesture is deliberately misinterpreted as a marriage proposal. In this case, the Kennedy brothers were responding to Khrushchev's two proposals in the way that suited them best, by all but ignoring the second one.

obsolete and due to be replaced by Polaris submarines in the Mediterranean, the Turkish government also wanted the decision to get rid of them kept quiet.[35] The Trollope Ploy was therefore strictly secret. Aside from the Kennedy brothers, eight other members of the ExComm were in on it; neither Johnson nor McCone was informed.[36] Indeed, it was not officially confirmed until the 1980s.

Khrushchev was asleep on his Kremlin sofa while all this was happening. His ambassador's report—sent, incredibly, by Western Union—did not reach the Soviet foreign ministry until the following morning (Sunday the twenty-eighth). As soon as Khrushchev was briefed about what Bobby Kennedy had said, he told his colleagues on the Presidium that they were "face to face with the danger of war and of nuclear catastrophe, with the possible result of destroying the human race. . . . In order to save the world, we must retreat."[37] Another public letter was drafted and duly broadcast at five p.m. Moscow time, nine a.m. eastern standard time. (It should have been earlier, but the courier got stuck in rush-hour traffic.) This time Khrushchev merely said that the missiles in Cuba would be dismantled, crated, and returned home.

It was over. "I felt like laughing or yelling or dancing," recalled one intensely relieved member of the ExComm. The British journalist Alistair Cooke watched a seagull soar in the sky above him and wondered why it was not a dove. Yet a gull was perhaps the right bird. For at the same time Khrushchev sent two private messages to Kennedy. The second said that the missiles were only being withdrawn "on account of your having agreed to the Turkish issue." Adlai Stevenson, the American ambassador to the United Nations, would later be accused of having offered to swap Turkish for Cuban missiles. This was a smear; it was the Kennedy brothers who had done it. Nor was the crisis quite at an end. The Pentagon continued to prepare its invasion of Cuba, still unaware that there were four times more Soviet troops on the island than they had estimated and that they were armed with battlefield nuclear missiles. It was not until November 20, when Khrushchev agreed also to withdraw the Il-28 bombers, that the crisis was really at an end.

III

The Cuban Missile Crisis was a game of chicken, but it was not only Khrushchev who swerved.[38] In the final analysis, Kennedy triumphed because of a mixture of luck, risk aversion, and deft public relations. He was lucky that he did not heed those who urged an amphibious invasion, because Khrushchev's initial instruction to the Soviet commander in Cuba, General Issa Pliyev, on the night of October 22–23 was unambiguous: "If there is a [U.S.] landing, [use] the tactical atomic weapons, but [not] the strategic weapons until [there is] an order." True, under pressure from the more cautious Deputy Premier Anastas Mikoyan and Defense Minister Rodion Malinovsky, he later changed this to an order to use the missiles but without nuclear warheads. Even so, he might have changed his mind in the face of a U.S. invasion, or Pliyev might have changed it for him if communications had been cut off.[39]

Kennedy was soft in agreeing to trade the Jupiters in Turkey for the Russian missiles on Cuba—a trade strongly opposed by Walt Rostow and others in the administration.[40] Just how far the president was prepared to bend is clear from the fact that on October 27 Kennedy had asked Rusk to contact Andrew Cordier—dean of Columbia University, and the former executive assistant to U Thant—and dictate to him a statement proposing the removal of the Jupiters from Turkey and the Soviet missiles from Cuba. If all else failed, Cordier was to hand this statement to Thant, who would then propose the reciprocal withdrawal as a UN initiative—a proposal that Kennedy would promptly have accepted.[41] Khrushchev did not need to fold as readily as he did on the twenty-eighth. Again, Kennedy was lucky.

By accepting the Turkish-Cuban deal privately but not publicly, Khrushchev handed Kennedy a public relations victory. As the Soviets dismantled their missiles, the Americans could pose as the tough guys who had not "blinked." Khrushchev, by contrast, suffered irreparable domestic damage: his gamble to tilt the balance of power decisively in favor of Moscow had failed.[42] At a meeting of the Central Committee on November 23, he sought to make the best of it. Had not a Soviet missile downed an American plane? Had not the United States pledged not to invade Cuba? But his colleagues felt that he had acted recklessly for little net benefit. In October 1964, two years after trading Cuban missiles for Turkish, Khrushchev himself would be traded in for Leonid Brezhnev. In truth, Castro was the sole beneficiary of the crisis—and he was the only one of the three leaders who was disappointed by the peaceful outcome, so much that he had to be strong-armed by Mikoyan into accepting the withdrawal of nearly all the Soviet arms.[43]

In some ways, the outcome of the Cuban Missile Crisis represented the triumph of psychological warfare over flexible response. Khrushchev had been half right. When presented with conventional military options to deal with the Soviet threat in Cuba, Kennedy had been willing to go no further than "defensive quarantine." Yet the resolution of the crisis was hugely to Kennedy's advantage in psychological terms. François de Rose, who had been so critical of U.S. policy just a few months before, now wrote Kissinger a euphoric letter congratulating him on the "masterly fashion" with which Kennedy had handled the "whole affair." "You must all feel very proud," de Rose wrote.[44] But the congratulations were due to others; Kissinger humbly passed the letter on to Schlesinger in the White House.[45] The harsh reality was that the author of *Nuclear Weapons and Foreign Policy* was so completely out of the loop in October 1962 that the only crisis he had to deal with was a crisis of secretarial staffing in Nelson Rockefeller's research department.[46] While his former colleagues were grappling with the danger of World War III, Kissinger was negotiating with the "Brownies" about their salaries. While Bundy reflected on an extraordinary victory for the NSC apparatus he had built, Kissinger was hearing a sob story from a cab driver about "a girl from Minnesota who is trying to get a typing job in New York." (Despite not knowing the girl, he passed her name on to June Goldthwait because "sometimes it is pleasant if unexpected things happen to people.")[47]

The truly unexpected thing that had happened was, of course, that Kennedy had triumphed, as Kissinger frankly acknowledged in his commentary on the Cuban crisis in *The Reporter*. The president had "exploded the myth that in every situation the Soviets were prepared to run greater risks than we." But how exactly had he succeeded?

Kissinger's answer was twofold. First, Khrushchev had made a "colossal error" that made no military sense:

> If the Soviets felt that missiles based on Cuban territory were necessary to redress the over-all strategic balance, then the Soviet arsenal of intercontinental rockets must be much smaller than had generally been believed. If, on the other hand, the Soviets consider their arsenal of intercontinental rockets adequate, then nuclear bases in Cuba were irrelevant to the security problem in Cuba.[48]

Second, the Soviet climbdown had confirmed that there truly was no missile gap; rather, it was the United States that enjoyed nuclear superiority:

> The crisis could not have ended so quickly and decisively but for the fact that the United States can win a general war if it strikes first and can inflict intolerable damage on the Soviet Union even if it is the victim of a surprise attack. Whatever one's reservations about the counterforce strategy enunciated by Secretary McNamara for the long term, it proved its efficacy in the Cuban crisis. The Soviet leaders did not dare invoke the threat of nuclear war against our blockade. . . . [F]or this crisis at least, the credibility of our deterrent was greater than theirs.[49]

In fretting about the missile gap and then berating Kennedy for being soft on Berlin and much else, Kissinger had been wrong, and he had no hesitation in admitting it.

Yet in common with nearly everyone outside the president's innermost circle, Kissinger was still under the impression that "the demand for dismantling our Turkish bases" had been "turned down." Had he been aware that the deal had in fact been done, he would surely have been more critical. Even without this knowledge, he could not resist a private dig. "Cuba was a case of the Communists overreaching themselves," he told Rockefeller, "but also an example of the disdain in which they held the Administration. And even there, the Administration did not press its advantage."[50] This may have been what tempted Rockefeller into an ill-judged "sideswipe" at Kennedy for allowing a continued presence of Soviet troops on the island.[51] By July 1963, however, he and Kissinger had worked out a more convincing position.[52] His draft resolution for the 1963 Governors' Conference—designed to appeal to the increasingly influential Cuban exile community— called on the government to use all means to get the Soviet troops out of Cuba and uphold the Monroe Doctrine.[53] "I do not believe that Cuba marks the end of Soviet imperialism," Kissinger wrote in November 1963.[54] The question was where in the world the United States was actually prepared to fight it, if not on an island off the Florida coast.

IV

"Does a full professor have to be dignified?" asked Nancy Hanks archly, on hearing that Harvard had promoted Kissinger to that rank in April 1962.[55] Once a full professorship had seemed to him like the most brightly glittering of prizes. Now, however, the lecture halls and seminar rooms had lost much of their luster. After the White House, the Center for International Affairs seemed a dull place. After writing so many confidential memcons, it was hard to go back to coauthoring a worthy book on West German politics with Karl Kaiser. And compared with the high-octane decision making of the ExComm, the abstract theorizing of Thomas Schelling at the Harvard-MIT Arms Control Seminar seemed maddeningly dry.[56] When Kissinger was asked to contribute to a conference in honor of his old mentor Bill Elliott in July 1963, the result was a rather unacademic talk that, at first sight, was almost wholly focused on the practice rather than the philosophy of national security. On closer inspection, however, this turns out to have been a profound meditation on what he had learned from his firsthand encounter with high-level decision making.

Kissinger's theme was "the problem of conjecture in foreign policy," a phrase he had first used in his 1959 essay "The Search for Stability."[57]

[On] the one hand policy requires prudence and caution and intelligent qualities of manipulating the known. But it also requires ability to project beyond the known. And when one is in the realm of the new, then one reaches the dilemma that there's really very little to guide the policy-maker except what convictions he brings to it. . . . [E]very statesman must choose at some point between whether he wishes certainty or whether he wishes to rely on his assessment of the situation. . . . [T]his does not mean that every time one acts on the basis of an assessment in an uncertain situation one is right. It simply means that if one wants demonstrable proof one in a sense becomes a prisoner of events.

To illustrate his point, Kissinger gave a series of counterfactual examples. If the democracies had moved against the Nazis in 1936, for instance, "we wouldn't know today whether Hitler was a misunderstood nationalist, whether he had only limited objectives, or whether he was in fact a maniac. The democracies learned that he was in fact a maniac. They had certainty but they had to pay for that with a few million lives." By the same token, it was "not inconceivable that Khrushchev all his life has hankered after the increased production of consumer goods and that he's really a frustrated Midwestern businessman (although he's chosen an odd career to bring this desire to the forefront)."

All I'm saying is we can't know. I'm saying that alternative hypotheses are also conceivable, which also cannot be proved. . . . [I]t is also possible that it is consistent with Soviet tactics that there is a period of consolidation following a period of expansion. It is possible in this period that the Soviet Union may want to encourage a race to Moscow [of European leaders seeking bilateral deals]. . . . The danger we face is that we will assume that . . . our own materialism motivates the Soviet revolutionaries, and that because we like plenty of iceboxes this is the predominant aim of people who, after all, managed to survive under Stalin.

A similar argument could be made about the debates on European integration between federalists and Gaullists. The key point for Kissinger was the uncertainty that must inevitably surround such choices. For that reason it was "the philosophical assumptions one makes about the nature of reality, the nature of historical trends that one is facing," that were bound to be "the determining features in the practice of foreign policy." Intellectuals had a tendency to forget that the "purely analytical approach operates on material which is known, and . . . doesn't have the dimension of time; while the policy-maker is part of an historical process and is making irreversible decisions, each of which becomes the factual basis for the next decision."

The period after the Cuban Missile Crisis was a time of marked relaxation in the Cold War; some have even seen in it the origins of détente. Rusk, for one, was already bandying that word about.[58] Yet the very "pragmatism" that was being exalted in 1963 struck Kissinger as perilous.

> The pragmatists who pride themselves so very much on their flexibility, and who always say that they're steering the precise middle course between extremes, and who say that if two sides take a position they have both to be wrong, and the fellow in the middle must be right—this exaltation of the middle ground is bound to produce the extremes which everybody deplores, because when you are dealing with the perfect pragmatist the only way you can get what you want is to produce the kinds of pressures which will force him to adjust, and everybody has the highest degree of incentive to create pressures. . . . The very flexible people, the very "pragmatic" people, are really as international phenomena absolutely unreliable people, because one cannot be sure what they're going to do until one knows what the situation is.[59]

This was nothing if not a veiled indictment of the Kennedy administration and the practice, if not the theory, of flexible response.

Kissinger was, of course, never likely to skulk in Cambridge for long. In November 1962, having secured reelection as governor of New

York but while not declaring any intention of running in 1964, Nelson Rockefeller asked him to "assume responsibility for preparing . . . positions in the international and security fields, arranging contacts with the intellectual community . . . and with foreign leaders" in order that he be "acquainted with the entire spectrum of responsible opinion."[60] Among the people Kissinger arranged for Rockefeller to meet in the subsequent months were General Lauris Norstad (the former SACEUR), Max Ascoli (editor of *The Reporter*), Frank Meyer (editor of *National Review*), Admiral Arleigh Burke (the former chief of naval operations), U Thant (the UN secretary general), the Tanzanian president Julius Nyerere, and Juan Bosch, the newly elected president of the Dominican Republic. By the fall, the research staff were frantically organizing Rockefeller quotes on every conceivable foreign policy issue. Much of this work was drudgery. In particular, Kissinger cannot have relished the chore of drafting Rockefeller's replies to letters from members of the public about international issues. Nevertheless, he stuck to it. When Bundy approached him in January 1963 with yet another request to go to Germany in a semiprivate capacity, Kissinger firmly declined—"like Caesar's wife," as he put to George Hinman, another Rockefeller adviser, he needed to be above reproach. "To claim . . . that I am visiting as a private citizen would only bewilder the Germans," he told Bundy. If he were asked for his own opinions, it "would again lead to the embarrassment which produced our decision last September to remove the ambiguity of my posture."[61] The most Kissinger was prepared to do was to send Bundy memcons of his key meetings when he visited France and Italy in early 1963.[62]

To advise a politician aspiring to the highest office is at once liberating and constraining. Kissinger was now free to write speeches and position papers that were harshly critical of the Kennedy administration. As the words would be uttered by Rockefeller rather than himself, there was no disloyalty. On the other hand, Kissinger could write only words that Rockefeller could credibly utter, and so it is important not to read the documents of this period as unambiguous statements of Kissinger's personal opinions. That said, the vehemence of his critique of Kennedy was startling. In a twenty-five-page memorandum written on January 8, 1963, Kissinger lambasted the administration he had once worked for. It had "demoralized the bureaucracy and much of the military." It had engaged in "government by improvisation and manipulation." It relied on "public relations gimmicks and . . . a superficial, somewhat managed press." Its idea of leadership was "the registering of public opinion as expressed in the editorials of our leading newspapers." It was a government that had "no respect for personal dignity and which treats people as tools. Strong-willed intellectuals, intoxicated with their first taste of power, push their theories regardless of the impact on the morale of the bureaucracy or the professional military." Here was more than a hint of the personal animus Kissinger now felt against Bundy.

Yet Kennedy's administration was "demoralizing" not just for America but for America's allies.

> Its manipulativeness makes it particularly dangerous for all those who have an emotional relationship to this country: the only group relatively impervious to it are our enemies, who can use its opportunism to move us from one position of disadvantage to another. . . . We have brutalized our allies within NATO, in West New Guinea and in the Congo to score points unrelated to any overriding conception. . . . We do not seem to be able to distinguish between friends and opponents. From Laos to Yemen to the Congo, we have taken the position that if our friends are not perfect we will line up with our enemies to destroy them.

Nor was that all. Brazil was "on the edge of anarchy." Iran "could go any day." In Vietnam the scale of Communist attacks was "increasing." The administration was undermining the U.S. reputation for reliability—"the most important asset any nation has." All this was partly a result of the way policy was made. The State Department was "a shambles, demoralized by the weakness of the Secretary of State and the interference of the White House." The administration's "extraordinary pragmatism" led inevitably to "an extremely fitful policy," in which "periods of lethargy alternate with sudden moves to impose some rapid solution, usually on our allies." But there was also a fundamental lack of strategic clarity, something that was desperately needed in "a period of revolutionary change." In short, Kennedy's foreign policy was "essentially a house of cards." Its weakness had merely been obscured by "three factors: (a) we are still so strong that we can impose even wrong policies on many parts of the world; (b) fortuitously for us, the Communist movement has been rent by internal schisms. . . . (c) an enormously skillful use of public relations stifles debate and has neutralized any possible focus for opposition." The conclusion was bleak: "If the present policies do not produce an impasse Kennedy will be unbeatable in 1964. But sooner or later they must produce an impasse. And then those who warned in time will be as desperately needed as Churchill was in 1940 and De Gaulle in 1958."[63]

To say that Kissinger wanted Rockefeller to win in 1964 would be an understatement. He also badly wanted Kennedy to lose. Among the most remarkable passages of this memorandum are those directed at the Kennedy family's political methods, which he likened to those of Napoleon, who "confounded his opponents by the dexterity of his movements, based on thorough, meticulous organization.

> The same is true of the Kennedys. The old-style politicians rely on good fellowship and temporary alliances for limited purposes. They tend to play hunches; they try various measures to see which works. Even the full-time politicians are in a deep sense amateurs.
>
> The Kennedys are different. They never depend on good fellowship; they never play hunches. They have succeeded because they know. They have understood that luck is the residue of design. Their research is meticulous; their organization all-embracing. State by state—and in Massachusetts county by county—they know who the key people are; what issues concern the voters; what bargains have to be struck; what solutions can be imposed.

If Rockefeller was to take on the eldest Kennedy and win, Kissinger argued, he would need "meticulous preparation" and "maximum flexibility" (a quality seemingly at more of a premium in the domestic arena). In particular, Kissinger recommended the "creation of a group among your advisors to recommend positions to you on a more policy-oriented level" as well as the appointment of a "chief of staff on national matters, to plan and implement substance, organization, and strategy." Above all, Rockefeller needed his advisers to provide him with "a clear strategic concept . . . of a notion of how victory could be achieved." Otherwise, he warned, "each of your advisors will continue to attempt to get your approval for specific courses of action which, however meritorious in themselves, will lack coherence."[64]

This diatribe was in fact almost as critical of Rockefeller as it was of Kennedy, even if the criticism of the former's lack of strategy was implicit (and indeed largely disguised as a critique of George Lodge's unsuccessful Massachusetts campaign against Edward Kennedy). Nancy Hanks worried Kissinger would have his "head cut off because of the memo."[65] But Fritz Kraemer, to whom Kissinger showed an early draft, expressed a more profound concern. While impressed by the memo's frankness, he remained skeptical that Rockefeller had the qualities of a president. Indeed, he confessed to "a feeling of tragedy" as he read: "Your 26 pages are just one long wake-up call addressed to the King: 'Sire, be great!' But he is probably only 'near-great' and yet *too* great" to wage the kind of ruthless political warfare at which the Kennedys excelled.[66] This was astute. Henry Kissinger has often been portrayed as very ruthless and calculating in his pursuit of power. But in committing himself again and again to Nelson Rockefeller, he failed to see that he was backing a man who would never be president of the United States.

V

John F. Kennedy had been elected partly because of a spasm of public anxiety that the Soviet Union was winning the nuclear arms race. This fear was, as we have seen, greatly exaggerated. But even if it had been better founded, by the end of Kennedy's first term as president, it would have been expunged. Despite much talk of disarmament, by 1964 the United States had increased its number of available nuclear weapons by 150 percent and its "deliverable megatonnage" by 200 percent, thanks in large part to the commissioning of ten Polaris submarines and an additional four hundred Minuteman missiles.[67] Yet the bigger the U.S. arsenal grew, the more uneasy America's European allies felt. "Our relations with Europe have deteriorated alarmingly," Kissinger told Rockefeller. "Europe . . . may well turn into our most difficult foreign policy problem."[68]

The problem was partly that advances in technology were making it harder and harder for the British and the French to maintain their independent nuclear capability. The U.S. decision to cancel the AGM-48 Skybolt—an air-launched missile that had been promised to the United Kingdom as a way of extending the life of British strategic bombers—left Harold Macmillan's government floundering. As a sop, when Kennedy met Macmillan in Nassau in December 1962, the British were offered Polaris missiles but only as part of the projected Multilateral Force (MLF) within NATO; they could be used independently only when "supreme national interests" were at stake. For Kissinger, this was a perfect illustration of the way the Kennedy administration antagonized its allies.[69] It was also the product of "a strategic theory which is almost a caricature of push-button warfare"—a supposedly "pure" strategy that "subordinates all considerations of psychology, policy, and the morale of our services to abstract and technical considerations of command and control."[70]

When Kissinger visited France—which had also been offered Polaris on the same terms—he was not surprised to hear Kennedy's policy attacked from all sides. According to Jean-Daniel Jurgensen, the deputy chief of the French NATO mission, the Nassau agreement confirmed not only that Britain "preferred an arrangement with the United States at any price to common action with Europe" but also that U.S. strategy implied turning Europe into "a battleground."[71] The foreign minister, Maurice Couve de Murville, rejected the "integration or multilateralism . . . we were pushing" as "unacceptable."[72] According to de Rose, the new talk of détente was interpreted by de Gaulle as the prelude to a superpower condominium that would reduce France and indeed Europe to second-class citizenship, a view echoed by Jean Laloy.[73] The Germans, too, were up in arms as usual. Every American initiative they invariably saw as "the first step towards atomic disengagement."[74] On January 10, 1963, Kissinger met with General Hans Speidel, a veteran of both world wars and now commander in chief of the NATO ground forces in Central Europe. Speidel revealed the roots of German unease: that Germany could not depend on French support (hence his advice to Adenauer to beware of de Gaulle's secret offer of nuclear cooperation); and that NATO's current conventional forces "would permit a defense against Soviet forces now deployed in Eastern Germany only along the line of the Weser[,] . . . would require the utilization of tactical nuclear weapons from the outset[,] . . . [and] would permit a defense for only an average of nine days."[75] In Italy, too, there was disquiet. The Italians Kissinger met with—including the president, Antonio Segni; the prime minister, Amintore Fanfani; the defense minister, Giulio Andreotti, and the head of the diplomatic service, Attilio Cattani—had by now worked out that the Jupiter missiles were being withdrawn from Turkey as part of a secret deal with the Soviets over Cuba. Would theirs be the next to go?[76] Though more enthusiastic than the French about the MLF, the Italians had their doubts about how it would work in practice. According to Fanfani, "the United States would probably propose placing Italian cooks on the submarines and call it joint control."[77] This was one of many subtle ways in which the deal to end the Cuban crisis indeed had negative repercussions for NATO. As the truth came out, trust in American leadership was diminished.

Despite Kissinger's break with Bundy, the Italian press still billed him as "a special adviser to President Kennedy on military affairs."[78] In fact, as we have seen, he was doing no more than send Bundy copies of his memcons, including the details of his conversation with Speidel, despite the fact that—as Kissinger made clear—the general had spoken "in the strictest confidence" and "implored me not to make any use of the information he gave me."[79] Writing to Bundy after his return from Europe, he remained constructive. "I had not seen eye-to-eye on a number of occasions with the Administration," he conceded. "However, I was convinced that the Nassau offer [of Polaris to the French] was serious. To be sure, there would be many technical problems to be ironed out. It seemed to me, however, that they would prove soluble if France entered the discussions with an open mind and on the basis of give-and-take."[80] Writing to Rockefeller, by contrast, he was scathing. The Kennedy administration's European policy was in "disarray" because of its "erratic and vacillating nature."[81] The conclusion he had now firmly reached was that the MLF was doomed to fail because the Europeans knew that behind the word *multilateral* lay increased U.S. dominance of NATO strategy. Instead, "[w]e should leave to the Europeans the internal organization of the European nuclear forces and aim to coordinate such a European force with our own."[82]

As so often, Kissinger took to the pages of *Foreign Affairs* to spell out his new position. "Strains on the Alliance" set out to explain German and French disillusionment with U.S. foreign policy in characteristically psychological terms. In the German case, the Berlin issue was crucial "not primarily because the city is physically vulnerable, but because all Germany is psychologically vulnerable." The Kennedy administration had sought to cut a deal over access to West Berlin by effectively giving East and West Germany equal status. But "no German political leader can accept as permanent the subjugation of 17,000,000 Germans by Communist guns," so the American proposal was unpalatable, even if practicable. In the French case, too, "we have treated what is essentially a political and psychological problem as if it were primarily technical . . . [showing] little understanding for the concerns of some of our European allies that their survival should depend entirely on decisions made 3,000 miles away." The unintended result of misreading both the German and the French national psyches had been to "encourage the Franco-German entente." The administration's vision of a multilateral force was unlikely to be realized under these circumstances. Better "to urge a European political control mechanism for its national forces and then to coordinate them with our strategic force," while at the same time establishing some form of "Atlantic coordinating body."[83]

In characterizing the strategic thinking of Adenauer and de Gaulle, Kissinger revisited the distinction between idealism and realism. Clearly, neither man was an idealist. (Indeed, de Rose had memorably told him that "to De Gaulle, states were unfeeling monsters operating only on the basis of self-interest.")[84] He and Adenauer were archrealists. But "their reality is their concept of the future or of the structure of the world they wish to bring about.

The overly pragmatic approach of many of our policy makers seems to many Europeans to involve the risk of latent unsteadiness, just as the Europeans' conceptual tendency appears to our officials as overly legalistic and theoretical. . . . [T]he generation which follows [Adenauer and de Gaulle] stands as much in danger of exalting technique over purpose as do their contemporaries in the United States. But on both sides of the Atlantic we should remember that there are two kinds of realists: those who manipulate facts and those who create them. The West requires nothing so much as men able to create their own reality.[85]

The antithesis of this kind of visionary realism was the kind of technocratic reductionism favored by McNamara's Defense Department. In a parallel article for *The Reporter,* Kissinger opened a new front in his own intellectual war: against the RAND Corporation and in particular Albert Wohlstetter. It had been Wohlstetter's argument that the nuclear balance of terror was "delicate" and that a war could be won by the United States even after a Soviet surprise attack so long as the United States still had the capability to destroy the remaining Soviet nuclear forces.[86] McNamara and Gilpatric had embraced this argument and had drawn the logical conclusion that all that therefore mattered was the American strategic retaliatory force. All other nuclear forces—tactical missiles, the French and British deterrents—were irrelevant. Therefore "all nuclear weapons of the Alliance had to be under tight control, indeed under a single command, which in effect meant U.S. command."[87] NATO's "nuclear dilemma," in Kissinger's view, was twofold. First, over time the Soviets might adopt and implement the same doctrine, reducing the advantage currently claimed by McNamara. Second, insisting on a U.S. monopoly on nuclear arms had the unintended consequence of alienating the country's principal European allies. Calling for a multilateral force that was in reality designed to subordinate all nuclear forces to the U.S. chain of command was merely disingenuous. Simultaneously telling the Europeans to build up their conventional forces made no sense. As Kissinger put it sardonically, "Europeans, living on a continent covered with ruins testifying to the fallibility of human foresight, feel in their bones that history is more complicated than systems analysis."[88]

Kissinger's plea to "accept the British and French national efforts and encourage first a common Franco-British and ultimately a European program" elicited widely differing reactions. His Francophile Harvard colleague Stanley Hoffmann was delighted. "You are inimitable and unrivalled," he gushed. "I only wish they'd listen to you more down there, in Washington."[89] But "down there," as Kissinger noted, his articles did not make him "too many friends."[90] The whole point of the MLF, Henry Owen argued in a critique for the NSC, was to resist "German pressures for a *national* nuclear role," which Owen argued the Kissinger scheme would only magnify.[91] The most combative public rejoinder came from none other than Robert Bowie, Kissinger's titular boss at the CFIA and a staunch proponent of the MLF.[92] Both seemed to miss Kissinger's central point. As he put it to Schlesinger, "my specific solutions are much less important than the fact that our approach so far has not managed to establish any real confidence [in Europe]. This alone dooms our specific proposals."[93] He was prepared to defend his former colleagues against French charges of "lying and insincerity."[94] He was even prepared to keep the State Department informed of his conversations when he visited Bonn in May 1963: as he told Bundy, "my disagreements with the Administration stop at the water's edge."[95] But he remained convinced that the administration's European policy was fundamentally "ill-conceived."

Was Kissinger's line to be interpreted as Rockefeller's line? That was the question posed by the London *Observer*. Haughtily, Kissinger denied it:

> I alone am responsible for my public statements. Neither Governor Rockefeller nor any of his associates even knew I was writing an article. They saw no advance text either in manuscript or galley or print. They have not discussed the article with me since its publication.
>
> In this respect, we have simply followed the procedure which has characterized a friendship extending over nearly a decade. Neither Governor Rockefeller nor any of his associates

have ever sought to influence my writings directly or indirectly. I have never given them advance information about my publications. Both sides have recognized, without it becoming an issue, that the manipulation of ideas is degrading, and that a professor's primary obligation is to his conception of the truth.[96]

Something similar happened a month later during a panel discussion at the Chamber of Commerce, which pitted Kissinger and Walter Judd, the Republican congressman from Minnesota, against Bundy and Thomas J. Dodd, the Democratic senator from Connecticut. When the moderator, Lawrence Spivak of *Meet the Press,* described Kissinger as a "Rockefeller spokesman," Kissinger replied stiffly,

> I am here as a Professor at Harvard and not as a spokesman for Governor Rockefeller. Governor Rockefeller is a friend of mine and I admire him. When he asks my opinion, I respond to it. However, my appearance before the Chamber of Commerce is in my capacity as a Professor of International Relations and nothing I say should be considered as reflecting anybody else's views.[97]

This distancing was somewhat at odds with reality. Rockefeller was by now closely following Kissinger's scripting on most foreign policy issues. A speech to the Newspaper Publishers Association in New York on April 25 was more or less a digest of Kissinger's two articles on Europe,[98] as was Rockefeller's argument for "a permanent body at the highest level charged with exploring the means of strengthening the cohesion of the nations bordering the North Atlantic." Also somewhat Kissingerian was Rockefeller's stock line to journalists at around this time: "Men are moved by ideals and values and not simply by cold calculation. There is nothing automatic about the shape of the future. It is compounded of the vision and the daring and the courage of the present."[99] He and Rockefeller were in regular contact. "We have to face the issue directly," he told the governor in April 1962, "whether [or not] we are prepared to see an independent center of nuclear decision in Europe and coordinate its action with ours through the process of

political consultation. Our present course . . . tends towards the denuclearization of Europe. This, I fear will eventually produce neutralism."[100] Kissinger was now deeply involved in developing Rockefeller's
policy positions ahead of his planned 1964 run for the presidency.

Yet it made little tactical sense for Kissinger publicly to commit
himself to Rockefeller at this early stage. The challenge to Rockefeller
from the conservative Arizona senator Barry Goldwater was already
growing.* When Wisconsin congressman Melvin Laird, an "unannounced" Goldwater supporter, asked Kissinger to contribute to a collection of essays entitled *The Conservative Papers,* Kissinger allowed his
two articles on Europe to be combined and abridged as "The Essentials
of Solidarity in the Western Alliance." Moreover, there seemed little
chance that either Rockefeller or Goldwater would defeat Kennedy in
1964. "Practically the President's term was eight years," Kissinger told
Adenauer when he visited Bonn again in May 1963. "Short of an inconceivable calamity . . . President Kennedy would be reelected."[101]

In any case, it did not hurt Kissinger's ability to walk the corridors
of power on the other side of the Atlantic that he continued to be identified as a White House adviser. As soon as classes finished at Harvard,
he returned once again to Europe, where he met key German, French,
Belgian, and British policy makers. Opinion on the MLF remained
mixed. The Belgians were willing to go along with it "so that Germany would not develop its own nuclear arms," according to the Belgian defense minister, Paul-Willem Segers.[102] The Germans would join
it, said Adenauer, "in order not to lose contact with America."[103] But
Franz Josef Strauss, who had been forced to resign for his role in the
Spiegel affair, begged to differ: in his view the MLF was "a fraud."[104]
Even more forthright was Lord Mountbatten, the last viceroy of India,
now serving as chief of the Defence Staff, who told Kissinger the MLF
was "a nonsense." In particular, "he had commanded enough ships in

---

*Though he was not a strong social conservative—he would later resist the Christian
right's pressure to politicize abortion and gay rights—Goldwater's campaign for the
Republican nomination benefited from the scandal surrounding Rockefeller's divorce
and remarriage. More substantive was the contrast between Goldwater's anti–New
Deal economic libertarianism and Rockefeller's tax-and-spend record as governor of
New York.

his lifetime to know that the notion of crews of mixed nationality was rubbish."[105] Not much more polite was the Labour shadow defense secretary, Denis Healey.[106] The most negative views, however, came from the French. Stehlin and de Rose warned that de Gaulle was taking decisive steps to reduce France's integration into NATO.[107] These and other insights Kissinger relayed to Bundy, with the sole comment that he should handle the French intelligence "particularly discreetly."[108]

The problem with attacking John F. Kennedy was that he retained the ability to snatch political success from the jaws of strategic failure. The administration's handling of the Berlin problem had been less than ideal; it had made concessions to the Soviets; it had left the city divided under an anachronistic four-power arrangement, and divided it would remain until 1989. Yet when Kennedy traveled to the city in June 1963 as Willy Brandt's guest, it was to deliver one of the greatest speeches of his career.[109] Like millions of Germans, the industrialist Kurt Birrenbach was deeply moved by Kennedy's *"Ich bin ein Berliner"* address, delivered at the Schöneberg Rathaus, seat of the West Berlin Senate, on June 26. Kennedy's challenge to those who saw Communism as "the wave of the future"—*"Lass' sie nach Berlin kommen!* Let them come to Berlin!"—was thrilling in a way that no Rockefeller speech had ever been or ever would be. The key arguments could scarcely have been better put. His contempt for the wall was coruscating. His allusion to ancient Rome—*civis Romanus sum,* Kennedy said, had once been the equivalent of "I am a Berliner"—was a subtle affirmation of the transatlantic *Pax Americana.* And his affirmation that his ultimate goal was the reunification of Germany, not just of Berlin, was manifestly sincere as well as stirring. The speech had, Birrenbach told Kissinger, "moved the masses in a way which I have not seen in decades," as well as providing "immunization to the French temptations." ("I am not so sure I like the 'decades' implication," Kissinger wryly noted in a postscript to Schlesinger. "But then we can't have everything.")[110]

Kennedy was a hard act to follow, but follow him Rockefeller did, embarking just a few months later on a two-week tour of Europe, at Kissinger's suggestion and with Kissinger by his side. (As the trip took place at the beginning of the Harvard semester, Kissinger requested that there be no press release about it lest "the governing boards of

Harvard might wonder what one of the faculty members is doing jun-keting around Europe with a political figure.")[111] Significantly, how-ever, the two men avoided Germany. Indeed, they carefully avoided meeting anyone Kissinger had seen when working as a White House consultant.[112] (As he explained to Rusk, this was "to avoid any possible embarrassment to the Government" and "because it involves a some-what delicate point of honor.")[113]

The problem for Rockefeller was not just that Kennedy was a more gifted orator, nor that Kennedy had been able to make better use of Kissinger's European contacts. The problem was that on key foreign policy issues, Kennedy was succeeding. After the Soviets resumed atmospheric nuclear testing in August 1961, Kennedy had overridden Bundy's advice not to do the same.[114] At the same time, however, Ken-nedy proposed a ban on tests in the atmosphere to be monitored by national inspection systems. Kissinger at first urged Rockefeller not to show his hand on the issue, but on reflection he and Teller decided it would be better to support the Kennedy proposal.[115] From August 1962 until July 1963, Rockefeller and his team wriggled on the hook. In January 1963 Rockefeller issued a statement cautioning against a pro-longed unilateral test ban but was dismayed by the number of hostile letters from constituents it elicited.[116] Four months later Kissinger pro-posed an alternative scheme involving "fix[ing] an upper limit on fall-out and assign[ing] quotas to countries," but that was plainly too complicated to be politically viable.[117] In addition to Teller, Rockefeller picked the brains of Stanley Hoffmann, Bernard Brodie and Malcolm Hoag from RAND, and even Walt Rostow.[118] In the end—after Khru-shchev had unexpectedly dropped his opposition to Kennedy's proposal—Rockefeller came down, grudgingly, in favor of the partial test ban, which prohibited tests in the atmosphere, in outer space, or underwater but not underground.[119]

Along with the Partial Test Ban Treaty, the creation of a hotline to the Kremlin and the revival of disarmament talks at Geneva made the idea of détente a reality. It was difficult to oppose. In an interview with *US News & World Report,* Rockefeller attempted a comprehensive demolition of Kennedy's record on Cuba, NATO, Latin America, over-seas aid, and even Vietnam, charging him with "indecision, vacillation and weakness."[120] As we shall see, however, it was not as if Kennedy was backing away from the U.S. commitment to South Vietnam; rather the opposite. Another line of attack was the "Opening to the Left" in Italy, Fanfani's attempt to bring elements of the left into government at the national as well as the local level, which Kennedy supported. But the claim that this was opening the door to a "disastrous" Communist takeover seemed overblown.[121] The only way forward for Rockefeller seemed to be to "hit . . . the general cynicism and double talking of the Administration."[122] "In the realm of foreign policy," stated the campaign's "Press Kit Material," dated November 21, "Governor Rockefeller finds the Kennedy Administration 'bewildered, floundering in a sea of expedients.'" How could "an administration composed of so many knowledgeable people . . . stumble from crisis to crisis"? The answer was "a lack of understanding as to the nature of international politics" and a tendency "to place expediency above principle."[123]

There was no longer any point in being coy. Kissinger was now being referred to as "Rocky's military adviser" in *The Washington Post*.[124] But the campaign itself was ailing. Teller reported from California that Rockefeller was "finished," to which Kissinger could only reply, "My disgust at what is happening is as great as yours."[125] With the first Republican primary in New Hampshire still four months away, his life was already "hectic beyond description."[126] But so far as Kissinger could judge, in the crucial state of California Rockefeller was "almost completely unknown, except for his personal life." Most West Coast Republicans were "for Goldwater, but not in a way that could not be changed if they knew what the Governor stands for."[127] Kissinger's hope had been that he and Rockefeller's inner circle could establish exactly what Rockefeller did stand for before the presidential race got under way in earnest. Thus far they had not succeeded.

VI

John F. Kennedy's assassination by Lee Harvey Oswald in Dallas on November 22, 1963, changed the course of American history in ways that can never be known for certain. A second-term Kennedy administration might have been less inclined to escalate the war in Vietnam than Lyndon Johnson's was—might even have reversed course by withdrawing rather than reinforcing the twelve thousand American personnel who were already in South Vietnam when Kennedy died.[128] It probably would have been less bold in enacting the civil rights and "Great Society" legislation that were Johnson's most important domestic achievements.* In other respects, there would surely have been continuity.[129] What Kennedy's sudden and violent death ensured was that criticism of his presidency would be very difficult for years to come. It also had the effect of silencing, if only temporarily, those who had most consistently attacked his foreign policy. As soon as he heard the news, Kissinger telegraphed Bundy, "I WANT YOU TO KNOW THAT I AM THINKING OF YOU WITH DEEP SYMPATHY AT THIS SAD MOMENT."[130] It was a prosaic, even bathetic message, to be sure. But perhaps the noteworthy thing was that Kissinger felt the need to send Bundy a message at all, after the frustrations and disappointments of the previous three years.

In the thirty-day campaign moratorium that followed Kennedy's death, Kissinger had time to ponder how best Rockefeller should respond. Interestingly, he included in his draft an explicit affirmation of support for civil rights: "To the members of my own Party," Kissinger wrote, "I say that . . . we must choose to lead in the fight for civil rights. We must choose to lead in securing a better education, a decent job, a safe home and a healthy body for all men." The nation had suffered a "deep shock" as a result of the "senseless and violent attack" on the president. But "we have seen that men can vanish but our institutions survive. No bullets can destroy our constitutional process. . . . We have suffered a loss. But life goes on."[131] It was already clear to Kissinger that, on foreign policy issues, Rockefeller could not hope to outbid the hawkish Goldwater—a fierce proponent of "rollback," uncompromising in his hostility to all Communist regimes.[132] But that

---

*The consequences of a less progressive domestic program are especially hard to imagine. In Stephen King's alternative-history novel *11/22/63*, a reelected Kennedy finds himself presiding over a nationwide backlash against the civil rights movement that culminates in the election of Governor George Wallace of Alabama as president in 1968. Wallace then escalates the Vietnam War to the point of using nuclear weapons, with disastrous consequences.

created an important gap in public debate that was to prove fateful. If Kennedy was, at least for a time, above criticism, then there would be little chance to assess the record of flexible response. Kissinger's analysis of its defects, both strategic and tactical, would go into abeyance; the concessions made over Berlin and Cuba would be overlooked, and the contradictions of counterforce doctrine would be set aside.

The United States under Kennedy had chosen not to fight a conventional war over Berlin, nor over Cuba, for fear that it might escalate into a nuclear war. But détente reduced the risk of such an escalation. The paradox was that the conventional war the United States chose to fight—the one John F. Kennedy had already chosen to fight, the one that would escalate relentlessly and calamitously for the remainder of the 1960s—was not over strategically pivotal Berlin nor over an American near-neighbor, Cuba, but over a distant and strategically inconsequential former French colony: Vietnam.

Book IV

Book IV

The Road to Vietnam

I opposed the war while Kissinger supported it.
—HANS MORGENTHAU, 1969[1]

Oriana Fallaci: But don't you find, Dr. Kissinger, that it's
been a useless war?

Henry Kissinger: On this I can agree.
—INTERVIEW, 1972[2]

I

Ten years after the United States had withdrawn its last man, ignominiously, from Saigon, the journalist Joseph Lelyveld observed
acutely, "When we talk about Vietnam, we are seldom talking about
the country of that name or the situation of the people who live there.
Usually we are talking about ourselves. Probably we always were,
which is one conspicuous reason our leaders found it so hard to shape a
strategy that fit us and our chosen terrain."[3] There are many ways of
explaining why the United States came to grief so spectacularly in
Vietnam. But the plain fact of it will always be astounding. The United
States was not only five times more populous than Vietnam, its economy was seventy-six times larger. In 1964 there were only around ten
countries in the world, aside from sub-Saharan Africa, that were poorer
than Vietnam in terms of per capita gross domestic product, at a time
when the United States came in second only to Switzerland.[4] Technologically the gap between the two countries—not least in the realm of
armaments—was so large as to be well nigh immeasurable. Yet America

lost. Small wonder the Vietnam War became a trauma not just for those men who served in it but for all Americans of that generation.

Robert McNamara, who was secretary of defense throughout the period of military escalation, looked back in shame on at least six different failures for which he took at least some responsibility. There was the failure to consult allies, despite the existence of the Southeast Asia Treaty Organization (SEATO) since 1954; the failure to appreciate how a people in arms could withstand and overcome the most sophisticated weaponry; the failure to see the limits of economic and military aid in the process of state building; the failure to uphold democratic principles in the governance of South Vietnam; the failure to understand the complex relationship between the application of military force and the achievement of political objectives; and above all, the failure of the American decision-making process itself. Policy makers "did not raise fundamental questions, did not address issues about policy choices, and did not recognize their failure to do so." To explain this, McNamara blamed lack of time, lack of institutional memory within the government, and "the incremental nature of decision-making about intervention in Vietnam [which] never allowed policymakers an opportunity to step back."[5]

Another member of the flagellant order of former Kennedy-Johnson officials was McGeorge Bundy. In a memorandum written as late as May 1967—a year after he had left the administration to run the Ford Foundation—Bundy could still assure the president, "The fact that South Vietnam has not been lost and is not going to be lost is a fact of truly massive importance in the history of Asia, the Pacific and the U.S." Nearly thirty years later Bundy added a simple marginal note: "McGB all *wrong*." His explanation for the American failure was a basic underestimation of "*the endurance of the enemy*."[6]

As John Gaddis has argued, an intervention like the one in Vietnam was a logical consequence of the strategy of flexible response. It was not necessary to subscribe uncritically to Eisenhower's domino theory to "believe deeply"—as Walt Rostow put it to Bobby Kennedy in August 1961—that the way to "save Southeast Asia and to minimize the chances of deep U.S. military involvement there is for the President to make a bold decision [for *limited* military involvement] very soon." Moreover, flexible response implied precise calibration of the use of force: what seemed a small threat could be met by a small intervention, and if the threat turned out to be bigger than expected, then military pressure could simply be turned up like the volume on one of those transistor radios that were ubiquitous in the Vietnam era. But the result in practice was "not 'fine tuning' but clumsy overreaction, not coordination but disproportion, not strategic precision, but, in the end, a strategic vacuum."[7]

Systems analysis gave the technocrats who infested the Pentagon the illusion that progress toward victory could be measured as accurately as the output of vehicles from a General Motors plant. The most dogged adherents of the strategy of escalating the U.S. military involvement were those, like Walt Rostow, who suffered most from what behavioral psychologists call confirmation bias—the "automatic mental filter [that] . . . accepted only reinforcing data, while systematically and totally rejecting all contrary evidence no matter how compelling."[8] There will doubtless continue to be books written, showing how the United States was capable of winning the Vietnam War. But such arguments invariably rest on too narrow a conception of victory. They focus on operational successes and overlook the massive strategic misjudgment that lay behind each and every operation.[9] Clausewitz taught us that war is "not merely an act of policy but a true political instrument, a continuation of political intercourse, carried on with other means" (*On War*, book 1, chapter 1).[10] On that basis, any argument that represents Vietnam as a military victory but a political failure collapses.

It has long been assumed—since Hans Morgenthau first asserted it in 1969—that Henry Kissinger "supported" the Vietnam War throughout the 1960s and that this was indeed one of the key reasons Richard Nixon offered him the job of national security adviser. This view is incorrect. While Kissinger certainly began by thinking—like McNamara, like Bundy, like Rostow—that South Vietnam needed to be defended against Communist aggression, he realized far sooner than they did that the Kennedy and Johnson administrations were bungling that defense. In public, on the few occasions he was called upon to do so, he defended the Johnson administration. But in private, as the archival records show, he was a scathing critic. Why then did he keep his criticism private? The answer is that Kissinger was not content to carp from the sidelines. Beginning in 1965, when he made the first of three trips to Vietnam in a sustained attempt to improve his understanding of the war, he sought to salvage the situation, first by recommending improvements to the American counterinsurgency strategy, then—to an extent never previously recognized by scholars—by seeking to broker some kind of peace agreement with the North Vietnamese, using a variety of indirect channels of communication to Hanoi that passed through not only Paris but also Moscow.

II

The origins of the Vietnam War can be traced back as far as 1956, though it is always important to remember that the United States could have changed course at almost any time between then and 1965—the crucial year when Lyndon Johnson increased the U.S. military presence beyond the level at which a unilateral withdrawal could have been achieved at a modest cost.

It was the Eisenhower administration that opted not to sign the 1954 Geneva Accords* and, for fear of a Communist victory, winked at the South Vietnamese government's decision to cancel the election that was due to take place in July 1956. The goal was to "support a friendly noncommunist South Vietnam,"[11] but in practice that meant open-ended military and economic aid to the Catholic, conservative, and corrupt president Ngo Dinh Diem and his brother and chief adviser, Ngo Dinh Nhu, who between them had ousted Emperor Bao Dai after a rigged referendum.

Part of what constrained U.S. policy makers in the case of Vietnam

---

*Under the agreements reached at the end of the 1954 Geneva conference, France agreed to withdraw its troops from Indochina, which was split into three countries: Laos, Cambodia, and Vietnam. Vietnam was to be temporarily divided along the 17th parallel until elections could be held, after which the country would be united. However, the United States did not sign the document, and the elections never took place. Although Walter Bedell Smith, the U.S. representative at Geneva, appeared to commit Washington to abide by them, in practice the United States backed Ngo Dinh Diem's proclamation of South Vietnam as an independent state.

was the widespread perception that Eisenhower had been too soft on neighboring Laos. There American pressure had sufficed to keep the Communist Pathet Lao out of power, but not to prevent a neutralist government led by Prime Minister Souvanna Phouma from accepting substantial amounts of Soviet aid, including arms, designed to achieve "the liquidation of the sources of international intervention in this region and the neutralization of this country."[12] The usual Cold War standoff developed, with money pouring into the country from both superpowers, the Soviets backing Phouma, the Americans his rival, General Phoumi Nosavan. A military coup in 1960 seemed to set the stage for Nosavan to take over, but North Vietnamese incursions rapidly turned a large part of the country into a thoroughfare (the "Ho Chi Minh Trail") for supplies to support the Communist insurgents known as the Vietcong in South Vietnam.[13] The disintegration of Laos, Eisenhower warned Kennedy as he prepared to hand over the White House, was "the most important problem facing the U.S." and might necessitate military intervention.[14]

In the spring of 1961 preparations were actually begun to send at least some U.S.-led forces to Laos. But this was a bluff. Kennedy, smarting from the Bay of Pigs fiasco, was happy to accept a British initiative whereby an international conference in Geneva paved the way for a broadly based neutral government, again led by Phouma but now including the Pathet Lao.[15] Despite the reservations of McNamara and Bundy, Averell Harriman persuaded the president that a neutralist government, even with Communist ministers, was preferable to a civil war.[16] In the final analysis, Kennedy did not regard Laos as "worthy of engaging the attention of great powers," while Khrushchev was content to wait for the country to "fall into our laps like a ripe apple."[17]

When Kennedy first asked his deputy national security adviser, Walt Rostow, about Laos—which was on January 9, 1961—Rostow "told him I simply didn't know enough about the situation to give him a judgment."[18] For reasons that are not obvious, Rostow felt no such inhibition about giving the president overconfident judgments about Vietnam. "Surely we are hooked in Viet-Nam," he argued later that year; "surely we shall honor our . . . SEATO commitment."[19] Already Rostow was forming the view that bombing North Vietnam would bring the country's rudimentary economy to its knees.[20] Like so many in the administration, his unquestioned assumption was that the bloody guerrilla war and terrorist campaign being waged by the Vietcong in South Vietnam was sponsored and run by the North. NSC staffer Robert Komer agreed: "American reaction to continued aggression would be carefully calibrated to alert the communists that U.S. policy was firmly supportive of a noncommunist South Vietnam, that the United States was willing and able to retaliate militarily to any increased communist pressure on South Vietnam and that military reprisals would intensify if communist pressure persisted."[21] By May 1961, the NSC had reached a consensus: the U.S. commitment to a non-Communist South Vietnam was essential and irrevocable.[22] NSAM 52, dated May 11, defined the goals of policy as being "to prevent Communist domination of South Vietnam; to create in that country a viable and increasingly democratic society, and to initiate, on an accelerated basis, a series of mutually supporting actions of a military, political, economic, psychological and covert character designed to achieve this objective." It also authorized "full examination by the Defense Department . . . of the size and composition of forces which would be desirable in the case of a possible commitment of U.S. forces to Vietnam."[23]

A visit to Vietnam with General Maxwell Taylor in October 1961 confirmed Rostow as the ringleader of the "hard hawks."[24] When Assistant Secretary of State Averell Harriman proposed a negotiated settlement, as in Laos, Rostow shot back:

> If we postpone action in Vietnam to engage in talks with the communists, we can surely count on a crisis of nerve in Viet-Nam and throughout Southeast Asia. The image of U.S. unwillingness to confront Communism—induced by the Laos performance—will be regarded as definitely confirmed. There will be panic and disarray. . . . If we negotiate now—while infiltration continues—we shall in fact be judged weaker than in Laos.[25]

Only with difficulty was Dean Rusk able to resist the Taylor-Rostow recommendation that eight thousand American troops accompany the throng of advisers, experts, and military instructors who were now sent to clean up the regime in Saigon—a recommendation that McNamara, and even some State Department officials (notably Robert H. Johnson), had endorsed.[26] Bundy, too, had come to believe in the need for committing "*limited* U.S. combat units, if necessary for *military* purposes (not for morale), to help save South Vietnam." The issue, he told Kennedy, had already "become a sort of touchstone of our will."[27] The pressure on Rusk only grew as the hawks were emboldened by the apparent success of going "eyeball to eyeball" over the Cuban missiles. "The whole lesson of the cold war, including the recent Cuban crisis," Rostow explained as he sought to convince Rusk of the benefits of air strikes, "is that the communists do not escalate in response to our actions."[28]

Intervention in Vietnam was, in short, flexible response in action. In his "Basic National Security Policy" (March 1962), Rostow urged Kennedy to "expand our arsenal of limited overt and covert counter-measures if we are in fact to make crisis-mongering, deeply built into Communist ideology and working habits, an unprofitable occupation."[29] Conversely, major losses of territory would, he argued, "make it harder for the U.S. to create the kind of world environment it desires . . . generate defeatism among governments and peoples in the non-Communist world, or give rise to frustrations at home."[30] To be sure, there were dissonant voices. J. K. Galbraith foresaw "the consequent danger [that] we shall replace the French as the colonial force in the area and bleed as the French did";[31] even Douglas MacArthur warned Kennedy that "there was no end to Asia and even if we poured a million American infantry soldiers into that continent, we would still find ourselves outnumbered on every side."[32] It made little difference. From strategic hamlets to defoliation, key elements of the U.S. war effort were already in place before Kennedy's assassination handed the presidency to Johnson.

As an idealist committed to resisting the Communist advance and an advocate of "limited war," Kissinger might have been expected to favor a hard line on Vietnam. His first comments on the subject were certainly hawkish in tone. As early as June 1961 he dismissed as "disingenuous" Walter Lippmann's argument that "we should not get involved in Southeast Asia lest we weaken the defenses in Quemoy, Matsu and

Berlin."[33] Speaking about Laos while in Pakistan the following February, he expressed "an unorthodox view which is not shared by many in our military establishments . . . that Laos was a rather good place to fight a conventional action.

> I don't see how the Chinese could have maintained substantial forces over the one road that is available to them if our Air Force is capable of doing anything, and I am personally of the opinion that if you ask about an area where one could fight a conventional action, an area where the aggressor has only one or two communication lines, where he is pretty far removed from his industrial potential and which is unsuitable for a massive operation, Laos is not a bad place to fight it.[34]

By this time, Kissinger was on his way out of the Kennedy administration and had resumed his work as an adviser to Nelson Rockefeller. A February 1962 briefing document ahead of a Rockefeller TV appearance reveals again the conditional nature of Kissinger's position. In answer to the stock question "Do you approve of U.S. actions in South Vietnam?" Kissinger wrote,

> All history proves that there is no cheap and easy way to defeat guerrilla movements. South Vietnam has been plagued by Communist Viet Cong attacks ever since it became independent in 1954. Their defeat can only be accomplished by adequate military force. I hope that we are aware of this and have made the internal commitment to ourselves to see that a sufficient military effort is made to end the guerrilla attacks; we cannot be content with just maintaining an uneasy peace.
>
> However, merely physical security will not solve the problem. The people of South Vietnam must develop a long-term commitment to their government if they wish to attain political and economic stability. . . .
>
> I regret that the JFK Administration has seemingly reversed its position of demanding governmental reform prior to ad-

ditional assistance and is now giving the aid without evidence
of substantial reform.[35]

Many hands were involved in drafting Rockefeller's key position
papers as he geared himself up for another run for the presidency, but
it is clear that Kissinger's made some crucial amendments to an April
1962 paper on Vietnam, which again emphasized the difficulty of
fighting a guerrilla war:

a. The present U.S. military program seems half-hearted and
   inadequate and may combine the worst features of every
   course of action. It may get us slowly into a war that a
   decisive effort now might prevent.

b. There are risks involved in stepping up our military effort
   in South Vietnam. However, it is likely that if we do not
   use our strength here we will have to fight somewhere
   else in Southeast Asia [added:] under worse
   circumstances.

c. ~~Many~~ Some people ~~fear~~ argue that if the U.S. greatly
   increases its military aid effort the situation may escalate
   into a major war. However, ~~it must be taken into
   consideration that the present gradual increase in the use of
   small forces is in itself escalation.~~ the worst course is a
   commitment just large enough to contain the guerrillas but
   not large enough to defeat them. This almost certainly will
   get us into a big war.[36]

In a similar vein, Kissinger advised Rockefeller to emphasize that
the United States had been "outmaneuvered by the Soviets" in Laos,
with the result that the country was now being used as "a corridor for
supplies to S. Viet-Nam."[37] A May 1962 position paper even recommended the "commitment of U.S. military forces in Laos" with a similar argument Kissinger had already made about Vietnam: "if we do not
defend Laos, we may be forced later to fight under even worse circumstances elsewhere. . . . Either we must decide to defend Laos, and must

be willing to commit adequate military force to do so, or we must be willing to move back and draw our line of defense in South Vietnam, Cambodia and Thailand."[38] This warning that ineffectual action now might lead to a "big war" in another location "under worse circumstances" was rather different from uncritical support of the Kennedy administration's policy.

That policy reached a crisis point in the fall of 1963. By this time, Kennedy had in fact come to the view that, as his press spokesman put it on October 2, "the major part of the U.S. military task [in Vietnam] can be completed by the end of 1965 . . . [and] that by the end of this year . . . 1,000 military personnel can be withdrawn" out of a total of more than 16,700 Americans then in Vietnam.[39] This was McNamara's recommended "way to get out of Vietnam," based on a visit with Max Taylor, who was now appointed chairman of the Joint Chiefs of Staff. NSAM 263, dated October 11, explicitly referred to "the implementation of plans to withdraw" troops from Vietnam.[40] What went wrong? The answer "Kennedy was assassinated" is too simple, for it overlooks the disastrous sequence of events in Saigon that had been set in motion the previous August, when Roger Hilsman, who ran the East Asia desk at the State Department, drafted a cable addressed to the U.S. ambassador in Saigon stating that President Diem must "rid himself" of his brother Nhu or forfeit American support. Averell Harriman approved the text, including the menacing line, "If in spite of all your efforts, Diem remains obdurate and refuses, then we must face the possibility that Diem cannot be preserved."

It was high summer. The president was in Hyannis Port. Rusk was at the United Nations. McNamara, Bundy, Taylor, and McCone were all out of town. George Ball, Rusk's number two at State, was playing golf with Alexis Johnson, but Harriman and Hilsman tracked them down to secure Ball's approval. Though one of the administration's doves, Ball had nothing but contempt for Diem and Nhu, so—after a perfunctory call to Rusk—he toned down the language and called the president, with whom he "went over the whole thing." Kennedy's instruction was to send the cable provided Ros Gilpatric signed off on behalf of the Pentagon. Believing that Kennedy himself had already approved it, Gilpatric did not hesitate to do so.[41] When they found out about the telegram, McNamara and Taylor were incandescent, and Rusk immediately instructed Saigon to rescind the instruction. ("My God!" an exasperated Kennedy exclaimed to the journalist Charles Bartlett. "My government is coming apart.")[42] However, the newly arrived ambassador, who had formed a very low opinion of both Diem and Nhu, drew his own inference.[43]

Henry Cabot Lodge, Jr., had been Nixon's running mate in 1960. Kennedy's decision to appoint him ambassador to South Vietnam was one of his many attempts to build bridges to moderate Republicans. It was a mistake. Kissinger was fond of Lodge but was also aware of his intellectual and temperamental shortcomings. In Saigon, Lodge liked to show visitors the gun he always carried with him. He was appalled to learn that Nhu was an opium addict and even more appalled by the overbearing Madame Nhu. Lodge itched for action, and the idea of a coup against Diem offered just that. When the August 24 telegram was rescinded, Lodge protested to Rusk and urged that aid to Diem be cut off.[44] As rumors of a coup flew around Saigon, the president changed his mind. On October 6, he cabled Lodge that "the United States will not thwart a coup."[45]

On November 1, Diem telephoned Lodge to tell him that his own generals were threatening him. Lodge replied that it was four-thirty a.m. in Washington and that the "U.S. government could not possibly have a view," but if he could do anything "for your physical safety, please call me." Diem and his brother were shot, their hands tied behind their backs, their corpses mutilated. The plotters' claim that they had committed suicide was risible. When Kennedy heard the news, according to Taylor, he "leaped to his feet and rushed from the room with a look of shock and dismay." This was surely theater. Kennedy, by the admission of his own secretary of state, had as good as given the order for the coup. As Lodge told Kissinger when they met in Saigon two years later, the president had not just had foreknowledge of the coup; he had been directly responsible for it. Kissinger replied bluntly that "I thought many of the current difficulties stemmed from that period."[46]

The overthrow of Diem was not only a genuinely criminal act; it was also a strategic disaster. Far from strengthening the South Vietnamese state, it had precisely the opposite effect, increasing its dependence on the United States. In an act that wholly invalidated all the earlier talk of reducing troop levels, Kennedy had to all intents and purposes made it clear that the government in Saigon was as much a creature of the United States as that in Budapest was a creature of the Soviet Union. In both cases, the incumbents owed their power to a bloody superpower-sponsored coup.

At the time, unlike most observers, Kissinger understood the magnitude of the blunder. As early as September 1963, he had urged Rockefeller to condemn Kennedy for "apparently encouraging a military revolt and otherwise undermining the existing government."[47] A month later he had denounced "public attacks by the Administration on the Diem Government" as just the latest examples of "the unfortunate style of conducting policy by press releases and confusing public relations gimmicks with diplomacy."

> The chief object of any guerilla war is to demoralize the existing government. If we undermine the Diem regime, we are really doing the Viet Cong's work for them. Moreover, how can our encouragement of a military revolt against the Diem government be reconciled with our disapproval of military revolts in other parts of the world? . . .
>
> A public announcement by Secretary McNamara that we would withdraw 1,000 troops by the end of this year and the remainder by 1965 must give comfort to the Viet Cong. It must have proved to the Communists that if they hold out long enough, they are bound to prevail.[48]

Clearly, Kissinger was not advocating withdrawal from Vietnam at this stage. He remained committed to the strategy of winning the guerrilla war against the Vietcong. But he understood far better than anyone in the administration that such a war could not be won by firepower alone; it was a psychological war—and in those terms undermining Diem was a self-inflicted wound.

When the news broke of Diem's murder, Kissinger was indignant. In an angry letter to Rockefeller on November 6, 1963, he summed up his position:

a) There is a vague moral uneasiness about Vietnam which it seems to me somebody has to crystallize.

b) Our policy has been shameful and you would perform a great service to be the first national leader to speak out against it.

c) Conditions [*sic*] in Vietnam will, in my judgment, get worse. It would be important to warn against this.

d) You would have picked an issue on which you are morally right and at the same time should be able to unite many Republicans.

The counterargument is that Lodge will undoubtedly support the Administration. But if we take this seriously we are debarred from ever raising the Vietnam issue—one of the most effective issues we have.[49]

Convinced that a dire mistake had been made, Kissinger hastily composed a statement for Rockefeller, which—had it been issued—would have radically redefined the terms of the debate on Vietnam:

The government of an allied country—which had been established originally with strong U.S. support—has been overthrown by a military coup encouraged by our government. Its leaders have been assassinated. . . . A thinly disguised military dictatorship has been established. I am deeply worried about a U.S. policy which has given rise to such methods. The honor and the moral standing of the United States require that a relationship exists between ends and means. . . . Is it conceivable that the troop movements leading to the coup could have occurred without our knowledge? Would the leaders of the junta have revolted had they been given to understand, in their talks with Secretary McNamara less than a month ago, that our abhorrence of military coups was not confined to Latin America?

Kissinger drew a parallel between what had happened in Laos, where a neutralist coalition had been installed with Soviet support, and

what had happened in Vietnam. Neither case sent an encouraging signal to other U.S. allies. But the case of Vietnam was the more troubling. "For the Diem regime was not just any government. The United
States was largely responsible for its establishment in 1955 and backed it
in its struggle to establish a viable state in a partitioned country." Yet
now Diem's ouster was being justified "with the argument that the
Diem government was losing the war against the Communist guerrillas. This contrasts strangely with repeated, highly optimistic accounts
from the Administration about the struggle against the Vietcong."
Kissinger, as an "outsider," did not presume "to judge the effectiveness
of the war effort of the Diem regime," but he was able to identify the
"objective obstacles to an effective policy in South Vietnam, regardless
of which government is in power," namely the opening up of the Laos-
Vietnamese border to "guerrilla infiltration" and the innate advantages
of guerrillas fighting with outside support from a "privileged sanctuary." To these obstacles was now added a third that Diem had not
faced: the appearance of being a "U.S. puppet," which was likely to
"undermine the popular support essential to the successful prosecution
of a guerrilla war." In reality, and paradoxically, the new government
was in "an ever stronger position to be intractable towards us than its
predecessor" because, "having been publicly embroiled with one Vietnamese government, we are in a poor position to bring pressure on its
successor." All in all, principle had been sacrificed to expediency. And
Kissinger concluded in terms that once again marked him out as an
idealist compared with the unscrupulous pragmatists of Camelot:

> [N]o American can take pride that our government should
> have been associated with events leading to the assassination of
> two leaders with whom we were formally allied. I do not like
> our country to be thought of in terms of the cynical use of
> power. Our strength is principle not manipulativeness. Our
> historical role has been to identify ourselves with the ideals and
> deepest hopes of mankind. If we lost [*sic*] this asset, temporary
> successes will be meaningless.[50]

III

Lyndon Baines Johnson was not a very nice man. When Kennedy offered him the number-two spot on the 1960 Democratic ticket, he had got his staff to find out how many presidents in the previous hundred years had died in office. The answer was five out of eighteen. "Clare, I looked it up," he told Clare Boothe Luce, "one out of every four Presidents has died in office. I'm a gamblin' man, darlin', and this is the only chance I got."[51] Johnson was corrupt as well as base, as journalists investigating the business activities of his friend Bobby Baker discovered. He was also an alcoholic, like his father before him, with a fondness for Cutty Sark scotch on the rocks matched only by his addictions to coffee and cigarettes. He gave up only nicotine after his 1955 heart attack. Early in his career, Johnson had diluted his drinks on the basis that "[d]rinking makes you lose control." But he liked others to lose control. In his office, guests' drinks were always regular strength; his were not. It was only on his Texas ranch that Johnson would binge drink. As he rose to the top of the greasy pole, however, his consumption of alcohol in Washington grew. "I had seen people smoke and drink at dinner before," one journalist recalled, but Johnson "did it like a man trying to kill himself."[52] One day there will be a thorough study of the role played by lunchtime drinking in the escalation of the war in Vietnam—though at least one participant maintains that Johnson did not consume alcohol at the regular Tuesday lunches he held with his senior advisers.

Johnson's defining characteristic, honed in the Senate, was his ability to bend others to his will. Norman Mailer, among others, had been struck by the cool, detached quality of John F. Kennedy. There was nothing cool or detached about Johnson, who enjoyed imposing himself on others, beginning with a bone-crushing handshake. To Bobby Kennedy, who grew to hate him, he was "mean, bitter, vicious—an animal in many ways."[53] But even those who admired Johnson ought to have wondered how prudent it was to have such a bully just a few well-aimed bullets away from the most powerful office in the world.

At first, Johnson was content to continue Kennedy's Janus-faced policy. His first statement on the subject of Vietnam was unequivocally equivocal. The "central point" and "overriding objective" of U.S. policy on South Vietnam" was still "to assist the new government there in winning the war against the Communist Vietcong insurgents," but the goal of withdrawing a thousand U.S. military personnel also remained. That was also the essence of NSAM 273, though it added the possibility of "military operations up to a line up to 50 kilometers inside Laos."[54] The Kennedy foreign policy team was kept intact, even if it meant enlisting Bundy's mother to persuade her son to stay on.[55] George Ball had the impression that Johnson was more focused on the domestic legislative program he had inherited than on "the problems of Vietnam which were cranking along."[56] But as the news from South Vietnam deteriorated in the course of December 1963—to the point that McNamara warned that South Vietnam was heading for "neutralization at best, and most likely to a Communist-controlled state"—Johnson began to fret. Even more than for Kennedy, foreign policy for Johnson was the continuation of domestic politics by other means. "Do you want another China?" he asked, remembering the way the Republicans had taunted Truman for "losing China" after Mao's triumph in 1949. "I don't want these people around the world worrying about us, and they are . . . [t]hey are worried about whether you've got a weak President or a strong President."[57] As he explained to John Knight of Knight Ridder newspapers, if he opted to "run and let the dominoes start falling over . . . God almighty, what they said about us leaving China would just be warming up compared to what they'd say now."[58]

Johnson was bound to think about domestic politics, to be fair. 1964 was an election year, and although voters would be going to the polls less than a year after his predecessor's assassination, he was disinclined to count on sympathy votes. His best hope, as it turned out, lay in the divisions that threatened to tear the Republican Party apart. Rockefeller, once again, was the candidate of the liberally inclined Northeast—of the so-called "Establishment." The challenger was Barry Goldwater, an Arizona-born pilot who had been elected to the Senate in 1952 and had never been anything other than a red-in-tooth-and-claw conservative. (He had once argued for "lob[bing] one into the men's room of the Kremlin" and wanted to undo the New Deal.) Unlike Nixon, Goldwater was the darling of the ideological right. The Draft Goldwater Committee had been founded by Peter O'Donnell, the Texas State Republican chairman, F. Clifton White, the leader of the Young Republicans, and William Rusher of the *National Review,* all of whom regarded Nixon as an unprincipled trimmer.[59]

Each of the two front-runners had one great strength. Rockefeller had money. Goldwater had an army of eager young "suburban warriors," ready to knock on doors all over America, each of them clutching a copy of Goldwater's ghostwritten manifesto, *The Conscience of a Conservative,* with its heady mixture of small government, states' rights (code for opposition to civil rights),* and "liberty or death" anti-Communism. But each had a serious weakness. Goldwater's was his tendency to say things off the cuff—but on the record—that were extreme, even outlandish, on issues ranging from civil rights to the Cold War. Rockefeller's Achilles' heel was his private life. If it had been a simple two-horse race, Rockefeller might have won, despite his divorce, remarriage, and new baby. But it never was so simple. Nixon had ruled himself out but repeatedly hinted (like Rockefeller four years before) that he might accept the nomination if drafted by the party leadership. Despite being in Saigon, Henry Cabot Lodge entered the lists, encouraged by Eisenhower. So did the governor of Pennsylvania, William W. Scranton—also encouraged by Eisenhower, who never gave any candidate his unqualified backing. And so, finally, did Michigan governor George Romney. The net effect of these additional candidates proved fatal to Rockefeller.[60]

Much that Rockefeller did in the race for the nomination was ill advised. In the summer of 1963 he railed against "extremist elements"— "Birchers and others of the radical right lunatic fringe"—whose methods included "threatening letters, smear and hate literature, strong-arm and goon tactics, bomb threats and bombings, infiltration and takeover of established political organizations by Communist and Nazi methods"— in short, the "tactics of totalitarianism."[61] It didn't work: Goldwater

---

*Goldwater had voted against the 1964 Civil Rights Act on ground that Titles II and VII unduly extended the power of the federal government over business.

surged in the polls.[62] Rockefeller also wholly underestimated the effect on core Republican voters of his marital shenanigans: it was not yet "the Sixties" in rural New Hampshire, where the crucial first primary was to be held and where people still thought it wrong "for a man to throw away his old wife and take up with a younger woman."[63] And he made the mistake of worrying about Nixon—despite Kissinger's advice "to ignore Nixon completely until he declares himself"[64]—when the real threat was the absentee candidate Lodge, whose enthusiastic supporters ran such an effective write-in campaign on his behalf that he actually won the New Hampshire primary by a huge margin, a blow from which Rockefeller never fully recovered.[65] (Kissinger later reproached Lodge for not "get[ting] out of the race in New Hampshire and urg[ing] his supporters to support Rockefeller." Lodge said he hadn't expected to get so many votes.)[66]

Conventional wisdom dictated that all politics was local, and no politics was more local than party primaries in states like New Hampshire. It was true that foreign policy issues came at the bottom of the list of voters' priorities,[67] compared with domestic economic issues like Social Security and civil rights. But Goldwater seemed to go out of his way to provoke Rockefeller on international issues. He characterized Rockefeller's support for the administration's idea of selling U.S. wheat to the Soviet Union as the political equivalent of "Me Too."[68] He suggested on *Meet the Press* that diplomatic recognition of the USSR ought to be withdrawn.[69] He argued for arming the Cuban exiles to launch another invasion of their homeland.[70] He called on the administration to violate the Test Ban Treaty. He proposed that, in a crisis, the NATO commander should be empowered to use tactical nuclear missiles without reference to the president. He floated the idea of amending the UN Charter in order to get rid of the Soviet veto on the Security Council.[71] He even cast aspersions on the "dependability" of U.S. nuclear missiles.[72]

As Rockefeller's chief foreign policy adviser, Kissinger was kept busy knocking these idiosyncratic ideas on the head. It was disconcerting work. He had gone to considerable trouble to ensure that Rockefeller was briefed on international issues like the space race by heavyweights like George Kistiakowsky.[73] But Goldwater seemed to be getting his scientific briefings from *MAD* magazine's Alfred E.

Neuman. ("What, me worry?") The difficulty was that, as Kissinger admitted, there were some issues about which Rockefeller and Goldwater essentially agreed.[74] But where they parted company, it was Rockefeller and *The New York Times* who agreed.[75] There was something unconvincing to Republican voters about Rockefeller's characterizations of Goldwater's more extreme positions as "irresponsible," "dangerous," and "radical." "I don't believe," he told the *Times*, "that the answer to the failures in the foreign policy of the present administration is to be found in a reckless belligerance [*sic*]."[76] Many Republicans in 1964 firmly believed in belligerence.

It was on Vietnam that Kissinger believed Rockefeller should take a stand. To the right, there was Goldwater, arguing for "carrying the war to North Vietnam" and musing that ten years ago the United States could just have dropped a low-yield A-bomb on Hanoi. To the left was Johnson, continuing with the obviously self-contradictory policy of increasing control over Saigon while pledging to withdraw troops. Voters were uncertain. A poll of Republicans and Republican-leaning independents in early 1964 revealed that while 46 percent thought the United States was doing enough in Vietnam, 12 percent wanted to do more, 22 percent less, and 20 percent didn't know.[77] In the electorate as a whole, only around a third of voters wanted to step up the U.S. effort. Paradoxically, LBJ had a net approval rating of 68 percent on "keeping the country out of war."[78]

Beginning as early as October 1963, Kissinger bombarded Rockefeller with novel arguments about Vietnam, urging him to differentiate himself from the other candidates and exploit the public uncertainty. He should argue that it was time to press the Chinese to have "a restraining influence on the aggressive policies of the North Vietnamese." He should point out the disturbing resemblances between Laos and Cambodia, another weak monarchy that was already being used to supply the Vietcong and might end up being "neutralized."[79] On January 16, 1964, Rod Perkins and he produced a draft statement in which Rockefeller was to call on Johnson to tell "the American people frankly just what this Nation's policies and objectives in Southeast Asia really are." Once again, this was not a call for withdrawal; on the contrary, the line remained that "our failure to defeat the Communist guerrilla movement in Vietnam will lead to the extension of Communism throughout all of Southeast Asia." But at the risk of implying still further escalation, Kissinger now wanted Rockefeller to demand an admission from Johnson that the war was going badly, and to argue that it was going badly because the Vietcong enjoyed the inherent advantages of guerrillas with outside support.[80]

Kissinger was certainly right that Rockefeller's campaign for the Republican nomination was foundering. Whether adopting a more critical stance on Vietnam would have helped matters is another matter, but that is not really the issue. The striking thing is how early Kissinger parted company with the Kennedy-Johnson strategy: even before the coup against Diem. Unfortunately, the political professionals on the Rockefeller campaign regarded what he was proposing as altogether too risky. The January 16 statement on Vietnam went through eight drafts and was then buried when it was released on January 29. A second, more orthodox statement went through two drafts and was issued on February 23 despite Kissinger's "explicit object[ion]." A third was never used. Not until April 26 did the candidate make a Vietnam statement of which Kissinger approved. Three months previously, Kissinger was convinced, this would have been a remarkably prescient critique of the Democrats' policy.[81] Procrastinating was a blunder, he insisted, in terms of both campaign strategy and grand strategy. "Foreign policy," Kissinger argued, "is the area where your differences with the Administration are most obvious. It counteracts the likely Goldwater strategy of labeling you as close to the Democrats."[82]

Over dinner in early February 1964, Kissinger and Rockefeller had a heart-to-heart discussion of the campaign. After he returned to his desk, Kissinger resolved to unburden himself with an unvarnished memorandum. "Your chief opponent is not Goldwater," Kissinger argued, "but the so-called 'dark horses': Scranton, Lodge, Nixon. Goldwater will defeat himself." As for Johnson, "[t]he area in which [he] is most vulnerable is foreign policy. Here his instincts are least developed. He has inherited a terrible legacy. Many crises are beyond his control. His advisors are the very people who have produced the existing critical situation." Yet Rockefeller's other advisers had systematically thwarted Kissinger's repeated attempts even to "have a discussion of the Vietnam statement." Instead, the campaign had issued random documents on the UN, the space race, and the like, without any regard for the overall strategy. "The current process," Kissinger complained, "overemphasizes short-term public relations considerations at the expense of the fundamental moral concerns which are your primary raison d'etre. The quest for tomorrow's headline jeopardizes your capacity to lead six months from now."[83] "The greatest contribution you can make to our country is to advocate the programs which represent what you most deeply believe. The test of your role is not tomorrow's editorial but the one three or five years from now. Only such an attitude can reverse the collapse of values and of thought which has characterized so much of our post-war policy."[84]

This memorandum went through multiple drafts over several days, each iteration marked "strictly personal and confidential," and each ending with the recommendation that Rockefeller create "a group of senior advisers charged with coordinating strategy, substance and image." Kissinger accompanied the final version with a request that Rockefeller not show it to any other member of his staff and an ambiguous addendum about Rod Perkins.*[85] His advice was heeded. Shortly afterward Rockefeller created a six-man "Substantive Group." Among its members were both Kissinger and Perkins.[86]

Kissinger was now entirely caught up in the tactical battle for the Republican nomination. He offered to speak on Rockefeller's behalf on the West Coast (though he warned that "I generally do better in a non-partisan than on [*sic*] a partisan setting").[87] He opposed hiring the journalist Don Whitehead to mount a last-minute challenge in Massachusetts ("a political prostitute of the first order").[88] He favored targeting Johnson's "thin skin" and extolled the political benefits of "absolutely infuriat[ing] him."[89] But on the issue of content he was consistent. "I believe that the Vietnam situation is a mess," he wrote on January 24, "but I also think that Johnson will do something about it before too much time has passed. I would strongly urge that we assert

---

*"His view of priorities is not always mine. He is very literal minded and very aggressive in carrying out what he understands to be your wishes. His insistence sometimes makes me very nervous."

a leadership position here."[90] In deference to Rockefeller's greater knowledge of Latin America, he was willing to broaden the attack on the administration's policy to include Cuba, Brazil, and even Panama and to allege a general "leadership gap."[91] But the scripted answer for a Rockefeller press conference in New Hampshire kept Vietnam as the punch line: "Cuba is a Communist bastion and Panama is in turmoil. Laos is sliding under the Bamboo Curtain, Cambodia may follow, and in Vietnam the Communists are apparently winning the war."[92]

Nevertheless, Kissinger remained a lone voice on the issue. As late as March 17, 1964, there was still no consensus on Vietnam within the Rockefeller camp, beyond emphasizing "the importance of South Vietnam to all of Southeast Asia" and "the demoralizing effect . . . of American policy confusion."[93] As early as February 24, Kissinger declared impatiently that he "no longer [had] any confidence that my understanding of what is correct policy and that of those who clear these statements" coincided.[94] It was, he declared in April, an "appalling . . . confession of futility" that Rockefeller had failed to make a substantial statement on the subject in six months of campaigning, as Vietnam and Cuba were now "the two biggest issues we have in foreign affairs."[95] Frustrated, he sent Doug Bailey to be briefed on Vietnam by Dolf Droge and Donald Rockland of USIA. Their view of the situation only deepened Kissinger's conviction that the campaign against the Vietcong was going badly awry and that the Vietnam War was now a regionwide conflict in which Laos and Cambodia were both engaged, while the North Vietnamese were successfully playing the Soviets off against the Chinese to secure maximum aid with minimum strings attached.[96]

It was no good. Rockefeller's belated intervention in the Vietnam debate on April 26—he called for U.S. air strikes against Vietcong supply lines in Laos and Cambodia, which already seemed to Kissinger a military necessity—had minimal impact. Goldwater had won in Illinois on April 14, Lodge took New Jersey a week later, followed by his home state of Massachusetts on April 28. Scranton won Pennsylvania that same day. Goldwater then swept to victories in Georgia, Texas, and Tennessee, followed by Indiana and Nebraska. Rockefeller's first success came in West Virginia, an unlikely state for a multimillionaire to win. By this stage, Rockefeller was so far behind in the delegate count that he began to talk as if his sole purpose was to keep Goldwater within the "mainstream."[97] Despite also winning in Oregon on May 15—a major reverse for Lodge, who had seemed unstoppable in mid-April[98]—Rockefeller was narrowly defeated by Goldwater in the decisive California primary on June 2.

In part, Rockefeller lost because the "ground game" played by hundreds of Goldwater conservative volunteers trumped George Hinman's strategy of constructing the most impeccable list of delegates drawn from the Californian elite.[99] But the birth of Nelson Junior on May 30, just a year after the candidate's controversial remarriage, would likely have cost his father the nomination even if the campaigns had been identically run. (As Lodge later put it, "Only a rich man like Rockefeller could have believed that he could have both his love life and the Presidential nomination in the same year.")[100] An experienced journalist told Kissinger a few weeks later that "NAR lost the California primary partly because of Nelson, Jr.'s, birth, partly because his campaign had lacked any substance."[101] The latter deficiency was one Kissinger had tried, and failed, to remedy.

IV

Henry Kissinger's response to Rockefeller's admission of defeat was emotive. In a handwritten note, he told Rockefeller that he had "never admired you more than in these heartbreaking weeks when all [alone?] you fought for your principles. If the Republican party and our two-party system is saved the credit goes largely to you."[102] This might seem like hyperbole, perhaps calculated to cheer his vanquished patron. Yet it would be a mistake to underestimate how feverish Kissinger's mood at this time was. The Republican Party's 1964 national convention, held in San Francisco's Cow Palace in July, was the first such event he ever attended. Never before had he been in such close proximity to the American democratic process, from the smoke-filled rooms where the deals were done to the partisan throng of the convention chamber. It was a searing experience, recorded in a diary marked "Personal and Confidential."[103]

Kissinger arrived in San Francisco a week before the convention. He and the other members of Rockefeller's campaign team were not hopeful of achieving very much, but their boss remained convinced that he could somehow restrain Goldwater, if only by ensuring that the Republican Party platform was purged of the likely nominee's more extreme positions. Technically, there still had to be a vote to confirm Goldwater as nominee, as Scranton was still in contention, but it was all but a foregone conclusion. "The general atmosphere was one of dejection," Kissinger noted after an initial meeting. "This could have been NAR's show. As it is, everyone present had his own regrets and his own theory for the failure."[104] He was unimpressed by what he saw of the other also-rans—the disorganized and indecisive Scranton, the dapper but empty and egotistical Romney, the self-important but vacuous Lodge—"not one of whom . . . has the moral courage to draw an issue of principle and each of whom holds himself available either for the unexpected here or at least as the heir presumptive of the Goldwater following for 1968." Kissinger was all for taking a stand, urging Rockefeller to "use the argument that he did not want the party of Lincoln to be turned over to Goldwater's forces by acclamation" in order to force a floor fight if the party platform did not meet his minimum requirements. These should be "(a) maintenance of our membership in the U.N., (b) continued recognition of the USSR, and (c) no delegation of the decision to use nuclear weapons."[105] As he told the less excitable Perkins, "The anti-Goldwater group was running for history not only for the Convention."[106] Kissinger's most significant contribution was to try to get the convention to amend the Goldwaterite plank in the party platform that proposed delegating control over nuclear weapons to the NATO commander.[107] He spent long hours on the phone and in meetings trying to rally former Eisenhower administration officials, notably Allen Dulles, Thomas Gates, Christian Herter, and John McCloy—even Eisenhower's brother Milton—only for the former president himself to back away from a confrontation, Scranton to get cold feet, and Romney to defect altogether.[108]

Almost every aspect of the convention appalled Kissinger. There was Mel Laird, "showing the brass knuckles" as he ran the platform committee in anticipation of Goldwater's victory. There were the "so-called moderates . . . impotent, incompetent and selfish"—and worst of all, divided. There were the old boys of the Eisenhower administration, far too wily ever to commit themselves to one of Kissinger's principles. Worst of all were the Goldwater supporters. Far from being "old ladies in tennis shoes and retired colonels," Kissinger noted, they were "bright, eager young men" with a fondness for "semantic purism . . . intense, efficient, humorless, curiously insecure." Time and again Kissinger was reminded ominously of the politics of his German childhood. "The moderates behaved today in what has become characteristic vacillation," he wrote on July 9. "The whole behavior is reminiscent of that of the Democratic parties in the face of Hitler—an unwillingness to believe that their opponent is serious, a tendency to play for small stakes and to overlook the basic issues." The Goldwater supporters, by contrast, were "middle class and 'respectable.' They feel threatened and insecure. They crave the safety of total commitment. Whatever Goldwater's 'real' views, as a phenomenon his movement is similar to European fascism."[109] Nothing chilled Kissinger more than an encounter with a Goldwater supporter in the early hours of Monday, July 13, after a late-night meeting at which Rockefeller, Scranton, and Lodge had attempted to agree on the wording of the amendment to the nuclear weapons plank. "As we left the room," Kissinger recorded in his diary, "some Goldwaterite was checking off names on a list. I was not on it. But he knew me and said, 'Kissinger—don't think we'll forget your name.'"[110] Those were chilling words to a refugee from Nazi Germany.*

The convention itself opened later that same day. It was pandemonium, fully living up to the location's previous life as the California State Livestock Pavilion. The routed moderates pressed ahead with the idea of proposing amendments from the floor on three planks of the platform: not only presidential control of nuclear weapons but also civil rights (to which Goldwater was obliquely opposed) and "extremism." However, they found themselves outmaneuvered at every turn. The program had been changed so that the debate on the amendments did

---

*Later the same day Kissinger was "accosted in the street by Rep. [Graig] Hosmer, [the] ranking Republican House member on the Joint Atomic Energy Committee. He stopped me with the words: 'I notice you have gone over to the enemy.'" Kissinger had never previously met Hosmer.

not begin until nine p.m., ensuring that East Coast television viewers saw nothing of it. The heavily outnumbered Rockefeller supporters found they had been allocated seats in the far corner of the hall. By Kissinger's estimate, three-quarters of the doorkeepers and ushers were "Goldwater supporters and wore blatant Goldwater buttons"; even some of the police appeared openly to be backing "Barry." The chairman of the convention, the Kentucky senator Thruston Morton, was openly contemptuous of anyone standing in the way of the presumptive nominee. To cap it all, the antics of the Goldwater partisans were being orchestrated via walkie-talkie by Goldwater's campaign mastermind, Clif White, from his green-and-white communications trailer behind the convention hall.[111]

But it was the spontaneous behavior of the crowd that most appalled Kissinger. With a ticket to sit in Scranton's box, as well as a floor pass, he had not one but two ringside seats for one of the most unruly party conventions of modern times:

> I was immediately struck by the frenzy, the fervor and the intensity of most delegates and practically the entire audience. The atmosphere was more akin to a revival meeting than to a political convention. A revolution clearly was in the making. Neither spectators nor delegates had come to participate in a traditional victory. They were there to celebrate a triumph. They wanted to crush, not to integrate, their opponents. . . . It would be impossible to describe the witches' cauldron that was the Cow Palace on this evening. The roars of Ba-rry, Ba-rry filled the hall.[112]

When Eisenhower, in his opening speech, made his racially charged reference to criminals with switchblades,* "most [delegates] took it as a euphemism for a criticism of the civil rights movement and in this

---

*Eisenhower warned against "maudlin sympathy for the criminal who, roaming the streets with switchblade knife and illegal firearms seeking a helpless prey, suddenly becomes, upon apprehension, a poor, underprivileged person who counts upon the compassion of our society and the laxness or weakness of too many courts to forgive the offense."

spirit applauded any reference to it by subsequent speakers wildly." There were "frenzied cheers" when Senator John Tower read out those parts of the party platform that called for the "liberation" of the Baltic States and the breakup of Yugoslavia. But the nadir was Nelson Rockefeller's speech in favor of the extremism amendment, the text of which had been agreed to that morning:

> The Republican Party fully respects the contribution of responsible criticism, and defends the right of dissent in the democratic process. But we repudiate the efforts of irresponsible, extremist groups, such as the John Birch Society, the Ku Klux Klan, the Communist party and others, to discredit our Party by their efforts to infiltrate positions of responsibility in the Party, or to attach themselves to its candidates.

Greeted with catcalls, Rockefeller was howled down when he used the phrase "goon squads and Nazi methods" and for some minutes was almost entirely drowned out by chants of "We Want Barry!" Undaunted, he resumed by condemning "any militant doctrinaire minority, whether Communist, Ku Klux Klan or [John] Bircher" and calling on the Republican Party to "reject extremism from either the Left or the Right." Though these words were dutifully applauded by the New York and New Hampshire delegations, the booing from the rest of the hall grew louder when Rockefeller attacked an "alien" right-wing "minority" and affirmed his belief in "Republican liberalism." Finally, when he uttered the words "extremist threats," the Goldwaterites went berserk with a deafening cacophony of bullhorn honks and chants. Hurling a parting accusation of "outright threats of personal violence" at the mob, a furious Rockefeller abandoned the podium.[113] It was lucky most Americans had by this time turned off their televisions. This was as bad an advertisement for a political party as its opponent could have wished for. Clif White had in fact lost control of his own people.[114]

Kissinger was aghast:

> A TV rescreening I saw seemed to me but a pale reflection of the venomous, vicious, hysterical hatred which filled the Cow

> Palace. Before NAR could even begin to speak—introduced
> without any adjectives simply as the Governor of New York—
> there were minutes of booing, jeering and catcalls which the
> chair did nothing to restrain. The statement was interrupted
> every few words with disgusting, cheap and vicious outbreaks
> in which again the chair was anything but helpful.

It came as no surprise when the anti-extremism amendment was defeated amid further rowdy scenes; as was Romney's watered-down
version; as was a civil rights amendment; as was Kissinger's own laboriously crafted amendment on nuclear authority.

The culmination of the convention was Goldwater's bombastic
acceptance speech. Partly because it sent the audience so wild, the
speech is best remembered for the lines written for Goldwater by Harry
Jaffa, an academic best known for his conservative reinterpretation of
Lincoln. "I would remind you," Goldwater thundered, "that *extremism
in the defense of liberty is no vice.* And let me remind you also that moderation in the pursuit of justice is no virtue." (Not everyone cheered. "My
God," muttered a stunned reporter. "He's going to run as Barry Goldwater." A stony-faced Richard Nixon conspicuously did not applaud.)[115]
But the speech was significant in more ways than one. Goldwater's
scornful references to "the swampland of collectivism" and "the bullying of Communism" were nothing very new. But the few words he said
on foreign policy were calculated to goad Lyndon Johnson: "Yesterday
it was Korea. Tonight it is Vietnam. . . . We are at war in Vietnam.
[applause] And yet the President, who is the commander-in-chief of
our forces, refuses to say . . . whether or not the objective over there is
victory." Also significant were the hostile crowds outside the convention hall. As many as forty thousand civil rights demonstrators took
over City Hall Plaza to denounce Goldwater as the next Hitler.

The liberal press was a favorite target of the Goldwaterites. The
newspapers' coverage of the convention reciprocated. Some newspapers, apparently unaware of the Goldwater family's Jewish origins,
bizarrely reported that he was planning a visit to Berchtesgaden—
Hitler's Alpine retreat—after the convention. *Life* spoke of a "tide of
zealotry." Columnist Drew Pearson detected "the smell of fascism."[116]

One of those who had been present as an accredited Republican Party member was inclined to agree. Henry Kissinger was in no doubt about what he had witnessed:

> The frenzy of the cheering at the Cow Palace was reminiscent of Nazi times. . . . They [the Goldwater supporters] are the middle class gone rampant: the technocrats, the white collar workers impelled by an almost fanatical zeal. They are the result of a generation of liberal debunking, of the smug self-righteousness of so many intellectuals. . . . They have a faith not a party. The delegates walking around with stamp out Huntley and Brinkley* buttons are a new phenomenon. The delegate who said to me I am sorry the button is not big enough to include Howard K. Smith and all Eastern newspapers was a new form of delegate. This group once organized will be hard to dislodge. It will try to become the residuary legatee of all crises that are likely over the next decade. . . . The Goldwater victory is a new phenomenon in American politics—the triumph of the ideological party in the European sense. No one can predict how it will end because there is no precedent for it.

The coverage of this "tragicomedy" was enough to alarm Kissinger's father, then on vacation in the Swiss Alps, who wrote to his son warning that it would be a "tragedy for U.S.A. as well as the whole world" if "this man" were helped by "malcontents" and "reactionaries" to a victory in November.[117] But his son understood that there were other dangers, too. An equal and opposite force might also be gathering on the political left. "What may be ahead of us," he noted presciently, "was symbolized at the Cow Palace. Outside there were pickets calling for neutralization of Vietnam, for the end of NATO and CORE [Congress of Racial Equality] demonstrators. Inside were the extremists of the right."[118]

---

*David Brinkley and Chet Huntley were the liberal hosts of NBC's *The Huntley-Brinkley Report,* a nightly news broadcast. *Howard K. Smith: News and Comment* aired on ABC on Sunday mornings.

It had been, he told the British historian Michael Howard a few days later, a "shattering experience . . . worse than anything the newspapers could possibly report."[119] Howard sympathized. Such firsthand experiences of political life were "chastening." "The power of unreason is something which we academics know all about in principle," he wrote, "but it is pretty disagreeable when one meets it in practice, and it increases one's respect for the politicians who succeed in mastering it."[120] Yet Howard's comparison between the Goldwaterites and the Campaign for Nuclear Disarmament—then in one of its periodic upswings in the United Kingdom—was not the right one.[121] What was happening in the United States was something distinctive, and as Kissinger reflected more, it had at least something to do with the *trahison des clercs* that had characterized the Kennedy years, when the best and brightest of the Ivy League had rushed to Washington, convinced of the inexorable correctness of the liberal project.

> Every democracy must respect diversity [he wrote]. But it must also know what its purposes are. Tolerance does not have to be equated with moral neutrality. On the contrary, if relativism grows too rampant, pseudo-values will substitute for the real values which have been destroyed. Man cannot live by tired slogans and self-righteous invocations. The whole of truth was not revealed to mankind in the 1930's. The smug, patronizing condescension with which too many of my colleagues (and probably I as well) have treated those less sophisticated was bound to create an emotional vacuum. . . . If the Goldwater phenomenon passes both parties have an obligation to undertake some profound soul-searching. They should ask themselves why peace and prosperity proved not to be enough; why the middle class became radicalized during a period of material well-being. They must consider that democracy cannot survive unless it bases respect for diversity on a strong sense of purpose.[122]

It was the tragedy of the 1960s that those ruling the United States convinced themselves that the Vietnam War could provide that sense of purpose. The disastrous consequences of that war's escalation by the administration of Lyndon Johnson were the reason why, for the next fifteen years, it was not the extremists inside the Cow Palace but those outside it who appeared to be the leading actors in the American political drama, even when in electoral terms the Goldwaterites substantially outnumbered the extremists of the left.

V

The government of the Democratic Republic of Vietnam was very far from being an innocent victim of American aggression, as its propagandists—and its leftist apologists—liked to claim. It was in December 1963, a year and a half before Lyndon Johnson's fateful decision to commit U.S. troops to the war on a large scale, that the Ninth Plenum of the central committee of the Vietnam Workers Party passed the following resolution: "If we do not defeat the enemy's military forces, we cannot . . . bring the revolution to victory. For this reason, armed struggle plays a direct and decisive role."[123] The Hanoi regime committed itself to sending regular People's Army of Vietnam troops south down the Ho Chi Minh Trail in September 1964, six months before Johnson sent the marines ashore at Da Nang. Throughout the conflict, its goal was, in the words of a resolution passed at the Twelfth Plenum in March 1965, "to inflict a defeat on . . . American imperialism, to defend the North, to liberate the South, to complete the national-democratic revolution in the whole country."[124] It was therefore far from implausible that, on August 2 and 4, 1964, the U.S. destroyer *Maddox* should have come under attack from North Vietnamese torpedo boats in the Gulf of Tonkin. Nor was it unreasonable for President Johnson to accuse the North Vietnamese of "open aggression." The authorization he sought from Congress—to take "all necessary measures to repel any armed attack against the forces of the United States and to prevent further aggression"—was not without justification.[125]

What Johnson omitted to tell Congress was that the Gulf of Tonkin "incident" was a direct consequence of OPLAN 34-A—a South Vietnamese program of commando attacks along the North Vietnamese coast, which had been devised by the U.S. Department of Defense and supported by the CIA—and the parallel effort by the U.S. Navy to carry out its own reconnaissance missions (so-called "Desoto patrols," short for "DE Haven Special Operations off TsingtaO," where they had first been undertaken).[126] On August 2, 1964, North Vietnamese patrol torpedo boats certainly did attack the *Maddox* while the destroyer was in international waters; the attack was confirmed by air support sent from the aircraft carrier *Ticonderoga*. Johnson was therefore well within his rights to send the USS *Turner Joy* to join the *Maddox* on patrol. More dubious was the way he and other members of his administration handled the conflicting reports they received on August 4. While both ships reported what appeared to be renewed attacks by torpedo boats, to which they responded with shellfire, the U.S. airman who flew in support saw "nothing but black water and American firepower." The commander of *Maddox* sent a flash message to Honolulu blaming "freak weather effects on radar and overeager sonarmen," though he later changed his story. There was only one piece of intercepted signal intelligence to suggest that the North Vietnamese really had attacked. Nevertheless, Johnson and McNamara seized on this scanty evidence to retaliate with an initial air strike for what Johnson called "repeated acts of violence against the armed forces of the United States."[127]

Johnson was being Johnson. He had hoped to keep Vietnam out of the election campaign; indeed, his intention was to cut defense spending in 1965.[128] But this was just too good an opportunity. He was at breakfast with congressional leaders when he received the initial reports of the second attacks. "I'll tell you what I want," he snapped. "I not only want those patrol boats that attacked the *Maddox* destroyed, I want everything at that harbor destroyed; I want the whole works destroyed. I want to give them a real dose."[129] This was his chance to rebut conclusively Goldwater's allegation in San Francisco that the administration was soft on Vietnam.[130] On the eve of his August 4 address to the nation, Johnson called Goldwater to secure his support for "tak[ing] all the boats out that we can, and all the bases in which they come."[131] How could a good patriot possibly say no? From a narrowly electoral perspective, Johnson was doing the right thing.[132] Constitutionally, he did not need the Gulf of Tonkin resolution. But it strengthened his hand against Congress. As Johnson himself said, it "was like Grandma's nightshirt. It covers everything." Only Senators Wayne Morse (Oregon) and Ernest Gruening (Alaska) voted against giving the president what amounted to a completely free hand in Vietnam. It was all part of a brilliant campaign strategy to represent Johnson as leading the "frontlash" against Goldwater's "backlash."[133] The result was a landslide that gave Johnson the biggest percentage of the vote in history. Even Kissinger voted for him.[134] So incensed had he been by the Republican convention that he even published a scathing critique of Goldwater on the eve of the election.[135]

It had not been hard for Johnson to portray Goldwater as "crazy . . . just as nutty as a fruit cake"—"a wild madman—[a] mad dog."[136] The Republican candidate provided ample evidence of his bad judgment. Johnson's claim that "he wants to drop atomic bombs on everybody" had indeed been the basis for one of the most successful television attack ads of all time—the famous "Daisy" commercial, which depicted the nuclear incineration of a little girl.[137] But it was not only the presidential race that the Republicans lost in 1964. They also lost thirty-six seats in the House of Representatives, giving Democrats the biggest majority in the House any party had enjoyed since 1945, and dropped two seats in the Senate, resulting an another enormous Democratic majority (of 68–32), also the biggest since the war.[138] It was the nadir of Republican fortunes. Even liberal members of the party, like Nelson Rockefeller, seemed vulnerable to the leftward lurch: when Bobby Kennedy resigned as attorney general—Johnson having denied his request for promotion to vice president or secretary of state—Rockefeller fretted that Kennedy might run against him for the governorship of New York. The Democrats' triumph empowered Johnson in two ways. It allowed him to enact a raft of liberal legislation: the Voting Rights Act, Medicare, and Medicaid, as well as laws protecting consumers and the environment. It also appeared to remove all political constraints on his Vietnam policy. Never has the Democratic Party been more powerful than when the Vietnam War was being brought to the boil.[139] The irony is that one of Johnson's motives for increasing U.S. military involvement in the war was his fear of being labeled as "soft" by a conservative movement he had crushed.[140]

The steps to hell were many, as were the reasons for taking them. On September 7, Johnson ordered retaliatory air raids "on a tit-for-tat basis" in case of attacks on U.S. units. However, when the Vietcong attacked the American air base at Bien Hoa, he asked an NSC working group headed by McGeorge Bundy's brother William, now assistant secretary of state for East Asian and Pacific affairs, to consider two other options: a heavy air assault of the sort LeMay craved, or the more graduated bombing campaign advocated by Walt Rostow. The latter option easily won out, and March 1965 saw the first phase of Operation Rolling Thunder—the beginning of a bombing campaign against North Vietnam that would last, with sporadic intermissions, for eight years.[141] March 1965 was also the month when the first U.S. combat battalions came ashore near Da Nang. On April 1 the NSC decided to deploy these troops directly against the Vietcong. By May 1965, 47,000 American combat troops were already in Vietnam.[142] On June 7 Westmoreland increased his "ask" to forty-four battalions, which would have taken the total number of U.S. troops deployed to 175,000 by the end of the year. Though McNamara called this "rash to the point of folly," he nevertheless supported the decision to lift the total to 100,000.[143]

The decision to escalate the Vietnam War in a "slowly ascending tempo" (the words of NSAM 328)[144] rather than to devise an exit strategy was the worst strategic mistake the United States made in the Cold War. From the outset, Johnson had his own doubts about this strategy, as did other members of the administration, notably George Ball.[145] But the president went ahead for four reasons. First, direct U.S. action seemed the simplest way to contend with the chronic instability of South Vietnam, whose "squabbling politicos" seemed less and less likely to achieve military success by their own efforts. An attempt by General Nguyen Khanh to seize power was thwarted as students and Buddhist monks took to the streets, but Khanh was soon restored to power as the army reasserted itself and, having survived another coup attempt, was able to create a High National Council and, on the basis of the constitution it drew up, to establish a civilian government with the former mayor of Saigon, Tran Van Huong, as premier.[146] As Ball later put it, "there had been a whole sordid series of coups, a feeling that the whole political fabric of South Vietnam was beginning to disintegrate, and that we had to do something very fair and affirmative if we were going to keep this damned thing from falling apart." U.S. bombing of the other side was "a great bucker-upper for South Vietnam."[147]

Second, the military under General William Westmoreland was promising Johnson "limited war with limited objectives, fought with limited means and programmed for the utilization of limited resources."[148] Johnson believed that any greater commitment—in particular, an invasion of North Vietnam—would risk bringing the Chinese into the war; the fear of another Korea was never far from his mind. Indeed, this was why LeMay's arguments for overwhelming force stood no chance.[149] But the "search and destroy" strategy favored by Westmoreland was essentially attritional and exposed the American troops to casualties that proved demoralizingly high.* Not enough consideration was given to the alternative advocated by army chief of staff Harold K. Johnson and his deputy, Creighton Abrams, which was for the U.S. forces to clear and hold key villages, leaving the lion's share of combat operations to the South Vietnamese.[150]

Third, "slowly ascending" military force was the most Johnson could employ without jeopardizing his much more rapidly ascending domestic program. Indeed, so fast did Johnson move on both welfare and civil rights that he very nearly overreached, despite his party's control of Congress. On June 30 his bill to give poor families rent subsidies was very nearly defeated; the voting rights and Medicare bills, which were due for conference in late July, also looked vulnerable. An alliance of fiscally conservative Republicans and southern Dixiecrats seemed to menace the Great Society. Johnson therefore did not dare ask Congress for the things that his escalation of the war really required: a new resolution, authorization to call up the reserves, a large supplemental appropriation, and a tax hike. Instead of giving a prime-time television address, Johnson casually announced the increased troop deployment at a midday press conference, insisting that it did not "imply any change in policy whatsoever."[151] As he explained to McNamara, if he made "a larger request . . . to the Congress . . . this will kill [our] domestic legislative program." Johnson was determined not to

---

*Battle deaths per month were roughly 469 in Vietnam compared with 909 in Korea.

give Congress the choice between guns and butter, not least because they might choose the former over the latter. In this he had the support of the Senate majority leader, Mike Mansfield.[152]

Finally, and crucially, those who had doubts about the strategy of creeping escalation failed miserably to make their case. It was not that Johnson closed down debate, as has sometimes been suggested.[153] By the standards of more recent presidents, the debates in 1965 were remarkably freewheeling. In a memo dated April 2, 1965, John McCone accurately forecast "increasing pressure to stop the bombing . . . from various elements of the American public, from the press, the United Nations and world opinion"; correctly inferred that the North Vietnamese were "counting on this"; and warned that even with an "ever-increasing commitment of U.S. personnel," the administration would find itself "mired down in combat in the jungle in a military effort we cannot win and from which we will have extreme difficulty extricating ourselves." Another early skeptic was John T. McNaughton, assistant secretary of defense.[154] He returned dejected from a visit to Saigon in the spring of 1965 with the verdict that America had been "a 'good doctor' who had simply lost a patient that was beyond repair."[155] "Yellow men should settle yellow men's trouble," he noted bluntly in June 1965.[156] Clark Clifford warned as early as May 17, 1965, of a "quagmire" if substantial ground forces were committed.[157] "I hate this war," he told Johnson at Camp David on July 23. "I do not believe we can win. . . . It will ruin us. Five years, 50,000 men killed, hundreds of billions of dollars—it is just not for us."[158] For George Ball, who knew better than most American officials what the French had been through, having spent time in France after the war, Vietnam was just a "rotten country." He too questioned the wisdom of "gradually escalating the thing." At one of the key meetings in the White House on July 21, Ball unequivocally argued for "cutting our losses" for the simple reason that "a great power cannot beat guerrillas." Sending more U.S. troops would be like "giving cobalt treatments to a terminal cancer case." True, this would mean the loss of South Vietnam. But the "worse blow would be [revealing] that the mightiest power in the world is unable to defeat guerrillas."[159]

All these prognoses were to be vindicated by events. Yet as Ball later confessed, "I had a kind of sense of fatality that I wasn't going to keep it from happening. It would indeed happen. Once you get one of those things going, it's just like getting a little alcohol; you're going to get a taste for more. It's a compelling thing."[160] By contrast, Rostow was unflagging in his optimism, constantly reassuring Johnson that the war could be won.[161] And, fatally for his own reputation and future peace of mind, McNamara jumped the wrong way. It was he who clinched the crucial July 1965 debate by reviving the domino theory, predicting that defeat in Vietnam would lead to "Communist domination" not only in "Laos, Cambodia, Thailand, Burma [and] Malaysia" but also potentially in Japan and India. Pakistan, he warned darkly, "would move closer to China. Greece, Turkey would move to a neutralist position. Communist agitation would increase in Africa."[162]

Thus, with a wild prediction that the United States would lose the third world if it lost South Vietnam, was the die cast.

VI

Henry Kissinger could scarcely have been less responsible for the fateful decision to escalate the war in Vietnam. As chief foreign policy adviser to the two-time loser Nelson Rockefeller—the man whose speech against extremism had been drowned out by a baying mob at the GOP convention—Kissinger was emphatically out. Unlike his predecessor, Lyndon Johnson had no use for an adviser loyal to a rival.

In any case, even as Johnson was ruling out an exit strategy that would have gotten the United States out of Vietnam, Kissinger was preoccupied with an exit strategy of his own. In August 1964 he and Ann were granted a divorce in Reno, Nevada. Even such a "quick" dissolution of their marriage was inevitably time-consuming and distracting. His life, he complained more than once at around this time, was "terribly" or "unbelievably hectic" because of "a combination of personal and unforeseen professional problems."[163] Moving out of the family home in Cambridge—which meant removing all his books and papers from the purpose-built study above the garage—cannot have been pleasant. The biggest challenge was, of course, the children, who, though they were just five and three at the time of their parents' divorce, were old enough to recognize an irrevocable rift. Their grandparents worried that Kissinger would not see enough of them.[164] In fact, as is sometimes the case, divorce made him a more attentive father, because when he was with Elizabeth and David, he now had to give them his full attention.

Divorce brought Kissinger closer to his parents, too. "I appreciate the warmth which speaks from your lines," wrote his father in February 1964, thanking him for a birthday gift.

> I am happy that you do not seem to have the resentment towards us any more which you apparently had for some time.
>
> Henry believe me, we both feel the whole tragedy of your situation. We parents cannot expect that you make in consideration of us a decision which would not lead to your ultimate happiness. We know too well [that] nobody could give up lightheartedly without deepest inner reserves such a beautiful property with its wonderful study and all the comfort of an own home. . . .
>
> You are the only judge, what is best for you. Please God, you would soon find a way which would bring you to a life of inner satisfaction and happiness.
>
> You are burdened with great financial obligations at present. . . . We deeply feel with you and wished nothing more than that we would be able to help you.[165]

Though he could offer them little financial help, Louis Kissinger sought to give his sons emotional support. In particular, he strove to keep them connected to their German and Jewish heritage. A typical Hanukkah gift was a selection of vinyl recordings of German composers: Beethoven's Eighth and Ninth Symphonies, played by the Berliner Philharmonic under Karajan, Schubert's Fifth and Eighth (Unfinished) Symphonies, Schumann's Rhenish Symphony, and Mahler 2, with the New York Philharmonic conducted by Bernstein. A year later, it was two Haydn symphonies and Mozart's Sinfonia Concertante. At the same time, Louis urged his sons to give their children a "Jewish religious education in a Hebrew school."[166] But both men—Walter even more than Henry, to the great distress of his father—were moving decisively in the direction of an American secular lifestyle.

Divorce is indeed expensive, but it can be worth every penny. Henry Kissinger was now living in an elegant apartment at 419 Beacon Street in Boston. He was also making frequent trips to New York and Washington, and for a change, not all his trips were on business. His father would doubtless have preferred it if he had gone to Carnegie Hall; instead Kissinger got tickets to see the musical farce *A Funny Thing Happened on the Way to the Forum,* starring Zero Mostel. Kissinger's own sense of humor was becoming more visible. "I am only sarcastic to people I like and respect very much," he told a rookie Rockefeller assistant.[167] Lines like this turned out to work well at parties. His father took disapproving note of this new gregariousness. Two days before Kissinger's forty-second birthday, he wrote to express his regret that Kissinger would not be able to dine with him and Paula, as had once been the family custom. They had thought of phoning, but "I suppose you don't want me to publicize your anniversary at the cocktail party."[168] Others noticed the change, too. Tom Schelling had once described Kissinger to a colleague in London as "fat, dumpyish, pale, and sickish." But the Kissinger who arrived at Heathrow for a meeting of the International Institute for Strategic Studies did not answer to that description. He had lost weight, his face was tanned, and his suit was now worthy of Madison Avenue.[169] Frank Lindsay's wife, Margot, saw it too. The old Kissinger had "not [been] a barrel of laughs." The new, slimmed-down Kissinger was "fun and a gossip."[170]

Yet even as he deplored his son's new lifestyle, Louis Kissinger could not help taking pride in his achievements. When "our Rabbi Goldberg in our neighbourhood synagogue 'Fort Tryon Jewish Center' mentioned you in his sermon of last Sabbath and cited a few sentences of your new book," Louis was delighted.[171] He was especially impressed by Kissinger's appearance in the CBS debate on Vietnam in December 1965 (see page 671):

> People called us up or addressed me where I met them on the
> street, in our house, in the subway. The German Jews were
> proud that one of "them" had the distinction to represent this

country, others appreciated that you tried to explain American policy, but all were impressed by your performance, even those who don't agree with US actions in Vietnam. As a lawyer told me today: You were terrific. And I was happy that you spoke with so much moderation, not warlike at all.[172]

Kissinger reciprocated by ensuring his parents received the red-carpet treatment when they went on vacation to Switzerland.[173]

In nearly every respect, as we have seen, Kissinger's attendance at the 1964 Republican convention had been a miserable experience. But there was one thread of silver lining in the Goldwaterite cloud: it was there, on a summer's day in San Francisco, that Kissinger first got to know Nancy Maginnes, the beautiful, brilliant, and—relative to Kissinger—toweringly tall expert on French history who had begun working part time for Rockefeller three years before.[174] The fuse lit in San Francisco burned slowly. It was not until January 18, 1967, that he wrote to offer her a full-time job as a foreign policy researcher. "Let me say now," he concluded the letter, "that it will be a pleasure to be associated with you again."[175] We know now that their romance had in fact begun shortly after the 1964 Republican convention, where Kissinger had been so struck by her that he had searched for her, row by row, in the convention hall.[176] However, given how recently Kissinger had been divorced and his parents' likely reaction to their elder son's potentially marrying outside the Jewish faith, they had resolved to keep the relationship secret.

VII

When Louis Kissinger saw his son on television in December 1965, he little realized how hard he had worked to get back into the public debate on American foreign policy—and not only into the public debate, but also into the policy-making process. It might be thought that, having been so critical of both Kennedy and Johnson on the subject of Vietnam, Kissinger would have had difficulty in doing the latter. In one respect, however, his task was made easier. McNamara's clinching argument in the key debates of July 1965 had been a version of the domino effect: defeat in Vietnam would have a contagion effect, emboldening Communist insurgents all around the world. Quite independently, Kissinger had drawn a similar conclusion. In September 1964 he drafted a speech for Rockefeller that was still couched as a critique of the administration's "misunderstanding of the Communist challenge" and its "confusion, vacillation and lack of candor" in Vietnam, but that nevertheless paved the way for his rehabilitation in Washington.

Eisenhower's domino effect had implied that Communism spread across borders, marching like an army from one contiguous country to another. But now Kissinger proposed a different framework, an updated version that was more appropriate to the age of intercontinental jets and missiles.

> The hesitancy to be firm and unwavering in the face of Communist advances in Laos and Vietnam has increased the trend toward neutrality in our SEATO allies. . . . But it should also be clear that our failure to make Sukarno pay for his aggression has been an invitation to Nasser—that a weakness at the Wall in Berlin resulted in a further test of our strength over missiles in Cuba.
>
> Isolated problems or states no longer exist. Single, simple remedies are no longer available. Every event has worldwide consequences.[177]

This striking intimation of globalization led Kissinger to a paradox he would refer to repeatedly for the rest of his career. "While modern technology has created a community of peoples, political concepts and tools are still imprisoned in the nation states. . . . [T]he triumph of national self-determination, welcome as it is, has come at the precise moment in world history when the nation state can no longer exist by itself." The political fragmentation of the postcolonial world, in other words, ran counter to the technological and economic trends that were increasing international integration and interdependence. What this implied, Kissinger reasoned, was the need for a new "wider structure" of international order.

Kissinger remained more of an idealist than those he criticized. In principle, like Woodrow Wilson, he favored "a worldwide system of security and growth." But that was "prevented by Communist hostility." Therefore "the great challenge before our foreign policy" must be to create a "Union of the Free." A first step in this direction would be to establish a "permanent body at the highest level of NATO charged with the responsibility of developing common negotiating positions and a common policy for the West's future." Such an entity could "make clear to all the world, that the victims of aggression—in Malaysia, in South Vietnam, in Thailand, in Venezuela, in the Middle East—anywhere, anytime—can count on our support." No doubt it could also promote the economic development of those countries, but Kissinger made it very clear that he aspired to much more:

> Efficiency can never be the only goal for free peoples. By itself, materialism destroys liberty. Despite all wishful thinking, there is no inevitable connection between material well-being and democratic values. . . . [I]n each of the great Western democracies, the process of industrialization was *preceded* by the acceptance of democratic values.
>
> However fallacious they are, we cannot fight ideas by talk of material well-being. All people want values which give meaning to their physical existence. We cannot afford to let freedom and democracy fail.
>
> We should not be embarrassed to affirm our dedication to the goal of making democracy the wave of the future.
>
> • By making it a reality for all in our own land;
> • By demonstrating to the world a faith which is valid for the realization of human values everywhere;
> • By measuring its worth in spiritual and not in material terms;
> • By finding in it the cause for the imagination and initiative and industry that it gave our forefathers.[178]

This kind of high-flown language—intended, of course, for Rockefeller's use*—was at least superficially compatible with the terms Johnson and his national security team were now using to justify their escalation of the Vietnam War. (The fact that they were acting without any European support was the obvious difference. But, for now at least, that could be glossed over.)

In the spring of 1965, Kissinger made his move, bombarding serving and former members of the administration with invitations to speak, offers of dinner, and letters of encouragement. He invited McNaughton for a "loose-jointed give-and-take" on counterinsurgency warfare at the Defense Policy Seminar.[†179] He dined with Robert Kennedy, now senator from New York.[180] On March 30 he wrote to assure Bundy that "I think our present actions in Vietnam are essentially right and to express my respect for the courage with which the Administration is acting."[181] Two weeks later Bundy replied appreciatively, noting that his support for the administration might make Kissinger "somewhat lonely among all our friends at Harvard."[182] Kissinger saw his opening.

> At the risk of being misunderstood [he wrote the next day], I want to tell you that I thought the President's program on Vietnam as outlined in his speech was just right: the proper mixture of firmness and flexibility. I say this because the carping of some of your former colleagues at Harvard may create a misleading impression of unanimity. I will look for an early opportunity to state my views publicly.[183]

All was forgiven. "I have been using your name in vain," wrote Bundy on April 30, "with a few people who want to know whether any

---

*The reader may legitimately wonder if a draft speech such as this can be regarded as an expression of Kissinger's own views, as opposed to views that Kissinger understood Rockefeller to want expressed. But Kissinger was no mere speechwriter. While some of the language he used here was clearly intended to suit Rockefeller's lofty style as an orator, the ideas were clearly Kissinger's own. It was for his ideas that Rockefeller paid him, not for fine phrases.

†The Harvard Defense Policy Seminar had been started by Barton Leach at the Law School and continued to meet there even after Kissinger took it over.

respectable professors are with us."[184] Kissinger duly reiterated his "strong support for Administration policy in Vietnam" and condemned an "outrageous attack" by members of the academic society Phi Beta Kappa, who had accused Bundy of "contempt for critics, lay and academic," after Bundy had declined an invitation to a radical "teach-in."[185]

Yet it was a Republican, not a Democrat, who secured Kissinger his first government job since the debacle of his part-time consulting role under Kennedy. Though unsuccessful in his bid for the Republican nomination, Henry Cabot Lodge had been reappointed by Johnson to the post of ambassador in Saigon, a decision Kissinger enthusiastically welcomed.[186] As part of his charm offensive, Kissinger invited Lodge to his Defense Policy Seminar, but he had been forced to cancel as South Vietnam's internal politics took yet another turn for the worse. There was, however, another Lodge available: the ambassador's elder son, George, then a junior professor at Harvard Business School and author of a book on labor in developing countries. In 1962 Kissinger had supported the younger Lodge's unsuccessful campaign against the thirty-year-old Edward Kennedy for one of Massachusetts's two Senate seats. (At the time, Kissinger had half-seriously told Nancy Hanks that opposing a Kennedy probably meant "the end of my political career for eight years.")[187] Now Lodge came to mind as Kissinger looked around for a bright young academic to give his International Seminar some lectures on the rapidly intensifying generational conflict within the United States. The two men lunched at the Century Club to discuss it. Lodge, however, had a better idea. What if he and Kissinger themselves volunteered to serve in Vietnam—as consultants to Lodge's father?[188]

It was an invitation Kissinger jumped at. Almost at once he applied for and was granted a year of sabbatical leave from Harvard. (He would have left almost immediately for Saigon had not Bundy urged him to delay for a month and Lodge cabled that October "would be fine.")[189] Yet it cannot easily be argued that, in doing so, he was motivated by ambition, as the role of special consultant to the ambassador in Saigon was in no way a prestigious one. Moreover, as we shall see, the job was not without its risks; his parents had good reason to pray for his safety at a time when Vietcong terrorist attacks in Saigon were growing more frequent.[190] His Harvard colleagues were openly skeptical. As Tom Schelling sardonically told *The Harvard Crimson*, "No one at Harvard knows whether Kissinger will be working out of Saigon, tramping the jungles, or holed up on an aircraft carrier."[191] A few, like Stanley Hoffmann, were frankly curious and would press Kissinger for intelligence when he returned. But most were already convinced, as Kissinger put it, that the North Vietnamese were "poor, put-upon, innocent victims" and that to serve in Saigon was to sup with the devil.[192] Characteristic of the darkening mood in the summer of 1965 was the denunciation of U.S. policy published in the *Crimson* by three French participants in Kissinger's International Seminar. Just like the French in the 1950s, they argued, the Americans were deluding themselves by insisting they were fighting for freedom. In reality, they were effectively "defend[ing] the feudal structure of the local society, the oppression of peasants and the corruption of the leading class.

> The fact which we should consider is that Vietnam has been ravaged by war for more than twenty years, only because external powers don't approve a change in its social system, a change which is wished by most of the inhabitants of Vietnam. . . . [T]he major powers [must admit] that each nation must choose by itself its own destiny and the form of its government, whatever that form may be.[193]

Whatever else Kissinger hoped to gain by assisting the U.S. government's representative in South Vietnam, it was not popularity in Cambridge, Massachusetts. His real motivation seems to have been more straightforward. By the summer of 1965, Vietnam had become not just the most important foreign policy challenge facing the United States but the only one, and he thirsted to understand the problem better.

Henry Kissinger had never been to Vietnam. He knew little if anything about the country's history and not a word of its language. But in August 1965, as he began preparing for the long and arduous journey to Saigon, he already knew one thing. This was a war that could not be won by military means. The only question worth discussing was how to negotiate an end to it.

It was a question he was destined to spend the next eight years struggling to answer.

CHAPTER 17

The Unquiet American

KISSINGER suggested the following framework for
discussion:
(1) The conduct of military operations in relation to
negotiations.
　　　　—MINUTES of a discussion at Harvard, August 1965[1]

Let's face it. At some point on this road we will have to cut
the balls off the people we are now supporting in Vietnam,
and if you want to do a really constructive study you ought
to address yourself to the question of how we can cut their
balls off.
　　　　—JOHN MCNAUGHTON to Kissinger, September 1965[2]

I

In Graham Greene's novel *The Quiet American*—written when the
United States was still halfheartedly propping up the doomed French
colonial regime in Indochina—the character of Alden Pyle personifies
the American predicament in the Cold War. To the battle-hardened
British war correspondent who is the narrator, he seems comically
naïve:

He was talking about the old colonial powers—England and
France, and how you couldn't expect to win the confidence of
Asiatics. That was where America came in now with clean
hands.

"Hawaii, Puerto Rico," I said. "New Mexico." . . .

> He said . . . there was always a Third Force to be found free
> from Communism and the taint of colonialism—national
> democracy he called it; you only had to find a leader and keep
> him safe from the old colonial powers.[3]

Pyle fails to grasp that this search for indigenous collaborators is
quintessentially imperial. Nor does he see that to install such a "Third
Force" without a long-term commitment to the country is bound
to end in disaster. In an attempt to convince him of this, Greene's
narrator draws an explicit parallel with the British in India and
Burma.

> I've been in India, Pyle, and I know the harm liberals do. We
> haven't a liberal party any more—liberalism's infected all the
> other parties. We are all either liberal conservatives or liberal
> socialists: we all have a good conscience. . . . We go and invade
> the country: the local tribes support us: we are victorious:
> but . . . [in Burma] we made peace . . . and left our allies to be
> crucified and sawn in two. They were innocent. They thought
> we'd stay. But we were liberals and we didn't want a bad
> conscience.[4]

Pyle turns out to be less naïve than he at first appears. Yet the sinister
CIA operation he is engaged in is not sufficiently covert for him to
avoid a nasty death. *The Quiet American* is a prescient, even prophetic
work. Ten years before Lyndon Johnson ordered the combat troops and
B-52s into action, Greene already sensed what Vietnam had in store for
America.

It is tempting to portray the Henry Kissinger who flew to Vietnam
in November 1965 as another "quiet American," hoping to square the
circle of America's empire in denial, willing to use all available methods to achieve victory. Yet among the most striking aspects of Kissinger's first trip to Vietnam was his complete lack of that insufferable
self-assurance personified by Pyle. Kissinger traveled to Saigon with
questions, not answers.

II

It was August 4, 1965. The setting was a Harvard seminar room. Among those present were those members of the Harvard–MIT Arms Control Seminar who were not on vacation, notably the biochemist Paul Doty, the Sinologist John Fairbank, the political scientist Samuel Huntington, the international lawyer Milton Katz, and the economist Carl Kaysen, who was now back at Harvard after three years as Kennedy's deputy national security adviser. The topic for discussion was Vietnam, and in the chair was Henry Kissinger. The agenda he proposed was startling. Item number one was "The conduct of military operations in relation to negotiations." Under that heading, Kissinger posed three questions:

(a) Should negotiations await some change in the military situation?

(b) Can military operations be geared to support the object of bringing about negotiations?

(c) What non-military measures can we take during military operations to support the objective of negotiations?

To which a fourth, even more arresting question was appended in parentheses: "(What do we do if the Saigon regime collapses?)" The second item on Kissinger's agenda was some procedural questions, again about negotiations:

(a) Who should initiate proposals for negotiation? Would it be more acceptable to the Communist countries if powers other than the U.S. took the initiative?

(b) Who should participate in the negotiations?

Third and perhaps most important, Kissinger posed questions about the "substance and purpose of negotiations":

(a) Criteria—What are we trying to achieve? To show that wars of national liberation won't work? To curb Chinese expansion? To exploit the Sino-Soviet conflict? (These are not mutually exclusive.) Johnson and Rusk say we are trying to preserve free choice for the people of Vietnam. Are we fighting against a certain method of change (wars of national liberation) or the fact of change?

(b) Can we give content to the phrase "a free and independent South Vietnam"? Would South Vietnam alone be the subject of negotiation or should other problem areas be included?

(c) What guarantees are needed? Who must participate in the guarantees?[5]

In other words, Kissinger's starting point for discussing the Vietnam War—and indeed, the premise on which all his subsequent work on the war was to be based—was that there had to be a negotiated end to it. The victory repeatedly promised to Johnson by his commanders he already regarded as a chimera.

The discussion that ensued sheds fascinating light on how key members of the Harvard faculty's "brightest and best" were thinking about the Vietnam War on the eve of the great generational revolt that the war was about to unleash on university campuses all over North America and Western Europe. Three things are immediately apparent. First, no one in the room had the remotest inkling of the coming wave of student antiwar protest. Indeed, American public opinion was not even mentioned in the discussion. Second, the majority of participants were pessimistic, though not everyone went as far as the MIT political scientist Norman Padelford, whose sole contribution was to call Vietnam "the wrong war at the wrong time in the wrong place," a phrase first used by General Omar Bradley in 1951 as an argument against expanding the Korean War into China. Third, there was nothing remotely resembling a consensus on how the United State should proceed in Vietnam.

Discussion revolved around three main issues. First, what exactly would the object of negotiations be? Lucian Pye of MIT, who was the optimist in the group, suggested that "the first objective [of negotiations] was to get North Vietnam to cease their aid of the insurgency." In his view, the Vietcong were beatable; indeed the war against them was approaching a "real hard crunch." Perhaps, ventured Huntington, the aim should be "to separate the Viet Cong from Hanoi and negotiate with them on the creation of a government in Saigon with Communist participation but not domination." The worldly Kaysen, who had the most government experience of those present, argued that, as "we cannot find a viable free government for South Vietnam[, p]robably the best solution would be 'unending talk'—a mixed situation characterized by some talk, and some measured violence—like Laos." Marshall Shulman from Harvard's Russian Research Center agreed. "Negotiations for their own sake" should be started sooner rather than later, "and it is probably better not to be too precise about what we are after." But Pye disagreed. "We should consider the possibility," he noted, "that negotiations will make the parties adopt a hard line," especially if there was some kind of "linkage of bombing with negotiations." Milton Katz was emphatic: "If we enter negotiations without knowing what our objectives are, we will cut a sorry figure and we will fall flat on our face."

The second issue debated at the seminar was the idea of creating "secure enclaves [in South Vietnam], where the people who are counting on our protection can be protected," as one participant put it. Kaysen countered, with the old self-confidence of Camelot, that the United States could do better than that: "We can wall off South Vietnam if we are willing to pay the price. Seven or eight divisions on the frontier between North and South Vietnam and along the Laotian frontier would do it." But the consensus was that this would be too costly in blood and treasure. For Doty, it seemed obvious that "we are going to have to accept an enclave type of solution." That was "where we are heading." David Cavers, the Fessenden Professor of Law, countered that American enclaves in Vietnam would only "increase . . . tension." He preferred the idea of involving the United Nations.

The third bone of contention was the role of China. Fairbank made the essentially defeatist argument that "Vietnam, like Korea, is in the Chinese culture area. Both the DRV and the Government of North

Korea are built on the Chinese model. It is not Communism that is important, but China. The Chinese pattern, as often before in history, is being exported to the periphery of the Chinese cultural area. If there were no Mao, there would be no Viet Cong." According to Fairbank, it would make more sense to "set limits to Communist expansion" in Malaysia or Thailand. Even a permanently "divided Vietnam" might be impossible for the United States to sustain. "The main thing," he concluded, "is to try to get China into the act, to give her the idea that she has a responsible role in the world, to get her into the United Nations, and to establish contact with her at as many levels and in as many contexts as possible."

Katz essentially agreed. The United States had no "vital strategic interest" in Vietnam. Its presence there was simply due to "the specter of China [which] is a frightening domestic political factor in the US. . . . If we get our priorities straight, we will see that we can afford to cut our losses when we get in an untenable situation." A few others concurred. Even Pye was willing to contemplate Chinese representatives at "the conference table."

Kissinger listened carefully to all of this. He made only one intervention, about halfway through the discussion, but it was emphatic. "We cannot enter negotiations unless we know what our objectives are, at least within broad limits," he said. "We must know (a) what is desirable from our point of view and (b) what is bearable." As for "establishing enclaves—'new Hong Kongs,'" Kissinger was "not interested" as they would "only be a perpetual irritant. If it comes to that, we should get out."[6]

III

What was desirable? What was bearable? Unbeknownst to the professors in Cambridge, the Johnson administration had already begun looking for a negotiated way out of Vietnam.[7] The problem was that they and the North Vietnamese gave mutually incompatible answers to these questions. In December 1964, a working group set up by Johnson reported that the United States should "be prepared to explore negotiated solutions that attain U.S. objectives in an acceptable manner." But those objectives were to end North Vietnamese support and direction of the Vietcong and to "re-establish an independent and secure South Vietnam with appropriate international safeguards, including the freedom to accept U.S. and other external assistance as required."[8] The North Vietnamese regarded these goals as unacceptable. This became clear as soon as third parties sought to mediate. Blair Seaborn was the Canadian member of the International Control Commission that had been set up to implement the 1954 Geneva Accords. Between June 1964 and June 1965, Seaborn visited Hanoi five times and relayed what he heard there to Washington.[9] The message was blunt: the North Vietnamese wanted a unified Vietnam. The widely publicized but abortive attempt by UN secretary general U Thant to initiate talks in the autumn 1964 failed for much the same reason.[10]

Even as he was authorizing the bombing of North Vietnam, Johnson was trying to head off the mounting domestic hostility to the bombing by appearing open to peace talks. In a speech on March 25, 1965, he said he was "ready to go anywhere at any time, and meet with anyone whenever there is promise of progress toward an honorable peace."[11] He reiterated this message in an address at Johns Hopkins University on April 7, when he spoke of "unconditional discussions."[12] A day later Hanoi responded with its Four Points, the regime's first formal statement of peace objectives (or rather war aims). These were almost the exact opposite of Johnson's. U.S. forces must withdraw from South Vietnam. There should be no foreign alliances before Vietnamese reunification. The National Liberation Front (the Communist front organization in South Vietnam whose armed wing was the Vietcong) should have interim authority in Saigon, and reunification should follow on the basis of self-determination.[13] For domestic political reasons that Lucian Pye was right to question, Johnson decided to respond to this uncompromising document with a five-day pause in the Rolling Thunder bombing campaign.[14]

MAYFLOWER was the first of many misconceived and bungled attempts to link the administration's military and diplomatic efforts. It was misconceived because Johnson appeared to think the kind of tactics that worked in a Texas saloon would work in Vietnam: beat a man, then stop beating him and say, "Give in, or I'll beat you some more."[15] It was misconceived because, still fearful of criticism from the right, Johnson did not even publicize what he was doing: only Hanoi and Moscow knew of his offer that the United States would maintain the bombing halt provided that it led to productive discussions and that Hanoi did not seek to take military advantage of it (an offer later known as "Phase A–Phase B"). It was also bungled because, when the North Vietnamese responded by softening their third point, dropping all reference to the NLF to say merely that the United States should "let the South Vietnamese people decide their own internal affairs," American intelligence analysts missed it. And it was further bungled because William Bundy dismissed out of hand a potentially important message relayed from Paris by Étienne Manac'h, the Asian director at the Quai d'Orsay, who had got the North Vietnamese ambassador to France, Mai Van Bo, to accept that "the concrete realization" of American withdrawal would be "linked to the conclusions of a negotiation."[16] "We have got to keep peace proposals going," Johnson told Ball, Clifford, McNamara, and Rusk two months after the failure of MAYFLOWER. "It's like a prizefight. Our right is our military power, but our left must be our peace proposals."[17] He never really understood that diplomacy is not like boxing. Time and again Johnson's right hand acted as if it did not know what his left hand was doing. The military and diplomatic blows he landed on Hanoi tended to cancel one another out.

IV

Bundy and Lodge had been right to delay Kissinger's departure. It gave him time to deepen his knowledge and, in particular, to pick brains other than those of other Harvard professors. What he learned was not what he had expected. Before Kissinger even set foot in Vietnam, he received a shocking initiation into the Johnson administration's utter strategic disarray.

A somewhat cynical military briefing from Lodge's former assistant Colonel John M. ("Mike") Dunn was a foretaste of what lay ahead.[18] On September 13 Kissinger had lunch in Washington with William

Bundy, assistant secretary of state for East Asian and Pacific affairs. Kissinger asked how much confidence Bundy had in the intelligence reports on Vietcong infiltration of government-controlled areas. Bundy replied that he thought they were "off by a factor of three."[19] He then went to the CIA, where he was briefed by Deputy Director Ray S. Cline and William Colby, chief of the agency's Far East Division and a former Saigon station head. Puzzled by their relative optimism—they assured him they were having no difficulty recruiting 50,000 South Vietnamese operatives to work as pro-government cadres in provincial capitals—he was downright perturbed by their "uniformly hostile" comments about General Edward Lansdale, renowned as the grand master of counterinsurgency, who had returned to South Vietnam as a minister at the Saigon embassy.[20]

Kissinger's consternation was complete after an encounter with the agency's director, Admiral William Raborn, who treated him to

a *tour de horizon* of the international situation . . . of almost incredible simplicity, about the level of a sophomore. When he reached South Africa he said there "they are trying to get us to take the country away from the Whites and turn it over to the Niggers who have demonstrated that they cannot run any-thing," and he did not see why "one would have to turn things over to the Niggers when there were white anti-Communists capable of running the country." I finally got him focused on Southeast Asia. When he discussed Vietnam he confused the names of the major figures there; for example, he thought that General Ky, who is Prime Minister, was first corps commander, and that General Thi, who is first corps commander, was the leading man in the Directory—this in turn happened to be General Thieu. He also did not know the name of the Bud-dhist leaders. In short, on one of the toughest foreign policy questions the Director of Central Intelligence was amazingly badly informed.[21]

Raborn did, however, know that the CIA's operations in Laos were far more cost-effective than those of the Marine Corps. What his agency could not overcome was the fact that "in Southeast Asia there wasn't such a thing as an honest man." He and J. Edgar Hoover, he told Kissinger, regarded Vietnam—not to mention the Dominican Republic, where the Johnson administration had also sent U.S. troops—as "a God-damn Mess."[22]

Matters did not improve the following day, when Kissinger made his rounds of the Pentagon. John McNaughton gave him a doleful account of the situation. If any other crisis blew up in Asia, the United States would find itself hard pressed to respond, so great had its commitment become to South Vietnam. Yet even with 200,000 troops, McNaughton still saw a less-than-even chance of success:

> He showed me some papers which he had prepared for the contingencies of cease-fire, of things which the VC might do and the things which they could not do. I told him that my impression was that the package which he called Compromise Package B . . . in effect amounted to a division of the country and the recognition of the NLF as a legitimate unit. He said that this was so.

Nothing he had hitherto read had prepared Kissinger for this. But there was more:

> He then showed me a paper which he had prepared in which he had assigned probabilities to various outcomes at various force levels. In no case and at no level of force did he give the probability of win of higher than 40%. In every case he gave the highest probability to a compromise outcome which would then have the essential characteristic of recognized VC areas.

When Kissinger spluttered that "the VC in these conditions might well take over the country," McNaughton's reply was shattering. "Let's face it," he said. "At some point on this road we will have to cut the balls off the people we are now supporting in Vietnam, and if you want to do a really constructive study you ought to address yourself to the question of how we can cut their balls off."[23]

To go from this meeting to an afternoon rendezvous with Walt Rostow at the State Department can only have been surreal, for Rostow was as "bubbling over" with optimism about the war as McNaughton was dissolving into despair. The "main forces" of the Vietcong just had to be "smashed." The North Vietnamese simply had to be "got . . . to cease their direction and supply" of the Vietcong. After those things were achieved, the guerrillas "would eventually wither away." Then the NLF could be divided by allowing Communists to participate in the South Vietnamese politics "as individuals" but not as an organized group. A sense of realism returned with Leonard Unger, who had recently returned from Laos to lead the State Department's Vietnamese task force. Unger warned that "any negotiation would be extremely difficult because the South Vietnamese government did not have enough cohesion and because the Vietnamese mind was so complicated that they would surely assume that this was the beginning of an American sell-out." Worse, there was "no clear idea" of what the American side wanted to achieve from negotiation.

In short, wherever Kissinger turned in Washington, he encountered backbiting of varying degrees of viciousness. Max Taylor was now a special consultant to the president, but he had also served as chairman of the Joint Chiefs of Staff as well as ambassador in Saigon. He could not resist having a dig at McNamara, "who wanted to take over the whole country" and involve the United States in "an imperial adventure for an indefinite number of years."

Kissinger cannot have expected to encounter perfect harmony. There had been no shortage of recrimination when the U.S. war effort had got bogged down in Korea, after all. Yet the thing that dismayed Kissinger the most was the way senior officials were concealing information from one another. William Bundy admitted over lunch that "the significant documents . . . were being kept in his office and not circulated in the [State] Department."[24] He heard a similar story from McNamara's aide Adam Yarmolinsky, who offered to show him a "rather closely held" report McNamara had written on Vietnam.[25] When he went to see McNaughton, he too produced "a file of looseleaf notebooks which are never permitted to leave his office and had never been shown to the State Department. Indeed, the copies had been seen only by Mac Bundy, McNamara, and McNaughton." To the young Kissinger, ironically, all this secretiveness seemed bizarre. "It is not clear to me," he noted in the diary he had begun to keep, "how one can make national policy with each of the key sub-Cabinet officials guarding their documents for their own personal use without sharing them either with their staff or with the key department."[26]

McNaughton offered an explanation. While McNamara "shared to some extent" his "notions of compromise," they had to be "extremely closely held because the Chiefs of Staff were violently opposed to any such notion and he, therefore, implored me never to mention anything like this to the military leaders." Kissinger was beginning to grasp that U.S. policy in Vietnam was the product not of grand strategic thinking but of "bureaucratic struggle." There was no overall plan, no central concept, only "pieces of paper" produced by "essentially autonomous operations." Thus "it was quite possible for different agencies to follow different philosophies and simply avoid overt competition." Admiral Raborn had talked a lot of nonsense, but he had been right about one thing, Kissinger concluded. What was needed was a "management-consultant-type of approach in which the component parts were studied and the whole puzzle put together." As he told Lodge, who cannot have been surprised to hear it, "[I]n Washington there does not seem to exist any long-range integration of the many diverse operations now taking place. What goes under the name of inter-agency planning is really a device for coordinating essentially autonomous efforts which may be based on different concepts and assumptions."[27]

If this was the state of Washington, what would Saigon be like? On September 7, in a preliminary report for Lodge, Kissinger attempted to summarize his initial thoughts. First, the government of South Vietnam (the acronym GVN was preferred in official documents) must be strengthened, not undermined. There must be no more talk of coups, and much less of an "an attitude of disdain" toward the Vietnamese. By the same token, the Vietcong should not be dignified with the propagandistic name of National Liberation Front (NLF). Second, the administration must stop talking about "negotiations" without saying what the word actually meant; "a concrete program" was urgently needed. This was doubly important. Too blanket an offer to negotiate gave the North

Vietnamese a free option: "If they know that they can always get to the conference table and that the terms will remain essentially the same they will have every incentive to continue military operations." In any case, it would be wrong to expect the Communists to enter into negotiations with the intention of "settling"; they would do so "with the aim of winning at the conference table the prize which eluded them on the battlefield." At the same time, too much talk of negotiation would likely demoralize the South Vietnamese government and people. Kissinger had learned some valuable lessons about this kind of peace process from the Berlin Crisis:

> "Unconditional negotiations," "cease fire," "tacit mutual concessions" are useful phrases if some concrete meaning attaches to them. Otherwise they can be turned against us, and confuse and demoralize our friends. It is true that we cannot know all the elements of a negotiating position in advance. But we do know that we will have to adopt an attitude towards the NLF; we must know whether we will strive for an all-Vietnamese or simply a South Vietnamese solution; we must have ideas on how to police an agreement. If we cannot be precise on these issues, there is a grave danger that negotiations will primarily concern the extent of our concessions. . . . [We] must recognize that they begin a new phase of the struggle rather than mark its end.[28]

The third and perhaps most important insight Kissinger had arrived at before his departure for Saigon was that the Vietnam War was, first and foremost, a civil war. This mattered because civil wars were "the most difficult to end by negotiations and 'settlements' which preserve a rough equilibrium are likely to be fragile.

> This is no accident. Civil wars usually evoke the most intense passions. Involving people of the same backgrounds and culture, inhabiting the same area, the terms are extremely difficult to enforce. This is why those civil wars which have ended since World War II have usually been concluded with the predomi-

nance of one side or the other—as in Greece, Malaya, the Philippines, or China—without formal acknowledgment by the defeated side. Formal settlements as in Laos or Cyprus have almost invariably been the starting point of new conflict.

The conclusion he drew from this analysis was striking, namely that "an outcome in which we achieve a major pacification without a formal settlement might not be the worst result of the Vietnamese war."[29]

As Lodge said, Kissinger's report was "a remarkable contribution from someone who has never been here."[30] But what was most remarkable about it was its *ex ante* pessimism. A second report, written nearly three weeks later, was not much more cheerful.[31] By the time Kissinger packed his suitcase, he had conducted a further seventeen interviews with experts inside and outside the government, covering everything from grand strategy to the nitty-gritty of operations against the Vietcong. Though only fragmentary notes of these interviews have survived, and though some of those interviewed can no longer be identified (in his notes, Kissinger identified individuals by a single letter), a number of points helped shape his thinking. "A"—clearly a senior military man—underlined the "question mark" over "the ability to maintain control over countryside" and the "rivalry in VN among various American agencies."[32] "B" asked two difficult questions: "Why are we not controlling more roads? How can one be convincing at a distance of 10,000 miles that one is prepared to stay as compared to indigenous people who have no place to go."[33] "C"—who was Alexis Johnson, only recently returned from Saigon to become deputy undersecretary for political affairs—warned Kissinger of five distinct problems about South Vietnam.

> As far as generals are concerned, they will go along [with any negotiation] without understanding it. What they fear most is peace. They are right. . . .
>
> Utter lack of political experience of Vietnamese leaders. Experience such as it is is conspiratorial. . . .
>
> Vietnamese have Samson complex: pulling temple down around themselves. . . . Overwhelming fact of situation is

regionalism. . . . Degree of control of central government is tenuous. Corps commanders and province chiefs carry out orders if they feel like it. . . .

Americans should not do pacification (i.e. clearing and holding a guerrilla infested area by rooting guerrillas out of population). It is a hopeless role for foreigner.[34]

Johnson also had three specific things he thought Kissinger should seek to avoid: a "full dress Geneva" conference, as the outcome of such an international gathering would inevitably be worse than that in 1954; a cease-fire as a preliminary to negotiations, which would be equivalent to "throwing in the sponge"; and insisting as a quid pro quo that the North Vietnamese end the infiltration of forces into South Vietnam, as this would be all but impossible to verify.[35]

A final striking feature of Kissinger's preparation for his trip to Vietnam was that there was no shortage of good advice from officials. "D" (Allen Whiting, a State Department China hand) astutely noted that it had been a mistake in 1965 "to step-up air operations while DRV was deliberating—[which] gave them the feeling we were trying to bomb them into negotiations." The Communists, he added, "never doubted our resolve in the short run. Do doubt our ability to last five years."[36] Chester Cooper from the NSC clearly saw the need to manage American expectations:

Need public support for proposition that this kind of war has no victory and if we come out where we came in we do well.

Must recognize that even a settlement implies

(1) Continued existence of DRV

(2) Continued existence of VC.

"Must realize," Kissinger jotted down, "that only possible outcome is limited one . . . in which VC have some kind of role." Such a compromise solution was the only good option available. Outright victory in South Vietnam was unattainable because "we know nothing about nation-building."[37] The puzzle—not for the last time in history—remains why American strategy could have gone so disastrously awry when so many highly placed public servants understood so well the nature of the problem they faced.

Far from arriving in Saigon an *ingénu*, then, Henry Kissinger was already a sadder and wiser man on the subject of Vietnam on his way home from Washington. He had been especially impressed by the views of Deputy Undersecretary Alexis Johnson, whose best-case scenario was that there might be a "technical military meeting" between representatives of the Hanoi and Saigon governments, at which the latter would demand the withdrawal from their territory of Vietcong "mainforce" units. But for this to happen, two things were essential: a competent government in Saigon and a defeated government in Hanoi. In the fall of 1965, neither looked very likely. "My only problem," Kissinger told him "is that I find myself in so much agreement with you that I do not know what I will be able to add to your own report."[38] From Saigon, Philip Habib—Lodge's counselor for political affairs—wrote to reinforce the extreme difficulty of Kissinger's mission. The "Ultimate Long-Term Objectives" of the United States "as stated by the President" boiled down to "an independent South Viet Nam, securely guaranteed, free to shape relations, etc." If a negotiated settlement were to achieve that, conditions on the ground would need to improve drastically "in terms of pushing back Viet Cong units and destroying overt [National] Liberation Front apparatus, restoring local government and self-defense capacity."[39]

In the long-running CBS series *Mission: Impossible,* which first aired in 1966, cerebral middle-aged men in civilian attire battled nebulous authoritarian regimes. Henry Kissinger's mission to Vietnam in 1965 had something of the same quality.

V

It was a long way. Kissinger left Boston on October 7. His itinerary was a grueling one requiring no fewer than five layovers: New York, Pittsburgh, San Francisco, Honolulu—where he paused for briefings at

CINCPAC* headquarters—and Hong Kong. He arrived on October 15. As a State Department consultant, he was required to fly economy the whole way, though he paid for his own upgrades on the longer legs of the trip. The planned duration of his stay in Vietnam was just three weeks.[40] But as he told Lodge, "I do not mind—indeed I prefer—to work fifteen hours a day every day that I am in Vietnam (including the week-ends)."[41] To judge by the exhaustive list of key people he met—Americans and Vietnamese, civilians and soldiers—he was as good as his word.[42] The mission might well prove to be impossible, but Henry Kissinger was determined to give it his best shot.

The unquiet American's preferred method was to ask disquieting questions. In Honolulu he was briefed on U.S. operational planning for Vietnam by Lieutenant General Paul S. Emrick, the Pacific Command chief of staff. A major thrust of the American effort in late 1965 was to destroy Vietcong "mainforce" units. Kissinger's question was simple: "I asked him about what would happen if the Vietcong would not fight in battalion-size units." Then, replied the general, the problem would become one of "pacification" rather than combat. But was that not precisely the same challenge the South Vietnamese had faced in 1961? Kissinger asked.

> General Emrick then said that all the soldiers in Vietnam were being trained to be good will ambassadors handing out candy and defending the villages. There was an enormous distinction between American soldiers and French soldiers since the French had a stand-offish colonial attitude, but the American soldiers came as friends. I suggested that perhaps the problem was not only friendship but physical security against assassination. Many people in American cities are paying for protection against gangsters. This doesn't mean that they love the gangsters; it simply proves that the police are not able to protect them.[43]

---

*Commander in chief, Pacific Command.

Unlike Greene's Pyle, Kissinger was never under the illusion that there was some profound moral difference between the Americans in Vietnam and the French in Indochina.

Emrick was a defender of the American bombing of North Vietnam, arguing that it had cut by half the number of enemy forces that could be put into the South. But the most illuminating—and shocking—analysis of the bombing came from General John W. Vogt, a former fellow at the Harvard Center for International Affairs. It was extremely unlikely, he told Kissinger, that the B-52 raids "hit absolutely nothing." In any case, the raids were not being carried out for the purpose of destroying enemy forces. "The B-52 raids represent some of the cheapest methods of using our power. The bombs were in practically unlimited supply; the B-52s would be on training missions of similar duration anyway and this gave them extremely good practice in targeting under nearly perfect conditions. . . . In other words, for supporting the Vietnam war SAC was paying no more than it would have to pay for its training anyway." In reality, the bombing was "not really designed to support the immediate tactical situation in South Vietnam but to achieve the political objective of forcing the Vietnamese to the conference table."

Kissinger left Honolulu reassured on only one point. The probability of a Chinese intervention in the war, on the Korean model, was vanishingly small. Though there were concentrations of People's Liberation Army troops and aircraft in the vicinity of the Vietnamese border, they would be easily defeated by U.S. counterstrikes (especially, Kissinger noted, "if nuclear weapons were used"). But in all other respects, the military briefings unnerved him. The fact was that "no one could really explain to me how even on the most favorable assumptions about the war in Vietnam the [war] was going to end." No one really had a plan for pacification. No one really knew how infiltration was happening. His conclusion was as bleak as it was prescient:

I am quite convinced that too much planning in the government and a great deal of military planning assumes that the opponent is stupid and that he will fight the kind of war for

which one is best prepared. However . . . the essence of guerrilla warfare is never to fight the kind of war your opponent
expects. Having moved very many large units into Vietnam . . .
we must not become prisoners now of a large-unit mentality.
Otherwise I think that we will face the problem of psychological exhaustion.

Perhaps most unnerving of all was Vogt's warning to Kissinger to stick
close to the U.S. embassy and other secure installations as "the losses to
the terrorist activity in Saigon were much greater than was being
announced."[44]

VI

Saigon in the 1960s was hell. That, at least, was the impression that
many American journalists liked to convey. Beverly Deepe Keever of
The Christian Science Monitor had first seen the city in 1962 and had been
enchanted by its Parisian boulevards, high-steepled cathedral, and
"relaxed pace necessitated by muggy days." As the war escalated, however, Saigon became "electric with an air of uncertainty mixed with
danger." Life there became a blur "of fleeting acquaintances, hidden
dangers, and unknown tomorrows." Soon, as refugees flooded into the
city, its streets became "cluttered" with "beggars, black marketers, and
destitute women selling themselves . . . creating a slum-like sprawl that
overshadowed the captivating, Frenchified city. . . . Huddled outside
swank hotels were ragamuffin children called *bui dui*—'dust of life.'"[45]
"In the monsoon season," wrote *New Yorker* contributor Frances
Fitzgerald, "whole quarters of the city sink into the marsh. Some districts are little more than gigantic sewers, lakes of filth above which
thatched huts rise on stilts, connected only by rotting boards. In other
quarters where the refugees have not had time to built stilts, the sewage
inundated even the houses."[46] Recruited from a huge population of
orphans, street gangs "roam[ed] like wolf packs, never sleeping in the
same place twice, scavenging or stealing."[47]
Michael Herr was covering Vietnam for *Esquire* magazine. (Admit-

tedly, he got to Saigon two years after Kissinger, but the city cannot have changed much in so short a time.) Herr felt himself in an inferno:

> By 7:30 it was beyond berserk with bikes, the air was like LA on short plumbing, the subtle city war inside the war had renewed itself for another day . . . with thousands of Vietnamese . . . plugging the feed tube into their own hearts, grasping and gorging; young Americans in from the boonies on TDY, charged with hatred and grounded in fear of the Vietnamese; thousands of Americans sitting in their offices crying in bored chorus, "You can't get these people to do a fucking thing, you can't get these people to do a fucking thing."

There were the families of refugees living in cardboard boxes and on trash heaps. There were the unemployed "students" in cafés like La Pagode, reading Pléiade editions of Proust, Malraux, and Camus and comparing the American empire with the Roman. There were the ferocious bag and watch snatchers of Lam Son Square, who could "snap a Rolex off your wrist like a hawk hitting a field mouse." There were the drunken civil engineers in the Hotel Continental bar, to whom the locals were simply "nigs." There were the "four known VC sapper battalions in the Saigon-Cholon area, dread sappers, guerrilla superstars, [who] didn't even have to do anything to put the fear out." There was the "serious tiger lady going around on a Honda shooting American officers on the street with a .45." Saigon, Herr wanted his readers to understand, was both exotic and potentially fatal:

> Sitting in Saigon was like sitting inside the folded petals of a poisonous flower, the poison history, fucked in its root no matter how far back you wanted to run your trace. . . . Saigon . . . breathed, expelled it like toxin, Shit Piss and Corruption. Paved swamp, hot mushy winds that never cleaned anything away, heavy thermal seal over diesel fuel, mildew, garbage, excrement, atmosphere. A five-block walk in that could take it out of you, you'd get back to the hotel with your head feeling like one of those chocolate oranges, tap it sharply in the right

spot and it falls apart in sections. Saigon . . . You'd stand nailed
there in your tracks sometimes, no bearings and none in sight,
thinking, *Where the fuck am I?*[48]

Copy like this sold well in the second half of the 1960s, reinforcing as
it did the liberal media's increasingly explicit message that the Vietnam
War was an unmitigated bad thing.

Kissinger's Saigon, as recorded in the pages of the personal diary he
kept for his own use, was altogether less hellish—and more plausible.
As a veteran of a much bigger, much deadlier war (where he had also
seen war correspondents in "action"), he had little time for self-
dramatizing journalists aspiring to be the next Tom Wolfe. Indeed, he
could scarcely conceal his contempt when, at the airport in Pleiku, he
encountered "an absolutely absurd collection of newspaper men who
had been helicoptered to the battle field [at Plei Me] which was absolutely secure and who were comporting themselves as if they had just
been saved from a horrible ordeal. They looked dirty, disheveled,
unshaven and they must have spent all of their time shoveling dirt on
each other because the combat troops looked crisp and clean." He had
no time at all for these "absurd caricatures of Ernie Pyle," the most
famous American war correspondent of World War II.[49]

To Kissinger, Saigon was not hell; it was just "like Washington in
August . . . though for some reason [the humidity] does not have quite
the enervating effect that it does in a heat wave in the United States."
He found the late summer heat "soft and all enveloping . . . almost as if
you could feel the air physically." The only problem was that the "constant alteration between air conditioned individual offices and the
slightly steamy atmosphere outside causes almost everybody to suffer
from a cold."[50] Kissinger went for a swim at the Cercle Sportif, "which
is what passes for the exclusive swimming club in Saigon." It was "like
everything else here . . . run down and somewhat dilapidated," but it
offered a pleasant relief from the heat. He was disappointed to hear
from a French girl he met at the pool that the magnificent beaches to
the north of Saigon were no longer safe because they were being used
"as a rest and recuperation area for the Vietcong."[51] To a man who had
seen entire towns laid waste in northern Europe in 1944–45—and

similar scenes of devastation in Korea in the early 1950s—the atmosphere of Saigon was perplexingly unwarlike:

> When I was in combat during World War II, or when I visited Korea for the Department of the Army in 1951, one knew precisely when one was in a danger zone and while one was in the danger zone the chances of attack were more or less constant, say 10–20%. In Saigon and throughout Vietnam, one is in a way constantly in a danger zone but there is no appearance of physical danger whatever. At the front in World War II or in Korea one heard the guns and one could almost sense the physical approach of danger. In Saigon everything appears perfectly normal and there is really no choice except conducting one's business as if one were in downtown New York. If danger should ever materialize, it will be sudden, unexpected, and would have an almost 100% certainty of success. The result is, curiously enough, that there is never any particular fear.

The only sign of insecurity he saw on his first day was that "when cars stop at intersections people look around into adjoining cars and start tensing when people walk up . . . because it would, of course, be an easy matter to drop a grenade into the car and one would never know whether the Vietnamese driver had not brought one to an ambush deliberately." Kissinger himself felt safe. It was everyone else who was jumpy. He was woken up one night by "a fusillade of shots," but this was because one of the embassy guards had discharged his rifle by accident, "whereupon all the guards, and above all the Vietnamese on the outside of the compound, began firing like mad, even though there were no targets." He was struck by the fact that the security measures at the embassy were so patchy, with heavy protection at the front entrance but absolutely no defenses at the other end of the street. "Nothing would be easier than to set up a mortar and start shooting at the house." But nobody did.[52] The worst thing that happened to him on this trip was to have his pocket picked and his wallet stolen, along with the $247 in cash he was carrying.[53] Others left Saigon with memories that gave them nightmares. Kissinger took home a lacquer box, an "awful" Hue vase (to be made into a lamp), and a few "little montagnard things," worth in all $40.[54] (He admitted to having "gaudy tastes.")[55]

Nor was Kissinger content to remain in Saigon, as many American civilians felt safer doing. On October 26 he flew to Hue, the capital of Vietnam from 1802 until 1945 and one of the most attractive cities in Southeast Asia, nestling on the banks of the Perfume River in a valley ringed by high mountains. As they explored the town on foot, he could not fail to notice that he and his State Department escort were the only Americans in the street.[56] Hue was just over sixty miles south of the demilitarized zone that separated North and South Vietnam, running just below the 17th parallel. Kissinger was not foolhardy, at least not at first. When the dean of Hue University urged him to visit an imperial tomb less than three miles outside the city—an area of such heavy Vietcong concentration that he was advised it would take three platoons to get him there—he declined. "As it happened," he noted in his diary, "I did not have the time to test it and I am probably not heroic enough . . . in any event."[57] But there is no gainsaying his courage. One of the Buddhist leaders he wanted to interview insisted on meeting at a pagoda some distance from the town center. Kissinger bleakly noted that "if the VC were in fact as pervasive as the situation indicated it would be an easy matter to knock us off on the way there." The young John Negroponte—who was his escort from the embassy— replied that "the VC never engaged in indiscriminate assassination, that if they shot at us we would have the consolation of knowing that we had been singled out for specified targets."[58]

Kissinger also flew—through a thunderstorm in a twin-engine Beechcraft Model 18—to the "hair-raising" airstrip at Pleiku, which had been the scene of a heavy mortar attack earlier that year (a key incident in the Johnson administration's narrative of escalation). The terminus of the strategically vital Route 19 from the coast, Pleiku was the headquarters of the South Vietnamese Second Corps and was occupied at the time of Kissinger's visit by two Vietnamese divisions, one American division, and one South Korean division. It was essentially besieged: beyond a radius of only ten miles from the town center, it was too dangerous to drive at night. The American compound was surrounded by sandbags, barbed wire, and mortar shelters. As Kissinger noted, it looked "like one of these frontier towns inside a stockade [from] the movies about the West on television." At the time of his visit, a major battle had just taken place at Plei Me, around twenty-five miles to the south, where the 33rd and 320th PAVN regiments had attacked a Special Forces camp, only to be repulsed by ARVN forces supported by the U.S. First Air Cavalry Division.* Not content with this, Kissinger then proceeded with a CIA escort to an even more remote Special Forces outpost, seventy miles north of Pleiku and twenty miles from the Laotian border, in order to see for himself how North Vietnamese infiltration was being countered.[59]

Kissinger saw a lot of Vietnam in just three weeks. He saw a lot of key decision makers too, beginning right at the top on October 16 with General William Westmoreland, the commander of Military Assistance Command, Vietnam (MACV)—a force that by the end of his posting in 1968 would have grown to more than half a million men. As far as Westmoreland was concerned, the only question Kissinger needed to address was "how long it will take our programmed military efforts to accomplish the objective of pacifying the country." The answer was that 60 percent of the population would be under government control within 19 months—not 18 or 20—and that after another 18 months that proportion would have risen to 80 percent.[60] Kissinger heard similar things from other senior officers. "If I listened to everybody's description of how they were succeeding," he remarked to Lodge, "it was not easy for me to see how the Vietcong were still surviving."[61] It was the same story at Pleiku, where "briefers at the Second Corps headquarters claimed [that] 68% of the population was under government control." Kissinger was disgusted. "Since I have last had contact with it," he noted scornfully, "the Army has degenerated. They have produced a group of experts in giving briefings whose major interest is to overpower you with floods of meaningless statistics and to either kid themselves or deliberately kid you." When he asked the Pleiku briefers

---

*PAVN: People's Army of Vietnam—North Vietnamese army. ARVN: Army of the Republic of Vietnam—South Vietnamese.

"how much of the population which was technically under their control was also under their control at night," they answered only 30 percent. Kissinger did not believe this either, but even if it were true, "it indicates the enormity of the problem. It also indicate[s] that we can go from technical victory to technical victory and not really advance in the major problem of establishing control over the population."[62]

In fact, the majority of Americans Kissinger spoke to in Vietnam were much less optimistic than Westmoreland and his MACV mouthpieces. Lansdale was obviously being marginalized, but at least he was frank—which was probably why he was being marginalized. He told Kissinger "he found conditions in Vietnam infinitely worse than he had expected." The Vietnamese government "could not be called a government in any normal sense"—their "writ ran hardly outside of Saigon." As for the army reports of pacification, these "were based on an entirely formalistic criteria [sic] having to do with the number of incidents and large unit engagements." The real problem that was not being overcome was "highly organized Vietcong political apparatus which penetrated every aspect of Vietnamese life and which existed in every village as a de facto government." In Lansdale's view, it would take a minimum of five years to break the Vietcong political apparatus.[63] Kissinger heard a roughly similar analysis from the CIA station chief, Gordon Jorgensen. Whereas official reports indicated that only a quarter of the population was under Vietcong control, in reality the proportion was closer to half, "in the sense that the Vietcong were operating in the villages at night and were in the position to impose their will selectively." The visitor asked his usual uncomfortable question: whether they had "any indications that in the areas where the United States had established base areas the hold of the Vietcong was being broken." The answer was no. There was a political battle still to be won against the Vietcong in the villages "through careful tough detailed operation," but it would take a minimum of three years. Who exactly were the Vietcong? inquired Kissinger innocently. "They said they knew the Vietcong at the province level but they did not know the names of the Vietcong at the district and fighting level and that in many cases they knew only the code names."[64] The CIA agents Kissinger met in Hue were even more pessimistic. As far as they could establish, 80 percent of the province's population was under VC control at night, while in the hamlets listed as pacified, "the authorities hole up with their protective forces in their houses and pray that the VC will not attack them."[65] A peace deal based on an end to infiltration would be impossible to verify. A cease-fire would simply mean collapse.

Just as in Washington, so in Saigon, the CIA blamed the military for being "too pedantic and . . . operating much too slowly and much too carefully and from the Vietcong's point of view much too predictably," while the embassy blamed the CIA for "spending their time on what was really a job of rural reconstruction in order to justify their existence."[66] Yet the political section of the embassy was largely unanimous in agreeing with the CIA that negotiations would be a mistake that would backfire. "If Ky tried to negotiate," Habib and his twenty-man team told Kissinger, "there would be a coup within seventy-two hours. . . . [I]f the NLF was formally recognized it would take over the government in a very short time. . . . [A]ny amnesty of VC with freedom to participate in the political process, would lead to collapse. . . . [I]t would take at least nine months to have a government stable enough so that one could mention the idea of negotiations and . . . three [to] five years to strengthen the political structure enough to be able to compete with the Communists peacefully."[67] Nor were lower-level army officers any more sanguine. As one at Pleiku pointed out to Kissinger, "they had managed to assemble six battalions or two regiments twenty miles from Pleiku at Pleime. We did not know it until they had attacked us. The terrain was such that it was simply impossible to check infiltration routes. I asked the briefers how long they thought it would take to finish the job; they said a minimum of five and more likely ten years."[68]

As before his trip, Kissinger noted with disapproval the extent of American prejudice toward the Vietnamese. To the CIA head of station, "the Vietnamese were the most devious people in the world," compared with whom "the Chinese were models of straightlacedness and directness." According to Habib's team at the embassy, the South Vietnamese "never believe[d] anything that they were being told and [always] assumed that there was some devious reason" for everything. Walter Lundy, the weary American consul in Hue, said simply that in Vietnam "anything could happen"; or as Kissinger put it, he had "accepted the

Vietnamese attitude . . . in which a miracle becomes an ordinary event."[69] Yet Kissinger himself had an altogether different reaction to the Vietnamese he met. He was struck "by the dignity of the average Vietnamese. One never sees the squalor and . . . frenzy of India. One never sees a vulgar Vietnamese. This is a tough and impressive people; if not necessarily an extremely attractive one."[70] Kissinger's readiness to show the Vietnamese respect did not go unnoticed. When he flew home, the South Vietnamese foreign minister spontaneously came to see him off at the airport (though he failed to locate him).

Kissinger based his positive view of the Vietnamese on around a dozen meetings with members of both the government and the non-Communist opposition. What they had to say to him was character-ized more by candor than by deviousness. One spoke for many in South Vietnam when he said that "when peace is achieved you will suddenly lose interest in us and you will leave us to our own devices; you will reduce your aid; you will bring back your people, and then what are we going to do[?]"[71] Tran Ngoc Ninh, the commissioner for education, asked Kissinger outright if it was true that "the U.S. government is try-ing to bring about a civilian government which would be willing to negotiate with the DRV, and that economic pressures are being applied by the U.S. government to bring this change about?"[72] These were fair questions. Even at this early stage, the South Vietnamese government knew—just as McNaughton had said—that negotiations would not bode well for them.

As Prime Minister Ky tried to explain to Kissinger over lunch at Nha Trang, South Vietnam was chronically weak in two respects. First, the country was politically divided because of "the age-old problems of regionalism and religious differences." (The only element capable of transcending these divisions was, of course, the army.) Second, the gov-ernment had not yet worked out how to "compete with the Viet Cong in many parts of the countryside—not because [the] VC are popular, but because of their ruthless organization." For that reason, even "the announcement of the acceptance of negotiations could weaken the morale and will to resist Communism to a dangerous extent—even to the point where the ARVN could lose its will to fight with 'many sol-diers giving up and going home.'" Moreover, a cease-fire would only "provide a means by which the Viet Cong would further consolidate their hold over those areas of the country which they now controlled," effectively partitioning South Vietnam.[73]

The Vietnamese minister who impressed Kissinger the most was Foreign Minister Tran Van Do, "a slight man with [the] delicate and almost ethereal features of the educated Vietnamese." He too emphasized the internal divisions of South Vietnam, particularly the rift between southerners and northerners, which he feared could only be overcome by an organization like India's Congress Party. Kissinger asked him "whether he thought that the NLF contained some nationalistic elements that could be won over." Do's reply was blunt: "The NLF are the Vietcong; there is no distinction between them." Kissinger asked "whether there might be any sense in talking to them anyway." Do "utterly rejected this notion and said that this would be the end of Vietnam."

> I asked Tran Van Do how he visualized the war ending. He said that this was absolutely not the time for negotiations. The country was not ready for it and . . . the South Vietnamese government could not stand facing the Vietcong in a political contest. They needed many years in order to resurrect the whole structure of the society which had been smashed.[74]

When Do and Kissinger met again shortly before the latter's departure, Do made clear that his government did not feel bound by the Geneva Accords and was in no way committed to reunification through elections. Reunification, he argued, "was something for the distant future and . . . for an indefinite time the division of Vietnam into two separate states should be maintained," meaning "that South Vietnam had to retain the right to police its own territory . . . the right to take action against the rebels within its borders without hindrance from the North. If the North would withdraw its military units and its aid to the Viet Cong, that could be done. Then one could think of stopping the bombing in the North."[75]

In another meeting, the minister for rural reconstruction enlarged on the difficulty of "restoring civil authority" in rural areas. "The problem was that the Vietcong had started ten years earlier to infiltrate the countryside and had built up an infrastructure throughout the country. It was now necessary for the government to begin where the Vietcong had been ten years ago and try to win back the country from the Vietcong."[76] Matters were not made easier by the refugee crisis. As General Nguyen Van Chuan, the commander of the First Infantry Division, explained to Kissinger in Hue, people who had fled south to escape the conflict were in turn becoming targets of Vietcong recruitment "to foment unrest and insurrection."[77]

The problem was that, as became clear in a meeting with Major General Pham Xuan Chieu, the South Vietnamese military regime was hazy about its own objectives, beyond basic survival. Chieu acknowledged that the government needed to present "a 'new doctrine' to the people which will provide an alternative to Communism," but he "stated quite frankly that he hoped to obtain *Quelques éclaircissements* from the Professor [before he left Vietnam], and it seemed obvious that he was thinking in terms of the formulation of his policy doctrine."[78] There was certainly little hope of an *éclaircissement* from the U.S. ambassador. At a dinner in honor of Foreign Minister Do, Kissinger listened with incredulity as Lodge insisted that "the American system of elections was equally applicable to Vietnam and that even a North-South split was not unheard of in the United States." Habib suggested that the South Korean electoral system might be preferable. (Although Park Chung Hee had come to power in a military coup, parliamentary elections had been held in 1963.) Through all this, as Kissinger noted in his diary, "Tran Van Do was sitting there with a resigned face while Lodge and Habib were arguing whether the Massachusetts system of election or the Korea system of election was more applicable in a country where the Vietcong happen to control over 50% of the population."[79]

The obvious question arose: if the existing Vietnamese military government was uniformly hostile to the idea of any kind of negotiation, might there be other elements in South Vietnam more willing to compromise? The answer appeared to be no. The veteran civilian politician Phan Huy Quat, who had briefly served as prime minister that year, conveyed "with considerable force his complete and absolute conviction that the non-communist forces in South Vietnam were totally unprepared for a peaceful political confrontation with the communist

U.S. ambassador Henry Cabot Lodge, Jr., meets the president of South Vietnam, Ngo Dinh Diem, 1963. The Kennedy administration connived at Diem's overthrow and execution. The unintended result was to increase Saigon's dependence on Washington.

Economist and game theorist Thomas C. Schelling in 1964. Though he and Kissinger were on friendly terms during the 1960s, their relationship would later deteriorate as Schelling sought to distance himself from the Vietnam War.

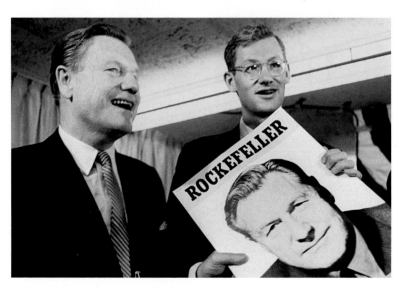

Second time unlucky: Nelson Rockefeller and his eldest son, Rodman Rockefeller, with a campaign poster, June 1, 1964. Kissinger supported each of Rockefeller's three unsuccessful bids for the Republican presidential nomination.

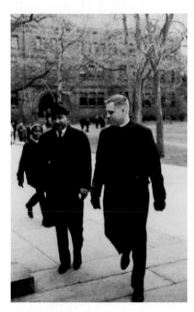

Martin Luther King, Jr., in Cambridge as a guest preacher at the
Harvard Memorial Church, January 1965.

ABOVE: Supporters of Barry Goldwater, the successful candidate for the nomination at the 1964 Republican National Convention in San Francisco.

LEFT: The last Prussian: Marion Countess Dönhoff, editor and later publisher of the West German weekly *Die Zeit*.

Kissinger among the Germans: briefing Bundeswehr officers including the commanding officer of the 5th West German armored division, circa 1965.

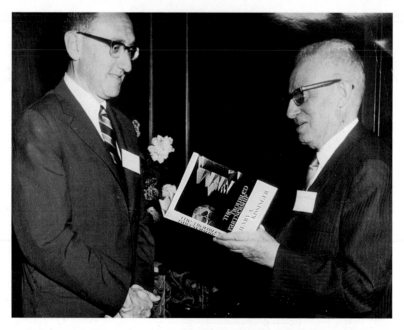

A less troubled partnership: Henry Kissinger with his father, Louis, at an event marking the publication of Kissinger's book *The Troubled Partnership*, 1965. "It is a pity," his father remarked, "that this book was published at a time when all attention is focused to Asia and not to Europe."

McGeorge Bundy and Lyndon Johnson at the White House. The former dean of the Harvard Faculty of Arts and Sciences served both Johnson and Kennedy as "special assistant to the president for national security affairs"— or national security adviser, for short.

McGeorge Bundy is met by Ambassador Maxwell Taylor (behind Bundy) at Tan Son Nhut Air Base, Saigon, February 4, 1965.

The bombing of the U.S. embassy, Saigon, by Vietcong terrorists, March 30, 1965.

A South Vietnamese soldier kicks a suspected Vietcong guerrilla, Xom Chua, Vietnam, October 1965.

LEFT: Kissinger in Vietnam in 1965. His first trip there convinced him that the United States had got itself into an untenable position. "The mere fact that many high sounding programs have been initiated and then collapsed," he noted, "has induced a general atmosphere of cynicism and demoralization."

BELOW: Daniel Ellsberg in Vietnam, where he worked with General Edward Lansdale, the grandmaster of American counterinsurgency. Ellsberg had first become interested in national security issues at Kissinger's Defense Policy Seminar at Harvard. He would later leak the classified documents about the war that became known as the Pentagon Papers.

The agony of Vietnam: American Marines carry a wounded comrade during an operation south of the demilitarized zone between North and South Vietnam, October 1966.

A wounded American soldier receives treatment in the field, October 1966. As Kissinger noted after visiting a Marine base three months earlier, "The job here was a slow, dirty grinding one."

Kissinger with South Vietnam's president, General Nguyen Van Thieu, Saigon, July 28, 1966. At this point Thieu was regarded as the second man in a duumvirate led by the prime minister, Nguyen Cao Ky. A French-trained Roman Catholic army officer, Thieu had an aptitude for political machination. But, as Secretary of State Dean Rusk admitted, he had "every right to be suspicious of Hanoi's purposes" in the subsequent Paris peace talks.

Ho Chi Minh holding his goddaughter, Babette Aubrac, with her mother, Lucie Aubrac, Paris, 1946. Babette's father, Raymond Aubrac, would later act as one of two French intermediaries seeking to establish a channel of communication between Kissinger and the North Vietnamese government.

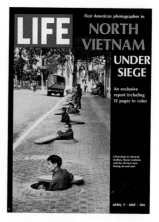

"North Vietnam Under Siege": *Life* magazine's cover of April 7, 1967, showing residents of Hanoi taking shelter from U.S. bombing raids. The argument that American bombing aborted a possible peace settlement in 1967 presupposes that the North Vietnamese government was sincere in wanting a negotiated end to the war at this time.

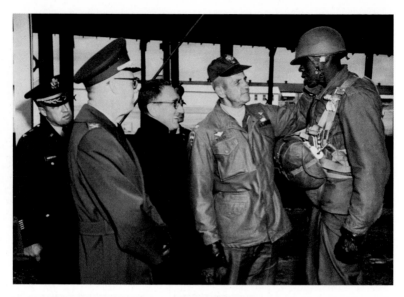

With senior officers and a trainee parachutist at Fort Benning, Georgia.

The West German president, Heinrich Lübke, attempts to get President Lyndon
Johnson and President Charles de Gaulle to shake hands at the funeral
of Konrad Adenauer, April 25, 1967.

ABOVE: Richard Nixon being interviewed near the Vltava River in Prague, March 1967. Two months before, his host, Antonín Šnejdárek—the director of the Czech Institute of International Politics and Economics—had given Kissinger revelatory insights into Sino-Soviet relations.

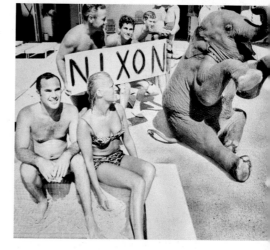

RIGHT: Sunbathing Nixon supporters with a baby elephant at the 1968 Republican National Convention in Miami.

Richard Nixon accepting his nomination as the Republican candidate for the presidency, watched by Congressman (and future president) Gerald Ford, August 7, 1968.

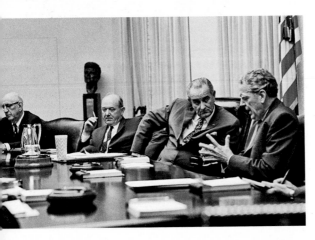

Michael Foot (far left) speaks, Tariq Ali (far right) expostulates, London School of Economics, 1969. The two firebrands of the British left had got the better of Kissinger in a televised debate on Vietnam in 1965.

Dean Rusk smokes, Lyndon Johnson listens, Secretary of Defense Clark Clifford holds forth in the cabinet room, October 14, 1968. Also present at left: Senator Richard Russell.

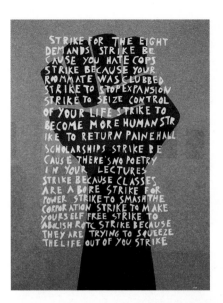

STRIKE FOR THE EIGHT DEMANDS STRIKE BE CAUSE YOU HATE COPS STRIKE BECAUSE YOUR ROOMMATE WAS CLUBBED STRIKE TO STOP EXPANSION STRIKE TO SEIZE CONTROL OF YOUR LIFE STRIKE TO BECOME MORE HUMAN STRIKE TO RETURN PAINE HALL SCHOLARSHIPS STRIKE BE CAUSE THERE'S NO POETRY IN YOUR LECTURES STRIKE BECAUSE CLASSES ARE A BORE STRIKE FOR POWER STRIKE TO SMASH THE CORPORATION STRIKE TO MAKE YOURSELF FREE STRIKE TO ABOLISH ROTC STRIKE BECAUSE THEY ARE TRYING TO SQUEEZE THE LIFE OUT OF YOU STRIKE

LEFT: The Harvard fist, 1969: a symbol of the campus revolt against the Vietnam War, and much else.

BELOW: Preceded by Nixon and followed by Richard V. Allen, Kissinger prepares to be presented to the press corps. Allen had advised Nixon on foreign policy during the campaign for the presidency and resented Kissinger's appointment over his head.

With Richard Nixon at the Pierre Hotel, New York City, on the day of his nomination as national security adviser.

With Nixon, who is facing W. Averell Harriman, and Robert Murphy at the Pierre, New York City, late 1968. Harriman, the veteran diplomat, had been picked by Johnson to lead the U.S. delegation to the Vietnam peace talks in Paris. Murphy was a Nixon adviser who had been undersecretary of state for political affairs under Eisenhower. Though seemingly a novice by comparison with these old hands, Kissinger had already won Harriman's praise as "a kindly but firm teacher" on the subject of Vietnam.

Reintroduction to the White House: with Lyndon Johnson and his outgoing national security adviser, Walt Rostow, December 5, 1968. "Read the columnists," Johnson told Kissinger, "and if they call a member of your staff thoughtful, dedicated, or any other friendly adjective, fire him immediately. He is your leaker."

Listening patiently to the voluble former German finance minister Franz Josef Strauss in 1969.

RIGHT: The public intellectual as budding media star: the newly appointed national security adviser photographed for *Life* magazine in 1969.

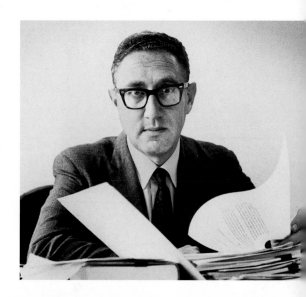

BOTTOM: Henry Kissinger with Nancy Maginnes in 1973. They successfully kept their romance a secret for nearly ten years. She, more than the faint hope of starting negotiations with Hanoi, was the reason Kissinger spent so much time in Paris in 1967.

minority." Far from being interested in peace, he urged the United States to "step up" both the air attacks on the North and the ground war in the South. "When our military effort had dashed the last communist hopes of victory, they would make peace."[80] When pressed on the subject of negotiations, Quat said "quite flatly that his first preference would be for bi-lateral conversations, with minimum of fanfare, between the Governments of North and South Vietnam." But the United States should not suspend its bombing for anything less than the withdrawal of all identifiable PAVN units from the South.[81] Tran Quang Thuan, the former minister of social welfare, was not much less intransigent. South Vietnam simply lacked the social cohesion to negotiate a peace agreement; a "social revolution" would be necessary for that to change. Unlike everyone else Kissinger talked to, Thuan was open to the idea of the United States engaging in secret bilateral negotiations with Hanoi, to which Kissinger replied that "he felt very strongly that the US could not do this, that we could not use small countries as pawns in this way, and that any discussions with the other side would have to involve the GVN."[82] This can only have struck the South Vietnamese as naïve (or mendacious). As Tran Van Tuyen, the former deputy prime minister, explained to Kissinger, there already were regular contacts between Hanoi and Saigon:

> Outside of Saigon . . . he was certain that there was much interchange. There was also much contact through third parties in Paris. (He did not exclude the possibility that he might be in contact with [National Liberation] Front representatives in this fashion, and, in fact, mentioned that friends of his had such contact.) In Paris, Vietnamese allied to both sides met freely in order to "exchange ideas." There was no effective restriction on this sort of interchange and it was going on all the time.[83]

Here, truly, was food for thought.

Kissinger did not confine himself to meeting politicians and generals. Learning as he went along about South Vietnam's complex religious makeup, he also met with Catholic and Buddhist leaders. Father Ho Van Vui was pessimistic about both Vietnamese politics and the war and saw no chance of a military victory over the Vietcong.[84] Mai Tho Truyen, the president of the Buddhist Southern Studies Association, alarmed him by predicting that "either the communists would agree to sign a peace analogous to the 1954 Geneva Accords or the war would accelerate into a third world war."[85] (The fact that this did not happen is perhaps the only respect in which Johnson's policy can be considered successful.) Another Buddhist, Thich Tri Quang, advised him that "China was a better target for American bombers than the people of Vietnam" but added that "everything [in South Vietnam] depended on corruption and on influence and the society was rotten to the core."[86] At times Kissinger's interviews seemed like a competition to see which expert could be the most pessimistic. Among the contenders for first place was Dang Van Sung, publisher of *Chinh Luan* daily, who dismissed the government in Saigon as "a military junta unrepresentative of anything save its members" and "lack[ing] any popular base or rapport with the people."[87]

As Kissinger prepared to leave Vietnam, his mood was despondent. The entire predicament of the United States in Vietnam was summed up by a tirade from the rector of Hue University, Bui Tuong Huan. As Kissinger noted in his diary,

> He never once expressed the slightest appreciation for the fact that the building had been put up by American funds. On the contrary he complained about the architectural style which he claimed was inconsistent with Vietnamese tradition. . . . At one point in the conversation we discussed the general problem of American aid and I told him that some Americans were of the view that really the major effort in Vietnam should be in the economic field and that economic assistance would create a sense of mutual appreciation. The Rector of the University thereupon said the only American aid that the average Vietnamese is getting are American bullets and American shells. Whatever is reconstructed or constructed by American [aid] is . . . made necessary by what they have destroyed.[88]

It was nearly time to leave.

VII

It is best not to sneer at journalists. It is also wise not to speak too frankly with them. Henry Kissinger had first experienced the perils of the press on his trip to Pakistan in 1962. A few ill-judged remarks had landed him in enough hot water to teach him a painful lesson. On his trip to Vietnam in 1965, he had therefore done his best to avoid reporters. But on November 1, under pressure from Ambassador Lodge and his chief spokesman, Barry Zorthian, Kissinger relented. He agreed to attend a lunch at Zorthian's home, to which the chief American correspondents in Saigon had been invited. Among those in attendance were Keyes Beech of the *Chicago Daily News*, Malcolm Browne of ABC, Peter Kumpa of *The Baltimore Sun*, Charles Mohr of *The New York Times*, John Maffre of *The Washington Post*, Robert Shaplen of *The New Yorker*, and William Tuohy of *Newsweek*. The last to arrive was Jack Foisie of the *Los Angeles Times*. As Dean Rusk's brother-in-law, Foisie might have been expected to pose the smallest threat to a consultant working for Rusk's own department. In fact, Foisie came very close to wrecking Kissinger's return to government work.

Immediately after the lunch, Foisie filed a story that appeared the next day under the headline: "Viet Regime Shaky, Johnson Envoys Find."

Recent emissaries from the White House are reporting that there is an almost total lack of political maturity or unselfish political motivation among the current leaders of the South Vietnamese government.

Although they themselves are not talking, these are known to be the findings of Prof. Henry Kissinger, the noted political scientist, and Clark Clifford, the Washington lawyer and adviser to Presidents—both of whom have been recent visitors to Saigon.

Clifford and Kissinger were sent here by President Johnson to make independent appraisals of the direction American political policy should take in South Vietnam.

There are authoritative reports that Kissinger will tell the White House that there is not yet a cohesive national government here primarily because nowhere among the nation's leaders is there a true sense of dedication to the nation. Kissinger's studies indicate there is loyalty to the family and the clan before there is any sense of responsibility to the country.

There then followed detailed criticism of the Ky government's corruption, its mishandling of the refugee problem, and its contempt for the peasantry. Foisie used all the tricks of his trade to put words in Kissinger's mouth. "Although Kissinger has not indicated his reactions to the current trend of U.S. aid," he wrote, "he has been made aware that many U.S. policymakers here believe the time has come to impose their will on Vietnamese officialdom. . . . Kissinger, it is known, has been bombarded with suggestions for changes in the American attitude to exert pressures aimed at remedying some of the defects in the Vietnamese government. He has gone out of his way, it is said here, to listen to divergent views.

Kissinger listens. Diplomatic observers who have watched him since he came here at President Johnson's request are impressed by his willingness to listen. . . .

Those who have been closest to Kissinger while he has been here believe that he will carry back the summation that . . . the Vietnamese government is not yet effective and has only surface stability.[89]

A version of the same story also appeared in *The Washington Post* under the headline "LBJ Envoys Find Almost Total Lack of Political Maturity in Saigon."

Kissinger was aghast. Before leaving Saigon, he fired off two furious telegrams to Washington, hotly denying that the story accurately represented his views. But worse was to come. On landing in San Francisco, he read with "astonishment" a White House statement (made by Bill Moyers) about his trip to Vietnam, which denied that he had any official role. Now beside himself, Kissinger scrawled a two-page letter to Mac Bundy:

> I was determined to carry out my first government assignment in three years quietly and unobtrusively. Therefore, throughout my stay in Vietnam I refused to see the press. Finally on the next to last day at the insistent request of the ambassador and Zorthian I did meet with a few with the promise that they tell *me* their views on Vietnam. I doubt that I spoke three sentences during that lunch. . . . The views ascribed to me were . . . inventions.
>
> Throughout my stay . . . I went out of my way to endorse Administration policy. With respect to the Saigon government, I did my utmost to stress the importance of governmental stability. . . . In attacking the things I did not say the White House may have unwittingly undermined the credibility of what I did say. In view of the fact that I travelled on government orders and worked from an office in the Embassy I do not know what the Vietnamese will make of the statement that I was there unofficially.

Kissinger conceded that his view of the situation in Vietnam was "less encouraging" than he had believed before going there. But the problem was not the weakness of the Saigon government, which was merely "a symptom." In any case, the present government was "as good as any available alternative." He could not understand why the White House had so reflexively decided to disown someone who had "consistently supported Administration policy in Vietnam." As much wounded as indignant, he demanded an official correction.[90]

It is not clear why Kissinger had believed himself to be immune to those pathologies of the Johnson administration that he himself had observed in Washington and in Saigon—in particular, the tendency for each of the different branches of government to blame the others for the deteriorating situation in Vietnam. Doubtless thinking to himself, "Here we go again," Bundy forwarded Kissinger's "angry blast" without comment to his brother, William.[91] The fact that Saigon embassy personnel had been present at all Kissinger's meetings helped, as did a telegram from Lodge defending his conduct.[92] But there was to be no White House correction.[93] Kissinger therefore took the decision to issue his own public denial.[94] And he pressed Bundy to clear him of having been "at least indiscreet and perhaps disloyal" by speaking to people whose opinion he valued, including Hamilton Fish Armstrong, the editor of *Foreign Affairs*. (Bundy obliged.)[95] The only other satisfaction Kissinger received was a note from Moyers expressing his "regret" at the "embarrassment" his statement had caused.[96] By November 11, when Kissinger went to Washington, he was able to report to Lodge that "the Foisie story had blown over."[97]

Clark Clifford's name had been mentioned by Foisie as if to imply that he shared the negative views attributed to Kissinger. This was what really sent Johnson "off the wall," as there was no denying that Clifford was reporting directly to the president.[98] Kissinger wrote a lengthy letter to Clifford, defending his own conduct. But there was a crucial difference. He had gone to lunch with the press corps; Clifford had not. According to Kissinger, he had begun the discussion at Zorthian's by saying that

> it seemed to me inappropriate to state any conclusions before I had done so to the Ambassador; indeed, I was still in the process of sorting out my impressions. I would be grateful, however, for the views of experienced men about the situation in Vietnam, especially with respect to the problem of strengthening governmental legitimacy and continuity. For the rest of the lunch I said, to all practical purposes, nothing and listened instead to an often passionate debate among the newsmen.

He had never so much as mentioned Clifford's name. His main recollection of the lunch was of being "shocked by the violence of the press comments against the Saigon government." He was "deeply sorry" and "depressed and shaken that my effort to be helpful to the Administration and to Ambassador Lodge has ended so ignominiously.

I have tortured myself these past few days to decide what I could have done otherwise and I still cannot understand what happened."[99]

So what had happened? There are two possible explanations. Clifford's was that Foisie had arrived late to the Kissinger lunch and so was never informed that the conversation was off the record.[100] Zorthian, however, had a different recollection. "Henry did a lot of talking and expressed deep pessimism about the Saigon leadership, which he said did not have popular appeal and was corrupt," he later told Walter Isaacson. "I must say, Foisie's story was accurate. So was Henry's pessimism."[101] In other words, Kissinger had once again blundered by speaking too frankly to the press. The reason this seems plausible is that it simply was not the case, despite what Kissinger told Clifford, that his own views, as expressed in his reports to Lodge, were "wholly at variance with" and "diametrically opposed to" those attributed to him by Foisie. As we have seen, scarcely a word of what Kissinger wrote about his trip to Vietnam suggested a "strong belief in governmental stability in Saigon."[102] Quite the opposite. His mistake was a classic one: to reveal to journalists what he really thought, then to flail around with denials that only drew more attention to the mistake.

VIII

What on earth was to be done about Vietnam? In his initial debriefing meetings with William Bundy, Alexis Johnson, and Len Unger at State, McNamara, McNaughton, and Yarmolinsky at Defense, and Raborn and his senior staff at CIA, Kissinger found himself competing with Clifford, who had got to Washington before him. "Before his departure," Kissinger reported to Lodge, "Clifford had been the most extreme of 'doves.' Since his return, he has been saying that the phrase 'unconditional negotiation' was neither diplomatically wise nor politically prudent. We need, according to Clifford, a slogan more focused on outcomes and on Communist concessions. To paraphrase an old saying: plagiarization is the sincerest form of flattery."[103] Kissinger had been persuaded by the South Vietnamese: it was not enough—indeed it was positively dangerous—just to talk about talking to the North Vietnamese. Washington was "intellectually unprepared for negotiations," despite claiming to want them. His other main conclusion from his trip was that the CIA's program of pacification—a euphemism for the counterinsurgency campaign to drive the Vietcong out of the villages they held—needed to be built up gradually, as a hasty expansion of People's Action Teams (PATs, anti-Vietcong cadres loyal to Saigon) might "wreck the whole program."[104]

Kissinger was now positioning himself as Saigon's man in Washington. His reports to Lodge were welcomed as "sagacious and helpful."[105] William Porter urged him to "stay close to the problem," adding, "We need you."[106] Philip Habib called his visit "a good clean breath of air" and urged him to return the following summer. "No other project can be half as fascinating, not even the circus you run," he wrote, presumably a reference to the International Seminar. "This is the Big Casino, and no player can afford to stay away."[107] Habib was eager to see Kissinger's final report to Lodge—"or was it so horrendous that the Boss kept it away from my inquiring eye?" The answer was that Kissinger's report on Vietnam was so horrendous that he did not even send it to Lodge. The "rough draft," of which Kissinger retained the only copy, makes it clear just how negative his views were in the aftermath of his first Vietnam trip. It is a damning indictment of the American predicament, tempered only by Kissinger's hope of somehow making it palatable to Lodge.

It was possible, Kissinger wrote, that the military situation would improve, even allowing for the "overoptimistic" predictions of the military. Success, however, would depend on "the ability to create a political structure to fill the void created by twenty years of civil war, ten years of systematic Vietcong assassination of key officials and two years of political upheavals in Saigon." The Saigon government was "in a precarious position," lacking cohesion, its authority in the countryside "still weak," its centralized bureaucracy "cumbersome."

> In the provinces, civil war and political turmoil in Saigon have produced a combination of . . . demoralization and lethargy. Assassinations, incompetence, governmental change all place a

premium on hedging bets. As one follows programs from Saigon into the provinces one is struck by how many peter out and how many of those of which remnants can be detected are beside the point. . . . The mere fact that many high sounding programs have been initiated and then collapsed has induced a general atmosphere of cynicism and demoralization.

This weakness was the key to the Vietnamese conundrum, for it explained the extreme difficulty of defeating the Vietcong, whose nocturnal control over rural areas Kissinger now put as high as 85 percent. Indeed, Kissinger suspected that "in many areas government survives only by means of a tacit agreement with the Vietcong whereby both sides coexist without getting into each other's way." In these areas, counterinsurgency resembled "a professional wrestling match." Elsewhere, South Vietnamese corps commanders enjoyed "an autonomy verging on war-lordism." Provincial government was "the weakest link in the chain."

Under these circumstances, American efforts were more likely to be counterproductive than productive. "Our exploding bureaucracy leads to a proliferation of programs," he wrote, which tended at once to overwhelm and to undermine the South Vietnamese regime's own efforts. In Alexis Johnson's image, U.S. aid was a fire hydrant; South Vietnamese state capacity was like a garden hose. Kissinger went through the complete list of U.S. agencies involved in South Vietnam, rating them on the basis of his observations, beginning with USOM (United States Operations Mission), which was run by AID (the Agency for International Development). Its top personnel he thought "excellent," but its people in the provinces were "the least able American group," and its "ever-growing bureaucracy" was attempting overambitious nationwide development projects that were not only beyond the capacity of the Vietnamese bureaucracy but, in Vietcong-controlled areas, might simply be "extend[ing] the Communist tax base." The CIA's chief of station impressed Kissinger, but on the ground the "penetration of the VC apparatus was on the whole extremely poor . . . only about 30% of the [pacification] teams are really operating as designed." MACV—the military operation under Westmoreland's command—was trying "to do too many things simultaneously"; it was excessively bureaucratic; and it focused too much on outcomes that could be "expressed numerically." As a result, there was a neglect of "efforts which depend on intangible qualities such as the discovery of local leadership groups." In particular, it lacked the skills to carry out pacification effectively—or as Kissinger politely put it, "the special qualities developed in a decade or more of combat training do not include discriminating political judgment in volatile and complex circumstances."

By contrast, Kissinger was impressed by Lansdale—"an artist at dealing with Asians . . . patient, inspirational, imaginative"—and by his young team, which included a brilliant Harvard game theorist named Daniel Ellsberg, who had first become interested in national security issues at Kissinger's Defense Policy Seminar. But their "artistic and highly individualistic temperament," as Kissinger nicely phrased it, had alienated other agencies. He also noted, shrewdly, that Lansdale was exaggerating the similarities between Vietnam in the 1960s and the Philippines in the 1950s (where Lansdale had helped the government defeat the Communist Hukbalahap insurgency). Finally, Kissinger turned to the U.S. embassy itself. Perhaps inevitably, given his intended audience, he was relatively positive about what he called "one of the strongest—if not the strongest—American mission that I have encountered anywhere." But here, too, he had criticisms, in particular the Saigon mission's tendency to pursue multiple programs "devised in isolation from each other and not fully related to overall criteria generally accepted by all members of the country-team," as opposed to "the personal predilections of some individual in Saigon or some provincial officer."

Kissinger's overall assessment of the U.S. effort was in equal measures shrewd and scathing. There was, quite simply, a woeful lack of interagency cooperation:

> Because each agency is above all eager to push its own programs there is a tendency to operate through what is in effect a series of non-aggression treaties. Unless one agency's program directly impinges on another element of the mission, there is a premium on not challenging it for fear of submitting one's own

cherished projects to general scrutiny. This process avoids
direct competition; it also encourages proliferating bureaucracies and a tendency to try to avoid choices by attempting to
carry out every available option, a course which given the scar-
city of available resources—especially in trained manpower—
is bound to produce disappointments.

The challenge the United States had taken on was to try to "build a
nation in a divided society in the middle of a civil war." But there was
a chronic gap between conception and execution because of the "virtual collapse of Vietnamese civilian administration in the provinces and
the American tendency to do too much too quickly on too vast a scale."
Kissinger did his best to conclude with some positive recommendations: more carefully calibrated pilot projects, better follow-through
once projects had been initiated, a thorough survey of provincial manpower, and the creation of a Program Review Committee of agency
deputy heads. But his best ideas were the simplest. It was time someone
drew a map of South Vietnam that "reflects the security situation not
as it applies to military units but as it affects the civilian population."
And it was time to drop the word *pacification*. "It has an excessively passive, perhaps even condescending, sound to it," Kissinger noted, "too
reminiscent of colonial wars when one pacified the 'natives.'"[108] Too
reminiscent indeed—just as Graham Greene had foreseen.

Kissinger's draft report was altogether too hard-hitting to be sent.
Two days later he sent Lodge a heavily edited version, with some of the
harsher criticism edited out and a slightly different conclusion, including a dutiful affirmation conspicuously absent from the first version: "I
am deeply persuaded that Vietnam is the hinge of our national effort
where success and failure will determine our world role for decades to
come."[109] After finishing the revised report, Kissinger added two after-
thoughts. Could a Vietnamese version of the Peace Corps be created to
combat "the lack of commitment of students and intellectuals in general to the war effort" by sending them to help with pacification in the
countryside? And to the same end, might it not be a good idea to establish "close ties" between South Vietnamese and American universities?

Kissinger was right about one thing: a "fundamental problem" facing the United States was "to develop an ideology which can enlist popular and especially intellectual support . . . something to affirm, not only to reject."[110] But it was his turn to dream if, as 1965 drew to a close, he seriously believed that such an ideology might emerge from an academic exchange between Harvard and Hue. Both were already too far gone.

CHAPTER 18

Dirt Against the Wind

We [are] simply shuffling dirt against the wind.
    —DANIEL ELLSBERG to Henry Kissinger, July 1966[1]

I never had any doubt that the Vietnamese were capable of
organizing complicated things. What I am not so sure about
is whether they can organize simple things.
    —HENRY KISSINGER to Michael Burke, September 1966[2]

I

It was a different Henry Kissinger who addressed the Harvard–MIT
Arms Control Seminar at the beginning of the spring semester. In
August 1965, Kissinger had asked the questions and listened to his colleagues' answers. On January 12, 1966, he was the one with the answers.
Unlike nearly everyone else in the room, he had been to Vietnam and
seen the American predicament there for himself. It is striking how
freely he spoke, considering that this was an academic gathering with
no real guarantee of confidentiality and considering his unhappy experience of speaking freely in Saigon the previous November.

The good news, he told the group, was that "it was clear that we
would not be militarily defeated, that no Dien-Bien-Phu type of disaster was in sight, in view of our tremendous superiority in air power
and other forms of technical equipment." That, unfortunately, was the
end of the good news. The bad news was much as he had outlined it
for Ambassador Lodge. First, it was not clear that the Vietcong would
oblige the U.S. military by engaging in classic combat operations or
taking full control of a key provincial capital that the Americans could

then drive them out of. "Our military tend to expect to fight this war as they have studied war at Fort Leavenworth," he explained, "while the other side is not doing anything of the kind. The Viet Cong is using political and psychological criteria where we are applying some very traditional military criteria." Indeed, increasingly he feared that "we were being lured into the role of a bull in a bullfight, who always forces the other side to give way, but in the process slowly has his strength drained." So long as U.S. forces were focused on fighting in the way they had been taught to fight, they were not advancing the pacification of the countryside. The United States might not lose this way, but it could not end the war either.

Second, South Vietnam was deeply "fragmented and disorganized," with a government that had no coherent positive program and a destructive custom of internecine strife between ministers. Meanwhile, there had been "a substantial disintegration of political presence and cohesion" at the provincial level, to the point that in some areas the civil government was in cahoots with the Vietcong, who levied taxes and even profited from U.S. economic aid. Third, the United States "lacked any overall concept for the conduct of military operations against the guerrillas, and for the building of a nation." Its stock recipe of copious resources and complex bureaucracy was disastrously inappropriate.[3]

Kissinger openly conceded that he had presented "a grim picture." Equally grim was the naïveté of some of the questions he was asked. Milton Katz asked why there could not be "full scale occupation and military government of South Vietnam by the United States," as in Germany and Japan after the war. Kissinger dismissed this by pointing out the absence of an administrative structure for the United States to take over, even were it militarily conceivable, which it was not. Seymour Martin Lipset wanted to know why helicopters did not "allow us to surround the Viet Cong rather than to chase them." Kissinger patiently explained how the jungle-covered terrain lent itself to concealment. Tom Schelling sought to look on the bright side, in that "Kissinger's picture [was] gloomy for the Viet Cong too . . . In terms of pain, cost, etc., we must remember that life is tough for the Viet Cong too. Life in Hanoi is just as bad as life in Washington these days. . . . [W]e should not underestimate the desperation of the other side." As things stood, neither side could achieve its objectives by military force, but escalation of the fighting posed a relatively bigger threat to the Vietcong. This perfectly illustrated the difference between game theory and knowledge gained from the ground up. Kissinger retorted that the real issue was the prolongation, not the escalation, of the conflict. "Perhaps they are more patient then we are, or feel more exhilaration for the period of struggle than for its completion. We must frustrate their expectations that they can outlast us, by showing a staying power rather than merely chasing after quick crash programs." As he had already shown, however, that was more easily said than done.[4]

From the moment he returned from Vietnam, Kissinger found himself in an invidious position. Privately, in gatherings of experts in Cambridge and Washington, he could give vent to his deep anxieties about the course of the war in Vietnam. In public, however, he had committed himself—to Bundy, to Lodge, and to others—to defending the administration. The chairman of the Joint Chiefs of Staff, Earle Wheeler, noted in December 1965 that Kissinger was "very persuasive in private with intelligent, well-informed men" but "would not be suitable for television."[5] Under the circumstances of 1965 and 1966, that was a correct assessment, because whatever public defense Kissinger might mount of the American strategy in Vietnam was bound to be halfhearted. For a man so often accused of being duplicitous, Henry Kissinger was remarkably bad at lying about the debacle that was unfolding in Southeast Asia. Shortly after his return to the United States, for example, he found himself sharing a platform with Tom Wolfe, who had just published *The Kandy-Kolored Tangerine-Flake Streamline Baby* and was about to hit the road with the LSD-addled Ken Kesey,* and the caustic *New Yorker* writer Marya Mannes, whose antiwar poem "Assignment" would be published the following year ("show us the wombs / of village mothers, seeded to replace / the small lives spindled, folded stapled mutilated / by this war").[6] Suddenly Kissinger was the archetypal square, hair

---

*Kesey is the central figure of Wolfe's later *Electric Kool-Aid Acid Test*. In the fall of 1965 he delivered an incoherent ramble on the subject of Vietnam, which ended, "There's only one thing to do. There's only one thing's gonna do any good at all. . . . And that's everybody just look at it, look at the war, and turn your backs and say . . . fuck it."

short, collar buttoned, telling Mannes that she was "very wrong to criticize the anguished people who are making the decisions [about Vietnam]." Intellectuals were in an easy position to talk about ideal policies, he insisted. "The harassed, hard-pressed officials are not in the same fortunate position."[7] Three weeks later Kissinger spoke at a public forum in Boston. "Our failure [to defend South Vietnam]," he told the audience, "would be considered by other nations as symbolic of our inability to protect them from this kind of Communist attack." But this retread of the domino theory had lost whatever power it ever had to convince an American audience. A member of the audience asked a simple question:

"As a result of your trip to Viet Nam, Dr. Kissinger, do you believe a final settlement can be reached? And if not, what steps would you recommend?"

Kissinger shrugged his shoulders, smiled, and said: "I'm sorry, but I really can't answer that."[8]

The mood was darkening on American campuses, Harvard included. A branch of Students for a Democratic Society (SDS) had been established in 1964, and by the fall of 1965 its representatives were making themselves heard with calls to defy the draft.[9] Students and a few faculty members were traveling to Washington to participate in the major antiwar demonstrations of that year. Whatever his private misgivings about the conduct of the war, Kissinger had no doubt where he stood as the antiwar movement picked up speed. To a man who had fought in World War II, this was defeatism. On December 10, 1965, he was one of 190 academics who published a letter in *The New York Times,* expressing their support for the administration's policy and their concern that the noisy tactics of a "small minority of the intellectual community" could prolong the war by causing "Peking and Hanoi to underestimate seriously the extent of the American commitment." Conspicuously, the only other Harvard signatories were Sam Beer and Morton Halperin.[10] As future Harvard president Derek Bok later put it, the faculty was beginning to fracture into leftists, "retreatists," conservatives, and a tiny few who "didn't lose their bearings."[11]

The nadir of Kissinger's public defense of the administration came eleven days later in a televised Harvard v. Oxford debate that pitted him and two Harvard Law School students—Robert Shrum, later a speech-writer for George McGovern, and Lawrence Tribe, later a law professor at Harvard—against the Labour MP Michael Foot and two young Oxford graduates: the Pakistani-born Tariq Ali, a recent president of the Oxford Union, and Stephen Marks, the former chairman of the Oxford Labour Club. The Americans were for the motion that "the United States should carry out its commitment in Vietnam." Although it was a CBS production, in the series *Town Meeting of the World,* the debate was conducted on a version of Oxford Union rules, and unfortunately for Kissinger, his adversaries included two masters of adversarial debate. He began with the official line: the U.S. commitment was to give the people of South Vietnam "an opportunity to decide their own future, free of outside interference." To abandon that commitment now would be to "leave countless thousands to a brutal fate." True, the war was a "grim and desperate struggle," but "[w]e are not in Vietnam because we want to stay. We are in Vietnam because we want to withdraw, and we will do so as soon as free choice is guaranteed to the people of South Vietnam." The British team countered that the United States was in breach of the 1954 Geneva Accords and was ducking opportunities to negotiate with Hanoi. The second point was easily enough rebutted. Hanoi had repeatedly refused UN mediation; the "feel through U Thant" had not been "a clear offer to negotiate"; and "there have been more than fifteen American proposals since then which surely could have provided an opening for another conversation."

But on Geneva Kissinger stumbled. "It is my belief," he said, "that the United States should accept the Geneva settlement as a basis for the settlement of the present war . . . and it is my impression that the American Government has indicated its readiness to do so." Foot pounced:

> FOOT: I think for an expert of Professor Kissinger's emi-
> nence to say that it's his impression that they accept
> it—why does not the United States say quite clearly
> they will accept the whole of the Geneva settlement?
> KISSINGER: I used the word "it is my impression" in defer-
> ence to the debating skill of the—of my British friends.
> I have every reason to believe that the American

> Government accepts the Geneva settlement, whatever
> may have happened in the past. I simply do not have
> the document in front of me in case I am challenged to
> produce the exact words.

At this point, Foot knew his side had won. For, as he triumphantly pointed out, Dean Rusk had said only a few days before that "the United States still wants peace talks on Vietnam, but only if South Vietnam's independence and territorial integrity is guaranteed." That, crowed Foot, was "contrary to the Geneva settlement."[12] In suggesting that the United States would accept the Geneva Accords—which had envisaged a united Vietnam—as the basis for peace in Vietnam, Kissinger had tripped up in a way that a truly convinced defender of Johnson's policy would not have.

Debating against the likes of Michael Foot and Tariq Ali was no fun. With their flowing locks and their fiery rhetoric, they were all but impossible to beat, especially in front of a crowd. They soon had American counterparts. Debating alongside George Lodge at an event at the University of North Carolina in June 1966, Kissinger found himself up against "a highly objectionable pacifist."[13] The problem was that the case for the defense of American policy in Vietnam left audiences stone cold. "We have no choice now but to maintain our commitment to prevent a Communist takeover in the south," Kissinger had told an audience in Winston-Salem, North Carolina, a few months previously, assuring them that "if we can only develop the psychological staying-power, we can prevent a Communist takeover indefinitely." As the local newspaper put it, "One is left, then, not with a justification for our involvement in Viet Nam in high-sounding terms like 'the defense of freedom,' but with a choice among evils, and a selection, presumably, of the least evil."[14] It was all too true. Yet as Kissinger observed in an article for *Look* magazine that August, the war in Vietnam was now "a crucial test of American maturity. . . . We do not have the privilege of deciding to meet only those challenges which most flatter our moral preconceptions."[15] In his eyes, to imply that the United States could simply walk away from South Vietnam was not idealism. It was irresponsibility—a betrayal of American ideals.

II

The most conspicuous absence from Kissinger's report on his first trip to Vietnam—absent even from his devastating first draft—had been any discussion of negotiations as a way to end the war. Essentially, Kissinger had ruled them out. As he put it, in his only allusion to the possibility of a diplomatic end to the conflict, the Saigon government was so weak that it was liable to be weakened further "by the mere act of making a proposal to it (this is particularly relevant in the area of negotiations)."[16] Speaking at Harvard, he could hardly duck the issue so easily, especially as his stated assumption before going to Vietnam had been that only negotiation would end the war.

> He agreed . . . that we probably should negotiate if possible. But we must also see the complexities involved, complexities that would not arise with a more stable government. . . . [A]s long as it is not clear that there is any line separating territory which is entirely controlled by the Viet Cong from territory which is entirely controlled by our side, a simple notion of a cease fire may lead to a great deal of turmoil.[17]

When Donald Brennan (cofounder with Herman Kahn of the Hudson Institute) asked what was preventing negotiation, Kissinger suggested that it might be "the North Vietnamese demand for prior withdrawal of U.S. forces, which at times they have left vague, and which possibly could therefore be negotiated." A second stumbling block was that "on both sides, we have a problem of constantly reassuring our allies," implying that there might be the same kind of constraint on Hanoi (from Beijing?) as there was on Washington from Saigon. But the principal obstacle in the short run was that the United States seemed unable to "specify in detail what conditions we would agree to in negotiations." Moreover, if the United States "gave the impression that a Viet Cong takeover was imminent and expected," then it could lead to "the collapse of the South Vietnamese regime. . . .

The danger is that if we do offer the Viet Cong our slow retreat, this will perhaps stampede our side into a fast retreat."[18]

This created a kind of catch-22: negotiations were necessary because the South Vietnamese government was so weak, but they also could not happen because the South Vietnamese government was so weak. In his *Look* magazine article—a broadly pro-Johnson piece that appeared alongside more critical pieces by Arthur Schlesinger and Hans Morgenthau—Kissinger spoke of "The Impossibility of Withdrawal" and "The Inevitability of Negotiation." But he added a crucial rider. Negotiations would be possible only "when Hanoi realizes that its political apparatus in the countryside is being systematically reduced, and that this process will accelerate the longer the war lasts." On this basis, he now argued, "the primary goal of military operations should be the creation of secure areas." After all, it was "better to have 100 per cent control in 40 per cent of the country than 40 per cent control in 100 per cent of the country." Meanwhile, the diplomatic way forward was not to try "to settle the war at a large conference which deals with all issues simultaneously" but rather "to segment the issues into their component elements, each of which is settled by the parties primarily involved."[19] It is striking to compare this formulation with Kissinger's position in August 1965, before his visit to Vietnam, when he had categorically rejected the idea of U.S.-controlled enclaves in South Vietnam. It also contrasted oddly with his statements elsewhere that time was on Hanoi's side.

At this juncture, Kissinger was still a bit-part actor in Washington. But his name was increasingly invoked as the Johnson administration struggled to square the circle of its unwinnable war. George C. Denney, the deputy director of the Bureau of Intelligence and Research, cited him to Rusk to support his argument that, as Marxists and as Vietnamese—whose "profoundly suspicious character and instrumental attitude toward 'truth' . . . foreign observers . . . have long remarked (most recently Professor Kissinger)"—the other side would never enter into negotiations in good faith.[20] The chairman of the Joint Chiefs wanted to have Kissinger explain to "Senator Mansfield, Senator Fulbright, and so forth" why a bombing halt would do no good.[21] Confident that "pacification" was making progress, Lodge, too, opposed an end to the bombing of the North.[22]

Unbeknownst to Kissinger, a heated debate was going on within the administration about what the next U.S. move should be. On one side were the generals, who saw no alternative but to ramp up both U.S. ground forces in the South and air attacks on the North. When McNamara saw Westmoreland in Saigon at the end of November 1965, the "ask" was for 400,000 troops by the end of 1966 and perhaps another 200,000 in 1967. On the other side were the doubters. "*Where the hell are we going?*" asked Clark Clifford in early December 1965. "I have the feeling we are getting further and further into this war with no prospect of a return. We are fighting the kind of war that Mao Zedong would have us fight. I agree we must do the job—I am sure of that. But couldn't we just use air power while holding our ground troops in more defensive positions? Can we avoid sending six hundred thousand men to fight in these jungles? We *must* try to get the job done with less costly means."[23] McNamara, too, was now assailed by doubts, unexpectedly arguing that "we should be prepared—in the dialogue during a pause, in negotiations or unilaterally . . . to present the other side with a ceasefire."[24] On December 18 he stunned Johnson by stating that "a military solution to the problem is not certain—I estimate it to be one out of three or one out of two." "You mean that no matter what we do in the military field, you think there is no sure victory?" asked Johnson. "That's right," McNamara replied.[25]

McNamara was wilting, encouraged in his despondency by John McNaughton's growing contempt for the South Vietnamese. ("[T]he ground beneath us is mush out there . . . the South Vietnamese Government['s] . . . total incapacity to behave themselves should amount to at least a minimum justification for our dumping them.")[26] Mac Bundy had been coming around to the same view. But in December 1965 Bundy left the White House, and Johnson—to Bundy's dismay—opted to replace him with the most hawkish of all the civilians in the administration: Walt Rostow, a man who believed (as Bundy later put it) he had to decide an issue "before he thought about [it]."[27] In Johnson's inimitable words, Rostow was going to be "*my* goddamn intellectual and I'm going to have him by the short hairs. . . . We're not going to have another Bundy round here"—in other words, another man whose first loyalty in politics was still to John F. Kennedy.[28] Rostow's appointment as national security adviser ensured that Johnson would continue to think of the Vietnam War as a prizefight that could be won if he slugged his opponent with sufficient force and then handed him a towel to throw in.[29]

It was not a prizefight at all. There were all kinds of other actors involved, each of which had at least the potential to exercise leverage in Hanoi. The Johnson administration was somewhat slow to grasp that neither the Soviet Union nor the People's Republic of China was unequivocal in its support for Hanoi. The Soviets had distinctly mixed feelings about the uncompromising North Vietnamese ambition to unify Vietnam under Communist rule, not least because they attributed it to Beijing; they would not have been unhappy with a negotiated compromise. Although they had firmly declined Dean Rusk's attempt to enroll them as messengers to Hanoi in the May 1965 bombing pause, the Soviets hinted that one of their Eastern European satellites might play that role.[30] Four months later Rusk had what seemed like an encouraging encounter with János Péter, the Hungarian foreign minister,[31] though the Hungarian chargé d'affaires, János Radványi, revealed after his defection that in reality Péter was "not in an effective contact with Hanoi."[32] The Chinese were indeed more inclined to egg Hanoi on— Mao saw Ho Chi Minh's struggle as a version of his own in the 1940s— but Zhou Enlai took care to signal that there would be no direct intervention by Beijing unless Chinese territory came under attack.[33]

Then there were the French, who were incredulous that the United States was attempting to do what they themselves, with all their knowledge of Indochina, had failed to. They had by far the best Western contacts in Hanoi. (The North Vietnamese leadership from Ho Chi Minh down was largely French-educated, after all.)[34] It was the North Vietnamese ambassador, Mai Van Bo, who was the point of contact when Edmund Gullion ("X"), a veteran diplomat who knew Vietnam, sought to revive the moribund Geneva institutions—an abortive initiative code-named XYZ.

Beginning on Christmas Eve 1965, another bombing "pause" was tried. Always more attuned to the domestic mood than to the geopolitical realities, Johnson declared a "peace offensive," dispatching Averell Harriman to Budapest and Warsaw, adding Belgrade, Cairo, and

Delhi for good measure. Also deployed in this scattergun effort were Vice President Hubert Humphrey and Assistant Secretary of State G. Mennen Williams. The United States now had points of its own— fourteen of them, to the North Vietnamese four—which (as Rusk put it) "put everything into the basket of peace except the surrender of South Vietnam."[35] This time the significance of the bombing pause was conveyed through two channels: PINTA, the exchanges between the U.S. ambassador to Burma, Henry Byroade, and his North Vietnamese counterpart, Vu Huu Binh;[36] and LUMBAGO, the visit by the Polish special envoy Jerzy Michałowski to Hanoi via Moscow and Beijing.[37]

But Hanoi showed no interest whatsoever. As Michałowski reported from Hanoi, the representatives of the NLF were "very militant" and in "no mood to negotiate," convinced that they could inflict another Dien Bien Phu on this new foreign foe.[38] A foreign ministry statement denounced the bombing pause as a trick, while a letter from Ho Chi Minh, broadcast on state radio on January 28, 1966, accused the United States of deceit and hypocrisy, demanded the withdrawal of U.S. forces, and insisted that any settlement be based on the North Vietnamese Four Points, including the recognition of the NLF as the "sole representative of the people of South Vietnam." On January 31, having lasted thirty-seven days, the bombing pause ended.[39] In March the retired Canadian diplomat Chester A. Ronning tried again but got no further. The North Vietnamese premier demanded that the United States cease bombing "for good and unconditionally" before talks could begin; Washington replied by demanding that Hanoi commit itself to reciprocal de-escalation.[40] As George Ball later put it, all these maneuvers were "foredoomed efforts, because we weren't prepared to make any real concessions. Negotiation at that time still consisted pretty much of saying to Hanoi, 'Look, let's work out a deal under which you will capitulate.'"[41] But Hanoi was "pretty much saying" the same.

All kinds of diplomatic schemes were now doing the rounds. William Sullivan, the U.S. ambassador to Laos, suggested that the United States propose dual membership in the United Nations for both North and South Vietnam, combined with "dual reception" in the General Assembly for both China and Taiwan and perhaps also membership for East Germany too. Mike Mansfield suggested "face-to-face" talks with

China. None of these ideas got off the drawing board. It seemed increasingly clear, as even Rostow was forced to admit, that "our best chance of making negotiating progress [was] through very secret talks with Hanoi."[42] But on what basis? At the end of April 1966, Maxwell Taylor proposed a quid pro quo. In return for stopping its bombing of North Vietnam, the United States should demand "some degree of reduction or elimination of Viet Cong and . . . North Vietnamese activity in the South, or a cessation of infiltration from the North, or a combination of both."[43] This exchange of "blue chips," as it came to be known, seemed like the best bet. Indeed, its potential viability was confirmed by Jean Sainteny, the former French cabinet minister sent to Hanoi by President de Gaulle, after meetings with Ho Chi Minh and Premier Pham Van Dong.[44] The crucial thing, Sainteny told Chip Bohlen, the American ambassador in Paris, was that any such deal must be done through "a secret channel by an individual, not too well known, possibly here in Paris."[45]

Kissinger, however, was unconvinced. In May 1966 he attended a conference at Ditchley Park,* where he had a chance to discuss Vietnam with Michael Stewart, then foreign secretary under Harold Wilson. Somewhat startled by his interlocutor's candor, Stewart reported that Kissinger was "decidedly gloomy about the current political situation in the south:

> He saw no real future in the Ky Government and derided the optimistic impressions . . . [of] Walt Rostow to the effect that Ky was . . . a kind of South Vietnamese General Park.† In Kissinger's view the elections are unlikely to prove anything. There was no prospect of the Americans cooking them so as to achieve a regime favourable to themselves. . . .
>
> Kissinger said he was also concerned at the emphasis that the United States Government felt obliged to put on their

---

*Churchill's wartime retreat near Charlbury in Oxfordshire—originally built in the early eighteenth century for the Earl of Litchfield—had been established by Sir David Wills as a center for conferences on international (and especially Anglo-American) relations in 1958.
†An allusion to the South Korean dictator Park Chung Hee, who ruled his country from 1961 until his assassination in 1979.

willingness to enter a broad Geneva-type negotiation. Obviously this was a good public position to be in propaganda-wise, but in practice if the other side ever displayed willingness to get into such negotiation this would confront the United States Government with very serious problems. In the first instance there would be the question of Vietcong representation. . . . This led on to the possibility of an internal negotiation within South Vietnam between an elected South Vietnamese Government and the Vietcong. . . . He was clearly inclined to hope that some kind of international negotiation could emerge after the Elections and could be a better face-saving device to enable an eventual American withdrawal than any full Geneva-type conference.[46]

This was in very marked contrast to Kissinger's remarks in his television debate with Michael Foot and Tariq Ali, which had implied support for some kind of new Geneva.

Kissinger also had "severe misgivings" about Max Taylor's "blue chips" idea, which seemed to him essentially to propose "a general cease-fire as a substitute for a unilateral ending of United States bombing." This might easily backfire. Clearly, the beginning of any negotiations would put Washington under immense pressure—not least from domestic opinion and allied governments—to stop bombing. There would be no mistaking a cessation of American air strikes. By contrast, would it be possible to devise an inspection system capable of monitoring Vietcong tactics like assassination and sabotage? Would not a cease-fire leave the Vietcong in effective control of large parts of South Vietnam—meaning, in effect, the country's partition? A better quid pro quo for an end to the air war, Kissinger suggested, would be "if the North (a) forswears infiltration in the South [and] (b) agrees to the establishment of control posts along the Ho Chi Minh trail and on both sides of the Vietnamese-Laotian border." This, he added, would have "the advantage of relating the end of bombing to the interdiction of supplies which is its stated purpose."[47]

III

There was one place where Kissinger's argument against negotiation was welcome, and that was Saigon. On reading Kissinger's critique of the Taylor proposal, Lodge wrote marveling that they had both come "to so many of the same conclusions."[48] As early as April 1966, the two began discussing a second Kissinger trip to South Vietnam, an idea that found support from Len Unger at State.[49] As he told William Bundy, Kissinger intended to look into "three problems[:] (1) progress in the pacification field . . . (2) a survey of the internal political situation . . . and (3) problems of constitution drafting."[50] The official State Department instruction was in fact to discuss with Lodge the "scenario" of negotiations and "other questions arising in connection with possible initiation of negotiations, including ceasefires and cessations of hostilities, standfasts, inspection by ICC or other body, etc."[51] That was the theory. In practice, Kissinger was continuing to play the role of Saigon's man in Washington. "As you know," he told Habib, with whom he would stay on this visit, "my view and that of the Embassy are very close indeed. (I would say indistinguishable.)"[52] Neither Lodge nor Kissinger was yet convinced of the wisdom of negotiations; they remained of the view that South Vietnam was simply not ready. For that reason, Kissinger would spend most of his time reassessing the state of the regime in Saigon and the various U.S. agencies charged with assisting it.

Arriving on July 16, 1966, Kissinger was elated to be back in "weirdly fascinating South Vietnam," with its dirty streets, its hopeless traffic jams, and yet its "graceful" people.[53] Not much had changed. Lodge was "very chipper and described to me again as he had already in October that the war was practically won." Westmoreland, "tall, courteous, somewhat soft spoken, rather bureaucratic . . . [but] very honorable, and decent," explained how he was "keep[ing] the Vietcong main force units constantly on the move," while bombing North Vietnamese troop concentrations near the border.

I was struck by the fact that last year he was arguing for a build-up of forces to the present level with many of the arguments he is now using for a build-up to new levels. Last year he told me that if he got the forces he is now getting he would have a victory within a year or at most two. Now he is saying that he can, with present forces, avoid defeat but he cannot guarantee anything except a very slow progress.[54]

The MACV briefers rattled off the usual pacification statistics that divided areas into "clear," "undergoing clearing," "undergoing securing," or "under Vietcong control." The new CIA team assured him that "Vietcong morale was becoming shaky and that penetration would be easier in the next few months." The widespread—and "totally unrealistic"—assumption was that "very major American forces" would remain in South Vietnam after any peace settlement. Lansdale's "swashbucklers [and] adventurers"—"the one group that does have an understanding of how to deal with the Vietnamese, that does have the patience and dedication that is not bureaucratic"—had been "squeezed out of the operation." Other visitors from Washington, of which there was a regular cavalcade, were "complete[ly] divorce[d] from reality."

Meanwhile the South Vietnamese ministers were worse than ever, shrugging their shoulders about corruption and inefficiency as if such things were a "basic fact of life." The minister of rural reconstruction appeared intent on using the pacification program to build his own private army.[55] Tran Van Do, the foreign minister whom Kissinger had befriended on his previous visit, complained that he was "in the position of a man with 10 mothers-in-law," an allusion to the habit of the ten generals on the governing Directory to meet separately from the civilian ministers.[56] Kissinger now grasped that Do was just the front man: real power was in the hands of his secretary of state, the "sly operator" Bui Diem, "the McBundy of Prime Minister Ky."*[57] As for

---

*Bui Diem returned the backhanded compliment. After the dinner at which he and Kissinger first met, other Vietnamese guests "wondered what he was doing in the country, asking as many questions as he had in his strange-sounding English. Whatever his reasons, my own opinion, gained at the dinner and at a meeting between Kissinger

the situation in the countryside, Daniel Ellsberg "painted a grim picture." The cadre program was "almost totally useless." If Kissinger made a spot inspection, he would "find them strung out in hammocks." In effect, "another bunch of marauders" had been inflicted on the villagers, as the funds earmarked for the cadres were used for local patronage. The South Vietnamese army was "almost totally useless in operations against main forces." Without better provincial administration, "we were simply shuffling dirt against the wind."[38]

Never one to shirk the front line, Kissinger set off to see for himself. His first stop was Bien Hoa, the location of a major U.S. military base just sixteen miles from Saigon. Despite this proximity, his request to go there by road was denied because "there had been a sniper on the road and . . . it would be too risky." Unnervingly—"another sign of the situation"—his helicopter "had two machines guns on either side and a machine gun at the front. As we approached the [airstrip] . . . the machine guns were trained on the ground." The AID and CIA operatives he spoke to at Bien Hoa confirmed that the cadre system was a farce. When they were not "goofing off," the cadres were preying on villagers or deserting at the first sign of trouble; "as soon as [they] had moved out of a village the Vietcong moved right back in and then took terrible retribution." The CIA man in Bien Hoa was especially discouraging: "[H]e would have to say there wasn't one village in the whole province in which he as an individual would be prepared to sleep at night as a regular matter. And even though 50% of the hamlets were listed as pacified, he would not be prepared to sleep in more than 25% of them as a one shot affair."

As for the South Vietnamese army, there "seemed to be a fair amount of tacit accommodation going on" between them and the Vietcong. At a field forces command post, Kissinger received the now familiar operational briefing: "[B]ased on the proposition of forcing the opponent to fight constantly and, therefore, first exhausting their supplies and also to spoil any operations that they might be planning . . . I

---

and Ky that I had sat in on, was that the man was brilliant. For someone relatively ignorant of Vietnamese affairs, his questions had been practical and acute, not at all what I expected from an academic."

asked what would happen if the Vietcong would not stand and fight but rather engage in delaying actions. This was considered improbable because I suppose it was so much against their plans."[59]

Back in his helicopter, Kissinger flew on to the First Division's headquarters, which were in a rubber plantation thirty miles from the Cambodian border. Looking down, he could see Vietcong trails in the jungle, Vietcong roadblocks, and blown bridges along the Route 13 north-south highway.

It may well be wondered why a State Department consultant, supposedly in Saigon to sound out the locals about negotiations, felt the need to risk his neck in this way. But risk it Kissinger did. A few days later he spent the night with the Ninth Marines at Hill 55,* ten miles southwest of Da Nang, the focal point of an area "fifteen miles deep and maybe thirty miles long" that was supposedly under U.S. control.[60] A different kind of war was being waged here from the one Westmoreland had described to him: a counterinsurgency campaign aimed at rooting out bands of guerrillas rather than a "search and destroy" hunt for large Vietcong formations. As Kissinger noted in his diary, however, "the job here was a slow, dirty grinding one." Very slow: over breakfast, two Marine colonels admitted that "the mining was no less in the areas which had been held by the Marines since the beginning than in those newly pacified."[61] Kissinger than flew on to Quin Nhon on the coast, "a miserable little fishing village" that had been turned into "one huge honky-tonk" after becoming the chief supply base for the northern part of the country. Flying in a jet because the Beechcraft he was due to take had crashed, he narrowly avoided death—"by about three feet"—as hurricane-force winds swept in off the sea.

Looking back, Kissinger conceded that the decision to fly back to Saigon that evening had been "insane."[62] The truth was that Vietnam had awakened the man of action long dormant inside the professor. Compared with deadly dull Cambridge, Vietnam was pulsating with an authentic if deadly energy. Compared with the *longueurs* of Harvard

---

*The heavily mined hill was also known as Nui Dat Son or Camp Muir, after Lieutenant Colonel Joseph Muir, commanding officer of the Third Battalion, Third Marines, who had been killed there the previous September.

Yard, the American embassy offered both tragedy and farce. Why had Kissinger rushed back to Saigon anyway? For a dinner at Lodge's with the wholly inconsequential Dutch, Korean, and Italian ambassadors, an event enlivened only by the postprandial performance of one of Lodge's aides, who "took the guitar and sang two songs which he had composed in Hue, which were extraordinarily witty but which were [also] extremely bitter, being an amalgam of optimistic reports submitted by Americans and coupled with newspaper headlines of what actually happened. These songs hit rather too close to home."[63]

Just two days later Kissinger was back in a heavily armed chopper, flying at three thousand feet to avoid sniper fire, this time bound for the headquarters of the 25th Infantry Division in Hau Nghia province—essentially an enclave in Vietcong "bandit country," just south of the Ho Bo woods and the notorious "Iron Triangle."[64] After a visit to the provincial capital—"a beleaguered fortress" that in no way resembled the pacified town he had been led to expect—he was back in time for dinner with General Lansdale, who rounded off another surreal day by playing "some tapes of Vietnamese folk songs and of Vietnamese singing American folk songs in Vietnamese."[65] Kissinger was beginning to understand what the press corps found so compelling about Saigon. He even suggested that he and Frances Fitzgerald "form a society for picaresque tales of Vietnam."[66]

Back in Saigon, Kissinger dutifully made the rounds of the local politicians and religious leaders.[67] With elections to the Constitutional Assembly scheduled for September 11, the main topic of conversation was who would emerge as the country's next president. Although Kissinger was supposed to be sounding out the South Vietnamese political elite on the issue of negotiations,[68] he made little headway. While some members of the government insisted on wholly unrealistic conditions ("a withdrawal of all North Vietnamese troops north of the 17th parallel and the eventual liquidation of the VC elements that remain"), increasingly disaffected Buddhist leaders talked as if they could hardly wait to hand over power to the NLF. As if to underline the combustibility of the political atmosphere, Kissinger reported an altercation with a "wild looking Monk with rolling eyes carrying a canister under his robe" who subsequently set himself on fire. Almost as unnerving was his meeting with Colonel Nguyen Ngoc Loan, the head of the secret police. "He has practically no chin," Kissinger noted in his diary, "he has a mirthless laugh, [and] when an embarrassing issue is raised he practically doubles over laughing and seems to collapse as if he were made of putty."[69] Like others close to the levers of power, including Deputy Prime Minister Nguyen Huu Co, Loan predicted that the next president would be General Nguyen Van Thieu, a French-trained Catholic officer with an aptitude for political machination.[70] As if reading from a script prepared in Washington, the outgoing president, Ky, assured Kissinger that Thieu would be a president "of the Korean type."[71] As far as Kissinger could see, however, South Vietnam was further than ever from miraculously morphing into South Korea.

All in all, it was impossible to see the situation as anything other than worse than it had been a year before. Perhaps the most significant thing Kissinger learned on his second visit to Vietnam was that "several approaches [had been] made in Paris to NLF representatives" by Foreign Minister Do, who regarded "Paris . . . as the best place for the GVN to contact the NLF."[72] From this and other tidbits, Kissinger inferred two things, one of which proved to be correct. The first—the one that proved to be wrong—was that there might be some possibility of driving a wedge between Hanoi and the Vietcong. The second was that, if there was a road to a peace deal, it led through Paris. Unfortunately, it was the first insight he opted to emphasize on his return to Washington.

Responsibility for putting out peace feelers had now been entrusted to Averell Harriman, as chairman of a new negotiations committee, and it was to him and his aide Daniel Davidson that Kissinger reported on August 1. He had three recommendations. The first (as recorded by Davidson in his memcon of the meeting) was a fundamental change of military strategy:

> Kissinger thought that Hanoi and the VC could accept a 10–1 kill ratio almost indefinitely. . . . He thought the VC were still far from the bottom of the barrel. . . .
>
> [O]ur strategy was wrong. "The best way to exhaust ourselves," he said, "is to spend our time chasing main force units

near the Cambodian border." Only the Marines had learned
that the war had to be won against guerrillas and not against
the main force units. . . . [But] this was a slow hard job which
did not appeal to the generals of Saigon [and] . . . they were
just beginning to learn how to conduct anti-guerrilla operations. Our military was not well equipped by training or experience to fight this kind of war.[73]

This amounted to a call for Westmoreland to be replaced, and—correct
though it surely was—it went nowhere. Kissinger's second recommendation of longer tours of duty in Vietnam was also both correct and
politically infeasible: limiting tours of duty in Vietnam to just eighteen
months ensured that there was no accumulation of local expertise
"since it took about a year and a half to learn the situation well enough
to be able to influence it." No one was about to start lengthening overseas postings. It was Kissinger's third point that made Harriman prick
up his ears:

Kissinger said we should stop talking about "unconditional"
negotiations if we want to convince the world that we are serious
about trying to find a peaceful settlement. . . . We should . . .
state openly what our conditions were. . . . Kissinger argued that
negotiations with the NLF-VC offered greater chance of success
than negotiations with Hanoi or multilateral negotiations under
the umbrella of the Geneva Agreements. . . .

He agreed that the central problem was to conduct negotiations in the South which would not result in a take-over by
the NLF.

Here Kissinger was abandoning the role of "Saigon's ambassador in
Washington," for (as he readily admitted to Harriman) "it would be
extremely difficult to bring Ambassador Lodge to accept negotiations
with the NLF-VC. . . . Lodge was completely sold on Ky and did not
like twisting his arm."[74]

Washington is a city that speaks in Chinese whispers. Kissinger
thought Harriman was pinning too much hope on the upcoming South

Vietnamese elections.[75] Harriman took Kissinger to mean not only that there might be a way of dividing the Vietcong from Hanoi but also that there might be a way of getting members of the Vietcong to defect altogether from the Communist side. Two days later Lodge received a cable from Rusk that cannot have pleased him. "[R]ecent reports from Saigon," it read, "have raised intense interest here at high levels in possibility of generating GVN initiatives to foment divisions among VC/NLF, stimulate increasing scale of defection and ultimately pave way to GVN-VC/NLF talks to work out negotiated solution to Viet-Nam conflict on favorable terms." Bizarrely, Rusk referenced a conversation between Kissinger and the former deputy prime minister, Tran Van Tuyen, despite the fact that neither man had mentioned defections as a possibility. (They had mainly talked about whether the Buddhist Institute had been infiltrated by Communists.)[76] Unwittingly, Kissinger had started a wild-goose chase. Suddenly, Washington had the answer: the war was going to be ended by prevailing on Vietcong and NLF members to defect.[77] There was in fact already a program in place—known as Chieu Hoi*—to encourage defection. But its focus had been the battlefield, whereas Harriman now envisaged a broader effort "looking toward possible eventual reconciliation between substantial elements of the Viet Cong and the GVN." The hope, he told Johnson and Rusk, was that "after the elections, perhaps by early October, conditions will be ripe for a proposal by the GVN for a general amnesty with full social, economic and political status for those who come over. Our targets are the noncommunist VC."[78] This was pie in the sky.

IV

I always find it inspiring to visit Vietnam. I can imagine no more vital assignment in today's world. Vietnam has become

---

*Also spelled Chu Hoi, this is loosely translated as "Open Arms." Invitations to defect were scattered in combat zones in waterproof bags used to carry M-16 ammunition. By 1967, approximately 75,000 defections had been recorded, though not all of them were genuine.

the hinge of our national effort. If we fail there, I foresee decades
of mounting crisis. If we succeed, it will mark a historic turning
point in the postwar era. Just as the Cuban–Berlin confrontation
may have convinced the Soviets of the futility of seeking political breakthroughs by military means, so Vietnam can put an
end to Chinese expansionism by the use or threat of force.[79]

When Henry Kissinger wrote those words in August 1966, he was
not stating a heartfelt conviction. Rather, he was administering a balm to
Henry Cabot Lodge prior to conveying some painful home truths. The
first of these was that, in trying to "rebuild a political structure" in Vietnam, the United States was attempting the impossible. "In Europe the
transition from feudalism to the modern state took three centuries," and
that was without the additional complication of a "century of colonialism." Second, the United States was trying to do the impossible without
any of the advantages of colonizers. In his most recent visit, he had
"found almost no one who knew about conditions in October 1965."
There was simply "no collective memory. . . . New people start with
great enthusiasm but little sophistication. By the time they learn their job
it is time for them to leave." Third, pacification was an illusion: "[I]n one
province shown on our maps as 70% pacified I was told by our sector
advisor . . . that 80% of the population was subject to VC taxation."[80]

Nor was that all. Harriman and his colleagues had drawn up a
"working paper on negotiations," though they had yet to answer the
all-important question, "What bait could we offer Hanoi?" By the end
of August, they had reverted to the idea of an end to the U.S. bombing
of North Vietnam in return for an "undertaking" by Hanoi to stop
infiltration of forces into the South. The problem was that Thieu, now
installed as president, rejected the idea of negotiations out of hand.[81]
Five days after the South Vietnamese elections, Michael Burke wrote
excitedly from Saigon to tell Kissinger that this "most complicated
political exercise . . . [had] far exceeded my predictions."[82] Kissinger's
sardonic reply spoke volumes about how he really regarded the situation: "I never had any doubt that the Vietnamese were capable of organizing complicated things. What I am not so sure about is whether
they can organize simple things."[83]

Even Kissinger's students knew what he really thought about Vietnam. His lectures for Government 180, "Principles of International Relations," were now renowned at Harvard for being "strongly critical of both the Kennedy and Johnson Administrations' foreign policies."[84] Yet the worse things got, the more Kissinger yearned to be back in Vietnam. His third trip in October 1966 was for just ten days—entailing an absence from Harvard that had to be approved by the dean of the Faculty of Arts and Sciences, Franklin Ford.[85] Its stated purpose was to assist the embassy with the "national reconciliation program" that had now grown, like Topsy, out of his earlier remark to Harriman about the possibility of negotiations with the NLF.[86] This time he flew in style—albeit the brutalist variety—in the converted B707 tanker McNamara preferred to use on long-haul flights, complete with bunk beds. On board, besides the defense secretary himself, were Daniel Ellsberg, en route back to Lansdale, and Undersecretary of State Nicholas Katzenbach, who fondly remembered Kissinger dressed in a bright orange jumpsuit, lecturing on the Soviet Union, the Cold War, and related matters.[87] But despite his assurances to Harriman, Kissinger knew full well that this was another doomed initiative. It was not just that defections from the Vietcong were never likely to reach a level sufficient to alter the political balance in Vietnam. It was not just that Thieu and the kingmaker Bui Diem were against the idea, which threatened to trigger a showdown between the new government and the newly elected Constituent Assembly.[88] It was the fact that the task was simply beyond the multiple competing American agencies whose efforts Kissinger was supposed to be helping to coordinate.

"I am becoming increasingly concerned," he told Harriman after nine days of fruitless toil, "that in Viet-Nam it is relatively simpler to figure out what to do than how to do it." In theory, a successful program of national reconciliation would "separate the problem of the internal structure of Viet-Nam from its international aspects" and "greatly improve our diplomatic position." In practice, even the existing Chieu Hui program was "split up among USAID, JUSPAO,* MACV

---

*The Joint United States Public Affairs Office, which was supposed to coordinate "information operations" between the military and civilian authorities.

(in turn subdivided between Psywar* and J-33†), and CAS.‡" There was "no clear assignment of responsibility." And everything else was being "carried on in a random, unsystematic, and, above all, fragmented manner." Kissinger dutifully mapped out a plan for better interagency coordination, but the tone of his report was scarcely optimistic.[89] As he summed up the problem in a meeting with Harriman following his return, "The military had the organization but not the mentality; the Embassy had the mentality but not the organization"—and that applied only to the outgoing Habib, not to Lodge, who was still "inclined to describe NLF-VC as gangsters and murderers."[90] Kissinger cannot have been surprised to hear in late November that Thieu had postponed the planned proclamation on national reconciliation, nor that Zorthian, rather than Habib, had been put in charge of interagency coordination. That signaled as clearly as could be that the initiative—whatever was left of it—had descended into the realm of public relations.[91]

As Christmas approached, Harriman sent Kissinger an autographed photograph with the inscription: "To Henry Kissinger, A kindly but firm teacher from a grateful pupil. With my warm regards."[92] What Kissinger had taught him, in a few short months, was not to engage in wishful thinking about Vietnam.

---

*Special Forces and CIA operations classified as "psychological warfare," e.g., the Phoenix Program of assassination of NLF members.
†The Revolutionary Development Division of J-3, the Operations Division of MACV.
‡Close Air Support.

Book V

CHAPTER 19

The Anti-Bismarck

I . . . was a little puzzled by your suggestion that we should
return to a diplomacy like Bismarck's. Having once planned
to write a book on Bismarck's diplomacy and, indeed,
having finished half of it, I could think of few policies more
likely to lead to catastrophe in present circumstances.

— HENRY KISSINGER to Michael Howard, 1961[1]

All of French policy was geared to be on good terms with
Moscow. The official French theory . . . was that the world
was tri-polar. One center was at Washington, another in
Peking dominating East Asia, the third was Europe
dominated by Moscow-Paris. . . . De Gaulle had told
Kosygin: "Because of the war in Vietnam the United States
is becoming more unpopular in Europe every day. This is
the way for us to build Europe together."

— JEAN DE LA GRANDVILLE to Henry Kissinger, 1967[2]

I

Even the most acute students of Kissinger's work have made the
mistake of asserting that he identified closely with the first chancellor
of the German Reich, Otto von Bismarck. But Kissinger never aspired
to be "an American Bismarck . . . appl[ying] the principles of political
realism" on the world stage furnished by the Cold War.[3] In the summer
of 1961, his friend the British military historian Michael Howard had
suggested that the United States should consider taking a more Bismarckian approach to foreign policy. This was at a time when many in
Great Britain, not least the prime minister, Harold Macmillan, fretted

about what they saw (wrongly) as the impetuous idealism of John F. Kennedy. As Howard explained,

> I chose [Bismarck] as the usual counterpoise to Gladstone, as a man who believed in the realities of power politics as opposed to one who believed in the power of moral leadership in world affairs; and as a man who, for most of his time as Chancellor, used his power to preserve and adjust the balance on which the peace of Europe rested, having achieved his strictly limited aim. . . . That is what I meant when I said that what is needed is a cold calculation of interests, and that this will be far more intelligible to the outside world than any attempt to assert "moral leadership," which will quite certainly be misunderstood abroad. . . . What we want to see in America is not moral fervour, but a position of relaxed, courteous, confident strength, and it looks as if Kennedy is feeling his way towards it.[4]

Kissinger confessed to being "a little puzzled" by Howard's line of argument. "Having once planned to write a book on Bismarck's diplomacy," he replied, "and, indeed, having finished half of it, I could think of few policies more likely to lead to catastrophe in present circumstances."[5]

To understand the deep ambivalence with which Kissinger regarded Bismarck—whose genius he never disputed, but whose achievement he regarded as fatally flawed—one must do more than read the celebrated article he published on the subject in the summer of 1968. For "The White Revolutionary," brilliant though it is, does not provide a complete reckoning. As Kissinger told Howard, by 1961 he had in fact written "half of . . . a book on Bismarck's diplomacy," and most of that had probably been done in the later 1950s. (In February 1967, when he sent the unfinished draft to Marion Dönhoff to read, he urged her to "remember that this was written over ten years ago." But he also made it clear that he still intended "to work on it.")[6] This book was intended to be the first of two sequels to *A World Restored,* the second of which was to cover the period from Bismarck's dismissal in 1890 to the outbreak of the First World War. Put differently, the Bismarck volume would have been the centerpiece of a triptych "on the maintenance of a hundred-year peace in Europe through a system of alliances based on a balance of power." That, at any event, was what Kissinger's London publisher George Weidenfeld had been led to expect. After the "minuscule sales" of the first volume, he had "lost sight" of Kissinger, only meeting him again twelve years after the appearance of *A World Restored,* by which time the author had been named as Richard Nixon's national security adviser. "I had been tipped off by his American publisher," Weidenfeld recalled, "that he might be coming to the end of the Bismarck volume." But Kissinger had disappointing news for him. "I am burning the manuscript," he said. "Even a few weeks near the center of power have made me realize how much I still have to learn about how policy is really made."[7]

This was not quite true—though as Weidenfeld noted, it was "an elegant excuse for not completing the book." In fact, Kissinger never completed the book on Bismarck; nor, however, did he burn it. The incomplete manuscript survived, unread for more than half a century, in his private papers. Perusal of the draft chapters confirms that what Kissinger published as "The White Revolutionary" was only a part of the argument he had intended to make.

We know, to be sure, how Kissinger *later* thought of Bismarck, as the Iron Chancellor is discussed at length in both *Diplomacy* and *World Order.* In Kissinger's mature view, the European order established by Castlereagh and Metternich at the Congress of Vienna broke down in the wake of Bismarck's foundation of the German Reich, because "with Germany unified and France a fixed adversary, the system lost its flexibility."[8] After 1871 a more rigid pentarchy of great powers (to use Leopold von Ranke's term, referring to Austria, Britain, France, Germany, and Russia) depended on the virtuoso diplomat Bismarck to keep itself in equilibrium. There is no need here to dwell at length on the pyrotechnics of Bismarckian peacekeeping in the 1870s and 1880s. One stratagem, however, came to seem of extraordinary importance to Kissinger in the period after he himself had left office: the Secret Reinsurance Treaty that Bismarck signed with the Russian foreign minister, Nikolay Girs, in June 1887. Under its terms, Germany and Russia each agreed to observe neutrality should the other be involved in a war with a third country, unless Germany attacked France or Russia attacked Austria-Hungary. This committed Germany to neutrality if Russia sought to assert control over the Black Sea straits. But the real point was to discourage the Russians from seeking a mutual defense treaty with France, which was exactly what happened after Bismarck's fall from power led to the nonrenewal of the Secret Reinsurance Treaty. "Paradoxically," as Kissinger later put it, "it was precisely that ambiguity which preserved the flexibility of the European equilibrium. And its abandonment—in the name of transparency—started a sequence of increasing confrontations, culminating in World War I."⁹ After Bismarck had gone, Kissinger argued, the great power system "aggravated" rather than "buffered" disputes. Over time "political leaders lost control over their own tactics," and "in the end, the military planning ran away with diplomacy."¹⁰ Yet this late masterpiece of diplomatic artistry was not the facet of Bismarck's career that most interested the younger Kissinger.

As with *A World Restored,* "The White Revolutionary"—as it was published in the magazine *Daedalus*—is full of extraordinary aperçus.¹¹ "Too democratic for conservatives, too authoritarian for liberals, too power-oriented for legitimists," writes Kissinger of Bismarck's Europe, "the new order was tailored to a genius who proposed to restrain the contending forces, both domestic and foreign, by manipulating their antagonisms."¹² Or: "It was not that Bismarck lied—this is much too self-conscious an act—but that he was finely attuned to the subtlest currents of any environment and produced measures precisely adjusted to the need to prevail. The key to Bismarck's success was that he was always sincere."¹³ Bismarck's conception of German unification under Prussian leadership "was not the first time that revolutionaries succeeded because their opponents could not believe in the reality of their objectives."¹⁴ Was Bismarck an opportunist? But of course! "Anyone wishing to affect events must be opportunist to some extent. The real distinction is between those who adapt their purposes to reality and those who seek to mold reality in the light of their purposes."¹⁵ Bismarck denied that "any state had the right to sacrifice its opportunities to its principles."¹⁶ But "the blind spot of revolutionaries ["white" ones included] is the belief that the world for which they are striving will combine all the benefits of the new conception with the good points of the overthrown structure."[17]

Each of these lines is arresting. But they are incidental to, or rather decorative of, the main argument. There are three central themes. The first is that Bismarck was not only a genius but also a demon (the archaic word *demoniac* is applied to him repeatedly as an epithet).[18] This explains why Kissinger spends so much time on Bismarck's spiritual journey from deism and pantheism to Pietism under the influence of the Thadens and Puttkammers—a subplot that at first appears to have no obvious relevance to the argument. As Kissinger makes clear, Bismarck's religious awakening was a facade behind which he evolved into a geopolitical Darwinian:

> The Metternich system had been inspired by the eighteenth century notion of the universe as a great clockwork: Its parts were intricately intermeshed, and a disturbance of one upset the equilibrium of the others. Bismarck represented a new age. Equilibrium was seen not as harmony and mechanical balance, but as a statistical balance of forces in flux. Its appropriate philosophy was Darwin's concept of the survival of the fittest. Bismarck marked the change from the rationalist to the empiricist conception of politics. . . . Bismarck declared the relativity of all beliefs; he translated them into forces to be evaluated in terms of the power they could generate.[19]

The "white revolutionary"—a phrase first applied to Bismarck by the Jewish banker Ludwig Bamberger in 1867[20]—was therefore only outwardly a conservative.

The second theme is that Bismarck's new European order hinged on his ability to "manipulate the commitments of the other powers so that Prussia would always be closer to any of the contending parties than they were to each other"—a crucially important Kissingerian insight, as we shall see.[21] This was possible because Bismarck was no longer constrained by any Metternichian notions of legitimacy. He could ally with or attack whomsoever he chose. But it "required cool nerves because it sought its objectives by the calm acceptance of great risks, of isolation, or of a sudden settlement at Prussia's expense."[22]

The third theme is that Bismarck's achievement, though magnificent, was unsustainable because it could not be institutionalized. "Institutions are designed for an average standard of performance," writes Kissinger. "They are rarely able to accommodate genius or demoniac power. A society that must produce a great man in each generation to maintain its domestic or international position will doom itself." By contrast, "[s]tatesmen who build lastingly transform the personal act of creation into institutions that can be maintained by an average standard of performance." It was Bismarck's failure to achieve this that Kissinger saw as his tragedy. "His very success committed Germany to a permanent tour de force . . . [and] left a heritage of unassimilated greatness. . . . A system which requires a great man in each generation sets itself an almost insurmountable challenge, if only because a great man tends to stunt the emergence of strong personalities."[23] In particular, Bismarck's successors were not capable of "a proper analysis of . . . the requirements of national interest": "Because of his magnificent grasp of the nuances of power relationships, Bismarck saw in his philosophy a doctrine of self-limitation. Because these nuances were not apparent to his successors and imitators, the application of Bismarck's lessons led to an armament race and a world war."

True, by annexing Alsace-Lorraine, Bismarck had deprived himself and his successors of an option he had enjoyed as minister president of Prussia: the option to ally, however temporarily, with France. After 1871 there were only three powers with whom Germany could hope to align itself, and one of them, Great Britain, was already inclining toward "splendid isolation." Yet a leader of Bismarck's caliber might still have averted disaster. The problem was that his *epigoni* saw only the ruthlessness of Realpolitik and not the element of self-limitation. In seeking to combat the "nightmare of coalitions" by saber rattling, colony grabbing, and navy building, they ended up cementing the alliance between France and Russia. "Thus Germany tended to bring on what it feared most."[24] It was in this sense that "Germany's greatest modern figure . . . [had] sown the seeds of its twentieth-century tragedies."

The significance of "The White Revolutionary" is therefore very definitely not that Kissinger identified himself with Bismarck. Kissinger's own family had suffered more than most from precisely the "tragedies" he depicted here as Bismarck's hubristic legacy to Germany. On the contrary: Kissinger deplored the "demoniac" Bismarck at least as much as he admired him. The real point is that Kissinger identified Bismarck with Charles de Gaulle:

> Just as de Gaulle's brutal cynicism has depended on an almost lyrical conception of France's historic mission, so Bismarck's matter-of-fact Machiavellianism assumed that Prussia's unique sense of cohesion enabled it to impose its dominance on Germany. Like de Gaulle, Bismarck believed that the road to political integration was not through concentrating on legal formulae, but emphasizing the pride and integrity of the historic states. Bismarck urged that foreign policy had to be based not on sentiment but on an assessment of strength. . . . Policy depended on calculation, not emotion. The interests of states provided objective imperatives transcending individual preferences.[25]

No well-informed contemporary reading those lines in 1968 would have failed to grasp the point. Bismarck and de Gaulle were the supreme realists: men who saw their nation's "requirements as a great power" as transcending all other forces, and particularly ideology, whether nineteenth-century liberalism or twentieth-century Communism. Like de Gaulle, Bismarck "assumed the perfect flexibility of international relationships limited only by the requirements of national interest."[26]

That this is the correct reading of Kissinger on Bismarck becomes incontrovertible when the points above are related to the unfinished book manuscript of which the published article was but a rump.[27] Six chapters survive, some in more than one draft, of which the first four were in large measure the raw material for the *Daedalus* article. It is the fifth ("The Crimean War") and the sixth ("The Contingency of Legitimacy") that offer the best insight into the book Kissinger might have written, had not the lure of action in the present drawn him away from the tranquil study of the past. Here more than in the abridged essay,

Kissinger makes clear that he saw Realpolitik as dangerously amoral. "The practical consequence he drew [from the Crimean crisis] was invarying," writes Kissinger, "that only a sober calculation of power relationships, not sentimental attachments, should motivate Prussia's commitments. And for this reason all of Bismarck's dispatches from the very beginning of the . . . crisis could be reduced to a calculus of strength." Yet there was something very disturbing about "the nature of the new world which his [Leopold von Gerlach's] demoniac charge was conjuring up, a world in which only miscalculation was evil and only failure is a sin. It was a world without illusion in which only giants or nihilists could live." Bismarck, he writes, was "a scientist who had weighed the factors, considered the possible combinations, and sought to manipulate into being a structure which would reflect the real power-relationships."[28] After German unification, "the European consensus was derived if at all from a calculus of strength, the legitimacy of which depended on the preciseness of its calculation."

There is much more here, too, on the importance of optionality. Bismarck, Kissinger writes, had a "policy of keeping all options open until the last moment"; hence the paradoxes of his "confusing frankness" and "bold caution." At times, it is true, Kissinger seems to be lost in admiration. "A statesman is ultimately distinguished by his conception of alternatives. And it was Bismarck's skill that he perceived combinations which had been thought impossible for over a generation." The unprincipled Junker had somehow divined, a century before they were formulated, the Kissingerian maxims that the statesman must always act with "insufficient knowledge"—"for if he waits until all facts are in it will be too late to do something about them"—and that the art of statesmanship is "the art of finding the right moment for action."[29] Yet in the final analysis, Kissinger comes down on the side of the true conservatives against the white revolutionary. In the last, unfinished chapter, entitled "The Contingency of Legitimacy," Kissinger grapples with what he calls the "inextricable element of the debate between the conservatives and Bismarck." In two long paragraphs that were evidently sweated over—the deletions and handwritten* inser-

---

*The handwritten insertions are in fact in capital letters in the original.

tions are reproduced here because they are so revealing—he tries to articulate his reasons for siding with Bismarck's critics:

> Bismarck's was the point of view of an observer standing outside of the events, careful in assessing their qualities, rigorous in drawing conclusions, pitiless in applying them. The conservative position on the other hand involved the conviction almost instinctive and therefore clumsily stated, that the maxims of analysis do not necessarily supply imperatives of conduct. For the strength of analysis is the irrelevance of the personal attitude to the subject of analysis; but the impetus of action involves a personal commitment. To analysis man is a force among many, a means to be manipulated. To his intuition he represents an end. ~~To announce that self-interest always motivated man is to utter a platitude for the crucial question is precisely the nature of man's self-interest. To preach the value of commitments is equally hollow unless the commitment can be given some content.~~ It is the paradox of analysis that it may ~~evade~~ ERODE the convictions which animate conduct, that increased understanding may only lead to a paralysis of will. It is the paradox of action that it is unable to relate man to the forces outside himself whose makings he sees but whose motives he can grasp only by analogy. Conservatives have always insisted that the balance between these two ~~sides~~ ASPECTS of human conduct is derived from a sense of reverence, ~~a recognition of forces transcending man and~~ WHICH IS THE REVERSE SIDE OF A RECOGNITION of the limitations of the individual apprehension of reality. The great rebels have ~~denied this and~~ insisted on finding in their own demoniac nature a sufficient motive for commitment. To the conservative the bond of society is a myth which reconciles the point of view which treats man as a means and his experience of himself by an analogy superior to analytical truth; to the rebel a myth is the tool of weaklings.

The second paragraph Kissinger subsequently drew two diagonal lines through; it is nevertheless well worth reproducing:

But however self-evident the rebel's lesson may seem to him, it presupposes an almost superhuman capacity for abstraction, an ability not only to regard others but oneself ~~as a force, as an outsider,~~ AS AN OUTSIDER, lest personal predelicitions [*sic*] upset the finest calculations. ~~It was the essence of Bismarck's revolutionary quality that he drew the full consequences from his scepticism that all beliefs became to him only factors to be manipulated. It was no accident therefore that~~ THUS, the more Bismarck preached his doctrine the more humanly remote he grew; the more rigorous he was in applying his lessons the more incomprehensible he became to his contemporaries. Nor was it strange that the conservatives gradually came to see in him the voice of the devil. For the devil is a fallen angel using the categories of piety to destroy it. And however brilliant Bismarck's analysis, societies are incapable of the courage of cynicism. The ~~insistence on men as atoms, on societies as forces has always led~~ to a tour de force ~~evading~~ ERODING all self-restraint. Because societies operate by approximations and because they are incapable of fine distinctions, a doctrine of power as a means may end up by making power an end. And for this reason, although Bismarck had the better of the intellectual argument, it may well be that the conservatives embodied the greater social truth.[30]

This tortured disavowal of Bismarck is of a piece with all that Kissinger had hitherto written on the impossibility of basing strategy on pragmatism alone. The idealist still held out against realism. And yet it is surely significant that this passage was struck out; surely significant that the project of a book about Bismarck book ended here, in an uncharacteristically uncertain tangle of deletions and insertions.

II

At first sight, the case of Germany in the era of unification offers almost no analogy applicable to the case of the United States in the era of Vietnam. Bismarck, it might be thought, had more in common with

Ho Chi Minh than with Lyndon Johnson, in that both Bismarck and Ho forged a united country by means of blood and iron. Yet revisiting Bismarck as he did in the 1960s helped Kissinger think about the problem of Vietnam in four distinct ways.

First, it was obvious that the Johnson administration's most elementary blunder was to have allowed itself to become diplomatically isolated in a way that was anything but splendid. Aside from South Korea and distant Australia, almost none of its allies offered it meaningful support in Vietnam. (There were also modest contributions from the Philippines, Thailand, and Taiwan.) The obverse of escalation of the Vietnam War was the decay of the post-1945 system of American alliances. Not only did SEATO prove next to worthless; so, too, did NATO. By contrast, Hanoi was in the happy position of being able to play two powerful allies off against one another: the Soviet Union and China.

Second, Kissinger understood that the United States must extricate itself from a position of weakness with the same cold calculation of self-interest that had enabled Bismarck to get Prussia out of its situation of chronic disadvantage in the 1840s and 1850s. Everyone else in Washington saw de Gaulle as the European leader most dismissive of the ideals trumpeted by the United States as it sought to justify what it was doing in Vietnam. Yet Kissinger understood that, in terms of national interest, France had the greatest potential to assist the United States in a region it knew better than any other Western power.

Third, studying Bismarck renewed Kissinger's lifelong interest in the problem of German unity. Whereas most Americans saw de Gaulle as the principal threat to transatlantic harmony, Kissinger saw the real threat as the policy that became known as *Ostpolitik*—rapprochement with the Soviet bloc, including the German Democratic Republic. As with Vietnam, so with Germany: unification could not be understood independently of its geopolitical context. In either case, a unification that ended up producing an enlarged Soviet satellite had to be resisted.

Finally, Kissinger learned from studying Bismarck's success and his successors' failure—or rather, from studying the unsustainable nature of Bismarck's achievement—the crucial importance of maintaining a degree of flexibility in the system of great power relations. Bismarck's most ingenious device as chancellor of Germany had been the combination of two seemingly incompatible commitments: an alliance with Austria-Hungary based on mutual defense and the Secret Reinsurance Treaty with Russia. Could the United States somehow strengthen its position by establishing similar relationships with the other great powers, even at the risk of making contradictory commitments? Kissinger came to believe the answer was yes. The grand strategy he began to devise in the mid-1960s had three distinct phases. First, he sought to revive and rejuvenate the American alliance with Western Europe, NATO, trying to counteract the powerful forces of European integration by revivifying the bilateral relations between the United States and the three major European powers: France, Germany, and Great Britain. Then he sought to develop the idea of détente into something more than empty rhetoric by seeking practical objects for cooperation between the United States and the Soviet Union—beginning with Vietnam. Finally, he began to discern that, despite its obviously revolutionary character, the People's Republic of China could also be brought into the pale of the balance of power. Here as in much else, he was led by de Gaulle and by his historical precursor as a practitioner of realism, Bismarck.

In seeking to learn from de Gaulle, Kissinger was going against the grain of U.S. foreign policy in the 1960s. In the eyes of American decision makers in both the Kennedy and Johnson administrations, de Gaulle was part of the problem—particularly in Vietnam—not part of the solution. We have seen already that de Gaulle had reacted negatively to American initiatives like the Multilateral Force (MLF). He had also refused to adhere to the 1963 Limited Test Ban Treaty banning nuclear tests in the atmosphere. To the Kennedy administration, de Gaulle seemed intent on driving a wedge into the transatlantic alliance, deepening France's ties with Germany while loosening its ties with the United States and, at the same time, vetoing British membership in the Common Market.[31] Worse was to follow. As early as August 1963, de Gaulle had made it known that France wished to see Vietnam "independent . . . from the outside, in internal peace and unity and in harmony with [its] neighbors."[32] In April 1964 he appalled the U.S. ambassador to Paris, the veteran diplomat Charles Bohlen, by telling him that "any military stabilization would only come about with Chinese consent and that with Chinese consent there could be genuine neutrality." Despite American protestations, it was clear that de Gaulle envisaged a neutralization only of South Vietnam, not of all Vietnam.[33] Two months later it was the turn of George Ball to be told by de Gaulle that "he did not believe America could win [in Vietnam], despite its military edge, even if it decided to wage a full-scale war."[34] Increasingly, de Gaulle pressed for an international conference as a means to resolve the conflict. His stated goal was a four-power commitment by China, France, the Soviet Union, and the United States not to intervene in Southeast Asia. His thinly veiled intent was to acknowledge the former territory of French Indochina as part of a Chinese sphere of influence. (As early as January 1964, France formally recognized the People's Republic of China.) De Gaulle declined to assist with efforts to start negotiations between Hanoi and Washington until the Americans had explicitly committed to withdrawing their forces. The crowning insult was his September 1966 speech in Phnom Penh, which effectively blamed the United States for the continuation of the war. This came after de Gaulle had removed France altogether from SEATO as well as from the command structure of NATO. To nearly all American policy makers, this was an appalling pattern of disloyal behavior.[35]

If relations between de Gaulle and Kennedy had been strained, between de Gaulle and Johnson they were nonexistent. They met only three times, on each occasion at a state funeral: Kennedy's, Adenauer's, and Eisenhower's. (Senator Mansfield's proposal that the two men meet in Paris had gone down badly in the Élysée, Kissinger was able to report in January 1966, "particularly when Senator Mansfield said that de Gaulle and Johnson would make two beautiful figures together on the balcony.")[36] Those whose counsel Johnson heeded on Vietnam—notably Rusk, the Bundy brothers, and Lodge—were united in dismissing the French president's repeated calls for neutralization. Only David Nes— briefly Lodge's number two in Saigon before the 1964 election called the ambassador back to the United States—came to realize that de Gaulle was offering a choice preferable to military escalation.[37]

As we have seen, Kissinger had been critical, almost from the outset, of the Kennedy and Johnson administrations' handling of U.S. relations with the major Western European powers. "The North Atlantic Alliance is in disarray," he wrote in one of many speeches he prepared for

Nelson Rockefeller in 1964. "The Democratic Administration . . . has failed to appreciate the significant changes which have taken place in Europe. It has pursued inconsistent policies calling for allied unity at one moment and acting unilaterally at another."[38] On the one hand, Washington was acting without proper consultation with its allies (for example, in choosing to side with Indonesia against the Netherlands in their dispute over Dutch New Guinea). On the other, the American enthusiasm for the MLF was based on a fundamental misreading of European attitudes toward nuclear security. In particular, the tendency of Kennedy and Johnson to pursue détente with the Soviet Union on a bilateral basis was arousing an understandable fear on the part of the major European powers of a "U.S.-Soviet accommodation"—the phrase was François de Rose's—at their expense.[39] Kissinger heard the same complaint in Bonn from Klaus Ritter, the former deputy director of German Intelligence, and General Hans Speidel, the former commander of NATO ground forces.[40] In this context, half-baked American appeals for assistance in Vietnam were bound to fall on deaf ears.[41]

Kissinger's map of Europe was a Bismarckian one. When he traveled across the Atlantic, as he did every year (usually in May and June, when the Harvard spring semester was over), he went to Bonn and to Paris without fail; London came third, followed by Brussels, The Hague, and Rome. He seldom if ever visited the capitals of the other European countries. Scandinavia was terra incognita. So, too, was the Iberian Peninsula. Uninterested in the economic forces that were propelling the integration of Western Europe after the signing of the Treaty of Rome in 1957, Kissinger's Europe was still the Europe of the Rankean great power pentarchy: Britain, France, and Germany, with Italy an also-ran and neutral Austria an extinct volcano.[42] Of the three surviving powers, Germany interested him the most, Britain the least. Yet it soon became obvious that the road to Hanoi went through Paris, not Berlin.

It certainly did not lead through London. As Kissinger's televised debate with Michael Foot and Tariq Ali had revealed, hostility to the Vietnam War was growing almost as rapidly in the United Kingdom as in the United States. On a visit to London in February 1966, Kissinger—"speaking as an independent and respected observer"—did his best to make the administration's case in a series of meetings with parliamentarians and civil servants, but he encountered opposition not only on the left (notably the deputy prime minister, George Brown) but also on the right (the shadow defense secretary, Enoch Powell) and even in the center (the Liberal leader, Jo Grimond). Only a few "middle level civil servants"—presumably with memories of victory in Malaya, where the British had won their Vietnam by defeating Communist guerrillas at their own game of jungle warfare—thought the United States "should be tougher."[43] Kissinger tried to put on a brave face, reporting to Len Unger that "virtually without exception the British are willing to go along with our policy and actions in Viet-Nam even though they are not enthusiastic about what they realize has to be done. He noted that even the left wing Laborites echo this view and he found even the most negative among the British much easier to talk to than his Harvard academic colleagues." But that was not a high bar, given the increasingly antiwar mood in Cambridge. The reality was that even the Conservative opposition was against Vietnam. Over breakfast, the new Tory leader, Edward Heath, told him that "while he was generally hopeful . . . our military strategy in Viet-Nam made little clear sense to him." As shadow defense secretary, Enoch Powell was the "most negative and advocated our getting out of Viet-Nam now." While it was possible to make the argument in London that Vietnam mattered "not just in its own context but as related to our worldwide position and the future orientation and roles of India and Japan," there was no market whatever for the claim that the war was being fought "in order to stop the spread of worldwide communism."[44] The positive public response to Powell's later allegation that, in thinking of sending British forces to Vietnam, Harold Wilson was "perfectly clearly and perfectly recognizably [acting] as an American satellite," may even have sufficed to change Wilson's mind.[45]

III

The German debate of the mid-1960s was different. On the one hand, most Germans could see the resemblance between their situation and that of the Vietnamese. Both countries were divided; like East Germany, North Vietnam was a Communist-controlled state that posed a potential military and political threat to its non-Communist neighbor. Yet that argument was not sufficiently potent to make Germans want to help the United States. On the contrary, the many German political and military leaders with whom Kissinger spoke to on the subject made it perfectly clear that they regarded their own problems arising from Germany's division as so absorbing that they had neither the time nor the resources to worry about Vietnam.

Kissinger tended to be an alarmist about where West Germany was heading, but he generally got the direction of travel right. As early as November 1964, he warned McGeorge Bundy that by "pushing through the MLF" and "forcing matters to [a] head," the United States risked "wreck[ing] the CDU," the Christian Democrats. "This in turn will cause the SPD [Social Democrats] to veer into a more leftist and nationalist course," he predicted. "My real concern is not the MLF, but that in three or four years we may have a situation in Germany similar to that which today obtains in Italy"—in other words, a fundamental shift of the center of political gravity to the left.[46] This was two years before the entry of the Social Democratic Party into a grand coalition with the CDU and the appointment of Willy Brandt as foreign minister and vice-chancellor.

In April 1965 Kissinger had his first encounter with Brandt's press spokesman, Egon Bahr, the man who was to emerge as the architect of *Ostpolitik*. Born in Thuringia, a German state on the wrong side of the iron curtain, Bahr had joined the Social Democrats in 1956 not because he was a socialist but because he was a nationalist who (rightly) suspected that neither the Christian Democrats nor the Americans were sincere about pursuing German reunification. At Brandt's instigation, Bahr had been so eager to see Kissinger that he came to Boston specially. (Kissinger had in fact tried to avoid him.) As Kissinger reported, Bahr excitedly explained what his boss intended to do as soon as the SPD came to power in Bonn:

> Brandt was determined to move full speed ahead. I asked in
> what direction. Bahr said toward greatly increased contact
> with the East including East Germany. He added that one of
> the high priority goals would be the development of a draft

peace treaty. The scheme he and Brandt were considering
would have the following features: A unified Germany would
leave NATO. It would renounce ownership of nuclear weapons. Foreign troops would be withdrawn from its territory.
The German armed forces would retain their present size.
There would be a four power guarantee of the territorial integrity of Germany. In addition there would be a treaty of mutual
assistance by which the four powers would undertake to assist
each other against German aggression.[47]

Kissinger listened with horror. "I asked whether Bahr was worried
that the guarantee might justify constant Communist intervention in
German affairs. Bahr replied that I was still thinking in Cold War
terms." By this Bahr meant that Kissinger was assuming "an unlimited
desire of the Soviets to expand their sphere," whereas "the perspective
of the Berlin SPD . . . assumed that the Soviet Union would become
more and more national in character" and would come "to value
friendship with Germany rather than seek to bring pressure on it." If,
however, the Soviets did bring pressure, then "the existing German
army could fight a delaying action until help from NATO arrived."
Kissinger could not stand much more of this wild talk:

> I pointed out that if Bahr's scheme counted on a strong NATO,
> he was likely to be in for a disillusionment. In the circum-
> stances described by Bahr, not only would Germany leave
> NATO but NATO itself would probably disintegrate. It seemed
> inconceivable that it was possible to combine a treaty of mutual
> assistance with the Soviet Union with an alliance directed
> against an assumed Soviet danger. Bahr replied that he did not
> consider NATO as such very viable; its primarily significant
> element was the American guarantee which he thought could
> be maintained even without NATO.[48]

It got worse. Kissinger asked how Bahr proposed to achieve German
unification. Bahr's reply was "through the closest contacts with the
East including East Germany." Unification would need to wait until

the economic gap between the West and the East had been closed—to avoid "an intolerable humiliation" for the East Germans—but that could be achieved after "perhaps five years of substantial West German economic assistance to the GDR to equalize standards of living." Kissinger objected that "then the GDR would be able to be even more active in the underdeveloped countries," but Bahr replied that "this was a risk which he was prepared to run" because "the whole conception of the Berlin SPD was that the East Germans were German first and Communist second."[49]

Kissinger was so appalled by Bahr that he dashed off a powerful and in some ways prescient article on "The Price of German Unity" for *The Reporter*.[50] As a student of Bismarck, Kissinger needed no persuading that Germany was "the key to European equilibrium." As he put it in "The White Revolutionary," "If Germany was too centralized or too powerful, it would bring about a combination of expansionist France and Russia to counterbalance it. If Germany was too divided, it would tempt constant pressure." Germany had to be "strong enough to resist attacks from both East and West, but not so powerful as to disquiet Germany's neighbors, sufficiently unified to be able to mobilize for defense, but not so centralized as to become an offensive threat."[51] What Bahr envisaged might sound superficially alluring. Indeed, many Americans bought the idea that "increased contacts between the two Germanys will promote the erosion of the East German regime." But in practice *Ostpolitik* would be bound to push Germany in the direction not just of unity but also of "nationalism or neutralization or both."[52] In the first instance, Bahr's approach would tend to enhance the status of the East German regime. Either the division of Germany would become more entrenched, or there would be a "gradual, almost imperceptible acceptance of the Soviet framework for German unity: that it be negotiated directly by the two German states."[53]

Kissinger argued instead for a common NATO approach to the issue. If there was to be some kind of confederation of the Federal Republic and the Democratic Republic, there would need to be conditions, like a guarantee of free elections to choose its government and a total demilitarization of its territory, followed after fifteen years by a referendum on reunification. Both German states would have to commit themselves to the Oder-Neisse line as Germany's eastern border. In short, Kissinger reasoned, German reunification could occur only within a broad framework of transatlantic and pan-European integration:

> The long-term hope for German unity resides in an evolution in the West that will act as a magnet for the countries of Eastern Europe. As Western Europe achieves political unity, the fear of any one state will diminish. A united Europe, moreover, will be a powerful magnet for the countries of Eastern Europe. As ties between the two parts of Europe grow, the East German satellite could increasingly appear as a vestige of a passing era. This united Europe, in turn, should be part of a close and confident Atlantic relationship. A farsighted western policy will therefore seek to convert the so-called German problem into an effort to build structures, European and Atlantic, in which the Federal Republic can participate as a respected and equal member.[54]

From the vantage point of 2015, this passage has an almost prophetic quality. *Ostpolitik* would indeed be tried by Brandt; the Soviets would indeed seek to subvert and instrumentalize it; and twenty years later, reunification would indeed take place under a Christian Democratic chancellor on precisely the basis of a reaffirmed Atlantic alliance and a deeper and wider European Union.

Yet it would have taken a Doctor Pangloss to attach a high probability to such a happy outcome in the mid-1960s. Listening to the forebodings of Herbert Wehner, the chairman of the SPD in June 1965, Kissinger grew ever more alarmed. The hard-bitten ex-Communist began by eviscerating the leading West German politicians, including his own *Kanzlerkandidat*:

> Erhard—a pastry cook (*konditor*) who loves to bake large cakes and put candles on top; Schroeder—an obsession with a clean vest made him an anti-Nazi for esthetic, not ethical reasons. If we get into trouble we will find that he has a clean vest again. Brandt—when things get rough he starts bawling (*flennen*) on

the shoulders of whoever has strong nerves; Erler—he is so accommodating (*verbindlich*) that he sells everything twice; Mende—Wehner had been told that the American press had praised that nihilist for flexibility. This proves that Americans are political idiots."[55]

Then he moved on to the rest of Europe: the former Belgian prime minister Paul-Henri Spaak was "a balloon who will fly away unless tied down and who punctures at the slightest prick," while the recently deceased Labour leader Hugh Gaitskell had been "a pedant confusing a walk to the podium with the march of history." As for de Gaulle, he was "a vestige of past centuries." All this was a mere warm-up. Like Bahr, Wehner was a nationalist before he was a socialist. He passionately believed that "Germany would collapse morally if it remained divided" and agreed that the other Western powers were merely paying lip service to reunification. Unlike Bahr, however, Wehner deeply distrusted the Soviet Union. He agreed with Kissinger that

> [a]ny recognition of the East German regime would only lead to a competition of two nationalist states. Nevertheless, the Federal Republic would have to conduct a very active unification policy if it was not to lose all moral cohesion and if it did not want to see extremist parties emerge again on the left and on the right. He said that the new generation no longer had the morbid fear of Communists (*Kommunistenschreck*) and they might start playing with the East. People like "that dilettante" Bahr were already toying with such ideas.[56]

Wherever he went in Germany, Kissinger heard the same thing. "Vietnam was not war but a bottomless morass," Wehner told him. *Der Alte*—the retired but still coruscating Konrad Adenauer—agreed: "The war in Vietnam was a disaster. Europe was the decisive area and we

---

*The references are to the chancellor, Ludwig Erhard; the foreign minister, Gerhard Schröder; the mayor of Berlin and SPD candidate for chancellor, Willy Brandt; the parliamentary leader of the SPD, Fritz Erler; and the Free Democrat leader and vice-chancellor, Erich Mende.

were instead getting sucked deeper into the morass in South East Asia. I said that we were defending Europe in South East Asia. Adenauer replied that if we kept up our present pace we would lose both Europe and Asia."[57]

The German complaint—echoed by Eugen Gerstenmaier, the president of the Bundestag—was that Americans kept asking them "to choose between France and the United States," to which he felt like replying, "And after we have made the choice will France then disappear from Europe?"[58] As Kissinger tried to explain to McGeorge Bundy, it made no sense to use the Federal Republic "as the . . . battering ram for [the State Department's] one-sided, almost obsessive anti-French bias. . . . If Germany is constantly asked to choose between the United States and France it will ultimately opt for unification by methods which are bound to be disruptive. . . . Woo[ing] the Federal Republic in order to thwart France . . . will conclude by alienating both Paris and Bonn."[59]

Kissinger breathed a sigh of relief when he heard that McNamara was finally abandoning the MLF in favor of a proposal for an "executive committee on nuclear matters."[60] (The MLF was laid to rest for good when Johnson met Erhard in December 1965 and told him—as relayed back to Kissinger—"Ludwig, I'll do anything for you but don't complicate my life by asking for nuclear weapons.")[61] But he accused the "Grand Old Men of the early days of NATO" of seeking to sabotage the idea in the mistaken belief that the "long-term danger in Europe" was "the excessive assertiveness of European will." The real danger, Kissinger correctly foresaw, was "the opposite—a tendency to abdicate all responsibility. . . . [T]en years from now Europe may have lapsed into the situation of Italy—only too eager to turn over foreign policy to us but unreliable in any period of stress. I cannot believe that it is in our interest to be the only country in the West conducting a serious foreign policy."[62]

It was a theme he returned to a year later, after yet another twist in American policy had produced the so-called "hardware solution" whereby U.S. nuclear submarines were to be sold to NATO and placed under joint NATO control with eventual mixed manning. This was essentially a reheated MLF, and Kissinger was unsparing in his scorn.[63] The real problem of the Atlantic alliance could not be solved with forms of integration that were at once too narrowly military and not in any case meaningful. What was needed was for Europe to "assume a greater responsibility for its policy and defense:

> It is in neither our interest nor that of Europe that Europe become the Greece to our Rome—a political backwater, interesting culturally but unable to play an active role. This would not be healthy for us because hegemony is demoralizing in the long run. I am urging that the only way we can maintain our influence is by reducing our formal predominance. . . . The present system encourages too many of our allies to shift the costs and the responsibilities of the common defense to us.[64]

The United States had to stop fighting against European efforts to pool their defense capabilities, including their nuclear ones. In particular the argument that Germany could not be allowed even a share of a European nuclear deterrent had to be dropped. How could it possibly be "good for the cohesion of the Alliance to keep insisting that one of its primary functions is to restrain the potential menace of one of its key members"?[65]

This appeal went unheeded. Instead of moving in the direction Kissinger favored—of a more politically integrated and militarily balanced NATO—the Johnson administration continued to pursue the path of détente, seemingly putting more faith in Moscow than in Bonn. The announcement in 1967 that the United States would embrace the (originally Irish) idea of a nuclear nonproliferation treaty (NPT) provoked another paroxysm in Germany. The American reasoning, based on an exhaustive study by former deputy secretary of defense Roswell Gilpatric, was that there was no better way of preventing the world lurching from a world of four nuclear powers to a world of fifteen or twenty by the mid-1970s.[66] As Francis Gavin has shown, U.S. thinking on the issue of nonproliferation was as convoluted as it was global in its scope: "[T]he United States needed to fight a conventional war in an area of little strategic interest (Vietnam), during a period of détente and cooperation with its main adversary (the Soviet Union), to convince an ally (Japan) and a neutral state (India) not to develop nuclear weapons, because if they did, the pressures on West Germany would mount, tensions with the Soviets would escalate, and détente would be undermined."[67] From Johnson's point of view, it is hardly necessary to add, the NPT had a domestic political appeal; as soon as Bobby Kennedy expressed interest in the idea, Johnson had to make it his own. The West Germans were uninterested in the intricacies of American reasoning; all they could see was that they, as loyal allies, were somehow being bracketed with the Chinese—who had in any case already carried out a successful nuclear test in 1964. In January 1967 Swidbert Schnippenkötter, the senior German diplomat responsible for disarmament, told Kissinger that this was "the turning point in Germany's relations to the United States and in many ways the damage was already irreparable."[68] Franz Josef Strauss, now back in government as finance minister, was pugnacious as ever: "He said the non-proliferation treaty was a super-Yalta. . . . [T]he behavior of the United States reminded him of an acute alcoholic who was telling non-drinkers that if they took one small drink they would be sentenced to death. The non-proliferation treaty amounted to permanent hegemony of the United States and the Soviet Union in nuclear matters."[69] Adenauer, speaking with the brutal candor to which his ninety-one years entitled him, told Kissinger that

> President Johnson was proposing a hegemonial relation with the Soviet Union against the whole rest of the world. The two great "haves" are trying to divide up the world against all the "have-nots." The United States was engaged in Asia. The priorities for the United States were first, Asia, and second, detente; Europe was being used simply as sort of a convenience when it was not a nuisance. . . . It was outrageous that the United States was even considering making a treaty which would, for all eternity, inflict a discriminatory status on the Federal Republic.[70]

Der Alte warned that he would "speak out publicly against you."

While a few old hands in the United States—notably John McCloy and Robert Bowie—were inclined to agree with the Germans, Kissinger himself was ambivalent about nonproliferation. When he attempted to relate it to the issue of German reunification with Strauss, he was given short shrift: "He [Strauss] was sick and tired of being told all the time that German unification would be the result of detente. The fact of the matter was that it was in nobody's interest to achieve German unification. Bismarck was very lucky that he had managed to create a unified Germany because of the misunderstanding of all surrounding powers to the effect that Austria was stronger than Prussia."[71] That was, of course, the Bavarian perspective, but it was not without its historical merits.

With Adenauer, Kissinger tried to play the Vietnam card. Was it really in Germany's interests, he asked, "to have American prestige collapse so entirely that the most intransigent element in the Communist world would be encouraged[?] If the United States were defeated by North Vietnam, what could the Soviets reply to Ulbricht if he wanted to put pressure on Berlin?

> Adenauer looked at me and said, and do you think that I believe that you will protect us? I said, yes. He said, I no longer believe that you will protect us. Your actions over recent years have made clear that to you detente is more important than anything else. I do not believe that any American president will risk nuclear war for Berlin; the only thing that is saving us is that the Soviets cannot be sure of this.[72]

Kissinger tried asking about German unification. Adenauer retorted that as far he was concerned, "it could not be achieved with or through the United States." The reality was that "the Americans were the most unreliable people in politics." It was far more likely, in his view, that "perhaps France might obtain German unification for the Federal Republic," if only because "from the point of view of *raison d'etat* it was essential for France to push Communism as far away from the center of Europe as possible."

> The United States was doing everything in its power to break the political back of the Atlantic area and to destroy the self-confidence of those upon whom a Western security system

> could he built. He said he would pay a visit to De Gaulle in a
> few weeks, and would urge him to push European political
> union. A purely economic union was simply not enough and
> the nation-state inadequate.[73]

What was remarkable was to hear such sentiments right across the
political spectrum and right across the generations. Egon Bahr took
essentially the same dim view of the NPT as Strauss and Adenauer,
though in his eyes it was just a new argument for making West Germany "a bridge between the East and West"* as well as a new partner
for countries like Sweden, Japan, and India, against which the treaty
was clearly aimed.[74] Helmut Schmidt, the new chairman of the SPD
Fraktion in the Bundestag, took the same line: the United States, in his
view, "wanted détente for its own benefit at the possible expense of
one of its closest allies . . . the end of NATO was being hastened."[75] If
the United States had set out to devise a policy to cement the new alliance between Christian Democrats and Social Democrats—forged less
than two months previously with the formation of a grand coalition
under Kurt Georg Kiesinger—it could not have come up with anything better than the NPT.

West Germany, in short, had nothing to offer the United States,
least of all with regard to Vietnam. "I am not sure," Kissinger reported
back to John McNaughton after what can only have been a dispiriting
series of meetings, "that even these conversations do justice to the
mood of self-pity and incipient nationalism in Bonn today."[76]

IV

In only one respect did Kissinger approve of the direction West Ger-
many was going in. As he had said during his first meeting with Egon
Bahr, "the whole conception [of *Ostpolitik*] struck me as quite Gaullist.
Bahr replied that Brandt was fascinated by De Gaulle."[77] Paris, once

---

*Bahr had the good sense to laugh when Kissinger shot back that "there was always the
danger that a bridge is something everyone walks over."

again, was the key. When it came to issues other than the German Question, the men in Berlin and Bonn had little to offer. In 1965 the German minister Heinrich Krone (whom Kissinger described as "Adenauer's closest confidant and Chairman of the German version of the NSC") offered the typically banal "fear . . . that the United States might become so absorbed in South East Asia it would reduce its interest in Europe."[78] As Kissinger put it to Marion Dönhoff, he had for some time been "skeptical about putting so much weight on a purely German-American relationship."[79] Germany was too self-obsessed to offer much in return for American interest. The key was therefore France.

From as early as July 1964, Kissinger began to signal his contrarian sympathy for de Gaulle. In a penetrating critique of what was wrong with the Atlantic alliance, published in *Foreign Affairs,* Kissinger set out the case for Gaullism. The "new spirit" of political independence and "polycentrism" was perfectly intelligible after nearly twenty years in which nuclear weapons had exponentially grown more numerous and more destructive but had not actually been used. The very success of deterrence was inevitably loosening transatlantic ties as the threat of Armageddon appeared to recede. "Far from doubting America's military commitment to Europe," Kissinger argued, "President de Gaulle is so certain of it that he does not consider political independence a risk."[80] In any case, the French had legitimate grounds for criticizing the Johnson administration's policy. The Multilateral Force was a gimmick. It was "basically a device to make American nuclear hegemony acceptable." Under the theory of flexible response, the Europeans were supposed to acquiesce in "exclusive U. S. control of nuclear strategy," confining themselves to building up their own conventional forces. But de Gaulle had "put his finger on . . . the key problem of NATO. In the absence of a common foreign policy—or at least an agreed range of divergence—the attempt to devise a common strategy is likely to prove futile."[81] Kissinger not only approved of de Gaulle's earlier proposal for a "Directory" of the great powers; he also favored the French vision of European integration based on "institutionalized meetings of foreign ministers and sub-cabinet officials" rather than German-style federalism, not least because it was "the one most consistent with British participation."[82] Comments like this make it clear that Kissinger was never wholly persuaded by Rockefeller's scheme for transatlantic federalism as a solution to the problems of NATO.[83]

In a deliberately provocative article entitled "The Illusionist," Kissinger accused Americans of "misread[ing]" de Gaulle.[84] Even kindred spirits like Marion Dönhoff were dismayed. (She had stopped reading the article in disgust.) But Kissinger was adamant. "[M]uch as I disapprove of some of his answers," he told her, "he has asked some terribly important questions."[85] Kissinger's attempt to arrive at answers of his own was published in 1965 as *The Troubled Partnership*.[86] Dedicated to his children, the book grew out of a series of three lectures delivered at the Council on Foreign Relations in March 1964 and was published under the auspices of the CFR simultaneously with two other volumes, Zbigniew Brzezinski's *Alternative to Partition* and Timothy W. Stanley's *NATO in Transition: The Future of the Atlantic Alliance*. It was a book written in a hurry. Even the "enormously able" research assistance provided by a young Peter Rodman and the "incisive and brilliant advice" proffered by Tom Schelling could not compensate for the haste of its composition (betrayed by several *Britians* and at least one use of *Franco-German* where *Franco-American* was clearly meant). Too many of the chapters had their origins in earlier articles for an entirely coherent argument to emerge about the future of the Atlantic alliance. Still, one important theme was well articulated. The United States had to take Gaullism more seriously. The days when "America was predominant and Europe impotent" were over, but they had left a legacy of, on one side, "self-righteousness and impatience" and on the other "querulousness and insecurity."[87] De Gaulle was merely the first European leader to realize that, under conditions of de facto American dominance of nuclear strategy and U.S.-USSR détente, there was "little risk and considerable potential gain in political independence."[88]

Kissinger's chapter on de Gaulle makes it clear just how important the parallel with Bismarck had become in his thinking at this time. While Americans (not least George Ball at the State Department)[89] had come to the view that Europe should be integrated as a federal United States of Europe and that such an entity would make it a better partner for the United States of America, de Gaulle had seen through this. Though sincere about wanting European unity, he wanted only a confederation of nation-states, and one that was no longer dependent on the United States for its security. Kissinger sympathized with this vision:

> Though De Gaulle often acts as if opposition to United States
> policy were a goal in itself, his deeper objective is pedagogical:
> to teach his people and perhaps his continent attitudes of inde-
> pendence and self-reliance. . . . His diplomacy is in the style of
> Bismarck, who strove ruthlessly to achieve what he considered
> Prussia's rightful place, but who then tried to preserve the new
> equilibrium through prudence, restraint and moderation.[90]

Throughout the book, he endorsed each move the French president had made, even those that had caused outrage in Washington. Thus de Gaulle had been right to reject Britain's application for Common Market membership; he had been right to establish France as "guardian of the Federal Republic's interests" through the 1963 Franco-German treaty of cooperation; he had been right to hang on to France's independent nuclear deterrent ("Taking out fire insurance does not indicate a liking for fires"); he had been right to reject the MLF.[91] Kissinger's new proposal for an "Executive Committee of the NATO Council composed of the United States, Britain, France, the Federal Republic, Italy and a rotating representative of the smaller countries" was essentially a refinement of de Gaulle's stillborn idea of a tripartite Directory.[92] The only catch was that, like Bismarck, de Gaulle might be creating a structure that could not survive him.

> [A] statesman must work with the material at hand. If the
> sweep of his conceptions exceeds the capacity of his environ-
> ment to absorb them, he will fail regardless of the validity of
> his insights. If his style makes him unassimilable, it becomes
> irrelevant whether he is right or wrong. Great men build truly
> only if they remember that their achievement must be main-
> tained by the less gifted individuals who are likely to follow
> them. A structure which can be preserved only if there is a

great man in each generation is inherently fragile. This may be the nemesis of De Gaulle's success.[93]

Some books owe their success to good timing. That had been true of *Nuclear Weapons and Foreign Policy*. By contrast, *The Troubled Partnership* was terribly timed. "It is a pity," wrote his father with an authentically German lack of tact, "that this book was published at a time when all attention is focused to Asia and not to Europe."[94] The reviews, nevertheless, were kind. The *New York Times* review was by the newspaper's veteran reporter Drew Middleton, who had only recently finished a six-year tour of duty in Germany. "Mr. Kissinger is an expert," noted Middleton, with the time-honored reverse snobbery of a jack-of-all-trades, "and too often he seems to be writing for other experts." But he was broadly supportive of Kissinger's critique of the MLF and his analysis of the latest iteration of the German conundrum.[95] Bernard Brodie liked the book so much he reviewed it twice, calling it "probably Henry Kissinger's best book thus far and the best book I know of on the Atlantic Alliance."[96] Another reviewer praised Kissinger's "nose for political realities."[97] Perhaps the most serious criticism was that Kissinger had more or less entirely ignored the economic aspects of the transatlantic relationship. There was no reference whatsoever to the Paris-based Organization for Economic Co-operation, nothing on issues such as "aid to the underdeveloped nations, the intricacies of international monetary liquidity, or trade relationships and the GATT [General Agreement on Trade and Tariffs] negotiations."[98] Yet the most obvious weakness of the book went largely unnoticed, and that was the fundamental incompatibility between Kissinger's vision of "an Atlantic Commonwealth in which all the peoples bordering the North Atlantic can fulfill their aspirations"[99] and the reality of de Gaulle's vision as it was evolving in his grandiose yet increasingly isolated quarters in the Élysée Palace. By the time Kissinger was called to testify on the Atlantic alliance before the Senate Foreign Relations Committee—fully a year after its publication—*The Troubled Partnership* was out of date, and the partnership itself even more troubled.[100]

V

European despair about the transatlantic alliance came in multiple flavors. The prevailing mood in Paris in 1965 was of presidential hauteur. Jean de La Grandville, *ministre plénipotentiaire* at the Quai D'Orsay, told Kissinger in May that

> De Gaulle was determined to reduce American domination of NATO, perhaps even to change NATO into an old-style traditional Alliance. He would spend most of this year laying the ground-work for what De La Grandville feared would be an ever more insistent attack. . . . [I]t was his impression that De Gaulle thought that he could harass the American presence in Europe until we had reduced it to those forces that were required for immediate security rather than an establishment that in De Gaulle's eyes was intended to give us political domination. . . . In short, the major thrust of De Gaulle's policy at the moment was to reduce America's standing in the world. He had heard De Gaulle say "we will puncture the American balloon in Vietnam."[101]

De La Grandville admitted to being "in despair about trends in the West, especially about the policy of his country." Not only was de Gaulle intent on "puncturing the American balloon"; he was also resolved to halt further European moves in the direction of federalism and—most shocking of all—to deal directly with the Soviets on the subject of (as de Gaulle had very deliberately put it to Gromyko) "the two German states . . . I beg your pardon. I mean the American-occupied zone of Germany and the Soviet-occupied zone of Germany."[102] Kissinger was stunned. "As long as I had believed that De Gaulle was basically a man of the West," he told de La Grandville, "I had had sympathy for his efforts and even believed them to be in the long-term interests of all Allies. Now I had my doubts."[103]

Within a year, as we have seen, de Gaulle had pulled France out of the integrated NATO command structure. His refusal to sign the Non-Proliferation Treaty was not difficult to predict. When Kissinger returned to Paris in January 1967, he was regaled once again by de La Grandville with tales of Gaullism run mad:

> The official French theory—as written down in official documents—was that the world was tri-polar. One center was at Washington, another in Peking dominating East Asia, the third was Europe dominated by Moscow-Paris. Thus during Kosygin's visit, De Gaulle had said to him: "We must watch the Germans continually—if necessary by meeting twice a day. . . . The United States is becoming more unpopular in Europe every day. This is the way for us to build Europe together." Kosygin had replied: "I had been told you thought this but I wanted to hear you say it."[104]

Yet at the same time, de Gaulle was seeking to use "an—if necessary fomented—dislike of the United States to build an autonomous Europe. . . . De Gaulle had told [the German chancellor] Kiesinger that he had only preceded him on a road which Kiesinger would have to travel sooner or later." In de La Grandville's view, this was "madness because France would be the first victim of such a German policy."[105] Finally there was Asia, where "French policy would do nothing to challenge Peking's hegemony in East Asia."

> De La Grandville said we had to face the fact that France was not neutral on Vietnam. He had heard [the French foreign minister] Couve [de Murville] say that the United States must be taught a lesson in South East Asia and that this would help affect her pretensions elsewhere. French officials frequently saw Ho and were urging him to adopt a more flexible stance which the United States would find it more difficult to counter. Also the French were urging that the NLF constitute itself with a formal government and seek recognition.[106]

Here, then, was the ultimate test of Kissinger's newfound admiration for the French Bismarck. Not only had he set his face against the United States' grand strategy of détente, seeking to reestablish the old pre-1914 alliance between France and Russia. Not only had he determined to lure the West Germans out of the American embrace, while excluding the British from Europe. Worst of all, he was actively working to help the North Vietnamese defeat the United States in Vietnam. And his motive for doing so was to achieve an authentically Bismarckian division of the world that would leave China dominant in East Asia, the United States confined to the western hemisphere, and France restored to power in a pan-European partnership with the Russians. What if the road to Hanoi led not just through Paris but via Beijing?

Indifferent as he was to ideology, de Gaulle had been quicker than most to foresee the Sino-Soviet split and to assume that it could be exploited for France's benefit. The thought had also occurred to Henry Kissinger. In *The Necessity for Choice,* published in 1961, Kissinger had directly addressed "the frequently voiced view that we should conduct our diplomacy so as to bring about a rift between Communist China and the U.S.S.R." However, his position was one of skepticism: "Of course, the possibility of a rift must not be overlooked. And if it occurs, we should take advantage of it rather than force the erstwhile partners into a new alliance through intransigence. Yet this is a far cry from the proposition that we can promote a split."[107] And elsewhere in the book he was conventional in his condemnation of "a country which has shown so callous a disregard of human life." Indeed, Kissinger was one of the first American writers to make the argument that, if China acquired a nuclear capability, the consequences would be "terrifying."

> What has come to be called the balance of terror may seem less frightful to fanatics leading a country with a population of 600 millions. Even a war directed explicitly against centers of population may seem to it tolerable and perhaps the best means of dominating the world. Chou En-lai is reported to have told a Yugoslav diplomat that an all-out nuclear war would leave 10 million Americans, 20 million Russians, and 350 million Chinese.[108]

Asked in February 1962 "Which is more of a threat to peace—Russia or China?," Kissinger's answer was equivocal:

> I would say that in the long run probably Communist China is likely to be in more of an expansionist phase than Soviet Russia. At the same time, most of the recent crises have been commanded by the Soviet Union. . . . It is my view that both of them are a menace to world peace and partly because of Communist doctrine. . . .
>
> In their tactics, the Chinese Communists are probably the greater menace; in their potentiality, the Russians are the greater menace, and much of the debate between them has somewhat of the character of two thieves arguing whether they have to kill you to get your wallet or whether they can lift your wallet without hitting you over the head. You lose your wallet either way.[109]

Two months later, working on a position paper for Nelson Rockefeller that began, "Our policy . . . should be to test the interest of Communist China in improving relations with us," Kissinger was the one who sought to toughen up the language:

> ~~We should attempt to~~ IF COMMUNIST CHINA AGREES TO RENOUNCE THE USE OF FORCE IN THE FORMOSA STRAIT, WE COULD CONSIDER open[ing] up channels of non-official contact . . . journalists, students, tourists, etc.
>
> If these measures show progress, we ~~should attempt~~ MIGHT establish commercial contacts, ~~first~~ by ~~abandoning the arms embargo and~~ applying to Communist China the same restrictions we apply to other members of the Communist bloc.
>
> If Communist China proves it is a responsible member of the international community, and can do so by agreeing to arms control, the question of admission to the U.N. can be re-examined in a new light ON THE BASIS OF A TWO-CHINA SOLUTION.[110]

This became Rockefeller's line. The United States should not accept PRC membership in the United Nations until Beijing had renounced its "belligerent and expansionist foreign policy" in Southeast Asia and the Taiwan Strait.[111] The French decision to recognize "Red China" should, Kissinger recommended, "be deplored."[112]

Whatever Kissinger subsequently came to believe, after it had become clear to both him and Richard Nixon that an American opening to China could bring about a diplomatic revolution in the Cold War, his line in the mid-1960s was that the West could "take little comfort from the internal Communist split and . . . in fact, the split could as easily double our problems as halve them."[113] In a speech drafted for Rockefeller in October 1964, Kissinger argued that "the Sino-Soviet split has weakened Communism by creating rival factions all over the world. . . . By following a differentiated approach to the various Communist regimes, it [the "Atlantic world"] could accentuate the splits in the Communist world." Yet the new situation had its dangers. "Henceforth the West confronts not alternating periods of hostility and peaceful coexistence but both at the same time." Moreover, the Communist split would "create great temptations for bilateral Western approaches." This might "enable the Communists to escape their difficulties by playing the allies off, one against the other."[114] It is hard to believe that Kissinger was unmoved by Herbert Wehner's report that "the Soviet ambassador in Bonn had told Wehner that China was no longer a Communist state, but a Nazi state—the worst possible epithet in the Soviet vocabulary."[115] No reliable report coming out of China, especially as the Cultural Revolution got under way, could encourage optimism about Mao Zedong's future role in international relations.

The only hint of Kissinger's future position was an observation in his 1966 essay on "Domestic Structure and Foreign Policy" that, although the Chinese still "possess[ed] more ideological fervor" than the Soviets,

> paradoxically, their structure may permit a wider latitude for new departures. Tactical intransigence and ideological vitality should not be confused with structural rigidity. Because the leadership bases its rule on a prestige which transcends bureau-

cratic authority, it has not yet given so many hostages to the administrative structure. If the leadership should change—or if its attitudes are modified—policy could probably be altered much more dramatically in Communist China than in the more institutionalized Communist countries.[116]

Here was a classic example of what Kissinger liked to call the "problem of conjecture," which he illustrated once again with the example of Hitler in 1936, when no one could know for sure whether he was "a misunderstood nationalist or a maniac."

When the scope for action is greatest, knowledge on which to base such action is small or ambiguous. When knowledge becomes available, the ability to affect events is usually at a minimum. . . . The conjectural element of foreign policy—the need to gear actions to an assessment that cannot be proved true when it is made—is never more crucial than in a revolutionary period. Then, the old order is obviously disintegrating while the shape of its replacement is highly uncertain. Everything depends, therefore, on some conception of the future.[117]

But what was China's future? De Gaulle might be the French Bismarck, but what if Mao were the Chinese Hitler, his future crimes as hard to foresee in 1966 as Hitler's had been in 1936? What then?

VI

Studying Bismarck and de Gaulle had challenged Kissinger's idealism. For the first time, he had been forced to confront the possibility that a realist strategy, based on the pure calculation of power relationships—pure in the sense of ethically indifferent and ideologically neutral—might be the only way to extricate the United States from its absurd predicament in Vietnam: the most powerful nation in history, unable to defeat a tiny Communist republic in the third world. The constraint that remained—which Bismarck had transcended but which would bring de Gaulle low in 1969—was domestic politics. In "Domestic Structure and Foreign Policy," published in *Daedalus* in 1966, Kissinger offered some insights into the policy-making process that certainly could not have been arrived at by sitting in his Harvard study.

The first problem, Kissinger argues, is bureaucracy, which makes "a deliberate effort to reduce the relevant elements of a problem to a standard of average performance." This is only problematic when "what it defines as routine does not address the most significant range of issues or when its prescribed mode of action proves irrelevant to the problem." At this point, the bureaucracy begins to absorb the energies of top executives "in reconciling what is expected with what happens."[118] Attention is "diverted from the act of choice—which is the ultimate test of statesmanship—to the accumulation of facts," and what passes for planning degenerates into the "projection of the familiar into the future."[119]

The second problem is the ever-shortening time frame within which results are supposed to be achieved, or as Kissinger puts it, "The time span by which administrative success is measured is considerably shorter than that by which historical achievement is determined."[120] Decisions are taken hurriedly, under stress, leaving decision makers susceptible to the "theatrical" effectiveness of briefings. But "not everything that sounds plausible is correct, and many things which are correct may not sound plausible when they are first presented."[121]

Third and consequently, there is a tendency for "bureaucratic contests" to become the only means of generating decisions, or for the various elements of the bureaucracy to make "a series of nonaggression pacts with each other and thus reduce the decision-maker to a benevolent constitutional monarch." The chief significance of a foreign policy speech by the president may therefore be to "settle an internal debate in Washington."[122] In turn, presidents may respond by transferring responsibilities to special emissaries or envoys in order to circumvent the bureaucracy.

A fourth and final point Kissinger added in a separate essay a year later was the fact that a gap had opened up in many countries between the requirements for reaching high office and the qualities needed to exercise it:

Where eminence must be reached by endless struggle, leaders may collapse at the top, drained of creativity, or they may be inclined to use in high office the methods by which they reached it. When political leaders are characterized primarily by their quest for power, when they decide to seek office first and search for issues later, then their technique to maintain power is necessarily short-range and manipulative.[123]

If every modern state made foreign policy roughly along these lines, the chances of "meaningful consultation with other nations" would be low even if there were no ideological schisms. When "the bureaucratic-pragmatic type" of state (i.e., the United States) was trying to do business with "the ideological type" (the Soviet Union and China) and the revolutionary-charismatic type (e.g., Cuba), it was miraculous that any agreement was ever reached.

Here, Kissinger concluded—albeit obliquely—was the problem in Vietnam. On one side was the United States, whose negotiators tended to be "extremely sensitive to the tactical requirements of the conference table—sometimes at the expense of longer-term considerations." In internal discussions, American negotiators would "often become advocates for the maximum range of concessions, their legal background tempt[ing] them to act as mediators between Washington and the country with which they are negotiating," and to apply the maxim that "if two parties disagree the truth is usually somewhere in between."[124] This legalism went hand in hand with a "relatively low valuation of historical factors." ("American leadership groups show high competence in dealing with technical issues, and much less virtuosity in mastering a historical process.")[125] On the other side was North Vietnam. Contrary to the optimists like Rostow, the leadership in Hanoi had no great interest in "raising the gross national product . . . [which] can be achieved only by slow, painful, highly technical measures which contrast with the heroic exertions of the struggle for independence."[126] They were "convinced that an adventurous foreign policy will not harm prospects for economic development and may even foster it," a view based partly on the fact that the competition between the superpowers was bound to result in economic assistance from one side or the

other. ("[T]he more obstrusive [*sic*] their foreign policy the greater is
their prospect of being wooed by the chief contenders.")[127]

The scene was set. The two counterparties could not have had more
different modes of operation, quite apart from their stated goals. The
time had come to try to bring them together. To achieve that, Henry
Kissinger now understood, there was no point going back to Saigon.
His travels in pursuit of peace in Vietnam would take him to Warsaw,
to Vienna, and to Prague—but above all to Paris.

CHAPTER 20

Waiting for Hanoi

Henry finally said, "I cannot believe that the security of the United States will be endangered if for a little while we do not bomb within ten miles of the capital of a fifth-rate agricultural power." Johnson glowered at him and said, "OK, we will do it the professor's way. But (glaring at Kissinger) if it doesn't work, I will personally cut your balls off."

      —ARTHUR SCHLESINGER'S DIARY, December 1967[1]

The struggle toward the heights is itself enough to fill a man's heart. One must imagine Sisyphus happy. (*La lutte elle-même vers les sommets suffit à remplir un cœur d'homme. Il faut imaginer Sisyphe heureux.*)

      —ALBERT CAMUS, *Le Mythe de Sisyphe*, 1942[2]

I

Agatha Christie's *The Mousetrap* and Samuel Beckett's *Waiting for Godot* are, it might be said, the opposite poles of theater in the Cold War era. Though they were first performed within just a few months of one another—*The Mousetrap* in Nottingham in October 1952, *Godot* in Paris in January 1953—they were, in almost every way, antithetical works. True, both are mysteries, and both have proved enduringly popular, but there the resemblances end. In Christie's play, the mystery of who murdered Maureen Lyon and Mrs. Boyle is solved with an audience-pleasing "twist" at the end of Act II. In Beckett's, we never find out why Estragon and Vladimir (or "Gogo" and "Didi," as they call one another) are waiting for Godot. Nor, indeed, are their identities or relationship explained. *The Mousetrap* has action, including a murder (albeit one committed with the theater lights down). *Waiting for Godot,* as *The Harvard Crimson's* reviewer complained, "has nearly no action, only waiting and talk, the talk to make the waiting pass more quickly. . . . Gogo says, 'I can't go on like this,' and Didi replies, 'That's what you think.' And that's the point of the play."[3]

The diplomatic history of 1967 looks at first sight much more like Beckett than Christie. For long days, Henry Kissinger would sit in Paris and wait—not for Godot, but for the North Vietnamese envoy to France, Mai Van Bo. But their meeting never occurred. And though the dialogue that filled the time was not quite as nonsensical as some of Beckett's, there were times when it was almost as obscure. In countless telegrams, phone calls, and meetings, Kissinger struggled to find the magic words that would bring Bo onto the stage and start the direct negotiations—or rather, "talks"—between Washington and Hanoi that now seemed to him the only way to end the Vietnam War. At one point it was as if the peace of Southeast Asia hinged on the difference between the French words *pourraient* and *peuvent* ("they could" and "they can").

Yet it is now possible to see that the drama being enacted in Paris in 1967 was really an old-fashioned whodunit, in which the audience was left in suspense about the identity of the murderer not just until the end of the play but for the better part of half a century. For most of that period, historians—encouraged by Robert McNamara, among others— have tended to argue that it was the United States that "killed" what would be called the PENNSYLVANIA peace initiative, as well as MARIGOLD before it (see below). With his foul mouth and abrasive temperament, President Lyndon Johnson has always been the prime suspect, with overconfident Walt Rostow and overrigid Dean Rusk as his red-handed accomplices. The murder weapons were the B-52 bombers that kept raining down high explosives on North Vietnam at the most inopportune moments. Kissinger himself had explained in *A World Restored* that the art of diplomacy was to keep the threat of force "potential, to keep its extent indeterminate and to commit it only as a last resort," because once it had been "made actual" and had proved unavailing, the bargaining position was altogether destroyed.[4] The conventional view is that Johnson and his advisers committed this cardinal sin.

But this conventional view is wrong. In reality, the villain of the piece was none other than the charming Monsieur Bo.

As *Time* magazine described him, the North Vietnamese representative in Paris had "grown grey, stylish and somewhat stout on the haute cuisine of hostesses delighted by his foxy charm and affable wit." He was a connoisseur of art, spoke perfect French, and liked to quote Balzac. "Chain-smoking cigarettes and sipping pungent tea," Bo received visitors at his office in the rue le Verrier, agreeably situated in the sixth arrondissement, next to the Jardin du Luxembourg and "a short walk from the house where Alice B. Toklas and Gertrude Stein used to hold court."⁵ Bo was the very model of a modern Marxist-Leninist. A veteran of the Viet Minh's campaign to drive the French out of Indochina and a seasoned propagandist, he excelled at putting Western imperialists in the wrong and his own tyrannical and murderous government in the right. In studying Bismarck and admiring de Gaulle, Henry Kissinger had endeavored to understand better the Machiavellian mind. But nothing had prepared him for the deviousness and duplicitousness of Mai Van Bo. So eager was Kissinger to achieve a diplomatic breakthrough—to end the deadlock that seemed to condemn the United States to either an interminable stalemate or a hazardous expansion of the war—that he failed to discern how cynically, from the very outset, the North Vietnamese were stringing him along.

We know now from Vietnamese sources that the Hanoi regime had no intention whatever of making peace in 1967. And we know, too, that Bo and his confederates were doing more than merely playing for time. Throughout the long months of "talks about talks," they were waging psychological warfare on the Johnson administration, exploiting the split they had discerned between hawks and doves. More than that: they were adroitly camouflaging their carefully premeditated plan to launch a massive offensive that they hoped would decide the Vietnam War in their favor.

II

For a year, beginning in the fall of 1965, Kissinger had made himself a Vietnam expert on the basis of three sometimes hair-raising trips to South Vietnam. What he learned there had convinced him that the United States must extricate itself from that country by diplomatic means. It clearly could not hope to win a war against an externally supported guerrilla movement at an acceptable cost in an acceptable time frame. Worse, the very government it was seeking to defend showed little sign of being capable, much less worthy, of being preserved. Kissinger's role therefore had to change. He had begun with the questions: Can the American war effort be improved? Can Saigon be strengthened? Now the question was: How can we get out without being humiliated? From August 1966 until the fall of Saigon slightly less than nine years later, Kissinger would devote an enormous proportion of his time and energy to this problem. It should be acknowledged from the outset that it was an impossible task. But the principal stumbling block to an honorable peace was not the antiwar movement in the United States, as is sometimes thought. It was the ruthless resolve of the North Vietnamese, regardless of the losses inflicted on them, to settle for nothing less than total victory and the unification of the two Vietnams under Communist rule.

On August 17, 1966, Kissinger's Sisyphean labor began. First—though he now held no formal consulting position—he was tasked by William Bundy and his special assistant, Daniel Davidson, with making the American case for talks with Hanoi at the forthcoming Pugwash conference of Western and Soviet bloc academics in Poland.[6] The next day the negotiations committee chaired by Averell Harriman resolved that Kissinger was also "the right man" to talk to the former French minister Jean Sainteny,* who was known to have met with the North Vietnamese premier, Pham Van Dong.[7] The Johnson administration's

---

*It did not hurt that Jean Sainteny's wife was a favorite student of Kissinger's, having attended the International Seminar at Harvard.

position was, at first sight, straightforward: "The United States will withdraw its troops from South Viet-Nam just as soon as the independence of South Viet-Nam is secured." As President Johnson would make clear at the summit of Asian leaders held at Manila in October of that year, he did not want permanent bases in South Vietnam. The question, as Kissinger had come to see, was how far one or more of the other major powers could persuade or otherwise induce the North Vietnamese to accept a peace deal on this basis. There was prima facie evidence to believe that the United States and the Soviet Union had "a common interest in checking the expansion of mainland Chinese influence in Southeast Asia." It was also obvious that the French had better contacts in Hanoi than anyone else, even if it was hard to imagine General de Gaulle lending the United States a helping hand.[8]

Putting out peace feelers, as Kissinger gradually discovered, was not a simple matter. First there was the challenge of finding the right intermediary. To go through more than one might seem smart in theory, but in practice one channel might be compromised or blocked by the other. Second, secrecy was necessary—these were not maneuvers that one wanted to read about in *The New York Times* until after a deal had been done—but secrecy was also an impediment, making it more or less impossible to coordinate action across all the many agencies involved in the U.S. war effort. Third, as Kissinger had shown in his essay "Domestic Structure and Foreign Policy," all the main actors had their own internal politics to consider: not only public opinion but also rival parties, factions, or interest groups.[9] Fourth, there were the usual headaches of diplomacy: crucial concepts could get lost in translation when participants in the process spoke multiple languages (Czech, English, French, Polish, Russian, and Vietnamese were all involved). Fifth, the documents about which there would be so much haggling were being crafted not just for the purpose of negotiation but also for the purpose of swaying future historians and through them posterity, so that some things were said more for the record than for any pressing present reason. Finally, and as it proved crucially, there was the unknown quantity: "What Hanoi has in mind," in the words of William Bundy. Despite all the resources made available to the CIA, the Americans had the utmost difficulty finding this out, and in the absence of good information, they generally made incorrect inferences from the brute fact that their destructive capability was so much greater than the enemy's.

III

Sopot is one of those rather bleak seaside resorts on the Baltic coast, once Prussian, now Polish. It was here that the 1966 Pugwash conference was held, and it was here, in the course of a boat trip to Gdańsk harbor, that Kissinger learned the true extent of the Sino-Soviet rift. "China was no longer Communist but Fascist," the Soviet mathematician Stanislav Emelyanov told him. "The Red Guards reminded him of nothing so much as the Hitler Youth. The U.S. and the U.S.S.R. had a common interest in preventing Chinese expansion." Kissinger saw his opening: "I said that if this was true, I did not understand the Soviet reluctance to help end the war in Vietnam. Emelyanov said we had to be patient. He had not seen the Soviet government so confused since the aftermath of Khrushchev's de-Stalinization speech. Some Stalinists saw in the Vietnamese war a chance to make a comeback; others just did not know what to do."[10] Kissinger heard much the same story from other members of the Soviet delegation with whom he was able to speak outside the conference chamber. On September 16, General Nikolai Talensky told him,

> The real menace in the world was China. A war between the U.S. and the U.S.S.R. over Vietnam would be an absurdity. The real problem was to keep Southeast Asia out of Chinese hands. The Chinese were Fascists. "If they have two nuclear bombs operational, will they use both against us or one against you?" . . . [True,] there were still military men who thought war a possibility; Soviet memories of partisan warfare created an automatic sympathy for the Vietcong. Still[,] peace between the U.S. and the U.S.S.R. was essential to prevent domination of the world by China and to permit the U.S.S.R. to continue developing its consumer industry.

But as the Soviet diplomat Vladimir Shustov had admitted two days before, the United States "vastly overestimated the degree of Moscow's influence in Hanoi." Moreover, "the Chinese situation made moves by Moscow very difficult."[11] That explained why, in the Pugwash plenary session, the Soviet spokesmen reverted to their traditional "intemperate, highly emotional language," denouncing American imperialism in Southeast Asia and everywhere else, too.[12] As Shustov made clear to Kissinger, Moscow's main priority in the détente process was the Non-Proliferation Treaty, which they intended to use as a means to ensure the permanent exclusion of the Germans from the nuclear weapons club. Vietnam was a long way down their list of priorities.[13] Indeed, a recurrent weakness of the American position was precisely Vietnam's insignificance in Soviet eyes. They supplied Hanoi with weapons and advisers not because they cared about Vietnam but because it was an inexpensive way of tying up American resources, and because not doing so would have risked turning Vietnam into a Chinese client state.

The Soviets had earlier hinted that one or other of their Eastern European satellites might be better positioned than they to help with Hanoi. With that in mind, Kissinger traveled from Sopot to Warsaw, where he lunched (at the U.S. embassy) with Marian Dobrosielski, a former counselor at the Polish embassy in Washington who was now running the Polish equivalent of Policy Planning at the State Department. An authority on the philosophy of Charles Peirce, Dobrosielski assured Kissinger that "Hanoi want[ed] peace." Echoing what the Soviets had said at Sopot, he argued that Hanoi's insistence on treating the Vietcong as the sole legitimate representatives of South Vietnam (the third of its four points) was merely an "opening and bargaining gambit." More important, he said that "if [the] U.S. were gradually to reduce bombing North Viet-Nam and eventually stop completely, Hanoi would reciprocate and cease infiltration from North Viet-Nam."[14] To be precise, as Kissinger recorded in his own memcon, "[W]e should stop bombing without any announcement over a period of two weeks. We could then observe the roads to see whether what we called infiltration stopped. If not we could resume bombing. He thought infiltration would stop."[15]

Even more intriguing was what Kissinger heard in Prague the next day. He had been struck by how sympathetic the Czech scientists had been at Pugwash. The distinguished microbiologist Ivan Málek, the head of the Central Institute of Biology and a member of the central committee of the Czech Communist Party, had told him over lunch that "Czechoslovakia desperately wanted the war in Vietnam to end because it could only retard relaxation of tensions in Europe." But the situation was "difficult." The Czech government had made an unpublicized effort to urge North Vietnam to negotiate the previous February, only to have it "brutally rebuffed."[16] Under the pretext of attending a "discussion of Central European problems," Kissinger, Paul Doty, and Marshall Shulman traveled to Prague to meet with Antonín Šnejdárek, the former head of Czech intelligence operations in Germany who was now director of the country's Institute of International Politics and Economics.[17] After dinner on the nineteenth, Šnejdárek told Kissinger that a high-level Czech delegation was leaving the next day for Hanoi, intending to "press as hard as possible for a peaceful solution." However, the Czech was frank about how limited his government's freedom of action was:

> Czechoslovakia could go only so far in risking Soviet displeasure over Vietnam. During the Warsaw Pact meetings in Bucharest, Czechoslovakia had got into difficulties with the USSR by urging restraint over Vietnam. . . . Anything he told me was subject to a Soviet veto for Czechoslovakia could not risk losing Soviet support in Central Europe over Vietnam. The Czechs were not at all sure that the Soviets wanted a settlement of the Vietnamese war. A relaxation of tensions might bring about a loosening of Soviet control in Central Europe which made the Soviets most uneasy.
>
> As for Hanoi, all Czech diplomatic and party reports spoke of extreme intransigence.[18]

What the Czechs wanted to know was how sincere the United States was about seeking peace—"or were the peace offers a smokescreen for continued escalation?"—and what role an intermediary might play. When Kissinger replied that Washington was "undoubtedly sincere in seeking an honorable peace" and that there was a "definite use" for a third party, Šnejdárek came back with three more questions, evidently straight from the country's central committee:

(a) If North Vietnam agreed to end its infiltration in return for an end of bombing, what would happen to the United States build-up in South Vietnam?

(b) What guarantees other than a coalition government were available to prevent the members of the NLF suffering the fate of the Communist party in Indonesia [which had been wiped out after an abortive coup in 1965]?

(c) How could the Czechs communicate the results of their Hanoi trip to the United States?

Now clearly out of his depth, Kissinger improvised. While the United States "could not stop resupply and rotation of personnel," some "limitations on an increase in the number of troops" did seem to him "an appropriate subject for discussion," as did the idea of international guarantees. But when Kissinger suggested using the U.S. embassy in Prague for further communication, Šnejdárek put him right. Mindful of Soviet ambivalence, "the Central Committee wanted no official contact with Americans and it wanted these conversations kept to the smallest possible number of people." In other words, he wanted Kissinger to be the Czechs' back channel to Washington.[19]

Kissinger and Šnejdárek met ten days later in Vienna at the annual meeting of the London-based Institute for Strategic Studies.* The trip to Hanoi via Moscow had discouraged the Czech. The Soviets, he reported, "seemed to be extremely confused." At first he had thought that "the war in Vietnam was an obstacle to a détente which was desired by the Soviet Union." Now he was beginning to wonder "whether the

---

*Set up in 1958 by Kissinger's friend Michael Howard, along with the Labour politician Denis Healey and the journalist Alastair Buchan, the ISS (later renamed the International Institute for Strategic Studies) was both bipartisan and, like Pugwash, a way through the iron curtain, though not only for academics.

Soviet Union really wanted a relaxation of tensions—indeed whether they were really very interested in ending the war in Vietnam.

> According to the Soviet view, the United States was getting stuck deeper and deeper in the muck of Vietnam. Sooner or later the United States would get tired of it and then accept terms going far beyond anything now being conceived. I interjected that the war was no strain on us either economically or militarily and that we could continue it indefinitely. . . . However, the Soviet response was that the United States had never fought a long war even when the issues were clearer. They counted on American psychological exhaustion.

This might explain the cool reception the Czech delegation had received in Hanoi when it had attempted to move the North Vietnamese "in a more peaceful direction." "Prague's impression was that a major internal struggle was taking place in the NLF between a pro-Hanoi and pro-Peking faction. . . . Clearly the USSR wanted to use North Vietnam as a barrier to Chinese expansion and did not want to see it too badly weakened."

When Kissinger pointed out that "in this respect U.S. and Soviet interests seemed parallel," Šnejdárek explained that "this was the other horn of the Soviet dilemma; they could not admit to an identity of interests with the United States[,] all the less so as they were under constant attack by China on this score." Indeed, the crisis in Southeast Asia might end up being "a convenient pretext [for Moscow] to tighten control over Eastern Europe." Already there were stirrings of reform in Slovakia, where Alexander Dubček had been appointed first secretary in 1963. Little did Kissinger realize it, but his frank discussions with Šnejdárek were themselves an intimation of the coming Prague Spring, a political thaw that the Czech already suspected would be unacceptable to the Soviets.

By the end of 1966, there were at least four separate initiatives, three of which hinged on the Soviets—whom Harriman still regarded as "our best hope for getting negotiations underway"[20]—and all of which were secret. As Kissinger explained to one of the British delegates to the Vienna conference, "the more people knew about the prospects of any negotiation, and in particular the more well intentioned efforts were made by potentially helpful friends, the less prospect there was of any real negotiation emerging." Indeed, Kissinger "implied that the present tendency in Washington was to work for a small and secret" process.[21] The difficulty was that he was not one of the insiders who knew about all the different moving parts. He was aware of Šnejdárek and of Sainteny. But he knew nothing of the peace initiatives code-named MARIGOLD and SUNFLOWER.

MARIGOLD had its origins in June 1966, when Janusz Lewandowski—the Polish member of the International Control Commission (ICC)—approached the Italian ambassador in Saigon, Giovanni D'Orlandi, claiming that he had been asked to convey a "very specific peace offer" from Pham Van Dong. When he met Harriman in Italy in November, D'Orlandi praised Lewandowski as "a reliable channel and an accurate reporter." Henry Cabot Lodge, still in charge in the U.S. embassy in Saigon, was therefore authorized to meet D'Orlandi and Lewandowski at the former's apartment and to set out the latest iteration of the American proposal known as "Phase A–Phase B," whereby Washington and Hanoi would agree to a "reasonable measure of de-escalation," to be executed in two phases. Phase A would be a bombing suspension by the United States. This would be followed after "some adequate period" by Phase B, a series of pre-agreed de-escalation steps.[22] Lodge spelled this out to Lewandowski in the expectation that he would faithfully and accurately communicate his words to Hanoi. As expected, the channel ran through Moscow—or rather through Sofia, where the Polish foreign minister, Adam Rapacki, briefed the new Soviet leader, Leonid Brezhnev,* who then put the case for negotiations to Nguyen Duy Trinh, the North Vietnamese foreign minister. Brezhnev was enthusiastic. "This is maximum [*sic*] from the Americans," he told Trinh. It was "hard to predict the results, but the situation is favorable:

---

*Brezhnev had been one of the leaders of the plot to get rid of his fellow Ukrainian and patron Khrushchev in 1964. Brezhnev took over the more powerful party post of first secretary, while Alexei Kosygin became the head of the Soviet government (premier). Formally, there was something more like collective leadership after Khrushchev's removal; in practice, power tended to gravitate toward Brezhnev.

the US on the crossroads, Vietnam on the crossroads, the PRC busy with the 'cultural revolution.'"[23]

The North Vietnamese seemed interested. "No one was able to hide some surprise at learning about the content of the proposal," Trinh told Rapacki. He canceled his planned visit to Budapest and flew directly to Moscow, where another Politburo member, Le Duan, was to meet him.[24] Back in Hanoi, Lewandowski had another meeting with Pham Van Dong, who told him that if the U.S. government was now "ready to confirm the views expressed in the conversations between ambassador Lodge and ambassador Lewandowski, they should do so directly via talks with the DRV ambassador in Warsaw."[25] Excitedly, Lewandowski rushed to Saigon to inform Lodge, who then relayed the apparent breakthrough to Washington.[26]

American historians, notably James Hershberg, blame the United States for "murdering" MARIGOLD. If only the State Department had not quibbled about Lewandowski's somewhat free and easy "ten point" rendition of what Lodge had told him to tell the North Vietnamese, insisting that "several specific points are subject to important differences of interpretation," it might have been different.[27] If only Johnson had not ordered the resumption of bombing, targeting the Van Dien vehicle depot and the Yen Vien railroad yards on the outskirts of Hanoi, MARIGOLD might have flowered.[28] It is true that the Americans made heavy weather of the Polish initiative. First they confused Lewandowski with Bogdan Lewandowski, a Polish foreign office official in charge of UN affairs. Then there was an apparent mix-up about the meeting in Warsaw. John A. Gronouski, the U.S. ambassador to Poland, was supposed to come to meet the North Vietnamese representatives— his counterpart, Do Phat Quang, and the special envoy Nguyen Dinh Phuong—on December 6. But Gronouski never turned up, having been led by the Poles to believe that the Vietnamese were not yet ready.[29] Above all, it was already clear that the biggest problem with secret negotiations was that, by definition, they could not be vouchsafed to General Westmoreland and his commanding officers in Vietnam.[30]

Yet there is reason to be skeptical about the claim that Washington murdered MARIGOLD. Considering his own views, Lodge could scarcely have set out the American case in a more conciliatory way, as the Polish records make clear. He was, he told Lewandowski,

> aware that before the talks begin the bombing has to stop and that its stopping cannot be conditional. They would be ready to stop "any time" if they were sure that it would lead to real steps toward negotiations. They understand that Hanoi will not accept a situation in which the cessation of the bombings is presented as an American success since then the fact of bombing would be perceived as equal to compelling the Vietnamese to negotiate. Therefore they would be ready to accept unconditionality and begin talks only after some time [passes by]. . . .
>
> They [the Americans] understand that the Front and Hanoi have good reasons to distrust the United States. Because of it, they [the United States] would be ready to consider and potentially execute certain concrete measures to convince the Vietnamese that they really want to end the conflict.[31]

Lodge was even more forthcoming the next day, when he told Lewandowski that the Americans were specifying a six-month time frame to withdraw their troops from South Vietnam because "an 'Eastern-European source' had informed them that it would make negotiations easier." They would not intervene in future South Vietnamese elections and would leave "the question of Vietnam's unification . . . to be decided by the Vietnamese," so long as it remained neutral. Washington was ready, Lodge concluded, "to carefully consider all official or unofficial, but concrete, proposals. One cannot expect from them that they will simply say OK to the [North Vietnamese] 4 points."[32]

The Soviets agreed. So did the Poles. It was "fair to conclude," noted Rapacki, that the Americans had "extended their elasticity further than at any point in the past and perhaps as far as they could do so." Yet when they put the case for negotiations to the North Vietnamese, they got nowhere. Brezhnev complained that when he talked to individuals in the Hanoi government, he was "met with understanding," but the "collective decisions" were "at odds with the views of individuals." There was also the "very serious and very little known to us problem of the relations between the DRV and the Viet Cong."[33] The Poles chimed in, pressing the North Vietnamese to spell out their "concrete and realistic . . . goals in the current stage of the war." But Trinh remained noncommittal, saying only that he would "pass the information and my supplementary comments to Hanoi for further and in-depth analysis."[34] Back in Hanoi, Dong was more or less open about what he intended to do. He and his comrades were "patient." So long as the United States moved out of South Vietnam, there was "no reason to hurry. They are ready to wait." But "cessation of bombing" remained the "sine qua non before any talks can begin."[35]

The reality was that there was considerable opposition not only in Hanoi but also in Beijing to starting talks. The deputy foreign minister, Nguyen Co Thach, "declared himself categorically against accepting" the U.S. proposals; Zhou Enlai told Le Duan the time was "not ripe."[36] On December 7—the day after the Warsaw meeting had been supposed to take place—Pham Van Dong "angrily denounced the most recent American conduct" to the Polish ambassador in Hanoi as "insolent, deceitful behavior."[37] Walt Rostow was not wrong about everything. He was almost certainly right when he expressed his doubt that "the communists held any inclination to make the necessary concessions to facilitate negotiations."[38] On this occasion, as throughout 1967, the North Vietnamese were not in earnest. The fact that, less than a month later, Hanoi was telling *The New York Times* of its interest in beginning discussions should be regarded as evidence for, rather than against, this point, given the North Vietnamese insistence on secrecy throughout MARIGOLD.[39] Subsequently, Dean Rusk was inclined to dismiss the whole episode on the basis of the allegation by the Hungarian defector János Radványi that "Lewandowski was a Polish intelligence agent acting on his own and that the Marigold Initiative was a sham."[40] But a more accurate assessment was the one made at the time by the negotiations committee: "In the Marigold operation, Hanoi was trying to see how far it could go in getting U.S. concessions before being confronted with the necessity of talking to us."[41] The January exchange between the two embassies in Moscow was more of the same: the U.S. deputy chief of mission, John Guthrie, offered to discuss the full range of issues;

the North Vietnamese minister counselor replied that Hanoi would "exchange views" with Washington only when it halted "immediately and unconditionally the bombing and all other acts of war" against the North.[42]

None of this was known to Kissinger when he returned to Prague at the end of January 1967 for further discussions with Antonín Šnejdárek.[43] U.S.-Czech relations had been complicated by the case of Vladimir Kazan-Komarek, a Czech-born American citizen—who happened to be the head of the Harvard Travel Service—who had been arrested by the Czech authorities when a Soviet airline bound from Moscow to Paris made an unscheduled stop in Prague.* Šnejdárek's interpretation of the case was clear: it had been foisted on the Czechs by the Soviets "to arrest the thaw in East-West relations." The Soviet Union, he explained, "was becoming increasingly sensitive about the growing freedom of movement of the East European countries and especially the Czech effort to reduce their economic dependence on Moscow." Šnejdárek then asked a question that Kissinger had to admit (not quite accurately) "had never occurred to me": whether he thought a "U.S.-Chinese deal was in the making." The American was reduced to bluffing: "I decided to play it cool and said that every country always tried to develop the maximum number of diplomatic options. They would not expect me to discuss possible unannounced American moves." Unimpressed, Šnejdárek proceeded to explain why China was the key to the failure of Harriman's attempt to seek peace in Vietnam by way of Moscow. It was a geopolitical master class:

> The Soviets took the Chinese attack on them [a key feature of Mao's Cultural Revolution] extremely seriously. They could not easily reconcile themselves to the end of Socialist unity and even less to the challenge to their position as the chief

---

*Kazan-Komarek was charged with high treason, espionage, and murder, crimes allegedly committed in the late 1940s when he had helped people escape from Czechoslovakia. His trial began on January 30, 1967, the day of Kissinger's arrival in Prague. After diplomatic pressure from the United States, he was charged with the lesser crime of subversion and then expelled. Five years later his decomposed body was found in the Spanish countryside, near his home in the coastal village of Estepona.

interpreters of Leninism. The extent of their attempt to influence internal Chinese developments is therefore not always grasped. They supported the party apparatus against Mao by two methods both related to Vietnam: a) they sought to appeal to the party members to create a united Socialist front against the United States on Vietnam. This is one reason . . . the Soviet Union has been loath to do anything to end the war. b) They used the pretext of arms shipments to Vietnam to strengthen army units thought to be favorable to this point of view.

This in turn explained two related developments: 1) the ambivalence of Soviet policy and as long as there was a chance of using Vietnam to re-cement Socialist unity, the Soviets were reluctant to assist peace efforts and even to relax tensions in Europe. (Another limitation [2)] was the fear of too great independence by the East European countries.)

This was as fascinating as it was discouraging. The Soviets had backed the party apparatus in China against the Maoists, and they were losing. The Maoists, in turn, were now desperate "to expel the Soviets physically from China. Nothing less than a complete rupture with the Soviet Union will enable them to feel secure." True, the Cultural Revolution looked like an ideological rift, with the Chinese as the more radical Marxists. But

[w]hatever Mao's ideological fervor, the human material available to him will force him in a nationalist direction—assuming he is still in charge of his movement. Despite their wild talk, the Maoists might turn out to be more flexible toward the U.S. than their opponents. They will have to shut off China in any event to reconstitute governmental authority and a form of non-aggression treaty with the United States might fit this design very well. Of course they hate the U.S. too; but . . . no Communist can forget the Hitler-Stalin pact.

From a Czech point of view, such a "Johnson-Mao pact" was an alarming scenario because "if the United States settled with China it would step up the [Soviet] pressure in Europe." Fearful of isolation, the Soviets would clamp down on what Šnejdárek obliquely called "the prospects of East European national development."

Kissinger was reeling. Seldom in his career, before or subsequently, was an interlocutor so many moves ahead of him. Although he later downplayed Šnejdárek's political significance,[44] he could scarcely ignore the profound strategic importance of what he was being told. His Czech hosts were obviously in earnest; their fear of "a U.S.-Mao deal seemed genuine and deep." Speaking "as a professor," he countered with the official Washington line: "the key lay in Moscow" because "if the United States had the choice to settle either with Moscow or with Peking, it would probably prefer the former if only because it was more predictable." It was an argument he himself had made in print. But then he paused. "On the other hand, if Moscow attempted to organize world-wide pressures against us, humiliate us in Vietnam, and expel us from Europe, elementary self-protection would force us to seek to isolate it."

Šnejdárek had won the argument. Now Kissinger could understand why the Czech delegation had returned from Hanoi empty-handed, having suffered multiple rebuffs. As he summed up the North Viet-namese position: "Both Hanoi and the NLF proclaim certain convic-tion in their victory[,] speaking of a twenty-year struggle if necessary. They say that the Americans came by force and have to leave by force."[45] Hanoi was in no mood for negotiation because at this point neither of its major backers was interested in peace. The United States was wast-ing its time in Moscow. If American salvation lay anywhere, Šnejdárek was telling Kissinger, it lay in the madhouse that was Beijing at the height of the Cultural Revolution.

To give Kissinger his due, he faithfully reproduced Šnejdárek's argu-ment, uncongenial though it was to him at this time.[46] There is no sign that anyone in Washington got the message (though Richard Nixon almost certainly did when he visited Prague the following month, as Šnejdárek acted as his host, too). On the contrary, five months later Mac Bundy (no longer in the White House but still advising) was almost completely reversing the sense of what Kissinger had been told, telling Rusk that "the Czechs were claiming Hanoi did not necessarily reject reciprocity for the bombing stopping."[47] The steadily shrinking circle of people to whom the president listened had persuaded themselves that the Soviets would give them a break in Vietnam, and they screened out any evidence to the contrary. The result was SUNFLOWER, a wholly futile attempt to get the British government to join in the effort to sell "Phase A–Phase B" to Moscow.

Harold Wilson was an intelligent man; he had been an Oxford don before turning to politics. But that had also made him arrogant. "We have to use our ingenuity," he told the Soviet premier, Alexei Kosygin, "to divorce in presentation the stopping of the bombing from the consequential actions. Yet you and I know that the consequential actions are essential if we are to get the bombing stopped."[48] Once again, it was true, there was blundering in Washington, as Rostow attempted to row back from the earlier position—as Lodge had plainly stated it and as Chester Cooper now repeated it—that the United States would de-escalate first, on the understanding that any North Vietnamese reciprocal action would come in Phase B. On February 8, at Rostow's urging, Johnson wrote a personal message to Ho Chi Minh pledging that the United States would stop its bombing "*as soon as I am assured* that infiltration into South Vietnam by land and sea *has stopped*." At the last minute, Washington cabled London that this was the correct form of words. Wilson, whose Oxonian opinion of Americans was now confirmed, was beside himself.*

In historiography, as in Downing Street, the U.S. government got the blame for the failure of the initiative.[49] It occurred to no one that Hanoi would have replied no regardless of what Washington said.[50] The absurdity of the entire exercise was that Johnson had in fact agreed to suspend bombing during the Tet holiday and maintained the pause until February 13, by which time it was impossible to ignore the advantage the North Vietnamese were taking of it.[51] As so often, it was not necessarily the smartest men in the room who divined what was going on. "I think," concluded Wilson's bibulous foreign secretary, George Brown, "that the Russians were leading everybody up the garden [path], including us."[52] Rusk was right, too, about the irrelevance of the

---

*As George Brown remarked, "Never before or since has the 'hot line' between No. 10 and the White House been so hot as it was during that period."

words "has stopped": "Had Hanoi been seriously interested in talks, this kind of misunderstanding could have been ironed out."[53]

If Moscow was out—and with it Prague and Warsaw, not to mention London—and Beijing off limits, that left only Paris. By December 1966, Jean Sainteny was being referred to by Harriman as Kissinger's "friend in Paris." Sainteny had offered to go to Hanoi to find out what "important price" Pham Van Dong would demand for doing a deal on South Vietnam. The problem was de Gaulle, who, as Kissinger nicely put it, had "been known to do cynical and brutal things."[54] The French president's speech at Phnom Penh had "finished France as a formal mediator." He was "clearly pursuing the line that he is extorting a settlement from us, and there is the risk that he might use any formal approach for his own purposes."[55] The problem was that someone as senior as Sainteny could scarcely proceed to Hanoi without de Gaulle's approval.[56] And that was not forthcoming. Instead the French sent Bobby Kennedy home to Washington with the message that negotiations would follow an unconditional bombing halt (a story picked up by *Newsweek*). This was too much for Johnson. "I'll destroy every one of your dove friends in six months," he ranted at Kennedy. "You'll be dead politically in six months. . . . There just isn't a chance in hell that I will do that, not the slightest chance." As Kennedy said to a friend, "If he exploded like that with me, how could he ever negotiate with Hanoi?" But the real point was that Johnson had come extremely close to doing exactly what the French were recommending.[57] What was so infuriating was that he could not tell anyone that he had—and that it hadn't worked.

IV

We have undertaken dozens of probes. We have been in touch with the Pope, with Secretary General U Thant, and the United Nations. Our position is entirely clear and it is summarized in the fourteen-point paper which we have now made public. The other side is not interested. We have had no

> comeback from them. We have used third parties without suc-
> cess. . . . All our efforts have encountered silence. We have had
> no serious response, private or public. . . . There is no evidence
> that Hanoi is ready to stop the fighting. The North Vietnam-
> ese want sanctuary in the north without giving anything, at
> the same time continuing the war in South Vietnam.[58]

Thus Dean Rusk at a meeting of the NSC on February 8, 1967. It was all true. But where did it leave him and his colleagues? If the disparate members of the Johnson administration had been converging on the possibility of talks with Hanoi, the failure of talks to materialize caused a near disintegration. As early as November 10, 1966, John McNaughton had noticed "a diminution of power, of influence, in McNamara's hands" as the defense secretary and the president diverged on the question of further bombing of North Vietnam.[59] McNamara was fast mutating into a dove, recommending that the U.S. unilaterally dial down the bombing of Hanoi. As he put it acidly, "The picture of the world's greatest superpower killing or seriously injuring 1,000 non-combatants a week, while trying to pound a tiny, backward nation into submission on an issue whose merits are hotly disputed, is not a pretty one."[60] Rostow, meanwhile, was becoming ever more hawkish, exhorting Johnson to mine Haiphong harbor and generally to "apply more weight" on the North. "They should feel that the sheriff is coming slowly down the road for them," he declared, in a calculated appeal to presidential machismo, "not that we are in a spasm of anxiety or desperation."[61] Encouraged by the CIA and Westmoreland, Johnson agreed to expand U.S. action, targeting for the first time the infiltration routes in Laos, but he would not go as far as Rostow, who was now ready to invade North Vietnam itself—an option consistently rejected by Johnson for fear of triggering Chinese intervention and another Korean War, with himself in the role of Truman.[62]

By now Johnson's decision making seemed to consist of splitting the difference between the hawks and the doves. Starting on May 22, he accepted McNamara's advice to suspend the attacks on targets within ten miles of Hanoi, a suspension that lasted until August 9.[63] He then agreed to two more weeks of bombing directed against "a few significant targets," before once again halting activity in the Hanoi area on August 24. At the same time, he approved yet another troop increase, pushing total U.S. strength in South Vietnam above half a million for the first time. "Are we going to be able to win this goddamned war?" he asked after McNamara returned from yet another fact-finding trip to Vietnam. "The situation is not a stalemate" was Westmoreland's unreassuring answer. "We are winning slowly but steadily, and the pace can accelerate if we reinforce our successes."[64]

Outside the White House, however, the tide was turning. On March 2 Bobby Kennedy unveiled a three-point plan to end U.S. involvement in Vietnam, beginning with an unconditional bombing halt. While Rusk accurately responded that "proposals substantially similar" had been "explored prior to, during and since the Tet truce—all without result," Johnson furiously denounced Kennedy's plan as "a dishonorable settlement disguised as a bargain for popularity purposes," and briefed the *Washington Post* columnist Drew Pearson that Kennedy was motivated by guilt feelings because his plotting to assassinate Castro had "backfired against his late brother."[65]

It was 1967. It was the Age of Aquarius. It was the zenith of an extraordinary period of cultural creativity in the Anglophone world that had produced a musical fusion bomb composed of Celtic folk harmonies, the twelve-bar blues of the Mississippi delta, and a few sitar riffs knocked off, in the Great British Orientalist tradition, from Ravi Shankar. On both sides of the Atlantic, four increasingly shaggy Liverpudlians bestrode the charts with *Sgt. Pepper's Lonely Hearts Club Band* and "All You Need Is Love." The counterculture musical *Hair,* with its explicitly antiwar plot, nude scenes, drug references, and songs about interracial sex, opened off Broadway. The Velvet Underground, the New York band sponsored by Andy Warhol, was "Waiting for the Man." Pink Floyd released *The Piper at the Gates of Dawn.* And the Doors burst open with their eponymous debut album, the centerpiece of which was the hypnotic extended version of "Light My Fire."

True, the first antiwar protests had occurred as early as 1965, but now fires were being lit all over America. The clamor against the Vietnam War was growing louder, subsuming the other burning issues of the day into a single nationwide conflagration. At New York's Riverside Church on April 4, Martin Luther King, Jr., denounced the war for "taking the black young men who had been crippled by our society and sending them eight thousand miles away to guarantee liberties in Southeast Asia which they had not found in southwest Georgia and East Harlem."[66] Just over three weeks later, the heavyweight boxing world champion Muhammad Ali (a name he had adopted when he joined the Nation of Islam) refused to be drafted "in the light of my consciousness as a Muslim minister and my own personal convictions."* There were antiwar demonstrations in New York and San Francisco in April, Los Angeles in June, and Washington in October. (The last of these worried the administration so much that McNamara advised Johnson to leave town.)[67] In July there were race riots in Newark, Minneapolis, Detroit, and Milwaukee. So much for the "Summer of Love" proclaimed by the young people who had streamed to Haight-Ashbury ("Hashbury") to "turn on, tune in, drop out." (That phrase had been coined by Timothy Leary, the former lecturer in psychology who had been fired by Harvard for extolling the benefits of magic [psilocybin] mushrooms.)

There was no summer of love in Hanoi either. Had the minds of the hippies not been addled by pot and acid—had the antiwar protesters not been so certain that it was Johnson who was prolonging the war—they might have noticed that it was the North Vietnamese, not the Americans, who shot down U Thant's March peace initiative.[68] Two other attempts at mediation by the Swedish and Norwegian ambassadors in Beijing (ASPEN and OHIO) also came to naught.[69] Johnson gave the Soviet channel one last try at his meeting with Kosygin at Glassboro, New Jersey, in June 1967. The North Vietnamese reaction was once again negative, convincing the Russians that it was "fruitless to meddle in anything between Vietnam and the United States."[70]

What the antiwar protesters—and indeed the Johnson administration—could not know was that in June 1967 the North Vietnamese politburo had endorsed General Nguyen Chi Thanh's plan for a "General Offensive General Uprising"—a massive assault on the South Vietnamese regime that was designed to win the war in 1968.

---

*He was sentenced to five years in prison and a $10,000 fine, as well as being stripped of his world title and banned from boxing in the United States.

Responsibility for preparing what became the Tet Offensive was entrusted to General Vo Nguyen Giap. The remaining proponents of a pro-Soviet strategy within the Hanoi regime were ruthlessly eliminated in a series of purges masterminded by Le Duan and Le Duc Tho in July, October, and December 1967.[71] Only those accustomed to fighting Communism in Asia had the measure of the other side. When the Singaporean prime minister, Lee Kuan Yew, visited the newly renamed John F. Kennedy School of Government at Harvard in October 1967, he began a meeting with the senior faculty by inviting comments on the Vietnam War. As Kissinger later recalled, "The faculty, of which I was one dissenting member, was divided primarily on the question of whether President Lyndon Johnson was a war criminal or a psychopath." After hearing a litany of criticisms of Johnson's policy, the thrust of which was that the United States could not leave Vietnam a moment too soon, Lee responded simply, "You make me sick."[72] As he told *The Harvard Crimson,* the United States was performing a valuable service to the region in maintaining a "military shield" around South Vietnam. "Saigon can do what Singapore did," he argued. "If you leave, we'll soldier on," he told an audience of students at Dunster House. "I'm only telling you the awful consequence which withdrawal would mean."[73]

V

The orthodox view of the PENNSYLVANIA peace initiative, in which Henry Kissinger was to make his reputation as a practicing diplomat, is unambiguous: the principal obstacle to beginning negotiations was the American bombing of North Vietnam. Hanoi was clear that the bombing had to stop before negotiations could begin, while the United States demanded that in return for a cessation of bombing, Hanoi must take steps to end, reduce, or at least not increase the infiltration of men and supplies into South Vietnam.[74] Peace was at hand in 1967, the argument runs. But every time it seemed within reach, the Americans bombed Hanoi.

The alternative view, based on the evidence of North Vietnamese and other sources, is that there was never the remotest chance of peace in 1967 because the Hanoi regime was intently preparing the Tet Offensive. The Americans thought they were in *Waiting for Godot,* and that sooner or later Godot—in the form of Mai Van Bo—would come along. The North Vietnamese knew they were all in *The Mousetrap,* and they themselves were the culprits.[75]

It happened, mostly, in Paris. Kissinger traveled there in June 1967 to attend an augmented meeting of the Pugwash executive committee that had been convened by the Polish-born physicist Joseph Rotblat, the secretary general of Pugwash, and the French microbiologist Herbert Marcovitch, head of the Insitut Pasteur.*[76] Though the first item on their agenda was the Six-Day War that had just been fought between Israel and her Arab neighbors, the meeting also resolved to find a "formula to stop the escalation of the war" in Vietnam.[77] In fact, Kissinger already had the formula with him. It consisted of a subtly modified version of "Phase A–Phase B": "The conveyance to the other side (Hanoi and Moscow) through appropriate channels of our intention to suspend general bombing of North Vietnam (except possibly for limited sother [*sic*] areas directly involved in their infiltration operations) without reciprocal positive actions on their part but subject to our reconsideration on the basis of their subsequent actions."[78]

The meeting decided that the conveying would be done by Marcovitch, who would travel to Hanoi via Cambodia on the pretext of reestablishing scientific links between the Insitut Pasteur and its former affiliates in Southeast Asia.[79] At the suggestion of Étienne Bauer, Marcovitch would travel to North Vietnam with Bauer's old friend Raymond Aubrac, a senior official at the UN Food and Agriculture Organization in Rome. Ho Chi Minh had lived with the Aubracs in 1946 and was godfather to Aubrac's daughter Babette.[80] The American formula could therefore be discreetly delivered as part of a social call on the North Vietnamese president.

Three points need special emphasis at the outset. Aubrac—usually

---

*In addition to Rotblat, Marcovitch, and Kissinger, the participants were the Soviet economist Ruben Andreossian, Étienne Bauer (who worked at the French Atomic Energy Commission), Paul Doty, the MIT physicist Bernard Feld, the vice president of the Soviet Academy of Sciences Mikhail Millionshikov, and the French physicist Francis Perrin.

described in the Vietnam literature as "a hero of the Resistance"—was a committed Communist. The story of his escape from the clutches of Klaus Barbie, the notorious "Butcher of Lyon," remains famous in France, not least because of the romantic role played by Lucie Aubrac in setting her husband free. Born Raymond Samuel (the name "Aubrac" was one of several wartime aliases), Aubrac had already become involved in leftist politics as a student before the war, and after the fall of France he had joined the Resistance group Libération. His wife was already an avid Communist; as early as 1935 she had been selected by the Comintern for training in Moscow. Though allegations that Aubrac was the informer who betrayed the Resistance leader Jean Moulin in 1943 have never been substantiated, there is no question that Aubrac's first loyalty was to the French Communist Party. Having lost his parents as well as many friends to the Nazis, Aubrac could be forgiven for feeling vengeful. But his conduct as "commissioner" in Marseille during the postwar épuration (directed against former collaborators with the Germans) looked more like a Red Terror than a mere settling of scores; indeed, de Gaulle dismissed Aubrac, accusing the Communists of having established "an anonymous dictatorship."[81] The fact that Aubrac was a personal friend of "l'oncle Ho" was not a coincidence. He remained a devoted Communist throughout the postwar period and, as his memoir makes clear, was at best ambivalent about "transmit[ting] a proposal from the U.S. government"—even one he regarded as "decent."[82]

The second point to note is that the initiative for PENNSYLVANIA came from Kissinger himself. He had informed Dean Rusk of what was being attempted, but the State Department had been dismissive. So was the president. He and Rusk agreed: it was "just another of those blind alleys that lead nowhere. We've been down them before. Forget it." It was McNamara—now more or less convinced that the United States must cut its losses in Vietnam—who gave Kissinger the official backing he needed after he had been copied on one of the early cables to Rusk.[83]

The third point is that the timing of U.S. bombing sorties took on added significance in the case of PENNSYLVANIA because the intermediaries actually went to Hanoi and intended to return there. It was another horrendous American blunder when U.S. planes hit Hanoi and

Haiphong on August 20, just before Marcovitch and Aubrac were supposed to arrive in the North Vietnamese capital, and a day after Johnson had authorized Kissinger to say that "effective August 24 there would be a noticeable change in the bombing pattern in the vicinity of Hanoi to guarantee their personal safety and as a token of our good will."[84] Never did the left hand of Johnson's diplomacy and the right hand of his war-making seem worse coordinated than in August 1967. This greatly facilitated Hanoi's double-dealing.

Aubrac and Marcovitch arrived in Cambodia on July 19. It took two days to persuade the North Vietnamese embassy in Phnom Penh to issue them with visas to proceed to Hanoi. On the twenty-first, they flew there in a plane belonging to the International Control Commission. They saw Pham Van Dong and the aging Ho Chi Minh on the afternoon of the twenty-fourth.[85] The next day they met with Pham Van Dong and the minister of health, Pham Ngoc Thach (who was there, presumably, to keep up the appearance that this was a scientific visit). They also had time to see for themselves the devastating effect of the U.S. bombing on Hanoi. Immediately after their return to Paris, the two Frenchmen met with Kissinger and reported on their conversations in Hanoi, also providing Aubrac's notes of the meetings. Kissinger hastily but meticulously conveyed what they told him back to Washington.

In a number of ways, it did look like a breakthrough. After the predictable preliminaries (the Frenchmen relayed the latest version of "Phase A–Phase B," whereupon Pham Van Dong denounced the United States), the conversation became interesting. When Aubrac asked Dong if he wanted "an official declaration that the bombing had stopped, or would he be satisfied with a de facto end of bombing," the Vietnamese premier replied that "a de facto cessation would be acceptable." Aubrac then asked if there should be some delay between the end of bombing and the beginning of negotiations, to which Dong replied somewhat elliptically, "This is not a problem." When Aubrac followed up by asking what channels should be used, Dong answered that this, too, was "not a problem but it should be someone authorized by both parties." Initial negotiations, he told the Frenchmen, could be "on those matters affecting the U.S. and North Vietnam as principals";

only when issues affecting South Vietnam were raised would the NLF need to be present. Aubrac and Marcovitch inferred from all this that "the scenario envisaged by Pham Van Dong involved an end of U.S. bombing to be followed within a matter of days by the opening of negotiations under acceptable auspices." Dong was explicitly encouraging. "You may think your travels are useless. In fact you have given us much to think about."

In their meeting the next day, by contrast, Dong treated them to a defiant assertion of North Vietnamese military resolve:

> [T]he White House and Pentagon seem determined to continue the war against the North. Therefore we think that attacks on the North are likely to increase. We have made provisions for attacks on our dikes; we are ready to accept war on our soil. Our military potential is growing because of aid from the USSR and other Socialist countries. . . . As for the situation on the battlefield, it is improving all the time. . . . We fight only when we choose; we economize on our resources; we fight only for political purposes. . . . We could easily step up our actions inside [Saigon]. But we take only those actions which have political meaning and which economize human lives. . . . We have been fighting for our independence for four thousand years. We have defeated the Mongols three times. The United States Army, strong as it is, is not as terrifying as Genghis Khan.

But this was just a prelude to a reiteration of the previous day's points: Hanoi was "willing to settle for a de facto stoppage" without public acknowledgment of an end to the bombing. If the Americans halted their air strikes "and we understand that they are willing to talk," then there would be "no question of delay." The negotiations themselves could be kept secret. And as long as the negotiations did not touch on South Vietnam, the NLF could be kept out of them. Then Dong added a new point: "[H]e realized that some U.S. troops would have to stay until the end of the process of political settlement. . . . We do not want to humiliate the U.S." Nor was that all.

Our position is: North Vietnam is socialist and wants to remain so. As for the South, our goals are national independence, democracy, peace and neutrality. Some people think we want to impose Socialism on the South. We are convinced that the NLF will not make such an error. The NLF envisages a broad coalition government, including all significant groups and religions *without consideration of past activities including members du gouvernement fantoche* [puppet] *et cadres d'armée fantoche*. . . . The essential thing is to forget the past.

As for unification, we recognize that the important first step is a political settlement of the South. We agree not to push things toward unification. Once the war in the South is settled, we shall discuss with the South and find the best means.[86]

Sitting in Marcovitch's Saint-Cloud home, Kissinger listened to all this intently. French was not his strong suit, so periodically he had to ask for translation into English. When they had finished, he said simply, "You are bringing something new."[87] He filed his report and flew home. The negotiations committee reacted with even more excitement, detecting at least four reasons to regard the conversation with Pham Van Dong as being "of considerable potential significance."[88] McNamara went further, calling it "the most interesting message on the matter of negotiations which we had ever had."[89] Admittedly, Johnson, Rostow, and William Bundy were all skeptical (especially when they heard about Aubrac's "political orientation").[90] Indeed, Johnson was more focused on the planned escalation of the bombing campaign.[91] Nevertheless, Kissinger was sent back to Paris, accompanied by Chester Cooper as a kind of State Department minder, "to discuss certain aspects of their report and possibly to pose some questions for further clarification."[92]

The first draft of the reply Kissinger took with him for Aubrac and Marcovitch to give to the North Vietnamese was clear-cut:

The United States is willing to stop the aerial and naval bombardment of North Vietnam if this will lead promptly to productive discussions between representatives of the United States and the DRV looking toward a resolution of the issues between them. We would assume that, while discussions proceed either with public knowledge or secretly, the DRV would not take advantage of the bombing cessation or limitation.[93]

However, Kissinger was careful to explain that

(1) The phrase "take advantage" refers to "any increase in the movement of men and supplies into the south";

(2) The phrase "productive" discussions indicated the determination to avoid extended Korean-type negotiations during unabated military operations;

(3) The bombing pause might make it impossible to keep the fact of negotiations secret for more than three weeks at the outside, though we could of course guarantee secrecy as to their substance. Therefore it might be desirable to conduct preliminary talks while tonnage, geographic or sorty [sic] limitations or reductions in the bombing occurred, with a complete end of the bombing when final negotiations took place.[94]

The Frenchmen replied that they were willing to go back to Hanoi, but they wanted the word si (if) in the French version of the American reply to be replaced by en comprenant que. After a debate about how best to translate that phrase into English—"with the understanding that" was the winner—this was agreed.[95]

Now the waiting for Godot began. Aubrac and Marcovitch informed the North Vietnamese legation of their intention to travel to Hanoi again, but they were informed that ongoing U.S. bombing made this impossible. Not unreasonably, the Frenchmen pressed Kissinger to get an assurance that the bombing would at least temporarily be stopped. On August 18, as we have seen, Johnson agreed to a bombing halt in a ten-mile radius around Hanoi. As Rusk put it, "these fellows will get there on the 25th and it's not good to hit them when they get there." He now thought there was a one in fifty chance of Kissinger's establishing "secret contact"; McNamara put the odds at one in ten.[96] (It was an era of spurious probabilities.) The defense secretary therefore authorized Kissinger to say that "effective August 24 there would be a noticeable change in the bombing pattern in the vicinity of Hanoi to guarantee their personal safety and as a token of our good will." Kissinger was deliberately vague about both the geographic extent and the duration of the "change in the bombing pattern" in order "to avoid [the] impression of [an] ultimatum"—which both Aubrac and Marcovitch knew was a neuralgic point for the North Vietnamese—but McNamara insisted that he specify that the air raids on Hanoi would resume on September 4.[97] By now McNamara and Harriman had privately agreed that the United States should be ready to accept "a coalition government, including the VC, which would be non-communist and neutral" in South Vietnam.[98]

It was all academic. The North Vietnamese flatly declined to issue visas and adhered to this refusal despite an explicit indication that the Frenchmen were bringing an important message.[99] McNamara assumed this was a response to the wave of American air attacks that had been carried out between August 20 and August 23 because of an improvement in the weather over North Vietnam.[100] But it is highly doubtful that this was anything other than a pretext for the rejection of the visa applications. When Aubrac and Marcovitch met with Mai Van Bo on August 25, he showed "manifest interest" in the latest communications from Washington, as well as in Kissinger's role, but he sent them away with nothing more than an assurance that he would cable this information to Hanoi.[101] For the next week, scarcely a day passed without Bo communicating with Aubrac and Marcovitch, but it was always the "answer answerless." He had not heard from Hanoi (August 29). There was a technical break in communications with Hanoi (August 30). They could not receive visas because of the escalation of U.S. bombing, but Aubrac should nevertheless remain in Paris (August 31, September 2). On September 2, Bo asked for the suspension of bombing of Hanoi to be extended for "the next few days"; Kissinger was authorized to say it would be extended for seventy-two hours. On the fourth, Bo reverted to stalling and blaming the delay on the American air raids.[102] When Marcovitch saw Bo on September 6, he formed the impression that Bo regarded the three-day extension of the "Hanoi bombing hiatus" as having an "ultimative character," but this was an inference from Bo's "icy" reaction. The reality was that Bo would have stonewalled even if the hiatus had been two or three times as long.[103]

Kissinger did not wait for Godot in Paris. Forsaking the threadbare comforts of the Hotel Port Royal in the rue Montalembert, he was now back in Cambridge, preparing for the beginning of the Harvard semester. Aubrac returned to Rome. This created a bizarre communications problem, as—for fear of compromising his independence—Marcovitch refused to use the U.S. diplomatic bag to send written accounts of his meetings with Bo, so that at least one key message was sent by regular airmail. On the night of the eighth, however, Kissinger flew back to Paris, en route to give some previously arranged lectures in Germany. Crucially, Bo had told Marcovitch that if Kissinger was returning to Paris he would seek permission from Hanoi to see him.[104]

PENNSYLVANIA was now serious enough to merit the president's attention. On September 5 he requested "the entire file on the Kissinger Project,"[105] then asked Rostow to have it assessed by CIA chief Richard Helms.[106] Helms's assessment was mixed. The North Vietnamese delay in replying to Kissinger's message might reflect "a combination of factors of timing and interpretation, reinforced by its deep-seated distrust of US motives in the area." On the other hand, Hanoi "continue[d] to insist on an unconditional stop to the bombing and a settlement based on their four points. They show[ed] no sign yet of any readiness to compromise those objectives."[107] William Bundy was equally ambivalent. The U.S. message had "put Hanoi squarely on the spot," because "most people would regard [it]—if the exchange ever became public—as a reasonable proposal that reflected major movement from our past public positions." Then again, he could not "at all exclude the possibility that Hanoi is playing us for a sucker, and simply trying to stretch out the Hanoi [bombing] exemption."[108] Johnson was now "very much interested" in the Kissinger channel,[109] but Rostow and Rusk reminded him that while "there [was] still much noise on the staircase . . . no one [had] come into the room."[110] It was agreed that Kissinger should now turn up the pressure, communicating via Marcovitch the "increasing US impatience at failure to receive any reply from Hanoi" and "contrast[ing] US restraint to date with numerous attacks sustained by US in the South."[111] Kissinger was emphatic, telling Aubrac (who had returned from Rome at Kissinger's request) that "our officials have gained the impression that communication with Hanoi is a oneway street. We would not be asked to exercise unilateral restraints over a prolonged period without any signal from Hanoi about our overture."[112] But he added a sweetener, blaming the air raids on Hanoi in late August on a bureaucratic bungle and noting that "probably the only other government which could understand the full complexity of our decision-making process was the Soviet Union"—a dig at Moscow that doubtless went down well with Bo.[113]

Careful study of Bo's behavior in the succeeding days suggests that Bundy was right the second time: Hanoi was indeed playing Washington for a sucker. On the eighth, Bo asked Marcovitch how long Kissinger would remain in Paris; the answer was ten days. Bo's response was that "something could well happen" during that period, provided there was no bombing of Hanoi. On the ninth, when warned about mounting American impatience by Aubrac and Marcovitch, Bo "asked if Walt Rostow had cleared the message." The Frenchmen had no idea who that was. Bo explained that he was really asking if the August 25 message was "still valid." He then warned that any attempt by the Americans to create a "McNamara Line" (a Korean-style border between North and South Vietnam) would be viewed as a "political action to make the separation of brothers permanent."[114] Both points were clearly intended to convey to the American side that Hanoi had good intelligence—and to play for time.

On September 11, Bo finally handed the Frenchmen the official reply. It was wholly negative, accusing the United States of issuing an ultimatum and making the now-familiar demands for an unconditional end to the bombing, withdrawal of U.S. forces, and recognition of the NLF.

VI

The phrase *Stockholm syndrome* would not be coined for another six years. Inspired by the behavior of the hostages taken during the 1973 Kreditbanken robbery in the Swedish capital, where the victims became emotionally attached to their captors, it is now a familiar concept in evolutionary psychology. To be sure, Kissinger had compelling personal reasons for spending as much time as possible in Paris: he was in love with Nancy Maginnes, and she was studying at the Sorbonne. Indeed, she was living in the rue Monsieur le Prince, just a few blocks from Monsieur Bo's North Vietnamese legation. Nevertheless, Kissinger's conduct as a negotiator in 1967 was Stockholm syndrome *avant la lettre*. Curiously, in this case, the captive never met the captor. So invested was Kissinger in meeting Mai Van Bo that he became emotionally attached to him—or rather, to the diplomatic process he had set in train. Bo had said no. But Kissinger's commentary on the North Vietnamese reply to the American letter of August 25 was pure Stockholm:

> The last paragraph represents an advance over those previous exchanges with which I am familiar in three respects: (1) for the first time, Hanoi has answered an American proposal and not closed the door on further negotiations; (2) Hanoi demands the recognition of the National Liberation Front but seems to have dropped the previous insistence that the National Liberation Front be accepted as the "most authentic representative" . . . (3) it states that negotiations would follow a bombing cessation.

Rather than "tak[ing] the message at face value and end[ing] the A-M channel," he urged Washington "to treat the message as a first step in complicated bargaining process," seizing the opportunity to have "a fuller exploration of Hanoi's mood and intentions" and "to improve the public record."[115]

Here his diplomatic inexperience showed. For September 11 was the day to walk away. As Rostow observed, it was "barely conceivable" that Kissinger was right in regarding the response from Hanoi as a "first step."[116] Kissinger was "a good analyst . . . [but] he may go a little soft when you get down to the crunch." Rusk was inclined to agree. Kissinger was "basically for us," he said, but had been duped.[117] They were right. It was a clear show of weakness to keep begging Hanoi for a Kissinger–Bo meeting,[118] to keep making excuses for the bombing of Haiphong.[119] Kissinger was now so desperate to meet Bo that he devised an elaborate ruse whereby Marcovitch would hand the North Vietnamese envoy a note "in a sealed envelope on plain paper and unsigned" saying that Kissinger had with him not only a new American message but also a commentary on it, which, "because the commentary refers to other discussions with Hanoi which we have promised not to reveal," he had been "instructed to deliver . . . personally."[120] Bo clearly found this gambit highly amusing. He told Marcovitch that while he could not meet with Kissinger, he was happy to "keep the channel" going, if necessary with unsigned letters in sealed envelopes. "We may be edging up to some exchange" was Kissinger's ever-hopeful message to Washington.[121] Perhaps if the United States now slowed things down, holding back its "principal message," Bo would be lured by curiosity into a meeting.[122] Or perhaps if Marcovitch were to tell Bo that Kissinger was about to leave Paris . . . or would that just be interpreted by the hypersensitive North Vietnamese as another form of ultimatum?[123] The more Kissinger told Washington not to give Hanoi "the impression that we are excessively anxious," the more he himself did precisely that.[124]

The trouble was twofold. Not only did Bo have no intention whatever of meeting Kissinger; the French workhorses were also beginning to kick over the traces. On the thirteenth, Marcovitch—who had already threatened to reveal the negotiations to the French government—complained to Kissinger that "every time I brought a message we bombed the center of a North Vietnamese city. If this happened one more time he was no longer prepared to serve as channel." Aubrac was by far the tougher of the two men, and whenever he was in Rome, Kissinger missed his "political savvy."[125] His return to Paris sharpened up the discussions noticeably. ("A. commented that as far as he could tell Washington offered to stop bombing of [*sc.* if] Hanoi would promise to negotiate and Hanoi offered to negotiate if Washington would first stop bombing.")[126] But the reappearance of Uncle Ho's old friend gave Bo an opportunity to turn on the charm, offering whiskey, tea, and pastries when he and Marcovitch arrived with the "principal message" on September 16.[127] Aubrac warned Bo that he and Marcovitch were now "at the end of our tether (*au bout de notre rouleau*)," but Bo coquettishly implied that a meeting with Kissinger was now imminent. Marcovitch now threatened to reveal their talks to the Élysée (implying somewhat implausibly that the French authorities were oblivious to what was going on under their noses). Emollient, Bo advised him not to and assured him, "[Y]our channel is not at the end of its usefulness." As Aubrac prepared to return to Rome, Bo offered more reassurance: "Things may seem to move slowly. In fact, they are moving at their 'normal' speed for exchanges of this kind." This gave Aubrac fresh hope that Hanoi was in fact "tortuously groping its way to a dialogue with the U.S." Yet when he flew back to Paris on September 20, his suggestion that he, Bo, and Kissinger dine together elicited only laughter from Bo. The most he was prepared to say, even as Kissinger departed for Hanover and Cambridge, was that the channel was "very convenient for us."

Twenty-five days had now elapsed since Bo had been handed the initial American communication, and this was all he had to tell the weary Frenchmen:

> The Americans are playing a double game. On the one hand
> they are offering us peace; on the other they increase their
> bombing. . . . [But] I will accept a communication at any time.
> I will be in touch as soon as I have something to say. . . . Do not
> worry. If we come to the conclusion that we do not wish to
> communicate via Kissinger we shall tell you. If we ever think
> that you should no longer continue, we shall tell you without
> hesitation. But we want you and Kissinger to continue.[128]

Two days later he delivered yet another blistering condemnation of U.S. conduct, denouncing the continued bombing of targets outside Hanoi and the "two-faced policy" of seeking negotiations while actually escalating the conflict to the point of "extermination."[129] On

September 30 he was repeating once again that the American letter of August 25 was implicitly conditional and therefore unacceptable. Only if the United States halted the bombing altogether should Kissinger "put on his hat and come to Paris immediately."[130] Threats of "growing impatience in Washington" were like water off the proverbial duck's back. Bo could parry them by saying that "talks"—not to be confused with "formal negotiations"—could begin "almost immediately after the end of the bombing."[131]

Bo's meeting with Marcovitch on October 2—at the Frenchman's initiative—appeared to herald Godot's arrival. The note that Marcovitch wrote to relay Bo's statements to Kissinger was mailed by special delivery to Kissinger, since Marcovitch persisted with his refusal to use official channels. Its content did indeed seem to signify, as Rostow acknowledged, "the first movement we've had."[132] The note suggested, among three possible scenarios, that Hanoi would accept as an indication of an unconditional "stop" to the bombardment "an official declaration but non-public preceding the cessation of the bombardment" that could be "communicated by the channel K/A-M (officieusement)—not quite officially," a term carefully chosen by Marcovitch to capture Kissinger's semiofficial status. The Frenchman also inferred that "official contacts, public or non-public, could begin upon cessation of the bombardments, within a short time"—perhaps as few as three or four days.[133] Once again skepticism was wholly warranted. As Helms put it, "we had an American who does not understand much French talking to a Frenchman who does not understand much English over a trans-Atlantic phone call."[134] No sooner had Marcovitch sent his note to Kissinger than Bo began rowing back, denying he had ever used the phrase "solemn engagement," which Marcovitch swore he had. Bo also declined to confirm two of the three scenarios sketched by Marcovitch.[135] With good reason, Rostow's view changed: the latest communication from Paris was "obscure and thin" if not "a piece of monkey business."[136] "They are still weaseling on us," complained Rusk. As so often, Johnson's response to a diplomatic disappointment was to tell McNamara to "hit all [the targets] you can."[137] He persisted in seeing diplomacy and warfare as alternates, rather than elements of the same political process. ("They have escaped the bombing in Hanoi," he complained at one point, "just because two professors are meeting.")[138] Yet even a subtler and better schooled mind would have got little further.

In his novella *Worstward Ho* (1983), Samuel Beckett wrote one of his most famous lines: "Ever tried. Ever failed. No matter. Try again. Fail again. Fail better." This more or less sums up the final phase of PENN-SYLVANIA. From Paris came another barely coherent note addressed to "Henri" and dictated by Bo to Marcovitch in a mixture of French and English:

> I do not know at this stage if what I say is appropriate; you know better than me.
>
> Your Government . . . would send a first message through us announcing unequivocally the unconditional ~~halt~~ cessation of the action now taking place.
>
> Once this has been actually done, a second message, again sent through us, would suggest the opening of a dialogue, at the desired date and place.[139]

Late at night in the White House, Johnson, McNamara, Rostow, and Rusk struggled to draft a reply that would cover Johnson for the eventuality that the North Vietnamese would act in bad faith by escalating their military efforts as soon as the U.S. bombing ceased.[140] The result was a draft response that Kissinger was instructed to deliver to Bo:

> The United States Government understands the position of the Democratic Republic of Vietnam to be as follows: That upon the cessation by the United States of all forms of bombardment of the Democratic Republic of Vietnam, without expression of condition, the Democratic Republic of Vietnam would enter promptly into productive discussions with the United States. The purpose of these discussions would be to resolve the issues between the United States and the Democratic Republic of Vietnam.
>
> Assuming the correctness of this understanding of the position of the Democratic Republic of Vietnam, the United States Government is prepared, in accordance with its proposal

of August 25, to transmit in advance to the Democratic Republic of Vietnam the precise date upon which bombardment
of the Democratic Republic of Vietnam would cease and to
suggest a date and a place for the commencement of discussions.[141]

On this basis, then, Johnson was prepared to stop the bombing of
North Vietnam. He urged McNamara to sell the new pause to the
generals—"Otherwise, I am a man without a country." Rusk remained
doubtful. "I just want everybody to know," he declared as the meeting
wrapped, "that my sniffer doesn't smell peace yet."[142] But even he was
sufficiently optimistic to join in the discussion about where the historic
talks should take place. Bizarrely, the secretary of state suggested Moscow. Rostow came up with Rangoon. As to the person best suited to
represent the United States at the talks, McNamara favored replacing
the superannuated Harriman with the man of the moment: Henry
Kissinger.[143]

All this was of course premature. No sooner had Aubrac and Marcovitch seen the American reply than they began complaining that the
phrase "in accordance with our proposal of August 25th" would be
rejected by Bo, as Hanoi had already rejected that proposal.[144] When
the Frenchmen saw Bo on the morning of October 8, 1967, he immediately objected that "all that appeared after the opening phrase stating
US willingness to stop the bombing without conditions did in fact
constitute conditions. In particular B[o] characterized as 'conditions'
the words 'prompt', 'productive' and 'in accordance with the proposal
of August 25.'"[145] He flatly denied that there was "anything new" in the
October 8 message.[146] On October 17 he spelled out to Marcovitch that
they were back to square one: the American "proposals of peace" were
"double-faced."[147]

Rostow was disgusted. "Our intermediaries . . . are like a couple
of Mexican jumping beans," he complained to Johnson. "I wish they
could sit still for a bit."[148] Kissinger postponed his planned trip to
Paris.[149] The champagne was put back in the cooler. In the White
House, the mood turned black once again. Should they now go ahead
with the pause anyway, if only because it would be a "domestic plus"?

DIRECTOR HELMS: I do not think anything will come out
of the Pennsylvania channel. It will get information back
to Hanoi. But I do not expect to get anything out of it.

SECRETARY RUSK: The proposal we made to them was
almost too reasonable.

THE PRESIDENT: How are we ever going to win?

SECRETARY MCNAMARA: We are making progress. But it
is slow. I have no idea how we can win it in the next 12
months.

    We have to do something to increase the support
for the war in this country. I know of no better way to
do it except by a pause.

THE PRESIDENT: We may lose if we have a pause. I do not
think it would change any of these folks.[150]

All that was left to do, it seemed, was to leak the Paris initiative to the
press and try to get the credit.

Yet Stockholm syndrome is a powerful thing. On October 17 Kissinger called Rostow in a last desperate bid to salvage PENNSYLVANIA.
He "wholly disagreed with the . . . wholly negative . . . interpretation"
of the latest communication from Paris:

> When asked what he found positive in the message, he said:
> "Discussions can take place" as opposed to "could" take place
> [the supposedly key distinction between *peuvent* and *pourraient*].
> He went on to say that if you assume North Vietnam is a small,
> uncertain power, with a split government, facing an immense
> power whose intentions it does not understand or trust, the
> message could be read as follows: We will talk if you end your
> bombing without condition; and we might explore your proposition further if you de-escalate in degree.

Kissinger recommended telling Bo:

> We interpret your message to mean that you are willing
> to enter productive discussions when bombing has ceased

unconditionally; and that you are willing to regard a period of de-escalation as the occasion to explore the time and place for such discussions. On this basis we have cut back our bombing to, say, the 20th parallel; and we are prepared to cease bombing unconditionally if you confirm that our interpretation is correct.[151]

His hypothesis was that "what appears to the outsider as deliberate delay may in reality reflect uneasy navigating between Peking and Moscow, coupled with uncertainty about internal cohesion under the stress of negotiations (especially as Peking disapproves)." North Vietnamese policy was "a set of compromises between individuals jockeying for political survival"; it was bound to be "tortuous and complicated rather than clear cut."[152]

On the evening of October 18, Kissinger was invited to the White House for what proved to be a remarkable meeting of Lyndon Johnson's inner circle. Present were Clark Clifford and Supreme Court justice Abe Fortas, along with Katzenbach, McNamara, Rostow, Rusk, and Maxwell Taylor. Kissinger made the case that "Bo is eager to keep this going" and that there had been "a slight movement in their position." The president's response was, as usual, unsubtle, but quite probably correct:

> My judgment is that they are keeping this channel going just because we are not bombing Hanoi. I know if they were bombing Washington, hitting my bridges and railroads and highways I would be delighted to trade off discussions through an intermediary for a restriction on the bombing. It hasn't cost him one bit. The net of it is that he has a sanctuary in Hanoi in return for having his Consul talk with two scientists who talked with an American citizen.

In the discussion that followed, Rusk, Taylor, Clifford, and Fortas argued for abandoning PENNSYLVANIA, while Katzenbach and McNamara pressed to keep it going by once again pausing the bombing. Rostow was the surprise swing vote in favor of keeping the Paris process going, not because he believed there would ever be a breakthrough but because he felt a bombing pause was essential for domestic political reasons. (As he put it, "Domestic politics is the active front now.") The trump card was a memo from Mac Bundy that Johnson produced (without revealing its authorship), suggesting that the president had all along intended to give Kissinger one last chance.[153] Being Johnson, however, he had to end the meeting with a boorish threat. Arthur Schlesinger recorded in his diary Kissinger's version of the exchange:

> Henry finally said, "I cannot believe that the security of the
> United States will be endangered if for a little while we do not
> bomb within ten miles of the capital of a fifth-rate agricultural
> power." Johnson glowered at him and said, "OK, we will do it
> the professor's way. But (glaring at Kissinger) if it doesn't work,
> I will personally cut your balls off."*[154]

VII

Clearly, the PENNSYLVANIA channel's principal "convenience" for Mai Van Bo consisted in camouflaging Hanoi's true intentions, as well as providing a chance to pick, albeit at one remove, an influential American brain.[155] The domestic political situation in the United States was of growing interest to Hanoi, given that a U.S. presidential election was now just over a year away. As if to mock Kissinger, Bo continued throughout this period to give interviews to American journalists, notably the syndicated columnist Joe Kraft.[156] It was just that, as he smilingly explained to Marcovitch, he had no authorization from Hanoi to see "any officially connected American." What Bo may not have realized was that he was himself indirectly and dramatically affecting the political situation in Washington.

From the vantage point of Washington, Kissinger was performing

---

*Kissinger also described to Schlesinger a comparable scene he had "witnessed in the Cabinet Room: Johnson harrying McNamara, saying to him insistently: 'How can I hit them [the North Vietnamese] in the nuts? Tell me how I can hit them in the nuts.'" As a devout Kennedy loyalist, Schlesinger was the perfect audience for such anecdotes.

"quite correctly . . . the complicated dance between Mr. Bo and Mr. Kissinger," as Rostow put it.[157] McNamara praised Kissinger's "superb" handling of the nonnegotiation.[158] As Katzenbach told Johnson, it was "the closest thing we have yet had to establishing a dialogue with North Vietnam."[159] Johnson wrote to Kissinger to express his "great respect [for] the skill and dedication with which you are seeking the road to peace."[160] But there was also a growing awareness that time was running out for Johnson. As Katzenbach put it, "The chances of getting Vietnam resolved before November 1968, depends on our ability to get talks going."[161] Unfortunately, that was about all the president's closest advisers agreed about. McNamara was increasingly convinced that nothing short of an unconditional halt to the bombing would allow the negotiations to commence, and that the U.S. side would have to accept Vietcong participation in a coalition government in Saigon. Katzenbach, too, favored a generalized bombing pause if only to "eliminate all possible doubt with respect to the Kissinger negotiations." Rostow and Rusk were adamantly against both moves. Johnson, the tough-as-nails Texan, was being slowly, agonizingly torn apart. His instinct was to side with the hawks and to smell a rat in Paris. But where was the evidence that further military escalation would work? And how could he contain the escalating mutiny within his own party, even among old loyalists to his cause?[162] The annals of American government offer few better illustrations than this of what it means for a leader to be of two minds:

> PRESIDENT: I see nothing coming from this.
>
> ROSTOW: I do not see any connection between bombing and negotiations.
>
> KATZENBACH: I do not think we are going to get negotiations by bombing.
>
> PRESIDENT: I do not see [the case for] holding off again. What have we gotten out of this so far[?]
>
> KATZENBACH: We have gotten into communications with them. There have been no communications since February of this year. . . . I favor a pause between now and February.

PRESIDENT: I do too. But we are too quick to pick up what any professor may get going. I think we should get those targets now.

A pause won't change the political situation. It will give them an answer though that we are prepared to go the last mile.

But I do want to get all those targets before a pause.

MCNAMARA: We are not going to be able to have a pause without the military saying there still are targets to be hit.

KATZENBACH: Don't step up the bombing and then pause.

HELMS: I do not agree that by not bombing in a particular location it will have any effect on talks.

PRESIDENT: History may make us look silly on this whole thing.

We pull out of Hanoi any bombing for six weeks to let people get in [to negotiations]. Then they never go in. . . . I think they are playing us for suckers. They have no more intention of talking than we have of surrendering. In my judgment everything you hit is important. It makes them hurt more.

Relatively few men are holding down a lot of men. I think we should get them down and keep them down. We will give them an opportunity to speak and talk if they will.

If we believe that we should bomb, then we should hit their bridges, their power plants, and other strategic targets outside the ones which we have ruled off-limits.

We get nothing in return for giving all we have got. But I guess a pause won't hurt because the weather is bad anyway. But I do want to get all the targets hit that we dare approve. . . . If they do not talk we will have to go to more drastic steps.

We are losing support in this country. The people just do not understand the war. But nobody can justify holding off for five weeks. We must look at this thing very carefully.

> I agree with Dick Helms. It makes no difference in their minds where we hit.
>
> Hanoi alone will not do it. They still want permanent cessation, their four points, and what they have said.
>
> How do you wrap up the channel if it is getting us nowhere[?] . . .

KATZENBACH: Bo could say I'll talk with Kissinger. It makes a difference what we do and say. We should adjust our messages so they can do something or call it off.

PRESIDENT: Nick, give me a paper on what hopes you and State see in this thing. I just do not see them. But I want a paper on this. You already have given them five weeks.

KATZENBACH: But it did not cost us anything.

PRESIDENT: You built a big umbrella which gives them a chance to rebuild. I would deny them that. But let me see it. Write down what we have to gain. . . . I want Katzenbach to prepare me a memo on why he thinks we should continue this channel, a scenario for wrapping it up, because we have met twice with a firm no.[163]

It was in this pitifully conflicted state that Johnson delivered his San Antonio speech, an attempt by Rostow to square the circle by couching in Texan braggadocio a new American concession—the first public statement of what Kissinger had told Mai Van Bo more than a month before: "The United States is willing to stop all aerial and naval bombardment of North Vietnam when this will lead promptly to productive discussions. We, of course, assume that while discussions proceed, North Vietnam would not take advantage of the bombing cessation or limitation."[164] (Bo curtly dismissed Johnson's speech as "insulting.")

The debate resumed with even greater intensity on October 3, prompted by the latest false positives from Paris. After Rostow and McNamara had once again locked horns over the wisdom of stopping the bombing, Johnson stunned his advisers by asking "what effect it would have on the war if he announced he was not going to run for another term. He said if it were set either way today, the decision would be that he would not run." Rusk was aghast. "You must not go down," he exclaimed. "You are the Commander-in-Chief, and we are in a war. This would have a very serious effect on the country. . . . Hanoi would think they have got it made." McNamara did his usual cool cost-benefit analysis:

> Of course, there would be no worry about money and men. We could get support for that. I do not know about the psychology in the country, the effect on the morale of the men, and the effect on Hanoi.
>
> I do think that they would not negotiate under any circumstances and they would wait for the 1968 elections.

It is clear from the minutes of this meeting that Johnson's principal concern was domestic. All he was hearing from Democrats in Congress was that "we will lose the election if we do not do something about Vietnam quick," which (as Rusk drily observed) had much more to do with the recent tax hikes than with the antiwar protests. Yet Johnson's willingness to contemplate abdication also reflected his despair at the seeming impossibility of "do[ing] something about Vietnam quick."[165] It was a feeling of despair that Mai Van Bo had been doing his utmost to accentuate.

From Hanoi's point of view, the beauty of PENNSYLVANIA was exquisite. As Johnson and his advisers came to realize, they had extended a bona fide olive branch, but because secrecy had been insisted on and maintained, and because a tiny chance remained that the Paris channel might be reactivated in future, they could not derive any domestic benefit from their efforts by publicizing them. Johnson itched to go public. His "political instinct" told him that this was the way to respond to the antiwar protests, by making his own proposals and the North Vietnamese answers "so clear . . . that we can tell a farmer what has taken place and be able to have him understand it." But as Rusk pointed out, "The doves will make trouble if we publicize the message. In addition we may want to talk some serious business through this channel at a later time."[166] Moreover, the PENNSYLVANIA files contained "a lot of material which could prove to be embarrassing."[167]

The full horror of Johnson's predicament—and the tragic nature of the American predicament—was now laid bare, as he lamented incoherently to McNamara, Rostow, Rusk, and Wheeler, the chairman of the Joint Chiefs.

It doesn't seem we can win the war militarily. I asked the JCS [for] suggestions on how to shorten the war but all of their proposals related to suggestions outside South Vietnam.

We can't win diplomatically either. . . . We've tried all your suggestions. We've almost lost the war in the last two months in the court of public opinion. These demonstrators and others are trying to show that we need somebody else to take over this country.

People who want us to stop the bombing should know all we have gone through in this exchange. There are men at this table who do not know what all has taken place. We have not seen one change in their position. They are filling the air waves with this propaganda. . . . The hawks are throwing in the towel. Everybody is hitting you. San Antonio did not get through. I cannot mount a better explanation.

If we cannot get negotiations, why don't we hit all the military targets short of provoking Russia and China. It astounds me that our boys in Vietnam have such good morale with all of this going on.

We've got to do something about public opinion.

I want to make sure that Kissinger is on board. We ought to have a sentence every farmer can understand and the enemy say no to it.

We must show the American people we have tried and failed after going the very last mile.

What about the reserves?

It was not quite *Krapp's Last Tape,* but it was close.

VIII

PENNSYLVANIA was a long time dying. On October 20, Kissinger arrived once again in Paris with a lengthy and indignant set of instructions from the State Department that boiled down to this: The United States had "for eight weeks unilaterally refrained repeat unilaterally refrained from bombing in the immediate vicinity of Hanoi," but at no point in that period had the North Vietnamese government made any attempt "(1) to indicate in this channel or otherwise that for its part it will engage in discussions with the US even if the bombing had stopped in accordance with US proposals; or (2) to make any substantive counter proposal on how to proceed to discussions leading to peaceful settlement of differences."[168] To his amazement, Kissinger found Marcovitch "in a state of advanced euphoria.

> According to him, the last message from Bo made all the frustrations worthwhile. When I asked him for the cause of his optimism, he called attention to the distinction between escalation and bombing and the change of tense in the last sentence. I quickly disillusioned him. I said that the issue was really quite simple. If Hanoi wanted to negotiate it should be able to find some way of expressing this fact by means other than subtle changes in tense and elliptical references full of double meanings.[169]

When Aubrac arrived from Rome, he seemed equally delusional. "He [Kissinger]'s got a problem with the two amateurs M and A," Rostow sneered.[170] Strangely, neither he nor his boss appears to have considered the obvious possibility that neither Aubrac nor Marcovitch was the neutral intermediary that both posed as. In view of Aubrac's record as a committed Communist, he was anything but neutral: from the outset he had made no secret of his sympathy with Hanoi. It is of course possible that he and Marcovitch sincerely hoped that Mai Van Bo would finally agree to meet with a representative of the U.S.

government. It is more probable that at least one of the men was in cahoots with Hanoi or, at the very least, was keeping Moscow abreast of developments. Did Raymond Aubrac really want PENNSYLVANIA to succeed? Or was he as well aware as Bo of the nature of the play in which they were acting? We cannot be sure. But by not pausing to ask himself this question, Kissinger revealed that, if any member of the cast was an amateur, it was he.

The final scene, too, had its Beckett-like quality. That same night (October 20) Aubrac and Marcovitch set off to see Bo, armed with yet another artfully drafted document. But Bo would not even see them. When they telephoned, he stonewalled.

A[UBRAC]: We would like to see you urgently.

BO: There is nothing new to say. The situation is worsening. There is no reason to talk again.

A: There is something new and very important.

BO: Repeated word for word the same phrase as before.

A: There is something very important—perhaps the most important juncture of our exchanges.

BO: Repeated word for word the same phrase but then added: What is the important matter[?]

A: It has to do with the meaning of the last sentence of your last message and the sequence with which steps have to be taken.

BO: Our position is perfectly clear.* . . . Bo then repeated word for word the original phrase.[171]

---

*Bo referred them to an article published in the *National Guardian* by the Australian journalist Wilfred Burchett, based on an interview with Nguyen Duy Trinh, which stated, "Hanoi is in no mood for concessions or bargaining and there is an absolute refusal to offer anything—except talks—for a cessation of the bombardment. The word stressed is 'talks,' not negotiations. . . . It is repeated at every level that total independence with complete American withdrawal from South Vietnam is the unalterable aim of the Hanoi government and the Liberation Front for South Vietnam. They are prepared to fight 10 or 20 years to achieve this, and life is being reorganized on this basis." Burchett was not only a Communist Party member but also a KGB operative.

As Kissinger reported to Washington, the Frenchmen were dis-traught: "M was close to tears and A, too, was extremely depressed.

> In these circumstances I confined myself to thanking them for
> their dedication and meticulousness. The channel failed, not for
> lack of goodwill or imagination, but because Hanoi either could
> not or would not talk. M said that at least we had learned what
> Hanoi meant by unconditional. I replied that no serious person
> could believe in an absolutely unconditional relationship.[172]

Rostow dropped Johnson one of those laconic notes that were his forte: "Herewith Kissinger brings M and A closer to the facts of life."[173] It was, he reflected, "the end of the Paris channel." There were two pos-sible explanations, he theorized: either "they regard U.S. politics and world diplomacy as too attractive to begin talking now," or "their talks with Communist China involve a new deal for support or, even, Chi-nese military action." A third possibility, which he did not at first con-sider, was that the entire episode had been a charade.[174] Reviewing the files, he calculated that the North Vietnamese had refused to talk to Kissinger no fewer than fifteen times: that indicated "a clear policy—if nothing else."[175] Helms applied Ockham's razor: Hanoi had never really moved, and Kissinger had been engaged in "an effort to look for some-thing that simply [was] not there."[176] "In short, Mr. President," he told Johnson, "you ended up where you began."[177]

Success has many fathers; so, sometimes, has failure. Aubrac and Marcovitch laid the blame at Johnson's door. They found it "difficult to believe" that the coincidence of their visit to Hanoi and the contin-ued American bombing had been "accidental" as "these two 'deliveri-ies' came from the same 'sender.'"[178] Marcovitch always stuck to the view that Kissinger had been defeated by the hawks around Johnson.[179] Later, to be sure, Aubrac was critical of Kissinger himself, accusing him of leaking the whole story of PENNSYLVANIA to the *Los Angeles Times* in order to burnish his own reputation.[180] (Indeed, in his dotage Aubrac went so far as to claim that he had "no idea about the connec-tion between Henry and the State Department or the White House"— either an astonishing lapse of memory or a barefaced lie.)[181] But it was

Johnson whom the world preferred to blame for the failure of peace to break out in the Summer of Love.

The story had of course leaked. Two journalists—David Kraslow of the Cox newspaper group and Stuart H. Loory, who had been the *New York Herald Tribune*'s Moscow correspondent—put together enough pieces of the jigsaw to write *The Secret Search for Peace in Vietnam,* published in 1968.[182] They tracked down Marcovitch. They quizzed John Gunther Dean, the first secretary of the U.S. embassy in Paris. They managed to work out that "Kissinger had been involved with two leftist Frenchmen in conveying messages to Mai Van Bo in the fall of this year" and that "one of the messages conveyed to Bo included a guarantee that Hanoi would not be bombed for a certain period of time as proof of our good faith and willingness to enter into discussions." Contrary to Aubrac's claim, however, Kissinger refused to see Kraslow and Loory, despite four requests for an interview.[183] Cruelly, from the administration's point of view, the thesis the two journalists advanced was that "the President and Secretary Rusk were misleading the American public on Vietnam and that . . . the North Vietnamese had been receptive to U.S. efforts to enter into negotiations with us, something the Administration denies."[184] They could not have got the story more wrong. But of course their interpretation dovetailed perfectly with the antiwar mood. Senators Fulbright and Mansfield—with support even from Republicans like John Sherman Cooper of Kentucky—kept pressing for a full bombing halt, oblivious to the fact that this was Johnson's last remaining bargaining chip and that Hanoi had repeatedly refused it.[185]

Meanwhile Hanoi prepared to launch its onslaught, following Mao's advice to Ho Chi Minh to pursue a strategy of "annihilation." In October 1967—as Henry Kissinger sought peace in the difference between *pourraient* and *peuvent*—the Vietnamese politburo took the decision to go ahead with the Tet Offensive: "the phase of winning decisive victory" in South Vietnam, in the words of the resolution issued two months later and affirmed at the fourteenth plenary session of the central committee. The "General Offensive General Uprising" was designed to unleash the Vietcong in an all-out assault on the South's major cities—Saigon, Hue, and Da Nang. In the words of Truong Cong Dong, a member of the NLF's mission in North Vietnam,

"The talks will begin when the Americans have inflicted a defeat on us or when we have inflicted a defeat on them. Everything will be resolved on the battlefield."[186] This gives the lie to the notion that Hanoi was in any way sincere about peace talks in 1967. No doubt it was true, as Nguyen Khac Huynh of the North Vietnamese foreign ministry later told McNamara, that "those of us [in Hanoi] who were at that moment working on a negotiating strategy" had been "very encouraged" by PENNSYLVANIA—encouraged in their assumption that genuine talks would be easy to start *after* the Tet Offensive. To say that Kissinger's efforts had "provided the basis for beginning the Paris peace process" is therefore misleading. In the words of Luu Doan Huynh, who was one of Hanoi's men in Beijing at the time, the North Vietnamese aim had all along been "to establish conditions that are best for negotiations—but *after Tet!*"[187]

This explains why the peace feelers extended in the final months of 1967—like PACKERS, a Romanian initiative to broker peace talks—were not simply rebuffed. In the words of George Herring, PACKERS should be understood as "an exercise in deception designed to lull the United States into a false sense of military security and to increase domestic and international pressures for negotiations on the eve of the military blow to be delivered at Tet."[188] The same can be said not only of the statements issued by Nguyen Duy Trinh on December 29 and by Mai Van Bo on January 1 but surely also of PENNSYLVANIA itself. Contrary to McNamara's recollection, the French connection remained open until the very eve of Tet. In early December 1967, Kissinger asked Marcovitch to make one final attempt "to contact Paul" (their code name for Bo). Marcovitch replied that he could do this only if he could bring two dates: "the first announcing the halting, purely and simply, of the bombings and of all acts of war against the DRVN; the other, a later date, within a reasonable period of time, mentioning a rendez-vous for discussions." With Cartesian elegance, he added that "the word 'fruitful' must be strictly avoided, for, to be completely logical, one cannot tell in advance if a discussion that is to take place will be fruitful."[189] At nine p.m. on January 16, Marcovitch was startled to receive a call from Bo, inviting him over for what turned into a two-hour conversation. The "breakoff in conversations . . . last October,"

Bo said, had been "occasioned by general conditions"; his government still "held both of them [Aubrac and Marcovitch] in high personal esteem." In fact, Hanoi stood ready to begin talks at "an appropriate time after cessation of the bombing . . . just as soon as it will be established that the cessation is effective." So would Bo now finally consent to receive Kissinger? Bo replied, with his customary opacity, that "under existing circumstances any such request would be taken into consideration." Marcovitch called Kissinger to relay this new noninvitation. Kissinger sent him a brusque response, offering to "make an effort to come [to Paris] although my schedule is full" if Bo wished "to see me directly."[190] On the morning of January 18, Marcovitch passed this message to Bo in yet another sealed envelope. Bo opened it but said only that he hoped "things were going somewhere this time." The atmosphere, Marcovitch reported, was "cordial."[191]

The Tet Offensive began twelve days later.

IX

What had been born at Pugwash died at Pugwash. On December 28, 1967, Henry Kissinger found himself in the belly of the beast of world Communism: in Moscow, for a meeting of Soviet and American scientists, most of them regular attendees at Pugwash conferences. Indeed, the lineup was more or less the same as at Sopot fifteen months before. Much else had changed in the intervening months, however. The Soviet delegates were noticeably more restrained in their denunciations of American policy. For his part, Henry Kissinger now knew much more than he had in 1966 about the character of America's foe in Vietnam. As he told the Soviet delegates, "Hanoi was reluctant to give up its posture of inflexible ferocity. Hanoi looked at events only in a local context. Distrust on both sides was very deep."[192] Was there not some way for Moscow to act as an intermediary? The most senior participant on the Soviet side, Mikhail Millionshikov, dutifully put forward yet another mediation plan (communicated to Kissinger by the Academy of Sciences interpreter Igor Pochitalin). It was an exceedingly elaborate five-stage scheme. First Millionshikov would meet

Kissinger and Paul Doty and would inform them that "Hanoi was prepared to agree to talk promptly and productively." Then within ten days, the United States would "reduce the bombing of North Vietnam significantly, preferably by stopping attacks on Hanoi and Haiphong." Within another ten days, preliminary "talks would begin through this channel about the technical preparation of a conference including such items as agenda, time, place, etc." Within ten days of the successful conclusion of these technical talks, the United States would stop bombing altogether. Finally, after another thirty days, "a formal, official conference with Hanoi would follow."

Maybe it was true, as Kissinger was assured by the man he suspected was the KGB contact at the academy, that "Moscow definitely wanted a settlement [while] Peking clearly wanted the war to continue." But maybe it was not. Perhaps Moscow was merely adding another acrid cloud to the pre-Tet smoke screen. The nearest thing to an honest exposition of the Soviet position came from the economist Stanislav Menshikov, of the Institute of the World Economy and International Relations. Rather than discuss Vietnam at the official conference, Menshikov took Kissinger for a three-hour drive around the great, empty boulevards of Moscow in his car, the nearest thing to a private place that existed in the Soviet Union at that time. It was New Year's Eve, a good time for a revelation. The truth, Menshikov explained—"speaking purely privately"—was that the Soviets had next to no influence over Hanoi. The North Vietnamese were, as he put it, "not easy to deal with." Moreover, "the extent of distrust of our motives [in Hanoi], and the precariousness of the Soviet position vis-a-vis China inspired the Soviet leaders with great caution."

> The Soviet government had a morbid fear of having the wool pulled over its eyes. It was simply not certain of US intentions. . . . Moreover, the Soviet difficulties were no less than our own. The war in Vietnam had worsened Sino-Soviet relations. Nothing short of a direct US attack on Communist China was likely to restore them. . . . His institute was undertaking a projection of trends to the year 1980. It had come to the conclusion that at no time in that time frame would

Sino-Soviet relations be good, even though Mao would, no doubt, have died by then.

This was extraordinary stuff—almost as extraordinary as what Kissinger had heard from Antonín Šnejdárek in Prague nearly a year before. But Menshikov had another bomb to drop:

> [He] asked whether we were concerned about Soviet intervention [in Vietnam]. I said that, of course, there was . . . deep concern about a conflict with the Soviet Union. At the same time, a look at the map indicated that Soviet military action in South East Asia was not simple. Menshikov said: "We could make trouble where the situation is more favorable, such as in Berlin." I replied, "Only at the risk of a general war." Menshikov said[,] "You see we have our own credibility problem."[193]

Scholars have long speculated as to which American strategist conceived of the opening to China that would so transform the geopolitical landscape in 1972. But it was not Americans who thought of it first (though, as we have seen, Kissinger had toyed with it as early as 1964, only to reject it). It was the strategic thinkers of the Soviet bloc—perhaps because they generally preferred chess to amateur theatricals—who foresaw the new world conjured up by the Sino-Soviet split. As Menshikov understood, nothing short of a war between the United States and China would restore the old unity of the Communist bloc, and the probability of that was dwindling to zero as it became ever clearer that Vietnam was not Korea. The rift between Moscow and Beijing created the potential for an American-Chinese deal, as Šnejdárek explained: an analogue to the Nazi-Soviet Pact of 1939, but this time directed against Moscow—a partnership of opposites that would represent a triumph for realism over idealism, for pragmatism over ideology. Yet Menshikov understood that such a pact would not exclude a continuation of détente between Moscow and Washington.

The United States might have been humiliated, abjectly, in the quagmire that was Vietnam. One of its best and brightest might have been played for a sucker and led up the longest garden path in Paris. But mistaking *The Mousetrap* for *Waiting for Godot* was not a fatal error if, while waiting in vain for Mai Van Bo, Henry Kissinger had glimpsed the script for a much grander drama—a drama that would be enacted not in some dowdy Paris salon but five years later in a cavernous Beijing banqueting hall.

CHAPTER 21

1968

Each time I go there [to Washington], I am struck by how
unique your position there is, regardless of whether I am
meeting with Republicans or Democrats, politicians or
bureaucrats. Actually it seems to me that your renown
remains the same in the eyes of everyone and—perhaps
even more impressively—in every phase. And that really
counts for a lot in a world that seems to value only novelty.
—MARION DÖNHOFF to Henry Kissinger, March 1968[1]

The combination was unlikely.
—RICHARD NIXON, 1978[2]

I

Nineteen sixty-eight was the *annus horribilis* of modern American history. Beginning on the Vietnamese lunar New Year, the Tet Offensive—though it looked much worse to television viewers than it did to U.S. military planners—was the first of a cascade of calamities. Nineteen Vietcong sappers broke into the U.S. embassy in Saigon, killing five American soldiers. For weeks Hue was the scene of bloody house-to-house fighting. Eddie Adams's photographs of the cold-blooded execution of the captured Vietcong officer Nguyen Van Lem by a South Vietnamese police officer summed up the ruthlessness of the counterattack. The violence seemed to seep from television screens into the United States itself. On April 4, James Earl Ray shot Martin Luther King, Jr., dead as the civil rights leader stood on the balcony of his room in a Memphis motel. Two months later Robert Kennedy was fatally wounded by the Palestinian immigrant Sirhan Sirhan as he walked through the kitchens of L.A.'s

Ambassador Hotel. There was even an attempt on the life of Andy Warhol by an unhinged radical feminist writer named Valerie Solanas.

Student protests swept universities all across America, beginning in
Berkeley and then spreading to New York University and Columbia;
by December the craze for antiwar "sit-ins" had reached even Harvard.
Two black students from South Carolina State University were shot
dead by police during a demonstration against segregation in Orange-
burg. In the streets outside the Democratic National Convention in
Chicago, there were pitched battles between police and protesters led
by the Youth International Party ("Yippies"), Students for a Democratic Society (SDS), and the National Mobilization Committee to End
the War in Vietnam. There were fresh race riots as young African
Americans took to the streets after Martin Luther King's assassination,
which they blamed on a government conspiracy. Black Panthers and
other militant black power groups fought gun battles with the police in
Oakland, California, and Cleveland, Ohio.

Abroad, the world went to hell in a handcart. Though the Tet
Offensive was halted and heavy losses were inflicted on the Vietcong
and their North Vietnamese allies, discipline among U.S. and South
Vietnamese forces threatened to collapse in a wave of massacres of
civilians. In June the Malayan Communist Party launched the second
Malayan insurgency. In August a huge Soviet-led force invaded
Czechoslovakia to crush the Prague Spring and overthrow Dubček's
reformist government. There were coups in Iraq, Panama, and Mali.
Even in placid Britain there were intimations of bloodshed, from the
Royal Ulster Constabulary's beating of Catholic marchers in Lon-
donderry to Enoch Powell's prophecy that immigration from Britain's
former colonies would end in racial violence. Though he quoted the
Aeneid ("I seem to see 'the River Tiber foaming with much blood'"), it
was the American experience of race riots that inspired Powell's speech.
Everywhere the phrase *Pax Americana* seemed an oxymoron. The American ambassador was gunned down in the streets of Guatemala City.
North Korean forces boarded and captured the USS *Pueblo*. The nuclear
submarine *Scorpion* sank off the Azores. Not even the skies were safe. In
November 1968 a wave of hijackings began when armed men seized
control of Pan Am Flight 281, bound from New York's Kennedy

Airport to San Juan, Puerto Rico. Between 1961 and 1967 there had been just seven attempts to hijack U.S. aircraft. Between 1968 and 1971 the number soared to seventy-one. Nearly all were redirected to Cuba, making "Take me to Havana" one of the catchphrases of the era.

Small wonder Lyndon Johnson feared Robert McNamara might commit suicide.[3] Small wonder that for his secretary of state, Dean Rusk, 1968 was a "blur." "I was bone-tired," he later recalled, and surviving on a daily diet of "aspirin, scotch, and four packs of Larks." "I don't remember too much of what happened that year," he told his son.[4] But it was his son's generation who were the principal source of trouble in the world. The postwar baby boomers were entering their twenties, and there were lots of them, especially in North America, where the share of the population aged between fifteen and twenty-four was rising toward its mid-1970s peak of nearly 19 percent. It was not only young Americans who were taking to the streets, however. There were significant student protests in Bonn, Paris, Rome, Stockholm, and West Berlin. Nor was the phenomenon confined to the Western democracies. Students rioted in Mexico City and in Kingston, Jamaica. There were also protests in authoritarian states (Spain and Brazil). And there were student protests in the Communist world, too, in Warsaw (January and March), Belgrade (July), and above all, in Mao's China, where the Cultural Revolution was a kind of state-sponsored generational revolt.[5]

For radical students in search of a target, the Harvard Center for International Affairs—where Henry Kissinger was still associate director—cried out for direct action and not merely sit-ins. In October 1968 the Marxist November Action Committee began what was to be a protracted and increasingly violent campaign against the "imperialist facilities" at 6 Divinity Avenue. In September the following year, a group of between twenty and thirty members of the SDS faction that later became the Weather Underground stormed the building and forcibly expelled its occupants, leaving one staff member with a gash that required several stitches. A flyer published by the group gives a flavor of the period:

> The people who run the C.F.I.A. are hired killers. They write
> reports for the government on how to keep a few Americans

rich and fat by keeping most people poor and starving. You might think these vicious pimps would rush off to Vietnam to fight since they dig the war so much. But these are smart pigs. They prefer to stay at Harvard while Black people from Roxbury and white working kids from Dorchester and Jamaica Plain are sent off to die.[6]

Another pamphlet in the same vein accused the center of producing "ideas which maintain the international power of the United States at the expense of the majority of the world's people."[7] The CFIA was "a particularly blatant example of university complicity with U.S. economic penetration abroad at the expense of oppressed peoples."[8]

There were recurrent attacks on the CFIA offices—notably in April 1970, when the offices were "trashed," and six months later, on October 14, 1970, when a bomb exploded on the third floor. The building was ransacked once again in April 1972 in a protest against "America's genocidal war against the people of Indochina."[9]

Henry Kissinger had more than one reason to accept a job in Washington in 1968. To the eyes of a man who had been a teenager in Nazi Germany, the self-proclaimed New Left looked familiar in a number of disturbing ways. In a review of a book about the Nazi Nuremberg rallies, published in March 1968, Kissinger made this parallel explicit:

> There is a danger that modern mass society starves the individual emotionally. Among the careful calculations of the bureaucratic state there is often no residue for commitment. But when all the normal avenues of commitment are closed, the need to belong may break forth in elementary ways. *It is no accident that in the beginning the Nazi party was especially attractive to students, the very group which has felt increasingly unfulfilled by modern society.* Fortunately the Nuremberg party rallies belong to the past. Still, we should read them . . . as a warning.[10]

Shortly after Robert Kennedy's assassination, Kissinger drafted a speech for Nelson Rockefeller that developed this theme, which provides a reminder that Kissinger's historical imagination never confined itself strictly to the realm of diplomacy, and that his idealism remained rooted in a rejection of the materialism so dear to the Marxists. The problem of youthful unrest was a pathology of a "highly industrialized, heavily bureaucratized society," he wrote. Although most pronounced in the most advanced societies, it was a global phenomenon.

> One difficulty is the unprecedented pace of change. Familiar patterns are destroyed everywhere. But nothing integrating replaces them. Modern society exalts specialization. The industrial process is based on an elaboration of individual functions. The day-to-day experience of most men emphasizes the particular, while the complexity of our problems suggest[s] the need for some general principles. The day-to-day experiences of the individual have grown discontinuous with his moral and psychological needs. . . .
>
> The sense of reverence for the individual tends to be threatened by the vast scale of modern life. Our young people see administrative structures operating with great efficiency. But the seeming automaticity of their operation apparently reduces the need for the individual, for his creativity and concerns. They answer the need for efficiency; they leave open the need for commitment. . . . What is at issue is nothing less than whether life can be given meaning . . . in an environment which seems to dwarf the individual.

The answer to this problem was not the favorite remedy of the modern age: growth and jobs. As Kissinger pointed out, the "contemporary uneasiness—especially of our young generation," was in part a "rebellion against the emptiness of a life which knows only 'practical' problems and material goods and lacks a deeper purpose. . . . The contemporary disquiet proves among other things that man cannot live by economics alone; he needs quality and purpose in addition to material well-being."[11] The idealist despised the pat palliatives of the materialists of his own generation almost as much as the fake idealism of a rebellious youth willing to align itself with Hanoi and Havana.

II

Nevertheless, for many Americans—to this day—the worst thing to happen in 1968 was none of the events described above. It was the election as president of the United States of America of Richard Milhous Nixon.

In the demonology of Nixon's rise, a peculiar but significant role has been attributed to Henry Kissinger. Beginning with the journalist Seymour Hersh, a succession of writers have alleged that Kissinger conspired to help Nixon win the 1968 election by leaking secret and vital information about the official peace talks between the United States and North Vietnam that began in Paris in May. The case made by Hersh is that, after the failure of Rockefeller's third bid for the Republican nomination, Kissinger offered his services to the Nixon campaign. According to Hersh, on September 10, 1968, Kissinger phoned Richard V. Allen, one of Nixon's foreign policy advisers, and told him he "had a way to contact" his friends in the administration involved in the Vietnam talks.* He then "funneled information" to Nixon "betraying people with whom he had worked on the still-secret Vietnam negotiating efforts," notably Daniel Davidson and John Negroponte. Indeed, on September 17, he went to Paris in order to be as close as possible to the negotiations. Well aware that he was leaking classified information, Kissinger conveyed what he knew to Allen by calling him on pay phones and speaking partly in German. To cover his tracks, he simultaneously offered his former Harvard colleague Zbigniew Brzezinski—who had served in Policy Planning under Rusk and was now working for the Humphrey campaign[12]—Rockefeller's "shit file" of incriminating information about Nixon, telling Brzezinski, "Look, I've hated Nixon for years."

Kissinger was hedged, so the story goes: whether Nixon or the

---

*Allen later stated that Kissinger had "volunteered information to us through . . . a former student, that he had in the Paris peace talks." It is not clear who this can have been.

Democratic nominee, Vice President Humphrey, won, he could count on being made national security adviser, as he had also offered his services to Humphrey. Indeed, he made a job offer to Davidson on that basis. But he did more for Nixon. On September 26 he told Allen that "something big was afoot regarding Vietnam." A few days later he told him there was "a better than even chance that Johnson will order a bombing halt at approximately mid-October." On October 12 he reported "a strong possibility that the administration would move before October 23" and that there was "more to this than meets the eye." On the thirty-first, twelve hours before Johnson finally ordered an end to the bombing of North Vietnam, Kissinger told Allen he had "important information," namely that Harriman and his deputy, Cyrus Vance—formerly deputy secretary of defense—had "broken open the champagne" to celebrate doing a deal with Hanoi. This information, we are told, was invaluable to Nixon, who was briefed about it by H. R. "Bob" Haldeman, who would later become his chief of staff, and by John Mitchell, the future attorney general. In turn, Nixon gave Kissinger his reward by appointing him as his national security adviser.[13]

Hersh's story has become canonical. Walter Isaacson toned it down somewhat but still concluded that Kissinger had "curried favor by sharing secrets" with Nixon.[14] Christopher Hitchens ramped it up by calling Kissinger "an informant within the incumbent administration" whose information was then fed by Nixon to the South Vietnamese government, thereby "sabotag[ing] the Paris peace negotiations." Kissinger's leaks were one half of Nixon's alleged skullduggery; Anna Chennault, who acted as a channel between Nixon and the South Vietnamese ambassador Bui Diem, was the other.[15] The notion of a Nixonian conspiracy in which Kissinger was complicit has recently been reinforced by Ken Hughes.[16]

That Nixon was eager to know how the negotiations in Paris were progressing is clear. More debatable is Clark Clifford's claim that "the activities of the Nixon campaign constituted a gross, even potentially illegal, interference in the security affairs of the nation."[17] Still, the verdict has stuck that Nixon "played politics with peace to win the 1968 election."[18] According to one study of the election, "Republican actions delayed the opening of expanded talks during 1968, and helped to prevent a Democratic victory which would have led to a peace settlement in 1969."[19] It was Nixon, argues Anthony Summers, who "encouraged [South Vietnam's] President Thieu to believe he would get a better deal from a Nixon administration [and] actually urged him to boycott the talks."[20]

As we shall see, it is highly doubtful that President Thieu would have behaved any differently if Nixon had regained his Quaker faith, lost his will to win, and canceled the final two months of his campaign. It seems just as doubtful, moreover, that the North Vietnamese would have accepted a compromise peace settlement in 1969 even if Thieu had decided not to boycott the 1968 talks—indeed, even if Hubert Humphrey had won the presidency. For now, however, it is the Hersh-Hitchens account of Kissinger's role that needs to be scrutinized.

There are two obvious weaknesses to the allegation that Kissinger conspired to leak information to Nixon. The first, as even so sympathetic a reviewer as Kissinger's former colleague Stanley Hoffmann could not overlook, is that Hersh simply "does not prove that it was Mr. Kissinger who gave the secrets of the Paris negotiations to the Nixon camp."[21] William Bundy—who by the 1990s was no friend of Kissinger's—was equally skeptical that Kissinger could have obtained "inside information" during his visit to Paris on September 18–22.[22] We shall see that there is no documentary evidence whatever that Kissinger made any effort to obtain confidential information about the Paris talks; such information as existed was being liberally made available to the press corps in any case.

This brings us to the second weakness of the Hersh-Hitchens narrative. It is based almost exclusively on interviews or remarks made some time after the fact by people who had obvious incentives to present Kissinger in a bad light. An example is Daniel Davidson. Kissinger did indeed offer a government job to Davidson in 1968, but his appointment to the NSC staff was not a success; Davidson went on to have a moderately successful career as a Wall Street lawyer, but any hopes he had of a career in government were dashed. The key witness in the case—Richard Allen—was even less likely to speak kindly of Kissinger by the time he was interviewed by Hersh. In a lengthy 2002 interview, Allen claimed that he had "recommended that Kissinger be appointed

National Security Adviser because I didn't have any designs on that job myself, though it is often said that I did. . . . I had no intention whatever of doing that. I wanted to go back to Palo Alto," where he was on the staff of the Hoover Institution.[23] Perhaps, but when Nixon offered him the position of deputy national security adviser, Allen accepted—on condition that he was appointed by the president rather than by Kissinger. It was not a happy arrangement.

> Immediately . . . I found myself thwarted at almost every level.
> My memos were ostensibly going to the President, but Henry
> organized the National Security Council in such a way that no
> one could write to the President and his name went on memo-
> randa that were prepared by others. . . . Then Henry pro-
> ceeded to staff the NSC with a group of people who could at
> best be described as Nixon critics and at worst as Nixon haters,
> and it puzzled the Dickens out of me. So I was in the NSC,
> number two man, alive in a sea of hostility.

Allen was given the job of acting as "the listener" for low-level people who wanted to lobby the president, but his reports "never got to" Nixon because they were "headed off" by Kissinger. Allen left the administration after less than a year, in December 1969, following a row about secret U.S. military bases.

Allen later worked for Ronald Reagan, whose approach to the Cold War—to "win" it rather than to "manage" it—he much preferred. As one of the founders of the bipartisan Committee on the Present Danger, Allen was a vociferous critic of Kissinger's continuation of détente, as well as of Kissinger himself. ("Most of the world Kissinger didn't know anything about at all. He knew about Metternich and Castlereagh, and he knew about Vietnam, but not much.")[24] In 1981, Allen appeared to have achieved revenge when Reagan appointed him as his national security adviser. The following year, however, he was forced to resign over a payment he had allegedly received from a Japanese journalist to set up an interview with the first lady. John F. Lehman also served both Nixon and Reagan. As a staff member of the National Security Council, he had a ringside seat for Kissinger's duel with Allen, and he later recalled how Kissinger had squeezed out his unwanted deputy, marooning him in a grand office in the Executive Office Building, far from the main NSC offices in the West Wing, and then brought in Alexander Haig to be his effective number two.[25] Kissinger won the bureaucratic battle but made a lifelong enemy.

The second most important witness for the Hersh-Hitchens case is Richard Nixon himself, a man both writers spent much of their careers denouncing as a liar but whom they nevertheless—on this one subject— quote as a reliable authority. The key text is Nixon's memoir, *RN*.[*] Nixon's account of the events of 1968 in fact acknowledges that it was Rockefeller, rather than Kissinger himself, who had been "urging" Nixon to make use of him as a foreign policy adviser. He also writes that Kissinger "was completely circumspect in the advice he gave us during the campaign. If he *was* privy to the details of the negotiations he did not reveal them to us." True, Kissinger went to impressive lengths to "protect his secrecy," a trait Nixon admired. But that was understandable when the most powerful job in the world was at stake— and when, moreover, Kissinger was advising a man he had criticized on multiple occasions. The atmosphere was one of collective paranoia. Nixon asked himself the characteristically devious question, "What if Johnson's people knew that [Kissinger] was passing information to me and were feeding him phony stories?" He also shows that he and his campaign team sought to get intelligence about the Paris talks from multiple sources, including Everett Dirksen, the Republican minority leader in the Senate, Dean Rusk, General Andrew Goodpaster, and— on October 22—"someone in Johnson's innermost circle" (i.e., clearly not Kissinger), who very accurately reported the president's plan to

---

*It should be recalled that publication of this memoir sparked a widespread protest led by the Committee to Boycott Nixon's Memoirs (slogan: "Don't Buy Books by Crooks"). The verdict of J. K. Galbraith bears repeating. "That Nixon was a rascal is now generally accepted. But, as . . . this book superbly affirms, he was and remains a rascal who either considers himself a deeply moral man or, at a minimum, believes that he can so persuade any known audience. . . . Nixon's belief [is] here affirmed, that the misuse of FBI, IRS, and other federal agencies is one of the accepted rights of incumbency." "The Good Old Days," *The New York Review of Books*, June 29, 1978.

"pull the election out for HHH [Humphrey]" by announcing a deal with Hanoi on prime-time television.

There was in fact nothing very secret about what was happening in Paris. Unlike the Kissinger channel through Aubrac and Marcovitch, the 1968 talks were public and took place amid a veritable media circus. By mid-October, as Nixon recalled, "rumors became rampant that something big was about to happen in Paris." What remained secret were the separate decision-making processes in Washington, Hanoi, and Saigon, and Kissinger was no better informed about those than the average journalist. As Nixon's memoir makes clear, the vital tip-off about Johnson's October 31 bombing halt announcement came not from Kissinger but from a mole inside the administration. Nor was Kissinger in any way involved in the decision of the South Vietnamese not to participate in the negotiations when invited. The most that can be gleaned from Nixon's account is that Kissinger more than once "warned [Nixon] against making any statement that might be undercut by negotiations I was not aware of." To judge by this evidence, Kissinger was doing no more than helping his own party's candidate avoid an October surprise that, as we shall see, he had every reason to fear from Johnson.[26] Perhaps Nixon's account should simply not be believed. But Hersh and Hitchens want us to believe it, apparently unaware that Nixon's account contradicts their central claim against Kissinger.

If the evidence for the case against Kissinger is either unreliable or nonexistent, so too is the logic of the case itself. If Henry Kissinger really was so keen for a government job after the 1968 election, was leaking sensitive information about the Vietnam negotiations to Richard Nixon—who was by no means guaranteed to win—the obvious way to get it? A rather more obvious way would surely have been for Kissinger to lend his support to the Republican front-runner from the outset, seeking to build a reputation for competence and reliability as a foreign policy expert. Those, after all, are the qualities a president looks for in a national security adviser. Yet Kissinger had done the very opposite. Yes, he dreamed of a job in government; he had spent much of the 1960s vainly seeking one. Yes, he had every reason to get out of Harvard as the campus descended into pandemonium. And yes, he

sincerely believed he was the man best qualified to succeed Walt Rostow as the next national security adviser. But he scarcely went about
getting that job in a rational way. Indeed, so indifferent to his own
career prospects was he in early 1968 that he once again enlisted as
foreign policy adviser to Nelson Rockefeller—the two-time loser who
never for a moment looked likely to stop Nixon from securing the
Republican nomination.

III

Rockefeller liked to sublet his advisers. Having initially decided
against running in 1968, he made Henry Kissinger and the rest of his
campaign team available to the man who seemed to have the best
chance of beating Nixon: George Romney, the favorite of his fellow
Republican governors. According to the recollections of Bill Seidman,
one of Romney's Michigan business associates, Kissinger had been sent
by Rockefeller to brief Romney on the issue of Vietnam, about which
the putative candidate was having doubts. It was no good. In an interview for a Detroit radio station at the end of August 1967, Romney
remarked that when he visited Vietnam in November 1965, he had
"just had the greatest brainwashing [by U.S. military spokesmen] that
anybody can get."[27] The fact that there was probably some truth in this
was what made it so disastrous. Romney soldiered on but his poll numbers never recovered.

Any serious candidate aspiring to run for the presidency in 1968
clearly had to have a view on Vietnam, and it almost certainly had to
be different from his view four years before. Though Rockefeller still
said he was not running, he was clearly already working out his position. Nine days before Romney's self-immolating interview, Kissinger
drafted for Rockefeller a mock interview on Vietnam anticipating a
"Rockefeller Call for a New Vietnam Policy." Although it was never
released, this document is nevertheless remarkable in the scope of its
challenge to the Johnson administration's policy. The problem, Kissinger proposed that Rockefeller say, was that

we are seeking to apply techniques of conventional war to a situation which is ultimately political and psychological. There is no purely military solution to the Vietnam problem. The insecurity of the average Vietnamese peasant is produced above all by guerrilla units. The costly "search and destroy" operation—which sees American troops rushing from one area of Vietnam to another without a guarantee to the local population that they will remain to protect them—should be replaced by "clear and hold" action which seeks to give as permanent security as is possible to that part of the population our military force are able to protect.[28]

Nor was economic aid a sufficient solution in a country that was "lacking the very concept of political legitimacy, that is acceptance of governmental authority based on legal processes and an effective administration." In such a context, "economic development unaccompanied by the creation of political structures" simply tended "to multiply dislocation." What was to be done? Unilateral withdrawal was clearly "unthinkable," but a total American victory seemed "unattainable": "Our path falls, then, between these extremes: a limited use of power to secure a compromise settlement." Kissinger wrote that it was "difficult to believe that a little more of the same military medicine will miraculously cure a situation which has proved resistant to two years of constant escalation" and concluded that the United States should

confine the bombing to the access roads into the South and make clear that we would reduce our bombing if Hanoi limits its infiltration . . .

seek alternatives to bombing in cutting off supplies from the North . . .

give high priority to the development of a concept of political stability and to its implementation in the countryside [and] . . .

pursue all efforts for a negotiated peace . . . by spelling out in detail exactly what we are trying to accomplish [regarding] . . . the future state of South Vietnam, the presence of American troops there, and the role of the NLF.[29]

Perhaps the most striking part of this unpublished document was Kissinger's argument that it was not just the policy in Vietnam that was flawed but the way it was being developed and implemented:

> We are conducting the war in Vietnam with an organization which is barely adequate [and] . . . which breaks down under stress. There exists no focus to coordinate the action of the various agencies, short of the President who does not have the time to deal with any but crisis decisions. As a result, each agency pursues its own program with no guiding doctrine or plan. Thus our efforts to negotiate have sometimes been defeated by military escalations, and our diplomatic moves have occasionally had a characteristic of anxiety that deprived them of their ultimate impact.[30]

A key recommendation was therefore institutional reform in Washington, which meant creating "a focus for relating our actions to each other. Our diplomatic, military and economic moves should form part of a pattern." That pattern must include a more intelligent policy toward Moscow and Beijing.[31]

Four years previously, Kissinger had tried and failed to persuade Rockefeller to adopt a more critical stance on Vietnam. In 1967 he failed again. When *The New York Times* ran a speculative story in which Kissinger was quoted as refusing to be quoted ("Someone in an advisory position shouldn't say what he's advising"), Rockefeller issued an immediate denial that he was (as the *Times* had put it) "shifting toward a more moderate position."[32] Yet the issue refused to go away, and it was an issue for the Republican front-runner just as much as it was for Romney and Rockefeller.

Richard Nixon had not abandoned politics entirely for the law. In his wilderness years after his defeat for the governorship of California in 1962, he had continued to write and speak on political issues. Indeed, in 1965 Kissinger had found himself writing to thank Nixon on Rockefeller's behalf for sending no fewer than three statements on Vietnam (which one suspects Rockefeller had not read).[33] Then, on election day 1966, as Rockefeller waited to hear if he had won a third term as governor of New York, came a remarkable letter from Nixon—as he put it, from one "authentic big leaguer" to another. Nixon claimed to be "deeply distressed by the fact that the Johnson administration has failed to come up with one single new idea in the field of foreign policy" despite situations "which simply cry out for new initiatives."

> What I am trying to say is that I do not see new leadership coming from the Democratic side due both to the division within the Democratic Party and [to] Johnson's complete inability to project his policies in idealistic terms. As far as the Republicans are concerned, no fresh ideas seem likely to emerge from the House and Senate group. My suggestion is so way out that nothing may materialize from it, but it would be quite exciting and intriguing if the two of us could sit down, as we did in times gone by, and provide some much needed leadership in the foreign policy area.[34]

Whatever Nixon's motivation, the meeting did not take place. But the fact that Nixon could even suggest it showed how the failure of Johnson's foreign policy was creating an opportunity for a new configuration on the Republican side.

On the surface, Rockefeller and Nixon were still rivals. By the end of November 1967, Kissinger was back in harness as Rockefeller once again prepared to challenge Nixon for the Republican nomination, once again coming late into the race, once again hoping to be drafted at the convention.[35] It was the usual drudgery: answering letters from fans and cranks, reading draft speeches, laboriously arranging a series of expert breakfast and lunch briefings with inter alia Bernard Brodie, Mac Bundy, Stanley Hoffmann, Herman Kahn, Richard Neustadt, and the young Joseph Nye—not to mention a rising star of the French left named François Mitterrand.[36] Yet beneath the surface Rockefeller and Nixon were converging. In some ways it was Vietnam that was bringing them together. In an important albeit indirect way, however, it was Kissinger.

Throughout the campaign, Kissinger chipped away at Rockefeller's position on Vietnam (which was that the policy of defending South Vietnam was right in principle, and that it would be presumptuous to criticize the president, who alone was in full possession of the military and diplomatic facts). Over lunch at the Century Club, Arthur Schlesinger was reassured by Kissinger that "Nelson's views were identical with his own:

> [Kissinger] made absolutely clear his own opposition to further escalation and his own skepticism about the administration's attitude toward negotiation. He had seen Johnson a few times this winter in connection with a Hanoi peace feeler with which he became accidentally but deeply involved; and he had come away with a conviction that LBJ's resistance to negotiation verges on a sort of madness. Henry feels that practically anyone would be better than Johnson.[37]

Invited to meet Rockefeller himself, Schlesinger was pleased to have this confirmed. Although "Nelson did not state any positions on Vietnam . . . the conversations skirted the subject a great deal of the time, and the tacit assumption of the talk was that he agreed with Henry and me on the futility of the present policy and the illusions of the Johnson administration."[38]

A more significant meeting had taken place two months earlier. On December 10, 1967, Clare Boothe Luce decided to bring together Henry Kissinger and Richard Nixon at a pre-Christmas cocktail party in her elegant apartment at 933 Fifth Avenue. Kissinger arrived early and (as she later recalled) "with his limited talent for small talk, the 'objective conditions,' to use a favorite phrase of his, indicated a hasty disengagement." Just as he was about to leave, Nixon appeared. They spoke for "no more than five minutes"—not about politics but about Kissinger's writings, specifically *Nuclear Weapons and Foreign Policy* (which, as we have seen, Nixon had read and admired at the time it was published).[39] This was their one and only meeting before November 25,

1968. What is not recorded is whether the two men also discussed Nixon's writings, specifically the article he had just published in *Foreign Affairs*. It is inconceivable that Kissinger had not read it or appreciated its significance.

"Asia After Viet Nam" was published in October 1967 and is more frequently cited than read by people who see in it a harbinger of Nixon and Kissinger's opening to China in 1971–72.[40] That is not at all what the article is about. Nixon's main point is in fact that China represented a mortal "danger" to the rest of Asia, and that, in the wake of Vietnam, the United States could not contain that threat single-handedly. "During the final third of the twentieth century," wrote Nixon, "Asia, not Europe or Latin America, will pose the greatest danger of a confrontation which could escalate into World War III." The "American commitment in Vietnam" had been "a vital factor in the turnaround in Indonesia . . . [and had] diverted Peking from such other potential targets as India, Thailand and Malaysia."[41] As Nixon put it, in an incongruous comparison, "Dealing with Red China is something like trying to cope with the more explosive ghetto elements in our own country. In each case a potentially destructive force has to be curbed; in each case an outlaw element has to be brought within the law; in each case dialogues have to be opened; in each case aggression has to be restrained while education proceeds."[42] True, Nixon wrote the famous lines "[W]e simply cannot afford to leave China forever outside the family of nations, there to nurture its fantasies, cherish its hates and threaten its neighbors. There is no place on this small planet for a billion of its potentially most able people to live in angry isolation."[43] True, he spoke of "the struggle for influence in the Third World [as] a three-way race among Moscow, Peking and the West." But Nixon's proposal was not diplomatic engagement with China. The United States should not be "rushing to grant recognition to Peking, to admit it to the United Nations and to ply it with offers of trade—all of which would serve to confirm its rulers in their present course." Rather, China had to be "persuade[d] . . . that it must change" by placing the other nations, backed by the ultimate power of the United States[,] . . . in the path of Chinese ambitions." And that meant building up ASPAC: a grouping of countries that already included Australia, Japan, Malaysia, New

Zealand, the Philippines, South Korea, Taiwan, and Thailand—not forgetting South Vietnam and Laos. All were acutely conscious of the Chinese threat, and all except Malaysia had military ties with the United States.

ASPAC sank without a trace. But in one crucial respect Nixon's argument was brilliantly perceptive. As he said, the spectacular growth of economies like those of Japan, Hong Kong, Singapore, South Korea, and Taiwan represented "a new chapter . . . in the winning of the West: in this case, a winning of the promise of Western technology and Western organization by the nations of the East." The rapidly industrializing Asian economies had indeed "discovered and applied the lessons of America's own economic success."[44] And this was the key reason why—though Nixon did not say it explicitly—ultimate American failure in Vietnam did not really matter that much. Communism had succeeded in China, North Korea, and North Vietnam. South Vietnam, Cambodia, and Laos still hung in the balance. But everywhere else it had lost. Not only that, but capitalism was succeeding in what would come to be called the East Asian "tigers" as it had never succeeded anywhere before, as Western technology was combined with an Asian work ethic to generate some of the highest growth rates ever recorded. The dogmatic antimaterialist Henry Kissinger could hardly ignore the statistics Nixon cited. Rapid growth might not translate into spiritual fulfillment, especially for teenagers; but for their parents, who remembered the miserable poverty of the entire region in 1945, it was vastly preferable to the alternative. Nixon was right: this was the fantastically good news about Asia that their fixation on Vietnam was causing Americans to overlook.

The rethinking of U.S. policy toward Asia was only one of two things that brought Kissinger and Nixon together, however—and arguably it was the less important. The other was their common recognition that the disastrous performance of the Johnson administration in Southeast Asia was itself merely a symptom of a more profound problem: the chronically dysfunctional condition of the foreign-policy-making machine. It was to this problem—not to the seemingly gridlocked negotiations in Paris—that Kissinger devoted a rising proportion of his time and energy in the course of 1968. That there was a problem had gradually become apparent to him, beginning with his first briefings before going to Vietnam in 1965. The breakdown of communications between the major departments and agencies in Washington was mirrored on the ground in South Vietnam. Then there was the ultimate horror of participating in one of the chaotic bull sessions that passed for meetings about national security in the twilight of the Johnson administration. In an extraordinary paper he wrote for Rockefeller in January 1968, Kissinger sought to define the problem in technocratic terms. There were, he argued, two basic problems: "(a) the capacity of the governmental machinery to receive, absorb or retrieve the relevant data, [and] (b) the ability to bring the available information to bear on immediate issues or even more importantly on long-range planning." The problem of information overload was comparatively new: "In the past, governments suffered mostly from an insufficiency of information.

> The U.S. government is [now] overwhelmed by it. . . . The top policy-maker in turn has so much information at his disposal that in crisis situations he finds it impossible to cope with it. As for planning, while a commitment to it exists in theory, in practice it is defeated by the action-orientation of the top policy maker and the absence of criteria for what is relevant. . . . [O]ne of our chief problems in national policy making [is] how to bring policy makers naturally into contact with the issues of most concern before a crisis takes away the scope for reflection.[45]

Kissinger identified three needs. First, he argued, "if top policy makers could be consistently briefed on likely trouble spots, crisis situations could be handled within an over-all conceptual framework. The time now devoted to determining where we are could be spent on deciding where we wish to go. Such a process would enable us to avoid many crises altogether. Purpose could shape technique instead of the opposite." Second, "the system . . . should be able to give an indication of potential trouble spots even when they have not been assigned top priority. Almost as important as collecting the information and keeping problem areas under surveillance is the ability to present in 'real time,' that is the time actually available to the top policy makers and in a manner that they are able to absorb." Third, policy makers should be given "a set of action-options . . . outlin[ing] the major alternatives in response to foreseeable circumstances with an evaluation of the probable consequences, domestic and foreign of each such alternative." As Kissinger noted, to meet these needs would require major investments in programming, storage, retrieval, and graphics. Fortunately, the "hardware technology" now existed to perform all four of these functions:

> [W]e can now store several hundred items of information on every individual in the United States on one 2,400 foot magnetic tape. . . . [T]hird-generation computers are now capable of performing basic machine operation in nano seconds, i.e., billionths of a second. . . . [E]xperimental time-sharing systems have now demonstrated that multiple-access capability for large-scale digital computers is possible to allow for information input/output at both the executive and operator stations distributed around the world. . . . [And] very shortly color cathode ray tube display will be available for computer output.[46]

The modern reader is of course struck by the prescience of all this—as well as by the evidence of Kissinger's early interest in data on tape. But his point was more about data analysis than about storage. What was lacking was the conceptual framework that would enable his proposed information retrieval and display system actually to be used. Which data relevant to high-level foreign policy decisions would actually be input? How could the "cardinal rule" of all information systems—"Garbage in, garbage out"—be enforced? Clearly, pilot studies would need to be carried out. (He suggested the cases of Berlin, Cyprus, and Haiti as suitable for trial.) But it was hard to believe this approach would not produce an improvement "on the present system of individual memories, files of position papers, ad hoc group discussions, and so on.'[47]

The 1960s were, after all, about more than just flower power; they were also about processing power. Four years before, IBM had introduced its System/360, the first time that it had been possible to have multiple compatible computers connected together in a network. The New York–based company's computers were already handling the American Airlines SABRE system for flight reservations as well as the guidance systems for NASA's Gemini space program, the precursor of Apollo. By 1968 the IBM System/4 Pi was standard on B-52 bombers, its dynamic random-access memory chips allowing a major increase in programming capability. It might be thought odd that Henry Kissinger—a man whose Ph.D. had "restored" a lost world of handwritten diplomatic dispatches—should have been an early advocate of computerized foreign policy. But his point was precisely that the excessive flow of information created by the combination of bureaucracy, the typewriter, and the telegraph had made Metternichian strategic thinking impossible.

Of course, Kissinger was not so naïve as to think that information technology could solve all the problems of the U.S. government. In an obscure but iconoclastic paper entitled "Bureaucracy and Policy Making," first presented at a seminar at UCLA in the spring of 1968, Kissinger mapped out a complementary argument about the need for a transformation of the institutional structure of decision making. "[T]here is no such thing as an American foreign policy," he began. There was only "a series of moves that have produced a certain result" that they "may not have been planned to produce" and to which research and intelligence organizations, either foreign or national, attempt to give a rationality and consistency . . . which it simply does not have."[48] The "highest level in which people can still think" in a government department was "the middle level of the bureaucracy—that of the assistant secretary and his immediate advisers. . . . Above that, the day to day operation of the machine absorbs most of the energy." Bureaucracy, Kissinger argued, was the dominant institution of the U.S. government, altogether more powerful than any president or secretary. This point had been made before (notably by Arthur Schlesinger), but Kissinger drew several original inferences. First, "decisions do not get made until they appear as an administrative issue." Thus "[t]here is no such thing, in my view, as a Vietnam policy; there is a series of programs of individual agencies concerned with Vietnam. These programs are reconciled or not, as the case may be, if there is a conflict between the operating agencies."[49] The system worked only when there were two opposing agencies, one on either side of an issue; it went awry when a small, dedicated, unopposed group got to work.

Second, there could be no planning because no one had time for it. ("Planning involves conjectures about the future and hypothetical cases. They are so busy with actual cases that they are reluctant to take on theoretical ones.") Third, policy makers were plagued by a "congenital insecurity" because they lacked the expertise of their advisers; they therefore sought refuge in "a quest for administrative consensus." Often they were the victims of theatrically talented briefers. To avoid being taken for a ride, some decision makers sought to take key issues away from the bureaucracy, deciding them in small groups or bringing in outsiders.[50] In the case of foreign policy, however, there was always a temptation not to make a decision at all but simply to see, after a negotiation had begun, "what the other side had to offer."

> Therefore, in periods of preliminary diplomacy, our position is very rigid and tough, but this changes rapidly when a negotiator has been appointed because he acts as spokesman for the other side. It is not his problem to worry about the overall picture. He worries about the success of the negotiations, and you make the negotiations succeed by taking very seriously into account what the other side has to say.[51]

Kissinger had, as we have seen, some firsthand experience in this regard. Here, however, he averred that "if you don't know what is desirable and operate only on the basis of what is negotiable, you really encourage the other side to take a very extreme position." For all these reasons, he argued, "a new President, in the areas where he wants to effect change, must do so within the first four months. He . . . must give enough of a shake to the bureaucracy to indicate that he wants a new direction and he must be brutal enough to demonstrate that he means it."[52] Kissinger made it clear that a new president should reserve an especially large shake for the State Department.

Kissinger's most telling point focused on the decline and fall of Eisenhower's highly formalized use of the National Security Council, which he contrasted with Kennedy's attempt to "substitute for it a sort of nervous energy and great intellectual activity" and Johnson's model, which combined "the disorganization of Kennedy without the intellectual excitement, and with somewhat of a fear of the President superimposed on it"—not to mention Johnson's own "compulsive secretive[ness]."[53] True, Eisenhower's system had produced policies that were (or sounded like) little more than "platitudes." But that was still preferable to the system of 1968. The ideal, Kissinger suggested, would be "a National Security Council with a staff of McGeorge Bundy qualities" or "something similar to what McNamara did in the Defense Department, that is, to try to establish some criteria by which to judge success and failure."[54]

His final point was that Vietnam had laid bare the paucity of criteria for judging the national interest because "most of the traditional concepts of balance of power just don't apply."

> All the thinking of balance of power has been related to territorial control. You could judge whether there was an equilibrium by what country changed allegiance. We live in a curious period in which territorial control may not be that important. We have good categories for resisting what we call aggression. [But] leaving the issue of whether we are correct in our assessment that the Vietnamese war was Chinese instigated—which I don't happen to believe—one would still be able to argue that no conceivable territorial gain of Communist China in Vietnam, or for that matter in Southeast Asia, could compare in terms of augmentation of its strength with the acquisition of nuclear weapons so far as concerned its impact on the international situation. We have some criteria for judging one, and none for the other.[55]

Unfortunately, the last man likely to make that kind of judgment would be a successful candidate for the presidency, because "the typical political leader of the contemporary managerial society is a man with a strong will, a high capacity to get himself elected, but no very great conception of what he is going to do when he gets into office." Hence the "curious phenomenon of people deciding to run for high office first and then scrambling around for some intellectuals to tell them what their positions ought to be"—a phenomenon with which Kissinger was all too familiar.

It was around this time that an important new initiative was taken at Harvard with the formation of the Study Group on Presidential Transition, 1968–69, at the newly established Institute of Politics.[56] The members of the group were Phillip E. Areeda* of the Law School, Kissinger himself, Frank Lindsay of the defense company Itek, and the historian Ernest May, author of an award-winning study of American isolationism before 1917. Their mode of operation was to invite expert guests to Harvard and pick their brains: the roster of speakers in the spring semester of 1968 was General Andrew Goodpaster—the man widely credited with the success of Eisenhower's NSC—McGeorge Bundy, General Matthew Ridgway, and Henry Cabot Lodge; they were followed in the fall by General Lauris Norstad, Adam Yarmolinsky, and Richard Neustadt. Although Kissinger "dropped out" during the late spring to work on Rockefeller's campaign, he was able to "rejoin us later," as Lindsay explained to the man to whom, in the course of 1968, all the study group's reports would be sent—a man he had known since their work together on the Herter Committee twenty years before. That man was Richard Nixon.[57]

IV

The unraveling of Lyndon Johnson's presidency offered the perfect illustration of all that Henry Kissinger and his colleagues were saying was wrong with the American way of government. This is a vitally important point in two respects. First, it helps to identify Nixon's real motive for choosing Kissinger as his national security adviser. Second,

---

*Areeda had been White House assistant special counsel in Eisenhower's second term.

it clarifies that there was not the slightest chance of a quick and easy termination of the Vietnam War in 1968.

For the Hersh-Hitchens case against Kissinger—and indeed the same authors' case against Nixon—to be historically significant, it needs to be shown that (a) the probability of peace in Vietnam was significantly higher in 1968 than it had been the previous year and (b) but for the actions of Kissinger and Nixon, peace would have been concluded. Superficially, it certainly looked as if peace had come closer in 1968. The Tet Offensive did not win the war. The North Vietnamese agreed to enter into negotiations in Paris. But there were three problems. First, the North Vietnamese had not given up hope of achieving outright military victory even as they went to Paris. They continued to fight even as they talked, and indeed they regarded the talks as a new front in the psychological war against the United States. Second, the Johnson administration had not radically altered its approach either. Swayed alternately by doves and hawks, Johnson still itched to extract a meaningful quid pro quo for stopping the bombing and, when Hanoi dragged its feet, itched to "hit them in the nuts." Third and most important, the South Vietnamese had every incentive, if they suspected the United States of selling them down the river, to sabotage the talks. The idea that they were entirely reliant on Richard Nixon for evidence of such a sellout—and for that matter that Nixon was entirely reliant on Kissinger for it—is self-evidently not credible. The existence of the Saigon regime was at stake. Bui Diem's job in Paris was to find out whatever he could about what was going on from every available source—and there were much better sources than the Nixon campaign. But even if Diem had found out nothing, it would still have been easy to guess what was coming. The real significance of Nixon to Saigon was not as a source of intelligence but as a future president. So long as he looked likely to beat Humphrey, they had no need to rush into negotiations, since he was plainly going to be tougher on Hanoi than Johnson. If Humphrey was going to win, the outlook was less bright for South Vietnam but not markedly gloomier than it was under Johnson.

Johnson was not denied peace by Nixon. Johnson was denied peace by Johnson, in that Johnson had failed to break the North Vietnamese regime's resolve. As Kissinger noted in his article on bureaucracy, McNamara—the greatest of the whiz kids—had failed. He was sufficiently aware of the scale of his own failure to commission a huge forty-seven-volume internal Pentagon study on "the background of the Vietnam War": the files that were later leaked to *The New York Times* by Daniel Ellsberg and made famous as the "Pentagon Papers."[58] Before the study was even complete, McNamara had convinced himself that it was time to stop increasing U.S. combat forces, to implement a bombing halt, and to raise South Vietnam's share of the military operations and therefore of the casualties. The true measure of his failure as defense secretary was that he could convince no one else that mattered: not the Joint Chiefs of Staff, who had closed ranks against him, and not the president himself.[59] Though he asked Rostow to run McNamara's proposal past six of his most trusted advisers, Johnson did not even reply to it, much less relay their mostly negative comments.[60] The president's view was that stopping the bombing at this stage—or indeed putting a ceiling on U.S. troop levels—would be "read in both Hanoi and the United States as a sign of weakening will."[61] Peremptorily he announced that McNamara would be moving to the presidency of the World Bank, though with Johnsonian ambiguity he did not specify when.[62]

That the Tet Offensive came as a surprise was one of countless intelligence failures during the Vietnam War. But there was also a strategic failure, symptomized by Westmoreland and Wheeler's request for 206,000 additional men. They had got the better of McNamara; now they would get the better of Johnson by putting the onus on him to refuse the extra troops, thereby giving themselves an alibi for losing the war.[63] Johnson was now in what seemed to him an impossible position. It is important to stress that the hippies and Yippies running amok on campuses were in no way representative of ordinary Americans: this was an era when just over 3 percent of the population was attending university. A poll conducted for Rockefeller in March 1968—after the launch of the Tet Offensive, in other words—made clear how difficult it was for any American politician to abandon the commitment to Saigon. Only 24 percent of voters canvassed favored "discontinu[ing] the struggle to win the war and begin[ning] to pull out of Vietnam gradually in the near future." Nearly the same proportion (25 percent) favored "gradually broaden[ing] and intensify[ing] our military effort," while 28 percent said they would support "an all-out crash effort in the hope of winning the war quickly even at the risk of China or Russia entering the war." Republicans were somewhat more hawkish than Democrats, but 49 percent of Democrats still backed the two escalation options. A staggering 59 percent of voters in their twenties favored escalation. A majority of voters said they were leaning more toward escalation than a year before. Only African American voters overwhelmingly favored peace, with fully 45 percent in favor of "pulling out" altogether. But the key questions were the last ones in the poll. Just under half of respondents answered yes to the question "In view of the developments since we entered the fighting in Vietnam, do you think the U.S. made a mistake sending troops to fight in Vietnam?" And very nearly three-quarters said they expected the war to end not with victory or defeat but with a "compromise peace." Rockefeller's pollster correctly inferred that escalation was favored by a majority of voters "not because a war-like spirit is predominant in the country, but because escalation is seen as one way of getting the war over with as quickly as possible."[64] Yet the one option Johnson and his advisers no longer believed in was further escalation of the sort requested by Westmoreland.

Kissinger's advice to Rockefeller was as before: stake out a new and popular position. Tet had increased the probability of peace talks "before July," he predicted, because of the losses the Vietcong had sustained as their offensive was repulsed. Hanoi would gain from negotiations because—"especially if accompanied by a cease-fire, or even [a] reduction of hostilities"—they would make it difficult for the Saigon government to regain control in the countryside. Rockefeller should take the opportunity to "make some unilateral changes in strategy," explaining to voters how he would "bring about a negotiated solution" that would "move towards winding up the war under honorable conditions."[65] Still Rockefeller hesitated. On March 19 the *Times* reported that his advisers were "deeply divided" over Vietnam, with Gavin and Javits favoring a "moderate dove" stance between Nixon and Robert Kennedy.[66] Nixon, meanwhile, was on the brink of making just the kind of move Kissinger was recommending.

He did not need to. Johnson had decided to take the drastic step he had threatened the year before. Visibly depressed by his new defense secretary Clark Clifford's report, which rejected the military's demand for yet more troops,[67] by a run on the dollar as European banks converted U.S. currency into gold, and by Westmoreland's warning that the Vietcong were about to launch a new offensive against civilians, the president went on television to announce three things: a partial bombing halt (north of the 20th parallel) as an incentive to Hanoi to start peace talks; the appointment of Averell Harriman to conduct negotiations as soon as possible; and his own withdrawal from the presidential contest.[68]

Here was another decision that no one had properly thought through. To the North Vietnamese, here was fresh evidence that "the US must be in great difficulty"—a consoling thought after the failure of Tet. The decision to agree to preliminary discussions was an easy one. Le Duan argued that outright rejection would hurt Hanoi's international image after Johnson's abdication, but that there was no need for substantive discussions; they could continue to argue, as before, that these could begin only after the unconditional cessation of all bombing.[69] As yet another secret initiative (code-named KILLY) was already under way, this time with the Italians as the intermediaries, it was more a matter of making public what was already going on undercover.[70] The South Vietnamese leaders Thieu and Ky, conversely, were appalled at the prospect of a slippery slope leading to American withdrawal. They might have been reassured if they had known how much more the U.S. side planned to ask of the North Vietnamese delegates than they were ever likely to yield. As Rusk put it, "We wanted the North Vietnamese to agree to a cease-fire, accept the South Vietnamese regime at the conference table, negotiate a mutual withdrawal of American and North Vietnamese forces, respect the demilitarized zone, stop attacking South Vietnamese cities, release American prisoners of war, and comply with the Laos Accords of 1962." As he later acknowledged, this was "somewhat naïve." It took weeks to agree even on the location of the talks: Hanoi turned down Geneva, Vienna, New Delhi, Jakarta, and Rangoon. Finally, Rusk proposed Paris. It was agreed, and Harriman prepared to fly to France, along with Cyrus Vance.[71] But those who had tried and failed to broker piece in Paris the year before were not forgotten. "I wanted to tell you," Harriman wrote to Kissinger, "that I believed all your hard work had laid a sound foundation for our discussions that may now take place & to express my profound gratitude."[72]

The choice of Paris in May 1968 as the location for peace negotiations—particularly negotiations with a Communist regime—could scarcely have been worse. Student violence had begun on the outskirts of the city in March, on the ugly concrete campus of the University of Paris X Nanterre, where an absurd argument about male access to female dormitories had somehow become the spark for red revolution. By May the trouble had reached the Sorbonne and therefore the city center. On the night of the fifth there were clashes between cobble-throwing students and truncheon-wielding police in St.-Germain-des-Prés that left the streets strewn with overturned cars and vandalized buses.[73] By May 13, when the students joined forces with the trade unions to proclaim a general strike, Paris appeared on the brink of an authentic French revolution. With dreadful timing, this was also the first day of the Vietnam talks. There were so many red flags on the Sorbonne and the place de la République that the delegation from Hanoi must have felt quite at home. Fortunately, the Hotel Majestic in the avenue Kléber—where the first talks were held—was a good fifteen-minute drive from the principal battleground. Nevertheless, the ambience can scarcely have been conducive to peace talks. Prime Minister Georges Pompidou likened the condition of France to the waning of the Middle Ages in the fifteenth century.[74] Without informing him, de Gaulle fled across the border to Baden-Baden to rally the army behind him. It seemed for a time as if Harriman and Vance had flown into an incipient French civil war.

Predictably, the talks went nowhere. It was the old story. The North Vietnamese wanted an unconditional halt to the bombing. Harriman had been told to get something in return.[75] It was a reenactment of Kissinger's nonmeeting with Mai Van Bo, complete with the obligatory two-phase proposal and a great deal of verbal gymnastics. (Were "circumstances" different from "conditions"?) Talk of de-escalation was in any case rendered absurd by the launch of the second phase of the Tet Offensive on May 4 (it lasted until August 17, to be followed by Phase

III until September 30). We now know that the leadership in Hanoi had no serious intention of reaching an agreement with the Americans and indeed regarded the negotiations as just "a war around a green carpet" until their losses in battle finally began to make a bombing halt seem worth a concession.[76] Bui Diem watched the charade with skepticism, "convinced that nothing of substance would happen."[77] He busied himself by giving interviews. There was nothing else to do but talk to the press. Kissinger called on Harriman on June 23,[78] on his way to Bonn.[79] Unusually, Kissinger apparently made no record of his conversations on this trip to Europe. That may be because the records have been lost or destroyed. Or it may be that there was nothing worth writing down.

In Washington, too, it was the familiar story. Frustrated by the lack of progress, Johnson leaned back to the hawks and began to contemplate increased bombing. Vance and Clifford took the other side. Among the doves, the old vain hope of some kind of Soviet assistance resurfaced. Rostow retaliated by trying to cut the Defense Department out of the Paris cable traffic. Clifford countered by claiming—with no basis whatsoever—that there were "straws in the wind" intimating progress in Paris, to which brazen lie the North Vietnamese negotiators Xuan Thuy and Ha Van Lau not unreasonably objected.[80] On June 26 Vance tried a secret meeting with Lau in a safe house in the suburbs. It made no difference. By mid-July the press was complaining that the public sessions were "two monologues rather than talks" or a "dialogue of the deaf." The most that could be said was, as *The New Republic*'s correspondent put it, that "both sides—like lovers who, though unsuccessful, still possess desire—have a tacit agreement to stick at it despite the apparent barrenness."[81] Meanwhile a desultory trip to Honolulu to meet with Thieu did not sufficiently alert Johnson, Clifford, Rostow, and Rusk to the fact that the leadership in Saigon had no intention of swallowing a disadvantageous deal. Harriman kept wishing Johnson would stop the bombing altogether, a difficult position to sell in Washington as Red Army tanks rolled through the streets of Prague.[82] "We are not going to stop the bombing just to give them a chance to step up their bloodbath," thundered Johnson at the annual convention of the Veterans of Foreign Wars on August 19.[83] Rostow urged him to consider "bombing Cambodia . . . bombing Hanoi-Haiphong, mining Haiphong . . . and [launching] ground attacks north of the DMZ."[84]

On July 17, as if to cheer him up, Kissinger sent Harriman a copy of his newly published Bismarck article.[85] The two had at least one lunch together in Paris that summer, but it is not clear from Kissinger's "belated" thank-you letter when it took place.[86] "All is forgiven," wrote Harriman jestingly on August 9, on hearing the news that Nixon had won the Republican nomination and Kissinger was washing his hands of party politics. "Welcome back into the fold."[87] But aside from suggesting another lunch around September 17, when he would next be in Paris, Kissinger was not in contact with him or any other member of the American delegation in Paris.[88] If he was informed about the private conversations Harriman and Vance had held with Xuan Thuy and the key figure of Le Duc Tho on the fourteenth and fifteenth—when the North Vietnamese finally agreed to allow a South Vietnamese presence at the Paris talks—he kept no record of the fact.[89] The only substantive communication from a U.S. diplomat Kissinger received in this period came from Henry Cabot Lodge, who repeated his tired old line that letting the Vietcong into the government would be like "putting the fox into the chicken coop."[90] But Lodge was writing from the U.S. embassy in Bonn. He, like Kissinger, was now out of the Vietnam loop.

V

There were three reasons Henry Kissinger took no interest in the Paris peace talks. The first and obvious one was that he was not invited to them. The second was that Nancy Maginnes was now back in the United States. And the third was that, from April until August 1968, he was largely preoccupied with Nelson Rockefeller's third bid to become the Republican Party's candidate for president of the United States.

On April 10 *The New York Times* reported that Rockefeller had "hired" Emmet Hughes to be his chief of staff, along with Oscar Ruebhausen, the economist Richard Nathan, and Kissinger on foreign affairs. In other words, he was going to run if, as seemed likely, Rom-

ney could not go the distance.[91] Kissinger was indignant, telling Kraemer (who had teased him about it), "My status is precisely what it has
always been; an outside consultant who determines for himself the
extent of his participation."[92] This was true as far as it went. When the
Times reported that Rockefeller was going to make a dovish Vietnam
speech drafted by Hughes, Kissinger made sure that he was the one
who actually wrote the speech.[93] Again Rockefeller hesitated, delivering instead a speech on urban crises so dull that Hugh Morrow called it
"the biggest bomb since Hiroshima."[94] On April 30, a week after President Johnson had urged him to "abandon his coy stance and become an
active candidate"—if only to keep Nixon out of the White House—
Rockefeller declared his candidacy and promptly won the Massachusetts primary.[95] The next day he delivered a speech entitled "The
Building of a Just World Order" that was vintage Kissinger. He framed
the crisis in Vietnam as part of a generalized crisis of world order due to
the relative decline of the United States both in nuclear and financial
terms; the fragmentation of the Communist world; and the growing
awareness that "the deepest division of our earth may not be between
East and West—but between North and South, between rich and poor."
In this context, it was time for a "sober assessment" of the war in Vietnam. Militarily, the United States had "applied the maxim that victory
depended on control of territory." But the enemy objective in Vietnam
had not been "to seize terrain but to disrupt orderly government. Our
misconception led to open-ended escalation . . . and a stalemate at an
ever-higher level of violence." Meanwhile the South Vietnamese war
effort had become ever more "Americanized." Politically, too, there
had been failure: the pacification effort simply did not give the villagers
of Vietnam adequate security. "From all this," Rockefeller declared,
"the great majority of our people have rationally concluded that there
can be no purely military solution. This seems wholly clear." Admittedly, the long list of proposals that followed contained little that was
new or startling. But the speech did end with a flourish that Nixon
must have recognized as a nod in his direction:

> [W]ith respect to Communist China, we gain nothing, and we
> prove nothing, by aiding or encouraging the self-isolation of

so great a people. Instead, we should encourage contact and communication—for the good of us both.

This could significantly affect the whole future of our relations with the Communist world. *For in a subtle triangle with Communist China and the Soviet Union, we can ultimately improve our relations with each—as we test the will for peace of both.*[96]

The campaign trail had its own indignities. For a man who, less than a year before, had been clandestinely seeking peace in Vietnam in the streets of Montparnasse, the "Candidates Roll Call"—organized by the Massachusetts Junior Council on World Affairs and held at Boston Latin School on May 29—cannot have been very exhilarating.[97] Nevertheless, the appeal to youth was a key part of Rockefeller's strategy, especially after the murder of Bobby Kennedy, and a surprising number of Kennedy supporters rallied to his side, including Martin Luther King's father.[98] Kissinger threw himself enthusiastically into the fray. Conscious that his candidate's campaign had yet to catch fire, Kissinger tried his hand at the dark art of winning votes, proposing a new "popular tag, i.e. along the lines of 'New Deal,' 'Let's Get America Moving Again' [or] 'Great Society.'" The "tag" should simultaneously convey "trust, or integrity; this is aimed at Nixon, whom many people regard as not credible and lacking integrity," and "a new politics of fairness, aimed at the record of the Democratic party." Kissinger knew electoral politics was not his forte ("Other people are no doubt better at this than I am"), but he still threw out "Fair Society" as a possible slogan—a cross between Truman's Fair Deal and Johnson's Great Society. He also suggested a "mass advertisement" that "might lead off with the Santayana quote about those who ignore history being doomed to repeat it"—surely the first time that the Harvard philosopher had been drafted into Republican Party politics.[99]

Not surprisingly perhaps, Kissinger's primary responsibility remained the drafting of Rockefeller's foreign policy speeches. On June 15 he drafted another important one on "Government Organization for the Conduct of Foreign Policy," which set out concrete proposals for improving the decision-making process in Washington. A new Office of International Policy and Programs in the Executive Office of the President should be created to take over the work of the moribund National Security Council staff on long-range planning, coordination, and program evaluation. A new National Security Review Board should also be set up in imitation of the National Intelligence Review Board "to make sure that strategy guides tactics instead of the opposite."[100] And he also mapped out the Rockefellerite platform on foreign policy, building on themes of earlier speeches. Under the changed circumstances of the late 1960s, Kissinger argued, five points needed to be clearly understood:

1. We cannot act as the world's policeman. America should commit itself only when there is a genuine international threat to peace and our own national interest is directly involved.

2. We must carefully measure and allocate our own resources according to well-defined priorities. Our commitments cannot be open-ended, one-sided, and interminable.

3. Before we commit even small forces, all the far-reaching implications of this act must be faced—as they were not faced in Vietnam. We must not find ourselves with a commitment looking for a justification.

4. We must insist that local resources are used to the maximum, and that we support our allies and not substitute for them.

5. We must assure the widest possible international cooperation through the United Nations where possible. Unilateral U.S. intervention should only be a last resort and only in response to overwhelming danger.

As for the Vietnam War—the conduct of which the five points implicitly repudiated—the United States now needed to "achieve an honorable peace" based on the principle that "any group willing to abide by democratic processes should be free to participate in South

Vietnam's political life." In the meantime, the United States should "de-Americanize the war as rapidly as possible."[101]

It will be seen at once how much of this program would subsequently become the policy of the Nixon administration. But it is important to emphasize how committed Kissinger remained at this point to serving not Nixon but Rockefeller—and also how far the two candidates still differed. A case in point is Kissinger's rare (and presumably coauthored)* foray into "foreign economic policy," a speech that explicitly addressed the problem of waning foreign confidence in the dollar and made some distinctly un-Nixonian recommendations. "It cannot be stated too strongly," Rockefeller was supposed to say, "that our success in meeting our fiscal and social problems at home will determine whether we can fill the role of leadership in the free world . . . [as] domestic and international factors are closely integrated." But "the fundamental source of the balance of payments problem" was "inflation," which had led to "a loss of credibility and practices of creeping controllism." The specific remedies he listed were "[a] reduction in public spending, increase in income taxes at least as large as the ten percent surcharge, review of U.S. commitments around the world, and avoidance of further controls and restrictions. These basic steps will allow us to avoid extreme and undesirable acts such as wage and price controls, direct subsidies to U.S. exports, as well as devaluation."

On top of that, Rockefeller was to propose a European-style "value added tax, for part of what is raised through corporate income taxes, [as well as] remitting the tax on exports and applying it on imports."[102] The speech also endorsed the then-fashionable idea of shifting from having the dollar as the world's reserve currency to using the International Monetary Fund's Special Drawing Rights (SDRs).[103] While the case for switching to SDRs was never very strong—the net benefits to the United States of owning the world's reserve currency were to become steadily more obvious in future decades—the remainder of Rockefeller's foreign

---

*Rockefeller's speechwriter Joseph Persico may also have played a part, along with economics adviser Richard Nathan, a Harvard Ph.D. who was then a researcher at the Brookings Institution. However, Nathan's expertise was in domestic economic policy, not in the international issues addressed in this speech.

economic policy compares very favorably with the stagflationary, protectionist, price-fixing mess that was to come under Nixon.

Clearly, there were no votes—or convention delegates—in SDRs, much less in an income tax hike. Everything came down to Vietnam. In 1968 it *was* American foreign policy. On July 13, with the Republican convention just over two weeks away, Rockefeller unveiled his four-stage plan to end the war "within six months or so"—the product, as we have seen, of four years of intermittent internecine warfare between Kissinger and his other advisers. Stage I was to see "a mutual pull-back" of U.S. and North Vietnamese forces and the insertion between them of "an international force of neutral—and largely Asian—nations" as a buffer to enforce a cease-fire. Once the North Vietnamese had withdrawn their troops to their own territory, the United States would begin withdrawing its forces as a "token of good faith." Stage II would see the United States withdraw "the bulk of its forces," leaving only a small number of troops confined to their bases, while an expanded international force would move into the populated areas of the country. If the NLF renounced force, it would be able to participate in politics. Stage III would see free elections under international observation and the departure of the last U.S. troops. Stage IV would see direct negotiation over reunification between the two Vietnamese states, followed by the departure of the international force.[104]

The obvious defect of this plan, which the North Vietnamese were quick to point out, was that it said nothing about when the air campaign against their country would cease. Yet the plan's most bitter critic proved to be Hans Morgenthau, the grand master of foreign policy realism, who savaged it as "the most elaborate attempt to date on the part of supporters of the war to cover their tracks." This cut Kissinger to the quick.[105] But Morgenthau—who had been consistently critical of U.S. policy in Indochina since 1956, and who had paid a price by being fired as a Pentagon consultant in 1965[106]—stuck to his guns:

> Both of you [i.e., Rockefeller and Kissinger] have supported the
> war in public and lent your considerable prestige to it. Both of
> you realize now, as does almost everybody else, that the war

cannot be won and must be liquidated. But it is impossible to do this while maintaining one's original justifications for the war.

The real issue in South Vietnam is, who shall govern, the Communists or the opponents? Both of you have assumed that the Saigon government is the legitimate government of South Vietnam which has been the victim of foreign aggression and internal subversion. . . . [But] the Vietcong have naturally no intention to surrender at the negotiating table what they have been able to defend on the battlefield, that is, the military and political control of a large proportion of the territory of South Vietnam.[107]

Like many commentators who have been vindicated by events, Morgenthau was eager to exclaim "I told you so!" Like many who have not been so prescient, Kissinger was just as eager to remember selectively. "I never supported the war in public," he replied in November 1968—forgetting, among other things, his debate with Michael Foot and Tariq Ali and his article for *Look*.

Before 1963, this was because I did not know enough about it and because I tended to believe the official statements. After the assassination of Diem I thought the situation was hopeless. In 1965 when I first visited Vietnam I became convinced that what we were doing was hopeless. I then decided to work *within* the government to attempt to get the war ended. Whether this was the right decision we will never know, but it was ineffective.

Kissinger added that his view now was "not very different" from Morgenthau's—"though as a practical matter I might try to drag on the process for a while because of the international repercussions."[108] This was not a defense that Morgenthau ever accepted, although we can now see that Kissinger's account of his own thinking about Vietnam, though not of his public statements on the subject, was accurate. The striking point, however, is that the two men could disagree so bitterly over the single biggest foreign policy error of the entire Cold

War. It was not just that Morgenthau had gone public with his criticism,[*] while Kissinger had operated within the corridors of power. Morgenthau had got it right by being a realist, discerning what was wrong with the South Vietnamese regime, why U.S. policy was driving Hanoi and Beijing together despite their historic enmity, and why starveling guerrillas would defeat systems analysis and B-52s. Kissinger had—initially—got it wrong, and he had got it wrong precisely by being an idealist who, for a time, genuinely believed that South Vietnam's right to self-determination was worth American lives.

VI

August is not the best month to visit Miami. On Monday, August 5, 1968—the first day of the Republican National Convention—it was 89 degrees Fahrenheit and oppressively humid, suffocating "like a mattress," as a veteran journalist recalled. William F. Buckley, Jr., was not surprised when Henry Kissinger asked him for a meeting; the editor of the *National Review*—now a national figure thanks to his television show *Firing Line*—knew Kissinger was working for Rockefeller; indeed, the three men had met that spring so that Rockefeller could lecture Buckley about his role in the founding of the United Nations. Matters were now more earnest. "If Rockefeller was nominated" by the convention, Kissinger explained, "he could not possibly win the election if there were substantial defections from the right wing." Buckley's "responsibility," Kissinger argued, "was to demonstrate to American conservatives that the country would be better off with Rockefeller as President, than with a Democratic President."

There is idealism; then there is naïveté. Buckley, with his extensive experience of American domestic politics, could tell one from the other:

---

[*]In an interview for the *San Francisco Chronicle* in March 1965, Morgenthau declared, "If I could use a certain four letter word on this campus, I could sum up our policy in Vietnam."

I twitted him that the question was entirely academic, inasmuch as Nixon was going to be nominated; I told him that if Nixon suddenly disappeared from the face of the earth, Reagan, not Rockefeller, would be nominated; and I told him, further, that Nixon had told me, accurately I believed, that even if he, Nixon, came out in favor of Rockefeller's nomination, the convention would not accept him, that only one man could effect such a nomination, and that was [Barry] Goldwater; and Goldwater had no intention of doing that. And anyway, it was all sewn up for Nixon. Kissinger told me not-to-be-so-sure, but . . . I knew . . . that his contingent operation . . . was either formalistic or—more likely—evidence of his dogged ignorance of American politics.[109]

There was never the remotest chance, as Buckley correctly told Kissinger, that Rockefeller would leave Miami as the Republican nominee. Only four years before, he had been howled down in San Francisco by the Goldwaterites. The conservative backbone of the party had seen nothing in the intervening years to alter their view of Nelson Rockefeller as a privileged philanderer with a penchant for big government. Theodore White was sympathetic to Rockefeller, but he too knew a lost cause when he saw one. Nixon was nominated on the first ballot by 692 votes to 277 votes for Rockefeller and 182 votes for Ronald Reagan, the governor of California and the new darling of the right-wingers. Asked why he thought he had lost, Rockefeller responded acidly, "Did you ever see a Republican convention?" In reality, Miami 1968 was the antithesis of San Francisco 1964. After the mayhem of the Goldwater nomination, the party faithful wanted "caution, quiet, and a winner. Richard Nixon was the One."[110]

Yet in one respect Kissinger and Rockefeller had a meaningful role to play. Unlike Nixon, who had remained carefully noncommittal, they had a plan for Vietnam—and it was clear that Vietnam was going to be the key foreign policy issue in the election, especially if the Paris talks were to spring into life before election day. Clueless he might be about American domestic politics, but Kissinger was the Republican go-to guy on Vietnam, and Nixon knew it.[111] Compared with Kissinger, his own foreign policy adviser, Richard Allen, was a nonentity at best. At the time of the convention, his prediction that the Soviets would invade Czechoslovakia had not yet come true; meanwhile the press was still making fun of the reckless statement he had drafted for Nixon, following the forced landing of an American airliner that had strayed into Soviet airspace, in which the phrase "flying Pueblo" had appeared (an allusion to the USS *Pueblo,* which the North Koreans had seized the previous January).[112]

It is in this context that we should read with skepticism Allen's colorful account of his clandestine meetings with Kissinger in Miami. It was certainly the case that drafts of the Vietnam plank for the party platform were being exchanged in the weekend before the conference. It is highly likely that Allen wished to avoid being seen talking to Kissinger by journalists on the lookout for another Nixon-Rockefeller deal like the 1960 "Compact of Fifth Avenue." There is no reason to disbelieve his entertaining recollection of their being spotted by Robert Novak of the *Chicago Sun-Times* and taking evasive action, only to run into Daniel Schorr of CBS. (As Novak did not recognize Kissinger and Schorr did not recognize Allen—who pretended to be one of Kissinger's students—they got away with it.)[113] But in reality Allen was not a key player—and in any case *The New York Times* had already got the story. The Vietnam plank was the result of a weekend of furious negotiation in room 1083 of the Fontainebleau Hotel—the Rockefeller "command post." On Rockefeller's side were Kissinger, Alton Marshall (another Rockefeller aide), Senator Jacob K. Javits of New York, and the New Jersey congressman Peter Frelinghuysen; on the other side were the Nixon supporters Senator John G. Tower of Texas and Senator Everett Dirksen, who chaired the platform committee and whose initial draft the Rockefellerites had considered unacceptably hawkish. After much wrangling, the result was a compromise that pledged the party to "a program for peace in Vietnam—neither peace at any price nor a camouflaged surrender of legitimate United States or allied interests—but a positive program that will offer a fair and equitable settlement to all based on the principle of self-determination."[114] This contrasted markedly with the equivalent plank of the Democratic Party platform, adopted in the chaos of Chicago in late August, which authorized Humphrey to "stop all bombing of North Vietnam, when this action would not endanger the lives of our troops in the field."

For Kissinger, the compromise at the convention was scant consolation for Nixon's victory. He left Miami in a bitter frame of mind, telling Casper Citron, the New York radio host, "I'm not a Republican. I consider myself an independent. My view was very deeply that Rockefeller was the only candidate at this time who could unite the country." He had, he said, "grave doubts" about Nixon. He was saying similar things to Oscar Ruebhausen and Emmet Hughes. "The man is, of course, a disaster," he told Hughes. "Now the Republican Party is a disaster. Fortunately, he can't be elected—or the whole country would be a disaster." Kissinger's view of Nixon remained as it had been in 1960, when he had declined even to answer Nixon's questions about "Optimum Organization for National Security": "That man is unfit to be president."[115] In this respect, as we have seen, Kissinger shared the conventional wisdom of both Cambridge and Manhattan: Nixon was just disreputable. It therefore seems reasonable to take his August 15 note to Harriman at its face value: "I am through with Republican politics. The party is hopeless and unfit to govern."[116] He said much the same to Daniel Davidson in Paris. "Six days a week I'm for Hubert," he said, "but on the seventh day, I think they're both awful." The idea that all this was a smoke screen to conceal a secret intention to work for Nixon is simply not plausible. On the contrary, Kissinger's first impulse after Miami was to offer his services to Hubert Humphrey. After all, two close and far-from-dovish former colleagues—Samuel Huntington and Zbigniew Brzezinski—were already on Humphrey's team. Visiting Huntington on Martha's Vineyard with his children later in the summer, Kissinger described the Rockefeller file of damaging stories about Nixon, of which he had a copy. "Look, I've hated Nixon for years," Kissinger told Brzezinski.[117] Kissinger's offer of assistance evidently reached the candidate. "Henry Kissinger should be in the White House," Humphrey wrote in his diary on election day. "I hope he'll come. Sam Huntington, too. . . . That Boston bunch is bright. I can understand why John Kennedy used them."[118]

Yet at the same time, we are told by Hersh and others, Kissinger was wooing the Nixon campaign. This, too, is not quite accurate. It was

Allen who invited Kissinger "to serve on Nixon's foreign policy advisory board," an invitation Kissinger declined. The most he would do, according to Allen, was to "provide advice privately . . . than publicly," telling him, "I can help you more if I work behind the scenes."[119] Over lunch Kissinger told Buckley that "he had a few ideas he thought would be interesting to Nixon, in framing his foreign policy campaign speeches," but that this would have to be done "discreetly, as he would not wish it to appear, having just now left the dismantled Rockefeller staff, to be job-seeking." Buckley relayed the offer to Frank Shakespeare at Nixon's new headquarters in the Pierre; Shakespeare passed the name on to John Mitchell. "There was," Buckley added, "no question about the disinterestedness of the advice he sought to convey to Nixon."[120] The evidence that this was indeed the case is a letter from Kissinger to Rockefeller dated August 20, in response to an unspecified offer from Nixon to Rockefeller to bury the hatchet. Kissinger agreed that nothing had "changed in the last two weeks to alter one's views about the candidate's suitability for the Presidency." But Rockefeller had to reflect that "every moderate Republican, including most of your key supporters, have endorsed the ticket." Second, "[t]he next Presidency is likely to be tragic. Nothing suggests that any of the prospective candidates can unify the country or restore America's position in the world. The next four years are likely to witness mounting crises—disorder at home, increasing tension abroad."

Under these circumstances, Rockefeller's priority must be to "preserve" himself as a "national asset who has stood for a large, humane, forward-looking, program throughout his public life." Of course, he should not allow himself to become "simply an instrument of Nixon." Nor, on the other hand, should he "appear as a quarrelsome loser who can be blamed for a defeat." Should Rockefeller ask as a condition of support that Nixon "renounce Senator Thurmond and the Southern strategy"—the play for southern votes that had led Nixon to heed the segregationist Thurmond's preference for Governor Spiro Agnew as the vice-presidential nominee? Kissinger advised against this, as it would lead Rockefeller down a political dead end. Instead, he "strongly recommend[ed] that, rather than wait for Nixon to take the lead," Rockefeller should say that he was "prepared strongly to campaign for the platform" to which he and his staff had made "a major contribution." In a covering note, Kissinger added, "The attached memorandum goes against my grain but I believe strongly that it is right." If Rockefeller decided to campaign for Nixon, Kissinger would stand ready to assist him. "I need not tell you," he concluded, "that our feelings will be quite similar."[121] It is against the background of this letter that we should understand Kissinger's subsequent dealings with the Nixon campaign. He and Rockefeller had taken a decision to hold their noses and back Nixon because they had effected enough of a change to the Republican platform to believe in it—and to believe, in Kissinger's words, that "only the Republican ticket can implement it." They may even have begun to contemplate that Rockefeller might accept a cabinet-level post if Nixon beat Humphrey.

No records survive* in Kissinger's hand of his September trip to Paris, from where he sent the intelligence that there was "a better than even chance that Johnson will order a bombing halt at approximately mid-October."[122] This quotation originates in a report from Haldeman dated September 17, which refers only to a "top diplomatic source who is secretly with us and has access to the Paris talks and other information.

> Our source feels that there is a better than even chance that Johnson will order a bombing halt at approximately mid-October. This will be tied in with a big flurry of diplomatic activity in Paris which will have no meaning but will be made to look important.
>
> He feels also there is a one-third likelihood of movement by LBJ before the election on the program that was discussed with RN at the ranch. In the European area, the Russians are pushing hard to get Johnson into some program that will help the Russian world image and our source thinks Johnson will fall for this. It would relate to the Mid-East situation and to the disarmament program. . . .

---

*It is of course conceivable that Kissinger subsequently destroyed or simply did not record evidence of his activities.

Our source feels Johnson has a compulsion to do some such thing and that he will do it. He thinks this may have some relation to the [George] Ball resignation which might have been done to give Johnson a chance to appear personally to be directing our efforts at the UN.

Our source does not believe that it is practical to oppose a bombing halt but does feel thought should be given to the fact that it may happen—that we may want to anticipate it—and that we certainly will want to be ready at the time it does happen.

He seriously questions whether Nixon and Agnew are actually getting anywhere near the briefing that they should have. (He also feels Humphrey is not being thoroughly briefed either although Ball may have considerable information for him.)

He says the Russians are now much more flexible on the Mid-East and are eager to get out the word that they are willing to move on disarmament.

Our source is extremely concerned about the moves Johnson may take and expects that he will take some before the election.[123]

Haldeman's source was surely Kissinger, with Mitchell as the likely intermediary. But the crucial point is that none of this was intelligence leaked from a member of Harriman's delegation in Paris. It was analysis of the sort Kissinger excelled at, and it was—as its source did not hesitate to point out—better than anything Nixon was getting from Allen or anyone else. As Kissinger later reminded Bob Haldeman, "I wasn't in on the discussions. . . . I just saw the instructions to Harriman"—presumably the ones the ambassador had been given by Johnson with his latest list of corollaries for a bombing halt, the details of which Kissinger did not divulge.[124] The other point to note is that Kissinger was only one of numerous outside sources Nixon was now tapping in a desperate effort to avoid being stymied by the October surprise he knew Johnson was plotting.

It is possible to argue that Nixon should not have been in touch with the South Vietnamese representative at the Paris peace talks, Bui

Diem, whom he met in New York on July 12.[125] It is also possible to question the wisdom of using the energetic if unsubtle "Dragon Lady" Anna Chennault* as a go-between.[126] Certainly, Nixon wanted Saigon to know that his position would be tougher than Humphrey's. But any reader of *The New York Times* could have found that out. It is hard to see that the NSA found anything incriminating or indeed surprising in Diem's cables to Saigon.[127] Also keeping Nixon abreast of developments were former CIA director John McCone,[128] Senator Dirksen,[129] Dean Rusk,[130] and even Lyndon Johnson himself, who called all three candidates on October 16.[131] What is clear is that, with all the information that was reaching him—not least Johnson's announcement of a breakthrough on the sixteenth—Nixon was not heavily reliant on Kissinger's insights from Paris.

In some ways the sequence of events was predictable without inside information. First, Humphrey moved to the left, offering to take "an acceptable risk for peace" by stopping the bombing of the North in return for nothing more than "evidence—direct or indirect, by deed or word—of Communist willingness to restore the demilitarized zone."[132] By October he was talking about a "systematic reduction of the American forces" in South Vietnam, again on a more or less unilateral basis.[133] True, Johnson was deeply ambivalent about Humphrey as a candidate.[134] However, as Humphrey began to gain on Nixon, Johnson's loyalty to his own party kicked in—not to mention his compulsion to play domestic politics with all foreign policy issues.[135] Also predictable was the mounting anxiety of Thieu and Ky as Humphrey simultaneously became more dovish and more popular, and the pressure from Washington grew on them to make concessions to help his cause.[136] Less predictable was what was going on in Hanoi. The decision on the part of the North Vietnamese to agree to Harriman's "our-side, your-side" formula—whereby, if the bombing stopped, the South Vietnamese (along with the NLF) would be admitted to expanded talks—was

---

*Chennault, née Chan, was the widow of General Claire Chennault, leader of the "Flying Tigers," a volunteer air force that fought on the Chinese nationalist side in World War II. Madame Chennault had close links to Chiang Kai-shek's regime in Taiwan. She was cochair, along with Mamie Eisenhower, of Republican Women for Nixon.

meaningful and reflected the pressure they were under in the battle-field and from their Soviet suppliers.[137] But did it really portend peace?

It was the president who was playing political offense; Nixon was on the defensive. Everyone in the White House knew it, as the lunch-time badinage on Tuesday, October 22, makes clear:

> THE PRESIDENT: Nixon will ask me if this isn't like put-ting a fox in the chicken coop. [Laughter].
>
> SECRETARY CLIFFORD: It seems Thieu gains enormously to have the GVN at the Table.
>
> THE PRESIDENT: We do, in effect, recognize them [the NLF] by letting them sit down with us.
>
> SECRETARY RUSK: It's about [sc. a bit] like letting Stokely Carmichael [the Black Panther leader] sit at [a] Cabinet meeting.
>
> SECRETARY CLIFFORD: It still seems like greater benefit than detriment.
>
> THE PRESIDENT: Factually, that's correct.
>
> SECRETARY RUSK: Emotionally, that's not correct.
>
> WALT ROSTOW: The South Vietnamese are afraid of how we play them in Conference—push them toward accepting a slippery slope—jam [them] into [a] coali-tion government.[138]

The locker room tone spoke volumes. Nixon was of course fighting dirty four days later when he implied (by saying he did "not believe" it) that Johnson was making a "cynical, last-minute attempt . . . to salvage the candidacy of Mr. Humphrey."[139] But the evidence is unambiguous that Johnson was doing exactly that. Moreover, Johnson thought noth-ing of authorizing the FBI to spy on and wiretap Chennault.[140] Equally clear is that the North Vietnamese concession was just another gambit; they had in no way abandoned their goal of annexing South Vietnam and crushing the non-Communist elements in that country. Would a lasting peace deal have been concluded if Nixon had just sat and watched? The answer must be no, for Thieu would surely have thrown a monkey wrench into the works even if he had received no tip-off from the Nixon camp via Chennault. Would it have made a difference if *The Christian Science Monitor* had run its correspondent Beverly Deepe's story that Thieu had decided to wait for the Nixon presidency?[141] Probably not. It was an open secret on Wall Street that Nixon was "trying to frustrate the President, by inciting Saigon to step up its demands, and by letting Hanoi know that when he took office 'he could accept anything and blame it on his predecessor.'"[142] Ky told it to Ellsworth Bunker, the new ambassador in Saigon, like it was: "Although the U.S. wants a bombing halt in the interest of the number of votes for Vice President Humphrey, it is impossible without the concurrence of the [redacted—South?] Vietnamese government, and there cannot be the ruination of [redacted] person for the sake of one person."[143]

In his television address on the night of October 31, Johnson told the American public exactly what a substantial proportion of voters wanted to hear: that the U.S. bombing of North Vietnam would stop immediately and that serious talks, in which Saigon would be "free to participate," would start the day after the election.[144] That same day, before the address had even gone out, Thieu had made clear to Bunker that he would not go along with the plan; on November 2 he gave the same defiant message to the South Vietnamese National Assembly, to rapturous applause.[145] Johnson's own defense secretary acknowledged that Saigon had at least five incentives "not . . . to move."[146] His own secretary of state conceded that "Thieu had every right to be suspicious of Hanoi's purposes in the Paris talks."[147] He also had every right to be suspicious of Lyndon Johnson. Thieu did not need Spiro Agnew or John Mitchell to tell Anna Chennault to tell Diem to tell him to "hold on."[148] Nor was Johnson justified in accusing the Nixon campaign of "treason," as he did on November 2.[149] That was what made the telephone conversation between the two men on November 3 so hilarious. It was like a game of poker in which the chips were lies:

> NIXON: [M]y God, I would *never* do anything to encourage Hanoi—I mean Saigon not to come to the table. . . .
> JOHNSON: Well, I'll tell you what I say I say it doesn't help—doesn't affect the election one way or the other—
> NIXON: I don't think it does.

JOHNSON: . . . I don't think it'll change one vote.

NIXON: Well, anyway, we'll have fun [laughs].

JOHNSON: Thank you, Dick.

NIXON: Bye.[150]

The idea that if Johnson had revealed his knowledge of Chennault's activities, Humphrey might have won in a wave of public revulsion at Nixon's skullduggery is not plausible, precisely because Johnson would simultaneously have been revealing his own skullduggery.[151] As Rusk put it, "we get information like this every day, some of it very damaging to American political figures. We have always taken the view that with respect to such sources there is no public 'right to know.' Such information is collected simply for the purposes of national security . . . [and] even if the story breaks, it was . . . too late to have a significant impact on the election."[152] As Chennault later ruefully acknowledged, "Politics is a very cruel game." No sooner had Nixon won the election than he all but repudiated her.[153] By the time *The Boston Globe* broke the story in January 1969, nobody cared.[154] When the subject later resurfaced in the White House, the suggestion was that Nixon could blackmail Johnson with evidence that he had "used the bombing halt for political purposes."[155] When the Watergate scandal began to look dangerous for Nixon, his first thought was to expose the evidence that Johnson had done "the bugging on us in '68."[156]

VII

In the battle of the bad guys, Nixon won. But he did not win the 1968 election because Henry Kissinger betrayed classified information about the Paris talks. Nor did he win because Anna Chennault—of whom, it might be added, Kissinger knew nothing—encouraged Nguyen Van Thieu to boycott those same talks. Nixon won, as we shall see, partly for the same reason that Georges Pompidou won the June election in France and de Gaulle was able to return to Paris and, a year later, to a dignified retirement at Colombey-les-Deux-Églises; for the same reason that, in December, Mao decided to rein in the Red Guards by sending a generation of Chinese students "down to the countryside." All over the world, as if by some law of political physics, the violent actions of the young in 1968 generated equal and opposite reactions. It was in the context of that reaction that Henry Kissinger found himself named, before the year was out, as Richard Nixon's national security adviser. We can see now that this appointment had nothing to do with mythical leaks from Paris. Yet Nixon's choice of Kissinger—and Kissinger's decision to accept—still requires some explanation. After all, as we have seen, there had been no love lost between these two men, infrequently though their paths had crossed. It was, as Nixon himself acknowledged, an unlikely combination. Indeed, as recently as the time of the Republican convention in Miami, few scenarios would have struck Kissinger himself as less likely. His own extraordinary bildungsroman—the forty-five-year-long story of his personal, philosophical, and political education—ended with a true twist in the tale.

CHAPTER 22

The Unlikely Combination

> You have to know what history is relevant. You have to
> know what history to extract.
> —HENRY KISSINGER, September 1968[1]

I

By 1968 Henry Kissinger knew better than most the difference between public intellectual and government official, between outsider and insider. Had he anticipated appointment to high office in a Nixon administration, it seems unlikely that he would have written two controversial articles certain to be published in the highly sensitive period of transition from one administration to the next.

The first was a wide-ranging essay entitled "Central Issues of American Foreign Policy," published by the Brookings Institution in December 1968, an article that inevitably came to be read as a manifesto for the Nixon administration's foreign policy.* The Economist noted superciliously that the author's "yearning for philosophical order" would soon pass once he set to work "grappling with the immediate."[2] It was in fact more retrospective than prospective, and its content strongly suggests that he can have had no idea when he wrote the piece that he would be appointed national security adviser within three weeks of its publication.

---

*The least interesting parts of the essay were the prescriptive sections calling, wearily, for "a new look at American national security policy," burden-sharing between the United States and the other members of NATO, and the "overriding need for a common [transatlantic] political conception." Kissinger had been saying such things for years.

Writing in 1968, Kissinger could hardly overlook "the contemporary unrest," and he began by offering the arresting thought that, while it was "less apocalyptic than the two world wars which spawned it," the crisis of the late 1960s was "even more profoundly revolutionary in nature." By this Kissinger did not intend to compliment the student radicals of the time, however. On the contrary, he took the opportunity to direct some well-aimed barbs at "the younger generation [who] consider the management of power irrelevant, perhaps even immoral," and whose "new ethic of freedom is not 'civic'; it is indifferent or even hostile to systems and notions of order." As Kissinger observed, there was something unforgivable about the way the "protest movements [had] made heroes of leaders in repressive new countries," oblivious to "the absurdity of founding a claim for freedom on protagonists of the totalitarian state—such as Guevara or Ho or Mao." But theirs was not the revolution he had in mind. Rather, reverting to themes he had first discussed in *A World Restored,* he meant the revolutionary challenge that was being mounted against the postwar international order, based as it had been since the late 1940s on a bipolar division of the world between the United States and the Soviet Union. "The age of the superpowers," Kissinger announced, "is drawing to an end." This represented a revolution as profound as the French Revolution. And, just as in the 1790s and 1800s, the revolution had created a desperate need for "an agreed concept of order" because, without that, the "awesome available power" was "unrestrained by any consensus as to legitimacy." In particular, there was a chronic "problem of political legitimacy . . . in regions containing two-thirds of the world's population."[3] The third world's wars might look like civil wars. But their sheer number and violence were making international order impossible.

A striking feature of Kissinger's analysis was that the revolution he discerned was impersonal in nature. Far from being the work of "Guevara or Ho or Mao," its causes were "deep-seated" and "structural" trends. The first of these was what was already occasionally referred to as globalization: the multiplication of nation-states since the breakup of the European empires, combined with the unprecedented economic integration of the postwar era of trade liberalization and container ships, and the emergence of new problems faced by "all modern states . . . problems of bureaucratization, pollution, environmental control, urban growth . . . [that] know no national considerations.'[4]

The second was the tension between the multipolarity of the post-colonial world and the rigid military bipolarity of the Cold War, combined with the "gargantuan" increase in destructive power made possible by innovations in nuclear technology, which paradoxically tended to reduce the superpowers' influence over smaller countries. This was not only because the superpowers seemed less and less likely ever to use their vast atomic arsenals; it was also because each new power that joined the nuclear club substantially reduced the value of membership. (The new Non-Proliferation Treaty might turn out to work, but then again it might be too transparently a superpower cartel.) In this post-superpower world, "a radio transmitter [could] be a more effective form of pressure than a squadron of B-52s," while annexing territory counted for less than acquiring nuclear weapons.[5] In any case, nuclear deterrence itself was losing its credibility.

> Deterrence is tested negatively by things which do *not* happen. But it is never possible to demonstrate *why* something has not occurred. Is it because we are pursuing the best possible policy or only a marginally effective one? . . . The longer peace is maintained—or the more successful deterrence is—the more it furnishes arguments for those who are opposed to the very premises of defense policy. Perhaps there was no need for preparedness in the first place.[6]

Because people are always reluctant to think counterfactually—to consider the importance of the things that do not happen—it was getting easier every day to talk about "banning the bomb," especially if the bombs kept getting more destructive. The longer the "long peace" between the superpowers lasted, the less their citizens understood their debt to the balance of terror.

This was the world the thirty-seventh president of the United States would inherit—a president who, if he secured reelection in 1972, could expect to be in the White House as the republic celebrated the bicentennial of its birth. Kissinger offered his fellow citizens no facile solutions. He merely urged them to answer two simple questions: "What is it in our interest to prevent? What should we seek to accomplish?" If the Vietnam War had done nothing else that was good, it had at least proved that the answer to these questions could not be "Everything"—for a United States that was "the trustee of every non-Communist area" would very soon "exhaust its psychological resources." Nor, however, could the answers to Kissinger's questions be "Nothing." Generation gap or no generation gap, it was time for "the American mood" to stop "oscillat[ing] dangerously between being ashamed of power and expecting too much of it."[7]

All this helps us begin to understand why it was that Richard Nixon chose Henry Kissinger to be his national security adviser. It was not, as his perennial graduate student Guido Goldman* once joked, because "Henry was the only thing of Nelson's that Nixon could afford."[8]

II

If Kissinger had been remotely aware in the fall of 1968 that, if elected, Nixon might invite him to join his administration, it seems equally unlikely that he would have written another classic article, "The Viet Nam Negotiations," which appeared in *Foreign Affairs* in the very month of Nixon's inauguration, and which must therefore have been written at around the time of the presidential election. Indeed, when he realized that Nixon wanted him in the White House, Kissinger tried vainly to stop the article's publication, for the obvious reason that it, too, would be seized upon as a blueprint for policy.[9] In fact the article had the unanticipated effect of validating Nixon's judgment. For it proved to be one of the most brilliant analyses of the American predicament in Vietnam that anyone has ever written.[10]

Written with a brio Kissinger had seldom achieved since the publication of *A World Restored*, the article began by defining what he called

---

*At that time Goldman was running the German Research Program at CFIA, as well as the Kennedy School's German Program. "How long have you been a graduate student?" asked Kissinger one day. Goldman replied that he was in his ninth year. "No graduate student of mine," retorted Kissinger, "goes into double figures."

"the Vietnamese syndrome: optimism alternating with bewilderment; euphoria giving way to frustration," based on the fundamental problem that "military successes . . . could not be translated into permanent political advantage."[11] Why was this? Partly, he acknowledged, it was because of a "vast gulf" in cultural terms: "It would be difficult to imagine two societies less meant to understand each other than the Vietnamese and the American."[12] But mainly it was because American strategy had all along been misconceived. From the outset of military intervention under Kennedy—as Morgenthau had seen, but he had missed—there had been a "failure . . . to analyze adequately the geopolitical importance of Viet Nam," by which Kissinger subtly implied its relative unimportance.[13] Then there was the fundamental problem that the American military had sought to wage a conventional war against guerrillas, following "the classic doctrine that victory depended on a combination of control of territory and attrition of the opponent." The generals had reasoned that defeating the Vietcong's "main forces would cause the guerrillas to wither on the vine." They would achieve victory by "inflicting casualties substantially greater than those we suffered until Hanoi's losses became 'unacceptable.'" But this strategy was doubly flawed. First, it misunderstood the nature of guerrilla warfare:

> Guerrillas rarely seek to hold real estate; their tactic is to use terror and intimidation to discourage cooperation with constituted authority. . . . Saigon controlled much of the country in the daytime . . . the Viet Cong dominated a large part of the same population at night. . . . The guerrillas' aim was largely negative: to prevent the consolidation of governmental authority. . . .
>
> We fought a military war; our opponents fought a political one. We sought physical attrition; our opponents aimed for our psychological exhaustion. In the process, we lost sight of one of the cardinal maxims of guerrilla war: the guerrilla wins if he does not lose. The conventional army loses if it does not win. The North Vietnamese used their main forces the way a bullfighter uses his cape—to keep us lunging in areas of marginal political importance.[14]

Second, the "kill-ratios" of U.S. to North Vietnamese casualties, while pleasing to the systems analysts in the Pentagon, were "unreliable indicators. Even when the figures were accurate they were irrelevant, because the level of what was 'unacceptable' to Americans fighting thousands of miles from home turned out to be much lower than that of Hanoi fighting on Vietnamese soil."[15]

The line about guerrillas winning if they do not lose has justly become one of Kissinger's most quoted. But his article made an equally telling point about the nature of American assistance to South Vietnam that repeated a point he had made often enough in the past: economics is not everything.

> In Viet Nam—as in most developing countries—the overwhelming problem is not to buttress but to develop a political framework. Economic progress that undermines the existing patterns of obligation—which are generally personal or feudal—serves to accentuate the need for political institutions. One ironic aspect of the war in Viet Nam is that, while we profess an idealistic philosophy, our failures have been due to an excessive reliance on material factors. The communists, by contrast, holding to a materialistic interpretation, owe many of their successes to their ability to supply an answer to the question of the nature and foundation of political authority.[16]

Kissinger also exposed the principal defect of American diplomacy, showing how "our diplomacy and our strategy were conducted in isolation from each other"—Johnson's mal-coordinated left and right fists in the prizefight of his imagination. Hanoi, by contrast, did not "view war and negotiation as separate processes." Misunderstanding that war and diplomacy form part of a continuum, the president had made multiple unforced errors. First, Johnson "had announced repeatedly that we would be ready to negotiate, unconditionally, at any moment, anywhere. This, in effect, left the timing of negotiations to the other side." Then he had got sucked into point-scoring: "Hanoi announced Four Points, the NLF put forth Five Points, Saigon advanced Seven Points and the United States—perhaps due to its larger bureaucracy—promulgated Fourteen," as if lengthening the agenda for talks would somehow help get them started. Third, in putting out his peace feelers, Johnson had failed to anticipate how the North Vietnamese would coquette with him—"many contacts with Hanoi which seemed 'abortive' to us, probably served (from Hanoi's point of view) the function of defining the terrain."[17] Fourth, the United States had failed—partly for its own systemic reasons—to formulate a coherent negotiating position. "Pragmatism and bureaucracy," as Kissinger put it, had "combine[d] to produce a diplomatic style marked by rigidity in advance of formal negotiations and excessive reliance on tactical considerations once negotiations start." Americans prepared for talks by engraving preconditions in stone; but as soon as they sat down at the conference table, they began splitting the difference. Fifth, Johnson had simply been too unsubtle to appreciate the significance of changes of tense and mood in Hanoi's communications (the unhappy memory of "waiting for Godot" in Paris was still fresh). Sixth, Johnson had agreed to suspend the bombing of North Vietnam on a condition—never accepted by Hanoi—that the talks would be productive. But if they were not, could bombing actually be resumed without a domestic political uproar? Finally, by bringing Saigon into the talks, Johnson had inadvertently exposed "the potential conflict of interest between Washington and Saigon," a new weakness for his foes to exploit.

What now? Kissinger ruled out unequivocally a unilateral withdrawal, using terms that would define the next four years of American foreign policy:

> [T]he commitment of 500,000 Americans has settled the issue of the importance of Viet Nam. For what is involved now is confidence in American promises. However fashionable it is to ridicule the terms "credibility" or "prestige," they are not empty phrases; other nations can gear their actions to ours only if they can count on our steadiness. The collapse of the American effort in Viet Nam would not mollify many critics; most of them would simply add the charge of unreliability to the accusation of bad judgment. Those whose safety or national goals depend on American commitments could only be dismayed. In many parts of the world—the Middle East, Europe, Latin America, even

Japan—stability depends on confidence in American promises. Unilateral withdrawal, or a settlement which unintentionally amounts to the same thing, could therefore lead to the erosion of restraints and to an even more dangerous international situation. No American policymaker can simply dismiss these dangers.[18]

One can readily imagine the joy with which those words were read in Saigon—though it must also be recognized that they were read with considerable enthusiasm in Japan, South Korea, and Taiwan, too, as well as in Israel and at least some quarters in West Germany.* This much, then, was clear: Kissinger would not cut and run. He also indicated that he would favor bilateral negotiations rather than involving the NLF and Saigon (to keep the vexed question of South Vietnam's political future off the agenda); that he would not agree to a cease-fire that, given the "crazy quilt" of current territorial holdings, would "predetermine the ultimate settlement and tend toward partition"; and that he would not be "party to an attempt to impose a coalition government" including the NLF on Saigon, as this would likely "destroy the existing political structure of South Viet Nam and thus lead to a communist takeover."[19] He did, on the other hand, favor a "staged withdrawal of external forces, North Vietnamese and American"—a position that he had already set out for Nelson Rockefeller the previous July. He at least implied that he would be reluctant to resume bombing. And he also repeated Rockefeller's recommendation for "an international presence to enforce good faith" in South Vietnam as well as an "international force . . . to supervise access routes" into the country, ideally equipped with "an electronic barrier to check movements" across its borders (McNamara's old and characteristically technocratic fantasy).

The most positive recommendation Kissinger made, however, was to step back and locate the Vietnamese negotiations in their broader context, taking account of the world's other crises in the Middle East and Eastern Europe. Here there were at least some grounds for hope:

---

*Whether there was any real merit in the credibility argument will be among the questions addressed in volume 2.

"[T]he Soviet doctrine according to which Moscow has a right to intervene to protect socialist domestic structures [has] made a Sino-Soviet war at least conceivable. For Moscow's accusations against Peking have been, if anything, even sharper than those against Prague. But in case of a Sino-Soviet conflict, Hanoi would be left high and dry." The fact that hostilities broke out along the Ussuri River within just two months did much to confirm the strategic direction Kissinger and Nixon would take. "However we got into Viet Nam, whatever the judgment of our actions," Kissinger concluded, "ending the war honorably is essential for the peace of the world. Any other solution may unloose forces that would complicate prospects of international order. A new Administration must be given the benefit of the doubt."[20] Kissinger little realized as he wrote those words that he was requesting that benefit for himself.

"The Viet Nam Negotiations" is arguably the most penetrating article Kissinger ever wrote. Subsequent events would determine how far what he proposed would suffice to achieve the honorable peace* he sought. Yet it would be a mistake to assume that Henry Kissinger's main preoccupation in 1968 was with Vietnam. Rather, as is abundantly clear from his own papers, it was with improving the process of decision-making in Washington. Kissinger's insight, after nearly three years of trying to understand and somehow resolve the Vietnam imbroglio, was that the United States was in a mess because of fundamental defects of the system of formulating and executing national security strategy. This was the true focus of his energies in late 1968, and—even more than his perceptive thinking about Vietnam, and far more than his "yearning for philosophical [world] order"—it provides the key to his appointment by Nixon.

---

*The allusion was probably to Benjamin Disraeli, who used the phrase "peace I hope with honor" in a speech on July 27, 1878, following his triumphant return from the Congress of Berlin, where he had not only averted war with Russia but had largely reversed the gains Russia had made from its attack on the Ottoman Empire and acquired Cyprus for the British Empire into the bargain. It is doubtful that Kissinger intended to evoke Chamberlain's use of the phrase after Munich; it is also doubtful that he knew of Edmund Burke's use of it in his pro-American speech of 1775. Its first use in English is in fact in Shakespeare's *Coriolanus*, act 3, scene 2.

III

Richard Nixon's election victory in November 1968 was due less to his machinations around the Paris peace talks than to the fundamental rift within the Democratic Party created by Johnson's push to enact civil rights at maximum speed. It was indeed a close race—Humphrey won Pennsylvania, Michigan, New York, and Connecticut by more votes than expected, and Nixon's margin of victory in the popular vote was just 0.7 percent. Nixon did not appear in the ballroom of the Waldorf Astoria to claim victory until twelve-thirty in the afternoon on November 6, half an hour after Humphrey had conceded defeat.[21] The key was the forty-five Electoral College votes won by the segregationist candidate George Wallace, most of which would surely have gone to the Democratic candidate had it not been for the civil rights split. As it was, the Democrats retained their control of both houses of Congress, making Nixon the first president not to carry at least one of them since Zachary Taylor in 1848; the Democrats also retained their dominance of state legislatures.

What had happened between 1964 and 1968 was one of the biggest reshapings of the voting landscape in American history. Though generational conflict was a factor, race was the key. Among whites who voted in both elections, fully one-third switched party. Around one Goldwater voter out of every five turned either to Humphrey or to Wallace in 1968, with Wallace taking three-quarters of them; at the same time, three out of every ten white Johnson voters in 1964 switched to Nixon or Wallace in 1968, with Nixon securing the votes of four-fifths of them. An astonishing two-fifths of Nixon's votes came from citizens who had supported Johnson in 1964. Fully 97 percent of black voters cast their ballots for Humphrey, while fewer than 35 percent of white voters did.[22] Vietnam's significance was that, especially since Martin Luther King's interventions on the subject, not to mention those of Stokely Carmichael, "Hell no—we won't go!" had become a succinct response to the disproportionate drafting of African Americans. The converse position was that of Wallace's running mate, General

Curtis LeMay, the former chief of Strategic Air Command, who would gladly have ended the Vietnam War by dropping an atomic bomb on Hanoi. It was Wallace, not Nixon, who defeated Humphrey, securing 13.5 percent of the popular vote and actually winning in five southern states—fewer than he had hoped for, but enough to determine the outcome.[23]

This meant that Richard Nixon entered the White House an exceptionally weak president, doomed to spend a minimum of two years with a hostile Congress at the other end of Pennsylvania Avenue, as well as an alienated African American community in the nation's big cities. It was fortunate for him, therefore, that a small group of Harvard professors had been working since August to ensure that he had the smoothest transition into office of any president in history. A member of that group was Henry Kissinger.

As we have seen, Kissinger had been one of the founding members, along with Phillip Areeda, Frank Lindsay, and Ernest May, of the Harvard Study Group on Presidential Transition. Kissinger had dropped out temporarily to assist Nelson Rockefeller's campaign, but after his candidate's defeat in Miami, he could rejoin the group, which was now tailoring its research ever more carefully to meet Nixon's needs. On August 15, 1968, Lindsay wrote directly to the Republican nominee, offering to make available to him all the study group's findings on past transitions, its recommendations on how best to proceed, and perhaps also some "names (especially of younger men)" whom Nixon might consider as appointees. As Lindsay pointed out, if Nixon won the election, he would have just ten weeks until his inauguration to fill around two dozen of the most important posts in his administration—far less time than would be typical for a business or even a university engaged in an analogous search for executive talent. He should therefore consider appointing, with immediate effect, a personnel adviser to begin drawing up the list of potential hires; he should also consider commissioning "substantive studies on issues which may be in crisis" in the first phase of his administration. He should appoint a screening committee to draw up shortlists for the key jobs and encourage its members to look beyond the political class to foundations, universities, and investment banks. Rather than interview candidates, he should use seminars to see how well they performed in a group setting. And his goal should be to have all the key positions filled by mid-December.

But what *were* the key positions? The study group's August report listed three staff jobs that Nixon should prioritize: appointments secretary, press secretary, and the post of "national security liaison and advice—a role similar to that played by Rostow for Johnson, Bundy for Kennedy and Gray and Goodpaster for Eisenhower."[24] In filling this third post, Nixon should bear in mind the potential for friction between this individual and the State Department: in the words of the report, "the lack of confidence, communication and team-spirit at the top level of the Kennedy-Johnson State Department is not a happy precedent."[25] The future president would need to make a choice, even before he was elected, as to who would be his "principal adviser on all foreign policy problems, including military, financial and economic policy." Would it be the secretary of state, or would it be the national security adviser? "This decision," the authors noted, "will affect both the qualities you will seek in a Secretary, and the breadth of the charter you will assign to the National Security Adviser on your staff."[26] Without stating flatly that it should be the latter, the study group made it perfectly clear that they saw the State Department as the wrong institution for this broader role because of its "perennial organizational problems," which in the past had "prevented it from being as useful to the President as it might be."[27]

Nor was this all. Two months later Lindsay followed this up with a long report on "Dealing with the Old Administration," which reinforced the argument for a strong national security adviser. "One of your most difficult and critical problems during the transition," the group's next report told Nixon, "will be the gaining of mastery (insofar as mastery is possible) over national security affairs." He must make sure no "eyes only" files relating to negotiations with the North Vietnamese vanished out the door of the White House in Lyndon Johnson's luggage. And he must make haste: "Unlike McGeorge Bundy [under Kennedy] . . . your national security staff should be appointed early and begin performance as soon as possible."[28] It is conceivable, of course, that Kissinger had himself in mind as he and his colleagues drafted these lines for Nixon. But it seems more likely that he was offering impartial advice on the basis of past experience.

On November 1, with just four days to go before the nation voted, the study group sent a third report specifically focused on transitional organization in the area of national security. Unlike the first reports, this one bore Kissinger's name, as well as his metaphorical fingerprints. The study group assumed Nixon would be his "own Secretary of State in the sense of retaining control over policy," leaving whomever he appointed to "mobilize and manage the diplomatic corps and related groups." He should aim to "preserve [the] centralized control of the military establishment" that had been Robert McNamara's principal achievement, keeping the tight budgetary control that McNamara had established through the Office of the Secretary of Defense. Nixon did not need to worry about the CIA, which was "comparatively efficient." The one institution that presented "an immediate problem for your administration" was—once again—the State Department, which was "ineffectual as compared with CIA [or] Defense" and seemed to excel only in generating a "stupefying . . . flow of written matter." When the study group recommended that Nixon "strengthen the Secretary of State," they meant strengthening him relative to the State Department, for example by making the secretary "interchangeable" with the under-secretary of state and empowering them both to appoint not only the assistant secretaries but also key ambassadors, to give them some lever-age over the career diplomats and desk officers.[29]

The most important proposal in the Harvard study group's November 1 report, however, was that Nixon should consider reviving the National Security Council rather than having a free-floating special assistant in the mold of Bundy and Rostow. Downgrading the NSC had led to excessive informality under Kennedy and Johnson. True, as the authors noted, Johnson's administration had sought to reimpose some kind of bureaucratic structure on national security with the cre-ation in 1966 of the Senior Interdepartmental Group (SIG) as a coordi-nating body composed of the undersecretary of state (who chaired it), the deputy secretary of defense, the chairman of the Joint Chiefs of Staff, the special assistant, and the heads of CIA, AID, and USIA.

There were also now interdepartmental regional groups (IRGs) chaired by the regional assistant secretaries of state. Though this system had at first seemed "a total failure," it was now working quite smoothly thanks to the efforts of Nick Katzenbach. The study group was therefore open to "giv[ing] the SIG-IRG system a trial before reinstituting NSC or other formal consultative machinery." But the report strongly "caution[ed] against the other extreme—concentration of the coordinating function under a single Special Assistant," unless Nixon was willing to consider having a very strong deputy in the role (as Carl Kaysen and Francis Bator had been to Bundy and Rostow). The key thing was to ensure that the White House national security staff, however organized, had adequate staff and resources to cope with the volume of cable traffic, as well as an expanded research staff.[30]

"As we read the history of the presidency in the last quarter-century," the authors concluded, "it contains many fewer examples of decisions unsoundly based than of decisions misinterpreted, misunderstood or accidentally or deliberately not carried out." Nixon would be "well advised not to adhere too closely to the often-stated rule that a President should keep as many options as possible open for as long a time as he can" (a Bismarckian vice, as we have seen). This had been seen as a virtue by Kennedy and Johnson. Yet "by maintaining until the last moment the impression that they might choose any one of a number of courses, they [had] encouraged the build-up of bureaucratic lobbies"— notably over the Vietnam bombing pause and the Multilateral Force. The president had to take decisions, often sooner than was comfortable. Above all, the president had to make clear the strategic concept behind his decisions, something Johnson had never been able to do.

> The great statesmen of nineteenth-century Europe—Metternich, Castlereagh, Palmerston, Bismarck, Salisbury—all had to write out explanations for their actions because they were responsible to monarchs. You face a similar necessity, of course, in having to respond to press conference questions and deliver messages to Congress and the public, but, in statements which all the world can hear, you can seldom be as explicit and candid as you might be *in camera*. And for the next four years you have as great a stake

> in winning understanding among the managers of your bureau-
> cracy as among the electorate.[31]

There can surely be no doubt which member of the study group wrote that paragraph.

The Harvard study group saved its final report, on staffing the White House, for November 6, the day after Nixon's victory. Once again deploying their intimate knowledge of recent administrations, the authors advised against appointing a powerful chief of staff control-ling access to the president, as a successful chief executive needed to mix "elements of hierarchy and diffused access." What the president most needed was to have loyal assistants in the West Wing. These assis-tants must not represent their own views as the president's or conduct their "own policy on any issue." They should not be briefing the press other than on condition of anonymity, as there had been "cases where a publicized staff member has exaggerated his role." They should be prepared to engage in "effective devil's advocacy" to resist the tempta-tions of groupthink.* They should not be too specialized, though Nixon should resist Roosevelt's penchant for duplicating assignments in order to promote competition among his subordinates. Finally, the authors offered a suggestion: "We would call an adviser simply 'Special Assistant' and assign him to, say national security affairs rather than designating him 'Special Assistant for National Security Affairs.'" A strong argument for this kind of generalism was that "a foreign rela-tions adviser should bring congressional or domestic political factors into his thinking and recommendations before he comes to you."[32]

The reports of the Harvard study group were the first shots in a battle over the structure of Nixon's administration—and in particular over the question of whether to revive the NSC—that would rage into 1969, inviting expert commentaries from such experienced former officials as John Eisenhower (who carefully characterized the role Andrew Goodpaster had played as Eisenhower's staff secretary)[33] and Roswell Gilpatric (who as Kennedy's former deputy defense secretary

---

*The term had first been used by William H. Whyte, Jr., best known for his book *The Organization Man*, in an article for *Fortune* in 1952.

was naturally against NSC restoration).[34] The outcome would have a profound impact on the way Nixon's administration functioned, especially in its first two years. For now, we need reflect only on its significance for Nixon's decision to appoint Kissinger. Without perhaps being fully aware of it, Kissinger had coauthored one of the most sophisticated job applications in the history of American foreign policy. He had not only set out his strategic stall with the *Foreign Affairs* article on Vietnam, which it seems reasonable to assume Nixon saw before its publication. More important, Kissinger and his Harvard colleagues had applied modern American history to explain to the president-elect, with extraordinary acuity, exactly how he should go about *implementing* his national security strategy.

IV

Kissinger did not think Nixon would hire him directly. He did think Nixon might hire Rockefeller—most likely as defense secretary—and that Rockefeller would then hire him. That Rockefeller would be part of Nixon's cabinet was indeed a widespread general assumption in the immediate aftermath of the election. The reporter Gene Spagnoli suggested to Nixon that Rockefeller might make a good secretary of state. Nixon's speechwriter William Safire even suggested putting Rockefeller's brother David at Treasury and Nelson at State. "No," Safire said after a moment's reflection, "you can't have two Rockefellers in the Cabinet." "Is there any law that says you have to have one?" snapped Nixon.[35]

Unaware that Nixon had no intention of appointing his perennial rival, Rockefeller convened his advisers to discuss how he should respond to a Nixon offer. The conversation was in full swing when the phone rang. It was Dwight Chapin, the youthful Haldeman sidekick and future perjurer whom Nixon had appointed as his appointments secretary. He wanted to speak to Kissinger.[36] To everyone else at the table, this was such a bolt from the blue that no serious consideration was given to the possibility that Nixon might actually want to offer Kissinger a job.[37] Indeed, Kissinger himself may have assumed that the president-elect merely wished to discuss with him his hypothesis that

Clark Clifford was contemplating a coup in Saigon before the inaugu-ration, a theory Kissinger had run past Buckley not long before.[38]

Nixon himself later described his decision as a meeting of minds. He knew, of course, of Kissinger's earlier "disparaging comments" about his "competence in the field" of foreign policy, but he "expected this from a Rockefeller associate, and . . . chalked it up to politics." When he and Kissinger met in Nixon's transition office on the thirty-ninth floor of the Pierre Hotel at ten a.m. on Monday, November 25, it was to discuss future strategy, not past politics.

> I knew that we were very much alike in our general outlook in that we shared a belief in the importance of isolating and influ-encing the factors affecting worldwide balances of power. We also agreed that whatever else a foreign policy might be, it must be strong to be credible—and it must be credible to be successful. I was not hopeful about the prospects of settling the Vietnam war through the Paris talks and felt that we needed to rethink our whole diplomatic and military policy on Vietnam. Kissinger agreed, although he was less pessimistic about the negotiations than I was. I said that I was determined to avoid the trap Johnson had fallen into, of devoting virtually all my foreign policy time and energy to Vietnam, which was really a short-term problem. I felt that failing to deal with the longer-term problems could be devastating to America's security and survival, and in this regard I talked about restoring the vitality of the NATO alliance, and about the Middle East, the Soviet Union, and Japan. Finally I mentioned my concern about the need to re-evaluate our policy toward Communist China, and I urged him to read the *Foreign Affairs* article in which I had first raised this idea as a possibility and a necessity. Kissinger said he was delighted that I was thinking in such terms. . . . I had a strong intuition about Henry Kissinger, and I decided on the spot that he should be my National Security Adviser.[39]

Kissinger's recollection was somewhat different. Nixon struck him as "almost diffident: his movements were slightly vague, and unrelated to what he was saying, as if two different impulses were behind speech and gesture. He spoke in a low, gentle voice. While he talked, he sipped, one after another, cups of coffee that were brought in without his asking for them." The president-elect proceeded to talk not about strategy but about the "massive organizational problem" he faced:

> He had very little confidence in the State Department. Its personnel had no loyalty to him. . . . He was determined to run foreign policy from the White House. He thought that the Johnson Administration had ignored the military and that its decision-making procedures gave the President no real options. He felt it imperative to exclude the CIA from the formulation of policy: it was staffed by Ivy League liberals. . . . They had always opposed him politically.

Kissinger replied innocuously that a "President who knew his own mind would always be able to dominate foreign policy." He agreed that the Johnson administration's methods had been slapdash, especially as decision making had devolved to the notorious Tuesday lunches. "A more systematic structure seemed to me necessary," he said, though it should avoid the "rigorous formalism" of the Eisenhower era. Only then did the subject turn to foreign policy itself. In his own account, Kissinger offered the vague reflection that policy had to be "related to some basic principles of national interest that transcended any particular Administration," language more suggestive of realism than his usual idealism.[40]

It was from this point onward that a confusion arose. Nixon appeared to be inviting Kissinger to join the administration "in some planning capacity," though he was not specific about the role he had in mind. Kissinger assumed he was being asked to serve under Rockefeller if he was offered a cabinet post. The conversation drew to an abrupt close. To Kissinger's surprise, Nixon ordered Haldeman to install a direct phone line to his Harvard office. Haldeman then told Kissinger about his own role as chief of staff and how the titles of "Special Assistant to the President" were to be shorn of the word "Special."

Somewhat mystified, Kissinger returned to Harvard in time to teach his four o'clock seminar.

That Kissinger genuinely thought he was being asked to serve under Rockefeller is clear. On the same day he saw Nixon—presumably after his seminar was over—he drafted a note to Rockefeller sketching how he thought the Department of Defense might be reorganized to retain the best features of McNamara's time as secretary, notably the direct access to the president unmediated by the national security adviser, while at the same time repairing relations with the military chiefs, "where Secretary McNamara left lasting scars." The note implicitly suggested that a new post of deputy secretary for policy and programs be created for Kissinger, with responsibility for "(a) representing the Secretary on interdepartmental sub-cabinet committees dealing with national security and intelligence; (b) dealing on behalf of the Secretary with the Joint Chiefs on contingency planning and on the preparation of the draft presidential memoranda establishing force levels."[41] It was a complete waste of effort. The next day Rockefeller phoned to tell Kissinger he had been dropped by Nixon; he was to stay put in Albany as governor of New York. An hour later John Mitchell called to invite Kissinger back to New York to discuss "his position in the new Administration." Still unclear what role he was being offered, Kissinger consulted McGeorge Bundy, his onetime mentor, now the head of the Ford Foundation. Never slow to condescend, Bundy assumed he was being considered for a mere assistant secretaryship at the State Department and advised him to press instead for George Kennan's old post of director of Policy Planning.[42] This too was beside the point. When Kissinger got to New York on the twenty-seventh, Mitchell's first question was, "What have you decided about the National Security job?" Kissinger said he did not know he had been offered it. "Oh, Jesus Christ," muttered Mitchell, "he has screwed it up again." Mitchell stomped down the hall to Nixon's office and then returned to fetch Kissinger. Finally the president-elect spat it out. He wanted Kissinger to be his national security adviser.[43]

Had Kissinger plotted all along for this job, presumably he would have accepted without hesitation—especially as it was clear that at least three other candidates were being considered.* Instead, he asked for time to consult his colleagues, an "extraordinary request" about which he subsequently felt embarrassed. (With a bizarre humility, Nixon suggested Kissinger speak with Lon L. Fuller, the Carter Professor of Jurisprudence at Harvard, who had taught him when he was at Duke Law School—as if the president-elect required a character reference.) Yet Kissinger's hesitation was a true reflection of his continuing doubts about Nixon—the man who "for more than two decades had been politically anathema."[44] He had foreseen the dilemma when imagining serving under Rockefeller in the Pentagon—to the extent of discussing with Gloria Steinem a piece for *New York* magazine on "The Collaboration Problem," an old preoccupation dating back to the days of *Confluence*.[45] When Joseph Kraft got wind of Nixon's offer, Kissinger was thrown into a panic, pleading with Kraft not to mention it to anyone, much less to print it. Though other Rockefeller staffers reacted to the news with dismay (some mockingly sang "I Wonder Who's Kissinger Now?"), Rockefeller himself urged him to accept at once—just as he had eight years before, when the offer to Kissinger had come from Kennedy.[46] Arthur Schlesinger said the same.[47] On the afternoon of Friday, November 29, Kissinger called Chapin and said yes. The following Monday, Nixon presented him to the crowd of reporters gathered expectantly at the Pierre.

The president-elect made it clear that Kissinger would have a different role from the one played by Rostow and Bundy before him. His first task would be "to overhaul the operations of the National Security Council" so that it could do more contingency planning "so that we may not just react to events when they occur." "Dr. Kissinger is keenly aware," Nixon declared, "of the necessity not to set himself up as a wall between the president and the Secretary of State or the Secretary of

---

*The others interviewed were Robert Strausz-Hupé, founder of the Foreign Policy Research Institute; William Kintner, the specialist in psychological warfare; and Roy L. Ash, the president of Litton Industries, the Wisconsin defense contractor. Strausz-Hupé became ambassador to Sri Lanka, suggesting that he had singularly failed to impress Nixon or his staff. Kintner succeeded him at FPRI. Ash went on to serve as director of the Office of Management and Budget, the creation of which he recommended as chairman of Nixon's Advisory Council on Executive Organization.

Defense. I intend to have a strong Secretary of State." Nixon then spelled out how he envisaged the new national security regime.

> I am one who likes to get a broad range of viewpoints expressed and Dr. Kissinger has set up what I believe—is setting up at the present time a very exciting new procedure for seeing to it that the President of the United States does not just hear what he wants to hear, which is always a temptation for White House staffers. . . . Men in positions of responsibility and men who really have the ability to do creative thinking too often get bogged down in reading the interminable telegrams, most of which are not really relevant to the problems they are concerned with. I don't want him [Kissinger] to get down to the situation room in the White House and spend too much time there going through cables.[48]

"Kissinger has set up . . .—is setting up . . ." Nixon's slip provides a clue as to what had really happened. Nixon had read not only Kissinger's *Nuclear Weapons and Foreign Policy.* He had read much else, and he had been impressed. Most of all he had been impressed by the Harvard study group's advice on how best to manage his transition. They had done their work well. The day before Nixon's unveiling of Kissinger, in the St. Regis Hotel—just six blocks away from the Pierre—the study group had reconvened, minus Kissinger, to discuss a new paper on "Revitalizing and Streamlining the NSC."[49] The next day Areeda wrote to Haldeman, setting out the group's ideas on the need for a central program planning staff in the White House.[50] The former Massachusetts attorney general Elliot Richardson was also now drawn into the discussion. (Nixon would later name him as undersecretary of state.)[51] On December 4 a copy of the group's key paper on "Revitalizing and Streamlining the NSC" was sent to Kissinger.[52] Although others weighed in,[53] NSC revival was indeed the direction that Nixon took.[54]

Kissinger's appointment thus needs to be understood as more than just a meeting of minds, though it was certainly that. It was part of a radical overhaul of the machinery of foreign policy making, an overhaul for which Kissinger himself had coauthored the blueprint. At their press conference, it was Nixon who conspicuously did most of the talking. What none of those listening appreciated was that he was reciting from Kissinger's script.[55]

Perhaps the most interesting feature of that blueprint was its deeply historical character. It was no coincidence that one of the study group's reports, by Ernest May, was entitled "Historians and the Foreign Policy Process" and argued for the introduction of a British-style rule for automatic declassification—but after only twelve or twenty years rather than the British thirty—to allow scholarly history to be done on the recent past.[56] A recurrent theme of Kissinger's critique of Johnson's administration had been its historical ignorance, extending all the way down from the president himself to the lowliest "grunt" in Vietnam. No one in the entire chain of command appeared even dimly aware of the lessons they might learn from the past, even the very recent past. This reflected partly a failure to institutionalize the learning process, partly the shortness of tours of duty in Vietnam. But it also reflected the innate bias of the American bureaucracy in favor of legal training. In a revealing clash with the Tufts political scientist John P. Roche*—who had served as a special adviser to Johnson between 1966 and 1968— Kissinger derided Roche's claim that "all the history in the world doesn't make any difference if the Russians decide to bail out their clients."

> You have to know what history is relevant [Kissinger replied]. You have to know what history to extract. I am sure an apple grower would tell Newton he did not know all there is to be known about the apple. History is not a cook book you can open. Some history is relevant to many situations. . . . [Lawyers are] the single most important group in Government, but they do have this drawback—a deficiency in history.[57]

The Nixon administration would come to grief for reasons other than ignorance of the past.

---

*The context was a panel on "The Intellectual and the White House Policy Maker" at the American Political Science Association's September 1968 conference.

V

The story broke on November 29.[58] It was confirmed, as we have seen, on December 2.[59] Seldom has a presidential appointment elicited such widespread enthusiasm. The Associated Press liked the look of Kissinger: "compact, square-jawed and circumspect" was how it described Nixon's pick to succeed Walt Rostow.[60] James Reston in *The New York Times* called the appointment "a reassuring sign that the new administration [was] going to make a serious and objective reappraisal of its security problems and priorities." Kissinger was "intelligent, articulate and remarkably industrious."[61] His newspaper profiled Kissinger as "brisk and businesslike but demanding," though with a "self-deprecatory sense of humor," while a leading article singled out for praise his "absence of intellectual or ideological rigidity."[62] "Not since Florence Nightingale," joked Buckley, "has any public figure received such universal acclaim."[63]

Abroad, there was a more mixed welcome. The London *Times* praised him as "a leading intellectual advocate of American military preparedness,"[64] who was "known for his toughness and the cold realism that he brings to the study of east–west relations"[65] But the newspaper of the British Establishment did not expect "Dr. Kissinger . . . to be so influential [as Rostow] because he will not be so sure of himself. He is less likely to be the source of policy than the exposer of difficulties and the advocate of caution."[66] *The Economist* begged to differ. In Kissinger's writing, the magazine found "an excellent resistance to the *clichés* of the day and, on occasion, a proper and likeable capacity to admit that he might have been wrong. . . . He does bring to the new Administration a touch of the intellectual arrogance which it might otherwise be sadly short of."[67] On the left, the *Guardian* identified him as a "hardliner,"[68] in "the same tough, slightly hawkish mould as his two immediate predecessors."[69] Always sympathetic to immigrants, the newspaper noted with satisfaction that Kissinger's mother was "an amiable German lady who occasionally helps to serve at dinner parties in a wealthy New York home."[70] *Le Monde* praised Kissinger as "a man of dialogue, who listens, who is not satisfied with preconceptions."[71] In the eyes of *Die Zeit,* it was a cause for celebration that Nixon had hired not just one but two intellectuals, the other being Daniel Patrick Moynihan, who was to advise on urban affairs (code for the mounting racial violence in American cities).[72] On the other side of the iron curtain, however, Kissinger was predictably denounced for his "Cold War philosophy."[73]

Admittedly, the warm welcome from the American media was just part of an unexpected (and short-lived) honeymoon between Nixon and his old foes in the press corps.[74] But academia too was delighted by Kissinger's elevation. Adam Yarmolinsky seemed to speak for the entire Harvard faculty when he said, "I will sleep better with Henry Kissinger in Washington." Stanley Hoffmann called his colleague "a man with a great deal of character and wisdom" who was "not the kind of person who will allow himself to be used." John Kenneth Galbraith, Carl Kaysen, and George Kennan were also enthused.[75] Though Schlesinger damned Nixon's initial cabinet appointments with faint praise— "nondescript but not disastrous"—he was in no doubt that "the best appointment" was Kissinger.[76] Kissinger was the toast of the East Coast intelligentsia as he swept into Princeton to put in an appearance at a big political science conference on "The United States: Its Problems, Impact and Image in the World" that was held there in early December.[77] The left-wing Princeton historian Arno Mayer was a rare dissenting voice at this early juncture, criticizing Kissinger for "persisting in stereotypical views of the foreign-policy behavior of Soviet political actors [and] for still stressing that a Communist regime anywhere in the non-Western world, including Latin America, would 'inevitably become a center of anti-Western policy' and should therefore be prevented."[78] This was nicely complemented by the complaint of Robert Welch of the John Birch Society that Nixon's new adviser had an "urge—and possibly an idealistic one—to see the United States and Germany and all other countries become simple geographical entities in a one-world empire . . . run by the Communists."[79] In short, only those on the political fringes could seriously object to Kissinger's appointment.

At Harvard there was an authentically celebratory atmosphere as Kissinger conducted his last seminar on December 16.[80] Harvard loves power more than most universities and, for one glad, confident morning, it seemed as if Camelot's brain trust was back in business. Kissinger was even given a standing ovation. ("This will do wonders for my megalomania" was the first wisecrack of the new era.) The speaker at that last seminar, Morton Halperin—whose topic was "Asian Security After Vietnam"—had already begun work for Kissinger in his new role. Having served under McNamara at the Pentagon before returning to the CFIA, Halperin seemed the ideal man to ask "how one could apply the techniques which Bob McNamara used in Defense to the entire range of foreign policy problems." He obliged with a classic Pentagon diagram, showing the assistant to the president for national security in a box of his own at the apex of a pyramid composed of the NSC staff, assistants for planning, and a planning staff.[81] His recommendation was to replace the Senior Interdepartmental Group, chaired by the undersecretary, with a new Review Group chaired by the national security adviser. Halperin's was one of many brains lining up to be picked: Jerome Wiesner, provost of MIT, offered a list of twelve names for an arms control briefing. Most were old friends or colleagues, veterans of the Harvard-MIT Arms Control Seminar like Paul Doty, Carl Kaysen, and Bernie Feld.[82] Richard Neustadt was already hard at work on the NSC overhaul.[83] Frank Lindsay's now-much-expanded study group cranked out its final report, providing yet more grist to the mill of executive branch reform.[84] Zbigniew Brzezinski offered his two cents' worth on the State Department.[85] By Christmas Eve, Kissinger had also taken delivery of Andrew Goodpaster's inside account of the functioning of the Eisenhower NSC.[86] By New Year's Eve, he was writing to Ernest May to apologize for not replying to his list of suggested appointees with Latin American expertise. "Needless to say," he confessed, "the pace here in New York has been more hectic than I ever imagined when I accepted the job. Hopefully, things will settle down after the 20th"—the date set for Nixon's inauguration.[87] Did Kissinger really cling to such an obviously forlorn hope? No, he was just trying to make a slighted colleague feel better about his place in the pecking order.

All this the members of the outgoing administration watched with the jaundiced eyes of men hardly likely to admit that their own mode of operation could be improved upon. On December 3, at one of

Johnson's last Tuesday lunches, the subject of the new national security adviser came up:

> THE PRESIDENT: What is your impression of Kissinger?
> SECRETARY RUSK: Theoretical more than practical. . . . [But he] handled himself in an honest fashion on the Paris talks.
> WALT ROSTOW: . . . Henry is a man of integrity and decency . . . [though he] doesn't understand [the] emergency [in] Asia.[88]

Others were more gracious. If Averell Harriman had any suspicion that Kissinger had betrayed Parisian confidences, he showed no sign of it. On December 3, he offered Kissinger his New York apartment should he need it during the transition.[89] It was not long, however, before Harriman needed it back: on January 5, 1969, Nixon announced that Harriman would be replaced at the Paris talks by Henry Cabot Lodge. Cyrus Vance was also out; his parting shot to Kissinger was "to avoid a situation in which every move the negotiators wish to take must be approved in Washington and Saigon."[90] That was another forlorn hope. Katzenbach, too, left office gracefully, responding to Kissinger's request for a list of "a dozen or so outstanding Foreign Service officers" and adding the plans he had been hatching "to devise some small but positive steps toward restoring relations with China."[91] With the simultaneous announcement of Philip Habib's retention as a member of the Paris negotiating team and Alexis Johnson's promotion to undersecretary of state, Kissinger could count on at least three key allies on the State Department side.[92] He was already preparing the ground for the long-planned marginalization of the secretary of state. The fact that Nixon appointed William P. Rogers—a former attorney general with almost no foreign policy experience—was neither here nor there. Any secretary of state would have been sidelined by Kissinger (though having a lawyer as his victim added a certain piquancy).

Washington beckoned. Kissinger knew the White House from his time as a consultant to Kennedy, but much had changed since 1961, and his one visit to brief Johnson about PENNSYLVANIA in 1967 had not included a guided tour. Bundy wrote, somewhat coldly but not unhelpfully, with detailed advice about the facilities Kissinger could expect to find in the White House West Wing. It was in the basement that Kissinger would be located, next to "the complex of files and communications and watch officers called the Situation Room. . . . It is really an information and reporting center—very occasionally also a command center." There he would find the "hotline," established after the Cuban Missile Crisis, that could connect the White House to the Kremlin in a crisis: not a red telephone but a teletype system, manned round the clock (and tested daily) by a staff of "bright young watch officers." As Bundy noted, the hotline was at once the most important tool at his disposal and the least used. The Situation Room's real utility, he suggested, was "for highly classified briefings . . . with good screens and built-in blackboards"—though he had to concede that neither Kennedy nor Johnson had used it for this purpose. All in all, Bundy was bound to report, Kissinger's new work premises were, for all the prestige associated with them, "mostly windowless underground space with inconvenient access." Still, the special assistant, along with the Situation Room, were "the President's immediate instruments of action in meeting his responsibilities for peace and war." Bundy's most constructive suggestion was to add "a really fast system of document transmission from the State Seventh Floor" to "maintain the immediacy and the range of communication between the Assistant and the crowd at State"—a recommendation unhesitatingly ignored by Kissinger.[93]

Characteristically overconfident, Bundy's successor, Walt Rostow, recommended that Kissinger change nothing. In a memorandum he drafted for Johnson before the outgoing president welcomed Kissinger back to the White House, Rostow defended the Tuesday lunches for their informality. They were, he wrote,

> an informal version of the old NSC—in effect a regular NSC
> meeting with carefully prepared staff work, plus the advantage of
> bringing together in a human setting the President and his chief
> national security advisers. Nothing is more important than that
> this group be close; feel free to debate openly with each other in
> the presence of the President; be loyal to each other as well as to

> the President. . . . The President's National Security Adviser can
> play one of his most important roles in keeping this decisively
> important group close to each other and to the President. . . .

"It is," he added—almost as an afterthought—"a challenging but reward-ing job."[94] The best advice he gave was not to underestimate how much of his time would be consumed by the humdrum: "Rose Garden speeches that do not justify full consultation with the secretaries involved; infor-mal meetings with the press . . . the planning of visits by foreign digni-taries to the White House and of Presidential trips abroad; the drafting of letters to congressmen and others; etc."[95] His worst advice was "to seize all of Laos, bypassing South Vietnam."[96] The outgoing president contented himself with a typical piece of cynicism: "Read the colum-nists, and if they call a member of your staff thoughtful, dedicated, or any other friendly adjective, fire him immediately. He is your leaker."[97]

Kissinger did not underestimate the scale of the challenge. No one would let him. In an act that was at once one of generosity and of emancipation, Rockefeller wrote him a check for $50,000, "as a token of my friendship and my appreciation for the work you have done in service to the people of this country."[98] (Having checked that it was legal for him to do so, Kissinger accepted the gift. He was, after all, a divorced professor on extended sabbatical leave from Harvard who was now being paid a government salary. He needed the money.) Always curious, Arthur Schlesinger asked him

> whether Nixon was turning out to be the kind of man Henry
> expected him to be. Henry replied enigmatically that he had
> been reassured on certain things that had previously worried
> him but was encountering other and unexpected qualities
> which might create problems. When I said how glad I was that
> he had been appointed, Henry said ruefully: "All I can say is I
> hope you will feel equally glad about it a year from now."[99]

Galbraith had put it somewhat similarly. The real test of Kissinger's popularity, he told *The New York Times*, "will be how people will react four years from now when Henry comes back"—implying slyly that Nixon would be a one-term president.[100]

But it was left to Fritz Kraemer to play the part of the *auriga,* the slave whose role was to whisper *Memento homo* in the victor's ear at a Roman triumph: you are only a man. On December 9, 1968, Kraemer added to the mounting pile of recommendations for appointments in the new administration with an extraordinary paean of praise for a forty-four-year-old army officer who had recently returned a hero from Vietnam, but whom Kraemer had got to know while he was working at the Pentagon. Cleverly, Kraemer made his point to Kissinger indirectly, by praising the qualities in this young officer that he implicitly wanted his former protégé to evince in his new role:

> The lieutenant colonel (and this really means something in a hierarchical world) stood his ground with absolutely extraordinary courage and presented his counter-arguments tirelessly in writing and in informal conversations with his superiors. Because of his unaggressive, quiet manners he was, surprisingly enough, able to do so without arousing anybody's antagonism. The latter feat is perhaps even more remarkable than his independence in thought and action.

Moreover, as he rose through the Pentagon ranks—reaching the position of military assistant to McNamara himself—this paragon of virtue never allowed power to corrupt him.

> In the end [he] sat in McNamara's inner office and very often was the only military person to accompany the Secretary to White House and NSC meetings. In this position, peculiarly tempting for a young officer, [he] retained his utter integrity to an extent which even aroused the admiration of McNamara himself, whose general capability for admiring others is decidedly underdeveloped. . . . McNamara . . . remarked . . . "This is one of only two Army officers who dare to contradict me to my face." Again [he] had succeeded in making his points

fearlessly and yet, at the same time, gaining the respect and
trust of a most difficult, near-dictatorial man.

Individuals with these characteristics, wrote Kraemer, had become very
rare. "Our mass age," he noted in language he knew would resonate
with Kissinger, was "not conducive to producing the type."

Then he came to the point: "In your fearsomely responsible new position you will be a lonely man and you need at least a very few on whose
unshakable human reliability, integrity, and profound understanding you
can rely."[101] The man he was recommending to Kissinger was Alexander
Haig, whom Kissinger without hesitation appointed as his military
adviser (and who, twelve long years later, would follow in his footsteps
by becoming secretary of state). For Kissinger, Haig met a need. His own
Harvard study group had specifically advised Nixon that "at least one
man in your White House staff should know the ins and outs of the Pentagon."[102] But Kraemer was writing as much about Kissinger as about
Haig. ("In fact," he wrote to make it clear that he was not seeking a favor,
"he and I are not close friends but merely respect each other.")

> I have known you for some time and I am convinced that you
> will be more than well served by this man. At this moment
> everybody is trying to obtain something from you, because
> you have risen so high. . . . The country, however, is in a very
> difficult and dangerous situation, and it is necessary that the
> few talents we have get into positions where they can be objec-
> tively most useful, and where they can be loyal and effective
> helpers of men like yourself on whose performance so very
> much depends.[103]

The first half of Henry Kissinger's life was at an end. The time of
becoming was over; the time of being had at last begun. But Kissinger's
first teacher—his Mephistopheles—had earned the right to the last
admonition.

Epilogue:
A Bildungsroman

> Every thing that happens to us leaves some trace behind it;
> every thing contributes imperceptibly to form us.
> —GOETHE, *Wilhelm Meister's Apprenticeship*[1]

The story of the first half of the life of Henry Kissinger is a true bildungsroman: like Goethe's seminal *Wilhelm Meister's Apprenticeship,* it is the tale of an education through experience, some of it bitter.

It was an education in five stages, rather than Wilhelm Meister's seven. The first was Kissinger's youthful experience of German tyranny, American democracy, and world war. The second was his discovery of philosophical idealism and then historical knowledge at Harvard, and his first application in "Boswash" of these academic insights in the new field of nuclear strategy. The third stage was the harsh lesson in political reality he received in Washington, D.C., during the giddy, risky years of the Kennedy administration. Then came the exposure, from the ground up, to the new kind of warfare that was being waged in Vietnam. Finally, in Paris, Kissinger learned what it was to be diplomatically hoodwinked.

At all but the last stage of his educational progress, there was a mentor: first, Fritz Kraemer, the monocled Mephistopheles in olive-green fatigues; then William Elliott, Dixie's Oxonian idealist; then McGeorge Bundy, the WASP in the White House; then Nelson Rockefeller, a would-be Medici to Kissinger's anti-Machiavelli, as naïve in his pursuit of power as Kissinger was idealistic in his counsel. Each man, in his different way, encouraged and developed Kissinger's idealism, which evolved from the rarefied Kantian philosophy of the Harvard years into the more accessible slogans of the better Rockefeller speeches. In the final phase, however, Kissinger was alone, wrestling with the dilemmas of Vietnam and learning to respect the alternative realist paradigm personified by Bismarck, de Gaulle, and Morgenthau.

Between 1945 and 1969, Kissinger saw four men hold the most powerful office in the world: Truman, the indestructible executor of the strategy of containment; Eisenhower, the unflappable administrator of atomic deterrence and brinkmanship; Kennedy, the charismatic but double-dealing master of flexible response; and Johnson, the unscrupulous blowhard who turned the theory of limited war into the practice of unlimited political disaster. Kissinger cut his teeth as a policy adviser by criticizing each of them in turn. For most of the period, he clung to the hope that the presidency would pass to Nelson Rockefeller, whom he idealized as an American aristocrat, a moderate Republican, and an enlightened ruler. The least likely outcome in Kissinger's own mind was that he would end up as national security adviser to the darkly devious Richard Nixon, a true realist in both theory and practice. Any account of Kissinger's life that depicts him clawing his way up the greasy pole of American politics therefore misrepresents the loyalty and naïveté that made him stick to Rockefeller, despite ample evidence that the governor of New York would never stoop to conquer in the way necessary to secure his party's presidential nomination. True, Rockefeller's rivals kept coming to Kissinger for advice, and usually he gave it. Of all of them, however, it was Nixon whose advances he resisted the most. Not until Nixon made his wishes unambiguously clear did Kissinger realize that he was being offered the post of national security adviser—and even then he hesitated to accept, despite the fact that Nixon had been more receptive than any other candidate to the proposals jointly authored by Kissinger to reform the system of national security policy making.

At every stage of his *Lehrjahre,* Kissinger learned something new about the nature of foreign policy, cumulatively building an understanding of international relations that, by the end of the 1960s, had few rivals. What had he learned from living as a Jew under Hitler, from fleeing Germany as a refugee, from returning there as an American soldier, from discovering the horror of the Holocaust? Earlier writers lacked the knowledge to answer these questions, so they speculated about trauma or repression. But as Kissinger himself told his parents, "not everybody came out of this war a psycho-neurotic."[2] His experiences changed him profoundly, but in the Nietzschean sense: what did not kill him made him stronger. "I am tough, even ruthless, with the persons whose participation in the party is responsible for all this misery," he told his father, who had urged him to be "tough" on the Germans. "But somewhere this negativism must end, somewhere we must produce something positive or we'll have to remain here, as guardians over chaos, forever."[3] Or, as he put it to his friend Robert Taylor on the night they heard of Hitler's death, "We would stay to do in our little way what we could to make all previous sacrifices meaningful. We would stay just long enough to do that."[4] As a counterintelligence officer carrying out denazification, he told his men, "We must . . . prove to the Germans by the firmness of our actions, by the justness of our decisions, by the speed of their executions that democracy is indeed a workeable [*sic*] solution. . . . Lose no opportunity to prove by word and deed the virility of our ideals."[5]

Other men came back from World War II psychologically broken. Kissinger came back feeling like a victor—but a victor not only over the Germans but also over the constraints of his Orthodox Jewish heritage. As he told his parents, "Certain ties bound in convention [now] mean little to me. I have come to judge men on their merits."[6] The war taught Kissinger not only strength but also, under Kraemer's influence, how to live. He threw himself with relish into his work, whether he was interrogating suspected Nazis or teaching his fellow Americans. But he also learned to seize the moment of pleasure: "What is life if not an ability to enjoy what is beautiful and fine while one can?"[7]

Yet the most important lesson he learned from the war was the one he expressed in his letter of July 1948, a year after he returned from Germany to the United States, in which he explained that "there is not only right or wrong but many shades in between," and that "the real tragedies in life are not in choices between right and wrong," because "only the most callous of persons choose what they know to be wrong. . . . Real dilemmas are difficulties of the soul, provoking agonies."[8] After 1941, World War II was itself a war between evils, with Hitler on one side and Stalin on the other. The dilemma had been to choose between those evils and the challenge was to recognize that the Soviet Union was a lesser evil than the Third Reich. A good example of the kind of choice between incommensurate evils was that which had faced people in German-occupied Europe or, for that matter, within the great dictatorships. "Should, in such a situation, the individual concerned about his values go immediately into open opposition; or can the opposition become most effective by operating within the apparatus?" This was a question the young Kissinger had the self-confidence to put to Albert Camus. The question, as Kissinger put it, raised "subtle problems which only those who have lived through them [foreign occupations or totalitarian dictatorships] have a moral right to discuss." He had lived under Hitler, of course, and so he could hazard the answer that "very often the knave and the hero are distinguished less by their action than by their motivation, and this may contribute to the erosion of all moral restraints during totalitarian periods."[9] It was a theme he reverted to in his doctoral dissertation. Sometimes, he observed, "to show one's purpose is to court disaster." In periods when a foe has to be conciliated because a state lacks the power to resist, it may be necessary to feign collaboration. Here again the "the knave and the hero, the traitor and the statesman," could be distinguished "not by their acts, but by their motives."[10]

The argument that most strategic choices are between evils is one of the leitmotifs of Kissinger's life. In *Nuclear Weapons and Foreign Policy,* for example, he argued that "to maintain at least an equilibrium of power . . . may require some very difficult choices.

> We are certain to be confronted with situations of extraordinary ambiguity, such as civil wars or domestic coups. . . . There can be no doubt that we should seek to forestall such occurrences. But once they have occurred, we must find the will to act and to run risks in a situation which permits only a choice among evils. While we should never give up our principles, we must also realize that we cannot maintain our principles unless we survive.[11]

If Kissinger knew all this already before he even returned from occupied Germany, what did he learn at Harvard? First, he learned about the nature of individual freedom. In his senior thesis he documented his own realization that "all the seemingly limitless possibilities" of his youth had been reduced to "one actuality"—his first encounter with "the problem of Necessity and Freedom, of the irrevocability of our actions, of the directedness of our life."[12] In the "tired times" that followed the exaltation of 1945's victories, there was solace in the realization that freedom was "an inner experience of life as a process of deciding meaningful alternatives," for it was this that enabled the individual "to rise beyond the suffering of the past and the frustrations of history" and to achieve "the self-transcendence which gives peace."[13]

At Harvard, Kissinger also learned about history itself. He learned to use historical analogies, always remembering that "whatever relationship exists [between two historical events] depends, not on a precise correspondence, but on a similarity of the problems confronted," because "history teaches by analogy, not identity." In the study of foreign affairs, an awareness of the historical context was indispensable. In particular, because a people defined its identity "through the consciousness of a common history," history could be understood as "the memory of states." Its study was therefore a guide to the self-understanding of other states.[14] Working on this basis, Kissinger could see both the similarities and the differences between the world of 1815 and the world of 1945. In both cases it was imperative to reconstruct a legitimate international order. In both cases the major obstacle was the existence of a revolutionary power (after 1949 two of them). The lesson of history was that the United States now stood in relation to the whole of Eurasia much as Great Britain had once stood in relation to Europe. Simply acting as the balancer was not enough; it was necessary simultaneously to build a legitimate international order by sapping the revolutionary power of its dangerous energy.

In *Nuclear Weapons and Foreign Policy,* Kissinger acknowledged that the world had been changed by Hiroshima, but not changed as much as most of his contemporaries assumed. Just as Clausewitz had come to realize after 1815 that not all future wars would be of the absolute variety waged by Napoleon, so Kissinger argued that limited wars could still be fought in an age of superpowers and thermonuclear weapons. We should not understate what a shocking argument this was and remains. Nor should we overlook its fundamental frailty in strictly strategic terms: neither Kissinger nor subsequent NATO strategists could explain away the obvious risk that any use of nuclear missiles, no matter how limited in intent and scale, would be likely to escalate into full-blown Armageddon. Yet Kissinger was always more concerned with the principle that one needed still to be able to threaten the use of force credibly than with the actual practicalities of a limited nuclear war; that indeed was the argument's core weakness.

Kissinger was a Kantian idealist, not a Wilsonian idealist. To the Wilsonian argument that the United States should "confine our actions to situations in which our moral, legal and military positions are completely in harmony," Kissinger had a consistent reply: "To deal with problems of such ambiguity presupposes above all a moral act: a willingness to run risks . . . for a less than perfect application of one's principles." The naïve insistence on absolutes, so characteristic of the liberal tradition in American foreign policy, was "a prescription for inaction."[15] As he put it to Stephen Graubard in 1956, "the insistence on pure morality is in itself the most immoral of postures."[16] Yet Kissinger was even more wary of the realists or, as he more accurately called them, the pragmatists: those who would quietly surrender Cuba, East Berlin, Laos, and South Vietnam to Communist control rather than risk a confrontation with Moscow or Beijing. Though Kissinger did not overuse the analogy with the 1930s—he knew well enough that in foreign policy Stalin and his successors were no Hitlers—he could not resist pointing out that Baldwin and Chamberlain had thought of themselves as "tough realists" in the 1930s.[17] Kissinger was never a Machiavellian. Indeed, a striking feature of his Harvard career is how little attention he paid to the Florentine and to those, like Isaiah Berlin, who sought to reinterpret him for a modern audience.[18] In this regard, what Kissinger did not read (Tolstoy's *War and Peace* was another notable omission) was almost as important as what he did read.

As a political doctrine, Kissinger's idealism was nowhere more clearly stated than in his 1958 interview with Mike Wallace, where he argued for an American "spiritual offensive in the world" that would identify the United States with, rather than against, the postcolonial revolutions of the era:

> We should say that freedom, if it is liberated, can achieve
> many ... things. ... Even when we have engaged in con-
> structive steps ... we have always justified them on the basis of
> a Communist threat, very rarely on the basis of things we
> wanted to do because of our intrinsic dynamism. ... [W]e
> should have said, ". . . These are things we want to do because
> of the values we stand for, not because we want to beat the
> Communists."[19]

Such are the positions the public intellectual can easily take. In the third phase of Kissinger's education, he came to see that the policy maker must do more than make fine speeches. It was in the 1960s that he formulated perhaps his most important insight into the nature of statesmanship: what he called "the problem of conjecture." In its first iteration, Kissinger distinguished between two options: "the assessment which requires the least effort" and "an assessment which requires more effort." If a political leader took the line of less resistance, "then as time goes on it may turn out that he was wrong and then he will have to pay a heavy price." But if he took the more difficult option "on the basis of a guess, he will never be able to prove that his effort was necessary, but he may save himself a great deal of grief later on." Here was the crux of the matter: "If he acts early, he cannot know whether it was necessary. If he waits, he may be lucky or he may be unlucky. It is a terrible dilemma."[20]

In a later formulation, Kissinger put it slightly differently. Policy, he argued, required the "ability to project beyond the known." But

> when one is in the realm of the new, then one reaches the
> dilemma that there's really very little to guide the policy-
> maker except what convictions he brings to it. ... [E]very
> statesman must choose at some point between whether he
> wishes certainty or whether he wishes to rely on his assessment
> of the situation. ... [T]his does not mean that every time one
> acts on the basis of an assessment in an uncertain situation one
> is right. It simply means that if one wants demonstrable proof
> one in a sense becomes a prisoner of events.

The key point for Kissinger was the uncertainty that must inevitably surround all strategic choices. For that reason, it was "the philosophical assumptions one makes about the nature of reality, the nature of historical trends that one is facing," that were bound to be "the determining features in the practice of foreign policy." Unike the intellectual, the policy maker "is part of an historical process and is making irreversible decisions, each of which becomes the factual basis for the next decision."[21] Inherently, the payoffs for *ex ante* "right" decisions were modest relative to the penalties for *ex post* wrong ones. If the democracies had stood up to Hitler in 1936, perhaps World War II might have been averted. But no one living in that particular parallel world would ever experience World War II, so they would never know what had been averted; by contrast, any unintended adverse consequences of a showdown in the Rhineland in 1936 would be blamed on the proponents of preemption. Conversely, if Johnson had followed the advice of George Ball and simply abandoned South Vietnam to its fate in 1965, the outcome might have been even worse than the Vietnam War, with all of Southeast Asia succumbing to Communist rule, as Lee Kuan Yew feared. Yet almost no one today is grateful to Johnson for escalating the war against Hanoi.

The problem of conjecture in foreign policy is also, as Kissinger clearly understood, the single biggest philosophical problem that confronts the historian. As Kissinger put it, "The historian . . . deals only with successful elements, and the blatantly successful ones at that. He has no way of knowing what was most significant to the participants: the element of choice which determined success or failure." Just as the policy maker can never know, once Option A has been selected, what would have happened had he chosen Option B, so the historian cannot know. Yet to reconstitute the past thought of the policy maker, the historian must imagine the moment before the decision, when both options existed side by side, each with its merits, each with its imaginable and unknowable consequences. The historical process thus "proceeds not in a straight line but through a series of complicated variations." There are turns and forks at every step of the road and the choices between routes "have to be taken for better or worse.

The conditions governing the decision may be of the most delicate shading. The choice may appear in retrospect to be nearly random or else to be the only option possible under the prevailing circumstances. In either case, it is the result of the interaction of the whole sum of previous turnings—reflecting history or tradition or values—plus the immediate pressures of the need for survival.[22]

Nothing illustrates this point better than the twisted road that led the United States from the minimal commitments made by Eisenhower to South Vietnam to the full-scale military involvement of Johnson. Kissinger learned two things from his experiences in Vietnam. First, war from the ground up was a radically different thing from war as envisioned at the White House lunch table. If he had arrived in Vietnam in 1965 with the idea of helping to improve the American war effort, he soon came to appreciate that the only viable course of action was to find a diplomatic way out of the quagmire. It was in Vietnam that Kissinger grasped just how dysfunctional the U.S. government could be, for this was not Germany in 1945 nor Korea in 1951. The lack of capacity for countering guerrilla methods, the overreliance on bombing, and the absence of interagency cooperation, combined with the chronic weakness of the South Vietnamese regime, patently made the war unwinnable. Kissinger saw this early. Yet there was no gainsaying that Hans Morgenthau had seen it earlier; in the end, his realism had been a better guide to Vietnam than Kissinger's idealism. This lesson was a pivotal one. As Kissinger sought strategic combinations to unlock the gate that trapped the United States in Vietnam, he found himself thinking in increasingly Bismarckian terms. De Gaulle was a chronic Anglophobe, but might he hold the key to a route out of Saigon that went through Paris? The Soviets were ideological adversaries, but might the way home lead through Moscow? Finally, and tentatively, Kissinger began to contemplate the most daring answer of all: that the key to peace with honor might be found in Mao's Beijing.

There is no single moment that one can point to and say: that was when the idealist became a realist. Rather, as John Gaddis suggested to me when he read the first draft of this volume, it may be better to regard idealism and realism "not as the biographical equivalent of positive and negative electrical charges—either one or the other—but rather as the opposite ends of a spectrum along which we act as circumstances require.

> Some people gravitate to one pole or the other throughout their lives. Others zig zag erratically. Still others achieve Scott Fitzgerald's standard for a "first-rate intelligence"—they hold opposing ideas in mind simultaneously, and adjust in line with life's unpredictabilities. This last, I think, is the essence of strategy: your skill in adjusting depends on having long-term objectives for short-term improvisations. Or, as Lincoln says to Thaddeus Stevens in Tony Kushner's screenplay [for the film *Lincoln*], you consult your compass *and* you avoid swamps.*

Kissinger the academic and public intellectual—not to mention the veteran of World War II—was deeply reluctant to face this, yet in Vietnam he found that his initial support for Kennedy and Johnson's policy had led into the swamps. Indeed, he might have found himself in an even deeper swamp had his uncompromising advice on Berlin been heeded by Kennedy and Bundy (though it could equally well be argued that a tougher stance on Berlin in 1961 might have averted the Cuban crisis the following year). Idealism had its perils. Perhaps that was why at some point Kissinger deleted his most penetrating critique of Bismarck in his unfinished and unpublished book manuscript about the Iron Chancellor:

> It was the essence of Bismarck's revolutionary quality that he drew the full consequences from his scepticism that all beliefs became to him only factors to be manipulated. It was no

---

*"A compass, I learnt when I was surveying, it'll . . . point you True North from where you're standing, but it's got no advice about the swamps and deserts and chasms that you'll encounter along the way. If in pursuit of your destination you plunge ahead, heedless of obstacles, and achieve nothing more than to sink in a swamp, what's the use of knowing True North?"

accident therefore that the more Bismarck preached his doctrine the more humanly remote he grew; the more rigorous he
was in applying his lessons the more incomprehensible he
became to his contemporaries. . . . [For] however brilliant Bismarck's analysis, societies are incapable of the courage of cynicism. The insistence on men as atoms, on societies as forces has
always led to a tour de force eroding all self-restraint. Because
societies operate by approximations and because they are incapable of fine distinctions, a doctrine of power as a means may
end up by making power an end.[23]

Power in the end came to Kissinger. As early as 1953, Bill Elliott had
argued that the president needed at his side a quasi deputy—"an Executive Director or a Staff Director of the National Security Council
who will be more than a Secretary"—a man possessing sufficient diplomatic skill and capacity to broker agreement between agencies and to
present the president with a "fair assessment of the real alternatives of
policy."[24] The crooked path of history ultimately led his sorcerer's
apprentice Henry Kissinger to play just such a role under Richard
Nixon, by 1973 if not before. But as Kissinger had foreseen in wrestling
with Bismarck's legacy, the power he would acquire came at a price: the
more Bismarckian he was in its utilization, the more he risked estrang-
ing himself from his fellow Americans by appearing to "make power an
end" in itself.

Fritz Kraemer had an intuition all along that something like this
might happen. Though he had played the part of Mephistopheles to
Kissinger's Faust, he could offer only intellectual, not worldly, power.
Indeed, he exhorted Kissinger *not* to pursue the latter. "[T]he secret of
independence," Kraemer had explained early in their friendship, "lies
in acting independently; one may not even *aim* for success. . . . Only if
you do not 'calculate' will you have the freedom which distinguishes
you from the little people."[25] More than once Kraemer warned his protégé that the pursuit of power might corrupt him, even if his motive for
pursuing it was noble. "Until now," he told Kissinger in 1957, "you had
to resist only the wholly ordinary temptations of the ambitious, like
avarice, and the academic intrigue industry. *Now* the trap is in your own

character. You are being tempted . . . with your own deepest principles: to commit yourself with dedication and duty."[26] Within six months, the temptation had been yielded to as Kissinger grew ever closer to his patron Rockefeller: "You are beginning [Kraemer cautioned him] to behave in a way that is no longer human and people who admire you are starting to regard you as cool, perhaps even cold. You are in danger of allowing your heart and soul to burn out in your incessant work. You see too many 'important' and not enough 'real' people." [27] It was that concern that prompted Kraemer's final admonition to Kissinger, as he prepared to come to Washington at the end of 1968. "At this moment everybody is trying to obtain something from you, because you have risen so high," he wrote. "In your fearsomely responsible new position you will be a lonely man." His only chance was to uphold "utter integrity" and to seek it in others.[28]

The bildungsroman thus concludes with a strange scene: Mephistopheles warning Faust against the corrupting effects of power. Of course, as is often the case with the mentors of successful men, Kraemer's pious admonitions belied the pangs of estrangement, if not jealousy, that he felt as he watched his protégé soar out of his gravitational field.* Still, there was a kernel of truth in what he was saying. In forty-five years, Henry Kissinger had learned much. He had learned the far-from-simple truth that decision makers have free will, though they must exercise it under conditions of uncertainty, and that their choices are usually between evils. He had learned that the self-understanding of actors on the world stage is historically derived and that historical analogies may be the statesman's best guide. He had learned that the mental habits of pragmatism and materialism—of taking the world as one finds it, and basing all decisions on "the data"—could lead at best to dirty deals, at worst to paralysis. Better by far to acknowledge the problem of conjecture and to accept that, if it seems historically advisable, then bold preemption is morally preferable to inert procrastination, even if the political payoffs are skewed in favor of the latter. What Kissinger had yet to learn was the answer to Kraemer's—and his

---

*As Kissinger later put it, less reverently, he was "like a Jewish mother who worried when I got out of his jurisdiction."

own—most difficult question. Could the idealist inhabit the real world of power and still retain his ideals?

Kissinger was the first to acknowledge the difference between the world of the intellect and the world of power. "I am burning the manuscript [of the Bismarck book]," he would tell George Weidenfeld not long after his arrival in the White House, as we have seen. "Even a few weeks near the center of power have made me realize how much I still have to learn about how policy is really made."[29] Yet the lesson he was to learn was not—as we shall see—Lord Acton's banal one that "power tends to corrupt and absolute power corrupts absolutely"*—an idea that remains irresistible to academics who have never ventured beyond the low-stakes realm of academic politics. Rather, what Kissinger was to learn between 1969 and 1977—when he would leave Washington,

---

*Acton's argument in his letter to Mandell Creighton of 1887 was that historians should not judge the "great men" of the past—he had in mind the popes of the pre-Reformation era—by less exacting standards than those of Victorian law. "I cannot accept your canon," he wrote, "that we are to judge Pope and King unlike other men, with a favourable presumption that they did no wrong. If there is any presumption it is the other way against holders of power, increasing as the power increases. Historic responsibility has to make up for the want of legal responsibility. Power tends to corrupt and absolute power corrupts absolutely. Great men are almost always bad men, even when they exercise influence and not authority: still more when you superadd the tendency or the certainty of corruption by authority." Creighton was himself a bishop, whereas Acton—aside from a brief and undistinguished period as an MP—was only ever an academic and public intellectual. "[A]nyone engaged in great affairs occupied a representative position," Creighton replied, "which required special consideration. Selfishness, even wrongdoing, for an idea, an institution, the maintenance of an accepted view of the basis of society, does not cease to be wrongdoing: but it is not quite the same as personal wrongdoing. . . . The acts of men in power are determined by the effective force behind them of which they are the exponents. . . . [T]he men who conscientiously thought heresy a crime may be accused of an intellectual mistake, not necessarily of a moral crime. . . . I am hopelessly tempted to admit degrees of criminality, otherwise history becomes a dreary record of wickedness. I go so far with you that it supplies me with few heroes, and records few good actions; but the actors were men like myself, sorely tempted by the possession of power, trammeled by holding a representative position (none were more trammeled than popes), and in the sixteenth century especially looking at things in a very abstract way. . . . I cannot follow the actions of contemporary statesmen with much moral satisfaction. In the past I find myself regarding them with pity—who am I that I should condemn them?" Which man was the wiser? Acton, after all, had urged Gladstone to back the Confederacy in the American Civil War and lamented its defeat.

D.C., after eight tumultuous years—was how wise his father had been, on returning to his sons' birthplace, to cite Aristophanes's *Peace*.

In the play, the ironical and genial Trygaeus succeeds in ending the Peloponnesian War after ten years of conflict between Athens and Sparta. He achieves this by flying to Mount Olympus on the back of a giant dung beetle (following the example in one of Aesop's fables). He finds the home of the gods all but deserted, apart from Hermes, who explains that the goddess Peace has been thrown into a deep pit by the monster War and that the prolongation of her captivity is the fault of certain Athenian politicians—the human "pestles" with which War grinds up the Greek people in his bloody mortar. Assisted by a chorus of his fellow citizens, as well as by Hermes, Trygaeus succeeds in liberating Peace. But his success—though crowned by his marriage to Harvest (symbolizing postwar prosperity), and celebrated by the farmers who can return to their fields—is not unalloyed. For Aristophanes's real theme is not peace at all. It is how hard war is to stop:

> CHORUS: Yes, a man like this one is good for all the citizenry.
>
> TRYGAEUS: When you gather your vintage, you'll realize much better what a man I am.
>
> CHORUS: Even now we plainly see, for you've become a saviour for all mankind.
>
> TRYGAEUS: That's what you'll say when you drink off a cup of new wine![30]

Acknowledgments

This book could not have been written without the research assistance of Jason Rockett, whose dedication to both the philosophy and the practice of history is second to none. It was he who laboriously assembled the documents from archives all over the world. He was very ably assisted in the battle to tame the published material by Sarah Wallington. The technical challenge I set myself was to acquire the maximum number of documents and to integrate them into a digitized database. This would not have been possible without the efforts of a succession of undergraduates, who spent long hours proofreading the documents to ensure that the optical character-recognition software had not garbled the original text. I would like to thank Nelson Barrette, Ebony Constant, Taylor Evans, Winston Shi, Gil Highet, Danyoung Kim, Keith MacLeod, Sarah Pierson, Will Quinn, Jason Schnier, Cody Simons, Lilias Sun, Sara Towne, Brett Rosenberg, Helen Tu, and Esther Yi.

I was also assisted in a multitude of ways by various associates and employees of Kissinger Associates, as well as friends and advisers to Dr. Kissinger. Special thanks are due to the late William D. Rogers; his wife, Suzanne "Suki" Rogers; and their son Daniel R. Rogers. After Bill Rogers's death, it fell to Ambassador Richard Viets to play the role of intermediary and occasional peacemaker between author and subject. Dr. Kissinger's assistants also deserve my gratitude, notably Theresa Amantea, Louise Kushner, Jessee Leporin, and Jody Williams. Also helpful at critical junctures have been Dennis Gish, Rosemary Niehuss, Joshua Cooper Ramo, J. Stapleton Roy, Schuyler Schouten, and Allan Stypeck. In the course of writing this volume, I have come to have a particular appreciation of the work done by Dennis O'Shea.

It would be impossible in the space available to express gratitude to all the archivists and librarians at the more than a hundred archives that

Jason or I visited. All those listed in the sources are hereby thanked. Those who went above and beyond the call of duty to help us included Karen Adler Abramson, director of archives at the Kennedy Library; Sahr Conway Lanz, formerly at the National Archives and Records Administration and now at Yale University; Gregory Cumming at the Nixon Library; John E. Haynes at the Library of Congress; Timothy Naftali, formerly director of the Nixon Library; Amanda Seigel of the New York Public Library's Dorot Jewish Division; Diane Shaw, director of special collections at Lafayette College; and Matthew Turi, research librarian at the University of North Carolina.

Historians who were helpful during the research process included Tomasz Blusiewicz, Sandra Butcher, Peter W. Dickson, Hubertus Hoffmann, Mark Kramer, Stefan Link, Charles Maier, Ernest May, Alan Mittleman, Lien-Hang Nguyen, Luke Nichter, Glen O'Hara, Daniel Sargent, Laura Thiele, Nicholas Thompson, Maurice Vaïsse, Kenneth Weisbrode, Jeremy Yellen, and Jennifer Yum. Other individuals who were of assistance included Samuel Beer; Christopher Buckley; Abigail Collins; Ariella Dagi; David Elliott and his wife, Mai Elliott; Ward Elliott and his wife, Myrna; Frank Harris and his wife, Beri Harris; Tzipora H. Jochsberger; Robert McNamara and his wife, Diana Masieri Byfield; David Houpt; Rabbi Moshe Kolodny; Steven Lowenstein; Errol Morris (and his assistant Josh Kearney); Herman Pirchner, Jr.; Edward Roney; Alexandra Schlesinger; Arthur Schlesinger; James Tisch (as well as his assistant Laura Last and his employees at Loews Hotels); Justin Vaïsse; and Gerald Lee Warren.

I owe a special debt to the following for agreeing to be interviewed by me: Derek Bok, Zbigniew Brzezinski, Guido Goldman, Morton Halperin, Walter Kissinger, Margot Lindsay, Edward Nixon, Roswell Perkins, Henry Rosovsky, Thomas Schelling, Andrew Schlesinger, Marian Cannon Schlesinger, Stephen Schlesinger, and George Shultz.

Harvard University has helped this project in numerous ways. I would like to thank Steven Bloomfield, who, as executive director of the Weatherhead Center for International Affairs, has been a consistent source of encouragement and research funding. His colleague Ann Townes also deserves thanks. At the Center for European Studies (CES), I was also ably assisted over the past decade by Lori Kelley, Zac

Pelleriti, Sarah Shoemaker, and Michelle Weitzel. A crucial role was played by Paul Dzus, who has acted as my information technology guru, as well as by his predecessor, George Cummings. Other CES staff who have been helpful in my endeavor include Filomena Cabral, Amir Mikhak, Elaine Papoulias, Anna Popiel, and Sandy Selesky. I owe thanks to successive directors of the center, too.

I would like to thank all my colleagues in the Harvard history department, particularly my dear friend Charles S. Maier. A valuable contribution came from the teaching fellows who helped me teach my seminar on Kissinger's theory and practice of statecraft, Greg Afinogenov and Barnaby Crowcroft. Thanks also go to all the students who took the class.

At the Hoover Institution, Stanford, I always find a haven to write. In addition to Secretary Shultz, I would especially like to thank John Raisian, Condoleezza Rice, Richard Sousa, Celeste Szeto, and Deborah Ventura for their encouragement and help.

Interviewing Henry Kissinger was in itself no easy task. My friends at Chimerica Media—Melanie Fall, Adrian Pennink, Vivienne Steele, and Charlotte Wilkins, along with the peerless cinematographer Dewald Aukema—ensured that the experience was a truly memorable one. Also deserving of thanks are my colleagues at Greenmantle LLC, particularly Pierpaolo Barbieri, Joshua Lachter, and Dimitris Valatsas, all of whom showed understanding when the writing of this book took precedence over everything else. In the final phase of the project, Charlotte Park has provided invaluable assistance, ably reinforced by Ebony Constant.

Andrew Wylie and everyone at the Wylie Agency, notably James Pullen, have been—as always—superbly professional. I have also been exceedingly fortunate in having as my editors at Penguin two of the finest in the business: Scott Moyers in New York and Simon Winder in London.

If there is one historian who can justly claim mastery of the history of the Cold War, it is John Gaddis. I was helped hugely by his comments on the first draft of the manuscript, which not only saved me from errors but also helped shape the conclusion I subsequently wrote. I would also like to thank my colleagues Graham Allison, Charles Maier, Erez Manela, and Joe Nye, all of whom found time at a very busy stage of the spring semester to read and react to the fourth draft of the manuscript, as did my friend Robert Zoellick. Later drafts were read and improved by Teresita Alvarez-Bjelland, Emmanual Roman, and Kenneth Weisbrode. Jim Dickson kindly read the proofs.

Finally, I want to express my most heartfelt thanks to my family, who for more than ten years have had to contend with the shadowy presence in their lives of a former secretary of state. Susan Douglas will recollect the genesis of the enterprise. We have gone our separate ways but not, I hope, on terms of enmity. I also hope that my children, Felix, Freya, Lachlan, and Thomas, will one day read this book and that doing so will in some small measure compensate them for their father's many absences while writing it. Last but very far from least, I thank my wife, Ayaan, the greatest source of inspiration I could ever imagine.

I dedicate the book to my tutors at Magdalen College, Oxford, who taught me to be a historian.

Notes

Preface

1. Boswell, *Life of Johnson*, 1f.
2. Jorge Luis Borges, "A Lecture on Johnson and Boswell," *New York Review of Books*, July 28, 2013.
3. Cull, *Cold War and USIA*, 294.
4. Henry Kissinger [henceforth HAK] to the author, Mar. 10, 2004.
5. Collingwood, *Autobiography*, 111–15.
6. Isaacson, *Kissinger*, Kindle location [henceforth KL] 2200–203.
7. Ibid., KL 6932.
8. Lee Dembart, "80 Toast Kissinger for 50th Birthday," *New York Times*, May 28, 1973, 8.
9. Judy Klemesrud, "Kissinger's Dinner Honors U.N. Colleagues," *New York Times*, Oct. 5, 1973.
10. "Doctor Weds, Nixon Delays Test," *New York Times*, Dec. 22, 1973.
11. "Prince Charles Goes to Sea," *Washington Post*, Jan. 4, 1974.
12. "Ducking Out to Dine," *Washington Post*, Jan. 5, 1974, D3.
13. "Kissinger Weds Nancy Maginnes," *New York Times*, Mar. 31, 1974, 1.
14. Marilyn Berger, "Kissinger, Miss Maginnes Wed," *Washington Post*, Mar. 31, 1974, A1.
15. Isaacson, *Kissinger*, KL 7214–24.

Introduction

1. Oriana Fallaci, "Henry Kissinger," in *Interview with History*, 42, 44. For the original, see "An Interview with Oriana Fallaci: Kissinger," *New Republic*, Dec. 16, 1972.
2. Fallaci, "Henry Kissinger," 17.
3. Mazlish, *Kissinger*, 3f.
4. Fallaci, "Henry Kissinger," 18.
5. Eldridge, "Crisis of Authority," 31.
6. "Episode 70: Carousel," *You Miserable Bitch*, http://bit.ly/1HAIitm.
7. "Freakazoid Episode 21—Island of Dr. Mystico," *Watch Cartoon Online*, http://bit.ly/1EntSvb.
8. "$pringfield (Or, How I Learned to Stop Worrying and Love Legalized Gambling)," tenth episode of the fifth season of *The Simpsons*, first broadcast on Dec. 16, 1993.
9. "April in Quahog," http://bit.ly/1Gpo2Jc.
10. Fallaci, "Henry Kissinger," 40f.
11. Barbara Stewart, "Showering Shtick on the White House: The Untold Story; Woody Allen Spoofed Nixon in 1971, but the Film Was Never Shown," *New York Times*, Dec. 4, 1997.
12. Lax, *Woody Allen*, 112–14. See also Day, *Vanishing Vision*, 224–26.
13. "Men of Crisis: The Harvey Wallinger Story," http://bit.ly/1z1ezrV.
14. Lax, *Woody Allen*, 114.
15. "Did Tom Lehrer Really Stop Writing Protest Songs Because Henry Kissinger Won the Nobel Peace Prize?," *Entertainment Urban Legends Revealed*, Dec. 5, 2013, http://bit.ly/1CWjcOS.
16. David Margolick, "Levine in Winter," *Vanity Fair*, Nov. 2008.
17. Heller, *Good as Gold*, 38.
18. From the album *Monty Python's Contractual Obligation* (1980), http://bit.ly/1aYjqyv.
19. Idle, *Greedy Bastard Diary*, KL 1827–32.
20. Fallaci, "Henry Kissinger," 25–27.
21. Those interested can find many examples of the genre at http://theshamecampaign.com and http://www.globalresearch.ca, just two of many such websites.
22. Quigley, *Tragedy and Hope*; Quigley, *Anglo-American Establishment*.
23. Lyndon H. LaRouche, Jr., "Sir Henry Kissinger: British Agent of Influence," *Executive Intelligence Review* 24, no. 3 (Jan. 10, 1997): 27f.
24. Lyndon H. LaRouche, Jr., "Profiles: William Yandell Elliott," *Executive Intelligence Review* 24, no. 49 (Dec. 5, 1997): 29–33; Stanley Ezrol, "William Yandell Elliott: Confederate High Priest," ibid., 28f.
25. Allen, *Kissinger*.
26. Schlafly and Ward, *Kissinger on the Couch*.
27. Marrs, *Rule by Secrecy*.
28. Wesman Todd Shaw, "Henry Kissinger: Architect of the New World Order," Nov. 12, 2012, http://bit.ly/1JQkC3k.
29. Len Horowitz, "Kissinger, Vaccinations and the 'Mark of the Beast,'" Dec. 12, 2002, http://bit.ly/1DrKi1Z.
30. Alan Watt, "Kissinger, Depopulation, and Fundamental Extremists," http://bit.ly/1FkhFbq.
31. Brice Taylor, *Thanks for the Memories: The Memoirs of Bob Hope's and Henry Kissinger's Mind-Controlled Sex Slave*, http://bit.ly/1KcZkgy.
32. David Icke, "List of Famous Satanists, Pedophiles, and Mind Controllers," http://bit.ly/1HA9PuD.

33. Zinn, *People's History of United States*, 548.
34. Zinn, *Declarations of Independence*, 14.
35. Stone and Kuznick, *Untold History*, KL 7983.
36. Hunter S. Thompson, "He Was a Crook," *Rolling Stone*, June 16, 1994.
37. Kevin Barrett, "Arrest Kissinger for Both 9/11s," Sept. 10, 2014, http://bit.ly/1aYk4Mi.
38. Hitchens, *Trial of Kissinger*, KL 348–59.
39. Shawcross, *Sideshow*, 391, 396.
40. Bass, *Blood Telegram*.
41. Ramos-Horta, *Funu*.
42. Haslam, *Nixon Administration and Chile*; Kornbluh, *Pinochet File*.
43. Chomsky, *World Orders*, 209f.
44. Bell, "Kissinger in Retrospect," 206.
45. William Shawcross, "Chronic Terror: The New Cold War," Hoover Institution Retreat, Oct. 28, 2013.
46. Peter W. Rodman and William Shawcross, "Defeat's Killing Fields," *New York Times*, June 7, 2007.
47. Christopher Hitchens, "A War to Be Proud Of," *Weekly Standard*, Sept. 5–12, 2005.
48. Kalb and Kalb, *Kissinger*, 13.
49. Blumenfeld, *Kissinger*, 232.
50. National Security Archive, Memcon Elekdag, Esenbel, Tezel, Yavuzalp, Barutcu, Kissinger, Sisco, Hartman, Rodman, Mar. 10, 1975.
51. Kalb and Kalb, *Kissinger*, 10.
52. Fallaci, "Henry Kissinger," 43.
53. Kraft, "In Search of Kissinger," 61.
54. "Henry Kissinger, Not-So-Secret Swinger," *Life*, Jan. 28, 1972.
55. Evans, *Kid Stays in the Picture*, 228. See also Feeney, *Nixon at the Movies*, 168.
56. Feeney, *Nixon at the Movies*, 167.
57. Kraft, "In Search of Kissinger," 54.
58. Thomas Schelling, interview by author.
59. Shawcross, *Sideshow*, 150.
60. Isaacson, *Kissinger*, KL 5476; Mike Kinsley, "Twelve Professors Visit Washington," *Harvard Crimson*, June 11, 1970.
61. Suri, *Kissinger*, 125. See also Mazlish, *Kissinger*, 113.
62. Blumenfeld, *Kissinger*, 14.
63. Stanley Hoffmann, "The Kissinger Anti-Memoirs," *New York Times*, July 3, 1983.
64. Safire, *Before the Fall*.
65. Lasky, *It Didn't Start*.
66. Dallek, *Nixon and Kissinger*.
67. Haldeman and Ambrose, *Haldeman Diaries*, 8.
68. Anthony Lewis, "Kissinger in the House of Horrors," *Eugene Register-Guard*, Apr. 21, 1982.
69. Ball, *Memoirs*, 173.
70. Garthoff, *Détente and Confrontation*.
71. Morgenthau, "Henry Kissinger," 58.
72. "Morgenthau Accuses Kissinger of Two-Faced Diplomacy; Says U.S. Seeking to Woo Arab World," Jewish Telegraphic Agency, Mar. 14, 1974.
73. Stoessinger, *Henry Kissinger*, 224, 217.
74. Falk, "What's Wrong with Kissinger's Policy?"
75. Landau, *Kissinger*, 130.
76. Suri, *Kissinger*, 2f., 38, 44, 47, 50.
77. Ibid., 222.
78. Mazlish, *Kissinger*, 36f., 46.
79. Heller, *Good as Gold*, 348–49.
80. Mazlish, *Kissinger*, 128; Suri, *Kissinger*, 97.

81. Anthony Lewis, "The Kissinger Doctrine," *Telegraph*, Mar. 6, 1975.
82. Kalb and Kalb, *Kissinger*, 6f.
83. Stanley Hoffmann, "The Case of Dr. Kissinger," *New York Review of Books*, Dec. 6, 1979.
84. Stanley Hoffmann, "The Kissinger Anti-Memoirs," *New York Times*, July 3, 1983.
85. Isaacson, *Kissinger*, KL 242.
86. Gaddis, *Strategies of Containment*, 297.
87. Suri, *Kissinger*, 43f.
88. Ibid., 128.
89. For an early example, see I. F. Stone, "The Education of Henry Kissinger," *New York Review of Books*, Oct. 19, 1972; "The Flowering of Henry Kissinger," *New York Review of Books*, Nov. 2, 1972.
90. Courtois et al., *Black Book of Communism*.
91. Dikötter, *Tragedy of Liberation*; Dikötter, *Mao's Great Famine*.
92. Rummel, *Lethal Politics*.
93. Applebaum, *Iron Curtain*.
94. See Williams, *Tragedy of American Diplomacy*; Williams, *Empire as a Way of Life*. Also influential in this vein, Kolko and Kolko, *Limits of Power*.
95. Andrew and Mitrokhin, *Sword and the Shield*; Andrew and Mitrokhin, *World Was Going Our Way*.
96. Westad, *Global Cold War*.
97. Lundestad, *United States and Western Europe*.
98. Magdoff, *Age of Imperialism*, 42.
99. Lundestad, *American "Empire*," 54.
100. Ibid., 65.
101. Pei, "Lessons of the Past," 52.
102. "X" [George F. Kennan], "The Sources of Soviet Conduct," *Foreign Affairs* 25, no. 4 (July 1947): 566–82.
103. Kaplan, "Defense of Kissinger."
104. Mazlish, *Kissinger*, 92f.
105. Starr, "Kissinger Years."
106. HAK, *White House Years* [henceforth *WHY*], 27.
107. Quoted in Mazlish, *Kissinger*, 50.
108. Stoessinger, *Kissinger*, 3.
109. Fallaci, "Kissinger," 39f.
110. Dickson, *Kissinger and Meaning*, 52, 57.
111. Ibid., 129.
112. Ibid., 156f.
113. HAK, *World Order*, 39f., 258.
114. Osgood, *Ideals and Self-Interest*.
115. U.S. Department of State, Office of the Historian, *Foreign Relations of the United States* [henceforth *FRUS*], *1969–1976*, vol. 38, part 1, *Foundations of Foreign Policy, 1973–1976*, Doc. 17, Address by HAK, "A Just Consensus, a Stable Order, a Durable Peace," Sept. 24, 1973. All *FRUS* documents cited below are available online at http://1.usa.gov/1GqRstv.
116. Max Roser, "War and Peace After 1945" (2014), published online at OurWorldInData .org, http://bit.ly/1Jl6oeO.
117. Dickson, *Kissinger and Meaning*, 149f., 154, 157.
118. Ferguson, *Cash Nexus*.
119. Ferguson, *Colossus*.
120. See, e.g., Niall Ferguson, "A World Without Power," *Foreign Policy*, Oct. 27, 2009, http://atfp .co/1PvdH2D.

Chapter 1: *Heimat*

1. "Fürth ist mir ziemlich egal," *Stern*, June 7, 2004.
2. Mazlish, *Kissinger*, 29, 32.
3. Suri, *Kissinger*, 20, 30, 146, 198, 221, 252.
4. "Der Clausewitz Amerikas hatte in Fürth Schulverbot," *Fürther Nachrichten*, Nov. 22–23, 1958, 9.
5. Blumenfeld, *Kissinger*, 3.
6. HAK, *WHY*, 228f.
7. "Fürth ist mir ziemlich egal," *Stern*, June 7, 2004.
8. HAK, interview by author. Cf. Kasparek, *Jews in Fürth*, 46f.
9. "Kissinger besucht Fürth," *Fürther Nachrichten*, Dec. 30, 1958.
10. "Grosser Bahnhof für Henry Kissinger," *Fürther Nachrichten*, Dec. 15, 1975.
11. "Henry A. Kissinger in Fürth," *Amtsblatt der Stadt Fürth*, Dec. 19, 1975, 338.
12. Kissinger family papers, Louis Kissinger, Rede anlässlich die Verleihung der "Goldenen Bürgermedaille" an Dr. Henry Kissinger, Dec. 15, 1975.
13. "Beide Parteien distanzieren sich," *Fürther Nachrichten*, Dec. 15, 1975.
14. "Henry A. Kissinger in Fürth," *Amtsblatt der Stadt Fürth*, Dec. 19, 1975, 339.
15. HAK to Bürgermeister of Fürth, Dec. 18, 1975, *Amtsblatt der Stadt Fürth*, Jan. 9, 1976.
16. Wassermann, *Life as German and Jew*, 5.
17. Ibid., 242.
18. Ibid., 26.
19. Ibid., 242.
20. Ibid., 27.
21. Baedeker, *Süd-Deutschland und Österreich*, 171f.
22. Bell and Bell, *Nuremberg*, 153.
23. Anon., "Dragon of Fürth."
24. Strauss, *Fürth in der Weltwirtschaftskrise*, 261.
25. Schaefer, *Das Stadttheater in Fürth*.
26. Strauss, *Fürth in der Weltwirtschaftskrise*, 8–16.
27. Schilling, "Politics in a New Key." See also Mauersberg, *Wirtschaft und Gesellschaft*.
28. Barbeck, *Geschichte der Juden*, 45–48.
29. Kasparek, *Jews in Fürth*, 6.
30. Israel, "Central European Jewry."
31. Ophir and Wiesemann, *Die jüdischen Gemeinden*, 179.
32. Ibid.
33. Kasparek, *Jews in Fürth*, 10f. See also Ferziger, *Exclusion and Hierarchy*, 84.
34. Mümmler, *Fürth*, 125.
35. Ophir and Wiesemann, *Die jüdischen Gemeinden*, 13f.
36. Edgar Rosenberg, "Kristallnacht Memories," http://bit.ly/1DrLCSu.
37. Wassermann, *Life as German and Jew*, 5.
38. Ibid., 6f.
39. Ibid., 12f., 14f.
40. Ibid., 17.
41. Ibid., 22.
42. Ibid., 24.
43. Ibid., 11.
44. Ibid., 64.
45. Ibid., 220f.
46. Hellige, "Generationskonflikt, Selbsthaß und die Entstehung antikapitalistischer Positionen."

47. Kissinger family papers, Martin Kissinger to Charles Stanton, Jan. 27, 1986.
48. Ibid., Martin Kissinger to Charles Stanton, July 3, 1980.
49. Stadtarchiv Fürth, Biographische Sammlung Henry Kissinger, Herkunft der Familie Dr. Henry Kissinger, Friedrich Kühner to E. Ammon, June 24, 1974.
50. Kurz, *Kissinger Saga*, 45–49.
51. Ley, "Die Heckmannschule," 68.
52. Stadtarchiv Fürth, Biographische Sammlung Henry Kissinger, E. Ammon to Dr. W. Mahr, Jan. 18, 1974.
53. See the 1932 photograph of him at the Handelsschule Fürth preserved in the Stadtarchiv Fürth.
54. Kurz, *Kissinger Saga*, 50f. Cf. Strauss, *Fürth in der Weltwirtschaftskrise*, 103f.
55. HAK, interview by author. See also Isaacson, *Kissinger*, KL 285, quoting interviews with Paula and Arno Kissinger.
56. Kurz, *Kissinger Saga*, 92.
57. On Zionism in Fürth, see Zinke, "Nächstes Jahr im Kibbuz."
58. New York Public Library, Dorot Jewish Division: P (Oral Histories), Box 90, no. 5, Paula Kissinger interview, 13. See also Kurz, *Kissinger Saga*, 92.
59. New York Public Library, Dorot Jewish Division: P (Oral Histories), Box 90, no. 5, Paula Kissinger interview, 5.
60. Ibid., 3, 11.
61. Strauss, *Fürth in der Weltwirtschaftskrise*.
62. Stadtarchiv Fürth, Biographische Sammlung Henry Kissinger, E. Ammon to Wilhelm Kleppmann, June 12, 1973.
63. New York Public Library, Dorot Jewish Division: P (Oral Histories), Box 90, no. 5, Paula Kissinger interview, 6.
64. Stadtarchiv Fürth, Biographische Sammlung Henry Kissinger.
65. "Kissinger's Boyhood Buddy," *Hadassah*, no. 35, Mar. 1974.
66. "Als US-Henry Noch Heinz Alfred war," *Wiener Kurier*, Aug. 12, 1974.
67. "Kissinger's Boyhood Buddy," *Hadassah*, no. 35, Mar. 1974.
68. Ibid.
69. Isaacson, *Kissinger*, KL 400.
70. Blumenfeld, *Kissinger*, 4.
71. "Henry A. Kissinger in Fürth," *Amtsblatt der Stadt Fürth*, Dec. 19, 1975, 342.
72. Kilmeade, *Games Do Count*, 63f.
73. "Kissinger's Boyhood Buddy," *Hadassah*, no. 35, Mar. 1974. Lion's parents went to Palestine in 1938. The former friends met again in 1963, when Kissinger came to lecture at Israel's Foreign Ministry.
74. Kissinger family papers, Paula Kissinger to HAK, Mar. 3, 1964.
75. Mazlish, *Kissinger*, 24.
76. Walter Kissinger, interview by author.
77. Ophir and Wiesemann, *Die jüdischen Gemeinden*, 19, 179.
78. Ibid., 20.
79. Zinke, "An allem ist Alljuda schuld," 89–94.
80. Strauss, *Fürth in der Weltwirtschaftskrise*, 381f.

81. Zinke, *"An allem ist Alljuda schuld,"* 96ff.
82. Strauss, *Fürth in der Weltwirtschaftskrise,* 165–206.
83. Ibid., 207, 223.
84. Ibid., 457ff.
85. Ibid., 263, 275.
86. Ibid., 280.
87. Ibid., 289–94. See also 400, 408 for examples.

88. Mierzejewski, *Ludwig Erhard,* 2f.
89. Strauss, *Fürth in der Weltwirtschaftskrise,* 393–96.
90. Zinke, *"An allem ist Alljuda schuld,"* 100.
91. Ibid., 94f.; Strauss, *Fürth in der Weltwirtschaftskrise,* 402f.
92. Mümmler, *Fürth,* 11–15.
93. Strauss, *Fürth in der Weltwirtschaftskrise,* 419.

Chapter 2: Escape

1. HAK to his parents, 1945, quoted in Isaacson, *Kissinger,* KL 899.
2. Mümmler, *Fürth,* 105.
3. Ibid., 49–52.
4. Ibid., 95–104.
5. Ibid., 21, 23, 80.
6. Strauss, *Fürth in der Weltwirtschaftskrise,* 439.
7. Ophir and Wiesemann, *Die jüdischen Gemeinden,* 22.
8. Grete von Ballin, "Chronik der Juden in Fürth," ed. Hugo Heinemann (n.d.), 5.
9. Strauss, *Fürth in der Weltwirtschaftskrise,* 442.
10. Ballin, "Chronik," 19.
11. Mümmler, *Fürth,* 86, 138–43.
12. Ballin, "Chronik," 5–9, 19.
13. Mümmler, *Fürth,* 215.
14. Ballin, "Chronik," 11.
15. Ibid., 12f.
16. Suri, *Kissinger,* 41.
17. Ophir and Wiesemann, *Die jüdischen Gemeinden,* 182.
18. Ballin, "Chronik," 13.
19. Strauss, *Fürth in der Weltwirtschaftskrise,* 444.
20. Ophir and Wiesemann, *Die jüdischen Gemeinden,* 182.
21. Mümmel, *Fürth,* 122; Kurz, *Kissinger Saga,* 89.
22. Walter Kissinger, interview by author.
23. New York Public Library, Dorot Jewish Division: P (Oral Histories), Box 90, no. 5, Paula Kissinger interview, 8. For a different view see "Sie kramten in der Erinnerung," *Fürther Nachrichten,* n.d., c. 1974, describing Louis's return to what was now the Helene-Lange-Gymnasium. Louis is quoted as saying, "Even those who had sympathy with the then [political] tendency were always friendly to me."
24. Stadtarchiv Fürth, Biographische Sammlung Henry Kissinger, E. Ammon, Betreff. Schulbesuch von Henry A. Kissinger, July 19, 1974.
25. HAK, interview by author.
26. Thiele, "Leben vor und nach der Flucht aus dem Regime des Nationalsozialismus," 10f.
27. New York Public Library, Dorot Jewish Division: P (Oral Histories), Box 90, no. 5, Paula Kissinger interview, 7.
28. Kalb and Kalb, *Kissinger,* 33.
29. Ballin, "Chronik," 21.
30. Kilmeade, *Games Do Count,* 63f.
31. Jules Wallerstein, "Limited Autobiography of Jules Wallerstein," MS, n.d.
32. Thiele, "Leben vor und nach der Flucht," 12.
33. National Archives and Records Administration, RG 59, Box 7, Folder "Soviet Union, May–Sept. 1976," 02036, Memcon HAK, Sonnenfeldt, Rabbi Morris Sherer, Aug. 23, 1976.

34. For details on the Jewish youth groups Esra and Zeirei Agudath Israel, see Breuer, *Modernity Within Tradition.*
35. Agudath Israel of America, Orthodox Jewish Archives, Herman Landau Papers, HAK handwritten note and transcriptions, July 3, 1937.
36. For a good recent account, see Sinanoglou, "Peel Commission," in Miller, *Britain, Palestine and Empire,* 119–40.
37. New York Public Library, Dorot Jewish Division: P (Oral Histories), Box 90, no. 5, Paula Kissinger interview, 8.
38. Isaacson, *Kissinger,* KL 415.
39. Ibid., KL 459.
40. New York Public Library, Dorot Jewish Division: P (Oral Histories), Box 90, no. 5, Paula Kissinger interview, 9; Kurz, *Kissinger Saga,* 96.
41. Staatsarchiv Nuremberg, Bestand Polizeiamt Fürth, Nr. 441, "Personal-Akt über Louis Kissinger," Bescheinigungen, Apr. 21, 1938.
42. Ibid., Louis Kissinger to Polizeiamt Fürth, Apr. 24, 1938.
43. Ibid., Geheime Staatspolizei to Polizeipraesidium Nürnberg-Fürth, May 5, 1938.
44. Ibid., Finanzamt Fürth to Geheime Staatspolizei to Polizeipraesidium Nürnberg-Fürth, May 6, 1938.
45. Ibid., Zollfahndungsstelle to Geheime Staatspolizei to Polizeipraesidium Nürnberg-Fürth, May 9, 1938.
46. Ibid., Polizeiamt Fürth, May 10, 1938.
47. Isaacson, *Kissinger,* KL 466–67.
48. HAK, interview by author.
49. Kurz, *Kissinger Saga,* 98.
50. HAK, interview by author.
51. Ophir and Wiesemann, *Die jüdischen Gemeinden,* 25.
52. Edgar Rosenberg, "Kristallnacht Memories," http://bit.ly/1DrLCSu.
53. Mümmel, *Fürth,* 150ff.
54. Edgar Rosenberg, "Kristallnacht Memories."
55. Ibid.
56. Thiele, "Leben vor und nach der Flucht," 14.
57. Ophir and Wiesemann, *Die jüdischen Gemeinden,* 183f.; Ballin, "Chronik," 27–41.
58. Wiener, *Time of Terror,* 252.
59. Yale Fortunoff Archive for Holocaust Testimony, Alfred Weinbeber interview, HVT-2972, Mar. 29, 1995.
60. Rosenberg, *Stanford Short Stories 1953,* 163.
61. Mümmler, *Fürth,* 184.
62. Gregor, "Schicksalsgemeinschaft?"
63. Mümmler, *Fürth,* 89.
64. Baynes, *Speeches of Hitler,* 1:741.
65. Ballin, "Chronik." This chronicle was compiled in 1943 at the orders of the Gestapo. When it

ended (with the author's own deportation) only 88 Jews remained, of whom 55 were originally members of the Fürth Jewish community. For somewhat different estimates, see Mümmler, *Fürth*, 89, 156, 220. A complete list of all the deported can be found at Leo Baeck Institute, 7, List of 1841 and Lists of Jews who were deported or emigrated, Oct. 7, 1974.

66. Kasparek, *Jews in Fürth*, 34.
67. Thiele, "Leben vor und nach der Flucht," 20.
68. Ophir and Wiesemann, *Die jüdischen Gemeinden*, 186.
69. New York Public Library, Dorot Jewish Division: P (Oral Histories), Box 90, no. 5, Paula Kissinger interview, 9.

70. HAK, interview by author. Kissinger remembered that she was sent to Auschwitz, but Belžec seems more likely.
71. Yad Vashem Central Database of Shoah Victims' Names. See also *Gedenkbuch: Opfer der Verfolgung der Juden under de nationalsozialistischen Gewaltherrschaft in Deutschland, 1933–1945*, 2 vols. (Koblenz: Bundesarchiv, 1986). Cf. Kurz, *Kissinger Saga*, 103f.
72. Stadtarchiv Fürth, Biographische Sammlung Henry Kissinger, Überreichung der Goldenen Bürgermedaille seiner Vaterstadt an Herrn Aussenminister Professor Henry A. Kissinger, Dec. 15, 1975.
73. Isaacson, *Kissinger*, KL 487.
74. HAK, interview by author.
75. Ibid.

Chapter 3: Fürth on the Hudson

1. Kissinger family papers, HAK to Hilde, July 29, 1939.
2. Moore, *At Home in America*, 30, 86.
3. Appelius, *"Die schönste Stadt der Welt,"* 30–34, 151, 127.
4. David Kennedy, *Freedom from Fear*, KL 6342–441, 13940–41.
5. Ibid., KL 3543.
6. Ibid., KL 13515–16.
7. Ferguson, *War of the World*, 273f.
8. David Kennedy, *Freedom from Fear*, KL 5964, 6207.
9. Ibid., KL 6332–33.
10. Ibid., KL 5655–57, 6326.
11. "Mayor Arranges Trucking Parley as Tie-Up Spreads," *New York Times*, Sept. 18, 1938.
12. "Bombs Shatter Windows of 7 Fur Shops," *New York Times*, Sept. 12, 1938.
13. Bayor, *Neighbors in Conflict*, 41–45.
14. Milton Bracker, "Football Comes to the Gridiron of Asphalt," *New York Times*, Nov. 6, 1938.
15. Horowitz and Kaplan, "Estimated Jewish Population of the New York Area, 1900–1975," 14f.
16. Ibid., 22.
17. Moore, *At Home in America*, 30.
18. Leventmann, "From Shtetl to Suburb," in Rose, *Ghetto and Beyond*, 43f.
19. Moore, *At Home in America*, 36ff.
20. Ibid., 65, 85.
21. Strauss, "Immigration and Acculturation of the German Jew."
22. Lowenstein, *Frankfurt on the Hudson*, 47.
23. Appelius, *"Die schönste Stadt der Welt,"* 30–34, 151.
24. Moore, *At Home in America*, 8, 13.
25. Bayor, *Neighbors in Conflict*, 20.
26. Moore, *At Home in America*, 5.
27. Bayor, *Neighbors in Conflict*, 10–13, 20.
28. Ibid., 25f. See also ibid., 127, 130, for the Jewish vote in 1933.
29. Moore, *At Home in America*, 215.
30. Bayor, *Neighbors in Conflict*, 51.
31. Ibid., 33ff., 137, 143, 147.
32. Ibid., 29, 31f.
33. Ibid., 39.
34. Ibid., 89, 92f.
35. Moore, *At Home in America*, 204.

36. Bayor, *Neighbors in Conflict*, 41.
37. Moore, *At Home in America*, 223.
38. Ferguson, *War of the World*, 527.
39. David Kennedy, *Freedom from Fear*, KL 7478–79, 7499–500, 7505–6, 7503–4, 7507–9.
40. Ferguson, *War of the World*, 527.
41. "Asks Red Inquiry at N.Y.U., Hunter," *New York Times*, Oct. 6, 1938.
42. Appelius, *"Die schönste Stadt der Welt,"* 23–29.
43. Bayor, *Neighbors in Conflict*, 97f.
44. Ibid., 61.
45. Ibid., 57.
46. Ibid., 71–78.
47. Ibid., 113, 116, 121.
48. Epstein, *Oblivious in Washington Heights*, 1f.
49. Lowenstein, *Frankfurt on the Hudson*, 107, map 5.
50. Ibid., 178; Appelius, *"Die schönste Stadt der Welt,"* 177.
51. Appelius, *"Die schönste Stadt der Welt,"* 23–29.
52. Lowenstein, *Frankfurt on the Hudson*, 66. Cf. Moore, *At Home in America*, 82. See also Yeshiva University Museum, *German Jews of Washington Heights*; Lendt, *Social History of Washington Heights*.
53. Lowenstein, *Frankfurt on the Hudson*, 86.
54. Moore, *At Home in America*, 66, table 4.
55. Appelius, *"Die schönste Stadt der Welt,"* 171.
56. Bayor, *Neighbors in Conflict*, 150f.
57. Stock, "Washington Heights' 'Fourth Reich,'" 581.
58. Ibid., 584.
59. Appelius, *"Die schönste Stadt der Welt,"* 165f.
60. Stock, "Washington Heights' 'Fourth Reich,'" 582.
61. Ibid., 583.
62. Lowenstein, *Frankfurt on the Hudson*, 49.
63. Ibid., 126.
64. Appelius, *"Die schönste Stadt der Welt,"* 162f.
65. Moore, *At Home in America*, 124–47.
66. Ibid., 178–99.
67. Lowenstein, *Frankfurt on the Hudson*, 152f., 158, 163–67.
68. Ibid., 148, 149, tables 25 and 26.
69. Ibid., 19.
70. Stock, "Washington Heights' 'Fourth Reich,'" 584. For good images of Washington Heights in this period, see Stern, *So war es*.

71. Lowenstein, *Frankfurt on the Hudson*, 75, table 4, 78, table 6.
72. Ibid., 32–38.
73. Appelius, *"Die schönste Stadt der Welt,"* 185.
74. Ibid., 187.
75. Bloch, Marx, and Stransky, *Festschrift in Honor of Congregation Beth Hillel*.
76. See for insights into Breuer's thinking, Breuer, *Introduction to Rabbi Hirsch's Commentary*; Breuer, *Jewish Marriage*.
77. See for example *Mitteilungen: Organ der K'hall Adass Jeshurun und der K'hall Agudath Jeshorim*, [henceforth *Mitteilungen*], Jan. 1940.
78. Joseph Breuer, "Zur Jahreswende," *Mitteilungen*, Sept. 1940, 1. See also "Der 'zionistische' Aufruf des Propheten," *Mitteilungen*, July–Aug. 1943, 1.
79. Lowenstein, *Frankfurt on the Hudson*, 114–18, 122, 130. See also Appelius, *"Die schönste Stadt der Welt,"* 190f.
80. Lowenstein, *Frankfurt on the Hudson*, 141, 154.
81. HAK, interview by author.
82. Fass, *Outside In*, 73–79.
83. Moore, *At Home in America*, 96.
84. Fass, *Outside In*, 81, 92, 87 table 3, 94.
85. Greenspan, *Age of Turbulence*, 19–24.
86. Bayor, *Neighbors in Conflict*, 155f. Cf. Appelius, *"Die schönste Stadt der Welt,"* 174f.
87. Lowenstein, *Frankfurt on the Hudson*, 39–46. See also Appelius, *"Die schönste Stadt der Welt,"* 21, 52ff., 62ff., 104–9.
88. Appelius, *"Die schönste Stadt der Welt,"* 171.
89. Bayor, *Neighbors in Conflict*, 155f.
90. Lowenstein, *Frankfurt on the Hudson*, 241.
91. Appelius, *"Die schönste Stadt der Welt,"* 179–82, 204.
92. *WHY*, 229.
93. Mazlish, *Kissinger*, 7.
94. Suri, *Kissinger*, 44–47.
95. Appelius, *"Die schönste Stadt der Welt,"* 169.
96. Museum of Jewish Heritage, HAK interview by Louise Bobrow, Jan. 11, 2001.
97. New York Public Library, Dorot Jewish Division: P (Oral Histories), Box 90, no. 5, Paula Kissinger interview, 14.

98. Isaacson, *Kissinger*, KL 582.
99. Appelius, *"Die schönste Stadt der Welt,"* 167.
100. Greenspan, *Age of Turbulence*, 24.
101. Library of Congress [henceforth LOC], HAK schoolwork samples, June 6, 1939. Unless otherwise stated, all LOC references are the Kissinger Papers housed at the LOC.
102. Ibid., HAK school grades, Jan. 4, 1940, and June 27, 1940. Unless otherwise stated, all LOC references are to the Kissinger papers housed when I used them at the Library of Congress.
103. HAK, interview by author.
104. Museum of Jewish Heritage, HAK interview.
105. Kalb and Kalb, *Kissinger*, 36f.
106. Lowenstein, *Frankfurt on the Hudson*, 187.
107. Abraham Goldstein, "Our New Home," *Mitteilungen*, Apr. 1941, 5a.
108. Stock, "Washington Heights' 'Fourth Reich,'" 585.
109. Moore, *At Home in America*, 105. See also Mazlish, *Kissinger*, 39–41.
110. Isaacson, *Kissinger*, 37f.; Kalb and Kalb, *Kissinger*, 37.
111. Blumenfeld, *Kissinger*, 23, 42.
112. Isaacson, *Kissinger*, 35f.
113. HAK, interview by author.
114. Stock, "Washington Heights' 'Fourth Reich,'" 588.
115. Kissinger family papers, "Voice of the Union: *Eine Zeitung im Aufbau!*" May 1, 1939.
116. Ibid., HAK to Hilde, July 29, 1939.
117. Lowenstein, *Frankfurt on the Hudson*, 55, 56.
118. Blumenfeld, *Kissinger*, 249.
119. Kissinger family papers, HAK to Hilde, July 29, 1939.
120. Appelius, *"Die schönste Stadt der Welt,"* 130ff.
121. Kissinger family papers, HAK to Hilde, July 29, 1939.
122. Ibid., HAK to Dept. of Parks, New York City, July 9, 1942.
123. Isaacson, *Kissinger*, 35ff.
124. Kissinger family papers, HAK to Edith, Mar. 14, Mar. 31, 1940.
125. Ibid., HAK to Hilde, July 29, 1939.

Chapter 4: An Unexpected Private

1. Arndt Gymnasium Dahlem, Fritz Kraemer, "Der Pakt zwischen Mephistopheles und Faust (nach Goethes Faust)," Deutscher Aufsatz, Feb. 3, 1926.
2. LOC, G-14 Supp. (Kraemer), Kraemer to Prof. Robinson, Nov. 8, 1940.
3. Charles Lindbergh, "Des Moines Speech," PBS, http://to.pbs.org/1bAMey9.
4. Museum of Jewish Heritage, HAK interview by Louise Bobrow, Jan. 11, 2001.
5. HAK family papers, HAK to Dept. of Parks, New York City, July 9, 1942.
6. Isaacson, *Kissinger*, 38.
7. Breuer, "Our Duty Towards America," *Mitteilungen*, Jan. 1942, 1.
8. Franklin, "Victim Soldiers," 46.
9. Walter Kissinger, interview by author.
10. Franklin, "Victim Soldiers," 48, 52.
11. Appelius, *"Die schönste Stadt der Welt,"* 213.
12. Ibid., 211ff.

13. David De Sola Pool, "Immigrant and U.S. Army," *Aufbau*, Jan. 30, 1942, 1.
14. Samson R. Breuer, "A Pessach Message from Afar," *Mitteilungen*, Apr. 1944, 2.
15. Grailet, *Avec Henry Kissinger*, 8.
16. Isaacson, *Kissinger*, 39.
17. Ibid. For details on Camp Croft, see http://bit.ly/1z17fNd.
18. Franklin, "Victim Soldiers," 48.
19. Suri, *Kissinger*, 58.
20. Isaacson, *Kissinger*, 40f.
21. "Soldier Column," *Mitteilungen*, Apr. 1945, 2.
22. See Mailer, *Naked and the Dead*.
23. Suri, *Kissinger*, 62.
24. Keefer, *Scholars in Foxholes*, 81n.
25. Ibid., 221.
26. Ibid., 69. Elsewhere (ibid., 270) the total of men who entered the program is given as 216,000.
27. Ibid., 93.
28. Reid, *Never Tell an Infantryman*, 31.

29. Ibid., 36.
30. Charles J. Coyle, "Roommate Recalls Kissinger's Days at Lafayette," *Lafayette Alumnus* 44, no. 3 (Feb. 1973), 24f.
31. Ibid.
32. LOC, MCD-101, HAK Certificate of Attendance, Apr. 1, 1944; ASTP Student Record—Lafayette College.
33. Ibid., John H. Yundt letter of recommendation, Mar. 13, 1944.
34. Keefer, *Scholars in Foxholes*, 170.
35. Kalb and Kalb, *Kissinger*, 38.
36. Keefer, *Scholars in Foxholes*, 190, 157, 87n, 205, 215, 217, 218, 271.
37. Coyle, "Roommate Recalls," 24f.
38. Isaacson, *Kissinger*, 42.
39. *Camp Claiborne News*, http://www.campclaiborne.com.
40. Mazlish, *Kissinger*, 41f. Cf. Reid, *Never Tell an Infantryman*, 36.
41. Edwards, *Private's Diary*, 2.
42. Draper, *84th Infantry Division*, x.
43. Matson and Stein, *We Were the Line*, 9.
44. Ibid., 22.
45. Reid, *Never Tell an Infantryman*, 37–42.
46. Edwards, *Private's Diary*, 8.
47. Isaacson, *Kissinger*, KL 695.
48. Grailet, *Avec Henry Kissinger*, 7.
49. Isaacson, *Kissinger*, KL 755–57.
50. Coyle, "Roommate Recalls," 24f.
51. Isaacson, *Kissinger*, KL 726–29.
52. "Fritz Kraemer," *Daily Telegraph*, Nov. 10, 2003.
53. Arndt Gymnasium Dahlem, Fritz Kraemer, "Der Pakt zwischen Mephistopheles und Faust (nach Goethes Faust)," Deutscher Aufsatz, Feb. 3, 1926.
54. Frankfurt University Archives, Fritz Kraemer, "Lebenslauf," 1931.
55. Drucker, *Adventures of Bystander*, 141f.
56. Sven Kraemer, "My Father's Pilgrimage," in Hoffmann, *Fritz Kraemer on Excellence*, 80f.
57. Drucker, *Adventures of Bystander*, 141f.
58. Ibid., 142–47.
59. Ibid., 147.
60. Harley, *International Understanding*, 188.
61. London School of Economics Archives and Rare Books Library, C. A. Waterfield to E. V. Evans, July 24, 1926; Kraemer admission application, 1926; Kraemer certificate, Apr. 11, 1927; W. C. Dickinson to P. N. Baker, Dec. 3, 1926.
62. Frankfurt University Archives, Fritz Kraemer, "Lebenslauf," 1931. Cf. Link, *Ein Realist mit Idealen*.
63. Kraemer, *Das Verhältnis der französischen Bündnisverträge*, 92–95. See also 106, 123.
64. Ibid., 128.
65. Ibid., 41.
66. Luig, *Weil er nicht arischer Abstammung*, 244–47. See also Bergemann and Ladwig-Winters, *Richter und Staatsanwälte jüdischer Herkunft*.
67. A facsimile of his death certificate can be seen at "Krämer Georg," Holocaust.cz, http://bit.ly/1DYouxi. See also "Krämer Georg," Memorial Book, Das Bundesarchiv, http://bit.ly/1d9lXrn.
68. Drucker, *Adventures of Bystander*, 147f.
69. Ibid., 148.
70. Ibid.
71. *American Philosophical Society Year Book 1941* (1942). For what may have been part of this project see LOC, G-14 Supp. (Kraemer), "Territorial Changes in North Europe," n.d.
72. LOC, G-14 Supp. (Kraemer), Philip Jessup to Kraemer, June 6, 1943.
73. Ibid., Kraemer to Prof. Robinson, Nov. 8, 1940.
74. Ibid., Kraemer to Mr. Cornelison, n.d., c. 1952.
75. FBI, Fritz Kraemer file: 100-3778 [1942 investigation]; WFO 118-5366 [1951 investigation]; WPO 161-15133 [1981 investigation].
76. LOC, G-14 Supp. (Kraemer), "Story of Contacts with OSS, 1943/1944," n.d.
77. "Fritz Kraemer," *Guardian*, Nov. 12, 2003.
78. LOC, G-14 Supp. (Kraemer), Kraemer to Mr. Cornelison, n.d., c. 1952.
79. Ibid., Lt. Austin O'Malley to Prof. Fritz Marti, Feb. 28, 1944.
80. "Fritz Kraemer," *Guardian*, Nov. 12, 2003.
81. Isaacson, *Kissinger*, KL 772.
82. HAK, "The Prophet and the Policymaker" [eulogy for Fritz Kraemer, Oct. 8, 2003], in Hoffmann, *Kraemer on Excellence*, 10.
83. Mazlish, *Kissinger*, 47f., 50f.
84. Suri, *Kissinger*, 80.
85. Mazlish, *Kissinger*, 50.
86. Kalb and Kalb, *Kissinger*, 39.
87. HAK, interview by author.
88. Roberts, *Masters and Commanders*, 514–25.
89. Ibid., 511, 519.
90. Beevor, *Second World War*, 633–43; Hastings, *All Hell Let Loose*, 577–89.
91. Kershaw, *The End*.
92. Matson and Stein, *We Were the Line*, 24.
93. Edwards, *Private's Diary*, 19.
94. Ibid., 28.
95. Matson and Stein, *We Were the Line*, 25.
96. Ibid., 29, 35, 31.
97. Reid, *Never Tell an Infantryman*, 48–54; Matson and Stein, *We Were the Line*, 34–37.
98. Matson and Stein, *We Were the Line*, 43.
99. Edwards, *Private's Diary*, 61.
100. Kissinger family papers, HAK to his parents, Nov. 25, 1944.
101. Reid, *Never Tell an Infantryman*, 54f.
102. Edwards, *Private's Diary*, 64.

Chapter 5: The Living and the Dead

1. Kissinger family papers, HAK to his parents, Nov. 25, 1944.
2. LOC, A-19(b), HAK, "The Eternal Jew," n.d. [April or May 1945].
3. Matson and Stein, *We Were the Line*, 49.
4. Reid, *Never Tell an Infantryman*, 63.
5. Kissinger family papers, HAK to his parents, Nov. 25, 1944.
6. Draper, *84th Infantry Division*, 10.
7. Edwards, *Private's Diary*, 133.

8. Matson and Stein, *We Were the Line*, 56.

9. Draper, *84th Infantry Division*, 22, 34f.

10. Edwards, *Private's Diary*, 203.

11. Kissinger family papers, HAK to his parents, Oct. 16, 1944.

12. Draper, *84th Infantry Division*, 4f.

13. Ibid., 20.

14. Ibid., 74f.

15. Ibid., 40.

16. Matson and Stein, *We Were the Line*, 62f.

17. Draper, *84th Infantry Division*, 49–71.

18. U.S. Army Military History Institute, 335th Infantry, 2nd Battalion, HQ Company, "A Company Speaks," 5.

19. Matson and Stein, *We Were the Line*, 74.

20. Ibid., 73.

21. Ibid., 75.

22. Ibid., 77.

23. Edwards, *Private's Diary*, 171.

24. Ibid., 241.

25. Ellis, *World War II Databook*, 228, 255f.

26. Edwards, *Private's Diary*, 577, appendix 1.

27. Matson and Stein, *We Were the Line*, 207ff.

28. HAK, "The Prophet and the Policymaker." Isaacson has Kissinger becoming a driver-cum-translator for General Bolling, which seems improbable: Isaacson, *Kissinger*, KL 845.

29. LOC, MDC-101, HAK Application for Federal Employment, Nov. 17, 1945.

30. Kissinger family papers, HAK to his parents, Nov. 29, 1944.

31. Edwards, *Private's Diary*, 153.

32. Draper, *84th Infantry Division*, 77f.

33. Grailet, *Avec Henry Kissinger*, 9. See also Matson and Stein, *We Were the Line*, 84.

34. Draper, *84th Infantry Division*, 86.

35. Ibid., 87.

36. Ibid., 89.

37. Ibid., 86.

38. Grailet, *Avec Henry Kissinger*, 10f.

39. U.S. Army Military History Institute, 335th Infantry, 2nd Battalion, HQ Company, "A Company Speaks," 7.

40. Matson and Stein, *We Were the Line*, 92f.

41. Railsplitter Society (84th Infantry Division), Capt. Roger K. Taylor, 335th Infantry After Action Report, Dec. 31, 1944, http://www.84thinfantry.com.

42. Ibid., 335th Infantry After Action Report, Dec. 31, 1944.

43. Draper, *84th Infantry Division*, 95–103.

44. LOC, A-19(b), HAK to Walter, "On the Western Front," Feb. 5–8, 1945 [Jan. 1947], 1.

45. Edwards, *Private's Diary*, 266f.

46. See, e.g., ibid., 276.

47. LOC, A-19(b), HAK to Walter, "On the Western Front," Feb. 5–8, 1945, 2.

48. Draper, *84th Infantry Division*, 86.

49. Franklin, "Victim Soldiers," 69f.

50. LOC, A-19(b), HAK to Walter, "On the Western Front," Feb. 5–8, 1945, 3.

51. Ibid., 4. According to Kissinger, this passage of the letter was written by Kraemer. The worldly-wise comment about "the art of seduction" certainly sounds more like him than like Kissinger.

52. Ibid., 5.

53. Ibid., 6–7.

54. Ibid.

55. Ibid., 8.

56. Ibid., 8f.

57. Isaacson, *Kissinger*, KL 852.

58. LOC, A-19(b), HAK to Walter, "On the Western Front," Feb. 5–8, 1945, 10.

59. Draper, *84th Infantry Division*, 95–103.

60. LOC, A-19(b), HAK to Walter, "On the Western Front," Feb. 5–8, 1945, 11.

61. Edwards, *Private's Diary*, 284.

62. Matson and Stein, *We Were the Line*, 106f., 132.

63. Grailet, *Avec Henry Kissinger*, 19–21.

64. Ibid., 15f. Cf. Matson and Stein, *We Were the Line*, 103.

65. Edwards, *Private's Diary*, 284.

66. Matson and Stein, *We Were the Line*, 117.

67. Grailet, *Avec Henry Kissinger*, 36.

68. Ibid., 22ff., 27.

69. Ibid., 40.

70. Ibid., 420f.; Matson and Stein, *We Were the Line*, 140–48.

71. Draper, *84th Infantry Division*, 132–60.

72. Edwards, *Private's Diary*, 431ff.

73. Ibid., 443.

74. Draper, *84th Infantry Division*, 174f. Cf. Matson and Stein, *We Were the Line*, 148–53.

75. Draper, *84th Infantry Division*, 187; Matson and Stein, *We Were the Line*, 156.

76. Bommers, "Kriegsende," unpublished ms., 1–3, 11–15.

77. Draper, *84th Infantry Division*, 161–67.

78. Ibid., 183.

79. Matson and Stein, *We Were the Line*, 161.

80. Isaacson, *Kissinger*, KL 862. The story is repeated by Suri, *Kissinger*.

81. See, for example, the case of Eric W. Lange: "97-Pointer Gets Job That May Delay Him," *New York Times*, June 6, 1945, 3.

82. LOC, HAK, A & P, Kraemer letter of recommendation, Mar. 7, 1949. Cf. Elsässer, "Kissinger in Krefeld und Bensheim," 15–19.

83. Kremers, *Lucky Strikes*, 18f.; Bommers, "Kriegsende," 44.

84. Bommers, "Kriegsende," 5.

85. *Parade*, Mar. 24, 1945.

86. Pocock, *Alan Moorehead*, 197.

87. Stadtarchiv Krefeld 70, 565, "Die Verhältnisse im Bahnhofsbunker Krefeld während der letzten Tage des Krieges 1945," Nov. 1, 1946.

88. Bommers, "Kriegsende," 16.

89. Matson and Stein, *We Were the Line*, 153.

90. Ibid., 196.

91. Edwards, *Private's Diary*, 499f.

92. Kremers, *Lucky Strikes*, 8–10, 15, 16.

93. Bommers, "Kriegsende," 28.

94. Stadtarchiv Krefeld, 70, 565, "Aus dem Kriegstagebuch eines Linners," Mar. 3, 4, 26, 1945.

95. Ibid., Apr. 9, 1945.

96. Stadtarchiv Krefeld, 70, 565, "Aus dem Kriegstagebuch eines Krefelders," Mar. 7, 1945.

97. Ibid., 70, 565, "Aus dem Kriegstagebuch eines Fischbelners [Franz Heckmann]," Mar. 1, 1945.

98. Ibid., Apr. 1, 1945.

99. Ibid. Cf. Kremers, *Lucky Strikes*, 11.

100. LOC, MDC-101, HAK to Wesley G. Spencer, May 10, 1947.

101. Kickum, "Strukturen der Militärregierungen," 110f.
102. See in general Kershaw, *The End*.
103. Padover, *Experiment in Germany*, 284ff.
104. Stadtarchiv Krefeld, 70, 565, Heuyng to Lorentzen, Mar. 1, 1945.
105. Kickum, "Strukturen der Militärregierungen," 108; Bommers, "Kriegsende," 18–20.
106. LOC, A-19(b), 94–116, HAK and Robert S. Taylor, Memorandum to the Officer in Charge: Investigation of City Officials in Krefeld re: Political Fitness for Office, Mar. 17, 1945.
107. Stadtarchiv Krefeld, 70, 565, "Aus dem Kriegstagebuch eines Linners," Mar. 28, 1945.
108. National Archives and Records Administration, RG 319.270.84.[84.]20, Krefeld Gestapo XE 019212, Apr. 18, 1945.
109. Ibid., RG 319.270.84.20, 37, Darmstadt Gestapo XE 003411, July 26, 1945.
110. Hangebruch, "Emigriert—Deportiert," in Rotthoff, *Krefelder Juden*, 137–215.
111. Johnson, *Nazi Terror*.
112. Schupetta, "Die Geheime Staatspolizei."
113. Suri, *Kissinger*, 72. See also Mazlish, *Kissinger*, 41f.
114. Colodny and Schachtman, *Forty Years War*, 25.
115. Kissinger, "Prophet and the Policymaker." Cf. Colodny and Schachtman, *Forty Years War*, 25.
116. Matson and Stein, *We Were the Line*, 170f.
117. Draper, *84th Infantry Division*, 202ff. See also Edwards, *Private's Diary*, 516f.
118. Kershaw, *The End*, 280.
119. Matson and Stein, *We Were the Line*, 177.
120. Ibid., 181.
121. Kissinger family papers, HAK to his parents, May 6, 1945.
122. LOC, A-19(b), 86–88, Memorandum to the Officer in Charge: Chronological Activities of Investigation of Underground Activities, Members of the Gestapo and Gestapo Plot in Hanover, Apr. 16, 1945. For more details about Binder, see Paul and Mallmann, *Die Gestapo*.
123. LOC, A-19(b), 70–72, Translation of Life History and Underground Activities, Adolf Rinne, Member of the Gestapo, Hanover, Apr. 16, 1945.
124. Ibid., 90–93, Major General A. R. Bolling, General Orders No. 81, Apr. 27, 1945. For further details, see LOC, MDC-101, Paul H. Wyman, Report of CIC Activities of Special Agent Henry Kissinger, Nov. 18, 1945.
125. LOC, MDC-101, Letter of Recommendation Regarding Special Agent Henri [sic] Kissinger, Aug. 28, 1945.
126. Ibid., "Promotion of Enlisted Men," Aug. 28, 1945.
127. *Mitteilungen*, Dec. 1942, 1.
128. Breuer, "Der jüdische Hilferuf," *Mitteilungen*, Feb. 1944, 1.
129. Tott, "Ahlem Concentration Camp," unpublished ms., 140.
130. Gutmann, "KZ Ahlem," in Fröbe et al., *Konzentrationslager in Hannover*, vol. 1, 331–406.
131. Tott, "Ahlem Concentration Camp." More details are given in Anschütz and Heike, *"Wir wollten Gefühle sichtbar werden lassen."*
132. Tott, "Ahlem Concentration Camp," 11. See also Tott, *Letters and Reflections*.
133. Edwards, *Private's Diary*, 528f.
134. Ibid., 534.
135. Ibid.
136. Ibid., 528.
137. Tott, "Ahlem Concentration Camp," 4–7, 12–38. Tott's ms. assembles many survivors' accounts of their appalling mistreatment at Ahlem.
138. Tott, *Letters and Reflections*, n.p.
139. Edwards, *Private's Diary*, 532.
140. HAK, interview by author.
141. Anschütz and Heike, *"Wir wollten Gefühle sichtbar werden lassen,"* 33.
142. LOC, A-19(b), HAK, "The Eternal Jew," n.d.

Chapter 6: In the Ruins of the Reich

1. Harry S. Truman National Historic Site, Oral History #1992-3, Interview with HAK, May 7, 1992.
2. HAK, Kent papers [these are private papers in Dr. Kissinger's possession that he keeps at his house in Kent, CT], HAK to his parents, July 28, 1948.
3. Burleigh, *Moral Combat*, 539.
4. Ferguson, *War of the World*, 555ff., 581.
5. Ibid., 585.
6. Smith, *Papers of General Clay*, 143.
7. Backer, *Priming the German Economy*, 188, table 6.
8. Selby, *Axmann Conspiracy*, 141.
9. Wolfe, *Americans as Proconsuls*, 103.
10. See, e.g., Smith, *Papers of General Clay*, 174.
11. Wolfe, *Americans as Proconsuls*, 112f.
12. HAK, interview by author.
13. Blumenfeld, *Kissinger*, 59f.
14. Fussell, *Boys' Crusade*, 151–58.
15. Museum of Jewish Heritage, HAK interview by Louise Bobrow, Jan. 11, 2001.
16. HAK, interview by author.
17. LOC, A-19(b), HAK to Mrs. Frank, Apr. 21, 1946.
18. HAK, interview by author.
19. Kissinger family papers, HAK to his parents, May 6, 1945.
20. Museum of Jewish Heritage, HAK interview by Louise Bobrow, Jan. 11, 2001.
21. HAK, interview by author.
22. Museum of Jewish Heritage, HAK interview by Louise Bobrow, Jan. 11, 2001.
23. Harold R. Holocaust Testimony (HVT-4425). Fortunoff Video Archive for Holocaust Testimonies, Yale University Library.
24. Kilmeade, *Games Do Count*, 63f.
25. Mümmler, *Fürth*, 194. See also Fritz, *Endkampf*.
26. Kissinger family papers, HAK to his parents, Feb. 10, 1946. The newer Jewish cemetery in Erlangerstrasse had not been destroyed by the Nazis.
27. Draper, *84th Infantry Division*, 247. See also Edwards, *Private's Diary*, 571.

28. "Fritz Kraemer," *Daily Telegraph*, Nov. 10, 2003.
29. Draper, *84th Infantry Division*, 248.
30. U.S. Army Military History Institute, Carlisle Barracks, CIC School, "History and Mission of the Counter Intelligence Corps," MS, n.d., 1–9.
31. Jensen, *Army Surveillance*, 227.
32. Ibid., 228.
33. Ibid., 218.
34. CIC School, "History and Mission," 46.
35. For further insights, see Koudelka, *Counter Intelligence*, esp. 121–49.
36. Selby, *Axmann Conspiracy*, 50.
37. Slawenski, *Salinger*, esp. 131–34, 143f.
38. Selby, *Axmann Conspiracy*, 83.
39. Ibid., 84. See Melchior, *Case by Case*.
40. Selby, *Axmann Conspiracy*, 208f.
41. Ibid., 94.
42. LOC, George S. Patton Papers, 51, 8, Eisenhower, "Removal of Nazis and Militarists," Aug. 15, 1945.
43. Oppen, *Documents on Germany*, 20.
44. Kalb and Kalb, *Kissinger*, 40f.
45. Suri, *Kissinger*, 75.
46. Elsässer, "Kissinger in Krefeld und Bensheim," 29f.
47. Ibid., 18f.
48. Kissinger family papers, HAK to his parents, June 24, 1945.
49. Elsässer, "Kissinger in Krefeld und Bensheim," 28.
50. LOC, Rental agreement, Mar. 23, 1946. A photograph of a white Mercedes convertible does survive among Kissinger's papers at Yale, but he is not the proud owner pictured beside it.
51. Kissinger family papers, HAK to his parents, June 24, 1945.
52. LOC, HAK, MDC-101, Order issued by Charles Roundtree, July 10, 1945.
53. Ibid., Order issued by Frank Logan, Aug. 20, 1945.
54. Ibid., Capt. Frank A. Logan order, Dec. 3, 1945.
55. Ibid., Capt. Frank A. Logan order, May 22, 1946.
56. Kilthau and Krämer, *3 Tage fehlten*, 17.
57. Ibid., 19–21.
58. National Archives and Records Administration, 37, Darmstadt Gestapo XE 003411, HAK, Memorandum for the Officer in Charge, July 26, 1945.
59. Kilthau and Krämer, *3 Tage fehlten*, 27.
60. LOC, HAK, A-19(b), HAK report, Mar. 9, 1946.
61. Kissinger family papers, HAK to his parents, May 6, 1945.
62. LOC, HAK, MDC-101, HAK to Wesley G. Spence, Office of the Counselor for Veterans, May 10, 1947.
63. Ibid., Lieut. Paul H. Wyman, Report of CIC Activities of Special Agent Henry Kissinger, Nov. 18, 1945.
64. LOC, HAK, A-19(b), C.I.C. Team 970/59, Bensheim, Weekly Report, Dec. 24, 1945.
65. Ibid., "Promotion of Enlisted Men," Aug. 28, 1945.
66. LOC, HAK, MDC-101, Lieut. James A. Forsyth letter of recommendation, Apr. 29, 1946.
67. Ibid., HAK to Adjutant General (Civilian Personnel Section), Mar. 6, 1946.
68. Ibid., Lieut. James A. Forsyth letter of recommendation, Apr. 29, 1946.
69. Ibid., Lieut. Paul H. Wyman, Report of CIC Activities of Special Agent Henry Kissinger, Nov. 18, 1945.
70. LOC, HAK, A & P, Kraemer letter of recommendation, Mar. 7, 1949.
71. Smith, *Papers of General Clay*, 172.
72. Sayer and Botting, *America's Secret Army*, 296.
73. Douglas Porch, "Occupational Hazards," 37.
74. LOC, HAK, A-19(b), HAK report, May 16, 1946.
75. Ibid., Lieut. Col. Dale M. Garvey to 2nd Lieut. Irwin R. Supow, Nov. 16, 1945.
76. Ibid., HAK report, Jan. 8, 1946.
77. Stadtarchiv Bensheim, 16, 1, Klapproth to Kiesewetter, Sept. 22, 1945.
78. LOC, HAK, A-19(b), C.I.C. Team 970/59, Bensheim, Weekly Report, Oct. 13, 1945.
79. Ibid., Oct. 26, 1945.
80. Ibid., Oct. 13, 1945.
81. Ibid., Oct. 26, 1945.
82. Ibid., Dec. 24, 1945.
83. LOC, HAK, A-19(b), HAK report, Feb. 5, 1946.
84. Ibid., C.I.C. Team 970/59, Bensheim, Weekly Report, Oct. 26, 1945.
85. Ibid., Dec. 24, 1945.
86. Elsässer, "Kissinger in Krefeld und Bensheim," 26.
87. Stadtarchiv Bensheim, 16, 1, Wien to Lehmann-Lauprecht, Aug. 11, 1945.
88. LOC, HAK, A-19(b), Klapproth to Kiesewetter, Aug. 31, 1945.
89. Ibid., Klapproth to Kiesewetter, Sept. 1, 1945.
90. Ibid.
91. Ibid., HAK report, Jan. 8, 1946.
92. Ibid., Klapproth to Captain Leggatt, Sept. 10, 1945.
93. Stadtarchiv Bensheim, 16, 1, Klapproth to Leggatt, Sept. 17, 1945.
94. Ibid., Klapproth memorandum, Sept. 14, 1945.
95. Ibid., Klapproth to "Herr Henry," Aug. 11, 1945.
96. Ibid., August, Luise and Martha Sprengart, Eidesstattliche Erklärung, Nov. 5, 1945.
97. LOC, HAK, A-19(b), Polizeipräsident Dessau to Klapproth, Feb. 8, 1946.
98. Stadtarchiv Bensheim, 16, 1, Letter to Kiesewetter, Jan. 19, 1946. Cf. Elsässer, "Kissinger in Krefeld und Bensheim," 21ff.; Manfred Berg, "Bensheim nach dem Zweiten Weltkrieg," in Maasß and Berg, *Bensheim*, 390ff.
99. LOC, HAK, A-19(b), HAK report, Feb. 22, 1946.
100. See Ferguson, *High Financier*, 417–21.
101. Stadtarchiv Bensheim, 14, 1, Testimony of Otto and Minna von Humbert, Jan. 25, 1946; Klapproth to Capt. Nagy, Jan. 31, 1946; Klapproth to HAK, Jan. 31, 1946.
102. Elsässer, "Kissinger in Krefeld und Bensheim," 23f.; Berg, "Bensheim nach dem Zweiten Weltkrieg," 392f.
103. Berg, "Bensheim nach dem Zweiten Weltkrieg," 387.
104. Stadtarchiv Bensheim, 14, 12, Treffert report to CIC, Apr. 5, 1946.
105. LOC, HAK, MDC-101, HAK Application for Federal Employment, Nov. 17, 1946.
106. Ibid., HAK to Adjutant General (Civilian Personnel Section), Mar. 6, 1946.

107. Kissinger family papers, HAK to his parents, Feb. 10, 1946.
108. LOC, HAK, A-19(b), D. Donald Klous to HAK, July 22, 1946.
109. Ibid., Rosemary Reed to HAK, Apr. 8, 1946.
110. Stadtarchiv Bensheim, 14, 12, Treffert report to CIC, May 20, 1946, and July 5, 1946. Cf. Elsässer, "Kissinger in Krefeld und Bensheim," 25; Berg, "Bensheim nach dem Zweiten Weltkrieg," 389.
111. Kissinger family papers, HAK to his parents, Feb. 10, 1946.
112. Gaddis, *Kennan*, 221.
113. LOC, HAK, A-19(b), C.I.C. Team 970/59, Bensheim, Weekly Report, Dec. 24, 1945.
114. Ibid., Oct. 26, 1945.
115. LOC, HAK, A-19(b), HAK report, Feb. 5, 1946. Cf. Berg, "Bensheim nach dem Zweiten Weltkrieg," 391.
116. LOC, HAK, MDC-101, HAK to Wesley G. Spence, Office of the Counselor for Veterans, May 10, 1947.
117. LOC, HAK, A-19(b), HAK report, Oct. 16, 1945; Raymond L. Patten report, Oct. 26, 1945.
118. Duffy, "Third Century of Passion Play."
119. Shapiro, *Oberammergau*, 17.
120. Duffy, "Third Century of Passion Play," 669f.
121. Waddy, *Oberammergau in the Nazi Era*, 3–12.
122. Shapiro, *Oberammergau*, 57.
123. Ibid., 70.
124. Ibid., 76f.
125. Ibid., 147.
126. Waddy, *Oberammergau in the Nazi Era*, 153f.
127. Shapiro, *Oberammergau*, 149.
128. Waddy, *Oberammergau in the Nazi Era*.
129. Ibid., 141–44, 176f. See also 207f.
130. Ibid., 211, 217, 221.
131. Ibid., 184.
132. Shapiro, *Oberammergau*, 142.
133. Waddy, *Oberammergau in the Nazi Era*, 213.
134. Ibid., 223.
135. Piszkiewicz, *Nazi Rocketeers*, 221.
136. Ibid., 234.
137. Heaps, "Oberammergau Today," 1469.
138. Shapiro, *Oberammergau*, 148.
139. Heaps, "Oberammergau Today," 1469.
140. Waddy, *Oberammergau in the Nazi Era*, 243f.
141. Ibid., 235.
142. Shapiro, *Oberammergau*, 180f.
143. Waddy, *Oberammergau in the Nazi Era*, 250.
144. Shapiro, *Oberammergau*, 183.
145. Ibid., 6. Cf. Heaps, "Oberammergau Today," 1469.
146. CIC School, "History and Mission," 83.

147. Lüders, *Fürchte Dich nicht*, 151.
148. U.S. Bureau of the Census, *Statistical Abstract of the United States: 1962* (Washington, DC: U.S. Government Printing Office, 1962), 336, table 453.
149. LOC, HAK, A & P, Kraemer letter of recommendation, Mar. 7, 1949. Cf. LOC, HAK, MDC-101, Outline for Lectures: Role of Intelligence Investigator, Aug. 30, 1946.
150. LOC, HAK, MDC-101, European Theater School of Intelligence Lesson Plans, May 28, 1947.
151. Ibid., Col. Raymond letter, June 20, 1947.
152. Betty H. Carter Women Veterans Historical Project, University of North Carolina, Greensboro, Digital Collections, Interview with Jane Brister, 1999, http://bit.ly/1EyZQ9U.
153. LOC, MDC-101, HAK to Lieutenant Colonel Veazey, Oct. 1, 1946.
154. Ibid.
155. Ibid., Jane G. Brister special orders, Aug. 8, 1946.
156. Ibid., HAK and Springer report, Aug. 22, 1946.
157. Ibid., Oct. 26, 1946.
158. Ibid., HAK to Director of Training, Academic Division, U.S. Army, Mar. 5, 1947.
159. Mazlish, *Kissinger*, 44. See also Saalfrank, "Kissinger in Oberammergau," 36f., and Saalfrank, "Kissinger und Oberammergau."
160. LOC, HAK, MDC-101, HAK statement, Oct. 5, 1946.
161. Ibid., Capt. Edward F. Esken to Lieut. Col. Veazey, Feb. 9, 1947.
162. Ibid., HAK to Chenil de la Bergenne, Paris, Feb. 20, 1947, and reply dated Apr. 4, 1947.
163. LOC, HAK, A-19(b), Pan-Am Airway Bill, July 7, 1947.
164. Suri, *Kissinger*, 81. See also Saalfrank, "Kissinger in Oberammergau," 39.
165. HAK, interview by author. See also Henry Rosovsky, interview by author.
166. Kissinger family papers, HAK to his parents, Feb. 10, 1946.
167. Ibid., Apr. 2, 1947.
168. HAK, interview by author.
169. HAK, Kent papers, HAK to his parents, July 28, 1948.
170. Kissinger family papers, HAK to his parents, Apr. 2, 1947.
171. Ibid.
172. Ibid., HAK to his parents, Apr. 12, 1947.
173. Ibid.
174. Ibid., HAK to his parents, June 22, 1947.

Chapter 7: The Idealist

1. James, "True Harvard," in Bentinck-Smith, *Harvard Book*, 12.
2. Quoted in Menand, *Metaphysical Club*, 60.
3. HAK, "Epics Are Prescriptions for Action," in Anon., *William Yandell Elliott*.
4. Kissinger family papers, HAK to his parents, May 12, 1947.
5. Ibid., May 28, 1947.
6. LOC, HAK, MDC-101, HAK to the Registrar, Harvard, Apr. 2, 1947. See also HAK to Wesley G. Spence, Office of the Counselor for

Veterans, May 10, 1947. Cf. Blumenfeld, *Kissinger*, 81; Mazlish, *Kissinger*, 44; Kalb and Kalb, *Kissinger*, 42.
7. LOC, HAK, MDC-101, Spence to HAK, June 13, 1947.
8. Ibid., Spence to Louis Kissinger, May 23, 1947.
9. UNRRA, Office of the Historian, Staffing Authorization, July 16, 1948.
10. LOC, HAK, A & P, Kraemer letter of recommendation, Mar. 7, 1949.

11. Kissinger family papers, HAK to his parents, Apr. 12, 1947.
12. Ibid., June 18, 1947.
13. Ibid., Aug. 12, 1948.
14. LOC, HAK, A-18(a), Kraemer to HAK, Oct. 3, 1949.
15. Blumenfeld, *Kissinger*, 82–86.
16. Ibid., 81.
17. Ibid., 80.
18. Kalb and Kalb, *Kissinger*, 42.
19. Isaiah Berlin to his parents, Mar. 15, 1941, in Berlin, *Letters*, 1:367.
20. Trevor-Roper, *Letters from Oxford*, 34.
21. Morison, *Three Centuries of Harvard*, 1–19, 23.
22. Ibid., 22f., 60, 69ff.
23. Menand, *Metaphysical Club*, 6, 77, 61, 219, 227, 229, 350–57, 441.
24. Morison, *Three Centuries of Harvard*, 435.
25. Ibid., 419ff.
26. Rosovsky, *Jewish Experience*, 72.
27. Feder, "Jewish Threat," 45f.
28. Eaton, "Here's to the Harvard Accent," in Bentinck-Smith, *Harvard Book*, 13.
29. Feder, "Jewish Threat," 10.
30. Morison, *Three Centuries of Harvard*, 446, 449.
31. Feder, "Jewish Threat," 70.
32. Rosovsky, *Jewish Experience*, 7, 11.
33. Ibid., 9.
34. Feder, "Jewish Threat," 5.
35. Rosovsky, *Jewish Experience*, 55.
36. Feder, "Jewish Threat," 13.
37. Rosovsky, *Jewish Experience*, 15.
38. Ibid., 20.
39. Ibid., 23.
40. Stedman, "Born unto Trouble."
41. Ibid., 106.
42. Ibid., 104.
43. Ibid., 110. See also 36, 44, 61ff.
44. Kraus, "Assimilation, Authoritarianism, and Judaism," 19f., 35; tables 3, 4, 5, 6, 7, 8, 9, 13, 15.
45. White, *In Search of History*, 43f.
46. Ibid., 41.
47. Rosovsky, *Jewish Experience*, 31.
48. Schlesinger, *Life in the Twentieth Century*, 37, 54f.
49. Ibid., 510.
50. "Harvard College Class of 1950," Harvard Alumni, http://bit.ly/1yWyOGX.
51. See, e.g., Blumenfeld, *Kissinger*, 82.
52. "Housing Tight Again in Fall," *Harvard Crimson*, Aug. 15, 1947; "College May Discard 5400 'Limit' on Fall Enrollment," *Harvard Crimson*, Aug. 28, 1947. See also "President's Report," *Official Register of Harvard University* 46 no. 30 (Dec. 1, 1949), 5f.
53. "Gym Houses Students Overflow of 180," *Harvard Crimson*, Sept. 22, 1947.
54. "Entry System Boosts Appeal, Erases Stigma of Claverly," *Harvard Crimson*, Apr. 1, 1954; "Large Percentage of Claverly Hall Students Will Not Move to Houses," *Harvard Crimson*, Mar. 30, 1955.
55. Mazlish, *Kissinger*, 56.
56. "The Union United," *Harvard Crimson*, Oct. 15, 1947. See also Harvard Archives, HUB XXX, Box 30, 023.B.5, The Harvard Union.
57. See, e.g., Blumenfeld, *Kissinger*, 82.
58. Anon., *Gold Coaster*.
59. "Adams Presents Good Food, Pool, Location Near to Yard," *Harvard Crimson*, Mar. 24, 1950.

60. "Adams Forum to Discuss Schlesinger's 'Vital Center,'" *Harvard Crimson*, Dec. 1, 1949.
61. Graubard, *Kissinger*, 5; Mazlish, *Kissinger*, 57.
62. LOC, HAK, A-1(a), HAK to CIC Reserve Affairs Section, Mar. 26, 1950.
63. Ibid., A-18(a), Kraemer to HAK, Oct. 3, 1949.
64. Ibid., G-14 Supp. (Kraemer), Kraemer to HAK, Nov. 17, 1949.
65. Ibid., MDC-101, HAK to Hans-Joachim Hirschmann, Sept. 9, 1948.
66. Ibid., Victor Guala to HAK, Sept. 8, 1948.
67. Blumenfeld, *Kissinger*, 84.
68. Ibid., 90.
69. Isaacson, *Kissinger*, KL 1253–56.
70. LOC, HAK, A-18(a), Ann Kissinger to HAK, Sept. 26, 1949.
71. Isaacson, *Kissinger*, KL 1257–80.
72. Ibid., KL 1109–13.
73. See Kistiakowsky, *Scientist at the White House*.
74. LOC, HAK Kent 9, Harvard Report Card, July 21, 1949. Cf. Blumenfeld, *Kissinger*, 83.
75. White, *In Search of History*, 44f.
76. LOC, HAK, A & P, Kraemer letter of recommendation, Mar. 7, 1949.
77. Friedrich, *New Image of Common Man*.
78. Ibid., 117.
79. Ibid., 315.
80. Mazlish, *Kissinger*, 61. See also Isaacson, *Kissinger*, KL 1165–68.
81. Blumenfeld, *Kissinger*, 87.
82. Michael W. Schwartz, "On Professor Elliott's Retirement," in Anon., *William Yandell Elliott*. See Purdy, *Fugitives' Reunion*.
83. Stone, "New World Order."
84. Elliott, *Pragmatic Revolt in Politics*.
85. Ibid., 423, 469.
86. Gunnell, "Real Revolution in Political Science," 48. I am grateful to David Elliott for sharing some of his own research on his father's career.
87. Gunnell, "Political Science on the Cusp." For a critique, see Dryzek, "Revolutions Without Enemies."
88. Louis Hartz, "Elliott as a Teacher," in Anon., *William Yandell Elliott*.
89. Mazlish, *Kissinger*, 64.
90. *Dictionary of American Biography*, 214.
91. Hoover Institution Archives, William Y. Elliott Papers, Box 161, Elliott to Samuel Beer, Aug. 25, 1961.
92. Stone, "New World Order," 57.
93. Lincoln Gordon, "A Desire to Convey Understanding," in Anon., *William Yandell Elliott*.
94. *Dictionary of American Biography*, 214.
95. Harris, "Footnote to History," 8.
96. Harvard Archives, William Y. Elliott Papers, Elliott to Cordell Hull, Control of Raw Materials Through Joint Holding Companies, Sept. 29, 1941.
97. Harris, "Footnote to History," 7.
98. Harvard Archives, William Y. Elliott Papers, Elliott, Control of Strategic Materials in War and Peace, Institute of Public Affairs, July 7, 1942.
99. Heard Library, Vanderbilt, RG 300, 162, 21, Elliott to Harvey Branscombe, Apr. 14, 1952.
100. Ibid., RG 519, Elliott to Avery Leiserson, July 3, 1956.

101. Gunnell, "Political Science on the Cusp."
102. HAK, "Epics Are Prescriptions for Action," in Anon., *William Yandell Elliott*.
103. Ibid.
104. Blumenthal, *Kissinger*, 86ff. See also Kalb and Kalb, *Kissinger*, 43.
105. LOC, HAK, A & P, Elliott, letter of recommendation, Oct. 31, 1949.
106. Ibid.
107. "A Guide to Writing a Senior Thesis in Government," 36, http://bit.ly/1DrBetP.
108. Blumenfeld, *Kissinger*, 92.
109. Suri, *Kissinger*, 29f.
110. Weber, "Kissinger as Historian," 3.
111. HAK, "Meaning of History" [henceforth MoH].
112. MoH, 1f., 4.
113. MoH, 10.
114. MoH, 112.
115. MoH, 142, 213.

116. MoH, 276.
117. MoH, 260f.
118. MoH, 288.
119. MoH, 321.
120. MoH, 123.
121. MoH, 123.
122. Dickson, *Kissinger and Meaning*, 59f.
123. MoH, 127f. Emphasis added.
124. MoH, 249.
125. MoH, 321.
126. MoH, 348.
127. Dickson, *Kissinger and Meaning*, ix.
128. Ibid., 8, 43, 72f.
129. Curley, "Kissinger, Spinoza and Genghis Khan," in Garrett, *Cambridge Companion to Spinoza*, 315f.
130. MoH, 323.
131. MoH, 333.
132. MoH, 348.

Chapter 8: Psychological Warfare

1. Lucas, "Campaigns of Truth," 301.
2. *Confluence* 3, no. 4 (1954), 499.
3. John H. Fenton, "'Live and Let Live,' Acheson Bids Reds: Acheson at Harvard Yard for Commencement," *New York Times*, June 23, 1950.
4. "Peace Group Pickets Acheson at Harvard," *Boston Traveler*, June 23, 1950.
5. "Acheson Hits Reds' Trojan Moves," *Boston Evening American*, June 22, 1950.
6. "The Secretary Speaks," *Harvard Alumni Bulletin*, 760ff., 767.
7. Gaddis, *Kennan*, 404.
8. Leffler, *Soul of Mankind*, KL 540–41.
9. Ibid., KL 594–95.
10. Ibid., KL 603–4.
11. Ibid., KL 853–55.
12. Ibid., KL 928–40.
13. George F. Kennan to Secretary of State, telegram, Feb. 22, 1946, http://bit.ly/1DHuLu6.
14. Gaddis, *Kennan*, 203.
15. Gaddis, *Strategies of Containment*, 20.
16. Kennan to Secretary of State, telegram, Feb. 22, 1946, http://bit.ly/1DHuLu6.
17. Leffler, *Soul of Mankind*, KL 1078–79.
18. Ibid., KL 1014–19.
19. Gaddis, *Kennan*, 243f.
20. Ibid., 250.
21. Ibid., 260.
22. Ibid., 261.
23. Ibid., 273.
24. Ibid., 329.
25. See in general May, *American Cold War Strategy*. The full text is on 23ff.
26. Ibid., 34.
27. Chomsky, "Cold War and the University"; Robin, *Making of Cold War Enemy*, 57–71.
28. President James B. Conant, "Report to the Alumni," June 22, 1950.
29. "Conant, Eisenhower, 18 Educators Urge Ban on Communist Teachers," *Harvard Crimson*, June 9, 1949.
30. Winks, *Cloak and Gown*.
31. Ibid., 119, 247ff., 450, 453, 457ff.

32. Wilford, *Mighty Wurlitzer*, 128f.
33. Winks, *Cloak and Gown*, 447.
34. Suri, *Kissinger*, esp. 93–99, 109f.
35. Friedrich, *New Image of Common Man*, 319f.
36. Ibid., 330.
37. Elliott, "Time for Peace?"
38. Ibid., 166. See also William M. Blair, "Declares Russia Plans Atomic War: Prof. Elliott of Harvard Says Loans and Scientific Data Should Be Denied to Soviet," *New York Times*, June 15, 1946.
39. Hoover Institution Archives, Elliott Papers, Box 110, Elliott to William Jackson, Oct. 11, 1950.
40. See Winks, *Cloak and Gown*, 54.
41. See, e.g., Hoover Institution Archives, Elliott Papers, Box 110, Jackson to Elliott, Dec. 27, 1950; Joseph Larocque to Elliott, Jan. 15, 1951.
42. Ambrose, *Nixon*, vol. 1.
43. Lindsay, *Beacons in the Night*, 330. On the Herter Committee, see Chris Barber, "The Herter Committee: Forging RN's Foreign Policy," *The New Nixon* (n.d.), http://bit.ly/1aYeZnj.
44. Elliott, "Prospects for Personal Freedom," 182.
45. Elliott and Study Group, *United States Foreign Policy*.
46. Stone, "New World Order," 187.
47. Hoover Institution Archives, Elliott Papers, Box 30, "How Can We Have an Effective Coordination for Foreign Policy Under the Constitution of the United States?," May 22, 1951.
48. Truman Library, Psychological Strategy Board, Box 7, Sidney Sulkin to Raymond Allen, Feb. 14, 1952.
49. Hoover Institution Archives, Elliott Papers, Box 14, Elliott to Frank Barnett, Mar. 28, 1956. See also Elliott, "Proposal for a North Atlantic Round Table."
50. Hoover Institution Archives, Elliott Papers, Box 77, Elliott to Samuel Beer, Aug. 25, 1961.
51. Ibid., Box 166, Elliott to Richard M. Nixon [henceforth RMN], Sept. 11, 1958.
52. Eisenhower Library, NSC Series, WHO OSANSA: Records, 1952–1961, Box 6, Elliott to Charles Stauffacher, Nov. 19, 1952.

53. Ibid., Elliott, "NSC Study," Dec. 23, 1952; Memorandum for Arthur S. Flemming, Dec. 23, 1952. See also Edwin B. George to Elliott, Jan. 5, 1953.

54. Just three weeks after Eisenhower's inauguration, Elliott sent Nixon a proposal to "build up . . . U.S. airlift capabilities by the subsidy of a commercial fleet": Nixon Library, General Correspondence 239, R. E. Cushman, Jr., to Robert Cutler, Feb. 11, 1953.

55. Elliott et al., *Political Economy of American Foreign Policy,* 322f.

56. Hoover Institution Archives, Elliott Papers, Box 93, Elliott, Memorandum for Under Secretary of State Christian Herter, Some Suggested Areas for the Development of Policy Planning in the Department of State, n.d., 5.

57. Ibid., Box 112, Elliott to Under Secretary Robert Thayer, June 10, 1960.

58. Elliott, *Mobilization Planning,* 35–40.

59. Hoover Institution Archives, Elliott Papers, Box 93, Elliott, Memorandum for Under Secretary of State Christian Herter, Some Suggested Areas for the Development of Policy Planning in the Department of State, n.d., 4.

60. Eisenhower Library, Elliott to C. D. Jackson, "Organization of Psychological Defense Measures at Home," Apr. 24, 1953.

61. Ibid.

62. For a skeptical view of its efficacy, see Schlesinger, *Life in the Twentieth Century,* 297.

63. Gaddis, *Kennan,* 295.

64. Wilford, *Mighty Wurlitzer,* 7.

65. Lucas, "Campaigns of Truth." See also Lucas, *Freedom's War,* 128–62.

66. Lucas, *Freedom's War,* 131.

67. Wilford, *Mighty Wurlitzer,* 25.

68. Mazlish, *Kissinger,* 59.

69. LOC, A-18(a), HAK to Advisor to Overseas Students, Oxford, Nov. 5, 1949.

70. Isaacson, *Kissinger,* KL 1282–89.

71. LOC, A-18(a), HAK to "Head Tutor," Balliol, Aug. 30, 1950.

72. LOC, G-14 Supp. (Kraemer), Kraemer to HAK, Sept. 13, 1950.

73. LOC, MDC-101, Kraemer letter of recommendation, Feb. 16, 1951.

74. LOC, G-14, HAK to George van Santwoord, May 4, 1954; Lawrence Noble to Kraemer, June 10, 1954.

75. LOC, A-1(a), HAK to Commanding Officer, Camp Holabird, Mar. 26, 1950.

76. Defense Technical Information Center, Fort Belvoir, VA, "History of Fort Holabird: December 1917 to 29 June 1973," MS.

77. LOC, MDC-101, Hirsch to Assistant Commandant, Evaluation of MRA (66th) for June 1950, Jul. 6, 1950.

78. Ibid., George Springer to George S. Pettee, Apr. 19, 1951, and Apr. 30, 1951.

79. Schrader, *History of Operations Research,* 1:v. The ORO relationship with Johns Hopkins persisted until 1961, after which it became the Research Analysis Corporation.

80. LOC, D-4, HAK to Darwin Stolzenbach, July 17, 1951.

81. Kalb and Kalb, *Kissinger,* 49.

82. LOC, K-69, More Korea Diaries 1951. For details of the interviews, see ibid., MDC-101, HAK to Stolzenbach, Nov. 17, 1951.

83. HAK and Darwin Stolzenbach, Technical Memorandum ORO-T-184: "Civil Affairs in Korea, 1950–51" (Chevy Chase, MD: ORO, [Aug.] 1952).

84. LOC, D-4, HAK to Stolzenbach, Feb. 7, 1952. Two years later, Stolzenbach was able to say that their report had proved very valuable in practice and was widely regarded as a benchmark by ORO.

85. LOC, G-14 Supp. (Kraemer), HAK to Kintner, Nov. 20, 1951.

86. For Kraemer's 1951 memo "U.S. Psychological Warfare Campaign for Political, Economic, and Military Integration of German Federal Republic into Western Europe," see LOC, G-14, Kraemer to Rentnik, Dec. 9, 1951; Truman Library, Psychological Strategy Board, Box 24, 334 Panel "I," Harriman to Allen, Apr. 16, 1952.

87. Truman Library, Psychological Strategy Board, Box 6, Folder 1, Kissinger's Analysis of Germany, July 11, 1952. See also ibid., James W. Riddleberger memorandum, July 30, 1952. This paper may later have acquired the title "The Moral Failure of the Military Occupation of Germany."

88. Isaacson, *Kissinger,* KL 1513–17 [HAK to his parents, June 4, 1952].

89. LOC, D-4, HAK to Nancy Sweet, June 24, 1952.

90. Ibid., HAK to Richard Sherman, Oct. 19, 1951.

91. Ibid., HAK to Maj. A. M. Sears, Oct. 10, 1952.

92. Ibid., HAK to Otte Pribram, July 21, 1954.

93. Ibid., HAK to Stolzenbach, July 31, 1952.

94. Ibid., HAK to Stolzenbach, Nov. 12, 1952. See also Robert Sorensen to HAK, Oct. 22, 1952; HAK to Sorensen, Oct. 31, 1952.

95. LOC, A-18(a), Ann Fleischer to HAK, July 25, 1950.

96. LOC, A & P, HAK to Elliott, July 10, 1950.

97. LOC, A-1(a), transcript of a Harvard Government seminar, Mar. 2, 1953. See also the following week's transcript: Mar. 9, 1953. The later meeting was essentially taken over by Elliott for a reprise of the argument of his book *The Pragmatic Revolt.* Among the participants in the seminar was the young British political theorist Bernard Crick.

98. Wilford, *Mighty Wurlitzer,* 124f.

99. Ford Foundation Archives, Reel R-0492, John Conway to HAK, Apr. 19, 1951.

100. Ibid., Elliott to Carl B. Spaeth, Oct. 8, 1952.

101. Hoover Institution Archives, Elliott Papers, Box 2, HAK to Elliott, Aug. 22, 1951.

102. Ibid., Elliott to James Perkins, Oct. 20, 1953.

103. Ford Foundation Archives, Reel R-0492, Bernard L. Gladieux to Joseph M. McDaniel, Aug. 13, 1952.

104. Eisenhower Library, WHO–National Security Council Staff: Papers, 1942–1961, OCB Secretariat Series, HAK to Edward Lilly, Sept. 8, 1953.

105. Hoover Institution Archives, Elliott Papers, Box 2, Elliott to James Perkins, Oct. 20, 1953.

106. For grumbling on these scores, see Anne Cameron, "Seminar Is Crossroads for Diverse Ideas, Interests," *Harvard Crimson*, Aug. 6, 1963.
107. Graubard, *Kissinger,* 57f.
108. Ford Foundation Archives, Reel R–0492, Report by P. S. Sundaram, Nov. 22, 1954.
109. Blumenfeld, *Kissinger,* 98.
110. Ibid., 101.
111. Isaacson, *Kissinger,* KL 1310–16. Cf. Suri, *Kissinger,* 120ff.
112. Hoover Institution Archives, Elliott Papers, Box 110, Elliott to H. Gates Lloyd, Nov. 15, 1950.
113. Ibid., Elliott to Wisner, July 16, 1951.
114. LOC, HAK to H. Gates Lloyd, Apr. 20, 1951. Cf. Wilford, *Mighty Wurlitzer,* 123.
115. Ibid., HAK to H. Gates Lloyd, May 7, 1951.
116. Ford Foundation Archives, Reel R–0492, Bernard L. Gladieux to Joseph M. McDaniel, Aug. 13, 1952.
117. Kent papers, HAK to Allen Dulles, Oct. 28, 1952.
118. Ford Foundation Archives, Reel R–0492, Melvin J. Fox to Carl B. Spaeth, Aug. 1, 1952.
119. Hoover Institution Archives, Elliott Papers, Box 2, Elliott to Julius Fleischmann, Jan. 7, 1953, and Fleischmann's reply, Jan. 21, 1953.
120. Harvard Archives, 1953 Harvard International Seminar, Oct. 9, 1953.
121. Hoover Institution Archives, Elliott Papers, Box 2, Elliott to James Perkins, Oct. 20, 1953.
122. LOC, Kent 64, Elliott to Bundy, Nov. 3, 1953.
123. LOC, G–14 Supp. (Kraemer), HAK to Kraemer, Dec. 31, 1953.
124. Ford Foundation Archives, Reel R–0492, Elliott to Don K. Price, Feb. 13, 1954.
125. LOC, D–4, HAK to Stolzenbach, Feb. 25, 1954.
126. Ford Foundation Archives, Reel R–0492, Excerpt from docket, Oct. 29, 1954.
127. Harvard Archives, International Seminar, Elliott to John Marshall, Dec. 1, 1954.
128. Ibid., UAV 813.141.10, Robert Blum to HAK, Oct. 21, 1955.
129. Ibid., International Seminar, HAK to Don Price, Dec. 10, 1955.
130. Ford Foundation Archives, Reel R–1057, Elliott to Katz, Mar. 17, 1952.
131. Harvard Archives, Elliott to Rusk, Apr. 30, 1952; Elliott to Marshall, May 12, 1952.
132. Ibid., International Seminar, Bowie to Stone, Mar. 5, 1953.
133. Ford Foundation Archives, Reel R–0492, Stanley T. Gordon to Shepard Stone, Sept. 1, 1954.
134. See Lindsay, *Beacons in the Night.*
135. Thomas, *Very Best Men,* 70–73.
136. Ford Foundation Archives, Reel R–1057, Shepard Stone to James Laughlin, May 13, 1953.
137. Ibid., Laughlin to Frank Lindsay, July 16, 1953.
138. LOC, Kent 64, HAK to Bundy, May 20, 1954.
139. Ibid., Marie Carney to Bundy, Aug. 20, 1952.
140. See in general Wilford, *Mighty Wurlitzer.* See also Cull, *Cold War and USIA;* Saunders, *Who Paid the Piper?;* and Von Eschen, *Satchmo Blows Up the World.*
141. Isaacson, *Kissinger,* KL 1328–32.
142. Suri, *Kissinger,* esp. 124. See also Mazlish, *Kissinger,* 71.
143. Isaacson, *Kissinger,* KL 1378–79.
144. LOC, Kent 64, Bundy to Lippmann, Feb. 20, 1953; Harvard Archives, International Seminar, Bundy to Byron Dexter, Feb. 25, 1953. See also HAK to Stone, Mar. 17, 1953.
145. Leffler, *Soul of Mankind,* KL 1344–45.
146. Ibid., KL 1347–51.
147. William Fulton, "Harvard Makes It Easy to Air Red, Pink Views," *Chicago Tribune,* Apr. 10, 1951.
148. Boston Athenæum, National Council for American Education, "Red-ucators at Harvard University," ms.
149. William Fulton, "'I Am a Red' He Said; 'Also a Harvard Grad,'" *Chicago Tribune,* Apr. 8, 1951.
150. Isaacson, *Kissinger,* KL 1310–16; Sigmund Diamond, "Kissinger and the FBI," *Nation,* Nov. 10, 1979.
151. Diamond, *Compromised Campus,* 138–50. See also Suri, *Kissinger,* 127f.; Gaddis, *Kennan,* 496.
152. Kennedy Library, Schlesinger Papers, Incoming Correspondence, 1945–1960, Box P-17, HAK to Schlesinger, Mar. 16, 1953.
153. Harvard Archives, International Seminar, HAK to Camus, Jan. 26, 1954.
154. LOC, Kent 63, HAK to Schlesinger, Mar. 10, 1954.
155. Isaacson, *Kissinger,* KL 1358–61.
156. Kennedy Library, Bundy Papers, Harvard Correspondence, Box 14, HAK to Bundy, May 8, 1952.
157. LOC, E–2, HAK to Schlesinger, Sept. 28, 1953.
158. "Letters," *Confluence* 3, no. 3 (1954), 360.
159. William Yandell Elliott, "What Are the Bases of Civilization?," *Confluence* 1, no. 1 (1952).
160. Harvard Archives, International Seminar, HAK to Hessenauer, Jan. 3, 1952.
161. *Confluence* 2, no. 1 (1953), 10.
162. Ibid., 42.
163. *Confluence* 2, no. 3 (1953), 126.
164. *Confluence* 2, no. 4 (1953), 61–71.
165. *Confluence* 3, no. 3 (1954), 131f., 136.
166. Ibid., 295–306.
167. *Confluence* 3, no. 4 (1954), 497f.
168. LOC, G–14 Supp. (Kraemer), HAK to Kraemer, Nov. 19, 1954.
169. *Confluence* 3, no. 4 (1954), 499f.

Chapter 9: Doctor Kissinger

1. LOC, Kent 64, HAK to Bundy, Jan. 28, 1954.
2. Blumenfeld, *Kissinger,* 93.
3. LOC, MDC-101, Sargent Kennedy to HAK, June 2, 1954.
4. Fukuyama, "World Restored."
5. Kaplan, "Kissinger, Metternich, and Realism."
6. See, e.g., Kalb and Kalb, *Kissinger,* 46ff.
7. Isaacson, *Kissinger,* KL 1403–5.
8. Suri, *Kissinger,* 129.
9. Graubard, *Kissinger,* 17.
10. LOC, ORO & CIC-HAK Misc. Corr. (N–Z), HAK to George Pettee, Jan. 4, 1955. Cf. Weidenfeld, *Remembering My Friends,* 384–87.
11. Kalb and Kalb, *Kissinger,* 46.

12. Isaacson, *Kissinger*, KL 1445–50, citing HAK to Louis Kissinger, Jan. 31, 1954.
13. See, e.g., Birke, "World Restored."
14. HAK, *World Restored* [henceforth *WR*], KL 237–38.
15. *WR*, KL 3679–82.
16. *WR*, KL 3664–65.
17. *WR*, KL 2810–14.
18. *WR*, KL 349–50.
19. *WR*, KL 494–95.
20. *WR*, KL 2867–68.
21. *WR*, KL 3509.
22. *WR*, KL 4302.
23. *WR*, KL 1546–50.
24. *WR*, KL 1646–47.
25. *WR*, KL 1725–27.
26. *WR*, KL 1159–61.
27. *WR*, KL 948.
28. *WR*, KL 2300–2307.
29. *WR*, KL 2567–68.
30. *WR*, KL 3434–37.
31. *WR*, KL 5442–43.
32. *WR*, KL 6565–84. Emphasis added.
33. *WR*, KL 662–64, 747–48.
34. *WR*, KL 3472–74.
35. *WR*, KL 3939–76.
36. *WR*, KL 254–55.
37. HAK, "Conservative Dilemma," 1030.
38. *WR*, KL 230–31.
39. *WR*, KL 1701–5.
40. *WR*, KL 3521–24.
41. *WR*, KL 3802–3.
42. *WR*, KL 1803–4.
43. *WR*, KL 5741.
44. *WR*, KL 453–56.
45. *WR*, KL 1537–43.
46. *WR*, KL 2237–41.
47. *WR*, KL 281–85.
48. *WR*, KL 558–63.
49. *WR*, KL 281–85.
50. *WR*, KL 295–99.
51. *WR*, KL 1336–37.
52. *WR*, KL 4336–39.
53. *WR*, KL 6526–39, 6542–45.
54. *WR*, KL 719–20.
55. *WR*, KL 5621–26.
56. *WR*, KL 181–95.
57. *WR*, KL 172–81.
58. *WR*, KL 102–19.
59. *WR*, KL 172–81.
60. *WR*, KL 140–48.
61. *WR*, KL 119–40.
62. HAK, "Congress of Vienna: Reappraisal," 280.
63. *WR*, KL 702–8.
64. *WR*, KL 847–48.
65. *WR*, KL 1188–92.
66. *WR*, KL 1248–54.
67. *WR*, KL 1270–71.
68. *WR*, KL 1606–8.
69. *WR*, KL 2837–61.
70. *WR*, KL 2923–33.
71. *WR*, KL 2974–3022.
72. For a sympathetic modern account, see Bew, *Castlereagh*.
73. *WR*, KL 4178–85.
74. *WR*, KL 5377–78, 5389.
75. *WR*, KL 5396–99.
76. *WR*, KL 6398–400.
77. Most obviously in this passage: *WR*, KL 3685–98.
78. *WR*, KL 3478–505.
79. *WR*, KL 3812–19.
80. *WR*, KL 6416–43.
81. *WR*, KL 6633–53.
82. *WR*, KL 6604–29.
83. *WR*, KL 6633–53.
84. Fukuyama, "World Restored"; Kaplan, "Kissinger, Metternich, and Realism."
85. Webster, "World Restored."
86. Birke, "World Restored."
87. Maxwell, "World Restored."
88. Hans Kohn, "Preserving the Peace," *New York Times*, Oct. 13, 1957.
89. Wright, "World Restored."
90. LOC, Kent 64, HAK to Bundy, Jan. 28, 1954.
91. LOC, A & P, HAK to Elliott, July 10, 1950.
92. LOC, Kent 63, HAK to Elliott, Dec. 12, 1950.
93. Ibid.
94. LOC, Kent 63, HAK to Elliott, Mar. 2, 1951.
95. LOC, G–14 Supp. (Kraemer) HAK to Kintner, Nov. 20, 1951.
96. Ibid.
97. Ibid.
98. LOC, Kent 63, HAK, "Soviet Strategy—Possible U.S. Countermeasures," Dec. 1951.
99. Leffler, *Soul of Mankind*, 91f.
100. LOC, Kent 63, HAK, "The Soviet Peace Offensive and German Unity," June 3, 1953.
101. LOC, Kent 64, Bundy to HAK, June 23, 1953.
102. LOC, D–4, George Pettee to HAK, June 10, 1953.
103. Ibid., HAK to Pettee, June 12, 1953.
104. LOC, E–2, HAK to Schlesinger, June 10, 1953.
105. LOC, Kent 63, HAK to Schlesinger, Mar. 10, 1954.
106. Isaacson, *Kissinger*, KL 1518–23. According to Henry Rosovsky, it was the economist Carl Kaysen who blackballed him.
107. Mazlish, *Kissinger*, 50, 78f.
108. LOC, Kent 64, HAK to Bundy, Dec. 31, 1952.
109. Isaacson, *Kissinger*, KL 1456–99.
110. Blumenfeld, *Kissinger*, 93.
111. Harvard Archives, International Seminar, Leland DeVinney to Nathan Pusey, May 20, 1954.
112. The award is recorded in a card index held at the Rockefeller Archive Center.
113. LOC, Kent 64, HAK to Bundy, June 8, 1954.
114. Ibid., HAK to Bundy, Sept. 26, 1954.
115. National Archives, Nixon Presidential Materials, White House Tapes, Oval Office, Conversation Number: 699-1, Mar. 31, 1972.
116. Bentinck-Smith, *Harvard Book*, 24.

Chapter 10: Strangelove?

1. "A New Look at War-Making," *New York Times*, July 7, 1957.
2. LOC, Box 43, Oppenheimer to Gordon Dean, May 16, 1957.
3. Isaacson, *Kissinger*, KL 1536.
4. Marian Schlesinger, interview by author.
5. Stephen Schlesinger's diary, Oct. 6, 2008.
6. LOC, Kent 64, HAK to Bundy, Sept. 16, 1954.

7. HAK, "Eulogy for Arthur M. Schlesinger, Jr.," Apr. 23, 2007, http://bit.ly/1yWzxbl.

8. LOC, Kent 63, HAK, "The Impasse of American Policy and Preventive War," Sept. 15, 1954.

9. Ibid., HAK to Schlesinger, Dec. 8, 1954.

10. LOC, E-2, Schlesinger note on Harrison Salisbury's articles from Russia in *New York Times*, Sept. 23, 1954.

11. Ibid., Schlesinger to HAK, Sept. 22, 1954.

12. LOC, D-4, Pettee to HAK, Oct. 12, 1954.

13. LOC, Kent 63, HAK to Schlesinger, Dec. 8, 1954.

14. Ibid., Memorandum to Schlesinger, Dec. 8, 1954.

15. LOC, D-4, R. G. Stilwell to HAK, Feb. 25, 1955.

16. Ibid., HAK to Pettee, Mar. 1, 1955. Kissinger found McCormack "absolutely brilliant."

17. LOC, E-2, HAK to Schlesinger, Feb. 16, 1955.

18. HAK, "Military Policy and 'Grey Areas.'"

19. LOC, E-2, HAK to Schlesinger, Feb. 16, 1955.

20. See also HAK, "American Policy and Preventive War," *Yale Review* 44 (Spring 1955).

21. Finletter, *Power and Policy.*

22. HAK, "Military Policy and 'Grey Areas,'" 417.

23. Ibid.

24. Ibid., 418.

25. Ibid., 419.

26. Ibid., 428.

27. Ibid., 423f.

28. Ibid., 421.

29. Ibid., 422.

30. Ibid., 425.

31. Ibid., 426.

32. Ibid., 427.

33. Hart, *Revolution in Warfare*, 99. See also Hart, "War, Limited."

34. Osgood, *Limited War.*

35. See, e.g., Richard Leghorn, "No Need to Bomb Cities to Win War," *U.S. News & World Report*, Jan. 28, 1955.

36. Bernard Brodie, "Unlimited Weapons and Limited War," *Reporter*, Nov. 18, 1954; Brodie, "Nuclear Weapons: Strategic or Tactical?," esp. 226–29. See Brodie's later article "More About Limited War." However, Brodie's book *Strategy in the Missile Age* did not appear until 1959. See in general Larsen and Kartchner, *On Limited Nuclear War.*

37. HAK, "The Limitations of Diplomacy," *New Republic*, May 9, 1955, 7f.

38. LOC, G-13, HAK to Huntington, Apr. 29, 1955.

39. Ibid., Huntington to HAK, Apr. 24, 1955.

40. Bird, *Color of Truth*, 107.

41. Ibid., 142. See also Isaacson, *Kissinger*, KL 1550.

42. Gaddis, *Kennan*, 374.

43. NSC-68, 56.

44. Gaddis, *Kennan*, 377.

45. Rosenberg, "Origins of Overkill," 22.

46. Bowie and Immerman, *Waging Peace*, 224ff.

47. John Gaddis, "The Long Peace: Elements of Stability in the Postwar International System," in Lynn-Jones and Miller, *Cold War and After*, 1f.

48. For a compelling critique of this view, see Gavin, *Nuclear Statecraft*, 60f.

49. Chernus, "Eisenhower: Toward Peace," 57.

50. Gaddis, *Strategies of Containment*, 171ff.

51. Ferrell, *Eisenhower Diaries*, 210.

52. Gaddis, *Strategies of Containment*, 137.

53. Gaddis, *Cold War*, 68.

54. Gaddis, *Strategies of Containment*, 174. Cf. Craig, *Destroying the Village*, 69.

55. Bowie and Immerman, *Waging Peace.*

56. See Soapes, "Cold Warrior Seeks Peace."

57. Fish, "After Stalin's Death."

58. See Osgood, *Total Cold War*, 57ff.

59. Bowie and Immerman, *Waging Peace*, 193.

60. Rosenberg, "Origins of Overkill," 31.

61. Jackson, "Beyond Brinkmanship," 57.

62. Ibid., 60.

63. Ambrose, *Nixon*, vol. 1, KL 12757.

64. Gaddis, *Strategies of Containment*, 147f.

65. Ibid., 133.

66. Thomas, *Ike's Bluff*, KL 2772–75.

67. Parry-Giles, "Eisenhower, 'Atoms for Peace.'"

68. Hixon, *Parting the Iron Curtain*, 223.

69. Thomas, *Very Best Men*, 165–69.

70. Paul H. Nitze, "Limited War or Massive Retaliation?"

71. Osgood, *Total Cold War*, 167.

72. Greene, "Eisenhower, Science and Test Ban Debate."

73. For the panel's report, see http://1.usa.gov/1OkG4DA.

74. William L. Borden to J. Edgar Hoover, November 7, 1953, http://bit.ly/1ICqWfN.

75. Tal, "Secretary of State Versus the Secretary of Peace."

76. Hoover Institution Archives, Elliott Papers, International Seminar, HAK to RMN, May 12, 1955.

77. LOC, Kent 64, HAK to Bundy, Aug. 17, 1955.

78. Ibid., Bundy to HAK, Aug. 23, 1955.

79. Grose, *Continuing the Inquiry.*

80. Wala, *Council on Foreign Relations*, esp. 229–43.

81. Shoup and Minter, *Imperial Brain Trust.* See also G. William Domhoff, "Why and How the Corporate Rich and the CFR Reshaped the Global Economy After World War II . . . and Then Fought a War They Knew They Would Lose in Vietnam," http://bit.ly/1DFj0UG. For an especially fatuous version of the conspiracy theory, "Stuff They Don't Want You to Know—The CFR," http://bit.ly/1JEm63t.

82. LOC, Box 43, Franklin to Oppenheimer, Mar. 28, 1955.

83. Ibid., HAK to Oppenheimer, Apr. 1, 1955.

84. Kennedy Library, Bundy Papers, Box 17, Bundy to HAK, Apr. 14, 1955.

85. Harvard Archives, Bundy Papers, UA III 5 55.26 1955–1956, CFR Study Group meeting, unedited digest, May 4, 1955.

86. Kennedy Library, Schlesinger Papers, Box P-17, HAK to Schlesinger, Oct. 3, 1955.

87. Smith, *On His Own Terms*, KL 5699.

88. Ibid., KL 5894. See also Reich, *Life of Rockefeller.*

89. Lewis, *Spy Capitalism*, 21.

90. Rockefeller Archive Center, Gen. Theodor Parker to Nelson Rockefeller [henceforth NAR], Draft of Letter to Eisenhower, July 29, 1955. See also Parker to NAR, Aug. 4, 1955; Aug. 8, 1955; NAR to Charles Wilson, Aug. 9, 1955; Memorandum of Conversation with John Foster Dulles and Allen Dulles, Aug. 11, 1955.

On the failure of "Open Skies" as propaganda, see Osgood, *Total Cold War,* 194.

91. Hoover Institution Archives, Elliott Papers, Box 166, Elliott to Raymond Moley, Mar. 30, 1960.
92. Reich, *Rockefeller,* 614f.
93. Smith, *On His Own Terms,* KL 5995.
94. Rockefeller Archive Center, Panel Members, Aug. 16, 1955.
95. Ibid., Open Remarks to Panel by NAR, Aug. 23, 1955.
96. HAK, "Eulogy for Nelson Rockefeller," Feb. 2, 1979, http://bit.ly/1DHvpb1.
97. Harvard Archives, International Seminar, Sept. 9, 1955.
98. Rockefeller Archive Center, Fourth Session, Aug. 28, 1955.
99. Gavin, *Nuclear Statecraft,* 57.
100. LOC, Kent 63, HAK, "The Problem of German Unity," Oct. 10, 1955.
101. Eisenhower Library, HAK, "Psychological and Pressure Aspects of Negotiations with the USSR," NSC Series, 10, "Psychological Aspects of United States Strategy" (Nov. 1955).
102. LOC, E-2, HAK to NAR, Nov. 8, 1955.
103. Ibid., HAK to Operations Research Office, Dec. 21, 1955. Here, as elsewhere, I prefer to adjust relative to GDP rather than simply using the consumer price index: details in Lawrence H. Officer and Samuel H. Williamson, "Explaining the Measures of Worth," http://bit .ly/1I4ygkz.
104. LOC, E-3, HAK to NAR, Dec. 21, 1955.
105. Kennedy Library, HAK to Schlesinger, Dec. 15, 1955.
106. Ibid., Schlesinger Papers, Box P-17, HAK to Schlesinger, Jan. 25, 1955.
107. Ibid., HAK, Soviet Strategy—Possible U.S. Countermeasures, Dec. 15, 1955. See also LOC, Kent 13, HAK, Notes on the Soviet Peace Offensive, Apr. 4, 1956.
108. Kennedy Library, Schlesinger Papers, Box P-17, HAK to Schlesinger, Jan. 24, 1956.
109. HAK, "Force and Diplomacy," 350ff.
110. Ibid., 357.
111. Ibid., 360.
112. Ibid., 362.
113. Ibid., 365f.
114. Rosenberg, "Origins of Overkill," 42.
115. HAK, "Reflections on American Diplomacy," 38.
116. Ibid., 41.
117. Ibid., 46f.
118. Ibid., 40.
119. Falk, "National Security Council Under Truman."
120. Ibid., 53, 42.
121. Kennedy Library, Bundy Papers, Box 19, HAK to Bundy, Nov. 1, 1956.
122. LOC, Kent 64, HAK to Bundy, Nov. 8, 1956.
123. Harvard Archives, International Seminar, HAK to Graubard, Nov. 12, 1956.
124. Ibid., HAK to Graubard, Dec. 31, 1956.
125. Isaacson, *Kissinger,* KL 1627.
126. LOC, A-2, HAK to Kraemer, June 24, 1957.
127. Ibid., HAK to Teller, June 5, 1957.
128. LOC, Kent 69, HAK speech, "How the Revolution in Weapons Will Affect Our

Strategy and Foreign Policy," Economic Club of Detroit, Apr. 15, 1957.
129. HAK, "Strategy and Organization."
130. Eisenhower Library, Papers as POTUS, 1953–1961 [Ann Whitman File], Box 23, Eisenhower note, Apr. 1, 1957.
131. HAK, "Strategy and Organization," 380.
132. Ibid., 383, 386.
133. Ibid., 387.
134. Ibid.
135. Ibid., 388.
136. Ibid., 390–93.
137. Ibid., 389.
138. HAK, "Controls, Inspection, and Limited War," *Reporter,* June 13, 1957.
139. LOC, A-2, HAK to Bundy, Feb. 7, 1957.
140. HAK, *Nuclear Weapons and Foreign Policy* [henceforth *NWFP*], 7.
141. *NWFP,* 60.
142. *NWFP,* 84.
143. Ibid.
144. *NWFP,* 211, 214, 219.
145. *NWFP,* 128, 131.
146. *NWFP,* 144, 170.
147. *NWFP,* 360.
148. *NWFP,* 227f.
149. *NWFP,* 183f.
150. *NWFP,* 226.
151. Schelling, "Essay on Bargaining"; Schelling, "Bargaining, Communication, and Limited War."
152. *NWFP,* 157.
153. *NWFP,* 180–83.
154. *NWFP,* 194–201.
155. *NWFP,* 427–29.
156. LOC, F-3(c), HAK to Oscar Ruebhausen, June 11, 1956.
157. LOC, Box 43, Oppenheimer to Gordon Dean, May 16, 1957.
158. LOC, Oppenheimer Papers, Box 262, Kissinger Book, RO Statement, June 14, 1957.
159. Harvard Archives, International Seminar, HAK to Graubard, July 8, 1957.
160. "A Recipe Against Annihilation," *Washington Post and Times Herald,* June 30, 1957.
161. "An Atom Age Strategy," *Chicago Daily Tribune,* July 7, 1957.
162. Book Review, *New York Herald Tribune,* July 10, 1957.
163. "On the Problems of Preparedness in Today's World," *Christian Science Monitor,* June 27, 1957.
164. "A New Look at War-Making," *New York Times,* July 7, 1957.
165. *American Political Science Review* 52, no. 3 (Sept. 1958), 842–44.
166. "War Without Suicide," *Economist,* Aug. 24, 1957.
167. "Dilemma of the Nuclear Age in a Keen, Many-Sided View," *New York Herald Tribune,* June 30, 1957.
168. James E. King, Jr., "Nuclear Weapons and Foreign Policy, I—Limited Defense," *New Republic,* July 1, 1957, and "II—Limited Annihilation," ibid., July 15, 1957.
169. Paul H. Nitze, "Limited War or Massive Retaliation?"
170. Isaacson, *Kissinger,* KL 1682.
171. Nitze, "Atoms, Strategy, and Policy."

172. Morgenthau, "Nuclear Weapons and Foreign Policy." See also the journalist Walter Millis's somewhat similar critique: *Political Science Quarterly* 72, no. 4 (Dec. 1957), 608ff.

173. Brodie, "Nuclear Weapons and Foreign Policy."

174. Possony, "Nuclear Weapons and Foreign Policy."

175. Kaufmann, "Crisis in Military Affairs," 585, 593.

176. William H. Stringer, "State of the Nation: Is Limited War Possible?," *Christian Science Monitor*, July 24, 1957.

177. "USAF Policy Theorist Brands Limited War Escapist Language," *Globe and Mail*, Sept. 16, 1957.

178. LOC, A-2, Gavin to HAK, July 15, 1957; HAK to Gavin, July 27, 1957.

179. "Can War Be Limited?," *Des Moines Sunday Register*, July 21, 1957.

180. Chalmers M. Roberts, "Headaches for Ike . . . ," *Washington Post and Times Herald*, July 24, 1957. See also Roberts, "Kissinger Volume Stirs a Debate," ibid., Sept. 1, 1957.

181. Nixon Library, Pre-Presidential Papers, General Correspondence 414, RMN to HAK, July 7, 1958.

182. Lodge, *As It Was*, 202.

183. Eisenhower Library, Papers as POTUS, 1953–1961 [Ann Whitman File], Box 23, Lodge to Eisenhower, July 25, 1957.

184. Ibid., Box 25, Eisenhower to Acting Secretary of State Herter, July 31, 1957. In a private memorandum, however, Eisenhower made his own objections more explicit: "This man would say, 'We are to be an armed camp—capable of doing all things, all the time, everywhere.'" Thomas, *Ike's Bluff*, KL 7243–45.

185. Russell Baker, "U.S. Reconsidering 'Small-War' Theory," *New York Times*, Aug. 11, 1957.

186. Alistair Cooke, "Limited or World War? U.S. Debates the Odds," *Manchester Guardian*, Aug. 12, 1957.

187. Russell Baker, "The Cold War and the Small War," *Time*, Aug. 26, 1957.

188. Harvard Archives, International Seminar, HAK to Graubard, Dec. 5, 1956.

189. LOC, A-2, HAK to Bundy, Feb. 7, 1957.

190. Gaddis, *Strategies of Containment*, 178f.

191. Osgood, *Total Cold War*, 336f.

192. Ibid., 344.

193. Mieczkowski, *Eisenhower's Sputnik Moment*. For the text of Eisenhower's Nov. 7 speech, see http://bit.ly/1EnogkR.

194. "Man to Watch," *New York Herald Tribune*, Mar. 21, 1958.

195. "Kissinger Speaks," *New York Herald Tribune*, Oct. 14, 1957. See also "Dr. Kissinger Amplifies," ibid., Oct. 17, 1957.

196. Eisenhower Library, Records as POTUS—White House Central Files, Box 7, Leo Cherne to executive members of the Research Institute, Oct. 24, 1957.

197. "U.S. Warned to Prevent More 'Syrias,'" *Los Angeles Examiner*, Oct. 30, 1957.

198. LOC, *Face the Nation*, Nov. 10, 1957, transcript.

199. Eisenhower Library, CIA, Foreign Broadcast Information Service, Current Developments Series, Radio Propaganda Report, CD.78, Oct. 1, 1957.

200. Jackson, "Beyond Brinkmanship."

Chapter 11: Boswash

1. LOC, Kent 9, John Conway to HAK, Feb. 17, 1956.

2. HAK, "The Policymaker and the Intellectual," *Reporter*, Mar. 5, 1959, 30, 33.

3. LOC, G-13, Huntington to HAK, Apr. 14, 1956.

4. Ford Foundation Archives, Reel R-0492, Elliott to Don Price, n.d.

5. LOC, Kent 64, HAK to Bundy, June 14, 1956.

6. LOC, Kent 13, Rockefeller to HAK, Apr. 28, 1956.

7. LOC, F-3(c), HAK to Oscar Ruebhausen, June 11, 1956. On the genesis of the Special Studies Project, see Smith, *On His Own Terms*, KL 6096.

8. Harvard Archives, International Seminar, HAK to Graubard, June 25, 1956.

9. LOC, Kent 64, HAK to Bundy, Aug. 9, 1956.

10. Harvard Archives, International Seminar, HAK to Graubard, June 25 and July 9, 1956.

11. LOC, Kent 9, HAK to NAR, May 22, 1957.

12. Atkinson, *In Theory and Practice*, 18. Cf. Isaacson, *Kissinger*, KL 1762–70.

13. LOC, Kent 9, Robert Strausz-Hupé to HAK, July 24, 1957. On Strausz-Hupé, see Wiarda, *Think Tanks and Foreign Policy*, 14ff.

14. LOC, Kent 64, HAK to Bundy, Aug. 6, 1957; Bundy to HAK, Aug. 15, 1957. For evidence of Bundy's unease at the extent of Kissinger's extracurricular commitments, see HAK to Bundy, Sept. 11, 1957.

15. "Kissinger Talk Views U.S. Gov't Defense Program," cutting from unidentifiable newspaper, May 31, 1958.

16. LOC, E-2, HAK Resignation as Reserve Office (1959), Mar. 6, 1959.

17. LOC, G-13, HAK to Stanley Hoffmann, Sept. 13, 1957.

18. Graubard, *Kissinger*, 115.

19. LOC, HAK Papers, D-9, Kraemer to HAK, May 17, 1958.

20. Rockefeller Archive Center, Kraemer, Trends in Western Germany, June 1, 1958.

21. Ibid., HAK to Lt. Col. Robert Ekvall, July 7, 1956.

22. Andrew, "Cracks in the Consensus," 551.

23. Rosenberg, "Prospect for America," 2f.

24. Smith, *On His Own Terms*, KL 6096.

25. Rockefeller Archive Center, Special Studies Project, Oct. 31, 1956.

26. Ibid., Elliott draft, Nov. 1, 1956. See also the revised and retitled draft, Elliott to Robert Cutler, Nov. 2, 1956.

27. Hoover Institution Archives, Elliott Papers, Box 88, United States Democratic Process—The Challenge and Opportunity, Nov. 9, 1956.

28. See, e.g., Rockefeller Archive Center, HAK to Rusk, Nov. 27, 1956.
29. Reich, *Life of Rockefeller*, 653, 658f.
30. Smith, *On His Own Terms*, 6156.
31. Lewis, *Spy Capitalism*, 58.
32. Rosenberg, "Prospect for America," 20. Cf. Snead, *Gaither Committee*. See also Halperin, "Gaither Committee."
33. Gaddis, *Strategies of Containment*, 182f.
34. Osgood, *Total Cold War*, 345.
35. Lewis, *Spy Capitalism*, pp. 79ff.
36. Rockefeller Brothers Fund, *Prospect for America*, 96, 104.
37. Reich, *Life of Rockefeller*, 665.
38. Andrew, "Cracks in the Consensus," 541.
39. Rosenberg, "Prospect for America," 2f. See Isaacson, *Kissinger*, KL 1739–42.
40. Rosenberg, "Prospect for America," 2f.
41. Kennedy Library, Schlesinger Papers, Incoming Correspondence, 1945–1960, Box P-17, HAK to Schlesinger, Jan. 13, 1958.
42. LOC, HAK Papers, E-2, Schlesinger to HAK, Jan. 28, 1958.
43. Rosenberg, "Prospect for America," 22.
44. Ibid., 27ff.
45. Andrew, "Cracks in the Consensus," 544f.
46. Ibid., 542.
47. Ibid., 538, 548.
48. LOC, Kent 13, NAR to HAK, July 2, 1958.
49. Andrew, "Cracks in the Consensus," 549.
50. Rosenberg, "Prospect for America," 7, 27ff.
51. Collier and Horowitz, *Rockefellers*, 195.
52. Rosenberg, "Prospect for America," 5.
53. Persico, *Imperial Rockefeller*, 77.
54. Reich, *Life of Rockefeller*, 661.
55. Ibid., 663.
56. Smith, *On His Own Terms*, KL 6514.
57. HAK, interview by author.
58. Harvard Archives, International Seminar, HAK to Graubard, Nov. 12, 1956.
59. Ibid., HAK to Graubard, Dec. 5, 1956.
60. Rockefeller Archive Center, HAK to NAR, Dec. 27, 1956; NAR to HAK, Dec. 31, 1956.
61. Ibid., HAK to NAR, Jan. 9, 1957; LOC, Kent 9, HAK to NAR, May 22, 1957; LOC, Kent 64, HAK to NAR, Aug. 10, 1957.
62. LOC, Kent 69, Milton Katz to HAK, Jan. 6, 1961.
63. Isaacson, *Kissinger*, KL 1812–14.
64. Straight, *Nancy Hanks*, 57f.
65. Reich, *Life of Rockefeller*, 662.
66. LOC, F-3(c), Hanks to HAK, Sept. 22, 1961.
67. Isaacson, *Kissinger*, KL 1730–32.
68. On the relationship with NAR, see Straight, *Nancy Hanks*, 47–55. She went on to serve as the second chairman of the National Endowment for the Arts (1969–77).
69. Ibid., 57.
70. LOC, HAK Papers, E-1, HAK to Nancy Hanks, Nov. 6, 1958.
71. Ibid., E-2, HAK to Jamieson, Nov. 7, 1958.
72. LOC, F-3(c), HAK to Hanks, Jan. 12, 1960.
73. LOC, E-1, Hanks to HAK, Mar. 17, 1960.
74. Ibid., HAK to Hanks, Mar. 21, 1960.
75. Ibid., Hanks to HAK, Mar. 23, 1960.
76. LOC, F-3(c), HAK to Hanks, Sept. 26, 1961.
77. LOC, E-1, HAK to Hanks, June 16, 1960.
78. "Summertime . . . Busiest Season of All. Traveler Visits One of Nation's Outstanding Young Men," *Boston Traveler*, July 7, 1959.
79. Isaacson, *Kissinger*, KL 1907–18, citing HAK to his parents, Sept. 8, 1961.
80. "Man to Watch: Dr. Kissinger—Foreign Policy Expert," *Tribune* [?], March 21, 1958.
81. Walter Kissinger, interview by author.
82. LOC, Kent 64, HAK to NAR, Jan. 6, 1960.
83. Mazlish, *Kissinger*, esp. 84–88.
84. Suri, *Kissinger*, 133–37.
85. Smith, *Harvard Century*, 215f.
86. Schlesinger, *Veritas*, 209.
87. Smith, *Harvard Century*, 219f., 227.
88. Harvard Archives, International Seminar, Mar. 26, 1958. See also HAK to Don Price [Ford Foundation], Dec. 10, 1958.
89. LOC, Kent 64, Elliott to Bundy, Mar. 25, 1959.
90. Atkinson, *In Theory and Practice*, 7–10.
91. Bird, *Color of Truth*, 143. Cf. Kalb and Kalb, *Kissinger*, 57; Mazlish, *Kissinger*, 75f.
92. Bowie and Kissinger, *Program of the CFIA*, 1.
93. Atkinson, *In Theory and Practice*, 28f.
94. Bowie and Kissinger, *Program of the CFIA*, 4.
95. Atkinson, *In Theory and Practice*, 28–32.
96. Ibid., 28.
97. Ibid., 48.
98. Ibid., 44.
99. Ibid., 118.
100. Ibid., 119f.
101. Hoover Institution Archives, Elliott Papers, Box 166, Elliott to Raymond Moley, Mar. 30, 1960.
102. Mazlish, *Kissinger*, 77f.
103. Isaacson, *Kissinger*, KL 1807–10.
104. LOC, HAK Papers, E-1, Hanks to Corinne Lyman, Feb. 28, 1958.
105. Ibid., Corinne Lyman to Hanks, Mar. 3, 1958.
106. Kent papers, HAK to Bowie, n.d.
107. Isaacson, *Kissinger*, KL 1785–87; Thomas Schelling, interview by author.
108. Bird, *Color of Truth*, 143.
109. Isaacson, *Kissinger*, KL 1827–44.
110. LOC, Kent 64, HAK to Bundy, June 17, 1958; LOC, G-14 Supp (Kraemer), HAK to Kraemer, Dec. 22, 1961.
111. Atkinson, *In Theory and Practice*, 78.
112. See, e.g., Kennedy Library, Bundy Papers, Harvard Years Correspondence, Box 22, Joint Arms Control Seminar: Abstract of Discussion, Oct. 4, 1960; Second Meeting, Oct. 24, 1960.
113. Kennedy Library, Bundy Papers, Harvard Years Correspondence, Box 22, Joint Arms Control Seminar: Abstract of Discussion, Dec. 19, 1960.
114. Isaacson, *Kissinger*, KL 1844–52.
115. Fred Gardner, "The Cliché Expert Testifies on Disarmament," *Harvard Crimson*, Jan. 16, 1963.
116. Charles S. Maier, "The Professors' Role as Government Adviser," *Harvard Crimson*, June 16, 1960.
117. Charles W. Bevard, Jr., "Two Professors Called Militarists," *Harvard Crimson*, May 29, 1963.
118. Westad, *Global Cold War*; Ferguson, *War of the World*, 596–625.
119. Gaddis, *Strategies of Containment*, 128f., 179f.
120. Ibid., 138.
121. Gaddis, *Kennan*, 487.
122. Osgood, *Total Cold War*, 96–113, 124f.

123. Ibid., 118ff.
124. Ibid., 132, 136.
125. Ibid., 138–40.
126. Frey, "Tools of Empire."
127. Osgood, Total Cold War, 124.
128. Frey, "Tools of Empire," 543.
129. Gaddis, Strategies of Containment, 156.
130. Ruehsen, "Operation 'Ajax' Revisited."
131. Osgood, Total Cold War, 146ff.
132. Leary, Central Intelligence Agency, 62f.
133. Thomas, Very Best Men, 229–32; Grose, Gentleman Spy, 723f.

134. HAK, interview by Mike Wallace. The interview can be viewed at http://cs.pn/1GpkMou.
135. American Broadcasting Company, in association with The Fund for the Republic, Survival and Freedom: A Mike Wallace Interview with Henry A. Kissinger (1958), 3–7.
136. Ibid., 5.
137. Ibid., 9f.
138. Ibid., 10.
139. Ibid., 11.
140. Ibid., 11, 13.
141. Ibid., 14.

Chapter 12: The Intellectual and the Policy Maker

1. Smith, On His Own Terms, KL 9499–500.
2. Nixon Library, Pre-Presidential Papers, General Correspondence 239, Elliott to RMN, Jan. 11, 1960.
3. LOC, Louis Kissinger newspaper cuttings collection. See also "Kissinger, Among Top Ten Men, Real Expert," Boston Traveler, Jan. 7, 1959; "Harvard's Kissinger Worked Days, Studied Nights," Boston Sunday Globe, Jan. 11, 1959.
4. HAK, "Policymaker," 31, 33.
5. Ibid., 34.
6. Ibid., 35.
7. LOC, Kent 13, NAR to HAK, July 2, 1958.
8. LOC, Kent 64, HAK to NAR, Aug. 26, 1958.
9. Ibid., HAK to NAR, Sept. 19, 1958.
10. LOC, E-1, HAK to Nancy Hanks, Oct. 6, 1958.
11. LOC, Kent 64, HAK to NAR, Oct. 6, 1958.
12. Smith, On His Own Terms, KL 7353.
13. LOC, E-2, Schlesinger to HAK, Nov. 5, 1958.
14. Gaddis, Kennan, 522–27.
15. Osgood, Total Cold War, 199–205.
16. HAK, "Missiles and Western Alliance," 383–93.
17. Ibid., 398.
18. "Kissinger Urges Europe to Accept Missile Bases," New York Herald Tribune, Mar. 19, 1958.
19. Stephen S. Singer, "Limited War Concept Defended by Kissinger," unidentified newspaper from Hanover, NH, Mar. 19, 1958.
20. Kennedy Library, Schlesinger Papers, HAK to Schlesinger, Mar. 28, 1958.
21. Rubinson, "'Crucified on a Cross of Atoms.'"
22. Osgood, Total Cold War, 207.
23. Thomas, Ike's Bluff, KL 3995–4000.
24. Gaddis, Strategies of Containment, 191f.
25. LOC, G-15, HAK to Harvard Crimson, Oct. 27, 1958.
26. LOC, Harvard Crimson, HAK to Richard Levy, Oct. 2, 1958.
27. HAK, "Nuclear Testing and the Problem of Peace," 7, 16.
28. LOC, E-2, Teller to HAK, Nov. 5, 1958.
29. Osgood, Total Cold War, 208f.
30. "Truth Kept from Public," Evening World Herald, Oct. 23, 1958.
31. LOC, Kent 64, HAK to NAR, Feb. 9, 1959.
32. Ibid., NAR to HAK, Dec. 17, 1958.
33. LOC, E-2, HAK to Schlesinger, July 6, 1959.
34. "So wenig wie möglich vernichten," Die Welt, Jan. 12, 1959.
35. "Atomare Abschreckung genügt nicht mehr," Süddeutsche Zeitung, Jan. 14, 1959.

36. LOC, D-4, HAK to Dönhoff, Feb. 2, 1959. See also Dönhoff to HAK, Feb. 26, 1959. Die Zeit ran a version of his piece on "The Policymaker and the Intellectual."
37. Gavin, Nuclear Statecraft, 58.
38. Ibid., 65.
39. Trachtenberg, Cold War and After, 25, 32.
40. "Der Theoretiker des 'begrenzten Krieges,'" Frankfurter Rundschau, Jan. 17, 1959.
41. "Kissinger sprach vor Generalen," Die Welt, Jan. 24, 1959.
42. "Mit Panzern nach Berlin?," Der Spiegel, Feb. 11, 1959. See also "Harvard Professor Favors Total War as 'Last Resort' to Keep Berlin Free," Reuters, Feb. 10, 1959.
43. "Mr. Kissinger ist für den Krieg," Berliner Zeitung, Feb. 10, 1959; "Westberlin ist Zeitzünderbombe," Neues Deutschland, Feb. 10, 1959; "Wer bedroht wen?," Nationalzeitung, Feb. 14, 1959.
44. "Professors Express Varied Views on Current State of Berlin Crisis," Harvard Crimson, Mar. 13, 1959. This was shortly before the publication of Brzezinski's reputation-making book The Soviet Bloc: Unity and Conflict.
45. For an early draft, see LOC, A-1(a), HAK, Beyond the Summit (Office Copy), Apr. 20, 1959.
46. HAK, "Search for Stability."
47. Ibid., 542.
48. Ibid., 543, 549, 551, 555.
49. Ibid., 556.
50. LOC, Kent 64, HAK to NAR, Mar. 7, 1960; Mar. 23, 1960.
51. LOC, C-1, Hobbing/Kissinger, Position Paper A-5, Rev. 2 (Preliminary), Berlin, June 14, 1960.
52. Ambrose, Nixon, vol. 1, KL 7601–2.
53. Telegraph, Apr. 25, 1988.
54. Nixon, RN: Memoirs, KL 3860–61.
55. Ambrose, Nixon, vol. 1, KL 10161–64.
56. LOC, Kent 64, HAK to NAR, May 7, 1959.
57. LOC, E-1, Nancy Hanks to HAK, Apr. 14, 1959.
58. LOC, Kent 64, HAK to NAR, July 22, 1959; July 27, 1959.
59. LOC, F-3(c), Roswell B. Perkins to HAK, Aug. 18, 1959.
60. LOC, Kent 64, HAK to NAR, Aug. 21, 1959.
61. LOC, F-3(c), Perkins to HAK, Gertrude Hardiman, and Tom Losee, Oct. 22, 1959.
62. LOC, Kent 13, HAK to NAR, Sept. 3, 1959.

63. Ibid., Statement After Meeting with Mr. Khrushchev [draft], Sept. 3, 1959.

64. LOC, Kent 13, HAK to NAR, Sept. 4, 1959.

65. HAK, "The Khrushchev Visit: Dangers and Hopes," *New York Times*, Sept. 6. 1959.

66. Ambrose, *Eisenhower*, vol. 2, KL 10735. Cf. Gaddis, *Strategies of Containment*, 195.

67. *Harvard Crimson*, Nov. 30, 1959.

68. LOC, G-15, HAK to Michael Churchill, Nov. 30, 1959. The letter was published as "Clarification," *Harvard Crimson*, Dec. 1, 1959.

69. Ambrose, *Eisenhower*, vol. 2, KL 10735.

70. LOC, F-3(c), HAK to Perkins, Nov. 5, 1959; HAK to NAR, Nov. 9, 1959.

71. LOC, Kent 64, HAK to NAR, Dec. 28, 1959.

72. Ibid., HAK to Bundy, Oct. 14, 1959.

73. See, e.g., Nixon Library, Pre-Presidential Papers, 414, Kirk, RMN to HAK, June 10, 1959.

74. Nixon Library, RMN, "What Can I Believe: A series of essays prepared by Richard M. Nixon during his Senior year of study at Whittier College during the 1933–1934 School Year in the course 'Philosophy of Christian Reconstruction,'" Oct. 9, 1933–Mar. 29, 1934, 1.

75. Wills, *Nixon Agonistes*, 31.

76. Nixon Library, RMN, "What Can I Believe," 2, 32.

77. Ibid., 30f.

78. Frank, *Ike and Dick*, 213ff.

79. Safire, *Before the Fall*, 275.

80. LOC, HAK Newspaper Collection, RMN to HAK, Sept. 15, 1959.

81. Hoover Institution Archives, Elliott Papers, Elliott to RMN, Jan. 29, 1958; Nixon Library, Pre-Presidential Papers, Box 239, RMN to Elliott, Feb. 25, 1958.

82. Nixon Library, Pre-Presidential Papers, Box 239, RMN to George Caitlin, Feb. 21, 1958.

83. Ibid., General Correspondence, 239, Elliott to John F. Fennelly, Mar. 29, 1960.

84. Ambrose, *Nixon*, vol. 1, KL 10319–59.

85. Nixon Library, Pre-Presidential Papers, General Correspondence, 239, Elliott to RMN, Jan. 11, 1960.

86. Ibid., Elliott to RMN, Apr. 24, 1960.

87. Hoover Institution Archives, Elliott Papers, Box 166, Unlabeled, Elliott to RMN, Apr. 24, 1961.

88. Aitken, *Nixon*, 341.

89. Reeves, *President Nixon*, 11f.

90. Stans, *One of the President's Men*, 268.

91. Aitken, *Nixon*, 161.

92. Donovan, *Confidential Secretary*, 158.

93. Black, *Richard Milhous Nixon*, 221.

94. Aitken, *Nixon*, 334.

95. HAK Newspaper Collection, "Debating Military Policy: Extension of Remarks of Hon. Lyndon B. Johnson," *Congressional Record*, Feb. 16, 1960. Cf. "The Nation," *Time*, Feb. 15, 1960.

96. LOC, F-3(c), HAK to Perkins, Jan. 19, 1960.

97. Ibid.

98. Ibid., Laurance Rockefeller to HAK, Mar. 25, 1960.

99. LOC, A & P, HAK to Schlesinger, Re. NAR, Apr. 9, 1962.

100. Rosenberg, "Origins of Overkill."

101. Osgood, *Total Cold War*, 210.

102. Thomas, *Very Best Men*, 218.

103. Gaddis, *Strategies of Containment*, 195f.

104. LOC, F-2(a), HAK to NAR, May 23, 1960.

105. LOC, Kent 64, HAK to NAR, May 20, 1960.

106. LOC, F-2(a), HAK, Thoughts on Our Military Policy, May 28, 1960, 15.

107. Ibid., 19.

108. LOC, F-2(a), HAK, Additional Note on Military Affairs, June 1, 1960.

109. Ambrose, *Nixon*, vol. 1, KL 10831–45.

110. LOC, F-3(c), HAK to Perkins, June 8, 1960.

111. LOC, Kent 13, Perkins to HAK, June 17, 1960. Cf. LOC, F-2(b), Foreign Affairs: Summaries of Position Papers, July 1, 1960.

112. LOC, Kent 64, HAK to NAR, Sept. 26, 1960; LOC, E-2, HAK to Teller, June 1, 1960.

113. Smith, *On His Own Terms*, KL 8030–31.

114. Ibid., KL 10916–28.

115. HAK, "Do the New Nations Need Our Kind of Democracy?," *New York Post*, June 19, 1960.

116. "A 'New Look' Plan on Arms Opposed," *New York Times*, June 19, 1960.

117. HAK, "Arms Control, Inspection," 559, 568, 571f.

118. Atkinson, *In Theory and Practice*, 72f., 76.

119. HAK, "Limited War: Conventional or Nuclear?," 806f.

120. Ibid., 808.

121. Isaacson, *Kissinger*, KL 1990–95.

122. Walter Millis, "The Object Is Survival," *New York Times*, Jan. 15, 1961.

123. Martin, "Necessity for Choice."

124. Wright, "Necessity for Choice."

125. HAK, *Necessity for Choice* [henceforth *NFC*], 1.

126. *NFC*, 2–6, 32, 98.

127. Fursenko and Naftali, *Khrushchev's Cold War*.

128. *NFC*, 23.

129. *NFC*, 257, 122.

130. HAK, "For an Atlantic Confederacy," *Reporter*, Feb. 2, 1961.

131. LOC, Box 7, HAK to Caryl Haskins, Nov. 12, 1959. See also Haskins's reply, Nov. 25, 1959.

132. *NFC*, 122.

133. *NFC*, 300ff.

134. *NFC*, 303, 308.

135. *NFC*, 311, 318, 328.

136. LOC, Kent 64, Cushman to HAK, June 28, 1960.

137. Schlesinger, *Journals*, Aug. 30, 1960.

138. Ambrose, *Nixon*, vol. 1, KL 11155–97. See also Smith, *On His Own Terms*, KL 8159; Black, *Richard Milhous Nixon*, 396.

139. Schlesinger, *Journals*, Aug. 30, 1960.

140. LOC, Kent 64, George Grassmuck to HAK, Aug. 29, 1960.

141. Ibid., HAK to Grassmuck, Sept. 1, 1960.

142. LOC, F-3(c), HAK to Perkins, Nov. 30, 1960.

143. Ibid., HAK to Adolph Berle, Jr., Oct. 17, 1960.

144. LOC, A & P, HAK to NAR, Nov. 18, 1960.

145. LOC, F-3(c), HAK to Cort Schuyler, Dec. 20, 1960. See also Dec. 23, 1960.

146. Ibid., HAK to Schuyler, Jan. 11, 1961.

147. LOC, Kent 64, HAK to NAR, Feb. 24, 1961.

148. LOC, HAK Papers, Box 7, HAK to Haskins, Nov. 12, 1959. Cf. *NFC*, 313f.

149. Rockefeller Archive Center, Kraemer to HAK, Nov. 1, 1956. See the paper Trends in Western Germany, Nov. 1956.

150. Schlesinger, *Journals*, Aug. 30, 1960.

151. LOC, G-14, Kraemer to HAK, Dec. 2, 1957.

Chapter 13: Flexible Responses

1. Hoover Institution Archives, Elliott Papers, "Conference on the Marriage of Political Philosophy and Practice in Public Affairs in Honor of Professor Elliott," Harvard Summer School, Program and Proceedings, July 22, 1963.
2. Kennedy Library, Subject File, 1961–1964, Box WH-13, HAK to Schlesinger, Sept. 8, 1961.
3. Andrew Dugan and Frank Newport, "Americans Rate JFK as Top Modern President," Gallup, Nov. 15, 2013, http://bit.ly/1d9qLNh.
4. Frank Newport, "Americans Say Reagan Is the Greatest U.S. President," Feb. 18, 2011, http://bit.ly/1DYtthB.
5. Halberstam, Best and Brightest, 42.
6. Schlesinger, Thousand Days, 728f.
7. Caro, Passage of Power, KL 6294–98, 6301.
8. Smith, Harvard Century, 13.
9. Atkinson, In Theory and Practice, 126f.
10. Dwight D. Eisenhower, "Farewell Address," Jan. 17, 1961, PBS American Experience, http://to.pbs.org/1DYtEcw.
11. Atkinson, In Theory and Practice, 127.
12. LOC, J-10, John F. Kennedy [henceforth JFK] to HAK, Dec. 13, 1958.
13. Ibid., HAK to JFK, Dec. 23, 1958.
14. Ibid., JFK to HAK, Jan. 23, 1959.
15. Ibid., JFK to HAK, Feb. 6, 1959.
16. Ibid., HAK to JFK, Feb. 13, 1959.
17. Ibid., JFK to HAK, June 4, 1959.
18. "Kennedy Moves to Organize Campus Braintrust," Boston Sunday Globe, Dec. 11, 1959.
19. John F. Kennedy Library Oral History Program, Abram Chayes, recorded interview by Eugene Gordon, May 18, 1964, 39–45. See also Archibald Cox, recorded interview by Richard A. Lester, Nov. 25, 1964, 39.
20. LOC, F-3(c), HAK to Perkins, Jan. 19, 1960.
21. LOC, D-4, HAK to Sally Coxe Taylor, Feb. 10, 1960.
22. NFC, 6.
23. LOC, Kent 13, HAK to Happy Murphy, Jan. 21, 1960.
24. Arthur Schlesinger, Journals, Aug. 30, 1960.
25. LOC, F-3(c), HAK to Adolph Berle, Jr., Oct. 25, 1960.
26. LOC, J-10, HAK to JFK, Nov. 14, 1960.
27. Ibid., HAK to JFK, Nov. 16, 1960.
28. Rosenberg, "Prospect for America," 57ff.
29. Richard H. Rovere, "Letter from Washington," New Yorker, Jan. 21, 1961, 108f.
30. William Manchester, "John F. Kennedy: Portrait of a President," New York Post Magazine, Mar. 22, 1963.
31. Kennedy Library, Schlesinger Papers, Incoming Correspondence, 1945–1960, Box P-17, HAK to Schlesinger, Jan. 23, 1961.
32. LOC, Kent 64, Bundy to HAK, Jan. 28, 1961.
33. "Kennedy Expected to Name Dr. Kissinger to Key Post," Boston Sunday Globe, Feb. 5, 1961.
34. Kennedy Library, Staff Memoranda, Box 320, Bundy to JFK, Feb. 8, 1961.
35. LOC, Kent 64, HAK to Bundy, Feb. 8, 1961.
36. LOC, J-10, HAK to JFK, Feb. 8, 1961.
37. LOC, Kent 64, Bundy to HAK, Feb. 10, 1961.
38. Ibid., Bundy to HAK, Feb. 18, 1961.
39. Ibid., HAK to Bundy, Mar. 1, 1961; Bundy to HAK, Mar. 9, 1961.
40. Ibid., HAK to Bundy, Feb. 22, 1961.
41. Kennedy Library, Staff Memoranda, Box 320, Office of the White House Press Secretary, Feb. 27, 1961.
42. Bird, Color of Truth, 186. See also 143f.
43. Kennedy Library, Subject File, 1961–1964, Box WH-13, HAK to Schlesinger, Sept. 8, 1961. See also New York Public Library, Schlesinger Journal, July 28, 1961.
44. LOC, A & P, HAK to Schlesinger, Re. NAR, Apr. 9, 1962.
45. LOC, Kent 64, HAK to NAR, Feb. 10, 1961.
46. See, e.g., LOC, F-3(c), Hugh Morrow to NAR, Feb. 20, 1961.
47. LOC, F-3(c), June Goldthwait to HAK, Mar. 20, 1961.
48. See, e.g., HAK, "A Stronger Atlantic Confederacy," Japan Times, Mar. 22, 1961.
49. LOC, F-3(c), Cort Schuyler to HAK, Apr. 13, 1961.
50. Ibid., Mary K. Boland to HAK, Mar. 10, 1961.
51. Ibid., Boland to Perkins and HAK, Apr. 14, 1961.
52. LOC, Kent 64, HAK to NAR, Aug. 7, 1961.
53. LOC, F-3(c), Morrow to NAR, Apr. 30, 1961.
54. LOC, Kent 64, HAK to NAR, June 1, 1961.
55. LOC, Kent 63, HAK to NAR, May 3, 1961.
56. Giglio, Kennedy, 48.
57. Gaddis, Strategies of Containment, 200.
58. Ibid., 216.
59. Freedman, Kennedy's Wars, esp. 417ff.
60. Preston, "Little State Department," 639–43.
61. Nelson, "Kennedy's National Security Policy."
62. Preston, "Little State Department," 644.
63. Destler, Presidents, Bureaucrats, 96–100.
64. Ibid., 102f.
65. Daalder and Destler, Shadow of Oval Office, 40.
66. Preston, "Little State Department," 647f.
67. Salinger, With Kennedy, 110f.
68. Reeves, President Kennedy, 288.
69. Ibid., 289–92.
70. New York Public Library, Schlesinger Journal ms., Mar. 31, 1962.
71. LOC, Kent 64, HAK to NAR, Aug. 14, 1961.
72. Kissinger family papers, Louis Kissinger to HAK, Nov. 19, 1963.
73. Isaacson, Kissinger, KL 1940–41.
74. Bartle Bull, "Castro Cites Cuban Goals in Dillon Talk," Harvard Crimson, Apr. 27, 1959.
75. Higgins, Perfect Failure, 50.
76. Beck, "Necessary Lies, Hidden Truths," 43.
77. Ibid., 52.
78. Higgins, Perfect Failure, 67.
79. Ibid., 68, 71, 81, 91, 168, 75, 103, 108.
80. Schlesinger, Thousand Days, 222, 225, 231.
81. Giglio, Kennedy, 58; Daalder and Destler, Shadow of Oval Office, 21; Schlesinger, Thousand Days, 259.
82. Vandenbroucke, "Anatomy of a Failure," 487, 478.
83. Rasenberger, Brilliant Disaster, 386.
84. Salinger, With Kennedy, 196.
85. New York Public Library, Schlesinger Journal ms., Apr. 21–22, 1961, 174f.
86. Giglio, Kennedy, 63.
87. May and Zelikow, Kennedy Tapes, 27.
88. Ibid., 28.

89. Rasenberger, *Brilliant Disaster,* 334.

90. Rothkopf, *Running the World,* 85.

91. Daalder and Destler, *Shadow of Oval Office,* 23.

92. Preston, "Little State Department," 649. See also Rasenberger, *Brilliant Disaster,* 334ff.; Rothkopf, *Running the World,* 90.

93. Kennedy Library, Staff Memoranda, Box 320, Bundy to Allen Dulles, May 29, 1961; NSC to Bundy, May 29, 1961; Dulles to Bundy, May 30, 1961. Cf. Atkinson, *In Theory and Practice,* 129.

94. Kennedy Library, Subject File, 1961–1964, Box WH-13, HAK to Schlesinger, Sept. 8, 1961.

95. Kennedy Library, Staff Memoranda, Box 320, HAK to JFK, Feb. 28, 1961.

96. Ibid., HAK to Bundy, Mar. 14, 1961.

97. LOC, D-Series, HAK, "Memorandum for the President: Major Defense Options," Mar. 22, 1961.

98. Ibid.

99. Ibid., HAK, "Revisions of National Security Council document called 'NATO and the Atlantic Nations,'" Apr. 5, 1961.

100. Ibid., HAK to Bundy, May 5, 1961.

101. Fursenko and Naftali, *Khrushchev's Cold War,* 341.

102. Rueger, "Kennedy, Adenauer and Berlin Wall," 77.

103. Brinkley, *Kennedy,* 78. Cf. Gavin, *Nuclear Statecraft,* 64.

104. Gavin, *Nuclear Statecraft,* 65.

105. Ausland and Richardson, "Crisis Management," 294.

106. Ibid., 295.

107. Rueger, "Kennedy, Adenauer and the Making of the Berlin Wall," 95.

108. Ibid., 92f.

109. *FRUS, 1961–1963,* vol. XIV, *Berlin Crisis, 1961–1962,* Doc. 42, Record of Meeting of the Interdepartmental Coordinating Group on Berlin Contingency Planning, June 16, 1961; Doc. 49, Report by Acheson, June 28, 1961. Cf. Rueger, "Kennedy, Adenauer and the Making of the Berlin Wall," 102; Gavin, *Nuclear Statecraft,* 67; Schlesinger, *Thousand Days,* 345.

110. Kennedy Library, Box 462, Kissinger Chronological File 7/61, HAK to Rostow, Apr. 4, 1961.

111. Ibid., HAK, Visit of Chancellor Adenauer— Some Psychological Factors, Apr. 6, 1961.

112. Klaus Wegreife, "Adenauer Wanted to Swap West Berlin for Parts of GDR," *Der Spiegel,* Aug. 15, 2011, http://bit.ly/1KcVDHO.

113. Kennedy Library, Box 462, HAK, Visit of Chancellor Adenauer—Some Psychological Factors, Apr. 6, 1961.

114. Ibid., HAK to Bundy, Dec. 26, 1961. See also Bundy to Dowling, Dec. 30, 1961; Dowling to Bundy, Jan. 18, 1962; Kaysen to HAK, Jan. 20; HAK to Kaysen, Jan. 24; Kaysen to Dowling, Jan. 26; Dowling to Kaysen, Jan. 30; HAK to Kaysen, Feb. 2, Feb. 3; U.S. Embassy Bonn to Rusk, Feb. 7; Bundy to Dowling, Feb. 7.

115. New York Public Library, Schlesinger Journal ms., Apr. 21–22, 1961, 174f.

116. LOC, D-Series, HAK to JFK, May 5, 1961.

117. LOC, D-4, HAK to Rostow, May 5, 1961.

118. Patrick, "Berlin Crisis in 1961," 90–93.

119. Kennedy Library, Staff Memoranda, Box 320, HAK to Bundy, May 5, 1961.

120. Ibid., Bundy to HAK, May 5, 1961.

121. LOC, D-Series, HAK, Meeting with Minister of Defense Franz Josef Strauss, May 10, 1961. See also Kennedy Library, Box 462, U.S. Embassy in Bonn to Rusk, May 18, 1961. Strauss subsequently gave a newspaper interview in which he made some of his disagreements with Kissinger public. See also Rueger, "Kennedy, Adenauer and the Making of the Berlin Wall," 148–50.

122. *FRUS, 1961–1963,* vol. XIII, *Western Europe and Canada,* Doc. 111, Dowling to Rusk, July 5, 1961.

123. LOC, D-Series, HAK, Meeting with Adenauer, May 18, 1961. See also Kennedy Library, Box 462, U.S. Embassy in Bonn to Rusk, May 19, 1961.

124. LOC, D-Series, HAK, Conversation with François de Rose, June 13, 1961.

125. Ibid., HAK memorandum, May 25, 1961.

126. Kennedy Library, HAK to Bundy, June 13, 1961.

127. Kennedy Library, Box 462, U.S. Embassy in Bonn to Rusk, May 25, 1961. Cf. Patrick, "Berlin Crisis in 1961," 95f.; Anthony Verrier, "Kissinger's Five Points," *Observer,* May 21, 1961.

128. Joseph Wershba, "Is Limited War the Road to, or from, the Unlimited Kind?," *New York Post,* June 5, 1961.

129. Kennedy Library, Box WH-13, HAK to Schlesinger, June 9, 1961. Cf. Brinkley, *Kennedy,* 80f.; Freedman, *Kennedy's Wars,* 55; Reeves, *Kennedy,* 174.

130. Brinkley, *Kennedy,* 78; Kempe, *Berlin 1961,* 294f.

131. Preston, *War Council,* 69f. See also Schlesinger, *Thousand Days,* 349.

132. *FRUS, 1961–1963,* vol. XIV, *Berlin Crisis, 1961–1962,* Doc. 76, Bundy to JFK, July 19, 1961.

133. Ibid., Doc. 57, Schlesinger to JFK, July 7, 1961.

134. LOC, Kent 64, HAK to Bundy, June 5, 1961.

135. Ibid., HAK to Bundy, June 5, 1961.

136. Ibid., Bundy to HAK, June 8, 1961.

137. Ibid.

138. LOC, D-Series, HAK to Bundy, June 20, 1961.

139. LOC, A & P, HAK to Rostow, June 27, 1961; Kennedy Library, Box 462, HAK to Bundy, June 29, 1961.

140. Ibid., HAK to Rostow, June 27, 1961.

141. "The Administration: The Test of Reality," *Time,* June 30, 1961.

142. Fursenko and Naftali, *Khrushchev's Cold War,* 370.

143. Rueger, "Kennedy, Adenauer and the Making of the Berlin Wall," 180f.

144. Schlesinger, *Thousand Days,* 350f.; Kempe, *Berlin 1961,* 299f.

145. Kennedy Library, Box 462, HAK to Bundy, General War Aspect of Berlin Contingency Planning, July 7, 1961.

146. Ibid., HAK to Bundy, Status of Berlin Contingency Planning, July 7, 1961.

147. Kennedy Library, Box 81a, Germany—Berlin, Kissinger's Report on Berlin, July 7, 1961. At one point, Kissinger expressed doubt that his memoranda ever left Bundy's office, but this

was not the case. See also *FRUS, 1961–1963*, vol. XIV, *Berlin Crisis, 1961–1962*, Doc. 38, Bundy to JFK, June 10, 1961.

148. Kennedy Library, Box 462, HAK to Bowie, July 8, 1961.

149. Ibid., HAK to Bundy, July 14, 1961.

150. Ibid., HAK to Bundy, Negotiations with the GDR, Aug. 11, 1961.

151. Kennedy Library, Staff Memoranda, Box 320, HAK to Bundy, Aug. 11, 1961.

152. Patrick, "Berlin Crisis in 1961," 110.

153. Kempe, *Berlin 1961*, 311ff.; Rueger, "Kennedy, Adenauer and the Making of the Berlin Wall," 195f., 253f.

154. *FRUS, 1961–1963*, vol. XIV, *Berlin Crisis, 1961–1962*, Doc. 85, U.S. Embassy in Moscow to Rusk, July 29, 1961.

155. Ibid., Doc. 84, U.S. Embassy in Moscow to Rusk, July 28, 1961.

156. New York Public Library, Schlesinger Journal ms., July 28, 1961.

157. Kempe, *Berlin 1961*, 490.

158. Brinkley, *Kennedy*, 82.

159. Kempe, *Berlin 1961*, 490.

160. Ibid., 332.

161. Ibid., 349, 355f., 371.

162. Brinkley, *Kennedy*, 82.

163. Kempe, *Berlin 1961*, 486.

164. Freedman, *Kennedy's Wars*, 68–69.

165. Brinkley, *Kennedy*, 81.

166. Gaddis, *Cold War*, 115.

167. Kennedy Library, Box 462, HAK, Some Reflections on the Acheson Memorandum, Aug. 16, 1961.

168. Kennedy Library, Staff Memoranda, Box 320, HAK to Bundy, Aug. 16, 1961. See in general Hofmann, *Emergence of Détente*.

169. Kennedy Library, Box 462, HAK to Rostow, Aug. 16, 1961.

170. Kennedy Library, Staff Memoranda, Box 320, HAK to Bundy, Aug. 18, 1961.

171. LOC, D-Series, HAK to Maxwell Taylor, Aug. 28, 1961.

172. Ibid., HAK to Taylor, Aug. 29, 1961, enclosing a draft memorandum for Taylor to send to Bundy.

173. Kennedy Library, Box 462, Kissinger Chronological File 7/61, HAK to Bundy, Sept. 1, 1961.

174. LOC, D-Series, HAK to Bundy, Some Additional Observations Regarding the Call-Up of Reserves; Military and Disarmament Planning, Sept. 8, 1961.

175. Kennedy Library, Box 462, Kissinger Chronological File 7/61, HAK to Bundy, Sept. 6, 1961.

176. Kennedy Library, Subject File, 1961–1964, Box WH-13, HAK to Schlesinger, Sept. 8, 1961.

177. LOC, A & P, HAK, Memcon Bundy, Sept. 19, 1961, 5:15 p.m.

178. Stephen Schlesinger, diary, Oct. 6, 2008.

179. Kennedy Library, Subject File, 1961–1964, Box WH-13, HAK to Schlesinger, Sept. 8, 1961.

180. Ibid., Schlesinger to HAK, Sept. 27, 1961; HAK to Schlesinger, Oct. 3, 1961.

181. Kennedy Library, Staff Memoranda, Box 320, HAK, Memorandum of Conversation with Soviet Delegates at Stowe, Vermont, Sept. 13–19, 1961.

182. Hargittai, *Buried Glory*, 19.

183. Kempe, *Berlin 1961*, 415f.

184. LOC, D-Series, HAK to Taylor, Sept. 28, 1961.

185. Ibid., HAK to Bundy, Oct. 3, 1961.

186. LOC, G-15, HAK to editors of *Harvard Crimson*, Oct. 5, 1961.

187. Kennedy Library, Subject File, 1961–1964, Box WH-13, HAK, Random Thoughts About Speech, Oct. 9, 1961.

188. Ibid., HAK to Schlesinger, Oct. 15, 1961.

189. LOC, D-Series, HAK, NATO Planning, Oct. 16, 1961.

190. Ibid., HAK, Military Program, Oct. 17, 1961.

191. LOC, F-2(b), HAK to Bundy, Oct. 19, 1961.

192. Ibid., HAK to Bundy, Nov. 3, 1961.

193. Ibid., HAK to JFK, Nov. 3, 1961.

194. Ibid.; Kennedy Library, Subject File, 1961–1964, Box WH-13, HAK to Schlesinger, Nov. 3, 1961.

195. LOC, F-2(b), Bundy to HAK, Nov. 13, 1961.

196. Kennedy Library, Subject File, 1961–1964, Box WH-13, HAK to Schlesinger, Nov. 3, 1961.

197. LOC, Kent 64, HAK, Memorandum of Conversation with Mr. Conway of *Newsweek* Magazine, Nov. 17, 1961.

198. Kennedy Library, Staff Memoranda, Box 320, Lois Moock to Bromley Smith, Nov. 6, 1961; Charles Johnson, Memorandum for the Record, Nov. 28, 1961. See also Isaacson, *Kissinger*, 113; Atkinson, *In Theory and Practice*, 131.

199. "JFK Aide Tells of Soviet Goal," *Durham Morning Herald*, Oct. 27, 1961.

200. Thomas, *Robert Kennedy*, 139.

201. Fursenko and Naftali, *Khrushchev's Cold War*, 400.

202. Daalder and Destler, *Shadow of Oval Office*, 31f.

203. Kennedy Library, Subject File, 1961–1964, Box WH-13, HAK to Schlesinger, Nov. 3, 1961.

204. Ibid., Schlesinger to JFK, Nov. 10, 1961.

205. NAR, *Future of Federalism*.

206. LOC, A & P, HAK to NAR, Oct. 19, 1961.

207. LOC, Kent 64, HAK to NAR, Oct. 20, 1961.

208. LOC, F-3(c), Goldthwait to HAK, Dec. 5, 1961; LOC, F-2(b), HAK to NAR, Dec. 7, 1961.

209. LOC, Kent 64, HAK to NAR, Dec. 19, 1961; LOC, F-3(c), HAK to Perkins, Dec. 20, 1961.

210. LOC, F-3(c), Goldthwait to HAK, Feb. 20, 1962; see also Goldthwait to Perkins, Feb. 20, 1962.

211. Ibid., Perkins to HAK, Mar. 6, 1962, Apr. 4, 1962.

212. Ibid., Perkins to HAK, May 14, 1962.

213. Ibid., HAK to Perkins (draft), Mar. 12, 1962.

214. *FRUS, 1961–1963*, vol. XIV, *Berlin Crisis, 1961–1962*, Doc. 215, Bundy to JFK, Nov. 20, 1961; LOC, D-Series, HAK, Military Briefing for Chancellor Adenauer, Nov. 20, 1961; LOC, Kent 64, Bundy to HAK, Nov. 30, 1961; Kennedy Library, Box 462, Bundy to HAK, Dec. 17, 1961.

215. LOC, F-3(c), HAK to Perkins (draft), March 12, 1962.

216. Statistics at *Chronik der Mauer*, http://bit.ly/1JkZSDx.

Chapter 14: Facts of Life

1. Kennedy Library, Staff Memoranda, Box 320, HAK, "American Strategic Thinking," speech at Pakistan Air Force Headquarters, Feb. 2, 1962.
2. LOC, D-Series, HAK, Memcon in Paris on Feb. 5, 1962, Feb. 9, 1962.
3. Garrow, "FBI and Martin Luther King."
4. LOC, LOC-A & P, HAK to NAR, Oct. 19, 1961.
5. LOC, Kent 64, NAR Correspondence 1962, HAK to NAR, May 25, 1962.
6. Kennedy Library, Box WH-13, Schlesinger to Gilberto Freyre, May 25, 1962.
7. Kennedy Library, Box 321, Consular Memcon, The Brazilian Crisis, June 7, 1962.
8. LOC, Kent 64, HAK to NAR, June 21, 1962.
9. LOC, G-14 Supp. (Kraemer), HAK to Kraemer, Sept. 20, 1962.
10. Kennedy Library, Box WH-13, Schlesinger to HAK, Oct. 1, 1962.
11. Kennedy Library, Box 321, Consular Memcon, June 9, 1962.
12. Andrew, *World Was Going Our Way*. See also Ladislav Bittman, *The Deception Game* (New York: Ballantine Books, 1981).
13. LOC, F-3(c), HAK to NAR, Mar. 6, 1963.
14. Kennedy Library, Box 462, U.S. Embassy New Delhi to Rusk, Jan. 10, 1962.
15. Kennedy Library, Box 320, 1–62, U.S. Embassy New Delhi to Rusk, Jan. 12, 1962.
16. LOC, Kent 9, HAK, Memcon Krishna Menon (Jan. 8 and Jan. 10, 1962), Feb. 8, 1962.
17. Ibid., HAK, Memcon Nehru (Jan. 10, 1962), Feb. 8, 1962.
18. Kennedy Library, Staff Memoranda, Box 320, HAK, Summary of Conversation About Disarmament with Indian Officials, Feb. 13, 1962.
19. Kennedy Library, Box 462, Dept. of State to U.S. Embassy Tel Aviv, Jan. 3, 1962; U.S. Embassy Tel Aviv to Rusk, Jan. 9, 1962; Kissinger Statements Reaction, Jan. 9, 1962; U.S. Embassy Karachi to Rusk, Jan. 10, 1962; U.S. Embassy New Delhi to Rusk, Jan. 10, 1962; L. D. Battle to Bundy, Jan. 10, 1962; Kissinger Comments, Jan. 10, 1962.
20. Ibid., U.S. Embassy Karachi to Rusk, Jan. 11, 1962; U.S. Embassy Karachi to Rusk, Jan. 12, 1962, Jan. 15, 1962, Jan. 16, 1962.
21. Ibid., U.S. Embassy New Delhi to Rusk, Jan. 11, 1962; U.S. Embassy Damascus, Jan. 30, 1962.
22. Kennedy Library, Staff Memoranda, Box 320, HAK, "American Strategic Thinking," speech at Pakistan Air Force Headquarters, Feb. 2, 1962.
23. Kennedy Library, Box 462, U.S. Embassy Karachi to Rusk, Feb. 1, 1962.
24. Kennedy Library, Staff Memoranda, Box 320, HAK, "American Strategic Thinking," speech at Pakistan Air Force Headquarters, Feb. 2, 1962.
25. Ibid., LeRoy Makepeace to State Dept., Feb. 13, 1962.
26. Kennedy Library, Subject File, 1961–1964, Box WH-13, Transcript of Dr. Kissinger's Question-and-Answer Session at the University of the Panjab, Lahore, Feb. 3, 1962.
27. Ibid., HAK to Schlesinger, Mar. 22, 1962.
28. Kennedy Library, Staff Memoranda, Box 320, Bundy to Lucius Battle, Feb. 13, 1962.
29. Ibid., HAK, "American Strategic Thinking," speech at Pakistan Air Force Headquarters, Feb. 2, 1962.
30. LOC, LOC-A & P, HAK to Schlesinger, Apr. 9, 1962.
31. Gaddis, *Strategies of Containment*, 205, 217, 232.
32. LOC, D-Series, HAK, Memcon Stehlin, Feb. 5, 1962, Feb. 9, 1962.
33. Ibid., HAK, Memcon Paris, Feb. 5, 1962, Feb. 9, 1962.
34. Ibid., HAK, Memcon Jean Laloy, Feb. 9, 1962.
35. Kennedy Library, Box 462, Background Briefing Material for HAK, Feb. 13, 1962; U.S. Embassy Bonn to Rusk, Feb. 13, 1962.
36. Ibid., Kissinger Trips, State Dept. to U.S. Embassy Bonn, Feb. 13, 1962.
37. LOC, D-Series, HAK, Summary of Conversations in Germany About Negotiations, Feb. 21, 1962.
38. *FRUS, 1961–1963*, vol. XIV, *Berlin Crisis, 1961–1962*, Doc. 298, Dowling to Rusk, Feb. 17, 1962.
39. Ibid., Doc. 300, Memcon Ambassador Grewe, Feb. 19, 1962.
40. Ibid., Doc. 305, Dowling to JFK and Rusk, Feb. 23, 1962.
41. *FRUS, 1961–1963*, vol. V, *Soviet Union*, Doc. 186, Salinger to JFK, May 1, 1962.
42. Schwarz, *Konrad Adenauer*, 2:601–4. See also Chopra, *De Gaulle and Unity*, 116.
43. Kennedy Library, Box 462, Kissinger Trips, U.S. Embassy Bonn to Rusk, Feb. 13, 1962; LOC, D-Series, HAK, Note on Franco-German Relations, Feb. 20, 1962.
44. LOC, D-Series, HAK, Summary of Conversations in Germany About Negotiations, Feb. 21, 1962.
45. Ibid., HAK to Bundy, Mar. 6, 1962.
46. Ibid., HAK, NATO Nuclear Sharing, Apr. 2, 1962.
47. LOC, A & P, HAK to Schlesinger, Apr. 9, 1962.
48. Ibid., HAK to Schlesinger, Re. NAR, Apr. 9, 1962.
49. LOC, C-1, Briefing Book, Central Europe, Apr. 16, 1962.
50. LOC, F-2(b), NATO—Report No. 1, Apr. 16, 1962.
51. LOC, Kent 64, NAR Correspondence 1962, NAR to HAK, Apr. 23, 1962.
52. LOC, F-3(c), HAK to Hanks, July 24, 1962.
53. LOC, Kent 64, HAK to NAR, Aug. 3, 1962.
54. HAK, "Unsolved Problems of European Defense," 519, 520, 521, 523f, 526.
55. Ibid., 531, 538.
56. Kennedy Library, Box WH-13, HAK to Schlesinger, June 15, 1962.
57. Chalmers Roberts, "Kennedy Aide Proposes French A-Force Support," *Washington Post,* June 18, 1962.
58. Kissinger papers, At the White House with Pierre Salinger, transcript, June 18, 1962.

59. Kennedy Library, Staff Memoranda, Box 321, Some Brief and Passing Thoughts on Henry Kissinger's Article in "Foreign Affairs," Oct. 25, 1962.

60. Fursenko and Naftali, *Khrushchev's Cold War*, 447.

61. *FRUS, 1961–1963*, vol. XV, *Berlin Crisis 1962–1963*, Doc. 93, William Y. Smith to Maxwell Taylor, July 5, 1961.

62. Kennedy Library, Box WH-13, Kissinger, Strauss to HAK, Sept. 15, 1962; HAK to Schlesinger, Sept. 24, 1962.

63. Kennedy Library, Box 321, HAK, Memcon zu Guttenberg, July 13, 1962.

64. Kennedy Library, Staff Memoranda, Box 321, David Klein to Smith, July 9, 1962.

65. Kennedy Library, Box 321, HAK, zu Guttenberg and Wehnert Memcons, July 18, 1962.

66. Kennedy Library, Box WH-13, Schlesinger to Helen Lempart, Aug. 21, 1962; Schlesinger to HAK, Aug. 22, 1962.

67. New York Public Library, Schlesinger Papers, Schlesinger Journal ms., Aug. 19, 1962.

68. Kennedy Library, Box 321, Bundy draft to HAK, Sept. 12, 1962; LOC, Kent 64, Bundy to HAK, Sept. 14, 1962.

69. LOC, Kent 64, HAK to Bundy, Oct. 3, 1962.

70. Ibid., Bundy to HAK, Nov. 15, 1962. Cf. Atkinson, *In Theory and Practice*, 131f.

Chapter 15: Crisis

1. JFK, "Foreword," in Sorensen, *Decision-Making*, xxix.

2. Harry S. Truman National Historic Site, Oral History #1992-3, Interview with HAK, May 7, 1992.

3. "1953: It Is 2 Minutes to Midnight," *Bulletin of the Atomic Scientists*, n.d., http://bit.ly/1KcVSCC.

4. Graham Allison, "The Cuban Missile Crisis," in Smith, Hadfield, and Dunne, *Foreign Policy*, 256.

5. Arthur M. Schlesinger, Jr., "Foreword" to Kennedy, *Thirteen Days*, 7.

6. Allison and Zelikow, *Essence of Decision*.

7. LOC, C-1, NAR Briefing Book, Cuba, Apr. 12, 1962.

8. Bird, *Color of Truth*, 242f.

9. May and Zelikow, *Kennedy Tapes*, 37.

10. Rockefeller Archive Center, HAK to NAR, Sept. 19, 1962.

11. LOC, Kent 64, HAK to NAR, Sept. 25, 1962.

12. Ibid.

13. LOC, C-1, Briefing Book, Cuba, Sept. 28, 1962.

14. Fursenko and Naftali, *Khrushchev's Cold War*, 439.

15. Gaddis, *We Now Know*, 264.

16. Talbott, *Khrushchev Remembers*, 494.

17. Allison, "Cuban Missile Crisis," 263.

18. Fursenko and Naftali, *Khrushchev's Cold War*, 440.

19. Bird, *Color of Truth*, 244.

20. Gaddis, *We Now Know*, 265.

21. Ibid.

22. Fursenko and Naftali, *Khrushchev's Cold War*, 455f.

23. Paterson and Brophy, "October Missiles and November Elections," 98.

24. Gaddis, *We Now Know*, 264.

25. Naftali and Zelikow, *Presidential Recordings*, 2:583–84.

26. Rothkopf, *Running the World*, 95.

27. Giglio, *Kennedy*, 219.

28. Bird, *Color of Truth*, 232–35; Daalder and Destler, *Shadow of Oval Office*, 35f.

29. Caro, *Passage of Power*, vol. 4, KL 5597–98. Cf. Shesol, *Mutual Contempt*, 95f.

30. See Thomas, *Robert Kennedy*, 229. The exchange, like all ExComm meetings, was taped and can be heard at http://bit.ly/1d9rXAs.

31. Walker, *Cold War*, 171.

32. Allison, "Cuban Missile Crisis," 271.

33. Paterson and Brophy, "October Missiles and November Elections."

34. Tony Judt, "On the Brink," *New York Review of Books*, January 15, 1998.

35. Welch and Blight, "Introduction to the ExComm Transcripts," 17n.

36. Caro, *Passage of Power*, KL 5605–6.

37. Allison, "Cuban Missile Crisis," 272.

38. Poundstone, *Prisoner's Dilemma*, 197ff.

39. Fursenko and Naftali, *Khrushchev's Cold War*, 471, 474.

40. Milne, *America's Rasputin*, 118.

41. Bird, *Color of Truth*, 241. See also Welch and Blight, "ExComm Transcripts," 15f.

42. Fursenko and Naftali, *Khrushchev's Cold War*, 491f., 528.

43. Giglio, *Kennedy*, 28.

44. Kennedy Library, Box WH-13, De Rose to HAK, Oct. 29, 1962.

45. Ibid., HAK to Schlesinger, Nov. 2, 1962.

46. LOC, F-3(c), Goldthwait to HAK, Oct. 29, 1962.

47. Ibid., HAK to Goldthwait, Nov. 28, 1962.

48. HAK, "Reflections on Cuba," *Reporter*, Nov. 22, 1962, 21.

49. Ibid, 23.

50. LOC, A & P, HAK to NAR, Jan. 8, 1963.

51. "Rockefeller on Cuba," *Christian Science Monitor*, Apr. 15, 1963.

52. LOC, C-1, Cuba Briefing Book, Draft, July 8, 1963.

53. LOC, F-3(c), HAK, draft resolution on Cuba, July 18, 1963.

54. Ibid., HAK to Hinman, Nov. 13, 1963.

55. Ibid., Hanks to HAK, Apr. 23, 1962.

56. See Atkinson, *In Theory and Practice*, 57f., 89f.

57. HAK, "Search for Stability."

58. Leffler, *Soul of Mankind*, 176, 183, 190f.

59. Hoover Institution Archives, 1, Conference on the Marriage of Political Philosophy and Practice in Public Affairs in Honor of Professor Elliott, Harvard Summer School, Program and Proceedings, July 22, 1963.

60. LOC, Kent 64, HAK to NAR, Dec. 7, 1962.

61. Ibid., HAK to Bundy, Jan. 8, 1963; LOC, F-3(c), HAK to Hinman, Jan. 8, 1963; Bundy to HAK, Jan. 17, 1963.

62. LOC, Kent 64, Bundy to HAK, Feb. 23, 1963.
63. LOC, A & P, HAK to NAR, Jan. 8, 1963.
64. Ibid.
65. LOC, F-3(c), Hanks to HAK, Jan. 15, 1963.
66. LOC, D-9, Kraemer to HAK, Dec. 17, 1962.
67. Gaddis, *Strategies of Containment*, 217.
68. LOC, A & P, HAK to NAR, Jan. 8, 1963.
69. LOC, A-1(a), HAK, The Skybolt Controversy, Dec. 26, 1962; LOC, F-3(c), HAK to NAR, Jan. 8.
70. HAK, "The Skybolt Controversy," *Reporter*, Jan. 17, 1963, 15–19.
71. LOC, Kent 64, Memcon De Rose [Jan. 10, 1963], Jan. 21, 1963.
72. Ibid., Memcon Couve de Murville [Jan. 12, 1963], Jan. 21, 1963.
73. Ibid., Memcon De Rose [Jan. 11, 1963], Jan. 21, 1963; Memcon Laloy [Jan. 12, 1963], Jan. 21, 1963.
74. Ibid., Memcon Stikker [Jan. 12, 1963], Jan. 21, 1963.
75. Kennedy Library, Box 321, Memcon Speidel [Jan. 10, 1963], Jan. 22, 1963.
76. Ibid., U.S. Embassy in Rome to Rusk, Jan. 17, 1963; LOC, Kent 64, Memcon Segni [Jan. 16, 196?], Jan. 21, 1963.
77. Ibid., Memcon Cattani [Jan. 16, 1963], Jan. 21, 1963.
78. Ibid., U.S. Embassy in Rome to Rusk, Jan. 15, 1963.
79. Ibid., Memcon Speidel [Jan. 10, 1963], Jan. 22, 1963. In capitals in original.
80. LOC, Kent 64, HAK to Bundy, Mar. 5, 1963.
81. LOC, F-3(a), NAR Statement, Feb. 1, 1963.
82. Ibid., HAK [?], Our Troubled Alliance and The Future of Freedom, Feb. 9, 1963.
83. HAK, "Strains on the Alliance," 263, 276, 267, 280, 284.
84. LOC, Kent 64, Memcon De Rose [Jan. 11, 1963], Jan. 21, 1963.
85. HAK, "Strains on the Alliance," 285.
86. Wohlstetter, "Delicate Balance of Terror."
87. HAK, "Nato's Nuclear Dilemma," *Reporter*, March 28, 1963, 25.
88. Ibid., 27.
89. LOC, G-13, Hoffmann to HAK, Mar. 24, 1963.
90. LOC, Kent 64, Memcon Sir Harold Caccia [May 21, 1963], May 31, 1963.
91. Kennedy Library, Box 321, Henry Owen, Comment on "NATO's Dilemma," by HAK, Apr. 24, 1963.
92. LOC, F-3(c), Bowie to NAR, Oct. 18, 1963. See Bowie, "Tensions Within the Alliance," and Bowie, "Strategy and the Atlantic Alliance."
93. Kennedy Library, Box WH-13, HAK to Schlesinger, Apr. 19, 1963.
94. Kennedy Library, Box 321, HAK to Pierre Gallois, Apr. 19, 1963.
95. LOC, Kent 64, HAK to Bundy, May 10, 1963.
96. Kennedy Library, Box WH-13, HAK to Godfrey Hodgson, Apr. 2, 1963; HAK to Schlesinger, Apr. 3, 1963.
97. LOC, F-3(c), HAK to NAR, May 8, 1963.
98. Ibid., (Digest) Nuclear Partnership in the Atlantic Community, Apr. 25, 1963.
99. Ibid., NAR remarks to Newspaper Publishers Association, Apr. 25, 1963.
100. Ibid., HAK to NAR, Apr. 2, 1963.

101. LOC, Kent 64, Memcon Adenauer [May 17, 1963], May 30, 1963.
102. Ibid., Memcon Segers [May 15, 1963], June 3, 1963.
103. Ibid., Memcon Adenauer [May 17, 1963], May 30, 1963.
104. Ibid., Memcon Strauss [May 17, 1963], June 3, 1963.
105. Ibid., Memcon Mountbatten [May 20, 1963], May 31, 1963.
106. Ibid., Memcon Denis Healey [May 21, 1963], May 31, 1963.
107. Kennedy Library, Box 321, U.S. Embassy Paris to Dean Rusk, May 24, 1963; Memcon De Rose [May 23, 1963], May 28, 1963; LOC, Kent 64, Memcon Stehlin [May 25, 1963], May 28, 1963.
108. LOC, Kent 64, HAK to Bundy, May 29, 1963.
109. Kempe, *Berlin 1961*, 500f. The full text of the speech can be found at http://bit.ly/1Gfk4QQ.
110. Kennedy Library, Box WH-13, HAK to Schlesinger, July 12, 1963; LOC, Kent 64, HAK to Bundy, July 26, 1963.
111. LOC, F-3(c), HAK to McManus, Aug. 30, 1963.
112. Kennedy Library, Box 321, HAK to Schlesinger, Sept. 3, 1963.
113. Ibid., HAK to Rusk, Sept. 13, 1963.
114. Preston, *War Council*, 57.
115. LOC, Kent 64, HAK to NAR, Aug. 22, 1962, Aug. 23, 1962.
116. LOC, F-3(a), NAR, Nuclear Testing and Free World Security, Jan. 28, 1963.
117. Ibid., HAK to NAR, June 28, 1963.
118. LOC, Kent 64, Teller to NAR, July 30, 1963; LOC, F-3(a), Brodie to HAK, Aug. 8, 1963; LOC, F-3(a), Summary Memorandum on Briefings on Current NATO Policy, Aug. 8, 1963; HAK to Brodie, Aug. 15, 1963.
119. LOC, F-3(c), Robert McManus to Executive Chamber Staff, Aug. 20, 1963; LOC, F-3(c), Teller to HAK, Aug. 26, 1963; HAK to NAR, Aug. 30, 1963.
120. LOC, F-3(a), Q. and A. for US News and World Report, Sept. 5, 1963; Foreign Policy Proposals, Sept. 7, 1963.
121. Ibid., HAK, Background Information on the "Opening to the Left," Nov. 4, 1963.
122. Ibid., HAK to Perkins, Nov. 8, 1963.
123. Ibid., Press Kit Material–Foreign Policy, Nov. 21, 1963.
124. Chalmers M. Roberts, "The Men Around the Big Men," *Washington Post*, Nov. 10, 1963.
125. LOC, F-3(a), HAK to Teller, Nov. 5, 1963.
126. LOC, G-13, HAK to Howard, Nov. 18, 1963.
127. LOC, F-3(c), HAK, Impression of the political situation in California, Nov. 21, 1963.
128. See Blight and Lang, *Virtual JFK*. See also James K. Galbraith, "Exit Strategy: In 1963, JFK Ordered a Complete Withdrawal from Vietnam," *Boston Review*, Sept. 1, 2003.
129. Diane Kunz, "Camelot Continued: What If John F. Kennedy Had Lived?," in Ferguson, *Virtual History*, 368–91.
130. LOC, Kent 64, HAK to Bundy, Nov. 22, 1963.
131. LOC, F-3(a), HAK and Douglas Bailey, "Draft of a post-moratorium speech or statement," Dec. 16, 1963.
132. Ibid., HAK to NAR, Oct. 23, 1963.

Chapter 16: The Road to Vietnam

1. Hans J. Morgenthau, "Kissinger on War: Reply to Clayton Fritchley," *New York Review of Books*, Oct. 23, 1969.
2. Fallaci, "Henry Kissinger," 36.
3. Joseph Lelyveld, "The Enduring Legacy," *New York Times Magazine*, Mar. 31, 1985.
4. These ratings are based on Angus Maddison's dataset, http://bit.ly/1JBRRa3, 2013 version.
5. McNamara, *Argument Without End*, 384, 388.
6. Goldstein, *Lessons in Disaster*.
7. Gaddis, *Strategies of Containment*, 236, 247, 271.
8. Preston, *War Council*, 76.
9. See, e.g., Sorley, *Better War*.
10. Clausewitz, *On War*, 28.
11. Cuddy, "Vietnam: Johnson's War—or Eisenhower's?," 354.
12. Fursenko and Naftali, *Khrushchev's Cold War*, 334.
13. Schlesinger, *Thousand Days*, 295.
14. Karnow, *Vietnam*, 197f.
15. Giglio, *Kennedy*, 70.
16. Freedman, *Kennedy's Wars*, 299.
17. Schlesinger, *Thousand Days*, 301–4. See also Fursenko and Naftali, *Khrushchev's Cold War*, 351ff.
18. Rostow, *Diffusion of Power*, 284.
19. Gaddis, *Strategies of Containment*, 239.
20. Milne, "'Our Equivalent of Guerrilla Warfare.'"
21. Preston, *War Council*, 81.
22. Ibid., 83.
23. *FRUS, 1961–1963*, vol. 1, *Vietnam, 1961*, Doc. 52, National Security Memorandum no. 52, http://1.usa.gov/1JloV6h.
24. Preston, *War Council*, 87ff.
25. McNamara, *Argument Without End*, 107–8.
26. Preston, *War Council*, 93–98.
27. Ibid., 99.
28. Milne, *America's Rasputin*, 120.
29. Gaddis, *Strategies of Containment*, 213.
30. Ibid., 238.
31. J. K. Galbraith to JFK, Apr. 4, 1962: http://bit.ly/1HA7f7Z.
32. Kenneth O'Donnell, "LBJ and the Kennedys," *Life*, Aug. 7, 1970.
33. Kennedy Library, Subject File, 1961–1964, Box WH-13, HAK to Schlesinger, June 5, 1961.
34. Kennedy Library, Staff Memoranda, Box 320, HAK, "American Strategic Thinking," speech at Pakistan Air Force Headquarters, Feb. 2, 1962.
35. LOC, Kent 64, HAK to NAR, Feb. 10, 1962.
36. Ibid., Position Papers with HAK comment, South Vietnam, Apr. 11, 1962.
37. Ibid., Position Papers, Laos, Apr. 12, 1962.
38. LOC, F-2(b), Laos, May 17, 1962; HAK to NAR, May 21, 1962.
39. Caro, *Passage of Power*, KL 9868–70.
40. Galbraith, "Exit Strategy."
41. Johnson Library, Transcript, George Ball Oral History Interview I, July 8, 1971, by Paige E. Mulhollan.
42. Daalder and Destler, *Shadow of Oval Office*, 39.
43. Ibid., 39.
44. Rusk and Papp, *As I Saw It*, 438.
45. Ibid, 439f.
46. LOC, HAK, Trip to Vietnam, Oct. 15–Nov. 2, 1965, Personal and Confidential, n.d. [1964–5].
47. LOC, F-3(a), Q. and A. for US News and World Report, Sept. 5, 1963.
48. LOC, F-3(c), HAK to NAR, Oct. 23, 1963.
49. Ibid., HAK to NAR, Nov. 6, 1963.
50. Ibid., HAK, Statement on Vietnam, Nov. 6, 1963.
51. Caro, *Passage of Power*, KL 3036.
52. Caro, *Master of the Senate*, 334, 435, 614f, 615.
53. Beschloss, *Taking Charge*, 388n.
54. NSAM No. 273, Nov. 26, 1963, http://bit.ly/1HwGenj.
55. Preston, "Little State Department," 654.
56. Johnson Library, Transcript, George Ball Oral History Interview I, July 8, 1971, by Paige E. Mulhollan.
57. Caro, *Passage of Power*, KL 13022.
58. Ibid., KL 13041–42.
59. Middendorf, *Glorious Disaster*, KL 485–509.
60. Critchlow, *Conservative Ascendancy*.
61. Middendorf, *Glorious Disaster*, 705–21.
62. Ibid., 722–29.
63. White, *Making of the President*, KL 2286.
64. LOC, F-3(c), HAK to NAR, Dec. 10, 1963.
65. White, *Making of the President*, KL 2405.
66. LOC, HAK, Trip to Vietnam, Oct. 15–Nov. 2, 1965, Personal and Confidential, n.d. [1964–65].
67. LOC, F-3(a), Issues for New Hampshire, Dec. 13, 1963.
68. Ibid., HAK to NAR, Jan. 6, 1964.
69. Ibid.
70. LOC, C-1, Cuba Briefing Book, Jan. 8, 1964.
71. LOC, F-3(a), HAK to NAR, Jan. 8, 1964.
72. LOC, C-1, Defense Briefing Book, Jan. 23, 1964.
73. LOC, F-3(a), HAK to Keith Glennan, Dec. 11, 1963.
74. LOC, F-3(c), HAK to NAR, Jan. 27, 1963.
75. Matthews, "To Defeat a Maverick," 666.
76. Ibid., 667. Cf. Wallace Turner, "Rockefeller Makes 'I'm Like Ike' Plea," *New York Times*, May 27, 1964.
77. LOC, F-3(a), Lloyd Free to NAR, Jan. 9, 1964.
78. Ibid., Free to NAR, Mar. 31, 1964.
79. LOC, F-3(a), HAK to NAR, Jan. 8, 1964.
80. LOC, F-3(c), Perkins, draft statement by NAR, Jan. 16, 1964. At this time Kissinger also raised the possibility of "com[ing] out for universal [military] service" in place of the selective draft.
81. Ibid., Foreign Policy Research Group memorandum, May 5, 1964. See also Comment on the Importance of Timing, May 6, 1964.
82. LOC, F-3(a), HAK to NAR, May 21, 1964.
83. LOC, A & P, HAK draft memorandum to NAR, Feb. 3, 1964.
84. LOC, F-3(c), HAK to NAR, Feb. 5, 1964.
85. Ibid., HAK to NAR, Feb. 7, 1964.
86. Ibid., Perkins to NAR, Mar. 21, 1964.
87. Ibid., HAK to NAR, Jan. 23, 1964.
88. Ibid., HAK to Douglas Bailey, Feb. 6, 1964.
89. Ibid., HAK to Bailey, Feb. 17, 1964.
90. Ibid., HAK to Charles Moore, Jan. 24, 1964.
91. LOC, C-1, NAR Statement, Feb. 22, 1964.
92. LOC, F-3(c), NAR answers to *Manchester Union-Leader*, Feb. 22, 1964.
93. Ibid., Outline of Statement on Southeast Asia, Mar. 17, 1964.
94. Ibid., HAK to Perkins, Feb. 24, 1964.
95. Ibid., HAK to Perkins, Apr. 15, 1964.

96. Ibid., Bailey to HAK, Mar. 23, 1964.
97. White, *Making of the President*, KL 2531.
98. Johnson, *All the Way with LBJ*, 109f.
99. White, *Making of the President*, KL 2800–50. See LOC, F-3(c), Free to NAR, June 5, 1964.
100. LOC, HAK, Trip to Vietnam, Oct. 15–Nov. 2, 1965, Personal and Confidential, n.d. [1964–65].
101. LOC, Kent 9, HAK, A Personal Diary of the 1964 Republican Convention, July 7, 1964.
102. Rockefeller Archive Center, HAK to NAR, June 14, 1964.
103. LOC, Kent 9, HAK, A Personal Diary of the 1964 Republican Convention, July 7–15, 1964. Kissinger had seven copies of this document made, though it is not clear for whom they were intended.
104. Ibid., July 6, 1964.
105. Ibid., July 6–7, 1964.
106. Ibid., July 8, 1964.
107. Ibid., July 10, 1964, appendix.
108. Ibid., July 12–13, 1964.
109. Ibid., July 10, 1964.
110. Ibid., July 12–13, 1964.
111. White, *Making of the President*, KL 4356–435.
112. LOC, Kent 9, HAK, "A Personal Diary of the 1964 Republican Convention," July 14, 1964.
113. For Rockefeller's speech, see http://cs.pn/ 1zUL5H8.
114. White, *Making of the President*, KL 4356–435.
115. Dallek, *Flawed Giant*, 133.
116. Critchlow, *Conservative Ascendancy*, 68–72. For Goldwater's acceptance speech, see http://cs.pn/ 1Fkg1H5.
117. Kissinger family papers, Louis Kissinger to HAK, July 22, 1964.
118. Ibid., July 15, 1964.
119. LOC, G-13, HAK to Michael Howard, July 20, 1964.
120. Ibid., Howard to HAK, July 22, 1964.
121. Ibid., HAK to Howard, Aug. 18, 1964.
122. Ibid.
123. Bator, "No Good Choices," 39.
124. Gaiduk, "Peacemaking or Troubleshooting?"; Westad et al., "77 Conversations," 126.
125. Francis Bator, "No Good Choices," 31n.
126. Moise, *Tonkin Gulf*, 22. The USS *De Haven* was the lead ship in the operation.
127. Hanyok, "Skunks, Bogies, Silent Hounds," 1–50; Paterson, "The Truth About Tonkin."
128. Moise, *Tonkin Gulf*, 32.
129. Dallek, *Flawed Giant*, 144–53.
130. Ibid., 154.
131. Beschloss, *Taking Charge*, 504
132. Matthews, "To Defeat a Maverick," 665.
133. Johnson, *All the Way with LBJ*.
134. Isaacson, *Kissinger*, KL 2196.
135. HAK, "Goldwater and the Bomb: Wrong Questions, Wrong Answers," *Reporter*, Nov. 5, 1964, 27f.
136. Beschloss, *Taking Charge*, 231, 383.
137. Ibid., 383.
138. David Frum, "The Goldwater Myth," *New Majority*, Feb. 27, 2009.
139. Johnson, *All the Way with LBJ*, 302f.
140. VanDeMark, *Into the Quagmire*, 135f.
141. Ibid., 185.
142. Logevall, "Johnson and Vietnam."
143. Bator, "No Good Choices," 6.
144. NSAM 328, Apr. 6, 1965, http://bit.ly/ 1DHy3NJ.
145. Johnson Library, Transcript, George Ball Oral History Interview I, July 8, 1971, by Paige E. Mulhollan.
146. VanDeMark, *Into the Quagmire*, 20–22.
147. Johnson Library, Transcript, George Ball Oral History Interview I, July 8, 1971, by Paige E. Mulhollan.
148. Herring, *LBJ and Vietnam*.
149. Leffler, *Soul of Mankind*, 219f.
150. Bator, "No Good Choices," 9–10.
151. Ibid., 9–11, 6–7.
152. Ibid., 12. Cf. Barrett, *Uncertain Warriors*, 56f.
153. Destler, *Presidents, Bureaucrats, and Foreign Policy*, 105, 107–10, 116f.; Logevall, "Johnson and Vietnam," 101. See also Berman, *Planning a Tragedy*.
154. Harrison and Mosher, "McNaughton and Vietnam"; Harrison and Mosher, "Secret Diary of McNamara's Dove."
155. Harrison and Mosher, "McNaughton and Vietnam," 503.
156. Ibid., 509.
157. Clifford with Holbrooke, *Counsel to President*, 410.
158. Ibid., 419f.
159. Barrett, *Uncertain Warriors*, 52f.
160. Johnson Library, Transcript, George Ball Oral History Interview I, July 8, 1971, by Paige E. Mulhollan.
161. Milne, "'Our Equivalent of Guerrilla Warfare,'" 186.
162. Barrett, *Uncertain Warriors*, 58.
163. LOC, G-13, HAK to Michael Howard, June 29, 1964.
164. Kissinger family papers, Louis Kissinger to HAK, July 22, 1964.
165. Ibid., Louis Kissinger to HAK, Feb. 6, 1964.
166. Ibid., Louis Kissinger to HAK, Dec. 3, 1964.
167. LOC, F-3(c), HAK to Ann Whitman, May 24, 1965.
168. Kissinger family papers, Louis Kissinger to HAK, May 25, 1965.
169. Thomas Schelling, interview by author.
170. Ibid.
171. Kissinger family papers, Louis Kissinger to HAK, Sept. 15, 1965.
172. Ibid., Louis Kissinger to HAK, Dec. 25, 1965.
173. Ibid., Louis and Paula Kissinger to HAK, Aug. 14, 1966.
174. Isaacson, *Kissinger*, KL 2196.
175. LOC, J-6, Kissinger, HAK to Nancy Maginnes, Jan. 18, 1967.
176. HAK, interview by author.
177. LOC, F-3(b), HAK to NAR, Draft Foreign Policy Statement, Aug. 18, 1964.
178. Ibid., HAK to NAR, Draft Foreign Policy Statement, Aug. 18, 1964.
179. LOC, G-14, McNaughton to HAK, Jan. 14, 1965; McNaughton to HAK, Jan. 25, 1965; HAK to McNaughton, Apr. 13, 1965.
180. LOC, G-14, HAK to Robert F. Kennedy, Feb. 18, 1965; Robert F. Kennedy to HAK, Mar. 18, 1965.
181. LOC, Kent 64, HAK to Bundy, Mar. 30, 1965.
182. Ibid., Bundy to HAK, Apr. 12, 1965.
183. Ibid., HAK to Bundy, Apr. 13, 1965.
184. Ibid., Bundy to HAK, Apr. 30, 1965.

185. Ibid., HAK to Bundy, May 11, 1965; HAK to Bundy, June 26, 1965; Bundy to HAK, July 6, 1965. See Richard Cotton, "Bundy Addresses Phi Beta Kappa; Explains American Foreign Policy," *Harvard Crimson*, June 16, 1965.
186. LOC, G-14, HAK to Lodge, July 16, 1965.
187. LOC, F-3(c), HAK to Hanks, Sept. 26, 1962.
188. Mazlish, *Kissinger*, 124f.
189. LOC, F-2(a), Jonathan Moore to HAK, Aug. 30, 1965.
190. Kissinger family papers, Louis Kissinger to HAK, Sept. 15, 1965; Sept. 23, 1965.
191. Linda G. Mcveigh, "Lodge Calls Kissinger to Vietnam as Advisor," *Harvard Crimson*, Oct. 11, 1965.
192. LOC, F-2(a), HAK to Blair Seaborn, Nov. 22, 1965.
193. "Frenchmen Answer Panelists, Denounce US Vietnam Policy, Cite Own Mistakes," *Harvard Crimson*, Aug. 9, 1965.

Chapter 17: The Unquiet American

1. LOC, Minutes of a meeting held on Aug. 4, 1965.
2. LOC, HAK, Trip to Vietnam, Oct. 15–Nov. 2, 1965, Sept. 14, 1965.
3. Greene, *Quiet American*, 124.
4. Ibid., 96.
5. LOC, Minutes of a meeting held on Aug. 4, 1965.
6. Ibid.
7. See in general Herring, *Secret Diplomacy*.
8. David Kaiser, "Discussions, Not Negotiations: The Johnson Administration's Diplomacy at the Outset of the Vietnam War," in Gardner and Gittinger, *Search for Peace in Vietnam*.
9. Herring, *Secret Diplomacy*, 5.
10. Rusk and Papp, *As I Saw It*, 462f.
11. Herring, *Secret Diplomacy*, 46.
12. Kaiser, "Discussions, Not Negotiations."
13. Gettleman, Franklin, Young, and Franklin, *Vietnam and America*, 276f.
14. Herring, *Secret Diplomacy*, 47.
15. VanDeMark, *Into the Quagmire*, 137, Herring, *Secret Diplomacy*, 57–58.
16. VanDeMark, *Into the Quagmire*, 135f, 138, 141f.
17. Barrett, *Uncertain Warriors*, 55.
18. LOC, F-2(a), Dunn to HAK, Aug. 20, 1965. For Dunn's role in Vietnam, see Johnson Library, John Michael Dunn interview, July 25, 1984, http://bit.ly/1aYhZ37.
19. LOC, HAK, Trip to Vietnam, Oct. 15–Nov. 2, 1965, Sept. 13, 1965.
20. Nashel, *Lansdale's Cold War*.
21. LOC, HAK, Trip to Vietnam, Oct. 15–Nov. 2, 1965, Sept. 13, 1965.
22. For Kissinger's insincere letter of thanks, see LOC, F-2(a), HAK to Raborn, Oct. 4, 1965.
23. LOC, HAK, Trip to Vietnam, Oct. 15–Nov. 2, 1965, Sept. 14, 1965.
24. Ibid.
25. Ibid.
26. Ibid.
27. LOC, Vietnam Missions, 1965–1967, HAK to Lodge, Sept. 24, 1965.
28. Massachusetts Historical Society, Lodge Papers, Vietnam, Reel 20, HAK to Lodge, Sept. 7, 1965.
29. Ibid.
30. Massachusetts Historical Society, Lodge Papers, Vietnam, Reel 20, Lodge to HAK, Sept. 14, 1965.
31. LOC, Vietnam Missions, 1965–1967, HAK to Lodge, Sept. 24, 1965.
32. Ibid., "Conversation with A," Sept. 28, 1965.
33. Ibid., "Conversation with B," Sept. 28, 1965.
34. Ibid., "Conversation with C," Sept. 28, 1965.
35. Ibid.
36. Ibid., "Conversation with D," Sept. 28, 1965.
37. Ibid., "Conversation with E," Sept. 29, 1965.
38. LOC, F-2(a), HAK to Johnson, Oct. 1, 1965.
39. LOC, Vietnam Mission 1965, Habib to Lodge, Oct. 11, 1965.
40. LOC, HAK, Trip to Vietnam, Oct. 15–Nov. 2, 1965.
41. LOC, Vietnam Missions, 1965–1967, HAK to Lodge, Sept. 24, 1965.
42. LOC, HAK, Trip to Vietnam, Oct. 15–Nov. 2, 1965, Personal and Confidential, n.d.
43. Ibid., Oct. 11, 1965.
44. Ibid. This part of the diary ends abruptly on p. 24.
45. Keever, *Death Zones and Darling Spies*, 12f., 54f.
46. Fitzgerald, *Fire in the Lake*, 427.
47. Ibid., 431.
48. Herr, *Dispatches*, KL 598–671.
49. LOC, HAK, Trip to Vietnam, Oct. 15–Nov. 2, 1965, Oct. 28 [?], 1965.
50. Ibid., Oct. 17 [?]. 1965 [p. 75].
51. Ibid.
52. Ibid.
53. LOC, F-2(a), Misc. Corr., Consular report, Nov. 1, 1965.
54. Ibid., Smyser to HAK, Nov. 19, 1965.
55. Ibid., HAK to Smyser, Nov. 30, 1965.
56. LOC, HAK, Trip to Vietnam, Oct. 15–Nov. 2, 1965, Oct. 26 [?], 1965.
57. Ibid., Oct. 27, 1965.
58. Ibid.
59. Ibid., Oct. 28 [?], 1965.
60. Gibbons, *Government and Vietnam War*, 81n.
61. LOC, HAK, Trip to Vietnam, Oct. 15–Nov. 2, 1965, Oct. 18, 1965.
62. Ibid., Oct. 28 [?], 1965.
63. Ibid., Oct. 17, 1965.
64. Ibid.
65. Ibid., Oct. 26 [?], 1965.
66. Ibid., Oct. 18, 1965.
67. Ibid.
68. Ibid., Oct. 28 [?], 1965.
69. Ibid., Oct. 26 [?]. 1965.
70. Ibid.
71. Ibid., Oct. 17, 1965.
72. LOC, Vietnam Mission 1965, Memcon Sung, Oct. 30, 1965.
73. *FRUS, 1964–1968*, vol. III, *Vietnam, June–Dec. 1965*, Doc. 172, Saigon Embassy to State Dept., Oct. 20, 1965.
74. LOC, HAK, Trip to Vietnam, Oct. 15–Nov. 2, 1965, Oct. 17, 1965.
75. LOC, Vietnam Mission 1965, Memcon Thuan, Nov. 2, 1965.

76. LOC, HAK, Trip to Vietnam, Oct. 15–Nov. 2, 1965, Oct. 18, 1965.

77. LOC, Vietnam Mission 1965, Memcon Chuan, Oct. 26, 1965.

78. Ibid., Memcon Chieu, Oct. 20, 1965. See also Johnson Library, NSF Country File Vietnam, Box 24, Vietnam Memos (B) Vol. XLII 11–65, Oct. 20, 1965. Copies of all the memcons cited below are also to be found at the Johnson Library.

79. LOC, HAK, Trip to Vietnam, Oct. 15–Nov. 2, 1965, Oct. 17, 1965.

80. LOC, Vietnam Mission 1965, Memcon Quat, Oct. 30, 1965.

81. Ibid., Memcon Quat, Oct. 31, 1965.

82. Ibid., Memcon Thuan, Nov. 2, 1965.

83. Ibid., Memcon Tuyen, Oct. 23, 1965.

84. Ibid., Memcon Vui, Oct. 20, 1965.

85. Ibid., Memcon Truyen, Oct. 20, 1965.

86. LOC, HAK, Trip to Vietnam, Oct. 15–Nov. 2, 1965, Oct. 27, 1965. Cf. LOC, Vietnam Mission 1965, Memcon Quang, Oct. 27, 1965.

87. LOC, Vietnam Mission 1965, Memcon Sung, Oct. 29, 1965.

88. LOC, HAK, Trip to Vietnam, Oct. 15–Nov. 2, 1965, Oct. 27, 1965.

89. Jack Foisie, "Viet Regime Shaky, Johnson Envoys Find," *Los Angeles Times*, Nov. 2, 1965.

90. Johnson Library, NSF Files of McGeorge Bundy, Box 15, HAK to McGeorge Bundy, Nov. 6, 1965. See also telegram sent Nov. 8.

91. Johnson Library, NSF Files of McGeorge Bundy, Box 15, McGeorge Bundy to William F. Bundy, Nov. 6, 1965.

92. Massachusetts Historical Society, Lodge Papers, Vietnam, Reel 20, HAK to Lodge, Nov. 10, 1965.

93. Johnson Library, NSF Files of McGeorge Bundy, Box 15, McGeorge Bundy to William F. Bundy, Nov. 10, 1965. See also McGeorge Bundy to HAK, Nov. 14, 1965.

94. "Kissinger Denies Saigon Statement," *Arizona Republic*, Nov. 9, 1965.

95. LOC, D-4, HAK to McGeorge Bundy, Nov. 12, 1965.

96. Johnson Library, NSF Files of McGeorge Bundy, Box 15, Moyers to HAK, Nov. 12, 1965.

97. LOC, Vietnam Mission 1965, HAK to Lodge, Nov. 12, 1965.

98. Clifford, *Counsel to the President*, 429–32.

99. Johnson Library, NSF Files of McGeorge Bundy, Box 15, HAK to Clifford, Nov. 11, 1965.

100. Clifford, *Counsel to the President*, 432.

101. Isaacson, *Kissinger*, KL 2252–55.

102. Johnson Library, NSF Files of McGeorge Bundy, Box 15, HAK to Clifford, Nov. 11, 1965.

103. LOC, Vietnam Mission 1965, HAK to Lodge, Nov. 12, 1965.

104. Ibid., HAK to Lodge, Nov. 23, 1965.

105. LOC, Vietnam Mission 1965, Lodge to HAK, Nov. 30, 1965.

106. LOC, F-2(a), Porter to HAK, Nov. 30, 1965.

107. Ibid., Dec. 8, 1965.

108. LOC, Vietnam Mission 1965, HAK to Lodge, Dec 1, 1965.

109. Ibid., HAK to Lodge, Dec. 3, 1965.

110. Ibid.

Chapter 18: Dirt Against the Wind

1. HAK DC Office, DC-3, Vietnam diary, July 19, 1966.

2. LOC, F-2(a), Misc. Corr., HAK to Burke, Sept. 29, 1966.

3. LOC, Joint Arms Control Seminar, Minutes of the Seventh Session, Jan. 12, 1966.

4. Ibid.

5. *FRUS, 1964–68*, vol. III, *Vietnam, June–Dec. 1965*, Doc. 237, Chairman of JCS Wheeler to McNamara, Dec. 21, 1965.

6. Bibby, *Hearts and Minds*, 108.

7. Charlotte Buchen, "Anguish and Foreign Policy," *Arizona Republic*, Nov. 9, 1965.

8. Kenneth Botwright, "U.S. Right to Reject Hanoi Bid, Says Expert," *Boston Globe*, Nov. 29, 1965.

9. Richard Blumenthal, "Objectors to Vietnam Not Exempt, Says Hershey," *Harvard Crimson*, Nov. 20, 1965.

10. "Educators Back Vietnam Policy," *New York Times*, Dec. 10, 1965. Cf. Gibbons, *Government and Vietnam War*, 100.

11. Derek Bok, interview by author.

12. HAK Newspaper Collection, CBS Reports transcript, Dec. 21, 1965.

13. LOC, Averell Harriman Papers, Box 481, HAK to Lodge, June 7, 1966.

14. Thomas Pepper, "Can the U.S. Really Win for Losing in the Baffling Battle of Viet Nam?," *Winston-Salem Journal*, Feb. 20, 1966.

15. LOC, D-1, *Look* Magazine Statement, June 6, 1966. See Murray Marder, "Moderate Critics Offer New Plans for Vietnam," *New York Herald Tribune*, July 28, 1966.

16. LOC, Vietnam Mission 1965, HAK to Lodge, Dec 1, 1965.

17. LOC, Joint Arms Control Seminar, Minutes of the Seventh Session, Jan. 12, 1966.

18. Ibid.

19. LOC, D-1, *Look* Magazine Statement, June 6, 1966.

20. *FRUS, 1964–68*, vol. IV, *Vietnam, 1966*, Doc. 44, Denney to Rusk, Jan. 26, 1966.

21. *FRUS, 1964–68*, vol. III, *Vietnam, June–Dec. 1965*, Doc. 237, Chairman of JCS Wheeler to McNamara, Dec. 21, 1965.

22. Gibbons, *Government and Vietnam War*, 82–84.

23. Clifford, *Counsel to the President*, 433.

24. Harrison and Mosher, "McNaughton and Vietnam," 512.

25. Clifford, *Counsel to the President*, 434.

26. Harrison and Mosher, "Secret Diary of McNamara's Dove," 521.

27. Bird, *Color of Truth*, 348f.

28. Halberstam, *Best and the Brightest*, 627.

29. See Hoopes, *Limits of Intervention*, 59f.; Peters, *Johnson*, 135.

30. Gaiduk, "Peacemaking or Troubleshooting?"

31. Rusk and Papp, *As I Saw It*, 465. Cf. Guan, "Vietnam War from Both Sides," 104.

32. Johnson Library, Dean Rusk Oral History Interview II, Sept. 26, 1969, transcribed by Paige E. Mulhollan, at http://bit.ly/1yWCDMp. See also William Fulton, "Rusk Gets Nowhere in Viet Peace Moves," *Chicago Tribune*, Oct. 9, 1965; János Radványi, "Peace Hoax," *Life*, Mar. 22, 1968, 60–71.

33. Robert K. Brigham, "Vietnam at the Center: Patterns of Diplomacy and Resistance," in Gardner and Gittinger, *International Perspectives on Vietnam*, 102f.

34. Logevall, *Choosing War*.

35. Rusk and Papp, *As I Saw It*, 465; Herring, *Secret Diplomacy*, 117.

36. Brigham, "Vietnamese-American Peace Negotiations," 393f.

37. See Hershberg, "Who Murdered Marigold?," 10.

38. Ibid., 12.

39. Ibid., 13f.

40. Herring, *Secret Diplomacy*, 159ff.

41. Johnson Library, Transcript, George Ball Oral History Interview I, July 8, 1971, by Paige E. Mulhollan.

42. Gibbons, *Government and Vietnam War*, 389–91.

43. LOC, Averell Harriman Papers, Box 481, William Bundy to Rusk, May 4, 1966.

44. Guan, *Vietnam from Other Side*, 109f.; Sainteny, *Ho and Vietnam*, 161–66.

45. *FRUS, 1964–1968*, vol. IV, *Vietnam, 1966*, Doc. 182, Bohlen to State Department, July 21, 1966.

46. British National Archives, PREM 13/1270, Michael Stewart to D. F. Murray, May 3, 1966.

47. LOC, HAK Vietnam Missions 1965–67, HAK to Lodge, June 7, 1966.

48. Ibid., Lodge to HAK, June 15, 1966.

49. Ibid., HAK to Lodge, Apr. 8, 1966; Lodge to HAK, Apr. 13, 1966.

50. LOC, F-2(a), HAK to William Bundy, June 11, 1966.

51. LOC, Averell Harriman Papers, Box 481, Unger to Saigon Embassy, July 11, 1966.

52. LOC, F-2(a), Misc. Corr., HAK to Philip Habib, July 1, 1966. Lodge said at a meeting of the Mission Council that "the Saigon Embassy was the only Embassy in the U.S. that had an Ambassador in Washington."

53. HAK DC Office, DC-3, Vietnam diary, July 16, 1966.

54. LOC, July 19–21, 1966 (Vietnam Trip), Vietnam diary, July 21, 1966.

55. HAK DC Office, DC-3, Vietnam diary, July 16–18, 1966.

56. LOC, Averell Harriman Papers, Box 481, Memcon Do, July 18, 1966.

57. Diem and Chanoff, *Jaws of History*, 251.

58. HAK DC Office, DC-3, Vietnam diary, July 19, 1966.

59. LOC, July 19–21, 1966 (Vietnam Trip), Vietnam diary, July 20–21, 1966.

60. LOC, J-3, Colonel D. J. Barrett, Jr., to 3rd Marine Division, July 24, 1966.

61. HAK DC Office, DC-3, July 25–28, 1966 (Vietnam Trip), July 25, 1966.

62. Ibid.

63. Ibid.

64. LOC, July 25–28, 1966 (Vietnam Trip), Vietnam diary, July 27, 1966.

65. Ibid.

66. LOC, F-2(a), Misc. Corr., HAK to Frances Fitzgerald, Aug. 12, 1966.

67. See, e.g., LOC, Secret DOS-HAK memoranda, Memcon Sanh, Dan and Sung, July 19, 1966; LOC, July 19–21, 1966 (Vietnam Trip), Vietnam diary, July 20–21, 1966; LOC, Secret DOS-HAK memoranda, Memcon Giac, July 20, 1966; Memcon Truyen, July.20, 1966; Memcon Diem, July 23, 1966; Memcon Tuyen, July 23, 1966; Memcon Quynh, July 28, 1966.

68. LOC, Averell Harriman Papers, Box 481, Rusk to Saigon Embassy, July 22, 1966.

69. HAK DC Office, DC-3, July 25–28, 1966 (Vietnam Trip), July 26, 1966.

70. LOC, Secret DOS-HAK memoranda, Memcon Loan, July 26, 1966; Memcon Co, July 26, 1966.

71. HAK DC Office, DC-3, July 25–28, 1966 (Vietnam Trip), July 28, 1966.

72. LOC, Averell Harriman Papers, Box 481, Memcon Do, July 18, 1966.

73. Ibid., State Dept. Memcon, Aug. 2, 1966.

74. Ibid.

75. LOC, HAK Vietnam Missions 1965–67, HAK to Lodge, Aug. 9, 1966. See also HAK to Lodge, Aug. 12, 1966.

76. LOC, Secret DOS-HAK memoranda, Memcon Tuyen, July 23, 1966. See also Kissinger's report to Robert Komer, which made no reference whatever to the possibility of negotiations with the VC/NLF, much less to the possibility of defections: LOC, HAK Vietnam Missions 1965–67, HAK to Robert Komer, Aug. 8, 1966.

77. *FRUS, 1964–1968*, vol. IV, *Vietnam, 1966*, Doc. 203, Rusk to Lodge, Aug. 5, 1966.

78. Ibid., Doc. 213, Harriman to Lyndon Baines Johnson [henceforth LBJ] and Rusk, Aug. 18, 1966.

79. LOC, HAK Vietnam Missions 1965–67, HAK to Lodge, Aug. 18, 1966.

80. Ibid., 1966.

81. Gibbons, *Government and Vietnam War*, 396–99.

82. LOC, F-2(a), Misc. Corr., Burke to HAK, Sept. 16, 1966.

83. Ibid., HAK to Burke, Sept. 29, 1966.

84. "Kissinger Said to Be En Route to Vietnam," *Harvard Crimson*, Oct. 10, 1966.

85. LOC, State Dept. Telegram re. HAK Vietnam Mission 1966, Harriman to State Dept., Oct. 22, 1966.

86. LOC, Averell Harriman Papers, Box 481, HAK to Harriman, Oct. 11, 1966.

87. Katzenbach, *Some of It Was Fun*, 230f.

88. LOC, Averell Harriman Papers, Box 481, HAK to Harriman, Oct. 14, 1966, Oct. 17, 1966. See also *FRUS, 1964–1968*, vol. IV, *Vietnam, 1966*, Doc. 276, Harriman to Rusk, Oct. 19, 1966.

89. LOC, HAK Vietnam Missions 1965–67, HAK to Lodge, Oct. 19, 1966.

90. LOC, Averell Harriman Papers, Box 481, Memcon Harriman, HAK, Oct. 25, 1966.

91. Ibid., Lodge to HAK, Nov. 29, 1966.

92. Ibid., autographed photograph, dated Dec. 19, 1966.

Chapter 19: The Anti-Bismarck

1. LOC, G-13, HAK to Michael Howard, July 31, 1961.
2. LOC, Memcon de La Grandville [Jan. 28, 1967], Feb. 6, 1967.
3. Dickson, *Kissinger and Meaning*, 104f.
4. LOC, G-13, Michael Howard to HAK, Aug. 4, 1961.
5. Ibid., HAK to Michael Howard, July 31, 1961.
6. LOC, D-4, HAK to Dönhoff, Feb. 14, 1967.
7. Weidenfeld, *Remembering My Friends*, 384f.
8. HAK, *World Order*, 78.
9. Ibid., 233.
10. Ibid., 80, 82.
11. HAK, "White Revolutionary." It also contains a few surprising errors, notably the garbling of the name of Bismarck's junior school. This was not the "Max Plaman Institute" (892) but the Plamann Institute, founded in 1805 by Johann Ernst Plamann.
12. Ibid., 888.
13. Ibid., 898.
14. Ibid., 904.
15. Ibid., 910.
16. Ibid., 913.
17. Ibid., 919.
18. Ibid., 889.
19. Ibid., 909, 919.
20. Steinberg, *Bismarck*, 263.
21. HAK, "White Revolutionary," 912f.
22. Ibid., 913.
23. Ibid., 890, 921.
24. Ibid., 919f.
25. Ibid., 906f.
26. Ibid., 911.
27. Yale University Library, HAK Papers, MS 1981, Part II, Box 273, Folders 1-6, 14-15, HAK, unpublished ms. on Bismarck.
28. Ibid., Folder 2, The Crimean War, 12f, 14, 19.
29. Ibid., 21, 36, 26f.
30. Ibid., Folder 5, The Contingency of Legitimacy, 2f.
31. See in general on de Gaulle's foreign policy, Vaïsse, *La Grandeur*.
32. Logevall, *Choosing War*, KL 245.
33. Charles G. Cogan, "'How Fuzzy Can One Be?' The American Reaction to De Gaulle's Proposal for the Neutralization of (South) Vietnam," in Gardner and Gittinger, *Search for Peace in Vietnam*, KL 2169-414.
34. Vaïsse, "De Gaulle and the Vietnam War," KL 2449.
35. Cogan, "'How Fuzzy Can One Be?'"
36. Reyn, *Atlantis Lost*, 301.
37. Logevall, *Choosing War*, KL 1934-44.
38. LOC, F-2(a), NAR draft speech, May 22, 1964.
39. LOC, Kent 64, Memcon De Rose [May 26, 1964], June 10, 1964.
40. Ibid., Memcon Ritter and Speidel [May 25, 1964], June 10, 1964.
41. Ibid., Memcon Cattani [May 24, 1964], June 10, 1964; Memcon Müller-Roschach [May 25, 1964], June 10, 1964.
42. He did go to Vienna in September 1964, but en route to Prague: LOC, G-13, HAK to Hoffmann, Sept. 1, 1964.
43. LOC, 1966—Eurotrip, London Embassy to State Dept., Feb. 3, 1966.
44. Ibid., Leonard Unger, Memcon HAK, Feb. 4, 1966.
45. Heffer, *Like the Roman*, 440f.
46. LOC, Kent 64, HAK to Bundy, Nov. 27, 1964.
47. Johnson Library, Bundy Papers, Box 15, HAK, Memcon Bahr [Apr. 10, 1965], Apr. 12, 1965.
48. Ibid.
49. Ibid. Kissinger foresaw a "truly rocky time ahead in Germany after the election" if the views Bahr ascribed to Brandt were correct: LOC, Kent 64, HAK to Bundy, Apr. 13, 1965.
50. HAK, "The Price of German Unity," *Reporter*, Apr. 22, 1965 (published in *Die Zeit* as "Wege zur deutschen Einheit").
51. HAK, "White Revolutionary," 900.
52. HAK, "Price of German Unity," 13.
53. Ibid., 15.
54. Ibid., 17.
55. Johnson Library, Bundy Papers, Box 15, HAK Memcon Wehner, June 21, 1965.
56. Ibid.
57. Ibid., HAK Memcon Adenauer, June 25, 1965.
58. Ibid., HAK Memcon Gerstenmaier, June 22, 1965.
59. LOC, Kent 64, HAK to Bundy, July 20, 1965.
60. Ibid., HAK to Bundy, June 26, 1965. See also LOC, G-14, HAK to McNaughton, July 8, 1965.
61. Reyn, *Atlantis Lost*, 283.
62. LOC, Kent 64, HAK to Bundy, July 20, 1965.
63. Reyn, *Atlantis Lost*, 242.
64. HAK, "For a New Atlantic Alliance," *Reporter*, July 14, 1966, 21ff., 25.
65. Ibid., 26. See also his article "Deutschland unter dem Druck der Freunde," *Die Welt*, July 18, 1966.
66. Gavin, *Nuclear Statecraft*, 6-8, 75-93.
67. Ibid., 93.
68. LOC, Memorandum to McNaughton [re. lunch on Jan. 24, 1967], Feb. 13, 1967.
69. Ibid.
70. Ibid.
71. Ibid.
72. Ibid.
73. Ibid.
74. Ibid.
75. LOC, Kent 64, Memcon Schmidt, Feb. 13, 1967.
76. LOC, HAK to McNaughton, Feb. 14, 1967.
77. Johnson Library, Bundy Papers, Box 15, HAK, Memcon Bahr [Apr. 10, 1965], Apr. 12, 1965.
78. LOC, Kent 64, HAK Memcon Krone, Mar. 30, 1965. See also LOC F-3(c), HAK to NAR, Mar. 30, 1965.
79. LOC, D-4, HAK to Dönhoff, Feb. 12, 1965.
80. HAK, "Coalition Diplomacy," 530.
81. Ibid., 544.
82. Ibid., 543.
83. LOC, F-3(b), Bailey, NAR Post-Election Speech on Foreign Policy, Oct. 22, 1964. See also Oct. 26 draft and HAK's revisions of Oct. 27, Oct. 28, and Nov. 3. In his treatment of this issue, I suspect Suri confuses Kissinger's views with Rockefeller's, though their mode of operation makes the elision an easy one to make.

84. HAK, "Illusionist."
85. LOC, D-4, HAK to Dönhoff, Feb. 12, 1965.
86. HAK, *Troubled Partnership* [henceforth *TTP*].
87. *TTP*, 8.
88. *TTP*, 17.
89. Reyn, *Atlantis Lost*, 339–43.
90. *TTP*, 45, 47.
91. *TTP*, 72, 73f., 83, 166.
92. *TTP*, 170f., 246.
93. *TTP*, 63.
94. Kissinger family papers, Louis Kissinger to HAK, Sept. 23, 1965.
95. Drew Middleton, "Wanted: Warmer Hands Across the Sea," *New York Times*, May 30, 1965, BR3.
96. Brodie review of *TTP*, *Annals of the American Academy of Political and Social Science* 367 (Sept. 1966), 163f. See also Brodie review of *TTP*, *Journal of Politics* 29, no. 2 (May 1967), 424f.
97. Holmes review of *TTP*, *International Journal* 21, no. 2 (Spring 1966), 222f.
98. Curtis review of *TTP*, *Western Political Quarterly* 18, no. 3 (Sept. 1965), 711f.
99. *TTP*, 248.
100. LOC, A-5, HAK "Statement on the Atlantic Alliance" before the Senate Foreign Relations Committee chaired by William Fulbright, June 27, 1966. Cf. "France, Russia Agree to Establish Hot Line," *Washington Post*, June 29, 1966.
101. Johnson Library, Bundy Papers, Box 15, HAK Memcon de La Grandville, May 16, 1965.
102. Ibid.
103. Ibid.

104. LOC, Memcon de La Grandville [Jan. 28, 1967], Feb. 6, 1967.
105. Ibid.
106. Ibid.
107. *NFC*, 202.
108. *NFC*, 253.
109. Kennedy Library, Staff Memoranda, Box 320, HAK, "American Strategic Thinking," speech at Pakistan Air Force Headquarters, Feb. 2, 1962.
110. LOC, Kent 64, Position Papers, China, Apr. 11, 1962.
111. LOC, F-3(a), Q&A, Dec. 31, 1963.
112. Ibid., Summary Positions, Jan. 27, 1963.
113. LOC, F-3(c), HAK to NAR, Jan. 27, 1963.
114. LOC, F-3(b), Bailey, NAR Post-Election Speech on Foreign Policy, Oct. 22, 1964. See also Oct. 26 draft and HAK's revision of Oct. 27.
115. LOC, Memorandum to McNaughton [re. lunch on Jan. 23, 1967], Feb. 13, 1967.
116. HAK, "Domestic Structure and Foreign Policy," 521.
117. Ibid., 505.
118. Ibid., 507.
119. Ibid., 507f.
120. Ibid., 509.
121. Ibid., 510.
122. Ibid., 510f.
123. HAK, "Et Caesar, Et Nullus," *Reporter*, June 1, 1967, 51f.
124. HAK, "Domestic Structure and Foreign Policy," 517.
125. Ibid., 518.
126. Ibid., 522f.
127. Ibid., 523.

Chapter 20: Waiting for Hanoi

1. Schlesinger, *Journals*, Dec. 7, 1967.
2. Camus, *Mythe de Sisyphe*.
3. Allan Katz, "Wait for Godot," *Harvard Crimson*, Nov. 28, 1960.
4. *WR*, KL 3434–37.
5. "Mai Van Bo: Revolutionary with Style," *Time* 91, no. 19 (May 10, 1968).
6. LOC, Memcon, Kissinger's Conversations at Pugwash, Aug. 17, 1966.
7. *FRUS, 1964–1968*, vol. IV, *Vietnam, 1966*, Doc. 212, Meeting of the Negotiations Committee, Aug. 18, 1966.
8. Gibbons, *Government and Vietnam War*, 389–91 and n. See in general Maïsse, *Grandeur*, 521–36.
9. HAK, "Domestic Structure and Foreign Policy," 517.
10. LOC, HAK, Conversation with Soviet participants at Pugwash conference on the subject of Vietnam, Sept. 23, 1966.
11. Ibid.
12. LOC, HAK, Vietnam Resolution at the Pugwash Conference, Sept. 23, 1966.
13. LOC, Averell Harriman Papers, Box 481, Harriman and McNamara to Rusk, Sept. 19, 1966.
14. Ibid., Warsaw Embassy to State Dept., Sept. 19, 1966.
15. LOC, Secret Memorandum, Memcon Dobroscelski [Sept. 17, 1966], Sept. 23, 1966.

16. LOC, Secret Conversation with Snejdarek, Memcon Snejdarek [Sept. 19–20], Sept. 23, 1966.
17. On Šnejdárek, see Skoug, *Czechoslovakia's Lost Fight*, 11, 25.
18. LOC, Secret Conversation with Snejdarek, Memcon Snejdarek [Sept. 19–20], Sept. 23, 1966.
19. Ibid.
20. *FRUS, 1964–1968*, vol. IV, *Vietnam, 1966*, Doc. 300, Memorandum of meeting, Nov. 10, 1966.
21. British National Archives, PREM 13/1270, A. M. Palliser to C. M. MacLehose, Oct. 3, 1966.
22. *FRUS, 1964–1968*, vol. IV, *Vietnam, 1966*, Doc. 335, U.S. Embassy in Poland to State Dept., Dec. 9, 1966. See also Ang Cheng Guan, "The Vietnam War from Both Sides: Revisiting 'Marigold', 'Sunflower' and 'Pennsylvania,'" *War and Society* 24, no. 2 (Nov. 2005), 93–125.
23. Archiwum Polskiej Dyplomacji, Szyfrogramy z Sajgonu, 1966, Sygn. 6/77, w-173, t-558, Rapacki to Gomulka, Cyrankiewicz, Kliszko, Nov. 19, 1966.
24. Ibid., Szyfrogramy z Sajgonu, 1966, Sygn. 6/77, w-173, t-558, Michałowski to Malczyk, Nov. 19, 1966.
25. Ibid., Szyfrogramy z Hanoi, 1966, Sygn. 6/77, w-173, t-558, Lewandowski to Michałowski, Nov. 25, 1966. Cf. Hershberg, "Who Murdered Marigold?," 22f.

26. Archiwum Polskiej Dyplomacji, Szyfrogramy z Sajgonu, 1966, Sygn. 6/77, w-173, t-558, Lewandowski to Rapacki, Dec. 2, 1966.

27. Hershberg, "Who Murdered Marigold?," 25–28.

28. Ibid.,16. See also Guan, "Vietnam War from Both Sides," 98.

29. Ibid., 36.

30. Herring, *LBJ and Vietnam*, 106f.

31. Archiwum Polskiej Dyplomacji, Szyfrogramy z Sajgonu, 1966, Sygn. 6/77, w-173, t-558, Lewandowski to Michałowski, Nov. 14, 1966.

32. Ibid., Sygn. 6/77, w-173, t-558, Lewandowski to Michałowski, Nov. 16, 1966.

33. Ibid., Sygn. 6/77, w-173, t-558, Rapacki to Gomulka, Cyrankiewicz, Kliszko, Nov. 19, 1966.

34. Ibid., Sygn. 1/77, w-16, t. 39, Rapacki to Gomułka, Cyrankiewicz, Ochab, Kliszko, Nov. 21, 1966.

35. Ibid., Szyfrogramy z Hanoi, 1966, Sygn. 6/77, w-173, t-558, Lewandowski to Michałowski, Nov. 25, 1966. See also Lewandowski to Rapacki, Nov. 28, 1966.

36. Hershberg, "Who Murdered Marigold?," 22f.

37. Ibid., 42.

38. Milne, *America's Rasputin*, 184f.

39. Dallek, *Flawed Giant*, 445.

40. Rusk and Papp, *As I Saw It*, 467. Cf. Radványi, *Delusion and Reality*, 194f.

41. *FRUS, 1964–1968*, vol. V, *Vietnam, 1967*, Doc. 7, Memorandum of meeting, Jan. 5, 1967.

42. Guan, "Vietnam War from Both Sides," 106f.

43. LOC, Conversations in Prague with Snejdarek and others [Jan. 30–31, 1967], Feb. 6, 1967.

44. LOC, Harriman Papers, Box 481, U.S. Embassy Paris to Rusk, May 26, 1967.

45. LOC, Conversations in Prague with Snejdarek and others [Jan. 30–31, 1967], Feb. 6, 1967.

46. LOC, Harriman Papers, Box 481, Memcon Harriman, Kissinger, Feb. 9, 1967.

47. *FRUS, 1964–1968*, vol. V, *Vietnam, 1967*, Doc. 227, Bundy to Rusk, June 30, 1967.

48. Guan, "Vietnam War from Both Sides," 110.

49. Herring, *Secret Diplomacy*, 374f.

50. Milne, *America's Rasputin*, 185–88.

51. Guan, "Vietnam War from Both Sides," 113.

52. Ibid, 138f.

53. Rusk and Papp, *As I Saw It*, 469f.

54. LOC, Harriman Papers, Box 481, HAK to Harriman, Dec. 30, 1966.

55. LOC, HAK to Harriman, Jan. 3, 1967.

56. LOC, Harriman Papers, Box 481, Memcon Harriman, Kissinger, Feb. 9, 1967.

57. Dallek, *Flawed Giant*, 447.

58. *FRUS, 1964–1968*, vol. V, *Vietnam, 1967*, Doc. 43, Summary Notes of the 568th Meeting of the National Security Council, Feb. 8, 1967.

59. Harrison and Mosher, "Secret Diary of McNamara's Dove," 528f.

60. Milne, *America's Rasputin*, 192.

61. Ibid., 18.

62. Dallek, *Flawed Giant*, 459ff.; Milne, *America's Rasputin*, 189f.

63. Johnson, *Vantage Point*, 368.

64. Dallek, *Flawed Giant*, 470.

65. Ibid., 453f.

66. Martin Luther King, Jr., "Beyond Vietnam," Address Delivered to the Clergy and Laymen Concerned About Vietnam, at Riverside Church, April 4, 1967, http://stanford.io/1KcXUm6.

67. *FRUS, 1964–1968*, vol. V, *Vietnam, 1967*, Doc. 341, Notes of the meeting, Oct. 3, 1967. See Gardner, *Pay Any Price*, 390.

68. Guan, "Vietnam War from Both Sides," 115.

69. Herring, *Secret Diplomacy*, 521.

70. Dobrynin, *In Confidence*, 161.

71. Guan, "Vietnam War from Both Sides," 117.

72. HAK, "The World Will Miss Lee Kuan Yew," *Washington Post*, Mar. 23, 2015.

73. Joel R. Kramer, "Lee Kuan Yew," *Harvard Crimson*, Oct. 23, 1967.

74. Robert K. Brigham and George C. Herring, "The Pennsylvania Peace Initiative, June–October 1967," in Gardner and Gittinger, *Search for Peace in Vietnam*.

75. Guan, "Vietnam War from Both Sides," 118.

76. Brown, *Keeper of Nuclear Conscience*, 201.

77. Braun, *Joseph Rotblat*, 77.

78. LOC, F-2(a), Vietnam Material, Draft of a Memo to the Files, July 10, 1967.

79. LOC, Harriman Papers, Ordre de Mission, July 7, 1967.

80. Aubrac, *Où la mémoire s'attarde*, 255f.

81. Marnham, *Resistance and Betrayal*.

82. Aubrac, *Où la mémoire s'attarde*, 258.

83. McNamara, *Argument Without End*, 292f.

84. Brigham and Herring, "Pennsylvania Peace Initiative," 63.

85. Aubrac, *Où la mémoire s'attarde*, 261–69.

86. Johnson Library, 10, Pentagon Papers, Visit to Hanoi by Two Unofficial French Representatives, Aug. 2, 1967.

87. Aubrac, *Où la mémoire s'attarde*, 272.

88. *FRUS, 1964–1968*, vol. V, *Vietnam, 1967*, Doc. 267, Memorandum of meeting, Aug. 3, 1967.

89. McNamara, *In Retrospect*, 298; Dallek, *Flawed Giant*, 477.

90. *FRUS, 1964–1968*, vol. V, *Vietnam, 1967*, Doc. 272, Bundy to Negotiations Committee, Aug. 9, 1967.

91. Dallek, *Flawed Giant*, 477f.

92. *FRUS, 1964–1968*, vol. V, *Vietnam, 1967*, Doc. 267, Memorandum of meeting, Aug. 3, 1967.

93. Johnson Library, 10, Pentagon Papers, Pennsylvania, n.d. Aug. 1967. McNamara told Harriman he had personally dictated the text.

94. Ibid., revised and supplemented after review by Kissinger, Sept. 8, 1967.

95. Johnson Library, NSF Country File Vietnam, 140, Pennsylvania, HAK to Rusk, Katzenbach and Harriman, Aug. 17, 1967; HAK to Rusk, Katzenbach and Harriman, Aug. 18, 1967, 06.59; HAK to Rusk, Katzenbach and Harriman, Aug. 18, 1967, 14.58.

96. Gibbons, *Government and Vietnam War*, 777–79.

97. Johnson Library, NSF Country File Vietnam, 140, Pennsylvania, HAK to McNamara, Aug. 19, 1967, 06.49.

98. *FRUS, 1964–1968*, vol. V, *Vietnam, 1967*, Memcon Harriman, McNamara, Aug. 22, 1967.

99. Johnson Library, NSF Country File Vietnam, 140, Pennsylvania, Cooper memorandum, Aug. 22, 1967.

100. At this point, knowledge of PENNSYLVANIA was confined to Bundy, Cooper, Habib, Harriman, Katzenbach, McNamara, and Rusk.

101. Johnson Library, NSF Country File Vietnam, 140, Pennsylvania, Walsh memorandum, Aug. 25, 1967.

102. Ibid., 140, Pennsylvania, Read memo, Sept. 5, 1967.

103. Ibid., 140, Read memo, Sept. 6, 1967.

104. Ibid., 140, Read memo, Sept. 7, 1967, 12:30 p.m.

105. Ibid., 140, Pennsylvania, Rostow to LBJ, Sept. 5, 1967.

106. Ibid., 140, Pennsylvania, [Helms] note to Rostow, Sept. 7, 1967.

107. Ibid., 140, Helms to Rostow, Sept. 7, 1967.

108. Ibid., 140, William Bundy memorandum for the President, Sept. 7, 1967.

109. *FRUS, 1964–1968,* vol. V, *Vietnam, 1967,* Doc. 311, Memcon Rusk-Rostow, Sept. 9, 1967.

110. Johnson Library, NSF Country File Vietnam, 140, Rostow to LBJ, Sept. 9, 1967, 6:38 p.m.

111. Ibid., 140, Instructions for Mr. Henry Kissinger, Sept. 7, 1967.

112. Ibid., 140, HAK to Rusk, Sept. 9, 1967, 11:07 a.m.

113. Ibid., 140, HAK to Rusk, Sept. 9, 1967, 4:00 p.m.

114. Ibid.

115. Ibid., 140, HAK message, Sept. 11, 1967.

116. Ibid., 140, Rostow to LBJ, Sept. 11, 1967, 12:15 p.m.

117. Dallek, *Flawed Giant,* 484. See also Gardner, *Pay Any Price,* 387.

118. Johnson Library, NSF Country File Vietnam, 140, Rusk to HAK, Sept. 12, 1967. See also HAK to Rusk, Sept. 13, 1967, 7:49 a.m., for Kissinger's request that the U.S. response to Hanoi be toned down.

119. Johnson Library, NSF Country File Vietnam, 140, Rusk to HAK, Sept. 13, 1967.

120. Ibid., 140, HAK to Rusk, Sept. 13, 1967, 7:57 a.m.

121. Ibid., 140, HAK to Rusk, Sept. 13, 1967, 4:10 p.m.

122. Ibid., 140, HAK to Rusk, Sept. 14, 1967, 2:54 p.m.

123. Ibid., 140, HAK to Rusk, Sept. 15, 1967, 8:56 a.m.; Rusk to HAK, Sept. 15, 1967; HAK to Rusk, Sept. 15, 1967, 9:19 p.m.

124. Ibid., 140, HAK to Rusk, Sept. 19, 1967, 2:39 p.m.

125. Ibid.

126. Ibid., 140, HAK to Rusk, Sept. 16, 1967, 8:46 a.m.

127. Aubrac, *Où la mémoire s'attarde,* 278.

128. *FRUS, 1964–1968,* vol. V, *Vietnam, 1967,* Doc. 334, HAK to Rusk, Sept. 21, 1967.

129. Johnson Library, NSF Country File Vietnam, 140, Telcon Read-HAK, Sept. 25, 1967, 8:25 a.m.

130. Ibid., 140, Telcon Read-HAK, Sept. 30, 1967, 9:00 a.m.

131. Ibid., 140, Telcon Kissinger-Read, Oct. 3, 7:30 a.m.

132. Ibid., 140, Rostow to LBJ, Oct. 3, 1967, 10:15 a.m.

133. Ibid., 140, Marcovitch to HAK, Oct. 2, 1967; Note drafted by MA after M's conversation with Paul [Bo], Oct. 2, 1967; NSF Files of Walt Rostow, 9, Telcon Kissinger-Read, Oct. 3, 1967, 1 p.m. Slight variations in wording from one version to another reflect differences in translations from the French.

134. *FRUS, 1964–1968,* vol. V, *Vietnam, 1967,* Doc. 341, Notes of the meeting, Oct. 3, 1967. See Gardner, *Pay Any Price,* 390.

135. Johnson Library, NSF Country File Vietnam, 140, Telcons Read-Kissinger, Oct. 4, 1967, 4:15 and 4:30 p.m.; Oct. 4, 1967, 8:30 p.m.

136. Ibid., 140, Rostow to LBJ, Oct. 4, 1967; Rostow to LBJ, Oct. 4, 1967, 6:10 p.m.

137. *FRUS, 1964–1968,* vol. V, *Vietnam, 1967,* Doc. 346, Notes of the meeting, Oct. 4, 1967.

138. Ibid., Doc. 348, LBJ meeting with Rusk, McNamara and Rostow, 6:55–8:25 p.m. Cf. Gibbons, *Government and Vietnam War,* pt. 4, 783–86.

139. Johnson Library, NSF Country File Vietnam, 140, Text dictated by Mai Van Bo to Marcovitch, Oct. 5, 1967, 9:30 p.m.–midnight.

140. *FRUS, 1964–1968,* vol. V, *Vietnam, 1967,* Doc. 348, LBJ meeting with Rusk, McNamara and Rostow, 6:55–8:25 p.m.

141. Johnson Library, NSF Files of Walt Rostow, 9, Rusk [?] to HAK, Oct. 5, 1967; NSF Country File Vietnam, 140, Rusk to U.S. ambassador in Paris, Oct. 6, 1967.

142. *FRUS, 1964–1968,* vol. V, *Vietnam, 1967,* Doc. 348, LBJ meeting with Rusk, McNamara and Rostow, 6:55–8:25 p.m.

143. Johnson Library, NSF Files of Walt Rostow, 9, Rostow to LBJ, Oct. 6, 1967, 4:50 p.m.

144. Ibid., 9, Telcon Rostow-Kissinger, Oct. 8, 1967.

145. Johnson Library, NSF Country File Vietnam, 140, Telcon Read-Kissinger, Oct. 8, 1967.

146. Ibid., 140, Telcon Read-Kissinger, Oct. 9, 1967.

147. Ibid., 140, Telcon Read-Kissinger, Oct. 17, 1967, 7:45 a.m.

148. Ibid., 140, Rostow to LBJ, Oct. 9, 1967, 1:55 p.m.

149. Ibid., 140, Telcon Read-Kissinger, Oct. 10, 1967, 2:00 p.m.

150. *FRUS, 1964–1968,* vol. V, *Vietnam, 1967,* Doc. 353, LBJ meeting with Rusk, McNamara, Rostow, Helms and Christian, Oct. 16, 1967.

151. Johnson Library, NSF Country File Vietnam, 140, Telcon Rostow-Kissinger, Oct. 17, 1967, 6:00 p.m.

152. Ibid., 140, Kissinger memo, Oct. 17, 1967.

153. Johnson Library, Tom Johnson's Notes of Meetings, 1, Notes of the President's Wednesday Night Meeting, Oct.18, 1967. Cf. Gardner, *Pay Any Price,* 391ff.; Clifford, *Counsel,* 453f.

154. Schlesinger, *Journals,* Dec. 7, 1967. This story has a different setting in Isaacson, who (on the basis of an interview with Paul Doty) sets it in October as a phone call to Doty's Vermont farmhouse, where Kissinger was spending the weekend: Isaacson, *Kissinger,* KL 2320–25.

155. Johnson Library, NSF Country File Vietnam, 140, HAK to Rusk, Sept. 16, 1967, 3:27 p.m.

156. Ibid., 140, HAK to Rusk, Sept. 22, 1967, 5:57 p.m.

157. Ibid., 140, Rostow to LBJ, Sept. 14, 1967, 8:20 p.m.

158. *FRUS, 1964–1968,* vol. V, *Vietnam, 1967,* Doc. 330, Memcon Harriman-McNamara, Sept. 19, 1967.

159. Johnson Library, NSF Files of Walt Rostow, 9, Rostow to LBJ, Sept. 26, 1967.

160. LOC, D-4, LBJ to HAK, Oct. 4, 1967.

161. *FRUS, 1964–1968*, vol. V, *Vietnam, 1967*, Doc. 336, Notes of Meeting, Sept. 26, 1967, 1:15–2:35 p.m. Cf. Gardner, *Pay Any Price*, 387f.

162. Gardner, *Pay Any Price*, 388f.

163. *FRUS, 1964–1968*, vol. V, *Vietnam, 1967*, Doc. 336, Notes of Meeting, Sept. 26, 1967, 1:15–2:35 p.m. Cf. Gardner, *Pay Any Price*, 387f. Cf. McNamara, *In Retrospect*, 298–301.

164. Lyndon B. Johnson, Address on Vietnam Before the National Legislative Conference, San Antonio, TX, Sept. 29, 1967, http://bit.ly/1aYigDa. Cf. Johnson Library, NSF Files of Walt Rostow, 9, Rostow to LBJ, Sept. 26, 1967; Gardner, *Pay Any Price*, 389.

165. *FRUS, 1964–1968*, vol. V, *Vietnam, 1967*, Doc. 341, Notes of Meeting, Oct. 3, 1967. See Gardner, *Pay Any Price*, 390.

166. *FRUS, 1964–1968*, vol. V, *Vietnam, 1967*, Doc. 363, Notes of Meeting, Oct. 23, 1967. Cf. Gardner, *Pay Any Price*, 395; Gibbons, *Government and Vietnam War*, 789–94.

167. *FRUS, 1964–1968*, vol. V, *Vietnam, 1967*, Doc. 420, Notes of Meeting, Nov. 29, 1967.

168. Johnson Library, NSF Country File Vietnam, 140, State Dept. to American Embassy, Paris, Oct. 19, 1967.

169. Ibid., 140, HAK via American Embassy, Paris, to State Dept., Oct. 20, 1967, 7:20 a.m.

170. Ibid., 140, Rostow to LBJ, Oct. 20, 1967, 10:50 a.m.

171. Ibid., 140, HAK to State Dept., Oct. 20, 1967.

172. Ibid. See also Aubrac, *Où la mémoire s'attarde*, 279f.

173. Johnson Library, NSF Country File Vietnam, 140, Rostow to LBJ, Oct. 20, 1967.

174. Ibid., 140, Rostow to LBJ, Oct. 21, 1967.

175. Ibid., 140, Rostow to LBJ, Oct. 27, 1967.

176. Ibid., 140, Helms to Rostow, Oct. 23, 1967.

177. *FRUS, 1964–1968*, vol. V, *Vietnam, 1967*, Doc. 363, Notes of Meeting, Oct. 23, 1967. Cf. Gardner, *Pay Any Price*, 395; Gibbons, *Government and Vietnam War*, 789–94.

178. Johnson Library, NSF Country File Vietnam, 140, Aubrac and Marcovitch to HAK, Oct. 25, 1967.

179. Ibid., 140, Marcovitch to HAK, Dec. 15, 1967.

180. Aubrac, *Où la mémoire s'attarde*, 282.

181. Butcher, "Questions About the Nature of Transfer in Track Two."

182. Loory and Kraslow, *Secret Search for Peace*.

183. Johnson Library, NSF Country File Vietnam, 94, Read memo, Dec. 11, 1967.

184. Ibid., 140, Memcon Gunther, Cook, Kraslow, Dec. 6, 1967.

185. Herring, *LBJ and Vietnam*.

186. Guan, "Vietnam War from Both Sides," 121–23.

187. McNamara, *Argument Without End*, 299–301.

188. Herring, *Secret Diplomacy*, 522f.

189. Johnson Library, NSF Country File Vietnam, 94, Marcovitch to HAK, Dec. 6, 1967.

190. Ibid., 140, Memcon Read, Kissinger, Jan. 17, 1968, 7:30 a.m. and 6 p.m.; Rostow to LBJ, Jan. 17, 1968.

191. Ibid., 140, Memcon Read, Kissinger, Jan. 18, 1968, 9:00 a.m.

192. Ibid., 140, HAK to Rusk [three telegrams], Jan. 4, 1968.

193. Ibid.

Chapter 21: 1968

1. LOC, D-4, Dönhof to HAK, March 22, 1968.

2. Nixon, *RN: Memoirs*, KL 6520–47.

3. McNamara, *In Retrospect*, 313.

4. Rusk, *As I Saw It*, 417.

5. See in general Suri, *Power and Protest*.

6. Atkinson, *In Theory and Practice*, 139.

7. Ibid., 143.

8. Ibid., 149.

9. Ibid., 150, 153.

10. HAK, "The Need to Belong," *New York Times*, Mar. 17, 1968.

11. LOC, F-2(a), HAK, Outline of Remarks [by NAR] at Rensselaer Commencement, June 6, 1968.

12. Vaïsse, "Zbig, Henry, and the New U.S. Foreign Policy Elite," KL 3–26.

13. This paragraph is based on the first chapter of Hersh, *Price of Power*.

14. Isaacson, *Kissinger*, 2451–71.

15. Hitchens, *Trial of Kissinger*.

16. Hughes, *Chasing Shadows*, esp. the circumstantial evidence in footnote 7, KL 4133–4182.

17. Clifford, *Counsel to the President*, 581f.

18. Hughes, *Chasing Shadows*, KL 4079–81.

19. Seig, "1968 Presidential Election," 1062.

20. Summers, *Arrogance of Power*, 298.

21. Stanley Hoffmann, "The Kissinger Anti-Memoirs," *New York Times*, July 3, 1983.

22. Bundy, *Tangled Web*, 39f.

23. Miller Center of Public Affairs, University of Virginia, Ronald Reagan Oral History Project, interview with Richard F. Allen, May 28, 2002, 13.

24. Ibid., 32.

25. Lehman, *Command of the Seas*, 67f.

26. Nixon, *RN: Memoir*, KL 6170–314.

27. Smith, *On His Own Terms*, 496–97.

28. LOC, F-2(a), "A Rockefeller Call for a New Vietnam Policy," Aug. 22, 1967.

29. Ibid.

30. Ibid.

31. Ibid.

32. Richard Witkin, "Rockefeller Turning Away from Johnson on Vietnam," *New York Times*, Oct. 4, 1967; "Rockefeller Bars Vietnam Comment," Oct. 4, 1967.

33. LOC, F-3(c), NAR to RMN [draft], Apr. 2, 1965.

34. Rockefeller Archive Center, RMN to NAR, Nov. 8, 1966.

35. Smith, *On His Own Terms*, 527.

36. LOC, F-2(a), Nancy Maginnes to Ann Whitman, Nov. 22, 1967.

37. Schlesinger, *Journals*, Dec. 7, 1967.

38. Ibid., Feb. 19, 1968.

39. Kalb and Kalb, *Kissinger*, 14f.

40. RMN, "Asia After Viet Nam," *Foreign Affairs* (Oct. 1967), 111–25.

41. Ibid., 111f.

42. Ibid., 123.

43. Ibid., 121.
44. Ibid.
45. LOC, F-3(c), HAK to NAR, Jan. 26, 1968.
46. Ibid.
47. Ibid. It seems likely that Kissinger had read Fisher Howe's pamphlet *The Computer and Foreign Affairs: Some First Thoughts* (1966).
48. HAK, "Bureaucracy and Policy Making: The Effect of Insiders and Outsiders on the Policy Process," in HAK and Brodie, *Bureaucracy, Politics and Strategy*.
49. Ibid., 3.
50. Ibid., 6.
51. Ibid., 6f.
52. Ibid., 8, 11.
53. Ibid., 9.
54. Ibid.
55. Ibid., 10.
56. LOC, K-2, Study Group on Presidential Transition, 1968–1969.
57. Ibid., Lindsay to RMN, Aug. 15, 1968, enclosing report signed by Areeda, Lindsay and May.
58. Prados and Porter, *Inside the Pentagon Papers*.
59. Johnson, *Vantage Point*, 373. For Rusk's reply see *FRUS, 1964–1968*, vol. V, *Vietnam 1967*, Doc. 403, Rusk to LBJ, Nov. 20, 1967.
60. McNamara, *In Retrospect*, 309f.
61. Johnson, *Vantage Point*, 600f.
62. McNamara, *In Retrospect*, 310f.
63. Robert Buzzanco, "The Myth of Tet: American Failure and the Politics of War," in Gilbert and Head, *Tet Offensive*, 232f.
64. LOC, F-2(a), Lloyd Free, American Opinion About Vietnam, Preliminary Report on American Opinion About Vietnam, Lloyd Free, Mar. 15, 1968.
65. LOC, Kent 64, HAK to NAR, Mar. 27, 1968.
66. Richard Reeves, "Governor to Run; He Will Disclose Plans Thursday," *New York Times*, March 19, 1968.
67. Buzzanco, "Myth of Tet," 245.
68. Gilbert and Head, *Tet Offensive*, 242, 246f.
69. Guan, *Ending Vietnam War*, KL 222. See also Herbert Y. Schandler, "The Pentagon and Peace Negotiations After March 31, 1968," in Gardner and Gittinger, *Search for Peace in Vietnam*.
70. Herring, *Secret Diplomacy*, 524f.
71. Rusk, *As I Saw It*, 484.
72. LOC, Harriman Papers, Box 481, Harriman to HAK, Apr. 15, 1968.
73. Joseph Carroll, "Paris, May 1968," *Guardian*, May 6, 1968.
74. Joseph A. Harris, "Letter from Paris. May 1968: Something Happened (but What?)," *American Spectator* (Nov. 2008).
75. Schandler, "Pentagon and Peace Negotiations"; Rusk, *As I Saw It*, 485.
76. Details in Guan, *Ending Vietnam War*.
77. Diem and Chanoff, *Jaws of History*, 230f.
78. LOC, Harriman Papers, Box 481, HAK to Harriman, May 31, 1968.
79. LOC, G-14, HAK to Lodge, June 28, 1968.
80. Milne, "1968 Paris Peace Negotiations," 589f.
81. Ross Terrill, "A Report on the Paris Talks," *New Republic*, July 13, 1968.
82. Seig, "1968 Presidential Election," 1063. See also Rusk, *As I Saw It*, 486f., 490.

83. LBJ, Remarks in Detroit at the Annual Convention of the Veterans of Foreign Wars, Aug. 19, 1968, http://bit.ly/1yWCUyR.
84. Milne, "1968 Paris Peace Negotiations," 592.
85. LOC, Harriman Papers, Box 481, HAK to Harriman, July 17, 1968; see also Harriman to HAK, Aug. 30, 1968.
86. Ibid., HAK to Harriman, Nov. 15, 1968.
87. Ibid., HAK to Harriman, Aug. 9, 1968.
88. Ibid., Harriman to HAK, Aug. 15, 1968.
89. Milne, "1968 Paris Peace Negotiations," 592.
90. LOC, G-14, Lodge to HAK, May 8, 1968.
91. James F. Clarity, "Rockefeller Hires Campaign Chief," *New York Times*, Apr. 10, 1968.
92. LOC, G-14 Supp. (Kraemer), HAK to Kraemer, Apr. 10, 1968.
93. LOC, F-2(a), HAK to NAR, Apr. 20, 1968.
94. Smith, *On His Own Terms*, 528.
95. Ibid., 529.
96. LOC, F-2(a), Remarks by Governor Nelson A. Rockefeller, Prepared for Delivery at the World Affairs Council of Philadelphia Luncheon, May 1, 1968; emphasis added. See Isaacson, *Kissinger*, KL 2378–91.
97. Ibid., Excerpts of Remarks by Governor Nelson A. Rockefeller, Prepared for Delivery at Kansas State College, Manhattan, Kansas, May 9, 1968.
98. Smith, *On His Own Terms*, 532f.
99. LOC, F-2(a), HAK to Thomas Losee, July 1, 1968.
100. Ibid., NAR draft speech on Government Organization for the Conduct of Foreign Policy, June 15, 1968. See also LOC, D-4, NAR Related, Government Reorganization, June 21, 1968.
101. Ibid., HAK, Outline of Suggestions for the Republican Platform: Foreign Policy, HAK to Alton Marshall, June 30, 1968.
102. Ibid., NAR Statement on Foreign Economic Policy, July 1, 1968.
103. Ibid.
104. Ibid., NAR 4 stage VN peace plan, News from Rockefeller for President, July 13, 1968. Cf. R. W. Apple, Jr., "Rockefeller Gives Four-Stage Plan to End the War," *New York Times*, July 14, 1968.
105. Leo Baeck Institute, AR 4198, Hans Morgenthau Collection, Box 4, Folder 1, HAK to Morgenthau, Oct. 9, 1968.
106. Zambernardi, "Impotence of Power."
107. Leo Baeck Institute, AR 4198, Hans Morgenthau Collection, Box 4, Folder 1, Morgenthau to HAK, Oct. 22, 1968.
108. Ibid., HAK to Morgenthau, Nov. 13, 1968.
109. Buckley, *United Nations Journal*, 55f.
110. White, *Making of the President 1968*, 285.
111. Isaacson, *Kissinger*, KL 2402–6.
112. Hedrick Smith, "Nixon Research Aide Warned of Prague Invasion by Russians," *New York Times*, Dec. 14, 1968.
113. Miller Center of Public Affairs, University of Virginia, Ronald Reagan Oral History Project, interview with Richard F. Allen, May 28, 2002, 7f. Cf. Isaacson, *Kissinger*, KL 2409–32.
114. John W. Finney, "Rockefeller Coup Gave Platform a Dovish Tone," *New York Times*, Aug. 6, 1968.

115. Isaacson, *Kissinger*, KL 2409–32. Cf. Nixon Library, 414, Kirk, Brent-Kittens, 1960, George Grassmuck to HAK, Aug. 29, 1960.

116. LOC, Harriman Papers, Box 481, Harriman to HAK, Aug. 15, 1968. For the widely repeated claim that this was a lie, see, e.g., Milne, "1968 Paris Peace Negotiations," 592.

117. Isaacson, *Kissinger*, KL 2513–30.

118. Humphrey, *Education of Public Man*, 9.

119. Isaacson, *Kissinger*, KL 2443–45.

120. Buckley, *United Nations Journal*, 56.

121. LOC, D-4, HAK to NAR, Aug. 20, 1968.

122. See Ambrose, *Nixon*, vol. 2, KL 3760–85. Cf. Isaacson, *Kissinger*, KL 2492–95. Isaacson's information is nearly all based on interviews conducted between 1989 and 1991, more than twenty years after the event. Davidson also went on the record to repeat his story in the 2002 documentary film *The Trials of Henry Kissinger*, http://bit.ly/1bATfzh.

123. Nixon Library, White House Special Files Collection, Folder 11, Haldeman to RMN and Harlow, Sept. 27, 1968.

124. Hughes, *Chasing Shadows*, KL 127–55. In his footnotes, Hughes makes much of this, but Kissinger had seen such lists before, and in any case, there is no evidence that he communicated the specifics to anyone on the Nixon campaign.

125. Diem and Chanoff, *Jaws of History*, 237.

126. See, e.g., Summers, *Arrogance of Power*, KL 1067–70.

127. Diem and Chanoff, *Jaws of History*, 237.

128. Nixon Library, White House Special Files Collection, Folder 11, McCone to RMN, Sept. 21, 1968.

129. Ibid., Harlow to RMN, Sept. 24, 1968.

130. Ibid., Haldeman to RMN and Harlow, Sept. 27, 1968.

131. Ambrose, *Nixon*, vol. 2, KL 4096.

132. Seig, "1968 Presidential Election," 1067; LaFeber, *Deadly Bet*, 158.

133. LaFeber, *Deadly Bet*, 159f.

134. Milne, "1968 Paris Peace Negotiations"; White, *Making of the President 1968*, 325.

135. LaFeber, *Deadly Bet*, 162f.

136. Diem and Chanoff, *Jaws of History*, 238–40.

137. See also Rusk, *As I Saw It*, 487f.

138. *FRUS*, vol. VII, *Vietnam, Sept. 1968–Jan. 1969*, Doc. 104, Minutes of the meeting, Oct. 22, 1968.

139. Ambrose, *Nixon*, vol. 2, KL 4041.

140. Powers, *Man Who Kept Secrets*, 198–200. Hoover even claimed Nixon's plane had been bugged, though this was a lie.

141. Keever, *Death Zones and Darling Spies*, 223–26. On this incident see Diem and Chanoff, *Jaws of History*, 243.

142. Johnson Library, South Vietnam on U.S. Policies, Eugene Rostow memo, Oct. 29, 1968, forwarded to LBJ by Walt Rostow. Cf. Hughes, *Chasing Shadows*, KL 206–24.

143. Johnson Library, South Vietnam on U.S. Policies, Vice President Ky Expresses Opinions on Conduct of Bomb Halt, Oct. 29, 1968. Cf. Diem and Chanoff, *Jaws of History*, 240f.; Woods, *LBJ: Architect of Ambition*, 872–75.

144. Rusk, *As I Saw It*, 489f.

145. Berman, *No Peace, No Honor*, 33–36. See also Milne, "1968 Paris Peace Negotiations," 596f.

146. Ambrose, *Nixon*, vol. 2, KL 4157.

147. Rusk, *As I Saw It*, 490.

148. Witcover, *White Knight*, 270. See also Summers, *Arrogance of Power*, 306, who admits that "Thieu would very probably have balked at attending talks anyway, even without the Republican pressure."

149. The accusation can be heard in the recorded call between Johnson and Everett Dirksen, http://bit.ly/1boC8jl.

150. The most detailed account of the episode is Hughes, *Chasing Shadows*, KL 1138–298. See also Summers, *Arrogance of Power*, 303ff.

151. Hughes, *Chasing Shadows*, KL 1138–298. See also Keever, *Death Zones and Darling Spies*, 227f.; Humphrey, *Education of Public Man*, 8, 9, 14. According to Theodore White, the Nixon campaign was in fact filled with unfeigned "fury and dismay" when they realized what Chennault had been doing (or, at least, that she had been caught doing it by Johnson): White, *Making of the President 1968*, 445.

152. *FRUS*, vol. VII, *Vietnam, Sept. 1968–Jan. 1969*, Doc. 194, Rostow to LBJ, Nov. 4, 1968.

153. Summers, *Arrogance of Power*, 519. Cf. Rosen, *Strong Man*, 59–62; Safire, *Before the Fall*, 89f.

154. Tom Ottenad, "Was Saigon's Peace Talk Delay Due to Republican Promises?," *Boston Globe*, Jan. 6, 1969.

155. Hughes, *Chasing Shadows*, KL 127–55.

156. Haldeman, *Haldeman Diaries*, 565.

Chapter 22: The Unlikely Combination

1. Joseph A. Loftus, "Ex-Adviser Cites Problems of Presidential Power," *New York Times*, Sept. 7, 1968.

2. "Season for Blueprints," *Economist*, Dec. 7, 1968, 41f.

3. HAK, "Central Issues of American Foreign Policy," in *American Foreign Policy: Three Essays*, 52, 95, 85, 56, 57, 84.

4. Ibid., 77.

5. Ibid., 60.

6. Ibid., 61.

7. Ibid., 95.

8. Guido Goldman, interview by author.

9. Hedrick Smith, "Kissinger Has Parley Plan: Nixon Adviser's Article Asks 2-Level Talks," *New York Times*, Dec. 19, 1968.

10. HAK, "Viet Nam Negotiations."

11. Ibid., 211f.

12. Ibid., 220.

13. Ibid., 218.

14. Ibid., 213f.

15. Ibid., 214.

16. Ibid., 215.

17. Ibid., 216, 221.

18. Ibid., 218f.

19. Ibid., 227f.

20. Ibid., 230, 234.

21. White, *Making of the President 1968,* 460f.

22. Converse, Miller, Rusk, and Wolfe, "Continuity and Change in American Politics," 1084.

23. White, *Making of the President 1968,* 467.

24. LOC, K-2, Study Group on Presidential Transition 1968–1969, Frank Lindsay to RMN, Aug. 15, 1968, enclosing report signed by Areeda, Lindsay, and May, 11.

25. Ibid., 12.

26. Ibid., 28.

27. Ibid., Lindsay to RMN, Aug. 15, 1968, enclosing report signed by Areeda, Lindsay and May.

28. Ibid., Lindsay to RMN, Oct. 18, 1968, enclosing report.

29. Ibid., Lindsay to RMN, Nov. 1, 1968, enclosing report.

30. Ibid.

31. Ibid.

32. Ibid., Lindsay to RMN, Nov. 6, 1968, enclosing report.

33. LOC, K-2, John Eisenhower to Haldeman, Nov. 25, 1968.

34. LOC, Elliot Richardson Papers, Box I 64, Gilpatric to Lindsay, Nov. 24, 1968.

35. Safire, *Before the Fall,* 33.

36. Smith, *On His Own Terms,* 542.

37. Isaacson, *Kissinger,* KL 2557–73.

38. Buckley, *United Nations Journal,* 56f.

39. Nixon, *RN: Memoirs,* KL 6538–52.

40. *WHY,* 11f.

41. Rockefeller Archive Center, HAK to NAR, Nov. 25, 1968.

42. *WHY,* 14.

43. Isaacson, *Kissinger,* KL 2574–608.

44. *WHY,* 15.

45. Isaacson, *Kissinger,* KL 2534–44.

46. Ibid., KL 2613–22.

47. Robert Reinhold, "Scholars Praise 2 Nixon Choices: They See Encouraging Sign for New Administration," *New York Times,* Dec. 4, 1968.

48. R. W. Apple, Jr., "Kissinger Named a Key Nixon Aide in Defense Policy," *New York Times,* Dec. 3, 1968.

49. LOC, Elliot Richardson Papers Box I 64, Task Force on Organization of Executive Branch I, Revitalizing and Streamlining the NSC, Dec. 1, 1968.

50. LOC, K-2, Study Group on Presidential Transition 1968–1969, Program Planning for the White House, Areeda to Haldeman, Dec. 2, 1968.

51. LOC, Elliot Richardson Papers, Box I 64, Lindsay to Richardson, Dec. 2, 1968.

52. LOC, K-2, May to HAK, Dec. 4, 1968.

53. Ibid., Jerry Friedheim, Thoughts on National Security Council, Dec. 5, 1968.

54. Robert B. Semple, Jr., "Nixon to Revive Council's Power: Aims to Give Security Board," *New York Times,* Jan. 1, 1969. See Rothkopf, *Running the World,* 108–56.

55. James Reston was even fooled by Nixon into believing the ideas for NSC reform were the president's own: "The First Myth of the Nixon Administration," *New York Times,* Dec. 18, 1968.

56. LOC, K-2, Ernest May, Historians and the Foreign Policy Process, Dec. 4, 1968.

57. Joseph A. Loftus, "Ex-Adviser Cites Problems of Presidential Power," *New York Times,* Sept. 7, 1968.

58. Robert B. Semple, Jr., "Kissinger Called Nixon Choice for Adviser on Foreign Policy," *New York Times,* Nov. 30, 1968.

59. R. W. Apple, Jr., "Kissinger Named a Key Nixon Aide in Defense Policy," *New York Times,* Dec. 3, 1968.

60. "Nixon's National Security Aide," *Register,* Dec. 4, 1968.

61. James Reston, "Kissinger: New Man in the White House Basement," *New York Times,* Dec. 4, 1968.

62. "Nixon's Key Adviser on Defense Kissinger, Henry Alfred Kissinger," *New York Times,* Dec. 3, 1968; "The Kissinger Appointment," *New York Times,* Dec. 4, 1968.

63. "Kissinger: The Uses and Limits of Power," *Time* 93, no. 7 (Feb. 14, 1969).

64. Evelyn Irons, "Kissinger to Advise on Defence," *Times,* Dec. 3, 1968, 1.

65. Ian McDonald, "Mr. Nixon Picks Liberal Adviser on Science," *Times,* Dec. 4, 1968, 5.

66. Leonard Beaton, "The Strong European Bias of Dr. Kissinger," *Times,* Dec. 5, 1968.

67. "Season for Blueprints," *Economist,* Dec. 7, 1968.

68. Adam Raphael, "Nixon's Security Adviser," *Guardian,* Dec. 3, 1968, 1.

69. Scot Richard, "A Bonn–US Axis Under Nixon?," *Guardian,* Dec. 3, 1968, 2.

70. "Shepherds' Watch," *Guardian,* Dec. 11, 1968, 9.

71. "Lauded by Le Monde," *New York Times,* Dec 4, 1968.

72. "Amerikas neue Regenten: Nixons Kabinetts-Mannschaft: Nicht faszinierend, doch solide," *Die Zeit,* Dec. 20, 1968. See also Theo Sommer, "Der müde Atlas," *Die Zeit,* Jan. 17, 1969.

73. "Poles Criticize Kissinger," *New York Times,* Dec. 5, 1968.

74. Stephen Hess, "First Impressions: A Look Back at Five Presidential Transitions," Brookings, http://brook.gs/1d9uV7O.

75. Robert Reinhold, "Scholars Praise 2 Nixon Choices: They See Encouraging Sign for New Administration," *New York Times,* Dec. 4, 1968.

76. New York Public Library, Arthur Schlesinger Journal, Dec. 11, 1968.

77. Walter Goodman, "The Liberal Establishment Faces: The Blacks, the Young, the New Left," *New York Times,* Dec. 29, 1968.

78. "Letter: Foreign Policy Adviser," *New York Times,* Dec. 15, 1968.

79. John H. Fenton, "Nixon Naming of 3 Decried by Welch: Birch Head Scores Murphy, Moynihan and Kissinger," *New York Times,* Jan. 7, 1969.

80. "Kissinger Conducts His Last Seminar in Government Before Joining It," *New York Times,* Dec. 17, 1968.

81. LOC, K-2, Halperin to HAK, Dec. 11, 1968.

82. National Archives and Records Administration, Henry A. Kissinger Office Files, Arms Control, Jerome Wiesner to HAK, Dec. 12, 1968.

83. LOC, K-2, Neustadt to HAK, Notes of Dinner Meeting, Dec. 9, 1968.

84. Ibid., Lindsay to RMN, Report of Task Force on Organization of Executive Branch of the Government, Dec. 17, 1968. See also LOC, Elliot Richardson Papers, Box I 91, Lindsay to RMN, Dec. 20, 1968; Lindsay to RMN, Program Planning for the White House, Dec. 28, 1968.

85. LOC, J-3, Kissinger, Brzezinski to HAK, Dec. 18, 1968.

86. LOC, K-2, Goodpaster to HAK, The National Security Council Staff, Dec. 24, 1968.

87. Ibid., HAK to May, Dec. 31, 1968.

88. *FRUS, 1964–1968*, vol. VII, *Vietnam, Sept. 1968–Jan. 1969*, Doc. 244, Minutes of meeting, Dec. 3, 1968.

89. LOC, Harriman Papers, Box 481, Telcon Harriman-Kissinger, Dec. 3, 1968.

90. *FRUS, 1964–1968*, vol. VII, *Vietnam, Sept. 1968–Jan. 1969*, Doc. 266, Vance to Kissinger, Dec. 31, 1968.

91. Katzenbach, *Some of It Was Fun,* 290ff.

92. R. W. Apple, Jr., "Lodge Appointed to Head U.S. Team in Vietnam Talks," *New York Times,* Jan. 6, 1969.

93. LOC, K-2, Bund to HAK, Dec. 4, 1968.

94. Johnson Library, 43, Rostow 109 [1 of 2], Rostow to LBJ, Dec. 5, 1968.

95. Rostow, *Diffusion of Power,* 365. See in general on NSC organization, 358–68.

96. Ibid., 524.

97. *WHY,* 19.

98. Isaacson, *Kissinger,* KL 2613–22.

99. New York Public Library, Arthur Schlesinger Journal, Dec. 11, 1968.

100. "Kissinger Conducts His Last Seminar in Government Before Joining It," *New York Times,* Dec. 17, 1968.

101. LOC, G-14 Supp. (Kraemer), Kraemer to HAK, Dec. 9, 1968.

102. LOC, K-2, Study Group on Presidential Transition 1968–1969, Lindsay to RMN, Nov. 1, 1968, enclosing report.

103. LOC, G-14 Supp. (Kraemer), Kraemer to HAK, Dec. 9, 1968.

Epilogue: A Bildungsroman

1. Bk. VII, chap. 1.

2. Kissinger family papers, HAK to his parents, Apr. 2, 1947.

3. Ibid., HAK to his parents, May 6, 1945.

4. Ibid., HAK to his parents, Feb. 10, 1946.

5. Ibid., HAK to his parents, May 6, 1945.

6. Ibid., HAK to his parents, June 22, 1947.

7. Ibid., HAK to his parents, Apr. 12, 1947.

8. HAK, Kent papers, HAK to his parents, July 28, 1948.

9. Harvard Archives, International Seminar, HAK to Camus, Jan. 26, 1954.

10. *WR,* KL 453–56.

11. *NWFP,* 428f.

12. HAK, MoH, 1f., 4.

13. Ibid., 127f., 249.

14. *WR,* KL 6689–707.

15. *NWFP,* 428f.

16. Harvard Archives, International Seminar, HAK to Graubard, Dec. 5, 1956.

17. "Kissinger Speaks," *New York Herald Tribune,* Oct. 14, 1957. See also "Dr. Kissinger Amplifies," ibid., Oct. 17, 1957.

18. See, e.g., Isaiah Berlin, "The Originality of Machiavelli," in *Against the Current,* 25–79.

19. American Broadcasting Company, in association with the Fund for the Republic, *Survival and Freedom: A Mike Wallace Interview with Henry A. Kissinger* (1958), 11, 13.

20. Kent papers, HAK, "Decision Making in a Nuclear World" (1963), 4ff.

21. Hoover Institution Archives, 1, Conference on the Marriage of Political Philosophy and Practice in Public Affairs in Honor of Professor Elliott, Harvard Summer School, Program and Proceedings, July 22, 1963.

22. NFC, 300ff.

23. Yale University Library, HAK Papers, MS 1981, Part II, Box 273, Folder 5, The Contingency of Legitimacy, 2f.

24. Eisenhower Library, NSC Series, WHO OSANSA: Records, 1952–1961, Box 6, Elliott, "NSC Study," Dec. 23, 1952.

25. LOC, G-14 Supp. (Kraemer), Kraemer to HAK, Dec. 2, 1957.

26. Ibid.

27. LOC, HAK Papers, D-9, Kraemer to HAK, May 17, 1958.

28. LOC, G-14 Supp. (Kraemer), Kraemer to HAK, Dec. 9, 1968.

29. Weidenfeld, *Remembering My Friends,* 384f.

30. Aristophanes, *Peace.*

Sources

Archives

Agudath Israel of America, New York, NY

Alte Arndter: Freunde des Arndt-Gymnasiums, Berlin, Germany

Archiwum Polskiej Dyplomacji, Warsaw, Poland

Balliol College Archives, Oxford, UK

Betty H. Carter Women Veterans Historical Project, University of North Carolina at Greensboro, NC

Boston Athenæum, Boston, MA

Camp Claiborne Historical Research Center, Rapides Parish, LA

Carlisle Barracks Army Heritage and Education Center, Carlisle, PA

Central Archives of the History of the Jewish People, Jerusalem, Israel

Clemson University, Special Collections, Clemson, SC

Congregation K'hal Adath Jeshurun Archives, New York, NY

Defense Technical Information Center, Fort Belvoir, VA

Dwight D. Eisenhower Presidential Library and Museum, Abilene, KS

Federal Bureau of Investigation FOIA Reading Room, Winchester, VA

Ford Foundation Archives, New York, NY

Fortunoff Video Archive for Holocaust Testimony, Yale University, New Haven, CT

Frankfurt University, Germany

Harry S. Truman Library and Museum, Independence, MO

Harry S. Truman National Historic Site, Grandview, MO

Harvard Law School, Historical and Special Collections, Cambridge, MA

Harvard University Archives, Cambridge, MA

Hoover Institution Library and Archives, Stanford University, Palo Alto, CA

Jean and Alexander Heard Library, Special Collections and Archives, Vanderbilt University, Nashville, TN

John F. Kennedy Presidential Library and Museum, Boston, MA

Kissinger Family Papers, New York, NY

Lafayette College, Special Collections and Archive, Easton, PA

Leo Baeck Institute, New York, NY

Library of Congress [LOC], Washington, DC

London School of Economics, London, UK

Lyndon B. Johnson Presidential Library, Austin, TX

Massachusetts Historical Society, Boston, MA

Miller Center of Public Affairs, University of Virginia, Charlottesville, VA

Museum of Jewish Heritage, New York, NY

National Archives, London, UK

National Archives and Records Administration, College Park, MD

National Security Archive, The George Washington University, Washington, DC

New York Public Library, New York, NY

Princeton University, Mudd Manuscript Library, Princeton, NJ

Richard Nixon Presidential Library and Museum, Yorba Linda, CA

Rockefeller Archive Center, Sleepy Hollow, NY

Staatsarchiv Nuremberg, Germany

Stadtarchiv Bensheim, Germany

Stadtarchiv Fürth, Germany
Stadtarchiv Krefeld, Germany
United Nations Archives and Records
Management, New York, NY
United States Army Military History
Institute, Carlisle, Barracks, PA

University of North Carolina, Special
Collections, Raleigh, NC
Webb School, Bell Buckle, TN
Yad Vashem, Jerusalem, Israel
Yale University Library, Manuscripts and
Archives, New Haven, CT

Secondary Sources

Aitken, Jonathan. *Nixon: A Life.*
Washington, DC: Regnery, 1993.

Allen, Gary. *Kissinger: The Secret Side of
the Secretary of State.* Seal Beach, CA:
'76 Press, 1976.

Allison, Graham, and Phillip Zelikow.
*Essence of Decision: Explaining the
Cuban Missile Crisis,* 2d ed. New York:
Addison Wesley Longman, 1999.

Ambrose, Stephen E. *Eisenhower.* Vol. 2,
The President. New York: Simon &
Schuster, 1984. Kindle ed.

———. *Nixon.* Vol. 1, *The Education of a
Politician, 1913–1962.* New York:
Touchstone Books, 1987.

———. *Nixon.* Vol. 2, *The Triumph of a
Politician, 1962–1972.* New York: Simon
& Schuster, 2014. Kindle ed.

Andrew, Christopher, and Vasili
Mitrokhin. *The Sword and the Shield:
The Mitrokhin Archive and the Secret
History of the KGB.* New York: Basic
Books, 2000.

———. *The World Was Going Our Way:
The KGB and the Battle for the Third
World.* New York: Basic Books, 2005.

Andrew, John. "Cracks in the Consensus:
The Rockefeller Brothers Fund
Special Studies Project and
Eisenhower's America." *Presidential
Studies Quarterly* 28, no. 3 (1998):
535–52.

Andrianopoulos, Gerry Argyris. *Kissinger
and Brzezinski: The NSC and the
Struggle for Control of U.S. National
Security Policy.* New York: St. Martin's
Press, 1991.

Anon. "The Dragon of Fürth." *Western
Folklore* 7, no. 2 (1948): 192f.

Anon. *Gedenkbuch: Opfer der Verfolgung der
Juden unter der nationalsozialistischen

Gewaltherrschaft in Deutschland,
1933–1945.* Coblenz, 1986.

Anon. *Gold Coaster.* Published During the
War by the Members of Adams
House. Cambridge, MA, 1944.

Anon., eds. *William Yandell Elliott.*
Cambridge, MA: Samuel Marcus
Press, 1963.

Anschütz, Janet, and Irmtraud Heike.
*"Wir wollten Gefühle sichtbar werden
lassen": Bürger gestalten ein Mahnmal für
das KZ Ahlem.* Bremen: Edition
Temmen, 2004.

Appelius, Claudia. *"Die schönste Stadt
der Welt": Deutsch-jüdische Flüchtlinge
in New York.* Essen: Klartext,
2003.

Applebaum, Anne. *Iron Curtain: The
Crushing of Eastern Europe, 1944–1956.*
London: Allen Lane, 2012.

Aristophanes. *Peace.* Translated by Jeffrey
Henderson. Cambridge, MA: Loeb
Classical Library, 1998.

Atkinson, David C. *In Theory and in
Practice: Harvard's Center for
International Affairs, 1958–1983.*
Cambridge, MA: Harvard University
Press, 2007.

Aubrac, Raymond. *Où la mémoire
s'attarde.* Paris: Editions Odile Jacob,
1996.

Ausland, John C., and Hugh F.
Richardson. "Crisis Management:
Berlin, Cyprus, Laos." *Foreign Affairs*
44, no. 2 (1996): 291–303.

Backer, John H. *Priming the German
Economy: American Occupational Policies,
1945–1948.* Durham, NC: Duke
University Press, 1971.

Baedeker, Karl. *Österreich, Sud- und West-
Deutschland: Handbuch für Reisende.*

1868; reprint, Charleston, SC: Nabu Press, 2012.

Ball, George W. *Memoirs: The Past Has Another Pattern.* New York: W. W. Norton, 1973.

Barbeck, Hugo. *Geschichte der Juden in Nürnberg und Fürth.* Nuremberg: F. Heerdegen, 1878.

Barrett, David. *Uncertain Warriors: Lyndon Johnson and His Vietnam Advisers.* Lawrence: University Press of Kansas, 1993.

Bass, Gary. *The Blood Telegram: Nixon, Kissinger, and a Forgotten Genocide.* New York: Random House, 2014.

Bator, Francis M. "No Good Choices: LBJ and the Vietnam/Great Society Connection." Cambridge, MA: American Academy of Arts and Sciences, 2007.

Baynes, N. H., ed. *The Speeches of Adolf Hitler.* London: Oxford University Press, 1942.

Bayor, Ronald H. *Neighbors in Conflict: The Irish, Germans, Jews, and Italians of New York City, 1929–1941.* Urbana: University of Illinois Press, 1988.

Beck, Kent M. "Necessary Lies, Hidden Truths: Cuba in the 1960 Campaign." *Diplomatic History* 8 (1984): 37–59.

Beevor, Antony. *The Second World War.* London: Weidenfeld and Nicolson, 2002.

Bell, Arthur George, and Mrs. Arthur G. Bell. *Nuremberg.* London: Adam and Charles Black, 1905.

Bell, Coral. "Kissinger in Retrospect: The Diplomacy of Power-Concert." *International Affairs* 53, no. 2 (1977): 202–16.

Bentinck-Smith, William, ed. *The Harvard Book: Selections from Three Centuries.* Cambridge, MA: Harvard University Press, 1982.

Bergemann, Hans, and Simone Ladwig-Winters. *Richter und Staatsanwälte jüdischer Herkunft in Preußen im Nationalsozialismus.* Cologne: Bundesanzeiger Verlag, 2004.

Berlin, Isaiah. *Against the Current: Essays in the History of Ideas.* London: Pimlico, 1979.

———. *Letters.* Vol. 1, *1928–1946.* Edited by Henry Hardy. Cambridge: Cambridge University Press, 2004.

Berman, Larry. *No Peace, No Honor: Nixon, Kissinger, and Betrayal in Vietnam.* New York: Simon & Schuster, 2002.

———. *Planning a Tragedy: The Americanization of the War in Vietnam.* New York: W. W. Norton, 1984.

Beschloss, Michael R. *Taking Charge: The Johnson White House Tapes, 1963–1964.* New York: Touchstone Books, 1997.

Bew, John. *Castlereagh.* London: Quercus Books, 2011.

Bibby, Michael. *Hearts and Minds: Bodies, Poetry, and Resistance in the Vietnam Era.* New Brunswick, NJ: Rutgers University Press, 1996.

Bird, Kai. *The Color of Truth: McGeorge Bundy and William Bundy, Brothers in Arms.* New York: Simon & Schuster, 1998.

Birke, Ernest. "A World Restored." *Historische Zeitschrift* 198, no. 1 (1964): 238f.

Bittman, Ladislav. *The Deception Game.* New York: Ballantine Books, 1981.

Black, Conrad. *Richard Milhous Nixon: The Invincible Quest.* London: Quercus Books, 2007.

Blight, James G., and Janet M. Lang. *Virtual JFK: Vietnam If Kennedy Had Lived.* Lanham, MD: Rowman and Littlefield, 2009.

Bloch, Eric, Martin Marx, and Hugo Stransky, eds. *Festschrift in Honor of the 36th Anniversary of Congregation Beth Hillel of Washington Heights, New York, New York, 1940–1976.* New York: Congregation of Beth Hillel, 1976.

Blumenfeld, Ralph. *Henry Kissinger: The Private and Public Story.* New York: New American Library, 1974.

Bommers, Dieter. "Das Kriegsende und der politische und wirtschaftliche

Wiederaufbau in der Stadt Krefeld 1945–1948." Unpublished ms., n.d.

Boswell, James. *The Life of Samuel Johnson, LL.D.* 1791; reprint, Oxford: Oxford University Press, 1980.

Bowie, Robert. "Strategy and the Atlantic Alliance." *International Organization* 17, no. 3 (1963): 709–32.

———. "Tensions Within the Alliance— Atlantic Policy." *Foreign Affairs* (Oct. 1963): 49–69.

Bowie, Robert R., and Richard H. Immerman. *Waging Peace: How Eisenhower Shaped an Enduring Cold War Strategy.* New York: Oxford University Press, 1998.

Bowie, Robert R., and Henry A. Kissinger. *The Program of the Center for International Affairs.* Cambridge, MA: Harvard University Press, 1958.

Braun, Reiner. *Joseph Rotblat: Visionary for Peace.* New York: John Wiley, 2007.

Breuer, Joseph. *Introduction to Rabbi Samson Raphael Hirsch's Commentary on the Torah.* 2 vols. New York: Philipp Feldheim, 1948.

———. *The Jewish Marriage: Source of Sanctity.* New York: Philipp Feldheim, 1956.

Breuer, Mordechai. *Modernity Within Tradition: The Social History of Orthodox Jewry in Imperial Germany.* New York: Columbia University Press, 1992.

Brigham, Robert K. *Guerrilla Diplomacy: The NLF's Foreign Relations and the Viet Nam War.* Ithaca, NY: Cornell University Press, 1999.

———. "Vietnamese-American Peace Negotiations: The Failed 1965 Initiatives." *Journal of American–East Asian Relations* 4, no. 4 (1995): 377–95.

Brinkley, Alan. *John F. Kennedy: The American Presidents Series: The 35th President, 1961–1963.* New York: Henry Holt, 2012.

Brodie, Bernard. "More About Limited War." *World Politics* 10, no. 1 (1957): 112–22.

———. "Nuclear Weapons and Foreign Policy." *Scientific Monthly* 85, no. 4 (Oct. 1957): 206f.

———. "Nuclear Weapons: Strategic or Tactical?" *Foreign Affairs* 32, no. 2 (1954): 217–29.

Brown, Andrew. *Keeper of the Nuclear Conscience: The Life and Work of Joseph Rotblat.* Oxford: Oxford University Press, 2012.

Brown, Lord George. *In My Way.* Harmondsworth, UK: Penguin Books, 1972.

Buckley, William F. *United Nations Journal: A Delegate's Odyssey.* New York: Putnam, 1974.

Bundy, William. *A Tangled Web: The Making of Foreign Policy in the Nixon Presidency.* New York: Hill and Wang, 1998.

Burleigh, Michael. *Moral Combat: A History of World War II.* New York: HarperCollins, 2011.

Butcher, Sandra Ionno. "Questions About the Nature of Transfer in Track Two: The Pugwash Experience During the Cold War." Unpublished paper, 2014.

Camus, Albert. *Le Mythe de Sisyphe.* Paris: Gallimard, 1942.

Caro, Robert A. *The Years of Lyndon Johnson.* Vol. 3, *Master of the Senate.* New York: Vintage, 2003.

———. *The Years of Lyndon Johnson.* Vol. 4, *The Passage of Power.* New York: Knopf Doubleday, 2012. Kindle ed.

Chernus, Ira. "Eisenhower: Turning Himself Toward Peace." *Peace and Change* 24, no. 1 (1999): 48–75.

Chomsky, Noam. "The Cold War and the University." In *The Cold War and the University: Toward an Intellectual History of the Postwar Years,* edited by Noam Chomsky et al. New York: New Press, 1998.

———. *World Orders, Old and New.* New York: Columbia University Press, 1996.

Chopra, Hardev Singh. *De Gaulle and European Unity*. New Delhi: Abhinav Publications, 1974.

Clausewitz, Carl von. *On War*. Translated by Michael Howard and Peter Paret. Edited by Beatrice Hauser. Oxford: Oxford University Press, 2007.

Clifford, Clark, with Richard Holbrooke. *Counsel to the President: A Memoir*. New York: Random House, 1991.

Collier, Peter, and David Horowitz. *The Rockefellers: An American Dynasty*. New York: Holt, Rinehart and Winston, 1976.

Collingwood, R. G. *My Autobiography*. Oxford: Oxford University Press, 1939.

Colodny, Len, and Tom Shachtman. *The Forty Years War: The Rise and Fall of the Neocons, from Nixon to Obama*. New York: HarperCollins, 2009.

Converse, Philip E., Warren E. Miller, Jerrold G. Rusk, and Arthur C. Wolfe. "Continuity and Change in American Politics: Parties and Issues in the 1968 Election." *American Political Science Review* 63, no. 4 (1969): 1083–105.

Courtois, Stéphane, Nicolas Werth, Jean-Louis Panné, Andrzej Paczkowski, Karel Bartošek, and Jean-Louis Margolin. *The Black Book of Communism: Crimes, Terror, Repression*. Translated by Jonathan Murphy and Mark Kramer. Cambridge, MA: Harvard University Press, 1999.

Craig, Campbell. *Destroying the Village: Eisenhower and Thermonuclear War*. New York: Columbia University Press, 1998.

Critchlow, Donald T. *The Conservative Ascendancy: How the Republican Right Rose to Power in Modern America*. Lawrence: University Press of Kansas, 2011.

Cuddy, Edward. "Vietnam: Mr. Johnson's War—or Mr. Eisenhower's?" *Review of Politics* 65, no. 4 (2003): 351–74.

Cull, Nicholas J. *The Cold War and the United States Information Agency: American Propaganda and Public Diplomacy, 1945–1989*. New York: Cambridge University Press, 2008.

Curley, Edwin. "Kissinger, Spinoza and Genghis Khan." In *The Cambridge Companion to Spinoza*, edited by Don Garrett. Cambridge: Cambridge University Press, 1995.

Daalder, Ivo H., and I. M. Destler. *In the Shadow of the Oval Office: Profiles of the National Security Advisers and the Presidents They Served—from JFK to George W. Bush*. New York: Simon & Schuster, 2009.

Dallek, Robert. *Flawed Giant: Lyndon Johnson and His Times, 1961–1973*. New York: Oxford University Press, 1998.

———. *Nixon and Kissinger: Partners in Power*. New York: HarperCollins, 2007.

Day, James. *The Vanishing Vision: The Inside Story of Public Television*. Berkeley: University of California Press, 1995.

Destler, I. M. *Presidents, Bureaucrats, and Foreign Policy: The Politics of Organizational Reform*. Princeton, NJ: Princeton University Press, 1974.

DeVoto, Bernard. *The Hour: A Cocktail Manifesto*. Boston: Houghton Mifflin, 1951.

Diamond, Sigmund. *Compromised Campus: The Collaboration of Universities with the Intelligence Community, 1945–1955*. New York: Oxford University Press, 1992.

Dickson, Peter W. *Kissinger and the Meaning of History*. New York: Cambridge University Press, 1978.

Dictionary of American Biography. Supplement 10, *1976–1980*. New York: Scribner, 1995.

Diem, Bui, and David Chanoff. *In the Jaws of History*. Bloomington: Indiana University Press, 1999.

Dikötter, Frank. *Mao's Great Famine: The History of China's Most Devastating Catastrophe, 1958–1962*. New York: Walker and Co., 2010.

————. *The Tragedy of Liberation: A History of the Chinese Revolution, 1945–1957*. London: Bloomsbury, 2013.

Dobrynin, Anatoly. *In Confidence: Moscow's Ambassador to America's Six Cold War Presidents*. Edited by Lawrence Malkin. New York: Times Books/Random House, 1995.

Donovan, Robert J. *Confidential Secretary: Ann Whitman's 20 Years with Eisenhower and Rockefeller*. New York: Dutton, 1988.

Draper, Theodore. *The 84th Infantry Division in the Battle of Germany, November 1944–May 1945*. New York: Viking Press, 1946.

Drucker, Peter F. *Adventures of a Bystander*. Piscataway, NJ: Transaction Publishers, 1994.

Dryzek, John S. "Revolutions Without Enemies: Key Transformations in Political Science." *American Political Science Review* 100, no. 4 (2006): 487–92.

Duffy, Geraldine Gavan. "The Third Century of the Passion Play at Oberammergau." *Irish Monthly* 28, no. 329 (1900): 667–70.

Eaton, Walter Prichard. "Here's to the Harvard Accent." In *The Harvard Book: Selections from Three Centuries*, edited by William Bentinck-Smith. Cambridge, MA: Harvard University Press, 1982.

Edwards, Donald A. *A Private's Diary*. Big Rapids, MI: privately published, 1994.

Eldridge, A. "The Crisis of Authority: The President, Kissinger and Congress (1969–1974)." Paper presented at the International Studies Association annual meeting, Toronto, 1976.

Elliott, William Yandell. *Mobilization Planning and the National Security, 1950–1960: Problems and Issues*. Washington, DC: Government Printing Office, 1950.

————. *The Need for Constitutional Reform: A Program for National Security*. New York: McGraw-Hill, 1935.

————. *The New British Empire*. New York: McGraw-Hill, 1932.

————. *The Pragmatic Revolt in Politics: Syndicalism, Fascism, and the Constitutional State*. New York: Macmillan, 1928.

————. "Proposal for a North Atlantic Round Table for Freedom." *Orbis* 2, no. 2 (Summer 1958): 222–28.

————. "Prospects for Personal Freedom and Happiness for All Mankind." *Annals of the American Academy of Political and Social Science* 268 (Mar. 1950).

————. "A Time for Peace?" *Virginia Quarterly Review* 22, no. 2 (1946): 174ff.

————. *United States Foreign Policy: Its Organization and Control*. New York: Columbia University Press, 1952.

Elliott, William Yandell, and Duncan H. Hall. *The British Commonwealth at War*. New York: Alfred A. Knopf, 1943.

Elliott, William Yandell, and Neil A. McDonald. *Western Political Heritage*. New York: Prentice-Hall, 1955.

Elliott, William Yandell, et al. *The Political Economy of American Foreign Policy: Its Concepts, Strategy, and Limits*. New York: Henry Holt, 1955.

Elliott, William Yandell, and Study Group for the Woodrow Wilson Foundation. *United States Foreign Policy: Its Organization and Control*. New York: Columbia University Press, 1952.

Ellis, John. *The World War II Databook*. London: Aurum Press, 1993.

Elsässer, Brigitte. "Kissinger in Krefeld und Bensheim." *Deutsch-amerikanischer Almanach: Henry Kissinger* 1 (1994): 15–35.

Epstein, Michael. *Oblivious in Washington Heights and Loving It*. Bloomington, IN: AuthorHouse, 2007.

Eschen, Penny M. von. *Satchmo Blows Up the World: Jazz Ambassadors Play the Cold War*. Cambridge, MA: Harvard University Press, 2004.

Evans, Robert. *The Kid Stays in the Picture: A Notorious Life*. New York: HarperCollins, 2013.

Falk, Richard A. "What's Wrong with Henry Kissinger's Foreign Policy?" *Alternatives: Global, Local, Political* 1, no. 1 (1975): 79–100.

Falk, Stanley L. "The National Security Council Under Truman, Eisenhower, and Kennedy." *Political Science Quarterly* 79, no. 3 (1964): 403–34.

Fallaci, Oriana. "Kissinger." In *Interview with History*. Translated by John Shepley. New York: Liveright, 1976.

Fass, Paula S. *Outside In: Minorities and the Transformation of American Education*. Oxford: Oxford University Press, 1991.

Feder, Leslie Margaret. "The Jewish Threat to the Brahmin Ideal at Harvard in the Early Twentieth Century." Honors essay, Radcliffe College, 1981.

Feeney, Mark. *Nixon at the Movies: A Book About Belief*. Chicago: University of Chicago Press, 2012.

Ferguson, Niall. *The Cash Nexus: Money and Power in the Modern World, 1700–2000*. New York: Basic Books, 2001.

———. *Colossus: The Rise and Fall of the American Empire*. New York: Penguin Press, 2004.

———. "Crisis, What Crisis? The 1970s and the Shock of the Global." In *The Shock of the Global: The 1970s in Perspective,* edited by Niall Ferguson, Charles S. Maier, Erez Manela, and Daniel J. Sargent. Cambridge, MA: Belknap Press, 2010.

———. *High Financier: The Lives and Time of Siegmund Warburg*. London: Allen Lane, 2010.

———, ed. *Virtual History: Alternatives and Counterfactuals*. London: Macmillan, 1995.

———. *The War of the World: Twentieth-Century Conflict and the Descent of the West*. New York: Penguin Press, 2006.

Ferrell, R. H., ed. *The Eisenhower Diaries*. New York: W. W. Norton, 1981.

Ferziger, Adam S. *Exclusion and Hierarchy: Orthodoxy, Nonobservance, and the Emergence of Modern Jewish Identity*. Philadelphia: University of Pennsylvania Press, 2005.

Finletter, Thomas K. *Power and Policy: U.S. Foreign Policy and Military Power in the Hydrogen Age*. New York: Harcourt Brace, 1954.

Fish, M. Steven. "After Stalin's Death: The Anglo-American Debate Over a New Cold War." *Diplomatic History* 10 (1986): 333–55.

Fitzgerald, Frances. *Fire in the Lake: The Vietnamese and Americans in Vietnam*. Boston: Back Bay Books/Little, Brown, 2002.

Frank, Jeffrey. *Ike and Dick: Portrait of a Strange Political Marriage*. New York: Simon & Schuster, 2013.

Franklin, Joshua. "Victim Soldiers: German-Jewish Refugees in the Armed Forces During World War II." Honors thesis, Clark University, 2006.

Freedman, Lawrence. *Kennedy's War: Berlin, Cuba, Laos, and Vietnam*. New York: Oxford University Press, 2000.

Frey, Marc. "Tools of Empire: Persuasion and the United States' Modernizing Mission in Southeast Asia." *Diplomatic History* 27, no. 4 (2003): 543–68.

Friedrich, Carl. *The New Image of the Common Man*. Boston: Beacon Press, 1950.

Fritz, Stephen G. *Endkampf: Soldiers, Civilians, and the Death of the Third Reich*. Lexington: University Press of Kentucky, 2004.

Fröbe, Rainer, et al., eds. *Konzentrationslager in Hannover: KZ-Arbeit und Rüstungsindustrie in der Spätphase des Zweiten Weltkrieges*. 2 vols. Hildesheim: Verlag August Lax, 1985.

Fukuyama, Francis. "A World Restored." *Foreign Affairs* 76, no. 5 (1997): 216.

Fursenko, Aleksandr, and Timothy Naftali. *Khrushchev's Cold War: The*

Inside Story of an American Adversary. New York: W. W. Norton, 2006.

Fussell, Paul. *The Boys' Crusade: The American Infantry in Northwestern Europe, 1944–1945.* New York: Modern Library, 2003.

Gaddis, John Lewis. *The Cold War: A New History.* New York: Penguin Press, 2006.

———. *George F. Kennan: An American Life.* New York: Penguin Press, 2011.

———. "The Long Peace: Elements of Stability in the Postwar International System." In *The Cold War and After: Prospects for Peace,* edited by Sean M. Lynn-Jones and Steven E. Miller. Cambridge, MA: MIT Press, 1993.

———. *Strategies of Containment: A Critical Appraisal of American National Security During the Cold War.* New York: Oxford University Press, 2005.

———. *We Now Know: Rethinking Cold War History.* New York: Oxford University Press, 1997.

Gaiduk, Ilya V. "Peacemaking or Troubleshooting? The Soviet Role in Peace Initiatives During the Vietnam War." In *The Search for Peace in Vietnam, 1964–1968,* edited by Lloyd C. Gardner and Ted Gittinger. College Station: Texas A&M University Press, 2004.

Gardner, Lloyd C. *Pay Any Price: Lyndon Johnson and the Wars for Vietnam.* Chicago: Ivan R. Dee, 1995.

Gardner, Lloyd C., and Ted Gittinger, eds. *International Perspectives on Vietnam.* College Station: Texas A&M University Press, 2000.

———, eds. *The Search for Peace in Vietnam, 1964–1968.* College Station: Texas A&M University Press, 2004. Kindle ed.

Garrett, Don, ed. *The Cambridge Companion to Spinoza.* Cambridge: Cambridge University Press, 1995.

Garrow, David J. "The FBI and Martin Luther King." *Atlantic,* July 1, 2002.

Garthoff, Raymond L. *Détente and Confrontation: American-Soviet Relations from Nixon to Reagan.* Washington, DC: Brookings Institution, 1985.

Gati, Charles, ed. *Zbig: The Strategy and Statecraft of Zbigniew Brzezinski.* Baltimore: Johns Hopkins University Press, 2013. Kindle ed.

Gavin, Francis J. *Nuclear Statecraft: History and Strategy in America's Atomic Age.* Ithaca, NY: Cornell University Press, 2012.

Gettleman, Marvin E., Jane Franklin, Marilyn B. Young, and H. Bruce Franklin, eds. *Vietnam and America: A Documented History.* New York: Grove Press, 1995.

Gibbons, William C. *The U.S. Government and the Vietnam War: Executive and Legislative Roles and Relationships. Part 4, July 1965–January 1968.* Princeton, NJ: Princeton University Press, 1995.

Giglio, James N. *The Presidency of John F. Kennedy.* Lawrence: University Press of Kansas, 1991.

Gilbert, Marc Jason, and William Head, eds. *The Tet Offensive.* Westport, CT: Praeger, 1996.

Goldstein, Gordon M. *Lessons in Disaster: McGeorge Bundy and the Path to War in Vietnam.* New York: Henry Holt, 2008.

Grailet, Lambert. *Il y a 55 ans . . . avec Henry Kissinger en Ardenne.* Liège: SI, 1999.

Graubard, Stephen R. *Kissinger: Portrait of a Mind.* New York: W. W. Norton, 1974.

Greene, Benjamin P. "Eisenhower, Science and the Nuclear Test Ban Debate, 1953–56." *Journal of Strategic Studies* 26, no. 4 (2003): 156–85.

Greene, Graham. *The Quiet American,* 1955; reprint London: Vintage, 2001.

Greenspan, Alan. *The Age of Turbulence: Adventures in a New World.* New York: Penguin Press, 2008.

Gregor, Neil. "A Schicksalsgemeinschaft? Allied Bombing, Civilian Morale, and Social Dissolution in Nuremberg,

1942–1945." *Historical Journal* 43, no. 4 (2000): 1051–70.

Grose, Peter. *Continuing the Inquiry: The Council on Foreign Relations from 1921 to 1996.* New York: Council on Foreign Relations, 1996.

———. *Gentleman Spy: The Life of Allen Dulles.* Amherst: University of Massachusetts Press, 1985.

Guan, Ang Cheng. *Ending the Vietnam War: The Vietnamese Communists' Perspective.* London: RoutledgeCurzon, 2005. Kindle ed.

———. "The Vietnam War from Both Sides: Revisiting 'Marigold,' 'Sunflower' and 'Pennsylvania.'" *War and Society* 24, no. 2 (2005): 93–125.

———. *The Vietnam War from the Other Side: The Vietnamese Communists' Perspective.* Abingdon, UK: RoutledgeCurzon, 2002.

Gunnell, John G. "Political Science on the Cusp: Recovering a Discipline's Past." *American Political Science Review* 99, no. 4 (2005): 597–609.

———. "The Real Revolution in Political Science." *PS: Political Science and Politics* 27, no. 1 (2004): 47–50.

Gutmann, Christoph. "KZ Ahlem: Eine unterirdische Fabrik entsteht." In *Konzentrationslager in Hannover: KZ-Arbeit und Rüstungsindustrie in der Spätphase des Zweiten Weltkrieges,* edited by Rainer Fröbe et al., vol. 1, 331–406. Hildesheim: Verlag August Lax, 1985.

Halberstam, David. *The Best and the Brightest.* New York: Ballantine Books, 1993.

Haldeman, H. R. *The Haldeman Diaries: Inside the Nixon White House.* Edited by Stephen E. Ambrose. New York: Putnam, 1994.

Halperin, Morton. "The Gaither Committee and the Policy Process." *World Politics* 1, no. 3 (1961): 360–84.

Hangebruch, Dieter. "Emigriert—Deportiert: Das Schicksal der Juden in Krefeld zwischen 1933 und 1945." In *Krefelder Juden,* edited by Guido

Rotthoff, Bonn: Röhrscheid, 1981, 137–215.

Hanyok, Robert. "Skunks, Bogies, Silent Hounds, and the Flying Fish: The Gulf of Tonkin Mystery, 2–4 August 1964." *Cryptological Quarterly* (2000–2001): 1–55.

Hargittai, Istvan. *Buried Glory: Portraits of Soviet Scientists.* Oxford: Oxford University Press, 2012.

Harley, John Eugene. *International Understanding: Agencies Educating for a New World.* Palo Alto, CA: Stanford University Press, 1931.

Harris, Katherine Clark. "A Footnote to History? William Yandell Elliott: From the War Production Board to the Cold War." Honors essay, Harvard University, 2009.

Harrison, Benjamin T., and Christopher L. Mosher. "John T. McNaughton and Vietnam: The Early Years as Assistant Secretary of Defense, 1964–1965." *History* 92, no. 308 (2007): 496–514.

———. "The Secret Diary of McNamara's Dove: The Long-Lost Story of John T. McNaughton's Opposition to the Vietnam War." *Diplomatic History* 35, no. 3 (2011): 505–34.

Hart, Basil Liddell. *The Revolution in Warfare.* New Haven, CT: Yale University Press, 1947.

———. "War, Limited." *Harper's Magazine* 12, no. 1150 (Mar. 1946): 193–203.

Haslam, Jonathan. *The Nixon Administration and the Death of Allende's Chile: A Case of Assisted Suicide.* London: Verso, 2005.

Hastings, Max. *All Hell Let Loose: The World at War, 1939–1945.* London: HarperPress, 2011.

Heaps, Willard A. "Oberammergau Today." *Christianity Century* 63 (1946): 1468–69.

Heffer, Simon. *Like the Roman: The Life of Enoch Powell.* London: Faber and Faber, 2008.

Heller, Joseph. *Good as Gold.* 1979; reprint, New York: Simon & Schuster, 1997.

Hellige, Hans Dieter. "Generationskonflikt, Selbsthaß und die Entstehung antikapitalistischer Positionen im Judentum. Der Einfluß des Antisemitismus auf das Sozialverhalten jüdischer Kaufmanns- und Unternehmersöhne im deutschen Kaiserreich und in der k.u.k.-Monarchie." In *Geschichte und Gesellschaft* 5, no. 4: *Antisemitismus und Judentum* (1979): 476–518.

Herr, Michael. *Dispatches.* London: Picador, 2015. Kindle ed.

Herring, George C. *LBJ and Vietnam: A Different Kind of War.* Austin: University of Texas Press, 2010.

———, ed. *The Secret Diplomacy of the Vietnam War: The Negotiating Volumes of the Pentagon Papers.* Austin: University of Texas Press, 1983.

Hersh, Seymour M. *The Price of Power: Kissinger in the Nixon White House.* New York: Summit Books, 1983.

Hershberg, James Gordon. "Who Murdered Marigold? New Evidence on the Mysterious Failure of Poland's Secret Initiative to Start U.S.–North Vietnamese Peace Talks, 1966." Woodrow Wilson International Center for Scholars Working Paper no. 27 (2000).

Higgins, Trumbull. *The Perfect Failure: Kennedy, Eisenhower, and the CIA at the Bay of Pigs.* New York: W. W. Norton, 1987.

Hitchens, Christopher. *The Trial of Henry Kissinger.* New York: Verso, 2001. Kindle ed.

Hixon, Walter L. *Parting the Iron Curtain: Propaganda, Culture, and the Cold War, 1945–1961.* New York: St. Martin's Press Griffin, 1998.

Hoffmann, Hubertus, ed. *Fritz Kraemer on Excellence: Missionary, Mentor and Pentagon Strategist.* New York: World Security Network Foundation, 2004.

Hofmann, Arne. *The Emergence of Détente in Europe: Brandt, Kennedy and the Formation of Ostpolitik.* London: Routledge, 2007.

Hoopes, Townsend. *The Limits of Intervention: An Inside Account of How the Johnson Policy of Escalation in Vietnam Was Reversed.* Philadelphia: D. McKay Co., 1969.

Horowitz, C. Morris, and Lawrence J. Kaplan. "The Estimated Jewish Population of the New York Area, 1900–1975." Demographic Study Committee of the Federation of Jewish Philanthropies, ms., New York, 1959.

Hughes, Ken. *Chasing Shadows: The Nixon Tapes, the Chennault Affair, and the Origins of Watergate.* Charlottesville: University of Virginia Press, 2014. Kindle ed.

Humphrey, Hubert H. *The Education of a Public Man: My Life and Politics.* New York: Doubleday, 1976.

Idle, Eric. *The Greedy Bastard Diary: A Comic Tour of North America.* London: Orion, 2014. Kindle ed.

Isaacs, Arnold R. *Without Honor: Defeat in Vietnam and Cambodia.* Baltimore: Johns Hopkins University Press, 1983.

Isaacson, Walter. *Kissinger: A Biography.* New York: Simon & Schuster, 2005. Kindle ed.

Israel, Jonathan I. "Central European Jewry During the Thirty Years' War." *Central European History* 16, no. 1 (1983): 3–30.

Israelyan, Victor. *Inside the Kremlin During the Yom Kippur War.* University Park: Pennsylvania State University Press, 1995.

Jackson, Michael G. "Beyond Brinkmanship: Eisenhower, Nuclear War Fighting, and Korea, 1953–1968." *Presidential Studies Quarterly* 35, no. 1 (2005): 52–75.

Jacobs, Jack, and Douglas Century. *If Not Now, When?: Duty and Sacrifice in America's Time of Need.* New York: Berkley Caliber, 2008.

James, William. "The True Harvard." In *The Harvard Book: Selections from Three Centuries,* edited by William Bentinck-Smith. Cambridge, MA: Harvard University Press, 1982.

Jensen, Joan M. *Army Surveillance in America, 1775–1980.* New Haven, CT: Yale University Press, 1991.

Johnson, Eric A. *The Nazi Terror: The Gestapo, Jews and Ordinary Germans.* London: John Murray, 1999.

Johnson, Lyndon Baines. *The Vantage Point: Perspectives of the Presidency, 1963–1969.* New York: Holt, Rinehart and Winston, 1971.

Johnson, Robert David. *All the Way with LBJ: The 1964 Presidential Election.* New York: Cambridge University Press, 2009.

Kalb, Marvin, and Bernard Kalb. *Kissinger.* Boston: Little, Brown, 1974.

Kaplan, Robert D. "In Defense of Henry Kissinger." *Atlantic Monthly* (Apr. 2013): 70–78.

———. "Kissinger, Metternich, and Realism." *Atlantic Monthly* (June 1999): 72–82.

Karnow, Stanley. *Vietnam: A History.* New York: Viking, 1983.

Kasparek, Katrin. *The History of the Jews in Fürth: A Home for Centuries.* Nuremberg: Sandberg Verlag, 2010.

Katzenbach, Nicholas deB. *Some of It Was Fun: Working with RFK and LBJ.* New York: W. W. Norton, 2008.

Kaufmann, William W. "The Crisis in Military Affairs." *World Politics* 10, no. 4 (July 1958): 579–603.

Keefer, Louis E. *Scholars in Foxholes: The Story of the Army Specialized Training Program in World War II.* Jefferson, NC: McFarland, 1988.

Keever, Beverly Deepe. *Death Zones and Darling Spies: Seven Years of Vietnam War Reporting.* Lincoln: University of Nebraska Press, 2013.

Kempe, Frederick. *Berlin 1961: Kennedy, Khrushchev, and the Most Dangerous Place on Earth.* New York: Putnam, 2011.

Kennedy, David M. *Freedom from Fear: The American People in Depression and War, 1929–1945.* Oxford: Oxford University Press, 1999. Kindle ed.

Kennedy, Robert. *Thirteen Days: A Memoir of the Cuban Missile Crisis.* New York: W. W. Norton, 1999.

Kershaw, Ian. *The End: Hitler's Germany, 1944–45.* London: Allen Lane, 2011.

Kickum, Stephanie. "Die Strukturen der Militärregierungen in Krefeld der frühen Nachkriegszeit (1945/46)." *Die Heimat* 71 (2000): 107–12.

Kilmeade, Brian. *The Games Do Count: America's Best and Brightest on the Power of Sport.* New York: HarperCollins, 2004.

Kilthau, Fritz, and Peter Krämer. *3 Tage fehlten zur Freiheit: Die Nazimorde am Kirchberg Bensheim, März 1945.* Bensheim: Geschichtswerkstatt Jakob Kindinger, 2008.

Kissinger, Henry A. *American Foreign Policy: Three Essays.* New York: W. W. Norton, 1969.

———. "Arms Control, Inspection and Surprise Attack." *Foreign Affairs* 38, no. 4 (July 1960): 557–75.

———. "Coalition Diplomacy in a Nuclear Age." *Foreign Affairs* 42, no. 4 (July 1964): 525–45.

———. "The Congress of Vienna: A Reappraisal." *World Politics* 8, no. 2 (Jan. 1956): 264–80.

———. "The Conservative Dilemma: Reflections on the Political Thought of Metternich." *American Political Science Review* 48, no. 4 (Dec. 1954): 1017–30.

———. "Domestic Structure and Foreign Policy." *Daedalus* 95, no. 2 (1966): 503–29.

———. "Force and Diplomacy in the Nuclear Age." *Foreign Affairs* 34, no. 3 (1956): 349–66.

———. "The Illusionist: Why We Misread de Gaulle." *Harper's,* March 1965.

———. "Limited War: Conventional or Nuclear? A Reappraisal." *Daedalus* 89, no. 4 (1960): 800–817.

———. "The Meaning of History: Reflections on Spengler, Toynbee and Kant." Senior thesis, Harvard University, 1950.

———. "Military Policy and the Defense of the 'Grey Areas.'" *Foreign Affairs* 33, no. 3 (Apr. 1955): 416–28.

———. "Missiles and the Western Alliance." *Foreign Affairs* 36, no. 3 (1958): 383–400.

———. "Nato's Nuclear Dilemma." *Reporter* (Mar. 28, 1963): 22–33.

———. *The Necessity for Choice: Prospects of American Foreign Policy.* New York: Harper and Brothers, 1961.

———. "Nuclear Testing and the Problem of Peace." *Foreign Affairs* 37, no. 1 (Oct. 1958): 1–18.

———. *Nuclear Weapons and Foreign Policy.* New York: Harper and Brothers, 1957.

———. "Peace, Legitimacy, and the Equilibrium (A Study of the Statesmanship of Castlereagh and Metternich)." Ph.D. dissertation, Harvard University, 1954.

———. "The Prophet and the Policymaker." In *Fritz Kraemer on Excellence: Missionary, Mentor and Pentagon Strategist*, edited by Hubertus Hoffmann. New York: World Security Network, 2004.

———. "Reflections on American Diplomacy." *Foreign Affairs* 35, no. 1 (1956): 37–56.

———. "Reflections on Cuba." *Reporter* (Nov. 22, 1962): 21–24.

———. "The Search for Stability." *Foreign Affairs* 37, no. 4 (1959): 537–60.

———. "The Skybolt Affair." *Reporter* (Jan. 17, 1963): 15–18.

———. "Strains on the Alliance." *Foreign Affairs* 41, no. 2 (Jan. 1963): 261–85.

———. "Strategy and Organization." *Foreign Affairs* 35, no. 3 (Apr. 1957): 379–94.

———. *The Troubled Partnership: A Re-appraisal of the Atlantic Alliance.* New York: McGraw-Hill, 1965.

———. "The Unsolved Problems of European Defense." *Foreign Affairs* 40, no. 4 (July 1962): 515–41.

———. "The Viet Nam Negotiations." *Foreign Affairs* 11, no. 2 (1969): 38–50.

———. *White House Years.* Boston: Little, Brown, 1979.

———. "The White Revolutionary: Reflections on Bismarck." *Daedalus* 97, no. 3 (1968): 888–924.

———. *World Order.* New York: Penguin Press, 2014.

———. *A World Restored: Metternich, Castlereagh and the Problems of Peace, 1812–1822.* London: Weidenfeld & Nicolson, 1957. Kindle ed.

Kissinger, Henry A., and Bernard Brodie. "Bureaucracy, Politics and Strategy." Security Studies Paper no. 17. Los Angeles: University of California, 1968.

Kistiakowsky, George B. *A Scientist at the White House: The Private Diary of President Eisenhower's Special Assistant for Science and Technology.* Cambridge, MA: Harvard University Press, 1976.

Kolko, Gabriel, and Joyce Kolko. *The Limits of Power: The World and United States Foreign Policy, 1945–1954.* New York: Harper & Row, 1972.

Kornbluh, Peter. *The Pinochet File: A Declassified Dossier on Atrocity and Accountability.* New York: New Press, 2003.

Koudelka, Edward R. *Counter Intelligence, the Conflict, and the Conquest.* Guilderland, NY: Ranger Associates, 1986.

Kraemer, Fritz. "To Finish the Manuscript of the Historico-Juridical Reference Book on 'the Parliaments of Continental Europe from 1815 to 1914.'" *American Philosophical Society Year Book* (1942).

———. "U.S. Propaganda: What It Can and Can't Be." *Stanford Research Institute* 3 (1959): 151–59.

———. *Das Verhältnis der französischen Bündnisverträge zum Völkerbundpakt und zum Pakt von Locarno: Eine juristisch-politische Studie.* Leipzig: Universitätsverlag von Robert Noske, 1932.

Kraemer, Sven. "My Father's Pilgrimage." In *Fritz Kraemer on*

Excellence: Missionary, Mentor and Pentagon Strategist, edited by Hubertus Hoffmann. New York: World Security Network Foundation, 2004.

Kraft, Joseph. "In Search of Kissinger." *Harper's Magazine* (Jan. 1971).

Kraus, Marvin. "Assimilation, Authoritarianism, and Judaism: A Social-Psychological Study of Jews at Harvard." Honors essay, Harvard University, 1951.

Kremers, Elisabeth. *Lucky Strikes und Hamsterfahrten: Krefeld 1945–1948*. Gudensberg-Gleichen: Wartberg Verlag, 2004.

Kuklick, Bruce. *Blind Oracles: Intellectuals and War from Kennan to Kissinger*. Princeton, NJ: Princeton University Press, 2006.

Kunz, Diane. "Camelot Continued: What if John F. Kennedy Had Lived?" In *Virtual History: Alternatives and Counterfactuals,* edited by Niall Ferguson. London: Macmillan, 1995.

Kurz, Evi. *The Kissinger Saga: Walter and Henry Kissinger, Two Brothers from Fürth*. London: Weidenfeld and Nicolson, 2009.

Landau, David. *Kissinger: The Uses of Power: A Political Biography*. London: Robson Books, 1974.

Larsen, Jeffrey A., and Kerry M. Kartchner, eds. *On Limited Nuclear War in the 21st Century*. Palo Alto, CA: Stanford University Press, 2014.

Lasky, Victor. *It Didn't Start with Watergate*. New York: Dial Press, 1977.

Lax, Eric. *Woody Allen: A Biography*. Cambridge, MA: Da Capo Press, 1991.

Leary, William M., ed. *The Central Intelligence Agency: History and Documents*. Tuscaloosa: University of Alabama Press, 1984.

Leffler, Melvyn P. *For the Soul of Mankind: The United States, the Soviet Union, and the Cold War*. New York: Hill and Wang, 2007. Kindle ed.

Leffler, Melvyn P., and Odd Arne Westad, eds. *The Cambridge History of the Cold War.* Vol. 2, *Crises and Détente.* Cambridge: Cambridge University Press, 2012.

Lehman, John F. *Command of the Seas*. Annapolis, MD: Naval Institute Press, 2001.

Lendt, Lee E. *A Social History of Washington Heights, New York City*. New York: Columbia–Washington Heights Community Mental Health Project, 1960.

Leventmann, Seymour. "From Shtetl to Suburb." In *The Ghetto and Beyond,* edited by Peter I. Rose. New York: Random House, 1969.

Lewis, Jonathan F. *Spy Capitalism: Itek and the CIA*. New Haven, CT: Yale University Press, 2002.

Ley, Walter. "Die Heckmannschule." *Fürther Heimatblätter* 41 (1991): 65–74.

Lindsay, A. D. *The Philosophy of Immanuel Kant*. London: T. C. and E. C. Jack, 1919.

Lindsay, Franklin. *Beacons in the Night: With the OSS and Tito's Partisans in Wartime Yugoslavia*. Palo Alto, CA: Stanford University Press, 1993.

Link, Sandra. *Ein Realist mit Idealen: Der Völkerrechtler Karl Strupp (1886–1940)*. Baden-Baden: Nomos, 2003.

Lodge, Henry Cabot. *As It Was: An Inside View of Politics and Power in the '50s and '60s*. New York: W. W. Norton, 1976.

Logevall, Fredrik. *Choosing War: The Lost Chance for Peace and the Escalation of War in Vietnam*. Berkeley: University of California Press, 1999. Kindle ed.

———. "Lyndon Johnson and Vietnam." *Presidential Studies Quarterly* 34, no. 1 (2004): 100–112.

Loory, Stuart H., and David Kraslow. *The Secret Search for Peace in Vietnam*. New York: Random House, 1968.

Lowenstein, Steven M. *Frankfurt on the Hudson: The German-Jewish Community of Washington Heights, 1933–1983, Its Structure and Culture*. Detroit: Wayne State University Press, 1989.

Lucas, Scott. "Campaigns of Truth: The Psychological Strategy Board and

American Ideology, 1951–1953."
International History Review 18, no. 2
(1996): 279–302.

———. *Freedom's War: The American
Crusade Against the Soviet Union.*
New York: New York University
Press, 1999.

Lüders, Marie-Elisabeth. *Fürchte Dich
nicht: Persönliches und Politisches aus mehr
als 80 Jahren, 1878–1962.* Cologne:
Westdeutscher Verlag, 1963.

Luig, Klaus. . . . *weil er nicht arischer
Abstammung ist. Jüdische Juristen in Köln
während der NS-Zeit.* Cologne: Verlag
Dr. Otto Schmidt, 2004.

Lundestad, Geir. *The American "Empire"
and Other Studies of U.S. Foreign Policy
in a Comparative Perspective.* London:
Oxford University Press, 1990.

———. *The United States and Western
Europe Since 1945: From "Empire" by
Invitation to Transatlantic Drift.* Oxford:
Oxford University Press, 2003.

Lynn-Jones, Sean M., and Steven E.
Miller, eds. *The Cold War and After:
Prospects for Peace.* Cambridge, MA:
MIT Press, 1993.

Maaß, Rainer, and Manfred Berg, eds.
Bensheim: Spuren der Geschichte.
Weinheim: Edition Diesbach, 2006.

MacMillan, Margaret. *Nixon and Mao:
The Week That Changed the World.*
New York: Random House, 2007.

McNamara, Robert S. *Argument Without
End: In Search of Answers to the Vietnam
Tragedy.* New York: PublicAffairs, 1999.

McNamara, Robert S., and Brian
VanDeMark. *In Retrospect: The Tragedy
and Lessons of Vietnam.* New York:
Times Books, 1995.

Magdoff, Harry. *The Age of Imperialism:
The Economics of United States Foreign
Policy.* New York: Monthly Review
Press, 1969.

Mailer, Norman. *The Naked and the Dead.*
New York: Rinehart and Co., 1948.

Marnham, Patrick. *Resistance and Betrayal:
The Death and Life of the Greatest Hero
of the French Resistance.* New York:
Random House, 2000.

Marrs, Jim. *Rule by Secrecy: The Hidden
History That Connects the Trilateral
Commission, the Freemasons, and the
Great Pyramids.* New York:
HarperCollins, 2000.

Martin, L. W. "The Necessity for
Choice." *Political Science Quarterly* 76,
no. 3 (1961): 427–28.

Matson, Clifford H., Jr., and Elliott K.
Stein. *We Were the Line: A History of
Company G, 335th Infantry, 84th Infantry
Division.* Fort Wayne, IN: privately
published, 1946.

Matthews, Jeffrey J. "To Defeat a
Maverick: The Goldwater Candidacy
Revisited, 1963–1964." *Presidential
Studies Quarterly* 27, no. 4 (1997):
662–78.

Mauersberg, Hans. *Wirtschaft und
Gesellschaft Fürth in neuerer und neuester
Zeit.* Göttingen: Vandenhoeck und
Ruprecht, 1974.

Maxwell, A. J. "A World Restored."
World Affairs 120, no. 4 (1957): 123f.

May, Ernest R., ed. *American Cold War
Strategy: Interpreting NSC 68.* Boston:
Bedford Books of St. Martin's
Press, 1993.

May, Ernest R., and Philip D. Zelikow,
eds. *The Kennedy Tapes: Inside the
Cuban Missile Crisis.* Cambridge, MA:
Belknap Press, 2002.

Mazlish, Bruce. *Kissinger: The European
Mind in American Policy.* New York:
Basic Books, 1976.

Melchoir, Ib. *Case by Case: A U.S. Army
Counterintelligence Agent in World War
II.* Novato, CA: Presidio, 1993.

Menand, Louis. *The Metaphysical Club: A
Story of Ideas in America.* New York:
Farrar, Straus and Giroux, 2002.

Middendorf, J. William, II. *A Glorious
Disaster: Barry Goldwater's Presidential
Campaign and the Origins of the
Conservative Movement.* New York:
Basic Books, 2008. Kindle ed.

Mieczkowski, Yanek. *Eisenhower's Sputnik
Moment: The Race for Space and World
Prestige.* Ithaca, NY: Cornell
University Press, 2013.

Mierzejewski, Alfred C. *Ludwig Erhard: A Biography*. Chapel Hill: University of North Carolina Press, 2004.

Miller, Rory, ed. *Britain, Palestine and Empire: The Mandate Years*. Farnham, Surrey, UK: Ashgate, 2010.

Milne, David. *America's Rasputin: Walt Rostow and the Vietnam War*. New York: Hill and Wang, 2008.

———. "The 1968 Paris Peace Negotiations: A Two Level Game?" *Review of International Studies* 37, no. 2 (2010): 577–99.

———. "'Our Equivalent of Guerrilla Warfare': Walt Rostow and the Bombing of North Vietnam, 1961–1968." *Journal of Military History* 71 (2007): 169–203.

Mohan, Shannon E. "Memorandum for Mr. Bundy: Henry Kissinger as Consultant to the Kennedy National Security Council." *Historian* 71, no. 2 (2009): 234–57.

Moise, Edwin E. *Tonkin Gulf and the Escalation of the Vietnam War*. Chapel Hill: University of North Carolina Press, 1996.

Moore, Deborah Dash. *At Home in America: Second Generation New York Jews*. New York: Columbia University Press, 1981.

———. *GI Jews: How World War II Changed a Generation*. Cambridge, MA: Harvard University Press, 2004.

Morgenthau, Hans J. "Henry Kissinger: Secretary of State." *Encounter* (Nov. 1974): 57–60.

———. "Nuclear Weapons and Foreign Policy." *American Political Science Review* 52, no. 3 (Sept. 1958): 842–44.

Morison, Samuel Eliot. *Three Centuries of Harvard, 1636–1936*. Cambridge, MA: Belknap Press, 1936.

Morris, Roger. *Uncertain Greatness: Henry Kissinger and American Foreign Policy*. New York: Harper & Row, 1977.

Moynihan, Daniel Patrick. *A Dangerous Place*. Boston: Little, Brown, 1975.

Mümmler, Manfred. *Fürth: 1933–1945*. Emskirchen: Verlag Maria Mümmler, 1995.

Naftali, Timothy, and Philip Zelikow, eds. *The Presidential Recordings: John F. Kennedy*. New York: W. W. Norton, 2001.

Nashel, Jonathan. *Edward Lansdale's Cold War*. Amherst: University of Massachusetts Press, 2005.

Nelson, Anna K. "President Kennedy's National Security Policy: A Reconsideration." *Reviews in American History* 19, no. 1 (1991): 1–14.

Nitze, Paul H. "Atoms, Strategy, and Policy." *Foreign Affairs* 34, no. 2 (1956): 187–98.

———. "Limited War or Massive Retaliation?" *Reporter* (Sept. 5, 1957): 40–42.

Nixon, Richard M. "Asia After Viet Nam." *Foreign Affairs* 46, no. 1 (Oct. 1967): 111–25.

———. *RN: The Memoirs of Richard Nixon*. New York: Simon & Schuster, 1992. Kindle ed.

Ophir, Baruch Z., and Falk Wiesemann, eds. *Die jüdischen Gemeinden in Bayern 1918–1945: Geschichte und Zerstörung*. Munich: R. Oldenbourg, 1979.

Oppen, Beate Ruhm von, ed. *Documents on Germany Under Occupation, 1945–1954*. Oxford: Oxford University Press, 1955.

Osgood, Kenneth. *Total Cold War: Eisenhower's Secret Propaganda Battle at Home and Abroad*. Lawrence: University Press of Kansas, 2006.

Osgood, Robert E. *Ideals and Self-Interest in America's Foreign Relations: The Great Transformation of the Twentieth Century*. Chicago: University of Chicago Press, 1953.

———. *Limited War: The Challenge to American Strategy*. Chicago: University of Chicago Press, 1957.

Padover, Saul K. *Experiment in Germany: The Story of an American Intelligence Officer*. New York: Duell, Sloan and Pearce, 1946.

Parry-Giles, S. J. "Dwight D. Eisenhower, 'Atoms for Peace'

(8 December 1953)." *Voices of Democracy* 1 (2006): 118–29.

Paterson, Pat. "The Truth About Tonkin." *Naval History* (Feb. 2008).

Paterson, Thomas G., and William J. Brophy. "October Missiles and November Elections: The Cuban Missile Crisis and American Politics, 1962." *Journal of American History* 1, no. 73 (1986): 87–119.

Patrick, Mark S. "The Berlin Crisis in 1961: U.S. Intelligence Analysis and the Presidential Decision Making Process." Master's thesis, Tufts University, 1997.

Paul, Gerhard, and Klaus-Michael Mallmann. *Die Gestapo: Mythos und Realität.* Darmstadt: Primus Verlag, 1996.

Pei, Minxin. "Lessons from the Past." *Foreign Policy* 52 (July 2003): 52–55.

Persico, Joseph E. *The Imperial Rockefeller: A Biography of Nelson A. Rockefeller.* New York: Washington Square Press, 1982.

Peters, Charles. *Lyndon B. Johnson. The American Presidents Series: The 36th President.* New York: Henry Holt/ Times Books, 2010.

Pisani, Sallie. *The CIA and the Marshall Plan.* Lawrence: University Press of Kansas, 1991.

Piszkiewicz, Dennis. *The Nazi Rocketeers: Dreams of Space and Crimes of War.* Westport, CT: Praeger, 1995.

Pocock, Tom. *Alan Moorehead.* London: Vintage Books, 2011.

Porch, Douglas. "Occupational Hazards: Myths of 1945 and U.S. Iraq Policy." *National Interest* (2003): 35–47.

Possony, Stefan. "Nuclear Weapons and Foreign Policy." *Annals of the American Academy of Political and Social Science* 316 (Mar. 1958): 141f.

Poundstone, William. *Prisoner's Dilemma: John von Neumann, Game Theory, and the Puzzle of the Bomb.* New York: Random House, 1992.

Powers, Thomas. *The Man Who Kept the Secrets: Richard Helms and the CIA.* London: Weidenfeld & Nicolson, 1980.

Prados, John, and Margaret Pratt Porter, eds. *Inside the Pentagon Papers.* Lawrence: University Press of Kansas, 2004.

Preston, Andrew. "The Little State Department: McGeorge Bundy and the National Security Council Staff, 1961–65." *Presidential Studies Quarterly* 31, no. 4 (2001): 635–59.

———. *The War Council: McGeorge Bundy, the NSC, and Vietnam.* Cambridge, MA: Harvard University Press, 2006.

Purdy, Rob Roy, ed. *Fugitives' Reunion: Conversations at Vanderbilt May 3–5, 1956.* Nashville, TN: Vanderbilt University Press, 1959.

Quigley, Carroll. *The Anglo-American Establishment: From Rhodes to Cliveden.* New York: Books in Focus, 1981.

———. *Tragedy and Hope: A History of the World in Our Time.* London: Macmillan, 1966.

Radványi, János. *Delusion and Reality: Gambits, Hoaxes, and Diplomatic One-Upmanship in Vietnam.* South Bend, IN: Gateway, 1978.

Ramos-Horta, José. *Funu: The Unfinished Saga of East Timor.* New York: Random House, 1987.

Rasenberger, Jim. *The Brilliant Disaster: JFK, Castro, and America's Doomed Invasion of Cuba's Bay of Pigs.* New York: Scribner, 2011.

Reeves, Richard. *President Kennedy: Profile of Power.* New York: Touchstone Books, 1994.

———. *President Nixon: Alone in the White House.* New York: Simon & Schuster, 2001.

Reich, Cary. *The Life of Nelson A. Rockefeller: Worlds to Conquer, 1908–1958.* New York: Doubleday, 1996.

Reid, Robert. *Never Tell an Infantryman to Have a Nice Day: A History Book by*

Robert "Bob" Reid, 84th Division, 335th, H Company, WWII. Bloomington, IN: Xlibris, 2010.

Reyn, Sebastian. *Atlantis Lost: The American Experience with De Gaulle, 1958–1969.* Amsterdam: Amsterdam University Press, 2010.

Rich, Mark. *C. M. Kornbluth: The Life and Works of a Science Fiction Visionary.* Jefferson, NC: McFarland, 2010.

Roberts, Andrew. *Masters and Commanders: How Roosevelt, Churchill, Marshall, and Alanbrooke Won the War in the West.* London: Allen Lane, 2008.

Robin, Ron. *The Making of the Cold War Enemy.* Princeton, NJ: Princeton University Press, 2001.

Rockefeller, Nelson A. *The Future of Federalism.* Cambridge, MA: Harvard University Press, 1962.

Rockefeller Brothers Fund. *Foreign Economic Policy for the Twentieth Century.* New York: Doubleday, 1958.
———. *Prospect for America: The Rockefeller Panel Reports.* Garden City, NY: Doubleday, 1961.

Rose, Peter I., ed. *The Ghetto and Beyond.* New York: Random House, 1969.

Rosen, James. *The Strong Man: John Mitchell and the Secrets of Watergate.* New York: Doubleday, 2008.

Rosenberg, Brett Alyson. "Prospect for America: Nelson Rockefeller, the Special Studies Project, and the Search for America's Best and Brightest, 1956–1961." Senior thesis, Harvard University, 2012.

Rosenberg, D. A. "The Origins of Overkill: Nuclear Weapons and American Strategy, 1945–1960." *International Security* 7, no. 4 (1983): 3–71.

Rosenberg, Edgar. "Appendix." In *Stanford Short Stories 1953.* Palo Alto, CA: Stanford University Press, 1953.

Rosovsky, Nitza. *The Jewish Experience at Harvard and Radcliffe.* Cambridge, MA: Harvard University Press, 1986.

Rostow, Walt W. *The Diffusion of Power: An Essay in Recent History.* New York: Macmillan, 1972.

Rothkopf, David. *Running the World: The Inside Story of the National Security Council and the Architects of American Power.* New York: PublicAffairs, 2006.

Rotthoff, Guido, ed. *Krefelder Juden.* Bonn: Röhrscheid, 1981.

Rubinson, Paul. "'Crucified on a Cross of Atoms': Scientists, Politics, and the Test Ban Treaty." *Diplomatic History* 35, no. 2 (2011): 283–319.

Rueger, Fabian. "Kennedy, Adenauer and the Making of the Berlin Wall, 1958–1961." Ph.D. dissertation, Stanford University, 2011.

Ruehsen, Moyara de Moraes. "Operation 'Ajax' Revisited: Iran, 1953." *Middle Eastern Studies* 29, no. 3 (1993): 467–86.

Rummel, Rudolph J. *Lethal Politics: Soviet Genocide and Mass Murder Since 1917.* Livingston, NJ: Transaction, 1990.

Rusk, Dean. *As I Saw It.* Edited by Daniel S. Papp. New York: W. W. Norton, 1990.

Saalfrank, Maximiliane. "Henry Kissinger und Oberammergau: Unterwegs in geheimer Mission." *Garmish-Partenkirchen Journal* 4 (Aug.–Sept. 1993): 34–38.
———. "Kissinger in Oberammergau." *Deutsch-amerikanischer Almanach: Henry Kissinger* 1 (1994): 36–41.

Safire, William. *Before the Fall: An Inside View of the Pre-Watergate White House.* New Brunswick, NJ: Transaction, 2012.

Sainteny, Jean. *Ho Chi Minh and His Vietnam: A Personal Memoir.* Chicago: Cowles, 1972.

Salinger, Pierre. *With Kennedy.* New York: Avon, 1967.

Saunders, Frances Stonor. *Who Paid the Piper? The CIA and the Cultural Cold War.* London: Granta, 2000.

Sayer, Ian, and Douglas Botting. *America's Secret Army: The Untold Story of the Counter Intelligence Corps.* New York: Grafton, 1989.

Schaefer, Jacob. *Das alte und das neue Stadttheater in Fürth: Eine Wanderung durch die neuere Stadtgeschichte von 1816–1902.* Fürth: G. Rosenberg, 1902.

Schelling, Thomas C. "Bargaining, Communication, and Limited War." *Conflict Resolution* 1, no. 1 (Mar. 1957): 19–36.

———. "An Essay on Bargaining." *American Economic Review* 46, no. 3 (1956): 281–306.

Schilling, Donald G. "Politics in a New Key: The Late Nineteenth-Century Transformation of Politics in Northern Bavaria." *German Studies Review* 17, no. 1 (1994): 35–57.

Schlafly, Phyllis, and Chester Charles Ward. *Kissinger on the Couch.* New Rochelle, NY: Arlington House, 1975.

Schlesinger, Andrew. *Veritas: Harvard College and the American Experience.* Chicago: Ivan R. Dee, 2007.

Schlesinger, Arthur M., Jr. *Journals: 1952–2000.* London: Atlantic Books, 2007.

———. *A Life in the Twentieth Century: Innocent Beginnings, 1917–1950.* Boston: Houghton Mifflin, 2000.

———. *A Thousand Days: John F. Kennedy in the White House.* Boston: Houghton Mifflin, 1965.

Schrader, Charles R. *History of Operations Research in the United States Army.* Vol. I, *1942–1962.* Washington, DC: U.S. Army, 2006.

Schupetta, Ingrid. "Die Geheime Staatspolizei in Krefeld." *Die Heimat* 76 (2005): 115–27.

Schwarz, Hans-Peter. *Konrad Adenauer: A German Politician and Statesman in a Period of War, Revolution and Reconstruction.* Vol. 2, *The Statesman, 1952–1967.* Leamington Spa, UK: Berghahn Books, 1997.

Seig, Kent S. "The 1968 Presidential Election and Peace in Vietnam." *Presidential Studies Quarterly* 26, no. 4 (1996): 106–80.

Selby, Scott Andrew. *The Axmann Conspiracy.* New York: Berkley, 2013.

Shapiro, James. *Oberammergau: The Troubling Story of the World's Most Famous Passion Play.* New York: Pantheon, 2000.

Shawcross, William. *Sideshow: Kissinger, Nixon, and the Destruction of Cambodia.* New York: Simon & Schuster, 1987.

Shesol, Jeff. *Mutual Contempt: Lyndon Johnson, Robert Kennedy, and the Feud That Defined a Decade.* New York: W. W. Norton, 1998.

Shoup, Laurence, and William Minter. *Imperial Brain Trust: The Council on Foreign Relations and United States Foreign Policy.* New York: Monthly Review Press, 1977.

Sinanoglou, Penny. "The Peel Commission and Partition, 1936–1939." In *Britain, Palestine and Empire: The Mandate Years,* edited by Rory Miller, 119–40. Farnham, Surrey, UK: Ashgate, 2010.

Skoug, Kenneth N. *Czechoslovakia's Lost Fight for Freedom, 1967–1969: An American Embassy Perspective.* Westport, CT: Greenwood, 1999.

Slawenski, Kenneth. *J. D. Salinger: A Life.* New York: Random House, 2012.

Smith, Jean Edward, ed. *The Papers of General Lucius D. Clay, 1945–1949.* Bloomington: Indiana University Press, 1974.

Smith, Richard Norton. *The Harvard Century: The Making of a University to a Nation.* Cambridge, MA: Harvard University Press, 1986.

———. *On His Own Terms: A Life of Nelson Rockefeller.* New York: Random House, 2014. Kindle ed.

Smith, Steve, Amelia Hadfield, and Tim Dunne, eds. *Foreign Policy: Theories, Actors, Cases,* 2nd ed. Oxford: Oxford University Press, 2012.

Snead, David L. *The Gaither Committee, Eisenhower, and the Cold War.* Columbus: Ohio State University Press, 1999.

Soapes, Thomas F. "A Cold Warrior Seeks Peace: Eisenhower's Strategy for Nuclear Disarmament." *Diplomatic History* 4, no. 1 (1980): 57–72.

Sorensen, Theodore C. *Decision-Making in the White House: The Olive Branch or the Arrows.* 1963; reprint, New York: Columbia University Press, 2005.

Sorley, Lewis. *A Better War: The Unexamined Victories and Final Tragedy of America's Last Years in Vietnam.* New York: Harcourt Brace, 1999.

Stans, Maurice H. *One of the President's Men: Twenty Years with Eisenhower and Nixon.* Washington, DC: Brassey's, 1995.

Starr, Harvey. "The Kissinger Years: Studying Individuals and Foreign Policy." *International Studies Quarterly* 24, no. 4 (1980): 465–96.

Stedman, Richard Bruce. "Born unto Trouble: An Analysis of the Social Position of the Jewish Upperclassmen in Harvard House." Honors essay, Harvard University, 1942.

Steinberg, Jonathan. *Bismarck: A Life.* Oxford: Oxford University Press, 2011.

Stern, Bruno. *So war es: Leben und Schicksal eines jüdischen Emigranten.* Sigmaringen: J. Thorbecke, 1985.

Stock, Ernest. "Washington Heights' 'Fourth Reich': The German Émigrés' New Home." *Commentary* (June 1951).

Stoessinger, John G. *Henry Kissinger: The Anguish of Power.* New York: W. W. Norton, 1976.

Stone, Oliver, and Peter Kuznick. *The Untold History of the United States.* London: Ebury, 2012. Kindle ed.

Stone, Sean. "New World Order: An Imperial Strategy for the Twentieth Century." Senior thesis, Princeton University, 2006.

Straight, Michael. *Nancy Hanks: An Intimate Portrait—the Creation of a National Commitment to the Arts.* Durham, NC: Duke University Press, 1988.

Strauss, Heinrich. *Fürth in der Weltwirtschaftskrise und nationalsozialistischen Machtergreifung: Studien zur politischen, sozialen und wirtschaftlichen Entwicklung einer deutschen Industriestadt 1928–1933.* Nuremberg: Willmy, 1980.

Strauss, Herbert A. "The Immigration and Acculturation of the German Jew in the United States of America." *Leo Baeck Institute Yearbook* 16, no. 1 (1971): 63–94.

———. "Jewish Emigration from Germany: Nazi Policies and Jewish Responses." *Leo Baeck Institute Yearbook* 26, no. 1 (1981): 343–409.

Summers, Anthony. *The Arrogance of Power: The Secret World of Richard Nixon.* New York: Viking Press, 2000.

Suri, Jeremi. *Henry Kissinger and the American Century.* Cambridge, MA: Harvard University Press, 2007.

———. *Power and Protest: Global Revolution and the Rise of Detente.* Cambridge, MA: Harvard University Press, 2003.

Tal, D. "The Secretary of State Versus the Secretary of Peace: The Dulles-Stassen Controversy and U.S. Disarmament Policy, 1955–58." *Journal of Contemporary History* 41, no. 4 (Oct. 2006): 721–40.

Talbott, Strobe, ed. *Khrushchev Remembers.* Boston: Little, Brown, 1970.

Taylor, Brice. *Thanks for the Memories: The Memoirs of Bob Hope's and Henry Kissinger's Mind-Controlled Sex Slave.* Brice Taylor Trust, 1999.

Thiele, Laura. "Leben vor und nach der Flucht aus dem Regimes des Nationalsozialismus. Biographie des jüdischen Lehrers Hermann Mandelbaum." Unpublished ms., 2012.

Thomas, Evan. *Ike's Bluff: President Eisenhower's Secret Battle to Save the World.* New York: Little, Brown, 2012.

———. *Robert Kennedy: His Life.* New York: Simon & Schuster, 2013. Kindle ed.

———. *The Very Best Men: The Daring Early Years of the CIA.* New York: Simon & Schuster, 2006.

Tott, Vernon. "Ahlem Concentration Camp: Liberated by the 84th Infantry Division on April 10, 1945." Unpublished ms.

———. *Letters and Reflections from the Collection of Vernon L. Tott, the Angel of Ahlem.* Sioux City, IA: G. R. Lindblade, 2007.

Trachtenberg, Marc. *The Cold War and After: History, Theory, and the Logic of International Politics.* Princeton, NJ: Princeton University Press, 2012.

Trevor-Roper, Hugh. *Letters from Oxford: Hugh Trevor-Roper to Bernard Berenson.* London: Orion, 2007.

Vaïsse, Justin. "Zbig, Henry, and the New U.S. Foreign Policy Elite." In *Zbig: The Strategy and Statecraft of Zbigniew Brzezinski,* edited by Charles Gati. Baltimore: Johns Hopkins University Press, 2013.

Vaïsse, Maurice. *La Grandeur: Politique étrangère du général de Gaulle, 1958–1969.* Paris: Fayard, 1998.

VanDeMark, Brian. *Into the Quagmire: Lyndon Johnson and the Escalation of the Vietnam War.* New York: Oxford University Press, 1995.

Vandenbroucke, Lucien S. "Anatomy of a Failure: The Decision to Land at the Bay of Pigs." *Political Science Quarterly* 99, no. 3 (1984): 471–91.

Waddy, Helena. *Oberammergau in the Nazi Era: The Fate of a Catholic Village in Hitler's Germany.* New York: Oxford University Press, 2010.

Wala, Michael. *The Council on Foreign Relations and American Foreign Policy in the Early Cold War.* Providence, RI: Berghahn, 1994.

Walker, Martin. *The Cold War: A History.* London: Macmillan, 1995.

Wallerstein, Jules. "Limited Autobiography of Jules Wallerstein." Unpublished ms., n.d.

Wassermann, Jakob. *My Life as German and Jew.* Translated by S. N.

Brainin. New York: Coward-McCann, 1933.

Weber, William T. "Kissinger as Historian: A Historiographical Approach to Statesmanship." *World Affairs* 141, no. 1 (1978): 40–56.

Webster, C. K. "A World Restored." *English Historical Review* 73, no. 286 (1958): 166f.

Weidenfeld, George. *Remembering My Good Friends: An Autobiography.* New York: HarperCollins, 1995.

Welch, David A. "An Introduction to the ExComm Transcripts." *International Security* 12, no. 3 (1987): 5–29.

Westad, Odd Arne. *The Global Cold War: Third World Interventions and the Making of Our Times.* New York: Cambridge University Press, 2005.

Westad, Odd Arne, et al., eds. "77 Conversations Between Chinese and Foreign Leaders on the Wars in Indochina, 1964–1977." Cold War International History Project Working Paper no. 22 (Mar. 1998).

White, Theodore H. *In Search of History: A Personal Adventure.* New York: Harper & Row, 1978.

———. *The Making of the President 1964.* New York: HarperPerennial, 2010. Kindle ed.

———. *The Making of the President 1968.* New York: HarperPerennial, 2010.

Wiarda, Howard J. *Think Tanks and Foreign Policy: The Foreign Policy Research Institute and Presidential Politics.* New York: Lexington, 2010.

Wiener, Jacob G. *Time of Terror, Road to Revival: One Person's Story: Growing Up in Germany, Negotiating with the Nazis, Rebuilding Life in America.* New York: Trafford, 2010.

Wilford, Hugh. *The Mighty Wurlitzer: How the CIA Played America.* Cambridge, MA: Harvard University Press, 2008.

Williams, William Appleman. *Empire as a Way of Life: An Essay on the Causes and Character of America's Present Predicament Along with a Few Thoughts*

About an Alternative. New York: Oxford University Press, 1980.

———. *The Tragedy of American Diplomacy.* New York: W. W. Norton, 1959.

Wills, Garry. *Nixon Agonistes: The Crisis of the Self-Made Man.* Boston: Mariner Books, 2002.

Winks, Robin W. *Cloak and Gown: Scholars in the Secret War, 1939–1961.* New Haven, CT: Yale University Press, 1987.

Witcover, Jules. *White Knight: The Rise of Spiro Agnew.* New York: Random House, 1972.

Wohlstetter, Albert. "The Delicate Balance of Terror." *Foreign Affairs* 37, no. 2 (1959): 211–34.

Wolfe, Robert, ed. *Americans as Proconsuls: United States Military Government in Germany and Japan, 1944–1952.* Carbondale: Southern Illinois University Press, 1984.

Woods, Randall B. *LBJ: Architect of American Ambition.* New York: Free Press, 2006.

Wright, Esmond. "The Necessity for Choice: Prospects of American Foreign Policy." *International Affairs* 38, no. 1 (1962): 83.

Wright, Quincy. "A World Restored." *American Historical Review* 63, no. 4 (1958): 953–55.

Yeshiva University Museum. *The German Jews of Washington Heights: An Oral History Project.* New York: Yeshiva University Museum, 1987.

Zambernardi, Lorenzo. "The Impotence of Power: Morgenthau's Critique of American Intervention in Vietnam." *Review of International Studies* 37, no. 3 (2011): 1335–56.

Zinke, Peter. *"An allem ist Alljuda schuld": Antisemitismus während der Weimarer Republik in Franken.* Nuremberg: Antogo Verlag, 2009.

———, ed. *"Nächstes Jahr im Kibbuz": Die zionistische Ortsgruppe Nürnberg-Fürth. Hefte zur Regionalgeschichte.* Nuremberg: Antogo Verlag, 2005.

Zinn, Howard. *Declarations of Independence: Cross-Examining American Ideology.* New York: HarperCollins, 1990.

———. *Howard Zinn on War.* New York: Seven Stories Press, 2011.

———. *A People's History of the United States.* New York: HarperCollins, 2001.

Illustration Credits

Index

HIV-AIDS, 8

Hoag, Malcolm, 574

Hobbes, Thomas, 242

Ho Chi Minh, 22, 676, 677, 678, 703, 748, 754, 756, 780, 836

Ho Chi Minh Trail, 585, 611, 679

Höchster, Leo, 69

Hoffmann, Stanley, 20, 405, 407, 574, 625, 793, 858

Holbrook, W. S., 178

Holmes, Oliver Wendell, 209, 214

Holocaust, 79–80, 105, 160–61, 164–68, 170, 172–73, 292, 866

   HAK on survivors of, 173–75

   impact on HAK of, 80–81

   Kissinger family in, 173

Holy Alliance, 308

Holyoke, Edward, 213

Holy Roman Empire, 39

Hooge, Willi, 163

Hoover, J. Edgar, 130, 178, 282, 284, 477, 635

Horowitz, Len, 7–8

Horowitz, Schabbatai Scheftel, 42–43

Hosmer, Graig, 605n

Hottelet, Richard C., 383

House of Representatives, U.S., 84

   Foreign Affairs Committee of, 260

   Foreign Aid Committee of, 260

   Postwar Economic Policy and Planning Committee of, 260

   Un-American Activities Committee (HUAC) of, 84, 282, 283

   see also Congress, U.S.; Senate, U.S.

Ho Van Vui, 655–56

Howar, Barbara, 14

Howard, Michael, 406, 610, 693–94, 739n

Howe, Irving, 82

"How the Revolution in Weapons Will Affect Our Strategy and Foreign Policy" (Kissinger speech), 366

Hue, Vietnam, 23, 648, 650, 786

Hughes, Emmet J., 423, 446, 455, 816, 826

Hughes, Ken, 792

Hull, Cordell, 234

human dignity, 453–54, 465, 474

Humphrey, Hubert, 361, 454, 677, 793, 810, 825–26, 829, 830

   1968 presidential campaign of, 791–92, 844–45

Hungarian revolution, 367–68, 380–81, 383, 426

Huntington, Samuel P., 228, 235, 341, 386, 403, 628, 630, 826

Hussein, Saddam, 11

hydrogen bomb, 342

IBM, 403, 806

Ibn Saud, king of Saudi Arabia, 415

Icke, David, 87

idealism, idealists, 26, 727, 865

   HAK as, 28, 32, 111, 242, 243, 415–16, 430, 431, 454, 458, 459–60, 461, 462, 465, 471–72, 497–98, 502–3, 513, 594, 610, 622, 702, 789–90, 865–66, 870–71, 873–74

   philosophical definition of, 28

Ideology and Foreign Affairs (CFIA report), 404

Idle, Eric, 5

Île de France, 73, 82

I'll Take My Stand (Ransom), 230n

"Illuminati," 6, 8

"Illusionist, The" (Kissinger), 719

immigrants, in U.S., 89

   German, 89, 92–93

   Irish, 89, 90–91, 93

   Italian, 89

   quotas and, 72, 91

   unrealistic expectations of, 83

immigrants, in U.S., German-Jewish:

   in military, 114–15

   in New York City, 87–91, 94–96

   upward mobility of, 88–90

   in Washington Heights, 88, 94–96, 113–14

Immigration Restriction League, 218

"Impasse of American Policy and Preventive War" (Kissinger draft), 332–34

imperialism, British tradition of liberal, 31

India, 410, 617, 627

   China and, 520–21, 522

   in Kashmir dispute with Pakistan, 522

Indian Atomic Energy Commission, 521

Indochina, 339, 340, 346, 733

Indonesia, 37, 409, 519

industrial revolution, 40

information technology, HAK on, 804–6

In Stahlgewittern (*Storm of Steel*; Jünger), 288

The Rough Guide
Chronicle

England

Rough Guides online

www.roughguides.com

credits

Text editor: Andrew Dickson
Rough Guides series editor: Mark Ellingham
Production: Michelle Draycott, Helen Prior
Cartography: Katie Lloyd-Jones
Picture research: Sharon Martins
Proofreading: Diane Margolis

cover credits

Front – Statue of Nelson by Edward Baily
Back – Hadrian's Wall, northeast England by Getty Images

publishing information

This edition published October 2002 by
Rough Guides Ltd, 80 Strand, London WC2R 0RL

distributed by the Penguin Group

Penguin Books Ltd, 80 Strand, London WC2R 0RL
Penguin Putnam, Inc, 375 Hudson Street, New York 10014, USA
Penguin Books Australia Ltd, 487 Maroondah Highway, PO Box
257, Ringwood, Victoria 3134, Australia
Penguin Books Canada Ltd, 10 Alcorn Avenue,
Toronto, Ontario M4V 1E4, Canada
Penguin Books (NZ) Ltd, 182–190 Wairau Road,
Auckland 10, New Zealand
Typeset to an original design by Henry Iles
Printed in Spain by Graphy Cems

A catalogue record for this book is
available from the British Library.
ISBN 1-85828-799-5

The Rough Guide

Chronicle

England

by
Robin Eagles

with contributions by Andrew Dickson

Chronicles series editor
Justin Wintle

acknowledgements

This book has been from the outset a joint effort, and much of the credit truly belongs to my series editor, Justin Wintle. I am grateful to everyone at Rough Guides for their patience, but especially to Andy Dickson (who took the manuscript in hand and made it work), to Helen Prior for layout and to Sharon Martins for inspired picture research. I must say a special word of thanks also to my friends and family who have put up with me talking about nothing else for the last year or so, but most of all to Beverly Adams, Sarah Morpeth, Jonathan and Laura Eagles, and my parents. I am forever in their debt.

Robin Eagles
London 2002

contents

introduction

England forms part of the present-day United Kingdom, along with Scotland, Wales and Northern Ireland. Sometimes the union is called 'Great Britain', sometimes just 'Britain'. Formally it is known as the 'United Kingdom of Great Britain and Northern Ireland'. Within the UK, England is the dominant partner in terms of geographical size, population and influence. Some fifty million of the current United Kingdom's sixty million live in England; until very recently England's government and parliament provided the political hub for the entire UK; economically it continues to dominate its immediate neighbours.

But these modern details and distinctions belie the long history of the British Isles. In the beginning, of course, there was no England, no Scotland, Wales or Ireland. In the period of prehistory (about which little is known), first man's ancestors – the hominids – then *homo sapiens sapiens*, colonized the British Isles, creating settlements that were loosely and only locally confederated. The first tangible evidence of wider societies is provided by the remarkable remains at Stonehenge, whose scale and construction history suggest that it was a ritual centre for people living miles around. Yet despite Stonehenge's advanced design – first erected around 2000 BC, it is one of the great monuments of the European Neolithic era – its precise use and significance remain veiled, as does the identity of those who built it.

In all probability there must have been many waves of invaders and settlers over the centuries after the construction of Stonehenge. Of these many immigrants, it was the metal-working Celts who eased Britain out of prehistory into history proper. Although they left no early written records, they were observed, then overrun, by the Romans – who did. Following expeditions undertaken by Julius Caesar in 55 and 54 BC, the Romans attempted wholesale subjugation under the emperor Claudius almost a hundred years later. But they were unable to tame the Scottish highlands, made only marginally greater progress in the mountainous territory that was to become Wales, and Ireland – known as Hibernia ('winter quarters') – was left largely untouched. In the fertile lowlands, however, the Romans succeeded in transplanting their advanced civilization, and it is from Roman times that England, known then as 'Britannia', began to take shape as a territorial and political entity.

The same area formed the major part of kingdoms established by the Anglo-Saxons from the mid-5th century onwards. These soon converted to Christianity, and eventually became a single kingdom ruled by the House of Wessex. It is from this period that the name 'England' (Land of the Angles) derives. But England's identity remained in near-constant flux. The Anglo-Saxons were invaded on numerous occasions, first by the Vikings and then, in the 11th century, by the Normans.

The Norman Conquest was critical to England's evolution. In the two centuries before 1066 England had been increasingly influenced by Scandinavia – indeed much of northern England was for a time a Viking kingdom known as the 'Danelaw'. But the Normans realigned their new territories with a different area of the continent, and it was this involvement that would shape the next stage of England's history. Throughout the Middle Ages, English and French fortunes were closely entwined – politically, militarily, and through royal and aristocratic bloodlines. France sought to conquer England, and England France. The result was a

MODERN ENGLAND

SCOTLAND

Edinburgh

NORTHERN
IRELAND

Isle of
Man

Douglas

IRISH
SEA

REPUBLIC
OF IRELAND

Carlisle

Newcastle-upon-Tyne

Tyne

Tees

York

Bradford · Leeds

Liverpool · Manchester

Mersey

Chester

ENGLAND

Nottingham

Leicester

Trent

NORTH
SEA

Birmingham

Severn

Avon

WALES

Cardiff

Oxford

Bristol Thames

Great Ouse

Norwich

Cambridge

LONDON

Southampton

Exeter

Plymouth

Portsmouth Brighton

Isle of
Wight

Dover

Scilly
Isles

Penzance

ENGLISH CHANNEL

0   50 miles

patchy and uncertain conflict, the Hundred Years War, that extended the tug-of-war between the two powers over some four generations.

Gradually, though, the kingdom of England emerged as a clear force in its own right. It was this kingdom, which grew in prosperity and influence under the Plantagenets and continued to do so under the Tudors, that began to make headway internationally in both trade and military power. The eventual result was the acquisition of an extraordinary empire, which at its 19th-century zenith extended across Canada, India, the Far East, Australasia and Africa.

Closer to home, too, the English tried to establish colonies. Union with Wales was negotiated in 1536; Scotland joined in 1707; Ireland was brought into the fold in 1801. Despite some benefits for these three individual countries, England's own interests remained the reason for a united Britain. Divisions remained, and during the course of the 20th century separatist forces within the union began make themselves heard. Ireland was partitioned shortly after World War I, forming a southern (mainly Catholic) republic and six northern (mainly Protestant) counties that remained within the UK. Some eighty years later, regional legislatures were established in Scotland and Wales in an attempt to give people in both countries more control over their politics.

All this, it has been said, leaves Britain – and with it the dominance of the English – looking more fragile now than ever before. Some doubt that the United Kingdom will still be united, still less a kingdom, in years to come. By the same token, though, this fragmentation has encouraged some historians to concentrate their efforts on the study of national and regional identity, considering both ideals of Britain and Britishness as well as what it might mean to be English.

But who are the English? Racially as well as politically, the answer is complex. England is – and always has been – a melting pot. Today, the descendants of Celts, Romans, Angles, Saxons, Jutes, Vikings, Normans and other European peoples mix with those from further afield – in particular immigrants from former colonies, many of whom arrived in the latter half of the 20th century to supply low-wage labour for the postwar British economy. England is now more multi-cultural and multi-ethnic than ever before.

This long assimilative tradition is just one of many that continues to influence life in 21st-century England. The monarchy, of course, still looms large. Despite criticism of it in sections of society, the royal family continues to provide a popular national focus and – its defenders often claim – a much-needed centre of political stability around which the country's parliamentary democracy functions. Though England is often accused of being hidebound, obsessed by history, perhaps it is truer to say that its culture is continually involved in a dialogue between the past and the present – especially as the nation struggles to adapt to a world in which it is no longer one of the most powerful players.

In many ways the ongoing debate over 'Europe' – whether or not England should engage more fully with the European Union – embodies these kinds of anxieties, perhaps because it has such a long pedigree. England has always had a tempestuous and involved relationship with the rest of Europe, and the present-day arguments rehearse older ones too: whether it is better to function as a fully European country, or to remain in insular isolation (bolstered, of course, by a so-called 'special relationship' with the United States and by remaining close to former colonies through the British Commonwealth). At the cusp of the third millennium, that decision looks like one of the most momentous England and its people have had to face.

1
Prehistoric, Early and Roman Britain

Up to c.450 AD

The British Isles originally formed part of the Eurasian landmass before breaking off to form an archipelago. They did not remain separate, however: when sea-levels fell during the Ice Ages, a land bridge reappeared between Britain (the largest of the British Isles) and the northwest of what was to become the continent of Europe. It was probably across this land bridge that *homo erectus*, then **Neanderthal man** and finally *homo sapiens sapiens* travelled in search of new lands to settle.

In time, the land bridge became permanently submerged, but the inhabitants of mainland Europe gradually learned to build boats capable of navigating the waters around Britain. Fresh waves of settlers continued to arrive and make the most of its fertile and hospitable terrain – particularly in the low-lying southern and central sections of the island.

But Britain's north and west are dominated by highlands, which probably proved less hospitable to early settlers. While the precise circumstances surrounding the island's separation into three territories – **England**, **Scotland** and **Wales** – are naturally a matter of debate, it seems likely that its topography has a great deal to do with it: England is mainly low-lying, while Scotland and Wales are largely mountainous. Since the 'English' territory was more accessible and fertile, and capable of sustaining a greater population, it tended to dominate its two neighbours. However, England continued to attract the attention of European predators. Right up until the **Norman Conquest** of 1066 and beyond its history is one of conquest and attempted conquest.

While it is clear that waves of sea-borne migration continued to replenish Britain's human population once the European land bridge became submerged around 7500 BC, little is known about the early settlers. **Stonehenge** (see p.6) and other megalithic monuments indicate that by as early as 3000 BC powerful tribal kingdoms had formed, but these did not last and no trace remains of the language or languages they spoke. Only with the arrival of the **Celts** in the centuries preceding the Roman Conquest does linguistic evidence become available – albeit in a confusing way. Two variants of what is assumed to have been a common Celtic language, related to the widely diffused Indo-European language group, have survived into contemporary times. The first and oldest is called **Q-Celtic** or **Goidelic**, and forms the basis of modern Irish, Scottish Gaelic and Manx (spoken on the Isle of Man). The second and younger tongue is **P-Celtic**, known also as **Brythonic**: the basis of modern Welsh, Breton and Cornish.

That these languages share Celtic roots suggests that the Celts separated from the original Indo-European population in the Black Sea region, then moved into central Europe – possibly as a result of pressure from further east. In due course they inhabited parts of Britain, most of France and sections of the Iberian peninsula. But the exact sequence of their movements is uncertain. A remarkable feature of western Europe c.1000 BC is the existence of a lively sea-based trade along the Atlantic coast, stretching from southern Ireland and Cornwall down to the Straits of Gibraltar, and connecting with Greek and Phoenician trading communities in the Mediterranean. This extended trade network enabled the startling pan-European cultural transformation known as the **Bronze Age** to happen. Significant deposits of tin in Cornwall and copper in Ireland were integral to its development and, given that the Celts were renowned as fine metallurgists, it seems almost certain that the Irish and Cornish ends of the trade were already Celticized. In the case of Ireland, this must certainly be so – otherwise the survival there of the Q-Celtic language is difficult to explain.

Because Q-Celtic also survives in Scotland, it is widely assumed that the whole of Britain must have seen **Goidelic Celtic** communities at this relatively early stage. Whether this was in fact the case, or whether the early Celts were less thorough in their occupation, is not known for sure. The evidence merely suggests that there was a gap of some kind between this earliest settlement and a second wave of immigration, which arrived from middle Europe from the 8th century BC onwards. This secondary expansion, which coincided with the onset of the **Iron Age** in northern and western Europe, is usually divided into two cultural phases, named after the archeological sites in Germany and Switzerland where contrasting artefacts were discovered: **Hallstatt** culture and **La Tène** culture. Although very few Hallstatt artefacts have been excavated in England and Britain, more sophisticated La Tène artefacts have been found in abundance.

Taking all of this fragmentary evidence into account, the most likely scenario is that an early Celtic settlement of England was followed by a hiatus during which the various Celtic communities of western Europe ceased having very much to do with their parent peoples. Then a second Celtic settlement from the 4th century BC onwards largely swallowed up the first, at least on the British mainland.

By about 150 BC it is clear that a Celtic people called the **Belgae** dominated southern England while East Anglia, the north and the west were split between Brythonic-speaking tribes such as the **Iceni** and **Brigantes**. All formed separate kingdoms and all regularly fought against each other – something that greatly contributed to the ease with which the Romans managed to dominate in the 1st century AD. Although some Celtic tribes collaborated on defence – the **Catevellauni** and **Silures**, for instance – others like the Brigantes made their own bargains with the imperial invaders. This inherent lack of unity meant not only that the Celts of Britain were subjugated by the Romans in the lands south of the Scottish Highlands, but that they were to suffer much the same fate when the Anglo-Saxons arrived four centuries later.

The inhabitants of Britain's lowlands enjoyed the benefits of Roman civilization, or at least the spectacle of it, in a way that those in the hills simply couldn't or didn't. Yet too much can be made of the newly 'European' development of southern Britain by Roman rule. Though they set about it less overtly, the Celts too had brought the British Isles closer to mainland Europe. Nor was the Roman occupation unchallenged: a succession of uprisings showed that even the warring Celts could sometimes unite against a common enemy. And when it came down to it, the style of Roman government was predominantly one of strategic control, operating out of fortified camps and townships. Britain itself – and British society – remained decidedly tribal. It was Rome's inability to consolidate its control in the Welsh and Scottish highlands that marked the beginning of England as a distinct entity.

At the end of the Roman period, it is hard to know quite how 'Romanized' most Britons were, but there was undoubtedly a profound impact. Some British chieftains were heavily influenced by continental culture and became **Romano-Britons**, adopting Roman habits and dress and living in specially commissioned villas; one such may have been the client-king **Cogidubnus**, for whom the palace at **Fishbourne** in Sussex was probably built. The Britons who faced the Anglo-Saxon onslaught also seem to have employed Roman tactics to face off the invaders: the myths that surround **King Arthur** or **Ambrosius Aurelianus** most probably derive from a Romano-British leader, perhaps a holder of one of the military offices created by the Roman authorities. Arthur's knights employed the kind of cavalry tactics typical of Roman auxiliaries, which suggests that some of the civil and military structures survived the Roman departure. Significantly, too, most of the Britons living in what had been Roman Britain were **Christian**. Christianity was slow to take root, and it was probably not until the 3rd century that many urban British began to adopt its practices. By the time of the Roman withdrawal, however, the religion was firmly established, and it was only the incursion of the Saxons that forced it into the hinterlands. There it continued as a distinctive Celtic Christianity – later to be challenged and eventually overwhelmed by continental missionaries sent to convert the very people they had fled from.

c.300,000 BC Britain is colonized by *homo erectus*, taking advantage of an interglacial period of the Ice Age during which the island is joined to the European continent. Primitive humans hunt the mammoth and hippopotamus species prevalent in southeast England using simple wooden spears.

c.250,000 BC **Swanscombe Woman**, a member of this *homo erectus* community, lives in Kent. Hers are the oldest surviving human remains found in Europe.

c.70,000 BC The first **Neanderthals** settle in England. They inhabit caves and hunt wild animals for food and clothing.

c.35,000 BC The last Neanderthals are displaced by the ancestor of modern humans, ***homo sapiens sapiens***, who begins settling in Britain.

c.12,000 BC The last **Ice Age** comes to an end.

c.7500 BC The land bridge connecting Britain with Europe is covered by the sea and Britain is separated from the Continent.

Stonehenge

Described by the 18th-century antiquarian William Stukeley as 'that most noble and stupendous piece of Antiquity', **Stonehenge** is Europe's outstanding megalithic monument. It has also teased generations of researchers: the 17th-century architect and designer Inigo Jones reckoned it to be of Roman origin, while some Arthurian myths ascribe its construction to the wizard Merlin. Modern archeology, at any rate, shows it to be the outcome of three discrete stages of construction between around 2800 and 2000 BC, known as **Stonehenge I, II** and **III**.

Its precise function is still disputed, but it seems to be a ritual circle of great importance, its alignment with the rising sun of the summer solstice no accident. There is little more than speculation about the kind of worship that occurred there, though, nor is it clearly understood how the huge standing stones were transported to the site or raised. The discovery of similar stones off the coast of southern England have led some scholars to conclude that these were pieces intended for the Stonehenge complex lost at sea while en route. And strong claims have been put forward in favour of **Preseli**, two hundred miles away in southwest Wales, as the quarry from which the 'bluestones' for Stonehenge II would almost certainly have had to have been carried by sea. The stone is certainly not local to Wiltshire, and this suggests that social and trading relations extended across wide swathes of Neolithic Britain. It may even be that Stonehenge was a ritual centre for a number of British tribes, not just the vision of one local people.

c.4300 BC Causeway settlements and **long barrow** burials are developed by Stone Age Britons. The causeways may lead to burial chambers of high-ranking members of these communities or sites of ritual significance.

c.3500 BC The first circular ritual monuments, or **henges**, are built, important both as temples for local religious cults and as clear indicators of where tribal boundaries lie.

c.2800 BC The first work is undertaken at **Stonehenge** in Wiltshire.

c.2750 BC The **Beaker People**, possibly early Celtic migrants from Germany and the Low Countries, begin settling in Britain, bringing with them a metal-working technology that makes use of Irish copper and Cornish tin to make bronze. They derive their name from their custom

The Avebury stone circle, Wiltshire.

of burying their dead with pottery jars or beakers in the long **barrows** or **tumuli** that still dominate the West Country landscape.

c.2600 BC The ritual complex at **Avebury** and the man-made hill at **Silbury** are developed by the 'Wessex People'.

c.2100BC The Bluestone circle at **Stonehenge II** is erected.

c.2000 BC The Sarsen circle is added to **Stonehenge III**.

c.1000 BC As the Atlantic seaboard trade establishes itself, **hill forts** become a common feature of the southern British landscape, reflecting the prevalence of tribal structures and the growing wealth of a warrior aristocracy.

c.750 BC As new Celtic migrations originating in central Europe push westwards, **iron** begins to displace bronze as the principal metal used for making tools and weapons in Britain.

c.500 BC Trade between southern Britain, Ireland and Brittany in northern France flourishes.

c.325 BC The Greek adventurer and geographer **Pytheas of Massilia** (Marseille) circumnavigates Britain and visits tin mines in Cornwall. Although his findings are treated with suspicion by contemporaries, his visit coincides with a period when southern Britain and the Mediterranean are coming into renewed and increasing contact. His estimates of the British coastline and of the distance between Britain and Massilia are generally accurate.

c.300 BC As Celtic **La Tène** culture continues to spread through western Europe, the British are actively engaged in human sacrifice as part of their religious ceremonies.

Around this time the individual known as **Lindow Man** is killed and offered to a lake deity.

Lindow Man

In 1984 peat cutters working in Lindow marsh in Cheshire were astonished to discover a foot protruding from their equipment. Suspecting foul play, the police were summoned to investigate and unearthed a human body missing only part of its lower limbs, which had been severed by the cutting apparatus.

Subsequent carbon dating indicated that the naked, bearded victim (who became known as **Lindow Man** and who now resides in the British Museum in London) was reckoned to be of Iron Age vintage. Archeologists working on the corpse discovered a number of gruesome features that must have contributed to his death. He had been hit over the head with a mercy blow, garrotted and his throat had been slashed. He had then been pushed face-first into a pool. This 'triple death' of the knife, the noose and the drowning – a feature of Druidic ritual and associated with the death of Merlin in some romances – possibly identifies him as a sacrificial victim. Some researchers connected his death with the fall of the Druids' stronghold at Anglesey and the defeat of **Boudicca**, although more precise carbon-14 dating has since since suggested that he died later, possibly as late as 119 AD. The fact that he had rare mistletoe pollen in his stomach has been taken to imply that the sacrifice could have been part of the feast of **Beltain** and his execution an offering to a god such as **Belenos**, rituals in whose honour Caesar describes in his account of the Roman campaign. Ultimately, though, it seems unlikely that the mystery of Lindow Man's death will ever be fully solved.

c.200 BC An aggressive Celtic people called the **Belgae** begin to raid and colonize Britain, forcing earlier Celtic arrivals such as the **Iceni** out of the southeast – where the Belgae now form kingdoms of their own.

55 BC Julius Caesar, commanding the Roman armies in Gaul and concerned by the assistance given to his opponents by 'Britons', sends Commius, king of the Gaulish Atrebates, to Britain to persuade the Belgae and other tribes to submit to Rome's authority. Commius is captured and imprisoned. Caesar mounts his first **armed reconnaissance** of Britain, landing on the south coast with a force of around 2000 troops. He frees Commius, who returns with him to Gaul.

54 BC Caesar revisits Britain with a greater force, again accompanied by Commius, and 'pacifies' some of the tribes in the southeast. The British over-king **Cassivelaunus** is forced to surrender. As well as agreeing to pay tribute to Rome, Cassivelaunus is compelled to refrain from interfering with the neighboring Trinovantes who enter into an alliance with the Romans. Caesar is ill-equipped for a sustained occupation, however, and returns to Gaul.

50 BC Commius, having rebelled against Rome with the Gaulish chieftain Vercingetorix in 53, flees to Britain, where he becomes king of a British kingdom of Atrebates.

34 BC A projected invasion of Britain by **Octavius** (the future **First Emperor Augustus**) is abandoned as civil war breaks out inside the Roman empire

26 BC Invasion of Britain is again suspended, this time because of local rebellions in Spain and the Alps that force Augustus to change his plans.

c.10 AD Cunobelinus (Cymbeline) of the Catevellauni secures his position as over-king of much of southeast England.

c.40 Cunobelinus banishes his son **Adminius**, who flees to the Continent with a small band of followers and surrenders to the Romans.

The emperor **Gaius Caligula** plans an invasion of Britain, but calls it off at the last moment. Cunobelinus dies soon afterwards.

The Celts

The term **Celtic** is used in two main ways: to denote specific peoples and languages and to describe a style or styles of culture (political and artistic as well as material) that dominated central, northwestern and western Europe during the 1st millennium AD and before. But Celtic studies is a field rife with dispute. Even the distinguished historian Barry Cunliffe has struggled to come up with a watertight interpretation, commenting that 'perhaps the only real definition of a Celt, now as in the past, is that a Celt is a person who believes him or herself to be Celtic'. If we allow, though, that 'Celtic' can broadly describe the Germanic peoples who colonized Britain prior to the Roman invasion, then the final Celtic intruders into Britain were the several **Belgic** tribes that, originating beyond the Rhine, had already invaded northeastern Gaul during the 4th and 3rd centuries BC. The most powerful of these Belgae were the **Catevellauni** and **Atrebates**. These overran the south, displacing the tribes already settled there.

Warfare was a regular feature of Celtic society: complex hill fort defences and the use of the chariot emphasize the investment made by a warrior aristocracy in military security and offensive capability. The Celts were more than fighters, though. Their arrival in Britain led to a diversification of agriculture and trade and the developments of arts such as metallurgy, pottery, ornamented stone-cutting and jewellery. The term **Celtic Art** is most often applied to the finely crafted late La Tène artefacts associated with the Belgic warrior aristocracy. These pieces form the high-point of Celtic bronze production and indicate real prosperity, featuring intricate curvilinear engraving and enamelwork. Objects like the **Snettisham torc** and bracelet and the oblong shield recovered from the Thames near Battersea, London (all now in the British Museum) lend credence to the image of a cultured people able to spend surplus wealth on luxury items.

c.41 Cunobelinus is succeeded by his sons **Togdumnus** and **Caratacus**.

Verica of the Atrebates is exiled by the Catevellauni and flees to the court of the new Roman emperor **Claudius**.

43 Responding to Verica's plea, Claudius orders the **invasion** of Britain. An army of four legions is led by the capable **Aulus Plautius**, who becomes the first Governor of the new Province of Britain. The first year of conquest meets with considerable success: eleven British kings, clearly happier to accept Roman rule rather than subjugation by the Catevellauni, offer their submission. The Catevellauni hold out, though, and there is heavy fighting around the River Medway in Kent. The British retreat to the Thames, where a further battle is fought and **Togodumnus** is killed. It takes the arrival of Claudius himself later in the year to inspire the Romans to complete their operations against the Catevellauni by seizing **Camulodunum** (Colchester), although they fail to capture Caratacus.

44 The Romans divide their forces and pursue campaigns against the Durotriges of Devon and Dorset; there is fierce fighting at the hill forts of **Hod Hill** and **Maiden Castle**. **Vespasian**, a young commander and future emperor, is thought to have been responsible for overcoming a number of British fortifications.

45 The Durotriges are defeated, and most of southern Britain comes under Roman control.

47 Claudius's armies extend the Roman occupation to the **River Severn** in the west and the **Trent** in the midlands. The new governor **Ostorius Scapula** provokes a rising among the Iceni and other peoples of Norfolk by attempting to disarm them.

48 The revolt of the Iceni and others continues.

49 Greater resistance is offered by **Caratacus**, now operating from the territory of the Silures and Ordovices in Wales. A colony of Roman veterans is established at the old Catevellaunian capital of **Colchester**.

**ROMAN BRITAIN &
THE BRITISH TRIBES**

0   50 miles

Feet
3000
2000
1500
1000
500
250
0

Antonine
Wall

SELGOVAE   VOTADINI

NOVANTAE   Hadrian's Wall   Arbeia
(South Shields)

Corstopitum
(Corbridge)

Luguvallium   CARVETII
(Carlisle)

Clanoventa
(Ravenglass)   Isurium
Brigantum
(Aldborough)

Manavia   Eboracum   Petuaria
(York)   (Brough on
Humber)

OCEANUS
HIBERNICUS   BRIGANTES   PARISI   OCEANUS
GERMANICUS

Mona   Lindum
(Lincoln)

Deva
(Chester)

DEGEANGLI

ORDOVICES   CORNOVII   Venta Icenorum
(Norwich)

WATLING STREET   Ratae
Coritanorum   ICENI
(Leicester)

Viroconium
(Wroxeter)   CORITANI

FOSSE WAY

Moridunum   Glevum   Chedworth   Cumulodunum
(Carmarthen)   (Gloucester)   (Colchester)

DEMETAE   SILURES   Corinium   Verulamium   TRINOVANTE
Woodchester   Dobunnorum   (St Albans)
Venta Silurum   (Cirencester)   Caesaromagus
(Caerwent)   AKEMAN STREET   CATUVELLAUNI   (Chelmsford)

Isca (Caerleon)   DOBUNNI   Calleva-   Londinium
Atrebatum   (London)   Rutupiae
Aquae Sulis   ATREBATES   (Silchester)   (Richborough)
(Bath)   *Lullingstone*
BELGAE   Durovernum   Dubris
Venta Belgarum   (Canterbury)   (Dover)
DUROTRIGES   (Winchester)   CANTIACI

Isca   *Bignor*   REGNI   LITTUS
(Exeter)   Noviomagus   SAXONICUM
Regnensium
Durnovaria   *Fishbourne*   (Chichester)
DUMNONII   (Dorchester)   *Vectis*

N

50 A new township is founded at **Londinium** (London) to provide merchants with a safe deep-water port on the Thames.

51 Scapula **defeats** Caratacus who, betrayed by the Brigantes, is taken to Rome in chains. There he impresses Claudius with his 'noble bearing' and his death sentence is revoked.

58 Suetonius Paulinus is appointed governor of Britain. He continues the process of conquest, undertaking a major campaign against the tribes of South Wales.

> ❝ The Britons took no prisoners, sold no captives as slaves and went in for none of the usual trading of war. They wasted no time in getting down to the bloody business of hanging, burning and crucifying. It was as if they feared that retribution might catch up with them while their vengeance was only half-complete. ❞
>
> Tacitus, *Annals*, trans. Peter Salway

60 Perhaps in order to undermine Celtic morale, Suetonius Paulinus attacks a fortified Druid centre on the island of **Anglesey** in northwest Wales and slaughters several hundred Druidic priests.

King Prasutagus of the Iceni dies, leaving half of his property to the emperor. Agents of the Roman procurator flog his widow **Queen Boudicca** (Boadicea) and rape his daughters. Led by Boudicca, the Iceni and neighbouring Trinovantes revolt and brutally sack **Camulodunum** (Colchester), **Londinium** (London) and **Verulamium** (St Albans). Suetonius Paulinus, returning from Wales, is forced to take on Boudicca's troops despite being heavily outnumbered. But the overconfident British are defeated, perhaps near **Mancetter** (in present-day Warwickshire), and Boudicca flees. According to legend she and her two daughters subsequently poison themselves.

Around this time construction begins of an impressive Roman pleasure complex at **Aquae Sulis** (Bath), a city whose modern name refers to the hot mineral springs tapped by the Romans.

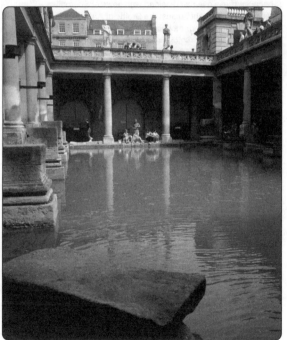

© GREG EVANS

The Great Bath, Bath.

Boudicca (d. c.60 AD)

Boudicca (Boadicea), widow of King Prasutagus of the Iceni tribe, was the leader of just one of several local rebellions against Roman rule in Britain – a short-lived revolt distinguished mainly by the atrocities committed by the troops under her command.

Boudicca's protests at Roman taxes after her husband's death led to her being flogged and her daughters raped. Perhaps because these events coincided with news of Suetonius Paulinus's onslaught against the Druids of **Anglesey** (see p.14), Boudicca was able to mobilize both her own Iceni and the nearby Trinovantes against **Colchester**, with its detested temple built in honour of 'the god' Claudius; they burnt it to the ground, massacring everyone in their path.

Suetonius hurried back from Wales ahead of his main force, but his appeal to the commander of the 2nd Legion for assistance was ignored and, unable to muster sufficient strength to hold **Londinium**, he abandoned it and **Verulamium** to Boudicca's followers. In Londinium alone the Iceni are reputed to have slaughtered some 70,000 inhabitants. Suetonius retreated to a position possibly near **Mancetter**, which may have had sacred significance for the Britons. Although heavily outnumbered, the legionaries' disciplined defence devastated Boudicca's army, which was trapped by their own baggage wagons.

Despite missing such a crucial military opportunity – and the brutality of her forces – Boudicca has passed into legend as the model of heroic British womanhood, even British nationhood: brave, resilient, proud. And despite the exaggerations and distortions of myth-makers, she was clearly an imposing person. The Greek historian Dio Cassius wrote: 'She was huge of frame, terrifying of aspect, and with a harsh voice. A great mass of bright red hair fell to her knees: she wore a great twisted golden torc, and a tunic of many colours, over which was a thick mantle, fastened by a brooch.'

70 The future governor of Britain, **Gnaeus Julius Agricola**, is given command of the 20th Legion at

Wroxeter in acknowledgment of his support for the new Emperor Vespasian (69–79). He arrives in Britain at a time of renewed unrest – the northern border is no longer secure, the Brigantes having recently **rebelled**.

The current governor of Britain, Vettius Bolanus, is replaced by the more dynamic **Petillius Cerialis**, who is determined to pursue an active policy of 'pacification'.

74 **Sextus Julius Frontinus**, succeeding Petillius as Governor, turns his attention to the problem territory of Wales, and is successful in subduing the **Silures**.

77 **Agricola**, having repeatedly shown military prowess, becomes governor. Immediately he is confronted by crisis as the **Ordovices** of north Wales revolt, wiping out a Roman cavalry detachment. He responds swiftly and decisively: overcoming the Ordovices, he seizes the opportunity to pacify the whole of **Wales**.

78 Moving his forces to the north, Agricola defeats the troublesome **Brigantes** and prepares for a campaign against the peoples of what is now Scotland. At the same time he seeks to consolidate Rome's hold over the territories already controlled, encouraging **Roman dress** among his Celtic subjects and the use of the **Latin** language.

80 Agricola begins campaigning in **northern Britain** (Scotland), in line with the expansionist policies of the new emperor, **Domitian**.

The British client king **Cogidubnus** – possibly the builder of **Fishbourne**, a palace near Chichester – dies. His territory is taken over and reorganized by the Romans into three new **civitates** (districts) administered from **Chichester**, **Silchester** and **Winchester**.

83–4 Agricola defeats a coalition of northern British tribes at **Mons Graupius**, an unknown battle site perhaps at Bennachie in Aberdeenshire. According to the historian

> Agricola had to deal with people living in isolation and ignorance, and therefore prone to fight; and his object was to accustom them to a life of peace and quiet by the provision of amenities. He therefore gave private encouragement and official assistance to the building of temples, public squares, and good houses. He praised the energetic and scolded the slack; and competition for honour proved as effective as compulsion. Furthermore, he educated the sons of the chiefs in the liberal arts, and expressed a preference for British ability as compared with the trained skills of the Gauls. The result was that instead of loathing the Latin language they became eager to speak it effectively. In the same way, our national dress came into favour and the toga was everywhere to be seen. And so the population was gradually led into the demoralizing temptations of arcades, baths, and sumptuous banquets. The unsuspecting Britons spoke of such novelties as 'civilization', when in fact they were only a feature of their enslavement.

Tacitus, *Agricola*, trans. H. Mattingly

Tacitus he achieves a complete rout, with the Romans suffering only 360 dead to the Britons' 10,000. Agricola is awarded triumphal decorations and a statue by Domitian, then recalled to Rome for other duties. Although he leaves Britain 'peaceful and secure' for his successor, in reality he has only succeeded in pushing the Roman frontier further north: the Scottish Highlands remain out-of-bounds.

85 Pressure on the **Danube** forces Rome to withdraw its troops from northern Britain. Its most northerly forts are dismantled.

90 A new **colonia** (colony) is established at **Lincoln**.

96 A new colonia is begun at **Gloucester**.

98 The historian **Tacitus** completes the *Agricola*, an account of his father-in-law's life and campaigns.

The new emperor **Trajan** (98–117) decides to concentrate Roman forces on expansion in the Middle East, leaving Britain to stagnate. During his reign what remains of the Roman presence in Scotland is lost.

c.103 The Romans suffer significant losses in the north. A number of their forward fortifications are damaged or destroyed by fire.

107–8 The famous **9th Legion**'s last posting at York is recorded. Possibly it is wiped out by a local rebellion, although there is some evidence that it may simply have been withdrawn to the Continent.

118 A revolt among the **Brigantes** is put down.

122 Visiting Britain, the Emperor **Hadrian** (117–138) encourages the construction of a clear barrier between 'Roman' Britain and the 'barbarian' north. Work on **Hadrian's Wall** (see p.22) commences, reflecting a wider policy of defensive rationalization across the Roman Empire undertaken by Hadrian.

131 The distinguished general **Sextus Julius Severus** is appointed governor of Britain.

139 Work begins on the **Antonine Wall**, commissioned by the emperor Antoninus Pius, some 160km to the north of Hadrian's Wall, reflecting a renewed will to extend the Roman frontier in Britain.

155–8 There is a revolt in the north against the Romans.

163 The Antonine Wall is **abandoned**, though a number of forts north of Hadrian's Wall continue to be manned.

175 Rome's British garrison is re-enforced with the arrival of 5500 Sarmatian cavalrymen.

Roman Britain

Between Julius Caesar's initial reconnaissance of 55 BC and the Claudian campaigns of the AD 40s nearly a century elapsed – and still the conquest of Britain was never satisfactorily completed. Rome's legions were reluctant to venture across the English Channel to an island full of warring tribes, and once they did make the journey they struggled to impose the emperor's authority uniformly. The territory that would one day become Scotland remained intractable, and not very much could be done about the Welsh interior either.

Yet once the limitations of Roman rule in Britain were given concrete expression by **Hadrian's Wall** (see p.22), all the trappings of a Roman colony were swiftly imported: fortified townships, temples, villas, public baths, straight roads to expedite the movement of troops in times of crisis. As the archeological record demonstrates, in England and southern Wales at least the Roman presence was both widespread and intended to last. The development of cities including **Londinium**, **Verulamium** and **Eboracum** created new urban communities, and in time many Britons seemed to adopt Roman values. From Rome's point of

180 The 'barbarian' **Picts** north of the Roman frontier and other British tribes revolt and break through Hadrian's Wall, killing a garrison.

c.185 The Antonine Wall is put back into operation.

197 Governor Lupus begins the reconstruction of forts along the **Pennines**, bribing the northern tribes to return beyond Hadrian's Wall.

205–7 Hadrian's Wall is **refurbished** by Governor Alfenius Senecio.

c.207 The Antonine Wall is **abandoned once more**.

view, the province became an important source not only of auxiliaries and front-line troops for its armies but also of grain and other products for its endless wars against the German tribes of central Europe. In the longer term, the Roman occupation underlined Britain's relationship with Europe, not least through the medium of **Latin** – which endured in its written form as the language of the Catholic Church.

However, the culture of the people conquered by the Romans did undergo a radical transformation. The Romans brought first their own religion, then **Mithraism** and **Christianity**. While social organization largely revolved around existing tribal units, some tribes adopted Roman military strategies – which persisted even as late as the 5th century and the defence of **Ambrosius Aurelianus** against the Saxons (see p.37). And during the 4th century the province was used as a stepping stone for several ambitious generals aiming for the imperial crown. Britain's island position may have made it geographically detached from the mainstream of empire, but it was a crucial political component nonetheless.

208–9 Emperor Septimius Severus visits Britain. In a bid to reconquer the far north, he advances his forces as far as Aberdeen.

210 Yet again the northern British rise in rebellion against the Romans.

211 Emperor Septimius dies at York.

Campaigning against the Picts and other northern peoples beyond Hadrian's Wall is **abandoned**.

c.211 Britain is divided into two provinces: **Britannia Superior** (administered from London) and **Britannia Inferior** (from York).

Hadrian's Wall

Hadrian's Wall expresses an early attempt to define the limits of 'England' within the island of Britain. As such, the 140-km Tyne–Solway line chosen by Hadrian and his planners has lasted well, although today it is more a psychological than a physical barrier. The present border between England and Scotland has crept further north, but frontier towns like **Carlisle** remained focal points for English expansion and were much fought over during the Middle Ages. Impressive as it is, though, Hadrian's Wall is scarcely unique. The much longer **Great Wall of China**, originally constructed at the end of the 3rd century BC, is the obvious example of a similar attempt to demarcate the 'civilized' and 'barbarian' worlds. And before either, the **Greeks** built walls and fortifications to keep Dorian invaders at bay.

Of the Roman walls, though, Hadrian's is the most impressive. Intended as a division between two rebellious tribes, the **Selgovae** to the north and the **Brigantes** to the south, it was constructed using two million tonnes of rock and soil. A ditch ten metres wide and three metres deep was dug to the north of the wall, providing material for the five-metre-high and two-metre-thick southern ramparts. Every mile was marked by the construction of a small fort, and in between each of these **mile-castles** were two further watch-turrets. In addition to these there were sixteen larger forts spaced along the length of the wall, providing accommodation both for troops and some civilian trading populations. Everything was constructed by some nine thousand legionaries, commemorated in a number of transcriptions along the wall's length.

The sheer scale of the project represents the seriousness of Roman investment in the province, but the development of Roman Britain was by no means settled by Hadrian's policy: under **Antoninus Pius** (138–161) expansion once more became the order of the day, and Roman forces again tried their luck in Scotland. After their failure, though, the frontier reverted to Hadrian's Wall – a rationalization which signalled the limitations of a wider imperial project.

212 Caracalla, formerly joint 'Augustus' with Septimius Severus, extends Roman citizenship to almost the entire Empire, including Britain. He builds the first coastal fort at **Reculver**, designed to repel the raids being mounted by the Picts and Saxon pirates.

269–73 As the Roman empire experiences civil war, Britain forms a short-lived **independent empire** based on France.

287 Coastal defences, designed to repel the increasingly frequent attacks of Saxon pirates and known as the 'Saxon Shore', are started.

The Channel commander, **Carausius**, is accused of colluding with the Saxons in order to share their booty. To avoid trial he declares himself 'Augustus' and establishes a **separatist empire** in Britain and northern Gaul.

293 Carausius is assassinated and replaced as Augustus in Britain by his chief financial officer, **Allectus**. In Rome, Emperor **Diocletian** reorganizes the Roman Empire, dividing it into **twelve dioceses**. Britain becomes one of the twelve and is divided into four provinces.

296 The emperor **Constantius I** defeats Allectus and reunites the province of Britain with the Roman Empire. The northern frontier, however, is subjected to attacks from Ireland and the Continent.

306 Constantius I dies at **Eboracum** (York). The Roman army in Britain, perhaps encouraged by the Germanic chieftain Crocus, proclaims Constantius's son **Constantine** the new Augustus.

312 Having marched on Rome and established his imperial authority, Constantine **converts to Christianity**, which becomes recognized and promoted throughout the Roman Empire. Three British bishops, including the Bishop of London, will attend the **Council of Arles** in 314, convened by Constantine to settle the 'Donatist heresy'.

The coming of Christianity

According to legend the Christian Church in Britain was founded by Christ himself, travelling in the company of his uncle **Joseph of Arimathea**, who later returned to Britain with the Holy Grail and established a church at Glastonbury. What seems more likely is that **merchants** working the Cornish tin trade routes brought the new faith to Britain, assisted later by the Romans, who began to enlist Christians into the ranks of their armies. In around 200 the early Christian theologian **Tertullian** was commenting that areas of Britain had been Christianized, and Origen, a theologian of the early Greek church, confirmed this some forty years later. In 304 Britain acquired its first martyr, **St Alban**, and by 314 there were at least three British **dioceses**, at York, London and Colchester. Their bishops attended the Council of Arles, though they were absent from the Council of Nicaea in 325.

With Emperor Constantine's decree freeing Christians from persecution in 312, the church in Britain was able to grow: Christian iconography begins to appear in villas and private chapels, demonstrating that it was permeating the upper levels of British society. Such too was the growing influence of British Christian thought that by the close of the 4th century Britain could boast its first renowned heretic. Casting doubt on St Augustine's doctrine of **Original Sin**, the British monk **Pelagius** (c.360–c.420) taught that man can attain salvation through his own efforts, irrespective of Divine Grace. To counter such unorthodoxy the Church of Gaul sent a stream of missionaries, among them the militant **St Germanus of Auxerre** (d.446), who demonstrated the validity of his case by leading the British to victory against the northern Picts and other wayward Pelagians. But the schism ultimately reinforced the separateness of Christianity in Britain and indirectly helped to bring about the formation of the so-called **Celtic Church**, at odds with mainstream continental Christianity. This division would last until the **Synod of Whitby** in 664 (see pp.42–43), but on a deeper level it points to the course that later religious developments would take.

343 The Emperor Constans visits Britain and creates the position of **Count of the Saxon Shore** to oversee the defence of the southern and southeastern coasts, which are increasingly threatened by Saxon raids.

360 Emperor Julian despatches one of his senior commanders, **Lupicinus**, to contain escalating attacks by Picts and Scots.

Britain is influenced by Julian's 'apostasy' as he renounces Christianity; many areas return to paganism.

367 An alliance of **Saxons**, **Picts** and **Scots** assault Roman Britain's coastal defences, killing the Count of the Saxon Shore. The northern frontier is again breached.

369 A fifth Roman province, **Valentia** (possibly in the northwest of England), is created in honour of the emperors **Valentinian** and **Valens**.

383 Following a period of domestic upheaval in Rome, **Magnus Maximus** is proclaimed the new Roman emperor in Britain.

395 The *Notitia Dignitarum* ('Roll of Dignitaries'), recording the officials of the Roman Empire, cites three commands in Britain: the **Dux Britanniarum** (duke of Britain); the **Comes Litoris Saxonici** (count of the Saxon Shore); and the **Comes Britanniarum** (count of Britain).

400 Hadrian's Wall is abandoned as the northern frontier disintegrates under the weight of persistent Pict attacks.

401 Rome's remaining legions and other troops are withdrawn from Britain in order to protect Italy from **Alaric** and the **Visigoths**.

406 The **Romano-Britons** unilaterally elect **Marcus**, and – following Marcus's murder – **Gratian** as emperor.

A detail from a wall painting at Lullingstone, Kent, depicting the Greek letters *chi* and *rho* – the first letters of Christ's name.

407 Gratian's successor, **Constantine III**, abandons Britain when he takes his small forces to Gaul.

Burgundians beyond the control of the empire advance into **France** and **Spain**, further weakening Britain's links with the Empire.

408 The first substantial force of **Saxons** invade southern Britain.

409 The last Roman troops **leave** Britain.

410 Some British chieftians appeal to the emperor **Honorius** for help, but are told to fend for themselves.

c.417 A Roman presence may very briefly be re-established around this time (lasting until c.425).

426 After the Roman withdrawal, a number of local Romano-British **chieftains** emerge, including **Vortigern** in the west.

429 St Germanus is sent to Britain by the bishops of Gaul at the request of members of the British church to combat the **Pelagian heresy** (see p.24).

431 St Patrick is at work in Ireland.

> " After the enemy's depredations had ceased, there was so great an abundance of corn in the island as had never before been known. With this affluence came an increase of luxury, followed by every kind of foul crime ... Not only were laymen guilty of these offences but even the Lord's own flock and their pastors. They cast off Christ's easy yoke and thrust their necks under the burden of drunkenness, hatred, quarrelling, strife, and envy and other similar crimes. In the meantime a virulent plague suddenly fell upon these corrupt people which quickly laid low so large a number that there were not enough people alive to bury the dead. Yet those who survived could not be awakened from the spiritual death of their kinsmen or by fear of their own death. For this reason a still more terrible retribution soon afterwards overtook this sinful people for their fearful crimes. They consulted as to what they should do and where they should seek help to prevent or repel the fierce and very frequent attacks of the northern nations; all, including their king Vortigern, agreed that they should call the Saxons to their aid from across the seas. As events plainly showed, this was ordained by the will of God so that evil might fall upon these miscreants. "
>
> Bede, *The Ecclesiastical History of the English People*, trans. Bertram Colgrave

432 **St Ninian**, missionary to Scotland, dies.

446 The Britons make a last appeal to the nominal emperor, **Aetius**, but are again refused assistance.

c.450 Vortigern, now a principal British chieftain, turns to the Angle mercenaries **Hengist** and **Horsa** from northern Germany to provide troops to help counter the Saxon and Pictish threats, offering them lands in the south and east as payment. But Hengist and Horsa take advantage of the British reluctance to fight by ousting them from their lands and expanding their own territories.

Further influxes of **Angles**, **Jutes** and **Saxons** add to the pressure on the British in the south, and they begin to carve out new kingdoms for themselves.

2
The Anglo-Saxons and the Vikings
450–1066

The Roman withdrawal from Britain left the Romano-British chieftains little chance to take stock before they were faced by the challenge of fresh invasions. Successive waves of Saxons, Angles and Jutes began to land on Britain's eastern shores, creating what became a significant and comprehensive settlement that eventually reached the Welsh and Scottish borders.

Retrospectively this colonization was given the collective name **Anglo-Saxon**, from which the term 'England' itself is derived. Significantly, the Angles and Saxons (and perhaps the Jutes) shared a roughly common Germanic language which, once it had bedded down in its new domain, emerged as what we now call **Old English**. This provided the foundation for Middle English, developed after the Franco-Norman Conquest of 1066 – which in turn evolved into Modern English.

In the two essentials of language and territory, then, the Anglo-Saxon settlement was integral to the emerging identity of England – and it is tempting to see the true history of the country as beginning now. As ever, though, the picture is blurred: although the political power of the Celtic British diminished under the Anglo-Saxons, not all Celtic people were forced to move. Substantial British enclaves remained, such as the kingdom of **Elmet** in Yorkshire and some areas of **East Anglia**, and here the Anglo-Saxons only gradually assumed control. The rarity of Anglo-Saxon graves in such places suggests, unsurprisingly, that England's new rulers eventually achieved pre-eminence by marrying into the existing hierarchy as much as through violent conquest.

Out of all this England derived an ethnically varied population, further enriched by Viking settlements from the 9th century onwards. The people eventually conquered by the Normans were of **Celtic-Romano-Anglo-Saxon-Jutish-Danish** descent, with perhaps a dash of pre-Celtic thrown in. For the historian trying to determine the precise proportions of these components the problem is an almost total lack of data – prior to the Domesday Book of 1087, there is practically no information regarding the numbers of settlers who crossed over from the Continent. In the future, **genetic sampling** – not just of today's British population, but of western Europeans in general – may provide some interesting clues. For now, our understanding of 'early England' is necessarily restricted to the written and material records.

Thus it is not even clearly understood when the first Angles and Saxons arrived. The *Anglo-Saxon Chronicle*, begun in the 9th century to record the progress of the Anglo-Saxon people, is a valuable source in this respect, but it relies heavily on hearsay and myth to explain the earliest events of the English kingdoms. Even so, the *Chronicle* makes clear that settlement was piecemeal and drawn out over a period of at least a century-and-a-half. In all probability both Angles and Saxons had been employed as auxiliaries in Roman armies since the 4th century or before, so there may have been a handful of both living in England at the time of the Romans' departure. By then, coastal raids were common occurrences; equally, the newly assertive British chieftains, who sometimes invited Anglo-Saxon mercenaries to assist them in their wars – just as the Romans had done – surely encouraged Angles and Saxons to begin thinking of Britain as a permanent home.

The best-known instance of this was King Vortigern's appeal to **Hengist** and **Horsa** to help fend off attacks by Scots and Picts around 450 (see p.34). But this coincided with a much wider migration of people across the Eurasian landmass, possibly triggered by a volcanic eruption on the island of **Krakatoa** in the Indonesian archipelago which caused climate changes damaging livestock productivity in Central Asia. This movement of Huns, Vandals, Goths and Visigoths directly encouraged the break-up of the Roman empire; indirectly it caused demographic change in lands they never saw. And it was from this time that the 'Anglo-Saxon Conquest' began in earnest.

The creation of Anglo-Saxon England 450–800

For the partly Romanized Britons left to fend for themselves, the Angle, Saxon and Jutish raiders were every bit as intimidating as the Vikings who terrorized later generations of settled Anglo-Saxons. While, as their name suggests, the Jutes arrived from an area of southern Scandinavia approximating to 'Jutland', the Angles and Saxons came from northern Germany. Once in England, all three peoples established domains of varying size and effectiveness, usually described as the **Heptarchy** ('seven kingdoms'). Among these, **Wessex**, **Mercia** and **Northumbria** vied for supremacy. But as time went by the smaller kingdoms were swallowed up, meaning that eventually half of England was unified – albeit only in the face of Viking aggression – under the **royal house of Wessex**.

Even early on, though, there appears to have been some notion of overkingship, as evidenced by the term **Bretwalda**

– the name generally adopted by the most powerful Anglo-Saxon king. While the actual authority exercised by a Mercian Bretwalda over, say, Kent or Northumbria is debatable, from the 8th century onwards the political will to establish a single kingdom strengthened. **Alfred 'the Great'** could justifiably be described as 'king of all the English' by his biographer Asser; and Alfred's successors **Edward the Elder** and **Athelstan** certainly achieved greater cohesion among the now-blended English peoples than at any point before.

Anglo-Saxon England was always something of a mongrel state, though. As time went by, under-kings and their families became powerful local earls and ealdormen who frequently challenged their king and pursued their own territorial vendettas. Contrary to the nostalgic views of 18th-century historians such as **Viscount Bolingbroke**, England was not yet a democracy guided by a wise, paternalistic monarch – even though some administrative structures, as well as a feudal system of land ownership, fell into place under Saxon rule.

The Angle and Saxon invaders of the 5th and 6th centuries worshipped an array of gods, among them **Thor** (Donner), **Wodin** and **Loge** (Loki), and the Celtic church, such as it was, was steadily forced into small pockets in the north and west by those who they called the 'fierce heathens'. With the exception of Cornwall, by 550 Christianity was all but extinct in England. The British monk **Gildas**, writing around 547 in the unambiguously entitled *De Excidio Britanniae* ('the ruin of Britain'), condemned his peers for their want of faith. Yet within a century the picture had once again been transformed. First from Ireland, then under the direction of the Roman papacy, a steady stream of missionaries strove to recover lost ground.

The most celebrated of these was **St Augustine**, who on

Christmas Day 597 reputedly baptized some 10,000 souls at Canterbury. While such figures sound implausible, the mere fact of Augustine's and others' success points to continuing connections with continental Europe. The fact that Christianity reappeared most rapidly in the south suggests the cultural influence of merchants plying the Channel trade.

The Midlands and northern England proved more difficult to persuade. **Penda**, the ruler of Mercia, permitted four missionaries to preach in his kingdom in 653 but declined communion himself. Only with the conversion of Penda's son Peada did the outcome of the Christian mission in England appear more certain. **Lindisfarne**, an island off the northeastern coast, became an important centre of Christian learning after a monastery was founded there in 635. Little by little the map of ecclesiastical England, with its episcopal dioceses and small parishes, took shape. In terms of its influence on rural society, this was among the longest-lasting of all the developments that took place in Anglo-Saxon England.

England changed continually in the Anglo-Saxon period. The advent of the Vikings gave rise to two major power-bases in England: the Saxon lands dominated by the kingdom of **Wessex** and the Viking kingdom known as the **Danelaw**. Yet others too were significant players in 'English' politics. The kings of Mercia sometimes made alliances with British princes in what came to be known as Wales, while the Northumbrians and Vikings of the Danelaw sometimes joined forces with the Scots and Britons of Strathclyde. The accession of **Edward the Confessor** as king of England further complicated matters. Edward's mother Emma was Norman, and with him came a number of Norman and Breton favourites – making Edward the first **Anglo-Norman** monarch. Yet while there was little sense of unity among the various factions vying for power, Anglo-Saxon rulers were expected to take regular advice from their council of wise men, the **Witan**, which was gathered from among the leading nobles and clerics of the day. The king was normally accompanied by a number of these advisers during his progress around the kingdom, but he would call larger council meetings – *witenagemots* – during major festivals such as Christmas and Easter, or to solve major disputes. It was also the Witan's responsibility to choose a new king. When they chose **Harold Godwinson** as Edward the Confessor's heir, in effect inviting Norman invasion, it was a decision which would have a larger impact than anyone could have realized.

c. 450 Vortigern, a British king, seeks help from the continent to contain incursions into his territories by Picts and Scots from the north. According to the *Anglo-Saxon Chronicle*, two brothers, **Hengist** and **Horsa** – leaders of three shiploads of Angles – respond to his invitation. After campaigning successfully on Vortigern's behalf, they decide to settle in Kent rather than return to their homelands.

455 Hengist and Horsa rebel against Vortigern, defeating his forces possibly at **Aylesford** in Kent. Horsa is killed in battle.

> ❝ The fierce Saxons, of ever execrable memory, [were] admitted into the island, like so many wolves into a sheep fold, to defend [the British] from the northern Nations. A thing more destructive and pernicious than ever was done in this Kingdom. O the mist and grossness of this sense of apprehension! O the dullness and blockishness of these souls! ❞
>
> Gildas, *De Excidio Britanniae*, trans. L. and J. Laing

The Heptarchy

Anglo-Saxon England developed slowly over a period of more than a century. During this time numerous bands of warriors and other settlers from Germany, Denmark and the Low Countries established settlements in southern Britain. These settlements gradually formed kingdoms, and out of these disparate realms grew what became known as the Heptarchy, the seven principal areas of early Anglo-Saxon England: Northumbria, Mercia, Wessex, Sussex, Kent, East Anglia and Essex. At times, though, there were more than that number. Middlesex and Hwicce were important settlements before being absorbed into Wessex, and Northumbria initially comprised three kingdoms: Lindsey, Deira and Bernicia. Alongside these, several British principalities also survived well into the 7th century. The last important British bastion in England was Elmet (near Leeds), but numerous British territories in Wales, Dumnonia (Cornwall) and Rheged (Strathclyde) also held out.

By the end of the 8th century there were effectively only four major Anglo-Saxon kingdoms: Mercia, Northumbria, Wessex and East Anglia. These vied with each other for ultimate supremacy, the ruler of the most powerful being accorded the title of overking or Bretwalda. This was in reality a fairly informal arrangement and for some leaders purely honorific, but for kings such as Offa of Mercia it represented a real determination to build political power outside his own borders. As tensions mounted between the Anglo-Saxon kingdoms and the remaining British enclaves (and later between Anglo-Saxons and Vikings), England became increasingly united. In the 7th century, King Penda of Mercia joined with the Christian Gwynedd of Wales against Wessex and Northumbria, and in the 8th century it was Mercia that had the upper hand. But it was Wessex that ultimately came to predominate, founding what became the first English royal house. By the time that the Danelaw began to unravel in the 10th century, Wessex held all the cards.

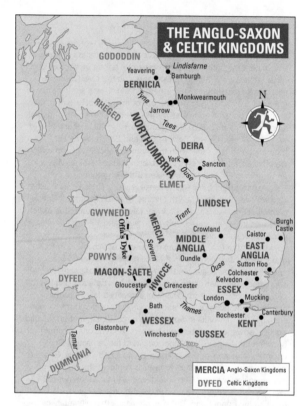

THE ANGLO-SAXON
& CELTIC KINGDOMS

GODODDIN

Yeavering *Lindisfarne*
Bamburgh
BERNICIA

RHEGED

Tyne
Monkwearmouth
Jarrow
Tees

N

NORTHUMBRIA

DEIRA

York Sancton
Ouse

ELMET

GWYNEDD

Offa's Dyke

LINDSEY

Trent

MERCIA

Crowland

Burgh
Castle

Caistor

**MIDDLE
ANGLIA**

**EAST
ANGLIA**

POWYS

Severn

MAGON·SAETE

Oundle

Ouse

Sutton Hoo

DYFED

Gloucester

HWICCE

Cirencester

Colchester
Kelvedon

ESSEX

Mucking

Bath

Thames

London

Canterbury

Glastonbury

WESSEX

Winchester

Rochester

KENT

SUSSEX

Tamar

DUMNONIA

| MERCIA | Anglo-Saxon Kingdoms |
| DYFED | Celtic Kingdoms |

456 Hengist and his son Esc drive the British out of Kent
and establish the **first kingdom** of Angles in Britain.

477 A Saxon community led by Elle settles in **Sussex**, displacing the British. According to Bede (see p.47), Elle
becomes the first **Bretwalda** or Anglo-Saxon overking.

> **❝** Amid the wreckage of deserted cities destroyed by the enemy, the citizens who had survived the enemy now attacked each other. So long as the memory of past disaster remained fresh, kings and priests, nobles and commoners, kept their proper rank. But when those who remembered died, there grew up a generation who knew nothing of these things and had experienced only the present peaceful order. Then were the restraints of truth so utterly abandoned that no trace of them remained, and very few of the people recalled their existence. **❞**
>
> Bede, *Ecclesiastical History of the English People*,
> trans. L. Sherley-Price and R. Latham

488 Hengist is succeeded as king of Kent by his son **Esc**, who rules for 24 years.

493 According to Bede, a Saxon army is defeated by Britons led by the Romano-British nobleman **Ambrosius Aurelianus**, a figure identified by some historians with the mythical King Arthur (see p.143).

495 Saxon settlers led by Cerdic and his son Cynric establish the kingdom of **Wessex**.

c. 500 As British resistance to Anglo-Saxon intrusion continues to stiffen, Saxons suffer another setback at **Mons Badonicus**, an unknown battle site possibly at or near Cadbury. According to tradition the British are led by **King Arthur**. In any event, the newcomers are temporarily restricted to the south and east.

501 Saxons led by **Port** establish a permanent camp at **Portsmouth**.

508 Cerdic and Cynric campaign westwards, defeating and killing a British king called **Natanleod**.

514 A Saxon band led by Stuf and Withgar establish a second kingdom in Wessex.

c. 539 According to legend, King Arthur is **killed** fighting his own followers, after his nephew (or illegitimate son) **Modred** rebels against him. In any event, it seems probable that renewed squabbling between Britons enables Angles and Saxons to **acquire more territory**.

c. 547 The British monk **Gildas** writes *De Excidio Britanniae* ('The ruin of Britain'), a diatribe detailing what he considers the fall of his people.

As the British continue to fight among themselves, the Anglo-Saxons make **further inroads** westwards and northwards.

560 Ethelbert becomes king of Kent, and is later accorded the title **Bretwalda**.

577 By defeating the British at **Dyrham**, the West Saxons (Saxon settlers in Wessex) secure control of the townships of **Bath**, **Gloucester** and **Cirencester**.

597 Pope Gregory I ('the Great'), eyeing the vibrant new kingdoms of the Anglo-Saxons, dispatches the Benedictine monk **Augustine** to Britain. Augustine's mission of forty monks lands on the island of **Thanet** off the Kent coast, and is welcomed by King Ethelbert, perhaps through the intercession of his Christian queen Bertha. After converting both the court and its followers to the Catholic faith, Augustine founds Christ Church at **Canterbury** after he is consecrated 'Bishop of the English' by St Virgilius of Arles. Canterbury consequently becomes the centre of Christianity in England and an important school for training later missionaries.

c. 598 Assembling at Edinburgh, northern British warriors march south to confront the Angles, but are comprehensively defeated at **Catreth** (Catterick). The northern

Brythonic bard **Aneirin** witnesses the carnage, and composes the elegiac *Y Gododdin*, destined to become a cornerstone of early Welsh literature.

601 Augustine is accorded 'metropolitan' jurisdiction over all the English by Pope Gregory as a new **archdiocese** is created.

604 Augustine establishes episcopal dioceses at **London** and **Rochester**, their bishops being subordinate to Canterbury. As Christianity spreads among the Angles and Saxons, further bishoprics are created. Augustine fails, though, to bring members of the British Celtic church back into the Roman fold after meeting Welsh church leaders at **Malmesbury** in Wiltshire.

605 St Augustine dies.

616 **Edwin** becomes King of Northumbria. His authority is quickly undermined when in the same year the Bretwalda, **Redwald** of East Anglia, attacks his territory having led his forces through Mercia. Briefly Redwald imposes his rule over the whole of Anglo-Saxon Britain.

624 Redwald dies, and is perhaps buried at **Sutton Hoo**. Edwin of Northumbria is acknowledged Bretwalda.

625 **Paulinus**, bishop of Kent and one of St Augustine's original companions, accompanies **Ethelburga**, daughter of King Ethelbert, to Northumbria.

627 King **Edwin** of Northumbria marries Ethelburga and converts to Christianity. Paulinus becomes bishop of a new diocese founded at **York**.

632 Edwin dies fighting **Cadwallon** (Cedwalla), the British king of Gwynedd. Cadwallon successfully joins forces with the king of Mercia, **Penda**, against the kingdom of Northumbria and its new king **Oswald**. Paulinus is forced to flee south, where he becomes Bishop of Rochester.

Anglo-Saxon craftsmanship

It was once thought that the Anglo-Saxons were culturally deficient, inhabitants of the 'Dark Ages' between the fall of Rome and the revival of learning in the 11th and 12th centuries. In fact they designed fine buildings and produced highly refined and

The Alfred Jewel.

633 Oswald of Northumbria regroups and defeats Cadwallon at **Heavenfield**, effectively bringing hopes of a British resurgence in the north to an end. The **alliance** between Gwynedd and Mercia, however, continues.

634 Paulinus is appointed **archbishop of Canterbury** by Pope Honorius I.

635 Influenced by King Oswald, King Cynegils of Wessex is elaborate ornaments. An outstanding example of the latter is the ship-burial discovered at Sutton Hoo in 1939. The site contained a 7th-century body – a warrior of high rank – buried in a long boat beneath a mound, together with his weapons and other treasures. The artefacts, including a ceremonial sceptre and an intricately engraved helmet, are among the finest of the period ever recovered. Also found was a well-constructed harp, symbolic of the importance attached to music and storytelling. Circumstantial evidence suggests that Sutton Hoo may well be the tomb of the Bretwalda Redwald.

A find of equal significance and beauty is the small pointer or *estal* known as the Alfred Jewel, discovered in 1693 in marshes near Athelney, Somerset, where King Alfred (see p.55) centred his resistance to the Vikings. A small golden oval with the figure of Christ (or perhaps Sight) in the centre picked out in precious stones, the Jewel is surrounded with rock crystal. Around the edge of the piece is the inscription *AELFED M/ED H/EH/T GEWYRCAN* – 'Alfred had me made'. Alfred's biographer Asser records that Alfred ordered several Bibles to be made for his bishops and abbots, and it is likely that a pointer like the Jewel would have accompanied each. While such discoveries are relatively few in number, they affirm literary descriptions of exquisitely crafted objects contained not only in the sagas of the time but also in the more prosaic *Anglo-Saxon Chronicle*.

baptized by the Roman missionary to Wessex, Birinus. He bases himself at Dorchester and enjoys modest success in converting Cynegils' Wessex men to Roman Christianity. **Aidan**, an Irish monk from Iona in the Inner Hebrides, founds a religious community on **Lindisfarne** (Holy Island), off the coast of Northumberland, at Oswald of Northumbria's invitation. Of the Anglo-Saxon kingdoms in England, only Mercia remains largely 'unconverted'.

642 King Oswald is killed fighting the British at **Oswestry**. He is succeeded by Oswy.

644 Death of St Paulinus.

653 **King Penda of Mercia** permits four missionaries to work among his people, although he does not himself convert to Christianity.

655 Penda **dies in battle** fighting Oswy of Northumbria. His son and successor, **King Peada**, who has already converted, encourages the spread of Christianity in his Mercian kingdom.

664 King Oswy convenes a **synod**, or council of churchmen, at **Whitby** to determine whether Northumbria should follow the Celtic or the Roman church. A Roman Catholic delegate, **Wilfrid**, persuades the synod to decide in favour of Rome; led by Colman, the Celtic Christians return to Ireland. But immediately after the synod, according to the *Anglo-Saxon Chronicle,* a **'pestilence'** sweeps across England, encouraging some Anglo-Saxon leaders to return to their previous beliefs. When the Archbishop of Canterbury **Deusdedit** dies, it is four years before the pope can find a willing replacement.

668 **Theodore**, originally from Asia Minor, is appointed Archbishop of Canterbury. Although he encounters some opposition from Wilfrid and other established figures, his reforming zeal strengthens the fabric of the Roman Anglo-Saxon church.

670 As the power of Mercia grows, Oswy of Northumberland is succeeded by his son **Ecgfrith**.

672 Theodore, Archbishop of Canterbury, convenes the **Council of Hereford** to resolve outstanding issues among Anglo-Saxon churchmen. It is agreed that Easter will be uniformly observed in all dioceses, and that bishops will meet annually at **Clofeshoh** (location now unknown). The

The Synod of Whitby (664)

The progress of Christianity in England was far from smooth. As St Augustine's mass conversion of 'ten thousand' souls at Canterbury in 597 suggests, much depended on winning over the ruler of the day. If a king could be converted then so too were all his subjects, but such an outcome was easily reversed by political or even environmental events – natural disasters or unfavourable portents were taken very seriously, and all sides traded in superstition.

Nor did it help that two separate and increasingly antagonistic churches vied for power. As this division of loyalties – between the Celtic north and west and the Roman south and east – hardened, King Oswy of Northumbria summoned a council or moot of churchmen at Whitby in 664 to determine which version his kingdom should adhere to. Much of the acrimony centred on the dating of Easter. The Celtic Church set it slightly later than its Roman counterpart, giving rise to a curious situation in which the queen of Northumbria, a Roman Christian, celebrated Easter whilst her husband, a Celtic Christian, was still observing Lent.

Under the supervision of Hilda, Abbess of Whitby, spokesmen from both sides were invited to argue their case. On the Celtic team were SS Colman and Cedd; on the Roman, James the Deacon and St Wilfrid. Colman and his followers eventually lost the war of words and retreated first to Iona, a religious community in the Hebrides, then to Ireland: it was decided that Northumbria would be Roman Catholic.

In the annals of English history, though (written and manipulated in its early phases largely by Roman Catholic monks), Whitby became synonymous with something grander – the triumph not just of Roman Catholicism but of Christianity itself.

bishops further agree to administer marriage laws and to establish rules governing the relations between themselves and monasteries and other religious foundations.

678 A Northumbrian army led by Ecgfrith is defeated by Mercia near the river Trent.

St Cuthbert (634–687)

One feature of Anglo-Saxon history is its roll-call of local saints, including two of royal pedigree, **Edmund of East Anglia** (c.841–869) and **Edward the Confessor** (c.1002–1066) – who were regarded as the patron saints of England until they were displaced by the Turkish hero St George.

But perhaps the best-loved of all was **Cuthbert**, probably a native of Northumberland. Raised as a shepherd, he experienced visions in early adolescence and entered the Celtic Northumbrian monastery of **Melrose** when he was sixteen. In 660, when Melrose was struck by plague, he became its prior and, aided by a reputation for bringing relief to plague victims, worked to spread the Christian message among the Northumbrian people. He attended the Synod of Whitby, and thereafter promoted Roman rather than Celtic practice. In 664 he was appointed prior of **Lindisfarne** under Bishop Eata, and was mainly responsible for instituting the monastery's exacting Benedictine disciplines. At the same time he continued his missionary work, and is traditionally credited with founding the Christian community at **Durham**, which became an important centre of the Roman Church in the northeast.

But for all his energetic proselytizing Cuthbert was by nature a recluse, and in 676 he retired to the island of **Inner Farne** to pursue a contemplative hermit life. In 684, however, Ecgfrith of Northumbria persuaded Cuthbert to become **Bishop of Hexham** and the following year Cuthbert returned to Lindisfarne as its **bishop-abbot**, dying two years later during another retreat to Inner Farne. His body, first buried on Lindisfarne, was exhumed in 875 to guard against Viking desecration and eventually came to rest in the cathedral at Durham, where the treasures of his richly carved coffin remain preserved.

685 The Saxon **Cedwalla** becomes King of Wessex and immediately begins expanding his territory into the southeast of England.

According to the *Anglo-Saxon Chronicle* during the course of the year it **rains blood**; milk and butter turn to blood.

686 Continuing his expansionist policy, Cedwalla, together with his brother Mul, lays waste to **Kent**. A **plague** kills many members of a newly founded monastic community at Jarrow in Northumbria, but its abbot **Ceolfrid** and the young **Bede** (see p.47) survive.

687 Mul and twelve of his followers are **captured and killed** by a Kentish war party; exacting reprisals, Cedwalla again ravages the southeastern kingdom.

Cuthbert, one of the foremost patron saints of the English church, dies on the islet of Inner Farne, close to Lindisfarne (Holy Island).

688 Cedwalla journeys to Rome and, a week before his death, is **baptized** by Pope Sergius. He is succeeded as King of Wessex by **Ine**, founder of the first abbey at **Glastonbury**.

690 Archbishop (later Saint) Theodore dies.

692 Behrtwald, a native Englishman and formerly Abbot of Reculver, is appointed archbishop in succession to Theodore. From now, English archbishops are generally recruited by Rome from amongst the English.

694 King Ine of Wessex is paid substantial **compensation** by the people of Kent for the murder of Mul in 687 (see p.45).

698 Around this time the **Lindisfarne Gospels**, a sumptuously decorated Latin text (with later Anglo-Saxon glosses), are consecrated at the island's monastery – possibly to celebrate the elevation of the relics of **St Cuthbert**.

710 As border conflicts continue, ealdorman **Beorhtfrith** fights against the Picts in the north; Ine of Wessex and his kinsman Nunna fight against **Geraint of Cornwall**.

The title page from the Gospel of St John, Lindisfarne Gospels.

St Bede (673–735)

The 'Venerable' Bede was a figure of European as well as national stature, and through his scholarly work he transcended a distinctly provincial background.

Born in Monkton in Jarrow, he began his schooling at the monastery of St Peter at Wearmouth in 679. He quickly fell under the influence of its cosmopolitan-minded Abbot, Benedict Biscop, who encouraged Bede to devote his life to learning and contemplation. In 685 he transferred to the sister monastery of St Paul at Jarrow, where he remained until his death, taking holy orders in 703.

From his pen flowed a steady stream of treatises, Biblical commentaries and historical writings. An early interest in the intricacies of dating events inspired Bede to devise the AD (*anno domini*) system for fixing a universal chronology from the birth of Christ. In this field his masterwork was *De temporam ratione* ('On the reckoning of time'), completed in 725, in which he endeavoured to solve the contentious issue of Easter's placement in the calendar. But although Bede also delved into grammar and orthography, in England at least he is best remembered for his *Historia ecclesiastica gentis Anglorum* ('Ecclesiastical history of the English peoples'), which detailed the progress of Christianity in what became the Anglo-Saxon kingdoms from Roman times onwards. Although Bede restricts his historical enquiry to religious developments and is fond of hagiography when recounting the lives of missionary saints, his scrupulous attention to chronology makes his an invaluable guide to the early Anglo-Saxon settlement, one which stands alongside the *Anglo-Saxon Chronicle*. But if Bede (and his mentor Biscop) seems to epitomize the growth of a more literate culture in late 7th- and early 8th-century England, his wider reputation was only gained after his death. That it developed at all is due to one of his own pupils, Alcuin, who travelled to the continent with copies of Bede's texts, where they were gradually disseminated through monasteries.

716 Ethelbald begins a 41-year reign as king of Mercia, which, under his rule, establishes itself as the pre-eminent Anglo-Saxon kingdom.

731 Bede completes his *History of the English Church and People* (also known as the *Ecclesiastical History*).

735 Bede dies.

757 Ethelbald of Mercia is succeeded by his son **Offa**. As well as extending Mercian authority over other Anglo-Saxon kingdoms, Offa either commissions or collaborates in the construction of extended defensive earthworks (known as **Offa's Dyke**) marking the boundary between Mercia and westerly Britons inhabiting modern Wales.

786 The first **papal legates** to arrive in England since St Augustine are welcomed at Offa's court.

787 Offa's son **Egfrith** is crowned king of the Mercians.

793 According to the *Anglo-Saxon Chronicle*, terrible **portents** appear in the skies over Northumbria. Heavy lightning and fiery dragons accompany the beginning of **Viking raids** on the monastic communities of **Lindisfarne** and **Iona**.

794 Offa asserts his authority over the East Anglians by beheading their king, **Ethelbehrt**.

796 Shortly before his death Offa is sent a **letter** – the only surviving missive from a European to an Anglo-Saxon ruler, and held to mark the high-point of Mercian ascendancy in England – from **Charlemagne** of the Franks praising his rule and describing him as 'a brother'.

Offa is succeeded by his son **Egfrith**, but soon afterwards Egfrith also dies – a double death interpreted by the monk **Alcuin** as a divine judgement.

798 King **Coelwulf** (Coenwulf) of Mercia attacks Kent. The Kentish king, **Edbert Praen**, is captured. After being taken to Mercia, he is blinded and his hands removed. Despite this, though, Mercian power is increasingly challenged by the growing prestige of Wessex and by the Viking attacks.

The Viking invasions and the expansion of Wessex 800-1066

Although the Anglo-Saxons continued to fight among themselves – and although Britons and Picts continued to challenge their borders – from about 600 Britain had enjoyed two centuries of respite from large-scale continental immigration. It was this period of relative stability that enabled England to become Christianized. But from the end of the 8th century a new and violent threat appeared: the **Vikings**. Their appearance was, as it happened, just the first stage in a gradual Scandinavian encroachment which would finish three centuries later with the arrival of the Normans – who were, as their name suggests, of Nordic origin. It was this that would bring an end to the unified Anglo-Saxon state finally achieved by the Wessex kings.

The Viking attacks on England have long been represented as indiscriminate assaults perpetrated by brutal pagans intent only on violence and destruction. Such at any rate was the view shared by Bede's disciple Alcuin, the compilers of the *Anglo-Saxon Chronicle* and other monastic witnesses of the time – hardly surprising given that monasteries were among the Vikings' first targets. But their testimony is only part of the truth: the Vikings, just like their Saxon and Angle predecessors, were also interested in acquiring territory and establishing peaceful permanent settlements.

In fact the Viking peoples went to extraordinary lengths to set up new settlements. **Harald Hardrada**, before he was killed at Stamford Bridge in 1066, had ventured as far as Russia and Byzantium in the search for land. The emperor Charlemagne's later years were regularly plagued by Viking raids, and Normandy itself was the price the western Franks had eventually to pay for peace. The Vikings also established colonies in Ireland, and – most famously of all – **Leif Ericson** explored what became America centuries before Christopher Columbus and other European settlers.

In England in particular the Vikings left a lasting impression. A Viking kingdom, the **Danelaw**, extended from the borders of Scotland to East Anglia, and other pockets of Viking influence are still to be found in northwest England. The Cumbrian dialect closely resembles some aspects of Norwegian, suggesting that it wasn't just Danish Vikings who travelled to mainland Britain. It was, though, a Dane – King Svein – who in the 11th century took control of the whole of England; and the accession of King Cnut (Canute) to the throne in 1016 might well have led to England's permanent attachment to Scandinavia – an outcome only prevented by the failure of his sons Harold Harefoot and Harthacnut to continue the family line.

Still, intermarriage and wrangling between the contending courts meant that Viking interests still played an integral part in the unfolding political drama. Edward the Confessor relied on a Viking Earl, **Siward**, to control Northumbria, and his successor, **Harold Godwinson**, owed his position as much to his Nordic as his Anglo-Saxon ancestry.

What is striking is the extent to which dynastic politics had, by the middle of the 11th century, become hugely important. Battles between different ethnic groups were as common now as they had been in the fifth and sixth centuries, but mass migration was no longer the principle instigator of conflict; rather it was the aims and objectives of individual power-brokers that began to shape events. If there is a single reason for the collapse of the Anglo-Danish state, it can be traced back to Edward the Confessor's penchant for

The Royal House of Wessex

Egbert 802–39
Ethelwulf 839–855
Ethelbald 855–60
Ethelbert 860–866
Ethelred I 866–71
Alfred ('the Great') 871–899
Edward the Elder 899–924
Athelstan 924–939
Edmund I 939–946
Eadred 946–955
Eadwig 955–959
Edgar 959–975
Edward the Martyr 975–979
Ethelred II ('the Unready') 968–1016
Edmund II ('Ironside') 1016
(Edmund b.1016)
(Edward the Exile d.1057)
Edward the Confessor 1042–1066
(Edgar the Atheling d.1125)

preferring Norman favourites such as his nephew **Earl Ralph** and the Breton **Robert FitzWimarc** – which in turn enabled Duke William of Normandy to seize power.

This development could not have happened without the emergence of a single polity under the Saxon House of Wessex. Under Alfred ('the Great') and Athelstan in particular the court of **Wessex** became the centre of Anglo-Saxon life. And although the same Viking assistance that helped the Wessex monarchs secure their expanded kingdom also led to their eventual undoing, by 1016 there was a sense in which 'England' existed as a unit – and a prize well worth having.

802 **Egbert** becomes king of Wessex. The Hwicce and the people of Wiltshire **meet in battle**. The Wiltshiremen win, putting an end to Hwicce as an independent kingdom.

815 Egbert campaigns in **Cornwall**, expanding the boundaries of the kingdom of Wessex and attacking the last outpost of the Celts in England.

825 Egbert turns his attention toward Mercia and defeats its king, **Beornwulf**, at **Ellandun**. The East Angles accept Egbert's overlordship and rebel against Mercian domination, killing Beornwulf.

Egbert's son **Ethelwulf** conquers Kent, Surrey, Sussex and Essex.

829 Egbert subdues Mercia and the lands south of the Humber, and becomes the **eighth Bretwalda**.

830 Egbert campaigns against the Celtic Britons of **Wales**.

835 Vikings, in their largest raid to date, lay waste to the island of **Sheppey** off Kent.

836 A Viking war-band defeats Egbert at **Carhampton** in Somerset.

A Viking ship, as depicted in the late 10th-century Anglo-Saxon chroniclers.

838 A Viking war-band joins forces with the Cornish Britons but is defeated by Egbert at **Hingston Down**.

839 Egbert is succeeded by **Ethelwulf**.

850 The *Anglo-Saxon Chronicle* records that for the first time Vikings stay in England during the winter months.

853 **Ethelwulf of Wessex** and **Burghred of Mercia** band together against the Welsh Britons.

855 Setting out on a pilgrimage to Rome with his youngest son **Alfred**, Ethelwulf divides his kingdom between his eldest sons **Ethelbald** and **Ethelbert**. En route father and son stay at the court of **Charles the Bald** of France. Ethelwulf marries Charles's daughter **Judith**.

In Wessex, **Ethelbald** attempts a coup to prevent his father's return. Although this fails, he is permitted to remain in power.

858 Upon Ethelwulf's death, **Ethelbald** succeeds to the throne of Wessex but creates unpopularity by immediately marrying his stepmother **Judith**.

The Danelaw

What began toward the end of the 8th century as little more than piratical raids had by the middle of the 9th developed into a more systematic process of colonization by the Vikings. The result was a relatively stable kingdom known as the **Danelaw** which grew to dominate **Northumbria**, **East Anglia** and **Mercia** from its capital at **Jorvik** (York) following the town's seizure in 919. This was just one part of a Viking expansion which covered parts of **Scotland**, **Ireland**, the **Isle of Man** and **Normandy** in northern France. Their presence also connected England with the wider limits of Viking exploration, which extended east into **Russia** and west as far as **Vinland** (America).

Alfred the Great's victory over Guthrum at **Edington** in 878 held on to Wessex, however, and his successors continued to expand their territory at Viking expense, Alfred's great-great-grandson **Eadred** finally expelling Eric Bloodaxe from York in 954. But by the 10th century the Vikings were once more gaining the upper hand, their control cemented in 1013 by the accession of the Danish **Svein I Haraldsson** as king of England. By then the Danes were accepted as part of the united kingdom created by Alfred's heirs: they were among Athelstan's forces at **Brunanburgh**, and leading Danish warlords such as **Siward** ruled the north on behalf of Saxon kings.

And it was not until **William the Conqueror**'s defeat of the rebellion against him in 1071 that he could be reasonably safe from Viking incursions (not to mention secure against the Saxon people he had conquered). But of course the Normans, as Viking descendants, also represented a tradition of Norse expansion which stretched all the way back to the 790s.

859 Ethelwulf dies and is succeeded by Ethelbert.

865 A **Viking army** lands in England and over the next four years carves out a northern kingdom – the **Danelaw** – from territories previously belonging to Mercia and Northumbria.

In Wessex, Ethelbert **dies** and is succeeded by his brother **Ethelred**.

869–70 Edmund, king of East Anglia, is brutally killed at **Hoxne** in Suffolk, shot to death with arrows – perhaps in parody of the martyrdom of St Sebastian. Subsequently Edmund is **canonized** and becomes one of the principal English saints. Having established the Danelaw, the Vikings take over **East Anglia** and what remains of **Mercia**.

871 The Vikings begin attacking **Wessex**. King Ethelred and his brother Alfred resist, but their forces are worn down. Ethelred **dies** in April, and **Alfred** becomes king of Wessex.

875 Viking pressure compels the **monks of Lindisfarne** to evacuate. Fleeing inland with the remains of **St Cuthbert** they eventually settle at Durham, where a new community is founded.

878 A Viking war-band takes the Saxons of Wessex by surprise at the royal manor of **Chippenham**. King Alfred, accompanied by a handful of followers, is forced into hiding at **Athelney** in Somerset while the Vikings, led by Guthrum, ravage his kingdom. In May, however, Alfred rallies his forces and defeats Guthrum at **Ethandun** (Edington). Guthrum is coerced into converting to Christianity, and pledges not to stray outside the Danelaw. Effectively England is divided between two main kingdoms: the **Danelaw** and **Wessex**.

891 Alfred orders the composition in 'English' (Anglo-Saxon) of an annal of principal events which will develop into the *Anglo-Saxon Chronicle*.

Anglo-Saxon literature

The three most significant British pre-medieval literatures – in Welsh, Gaelic and Anglo-Saxon – share some important similarities. They all have roots in ancient traditions of oral poetry; they were practised by bards and minstrels who worked at the courts of kings and other political leaders; and examples of their work were set down by monks schooled in Latin composition – and thus preserved in monastic libraries.

The chief poetic glory of Anglo-Saxon poetry (but one which makes no mention of Britain) is the 3000-line epic *Beowulf*, which recounts the exploits of the eponymous hero as he struggles against first the monstrous Grendel and then Grendel's equally monstrous mother. Probably composed in the early 8th century but almost certainly based on an earlier matrix, the version that has survived was transcribed around 1000. Other extant poems include *The Battle of Maldon* and *The Seafarer* and the more overtly religious work *The Dream of the Rood*. That the tradition of Anglo-Saxon poetry persisted until at least the end of the 10th century is proved by the *Battle of Brunanburgh*, which is inspired by the conflict of that name in 937 but imbued with the values of earlier epics. Typically such pieces combine heroic pagan values with a sense of Christian humility – the latter sometimes interpolated by monastic scholars. The constant adaptation of existing poems to suit altered circumstances and new audiences means that most Anglo-Saxon poets are anonymous. One of the few whose names we do know, Cynewulf, left no clear indication of when he was writing.

The authors of the most significant prose work in the vernacular, the *Anglo-Saxon Chronicle*, are likewise obscure. Its initial composition is usually associated with King Alfred, who ordered the creation of an annal in 891. Thereafter the *Chronicle* was regularly maintained until well after the Norman Conquest. Its earliest entries refer to the 5th century, and its span of almost 700 years is unique in Europe.

891 King Alfred dies and is succeeded by his son **Edward the Elder**. With his sister **Ethelfled**, 'Lady of the Mercians', Edward begins challenging the Danelaw.

920 After thirty years of campaigning Edward completes the '**reconquest**' of England. He accepts the submission of Regnald of York, Ealdred of Bamburgh, the Strathclyde British and Constantine, king of the Scots at Bakewell.

925 Edward is succeeded by his son **Athelstan**, known as '**King of All England**'.

927 The Scots and Strathclyde Britons take advantage of Edward's death to reassert their independence; Athelstan invades **Northumbria** and secures their submission.

934 Athelstan advances as far as **Kincardine** in Fife, but his success unites the northern peoples against him and he is forced to **abandon** the conquest of Scotland.

937 After his enemies form an alliance, Athelstan defeats a joint Danish, Scottish and Strathclyde army in the battle of **Brunanburgh** – events recounted in the Anglo-Saxon poem of that name.

937 Athelstan is succeeded as king of England by **Edmund I**.

> In this year king Edmund, lord of the English,
> Guardian of kinsmen, loved doer of deeds, conquered Mercia.
> As far as Dore and Whitwell Gap the boundary form
> And Humber River, that broad ocean-stream;
> The Boroughs Five he won, Leicester and Lincoln,
> Nottingham, Derby and Stamford too.
> Long had the Danes under the Norsemen
> Been subjected by force to heathen bondage,
> Until finally liberated by the valour of Edward's son,
> King Edmund, protector of warriors.
>
> *The Anglo-Saxon Chronicle*, year entry for 942, trans. G.N. Garmonsway

946 Edmund is succeeded by **Eadred**.

954 Eadred expels the Viking king **Eric Bloodaxe** from York.

955 Upon Eadred's death his kingdom is divided between his sons **Eadwig** (who gets Wessex) and **Edgar** (Mercia).

959 The English kingdoms are **reunited** when Eadwig dies and Edgar takes his brother's dominions.

975 Edgar dies, leaving behind two sons, Edward and **Ethelred**. Because there are doubts about Edward's

Ethelred (Aethelraed) 'the Unready' (968–1016)

It's somewhat ironic that one of the least successful Anglo-Saxon kings enjoyed one of the longest reigns in English history – nearly fifty years on the throne. The 'unready' nickname is deceptive, though: it is derived from the Anglo-Saxon for 'badly advised', so that 'Aethelraed Unraed' literally translates as 'Good Advice, Badly Counselled'.

To his credit it is true that he inherited a difficult situation that would have taxed someone far more able. From its beginning his rule was troubled by renewed Viking attacks, but in 991 he negotiated a treaty with Richard, Duke of Normandy which denied the raiders shelter across the Channel. But this success was effectively overturned a year later with the defeat of Byrhtnoth at Maldon. The huge implications of this catastrophe became apparent when Ethelred decided to renew the payment of Danegeld, a form of protection money that did little to temper the Vikings' appetite for adventure. Their raids escalated until finally, in 1013, Ethelred was forced into exile by King Svein of Denmark. Ethelred attempted a comeback in 1015, but was quickly undermined by Svein's successor Cnut and died in London a year later.

legitimacy there is dispute about which should succeed. Having secured the Church's backing, **Edward** becomes king but his short reign is politically turbulent.

979 Edward, who becomes nicknamed 'the Martyr', is **murdered** at Corfe Castle, probably by a supporter of Edward's brother Ethelred and perhaps with the connivance of Edward's family. Ethelred, known as 'the Unready', accedes to the throne.

991 Ealdorman **Byrhtnoth** and his followers are defeated, with heavy Saxon losses, by Viking raiders at the **Battle of Maldon** in Essex. In the same year, the Saxons offer to pay the Vikings money (**Danegeld**) in exchange for promises not to launch further attacks. This arrangement only encourages Viking raiders to extort greater sums, and so their raids continue.

993 The northeast of England is subjected to a series of particularly ferocious Viking attacks.

995 Halley's Comet crosses the skies above Britain, portending – in the minds of its interpreters at least – great adversity.

997 Viking raiders penetrate the west of England.

998 Establishing bases in Sussex and on the Isle of Wight, Viking war parties terrorize **Dorset**.

999 The **Kentish fyrd** (see box on p.62) is defeated in battle by a Viking army advancing on Rochester.

1001 Viking warriors wreak havoc in many parts of England. The **Hampshire fyrd** attempts resistance, but is badly mauled.

1002 In desperation Ethelred agrees to pay substantial amounts of **Danegeld** to Viking leaders. In the same year he marries **Emma**, daughter of **Duke Richard of Normandy** – the beginning of an association that will result in

Richard's descendant **William of Normandy** successfully laying claim to the English throne.

1004 King Svein of Denmark, at the head of a large Viking army, harries East Anglia and sacks Norwich. Breaking a **truce** with local ealdormen, he kills many English noblemen in savage fighting.

1005 England's troubles are compounded by a sizeable **famine**. The Vikings, however, temporarily **withdraw** to Denmark.

1007 Ethelred pays out more Danegeld.

1008 As it becomes apparent that Danegeld is unlikely to be anything other than a stop-gap measure, Ethelred orders a large **fleet** to be built so that the Vikings can be repulsed at sea.

1009 Ethelred's navy is all but **destroyed** during a dispute between two of his ealdormen, **Beorhtric** and **Wulfnoth**.

1010 The Vikings resume their attacks against East Anglia. Among many English nobles killed is Ethelred's son-in-law **Athelstan**.

1011 Ethelred again offers Danegeld to the Danish Vikings. He has little choice: they now control a large swathe of southern England from Essex and Kent all the way to Hampshire.

> ❝ All these misfortunes befell us by reason of bad policy in that tribute was not offered them in time; but when they had done their worst, then it was that peace was made with them. And notwithstanding all this truce and peace and tribute, they went about everywhere in bands, and robbed and slew our unhappy people. ❞
>
> *Anglo-Saxon Chronicle*, year-entry for 1011, trans. G.N. Garmonsway

1012 Again the Danish Vikings are bought off with Danegeld.

1013 No longer content to raid and extort Danegeld, King Svein of Denmark mounts a full-scale **invasion**. Ethelred **flees** to his wife's homeland in Normandy and Svein is acknowledged **king of England**.

1014 Svein is succeeded by his son **Cnut** (Canute). Ethelred returns to England and for a while fights successfully against the Vikings. Cnut returns to Denmark to raise a larger army.

1015 Cnut **re-invades** England, defeats Ethelred and secures his claim to the throne.

1016 Ethelred dies in London and is succeeded by **Edmund 'Ironside'** as the English claim to the throne. Edmund is defeated in battle by Cnut at Abingdon and dies shortly after, probably murdered. Cnut's authority is acknowledged by what remains of the English nobility, and England is added to Denmark's Scandinavian empire.

1017 Cnut marries Ethelred's widow, Emma of Normandy.

1018 Cnut is proclaimed **king of Denmark**.

1028 Cnut adds Norway to his domains by ousting **King Olaf**.

1031 Cnut accepts the submission of the **king of Scots**.

1035 Cnut dies at **Shaftesbury**. The succession is disputed between his designated heir **Harthacnut** and the illegitimate **Harold Harefoot**. Seizing the initiative, **Harold** is proclaimed king of England.

1036 Ethelred's second son Alfred is imprisoned by **Godwin**, the Earl of Wessex. Alfred is blinded and soon dies of his injuries.

The English shires and the fyrd system

The division of England into **shires** (counties) was completed relatively late in the Anglo-Saxon period. The first shires developed in Wessex, growing out of former kingdoms in the southeast such as Hampshire and Wiltshire and each presided over by a royal official, originally an **ealdorman** but later a **Shire Reeve** (Sheriff). The shires themselves were subdivided into **hundreds** or *wapentakes*. Like the shires, hundreds were far from uniform, their size and function depending largely on whether they were new administrative units – as was the case in the northern Danelaw – or rationalizations of previously existing units such as the Sussex 'rapes' and the Kentish 'lathes'.

By the 11th century each hundred had some common features. A court presided over by a Reeve was responsible for policing, tax collection and local defence. Landowners were also required to assist in creating a *fyrd* (army) when called upon, providing a quota of soldiers based on the size of their estates. The speed with which such militias were formed demonstrates the effectiveness of the system – **Harold Godwinson**'s ability to counter the invading forces of Harold Hardrada and Tostig at **Stamford Bridge** in 1066 being a case in point. But the system's flaws were dramatically displayed in 999 and 1001 when the Vikings attacked **Kent** and **Hampshire** respectively, wiping out the local armies – and of course when William, Duke of Normandy triumphed over Harold's *fyrd* at Hastings, a policy of rigid central control would come to predominate.

1040 Harold Harefoot dies and is succeeded by **Harthacnut**, who immediately has his half-brother's body exhumed and flung into a marsh.

1041 Harthacnut adopts Ethelred's son **Edward** (known as 'the Confessor' on account of his piety, and later regarded as one of England's patron saints) as his heir in England.

1042 Harthacnut **dies** during a drinking bout at the wedding of one of his nobles. The throne passes smoothly to

Edward the Confessor, an **Anglo-Norman** by virtue of his father's marriage to Emma of Normandy. To the chagrin of his English and Viking lords, however, Edward rapidly begins promoting Normans at his court. Led by the House of Godwin, the 'native' aristocracy will be driven to rebellion.

1043 Edward is crowned king of England at Winchester.

1043 In a bid to defuse the stand-off between his Norman retainers and the Anglo-Danish faction, Edward marries **Eadgyth**, daughter of the Earl of Godwin.

1046 Edward exiles Earl Godwin's son **Svein** for seducing the abbess of Leominster.

1048 England suffers an unusual series of earthquakes.

1049 Godwin's son Earl Svein causes further outrage by murdering his cousin **Earl Beorn** after returning from exile. He is declared *nithing* ('without honour') and re-exiled. Edward declares his lands forfeit, and awards some of them to his mainly Norman followers.

1050 Aided and abetted by his father, Svein returns to England and is restored to his earldom.

1051 Political tensions come to a head when some followers of Edward's brother-in-law, **Eustace of Boulogne**, intending to visit Edward, brawl with Godwin's supporters at the port of Dover. Earl Godwin and his sons Svein and Harold (known as **Harold Godwinson**) gather their forces and demand that Edward hand over Eustace. Edward in turn summons the earls **Siward of Northumbria** and **Leofric** of Mercia to his aid, and Godwin is forced to back down. Edward then orders Godwin to appear before a *witangemot* (council of elders) to answer charges of murder and treason. Rather than attend, Godwin and Svein flee to **Bruges**; Earl Harold escapes to **Ireland**. Edward strips the Godwins of their lands, and again redistributes them among his Norman favourites. Godwin's daughter and Edward's wife, **Queen Eadgyth**, is sent to a nunnery. At about the same time it is possible that Edward is visited by **William, Duke of Normandy**, and that Edward offers to make him his heir.

1052 Determined to regain their inheritance, Earl Godwin and his sons **return to England** at the head of an army of invasion. Siward and Leofric fail to intervene on Edward's behalf, and Edward is forced to **capitulate**. Lands and titles are restored to the Godwin family, and Queen Eadgyth returns to the court.

1053 Earl Godwin dies in April and is succeeded as earl of Wessex by **Harold Godwinson**. In order to balance the power of the two principal non-royal families, Edward arranges for Leofric's son **Elfgar** to replace Harold as earl of East Anglia.

1054 Earl Siward campaigns successfully against **King Macbeth** of the Scots. Macbeth is killed and replaced by **Malcolm III**. Siward's eldest son Osbeorn is killed fighting.

1055 Earl Siward dies and is succeeded as earl of Northumbria by Godwin's third son **Tostig**. Earl Elfgar is exiled for treason, but quickly returns with a Viking war party reinforced by the army of the Welsh prince **Gruffydd** (Griffith). They defeat **Earl Ralf** of Herefordshire, but are confronted by the stronger forces of Harold Godwinson and sue for peace. Elfgar is restored to his earldom and Gruffydd permitted to keep some territory.

1056 Harold Godwinson travels to Flanders to negotiate the return to England of Edmund Ironside's son **Edward Atheling**.

1057 Edward Atheling **dies** soon after his return to England. Earl Leofric of Mercia and Ralf also die. Edward endeavours to fill the ensuing power vacuum by making further gifts to the House of Godwin: Harold's brothers **Gyrth** and **Leofwine** are given East Anglia and the southern shires. In effect, this leaves the **Earl of Mercia** surrounded by the Godwins, and so is driven to seek help from amongst the Welsh princes.

1058 Earl Elfgar is **re-exiled**, and again returns with a Viking force under the military command of Harold Hardrada's son **Magnus**. Helped by Prince Gruffydd, Elfgar regains the earldom of **East Anglia** at the Godwins' expense, and Gruffydd marries Elfgar's daughter **Ealdgyth**.

1062 Elfgar is succeeded by his son **Edwin** as earl of Mercia.

1063 Harold Godwinson attacks Gryffydd's north Wales principality from the sea while his brother Tostig mounts a coordinated offensive on land. Gruffydd's forces are reduced by guerilla warfare; Gruffydd himself is betrayed by his followers and **murdered**. His head is sent to King Edward, but his lands are divided amongst other Welsh princes, restoring peace to the Welsh borders.

1064 Harold Godwinson visits **Normandy**, perhaps as an ambassador from King Edward to William. At any rate William compels Harold to swear an **oath of fealty**, later used by William to strengthen his claim to the English throne.

1065 In Northumbria there is a **rebellion** against the rule of Earl Tostig. To restore order King Edward exiles Tostig, replacing him with Earl Edwin's brother **Morkere**. In London, a new minster is completed at **Westminster**, and a *witangemot* summoned for its consecration on 28 December. King Edward, though, is too ill to attend.

1066 King Edward dies in January, and **Harold Godwinson** is chosen by the *witangemot* to succeed him. Almost immediately Harold is challenged by **Tostig**, who begins raiding the English coast. Tostig's forays are repelled by Earl Edwin of Mercia and Earl Morkere of Northumbria. In September Tostig joins an invasion force led by **King Harald Hardrada** of Norway. Together they defeat Edwin and Morkere at **Fulford** outside York. Rallying his army in the south, King Harold of England marches swiftly north and inflicts a decisive defeat on the Vikings at **Stamford Bridge** on 25 September; both Tostig and Harald Hardrada are killed. But King Harold has little time to celebrate: determined to assert his claim to the English throne, **William, Duke of Normandy** has raised his own army of invasion. On 27 September he crosses the Channel and lands at **Pevensea**.

3
The Normans
1066–1154

On 27 September, 1066, William, Duke of Normandy landed on the shores of England. Two weeks later he was **William I**, the country's king. This event had a number of far-reaching geopolitical consequences – not least of which was that England became directly embroiled in the affairs of continental Europe for the first time since the Roman era. For centuries English armies would regularly cross the Channel to campaign on the continent to defend or extend the Crown's territorial interests not just in Normandy but elsewhere in France. Somewhat less regularly, traffic flowed the other way, as French armies laid claim to the English Crown itself. The succession of **Henry II Plantagenet** in 1154 was the outcome of one such counter-campaign – belying the myth that 1066 was the last time England was invaded successfully.

The **Normans**, originally from Scandinavia, had been established in France for little over a century when they landed at Pevensea. But they had adopted the French language and brought it with them as the language of the court (and those who aspired to it) and thus the language of government – in fact it persisted in the form of 'law French', spoken in lawcourts, right up to the late 16th century. Although Anglo-Saxon survived, the vernacular was inevitably influenced by French, as well as by the continued survival of Cornish, Danish and of course ecclesiastical Latin. From this enriched hybrid form developed **Middle**

English, which in turn laid the foundations for Modern English.

William's victory had other consequences, too. Although England was already extensively Christianized, his reign was decisive in drawing English ecclesiastical institutions much closer to their French counterparts, and through those to Rome and the authority of the pope – a shift signalled by the imposing continental styles of architecture employed for building cathedrals, monasteries and churches such as those at **Durham**, **St Albans** and **Ely**. Equally imposing is the **Tower of London**, commissioned by William I: perhaps the most famous edifice of the Norman period, and a symbol of his dramatic sense of power.

The Normans also brought with them an exacting administrative genius, best expressed by the **Domesday Book** of 1087 – an example of royal record-keeping unrivalled in its scope and thoroughness. And it has been argued that the **feudal system** received systematic legal expression for the first time under Norman rule. The king took possession of all land, which he divided up amongst his leading followers and a handful of surviving Anglo-Saxon grandees. They in turn became feudal overlords, subdividing their estates among lesser barons and knights whose reeves oversaw villages and hamlets, in which narrow strips of land were allotted to villeins (serfs) and their families. Such land grants, whether hereditary or otherwise, were granted on carefully regulated terms – in return for military service, an amount of forced labour and other feudal duties. A significant exception to this top-down paradigm were the towns and cities, in part populated by freemen (later called 'yeomen') – although through the twin expedients of garrisons and charters the Norman regime also sought to bring these under its remit. Ecclesiastical lands, too, became increasingly anomalous. Although feudal dues were extracted from the serfs living on church lands, the fact that ecclesiastical estates were usually granted in perpetuity generated an inevitable source of tension between Church and Crown.

In the broader European context, the Norman conquest coincided with the emergence of two themes that dominate medieval politics and culture: the formation of well-defined **kingdoms** in which the arts of secular government were developed; and the consolidation of the **Roman Church**, not just as a spiritual authority but as a powerful organization with strong temporal interests. Even before the end of the 11th century the two had clashed head-on in England. The dispute was over the matter of who had the final say over church appointments, the king or the pope. Twice **Anselm,** the archbishop of Canterbury, was exiled by **William II**, sowing the seeds of a quarrel which would continue for many years to come and which would reach its climax in the schism of the **Reformation** (see p.2).

But arguably the greater threat to political stability came from the apex of the royal structure itself, an edifice the Normans did their best to reinforce. Each time a ruler died there were a number of rival candidates for the succession: first among **William I**'s sons, then among **Henry I**'s self-proclaimed heirs. And this too, though scarcely new to England, was set to define the political tone of the Middle Ages.

1066 Learning that **William of Normandy** has landed on the south coast and constructed a stockade at **Hastings**, King Harold Godwinson hurries south following his victory at Stamford Bridge. Without allowing his men time to recover or waiting for reinforcements, he takes up a position against the Norman invasion force on **Senlac Ridge** (Sandlake Ridge), a short distance from Hastings at what is now **Battle, Sussex**. In the ensuing battle, fought on 14 October, the Anglo-Saxons fight strongly for several

A detail from the Bayeux Tapestry.

hours, but towards the end of the day William's men gain ground. Harold is killed, as are his brothers **Gyrth** and **Leofwine** and many other English lords. The remaining English nobles elect **Edgar Atheling** king in Harold's stead, but their weakened armies swiftly submit to William after he ravages the southeast and seizes **London**; Edgar and his court formally surrender at **Berkhamstead**. Although earls Edwin and Morkere continue to offer resistance in the north, William – who has shrewdly gathered the support of the pope and the Holy Roman Emperor – becomes **king of England**. Seizing the estates of those Anglo-Saxon nobles who opposed him, he begins rewarding his senior followers with grants of sizeable **overlordships**, as Norman garrisons are imposed on many English counties.

1067 Encouraged by Count Eustace of Boulogne, **Kent** revolts against the new Norman rule, but the uprising is put down.

In the summer William returns to Normandy, leaving his

half-brother **Odo** (Bishop of Bayeux and newly created the earl of Kent) and **William Fitzosbern** to govern England as his regents. He returns in December.

> A strange manner of battle, where the one side works by constant motion and ceaseless charges, while the other can but endure passively as it stands fixed to the soil. The Norman arrow and sword worked on; in the English ranks the only movement was the dropping of the dead: the living stood motionless.
>
> William of Poitiers, *Chronicle*

1068 There is an **uprising** of William's English opponents, concentrated in the north of the country with **Edgar Atheling** as the nominal chief and supported by **Malcolm II of Scotland** and by a number of Welsh princes. Earls **Edwin** and **Morkere** soon surrender, however, and are restored by William to their existing lands and titles. Edgar Atheling and his remaining supporters flee to Scotland.

The Battle of Hastings

From the Anglo-Saxon perspective the **Battle of Hastings** was an unmitigated fiasco, its outcome less to do with William's military skill than the blunders of his opponent. Presumably exhausted by the hard-fought battle at **Stamford Bridge** and the march south again, Harold and his army would have been well-advised to wait for reinforcements before engaging William at what is now **Battle** in Sussex. Even so, on 14 October, at the beginning of the day Harold enjoyed what should have been a decisive advantage. His footsoldiers occupied the high ground on **Senlac Ridge**, looking down on the 5000-odd Normans, Bretons and French assembled below.

After the two sides exchanged arrows and slingshot, the Normans attempted an uphill cavalry charge. Despite the fact that men and horses alike struggled on the slope, the English shield-wall failed to hold when a group of soldiers decided to attack the retreating horsemen, only to be cut down in the mud. Traditionally they have been assumed to be members of the *fyrd* (see p.62), but the **Bayeux Tapestry** presents a different – though of course one-sided – view. It records that those killed included members of Harold's elite, including his brothers **Gyrth** and **Leofwine**, who fell in what may have been a Norman ruse. In any event, the Normans continued to charge and retreat, realizing that the English could be lured downhill. Despite rumours at one stage that William had been killed, as the day wore on this strategy began to pay off until the Norman cavalry reached Harold's close guard. As night approached, already severely wounded by an arrow in the eye – if the Tapestry is to be believed – the king was hacked to death. His leaders suffered the same fate: England's Anglo-Saxon warrior aristocracy was all but annihilated overnight. But had Harold risked an all-out assault on the Normans when they first seemed to be faltering, he would almost certainly have triumphed and Hastings would have gone down in history alongside Stamford Bridge as just another invasion averted.

1069 In January there is a renewed revolt in the north. William's appointee **Robert de Comines, Earl of Northumberland**, is killed along with his garrison in Durham. Edgar Atheling returns from Scotland, and is joined by rebels from York.

Just as **Vikings** are threatening the coast, two of Harold Godwinson's sons attempt an invasion of **Devon** from their base in Ireland and **King Svein** of Denmark contributes a fleet of 240 vessels under the command of his brother Osbern. **York** is sacked. William responds brutally: the rebellion is crushed and much of the north laid to waste. He accepts the submission of **Earl Gospatric**, however, and also of Old Siward's son **Waltheof** – who is betrothed to William's niece **Judith**.

1070 Still warring against English rebels, William ravages **Cheshire** and **Shropshire**.

King Svein arrives to take personal command of his forces on the Humber, but after briefly allying with the English rebel **Hereward 'the Wake'** ('the watchful one'), the Danes concede defeat and return home.

The surviving English archbishop of Canterbury **Stigand** is deposed, and replaced by William's candidate **Lanfranc** (formerly the abbot of Bec), who begins reforming the English Church to bring it more closely in line with its French counterpart and thus with Rome.

1071 Hereward sacks **Peterborough Abbey**. In April earls **Edwin** and **Morkere** flee William's court. Edwin is murdered by his own followers as he heads for Scotland, while Morkere joins Hereward at his stronghold on the **Isle of Ely**. Ely falls after a prolonged siege, and **Hereward** escapes to the continent with a band of followers. He will enter English folklore as the last Anglo-Saxon to offer resistance to the Normans – even though some sources suggest that he is reconciled to William.

The Domesday Book

Compiled shortly before William I's death and demonstrating the Norman genius for administration, the **Domesday Book** was so thorough in its investigation of the land he had conquered that, according to the *Anglo-Saxon Chronicle*, not an ox, cow nor pig slipped through its net. Though the precise reasons behind its commission remain unclear, the book gave an exact picture of England's wealth – and therefore the likely scope and limits of taxation – at a time when the country was threatened with foreign invasion. It also provided William with useful information as to where his forces might most effectively be garrisoned.

The Anglo-Saxons had conducted similar investigations since the time of **Alfred the Great**, and perhaps it is a tribute to existing local administrative systems that most of Domesday was assembled within a year. That said, nothing on this scale had been attempted before. William's agents were instructed to demand of every official in charge of a **hundred** (see p.62) an array of detailed questions: how many people lived in the area? what sort of people were they? what sort of land lay in the hundred? how much was it worth? But this wasn't all. Information had to be compiled for three separate periods: when Edward the Confessor was alive, when King William granted the local lord the estate, and at the present time (1086).

The resulting survey was so complete that it became likened to the Day of Judgement, when everything, living and dead, would be judged. Domesday provides a uniquely detailed portrait of an early medieval kingdom – and thoroughly deserves its awe-inspiring title.

1075 About this time the **Bayeux Tapestry**, probably commissioned by **Odo of Bayeux** and depicting the Battle of Hastings with the events immediately surrounding it, is woven – possibly by a group of women in Canterbury.

1077 In the same year that a new cathedral is completed at **Canterbury** under the auspices of Archbishop Lanfranc,

The Exon Domesday Book.

William of Warenne establishes the first **Cluniac monastery** in England. (Previously all monasteries have belonged to the Benedictine order.)

1078 Construction begins of the **White Tower**, the central keep of the **Tower of London** – a military and administrative complex designed to ensure Norman control over the country's largest city and its commercial capital.

1081 Anxious to extend Norman power westwards, William journeys through **southern Wales** and visits St Davids Cathedral. **Rhys ap Tewdwr** is acknowledged as ruler of the western principality of Deheubarth in return for paying William an annual tribute of £40. While the Normans have already begun erecting wooden castles in Wales, particularly along the border with England (known as **the Welsh Marches**), the Welsh are generally less amenable to the imposition of Norman rule and continue to resist in the mountainous interior.

1086 Threatened by an alliance between **Flanders** and **Denmark**, William imports the largest army ever seen in England. Partly to enable his administrators to raise sufficient taxes to maintain this force William orders the compilation of the **Domesday Book** at Gloucester, a hugely detailed survey of his English kingdom.

1087 William I dies campaigning in France against his rebellious eldest son **Robert Curthose** and King Philip I of France. Robert inherits Normandy while his second surviving son, **William Rufus** ('the red', so named because of his complexion), gets England. More cultivated than his father but capable of equal brutality, **William II** destablilized the close relationship William I had built up with the clergy and was not kindly viewed by contemporary chroniclers – who excoriated him for sexual depravity and accused him of homosexuality. A different perspective sees him as one of the early troubadours, a man open to the latest fashions and cultural developments on the continent.

1088 William II faces a rebellion orchestrated by his uncle **Odo of Bayeux** aimed at replacing William with Robert Curthose on the throne and reuniting England and Normandy. But when William gathers English support by promising to cut taxes and Robert fails to show up, the rebellion collapses.

1089 William begins a **seven-year campaign** against Robert Curthose to bring Normandy under England's control. Following **Lanfranc's death**, Canterbury remains without an archbishop for four years while a suitable candidate is sought.

1090 An attempted uprising against Robert in **Rouen** is foiled when William's youngest brother **Henry** sides with Robert and personally throws William's supporter **Conan** to his death from Rouen's battlements.

1091 Having led an army into Normandy, William makes a **temporary peace** with Robert. Each agrees that the other should become his heir, and that Henry should be barred from the succession.

Malcolm III of Scotland is compelled to acknowledge William II's overlordship, and the Norman presence in **Wales** is strengthened.

1092 William II again campaigns in northern England, stamping out rebellion in **Cumbria**.

1093 Malcolm III visits William II's court under safe conduct, but refuses to acknowledge Anglo-Norman jurisdiction in Scotland. Shortly afterwards Malcolm and his son Edward are ambushed and killed near **Alnwick** while mounting a raid against northern England; Malcolm is succeeded by his equally recalcitrant brother **Donald III** (known as 'Donald Bane').

William nominates **Anselm** as archbishop of Canterbury to settle what is becoming an ecclesiastical scandal. Anselm accepts only on condition that William restores lands previously confiscated and acknowledges **Urban II** as the true pope against the claims of Clement III. He is consecrated in December, but almost immediately falls out with William when he asks to be allowed to travel to Rome to fetch the **pallium**, the symbol of his spiritual authority;

Norman cathedral architecture

Though the motives behind William of Normandy's invasion of England are still hotly debated, it seems clear that his campaign was not simply a matter of personal aggrandizement backed up by a tenuous claim to the throne. For one thing, he had been careful to secure the backing of the pope for a 'holy war' to save the English Church from the peril into which it had fallen and to restore its links with mainstream Christianity.

To this end England's early Norman rulers were visibly pious – endowing dioceses and monasteries with significant lands and setting aside considerable funds for the building of new cathedrals, abbeys and churches along the grandest continental lines. What is striking about these commissions is the sheer contrast in scale compared with previous buildings. Anglo-Saxon England was not entirely devoid of imposing architecture – Edward the Confessor had made the creation of **Westminster Abbey** his pet project – but nothing could compare with what was created by William and his successors. Of the several cathedrals that have survived, **Ely** (begun 1083) boasts a 76-metre-long nave, although its Norman tower collapsed in 1322 and was replaced by the now-famous Octagon. **Peterborough** (1118) also demonstrates many distinctive features of the Anglo-Norman style. But perhaps the purest example is found at **Durham** (1099), in which massive Romanesque decorated pillars and arches support a triforium and above that a rib-vaulted ceiling, the first of its kind in Europe. Every bit as significant is its site, perched high on a rocky promontory with a commanding view of the surrounding landscape and flanked on one side by the equally huge Bishop's Palace. This grandeur was not merely an imitation of fashionable architecture; it also revealed the Normans' determination to overawe their new subjects. Although relations between Crown and Church quickly soured, initially they were partners in the same enterprise.

William refuses permission. Out of these circumstances arises the **investiture controversy** – a dispute about

The choir, Durham Cathedral.

whether Crown or Church has the final authority to appoint clerics.

Work begins on the cathedral at **Durham**.

1094 Now supported by his brother **Henry**, William Rufus again invades Normandy. As rumours of **rebellion** oblige the king to return to England, Henry assumes command in the war against Robert.

1095 Several of the rebels of 1088, dominated by barons from the Welsh marches, take up arms against William, intending to replace him with his cousin **Stephen of Aumerle**. The revolt is crushed, the rebels fined and mutilated.

As the investiture controversy intensifies, England's clergy side with the king against Anselm at the **Synod of Rockingham**. When a papal legate brings the pallium to England, Anselm refuses to accept it from William's hands. The king confiscates Anselm's lands, but gives him leave to travel to Rome – in effect sending him into exile.

Determined to bring about the recovery of the Holy Land from Islamic rule, **Pope Urban II** preaches the **First Crusade** at Clermont.

1096 To fund his participation in the First Crusade, Robert Curthose pawns the duchy of Normandy to his brother William II.

1097 William campaigns in Wales to defeat further rebellion.

1098 The **Council of Bari**, attended by Archbishop Anselm, confirms the papacy's view that only it has the right to invest prelates with the 'ring and the crozier', symbolizing their spiritual authority.

1099 In July, Jerusalem is recaptured by Christian crusaders. 40,000 Muslims, an unknown number of Jews and Eastern Orthodox Christians are **massacred**. In London, the new **Palace of Westminster** is completed by the king's unpopular chief minister, **Ranulf Flambard**.

William II campaigns in **Normandy** to quash further outbreaks of rebellion.

1100 William Rufus is **killed** by an arrow while hunting in the New Forest. The marksman – thought to have been **Walter Tyrel, Count of Poix** – is believed by some to have acted on behalf of William's brother **Henry**, who does little to quell the rumours by rapidly seizing the **royal treasury** at Winchester and staking his claim to the throne. Three days after William's death Henry is accepted as king by the nobility, and crowned at Westminster by the bishop of London. As **Henry I**, he immediately recalls Archbishop Anselm from exile in a move clearly designed to win clerical support against Robert Curthose, whose claim to the English throne is stronger than his own. As a gesture to the nobility he issues a 'Charter of Liberties', abolishing certain unpopular taxes.

In November Henry further consolidates his position by marrying **Edith** (known also as **Matilda**), the daughter of King Malcolm III of Scotland and Edgar Atheling's sister Margaret.

It is under Henry I that **crown justices** begin making regular tours, or circuits, of the English shires.

1101 Having returned to France, Robert Curthose lands with an army at **Portsmouth**. Among his supporters are **Eustace III** of Boulogne and the earls of **Surrey** and **Buckingham**. Civil war is averted when Henry agrees to surrender his claims to disputed territories in Normandy and to pay Robert an annuity of £2000. Eustace of Boulogne is restored to his English estates.

1102 Queen Edith gives birth to a daughter, **Matilda**. At an ecclesiastical council held in London, Archbishop Anselm attempts to enforce clerical celibacy, but the majority of clergy resist this and other reforms.

1103 Queen Edith provides Henry I with a male heir, **Prince William**.

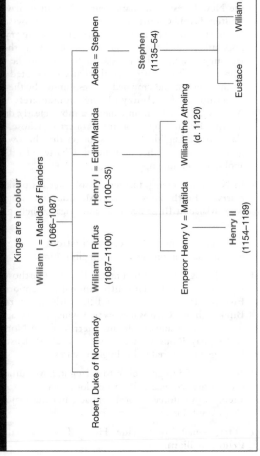

The Norman kings 1066–1154

Kings are in colour

Robert, Duke of Normandy

William I = Matilda of Flanders
(1066–1087)

William II Rufus
(1087–1100)

Henry I = Edith/Matilda
(1100–35)

Adela = Stephen

Stephen
(1135–54)

Emperor Henry V = Matilda

William the Atheling
(d. 1120)

Henry II
(1154–1189)

Eustace

William

Archbishop Anselm begins a second period of **exile**, having refused to confirm several episcopal appointments made by Henry I.

1104 Robert Curthose cedes territory to Henry in return for the king of England's help in crushing renewed rebellion.

1105 As relations between Henry I and Robert Curthose deteriorate, Henry invades **Normandy**.

1106 Henry defeats and captures Robert at **Tinchebrai**; among the estimated 400 knights and 10,000 soldiers taken prisoner is **Edgar Atheling**. But while Edgar is quickly pardoned and released, Robert remains in captivity as Henry seizes control of the whole of **Normandy**.

Archbishop Anselm returns from exile to Canterbury.

1107 **Louis VI** of France acknowledges Henry's claim to Normandy.

The investiture controversy is resolved – at least for the time being – when Church and king reach agreement at the **Synod of Westminster**. According to the agreement, the Crown renounces its right of investiture on condition that appointees render him feudal homage before being invested with the symbols of their office.

1109 Louis VI demands that Henry render homage for his 'French' lands and abandon his castle at **Gisors** in the Vexin district of Normandy; Henry refuses.

Archbishop Anselm dies on **21 April** – later to become his Saint's Day. The king and Church are unable to agree his successor.

1110 Louis VI captures **Meulan**, a county on the Seine belonging to Henry's active supporter **Robert of Beaumont**.

St Anselm (1033–1109)

Bitter disputes between Church and state were a defining feature of the early Middle Ages. At their heart was a debate about the nature of society itself – whether the advancing secular power of kings and princes or the spiritual authority of bishops, archbishops and ultimately the pope counted more. In reality, the best hope of survival for either side was compromise: in a superstitious age kings needed the moral sanctions offered by the Church quite as much as the Church needed the political and military support supplied by feudal courts.

In the post-Conquest period the first serious spat between Crown and Church in England centred on Anselm, William Rufus's unwilling appointee to the see of Canterbury. A pupil of the previous archbishop, Lanfranc, Anselm quickly began to agitate over the matter of investiture, insisting that only the Church had the right to select its own officials. William Rufus refused to make concessions, as at first did Henry I; as a result, Anselm was exiled twice. Henry I was the better strategist, however, and because he needed papal backing for his seizure of Normandy from his elder brother Robert Curthose, willingly agreed to the compromise enshrined in the Westminster agreement of 1107 in which the Church came out marginally ahead – at least on paper.

Fittingly, Anselm's canonization later in the century was engineered by Thomas Becket (see p.105), that most celebrated champion of ecclesiastical rights. But Anselm was the greater churchman: a formidable theologian, he is credited with fathering Scholasticism, the rationalistic movement which was the main theological foundation of the Catholic church until at least the Reformation. In his *Proslogium* he attempted to base belief in reason rather than in faith alone; his 'ontological proof' of God's existence, arguing that even a fool must concede that God could not exist as an idea without a greater reality to sustain it, is influential even now. Of less appeal is Anselm's satisfaction theory, presented in *Cur Deus Homo*, where God is depicted as the ultimate feudal overlord: mankind's debts, accrued through sin, are such that only God's incarnation as Christ can balance the books.

1111 Backed by Henry, Robert of Beaumont attacks the French king's capital, **Paris**.

1112 Henry arrests and imprisons Louis VI's envoy, **Robert of Bellême**.

1113 Louis VI and **Fulk of Anjou** sue for peace; Henry's son Prince William is betrothed to Fulk's daughter **Matilda**.

1114 Archbishop Thomas II of York dies of overeating and is succeeded by **Thurstan**, another prelate from Bayeux.

Henry I's daughter **Matilda** is married to the Holy Roman Emperor, **Henry V**.

1115 Henry I's ally **Theobald of Blois** ambushes and imprisons Louis VI's ally **William of Nevers**.

1116 Largely because of their quarrelsome barons, Henry I and Louis VI again find themselves at **war**. Henry supports his nephews **Stephen** and **Theobald**; Louis supports **Fulk of Anjou** and **Baldwin of Flanders**.

1118 Henry and Louis come to terms after Henry's forces are defeated by Fulk at **Alençon**.

Henry's wife **Queen Edith** dies.

1119 Fulk's daughter marries **Prince William**. Louis VI invades Normandy, but is repulsed by Henry's forces at **Bremule**. At once Louis VI attempts a second invasion, but Pope **Calixtus II** persuades the two sides to call a truce. Henry remains in possession of Normandy.

1120 Henry's successes in Normandy are overshadowed by the deaths of his only sons **William** and **Richard** when the *White Ship* is wrecked crossing the Channel, possibly because the crew was drunk. A number of barons and royal officials are also drowned.

1121 Desperate for an heir to replace William, Henry I marries **Adelaide of Louvain**.

Returning from the Crusades, **Fulk of Anjou** demands that his widowed daughter Matilda and the country of Maine be returned to him.

1123 His demands unmet, Fulk **declares war** on Henry.

In Normandy several nobles rebel in favour of Robert Curthose's son **William Clito**.

1124 Henry I defeats the Normandy rebels at **Bourgtheroulde** and persuades **Emperor Henry V** to invade France. The emperor's campaign is swiftly curtailed, however, when rebellion breaks out at **Wurms** in his own domains.

1125 Henry I enacts a law sentencing **moneyers** (illegal minters of coin) to have their right hands severed and to be castrated.

Emperor Henry V **dies**, temporarily giving Henry I a free hand in his negotiations with the French crown.

1126 Henry I's daughter, **Empress Matilda**, returns to the Anglo-Norman court at Christmas and is presented to Henry's barons.

1127 The barons, led by **David, King of Scots** and by Henry's illegitimate son Robert of Gloucester, promise **allegiance** to Matilda in the event that Henry dies without a legitimate male heir.

1128 Empress Matilda (aged 26) marries **Geoffrey Plantagenet**, heir to Anjou (aged 15).

William Clito, the titular duke of Normandy, dies of wounds received at the siege of **Alost**.

1129 Empress Matilda returns to her father after her marriage to Geoffrey of Anjou breaks down.

1131 Empress Matilda again accepts an **oath of allegiance** from a gathering of Henry's 'English' barons at **Northampton**.

1133 Having been reconciled to her husband Geoffrey, Matilda gives birth to a son who is called **Henry**.

1134 Robert Curthose **dies** in captivity in England. Matilda gives birth to a second son, named **Geoffrey**.

1135 Henry I **dies** at Lyons-la-Forêt in Normandy after quarrelling with his daughter Matilda and his son-in-law **Geoffrey of Anjou** on account of the latter's demands to be recognized as Henry's heir. The succession to Henry's crown is disputed between Matilda and Henry I's nephew **Stephen, Count of Blois**. While Geoffrey of Anjou has been specifically excluded from the throne by Henry I's will, it is probable that he intended Matilda to become queen. By invading southern Normandy, however, Matilda and Geoffrey alienate potential allies – who begin looking more favourably on Stephen's claims. Stephen crosses the Channel and is **accepted as king** by a significant proportion of England's nobility and London's merchants. Despite this, Stephen's reign will be marked by near-continuous civil war.

1136 Stephen confirms the Westminster Agreement of 1107, promising that the Church will be free from royal interference.

1137 **David, King of Scots**, seeking a restoration of his English earldoms, harasses the north.

1138 Stephen mounts a **counter-invasion** of Scotland. Discontented nobles in England, led by **Robert of Gloucester**, begin to rally to Empress Matilda's cause. Her husband, Geoffrey of Anjou, invades Normandy; as the year progresses, fighting between the two factions spreads in England. Stephen sends his queen, also called **Matilda**, to besiege Robert's stronghold at **Dover** while he campaigns against rebels in the West Country. An attempted invasion on 22 August by King David is halted by northern barons at the **Battle of the Standard**. But by the end of the year, Stephen has lost control of parts of both the north and the west. Geoffrey's attempted seizure of Normandy, however, fails.

1139 Stephen secures the Scottish border by the **Treaty of Durham**; David, King of Scots swears **fealty** to the English throne. In return David's son Henry is given the earldom of **Northumberland**. Empress Matilda, Geoffrey of Anjou and Robert of Gloucester remain at large, though, and now attempt to dispossess Stephen. Their supporter **Baldwin of Reviers** lands at Wareham and establishes a base at **Corfe**. Soon afterwards, Empress Matilda and Robert of Gloucester establish themselves at **Arundel**, where Stephen besieges them. When Robert escapes, the king unwisely allows Matilda to follow him. While the West Country remains in revolt, the Bishop of Ely adds to Stephen's difficulties by joining the rebellion.

1140 Stephen secures control over **Cornwall** and **Ely**. His opponents, angered by Stephen's Scottish policy and led now by the **Earl of Chester**, occupy **Lincoln** – which the king besieges toward the end of the year.

> ❝ England, once the seat of justice, the home of peace, the height of piety, the mirror of religion, became thereafter a place of perversity, a haunt of strife, a school of disorder, and the teacher of every kind of rebellion. ❞
>
> *Gesta Stephani*, trans. K.R. Potter and R.H.C. Davis

1141 As Stephen puts the pressure on Lincoln, a rebel relief force outnumbers and **captures** him. During the king's imprisonment, the Norman barons reluctantly acknowledge Geoffrey of Anjou's overlordship. But before the end of the year Stephen is **released** in exchange for Robert of Gloucester, captured by forces loyal to Stephen.

1142 Geoffrey of Anjou, still attempting to establish control over **Normandy**, declines to join his wife Empress Matilda in England. Instead he sends their son **Henry Plantagenet**, who joins forces with Robert of Gloucester.

Stephen and Matilda

Famously the reign of King Stephen has been called a time 'when God and his angels slept'. But this image of a period of unbridled anarchy following an era of peace and stability is hugely exaggerated: dynastic infighting among William I's heirs had continued intermittently since his death – even if the battles so far had taken place mainly in Normandy. Conversely, many senior Anglo-Norman barons, far from taking advantage of the Crown's difficulties, strove to resolve the outstanding issues.

In retrospect, it was the ambition of Geoffrey of Anjou – claiming the throne via his marriage to Henry I's daughter Matilda – that proved the flash-point. Matilda was far from popular, but her husband was massively opposed by the barons in Normandy as well as those in England. As a consequence the Crown was offered first to Henry I's nephew Count Theobald of Blois, then to Theobald's younger brother Stephen. That this supposedly weak man accepted and held on to it lays to rest another myth – though no one could describe the events of his reign as anything but unfortunate.

But Stephen's accession also reflected the growing authority of the Church. Another candidate for the throne was Henry's illegitimate son Robert the Bastard of Gloucester. Though not in England, illegitimate children had achieved success elsewhere in claiming their fathers' titles, and Robert might well have expected to do the same had it not been for the unanimous opposition of the bishops. With no love lost between him and Stephen, he had little choice but to support his half-sister Matilda in the hope of some great reward to come. This in turn encouraged less scrupulous barons with their own territorial ambitions to enter the fray; that Stephen lost control of the situation was hardly surprising.

1143 By attempting to curb the powers of the **earl of Essex**, the king merely encourages other barons to rebel.

1144 Unrest prevails in many parts of England and Normandy as the civil wars of Stephen's reign reach their fiercest stage yet. **Durham** falls to the Scots, and Robert of Gloucester ravages the **West Country**.

Towards the end of the year, though, Stephen **eliminates** several of his baronial opponents.

1145 Robert's son **Philip** abandons his father and pledges his loyalty to Stephen.

1146 The **Second Crusade** is preached, offering many English knights and nobles an alternative to warfare at home.

1148 **Henry Plantagenet** fails to revive the flagging rebellion in England.

His mother Empress Matilda crosses the Channel to **France**, never to return.

1149 Henry Plantagenet engineers an **alliance** between David, King of Scots and the earl of Chester, but their forces are swiftly routed by Stephen; Henry himself is chased out of the country by Stephen's son **Eustace**.

1150 Henry Plantagenet becomes **Duke of Normandy**, temporarily lost to the English crown.

1151 On the death of his father Geoffrey, Henry Plantagenet becomes **Count of Anjou**.

1152 Henry Plantagenet marries **Eleanor of Aquitaine**, recently divorced from Louis VII of France. In due course Eleanor will bear Henry eight children. Four sons will survive infancy: **Henry**, **Richard**, **Geoffrey** and **John**.

1153 Following a four-year lull in hostilities, Henry Plantagenet returns with an army to England. Renewed civil war is averted, however, by the death of Stephen's son and heir **Eustace**. It is agreed that Stephen should remain on the throne, but that Henry should succeed him.

1154 King Stephen dies of natural causes. Henry Plantagenet, known as **Henry II**, becomes king of England. The territories under his control stretch from **Scotland** in the north to the **Pyrenees** in southwestern France.

4
The Plantagenets
1154–1399

While their surname suggests that the Planatagenets are a separate dynasty from the Normans, this isn't technically the case. The founding monarch, **Henry II**, was the grandson of Henry I, albeit via his mother rather than his father. Indeed, right up until 1485 and the final collapse of the houses of Lancaster and York, it can be said that England was ruled by a single dynasty whose line reaches directly back to William I.

Even considered as a discrete unit, the Plantagenets were still England's longest-serving monarchical house – outdistancing the Tudors, the Stuarts, the Hanoverians and, to date, the Windsors. The argument in favour of looking at them separately is that under their stewardship – intermittent though it was – England found an identity to call its own. The French wars and the dynastic infighting continued, as did tensions between Crown and Church, but amid the upheavals there is a sense in which the English community gained focus – demanding to be heard in its own language, exerting pressure over England's political institutions and finding expression in indigenous works of art and literature.

An important aspect of this evolution is that the Anglo-Norman barony became gradually more Anglocentric – less willing to be drawn into the Crown's costly continental escapades, more eager to exert power in their English estates. This was an inevitable source of tension: Henry II and his immediate successors **Richard I** and **John** were every bit as preoccupied with politics outside England as their Norman predecessors had been.

The early Plantagenets 1154–1272

Where the king went his courtiers followed – both literally and metaphorically. This situation didn't change until the very end of John's reign when, in the wake of the king's military humiliation at the hands of Philip II Augustus of France, his barons managed to impose a contract securing their rights, **Magna Carta** of 1215.

In the early days of Plantagenet rule this seemed worlds away. Through a combination of circumstances Henry II's inheritance was unprecedentedly large. From Stephen he gained England and Normandy; from his father Geoffrey he acquired Anjou; and through his wife Eleanor he exerted control over Aquitaine. His domains, sometimes called the **Angevin Empire**, constituted the greatest swathe of territory in western Europe; and Henry, who was nothing if not determined in everything he did, was determined to hold on to each and every bit of it – even extend it further. England in 1154 was more tightly involved in continental politics than it had been at any point during the preceding century. In France Henry II may have been – technically at least – subordinate to the French king, but his independent kingdom with its supply of arms and men meant that he became a potentially useful (and much-courted) ally of France's European rivals. Significantly, of his 34-year reign, over 21 years were spent in France.

Richard I, Henry's third son but his immediate successor, spent even less time on English soil. He ruled for ten years but was absent for all but six months – crusading in the Holy Land, languishing in a German prison, attempting to recover

Normandy from the French king. Yet, paradoxically, the government of England benefited. Because Henry II often had to rule by proxy, he set up strong institutions headed by capable officials, and these continued under Richard. It was during Henry II's reign – and into the next – that something like a specifically English administration, supported by a reformed justice system, came into being.

Even so, it was a difficult inheritance for Henry's youngest son **John**, who came to the throne in 1199. John had to contend with the barons' growing disillusionment with the Crown's costly French campaigns and the warmongering of the French king, **Philip II Augustus**. Had John's forces triumphed against Philip domestic dissent would have been quelled, but losing Normandy permanently destabilized his power-base. He had little choice but to sign Magna Carta.

John had also fallen out with the pope by refusing to accept the papal candidate for the archbishopric of Canterbury, **Stephen Langton**. In this too he was not unlike his father, who had notoriously provoked Rome by his handling of **Thomas Becket**. Both kings suffered the indignity of excommunication – a serious obstacle, not only because the spiritual status of rulers was a matter of public anxiety but also because the pope himself was a key player in European power politics, someone whose favour could make or break an alliance between princes.

There followed the long and fractious reign of John's son, **Henry III**. With Magna Carta and half a century of greater involvement in central government behind them, England's barons were in no mood to be dominated by a ruler who was sometimes as inconsistent in his policies as he was undiplomatic in their execution. If the focal point of English politics of the mid-13th century was the rudimentary emergence of **Parliament** – the initiative not of the English barons themselves but of another Frenchman, **Simon de Montfort IV** – this is revealing of the way things stood. De

Montfort had two purposes in convening a consultative assembly made up of knights of the shire and burgesses as well as barons: to legitimize his usurpation of royal power, but also to provide a counterweight to the barons themselves.

In the short term his experiment failed. De Montfort's numerous opponents found in the heir to the throne, **Prince Edward**, a leader equipped to crush the 'foreign' interloper, even if the price for this was the revived prestige and authority of the Crown. Yet in a longer view de Montfort's parliament was surprisingly influential, if only because it suited Edward to retain it as a mechanism of political control. Although it is difficult to claim that it represents the first flowerings of popular democracy – as nineteenth-century critics were fond of arguing – it proved to have more resilience than anyone can have thought at the time.

1154 The addition of England to his portmanteau of territories means that **Henry II Plantagenet** rules a huge body of land stretching all the way from the **Scottish border** to the **Pyrenees** in southwestern France. While this makes him a principal player in western Europe, it also necessitates long absences from his English kingdom, where he will spend only fourteen years out of a 34-year reign. Despite this, his reform of the **English legal system** will constitute a lasting legacy. Henry rapidly assembles a team of outstanding officials, basing them in the **Exchequer** – so called because of the use of a board divided into squares for accountancy purposes. Among these are **Richard de Lucy**, **Robert de Beaumont** and the archdeacon of Canterbury **Thomas Becket**, whom Henry raises to the office of chancellor. In the early months of his reign Henry is aided by Becket in razing the castles of several rebellious barons.

Nicholas Breakspear is elected pope as **Adrian IV**, the only Englishman ever to become pontiff.

1155 Henry II thwarts a rebellion by the **earl of York**, and secures the submission of the troublesome marcher lord, **Roger of Hereford**.

1156 Henry pays homage to King Louis VII of France in respect of his French fiefdoms. While on the continent, he dispossesses his younger brother **Geoffrey** of most of his territories.

1157 Henry receives homage from **Malcolm IV** of Scotland (to whom he awards the **earldom of Huntingdon**), and the northern territories of **Northumberland**, **Cumberland** and **Westmoreland** are returned to the English Crown.

Campaigning in **Wales**, Henry brings prince **Owain Gwynedd** to heel and receives homage from him. His intrusion into Wales falls short of complete conquest, however.

1158 Becket heads a diplomatic mission to the French court on behalf of Henry II; in **Paris**, the excessive splendour of the chancellor's retinue attracts disapproving attention. The way is smoothed for the betrothal of Henry's three-and-a-half-year-old heir **Prince Henry** to Louis VII's six-month-old youngestdaughter **Margaret**. This too incites scandal – particularly among those aware that such a marriage could eventually lead to the union of the French and English crowns.

Soon afterwards the king crosses to the continent, where he will spend five years away from the English court. The death of his brother **Geoffrey** enables Henry to lay claim the remaining **Angevin lands**.

1159 Henry II quarrels with Louis VII, and the two kings' forces fight briefly and inconclusively until a **truce** is declared in November.

1160 A **papal schism** realigns European politics. While the Holy Roman Emperor supports the 'anti-pope' **Victor**

IV, Henry II gives his guarded support to the 'official' pope, **Alexander III** – who in return allows Prince Henry to marry the French infant princess Margaret. Fighting between the English and French resumes when Henry seizes Margaret's **dowry** for himself.

> ❝ He travelled incessantly, and in stages intolerable, like a public carrier, and, in this matter, showed scant consideration for his retinue. In dogs and birds he was most expert, and exceedingly fond of hunting. He passed nights without sleep and was untiring in his activities. Whenever in his dreams passion mocked him with vain shapes, he used to curse his body, because neither toil nor fasting was able to break or weaken it. I, however, ascribe his activities not to his incontinence but to his fear of becoming too fat. ❞
>
> Walter Map on Henry II, in *De Nugis Curialium* (c.1190), trans. F. Tupper and M.B. Ogle

1162 In May Thomas Becket, very much the king's candidate, is elected **archbishop of Canterbury** following the death of Archbishop Theobald in the previous year. Almost immediately Becket resigns as chancellor, and, in an apparently dramatic change of character, begins the defence of **ecclesiastical privileges** and rights that will occupy the rest of his life.

1163 Returning to England in January, Henry II begins a series of acrimonious arguments with Archbishop Becket. These chiefly concern Becket's insistence that clerics should be tried for any misdemeanours in **ecclesiastical courts**; also Becket's readiness to **excommunicate** a number of leading barons for ungodly behaviour also earns him royal displeasure.

1164 In January Henry II calls a council of senior ecclesiastics at **Clarendon** in Wiltshire to assert his 'ancestral' rights over the English Church. The resulting **Constitutions of Clarendon** specify that the king has the powers of recommendation and veto over the appointment of **bishops**; that clerics suspected of misdemeanours (called 'criminous clerks') are subject to trial in **royal courts**; that **vacant sees** should be held in custody by the Crown; that no royal official should be **excommunicated**; and that no appeal to **Rome** on any matter should be made without the king's consent. Archbishop Becket allegedly gives his verbal assent to these principles, but repudiates them soon afterwards. Matters are brought to a head in October, when Henry convenes a further council at **Northampton**, having pressured Becket in the interim by ordering him to provide a full set of accounts for the period he was chancellor. Supported by the bishop of London, **Gilbert Foliot**, the king reaffirms the Constitutions of Clarendon. In November Becket flees in disguise to the court of Louis VII of France, intending to appeal directly to **Pope Alexander III**. But while the pope welcomes Becket's pro-Church stance, he is nervous about pushing Henry II into an alliance with Emperor Henry V, who supports the rival 'anti-pope', and therefore keeps Becket at arm's length.

1165 Henry II fails to persuade Alexander III to repudiate Becket, despite threatening to give his allegiance to the new 'anti-pope' **Paschal**.

1166 Alexander III at last throws his weight behind Becket, appointing him a **papal legate**. Becket uses his increased ecclesiastical powers to **excommunicate** the bishop of London and other senior English churchmen. In the same year major judicial reforms are promulgated by Henry II at the **Assize of Clarendon**. As a result of the king's determination to create a tiered system of **courts** capable of delivering swift and impartial justice, crime and disorder

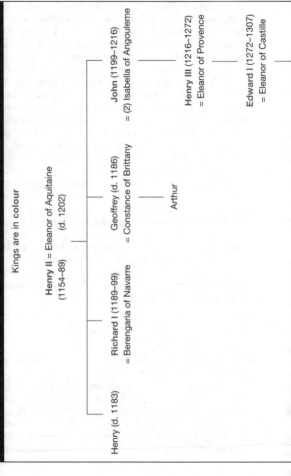

The Plantagenets 1154–1399

Kings are in colour

Henry II = Eleanor of Aquitaine
(1154–89)   (d. 1202)

Henry (d. 1183)

Richard I (1189–99)
= Berengaria of Navarre

Geoffrey (d. 1186)
= Constance of Brittany

Arthur

John (1199–1216)
= (2) Isabella of Angouleme

Henry III (1216–1272)
= Eleanor of Provence

Edward I (1272–1307)
= Eleanor of Castille

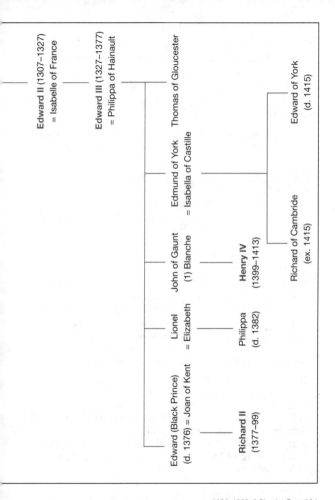

are significantly reduced in England.

1167 To limit the damage caused by Becket's exile, Henry II orders all English scholars living abroad to **return home**. Of those who obey, a number settle in **Oxford**, forming a community that will develop into England's first university.

Queen Eleanor gives birth to the youngest of Henry's surviving legitimate sons, the future king **John**.

1169 Eager to crusade, Henry II attempts a **reconciliation** with Becket at Montmirail, but the archbishop refuses to relent.

1170 In a move to clarify the succession – and in defiance of Becket – the king's heir **Prince Henry** is crowned as co-ruler by **Archbishop Roger of York**, who is promptly excommunicated by the exiled primate. In July, fearing that Pope Alexander III will issue a general interdict against England, the king meets Becket at **Fréteval**. Although little is done to resolve their dispute, Becket is encouraged to return to England.

On 2 December the archbishop resumes residence at Canterbury but refuses to lift the **excommunications** of Roger of York and Bishop Foliot. On 29 December, spurred into action by Henry's continuing frustration, four knights follow Becket into his cathedral and **murder** him – something that earns Henry papal excommunication and near-universal infamy as well as ensuring Becket's martyrdom.

Richard de Clare, the second earl of Pembroke, known as '**Strongbow**', initiates the English conquest of **Ireland** when he gains control of Leinster. Claiming that Pope Adrian IV had 'given' him Ireland, Henry II approves of Strongbow's intervention on condition that Henry himself is recognized as Leinster's overlord. In due course Henry will add '**king of Ireland**' to his titles. The greater part of Ireland, however, remains autonomous.

The medieval universities

Henry II's recall of English scholars studying in Paris had repercussions that lasted well beyond the immediate political crisis: it provided an incentive for the development of home-grown university education. A group of students from the continent formed an academic community at Oxford in 1185; everything went smoothly until 1209, when a group of disaffected clerks decamped for a fenland market town called Cambridge after brawling with local townspeople. Both universities were modelled on the Parisian schools, organized a curriculum based around study of the Seven Liberal Arts (Grammar, Rhetoric, Logic, Arithmetic, Geometry, Music and Astronomy) and offered degrees in Philosophy, Theology and Law.

Encouraged by the arrival of Dominicans and Franciscans – members of the new religious orders of mendicant friars – halls of residence, and eventually colleges, originally provided homes for poor students, enabling a limited social mobility otherwise hard to come by in early medieval England. At the outset it was the houses run by the friars that predominated: it wasn't until the 14th century that non-monastic scholars and secular colleges challenged the supremacy of the older foundations. And even then, the first responsibility of Oxford and Cambridge remained to prepare young men for holy orders – little or no education was provided for laymen as such, and the vast majority of students were either priests or were heading there.

Yet slowly the universities became centres of learning in their own right, eventually rivalling their continental competitors. It is significant that of the two intellectual heavyweights produced by England during the Plantagenet period, the first, Roger Bacon (see p.131), probably left Oxford for Paris, but the second, John Wyclif (see p.147), studied wholly in Oxford. And that students had become an established feature of the medieval social landscape is confirmed by Chaucer's wry portrait in *The Canterbury Tales* (see p.149) of the gaunt, earnest 'clerk of Oxenford', who spends so much money on his studies that he can't afford to keep himself – or his horse – properly fed.

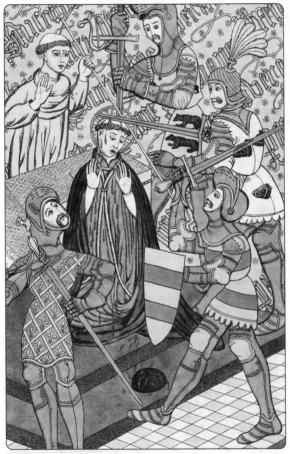

A 15th-century depiction of Becket's martyrdom.

Thomas Becket (c.1120–70)

The relationship between Henry II and Thomas Becket – as well as the quarrel that led to the latter's death – has fascinated generations of historians. It wouldn't be nearly so interesting were it not for Becket's seemingly abrupt change of character mid-career.

The son of a Cheapside merchant, Becket completed his education in Paris before joining the household of **Theobald**, the archbishop of Canterbury. The exceptionally able archdeacon was talent-spotted by the new king, who made Becket his chancellor. In the years that followed, Becket proved himself useful and was invaluable in helping Henry restore the Crown's authority after the mid-century civil wars. When Theobald died, it was natural for Henry to assume that Becket – his friend and confidant – would take over and continue as before.

Instead the archbishop took a different path. Resigning the chancellorship, which the king had expected him to keep, Becket immediately began championing **ecclesiastical autonomy** – particularly with regard to the question of whether miscreant clerics should be tried before Church courts (where punishment was generally lenient) or before the king's judiciary. Becket was forced into exile, from where he launched an unrelenting campaign against his former master. This ignited the sequence of events leading to Becket's murder at Canterbury in 1170, by four knights who had been present when Henry raged that he wanted to be 'rid of this turbulent priest'.

Noting Becket's love of wealth and ostentation during his time as chancellor, some critics have explained his seemingly abrupt transformation as the behaviour of a vain man unwilling to be outdone by his sovereign. More generous commentators have seen an individual who came to God in mid-life. Whatever the truth, in death he was even more influential than in life – his tomb become a focus of pilgrimage for nearly 400 years and his cult one of the most powerful of the European middle ages.

1171 Henry II's continental territories are placed under an interdict by the **archbishop of Sens** as a punishment for Becket's murder; in Canterbury itself, stories grow from Easter onwards of **miracles** associated with Becket's tomb.

Henry attempts to call the Church's bluff by leading a **crusade** to Ireland, but fails to extend English rule beyond Leinster.

1172 Henry II's personal excommunication is lifted on condition that he maintains **two hundred knights** in the Holy Land and himself undertakes to crusade against Islam for three years.

1173 Just three years after his death, Becket is **canonized**.

Prince Henry falls out with his father when Henry II proposes giving territories to his youngest and favourite son **John** (known as **Lackland**) at the expense of Prince Geoffrey. As the family feud deepens, **Queen Eleanor** and **Prince Richard** side with the younger Henry and Geoffrey, who are also supported by **Louis VII of France** and **William 'the Lion', King of Scots**. Such fighting as occurs is, however, mainly confined to the continent.

1174 On 12 July, in order to restore his ailing European reputation and atone for his mistreatment of Thomas Becket, Henry II performs **public penance** at Canterbury Cathedral.

William, King of Scots is captured at **Alnwick** on 13 July and is only released after agreeing to pay England homage.

Towards the end of the year Henry succeeds in overcoming his rebellious family; his sons are pardoned, but **Queen Eleanor** is arrested and spends the next eleven years in custody. Henry II initiates **divorce proceedings**, but they are never finalized.

1177 Henry II has Prince John proclaimed 'King of Ireland'.

1180 Differences between Henry and the Vatican still outstanding from the 1164 Constitutions of Clarendon are **resolved** on the basis of compromise.

The theologian **John of Salisbury** – who continued Becket's impassioned defence of ecclesiastical rights – dies. A committed advocate of Church poverty and a forward-thinking educationalist, his work influences the development of humanism three centuries later.

1181 Feuding again breaks out in the royal family when the princes Henry and Richard dispute territory in **Aquitaine**.

In England, Henry II decrees that all freemen should possess and maintain such weapons as are appropriate to their wealth and social position – an instrument known as the **Assize of Arms**.

1183 The death of Henry II's eldest son, **Prince Henry**, intensifies the rivalries between his younger sons Richard, Geoffrey and John.

1184 King Henry stokes further dynastic conflict by encouraging Prince John to seize **Aquitaine** from his brother Richard.

Richard wars against John and his father.

1186 The death of Prince Geoffrey during a jousting tournament seemingly strengthens Prince Richard's claim to his father's throne; but as Henry II blatantly favours his youngest son John, Richard forms an alliance with **King Philip II Augustus** of France against them. When Henry's forces are defeated, John joins Richard in rebellion.

1187 **Saladin**'s recapture of **Jerusalem** from the Crusaders casts a blight over Christendom.

The late Prince Geoffrey's heir, **Arthur**, is born.

Richard I (1157–99)

Richard I embodies the degree to which crusading came to dominate the minds – and the resources – of Europe's rulers during the 12th century. Partly it was a matter of chivalry, partly of faith, and partly of defending Christendom against the encroachments of Islam.

No sooner had Richard been crowned than he set about joining the **Third Crusade**, called in response to Saladin's capture of Jerusalem in 1187. **Acre** fell after a siege, but **Jerusalem** offered more resistance and the crusaders' objective remained beyond their grasp. When that happened, the Christian monarchs quickly began to squabble. In the aftermath Richard was seized by Leopold of Austria, and only released on the payment of a vast ransom. Even then, no sooner had Richard returned home than he left again to attend to his affairs in France.

Much as glamour and romance attached themselves to the king during his lifetime (the nickname *Coeur de Lion* appears as early as 1199), later historians have been quick to condemn Richard – not just for his mercilessness against Saladin's Muslims but for his apparent carelessness about the government of their own country. 'Richard I was rather a knight-errant than a king,' sniffed Sir James Mackintosh in his *History of England* (1830–32), continuing: 'His history is more that of a crusade than of a reign.' As usual, the truth lies somewhere in between. For a start, the French-speaking early Plantagenets had a wide view of their empire, of which England was just one part. Further, government did not collapse during Richard's absence. Thanks to the capable stewardship of the chief justiciar **Hubert Walter**, order was maintained, while the fact that Richard's ransom was easily raised indicates that his barons supported his activities abroad. Even so, his absence did provide England's earls and lords with a taste of power – as Richard's brother **John** discovered to his cost.

1188 Henry II and Philip Augustus meet and establish a **temporary peace**, but fighting between the English king and his sons in France continues.

1189 Henry II, grieved by his surviving sons' hostility toward him and still campaigning against them, dies at **Chinon** near Tours. Within a week Prince Richard succeeds to the English throne. As **Richard I**, known as *Coeur de Lion* ('Lionheart'), he grants his brother John substantial personal domains, but also exiles him from England for three years to prevent any seizure of his throne whilst he crusades in the Holy Land. Similarly Henry II's 'loyal' son, Geoffrey the Bastard, is compelled into taking holy orders, made **archbishop of York**, but also exiled. Having thus disabled his likeliest rivals, Richard earnestly sets about raising funds for his participation in the **Third Crusade**.

1190 Richard I leaves England for the **Holy Land**. He stops en route to lay claim to **Sicily**, the kingdom of his sister Joan's late husband, **King William II**. While travelling, he nominates **Arthur of Brittany** as his heir. On hearing this, John returns to England illegally and joins those opposed to Richard's chancellor **William Longchamp**.

1191 Richard marries **Berengaria of Navarre** and establishes his rule over the island of Cyprus. In the Holy Land he participates in the siege of **Acre**, which falls a month after the crusaders' arrival; its inhabitants, Jewish as well as Muslim, are massacred. Philip II Augustus of France abandons the crusade immediately afterwards, leaving Richard undisputed leader of the expedition. He marches towards Jerusalem, but although he defeats **Saladin** in open battle he is unable to close on his target.

In England, the monks of **Glastonbury** discover (or claim to discover) the graves of **King Arthur and Guinevere**.

1192 John succeeds in banishing the king's chancellor **William Longchamp** and briefly becomes effective ruler in Richard's absence, conspiring with Philip Augustus to take the throne for himself. Needing to return home,

Richard initiates **peace talks** with Saladin, and recognizes first **Conrad of Montferrat**, then **Henry II of Champagne** as king of the Latin kingdom of **Outremer**. Saladin agrees to a truce lasting three years, three months and three days, and guarantees Christian pilgrims access to Jerusalem. On his way back, Richard is taken prisoner by his enemy **Leopold of Austria** after being shipwrecked off **Venice**.

1193 **Emperor Henry VI** persuades Leopold to transfer Richard to his own custody. Encouraged by his brother's misfortune, John continues to build an **alliance** with Philip Augustus, who begins seizing Richard's lands in **Normandy**. In England the government remains loyal to Richard, though, and John is forced to flee to the continent.

1194 John allows Philip Augustus to take possession of all **Normandy** north of the Seine.

In Germany, Richard is finally **released** after his supporters agree to humiliating terms: England is to become a fief of the emperor, to whom it must pay a **ransom** of 150,000 marks. Returning to England, Richard swiftly defeats John's followers and destroys their castles; John himself is deprived of all his lands and **banished**. In May, Richard leaves once more for the continent, never to set foot in England again. He is warmly greeted in Normandy, and in July defeats Philip Augustus at **Freteval** – a victory that enables him to reclaim nearly all his lost territories in France.

1196 Richard consolidates his position in Normandy by embarking on a massive programme of castle-building, including the supposedly impregnable **Chateau Gaillard** on the Seine. The king and John are **reconciled**, the latter becoming heir to the English throne since Richard is childless.

1197 Hoping to secure the succession of his son Frederick, Emperor Henry VI releases Richard from vassalage.

1198 Henry VI dies and his brother **Philip of Swabia** is elected emperor. As factions within the empire begin feuding, Richard engineers the election of an alternative candidate – his nephew **Otto of Brunswick**. Richard's hand is strengthened by the election of **Innocent III**, a pope eager to prevent **Sicily** becoming part of the empire and to promote a new crusade.

1199 Richard I and Philip Augustus begin **peace talks** to end the fighting in Normandy, but before these can be concluded Richard is killed by a crossbow bolt at **Chalus** while attempting to subdue a rebellion led by **Audemar Taillefer of Angouleme** and his brother, the **viscount of Limoges**. The succession is disputed between his brother **John** and his nephew **Arthur of Brittany**. Reluctantly the barons of Normandy and England choose John, who is crowned at Westminster in May. Arthur is declared **count of Anjou**, and with the backing of Philip Augustus begins pressurizing John to make further territorial concessions in France. Forming an alliance with the counts of **Boulogne** and **Flanders**, John **declares war** against Arthur.

1200 Although John successfully defends England's northern counties against the **Scots**, he is unable to secure a meaningful victory in France and agrees instead to a peace concluded at **Le Goulet**. Although territorially the terms are favourable to Philip Augustus, Arthur of Anjou agrees to pay homage to the English Crown. The treaty is cemented by two marriages – between Philip's heir **Louis** and John's niece **Blanche of Castile**, and between John himself and **Isabella of Angouleme**. But while the latter extends John's influence in Aquitaine, it also provokes the **Lusignans** into rebellion, as Isabella has been previously promised to their count, **Hugh le Brun**. Crushed in battle by John, the Lusignans appeal to Philip Augustus to arbitrate.

1201 Philip II Augustus summons John as duke of Aquitaine to answer the Lusignan charge of mistreatment, and demands that he **surrender** several castles, including Chateau Gaillard. When John refuses to attend, King Philip declares him a 'contumacious vassal' and **confiscates** all his French lands.

> ❝ [John] was the worst of all our kings: a man whom no oaths could bind, no pressure of conscience, no consideration of policy, restrain from evil; a faithless son, a treacherous brother, an ungrateful master; to his people a hated tyrant. Polluted with every crime that could disgrace a man, false to every obligation that could bind a king, he had lost his inheritance by sloth, and ruined and desolated the rest. ❞
>
> Bishop William Stubbs, *The Constitutional History of England* (1874–78)

1202 Philip Augustus accepts the homage of **Aquitaine**, **Maine** and **Brittany** from Arthur. They then combine against John: Philip attacks Normandy and Arthur Touraine. Arthur is **captured**, along with Geoffrey de Lusignan and Hugh le Brun, while besieging Eleanor of Aquitaine at **Mirebeau**.

1203 As the Anglo-French war continues, John has Arthur **murdered** at Rouen; his maltreatment of Arthur and other prisoners persuades a number of allies to **desert** him.

Philip Augustus continues his campaigns in Normandy, besieging **Chateau Gaillard**. Contemporary chroniclers criticize John for failing to defend Normandy adequately.

1205 The death of **Hubert Walter**, the archbishop of Canterbury and John's chancellor, inspires the king to take a more active interest in the administration of England. John prefers to promote members of his own household to high office instead of making appointments from among the nobility. Together with an excessively harsh – not to mention efficient – **tax regime**, this progressively undermines such baronial support as John has.

1206 John, continuing to defend his possessions in the south of France at the expense of those in the north, mounts an expedition to **Poitou**. To the dismay of some English he begins promoting Poitevins as government officials in England.

> **❝** Unfortunately for his reputation, John was not a great benefactor to monasteries which kept chronicles. **❞**
>
> W.L. Warren, *King John* (1978)

John quarrels with **Pope Innocent III** over the choice of a new archbishop to replace Hubert Walter. When the pope's choice **Stephen Langton** is elected at Canterbury in December, John refuses to recognize him.

1208 As John continues to refuse to recognize Stephen Langton, England is placed under a **general interdict** by Innocent III, effectively excommunicating the country's entire population.

1209 John is **personally excommunicated** by Innocent III. Despite the ignominy of this, John profits by farming the revenues of vacant ecclesiastical appointments.

1212 In the summer John campaigns successfully in **Wales**, and foils a plot to murder him.

In November, anxious to form an alliance against Philip Augustus, he makes up with Innocent III by **acknowledging Langton** as archbishop.

1213 Relations with the papacy are fully restored when John 'surrenders' England to a **papal nuncio** at **Ewell** near Dover in May. The king's excommunication is **revoked**, as is the general interdict against England the following year.

To finance further campaigns in France, John attempts to levy heavy taxes on English knights and other men-at-arms in the form of **scutage** (fees in lieu of military service), but some northern barons refuse to contribute to a war that has nothing to do with them.

Magna Carta

Lauded by 18th-century historians and antiquarians as the cornerstone of the English constitution and a guarantee against monarchical oppression, Magna Carta was in fact a far more limited document.

Much of the charter deals with specific baronial grievances, among them such oddities as who held fishing rights on the River Thames. Mixed in with the ephemera, however, are more inspiring principles – notably the right to trial by jury and that of habeas corpus, whereby imprisonment without charge is deemed unlawful. Such clauses were sufficiently radical to prompt Pope Innocent III, a ruler himself, to declare the charter void. Yet in its intent Magna Carta was restricted to clarifying relations between monarch and lords alone, and only the imprecisions of its drafting allowed it to acquire the semblance of a contract between a king and all his subjects.

Even so, given that England's barons increasingly demonstrated an ability to act collectively (often in opposition to the throne), and that England's kings were frequently required to reaffirm Magna Carta, its libertarian reputation isn't too wide of the mark. While historically its beneficiaries were England's landowning elite, it articulated the bold statement that a king should be subject to the laws he made, and not – as many felt that John had attempted to rule – above them.

1215 Returning to England, John finds a majority of barons opposed to him. To buy time, he grants their demands by signing **Magna Carta** (the 'Great Charter') at Runnymede on 19 June. Almost immediately, however, the king appeals to the pope. Not wishing to be seen to support subjects against kings, Innocent III declares the charter **invalid**. As a result, **civil war** between king and barons breaks out.

1214 Although John enjoys initial successes against Philip Augustus at **Poitou**, his allies **Emperor Otto** and the **earl of Salisbury** are crushed at the climactic **Battle of Bouvines**, as a result of which Normandy is lost to the English Crown.

1216 Encouraged by some of John's enemies, Philip Augustus's heir, the **dauphin Louis** (later Louis VIII), invades England. Securing a bridgehead in the east, he gains control of London and lays siege to Dover Castle. John wages war against his northern barons and terrorizes the northern counties. Journeying south to confront Louis, however, he is either taken ill or poisoned, and dies at **Newark** on 19 October, having beforehand suffered the indignity of losing the royal baggage train – including the crown jewels – while attempting to cross the Wash. He is buried at Worcester Cathedral, and is succeeded by his eldest son **Henry III**, who is hurriedly crowned at Gloucester Abbey. The 9-year-old king immediately sets his seal to **Magna Carta**, as the much-respected **William Marshal**, Earl of Pembroke takes on the responsibilities of regent. Baronial discontent is further defused by the support for Henry III of a papal legate.

1217 Louis is forced to return to France after his supporters are defeated on land at **Lincoln** and at sea off **Dover**.

1218 **Judicial circuits** ('justices in eyre') are re-established to combat the lawlessness that has increasingly affected the English countryside during King John's reign.

1219 William Marshal dies, commending England to the care of a papal legate and complaining that 'there are no people in any land like those of England, where each person has his own opinion'.

As Henry III's minority continues, government is delivered by a **royal council** dominated by **Hubert de Burgh**.

1220 Henry III is **re-crowned** at Westminster by the archbishop of Canterbury, signalling a resolution of differences between Crown and Church.

1221 The first Dominican and Franciscan friars arrive in England.

1223 Pope Honorius III declares that Henry III, now aged 16, has **come of age**. But Hubert de Burgh continues as England's effective ruler.

1224 The Crown's previously loyal commander **Fawkes de Breauté** mounts an unsuccessful rebellion.

1225 Magna Carta is again affirmed by Henry III.

1226 A **general eyre** (tour of royal justices), lasting three years, is initiated to investigate unlawful confiscations of land and to attend the clearing of gaols.

1229 The French nobleman **Simon de Montfort** comes to England to make good his claim to the earldom of Leicester.

1231 De Montfort establishes himself as a royal favourite.

1232 Henry III, endeavouring to assert personal rule, replaces Hubert de Burgh with **Peter des Roches** and **Peter of Rievaux**, two ambitious Frenchmen whose promotion irritates England's barons.

1234 Under pressure from his barons, Henry III **dismisses** Peter des Roches and Peter of Rievaux. It is from this year that Henry's **personal rule**, lasting until 1258, is usually dated. Henry III will be remembered as one of England's weaker monarchs, a man eager to play up the symbolic mystery of (pre-Magna Carta) kingship despite – or because of – the political realities. His costly rebuilding of **Westminster Abbey** despite the worsening financial situation is unpopular, and his persistent favouring of officials recruited from France becomes so offensive to England's 'native barons' that they will endeavour to impose a form of **constitutional monarchy** in which royal appointments are taken out of the king's hands.

1236 Henry III marries **Eleanor of Provence**.

1237 Baronial disquiet is heightened by Henry III's appointment of his Savoyard relatives to high positions within his administration.

1238 Despite Henry III's sister, **Eleanor Plantagenet**, having taken an oath of chastity (and in the face of baronial opposition), the king arranges for her marriage to Simon de Montfort on 7 January.

1239 Protest against de Montfort's elevation continues, now led by Henry III's younger brother, **Richard of Cornwall**. Faced by the threat of revolt, Henry **exiles** de Montfort and Eleanor.

1240 Richard of Cornwall and Simon de Montfort find themselves fighting side-by-side during a crusade and are reconciled.

1242 Through his Lusignan relatives, Henry III is drawn into a humiliating and costly regional **war** in France in which he displays his lack of military skill; heavily defeated at **Saintes**, the king only escapes capture through de Montfort's intervention. De Montfort is allowed to return to England, where he re-establishes himself at **Kenilworth**, and where he forms friendships with **Robert Grosseteste** (the Bishop of Lincoln) and other progressive figures.

1244 Although de Montfort's loyalty to the Crown is still apparently intact, he is made a member of a **'committee of twelve'** in an attempt to resolve outstanding differences between Henry and his barons.

1248 When rebellion flares in **Gascony** (Henry's last remaining significant possession in France), de Montfort agrees to restore order there in return for being created **regent** for a term of seven years. But so brutally successful is de Montfort in crushing the Gascon revolt that leading Gascons petition Henry III for his removal; as a result, de Montfort is recalled to England to **stand trial**.

1252 De Montfort is **acquitted** by the barons. Almost immediately renewed rebellion in Gascony leads to his **reappointment** as commander of the king's forces in France.

1253 De Montfort returns to England when Henry III terminates his command.

1254 Henry III agrees a pact with **Pope Innocent IV**, offering to finance a papal war in **Sicily** to the tune of 150,000 marks, in return for the Crown of Sicily being bestowed upon Henry's infant younger son **Edmund**.

Henry's eldest son and heir, the 15-year-old **Prince Edward**, is married to **Eleanor of Castile**, the half-sister of **Alfonso X**, and is granted a portmanteau of titles by his father that includes **Gascony**, **Ireland** and the **'Four Cantrefs'** in north Wales.

1255 Prince Edward endeavours to impose his authority on **Wales**, but is swiftly defeated by **Llywelyn ap Gruffydd**.

1258 Pope Alexander IV threatens to **excommunicate** Henry III for failing to provide the Sicilian funds promised in 1254. In desperation Henry turns to his already discontented barons. In May the barons capitalize on this and impose upon the king a 24-member **'parliament'** made

Simon de Montfort (1208–1265)

Simon de Montfort was a charismatic French nobleman who was swift to stamp his seal on English politics in the 1250s. His father, also Simon de Montfort, had achieved fame throughout Christendom as the principal organizer of the Albigensian Crusade that, earlier in the century, had destroyed the Cathars and their Manichean 'heresy' in Provence. Through the usual complexities of advantageous marriage contracts, the de Montforts had a legitimate claim to the earldom of Leicester, and it was this that brought the younger Simon to England in 1229. Despite being regarded at first by Henry III's barons as yet another foreign interloper, de Montfort gradually emerged as the leader of their opposition. In 1258 he organized the so-called **'commune'** of barons that, in the same year, succeeded in imposing the **Provisions of Oxford** on Henry, formalizing an alternative to autocratic royal rule that for its time was revolutionary. Six years later, following his victory at **Lewes**, de Montfort established his own rule over England. Yet this was never likely to last long. Other barons resented his power, and enough of them supported the campaign of **Prince Edward** to ensure his downfall, and his death, in 1265.

In his years at the centre, well aware that many of the barons were suspicious of his continental background, de Montfort had sought to consolidate his power by appealing to a larger cross-section of English society. Accordingly he invited knights of the shire, then burghers, to attend two **'parliaments'** convened by him – the earliest template for the modern British parliamentary system. De Montfort's motives, though, were anything but democratic. What he wanted was merely a broad-based consultative body to rubber-stamp policies he had already determined. It was primarily as an instrument of central control that Parliament gradually became a fixture in later medieval England – in much the same way that the Cortes became a fixture in Castile, or the Etats-Generaux in France.

up of twelve of his own supporters and twelve of themselves – sometimes called **'the commune'** – led by Simon de Montfort.

In June, in return for the promise of necessary taxes, the king is obliged to accept the radical **Provisions of Oxford**, which greatly limit his powers. England is to be ruled by a 15-member **Privy Council**, part-elected by the 'commune' of barons but still led by de Montfort. The Provisions further determine that appointed officials should be made fully **accountable** to the Council, and that henceforward **'parliaments'** (in effect consultative assemblies composed of the great and good) should be held three times a year. Many of Henry III's appointees are dismissed from office and replaced by baronial candidates. As early as November, however, the king's position begins to recover when the Pope's Sicilian project is **abandoned**, releasing him from the need to raise further funds.

1259 Henry's hand is strengthened when a comprehensive treaty with France is concluded at **Paris**. Although **Gascony** is confirmed as the English Crown's only substantial French holding, the treaty reduces the likelihood of Henry having to make further financial requisitions on his English subjects.

At home, divisions appear within the ranks of the barons opposing him. In October the *communitas bacheleriae* (knights bachelor) petition the king and his barons, voicing grievances about the exactions made upon them by their feudal overlords. To placate the knights, the **Provisions of Westminster** – sometimes regarded as cementing the place of the lesser aristocracy within the medieval English system – are issued.

1261 In April the pope declares the Provisions of Oxford **invalid**. As his barons quarrel amongst themselves, Henry III renounces the Provisions and dismisses those officials imposed on him.

1262 Full-scale civil war between king and barons is averted by de Montfort's decision to withdraw from England.

1263 De Montfort returns to England towards the end of the year to lead those barons still determined to get their way with Henry III.

1264 In January Henry III appeals to **Louis IX of France** to resolve his baronial dispute. Louis obliges by issuing the **Mise of Amiens**, affirming Henry's right to appoint his own ministers.

In April de Montfort raises a rebellion, sometimes called the **barons' war**. In May Henry III and Prince Edward are captured at the **Battle of Lewes**, and imprisoned. De Montfort assumes dictatorial powers. In June he convenes an **expanded parliament**, which now includes four knights from each shire – ostensibly to set up a new form of government, but also to broaden his power-base within the realm.

1265 A **second parliament** convened by de Montfort is further expanded to allow wealthy representatives from England's towns and cities to attend. Among the barons, opposition to de Montfort spreads, led by **Gilbert de Clare, Earl of Gloucester**. In May, abetted by these dissidents, Prince Edward escapes captivity in Hereford and at once begins raising a royal army. The greater part of de Montfort's forces are besieged at **Kenilworth**. On 4 August de Montfort himself is defeated and killed at the **Battle of Evesham** by Prince Edward, who becomes *de facto* ruler on behalf of his ailing father.

1266 Prince Edward campaigns successfully against the remaining rebels and **re-establishes** Plantagenet rule. His excessively harsh policies against **London**, provoked by the city's previous alliance with the rebels, are moderated by the **Dictum of Kenilworth**, issued by Henry III.

Robin Hood

In the aftermath of Evesham, a handful of de Montfort's supporters took to the fens and forests of England to continue a guerilla-type resistance to the king. Out of this grew the legend of **Robin Hood**, an amalgam of medieval outlaw and folk hero who also bears the imprint of other rebel exiles such as **Hereward the Wake** (see p.72).

Tales of Sherwood Forest and of Robin's intimates – Maid Marian, Little John, Friar Tuck and the Merry Men – appeared from the 14th century onwards. His first literary reference occurs in a version of William Langland's *Piers Plowman,* while the earliest extant manuscript featuring him, *Robin Hood and the Monk,* dates from around 1450. Some of the orally transmitted ballads in which Robin Hood features go back further, however, and an attempt was made by the 18th-century antiquarian **William Stukeley** to establish a genealogy identifying Robin with the fictitious 13th-century rebel, **Robert, Earl of Huntingdon.**

Like all the best folk heroes, Robin has been flexible enough to champion a multiplicity of causes. Sometimes he appears as a loyalist defending 'Good King Richard'; elsewhere he stands up for Anglo-Saxon rights against Norman barbarism; by the 16th century he had become incorporated into the Mayday Rite as a personification of fertility. Overall, though, his profile has been relatively consistent – that of an all-purpose thorn in the side of corrupt and dastardly government, usually with the interests of the common man at heart. And, unlike King Arthur (see p.143), Robin seems to owe little to outside influence – the oak tree reputed to have been the centre of his Sherwood camp symbolizes the enduring glamour of 'English' justice and fair play.

1267 The **Statute of Marlborough**, issued by Edward and adopted by a parliament consisting of barons and commoners, confirms the Provisions of Westminster, but not the Provisions of Oxford. The same parliament also confirms the 'peace terms' that conclude the War of the Barons, but baulks at some of the taxes requested by Edward so that he can crusade in the Holy Land.

The **Treaty of Shrewsbury** is concluded with Llywelyn ap Gruffydd, effectively acknowledging that the Welsh prince has succeeded in creating an autonomous Welsh principality.

1270 Having raised sufficient funds to crusade, Edward entrusts England's government to four dependable ministers (among them **Robert Burnell**) and his Welsh territories to his brother Edmund.

1272 Henry III, having devoted his final years to rebuilding **Westminster Abbey**, dies on 16 November. Although Prince Edward is in Sicily at the time, on 20 November the barons swear **fealty** to him in his absence.

The later Plantagenets
1272–1399

The Plantagenets dramatically demonstrate the advantages and pitfalls of medieval kingship. A militarily capable monarch with a gift for administration could make the system work. But an overweening, militarily unlucky and tactless ruler could provoke civil discord – even civil war. Among the early Plantagenets Henry II proved himself strong; but John and Henry III, albeit in very different ways, demonstrated weakness. Among the later Plantagenets the story has been seen as much the same: two efficient monarchs, Edward I and Edward III; and two disasters, Edward II and Richard II.

Edward I had demonstrated his prowess before he came to the throne by containing Simon de Montfort and ending the **barons' war**. As king he fulfilled his promise, at least for the first twenty years of his reign. Accepting Parliament as a valuable means of generating (and enforcing) consent, he pushed through a far-reaching programme of administrative reform bolstering royal power, while at the same time acknowledging that England's merchant community now constituted an important component of his realm. And by defeating **Llywelyn** and successfully subjugating Wales, he reinvigorated the Crown's reputation. Edward I's latter years were less positive, however. An attempt to subjugate Scotland along the same lines was unsuccessful and, if anything, fed Scottish nationalism; while the cost of his campaigns – coupled with the crippling expense of erecting vast castles in Wales – bankrupted the Exchequer and made him hugely unpopular.

It would have taken an astute successor to repair the damage, but his son, the hapless **Edward II**, only added to it. By flaunting his attachment to Piers Gaveston and then adopting the Despensers as replacement favourites, he antagonized his barons to the point of rebellion. Nor, in pursuing his father's policy toward Scotland, was he able to make up for lost ground. A tide of patriotic fervour overran the northern kingdom, and Edward II's inadequacies in battle heralded a dismal failure for the English.

Edward III ascended the throne under the iron control of his mother **Queen Isabella** and her lover **Roger Mortimer**. Within three years, though, the young king had shaken off their influence and assumed power in his own right. Whereas his grandfather had limited his ambition to dominating Britain, the new king – on the pretext of a claim to the French throne via his mother – resumed the family's continental aspirations. Once again English armies crossed the English Channel, at first with astonishing success: in the opening phase of the so-called **Hundred Years War**, Edward III and his son (another Edward, known as the

Black Prince) scored devastating victories at **Sluys**, **Crécy** and **Poitiers**.

Almost the whole of France was theirs for the taking. But the French fought back, plague undermined England's economy, and by the end of Edward III's reign there was nothing to show for his campaigns other than the possession of four French towns. Once again the Crown was bankrupt and the country uneasy. At its zenith, Edward III's court – festooned with rituals partly derived from the myth of King Arthur – may have been the envy of Europe, but pomp and pageantry cost money.

Nor did things get easier. **Richard II**, besotted with unrealistic ideas about the grandeur of the Crown, lacked the realism or the political insight to retrench. Although 1381 saw him face down an uprising known as the **Peasants' Revolt** with a courage that won him support at the time, he was unable to deal with the complaints of his nobility. It was a failing that eventually cost him the throne – and which ignited a dynastic dispute that would plunge the country into civil war and last the best part of a century.

1272 At the time of his accession **Edward I** is virtually stranded abroad, and is able to return home only with the aid of a substantial loan advanced by the Italian bankers, the **Ricciardi of Lucca**. During his absence, **rebellion** flares in the northern counties. During his reign, however, Edward will provide the kind of military leadership – evidenced particularly by his subjugation of **Wales** – needed to maintain the authoritarian style of kingship favoured by the Plantagenets.

1274 Edward lands in England, and is **crowned** at Westminster on 19 August. Clearing the kingdom of rebels, he orders an investigation into the state of government locally, with a view to reclaiming royal lands usurped during his father's reign.

> **❝** But the chief advantage which the people of England reaped, and still continue to reap, from the reign of this great prince, was the correction, extension, amendment, and establishment of the laws, which Edward maintained in great vigour, and left much improved to posterity; for the acts of a wise legislator commonly remain, while the acquisitions of a conqueror often perish with him. This merit has justly gained to Edward the appellation of *the English Justinian*. **❞**
>
> David Hume on Edward I, in the *History of Great Britain* (1761)

1275 Edward I begins issuing a series of **statutes** that over the coming fifteen years will counterbalance England's **common law**, usually to the advantage of the throne.

Edward's queen, **Eleanor of Castile**, ejects **Jews** from her English estates.

1277 Determined to avenge himself on **Llywelyn ap Gruffydd** for his youthful humiliation, and supported by his marcher lords, Edward stages a major invasion of **Wales** by land and sea. Llywelyn, holed up in the mountains of Snowdonia, is forced to concede the **Treaty of Conway**, which confiscates territorial gains made since 1247, and makes him a vassal of the English Crown. In the wake of his victory, Edward begins imposing an English **administration** on Wales, now divided up into shires and counties for the first time. He also embarks on a programme of **castle-building** in north Wales to contain any further rebellion.

1278 Edward issues the **Statutes of Gloucester**, establishing the principle of *quo warranto*, by which royal feudal tenants are asked 'by what warrant' they hold their franchises. Those unable to prove their entitlement are dispossessed or obliged to pay compensation to the Crown.

Castle-building

The years of unrest under King Stephen had seen a proliferation of baronial castles in England, but by the beginning of the 13th century the increasing sophistication of siege warfare meant that only the king and a handful of magnates could afford the sort of massive structures now required for defence. **Simon de Montfort** (see p.119) invested huge sums in his modifications to **Kenilworth Castle**, enabling his supporters to hold out within its walls for a year after the Battle of Evesham. And Henry III dedicated equally vast resources to the development of **Dover Castle** following its lengthy – though abortive – siege by the dauphin Louis between 1216 and 1217.

Much of the new castle technology derived from the Holy Land, where the crusaders had experienced sustained assault by Islamic armies; aptly, it was on the way back from Palestine that Edward I met the Savoyard engineer known as **Master James of St George** whom he entrusted with his castle-building programme in Wales. Their partnership enabled a number of imposing fortresses that dominate the Welsh landscape to this day. At **Caernarfon**, the walls of Constantinople were deliberately evoked by the construction of polygonal towers surmounted by imperial eagles – a fitting assertion of Edward's desire for conquest. Technically, though, the most impressive of his castles is **Beaumaris** on the island of Anglesey, innovatively designed as a series of interlocking concentric circles with hardly a straight line in sight. But Beaumaris was the last of the Edwardine constructions, and it remained unfinished. Edward's lavish building spree had long since emptied the royal coffers.

1279 The **Statute of Mortmain** prohibits future gifts of land to the Church without royal approval.

1282 Llywelyn ap Gruffydd, having refused to pay Edward homage, joins a **revolt** against English rule led by his brother **Dafydd**. Known as the 'last prince of Wales', he is killed in an ambush at **Irfon Bridge**. His head is sent to London as proof of his death.

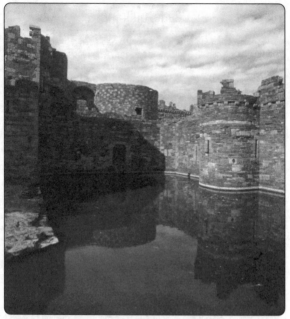

Beaumaris castle, Wales.

1283 The Edwardine conquest of Wales is completed when Llywelyn's brother Dafydd is **hung, drawn and quartered** at **Shrewsbury** – a symbolically brutal punishment invented specifically for him. But the huge cost of Edward's Welsh wars is such that the Crown falls further into **debt** with its Italian bankers.

1284 The **Statute of Wales** formalizes the new administration installed by Edward in Wales. As a sop to Welsh pride, Edward I gives his newborn son and heir, **Edward**, the title **earl of Caernarvon**, claiming that the infant 'speaks no other tongue' than Welsh. In future, male heirs to the English throne will be known as the **Prince of Wales**, although not all are ceremonially invested as such.

1285 The **Statute of Winchester** regulates England's law-enforcement system by declaring that counties will be held responsible for unsolved crimes and ordering highways to be widened and made safer.

1286 Edward I pays Philip IV of France homage for **Gascony** and other minor continental possessions, but Philip begins supporting local unrest that erodes some of the lands.

In **Scotland**, Alexander III dies, leaving **Margaret** (known as the 'Maid of Norway') as his only direct heir.

1289 Advised by **Robert Burnell**, Edward purges his government of corrupt and inefficient officials.

1290 **Eleanor of Castile** dies, depriving Edward III not only of his queen but a trusted adviser. Distraught by her death, the king orders the construction of **stone crosses** at each resting place along the route of her cortege. Perhaps also in her honour, and to the satisfaction of his other subjects, he expels all **Jews** from England.

The death of **Margaret of Scotland** leaves the Scottish throne without an heir.

In **Gascony**, French interference intensifies.

1291 By invitation of the Bishop of St Andrews, Edward presides over a 'Scottish parliament' convened at **Norham** to decide between thirteen candidates for the Scottish throne. Eventually Edward recognizes **John Balliol**, in preference to **Robert Bruce** (known as 'the Competitor') as king on condition that Balliol toes the line and recognizes Edward's overlordship.

1292 **Robert Burnell**, Edward's long-serving chancellor, dies. The ministers who follow are of lesser calibre, and unable to dissuade Edward – already financially hard-pressed – from pursuing the fruitless and costly policies of his later reign.

In December, John Balliol is crowned **king of Scotland**.

1293 By clever negotiation Philip IV dupes Edward's brother **Edmund**, sent to France to conduct negotiations, into surrendering **Gascony**. Preoccupied with **Scotland**, where he is determined to implant an English administration similar to that imposed on Wales, the English king fails to respond immediately.

1294 An attempted uprising in Wales is ruthlessly put down by Edward's forces.

1295 Under increasing pressure to adopt English institutions and with the backing of France, John Balliol **renounces** his allegiance to Edward I.

The English king convenes the **Model Parliament**, so called because the writs of attendance offer a clear statement of **'representation'** – a term that will become a keyword of parliamentary democracy.

1296 Determined to assert his control, Edward I invades and conquers Scotland. **Berwick** is sacked, a Scottish army is defeated by Earl Warenne at **Dunbar**, and John Balliol is forced to undergo ritual humiliation. Edward thanks Warenne with the words: 'A man who gets rid of a turd does a good job.' The **Stone of Scone**, used during the Scottish coronation ceremony, is removed to Westminster – it will stay there until 1996.

1297 Edward I assembles a task force to recover **Gascony** from Philip IV, but his English barons refuse to support him. In part they are motivated by a renewed outbreak of tension between Crown and Church; to raise money for

Roger Bacon (c.1214–92)

Nicknamed 'Doctor Mirabilis', teacher of wonders, Roger Bacon secured a reputation as the foremost scientific investigator of his day. Born in either Gloucestershire or Somerset, after studying at Oxford his formal education was completed in Paris. In 1247 he returned to England and, inspired by the natural philosophy of Aristotle, set about using his family's considerable wealth to establish a private research institute. His aim, largely achieved, was to acquire a complete knowledge of every aspect of 'science', stressing the need for experimental procedures. Although his own experiments were relatively limited, he carried out work in optics that almost certainly led to the invention of spectacles, and it seems likely that he understood the principles of the telescope. He also outlined more ambitious goals – predicting both mechanized flight and submarine travel.

After he joined the Franciscans in 1257, however, he began to confront serious obstacles. While Bacon believed that studying physical phenomena could only enhance human understanding of the divine, his superiors took a different view. Back in Paris, he was imprisoned for ten years, but managed to appeal secretly to the sympathetic Pope Clement IV. Clement responded by asking Bacon for a summary of his researches, out of which came the three books that established his reputation: *Opus Majus*, *Opus Minus* and *Opus Tertium* (the 'Greater', 'Lesser' and 'Third' Works). But no sooner were these completed than the pope died. Deprived of protection, Bacon – who was never reluctant to criticize his fellow scholars and religious authority – was again confined, and he remained imprisoned until shortly before his death. Although never condemned as a heretic, he was strongly suspected of necromancy and his name became something of a byword for magic.

In the larger view, he was a prodigious man whose passion for manuscripts helped the spread of scientific knowledge from Islamic countries (where Greek learning had been preserved) and, via those, from China – Bacon is credited with being the first European to give a precise recipe for gunpowder, a Chinese invention.

his wars Edward imposes taxes on the clergy, but the clergy are instructed by **Pope Boniface VIII** not to pay and consequently Edward outlaws them all. Notwithstanding these difficulties, Edward sails for **Flanders**. During his absence the barons collectively confirm existing **'charters'** upholding their rights, and add the proviso that 'arbitrary taxation' should not be allowed.

Rebellions break out in Scotland led by **Robert Bruce** (later Robert I) and by two charismatic knights, **Andrew Moray** and **William Wallace**, who defeat Warenne at Stirling Bridge. Edward returns home swiftly to tackle the new threat.

1298 Although Edward scores a significant victory over Wallace's forces at **Falkirk** on 22 July, resistance to English rule continues.

1299 Anglo-French differences are resolved by peace terms agreed between Edward and Philip IV. A diminished **Gascony** is returned to Edward, who agrees to marry Philip's sister **Margaret**. It is also proposed that **Edward of Caernarfon** marry Philip's daughter **Isabella**.

1304 In Scotland, Edward captures **Stirling Castle**. A majority of Scottish leaders come to terms with him.

1305 Edward's Scottish campaigns are seemingly crowned with success when **William Wallace** is captured, then hung, drawn and quartered.

1306 Pope Clement V, more favourably disposed toward Edward than his predecessor, allows the English king to exile **Robert Winchelsey**, the troublesome archbishop of Canterbury.

In Scotland Edward's victories fall apart when **Robert Bruce** is proclaimed king.

1307 On his way to another Scottish campaign, Edward I dies at **Burghly Sands** near Carlisle. Amid lingering tensions with the barons, he is succeeded by the Prince of Wales. But although **Edward II** attempts to placate his father's enemies by appointing some of them to high office, he earns their contempt by making his favourite, **Piers Gaveston**, earl of Cornwall. Nor is his position helped by severely depleted royal coffers.

1308 Edward II marries **Isabella**, daughter of Philip IV of France. Early fears about Edward's suitability are reflected in a new clause added to his coronation oath compelling him to uphold the 'rightful laws and customs which the community of the realm shall have chosen.' Rumours soon begin to circulate that Edward is more fond of Gaveston than of his 12-year-old bride, and Edward is forced to send his favourite into exile.

1309 Edward dismays his barons by allowing Gaveston to return, where he is again showered with honours.

1310 Edward undertakes his first major campaign in **Scotland**. It is a disaster and he is forced to agree to the appointment of 24 **Ordainers** to look into the question of reform of government

1311 Four years into his reign, Edward II is forced to give way to his barons. Edward concedes their terms, which severely limit his powers, and agrees to **exile Gaveston**. By the end of the year, though, Gaveston is back at Edward's court.

1312 Besieged in his castle at **Scarborough**, Gaveston surrenders to the earl of Pembroke. Despite being offered safe passage, he is recaptured by the earl of Warwick, who hands him over to the earls of Lancaster, Arundel and Hereford, by whom he is brutally murdered. While suspicion of foul play encourages some barons to remain loyal to the king, opposition to Edward centres on his cousin,

Trade and foreign communities

During the 12th and 13th centuries – and up until the Black Death of the late 1340s – Europe experienced sustained economic growth, marked by the development of great port cities such as Venice, Genoa, Barcelona, Seville and Antwerp. With their growth came sweeping social changes. Merchants, who had been on the fringes of society, gravitated toward its centre. England benefited from a thriving wool trade with the Low Countries, and London in particular – comfortably straddling the navigable Thames – emerged as an important centre, one populated by an assortment of foreign communities. French and Flemish merchants were joined by Jewish and Italian businessmen, the latter encouraged especially by Edward I's dependence on Italian bankers to finance his costly castle-building in Wales and campaigns in Scotland. First he relied on the Ricciardi, and then (after they had been forced out business by Philip IV of France in 1294) the Frescobaldi of Florence, accumulating debts that topped £200,000 by the time of his death. Edward I was also the first English king to provide a legal framework for merchants operating in London and other trade centres such as Bristol and Norwich. This, the Statute of Acton Burnell, established debtors' prisons for those with trade as well as other debts, while the *Carta Mercatoria* (Merchants' Charter) of 1303 granted foreign merchants the right to trade freely in England on condition they paid supplementary dues to the Crown. As a result of such measures London became increasingly cosmopolitan – as evidenced by names such as Lombard Street in the heart of today's City district.

Yet not all foreign communities profited from Edward's open-door policies. Jews were excluded from an early Statute of Merchants, and then in 1290 they were given three months to get out of England altogether; despite being guaranteed safe passage, many were attacked and robbed en route. Jewish communities were not permitted to return to the country until Cromwell's reign, some five hundred years later.

Thomas of Lancaster. Crucially, Queen Isabella and the king of France side with Edward – for the while.

1314 In an attempt to demonstrate military prowess, Edward II personally leads an army to crush Robert Bruce, but on 24 June is humiliated at **Bannockburn**, a battle that secures Scotland's independence.

1315 Effective government passes into the hands of **Thomas of Lancaster**.

In the country at large, a two-year **famine** begins.

1318 Thomas of Lancaster having failed to provide good government, **Aymer de Valence, Earl of Pembroke**, brokers a 'truce' between Edward II and some of the barons, enabling Edward to resume his rule.

The **Treaty of Leake** is agreed between Lancaster and Edward, allowing for a permanent council of seventeen members. The king swiftly regains unpopularity when he adopts a father and son, both called **Hugh Despenser**, as his favourites.

1321 Thomas of Lancaster, a great enemy of the Despensers, takes up arms against the king, plunging England into a fitful **civil war**.

1322 Edward II captures Thomas of Lancaster at **Boroughbridge** in Yorkshire and orders his beheading.

1324 The death of the **earl of Pembroke**, 'murdered suddenly on a privy seat', enables Edward II to centralize power within his Despenser clique.

Edward sends **Queen Isabella** as an emissary to **Charles IV** of France with Prince Edward. It is a crucial mistake. Angered by her husband's continuing favouritism for the Despensers, Isabella begins plotting with the banished baron **Roger Mortimer**, and begins an affair with him. Custody of the young heir strengthens their hand.

1326 With the support of the French Crown, Queen Isabella and Mortimer **invade** England, rapidly winning the allegiance of Edward's disaffected barons. Hugh Despenser the elder is captured and executed; the younger Despenser, also captured, is emasculated before being killed.

1327 In January, as the king's position becomes untenable, Edward II is deposed in favour of **Edward III**, his 15-year-old son by Isabella. Imprisoned, the ex-king is put to death in September at **Berkeley Castle**. As the new king is a minor, effective rule is supplied by Isabella and Mortimer.

1328 On 24 January Edward III is married to **Philippa**, daughter of the count of Holland and Hainaut. In the same year the **Treaty of Northampton**, concluded between the two crowns, affirms Scotland's independence from England.

1329 Robert I the Bruce of Scotland is succeeded by the young **David II**; the English Crown conspires with dissident Scottish lords to replace him with **Edward Balliol**. David flees to **France** where his faction gains the support of the French Crown.

1330 Edward III assumes **personal rule** by overthrowing the government of his mother Isabella and Mortimer. While Isabella is 'retired' to her estates, Mortimer is tried before the lords in Parliament and executed in November. Edward III's reign will be noted for a series of stunning but finally unproductive victories in **France** and also for the lavishness of his court, which for a while becomes the most glittering in Europe. He is routinely faced by bankruptcy as a consequence, and the end of his reign is marked by a steep decline. At **Woodstock**, Queen Philippa gives birth to Edward's eldest son and heir, also named Edward, but later known as the **Black Prince** – supposedly because of the colour of the armour he would choose to wear.

1333 An English victory over a Scottish force at **Halidon Hill** seemingly ensures Edward Balliol's tenure of the Scottish throne.

1337 As relations between the English and French thrones deteriorate and Philip VI 'confiscates' Gascony, Edward III leads an **expeditionary force** across the Channel, initiating a century-long but intermittent conflict known as the **Hundred Years War**. Edward's pretext for going to war is his claim, through his mother, to the French Crown itself. Other points of contention include Edward's persistent unwillingness to pay homage to Philip VI of France for his French possessions; French support for rebellious elements in the same possessions; Philip VI's support for David II of Scotland; and French aggression toward the Flemings, England's partners in the well-developed cross-Channel wool trade. Edward's opening campaign is cut short, however, when the king runs out of money.

The first 'English' **dukedom** is bestowed upon Prince Edward, now styled **duke of Gloucester**.

1339 A second invasion of France again falters as Edward runs out of money.

1340 Mounting his third campaign against France, Edward III annihilates the French fleet off the Flemish city of **Sluys** (Sluis). But he lacks the funds to follow up this victory.

1341 **David II**, now adult, is restored to the Scottish throne after Edward Balliol is deposed by Scottish barons resentful of his willingness to subordinate himself to Edward III.

As Edward requests money from his subjects, Parliament is able to win important **concessions** – including the right to approve royal appointments and audit royal accounts.

The Hundred Years War

The Norman Conquest and Henry II's accession to the English throne brought with it large tracts of French land, but at a time when the French Crown was trying to stabilize its boundaries. The problems were obvious: should the kings of England pay homage to the French monarchy for these continental territories? could the kings of France tolerate such powerful neighbours in even closer proximity? The situation was further complicated by the fact that the two royal houses were closely linked by marriage: it was only a matter of time before one throne would attempt to resolve matters by laying claim to the other.

This happened initially at the beginning of Henry III's reign, when the dauphin Louis attempted an invasion of England. And it occurred again in 1337 when Edward III decided to retaliate against Philip IV's seizure of Gascony. The immediate pretext for Philip's action was that Edward had offered shelter to the exiled Robert of Artois; Robert reputedly taunted Edward into claiming his inheritance by placing a heron (symbolizing cowardice) in front of the king at a banquet. So began what became known as the Hundred Years War, a term which only became current in the 1860s but which has been almost universally accepted since.

In its initial phase the French were stunned by a series of improbable victories – Edward III at Crécy in 1346, his son the Black Prince at Poitiers ten years later – which gave the English a reputation for invincibility. Yet by the end of Edward's reign his possessions in France had shrunk to a handful of towns. After years of indecisive wrangling Henry V launched the war's second main phase, triumphing at Agincourt in 1415 and briefly ruling the whole of France. As before, though, the French fought back. Inspired by Jeanne d'Arc (who led the army that liberated Orléans in 1429), they finally drove the English across the Channel in 1453. And despite attempts by Henry VIII to rekindle the conflict – with little success – the two kingdoms have remained separate ever since. For all that, it took the English monarchy over five hundred years to admit defeat: English kings called themselves 'king of France' until 1802.

1342 Edward III begins rebuilding **Windsor Castle** and, to foster martial and chivalric pride among England's knights, creates the **Order of the Garter**.

> **❝** In this season the king of Englande toke pleasure to newe reedefy the castell of Wyndsore, the which was begonne by King Arthure. And there first beganne the table rounde, whereby sprange the fame of so many noble knyghtes throughout all the worlde. Then Kynge Edwarde determyned to make an order and a brotherhood of a certayne nombre of knyghtes, and to be called knyghtes of the blue garter: and a feest to be kept yerely at Wynsore on saynt Georges day. **❞**
>
> Jean Froissart, *Chroniques*, trans. John Bourchier (1525)

1343 Prince Edward is proclaimed **prince of Wales**.

1346 After a six-year lull in hostilities, in July Edward III lands in **Normandy** with an army and marches on **Paris**. Yet again running short of funds, he withdraws toward the northeast. When Philip VI attempts to intercept his retreat, Edward comprehensively defeats the French army at **Crécy** in Ponthieu on 26 August. Integral to Edward's shock victory is his deployment of infantry armed with the **longbow**, of greater range and penetration than the conventional crossbow. In the same battle the youthful **Black Prince** gains his spurs, and adopts the crest and motto – an ostrich plume (four white feathers) and *Ich dien* ('I serve') – of the king of Bohemia. Encouraged by his success, in September Edward III lays siege to **Calais**, a main port on France's northern coast opposite Dover. In October David II, attempting to defend his Scottish throne, is defeated by an English army at **Neville's Cross**.

1347 Calais surrenders to Edward III in August, and will remain in English hands until 1558. Intending to make it a base for future campaigns, Edward expels its French inhabitants.

In September, however, insolvency forces him to come to terms with Philip VI. Nevertheless, on his return to England the king celebrates his victories in style.

1348 Edward III is offered the **Holy Roman Empire**, but declines.

Bubonic plague, known as the **Black Death**, reaches the British Isles having already ravaged much of Europe; over the coming year between a quarter and a third of England's population will die. The plague discourages any immediate resumption of the war against France, and creates an economic downturn the effects of which last a century and beyond.

1349 **William of Occam** (b. 1285), the leading thinker of the **nominalist** school of philosophy opposed to the 'realist' orthodoxy of Scholasticism, dies, perhaps of the plague. While his determined advocacy of logic and logical procedures at the expense of metaphysical speculation will earn the respect of 20th-century linguistic philosophers in particular, he is best known for **Occam's Razor**, a general injunction to avoid unnecessary complexity in philosophical argument.

1351 The **Statute of Labourers** attempts to fix wages and prices in the wake of the plague, but – in common with the rest of western Europe – market forces prevail. The **Statute of Provisors** restricts the access of foreign clergy to English clerical appointments.

1353 The **Statute of Praemunire** offers further protection for the English Church against papal interference in the matter of appointments.

The Black Death (1348–49)

An epidemic of the bubonic form of **plague** (*pasteurella pestis*) annihilated a huge portion of England's population in the space of just a few months between 1348 and 1349. The disease is thought to have originated in the Mongolian steppes, before being brought to Europe by transcontinental traders and spread by flea-infested rats. The 'Great Mortality', as the Black Death was also known, first appeared at **Melcombe Regis** (now Weymouth in Dorset) in July 1348 and crept northeast across the country at a rate of about one-and-a-half miles per day. It devastated huge swathes of land, creating ghost villages with hardly anyone left alive. **Newcastle**, already weakened by continual attack from Scotland, faced financial ruin; other towns had so few working men that they were unable to pay taxes; the village of **Ashwell** in Hertfordshire has a moving year-entry scrawled onto the church wall which describes 1350 as 'Miserable, wild, distracted. The dregs of the people alone survive to witness.'

While prices fell steeply in the immediate aftermath, a shortage of labour meant that working men could demand higher wages, so in the long term the Black Death arguably contributed to England's prosperity. Those who did survive were able to take advantage of changed circumstances and so improve their social standing. Relations between lord and tenant also became more sophisticated, with cash becoming more widely offered instead of feudal services. Such arrangements, known as **bastard feudalism**, had existed before the plague, but in its wake they became widespread, fuelling the 15th-century **Wars of the Roses** (see p.168). Though 1348 would never be forgotten, it would be remembered for a variety of reasons – a century later, the country was a place where 'Everyman' could create his own chances.

1355 Edward III resumes his **campaigns** against the French, but with little immediate success. In France, the Black Prince is given an **independent command** for the first time.

1356 In January and February Edward III harries southern

Scotland in a campaign known as the **Burned Candlemas**. Edward Balliol, having been persuaded by his followers to renounce Edward's overlordship, is forced to **surrender** Scotland to the English Crown.

The **Black Prince** campaigns in France, meanwhile, and on 19 September triumphs at **Poitiers**, where the longbow again proves decisive. In the company of many leading French nobles, **John II of France** is captured and sent to London.

1359 Having been royally entertained in captivity, John II concedes the **Treaty of London**, granting considerable French territories to Edward III. John is released on payment of a ransom of 1,500,000 gold crowns. In October Edward lands in France to enforce the terms of the treaty, but fails in his siege of **Reims**.

1360 Unable to make military headway, Edward III agrees by the **Treaty of Calais** to renounce his claim to the French throne in exchange for title to the whole of **Aquitaine**. Calais is also retained as an English possession.

1361 A fresh outbreak of **plague** ravages England.

In October the **Black Prince** marries **Joan**, the widowed countess of Kent – a union uncharacteristically based on love, not dynastic policy.

Jean Froissart joins the court of Edward III. Froissart, a cultivated Flanders scholar, will gain celebrity for his *Chroniques*, a stupendously detailed series of chronicles depicting contemporary events, most notably those of the Hundred Years War (though with a bias towards chivalry and courtly behaviour which is rather unrepresentative).

1362 Edward the Black Prince is granted the title of **prince of Aquitaine** by his father, and becomes ruler of the French territory for ten years.

King Arthur

King Arthur owes far more to the so-called 'Age of Chivalry' than he does to the 'Dark Ages'; in fact, it's during the early Middle Ages that he can really be said to arrive on the cultural scene. Historically he may have been one of several British chieftains who took advantage of Rome's withdrawal in the 5th and 6th centuries, but other than a few nebulous references in early Welsh writings there is no hard evidence of his existence. But following the discovery of his alleged remains by the monks of **Glastonbury** in 1191 he quickly became an icon whose fairytale court mirrored the ideals of royal government – not just in England but on the continent too.

In his verse romances, the French poet **Chrétien de Troyes** (fl. 1160–1191) knitted Arthur into a world of *gentilesse* (noble behaviour) and introduced French elements into the legend, among them Sir Lancelot and the quest for the Holy Grail. **Sir Thomas Malory** (d.1471), whose *Le Morte Darthur* is a glorious example of late medieval English prose, lends the Arthurian material fresh intrigue by introducing his own tempestuous career into the tale – claiming to write while in Newgate prison.

Inevitably, given the excitement aroused among the readers of such retellings (and the evidence suggests that Arthurian legends were hugely popular at court), Arthur emerged as a significant **political symbol**. England's Norman-French rulers, anxious to legitimize their kingship, were keen to adapt pre-Conquest legends to their own ends, encouraging stories that reworked the material within a continental tradition – and in the process changing them profoundly.

With Arthur, the Plantagenets certainly did both. While Glastonbury became a symbol of his revival, it suited the English throne that Wales's sometime (and theoretically future) king should be demonstrably dead. Meanwhile the mystical rituals and accoutrements of Arthur's court, including the Round Table, were incorporated into the living court – most notably by **Edward III** at **Windsor**. Yet the Celtic Arthur has the last laugh. The final royal house to invoke King Arthur were the **Tudors**, the 'Welsh' usurpers who finally ended the long line of Anglo-Norman monarchs.

A self-generated act of parliament, widely ignored by lawyers, decrees that **English**, not French, should be the language used in law courts. Parliamentary statutes and increasingly other official documents begin to be written in the native tongue.

1363 The Black Prince establishes his own court at **Bordeaux**. Like his father's it quickly earns a reputation for extravagance and the practice of chivalric manners. As a ruler, however, the Black Prince is less popular – an often-absent landlord who is notoriously oppressive of his French subjects.

1366 Edward III formally repudiates the papacy's **feudal overlordship** of England, originally proclaimed during the reign of King John.

1368 The Black Prince's subjects in **Aquitaine** are unhappy with his harsh rule and appeal to John II's successor, **Charles V of France**, who summons Prince Edward to Paris. The Black Prince ripostes that he will indeed come, but only with 60,000 men at his back. Charles repudiates the **Treaty of Calais** and dispatches troops to Aquitaine. Edward III's third son, **John of Gaunt**, the **duke of Lancaster**, campaigns in France.

The king's second son, **Lionel, Duke of Clarence**, dies.

1369 Supported by Charles V, Aquitaine **revolts** against the Black Prince. Relying upon mercenaries he can barely afford, the prince appals the French by the brutality of his assault upon **Limoges** in October.

Following the death of **Queen Philippa**, Edward III takes a mistress, the commoner **Alice Perrers**.

Plague again ravishes England; although it recurs at regular intervals, each epidemic is less severe than its predecessor.

c.1370 The poet **William Langland** completes the first of three versions of *Piers Plowman*, a visionary religious allegory and a masterpiece of Middle English.

1371 Having lost Aquitaine and other possessions, the Black Prince **returns** to England, perhaps suffering from dropsy.

John of Gaunt marries **Constance of Castile**, his second wife.

1372 Claiming he no longer has the funds to continue fighting, the Black Prince **'surrenders'** Aquitaine back to his father. In reality Aquitaine is already lost to the French.

1374 At loggerheads with his brother Prince Edward, **John of Gaunt** uses Alice Perrers to ingratiate himself with Edward III. As the king's faculties decline, Gaunt becomes England's *de facto* ruler. His harsh government inspires dissent among lords and commoners alike.

1375 Anglo-French fighting temporarily ceases when a **truce** is agreed between Edward III and Charles V. Only **Calais**, **Bordeaux**, **Bayonne** and **Brest** are left in English hands.

About this time *Sir Gawain and the Green Knight* is composed, a highly stylized Arthurian fantasy written by an unknown author in a northwestern dialect.

1376 Early in the year the **Good Parliament** seeks to redress various grievances against Edward III and John of Gaunt. In the Commons, opposition to the Crown is led by **Peter de la Mare**. Alice Perrers is **removed** from court, and **impeachment proceedings** are instigated against Gaunt's followers and corrupt officials. In a new departure, the Commons acts as prosecution, presenting their indictments to the Lords as judges. The death of the **Black Prince** on 8 June spares Gaunt further embarrassment, however, as it is acknowledged that of Edward III's surviving sons he is best suited to govern.

1377 In return for Gaunt agreeing to acknowledge the Black Prince's son **Richard of Bordeaux** heir to the throne, Parliament **rescinds** its legislation of the previous year. **Edward III** dies at Richmond, and Richard is proclaimed king. 10-year-old **Richard II** inherits a difficult situation: continuing tensions with France; a self-assertive, even subversive nobility; a depleted treasury; and general economic stagnation, stimulating unrest across the country. The early years of his government effectively stay in the hands of his bullying but experienced uncle John of Gaunt.

1380 The rector of Lutterworth, **John Wyclif** already in the public eye on account of his criticisms of ecclesiastical corruption and the Church's temporal ambitions – begins translating the **Bible** into a robust English designed to appeal to those with little education. He founds an order of **Poor Preachers** to disseminate his radical understanding of the scriptures, but it is a group of his followers, known as the **Lollards**, who will be better remembered for propagating his ideas.

1381 Against a background of economic hardship, Gaunt's attempts to apply the **Statute of Labourers** (1351) and to introduce a **poll tax** (levied on each head of the population) leads to a popular uprising known as the **Peasants' Revolt**. Peasants, members of the urban poor and artisans join forces to threaten the existing social order, primarily in the southeast but also in other areas of the country. The revolt is also coloured by an **anti–clericalism** derived from the teachings of John Wyclif, and captured in the uprising's celebrated slogan: 'When Adam delved and Eve span,/Who was then the gentleman?'. The revolt begins in May in Essex. In June, led by **Wat Tyler**, the men of Essex and Kent march toward London. On 13 June the Kentishmen enter **London**, massacre Flemish merchants and destroy John of Gaunt's **Savoy Palace**. A day later, Richard II 'courageously' meets the Essexmen at **Mile**

John Wyclif (c.1330–83)

John Wyclif – reformer, theologian and philosopher – was educated at **Oxford**, and became rector of **Lutterworth**, a parish just outside the city, in 1374. He cultivated a reputation as an outspoken troublemaker, arguing that the Church had fallen into sin by accumulating excessive wealth, and that only by returning to poverty could it recover moral authority. **John of Gaunt** was quick to spot the political potential of Wyclif's criticisms, encouraging his attacks on papal authority and providing protection when the pope condemned him in 1377. But Wyclif had different ambitions too: he resolved to translate the **Bible** into English, founded an order of **Poor Preachers** to preach the Gospel in a way ordinary people could understand, and his adherents, the **Lollards**, continued to agitate for reform after his death. Wyclif was no paragon, though – it was only in his last years that he spent time in his parish, and as a practical reformer he was too heavy-handed to bring about real change.

It was as a theologian that he made the greatest impact. His major work, the *Summa de Ente*, contains a sustained critique of **transubstantiation** – the doctrine that the bread and wine of holy communion actually become the body and blood of Christ. Wyclif never denied the **'Real Presence'** (the idea that Christ is present at the Eucharist) but he did reject the Church's teaching that the host was literally transformed. Such tenets were deeply heretical, and seen as undermining a society in which priests operated as intermediaries between humans and God. Wyclif grew too radical for many, and was eventually dropped by Oxford and the court after he glaringly failed to condemn the 1381 **Peasants' Revolt** (see p.146).

Yet Lollardism never quite died, despite its suppression under Henry IV, and its tenacity in certain areas of the country has led some to argue that it contributed to the ease with which the Reformation was accepted in England in the 16th century. As for Wyclif himself, he was fortunate to die before the full impact of his theology became widely understood. Once it was, he was immediately condemned, and his remains exhumed and burnt in 1428.

End outside London, and persuades them to disband by promising reforms – including an end to enforced feudal labour, the provision of affordable land and a free market as regards wages and fees. On the same day the Kentishmen seize the **Tower of London** and murder the perceived architects of the poll tax – the chancellor and archbishop of Canterbury **Simon of Sudbury**, and the treasurer **Sir Robert Hales**. The following day Richard II appears before the Kentishmen at **Smithfield**. When the enraged **Mayor of London** has Wat Tyler pulled from his horse and killed, the assembly threatens to get out of hand, but the king again persuades the crowd to disperse. The revolt rumbles on outside London during the early summer, but is finally crushed when the men of **East Anglia**, under the leadership of **John Lister**, are crushed by the **bishop of Norwich** (another Hugh le Despenser) in June. In its aftermath the king's assurances of redress are forgotten; but no further attempts to levy the poll tax are made.

1382 Richard II marries Princess **Anne of Bohemia**. Simon of Sudbury's successor as archbishop of Canterbury, **Thomas Courtenay**, orchestrates a campaign against Wyclif and the Lollards.

1383 In May Archbishop Courtenay convenes a synod at **Blackfriars**, which condemns many of Wyclif's writings. **Oxford University** follows suit by banning all Wyclif's works. Wyclif is left alone, however, and **dies** of a stroke at Lutterworth on 31 December.

1385 The barons' disquiet hardens as the king surrounds himself with courtiers who they regard as 'frivolous', among them **Richard de Vere, Earl of Oxford**. Opposition to Richard II is led by the earls of **Gloucester** (his uncle Thomas of Woodstock), **Arundel** (Richard Fitzalan) and **Warwick** (Thomas de Beauchamp).

Geoffrey Chaucer (c.1343–1400)

Had he never written a single one of *The Canterbury Tales'* 17,000 lines, **Geoffrey Chaucer** would still enjoy a reputation as the most celebrated poet of his time. Partly this is to do with the accessibility of his language, which is relatively close to modern English – certainly closer than that used in a poem such as *Sir Gawain and the Green Knight* (see p.145), whose gritty northwestern dialect is much harder to crack. Partly, too, it is a matter of national pride: generations of critics (beginning with poets such as **Thomas Hoccleve** and **John Lydgate**, a generation younger than Chaucer) have lauded him as the founder of a distinctively English poetic tradition.

But it is impossible to deny the range of his work, or the energy it must have taken to write so much while maintaining a successful career as a courtier and official. Chaucer was a busy man: as well as composing numerous poems including the *Book of the Duchess* (c.1370) and *Troilus and Criseyde* (c.1385), he translated the 6th-century philosopher Boethius and even found time to write a treatise on the astrolabe. Life was certainly made easier by John of Gaunt's patronage (he was married to one of the duke's sisters-in-law), and Chaucer was fortunate – or well-connected – enough to have been the recipient of a number of prestigious appointments, including being MP for Kent and clerk of the king's works to Richard II.

He is most well-remembered, though, for the huge verse-cycle, *The Canterbury Tales*, which he started in around 1372 and left unfinished at his death. If its premise is simple – 29 pilgrims heading to the shrine of St Thomas Becket at Canterbury (see p.105) meet at the Tabard Inn in Southwark and agree to tell each other tales on the way – its execution is virtuosic. Chaucer's various pilgrims and their varied stories permit the poet to show off an extraordinary range of subject matter and verse style. He mingles tragedy, comedy, tragicomedy, allegory, fable, philosophy, satire and classical learning, all brought together by an earthy sense of reality and a sharp eye for human detail. Though his status as 'the father of English poetry' is currently rather unfashionable, this poem continues to demonstrate his enduring appeal.

The Wilton Diptych

An exquisite example of late 14th-century art now housed in the National Gallery, the **Wilton Diptych** – named after Wilton House, where it was kept from the 18th century until 1929 – is a portable altarpiece. It depicts the young Richard II, supported by St Edward the Confessor and St Edmund, being presented by John the Baptist to the Virgin and Child, who are attended by eleven angels. The kneeling boy-king is being blessed by Christ, and is either about to receive – or has just offered as a gift – a banner of St George surmounted with an orb depicting England set in a silver sea.

The allegorical statement is unambiguous. King Richard is Christ's servant, England his realm, and his right to rule is divinely sanctioned. But the diptych also carries more subtle messages. Richard's kneeling posture recalls that of the Magi adoring Christ at the feast of Epiphany, which falls on 6 January (Richard's birthday). It is significant, too, that the host of angels all wear the king's badge of the white hart: an echo perhaps of Pope Gregory the Great's punning description of Saxon slaves as 'non Angli, sed Angeli' – angels, not Englishmen.

Why the diptych was commissioned, and by whom, remains uncertain. Possibly Richard instigated it himself, perhaps a wedding gift celebrating his second marriage to Isabelle of France – it was hoped the alliance might promote an Anglo-French crusade (for which a portable altar would have been essential). More probably, though, it was commissioned in 1397 to mark the twentieth anniversary of Richard's accession to the throne. Either way, the fact that within a few years of the diptych's crafting Richard was deposed and dead adds poignancy to its beauty.

1386 Richard II's position is further weakened by the departure of John of Gaunt for **Spain** to pursue a claim to the throne of **Castile**. Isolated at his own court, the king surrenders government to an eleven-man committee of barons who use Parliament to impeach and execute the chancellor,

The Wilton Diptych.

Michael de la Pole, **Earl of Suffolk**. Later in the year, Richard declares that the barons' actions constitute treason.

1387 Geoffrey Chaucer begins work on his great verse cycle, *The Canterbury Tales*.

1388 The king's baronial opponents, again using Parliament as their front, succeed in executing or outlawing many of Richard's closest associates. Richard himself is forced to give way to five **appellant lords**, including Gloucester, Arundel and Warwick, who assume the reins of government. The English are defeated by the Scots at **Otterburn**.

1389 In May Richard II, obsessed with what he considers the **divine right** supporting the throne, repudiates the appellants and proclaims himself **sole ruler**. Civil war between Crown and barons is averted by John of Gaunt's **return** to England, and the duke of Lancaster persuades

Richard and his barons to work together. But while the king submits to Gaunt's compromise, in secret he begins building up his own support.

1394 Richard II is devastated by the death of his queen, **Anne of Bohemia**.

1396 Partly as a means of extending the truce that prevails between England and France, Richard II marries **Isabelle of Valois**.

1397 After eight years' apparent quiescence, Richard II moves against his baronial opposition by having **Arundel** arrested, convicted of treason and executed. **Gloucester** is imprisoned and killed, **Warwick** exiled. Perhaps in celebration of his successful coup as well as to commemorate the anniversary of his coronation, the king commissions the **Wilton Diptych**.

1398 In September a quarrel between the two remaining lords appellant, **Henry Bolingbroke** (John of Gaunt's heir) and **Thomas Mowbray** (earl of Norfolk), encourages Richard II to banish both from England.

1399 John of Gaunt **dies** in February. When Richard II seizes Gaunt's sizeable **Lancastrian estates**, Henry Bolingbroke is deprived of his inheritance. Unwisely, the king leaves England to campaign in **Ireland** in May; during his absence Bolingbroke returns and rapidly secures the loyalty of many of the barons. In August Richard surrenders to Bolingbroke in Wales, and on 30 September **abdicates** in his favour.

5

Lancaster, York and the Wars of the Roses

1399–1485

Although the removal of Richard II from the throne left Henry Bolingbroke in a controlling position, the abdication of the last Plantagenet monarch was to introduce a prolonged period of political friction. The spectacular but brief reign of **Henry V** (1413–22) would provide some respite, but the country would not gain stability until some time after the 1485 accession of **Henry VII**, the first of the Tudors.

England's 15th century was dominated by infighting among Edward III's many male descendants and their various factions. Edward's grandson Bolingbroke was crowned **Henry IV**, the first of the House of Lancaster, but had to rely on the support of powerful nobles including **Henry Percy, Earl of Northumberland** in order to get there. When Percy became disenchanted with the new regime and convinced that he had not received sufficient credit, he quickly rebelled.

This set the pattern for much of what followed. During the lengthy reign of Henry IV's mentally unstable grandson **Henry VI**, several relations tried their luck, including Humphrey of Gloucester and Henry Beaufort, Bishop of Winchester. The greatest challenge to Henry, though, came from **Richard of York**. Although Richard narrowly failed to secure the crown for himself, his son **Edward IV** twice succeeded in supplanting the Lancastrian king – first following his dramatic victories at **Mortimer's Cross** and **Towton** and again after Henry was murdered, almost certainly on Edward's orders. But just as Henry's death removed one part of the problem, the kingdom was again jeopardized by rivalry between Edward's brothers, the **dukes of Clarence** and of **Gloucester**, and the family of his wife, **Elizabeth Woodville**.

In 1455 these internal squabbles boiled over into outright civil war, a conflict known as the **Wars of the Roses** after the red rose of Lancaster and the white rose of York – a picturesque description rooted in the Tudor propaganda of Henry VII, who proclaimed to unite the warring factions. As before, this brutal series of plots, rebellions and battles was perpetuated by dynasties from outside immediate royal circles. Private feuds merged with supposedly national causes to bring families such as the **Nevilles**, **Percies** and **Beauforts** into the political limelight.

The best-known of these 'over-mighty subjects' was **Richard Neville, Earl of Warwick**, nicknamed 'the Kingmaker' because he was the man to whom Edward IV owed both his crown and many of the difficulties he experienced holding on to it. This acute royal insecurity had a number of causes, among them what has been called **bastard feudalism** – a convenient term which describes the increasingly intricate relationships between lords and their retainers that developed after the Black Death and through the Hundred Years War. In such systems financial rewards and personal loyalties replaced the rigid hierarchical structures imposed by William I, meaning that magnates like Warwick could recruit large private armies with which they could threaten the monarchy itself.

Henry V's solution to all of this was simple: to revive the war against **France**. Risking his political credibility, he gambled on a foreign campaign and won – amazing not only his own subjects but also much of Europe by his victory at **Agincourt** in 1415. But like Crécy and Poitiers in the 14th century, the pay-out proved elusive. Henry V's early death, and the breakdown of England's alliance with Burgundy, destroyed the foundations of the 'dual monarchy' Henry had envisaged. Instead, France and Burgundy – and also Scotland – served to compound England's domestic troubles.

This crisis across the Channel encouraged the Wars of the Roses to worsen. Royal control in the country broke down, and a series of battles between the competing houses added to the upheaval. When **Richard of Gloucester** manoeuvred himself into the protectorship during **Edward V**'s minority, and from there to the throne, he created enough enemies for **Henry Tudor** to gain power relatively easily in 1485. It is largely because of Henry VII's propagandistic interventions – shoring up his somewhat distant claim to the throne – that Richard III has been so effectively demonized by historians, but there is little doubt that his two-year reign was controversial, then as now. Whether he was personally responsible for the deaths of the 'princes in the tower' (the uncrowned Edward and his brother Richard), as was widely suspected at the time, is a mystery that is unlikely to be solved – but the perception that he was a murderer of innocents did little to help him retain support.

After his triumph at Bosworth in 1485, **Henry VII** sought to draw a line under the political turmoil of the previous century – visibly seeking to build prosperity and develop his government rather than toying with military fireworks. To an extent this was happening already: the Tudors inherited an England which had already witnessed profound social and economic change. Although a majority of English people continued to live off the land, increasing numbers of them were doing so as tenants, paying rent to their overlords instead of rendering service. Equally as significant was the fact that England had ceased selling raw wool to Bruges and other continental markets, and instead began to produce woven cloths. As a result, some parts of the country became slowly richer – a new wealth evidenced by the building of many parish churches in the costly **English perpendicular** style, especially in East Anglia, the Cotswolds and Somerset, and the foundation of several large colleges at Oxford and Cambridge.

Technological developments continued, and at its close the period had witnessed the advent of printing in England. **William Caxton** simply used presses already available on the continent, but as a businessman-translator-publisher he heralded the emergence of a standard written language as well as laying the foundations for printed literature in the vernacular. Regional dialects persisted and varied spelling flourished, but on the printed page at least a truly common language had started to emerge.

1399 In September Henry Bolingbroke ascends the throne as **Henry IV**, the first monarch of the **House of Lancaster**. Although determined to reassert the authority of the throne, the earliest years of his reign are marked by near-continuous crisis and he will do little to overcome the Crown's chronic lack of money. His eldest son, also called **Henry** (sometimes known as 'Prince Hal') is created **earl of Chester**, and subsequently **prince of Wales** as well as titular **duke of Aquitaine**. In October the usurped king, Richard, is imprisoned at **Pontefract Castle** in Yorkshire.

1400 In January Henry IV defeats a **rebellion** by Richard's supporters. Richard himself dies at **Pontefract** shortly afterwards, probably murdered on Henry's orders.

In August a previously loyal Welsh courtier, **Owain Glyndwr**, leads Wales into its last major revolt against English rule. Over the next three years Henry campaigns against Glyndwr but fails to capture him. Seizing **Harlech Castle** and holding assemblies there, at **Machynlleth** and **Pennal**, Glyndwr forms alliances with English nobles opposed to Henry IV, among them **Henry Percy** – the **Earl of Northumberland** and formerly a close supporter of the king – and the French Crown.

1401 To suppress the **Lollards** – adherents of the ideas of John Wyclif (see p.147) – the first Parliamentary statute ordering the **burning of heretics** is enacted. Although an example is made of **William Sawtrey** even before the bill is passed, Lollardism continues as a focus of dissent.

1403 Northumberland and his son Henry Percy (nicknamed **Hotspur**), having openly rebelled against Henry IV, are defeated by the king and Prince Henry at **Shrewsbury** in July. Hotspur is killed in battle. Prince Henry is given command of the campaign against **Glyndwr** in Wales.

1405 **Thomas Mowbray, Duke of Norfolk** and **Richard Scrope, Archbishop of York**, having plotted further rebellion on Northumberland's behalf, are executed for treason. Northern England is also troubled by **Scottish incursions**, loosely coordinated with the activities of Glyndwr.

Henry IV shows the first signs of **ill health**; around this time he suffers a stroke.

1406 **James I of Scotland** is captured and imprisoned until 1424, giving Henry IV reasonable security on the Scottish border.

1407 The **Merchant Adventurers**, a company of English traders specializing in the export of cloths to markets in the Low Countries, is granted a royal charter. Although its turnover is slow to begin with, towards the end of the century it will contribute significantly to England's accumulating wealth.

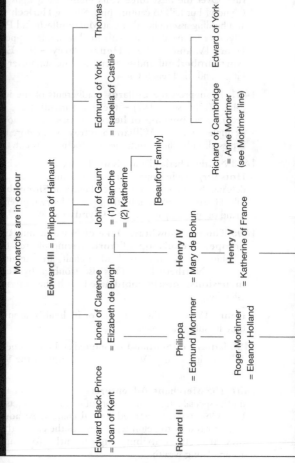

Lancaster and York (1399–1485)

Monarchs are in colour

Edward III = Philippa of Hainault

| Edward Black Prince = Joan of Kent | Lionel of Clarence = Elizabeth de Burgh | John of Gaunt = (1) Blanche = (2) Katherine | Edmund of York = Isabella of Castile | Thomas |

Richard II

Philippa = Edmund Mortimer

[Beaufort Family]

Henry IV = Mary de Bohun

Roger Mortimer = Eleanor Holland

Henry V = Katherine of France

Richard of Cambridge = Anne Mortimer (see Mortimer line)

Edward of York

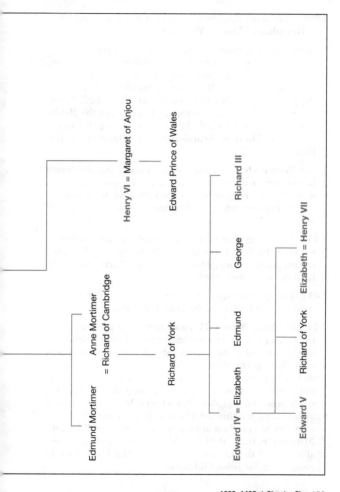

Edmund Mortimer

Anne Mortimer
= Richard of Cambridge

Richard of York

Edward IV = Elizabeth   Edmund   George   Richard III

Henry VI = Margaret of Anjou

Edward Prince of Wales

Edward V   Richard of York   Elizabeth = Henry VII

1408 Northumberland again rebels, but is defeated and killed at **Bramham Moor** in Yorkshire.

Although **Glyndwr** remains at large, Prince Henry deprives him of support through a combination of military action and diplomacy, and brings the Welsh campaign to a successful conclusion. Returning to his ailing father's court, the prince demands a place on the king's council. When this is refused he begins forming a faction with the **Beauforts** – Henry IV's half-brothers – against the king's chancellor **Thomas Arundel**, the archbishop of Canterbury.

1410 Prince Henry's faction ousts Arundel and the prince becomes **co-ruler** with his father, now incapacitated by illness. But the king resists his son's proposal to renew the war in **France**, which in any case the exchequer cannot afford.

1411 Intending to exploit increasingly volatile relations between the French throne and the emergent principality of **Burgundy**, Prince Henry takes a small army across the Channel but achieves little.

1412 Taking advantage of his son's French failure, Henry IV wrests power back from the prince of Wales.

1413 In March, **Henry IV** falls gravely ill; a prediction that the former crusader would 'die in Jerusalem' is fulfilled in one sense when the king is carried into the 'Jerusalem Chamber' at the Palace of Westminster, where he soon dies. The prince of Wales is immediately proclaimed king; but despite his general popularity among the nobility, it is not a peaceable kingdom that **Henry V** inherits. As well as renewed friction on the Scottish border, there are rumours of rebellion among those supporting **Edmund Mortimer**, the earl of March's claim to the throne, and also among the Lollards, now led by the king's former companion **Sir John Oldcastle**.

1414 An attempt by **Oldcastle** to raise rebellion is swiftly crushed by **Henry V**; harsh reprisals against the Lollards follow.

The king, determined to campaign in France, begins negotiating with the French Crown for the return of 'English possessions' including **Aquitaine**, **Normandy** and **Maine**. At the same time he tries to convince Parliament to grant the necessary taxes.

> 66 In the year of our lord 1415, Henry V King of England called together the prelates and lords of his kingdom, and asked their advice, on peril of their souls, whether he had a better grievance against the kingdom of Scotland or against the kingdom of France, to go to war about. 99
>
> From *The Book of Pluscarden*, late 15th century

1415 Following the 'collapse' of negotiations with France in June, Henry assembles his forces at **Southampton**. As he is preparing to embark, news reaches him of a plot to usurp his throne in favour of **Mortimer**. The principal conspirators – **Henry, Lord Scrope of Masham**, **Sir Thomas Grey** and Henry V's cousin, **Richard, Earl of Cambridge** – are seized and summarily executed. Other 'traitors' are rounded up and dealt with harshly, although Mortimer, having revealed the plot to Henry V, is spared. The king crosses to France and, assured of the neutrality of **John the Fearless of Burgundy**, captures the port town of **Harfleur** in September. Thus resumes the **Hundred Years War**. As the campaigning season draws to a close, Henry turns back toward England but is forced to engage the French at **Agincourt** on 15 October. Against huge odds (he has a depleted army of only five or six thousand against the French contingent of perhaps 20,000), Henry V turns a rearguard action into a comprehensive victory. Despite his **massacre** of French prisoners – against chivalric rules – this wins him domestic support and enables the king to borrow more funds from the banking community to fill his war chest.

Glyndwr disappears from view.

1416 An English fleet secures control of the Channel by destroying the main French fleet in the **Battle of the Seine**.

1417 Henry V campaigns in France to subjugate **Normandy**. In league with the Holy Roman Emperor **Sigismund**, he

Henry V (c.1386–1422)

Henry V owes much of his popular image to Shakespeare (see p.234), who, in his two *Henry IV* plays, represents him as a quick-witted but dissolute youth who metamorphoses into a paragon of princely virtue on the death of his father.

The reality was somewhat different. Henry shouldered many of the responsibilities that came his way as a young prince, notably against Glyndwr in Wales. Taken under Richard II's wing while his father was out of favour, his education was directed by his uncle Henry Beaufort, and he was the first English king to read and write in the vernacular with fluency; in government he would encourage the official use of English rather than French. As prince of Wales, however, he did make trouble for Henry IV, forming an alliance against Thomas Arundel and stage-managing a coup that temporarily made him England's co-ruler. Indeed, Shakespeare has difficulty squaring this ambitious young man with his depiction of the fast-living Hal.

The figure depicted in *Henry V*, though, is far more conventionally charismatic, and touches on important aspects of the real king while omitting less palatable truths. Deeply religious and a merciless persecutor of heretics, Henry V embarked on his secures the unopposed election of **Pope Martin V**, ending the papal schism that has lasted since 1378.

1419 In January Henry V captures **Rouen**, which becomes another English garrison. In September the murder of **John of Burgundy** by partisans of the French throne ends Burgundy's neutrality – to Henry's advantage.

1420 Outmanoeuvred militarily and politically, France concedes defeat. By the terms of the **Treaty of Troyes**, signed in May, Henry V is proclaimed heir to the French throne. The dauphin **Charles** is disinherited, and the king of France, **Charles VI**, acknowledges Henry as his regent – effectively giving the English king command of all of France.

French campaigns with an absolute conviction in the justice of his cause. Yet his slaughter of those taken prisoner at Agincourt, many of them nobles, tarnished his reputation. Equally, Shakespeare's portrayal of the king wandering from tent to tent on the eve of battle, raising his men's spirits and offering those without stomach for the fight free passage home, is far removed from the brutal disciplinarian who promised to amputate the right ear of any would-be deserter. But the fact that he invaded France with a deliberate and effective strategy of reducing key towns and leaving English garrisons in them demonstrates his military skill. It was this practicality as much as his dazzling victory at Agincourt that, within seven years of his accession, won him the French Crown.

What he did not foresee was his own early demise. Although his brother John of Bedford for a while successfully continued his strategy, the accession of Henry VI while still a minor only encouraged England's other princes and barons to squabble among themselves. Henry V's victories – just like Edward III's – finally counted for little.

To cement his position, in June Henry marries **Catherine of Valois**, Charles VI's daughter.

1421 As resistance to English rule in France begins, Henry V's brother **Thomas of Clarence** is ambushed and killed. Henry V resumes campaigning in France, laying siege to **Melun** and **Meaux**.

1422 Debilitated by constant warfare, **Henry V** dies aged 35 at **Bois de Vincennes** in September, and is succeeded by his infant son, **Henry VI**. In October Henry is also proclaimed **king of France**, following the death of his maternal grandfather **Charles VI** and according to the terms of the **Treaty of Troyes**. The government of England and those parts of France that remain loyal to the English Crown pass to the new king's uncles – **Humphrey, Duke of Gloucester**, **John, Duke of Bedford** and **Henry Beaufort, Bishop of Winchester**. The widowed **Catherine of Valois** soon marries **Owen Tudor**, a Welsh-born courtier.

1424 The **dauphin**, having repudiated the Treaty of Troyes, is heavily defeated by English forces at **Verneuil**.

1425 The erstwhile pretender to the throne, **Edmund Mortimer**, dies of plague in **Ireland**, making the House of Lancaster's controversial claim to the English throne somewhat easier. Further victories in France enable the English Crown to consolidate its territories in **Anjou** and **Maine**.

In England tensions between two of Henry VI's regents, **Gloucester** and **Henry Beaufort**, develop into a pitched battle between their followers on **London Bridge**.

1426 **John of Bedford**, responsible for England's continuing success in France, returns home to resolve the differences between his fellow regents.

1428 English fortunes in France prosper as **Normandy** is given its own Parliament; this means it is able to raise sufficient taxes in order to make the continuing English occupation financially workable. Against Bedford's advice, the ambitious **Earl of Salisbury** undertakes to campaign against the dauphin's power base in the south. In an attempt to secure a bridgehead over the river Loire he lays siege to **Orléans**.

1429 The dauphin's fortunes revive when a peasant girl, **Jeanne d'Arc** (Joan of Arc) convinces him that she has been sent from God to restore France and destroy the English. With her help the siege of Orléans is lifted, and an English army is defeated at **Patay**. The dauphin is crowned at **Reims** as **Charles VII**.

1430 Henry VI is taken to **Paris** to be crowned **king of France**; but since **Reims** is the traditional venue for a French coronation this move only heightens awareness of the House of Valois' revival.

1431 Jeanne d'Arc is captured by Burgundian forces, then handed over to the English. Charged with being a witch, a heretic and a transvestite, she is burned at the stake in **Rouen** marketplace in May.

With Henry VI and Beaufort both out of England, **Gloucester** accuses **Beaufort** of **Praemunire**, infringing royal rights by dealing with secular matters in an ecclesiastical court.

1433 Again **Bedford** is obliged to return to England to resolve the Gloucester–Beaufort dispute. The king's council implores Bedford to remain in **England**, thus depriving its forces in France of their most effective commander.

1434 Gloucester physically removes **Henry VI** to **Cirencester**, where the Council reconvenes in order to re-assert its authority.

1435 In France, the tide turns decisively against England when, following the breakdown of peace negotiations at

Arras, the Anglo–Burgundian alliance collapses and, later in the year, **John of Bedford** dies.

1436 After Charles VII captures **Paris**, England is left with few French possessions outside Normandy.

1437 Aged sixteen, **Henry VI** assumes the reins of government as his minority ends. Studious and retiring by nature, as well as mentally unstable later in life, he will be remembered as one of England's weakest kings, held responsible for losing his father's French conquests and for allowing his own country to become embroiled in three decades of civil war.

> This King Henry was chaste and pure from the beginning of his days... It happened once, that at Christmas time a certain great lord brought before him a dance or show of young ladies with bared bosoms who were to dance in that guise before the king ... but the king was not blind to it, nor unaware of the devilish wile, and spurned the delusion, and very angrily averted his eyes, turned his back upon them, and went out to his chamber, saying: 'Fy, Fy, for shame, forsother ye be to blame'.
>
> John Blacman on Henry VI, in the *Memoir* (c.1485)

1440 The 18-year-old Henry has the opportunity to fight in **Normandy**, but instead sends the **duke of York** as his lieutenant and busies himself with the founding of **Eton College** instead – one day to become the most famous of England's 'public' (ie, private) schools.

1443 Henry (now Cardinal) Beaufort's nephew **John, Duke of Somerset**, is despatched to France at the head of a force intended to recapture lost territories. But his appointment leads to a bitter feud with **Richard, Duke of York**, commander of the English in France and another descendant of Edward III.

1444 Henry VI, swayed by those seeking peace with Charles VII, concludes a truce at **Tours**. It is agreed he should marry Charles's distant and impoverished – but strong-willed cousin – **Margaret of Anjou**.

1445 Recalled to England, **Richard of York** is fobbed off with worthless promises when he claims campaign expenses, while his adversary **Edmund, Duke of Somerset** (brother of the late duke John) is rewarded with money and lands. York's resentment deepens when he discovers that Henry VI has secretly conceded **Maine** to Charles VII, apparently at the instigation of Queen Margaret.

1447 As divisions between the factions at Henry VI's court harden and Somerset gains ascendancy, **Humphrey of Gloucester** is arrested and imprisoned, then possibly murdered. While popular opinion holds Queen Margaret and Cardinal Beaufort responsible for the 'good duke's' death, Richard of York succeeds Gloucester as heir presumptive to the throne, and as such becomes leader of the main 'opposition' party within the Council.

In Cambridge, **King's College** is founded at Henry VI's behest, its chapel (finished under Henry VIII) a masterpiece of the **English perpendicular** style that now dominates ecclesiastical architecture in England.

1448 Under threat of French attack, English garrisons are **withdrawn** from Maine. In England, Richard of York turns against **William de la Pole, Duke of Suffolk**, Henry VI's chief adviser and a leader of the 'peace' faction. In Parliament there is mounting criticism of the king and his ministers.

1449 Henry VI is persuaded by Suffolk to resume hostilities against **Charles VII of France**.

1450 French forces defeat the English at **Formigny** in April, and complete the reconquest of Normandy in August. Suffolk is **attainted** by Parliament (condemned by parliamentary bill without trial) but, instead of agreeing to his execution, Henry VI exiles him. Suffolk's ship, however, is overtaken by 'pirates' and he is beheaded.

In **Kent**, a popular uprising led by an Irish mercenary, **Jack Cade**, erupts. Styling himself 'John Mortimer', Cade issues a manifesto against the king's 'evil advisers', calling for the restoration of such 'true' nobles as Richard of York. The rebels capture **London**, but disperse when Queen Margaret offers pardons to those agreeing to lay down their weapons. Cade himself is killed at **Rochester** while evading arrest.

1452 Richard of York openly rebels against Henry VI and the Beaufort faction, but lays down his arms on the understanding that the king will punish Somerset's excesses. Somerset remains in power, however.

1453 Somerset's position is seemingly strengthened when Henry VI lapses into a first bout of **insanity**, but a majority of councillors – distrustful of both Somerset and Margaret of Anjou – offer the **protectorship** to Richard of York. Shortly afterwards Queen Margaret gives birth to a royal heir, **Prince Edward**, rumoured to be Somerset's child.

John Talbot, Earl of Shrewsbury, is killed while charging enemy cannon at **Chatillon**. His death crushes any hopes of the English re-establishing their position in France and, as all remaining strongholds except Calais fall, the **Hundred Years War** effectively comes to an end.

1454 Recovering in December, Henry VI dismisses **Richard of York**. As Somerset is restored to favour, York gains important new allies among the influential and seemingly loyal **Neville** family.

1455 Richard of York, supported by the **Nevilles**, rebels against Henry VI and Somerset. The two sides clash at **St Albans**, generally considered the start of the **Wars of the**

Roses. Somerset and other of the king's favourites are engaged in violent street fighting. Henry VI is wounded in the shoulder by an arrow. York re-establishes his **protectorate** as Henry once more descends into madness.

The Wars of the Roses (1455–87)

Vicious though they were, the domestic conflicts that came to be known as the **Wars of the Roses** were more intermittent and localized than that title suggests. Most people in England would have had little clear idea of what was going on within the ruling elite, and only those who had the misfortune to be the tenants or retainers of the more enthusiastic participants would have experienced violence first-hand. Even most of the nobility steered clear of the fighting, and lawcourts continued to be the preferred means of resolving disputes.

Over the years the immediate causes of warfare also changed to match whichever political arguments were fiercest. The first round, between 1455 and 1460, surrounded the grievances of **Richard of York**. Once he was dead, the next episode of fighting (between 1460 and 1464) stemmed from the peculiarity of there being two crowned kings, **Henry VI** and **Edward IV**. The wars' brief – but bloody – resurgence between 1469 and 1471 was inspired by the **earl of Warwick**'s chagrin at his declining influence over **Edward IV**. And the culminating eruption of 1485 actually saw an alliance, led by Henry Tudor, of old Lancastrians and old Yorkists against the unpopular **Richard III**. Lesser conflicts continued until the mid-1490s – and Henry VIII was still executing Yorkist rivals in the 1530s – but his father's triumphs at **Bosworth** and **Stoke** marked the effective closure of three decades' tangled conflict.

Overall, the monarchy itself was the net beneficiary, if only because the more dangerous nobility had been culled. But as the Civil Wars of the mid-17th century were to demonstrate, the Crown could still be challenged by those of lesser pedigree – and in the process come seriously unstuck.

1456 As Henry VI again **recovers**, York is eased out of the protectorate for a second time. In the vacuum that ensues **Queen Margaret** assumes real power, but her attempts to punish York and his followers are resisted by a great council of the nobility convened at Coventry.

York's supporter **Richard Neville** – the **earl of Warwick** and known to history as **'the Kingmaker'** (see p.171) – becomes captain of **Calais**, later a pivotal Yorkist base.

1458 To reconcile the different factions of his court, Henry VI proposes a **'Loveday'**. But although York and Queen Margaret walk arm-in-arm through London to a service of reconciliation at **St Paul's Cathedral**, their mutual antipathy survives.

1459 Deprived of any say in government, Richard of York launches a fresh **rebellion**. After a stand-off with royalist forces at **Ludford**, York flees to **Ireland** with his second son, the **earl of Rutland**. His eldest son, **Edward, Earl of March**, is taken by Warwick to Calais. Queen Margaret summons the **'Parliament of Devils'** at **Coventry**. York and his followers are attainted in their absence, and their lands and titles confiscated in perpetuity. But these measures succeed only in drawing more support to the Yorkist cause.

1460 Warwick and Edward of March return to England from Calais and defeat a royalist force at **Northampton**. Warwick seizes London, and then in May captures the king himself. A fresh Parliament is summoned, and the attainders of the **Parliament of Devils** overturned.

In October Richard of York returns to England and astonishes his supporters by claiming the throne. Henry VI agrees to an **Act of Accord**, whereby the succession will pass to the House of York after his death. Queen Margaret dissents, however, and attacks York at **Sandal**, his stronghold near Wakefield. Badly prepared for a siege, York

Edward IV (1442–83)

The glamorous and handsome Edward IV came to the throne in 1461 on the back of his father Richard of York's persistent opposition to the House of Lancaster, but also thanks to the interventions of Warwick the Kingmaker. Unwisely, Edward elected to displace Warwick at court in favour of his wife's family, the Woodvilles, and in 1471 paid the price when Warwick combined with the Lancastrians to briefly restore Henry VI.

Like Henry VI, Edward got a second shot at the throne when he defeated his enemies the following year, but, unlike his predecessor, he learned from his mistakes. The second period of Edward's rule saw a restitution in the authority of royal government, even though it was marred toward its end by acrimonious rivalry between his brothers Clarence and Gloucester. Edward strengthened the judiciary and repaired the throne's finances; he also did much to advance the cause of English traders, repaying London for its staunch support for the House of York. But perhaps his greatest coup was to threaten France with a renewal of war in 1475, only to allow himself to be bought off with a handsome pension.

After 1475, due to the burgeoning success of the cloth trade in particular, prosperity returned to England, and increasingly historians have credited Edward IV with laying the foundations of the Tudor state, especially since 19th-century disapproval of his personal morals has been cast aside. But the popular rumour that he ordered his brother Clarence to be drowned in a butt of wine suggests his reputation for ruthlessness – and, like his reliance on a small circle of knightly intimates, points to something much more medieval in his outlook.

decides to leave his walls and fight, but is killed along with his second son Rutland and other supporters. His head, adorned with a paper crown, is impaled on Micklegate at **York**.

1461 Avenging his father, **Edward of March** defeats a Lancastrian army led by Henry VI's half-brother **Jasper Tudor**

at **Mortimer's Cross** in February. Among those executed is **Owen Tudor**, the king's stepfather. Edward's ally Warwick is defeated at the **Second Battle of St Albans** and forced to flee. Queen Margaret attempts to enter London, but is refused entry. As she retreats to the north, the Yorkists gain the capital, and Edward of March is proclaimed king on 4 March. As **Edward IV,** the first ruler of the **House of York,** he defeats the main Lancastrian force at **Towton** on 29 March. In a particularly bloody engagement, many of his opponents are slaughtered. Henry VI, Queen Margaret and Prince Edward **flee** to Scotland. While some of England's aristocracy, notably the **Percies** of Northumberland, declare their support for Henry, the queen's request for French assistance enables Edward to project himself as the patriotic choice. Warwick meanwhile takes the Lancastrian strongholds of **Alnwick**, **Bamburgh** and **Dunstanburgh**.

1462 The Lancastrian cause remains strong in **northern England**, where Warwick is obliged to continue siege warfare against its strongholds.

1463 Although Lancastrians revolt again in **Northumberland** – led by Somerset and Sir Ralph Percy – at the end of the year Edward IV isolates his opponents by concluding treaties with **France** and **Scotland**.

1464 In April, Percy is killed at **Hedgeley Moor** fighting a Yorkist force led by Warwick's brother **Lord Montagu**. In May Montagu caps his success by defeating a larger Lancastrian force at **Hexham**, for which he is created **earl of Northumberland**. Among those captured is the **duke of Somerset**, who is swiftly executed. As the Lancastrian movement in the north collapses, Warwick crosses to **France** to arrange a marriage between Edward IV and a French princess. During his absence Edward secretly marries **Elizabeth Woodville**, widow of the Lancastrian **Sir John Grey**. Her two sons, five brothers and seven sisters

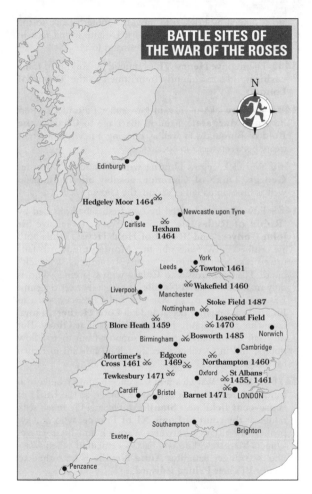

BATTLE SITES OF THE WAR OF THE ROSES

N

Edinburgh

Hedgeley Moor 1464

Newcastle upon Tyne

Carlisle Hexham 1464

York

Leeds Towton 1461

Wakefield 1460

Liverpool Manchester Stoke Field 1487

Nottingham Losecoat Field 1470

Blore Heath 1459

Birmingham Bosworth 1485

Mortimer's Cross 1461 Edgcote 1469 Northampton 1460 Norwich

Cambridge

Tewkesbury 1471 Oxford St Albans 1455, 1461

Cardiff Bristol Barnet 1471 LONDON

Southampton Brighton

Exeter

Penzance

are advanced by Edward to provide counterbalance to the influence of the Nevilles at court. Despite losing face in Paris, for the moment Warwick remains loyal.

1465 The fugitive **Henry VI** is captured by Yorkists in **Lancashire** and subsequently imprisoned in the **Tower of London**.

1467 To Warwick's dismay, in November Edward IV offers his sister **Margaret**'s hand in marriage to **Charles the Bold** of Burgundy, as well as agreeing a new commercial treaty between the two countries.

1468 Warwick begins plotting with Edward IV's brother **George, Duke of Clarence**, possibly offering him (as well as his own daughter's hand) the Crown itself.

1469 Edward is confronted by two fresh rebellions, led by **'Robin of Redesdale'** (probably Warwick's relative **Sir John Conyers**) and **'Robin of Holderness'**. While both are crushed by Warwick's brother **Montagu**, Edward's failure to take a firm grip on events strengthens Warwick's hand. The earl crosses to **Calais** with Clarence, who is duly married to **Isabel Neville**. Issuing a manifesto against Edward's 'evil advisers', Warwick and Clarence return to England. In July they defeat and kill **Lord Herbert**, a royal favourite, then capture Edward IV himself at **Olney**. But they fail to win any significant support from their fellow nobles, and in October agree to release Edward in return for a royal pardon.

1470 In March, Warwick and Clarence resume rebellion in Lincolnshire, but their forces are routed at the battle of **'Lose-coat field'** near **Stamford**. Fleeing, the rebels seek refuge at the court of **Louis XI of France**, who quickly brokers an alliance between Warwick and his relative, Queen Margaret. The compact is cemented when Warwick's younger daughter **Anne Neville** is betrothed to Henry VI's heir **Prince Edward**.

In September the rebels return to England, landing in **Devon** and wrongfooting King Edward, who is distracted by a secondary rebellion raised by Warwick's brother-in-law **Lord Fitzhugh**. Deserted by Warwick's hitherto loyal brother Montagu, Edward IV flees to **Burgundy** with his younger brother **Richard, Duke of Gloucester**. **Henry VI** is released from the Tower and nominally restored to the throne, though actual power stays in the hands of Warwick and Clarence. Their relationship is soon strained, however, when Lancastrians begin demanding the return of lands previously seized by Yorkists, and London's merchants resist Warwick's alliance with France at the expense of Burgundy.

Sir Thomas Malory completes his English prose romance *Le Morte Darthur*, possibly in prison, a year before his death; it will be printed by **William Caxton** (see p.178) in 1485.

1471 Supported by **Charles the Bold of Burgundy**, **Edward IV** and his followers return to England in March. Marching first to York, and unopposed by either Lord Montagu or the earl of Northumberland, he turns south again and besieges Warwick at **Coventry**.

In April **Clarence** defects to his brother's side, **Henry VI** is taken prisoner once more, and **London** opens its gates to Edward. On 14 April Warwick and his brother Montagu are killed in battle at **Barnet**.

On 4 May a second rebel army, headed by Queen Margaret, is crushed at **Tewkesbury**. As Margaret is captured, her son, Prince Edward, is killed attempting to flee. On 21 May King Edward returns to London; Henry VI dies on the same night, almost certainly murdered on his rival's orders. In the aftermath, Edward IV rewards both his brothers, Clarence and Gloucester, for their support – inadvertently sowing the seeds of contention between his siblings as each seeks greater power than the other.

> **Lord Wenlocke not having advanced to the support of the first line, but remaining stationary, contrary to the expectations of Somerset, the latter, in a rage, rode up to him, and beat his brains out with an axe.**
>
> Richard Brooke on Tewksbury,
> in *Visits to Fields of Battle in the Fifteenth Century* (1857).

1472 Clarence, married to Warwick's eldest daughter, attempts to prevent Gloucester marrying the younger daughter, **Anne Neville** (Prince Edward's widow). Gloucester strengthens his position by **imprisoning** his future mother-in-law under the pretence of protecting her from his brother. At the heart of the feud is the future of the substantial Warwick inheritance, which includes the lucrative estates of the **Beauchamp** family.

1473 Under pressure from the king, Parliament passes an **Act of Resumption**, returning alienated royal lands to the Crown.

1474 A further act of Parliament confirms a division of the **Neville estates** between Clarence and Gloucester in right of their wives; Warwick's widow is **disinherited**. In collaboration with Burgundy, Edward IV prepares to invade **France**.

A trading treaty is concluded with the powerful **Hanseatic League**, giving English cloth merchants access to new markets in the **Netherlands** and **Germany**.

1475 Edward IV lands in **France** with an impressive force, but Charles of Burgundy fails to give him promised support. The thrones of England and France instead conclude the **Treaty of Picquigny**, which promises Edward IV an annual pension of 50,000 gold crowns in return for withdrawing to England. France and England also conclude a **trade agreement**.

In **Bruges**, **William Caxton** publishes the first book to be printed in English.

1476 **Isabel Neville**, the duchess of Clarence, dies.

1477 Following the death of **Charles of Burgundy** in January, Clarence, seeking to lay claim to Burgundy itself, proposes marrying Charles's daughter **Mary**. As Mary is also Clarence's niece, **Edward IV** forbids the marriage to proceed – fearing that his brother will wreck his recently contrived peace with France. Clarence retaliates by seizing and executing two of his retainers, **Ankarette Twynyho** and **John Thursby**, having accused them of murdering Isabel and his young son. A summer rebellion in **Cambridgeshire** is also probably Clarence's inspiration. The king has Clarence arrested and imprisoned.

1478 In January Clarence is brought before Parliament and charged with **treason**. During his trial, eagerly promoted by the Woodvilles, the prosecution is masterminded by his brother **Gloucester**. Clarence is found guilty and dispatched to the Tower of London. There, on the king's orders, he is murdered – rumour has it, by being drowned in a butt of Malmesey wine.

1479 As the Woodvilles' influence grows, Edward grants one of the family the **earldom of Pembroke**, forcing the existing holder **William Herbert** to accept the inferior title of **Huntingdon** in compensation. Other families, including the **Berkeleys** and the **Howards**, are also eclipsed by the Woodvilles, and the young **duke of Buckingham** is forced to marry a Woodville against his will.

1480 As border clashes with **Scotland** escalate, Gloucester is appointed **lieutenant-general** in the north.

William Caxton (1422–91)

Although printing with movable type was introduced into Europe by Johann Gutenberg in 1458, it was seventeen years before the first printed book in English appeared. The man behind it was William Caxton, a London merchant who had spent nearly all his adult life on the continent. Arriving in Bruges in 1441, he rose to become governor of the Merchant Adventurers. After a spell attached to the household of the duchess of Burgundy, he travelled to Cologne in 1470, where it seems likely that he gained first-hand knowledge of the new technology for mass-producing the written word.

A true entrepreneur with an abiding interest in literature, he invested his own money to acquire a press, which he used initially to publish his own vivid translation of the *Recueil des histories des Troyes*. This and two other books were printed in Bruges before Caxton resettled in England in 1476, from where he went on to produce around a hundred titles. In the best traditions of London publishing – his press was housed near Westminster Abbey – his list contained a mixed bag of subject matter: as well as further translations, there were books about gaming and chivalric etiquette, and popular romances including Malory's *Morte Darthur*. Caxton also published devotional titles and – significantly for the poet's reputation – an edition of Chaucer's *Canterbury Tales* (see p.149). His object was to entertain, but also educate the affluent elite who could afford his products (his patrons included Edward IV). Not until well into the following century, when Protestant tracts began to circulate, would the subversive and radical potential of the printed word become fully apparent.

1482 A plan to place the rebellious **duke of Albany** on the Scottish throne appears. Gloucester invades Scotland in the summer, and succeeds in capturing both **Edinburgh** and **King James III**; but when Albany changes side, the English duke is forced to retreat, taking **Berwick** on his way back south.

Of eche of hem so as it semed me
And whyche they wern and of what degre
And in what aray eke they weren ynne
And at a knyght thenne I wyl begynne

A knyght ther was a worthy man
That fro the tyme that he first began
To ryden out / he loued chyualrye
Trouthe & honour fredom and curtesye
Ful worthy he was in hys lordis werre
And therto hadde he ryden noman ferre
And as wel in crystendom as in hethenesse
And euer hadde honour for hys worthynesse
At alisaundre he was whan it was wonne
Ful ofte tyme he hadde the bord begonne
Abouen alle nacions in pruce
In lettowe hadde he reysed and in Ruse

Chaucer's knight, from the *Canterbury Tales* (printed by Caxton c.1476).

1483 Gloucester is rewarded by his brother Edward IV for his Scottish services with a **palatinate** (area of special control) encompassing **Cumberland**, **Westmoreland** and any areas of **Scotland** he is able to conquer.

On 9 April **Edward** dies after catching a chill boating on the Thames. At once the **Woodvilles**, determined to see the king's adolescent elder son take the throne as **Edward V**, seize the royal treasury; **Richard of Gloucester** hurries swiftly south from York to assert his role as his nephew's protector. The uncrowned boy king, leaving Ludlow, is met by Gloucester at **Stony Stratford**; Gloucester arrests such members of the Woodville family as he can. Told of Gloucester's actions, the king's mother **Elizabeth Woodville** seeks sanctuary in **Westminster Abbey** with her other son Richard and her daughters. With Edward V in his custody, on 4 May Gloucester enters **London**, where the royal council confirms him as protector. Over the following weeks, as he arrests and sometimes executes opponents – and postpones Edward's coronation – it becomes apparent that Gloucester seeks the Crown for himself. Notwithstanding, he persuades Elizabeth Woodville to surrender **Prince Richard** into his safekeeping. Richard joins his brother the king apparent in a royal apartment in the **Tower of London**. The two boys quickly disappear from view, and are probably murdered.

On 26 June, following the execution of leading members of the Woodville faction at **Pontefract**, Gloucester proclaims himself king as **Richard III –** the second and last Yorkist monarch. In October dissent spreads among the nobility, and there is rebellion in **Kent**. Among those who desert the king is the **duke of Buckingham**, quickly captured and executed by Richard. And when the Kentish rebellion is also defeated, Richard's opponents transfer their allegiance to **Henry Tudor**, an obscure Lancastrian claimant living in exile in Brittany.

Richard III and the Princes in the Tower

Usually portrayed as a murderous, scheming monster, **Richard III** has not been kindly treated by posterity. The malevolent Richard that Shakespeare depicted evolved from Thomas More's *History of King Richard the Third*, an account which is predictably hostile to the 'croke backed' king because it was written for **Cardinal Morton**, Henry VII's archbishop of Canterbury – and, naturally, the Tudor regime had an interest in rubbishing Richard's reputation.

But Richard III deserves to be understood as a man of his time, someone who had to embrace whatever means it took to protect his own position. To his brother **Edward IV** he proved a loyal lieutenant, fighting for him in the north of England and campaigning in Scotland. Once Edward was dead, however, Richard's situation changed dramatically. The succession of a minor, **Edward V**, threatened a return to the sort of anarchy that had plagued the reign of Henry VI, and as the boy's uncle it was natural that Richard should become protector in order to defend against it. Yet his competitors at court, notably the **Woodvilles**, now wanted him out of the way.

In these circumstances, striking first was the only means of survival. It's unlikely that Richard intended to seize the throne all along, but as the summer of 1483 unfolded that became his best hope. Having made that decision, elimination of **Edward V** and his brother became a necessity. So murky are the circumstances surrounding their deaths, however, that even now we cannot be sure that Richard was directly responsible.

But many at the time thought he was. Soon a rumour surfaced that Richard had also poisoned his queen, **Anne**, and, despite Richard's public rebuttal of the charges, the mood against him hardened. Even so, when Henry Tudor challenged the king it was by no means a done deal; **Bosworth** was a battle Richard stood a good chance of winning until Thomas, Lord Stanley and his brother, Sir William Stanley, defected. Faced with an impossible situation, Richard was presented with a stark choice: flight or death. It is a testament to his courage that he chose to embrace the latter.

1484 The only **Parliament** convened during Richard III's reign attaints 104 members of the October rebellion. In April Richard's son and heir, another Edward, **dies**, raising doubts about the security of the succession.

> ❝ Richard, who was slender and not tall, had one shoulder a little higher than the other: a defect, by the magnifying glasses of party, by distance of time, and by the amplification of tradition, easily swelled to shocking deformity; for falsehood itself generally pays so much respect to truth as to make it the basis of its superstructure. ❞
>
> Horace Walpole, *Historic Doubts on Richard the Third* (1768)

1485 Rumours about Richard III intensify when his consort, **Queen Anne**, dies suddenly in March and the king expresses a desire to marry his niece, **Elizabeth of York**.

On 7 August **Henry Tudor** lands at **Milford Haven** in southwest Wales, then marches into England and northwards with his force. The king heads toward **Leicester** to confront him. On 22 August the two armies meet near Market Bosworth, at a battle site known as **Bosworth Field**. Initially Henry Tudor is outnumbered, but several of Richard's allies desert the king, among them **Lord Stanley**, Tudor's stepfather, while the **earl of Northumberland** refuses to engage his forces. **Sir William Stanley** goes one step further by switching sides midway through the engagement. Richard III himself is killed leading a desperate cavalry charge, and Henry Tudor is symbolically crowned by Stanley using the coronet from Richard's helmet. In October **Henry VII**, the founder of the **Tudor dynasty**, is formally crowned king of England at Westminster Abbey.

6
The Tudor Dynasty
1485–1603

Henry Tudor's victory at Bosworth gained him the throne, but there was little reason to suppose that his reign would be any longer than his predecessor's. Within two years, in fact, **Henry VII** faced rebellion when the first of many pretenders to his crown, **Lambert Simnel**, landed in England. When they faced each other at Stoke Henry's luck held, though, and the new dynasty began to look as though it might survive.

It was fortunate for the Tudors that they held power during an era of both national and European economic acceleration. As the disastrous consequences of the Black Death finally receded, England's population grew, replenishing old cities, towns and villages. Trade with the Low Countries and elsewhere boomed, and this had knock-on effects that were felt throughout society. But perhaps the greater beneficiaries of the new order were the **landed gentry**. In 1485 England was still dominated by a baronial elite; as time passed this aristocracy survived, adapted and held on to many of its privileges – but the class of gentry immediately below steadily enlarged and prospered.

One reason they did so was precisely because of the growth in population, assisted by a greater supply of money. After a century of depression, **rents** began to rise in line with increased demand. Those who had assets had learned to manage them skilfully and profitably. A visible sign of this was the change in England's countryside. The **enclosure** of common land for private agricultural purposes was a process that continued well into the 18th and even 19th centuries, often with dire consequences for the rural poor – who could be deprived overnight of traditional grazing for their few animals. But from the mid-16th century the hedgerows, fences and narrow lanes that are still a familiar feature of rural England were beginning to make their mark.

Nor did government attempt to resist these changes. On the contrary, it was Tudor policy to encourage the gentry's ambition as a counterweight to the interference of dukes, earls and lords. Again, it was during the 16th century that the system of provincial justice administered by **justices of the peace** drawn from the 'squirearchy' came fully into its own. And increasingly members of the gentry were expected to play a role in central government. For **Elizabeth I**, the last of the Tudors, the consequence was an increasingly ambitious House of Commons eager to flex its muscles. Yet this early emergence of institutionalized political dissent was scarcely her greatest concern. For much of her reign the most serious threats came from overseas, as they had done so often in the past.

In the wider picture, the most significant upheaval of the 16th century was the **Reformation**. Many thought that the Church had fallen into disrepute: prelates failed to control absentee priests; those near the top of the ecclesiastical edifice enriched themselves by acquiring multiple benefices (pluralism), and conferred appointments on often unqualified members of their own families (nepotism); clerics widely flaunted the rules of celibacy by keeping mistresses. The revolution against this began in Germany in 1517 when the Augustinian friar **Martin Luther** attacked the sale of **papal indulgences** (which enabled people to buy their way out of what the Church called sin), and then widened his assault to include key tenets of Roman Catholic doctrine. What emerged was a revolutionary theory that individuals should tend their own consciences and develop a more direct relationship with God, instead of depending on the intercession of the Church to attain salvation.

As reform gathered momentum, the political fallout was nothing short of spectacular. As old tensions and rivalries were realigned, the map of Europe was redrawn. In England, a number of scholars quickly joined the reformers by protesting against corruption and espousing their new ideas. Although the Roman Church rapidly regrouped – a backlash called the **Counter-Reformation** – every Christian ruler faced a stark choice between what soon amounted to opposing religions. The Reformation had scarcely begun to take root, however, when **Henry VIII** separated the English Church from Rome in what is usually interpreted as a purely political move. Thereafter England slowly entered the reformed fold, and increasingly found itself at odds with its former ally, **Spain**, a country that enthusiastically championed the revived Roman Catholicism and was determined to stamp out lutheranism along with any other type of 'heresy'.

The showdown came in 1588, with the launch of the **Spanish Armada**. Its failure gave England breathing space, and enabled it to develop as a European power – all the more so as England's traditional enemy, **France**, was plagued by a series of civil wars fought in the name of opposing faiths. Though the Reformation would scarcely leave England untouched, that level of large-scale violence was largely avoided by Henry VIII's pre-emptive move.

The Tudor kings
1485-1553

The first of the Tudors, **Henry VII**, was a cautious realist, committed to reconciling England's warring factions with a hands-on approach to government and avoiding costly foreign wars. It's sometimes said that he owed his success to three women. His mother, **Margaret Beaufort** – fortunate not to have been executed for her role in Buckingham's rebellion of 1483 – was instrumental in putting together the coalition of forces that secured his victory at Bosworth. Soon afterwards Edward IV's widow, **Elizabeth Woodville**, ensured both the survival of her own family and Henry's security as king by offering him the hand of her daughter, **Elizabeth of York**.

Since his advertised right to the throne was through his Lancastrian descent, Henry VII could claim to have united the two opposing houses. As a Tudor he also represented an advancement – albeit a symbolic one – for the people of Wales. Yet much of his reign was troubled by rebellion, most memorably in the shape of two impostors, **Lambert Simnel** and **Perkin Warbeck**, both supported by the Yorkist **Margaret of Burgundy**. It wasn't until the imprisonment of the earl of Suffolk in 1506, just three years before Henry's death, that the king could finally feel assured of no further threat. In the interim he worked enthusiastically to repair the machinery of government, and also sort out the royal finances. As a ruler he was far from innovative, but chose instead to resurrect policies and institutions that had worked well for Edward IV – and to that extent he was one of the more successful medieval kings.

The succession passed unchallenged to his more assertive and certainly more extravagant son, **Henry VIII**. Unlike his father, the younger Henry was prepared to delegate authority while seeking to cut a figure on the European stage. Emulating Henry V, and greatly assisted by his powerful lord chancellor **Cardinal Wolsey**, he endeavoured to re-establish an English presence in France beyond the confines of Calais. When this failed, he allied himself with France against the Emperor Charles V. Nearer home, Henry VIII strengthened English rule in Wales, proclaimed himself king of Ireland, and toyed with subjugating Scotland. There was nothing especially new in these policies: England's kings had often looked beyond the Channel to fulfil their wider ambitions while seeking control of the British Isles.

But in the middle years of his reign an extraordinary combination of circumstances set England on an entirely new path. At his succession in 1509 Henry VIII had married his brother Arthur's widow, **Catherine of Aragon**, six years older than he was. By the late 1520s it was clear she would not provide him with a male heir, and in any case he had fallen in love with **Anne Boleyn**. In the normal course of events the king could have expected the papacy, after a little horse-trading, to grant an annulment. But the sitting pope, **Clement VII**, held back: Catherine was **Charles V**'s aunt, and Charles had Clement in his pocket. A drastic solution to this impasse was developed by Henry's new adviser, **Thomas Cromwell**. Relations with Rome were gradually severed and an independent English Church created – one amenable to Henry VIII's wishes, of course, and with him as its supreme head. Although its immediate ramifications were obvious, Cromwell's intervention had two unforeseen effects. First, although Henry VIII wasn't interested in reforming the Church, Cromwell had radical leanings, and the destruction of the monasteries undertaken at his behest only increased suspicions among other European nations that England was actually taking part in Luther's Reformation. Second, Cromwell used parliamentary means to get the king his way. Though it was initially merely used to rubber-stamp royal policies, the **House of Commons** (now established as a chamber in its own right) gained a new and lasting profile.

For all that, during Henry's lifetime the **'Henrican Reformation'** was primarily an institutional, not a doctrinal, revolution. Although the king took four more wives following

Anne Boleyn's dramatic fall from favour, he continued in the Catholic faith and Catholic practice, promoting stern laws against Protestant 'heresy'. After his death in 1547, though, his young son **Edward VI** – the last of the Tudor kings – was entrusted to a council dominated by those sympathetic to the reformed religion. During Edward's reign England finally became what it was already assumed to be: a Protestant nation.

1485 Following his victory over Richard III at **Bosworth Field**, Henry Tudor is formally crowned **Henry VII** at Westminster on 30 October. Significantly, he dates his accession from the day before the battle in order to **attaint** those who fought against him for treason; Yorkist estates are confiscated. Basing his claim to the throne on descent from his Lancastrian ancestor **John of Gaunt** as well as by the 'judgement of God' shown in battle, in November Henry summons **Parliament** to legitimize his control still further. His anxiety to do so is perhaps symptomatic – much of his reign will be spent combating rebellion inside his kingdom, often in support of rival pretenders. Ruling through an **enlarged council** that includes lawyers and members of the gentry, Henry uses existing laws to curtail the powers of the barons.

1486 To strengthen his position among surviving Yorkists, Henry VII marries Edward IV's daughter, **Elizabeth of York**. During festivities held in York itself the **Tudor Rose** – an amalgam of the red and white roses of Lancaster and York – is displayed for the first time.

A rebellion mounted by **Francis, Lord Lovell**, formerly chamberlain to Richard III, is crushed.

1487 Henry VII's Yorkist opponents, led by Richard III's nephew the **earl of Lincoln** and his sister **Margaret**, the dowager **duchess of Burgundy**, encourage a rebellion by supporting the pretender **Lambert Simnel**. Simnel, an

Oxfordshire apprentice who bears a striking resemblance to **Edward, Earl of Warwick** (the duke of Clarence's son) is proclaimed king in **Dublin**, with the connivance of the Irish nobility. In England the Yorkist forces, including 2000 mercenaries sent by Margaret of Burgundy, are routed at **East Stoke**, Nottinghamshire in June. Lincoln and the mercenary commander **Martin Schwartz** are killed, but Simnel is pardoned and offered a junior position in the royal kitchens.

A royal statute for the first time refers by name to the **Court of Star Chamber**, named after the decorated ceiling of the room in which Henry's council meets as a judiciary to hear criminal cases. Under Henry's successors, Star Chamber develops a reputation as a formidable instrument of royal coercion.

1488 Henry VII signs the **Treaty of Medina del Campo** with Spain, beginning the Tudors' long association with Europe's emerging superpower.

1489 Following the death of the **earl of Northumberland** – lynched while trying to collect taxes in York – Henry VII fills the power vacuum in the north by promoting the **Howard family**, gradually returning lands and titles confiscated after Bosworth.

The king contemplates war against France in order to recover **Brittany**, now absorbed into French domains, but is deterred by the likely expenditure.

1491 **Perkin Warbeck**, trained by Margaret of Burgundy to impersonate Edward IV's younger son **Richard**, emerges as a fresh and more threatening Yorkist pretender to Henry VII's throne. His first attempt to invade England fails, though.

1492 Henry VII concludes the **Treaty of Etaples** with France, securing an indemnity of £159,000 – equivalent to

Henry VII (1457–1509)

Henry Tudor's claim to the throne was genuine enough, but it was remote. The founder of the Tudor dynasty was a curious, but not especially unusual, mix of Welsh, French and English lineages. His mother, Margaret Beaufort, was a great granddaughter of John of Gaunt's mistress Catherine Swynford, whom Gaunt married only after she had borne him children. Another source of royal blood was his paternal grandmother, Catherine of France, who married Owen Tudor after the death of her first husband, Henry V. Edmund, Owen's son and Henry's father, rose to become earl of Richmond, but it was Henry's uncle, Jasper Tudor, Earl of Pembroke, who raised the future king, removing him to Brittany after the Lancastrian debacle at Tewkesbury in 1471.

As king, Henry's preoccupation was to secure the throne against the continuing Yorkist challenge. In this he succeeded, and he proved an outstandingly successful monarch in other respects too. He ended up doubling royal revenues by cannily enforcing royal rights to feudal dues and legal fees, and by levying fines instead of other forms of punishment. Internationally his greatest triumphs were agreeing the Treaty of Etaples with the French Crown and securing the hand of Catherine of Aragon for Arthur, his eldest son. He also brokered important commercial treaties, not only with Spain and the Netherlands but Florence and Denmark too. At home he tried – though with limited success – to limit the power and influence of the nobility.

But perhaps the main ingredient of Henry VII's success was his unrelenting dedication to the task of government: few English kings have worked harder. Perceived as an unglamorous, even parsimonious ruler, he has sometimes been seen as the country's first 'modern' monarch. But it's more accurate to say that little was done to change or revolutionize the fabric of England: he left the country in a state of stability, albeit hard-won stability. His successor, Henry VIII, reaped the full rewards of that policy, in the process projecting himself as a 'Renaissance prince' in a manner that would have been wholly alien to his father.

twice the Crown's annual revenues at the time – in return for abandoning all his claims to French territories other than Calais. The treaty bolsters European recognition of Tudor rule in England.

1494 Henry VII's position in Ireland is strengthened by the passage of **Poyning's Law**, which requires all Irish legislation to gain the king of England's consent.

1495 **Perkin Warbeck** becomes the focus of renewed rebellion. Supported by the Holy Roman Emperor **Maximilian I**, James IV of Scotland and Margaret of Burgundy, Warbeck lands at **Deal**, but is soon forced to flee to Scotland.

1496 Although a Scottish army crosses the border in support of Warbeck, the pretender's cause is undermined when Henry VII joins the **Holy League** – an alliance promoted by King Ferdinand of Spain and Emperor Maximilian against French aggression in Italy – and signs the **Magnus Intercursus**, a trading and defence treaty with the Netherlands and Burgundy.

A royal charter is granted to an association of **Staplers**, responsible for collecting and distributing England's raw wool.

1497 Warbeck invades **Cornwall**, but soon afterwards his forces are defeated and Warbeck himself is captured at **Beaulieu** in Hampshire.

Henry VII concludes a **peace treaty** with James IV.

Armed with letters patent granted by Henry the previous year, and perhaps accompanied by his son Sebastian, the Italian navigator **Giovanni Caboto** (his name anglicized as **John Cabot**) sets out from **Bristol** with eighteen men on board the *Matthew* to cross the Atlantic in order to discover 'new lands' for the English crown. He lands in **Newfoundland**, and begins charting the upper eastern

The Tudors

Monarchs are in colour

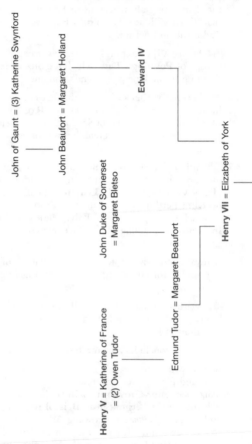

John of Gaunt = (3) Katherine Swynford

John Beaufort = Margaret Holland

John Duke of Somerset = Margaret Bletso

Edmund Tudor = Margaret Beaufort

Henry V = Katherine of France = (2) Owen Tudor

Edward IV

Henry VII = Elizabeth of York

Arthur

Henry VIII =

(1) Catherine of Aragon (2) Anne Boleyn (3) Jane Seymour

Mary I Elizabeth I Edward VI

Margaret = James IV of Scotland

James V

Mary, Queen of Scots

James VI & I

American coastline. On his return he is granted a £20 royal pension.

1498 **Cabot** sets out on a **second expedition**, this time with 200 men aboard five ships. Although there is no certain record of Cabot's return and no attempt is yet made to create an English colony in the Americas, Cabot's voyages lay the foundation for England's later settlement in **Canada**.

1499 **Warbeck** and the **earl of Warwick**, Clarence's real son, are beheaded, but opposition to Henry VII continues under the leadership of **Edmund de la Pole**, the **earl of Suffolk** and eldest surviving son of Edward IV's sister **Elizabeth**.

1501 Henry VII's prestige is greatly enhanced when, to further Anglo-Spanish relations, his son and heir **Prince Arthur** is married to **Catherine of Aragon**, daughter of **Ferdinand** and **Isabella of Spain**.

1502 The peace with Scotland is consolidated by the marriage of Henry VII's daughter **Margaret** to **James IV**. But the English succession is jeopardized by the death of **Prince Arthur**, making his sickly brother **Prince Henry of York** the king's heir. Arthur's widow Catherine and her dowry, worth 200,000 crowns, remain in England.

1503 The death of Henry VII's queen, **Elizabeth**, encourages **Suffolk** to extend his plots against the Crown.

1506 **Suffolk**'s imprisonment in the Tower of London effectively removes a major threat to Henry VII's throne.

1509 **Henry VII** dies, bequeathing his successor, the 18-year-old Prince Henry – now tall and renowned for his athletic ability – sound royal finances and a stable kingdom. **Henry VIII** reaffirms England's strategic alliance with an increasingly powerful Spain by marrying his brother's widow **Catherine of Aragon**, as his father had intended.

Unlike his father, however, Henry VIII displays his taste for spectacle by mounting elaborate **entertainments** at his court.

1510 Henry VIII executes his father's unpopular ministers **Sir Richard Empson** and **Edmund Dudley**.

1513 In alliance with his father-in-law **Ferdinand of Spain**, Henry VIII crosses the Channel to fight against France. He succeeds in capturing **Tournai**, which is held until 1518, but his campaign is a pale imitation of Henry V's conquests of a century earlier.

The Scots, in league with **Francis I of France**, attempt an invasion of northern England, but are routed by **Thomas Howard**, the earl of Surrey, at **Flodden**. James IV and many of his nobles are killed in battle. As a reward Surrey is granted the lost Howard duchy of **Norfolk**.

1514 Peace terms are concluded with France.

Thomas Wolsey is appointed archbishop of York and then lord chancellor, and so becomes the dominant figure in English politics for fifteen years.

1515 Wolsey's power is further increased when he is appointed a cardinal by the pope.

1516 Queen Catherine gives birth to **Princess Mary**, the only one of her children to survive infancy.

Utopia, a brief tract by **Thomas More** (see p.200) that recommends a form of communist theocracy as the ideal society, is published at **Louvain** (now in Belgium).

1517 More is invited to join the king's council.

In **Wittenberg**, Martin Luther sparks the Reformation with the publication of his **95 theses**, denouncing the Roman Church for its abuses. The **Lutheran religion** that follows holds that man can achieve salvation by 'faith alone', without recourse to the Church's intercession.

Cardinal Wolsey (c.1472–1530)

Thomas Wolsey was not the last churchman to play a leading role in English politics, but he was one of the more impressive. Reputedly the son of an Ipswich butcher, he became Henry VII's chaplain in 1507; noting his energy and appetite for work, the new king kept him on at court. It was after organizing the French campaign of 1513 that Wolsey rose to real prominence: by 1515 he was lord chancellor, in addition to being cardinal and archbishop of York. From then until the year before his death he was the most powerful man in the land after the king. Theirs was a close working relationship, and one Wolsey knew well how to manipulate: the Italian scholar **Polydore Vergil** observed that 'every time he wished to obtain something from Henry, he introduced the matter casually into his conversation; then he brought out some small present or another, a beautifully fashioned dish, for example, or a jewel or ring or gifts of that sort, and while the king was admiring the gift intently, Wolsey would adroitly bring forward the project on which his mind was fixed'.

Although Wolsey was appointed papal legate in 1518 to oversee reforms within the English Church, the cardinal concentrated his energies on solidly secular matters. He deployed the **Court of**

1518 Wolsey, now raised to legate *a latere* by the pope (resident ruler of the Church in England), scores a major but short-lived diplomatic triumph when he engineers the **Treaty of London**, a multilateral mutual security pact between Europe's leading powers.

1519 Following the death of Maximilian, **Charles V**, already king of Spain and duke of Burgundy – the latter giving him nominal control over the Netherlands – becomes **Holy Roman Emperor**, and so rules over a greater conglomeration of territories than has been seen in western Europe since the Roman Empire itself.

1520 As European politics realign to take account of Charles

Star Chamber to bring unruly barons to justice, and he created the **Court of Requests** to hear cases brought by poorer subjects. With the **Eltham Ordinances**, Wolsey radically downsized the court by expelling Henry's controversial young companions, his 'minions', from their sinecures. It was, however, in the international arena that Wolsey's star shone brightest – and where it finally fell. He endeavoured to promote Henry VIII's European reputation by opportunistically exploiting differences between Francis I of France and Charles V of Spain. The **Treaty of London** (1518) and the **Field of Cloth of Gold** (1520) marked the high points of this policy, but thereafter it unravelled. At the same time Wolsey was becoming widely unpopular, being blamed for high levels of taxation and resented for his deliberately ostentatious household.

It was the king's displeasure that brought about his downfall. A treaty between Charles V and Francis I in 1528 isolated England diplomatically, and in the following year Wolsey failed to deliver the promised divorce from **Catherine of Aragon**. The more serious accusation of treason followed, but – ever the statesman – Wolsey died before his trial.

V's unprecedented empire, **Henry VIII** and **Francis I** stage a reconciliation of their diplomatic interests, organized by **Wolsey**, at the **Field of Cloth of Gold** outside Calais – a huge (and hugely expensive) three-week cultural spectacle of feasting, jousting and wrestling.

1521 As the **Reformation** spreads in northern Europe and the Roman Church comes increasingly under doctrinal as well as institutional attack, Henry VIII writes and publishes *Assertio Septum Sacramentorum Adversus Martinum Lutherum* ('Defence of the seven sacraments against Martin Luther'). For this he is rewarded by the pope with the title **Fidei Defensor** ('Defender of the faith').

> **❝** Why come ye nat to court?
> To whyche court?
> To the kynges court,
> Or to Hampton Court?
> The kynges courte
> Shulde have the excellence;
> But Hampton Court
> Hath the preemynence. **❞**
>
> John Skelton, *Why come ye nat to court?* (c.1522)

1522 Henry VIII and Wolsey attempt a further invasion of **France**, but this proves an expensive failure.

1523 Parliament is summoned to raise new taxes, but those granted are insufficient to the Crown's requirements.

1524 Wolsey, appointed **papal legate** for life, declares **new taxes** without reference to Parliament, but is forced to rescind them.

1525 In Italy, **Francis I** is defeated and captured by Charles V's imperial army at **Pavia**. Wolsey, having supported France, is hard-pressed to defend his policies – the more so as England's trade with the Netherlands suffers as a consequence.

A combination of **economic depression**, **plague** and the growing impact of **lutheranism** makes the country restless.

1527 Having fallen in love with **Anne Boleyn**, the sister of a former mistress, Henry VIII initiates **divorce proceedings** against Queen Catherine on the twin grounds of her failure to provide him with a male heir, and that as the widow of his deceased brother his marriage to her is biblically illegal. Wolsey, still wishing to pursue an alliance against Catherine's nephew Emperor Charles V, supports the king's wishes. Difficulties arise, however, when an annulment petition is forwarded to **Pope Clement VII**, effectively Charles's prisoner in Italy.

1529 After protracted negotiations with the papacy, the pope's legate, **Cardinal Lorenzo Campeggio**, arrives in England to hear Henry VIII's divorce case alongside Wolsey. But Campeggio pronounces that the case must be heard in **Rome**, where a ruling against Catherine is unthinkable. In August, Henry's position is further weakened when Charles V and Francis I resolve their differences by the **Peace of Cambrai**. Losing patience with his chancellor, Henry dismisses Wolsey in October, stripping him of all his secular titles and property. **Thomas More**, known to be held in high esteem by the pope but opposed to the divorce, is appointed chancellor instead.

In November, aware that Wolsey's harsh measures have made the Crown unpopular, Henry summons a parliament, known as the **Reformation Parliament**, in an endeavour to refurbish his image. The mood of the **House of Commons**, sitting separately from the Lords, is notably anti-clerical. Over seven years the same Parliament will enact 137 statutes, many of them designed to destroy the power of the medieval Church.

1530 In November Wolsey is arrested in York on charges of treason, but dies later on the journey to London to face trial.

1531 The English Church grants Henry VIII a gift of £119,000 after the king threatens legal proceedings against the church's **'infringements'** of royal rights.

1532 Still unable to secure a papal annulment of his marriage to Catherine, Henry VIII turns to his councillor **Thomas Cromwell** (see p.204), a known Lutheran sympathizer, to further his divorce. Cromwell, who remains in power for the next eight years as Henry's principal minster, oversees the **Henrican Reformation**, relying heavily on Parliament to separate the Church in England from Rome. Cromwell also masterminds a comprehensive **reform of administrative departments**, leading to improved efficiency in government.

1533 In January Henry VIII secretly and bigamously marries **Anne Boleyn**, already pregnant with his child.

In April Parliament passes an **Act in Restraint of Appeals**. Forbidding appeals to be made to Rome in any matter whatsoever, this marks the beginning of England's formal repudiation of papal authority.

Thomas More (1477–1535)

Although the European Reformation had many root causes, it was nourished by a diffuse intellectual movement that became known as humanism, which was based on a revival of Greek learning that inspired a reappraisal of existing political, social and religious institutions. Although this 'new learning' germinated in Italy, its leading light in northern Europe was the Dutch Desiderius Erasmus, and one of its most celebrated literary creations, *Utopia*, was written by an Englishman.

Thomas More was a Londoner who began his career as a lawyer, becoming an under-sheriff for the City in 1510. From 1499 he enjoyed a close friendship with Erasmus, who described him as 'omnium horarum homo', a 'man for all seasons', and encouraged him to develop his literary work in print. Deploying similar ironic strategies to Erasmus's own *Moriae encomium* ('the praise of folly'), which itself puns on More's surname, *Utopia* outlines a supposedly ideal society located on a mythical island off the Americas – its title, coined by More, means 'no-place'. While the author's earthly paradise is described with a perfectly

In May **Thomas Cranmer**, elected archbishop of Canterbury in March and sympathetic to Henry's plight, presides over ecclesiastical hearings that result in the **unilateral annulment** of the king's marriage to Catherine of Aragon.

On 1 June, Boleyn is **crowned** Queen of England. On 7 September she gives birth to a girl, **Elizabeth**. In the same month Henry is **excommunicated** by the pope.

1534 Parliament passes three key statutes in rapid succession: an **Act of Succession**, enforcing recognition of Henry's marriage to Boleyn and legitimizing any male offspring as heir to the throne; an **Act of Supremacy**, confirming Henry VIII's status as 'supreme head of the English church' and abolishing papal jurisdiction in England; and an **Act of**

---

straight face, it offers an oblique critique of contemporary values, advocating a communal lifestyle in which everything from labour to dining is shared – a model of society which has been seen to foreshadow not only Marxist thinking but the communities some Puritans attempted to establish in the 17th century.

But as More's career advanced and lutheranism gathered pace, more serious business began to occupy him. He became increasingly concerned with combating the 'heresies' of the Reformists, publishing a steady stream of fierce attacks on the new religion. More entered royal service in 1517, and in October 1529 replaced Wolsey as lord chancellor. But his political usefulness to Henry VIII soon ended. In 1534 More refused to agree to the Act of Supremacy, and he refused to attend the king's wedding with Anne Boleyn; his resignation followed soon afterwards. After a swift show trial he was convicted of treason and sentenced to death. His last work, *A Dialogue of Comfort against Tribulation*, was composed while imprisoned in the Tower of London; the following July he was beheaded on Tower Hill. He was canonized in 1935.

Treason, expanding the definition of treason to cover seditious writing and talk. The last, framed against 'dissent', enables Cromwell to bring to trial and execute **Thomas More**, **John Fisher** (the bishop of Rochester) and other loyalists opposed to Henry's divorce.

> ❝ I pray you, Master Lieutenant, see me safe up, and my coming down let me shift for myself. ❞
>
> Thomas More, mounting the scaffold, 1535

1536 Catherine of Aragon dies in January. Shortly afterwards the king is **injured** whilst jousting, perhaps marking the beginning of the chronic ill-health that affects the remainder of his life.

Anne Boleyn **miscarries**; the allegedly deformed foetus encourages gossip that the eleven-fingered queen is a witch. But it is her failure to provide Henry (now in love with **Jane Seymour**) with a male heir that leads to her downfall. On 19 May, following accusations of treason, adultery and incest with her brother **Lord Rochford**, Anne is **executed**. In August Henry VIII marries Seymour, already pregnant with his child.

Guided by **Cromwell**, Parliament begins enacting legislation that, over the coming four years, will bring about the **dissolution of the monasteries**. The argument against the monasteries is that as international Catholic bodies they undermine the king's position as supreme head of the English Church; needless to say, confiscation of monastic lands also brings with it a vast windfall for the royal treasury.

Parliament passes an **Act of Union**, giving the people of Wales legal equality with the king's English subjects, but prohibiting Welsh-only speakers from holding office.

Towards the end of the year, a major Catholic uprising, known as the **Pilgrimage of Grace** – comprising those dismayed by the separation from Rome, but which is also fuelled by economic hardship – begins in **Lincolnshire** and **Yorkshire**.

1537 To Henry VIII's joy, Jane Seymour gives birth to a male heir, **Prince Edward**. To his grief, she dies in child-birth.

The **Pilgrimage of Grace** is crushed and Henry stamps his authority on the north, executing scores of local nobility and gentry and the rebels' principal spokesman, **Robert Aske**.

In a concession to Protestant feeling, a translation of the **Bible** into English by **Miles Coverdale** is 'authorized' by the king's government.

1539 To draw England closer to Germany's Lutheran princes, Thomas Cromwell 'arranges' a marriage between Henry VIII and **Anne of Cleves**. To whet Henry's appetite, Cromwell commissions **Hans Holbein the Younger** of Augsburg, then resident in England, to paint a flattering portrait of the unseen bride.

1540 Anne of Cleves arrives in England. Meeting her for the first time, Henry VIII likens her to a 'Flemish mare', but proceeds with the wedding. His disappointment, how-ever, provides an opportunity for Cromwell's enemies: by June the king is persuaded that Cromwell is both a traitor and a heretic. On 12 July king and queen are **divorced**; sixteen days later Cromwell is **executed** without trial. On the same day Henry VIII marries his fifth wife, **Catherine Howard**.

Parliament enacts the **Six Articles**, which broadly define the English Church's doctrines in traditional, neo-Catholic terms; Protestantism remains illegal in England.

Thomas Cromwell (c.1485–1540)

Sometimes called England's first parliamentary statesman, **Thomas Cromwell** was Henry VIII's second great minister. He was born in Putney, the son of a cloth-worker, and while his early career remains shadowy – he appears to have spent time in Italy and the Netherlands – he entered Wolsey's service around 1520. Following the cardinal's disgrace, Wolsey extricated himself from the fallout and entered Parliament, where he gained Henry VIII's attention. He was admitted to the Privy Council in 1530, and in 1532 emerged as the most powerful of the king's officials.

His greatest coups occurred simultaneously: he realized Henry VIII's divorce from Catherine of Aragon and brought about the creation of an English Church wholly separated from Rome. To do this he relied upon his own skills as a parliamentary fixer to ensure the approval of several key statutes, culminating in the **Act of Supremacy** in 1534. Using the same means, and against considerable opposition, he oversaw the dissolution of the monasteries. As a result the Reformation in England was achieved with relatively little bloodshed, at least in its early stages. As importantly, the House of Commons became an integral aspect of the English polity. Nor was Cromwell's strategy merely pragmatic:

As the **dissolution of the monasteries** reaches completion, the Crown begins selling off some of the confiscated lands in order to meet its debts. This increases the landshare of England's gentry.

1541 Henry VIII assumes the title **king of Ireland**.

1542 Archbishop Cranmer, supportive of Protestant elements at court and opposed to the 'conservative' Howards, writes in secret to Henry VIII accusing Catherine Howard of adultery. Catherine is executed after her supposed lovers 'confess' under torture.

A Scottish army, in league with France, is crushed at **Solway Moss**. James V of Scotland dies shortly afterwards, he nurtured constitutionalist ideas of a national sovereignty based on the king-in-parliament. During his ascendancy he also restructured the machinery of government, creating separate administrative departments outside of the king's household run by a more highly trained bureaucracy than had yet been seen in England.

Yet Henry's complex marital affairs proved, as for Wolsey, Cromwell's stumbling block. Fearing a hostile alliance between Charles V and Francis I, he pushed the king into a union with **Anne of Cleves** in 1540, attempting to promote a counter-alliance with the Protestant princes of Germany. Although he was created earl of Essex in the same year, seemingly assured of continuing royal favour, the increasingly unstable king had begun to listen to Cromwell's enemies. The Catholic-leaning dukes of Norfolk and Suffolk, suspecting that Cromwell wished to push reform of the Church further, seized their opportunity and arrested him. Cromwell's career was over, and he was beheaded in July. Yet Henry swiftly regretted the loss of his most able – and most faithful – servant. He never invested the same kind of power in a single minister again.

and is succeeded by his infant daughter, **Mary, Queen of Scots**.

To pay for his campaigns, Henry VIII fuels inflation by debasing the coinage.

A **Second Act of Union** provides for Welsh members to attend parliament, but also imposes full English administration throughout the principality.

1543 Anglo-Scottish hostilities are concluded by the **Treaty of Greenwich** which brokers the betrothal of Prince Edward and Mary, Queen of Scots. The treaty is quickly repudiated by the Scottish Parliament, however.

The English Parliament legislates an **Act for Abolishing Diversity of Opinion**, intended to discourage lingering loyalties to Rome.

Henry VIII marries his sixth and final wife, **Catherine Parr**.

1544 Charles V and Francis I, both loyal to Roman Catholicism, conclude a peace treaty without reference to Henry VIII, who launches a renewed attack on France. **Boulogne** is seized, and remains in English hands for eight years.

The king also orders a fresh assault on Scotland by way of 'rough wooing' on behalf of Prince Edward.

1546 Bereft of allies, Henry VIII finally abandons his French campaigns.

Anne Askew, burned at the stake for heresy, becomes England's first 'Protestant' martyr. **Sir Thomas Wriothesley** (later earl of Southampton) and **Sir Richard Rich** attempt to implicate the Protestant-leaning Catherine Parr as a member of Askew's circle, but when Wriothesley 'arrests' Catherine in front of the king, Henry intervenes.

1547 Henry VIII dies on 28 January, and is succeeded by his 9-year-old son **Edward VI**. Loose ends are rapidly tied: the king's maternal uncle **Edward Seymour** becomes Lord Protector, and is created **duke of Somerset**; Somerset's brother, **Thomas, Lord Seymour of Sudeley**, marries Catherine Parr and the younger of the king's two older half-sisters, **Princess Elizabeth**, lives with the couple.

Under Somerset's regency the regime is relaxed in some respects: a new **Treasons Act** significantly ameliorates the harsher measures introduced by Henry VIII to combat the spread of protestantism. Allowed to speak and think more freely, English Protestants – beginning to be influenced by the more extreme views of **John Calvin** as well as those of

Henry VIII (1491–1547)

There were many Henry VIIIs. One was the sickly child who unexpectedly inherited his brother Arthur's position as heir to the English kingdom. Another was the glamorous Renaissance prince who ascended the throne in 1509. Another was the husband who executed two of his six wives. Yet another was the Henry of his last years – paranoid, vicious, so overweight that he had to be moved around with the aid of machines.

In one way, though, Henry remained constant. Although the young king seemed eager to stamp his personality on the new regime by reversing a number of his father's policies and launching into war with France (with little success), his interest in work soon waned. He never enjoyed the day-to-day grind of politics, preferring to hunt or dabble in music and philosophy while his ministers laboured away. That his reign changed England so much is mainly due to the influence of two men, Thomas Wolsey and Thomas Cromwell, who alike realized that the king's personality allowed them unprecedented power to control and develop policy. Henry needed ministers who had the talent to realize his grand ambitions for the English throne: both Wolsey and Cromwell, in their different ways, provided that. But Henry's quixotic behaviour – which grew ever more erratic as he aged – was also their undoing. The king was his own master, and could not tolerate failure.

He certainly found it hard to tolerate his own failure to provide a male heir. He had acted decisively in marrying his brother's widow, Catherine of Aragon, in 1509, but as their relationship deteriorated with no son in sight, it was a decision he came increasingly to regret. Genuinely fearful that God was punishing him for marrying illegally, he decided to have the union annulled – with spectacular consequences. But a lasting solution to Henry's problem proved elusive. Though he died believing his succession to be secure at last, his son would survive only another six years. In the end Henry's legacy was that of political division.

Martin Luther – make use of print to disseminate their ideas more widely. But amidst the new climate of tolerance, other social and economic pressures create tensions in society and religion becomes a source of friction.

1548 Catherine Parr dies in childbirth. Thomas Seymour, seeking perhaps to oust his brother, endeavours but fails to marry **Princess Elizabeth**.

Somerset orders the removal of **religious images** and **statues** from churches and bans Catholic rituals such as the use of 'holy water'.

In the countryside, social unrest spreads as common land is **enclosed** by private landlords.

A group of twelve bishops and clergy, headed by **Archbishop Thomas Cramner**, is commissioned to draw up a uniform order of service for use throughout the English Church, which becomes known as the **Book of Common Prayer**.

The navigator **Sebastian Cabot**, son of John Cabot, having spent his career in Spanish and Imperial service, is given a naval command and becomes governor of the Merchant Adventurers. His attempt to establish a northeast passage to the Far East fails, but his expedition opens up a direct trade route between **England** and **Russia**.

1549 As religious dissent threatens to get out of hand, Somerset enforces an **Act of Uniformity** to impose the **Book of Common Prayer** on every church. **English** replaces Latin as the language of church services. Opposition to the Prayer Book, coupled with inflation and further land enclosure, sparks a **Catholic rebellion** in Cornwall, Devonshire and East Anglia.

Somerset also takes a more authoritarian line toward his brother **Thomas Seymour**, whom he executes for treason.

Somerset's troubles are compounded when war with **France** breaks out in the summer, following an unsuccessful intervention in Scotland. Blamed for the nation's troubles by fellow councillors, he is imprisoned in the Tower in October. In the ensuing power struggle, **John Dudley, Earl of Warwick** crushes **Kett's rebellion** in **East Anglia** and emerges victorious. Appointed lord president of the king's council, he swiftly terminates the war against Scotland.

1550 Warwick terminates the war against France by surrendering **Boulogne**. His decisive policies make him unpopular, though, when he presses for further reform of the Church. A dispute erupts when leading reformist **John Hooper** refuses to wear episcopal vestments for his consecration as bishop of Gloucester. Several 'conservative' bishops are imprisoned. In London, **Bishop Nicholas Ridley** orders altars to be replaced by simple tables. Although the young king becomes involved on the side of the reformists, his elder half-sister Mary refuses to use the Prayer Book.

1551 Warwick is created **duke of Northumberland**.

Somerset, released in 1550, is rearrested and returned to the Tower.

An exceptionally **bad harvest** adds to economic instability.

1552 To clarify 'official' religious policy, a **second Prayer Book**, again written by Cranmer, is promoted. Bishop Ridley's London practices are adopted across the country, and the church is stripped of its surviving wealth.

Somerset is **executed**.

1553 As it becomes apparent that **Edward VI** is suffering from a wasting illness, Northumberland easily persuades him to draw up a will that excludes his half-sisters Mary and Elizabeth from the succession in favour of his cousin **Lady Jane Grey**, married shortly beforehand to Northumberland's own son, **Guildford Dudley**.

On 6 July Edward VI **dies**, and Northumberland proclaims Lady Jane queen. Uncrowned, her 'reign' lasts barely nine days. Taking full advantage of Northumberland's unpopularity and banking on her Tudor pedigree, **Princess Mary** surrounds herself with followers at **Framlingham** (East Anglia), and marches on London. Northumberland is seized and executed; 'Queen' Jane and her husband are imprisoned.

The Tudor queens 1553–1603

Before 1553 no woman had ruled England in her own right; in the half-century that followed two unmarried women acceded to the throne. The brief reign of **Mary I** coincided with a low-point in Tudor fortunes, exacerbated by her struggle to resuscitate Roman Catholicism in England. As a result of her subsequent marriage to **Philip II of Spain**, she helped draw the nation into a prolonged European contest between the two religions which all but resulted in a Spanish invasion thirty years after her death.

Elizabeth I was Protestant but, unlike her sister, she played her religion to political advantage. Her settlement of the English Church took a middle course: the Anglican service set out in 1559 incorporated a revised version of Cranmer's Book of Common Prayer, blended elements of Catholic and Lutheran practice, but retained an episcopal structure. Archbishops and bishops continued to rule the roost, though now under the authority of the monarch. Elizabeth also displayed a degree of tolerance toward her

Catholic subjects. The Mass was officially banned, but in reality she turned a blind eye to its continued celebration in many parts of the country – at least until the religion presented a more palpable threat.

That threat was epitomized by **Mary, Queen of Scots**: the granddaughter of Henry VIII's sister Margaret and, until Elizabeth produced children of her own, heir presumptive to the throne. Indeed, in the eyes of some Catholics, Mary had an even stronger claim to the throne than Elizabeth. Because Elizabeth was the daughter of Anne Boleyn, who had 'illegally' displaced Catherine of Aragon as Henry VIII's queen, she could be considered illegitimate. Inevitably Mary became the focus of plots to depose Elizabeth, both before and after her imprisonment in 1568. But even her execution in 1587 did not resolve the central conundrum. Who would succeed Elizabeth?

As an unmarried monarch Elizabeth attracted the attentions of many suitors, both domestic and foreign. Yet, perhaps recognizing that the potential for long-term disadvantage outweighed any short-term gain, Elizabeth opted to remain single. And this was the trump card of her widely acclaimed statecraft: whatever her personal motives, by not marrying she retained her independence and with it the independence of her people.

That said, it was not an easy reign. In addition to the Spanish threat, Elizabeth had to contend with the intermittent hostility of France and with rebellions at home and in Ireland. The well-documented Catholic plots against her life were tangible and dangerous, and increasingly a new breed of English Protestant, the **Puritans**, challenged not only her view of religion but also the aspirations of the Tudor dynasty: the monarch might be equal to the pope, but God was still above them both. Well before the century was out the Puritans had established a foothold in the House of

Commons and began pressing for freedom of speech as well as further reform of the Church. Despite her carefully constructed image as the people's queen – 'Gloriana' – Elizabeth faced more dissent at the end of her rule than she did at its beginning.

And the Crown faced further difficulty with the Commons. Courtesy of Thomas Cromwell, the House had become an integral part of English politics and, as the more vociferous of the two parliamentary chambers, it learned how to flex what muscle it had – especially with regard to the granting of taxes. Yet Elizabeth had the political skill to hold her own.

Although the Elizabethan 'golden age' is more nostalgic gloss than fact (by the time of the queen's death she was deeply unpopular), it is undeniable that this era witnessed the belated flowering of Italianate Renaissance culture in England. Dazzling talents such as **William Shakespeare**, **Christopher Marlowe** and **Ben Jonson** filled London theatres with the latest dramatic spectacles; poets including **Edmund Spenser**, **Michael Drayton** and **Sir Philip Sidney** gave English verse new eloquence; composers such as **Thomas Tallis**, **William Byrd** and **John Dowland** built a distinctively English musical tradition.

It was also during the reign of Elizabeth that the English began to look beyond Europe. Francis Drake's circumnavigation of the globe did much to enhance his country's reputation. And although Walter Raleigh and others still struggled to found a colony in the Americas, after what seemed like a miraculous deliverance from the Spanish Armada in 1588 England's maritime future looked bright.

1553 Shortly after Mary I accedes to the throne, aged 37, Parliament debates the question of her marriage. The queen is urged to marry an Englishman, perhaps her cousin **Edward Courtenay**, but Mary persists with her ambition

Mary I (1516–58)

By remaining loyal to both her religious faith and her husband, Philip of Burgundy, **Mary I** rapidly forfeited the popularity that swept her to the throne in the wake of her half-brother Edward VI's death. It is as **'Bloody Mary'** that she is often remembered, responsible for the deaths of up to three hundred Protestants at the stake.

Yet that reputation is not entirely fair. Heretics had regularly been beheaded or burned since the days of Henry V's persecution of the lollards: her father Henry VIII had put dozens to death and so had the avidly Protestant duke of Northumberland, waging war against those Catholics who resisted Cranmer's Prayer Book. Such pogroms were a brutal part of the religious battles that dominated 16th-century Europe; in the Netherlands alone thousands went to their deaths. What singled Mary out for infamy was a combination of circumstances: a relatively high incidence of executions over a relatively short period; the brilliant propaganda of **John Foxe's** *Book of Martyrs* (1563), describing those killings in gory detail; and the bald fact that, under Elizabeth, Catholicism was decisively displaced in England. In reality, the burnings were probably not masterminded by Mary herself – who was devout rather than fanatical – but by her zealous co-religionists, bishops **Bonner** and **Gardiner**, under the supervision of **Cardinal Pole**.

In fact Mary's devastatingly unhappy personal life leaves much to sympathize with. The political pawn of her father, stigmatized as a bastard and at one point reduced to a lady-in-waiting to her younger half-sister Elizabeth, Mary fervently believed that she was returning England to the true faith. After her long wait for marriage, the disappointment of her miscarriage in 1555 (if indeed she had ever been pregnant) was crushing; so too was Philip's swift departure for the Netherlands later that year. At the end she died largely unmourned, even by Philip – who wrote coldly that 'I felt a reasonable regret at her death'.

to marry **Philip of Burgundy**, the staunchly Catholic son of **Emperor Charles V**.

Gory detail from Foxe' *Book of Martyrs*.

1554 Rejecting Parliament's advice, Mary concludes a peace treaty with **Spain**, part of Charles V's empire. As her forthcoming marriage to Philip becomes a certainty, she faces rebellion. A revolt led by Jane Grey's father the **duke of Suffolk** miscarries, as a result of which Jane and her husband **Guildford Dudley** are executed; Princess Elizabeth, also implicated in the plot, only escapes because of a lack of evidence. Another rebellion breaks out in **Kent** under the leadership of **Sir Thomas Wyatt**, and reaches London.

Mary proceeds with her marriage to Philip, and the expatriate **Cardinal Reginald Pole** arrives from Rome specifically to oversee the restoration of the Catholic Church in England.

1555 Parliament passes an Act restoring **papal supremacy**. To discourage further rebellion, the titles of former Church and monastic lands are guaranteed to their new owners. **Heresy laws** are revived, though, and enthusiastically applied. During Mary's reign some three hundred Protestants are eliminated: the first, **John Rogers**, is executed in February; **Bishop Hooper** is burned in the same month, and bishops **Ridley** and **Latimer** are burned in October. Thomas Cranmer, now imprisoned, is replaced as archbishop of Canterbury by **Reginald Pole** and persuaded to sign papers accepting Catholic doctrines.

England's first joint-stock company, the **Muscovy Company**, is founded.

1556 Philip of Burgundy becomes **Philip II of Spain** following the abdication of his father.

In March, **Cranmer** recants his statement of faith and is burned at the stake in Oxford.

Plots develop to replace Mary with her sister **Elizabeth**.

> ❝ With thoughts intent upon a far higher object than the empty threats of man, he reached the spot dyed with the blood of Ridley and Latimer. There he knelt for a short time in earnest devotion, and then arose, that he might undress and prepare for the fire. Two friars who had been parties in prevailing upon him to abjure, now endeavoured to draw him off again from the truth, but he was steadfast and immovable in what he had just professed and publicly taught. A chain was provided to bind him to the stake, and after it had tightly encircled him, fire was put to the fuel and the flames began soon to ascend. ❞
>
> John Foxe describing Thomas Cranmer's execution in the *Book of Martyrs* (1563)

1557 Philip II, intending to wage war against France, comes to England to raise troops; a French army is defeated by an Anglo-Spanish force at **St Quentin**.

As a result of a complex wrangle between the pope and Charles V, **Archbishop Pole** is deprived of his powers and investigated for heresy.

1558 The war in France turns against Philip, and England loses **Calais**, its last continental possession: 'When I am dead and opened,' Mary mourns, 'you shall find Calais in my heart'.

The queen dies on 17 November, followed twelve hours later by **Archbishop Pole**. Immediately her sister is proclaimed queen as **Elizabeth I**. Among her first acts is to appoint **William Cecil** secretary of state.

1559 As Mary I's Catholic restoration is overturned, Parliament passes new **Acts of Supremacy and Uniformity**, making Elizabeth **'supreme governor'** of the Church of England. Public celebration of the **Mass** is outlawed, although Catholics are permitted to continue their rituals privately upon payment of a monthly fine. All but two of Mary's bishops refuse to accept the **'Elizabethan settlement'** and are removed from their sees. **Matthew Parker** becomes archbishop of Canterbury.

Philip II of Spain offers to marry Elizabeth, but is rejected.

In Scotland, Protestants revolt against the Queen Regent **Mary of Guise**.

In France, Mary Queen of Scots' husband **Francis II** succeeds to the throne. The **Treaty of Cateau-Cambresis** brings the war with France to an end.

1560 Robert Dudley, son of Northumberland and a favourite of the queen, is damaged politically by the mysterious death of his wife **Amy Robsart**, leading to speculation that Dudley has murdered her in order to marry Elizabeth.

England gives **military assistance** to Scottish Protestants against Mary of Guise and her 'French' court. The French withdraw, taking Mary, Queen of Scots with them. The **Mass** is outlawed in Scotland.

1561 Elizabeth refuses Mary, Queen of Scots permission to travel through England on her way back to Scotland following the death of her husband **Francis II**. Negotiations take place for a possible marriage between Elizabeth and **King Eric of Sweden**.

1562 Elizabeth narrowly survives **smallpox**.

Robert Dudley is restored to favour and admitted to the Privy Council.

England intervenes in the **French Wars of Religion** on the side of the Huguenot Protestants.

John Hawkins voyages for the first time to the **Caribbean**, carrying slaves from West Africa to the Spanish colonies.

1563 The **Thirty-Nine Articles**, expressing a middle way between the Catholic and extreme Protestant faiths, are approved by Convocation, and so become the bedrock of the **Anglican** faith of the Church of England. A dissenting minority in Convocation, the first **Puritans**, argue for a more simplified form of worship.

1564 **John Dudley** is created **earl of Leicester**, fuelling speculation that Elizabeth intends to marry him. Along with **Henry Stuart, Lord Darnley**, Leicester is also mentioned as a possible husband for Mary, Queen of Scots.

Peace with France is brokered by the **Treaty of Troyes**, which confirms French possession of Calais.

Elizabeth I (1533–1603)

Elizabeth I has sometimes been accused of reacting to events rather than shaping them. Although this criticism contains a grain of truth, it's difficult to see how things could have been much different. During her reign England was threatened not only by the upheavals of the Reformation, but by the very real prospect of a Spanish conquest. These difficulties called for a flexible response, but they also demanded a commanding personality in control. Elizabeth provided both.

The settlement of the English Church during the early years of her reign struck a lucky balance between the main religious elements of the day. In civil matters, too, Elizabeth presided over a government that helped England attain unprecedented prosperity – she had a gift for identifying able administrators, among them **Burghley** and **Walsingham**. But her most remarkable achievement was to show that a woman could rule as well as any man. She was not the first successful European queen – Isabella of Spain was that – but unlike Isabella she had no Ferdinand at her side. Instead she manipulated her feminine allure, as well as her formidable intelligence, as an instrument of statecraft: her marital availability added an extra dimension to England's foreign relations.

She was fortunate, too, to have received an exceptional education: her tutor was the brilliant scholar and educationalist **Roger Ascham**, and she studied not only Latin and Greek but spoke French, Spanish and Italian. Her early life was far from uncomplicated, however. Her mother was beheaded when she was three, she was kept in seclusion at Hatfield House as a child and during Mary's reign she lived in constant fear for her life. The reasons behind her decision never to wed have been endlessly debated, but more certain than the gossip about her supposed lovers (**Robert Dudley** and **Sir Christopher Hatton** among them) is that, characteristically, she turned her marital status to political advantage. As 'Gloriana', England's 'virgin queen', she claimed to be married solely to her people.

1565 **Mary, Queen of Scots** marries **Lord Darnley**.

In a crackdown on Catholic ritual, Elizabeth launches an inquiry into the use of **vestments** in the English Church.

1566 Relations between Elizabeth and Parliament deteriorate as Parliament continues to press her to marry.

1567 In Scotland, **Lord Darnley** is murdered, probably with the connivance of Mary, Queen of Scots, who aggravates matters by marrying the supposed assassin, **Lord Bothwell**. A rebellion amongst Scottish lords leads to her defeat and capture at **Carberry Hill**. Imprisoned, Mary is forced to abdicate in favour of her infant son **James VI**.

1568 Mary, Queen of Scots **escapes** captivity. After her followers are defeated at **Langside** by her son's regent, the earl of Moray, she flees to England, where she is **arrested** pending an investigation of her activities in Scotland.

Relations between England and Spain deteriorate after Elizabeth condones the seizure at sea of a cargo of **Genoese bullion** bound for the duke of Alba's army in the Netherlands.

1569 During a year of domestic disturbances, a plot is hatched to marry Mary, Queen of Scots to **Thomas Howard, Duke of Norfolk,** who joins forces with Leicester in an endeavour to oust Elisabeth's senior minister **William Cecil**. Norfolk is arrested and sent to the Tower.

In October, the earls of **Northumberland** and **Westmorland** initiate armed rebellion in the north, but their revolt is crushed within three months.

There is a rising in **Ireland**, led by **James Fitzmaurice**.

1570 A further northern rebellion, led by **Lord Dacre**, is crushed.

Negotiations open between England and France with a

view to a marriage between Elizabeth and the **duc d'Anjou** (later Henry III of France).

To the discomfort of England's Catholics, **Pope Pius V** issues the bull *Regnans in Excelis*, calling for Elizabeth's overthrow.

The Schoolmaster, or Plain and Perfect Way of Teaching Children the Latin Tongue, a short educational treatise that – among other things – warns Englishmen to beware of Italian licentiousness, is published two years after its author **Roger Ascham**, a former tutor of the queen, dies.

1571 Elizabeth demonstrates her continuing faith in Cecil by making him **lord treasurer** and creating him **Lord Burghley**; **Sir Francis Walsingham** becomes **secretary of state**.

The **Ridolfi Plot**, aimed at replacing Elizabeth with the **duke of Norfolk**, is uncovered and shown to be supported by the Spanish Crown. Norfolk, released the previous year, is returned to the Tower.

The queen and Parliament continue to disagree over the question of her **marriage** and succession, now complicated by the claim of **Mary, Queen of Scots**.

Harrow School is founded.

The **Royal Exchange**, built by Thomas Gresham, opens.

1572 Norfolk is executed.

Against a background of gathering Spanish strength, England and France conclude a treaty of mutual defence at **Blois**. Relations between the two countries are strained, however, following the massacre of thousands of **Huguenots** on **St Bartholomew's Day** in August. Even so, the duc d'Anjou's brother, the **duc d'Alençon**, is put forward as a suitor for Elizabeth.

William Cecil (1520–98)

Cecil was an outstanding example of how far a member of the gentry could rise during the Tudor period. He served Elizabeth for forty years, from the time of her accession until his death, having previously served in the administrations of her three predecessors. As a young man he had been drawn towards Protestant circles and later developed some sympathy for radical Puritans. But ultimately he balked at the prospect of dismantling the Church's episcopalian structure, and is usually regarded as a contributing architect of the Elizabethan Settlement. As a court politician, he collided with the anti-episcopalian **Robert Dudley, Earl of Leicester** and also with the Catholic-minded **duke of Norfolk**, and it was not until 1571, when he was created **Lord Burghley**, that his position as the queen's closest adviser was secure.

He remained her most loyal minister, prepared to share dissenting opinions with his sovereign but always ready to subordinate them to her interests and the national good; his motto was 'to walk invisible'. Burghley's greatest triumph was to forward the execution of Mary, Queen of Scots, ensuring England's continuance as a Protestant nation. While this inevitably incurred the wrath of Spain, Burghley endeavoured to achieve a diplomatic outcome by negotiating with the **duke of Parma** in the Netherlands, at the same time prudently putting England's army and navy on a war footing. After the threat of the 1588 **Spanish Armada** had passed, Elizabeth's confidence in Burghley was unquestioned. When, later in the same year, in a rare emotional outburst she locked herself in her bedchamber after learning of her old favourite Leicester's death, it was Burghley who – knowing he was beyond rebuke – ordered the doors to be smashed open.

Francis Drake, acting independently but never reprimanded by Elizabeth, sets off on a voyage to the Americas to plunder Spanish shipping.

The **Society of Antiquaries** is founded.

1573 Edinburgh Castle, held by supporters of Mary, Queen of Scots, surrenders to an Anglo-Scottish army.

1574 Charles IX of France is succeeded by **Henry III**, Elizabeth's former suitor.

The first secret **Catholic missionaries** sent by Rome to overthrow Protestantism arrive in England. From about this time **Catholic recusants** are targeted by Elizabeth's government as possible agents of sedition. Those who retain the Catholic faith – especially prevalent in the more rural parts of the country – are obliged to worship in secret. In some houses **'priest holes'** are constructed to hide Catholic clergy.

Elizabethan drama

The ancestors of Elizabethan theatre stretch back into the early Middle Ages. Local pageants, aristocratic and university entertainments and the religious mystery and morality plays had entertained audiences (albeit socially segregated ones) for many years. But it took a surplus of educated university men, some curious restrictions and an architectural innovation to bring them all together into the distinctive form of professional Elizabethan drama.

Playhouses such as the Theatre (built 1576) and its descendants the Rose (1587), the Swan (1595) and the Globe (1599) offered all the world at least a view of the stage – galleried seating for the well-to-do, standing space for the groundlings. Although the earliest theatres were north of the Thames, Bankside in Southwark became the location of choice – timber from the dismantled Theatre even being carried across the river to construct the new Globe – perhaps because it had already become notorious for such nefarious pursuits as prostitution and bear-baiting. In any case the Puritan authorities would not license public stages within City limits, so players were forced into the 'liberties' beyond.

The open-air playhouses encouraged drama to flourish in

1575 Two Dutchmen, members of the extreme Protestant **Anabaptist** sect, are burned for heresy at **Smithfield**.

Edmund Grindal, sympathetic to Puritans, is elected to succeed Matthew Parker as archbishop of Canterbury.

William Byrd, perhaps the first English composer to gain a European reputation, is appointed organist to the Chapel Royal.

1576 Paul and **Peter Wentworth**, leaders of a growing faction of Puritans in the House of Commons, demand the right to discuss religious issues in Parliament, and are sent

Elizabethan London, with professional companies including the Admiral's Men and the Chamberlain's Men, named after their aristocratic patrons, competing for audience loyalty. Because religious subjects were firmly off-limits, writers plundered a variety of sources to construct not only tragedies and comedies on the classical model but a brand-new genre, histories – these last particularly encouraged by the authorities because they were felt to reinforce national unity. That this was a rather optimistic assumption is demonstrated by the fact that a history play called *Richard II* by one William Shakespeare (see p.234) was revived by the earl of Essex on the eve of his abortive rebellion in 1601, the story of one corrupt monarch presumably intended to rouse support for the removal of another.

Most of the time the theatre played safe, though – the main reason for its survival well into the next century. It launched the careers of Christopher Marlowe and Thomas Kyd (whose blockbusting *The Spanish Tragedy* was the most successful play of the 1590s) as well as later writers including Francis Beaumont, John Fletcher, Ben Jonson – and of course Shakespeare.

to the Tower after making disparaging comments about Elizabeth; the queen orders their release.

Martin Frobisher embarks on the first of three expeditions to discover a 'northwest' sea-passage to **Japan** and **China**. Although he doesn't succeed, and also fails to establish a colony in North America, his explorations of the **Newfoundland** and **Nova Scotia** coastline contribute to England's eventual conquest of the North American continent.

In London, **James Burbage** begins building England's first purpose-built playhouse, the **Theatre**, in Shoreditch.

1578 As negotiations continue for a marriage between Elizabeth and d'Alençon, her favourite, Leicester, secretly marries her cousin **Lettice Knollys**.

1579 Continuing unrest in Ireland culminates in the **Desmond Rebellion**, which takes four years to suppress.

Expectations of a royal marriage are raised when d'Alençon visits England, but Elizabeth's privy council advises Elizabeth against the marriage. **John Stubbs** has his right hand amputated for writing *The Discoverie of a Gaping Gulf*, a virulently anti-d'Alençon tract.

The **Jesuits**, leaders of the Counter-Reformation against the spread of Protestantism, found an English college in Rome.

1580 Pope Gregory XIII declares that 'it would not be a sin' to put Elizabeth 'out of the world'. Meanwhile two Jesuits, **Edmund Campion** and **Robert Parsons**, illegally enter England.

Francis Drake completes his **circumnavigation** of the globe.

1581 Fines against **recusants** are raised to £20 a month; **Edmund Campion** is arrested and executed.

A sketch of the Swan theatre by John de Witt, c.1596.

Francis Drake is knighted by Elizabeth.

The **Levant Company** is founded to trade east of Constantinople.

1582 D'Alençon returns to France after a second visit to Elizabeth's court, his marriage proposals rejected.

1583 In September **John Whitgift**, commanded by Elizabeth to halt the spread of Puritanism, succeeds Grindal as archbishop of Canterbury. Greatly trusted by Elizabeth, Whitgift will defend and extend the values of the Anglican church during the latter stages of her reign.

In October the secretary of state, **Walsingham**, uncovers a further Catholic plot against Elizabeth. Its organizer, **Francis Throckmorton**, is arrested and later executed.

Humphrey Gilbert voyages to North America to colonize **Newfoundland**, but is drowned on the return journey.

As London's enthusiasm for theatre-going grows, **Sir Edmund Tilney**, Master of the Revels, forms a new acting troupe called **The Queen's Players** to stage royal performances.

1584 The Spanish ambassador Bernardino Mendoza is expelled from England for complicity in the **Throckmorton Plot**. Relations with Spain deteriorate further when Elizabeth's Protestant ally in the Netherlands, **William I of Orange**, is assassinated.

A Franco-Spanish alliance forms aimed at preventing the Protestant **Henry of Navarre** succeeding to the French throne.

As threats against the queen multiply, representatives from every shire swear to avenge her in the event of an attempted assassination by Catholics in a **Bond of Association**.

Walter Raleigh sends an expedition to the Americas, leading in the following year to the first founding of **Virginia**, an English colony named in the queen's honour.

1585 Parliament passes an **Act for the Preservation of the Queen's Safety**, modelled on the Bond of Association.

As a **Catholic League** gains ascendancy in France, Elizabeth enters into the **Treaty of Nonsuch**, promising to assist Dutch resistance to Spanish rule in the Netherlands.

1586 A plot masterminded by **Anthony Babington** to replace Elizabeth with Mary, Queen of Scots is infiltrated by Walsingham's agents. In August Babington and his co-conspirators are arrested and executed. Both houses of parliament petition the queen to exercise her prerogative by executing Mary, Queen of Scots as well, to deter further attempts on her life. Elizabeth prevaricates, but agrees to the **Treaty of Berwick**, an Anglo-Scottish mutual defence pact.

In October Mary is arraigned by Parliament and found guilty of **treason**, but Elizabeth refuses to affirm her death warrant.

In the House of Commons the Puritan **Peter Wentworth** urges a bill to abolish the episcopacy. When ordered to desist, Wentworth speaks out in favour of free speech and is dispatched to the Tower for the second time.

In September, the adventurer **Sir Philip Sidney** dies three weeks after sustaining a musket-shot wound in the thigh while attacking a supply convoy on its way to the Spanish stronghold **Zutphen** in the Netherlands. In the years following his death Sidney's reputation as an outstanding courtier and poet is enhanced by biographical embellishments of his life and by the piratical publication of works such as *Arcadia* and *Astrophil and Stella*.

The Babington Plot

In the wake of Pope Pius V's bull of 1570 excommunicating Elizabeth and ordering that she should be deposed, a number of plots were hatched against her. One was the conspiracy led in 1586 by the young Derbyshire gentleman **Anthony Babington**. Babington had been a page to Mary, Queen of Scots and, having fallen deeply under her spell, conspired with his accomplices **Chideock Tichborne** and **John Ballard** to set her free and assassinate Elizabeth.

Unfortunately their plans had been infiltrated by Walsingham's spies. Messages to the imprisoned Mary had been concealed in the bungs of beer-barrels delivered to her prison, but these were intercepted and doctored to persuade the conspirators to release further information. Having taken the optimistic step of sitting for a group portrait to commemorate their intended coup, the plotters and their associates divided into two groups – one to kill Elizabeth, the other to release Mary. By the time they realized that they had been discovered, it was too late.

Babington attempted to switch sides, but was arrested anyway – though not before he had ordered an accomplice called **Savage** to go and kill the queen. This Savage might have done had he not lingered at a tailor's on the way, worried that without new clothes he would not gain entry to the palace. Tichborne, incapacitated by a bad leg, had no option but to sit at home and await arrest. Other associates fled to **Epping Forest** where they were soon rounded up and charged with treason.

When told all this, a furious Elizabeth asked Parliament whether, in the circumstances, the punishment of hanging, drawing and quartering could be made any more severe. Parliament replied that it had no authority to change the existing rules, but they were applied scrupulously. Babington, Tichborne, Ballard and Savage were dragged on a hurdle to the scaffold, hanged until they were unconscious, then revived, emasculated, disembowelled and finally cut up. When some spectators became distressed, Elizabeth decided to take pity on the remaining prisoners – they were hanged *before* being mutilated.

1587 Mary, Queen of Scots is executed on 8 February on the orders of the privy council. Elizabeth affects dismay when she is told, but is consoled when the bells of London's churches ring out for 24 hours. As the Queen had feared, however, news of Mary's execution incites Catholic Europe to redouble its efforts to remove her from the throne.

Drake is sent with a naval task force to **Spain**, where he 'singes the King of Spain's beard' by destroying a battle fleet in the harbour of **Cadiz**.

1588 A rebuilt **armada**, numbering some 138 ships, sails toward England in April. But a combination of optimistic timing (a plan to meet with reinforcements at Calais goes badly wrong) and bad weather makes the fleet vulnerable to attack. The English commander, **Lord Howard of Effingham**, is not slow to realize this, and launches a fireship attack on 7 August with devastating results. The armada heads north, but is pursued and heavily attacked at **Gravelines**; in deteriorating weather the Spanish are forced around Scotland and Ireland, many ships being wrecked en route.

The **earl of Leicester** dies in September.

1589 An English force is dispatched to **Portugal** to fight the Spanish, but achieves little.

> 66 I know I have the body of a weak and feeble woman; but I have the heart and stomach of a king, and of a king of England too, and think foul scorn that Parma, or Spain, or any prince of Europe should dare to invade the borders of my realm; to which, rather than any dishonour shall grow by me, I myself will take up arms, I myself will be your general, judge, and rewarder of every one of your virtues in the field. 99
>
> Elizabeth I, addressing her land forces at Tilbury
> in anticipation of a Spanish invasion, 1588

The Spanish Armada

Philip II's decision to invade England was not simply based on a desire to depose his sister-in-law and reinstate Roman Catholicism. Spanish shipping on its way to the Americas was regularly attacked by English pirates, whose activities Elizabeth did nothing to prevent. England also intermittently supplied and supported Protestant rebels in the **Netherlands** fighting against Spanish rule there. The Armada wasn't simply a crusade: it was an instrument of revenge.

But from the beginning the expedition was bedevilled by setbacks. Philip's most experienced admiral, **Santa Cruz**, died before preparations were completed, and his replacement, the **duke of Alva**, was far less equipped to see the operation through. To achieve its purpose, the Armada had first to sail to the Netherlands, where the **duke of Parma**'s army was waiting to embark. But as soon as the Armada entered the English Channel units of Elizabeth's smaller navy – commanded by **Lord Howard of Effingham**, supported by **Sir Francis Drake** and **John Hawkins** – began to harry its flanks. Philip's ships were simply too large to manoeuvre effectively against the smaller and more agile English vessels. But the real damage was done by bad weather. A storm blew up, and Alva failed to rendezvous with Parma. Seeking to escape the confines of the Channel, Alva turned north, but the English continued to fight (inflicting substantial damage off **Gravelines**) and the weather only got worse. Alva's plan was to round the British Isles then sail home, but one by one his ships were wrecked off Britain's and Ireland's coastlines – though contrary to Elizabethan propaganda, some two-thirds of the fleet eventually made it home. Nevertheless Elizabeth was confirmed in her people's minds as a semi-divine figure protected by God Himself.

England's immediate dangers are eased, however, when Henry III of France is assassinated, and is succeeded by the Protestant **Henry IV of Navarre**. As Henry's accession is resisted by the Catholic League, Elizabeth sends her co-religionist material support.

In Scotland, **James VI** marries the Protestant **Anne of Denmark**.

Archbishop Whitgift begins a campaign against **Presbyterianism** – an extreme, anti-episcopalian form of Protestantism given voice in a series of anonymous tracts purporting to be written by **'Martin Marprelate'**.

1590 **Sir Francis Walsingham** dies, and his office remains vacant.

Thomas Cartwright and other Puritan leaders are arrested for heresy, but Whitgift – anxious to deflect charges of bigotry away from the Anglican church – successfully urges them to be spared.

The American colony **Virginia** is found to be deserted by a relief and supply expedition.

The first three books of *The Faerie Queene* by **Edmund Spenser**, a chivalric epic celebrating Queen Elizabeth, are published.

1591 Lord Burghley's younger son **Robert Cecil** gains increasing prominence in government.

An army is dispatched to Brittany to assist **Henry IV** against the Catholic League.

1592 The text of *The Spanish Tragedy* by **Thomas Kyd** (a blockbusting drama of revenge and bloodshed), is published by its author during his lifetime – unusual for a play.

1593 **Robert Devereux, Earl of Essex**, the stepson of the earl of Leicester and Elizabeth's new favourite, joins the privy council.

In Ireland there is renewed unrest.

In May, **Christopher Marlowe** – author of *Tamburlaine*, *Dr Faustus*, *Edward II* and other outstanding stage-works, and possibly a government spy – is killed in a tavern brawl in **Deptford** in suspicious circumstances.

1594 Elizabeth's Spanish physician, **Dr Lopez**, is executed for attempting her assassination.

1595 The **earl of Tyrone** joins the burgeoning rebellion in Ireland.

Drake sets off on his last voyage to the **Caribbean**.

Sir Walter Raleigh sets out on his first voyage to **Guiana** in South America.

1596 A second **armada** sent from Spain to overthrow Elizabeth is dispersed by bad weather.

The ex-pirate and renowned explorer **Francis Drake** dies at sea off **Panama**. He is not mourned by the Spanish, who call him 'the master-thief of the unknown world'.

1597 Essex tries but fails to capture a Spanish treasure fleet; a third **armada** flounders off the French coast.

Pirated versions of **Shakespeare**'s plays *Romeo and Juliet*, *Richard II* and *Richard III* are published.

The theologian **Richard Hooker** completes *Of the Laws of Ecclesiastical Polity*, an eloquent defence of the Elizabethan Church and the main source of subsequent Anglican theology.

1598 Tyrone defeats an English army at **Yellow Ford** in Ulster.

> ❝ In the history of Essex, so perplexed in its issues, so desperate in its perturbations, so dreadful in its conclusion, the spectral agony of an abolished world is discernible through the tragic lineaments of a personal disaster. ❞
>
> Lytton Strachey, *Elizabeth and Essex: A Tragic History* (1928)

The Chancellors Seat

Elizabeth I addressing the House of Lords.

William Shakespeare (1564–1616)

The plays of Shakespeare have been read and performed in more countries, and translated into more languages, than those of any other dramatist. One reason for this extraordinary celebrity is that nearly all the plays were collected seven years after his death by his colleagues **John Heminges** and **Henry Condell**, in a groundbreaking volume entitled *Mr. William Shakespeare's Comedies, Histories, & Tragedies* but now referred to as the **First Folio**. Folios were large, prestigious and expensive books, and that the editors employed the format for Shakespeare – the first time that plays alone had been published in this way – indicates not just the esteem in which he was held but the amount of money that readers were being asked to pay for his work.

Shakespeare's fame during his lifetime is revealed by the success of his poems, one of which, *Venus and Adonis* (1594), was so popular that it went through ten editions by the time of his death – only one copy of the first edition survives, the rest having presumably been read to destruction. But it was as a playwright, not a poet, that Shakespeare chose to build his career. He is recorded in 1595 as a member of the **Chamberlain's Men**, and it was with them that he remained as an actor and a shareholder in the company, an exceptionally stable working relationship that lasted nearly two decades. During that time he wrote an average

France and Spain conclude a peace treaty at **Vervins** shortly before Philip II is succeeded by **Philip III**.

Lord Burghley dies soon after his son **Robert** (later **earl of Salisbury**; see p.241) is appointed secretary of state. **John Stowe** publishes the first edition of *A Survey of London*, which studies the city's history and antiquities.

1599 Against Robert Cecil's advice, Essex is appointed lord lieutenant in Ireland. He concludes a disadvantageous treaty with Tyrone and returns to London. Philip III begins planning a fourth *armada* against England. The **Globe**

of two plays a year, a pattern which seems to have suited him well. An extraordinary burst of creativity around the turn of the 17th century saw him produce some of his finest works, including *As You Like It*, *Twelfth Night*, *Measure for Measure*, *Julius Caesar*, *Hamlet*, *Othello*, *King Lear*, *Macbeth* and *Antony and Cleopatra*. As the title of the First Folio testifies, he was called upon to write in a variety of genres, and by all accounts did very well out of it – the only surviving piece of correspondence addressed to Shakespeare requests a loan of £30 from him, a tidy sum in 1598.

His impact on the course of English history, like so much else, has been immeasurable. The series of 'histories' he wrote in the late 1590s was hugely successful at the time and, despite the plays' unmistakably partisan view of history, they still shape popular perceptions of the past. His devilishly evil Richard III has been accused of obliterating the real king from the record, just as the dissolute but irresistible Prince Hal of the *Henry IV* plays possesses an enduring appeal for audiences and readers alike (perhaps more so than the canny careerist of reality). In his shaping of English history to form drama of remarkable power and depth, it's perhaps easy to agree with his fellow dramatist Ben Jonson that Shakespeare was 'not of an age, but for all time'.

theatre opens on **Bankside** in Southwark.

1600 Following his failure in Ireland, **Essex** is stripped of his offices and imprisoned in the Tower. Released in August, he determines to win back his position, if necessary by force.

Will Adams becomes the first Englishman to set foot in **Japan**.

The **East India Company**, a joint-stock venture destined to become the principal engine of Britain's eastern empire, is established by royal charter in London.

Richard Hakluyt publishes a second, enlarged edition of his *Principal Navigations, Voyages and Discoveries of the English Nation*, an enthusiastic account of English seafaring enterprises that encourages further expeditions.

The population of England and Wales is estimated at **four million**.

1601 Unable to win Elizabeth's favour, **Essex** half-heartedly attempts to stir **rebellion** in London but is quickly arrested. Tried for treason, he is **executed** in February.

When the House of Commons protests the grant of **monopolies** in important commodities to royal servants, Elizabeth agrees to abolish the most grievous of them and silences her critics by delivering her **'Golden Speech'** before parliament. In it she declares: 'Though God hath raised me on high, yet this I count the glory of my crown: that I have reigned with your loves.'

Spanish troops land in Ireland at **Kinsale**, but are besieged there by the new lord lieutenant, **Lord Mountjoy**. Tyrone, attempting to come to their rescue, is defeated, and the Spanish surrender the following year.

Ben Jonson's first solo play, *Every Man in his Humour*, is performed at the **Curtain** theatre.

1602 As Elizabeth, approaching her seventieth birthday, weakens, Robert Cecil enters into a secret correspondence with **James VI of Scotland** by way of preparing for the succession.

The first recorded performance of Shakespeare's *Hamlet* is given in July.

1603 Just hours before her death at **Richmond Palace** on 23 March, Elizabeth I resolves the succession issue – begun 45 years before at her accession – by affirming **James VI of Scotland** her heir.

7

The Stuart kings, the Republic and the Restoration

1603–1688

The peaceful accession of **James I** in 1603 accomplished what Edward I and Henry VIII had attempted by force: a conjunction of the thrones of England and Scotland. The two kingdoms remained administratively separate, however. Despite the king's wishes, attempts at greater integration were resisted on both sides of the border, and it was not until the reign of James's great-granddaughter **Queen Anne** in the early 18th century that a formal union was declared. And in England itself Elizabeth had bequeathed a complex situation. The country was financially weakened by its wars with Spain, the recent rebellion of the earl of Essex indicated a resurgence of aristocratic discontent and the Puritan movement was challenging the established Church, most vociferously in the House of Commons. These were the challenges that faced James when he crossed the border in the spring of 1603.

The new king did not cut an elegant figure: he was short (a full sixteen inches shorter than his queen), ruddy in complexion and some unflattering reports claim that he continually slavered because his tongue was too large for his mouth. He was, however, studious and intelligent and – perhaps most importantly – thoroughly Protestant. That said, he genuinely favoured religious tolerance and prevented England from becoming embroiled in foreign wars until almost the last year of his reign. But, lazy in temperament and a firm proponent of the **divine right** of kings – which held that kings were the images of God upon earth – he was less adroit at handling domestic affairs. It was widely believed that he was too dependent on a string of unpopular intimates, among them **Robert Carr** and **George Villiers**, and he was also contemptuous of the obstinate English Parliament. Despite a shortage of funds in the first years of his reign, he was reluctant to ask Parliament for money, and early in his reign authorized a sale of aristocratic titles that – whatever its short-term benefits – increased corruption and undermined the position of the Crown.

Charles I was certainly as cultured as his father – the collection of paintings he assembled was among the finest in Europe – but shared similar views about the divine status of the monarchy. And he could be equally stubborn, even autocratic, which made him many enemies over the course of his reign. When Charles attempted to initiate **personal rule** in 1629, dispensing with Parliament altogether, he failed to perceive that his enthusiasm for the **Arminians** was eroding his popular support. The Arminians, led by **Archbishop William Laud**, held high-church views and emphasized the importance of religious ritual – and as a consequence were treated with suspicion by many people, who regarded them as Catholics ('papists') in all but name. Despite his unpopularity Charles's personal rule lasted for eleven years, but he was eventually forced by lack of money to summon Parliament once more in 1640. The king's weakened position meant that he was also compelled to accept a number of humiliating restrictions on his power, among them the dismissal of Laud and his chief minister, the **earl of Strafford**, both of whom were later executed. When Parliament continued to make trouble, Charles took matters into his own hands and impeached his principal opponents for treason before marching into the House of Commons to arrest them. They had escaped beforehand, however, and as a consequence Charles decided to abandon London and set up base at the royalist stronghold of **Oxford**, in the process igniting what would become known as the **Civil Wars**.

The Civil Wars were vastly more complex than the simple image, often presented, of Royalist **Cavaliers** versus Puritan **Roundheads**. They were driven by social and economic as well as religious and political forces, and brought about domestic upheaval of unprecedented proportions. Ultimately, though, the overall political outcome began to seem inevitable: Charles only had enough money to fight a short war and, when it spiralled out of control after the 1645 defeat at **Naseby**, he was destined to lose his crown. After the army became convinced that peace was impossible while he was still alive, he also lost his head. A **Commonwealth**, controlled by a military junta headed by **Oliver Cromwell**, took his place.

As long as Cromwell survived, the Republic looked relatively secure. Despite a naval war against the Dutch, England allied itself with the other Protestant nations of northern Europe and trade continued to expand – as did colonization in **America**. But Cromwell's death in 1558 produced a vacuum at the centre of national politics which **General George Monck** exploited in 1660 when he made moves to restore **Charles II** to the throne. Yet the new king was faced by the same problems that had beset his father. Parliament failed to make adequate financial provisions for the Crown, and suspicions about Charles's involvement with Catholicism continued to dog the monarchy. Although addicted to the pleasures of life, among them a plethora of mistresses, Charles II dealt with the shifting sands of Restoration politics relatively successfully – and certainly more successfully than his brother and successor, **James II**. James's cataclysmic loss of support from all major factions in Parliament – and, crucially, the Anglican–dominated Army – led to his nervous breakdown and subsequent flight from England.

In retrospect the century was one of unusual commotion, private as much as public, but it was also a period of outstanding cultural achievement. It witnessed poets **Andrew Marvell**, **John Milton** and **John Dryden**; architects **Inigo Jones** and **Christopher Wren**; composers **Orlando Gibbons**, **William Lawes** and **John Blow**. In **Thomas Hobbes** the country could boast its first internationally significant – if somewhat idiosyncratic – political philosopher. And in the emerging sciences, too, **Isaac Newton**, **Francis Bacon**, **Robert Boyle** and **Robert Hooke** demonstrated that, in some respects at least, England was at the cutting-edge of intellectual progress.

1603 **James VI Stuart of Scotland** is warmly welcomed in England as he travels south to claim the throne – even if the risk of plague in London means that he is forced to avoid the elaborate public events celebrating his accession.

Sir Walter Raleigh is dismissed as captain of the guard and later imprisoned in the Tower on suspicion of conspiring to replace James with his Catholic cousin **Arabella Stuart**.

Father William Watson hatches the unsuccessful **'Bye Plot'** against the throne in response to the continuing collection of recusancy fines.

The war in **Ireland** ends in March following Tyrone's surrender.

1604 Parliament debates whether England, Wales and Scotland – now ruled by the same monarch – should be brought together in a single **union**, but although James I adopts the title **king of Great Britain** there is little enthusiasm for this move.

The **Treaty of London** formally ends hostilities with **Spain**, and James's heir by his wife Anne of Denmark, **Prince Henry**, is engaged to the Spanish infanta **Anna**, daughter of **Philip III**.

The **Hampton Court Conference** is convened by James to review the Church in England. The Elizabethan Settlement is retained, and existing anti-Catholic laws are kept in force. A new translation of the **Bible** is commissioned by royal authority.

1605 Robert Cecil, kept by James as the government's chief minister, is created **earl of Salisbury**.

The second session of James I's first parliament is disrupted in November by the discovery of the **Gunpowder Plot**.

Francis Bacon publishes *The Advancement of Learning*, an attempt to classify existing scientific disciplines and promote experimentation.

1606 Following the trial and execution of the Gunpowder Plot's conspirators, tougher **recusancy laws** are introduced and a new **Oath of Allegiance** to the king is imposed on English Catholics.

Although James I orders the creation of a new **national flag** symbolizing England and Scotland, the House of Commons continues to resist formal union.

An expedition sets out across the Atlantic to re-establish the colony of **Virginia**.

Perhaps in order to honour the king, **Shakespeare** (see p.234) writes his Scottish play, *Macbeth*, around this time.

1607 The king's favourite, **Robert Carr**, is knighted, the first of several honours bestowed on him to the chagrin of the 'Tudor' establishment.

Raleigh, still imprisoned, is stripped of his estates.

The Gunpowder Plot

When he came to the throne in 1603, James was determined to extend his policy of religious tolerance by relaxing existing laws that penalized Catholics for practising their religion. But the hard-line parliamentary response to his suggestion forced the king in the opposite direction: he had no option but to leave them as they were. One response to this decision would be infamous – the Gunpowder Plot.

The plan was simple enough: a group of Catholic gentlemen had decided to blow up the House of Lords during the state opening of Parliament on 5 November 1605, and with it the king and his entire government. The conspiracy was led by Robert Catesby and Thomas Percy, but the best-known conspirator was the explosives expert Guy Fawkes. Fawkes came from an established Yorkshire family, but had spent most of his adult life serving in the Spanish army after converting to Catholicism. He was recruited by Catesby in 1604, and was responsible for planting at least twenty barrels of gunpowder in a cellar that ran underneath the Parliament building. The plot was derailed, however, by another conspirator, Francis Tresham, who realized that a number of his friends and Catholic peers might die if not forewarned and wrote to persuade his brother-in-law Lord Monteagle not to attend the ceremony. The letter was passed to the Privy Council, and Fawkes was picked up on the day itself. Under torture he revealed the names of his co-conspirators, who were apprehended and charged with treason following a brief siege at Catesby's house. Following their trial in January 1606 all were condemned to execution – by the time-honoured method of hanging, drawing and quartering.

The plot proved to be the last serious attempt by militant English Catholics to overturn the Anglican settlement, but its memory – commemorated annually in firework displays on Guy Fawkes' Night and more personally by the burning of the 'guy' – demonstrated that there was continuing discord over questions of faith and toleration. When the Anglican settlement was suspended in the mid-century, it was not the Catholics but the Puritans who temporarily triumphed.

'Pray remember the 5th of November' – a Bowles & Carver catchpenny from the late 18th century.

Jamestown in Virginia becomes England's first permanent settlement in North America.

1609 To strengthen English rule in Ireland, commissioners are appointed to oversee the **'plantation'** of Ulster with English settlers.

1610 Salisbury endeavours to persuade Parliament to accept a **'Great Contract'** designed to ease the king's financial difficulties by the grant of regular subsidies, but the House of Commons rejects his initiative.

Prince Henry is created **prince of Wales**.

Arabella Stuart is imprisoned for marrying the **earl of Hertford**, another claimant to the throne.

1611 Parliament is **dissolved** in February. With a brief exception in 1614, James I rules without Parliament until 1621. To improve royal revenues, Salisbury devises the new title of **baronet** – a hereditary knighthood – which is widely sold for £1,095.

Arabella Stuart escapes captivity but is soon recaptured.

After four years' work by a team of 54 scholars, the so-called **'Authorized' Bible** is published (although it is never actually authorized as such). Drawing on unacknowledged previous translations made by **William Tyndale**, **John Wyclif** (see p.147) and others, the 'King James' Bible rapidly achieves scriptural status among Anglicans and other English-speaking Protestants.

1612 Two 'extreme' **Protestants** become the last heretics to be burned at the stake in England. The burning of **'witches'** – often distressed women ostracized by their immediate communities – continues, however.

Following the death of **Salisbury**, James I elects to become his own **secretary of state**.

In November, relations between king and aristocracy deteriorate when the popular **Prince Henry** dies; Henry's 12-year-old brother **Charles** becomes heir apparent.

1613 A scandal is created when the **countess of Essex** sues for divorce in order to marry **Sir Robert Carr** (created **earl of Somerset** later in the year) and the king intervenes in her favour.

James's daughter **Elizabeth** is married to the leading Calvinist prince in Germany, **Frederick the Elector Palatine of the Rhine**, dashing the hopes of 'conservatives' anxious to see a Spanish match. Anglo-Spanish relations and the standing of the pro-Spanish **earl of Northampton** are improved, however, when James I strikes up a convivial friendship with the newly arrived Spanish ambassador, **Diego Sarmiento** (later **count of Gondomar**).

1614 James I summons a new Parliament in the hope of raising badly needed taxes, but the **'Addled Parliament'**, as it becomes known, refuses his entreaties and is quickly dissolved.

Northampton dies, and is replaced as lord treasurer by his cousin, the **earl of Suffolk**; **Somerset** is appointed lord chamberlain. The future royal favourite, **George Villiers**, is presented at court and soon knighted.

Negotiations begin for a marriage between **Prince Charles** and a Spanish princess (infanta).

Sir William Cockayne persuades James to suspend the **Merchant Adventurers'** charter and prohibit the sale of unfinished cloth to the Netherlands. In the ensuing trade war with the Dutch, crisis is created in the English cloth industry when it fails to meet domestic demand.

1615 Somerset and his wife are arrested on suspicion of murdering **Sir Thomas Overbury**, an opponent of their marriage.

Villiers continues his rise to prominence by being appointed a **gentleman of the bedchamber**. The financier **Lionel Cranfield** is appointed surveyor-general.

A Spanish demand that any children born to Prince Charles and the infanta should be raised as **Catholics** creates widespread consternation, but James I persists with the marriage negotiations.

1616 Villiers is created a **viscount** and **knight of the garter**; Charles is made **prince of Wales**.

The Somersets are found guilty of Overbury's murder, but

Raleigh and Bacon

The two figures most famously associated with Jacobean England were products of the Elizabethan age. Both trained as lawyers, turned their hands to writing history and were damaged by a penchant for intrigue. Both, too, have been accused of failing to make best use of their diverse talents.

Sir Walter Raleigh (1554–1618) was the son of a Devonshire squire who climbed to become Elizabeth's favourite. A pirate and adventurer who tried unsuccessfully to create new colonies in the Americas, his career was interrupted by imprisonment in the Tower of London in 1588, when the queen discovered his secret marriage to Elizabeth Throckmorton (one of her maids of honour). Released, he became obsessed with the myth of El Dorado, and in 1596 he sailed past Spanish guns up the Orinoco to claim Guiana. In 1603 he was accused of plotting against James I and was returned to the Tower. His second incarceration lasted thirteen years, during which he wrote the grandly titled *History of the World* and indulged a passion for chemistry. In 1616 he was again freed and revisited Guiana, but his attacks on Spanish shipping at a sensitive moment landed him in further trouble, and Raleigh was executed shortly afterwards.

Francis Bacon, Viscount of St Albans (1561–1626) pursued a

spared the death penalty.

Sir Walter Raleigh is released from the Tower to prepare an expedition to **Guiana**.

Shakespeare dies, and is buried in his home town of **Stratford-upon-Avon** (see p.234). His younger colleague, **Ben Jonson**, publishes *Works*, a collection of his plays and poems.

1617 Villiers is created **earl of Buckingham**.

As the **'Cockayne scheme'** flounders, the Merchant

more sedentary but finally more useful career. Although appointed a clerk to the court of Star Chamber in 1582, his early career soon ground to a halt – partly because he opposed the grant of royal subsidies in Parliament and partly because of his support for the earl of Essex. His burning ambition for high office, though, dampened continuing scruples: under James I Bacon openly advocated a fuller union between England and Scotland, and defended the royal prerogative. As a result he was rewarded with the posts of solicitor-general (1607), attorney-general (1613) and finally lord chancellor (1618). Preferment came at the expense of his rivals, however, and in 1621 Bacon's enemies had their revenge when charges of bribery were brought against him. His sojourn in the Tower was brief, but his career was finished. His last years were spent adding to the already voluminous list of his writings, including a third edition of his popular *Essays* (1626). But his more important legacy was his contribution to English science (see p.278). Although he made no significant scientific discovery, his philosophical advancement of an experimental outlook, rooted in a belief that nature should be mastered for the benefit of man, helped establish an intellectual climate in which real breakthroughs could occur.

Adventurers' charter is restored and normal trading relations with the **Netherlands** resume.

1618 **Raleigh** creates a crisis in Anglo-Spanish relations by attacking a Spanish settlement in **Guiana**. Returning to England, he is imprisoned and executed despite widespread rioting on his behalf.

The king's popularity, already weakened by the favouritism extended toward Buckingham, is further damaged when **tax reforms** instituted by **Cranfield** begin to bite.

The philosopher and scientist **Francis Bacon** is appointed **lord chancellor**.

In Europe, the **Thirty Years War** commences after Bohemians reject their king-elect **Emperor Ferdinand II** in favour of **Frederick of the Rhine**, James I's son-in-law. As pressure on James to assist Frederick mounts, negotiations with Spain are suspended.

1619 James's queen, **Anne of Denmark**, dies. The king's financial problems are so acute that her embalmed body lies in state for ten weeks before sufficient funds can be found to pay for the funeral – even though her death reduces royal household expenditures.

Inigo Jones begins work on the **Banqueting House** at Whitehall, architecturally the most significant new building of James's reign because of its introduction of the pure Classical style into England.

The painter **Nicholas Hilliard**, renowned for his miniature portraits, dies.

1620 James I enters into a covert treaty with **Spain** agreeing to the marriage of Prince Charles to the infanta.

Frederick of the Rhine is driven out of Bohemia following the **Battle of the White Mountain** (outside Prague), and later in the year even loses control of his own Palatinate.

Economic depression and continuing tensions between Anglicans and Puritans inspire the **Pilgrim Fathers** to set sail in the *Mayflower* and found an English colony in what they call **New England**.

1621 James I calls his third **Parliament**.

Cranfield is appointed **lord treasurer**.

1623 Prince Charles travels to Spain incognito with **Buckingham** to arrange his marriage. The mission runs into severe difficulties when **Philip IV** insists on complete toleration of Catholics in England as part of the marriage settlement. Charles agrees to undertake instruction in Catholicism, but on returning to England in October he and Buckingham advocate that the marriage be broken off. His star now firmly in the ascendant, the earl is created **duke of Buckingham**, the first non-royal ducal creation since 1551.

1624 James I's **fourth Parliament** grants the king substantial subsidies in anticipation of war against Spain and the Holy Roman Emperor. But an army sent to restore **Frederick of the Rhine** is so badly equipped that most of its troops desert before even reaching the Netherlands.

A new marriage treaty for Prince Charles, this time with **Princess Henrietta Maria** of France, is swiftly negotiated.

As England's economy begins to recover, **Virginia** is made a royal colony.

1625 James I dies in March and is succeeded by **Charles I**, who marries **Henrietta Maria** in May.

Parliament grants the Crown **customs revenues** ('**tonnage and poundage**') for one year, but Charles will attempt to collect these for the rest of his reign without parliamentary approval.

As the **Thirty Years War** expands, England finds itself at

A detail from a 17th century map of Virginia.

war with Spain, but an expedition led by Buckingham to ransack **Cadiz** fails.

1626 Charles I summons a new **parliament**, but it refuses to grant fresh subsidies in protest at the king's continuing collection of tonnage and poundage, and instead attempts to impeach **Buckingham** for corruption. To finance the war against Spain, Charles orders a forced 'loan' to be raised – in effect an arbitrary tax.

Francis Bacon dies of a chill contracted during an experiment to refrigerate a hen by stuffing it with snow.

1627 Five knights, arrested for refusing to pay Charles's enforced loan, are refused the writ of **habeas corpus**. When their case goes before the courts, judgement is given in the king's favour on the grounds that the king's special command is sufficient cause to warrant imprisonment.

Buckingham leads a disastrous expedition to France, to relieve **Huguenots** besieged at **La Rochelle**.

1628 Charles I calls his **third Parliament**. Among new members of the House of Commons is **Oliver Cromwell**, MP for Huntingdon. Before it will consider the king's requests for subsidies the House presents him with the **Petition of Right**, outlining grievances against the Crown – including the arbitrary arrest of its subjects.

In August, **Buckingham** is assassinated by **John Felton**, a Puritan. Since Buckingham is known to be sympathetic to **Arminianism**, a high-church doctrine espoused by some church leaders, his murder is indicative of increasing religious tensions. Shortly afterwards **Bishop William Laud of Bath and Wells**, the leader of the Arminians, is elevated to the see of London. **Thomas Wentworth**, previously a stern critic of Charles I, is made a baron, and later becomes **earl of Strafford**.

The fall of **La Rochelle** to **Louis XIII** delivers a body-blow to French Huguenots, many of whom seek resettlement in England.

William Harvey, a physician at St Bartholomew's Hospital in London, publishes *De Motu Cordis,* which outlines his theory of the circulation of the blood in animals and of the heart as a pump.

1629 The House of Commons passes resolutions against Arminianism and against the king's continued levy of customs dues without parliamentary consent. Angered, Charles dissolves Parliament and embarks on an eleven-year period of **personal rule**. Lack of funds makes him wary of further involvement in Europe's wars, however: hostilities with France are brought to an end by the **Treaty of Susa**.

1630 The war with Spain is ended by the **Treaty of Madrid**.

A bad harvest encourages more Puritans to emigrate to New England.

1631 The **earl of Castlehaven**, a well-known peer, is tried and convicted for sodomy and rape in a trial that causes a national sensation.

1632 Strafford is appointed lord deputy in **Ireland**.

The Flemish artist **Anthony Van Dyck** settles in England and is appointed court painter.

1633 William Laud becomes archbishop of Canterbury, an elevation that prompts some to speculate that the throne may be contemplating a return to Catholicism.

The Puritan **William Prynne** publishes *Histriomastix*, a huge tract attacking the 'immorality' of the theatre. The following year he is hauled before the Court of Star Chamber for his none-too-subtle description of female actors as 'notorious whores', which is taken as an insult to the masque-loving queen. The fact that his ears are cut off as punishment does not deter him, though, and four years later he is sentenced to have the rest of his ears removed and his forehead branded.

The *Collected Works* of **John Donne**, erstwhile dean of St Paul's Cathedral, is published two years after his death – a volume containing, among much else, erotic lyrics that he was understandably eager not to see in print during his lifetime.

1634 Ship money, a royal tax aimed to supply the navy, is imposed on England's coastal counties.

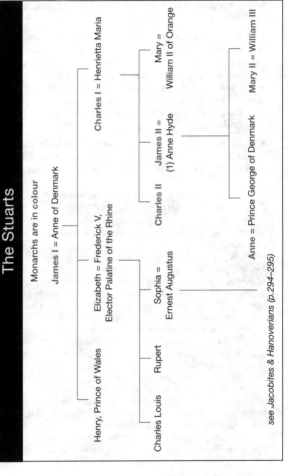

The Stuarts

Monarchs are in colour

James I = Anne of Denmark

Charles I = Henrietta Maria

Elizabeth = Frederick V,
Elector Palatine of the Rhine

Henry, Prince of Wales

Charles Louis

Rupert

Sophia =
Ernest Augustus

Charles II

James II =
(1) Anne Hyde

Mary =
William II of Orange

Anne = Prince George of Denmark

Mary II = William III

see Jacobites & Hanoverians (p.294-295)

1635 Ship money is extended to inland counties, causing widespread resentment and unrest.

1637 As **Arminianism** spreads, Puritan pamphleteers are increasingly sentenced to mutilation for speaking out against liturgical reforms introduced by Laud to promote the use of 'Catholic' ritual. The Calvinist bishop of Lincoln, **John Williams**, is sent to the Tower for criticizing the archbishop. Severe restrictions imposed on the press by the **Court of Star Chamber** only add to the growing tide of dissent.

1638 Serious differences erupt between Charles I and his Scottish subjects over whether the **Scottish Church** should follow an Anglican or Presbyterian path. **Strafford**,

Parliament and Puritans

Like its French and Spanish counterparts, the English Parliament grew out of an enlarged royal council, the purpose of which was to offer the throne advice and agree its policies. Initially nobles and others sat together in a single chamber, but as early as the 13th century Parliament began to divide into two houses. By Tudor times, the **House of Lords** and **House of Commons** were permanently separated. Those entitled to sit in the Lords by right were **barons**, **viscounts**, **earls**, **marquesses** and **dukes**, as well as **bishops** and – until the dissolution of the monasteries – some **abbots**. The 'other house' was made up of **knights of the shire** and **town burgesses**. Since these far outnumbered aristocrats, however, some sort of selection process had to exist. Out of this emerged **elective representation**, which in turn meant that the throne gradually lost control of who sat in the Commons.

In the 1530s, Parliament's independence was further enhanced by **Thomas Cromwell**'s deliberate strategy of using its power to realize the Henrican Reformation. The result, from the middle of Elizabeth's reign onwards, was institutionalized opposition. This became further entrenched when a group known as the **Puritans**, having gained a reputation for brutality in Ireland, urges stern reprisals against the rebellious Scots.

1639 Charles I raises an **army** to bring the Scots to heel, but no campaign is mounted. Faced by a chronic lack of money, the king reluctantly decides to summon a parliament. Before it can convene, a **'taxpayer's strike'**, aimed principally against ship money, spreads through England. Royal control over local government is seriously impaired.

1640 The **'short Parliament'** sits, but is dissolved within a month after it fails to agree new subsidies for the king.

Strafford is appointed the king's chief adviser and lord lieutenant in Ireland. In October, Charles I's deteriorating

who argued that the English Reformation had not gone nearly far enough, began to gain Parliamentary influence – and used it to demand 'purer' forms of worship.

In retrospect the Puritans were perhaps the first parliamentary party, though in reality they were united as much by their high-church enemies – who insisted on calling all advocates of plain worship 'Puritans' – as by common theological ground. When that enemy was weakened by the interregnum, the splits in the Puritan movement became wider than ever, with a number of different sects competing for freedom of expression. Some, such as the singularly named William Fiennes, Lord Saye and Sele, were sufficiently disgruntled with England to seek abandoning it altogether, and invested heavily in New England and the Bahamas in the hope of establishing godly aristocratic communities there. Even when these schemes failed they remained powerful – and it was out of these old, high-ranking Puritan families that the earliest manifestation of the Whig Party emerged to challenge another Stuart king, James II.

authority is further undermined when the Scots defeat an English force at **Newburn**. Charles is forced to concede the **Treaty of Ripon**, obliging him to pay the Scots £850 a day until a final agreement is reached – money he simply doesn't have. In desperation Charles summons a fresh parliament, known as the **'Long Parliament'**, in November. Such is the weakness of his position he is unable to prevent the impeachment of either **Strafford** or **Archbishop Laud**. Sensing their hour has come, **Puritans** launch fresh attacks against Arminian reforms. A body of Londoners submit their **'Root and Branch' petition** to the Commons, calling for the abolition of bishops.

1641 Parliament forces Charles I to accept the **Triennial Act**, stipulating that a parliament be summoned at least once every three years. Another act legislates that no parliament should be dissolved without its own consent. **Strafford** is executed by an **Act of Attainder**, and the **Court of Star Chamber** is abolished.

In November, as confidence amongst Charles's opponents swells, a **Grand Remonstrance**, denouncing the king's misgovernment and the subversive influence of bishops, is passed in the Commons by 159 votes to 148. The king travels to **Scotland**, but fails to remedy the situation there. There is also renewed unrest in Ireland, where Catholics massacre Protestants in Ulster.

1642 Charles I attempts to arrest five of his principal critics in the Commons – **John Pym**, **John Hampden**, **Denzil Holles**, **Sir Arthur Haslerigg** and **William Strode** – but they flee before his soldiers arrive. Relations between king and Parliament collapse and a broad coalition of opponents to Charles forms, including not just Puritans but merchants and members of the aristocracy too. As England slides into **Civil War**, Charles raises his standard at **Nottingham** on 22 August. The first significant encounter between Royalists (sometimes called **'Cavaliers'**) and the supporters of Parliament (**'Roundheads'**) takes place at **Edgehill** on 23 October, in an attempt to halt Charles's advance on London from his strongholds in the west. The king's nephew, **Prince Rupert of the Rhine**, commanding the Royalist cavalry, leads a devastating charge, but the effect of this is largely negated when Rupert's undisciplined soldiers begin looting the parliamentary baggage train. Led by the **Earl of Essex**, the parliamentary side counterattacks, and although by the end of the day Charles narrowly holds the field, the battle is inconclusive. The weakened Royalists push on toward London, but are checked at **Turnham Green**, and the king is forced to set

© HISTORICAL PICTURE ARCHIVE/CORBIS

A woodcut from a Civil Wars recruitment pamphlet.

up his headquarters at **Oxford** while the capital remains in parliamentary hands.

1643 Minor skirmishes between Royalists and Parliamentarians are fought throughout the year, but neither side is able to secure a decisive advantage. At the **First Battle of Newbury**, fought on 20 September, Charles is again prevented from seizing London. Parliament, hampered by a divided leadership and the reluctance of the earls of **Essex** and **Manchester** to fight too strenuously against the king, is weakened by the deaths of **John Hampden** in June and **John Pym** in December. Conversely the Scots, through a **Solemn League and Covenant**, agree to support Parliament. As a result the parliamentary position is consolidated, in the north especially.

1644 Charles I, unwilling to enter into negotiations with his enemies, summons a **royalist parliament** at Oxford. A Scottish army marches into England, and a major engagement is fought at **Marston Moor** on 2 July. Despite the flight of the Scots commander the earl of Leven – who is convinced that Parliament has been defeated – the Parliamentary army led by **Oliver Cromwell** defeats Charles's forces under the command of **Prince Rupert** and the **earl of Newcastle**. Charles loses the last vestiges of authority in the north, while royalist hopes are further dashed by Rupert's decision to surrender **Bristol** and another defeat at the **Second Battle of Newbury** on 27 October. Furious at his nephew's apparent cowardice in quitting his command, Charles orders Rupert into **exile**. It remains unclear at this stage, however, what the ultimate aims of the Parliamentarians are – whether to bring the king under control or remove him from the throne.

The poet **John Milton**, sympathetic to Parliament but opposed to its Presbyterian supporters, publishes *Areopagatica* – a sustained defence of freedom of expression.

> **EARL OF MANCHESTER:** 'If we beat the King ninety-nine times, yet he is King still and so will his posterity be after him; but if the King beat us once we shall be hanged, and our posterity be made slaves.'
>
> **CROMWELL:** 'My Lord, if this be so, why did we take up arms at first? This is against fighting ever hereafter. If so, let us make peace, be it never so base.'
>
> Calendar of State Papers, entry for 10 November, 1644

1645 King and Parliament attempt to come to terms at **Uxbridge**, but negotiations quickly break down.

Archbishop Laud is beheaded by Parliament on 10 January.

In response to criticisms of the poor quality and indiscipline of Parliament's troops, their commander **Sir Thomas Fairfax** creates the **New Model Army**, and it is this force – together with Cromwell's mounted **'Ironsides'** – that wins a convincing victory at **Naseby** on 14 June.

1646 Cromwell crushes a royalist army led by **Lord Ashley** at **Stowe-on-the-Wold** on 26 March.

On 5 May **Charles I** surrenders to the Scots and is imprisoned at **Edinburgh**. As Oxford capitulates, the **First Civil War** is brought to a conclusion.

Parliament, now controlled by Puritans, orders a **Presbyterian Church** to be established in England, and the offices of archbishop and bishop are abolished. But the problem of what to do about the king persists, and there are widening divisions among Parliament's followers. In the army, **Agitators** and **Independents**, and also an extra-parliamentary group called the **Levellers**, begin pressing for political reforms. Hoping to take advantage of his enemy's disunity, **Charles** rejects terms proposed at **Newcastle**, which would give Parliament control of the militia for twenty years.

The Civil Wars

The so-called **English Civil War** (1642–51) was really nothing of the kind. It was a series of conflicts that spanned nine grim years, and it spilled over into Scotland, Ireland and Wales. Nor were its divisions clear-cut: there were Puritans amongst the royalists, traditionalists amongst the parliamentarians. And even the armies themselves had difficulty identifying one another in battle; although individual regiments may have worn liveries, there were no set uniforms. Even the abusive nicknames that became attached to the opposing sides don't tell us much: not all those who fought for the king were libertine 'cavaliers' (from the Spanish *caballero*); nor were parliamentarians all 'roundheads' – a term coined by Queen Henrietta Maria, remarking on the Puritan Samuel Barnardiston's short-cropped hair.

Perhaps it's not surprising that historians have argued over the nature of the wars. Some see them as an essentially medieval battle between king and over-mighty subject, while others have interpreted the conflict in Marxist terms as part of a revolution led by the middle orders of society. What seems certain is that it was the army and those in charge of it that benefited. At the outbreak of the wars **Oliver Cromwell** (see p.268) was an obscure East

1647 **Charles I** is handed over by the Scots to Parliament, which orders its army to disband. Infuriated by Parliament's unwillingness to pay its wages, however, the **army revolts**, and on 4 June seizes the king from **Holmby House** in **Northamptonshire**. Joined by Cromwell and some other Parliamentarians, the army takes control of **London** in August. Supported by the Levellers, the army's Agitators form a deputation to meet with their commanders and representatives of Parliament. The ensuing **Putney Debates**, under Cromwell's chairmanship, open on 28 October, but no conclusion is reached about the future government of England. While the Levellers recommend extending the parliamentary franchise to all adult males,

Anglian landowner, but in the course of the conflict his genius as a cavalry commander came to the fore, and it was largely owing to his military success at **Naseby** and elsewhere that he ended up as leader of the **Commonwealth** and, later, **Protector** – king in all but name.

That Cromwell would end up in this position hardly seemed likely in the wars' immediate aftermath. The prospect of trying and executing the king was more than many on the parliamentarian side could stomach, and resolute old Puritans such as the **earl of Manchester** and **Lord Saye and Sele** retired to their homes rather than have anything to do with it. Nevertheless in January 1649 a court was established, and in spite of Charles's refusal to acknowledge it, he was tried and condemned to death. But the king went down fighting. In his final statement on the scaffold he declared: '[The people's] liberty and freedom consists in having government, those laws by which their lives and their goods may be most their own. It is not their having a share in the government, that is nothing appertaining to them. A subject and a sovereign are clean different things.'

'conservative' parliamentarians favour the retention of power among the landed elite. As a result, the Levellers inspire continued mutiny.

King Charles escapes custody on 11 November and flees to **Carisbrooke Castle** on the **Isle of Wight**, where, at the end of December, he signs an agreement with the **Scots**. In return for his agreement to abolish the episcopacy in Scotland, the Scots promise to restore Charles to his English throne by force.

George Fox forms the **Society of Friends** in **Leicestershire**, a puritanical sect dedicated to promoting 'inward' spiritual experience and later known as the **Quakers**,

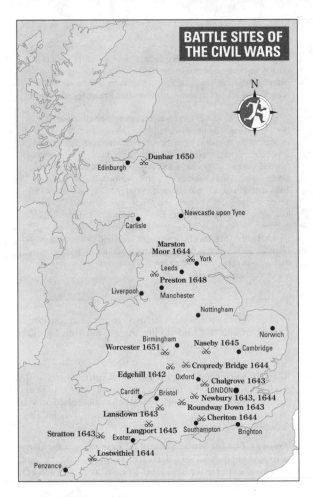

BATTLE SITES OF THE CIVIL WARS

N

Edinburgh ✂ Dunbar 1650

Newcastle upon Tyne

Carlisle

Marston Moor 1644 ✂ York

Leeds ✂
Preston 1648

Liverpool Manchester

Nottingham

Norwich

Birmingham **Naseby 1645** ✂
Worcester 1651 ✂ Cambridge

✂ Cropredy Bridge 1644
Edgehill 1642 Oxford ✂ **Chalgrove 1643**
Cardiff Bristol LONDON
✂ **Newbury 1643, 1644**
Lansdown 1643 ✂ **Roundway Down 1643**
✂ **Cheriton 1644**
Stratton 1643 ✂ **Langport 1645** Southampton Brighton
Exeter
✂ **Lostwithiel 1644**
Penzance

possibly because of their bodily shaking when possessed by the holy spirit.

1648 As news of Charles's actions spreads, royalists resume arms, sparking the **Second Civil War**. But the conflict is short-lived: a Scottish army of invasion under the **duke of Hamilton** is defeated in a three-day battle at **Preston** beginning on 17 August.

On 1 December the king is seized by the army, and a week later, with Cromwell's complicity, the Long Parliament is **purged** of the king's supporters by **Colonel Thomas Pride**. On 13 December the sixty-odd members who have not been purged – known as the **Rump Parliament** – vote that the king should stand trial.

In Europe, the **Thirty Years War** is brought to an end through the **Peace of Westphalia** (24 October).

1649 Charles I is tried by a specially convened court and sentenced to death by 59 signatories, known as **regicides**. Despite refusing to acknowledge the legitimacy of his accusers, the king is **beheaded** on an improvised scaffold outside the Banqueting House in Whitehall on 30 January. England becomes a **republic** under the military dictatorship of **Oliver Cromwell**. In Scotland and parts of Ireland, however, Charles's son **Charles II** is proclaimed king.

In May, as theatre, music and other forms of public entertainment are outlawed, England is declared a **'free commonwealth'**.

In the same month there is further Leveller-inspired **mutiny** in the army as it becomes apparent that Cromwell has no intention of extending political rights.

In September, Cromwell campaigns in **Ireland**. Storming **Drogheda** and **Wexford**, he orders the massacre of Catholics in revenge for previous Catholic atrocities against Protestants.

The Frontispiece to Charles I's *Eikon Basilike* (1648). The king kneels in prayer, clasping a crown of thorns while his earthly crown lies at his feet.

At **Walton-on-Thames** in **Surrey**, a spin-off group of the Levellers known as the **Diggers** endeavour to institute a communist society based on shared ownership of land and dwellings.

1650 Cromwell returns from Ireland and is appointed **lord general** and **commander-in-chief** of all the Commonwealth's armies in succession to Thomas Fairfax.

Charles II arrives in Scotland, where, despite the defeat of a Scottish army at **Dunbar** by Cromwell on 3 September and the subsequent surrender of **Edinburgh Castle** to the English, he is crowned at **Scone**.

A group of extreme Protestants known as the **Ranters** becomes active in London and other English cities, but are suppressed by Parliament. By the end of the year the **Digger** movement has also collapsed.

1651 Having lost Perth to Cromwell, **Charles II** crosses the border into England, but his small army is decisively beaten at **Worcester** on 3 September. He escapes to **France** in October.

Thomas Hobbes publishes *Leviathan*, perhaps the most brilliant work of political philosophy written in the English language.

1652 Cromwell continues with his brutal 'pacification' of **Ireland**.

The **First Anglo-Dutch War** breaks out as a consequence of England's assertion of maritime sovereignty. **Admiral Robert Blake** defeats a Dutch fleet in the **Battle of the Downs**, but the English fleet is subsequently defeated by the Dutch at **Dungeness**.

England's growing number of colonies in **North America** agree to recognize parliamentary authority.

Thomas Hobbes (1588–1679)

Hobbes was one of the most influential – and most controversial – thinkers in English political philosophy. His masterpiece, *Leviathan* (which means 'monstrous beast', a metaphor for the state), famously declares that human life is, in its natural form, 'solitary, poor, nasty, brutish and short'. Given that this is so, Hobbes proposes a stark solution: it is in the subject's interests to embrace a strong government that will safeguard his security, even if it curtails his liberty. In other words, authoritarian rule is better than anarchy.

Hobbes's thesis was unmistakably engaged in the political debates of his time, particularly the ongoing civil wars, and it twice landed him in trouble: first in 1640 when he was forced to flee to France because he was believed to support royal absolutism; once again when he was suspected of atheism after *Leviathan* was published. At the Restoration he was criticized for his defence of the Cromwellian regime – a charge which has some basis in fact, but which undervalues his careful delineation of how 'liberty' could be achieved and what it actually meant. He also argued that people must agree with each other to be ruled in this way (in effect, they must set up a form of social contract) and that it was in their interests to do so; thus his theory is in the truest sense interested in the 'common-wealth'.

And while life was certainly solitary, poor, nasty and brutish for many of his contemporaries, Hobbes demonstrated that perhaps he was too cynical about the last component of his most-quoted statement – he lived to the grand old age of 91. Or, as his acquaintance John Aubrey put it in a collection of biographical snippets, *Brief Lives*, 'he was against "too hasty concluding", which he did endeavour as much as he could to avoid.'

1653 Following further tensions with the army, Cromwell dissolves the **Rump Parliament** in April. He calls a fresh assembly, known as **Barebone's Parliament** (named after an MP for London, **Praise-God Barebone**), which sits from July until December. It produces an **Instrument of**

Government, outlining constitutional arrangements for an administration led by Cromwell under his newly proclaimed title of **Lord Protector**.

The English and Dutch navies fight inconclusively off **Portland** in February, but in July the Dutch are convincingly defeated in the **Battle of Texel**.

1654 In April, a formal union between England and Scotland is proclaimed. **George Monck**, previously a royalist, is appointed commander-in-chief in Scotland, and makes headway against the **'Glencairn'** rebellion.

The **Treaty of Westminster** brings to an end the Anglo-Dutch war and promotes a defensive alliance between England and the United Provinces, aimed partly at restraining **William II of Orange**, married to Charles I's daughter **Mary**. Further treaties are concluded with **Sweden**, **Denmark** and **Portugal**, to the benefit of the Commonwealth's international standing.

1655 **Cromwell** dismisses the first parliament to be convened under the Instrument of Government, and defeats a royalist uprising in **Wiltshire**.

Monck crushes the remaining Scottish rebels.

The government of Britain is modified so that each area is controlled by a **major general** given wide military and civil powers by Cromwell.

In the Americas, war breaks out with **Spain**. Cromwell dispatches a fleet to the **Caribbean** and **Jamaica** is seized.

A pact is concluded with **France** whereby the exiled Stuarts are excluded from French territory, forcing Charles II to seek refuge in the Netherlands.

Jews are admitted into England for the first time in three centuries.

Oliver Cromwell (1599–1658)

Oliver Cromwell rode his luck during times of upheaval and emerged as the undisputed controller of events. Yet he was also a man of deep inward convictions, someone who genuinely believed that God was on his side and that the republican government he pioneered was in England's best interests.

Cromwell converted to Calvinism in his thirties and by 1640, when he was elected **MP for Cambridge**, had gained a reputation as 'Lord of the Fens', attacking bishops in general and the bishop of Ely in particular. But Cromwell was not at the forefront of those opposed to the king in 1642, and at **Edgehill** in October he played only a minor role. In the immediate aftermath, though, he demonstrated his prowess as a military disciplinarian and organizer, and defeated a royalist army at **Gainsborough** the following January. Promotion rapidly followed, and by 1645 he had become second-in-command to **Lord Fairfax**. Crucially, when the army and Parliament fell out in June 1647, he sided with his troops. A signatory to the king's death warrant, he was appointed chairman of the **Council of State**, and strengthened the new republic by campaigns in **Scotland** and **Ireland** – where his savage reprisals against Catholics bequeathed a legacy of sectarian hatred.

In England, however, his reputation was assured, and in 1653 he assumed the title of **Lord Protector**, which gave him all the authority of the deposed king. Cromwell advocated religious toleration, encouraged education, opposed trade monopolies and created a written constitution. But his unpopular appointment of **major generals** to supervise regional government and his kowtowing to Puritan sentiment (which included the abolition of public festivals such as Christmas) provoked discontent. When he died his legacy quickly unravelled: government came back into the hands of the monarch and little remained of the sweeping changes he had made. Following the Restoration, his body was disinterred, mutilated and hurled into the Thames. His severed head, impaled on a pole, was exhibited in Westminster Hall for 25 years.

Cromwell's death mask.

> " Cromwell, our chief of men, who through a cloud,
> Not of war only, but detractions rude,
> Guided by faith and matchless fortitude,
> To peace and truth thy glorious way has ploughed,
> And on the neck of crowned Fortune proud
> Has reared God's trophies, and his work pursued,
> While Darwen stream with blood of Scots imbrued,
> And Dunbar field resounds thy praises loud,
> And Worcester's laureate wreath. Yet much remains
> To conquer still; peace hath her victories
> No less renowned than war: new foes arise,
> Threatening to bind our souls with secular chains:
> Help us to save free conscience from the paw
> Of hireling wolves whose gospel is their maw. "
>
> John Milton, 'To the Lord General Cromwell' (1652)

1656 The second parliament of the Protectorate attempts to limit **religious toleration**. Discontent with the **major generals** grows.

1657 Cromwell abolishes the **major generals** after Parliament refuses to supply funds. Parliament offers him the Crown in May in its **Humble Petition and Advice**, but Cromwell declines, concerned that this will limit his power.

A military alliance with France against Spain is formed. Blake annihilates the Spanish Caribbean fleet off **Santa Cruz** in April, but dies in August.

The first of a succession of bad harvests induces **economic depression**.

1658 An Anglo-French army defeats the Spanish in the **Battle of the Dunes** on 4 June, following which **Dunkirk** surrenders to the English.

On 3 September **Cromwell** dies, possibly of malaria; his son **Richard Cromwell** becomes Lord Protector.

1659 A new **parliament** convenes in January, but quickly falls foul of the army, which in April persuades Richard Cromwell to recall the **Rump Parliament** of 1648. In May he resigns. As political uncertainty continues, **John Lambert** suppresses a royalist uprising in Cheshire led by **George Booth** in August, but other rebellions proliferate, driven by fears among the well-to-do of a puritanical regime.

Abroad, tensions ease as **France** and **Spain** conclude the **Treaty of the Pyrenees**.

1660 Determined to restore order, **General Monck** marches south from Scotland, recruiting the Coldstream Guards along the way, and enters **London**. He recalls those members of the **Long Parliament** purged by Pride, but in March it is forced to dissolve; a **'Convention'** parliament is summoned by Monk a month later. The earl of Manchester and nine other peers take their seats in a reconstituted House of Lords. Although it has not been Monck's original intention to restore the monarchy, steadily this looks likely. Advised by **Edward Hyde**, Charles II issues the **Declaration of Breda**, promising as king of England he will promote liberty of conscience in religion, ensure that arrears in army pay are met and settle land disputes equitably. Following brief negotiations, on 8 May Charles is **proclaimed king**, and lands at **Dover** on 25 May. Four days later he enters London. On 29 August he issues an **Act of Free and General Pardon, Indemnity and Oblivion**, pardoning all those who have rebelled against the monarchy (except surviving regicides). **Edward Hyde** becomes lord chancellor.

The Restoration

After Cromwell's death in 1658 there was little debate about restoring the Stuarts, but his son and successor, **Richard Cromwell**, proved unable to resolve the underlying tensions between the military and Parliament. When he resigned the following year, only a limited set of options remained open. The public mood was turning against the political manoeuvring of the army (particularly after its recall and rapid dismissal of the Rump Parliament), and **General George Monck** seized the initiative by opening negotiations which paved the way for Charles II's restoration to the throne.

Despite the widespread rejoicing that greeted the king's carefully staged return – not to mention his guarantee that those responsible for his father's death would be treated fairly – a number of people had good reason to be nervous. The prospect of royalists returning from exile and demanding their confiscated lands back held little appeal. Even less attractive was the possibility that old parliamentarians might be brought to book for rebelling in the first place. In the end, Charles kept his word that only the surviving regicides would suffer, and old opposition peers were bought off with government offices. Ironically, it was diehard royalists who felt short-changed.

And restoring the monarchy (and with it the Commons, the Lords and the bishops) didn't simply return England to where it had been eleven years earlier. Rebellion and civil unrest were

1661 **Thomas Venner**, a member of the **Fifth Monarchist** sect dedicated to establishing a theocratic state in England, leads an unsuccessful **rebellion** against the Restoration.

A newly elected parliament, the so-called **Cavalier Parliament** (not dissolved until 1679), enthusiastically endorses the restitution of the monarchy, and initiates legislation to re-establish the **Church of England**. A **Corporation Act** enables boroughs to be purged of 'dissident' (ie Puritan) officials, while a **Militia Act** allows the king to tangible threats, and there was more open political debate than ever before. Throughout major towns and cities a lively press had begun to circulate, providing up-to-date news on the major affairs of state, while numerous coffee-houses had become the focus for discussion – so many that in the 1670s the government contemplated shutting them all down. Perhaps the greatest change, though, was at court. Charles II created an entirely different – and far more factionalized – government to the one presided over by his father. Instead of allowing himself to rely on Parliament for funds, he accepted the largesse of **Louis XIV** of France and relied on the prospect of a Catholic succession to keep the politicians divided. Least attractively, he was thoroughly disloyal to those who supported him. Both **Clarendon** and **Danby** were thrown to the dogs, and even his favourite son, **James, Duke of Monmouth**, was snubbed. This cut-throat environment was mirrored by a permissive (and, some said, utterly amoral) atmosphere. The admiralty official and diarist Samuel Pepys was frequently scandalized by the goings-on at the Stuart court, but took great delight in noting down its gossip. He exclaimed, describing supper with some of the 'merry gang' in 1688: 'Lord! What loose, cursed company was this that I was in tonight, though full of wit and worth a man's being in for once, to know the nature of it and their manner of talk and lives…'

maintain a standing army. In addition **Charles II** is granted permanent annual subsidies with a nominal value of £1,200,000. Difficulties in collecting this money, however, coupled with the king's extravagance, mean that the throne continues to be threatened by insolvency. **Edward Hyde** emerges as the king's chief minister, and is created **earl of Clarendon**.

Robert Boyle publishes *The Sceptical Chemist*, in which he demonstrates the existence of many different chemical elements rather than the Aristotelian matrix of four basic elements (earth, air, fire and water).

1662 Parliament passes further legislation in favour of the re-established **Church of England**, including the appointment of **archbishops** and **bishops**, and an **Act of Uniformity** that makes acceptance of a newly published **Book of Common Prayer** obligatory among England's school and university teachers.

Charles II's bride, the Portuguese infanta **Catherine of Braganza**, arrives in England. Astonished by her hair, arranged in wing-like ringlets, the king exclaims: 'They have brought me a bat'. But her dowry includes the port of **Tangier** in the Mediterranean and the island of **Bombay** in India, and the marriage goes ahead.

Dunkirk is returned to France in exchange for £400,000.

A royal charter is granted to a body known as the **Royal Society**, dedicated to the advancement of science.

1663 Attempts by Charles II to extend religious tolerance to **Nonconformists** and **Catholics** alike, in line with the **Declaration of Breda**, are rebuffed by Parliament.

As the number of English colonies in **North America** grows, colonists are forbidden to trade directly with other nations.

1664 In North America, the township that will become the city of **New York** is captured by English forces from the Dutch.

1665 The **Second Anglo-Dutch War** commences, much against Clarendon's wishes, as the two nations contest naval supremacy in northern waters.

In the autumn English cities are paralysed by what will be the last great attack of **bubonic plague**, severely hampering economic activity. In London alone some 70,000 citizens die and the court withdraws to **Oxford**.

Robert Hooke, professor of geometry at Gresham College in London, publishes *Micrographia*, which contains illustrations of the structure of the snowflake and close-up views of the flea generated by Hooke's experiments with the microscope.

A bluebottle, as depicted in Robert Hooke's *Micrographia*.

1666 **London** is dealt a second body-blow when the **Great Fire** breaks out on 2 September. Starting in **Pudding Lane**, it spreads quickly through the capital's closely packed buildings. The lord mayor Sir Thomas Bloodworth, somewhat underestimating the severity of the fire, is heard to comment that 'A woman might piss it out', but in all 13,200 houses, 87 churches and four bridges are destroyed and 100,000 people made homeless; some four-fifths of the City area is laid to waste. The architect **Sir Christopher Wren** puts forward a plan to rebuild London as a 'model city', but he is commissioned only to rebuild a number of churches and, most significantly, a new **St Paul's Cathedral**, the first new Protestant cathedral in the world.

> So down, with my heart full of trouble, to the Lieutenant of the Tower, who tells me that it begun this morning in the King's bakers house in Pudding Lane, and that it hath burned down St Magnes Church and most part of Fishstreete already. So I down to the waterside and there got a boat and through bridge, and there saw a lamentable fire. Poor Michells house, as far as the Old Swan, already burned that way and the fire running further, that in a very little time it got as far as the Stillyard while I was there. Everybody endeavouring to remove their goods, and flinging into the river or bringing them into lighters that lay off. Poor people staying in their houses as long as till the very fire touched them, and then running into boats or clambering from one pair of stair by the waterside to another. And among other things, the poor pigeons I perceive were loath to leave their houses, but hovered about the windows and balconies till they were some of them burned, their wings, and fell down.

Samuel Pepys, *Diary* (part of the entry for 2 September, 1666)

1667 England suffers an embarrassing defeat when Dutch war vessels penetrate the **River Medway** and reach the naval docks at **Chatham**. The war itself is ended by treaties drawn up in July. Despite his opposition to the war, the unpopular **Clarendon** is held responsible, and is dismissed as lord chancellor. In October the Commons, unsupported by the Lords, moves a motion for his impeachment. In November he flees to France, where he dies in 1674 after completing his monumental *History of the Rebellion*. In his wake government is placed in the hands of a group of five ministers known as the **Cabal** after the initials of their names: **Clifford**, **Arlington**, **Buckingham**, **Ashley** and **Lauderdale**. Charles II, however, undermines their efficiency by exploiting their differences.

John Milton publishes *Paradise Lost*, a poem which proclaims to 'justify the ways of God to men' and is often regarded as the finest verse epic in English.

1668 England enters into a Protestant **Triple Alliance** with **Sweden** and the **Dutch United Provinces**, ostensibly to counter the growing power of **Louis XIV**'s France. Privately Charles II maintains contacts with the French court.

1669 An admiralty official, **Samuel Pepys**, is forced to give up writing his *Diary*, which he began on 1 January 1660, due to failing eyesight. It will remain in cipher and unpublished until the 19th century.

1670 Charles signs the **Secret Treaty of Dover** with **Louis XIV**, agreeing to join France in an attack on the Dutch and also to convert to Catholicism as and when the political climate permits.

1672 An invasion of the Dutch United Provinces by **Louis XIV** is supported by English naval actions. In desperation the Dutch turn to **William of Orange**, appointing him their *stadtholder*. As Charles's secret dealings with the French are exposed – though not his promise to become a

The scientific revolution in England

The emergence of modern science was a Europe-wide movement spanning the 16th and 17th centuries, and was rooted in a number of developments: the thirst for new kinds of knowledge that accompanied the Renaissance, a revolution in mathematics and advances in technology. The declining authority of the Church probably played a leading role, too, though this has always been hard to quantify – despite the well-advertised face-off between Rome and Galileo Galilei.

England arrived on the scene later than Italy, France and the Netherlands, but during the Stuart period it saw a number of significant breakthroughs, culminating in the publication of Isaac Newton's *Principia Mathematica* in 1687 with the assistance of the astronomer Edmund Halley – a work that provided the ground rules of physics until Einstein's work in relativity at the beginning of the 20th century. For his numerous achievements, which included his 1704 study *Optics* and the invention of differential calculus, Newton was knighted in 1705, the first scientist to be so honoured.

But Newton's work was not isolated. His predecessor, Robert Hooke, claimed (not unreasonably) to have anticipated Newton's

Catholic – political opposition to the king grows in Parliament, coalescing into a faction that will become known as the **Whig Party** (see p.284). Charles responds by entrusting his affairs to his minister **Thomas Osborne**, who begins organising a 'loyalist' faction, the beginnings of the **Tory Party**.

1673 Although Charles II has fathered many illegitimate sons and daughters with his numerous mistresses, **Queen Catherine** fails to provide him with a legitimate heir. It becomes, therefore, a matter of widespread political concern when his brother (and heir apparent to the throne) **James, Duke of York** – a Catholic – marries the Catholic discovery of gravity. In the 1650s he had established the laws of **elasticity** and, taking full advantage of the **microscope**, went on to uncover cellular structures in natural materials. The Anglo-Irish **Robert Boyle** achieved even greater things. As well as suggesting the existence of chemical elements, Boyle experimented with gases, extrapolating the fundamentally important 'Boyle's Law', which stated that the pressure of a given quantity of gas is in inverse proportion to its volume.

Both men were intimately involved with the **Royal Society**, established at the beginning of Charles II's reign to encourage scientific research (and rival similar European institutions). But although English science became famously empirical under the Society's influence, in the 17th century the quest to unlock the 'laws of nature' was still closely tied to theology – those very laws, after all, were deemed to be devised by God. Newton himself spent much of his later life exploring prophecies contained in the biblical Book of Daniel, and Boyle's published works include lengthy attempts to define God's relationship with the physical universe. The stereotype of the scientist as an atheistical investigator belongs to a much later period.

princess **Mary of Modena**. Parliament hurriedly adds the **Test Act** to the statute book, obliging all office-holders – and by implication the monarch – to take Anglican sacraments.

Osborne becomes Lord Treasurer.

1674 Osborne is created **earl of Danby**. As his hold over government tightens his policies prevail: cautious opposition toward France; strict adherence to Anglicanism; and the upholding of royal authority. Hostilities with the Dutch are ended.

The Puritan divine **John Baxter** speaks out against the

shipment of black Africans to work as **slaves** on English plantations in the American colonies.

1675 The **Royal Observatory** at **Greenwich** is founded by royal charter to further astronomical observation and to investigate the problem of locating longitude at sea. **John Flamsteed** is appointed the first **astronomer-royal**.

> **"**To apply himself with the most exact care and diligence to the rectifying the tables of the motions of the heavens, and the places of the fixed stars, so as to find out the so much-desired longitude of places for the perfecting the art of navigation.**"**
>
> Instructions to John Flamsteed, the first astronomer-royal, 1675

1677 The marriage of Charles II's niece (and the duke of York's daughter by a previous marriage) **Mary** to **William III of Orange** goes some way to allaying fears about a Catholic succession. But Charles begins accepting secret **'subsidies'** from the French Crown to avoid becoming dependent on Parliament.

1678 Political tensions re-ignite when a London magistrate, **Sir Edmund Berry Godfrey**, is found murdered on London's Primrose Hill. **Titus Oates**, sometime Jesuit, testifies that Godfrey has been murdered by Catholic priests as part of a wider **Popish Plot** to assassinate Charles II, replace him with his brother James and restore Catholicism in England. In the ensuing panic five Catholic lords are imprisoned, many Catholics are executed and Parliament passes a **Disabling Act** barring 'papists' from public office. The crisis is exacerbated when **Louis XIV**'s financial support for Charles is exposed. Danby is held responsible, impeached, and later sent to the Tower. Oates's evidence also implicates Queen Catherine, but the king dissolves Parliament before she can be investigated. Investigation of Oates, however, shows his testimony to have been a tissue of lies, and he is placed in the stocks for perjury.

John Bunyan publishes the first part of *Pilgrim's Progress*, a Christian allegory that becomes an instant bestseller.

1679 Despite Oates's perjury, anti-Catholic feelings continue to run high, underpinning the **Exclusion Crisis** – an effort to bar the duke of York or any other Catholic from the succession. Hoping to revive his fading popularity and increase his revenues, Charles II calls the first of three short-lived **parliaments**. Each is dissolved when it becomes clear no compromise is possible. To ease his position, however, the king orders his brother to leave the country.

1680 The poet and libertine **John Wilmot, Earl of Rochester** – upheld by some as an icon of contemporary wantonness – dies aged 33.

> ❝ There is no doubt that Rochester is the most witty man in the kingdom; but then he is likewise the most unprincipled, and devoid even of the least tincture of honour... He applauds your taste, submits to your sentiments, and whilst he himself does not believe a single word of what he is saying, he makes you believe it all. ❞
>
> Miss Mary Hobart on John Wilmot, Earl of Rochester, c.1667

1681 Charles II dissolves his last **parliament**. Continuing French subsidies and a rigorous reform of the treasury enable the king and his privy council to govern England autonomously. Although Charles's popularity revives during his final years, political divisions remain. It is about this time that the terms **'Whig'** and **'Tory'** become common currency.

The poet and dramatist **John Dryden** writes *Absalom and Achitophel*, a verse satire that brilliantly captures the atmosphere of intrigue surrounding the king's court.

1683 Government ministers discover the details of the **Rye House Plot** – in fact two plots. One, supported by old Cromwellians, intends to assassinate the king at Rye House on his way back from the races at Newmarket. The second, the brainchild of **William, Lord Russell**, plans merely to capture the king and demand the formation of a government made up of MPs. Both plots are easily quashed, however, and Russell and his other conspirators are executed.

1684 **Danby** is released from the Tower.

> " Here lies a great and mighty king
> Whose promise none relies on;
> He never said a foolish thing,
> Nor ever did a wise one. "
>
> John Wilmot, Earl of Rochester, 'The King's Epitaph' (on Charles II)

1685 **Charles II** dies in London on 6 February, after professing the Catholic faith and supposedly begging: 'Let not poor Nelly starve' (referring to his favourite mistress, the actress **Nell Gwynn**). He is succeeded by his brother **James II** without immediate repercussions, at least in England. In Scotland, though, there is an uprising led by the **duke of Argyll**. Although this is crushed in June, it inspires Charles II's illegitimate son, **James, Duke of Monmouth**, known as the 'Protestant duke', to stage a second rebellion south of the border. Landing at **Lyme Regis**, Monmouth draws modest support in the West Country before his forces are defeated by Lord Feversham at **Sedgemoor** on 6 July. A few days later Monmouth is discovered in a ditch disguised as a shepherd. Refusing him clemency, James II orders his execution. **Judge George Jeffreys** is appointed head of a commission to root out Monmouth's supporters. As a result of Jeffreys' 'Bloody Assizes', hundreds are hanged in rows along the road connecting **Bridgewater** and **Chedzoy** in Somerset.

1686 Although James II honours his pledge not to forcibly impose Catholicism on England, suspicions are aroused when the Catholic **Lord Tyrconnell** is appointed lord lieutenant in **Ireland**. In response **Thomas, Lord Wharton** composes **'Lillibulero'**, a satirical poem warning of the dangers of popery. Set to music by **Henry Purcell**, it is embraced as a popular anthem by the king's opponents. Wharton will later claim credit for having 'sung King James out of three kingdoms'.

The **East India Company**, having failed to gain its commercial ends in India by diplomacy, begins using force to secure trading privileges – a pattern that will be replicated by the English throughout the Far East and other parts of the world.

1687 Hoping to re-introduce Catholicism by the back door, James II develops a **Declaration of Indulgence**, allowing free worship throughout his kingdoms.

Isaac Newton publishes *Principia Mathematica*, which identifies gravity as the mechanism of planetary motion.

1688 Fears about James II's true intentions deepen when the king orders his **Declaration of Indulgence** to be read from every pulpit. The crisis comes to a head when **Queen Mary of Modena** gives birth to a son on 10 June. The prospect of another Catholic succession, and James's

Whigs and Tories

Toward the end of Charles II's reign it started to become fashionable to refer to the two main political factions in England as **Whigs** and **Tories**. Both were racist terms of abuse. The 'Tories' were Irish bandits, while the 'Whigs' (originally 'Whiggamores') were Scottish cattle thieves.

In the political sense, Tories could be deemed loyalists. They stood for upholding the monarchy, and with it the Anglican Church. The Whigs, in contrast, were the opposition. They believed in a limited monarchy that respected the views of its subjects, and in the intertwined rights of liberty and property. Many Whigs were dissenters, or **Nonconformists**; and even those who were not extended sympathy toward dissent.

Inevitably, distinctions between Tories and Whigs tended to blur over specific issues, so that there were Tories with Whiggish leanings and vice versa. Where disagreement remained fundamental, however, was regarding the notion of protest. Tories, still haunted by the Civil Wars, could not countenance the idea of forcibly resisting the king – a tyrannical monarch was preferable to anarchy. Whigs, on the other hand, had no such qualms. Resistance in the name of liberty and property was not only right, it was necessary to maintain the rights of free Englishmen. And it was this cry of 'Liberty and Property' that was, above all others, to resound in the politics of the following century.

arbitrary replacement of a number of key officials, leads **Danby** and six other leading noblemen – among them the earls of **Nottingham** and **Devonshire** – to invite **William of Orange** to England to secure the election of a free Parliament and their Protestant rights. Driven by the 'Protestant wind', William lands with an army at **Torbay** on 5 November. Deserted by his army, James II flees to **France** on 23 December, throwing the Great Seal into the Thames as he goes.

8
The age of oligarchy

1689–1820

The period between the joint accession of **William III** and **Mary II** in 1688 and the death of **George III** in 1820 has sometimes been dubbed the 'long 18th century'. During this time England increasingly found itself playing a role on not just the European but the world stage, and with this some historians have detected a growing sense of 'English' or 'British' identity. At best, though, nationalism remained an ambiguous concept. England and Wales had been formally united in 1536, union with Scotland was finally achieved in 1707 and union with Ireland in 1801 resulted in the formation of a Parliament of Great Britain. Yet the Parliament continued to sit at Westminster, and the members from Scotland, Ireland and Wales were never left in any doubt that England remained the dominant partner.

The story of England in this period is tied in, as ever, with events in France. One of the motivating factors behind the union with Scotland and Ireland, in fact, was to forestall a French invasion through the back door. But the reasons for warfare changed as the century passed, and were indicative of England's internal politics. William of Orange had been eager to secure English support for his ongoing conflict with **Louis XIV**, and he was keen to establish a balance of power within Europe that would curb Louis' despotic tendencies. William had been accepted in England as the protector of the nation's liberties and protestantism against James II's francophile Catholic tendencies, and under **Queen Anne** the Whigs remained eager to see France humbled for the same reasons. A desire to curb the Jacobite threat posed by the exiled House of Stuart in part motivated the Hanoverians too to stand against France after 1714, but they were also heavily influenced by their interest in protecting their vulnerable German lands – which lay at the mercy of any passing army.

Increasingly colonial interests took on greater prominence, and it was these that came to the fore during the **Seven Years War** of 1756–63, which resulted in Britain driving the French out of Canada and adding India to its American and West Indian colonies. England and France clashed again during the **American War of Independence** (1775–83), which proved a costly embarrassment for Britain. But although colonial ambitions continued to motivate both sides, a new ideological flavour began to influence events too, first in the American War and later in the **French Revolution**. At its outset the Revolution seemed to promise England a more acceptable France stripped of its Bourbon absolutism – which for many conjured up images of torture and oppression – but as the country descended into bloodshed in the early 1790s many of the traditional hierarchies were torn down. They were replaced first by a republic, and then by the dictatorship of **Napoleon Bonaparte**, who was eager to dominate Europe. The **Napoleonic Wars** saw Britain ranged once more against France, in alliance from time to time with the other great European states: **Prussia**, **Austria** and **Russia**. These years were marked by the victories at **Trafalgar** (1805) and **Waterloo** (1815).

By the early years of the 19th century the British way of life had altered dramatically with developments in **industrialization**. People were moving to cities to find work in new industries, and the sweeping social changes that accompanied technological innovation would accelerate as the period drew to a close. **Colonialism**, at first driven by entrepreneurial private institutions as much as by government intervention, came to play a greater role in British finances with New World trades such as sugar, tobacco and slavery. This burgeoning global economy, based on overseas exploitation, created fresh domestic wealth and with it the support structure for continuing cultural development. **London** grew to be a world city (with a population to match) through the trade that passed through its ports, and the explosive growth of stately-home building at the latter end of the 18th century – employing the most fashionable architects, designers and painters – was in part financed by money made in colonies on the other side of the world.

Politically, for much of the period England was dominated by the **Whig Party**. It was they who took the credit for the **'Glorious Revolution'** of 1688–89, and who claimed to be the upholders of the ensuing settlement. Yet the monarch continued to exercise extensive power, as several politicians who earned royal displeasure – including the Whig **Thomas, Lord Wharton** and the Tory **Henry, Viscount Bolingbroke** – found to their cost. And, as the ideologies of the American and French revolutionaries began to take hold among some Whig factions, the Tory party, with its traditional ideals of upholding Church and monarch, came to be regarded as a safer pair of hands in dangerous times.

The Whig ascendancy: 1689-1759

Had James II not taken the decision to flee in 1688 he might well have remained in power, but it is likely that strong efforts would have been made to ensure that he was king in name only – and some form of regency would have wrested control from his hands. At any rate he had other reasons to quit: mass desertions from the army removed his military backing, and his political support within his own family was haemorrhaging. His effective 'abdication' allowed Parliament, after much soul-searching, to find a way of offering the throne to William and Mary as joint monarchs, though William himself held executive power. It was not a particularly happy compromise, however, and the 'Bloodless Revolution' was neither bloodless (several died during a skirmish between the Gloucestershire militia and Lord Lovelace as he attempted to fight his way through to William's army) nor the touchstone of liberty it later came to symbolize. In the 17th century 'revolution' meant 'restoration', not the creation of something new, and it was in this sense that the Whigs attempted to portray William of Orange's coup. And indeed his accession reopened old wounds. Over the next five years a steady outpouring of Whig legislation – including an **Act of Toleration** and the 1694 **Triennial Act**, committing the monarch to a fresh parliament every three years – endeavoured to limit the throne's room for manoeuvre, but the king remained a forceful presence and successfully made use of his new position to continue resisting Louis XIV.

Yet 1688–89 was an important watershed. It confirmed Parliament's role as the guarantor of the monarchy, and 25 years later, when William's successor **Queen Anne** died childless, it was Parliament that offered the throne to her German Protestant cousin, **George, Elector of Hanover**. The decision to adopt the House of Hanover over the heads of some fifty other candidates was perhaps the most significant outcome of the 'Revolution'. In William III's case it could be plausibly argued that his wife Mary was the legitimate heir to the English throne, but the accession of **George I** was the result of sheer expediency. Unable to speak more than a smattering of English and eager to keep in touch with his electorate at home (to which he often returned during the summer months), George surrounded himself with German favourites – among them his *kappelmeister*, **Georg Frederic Händel**.

The business of government came increasingly to be left to the king's ministers, which encouraged the office of **prime minister** to develop. There had been principal ministers before, but increasingly the 'first lord of the treasury', as the position was known, came to be seen as the effective head of government under the king. This was partly because it became more difficult for the monarch to rule in defiance of whichever faction held sway in Parliament. But the office of prime minister was mutually beneficial: a party lacking the monarch's support found it difficult to dominate Parliament. It was in these conditions that **Sir Robert Walpole**, generally regarded as Britain's first prime minister, came to dominate affairs. As first lord of the treasury between 1721 and 1742, Walpole headed an administration comprised almost exclusively of Whigs. In the meantime the Tories were forced into the political wilderness by their association with the Stuart cause. Their ambitions were disappointed twice: first with the accession of **George II**, who soon came to appreciate Walpole's abilities, and once again with the early death of his son **Prince Frederick**. It was not until **George III** came to the throne, proclaiming an interest in the traditional ideologies espoused by 'patriot' Tories, that the party's period in the wilderness appeared to be near its end.

In an age governed by the 'rage of party', political office (or the expectation of it) became increasingly important, creating a climate in which the pursuit of patronage added to the power of the aristocratic elite. Authors, artists and satirists such as the poet **Alexander Pope** and the erstwhile dean of St Patrick's, Dublin, **Jonathan Swift**, employed their talents to win favour by engaging in the political and personal feuds of the moment. The artist and engraver **William Hogarth** threw in his lot with the earl of Bute in defence of his government, as did the Scottish novelist **Tobias Smollett**; while **Laurence Sterne**'s comic travelogue, *A Sentimental Journey through France and Italy*, boasted a host of the great and the good among its subscribers – including the earl of Abingdon and the dukes of Buccleuch, Richmond and Grafton. Under the influence of such powerful patrons, literature in England witnessed a new development: the novel. But the success of **Daniel Defoe**'s *Moll Flanders*, **Samuel Richardson**'s *Clarissa* and **Henry Fielding**'s *Tom Jones* demonstrates that it was not merely those at the top of the social ladder who were interested in consuming culture – people from many backgrounds were eager to experience the pleasures of polite leisure.

1689 Following the flight of **James II** and **William III of Orange**'s largely unopposed march on London, a hastily gathered **Convention Parliament** offers the throne jointly to William and his wife and cousin **Mary**, subject to their agreeing to a **Declaration of Right**s, which lists James's wrongs and asks them to take the throne. They accept in February, and in April they are crowned as **William III** and **Mary II**. Although many English people welcome the new monarchs, there is resistance by some Scots and among Ireland's Catholic majority. William brings with him a commitment to opposing the expansion of French power under **Louis XIV**. Instead he recommends a balance of powers between Europe's leading states – a recipe that, over the following decades, draws England into a series of continental wars.

Parliament passes an **Act of Toleration**, enshrining the principle of 'liberty for tender consciences', but Catholics and dissenters (Nonconformists) remain barred from public office.

1690 Aided by Louis XIV, **James II** lands in Ireland in an attempt to recover his kingdoms, but is defeated by **William III** at the **Battle of the Boyne** in July and forced to return to France. As a result of William's victory, Ireland's Catholic majority continues to be ruled by a Protestant minority.

In England's Treasury (regarded as the most important department of state), the Whigs are displaced by three 'Tory' ministers: the **marquess of Carmarthen** (later **duke of Leeds**), **Sidney Godolphin** and the **earl of Northampton**.

The philosopher **John Locke** publishes his *Essay Concerning Human Understanding*, an attempt to explain the relations between knowledge and perception.

1692 English and Dutch forces defeat a French navy at **La Hogue**, but on land William III suffers a reversal at the **Battle of Steenkirk**.

1693 The **earl of Sunderland** begins reorganizing the Court party to further William III's control of government.

1694 Parliament limits the monarchs' scope for political manoeuvre by imposing the **Triennial Act** on William and Mary, obliging them to summon a new parliament every three years. **Mary II** dies of **smallpox** in December.

Greenwich Hospital is founded, its architect **Sir Christopher Wren**.

The **Bank of England** is founded on the initiative of **Charles Montague** (later **Lord Halifax**).

1695 **William Congreve** establishes himself as England's leading dramatist with the first production of his polished comedy *Love for Love*, to be followed five years later with the equally successful *The Way of the World*.

© NEIL SETCHFIELD

The Painted Hall at the Old Royal Naval College, Greenwich. James Thornhill's decoration, depicting William and Mary in triumph, took nineteen years to complete.

The eminent composer **Henry Purcell**, whose works include the opera *Dido and Aeneas* and the funeral music for Mary II, dies – after being locked out in the rain by his wife, if legend is to be believed.

1696 A plot by supporters of James II – known as **Jacobites** (see p.309) – to assassinate **William III** is uncovered. When **Sir John Fenwick**, one of the conspirators, accuses **Godolphin**, the **duke of Shrewsbury** and **Admiral Edward Russell** of secretly corresponding with James's court-in-exile at St Germain, **Thomas, Lord Wharton** and **Sir John Somers** rally the Whig forces to defend their friends. This group – Wharton, Somers, Shrewsbury, Russell and **Charles Montague** – comes to be known collectively as the **'Whig Junto'** and it forms one of the most powerful and well-organized cliques in parliament. Through their efforts the three ministers are exonerated and Fenwick is executed.

1697 Anglo-French hostilities are brought to an end by the **Peace of Ryswick**, in which Louis XIV agrees to recognize William III as **king of England**.

1700 The succession is thrown in doubt when the son of William III's sister-in-law, **William, Duke of Gloucester**, dies. To prevent a Catholic Stuart return, the eventual succession is offered to **Sophia, Electress of Hanover** – a descendant of James I's daughter Elizabeth and 56th in line to the succession.

The poet, dramatist and critic **John Dryden** dies.

1701 Parliament passes an **Act of Settlement**, disallowing any future Hanoverian monarch from leaving England without parliamentary approval and banning the appointment of foreigners to government posts.

James II dies in exile. His son, **James Edward**, is recognized as **James III of England** by Louis XIV in contravention of the Treaty of Ryswick.

The Jacobites and Hanoverians

Monarchs are in colour

James I

Charles I = Henrietta Maria

Elizabeth = Frederick V of the Rhine

Charles II

James II = (2) Mary of Modena

Sophia = Ernst Augustus of Hanover

James 'III' 'The Old Pretender'

George I = Sophia Dorothea of Brunswick & Zelle

Charles Edward 'Bonnie Prince Charlie'

Henry Benedict

George II = Caroline of Anspach

Frederick = Augusta of Saxe-Coburg-Altenburg

George III = Charlotte of Mecklenburg-Strelitz

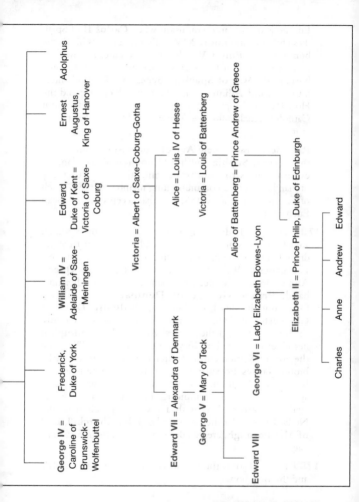

George IV =
Caroline of
Brunswick-
Wolfenbuttel

Frederick,
Duke of York

William IV =
Adelaide of Saxe-
Meiningen

Edward,
Duke of Kent =
Victoria of Saxe-
Coburg

Ernest
Augustus,
King of Hanover

Adolphus

Victoria = Albert of Saxe-Coburg-Gotha

Alice = Louis IV of Hesse

Victoria = Louis of Battenberg

Edward VII = Alexandra of Denmark

George V = Mary of Teck

Alice of Battenberg = Prince Andrew of Greece

George VI = Lady Elizabeth Bowes-Lyon

Edward VIII

Elizabeth II = Prince Philip, Duke of Edinburgh

Charles   Anne   Andrew   Edward

Europe is thrown into confusion when **Carlos II** of Spain dies childless, and **Louis XIV** of France supports his Bourbon grandson **Philip V** as Spain's new king. Following a French invasion of the Spanish Netherlands and the outbreak of the **War of Spanish Succession**, England enters into a **Grand Alliance** with the Dutch Republic and the Holy Roman Empire on 5 September, determined to limit Catholic French influence. The war will last another twelve years.

Parliament passes a new **Act of Succession**, nominating the electress **Sophia** and her Hanoverian descendants as eventual heirs to the throne, and stipulating that any monarch must be a communicating member of the Church of England (in other words, one that accepts the Anglican Eucharist).

1702 William III dies from internal bleeding on 8 March after his horse stumbles on a molehill. Thereafter Jacobites drink toasts to 'the gentleman in black velvet'. The succession passes to William's cousin and sister-in-law **Queen Anne**. Despite seventeen pregnancies, Anne and her husband, **Prince George of Denmark**, are childless following the death of their son, **William, Duke of Gloucester** in 1700, so a crisis over the succession looms. Ill-disposed toward the Whigs, Anne makes **Godolphin** her chief minister; but Tory hopes that Anne will rescind the Act of Settlement and offer the throne to her half-brother **James Edward** are dampened when he refuses to become an Anglican. Jacobite ambitions are further damaged when the queen indicates her support for the war against **France**. A British army is dispatched to the Netherlands under the command of **John Churchill, Earl of Marlborough**, created duke after a successful first campaign.

1703 Portugal joins the Grand Alliance against Louis XIV and the Bourbons.

1704 In July the Allies capture **Gibraltar**, which passes into English hands. Louis XIV attempts to bring hostilities to an end by ordering a daring march on **Vienna**. His army is comprehensively beaten, however, by an allied army under Marlborough at **Blenheim** on 2 August.

1705 In gratitude for his outstanding generalship, Parliament votes to reward Marlborough with the royal estate at **Woodstock** outside Oxford and the funds to build **Blenheim Palace**. Designed by **Sir John Vanbrugh** in the fashionable baroque style, the palace is considered one of England's architectural glories.

The Allies capture **Barcelona** in October.

1706 Marlborough again defeats a Bourbon army, this time on 23 May at **Ramillies**. In June the allies enter **Madrid**.

To strengthen British security, an **Act of Union** between England and Scotland is drawn up in July, and submitted to Scotland's Parliament in October.

1707 In January the Act of Union is approved by Scotland's Parliament.

1708 In Spain an allied army is defeated at **Almanza**, reviving Bourbon fortunes, but Marlborough delivers another crushing victory over the French at **Oudenaarde** in Flanders in July.

In March Louis XIV gathers an invasion fleet to carry the 19-year-old pretender, **James Edward**, to Scotland. After several delays the flotilla sails, but bad weather and the appearance of the English fleet under **Admiral Byng** force the Jacobites to head for home. One French ship, *The Salisbury* (previously taken by the French), is recaptured.

In May the **Act of Union** becomes law, creating a formal bond between England and Scotland. Some commentators, notably **Jonathan Swift**, protest Ireland's exclusion from the act.

The Act of Union

The union of England and Scotland had eluded countless rulers since the days of Agricola, but in 1707 it was enshrined in the **Act of Union**. Even then, any enthusiasm on either side of the border was conspicuously absent. The main impetus behind it was the matter of English security. Above all the Whigs feared that when Queen Anne died, the Scots might reject the planned Hanoverian succession and instead offer their throne to James II's Catholic-leaning son **James Edward**. The Calvinist Scots saw a similar danger, and so a deal was struck.

Scotland lost its own parliament, but in return was allocated 45 seats in the English House of Commons; sixteen Scottish peers, elected from within their own existing ranks, were provided places in the House of Lords. For most Scots, who had looked to the **duke of Hamilton** to negotiate a more advantageous settlement, these were less than inspiring terms – but at any rate they were preferable to the possible alternative. For a few, particularly in the Tory highlands, the settlement was unacceptable, and so encouraged the very thing the Whigs had been anxious to avert: hopes for a Stuart succession in Scotland.

But away from these sensitive political fronts, union brought with it significant benefits for both nations, mainly because the whole of mainland Britain (including Wales) was now a single economic zone, supported by a common currency. The Scots, who had never possessed foreign colonies of their own, began to participate in an expanding British empire, and with it Scottish businessmen were able to reap the lucrative rewards.

Following elections to the House of Commons, the Whigs under **Lord Wharton** gain a massive parliamentary majority and assume control of government in an uneasy alliance with **Harley** and **Godolphin**.

1709 Marlborough inflicts another heavy defeat on France at **Malplaquet** on 11 September.

On 5 November the Tory cleric **Dr Henry Sacheverell** causes outrage in the Whig ranks when he preaches against 'occasional' conformists and 'low' churchmen. The damaging thrust of his argument, though, is that by advocating the old 'high' church doctrine of 'non-resistance', he suggests that the 1688–89 settlement is unjustified. The Whigs call for his impeachment.

Richard Steele founds *The Tatler* magazine.

Construction of the main section of **Castle Howard** in Yorkshire, a grand new house built by Vanbrugh for the **3rd earl of Carlisle**, is completed.

1710 Sacheverell's trial opens on 27 February, but is brought to a halt within a week following the outbreak of

© EDMUND NAGELE

John Vanburgh's Castle Howard.

widespread rioting. The House of Lords is sharply divided along party lines – the Whigs voting for impeachment, the Tories for Sacheverell's acquittal.

In an October **general election** Tories gain from a swing against the Whigs, and secure a large majority in the House of Commons.

The **duke of Shrewsbury** and **Robert Harley** initiate secret negotiations with the French through the mediation of the English Jacobite **earl of Jersey**.

1711 The anti-French alliance falters when **Archduke Charles** becomes **Holy Roman Emperor**, threatening the Bourbons with an even greater Habsburg power bloc.

Following the machinations of his domestic (mainly Whig) enemies, **Marlborough** is dismissed as captain general on 9 December, accused of embezzling public funds.

Encouraged by Queen Anne's government, Tories set up the **South Sea Company** (see p.302), intended to provide alternative investment opportunities to those offered by the Whig-dominated Bank of England.

Richard Steele founds a second magazine, *The Spectator*, with politician and writer **Joseph Addison**.

1712 A duel between the **duke of Hamilton** and **Lord Mohun** – in which both combatants are killed – shocks society by underlining the violent disagreements between Whigs and Tories.

The German composer **Georg Frederic Händel** (Handel) settles in London, and will remain in England until his death in 1759. In that time he will produce an astonishing volume of work – including operas, oratorios, sacred music, concertos and ceremonial music (some of it for royalty).

1713 The **Treaties of Utrecht** bring to an end the **War of**

Spanish Succession. Although Philip V remains king in Spain, the treaties are favourable to British colonial expansion in the Americas and elsewhere.

1714 Following the death of **Queen Anne** on 1 August, Parliament offers the throne to **George Lewis, Elector of Hanover**. Speaking little English, **George I** arrives in England accompanied by two mistresses – the tall and thin **Ehrengard Melusina von Schulenberg** (created the duchess of Kendal) and the short and stout **Charlotte Sophia von Kielmannsegge** (later countess of Darlington). Together they are known as the 'Elephant and Castle'. George's wife, convicted of adultery, is left behind in Hanover.

Marlborough is restored as commander-in-chief of the English army, but plays little further part in public affairs.

1715 George I's tenure of the throne is threatened by the first **Jacobite Rebellion** after James Edward lands in Scotland. But James is beaten at **Sheriffmuir** and forced to flee back to the continent.

1719 A second **Jacobite Rebellion** is led by the exiled (Irish) **duke of Ormonde** and **Earl Marischal**, but it fails to attract sufficient support in either Scotland or England.

The sometime Tory propagandist **Daniel Defoe** publishes *Robinson Crusoe*, a fictionalized autobiographical account of a man shipwrecked on a desert island, perhaps based on a true story.

1720 The **South Sea Company**, set up in 1711, collapses in spectacular style after an attempt to drive competitors to the wall creates panic among investors – resulting in the **South Sea Bubble**. As catastrophe threatens, George I is forced to restore the Whig **Robert Walpole** (see p.307) to government. Walpole resolves the crisis, restores confidence in the economy, and in so doing lays the foundations for his 21-year domination of English politics.

1722 In a March **general election**, the Tories are heavily defeated by their Whig rivals, whose majority in the House of Commons now extends to over two hundred seats.

The South Sea Bubble

The South Sea Company was founded in 1711 with government backing to provide an alternative to the Whig-dominated Bank of England. Investors in the Bank had enjoyed good returns, and the Tories hoped to open up a little honest competition. At first the Company did well: an Anglo-Spanish Treaty of 1713 gave it a monopoly in the Spanish slave trade and a foothold in other European markets. But problems started with a 1719 scheme to redistribute the national debt – not a bad idea in itself, but one that came quickly unstuck as a result of unrealistic demands for profits from the Company's directors, investors, court interests and government ministers. As expectations rose, speculators piled in, creating an investment frenzy akin to that which preceded the Wall Street crash of 1929. As the bubble grew, more and more projects were devised, many of them fraudulently implausible.

And in 1720, after the Company spread bad rumours in the hope of destroying its competitors, confidence failed: the bubble had burst. Hundreds were bankrupted, including some who had sold their estates in the hope of multiplying their wealth. Parliament hurriedly pushed through emergency legislation regulating joint-stock ventures in the future, but for those who lost everything there was no compensation. Only the Whigs, swept back into power under Robert Walpole, could glean any immediate satisfaction. But while governmental integrity had suffered a severe blow, the long-term consequences of the South Sea Bubble, as it came to be known, weren't all bad. The introduction of tighter regulations and the recognition of a need for steady investment laid the foundations for sustained economic growth.

A Jacobite conspiracy is unmasked when **Walpole** is informed of a plot surrounding **Francis Atterbury, Bishop of Rochester**. Habeas Corpus is suspended, Atterbury is forced into exile and another conspirator, **Christopher Layer**, is executed.

1725 Fearful of the trade consequences of the **Treaty of Vienna** between Spain and Austria, Britain, France and Prussia enter into the **Alliance of Hanover**.

1726 As the Walpole administration extends its influence, Lord Bolingbroke – in alliance with a Whig faction led by **William Pulteney** (later **earl of Bath**) – launches a new Tory opposition journal, *The Craftsman*.

1727 In June **George I** dies while en route for Hanover. He is succeeded by his Tory-favouring son, **George II**. The new king attempts to replace Walpole with **Spencer Compton** but, backed by a Whig majority in Parliament, Walpole easily outmanoeuvres them both.

A **general election** in August results in further humiliation for the Tories.

Sir Isaac Newton (see p.278) dies.

1728 George II's first parliament votes to appoint **Arthur Onslow** as speaker of the House of Commons, a post he holds for 33 years.

The king's son **Prince Frederick** arrives in England from Hanover and is created **prince of Wales**.

Alexander Pope publishes *The Dunciad*, a scathing satire on his fellow poets.

John Gay's *The Beggar's Opera*, a vaudeville piece comparing the politics of the so-called 'Robinocracy' (see p.307) with the world of highwaymen and 'thief-takers' (bountyhunters), receives its first performance.

1729 John Wesley becomes leader of the small Oxford society of Nonconformists. Inspired by his teachings, **Methodism** – with its emphases on godliness and honest toil – grows to become one of Britain's principal religious denominations.

1731 Georgia is added to Britain's enlarging number of colonies in North America.

The *Gentleman's Magazine* is founded.

1732 The extent of **smuggling** around England's shores and attacks on customs officials is revealed in a report drawn up by a parliamentary committee and presented to the Treasury. The resulting **Excise Scheme** removes domestically consumed wine and tobacco – the main contraband goods – from the customs net, making them subject to **excise duties** (internal taxation) instead. Through *The Craftsman*, the Tories mount a vigorous attack against the perceived threat of all customs duties being replaced by excise.

1733 There are widespread **demonstrations** against the Excise Scheme.

Alexander Pope publishes his *Essay on Man*, a philosophical verse satire.

1734 The Whig administration suffers heavily at the polls during fresh **parliamentary elections**, largely as a result of the Excise controversy, but remains in power. **Walpole** continues to demonstrate his usefulness to George II by persuading Parliament to vote the Crown greater supplies for a larger army the following year.

1735 'Hogarth's Act', named after the artist and engraver **William Hogarth**, legislates in favour of copyright protection by making it illegal for pirated editions of engravings to be sold.

> Houses, churches, mixed together,
> Streets unpleasant in all weather,
> Prisons, palaces contiguous,
> Gates, a bridge, the Thames irriguous.
>
> Gaudy things enough to tempt ye,
> Showy outsides, insides empty;
> Bubbles, trades, mechanic arts,
> Coaches, wheelbarrows and carts.
>
> Warrants, bailiffs, bills unpaid,
> Lords of laundresses afraid;
> Rogues that nightly rob and shoot men,
> Hangmen, aldermen, and footmen.
>
> Lawyers, poets, priests, physicians,
> Noble, simple, all conditions;
> Worth beneath a threadbare cover,
> Villainy bedaubed all over.
>
> Women black, red, fair and grey,
> Prudes and such as never pray,
> Handsome, ugly, noisy, still,
> Some that will not, some that will.
>
> Many a beau without a shilling,
> Many a widow not unwilling;
> Many a bargain if you strike it:
> This is London! How d'ye like it?

John Bancks, 'A Description of London' (1738)

1736 Parliamentary tensions rise as the Whigs fail to achieve greater toleration for **Nonconformists**.

1737 George II's stormy relations with his son and heir **Prince Frederick** boil over into public view when the prince is expelled from **St James's Palace** in London. The prince establishes a rival 'court' at **Leicester House**, where he is wooed by members of the opposition.

1738 The exiled Tory **Viscount Bolingbroke** writes the *Idea of a Patriot King*, a political testament that inspires some of Prince Frederick's followers and which later influences **George III**.

1739 Tensions with **Spain** over illegal trading by British merchantmen in Spain's American colonies spill over into outright war – the conflict is called the **War of Jenkins' Ear**, after an incident the previous year in which the Royal Navy captain **Robert Jenkins** was disfigured during a clash with Spanish coastal vessels.

1740 As the Spanish war continues, members of the House of Lords warn of the consequences should **France** enter the conflict on Spain's side. Popular feeling against Spain rides high, however, and the patriotic chorus **'Rule Britannia'** from **Thomas Arne**'s new masque, *Alfred*, becomes a popular hit.

The **War of the Austrian Succession** begins in December as **Frederick the Great of Prussia** openly challenges the Habsburgs by invading **Silesia**.

1741 British naval assaults on the Spanish-held **Cuba** and **Carthagena** fail. The government's majority in Parliament falters, and Walpole begins to look insecure.

1742 Outnumbered in the House of Commons, **Walpole** resigns on 2 February. **Spencer Compton**, now **earl of Wilmington**, succeeds Walpole as First Lord of the Treasury.

Händel composes the first version of his oratorio *Messiah*.

Sir Robert Walpole (1676–1745)

Robert Walpole dominated politics during the reigns of the first two Georges, his enormous bulk an unmistakable presence in the House of Commons. In control of the nation's affairs between 1721 and 1741 almost without interruption, his supremacy was so complete that the age is often referred to as the "Robinocracy".

Appointed to the council of Queen Anne's husband, George of Denmark, in 1705, he maintained a cautious balance between moderate Tories such as Godolphin and the Whig Junto (see p.273), enabling him to climb the ladder of promotion with relative ease. The accession of George I ended Tory influence, and Walpole served in the ensuing Whig administration first as paymaster general and then, in 1715, as both first lord of the treasury and chancellor of the exchequer – a combination of offices that has led historians to call Walpole England's 'first prime minister'.

Party jealousies prompted his resignation in 1717, but he resumed office as paymaster general three years later, thanks in no small part to the influence of the King's mistress, the duchess of Kendal. The event that truly secured his return to power, however, was the South Sea Bubble (see p.302). Walpole was credited with being the only man capable of addressing the country's financial turmoil, and in 1721 he again became 'prime minister'. The accession of George II caused another brief hiatus in his career: the new monarch disliked Walpole, and replaced him with the ineffectual Spencer Compton. But Compton foolishly asked Walpole to assist him in arranging the civil list, giving the ousted leader a perfect opportunity to prove his value to the throne. Walpole guaranteed the monarch extensive subsidies, and, supported by Queen Caroline, he moved smoothly back into power.

Eventually, though, he fell foul of the Hanoverian habit of sons opposing their fathers. The Queen's death in 1737 left Walpole exposed to the machinations of Prince Frederick's circle (see p.310), who orchestrated an increasingly unruly House of Commons. Defeated in Parliament over a relatively minor issue involving a disputed election case, Walpole resigned two days after being created the earl of Orford.

1743 Following Wilmington's death in July, **Henry Pelham** becomes prime minister and forms a Whig administration.

Supporting the Austrian **Habsburg** cause, British contingents fight alongside Hanoverian and Hessian regiments against the French at the **Battle of Dettingen** in Bavaria on 23 June.

1744 As the European conflict widens, France enters the 'Family Compact' with Spain and declares war on Austria and Britain.

John Wesley's **Methodist Society** holds its first national conference.

The poet **Alexander Pope** dies.

1745 Jacobite rebellion is renewed when James Edward's son **Charles Edward Stuart** (known as 'Bonnie Prince Charlie') lands in Scotland and raises the clans against George II. A government force commanded by **Sir John Cope** is defeated by the pretender's highland army at **Prestonpans** on 21 September. The rebels progress toward **Edinburgh**, capturing the city but not its castle. As winter sets in, Charles Edward marches into England, recruiting a small regiment in **Manchester** and reaching **Derby** on 4 December. Unable to attract further followers, though, he is forced to retreat northwards two days later by his newly formed council of war.

1746 During a government crisis induced by the Jacobite rebellion, the Pelham administration resigns but is quickly reinstated after a replacement headed by the **earl of Bath** and the **earl of Granville** fails to attract public or political support. **William Pitt 'the Elder'** is appointed joint-vice-treasurer of Ireland.

Pursued across the Scottish border by government forces, the Jacobites mount a successful rearguard action at **Falkirk** on 17 January, but their main army is routed by George

Jacobitism

The cause of the exiled Stuarts attracted widespread support in Britain and on the continent, but a second Stuart Restoration was never truly on the cards. James II's son **James Edward**'s refusal to renounce Catholicism left him with insufficient parliamentary support for a peaceful return to be possible, and, despite French sympathies, no major European state was prepared to underwrite an armed invasion. Most English Jacobites were attached to the Stuarts only in an abstract way, their support seldom going beyond covert toasts raised to the 'king across the water'.

Even so, there were three Jacobite rebellions against the unpopular Hanoverians: in 1715, 1719 and, most famously, during 1745–46. Strictly speaking, the story of the last rebellion is a Scottish one: the majority of the action was fought on Scottish soil by Scottish participants. But it didn't always seem so – the last Stuart Pretender, **Charles Edward**, affectionately known as **'Bonnie Prince Charlie'**, assumed his invasion would be enthusiastically greeted in England and marched south, reaching as far as **Derby** and recruiting some 250 down-and-outs in **Manchester**. But no one else flocked to his banner, and his homesick Scottish and Irish commanders soon urged retreat. Harried by English forces, Charles Edward made it back to Scotland, but was ignominiously defeated at **Culloden**. His hopes dashed, he ended life an alcoholic.

1745 was a disaster for highland society, but it reassured the Hanoverians that although the English might grumble, actual revolt was far from a reality. In any case, after Bonnie Prince Charlie there were no more pretenders. When his brother **Henry Benedict** entered the Church, Jacobitism lost its *raison d'être*. It survived only as lively subject matter for romantic novelists, among them Sir Walter Scott.

II's younger son, the **duke of Cumberland**, at **Culloden Moor** on 16 April. **Charles Edward** spends five months in hiding before being spirited out of Britain.

1747 As the Whigs consolidate their hold on government, an increasing number of Tories turn toward **Prince Frederick**, who issues the **Carlton House Declaration** on 4 June, outlining a 'patriot' programme of reform. **George II** responds by dissolving Parliament and calling fresh **elections**, during which the Tories are heavily defeated and the government hand is further strengthened. The government, however, is divided on whether and how to pursue the war against **France** and **Spain**. Led by the dukes of **Cumberland** and **Newcastle** the war party wins the argument, and an army of 100,000 is raised. Cumberland is defeated at **Lauffeldt** by the **Marshal de Saxe**, but a French convoy setting out for the West Indies is destroyed

Frederick, Prince of Wales (1707–51)

Frederick, like his father, suffered from the traditional loathing Hanoverian fathers seemed to feel toward their eldest sons. George II and 'Fritz', as he was known inside the family, could barely endure to be in the same room, yet the king perversely blocked any attempt by his son to establish an independent household until he was expelled from St James's Palace in 1737. When the prince finally did get his own establishment, Leicester House, he used it with a vengeance. He gathered a motley collection of politically disaffected men and wits around him, and from this gathering flowed the re-invention of the 'patriot' cause in politics. Frederick's vision of a 'Patriot King', who would do away with oligarchy and end Whig dominance, was eventually taken up by his own son, George III, in the years immediately following George II's death.

But there was a seamier side to the prince's activities. Quite how involved he was with the peculiarities of the Hellfire Club (see p.325) is uncertain, but he was associated with several of its leading intimates, and members of the fraternity such as Bubb Doddington, Francis Dashwood and Lord Sandwich all found places in the new 'Patriot' ministry of their friend Lord Bute after by Admiral **Edward Hawke** off **La Rochelle**.

The first volumes of **Samuel Richardson**'s epistolary novel, *Clarissa*, are published (see p.290).

1748 The **War of the Austrian Succession** is brought to a close by the **Treaty of Aix-la-Chapelle**. **Prussia**'s possession of **Silesia** is confirmed, but in almost every other respect eight years' fighting has done little to resolve Europe's tensions, including those between Britain and the Bourbon nations of **France** and **Spain**. Even so, the peace is celebrated in London by the first performance of **Händel**'s *Music for the Royal Fireworks*. Prime minister **Henry Pelham** immediately begins reducing military expenditure,

1762. Set against this, Frederick was a passionate patron of the arts as well as a musician of some talent, and did much to champion the concept of a paid **Loyal Opposition** in Parliament. But his positive qualities are rarely remembered now, buried beneath a famous mock epitaph:

Here lies Fred,
Who was alive and is dead:
Had it been his father,
I had much rather,
Had it been his brother,
Still better than another;
Had it been his sister,
No one would have missed her;
Had it been the whole generation,
Still better for the nation:
But since 'tis only Fred –
Who was alive and is dead –
There's no more to be said.

and wins popularity for his government and the king by **lowering taxes**.

1749 To counter the success of French colonists in Canada, a British fort, backed by the government, is established at **Halifax, Nova Scotia**.

Henry Fielding publishes his novel *Tom Jones*.

1750 A split develops in the ranks of the Whig government between the Pelhamite **'Old Corps'** and **John Russell, Duke of Bedford**'s **'Bloomsbury Gang'**, but in effect little divides the various Whig factions – they all aim to uphold the Revolutionary Settlement.

1751 Hearing that **George II** is seriously ill and eager to assume power, **Prince Frederick** rushes to his father's bedside but catches a chill on the way and dies. As the Tory opposition is thrown into confusion by the loss of its figurehead, the king recovers his health. Frederick's own son, **Prince George**, created **prince of Wales**, becomes heir apparent.

An act to replace the Julian with the Gregorian calendar, already adopted by most of Europe, is passed in May to take effect the following September.

1752 With the introduction of the **Gregorian Calendar**, time in England jumps from 2 to 14 September. A confused population takes to the streets, riotously clamouring for the government to 'bring us back our eleven days'.

1753 Parliament passes a **Jewish Naturalization Bill** (permitting Jews the right to full citizenship in England), greeted in the country at large with mounting hostility.

The last significant Jacobite plot ends with the execution of **Dr Archibald Cameron** in June.

The library of **Sir Hans Sloane** and the remains of the **Harley collection** (containing some 7660 manuscripts)

> **Excise.** A hateful tax levied upon commodities.
>
> **Lexicographer.** A writer of dictionaries, a harmless drudge.
>
> **Network.** Anything reticulated or dessucated at equal distances, with interstices between the intersections.
>
> **Patron.** Commonly a wretch who supports with insolence, and is paid with flattery.

Some definitions in Samuel Johnson's
Dictionary of the English Language (1755)

are bought for the nation by the government and housed in what will become the **British Museum**.

1754 Following his death, **Henry Pelham** is succeeded as first lord of the treasury by his brother **Thomas Pelham-Holles**, the **duke of Newcastle**.

The government repeals the **'Jew Act'** of the previous year as parliamentary members fear its electoral consequences.

In **North America**, a critical situation develops after **Colonel George Washington** fails to capture **Fort Duquesne** from the French. A thousand British troops under **Edward Braddock** are dispatched to the colonies to bolster English interests.

1755 **William Pitt** (dismissed as paymaster later in the year) and **Prince Frederick**'s Leicester House grouping join forces in opposition to the **duke of Newcastle** and his government.

In **America**, Braddock's expeditionary force is annihilated by the French on the banks of the **Monongahela River** in July.

Lord Bute is appointed groom of the stole to **Augusta, Princess of Wales**, and **Henry Fox** becomes secretary of state for the Southern Department.

Dr Samuel Johnson sets new lexicographical standards with the publication of his *Dictionary of the English Language*, which uses citations from English authors to confirm the meanings of English words.

1756 As tensions between Europe's leading nations escalate – both as regards the balance of power in Europe itself and rivalry in the acquisition of overseas possessions and trading rights – Britain forms an alliance with **Prussia** by the **Convention of Westminster** on 16 January. In May **France** and **Austria** conclude a similar treaty at **Versailles**. On 18 May, its interests challenged in both America and India, Britain declares war on **France**, inaugurating the **Seven Years War**. But with previous spending cuts still in place, Britain is ill-prepared for hostilities, and experiences initial reverses.

In **India**, the **East India Company**'s trading settlement at **Calcutta** is overrun by **Siraj-ud-Daula**, the French-backed **nawab of Bengal**. There is a public outcry in Britain when it is learned that a number of Company officials have died following their incarceration in the guard room of **Fort Williams** – known as the **Black Hole of Calcutta**.

In June, **Admiral John Byng** fails to prevent the seizure of **Minorca** by the French, and in August the French commander **Montcalm** captures a British fort at **Oswego** on Lake Ontario.

Newcastle and **Fox** resign in November, and are replaced by a ministry headed by **Pitt** and the **duke of Devonshire**.

Russia joins the Versailles alliance against Britain.

There are **food riots** in the **Midlands** and the **West Country** following a bad harvest.

The East India Company

Europe's first overseas empires, belonging to Spain and Portugal, developed through sponsorship provided by the monarchies and governments of those countries. The British Empire, however, followed a different course, in which private enterprise was the guiding force. The American colonies were initially settled by adventurers funded by joint-stock companies, although they were quickly converted into 'Crown' colonies by the issue of royal charters. But in the eastern hemisphere the joint-stock principle held sway for almost two hundred years.

The East India Company was set up by royal charter in 1599, intended to create a monopoly among English traders plying the East Indies spice trade, but thereafter pursued a course very much its own. From around 1623 it focused on the Indian subcontinent, in time driving out all its European rivals. But the Company continued looking further afield, and periodically used brute force to open up the China market. By 1760, following Clive's victory at Plassey, the Company stood on the brink of assuming control over all of India, and was responsible for supplying England's growing thirst for Chinese tea.

Yet there were difficulties. China itself seemed uninterested in importing manufactured goods, and the cost of administering India threatened to get out of hand, even though these were supported by land revenues from the subcontinent. The solution to the first problem was to develop business between India and China, and from around 1770 Indian-grown opium – for which the Chinese did have an appetite – was traded for tea, silks and other goods. Then, when mills in England began processing American cotton, the Company began importing raw Indian cotton into Britain instead of finished fabrics. Both policies had catastrophic consequences: the Chinese became a nation of addicts, and India's garment-makers were dealt a body blow.

In 1784, in return for much-needed subsidies, an India Act brought the Company under governmental supervision, and by the mid-1830s it had lost its autonomy. The end eventually came after the Indian Uprising of 1857, when it was abolished for good.

1757 **Pitt** is ordered to resign from government on 5 April, and in Europe Britain's army continues to fare badly under the command of **Cumberland**.

National fortunes revive sharply in **India**, when **Robert Clive** recaptures **Calcutta**, defeats **Siraj-ud-Daula** at **Plassey** on 23 June and overruns the French settlement at **Charndernagor**. As a consequence of these victories – secured in part by Clive blackmailing the nawab of Bengal's Indian allies – Clive becomes **governor of Bengal**, the French are effectively driven out of India and India itself is opened up to British control.

Admiral Byng is court-martialled and shot for his failures of the previous year – in the words of the French philosopher **Voltaire**, 'pour encourager les autres'.

In June, following the failure of a British amphibious assault on **Rochefort**, **Pitt** and the **earl of Holderness** rejoin the government, and **Newcastle** is reappointed first lord of the treasury at the end of the parliamentary session.

> ❝ Out of the field of Plassey and the victors' 18 dead there spouted forth the power of the nineteenth century. Mammon now rode into supremacy to become the unchallenged god of the western world. Once in the lands of the rising sun western man had sought the Holy Sepulchre. That sun had long set, and now in those spiritually arid regions he found the almighty sovereign. What the Cross had failed to achieve, in a few blood-red-years the trinity of piston, sword and coin accomplished: the subjection of the East and for a span of nearly 200 years the economic serfdom of the Oriental world. ❞
>
> J.F.C. Fuller, *The Decisive Battle of the Western World* (1954–56)

1758 **Prince Ferdinand of Brunswick** wins major victories for the Anglo-Prussian alliance over the French at **Krefeld** (23 June), pushing the French back westwards across the **Rhine**. The tide of war also turns against the Versailles alliance in North America, where British contingents under **James Wolfe** and **Jeffrey Amherst** capture a number of French forts, including **Frontenac** on 27 August. Across the English Channel, British forces take **Cherbourg**, but are pushed back at **St Malo**.

Pitt breaks his ties with the **Leicester House group** and **Lord Bute**.

In line with a prediction made by the astronomer **Sir Edmund Halley** (see p.278) in 1705, a **comet** appears in the skies on Christmas Day.

1759 The **'Year of Victories'** begins with an English fleet repulsing a French attempt to seize **Madras** in southern India. In May the French surrender **Guadeloupe**, and on 1 August an Anglo-Prussian army led by **Frederick the Great** defeats a French army at **Minden**, although on 12 August Frederick himself is defeated by an Austro-Russian army at **Kunersdorf**. On 13 September **James Wolfe** comprehensively defeats the main French force under **Montcalm** on the **Plains of Abraham** outside **Quebec**, even though Wolfe himself is killed. British naval supremacy is assured by another victory in November, won by **Admiral Hawke**, over the **Brest** fleet in **Quiberon Bay**.

The first **Canal Act** is steered through Parliament by the **duke of Bridgewater**.

Josiah Wedgwood leases a pottery factory at Burslem.

The **British Museum** opens to the public.

1760 The French formally surrender their interest in **Canada** to the British at **Montreal** on 8 September.

On 9 October a Russian army sacks **Berlin**.

On 25 October **George II** dies aged 77, and is succeeded by his 22-year-old grandson **George III**, who will reign for sixty years.

Laurence Sterne publishes the first volumes of his experimental novel, *The Life and Opinions of Tristram Shandy, Gentleman.*

The reign of George III
1760–1820

George III came to the throne claiming that he 'gloried in the name of Briton'. He saw himself as a 'patriot king', embracing a creed espoused by his father **Prince Frederick** and drummed into him by his mother **Princess Augusta** and his tutor **John Mackenzie Stuart, Earl of Bute**. During his long reign, England underwent a radical transformation. It witnessed the humiliating loss of **America**, and found itself faced with a new ideological threat in the form of the **French Revolution**. Yet the bloodlettings across the Channel made the Tory party respectable again, while British prestige was restored with the final defeat of **Napoleon** at **Waterloo** in 1815.

Quite what George III hoped to achieve is hard to determine. His Whig opponents argued vociferously that he aimed to create a kind of continental-style absolutism, but the long tenure in office by both **Lord North** (1770–82) and **William Pitt the Younger** (1783–1801) demonstrate that, once satisfied with a ministry, George III wanted nothing better than to let it do its job. And even if he had intended to be an absolute monarch, his own mental instability rendered the ambition futile. In 1788, dejected at the loss of America, he suffered a mental breakdown caused by the hereditary disease **porphyria**; relapses followed until in

1810 he descended into permanent madness. When it became clear that he would not recover, Parliament transferred his authority to his son **George, Prince of Wales**, and thus the last ten years of George III's reign are known as the **Regency**.

In 1760, though, at his accession, hopes were high. George III seemed determined to do away with the oligarchical Whig groupings who dominated government and, like both William III and Anne before him, to attempt to create a non-party ministry. Crucially, too, George III wished to bring an end to the **Seven Years War**. A year after Britain's most significant wartime achievements, this policy attracted widespread criticism, and the king received still more by appointing his one-time tutor Bute prime minister. The appointment of a court favourite – and one, moreover, that bore the name of Stuart – gave rise to dire predictions of monarchical tyranny. Inexperienced and easily flustered, Bute was a poor choice and soon resigned, but not before the damage had been done.

Party in England was a diverse patchwork of factions and different interest groups and, although those calling themselves 'Whig' mostly attempted to uphold the Revolution Settlement, they didn't by any means all operate in harmony. One result of George III's apparent meddling in the 1760s, though, was the growth of a clearer sense of party ideology, and among one of the more coherent groups – those attached to the leadership of the **marquess of Rockingham** – an 'opposition manifesto' gradually developed. The outbreak of the **American War** gave greater impetus to the Rockinghams' concerns, and at their forefront was **Charles James Fox**, who became the King's especial *bête noire*. In 1783, Fox (in an unlikely alliance with George III's previous prime minister **Lord North**) forced the king to accept them as his government under the nominal leadership of the **duke of Portland**. Yet George was not finished, and at the close of the year engineered their defeat in Parliament and the appointment of the 24-year-old **William Pitt the Younger** as the new premier.

Pitt's eighteen-year period of office puts the lie to the suggestion that George III wished to rule as a despot, though the king did make it plain that he would not support any extensive reform of the political system. Between 1783 and 1789 Pitt busied himself with balancing the books, but his hour came with the outbreak of the **French Revolution**. Although this cataclysm was at first greeted by the Foxites as a glorious re-enactment of 1688, the onset of the guillotine showed that they had been mistaken and that Pitt's cautious suspicion was the wiser reaction. As fear of revolution in England spread, Pitt turned from his reforms of the economy, and instead instituted a wide-reaching programme of repressive legislation, restricting press freedom and the size of public gatherings. Pitt succeeded in keeping England safe from revolt at home, and free to pursue the continental war. He did not live to see the final triumph of **Waterloo**, but did return to power in time to reap the rewards of Nelson's victory at **Trafalgar** in 1805 before his own premature death the following year. And the Revolutionary War vindicated not only Pitt, but also served to restore the Tories' to respectability – from 1807 to 1832 Tory ministries dominated politics again, as the Whigs took their turn in the wilderness.

Yet despite the rejoicing Waterloo inspired, its aftermath proved a sour time for England. Unemployment, social unrest and economic stagnation affected much of society and calls for parliamentary reform became increasingly widespread. In the midst of the depression, the **Prince Regent**, addicted to the fine things in life and surrounded by an array of dandyish companions such as **George 'Beau'**

Brummell, attracted increasing criticism. The other royal dukes proved similarly disappointing, and as the mad, blind George III neared the end of his life, the future of the Hanoverian dynasty – and indeed of the monarchy itself – seemed in question.

1760 Influenced by his friend and ex-tutor the **earl of Bute**, the king endeavours to bring Britain's participation in the **Seven Years War** to an end. At the first meeting of his Privy Council, however, he is persuaded to modify his objections: a 'bloody and expensive war' becomes a 'just and necessary' one.

1761 The remains of the French army in India surrenders to the **East India Company** at **Pondicherry** in January.

Britain takes possession of the 'neutral' West Indian island of **Dominica**.

Belle Isle off the coast of Brittany is captured in June.

Bute, still determined to bring about peace, replaces the earl of Holderness as secretary of state, and the **duke of Bedford** is appointed to negotiate peace terms with the French.

George III marries **Charlotte of Mecklenberg–Strelitz** on 8 September, and is crowned king four days later.

On 19 December **Spain** declares war on Britain.

The **Bridgewater Canal**, built by **James Brindley**, is opened between **Worsley** and **Manchester**, initiating a network of canals that greatly improves trade and communications.

In an early manifestation of industrial unrest, 42 miners from **Northumberland** are killed by Yorkshire militiamen as they march toward **Hexham**, demonstrating against the **Militia Act** (in effect conscription).

1762 Admiral **George Rodney** and **General Robert Monckton** capture **Martinique** in the Caribbean. Later they occupy **St Lucia**, **St Vincent** and **Grenada**. Peace negotiations with **France** continue in secret as **Spain** invades Britain's ally **Portugal**.

The **duke of Newcastle** resigns as **first lord of the treasury**, a post now assumed by **Lord Bute**, who forms a ministry that includes members of the **Society of the Medenham Monks** (better known as the 'Hellfire Club'; see p.325) as well as some from the Leicester House grouping.

On the continent, French armies are defeated at **Wilhemsthal** and **Luttenberg** in June and July. British forces seize **Havana** as Spain sustains setbacks in Portugal. **Bedford** travels to Paris to finalize peace terms which **Henry Fox** is appointed to present to the House of Commons. The preliminaries are signed at **Fontainebleau** on 3 November, and approved by Bute's cabinet seven days later.

John Wilkes begins publishing the *North Briton*, a political newspaper set up to rival the pro-government *Briton* (edited by **Tobias Smollett** and backed by **William Hogarth**).

1763 As the **'King's Friends'** tighten their grip on power, the ousting of senior Whigs, masterminded by **Bute** and **Fox** and known as the **'Slaughter of the Pelhamite Innocents'**, draws to a conclusion.

The **Seven Years War** is formally ended when the **Treaty of Paris** is signed on 10 February. According to its terms, France cedes its **Canadian territories**, **Grenada** and **Senegal** to Britain, but retains **Guadeloupe**. Britain relinquishes **Cuba** in Spain's favour. The treaty is swiftly and strenuously attacked by **William Pitt the Elder**, who also campaigns against Bute's decision to tax **cider**. Bute suffers a nervous breakdown and, despite the king's annoyance, resigns as prime minister. **George Grenville** is appointed

John Wilkes caricatured by Hogarth, 1763.

in his place, and attempts to deflect Pitt's attacks by mounting an attack on **John Wilkes**. Wilkes is arrested for seditious libel on the basis that he made defamatory remarks about Bute and George III in an edition of the *North Briton*. On the orders of **Chief Justice Charles Pratt**, Wilkes is released, then re-arrested after Parliament votes that parliamentary privilege does not extend to publishing seditious libel. But he is released again when Pratt declares the **General Warrant** against Wilkes to be unconstitutional. He fights a duel with **Samuel Martin MP**, one of Bute's supporters, then flees to France.

1764 Wilkes is formally expelled from the **House of Commons** for his presumed authorship of the pornographic **'Essay on Woman'**.

Grenville puts forward plans to impose a **stamp duty** on such items as newspapers, pamphlets, legal documents and playing cards in the American colonies, but the scheme is delayed a year to give the colonists time to submit alternative proposals.

James Hargreaves invents the **spinning jenny**, the first step toward a fully mechanized loom, and the **Bolting Machine** is devised by John and Thomas Morris.

The painter and engraver **William Hogarth**, whose work depicted the foibles and vices of his age, dies.

1765 George III's endeavours to control government collapse with his first descent into madness. A **Regency Bill**, designed to provide security for the throne, is heavily opposed in both houses of Parliament.

In July, the **Grenville administration** falls, and is replaced by a cabinet headed by the **dukes of Cumberland** and **Newcastle** and the **marquess of Rockingham**.

The Stamp Act is passed on 22 March, but stamp duty is restricted in all thirteen of Britain's American colonies, led

Wilkes, 'Hellfire' and Liberty

In the middle years of the 18th century a group of politicians led by **Sir Francis Dashwood** formed a secret fraternity known as the **Brothers of St Francis of Medmenham**, taking their name from a ruined abbey at Medmenham in Berkshire where many of their meetings were held. Guided by their motto *Fay ce que vouldras* ('do as you will'), the brothers indulged in a variety of bizarre rituals, feasts and orgies, in the process shocking many in society. Among them were **Thomas Potter MP**, the rakish son of the archbishop of Canterbury, the **earl of Sandwich** and **George Bubb Doddington**. **Hogarth** too may have been a member, and possibly **Frederick, Prince of Wales**.

But the most notorious was **John Wilkes**, a strikingly ugly man and a brilliant conversationalist. For Wilkes, **'Hellfire'**, as the club came to be known, was a means to political office, which he needed to pay off his gambling debts. When **Bute** became George III's principal minister in 1762 the Brothers naturally benefited through their links with him, but Wilkes was left out in the cold. He responded by savagely attacking Bute's policies – and by implication George III – in the *North Briton*. Bute quickly resigned, but his successor, Lord Grenville, retaliated on Bute's behalf by having Wilkes arrested.

But this put Wilkes in his element, and he began inciting popular unrest in the name of 'liberty'. After being released on the orders of the lord chief justice he fled to France, returning to London in 1768 to battle his way into Parliament. Denied his place at Westminster, Wilkes became first an alderman of London, then its mayor – positions he skilfully exploited to embarrass the establishment still further. But it was the petitioning movement launched to support him, in the name of 'Wilkes and Liberty', that became his lasting legacy and which formed a direct antecedent of the dissident **Chartist** petitions of the 1830s and 1840s (see p.369).

by **Virginia**; there are riots in **Boston** and assaults on officials trying to collect the tax. A 'Stamp Act' Congress convenes in **New York** in October and votes a boycott of all British goods.

The death of **Cumberland** on 31 October means that Rockingham becomes *de facto* prime minister.

1766 Following the death of **James Edward Stuart**, known as the **'Old Pretender'**, the pope and other Catholic kings decline to recognize **Charles Edward Stuart** as **Charles III** of England.

Rockingham's government, supported by **Pitt**, endeavours to calm the situation in **America** by repealing the **Stamp Act**, but then makes the mistake of passing the **Declaratory Act**, which asserts Britain's right to impose direct taxes in the colonies. The **cider tax** is also repealed and **General Warrants** (by which people could be arrested without specific charges) are declared illegal.

The **duke of Grafton** resigns from the government, triggering four months of ministerial instability. The Rockingham–Newcastle faction disintegrates, and Rockingham himself resigns in July. **William Pitt**, now the **earl of Chatham**, becomes prime minister.

Henry Cavendish discovers hydrogen.

1767 In January **Charles Townshend** announces the government's intention to impose indirect taxation on the American colonies in the form of **import duties** on tea, paper and other goods. **Grenville**, the **Rockinghamites** and followers of the **duke of Bedford** unite in opposition. Notwithstanding, Townshend's **Revenue Act** is passed on 29 June, shortly before Parliament breaks for the summer. The legislation is greeted in **Boston**, **Philadelphia** and other American cities by renewed calls for a boycott of British goods. Bedford's followers are persuaded to join the government, thus isolating the 'Rockingham Whigs'.

As harvests fail and grain prices soar, there are further **food riots** in the **Midlands** and the **West Country**.

Joseph Priestley publishes *The History and Present State of Electricity*, an early attempt to explain **electromagnetic conductivity**.

1768 **John Wilkes** returns from France to stand for the **City of London** in parliamentary elections. Although he comes last in the poll, his name is also put forward for **Middlesex**, which he wins. Having regained membership of the Commons, he presents himself to answer the charges of blasphemy and pornography still outstanding. His outlawry (by which he is considered automatically a criminal and 'outside of the law') is overturned but he is remanded in custody pending trial, causing celebrations among his supporters – which soon turn into rioting in London amid the familiar cry of 'Wilkes and Liberty.' The government brings in soldiers to disperse the rioters, but their heavy-handed treatment results in the **'St George's Fields Massacre'** of 10 May which leaves seven dead and fifteen injured. The scale of the violence shocks the Wilkeites into quiescence, during which time Wilkes is convicted, fined £1000 and imprisoned for 22 months.

There is also rioting in **Boston**, after customs officials seize John Hancock's sloop *Liberty* on 10 June. Throughout the American colonies resistance to Townshend's duties stiffens.

In October **Chatham** resigns after the sacking of the **earl of Shelburne** from his government. He is replaced as prime minster by the **duke of Grafton**.

A Royal Navy lieutenant, **James Cook**, embarks on a series of great voyages in the southern Pacific aboard *HMS Endeavour* that open the way to British colonization of **Australia**, **New Zealand** and other islands in the eastern hemisphere.

1769 Released from prison, **Wilkes** attempts to take his seat in the Commons, but is thrown out. When voters in Middlesex re-elect him three times, the House finally declares his election illegal and confer his seat on his defeated opponent, **Henry Lawes Luttrell**. The Rockingham Whigs come out in Wilkes's support, and organize an unsuccessful **national petition** calling for his reinstatement.

As the **American colonies** teeter on the brink of rebellion, the government repeals all the Townshend duties, with the exception of the **import tax** on **tea**. The few Chathamites who remain in government resign their posts. Grafton's ministry is further damaged by the publication of scathingly critical letters published in the *Public Advertiser* and signed 'Junius'. They warn that Grafton is playing a 'foolish game' by taking on Wilkes, and one letter ominously ends: 'He rose by Mr Wilkes's popularity, and it is not improbable that he may fall by it.'

1770 Bowing to public pressure, **Grafton** resigns in January, and **Lord North** becomes prime minister. North, however, is unable to persuade Parliament to rescind the **import tax** on tea in America, and on 1 March, during an incident known as the **Boston Massacre**, three colonials are shot by British troops during renewed rioting.

The Irish-born writer and parliamentarian **Edmund Burke**, sometimes perceived as the greatest advocate of English liberties, publishes *Thoughts on the Present Discontents*, arguing for economic reform and warning of the dangers inherent in arbitrary monarchical government.

Priestley discovers **sulphur dioxide**.

1771 **Press freedom** in Britain becomes an important political issue when a number of **London printers** are summoned to the House of Commons accused of publishing details of parliamentary debates. The **lord mayor** and **city aldermen**, among them **Wilkes**, protect the printers by arresting the Commons' messenger. In riposte, the Commons arrests the **mayor**. The situation is defused by North's disinclination to insist on the secrecy of debates, and from 1774 onwards approved transcripts will be published by **Luke Hansard**. Wilkes becomes **high sheriff** of London.

Tobias Smollett publishes *The Expedition of Humphry Clinker*, a novel that satirizes the decrepitude of English society, and dies later in the year.

1772 Against the wishes of Rockinghamites and Chathamites alike, Parliament passes an act making all future **royal marriages** subject to the monarch's approval.

In India, **Warren Hastings** begins a thirteen-year stint as the **governor of Bengal** that will see the East India Company's hold on the subcontinent greatly consolidated.

Continuing poor harvests provoke **food riots** in all parts of England.

Daniel Rutherford isolates **nitrogen**.

1773 North's ministry pushes through legislation that grants the **East India Company** a monopoly on tea sales to the American colonies, but which also increases government control over the Company itself. On 16 December, in an event which becomes known as the **Boston 'Tea Party'**, dissident colonials disguised as 'Mohawks' board the Company's ships and throw 342 chests of tea into the harbour.

The **London Stock Exchange** is founded.

1774 **Charles James Fox**, dismissed at the king's bidding from a post at the Treasury, joins the **Rockingham Whigs**. The crisis in America mounts as the **First Continental Congress** is convened in **Philadelphia** in September to consider ways of resisting British interference. North's government raises the stakes by closing

Boston Harbour until the East India Company is compensated for its losses. The **Quebec Act**, extending religious toleration to Canadian Catholics, expands the frontiers of Quebec as far south as the **Mississippi** at the expense of **Massachusetts**, whose charter is revoked.

As a domestic crisis develops in **France**, English-speaking radicals on both sides of the Atlantic – including some Whigs – are vociferous in their condemnations of royal absolutism. Notwithstanding, the British government secures a substantial parliamentary majority following a general election.

Priestley isolates **oxygen** and discovers **ammonia**.

> ❝ You will doubtless soon after your return to England be a Member of one of the two Houses of Parliament; there you must take pains to distinguish yourself as a speaker. The task is not very hard if you have common sense, as I think you have, and a great deal more... The late Lord Bolingbroke had accustomed himself so much to a florid eloquence even in his common conversation (which anybody with care may do) that his real extempore speeches seemed to be studied. Lord Mansfield was, in my opinion, the next to him in undeviating eloquence, but Mr Pitt carried with him, unpremeditated, the strength of thunder, and the splendour of lightning... ❞
>
> The earl of Chesterfield, writing to his godson c.1773

1775 In the House of Lords **Chatham** proposes resolving the American crisis by returning to the original status quo, but his motion is defeated by 68 votes to 18. In response, North's ministry declares **Massachusetts** to be in a state of rebellion. An attempted reconciliation put forward by **Edmund Burke** is also rejected. The government orders **General Thomas Gage** to arrest **John Hancock** and his fellow patriot **Samuel Adams** in America, but as news of this leaks, armed colonials intercept his force of seven hundred British 'red coats' at **Lexington** and **Concord** on 19 April – two minor skirmishes that mark the beginning of the **American War of Independence**. But in the opening months of hostilities, neither side is able to secure a clear advantage.

1776 **Chatham** and **Rockingham** combine forces to reverse North's American policy, but are unable to defeat the government. As a result the Rockinghamites withdraw from Parliament.

John Wilkes attempts to introduce a parliamentary reform bill, but is unable to find anyone in the Commons to support it.

On 4 July the **Continental Congress of Philadelphia** adopts on behalf of the American colonies a **Declaration of Independence**, inspired by the English Quaker and radical **Thomas Paine**'s pamphlet *Common Sense* and drafted by **Thomas Jefferson**. **William, Viscount Howe** captures **New York** for the Crown, but the Americans gain victories at **Trenton** and (in January 1777) at **Princeton**, enabling them to take control of **New Jersey**.

Edward Gibbon publishes the first two volumes of his epic history, *The Decline and Fall of the Roman Empire*.

1777 The **Rockinghamites** return to Parliament to oppose – unsuccessfully – a bill to pay off **George III**'s debts. **Grafton**, supported by **Chatham**, also fails to persuade the Lords to adopt an address calling for an immediate cessation of hostilities in America. As the **Chathamite–Rockinghamite** alliance grows, **Howe** defeats the American general **George Washington** at the **Brandywine** and captures **Philadelphia**. General **John Burgoyne**'s army, however, is surrounded by the Americans at **Bemis Heights** and forced to surrender at **Saratoga** in October.

Edward Gibbon (1737–94)

If Britain's outstanding contributions to the 18th-century European Enlightenment were made by two Scotsmen – the philosopher **David Hume** and the economist **Adam Smith** – the Englishman Edward Gibbon provided a literary monument that is as readable and challenging today as it was when it was written.

The History of the Decline and Fall of the Roman Empire, published in six volumes between 1776 and 1788, spans the thirteen centuries up to the fall of Constantinople in 1453. It is not simply the story of the dying Roman court, but deals more widely with Islam and offers sympathetic portraits of the Slavs and Mongols. It also provides fascinating intellectual history, Gibbon taking mischievous delight in drawing out the squabbles of the early Christian sects – which earned him the loathing of several contemporary churchmen. Yet if Gibbon's conception of the past is sweepingly vast, his brushstrokes are detailed and intimate. Human foibles and corruption are lovingly depicted, and famously *Decline and Fall* is accompanied by eight thousand footnotes. The book is all the more remarkable for having been composed entirely while standing up: Gibbon constructed a writing lectern at one end of his London study with his library at the other end, and the tracks he made when pacing between them are still visible today.

The young Gibbon spent fourteen months at Oxford, but he was later to describe them as 'the most idle and unprofitable of my whole life'. He converted to Catholicism and left, whereupon his father sent him to Lausanne for corrective instruction. Much of the rest of his life was spent in Switzerland, although for a few years until the fall of North's ministry in 1782 he was MP for **Liskeard**. Gibbon also served as an officer in the Hampshire militia, at least according to his posthumously published *Memoirs* (1796). And although *Decline and Fall* guaranteed Gibbon personal celebrity, it was not received favourably by everyone. In words which are variously ascribed to the duke of Gloucester, the duke of Cumberland and even George III, the author was castigated for his labour: 'Another damned, thick, square book! Always scribble, scribble, scribble! Eh! Mr Gibbon?'

1778 As **France** enters the war on the Americans' side, Fox proposes to the Commons that no more troops be sent to the colonies, but is defeated by 259 votes to 165. Attacking the government's war policies in the House of Lords on 11 May, **Chatham** collapses and dies. While leadership of the Chathamites is assumed by the **earl of Shelburne**, Rockingham names his terms for joining the government, but is rejected by George III. The **earl of Carlisle** is despatched to **America** to explore peace terms with the rebels, but returns empty-handed. As the war in America continues to seesaw, the French and English fight an inconclusive naval battle off **Ushant**.

1779 **Admiral Augustus Keppel**, a supporter of Rockingham, is unsuccessfully court-martialled for his 'failure' at **Ushant**. On the day of his vindication **Fox** and other supporters travel to **Portsmouth** to encourage widespread rioting in celebration. Returning to London, Fox makes political capital by renewing his parliamentary attacks on the government's handling of the war.

Spain joins in on the American and French side, laying siege to **Gibraltar**. The **duke of Bedford**'s faction deserts the government in an attempt to force **North** to resign.

As the **national debt** grows, Burke introduces an **Economical Reform Bill**. His plan is to reduce the Crown's influence over Parliament by abolishing a number of sinecures that are a central part of government patronage, but he makes little progress as North's ministry succeeds in destroying it at the committee stage.

Samuel Crompton invents the **'spinning mule'**, improving on Hargreaves's 'spinning jenny', which enables the mass production of muslin cloth.

England's first **Iron Bridge**, a showcase construction that spans the Severn River at **Coalbrookdale**, is built by **Abraham Darby**. The area will become an epicentre for industry and a great iron manufacturing area.

Richard Brinsley Sheridan's tragedy *The Critic* receives its first performance in London's **Drury Lane**.

James Cook, now a captain, is killed while in **Hawaii**.

1780 As the Crown's forces fail to bring the rebels in **America** to heel, North's government finds itself under attack from all sides. The Rockingham Whigs too press for **Burke**'s economic reform programme, while the **Yorkshire Association**, formed by **Christopher Wyvill**, urges **parliamentary reform**. The government defeats the Rockinghamites over the economy, but in turn is defeated over a motion bemoaning the apparently increased influence of the king. North attempts to resign, but George III refuses him permission.

On 2 July a mob of 50,000 rampages through **London** in protest at an **Act of Catholic Relief**, passed in 1778 to restrict some of the injustices suffered by English Catholics. The so-called **Gordon Riots**, named after their leader **Lord George Gordon**, founder of the hardline **Protestant Association**, cause widespread dismay. Even radicals like **Wilkes** take to the streets against the protesters. After six days the rioters are dispersed and order is restored, but Lord George Gordon is acquitted of treason.

James Watt constructs a steam-powered flour mill.

1781 As the war in **America** turns against the Crown and North's government, a peace motion in the Commons fails by only 34 votes. On 19 October **General Charles Cornwallis** is forced to surrender at **Yorktown** when **Admiral Thomas Graves** fails to relieve his besieged army.

1782 North's ministry survives a further Commons motion to end the American war by a single vote, and two motions of no confidence by margins of nine and ten votes. But the

The loss of America

Despite its reputation, the American Revolution was a blown-up civil war rather than a grand anti-imperialist colonial uprising. And it was one that more or less excluded the original inhabitants of the American mainland: the native Americans had been conquered and displaced by the English, but they played little part in the unfolding drama, which was essentially a dispute between Britons on one side of the Atlantic and those on the other.

In England itself, political society was sharply divided over what should be done. The perceived despotism of George III – and the secretive Tory government that surrounded him – persuaded many in opposition that the colonists' grievances were entirely just. As the war developed, domestic opinion split three ways. First came the government line. Led by Lord North, and heavily influenced by King George, the government took the view that America was simply in a state of rebellion, and should be dealt with accordingly: the only solution was the reimposition of direct rule. A middle view, espoused by William Pitt the Elder, Lord Chatham, advocated that the Americans should be granted representation in the British Parliament, but that the colonies themselves should remain Crown territories. But a radical stance was taken by the Rockingham Whigs, who came to support the idea of full American independence. Various leading lights of this party (including Charles James Fox) took to wearing blue and bluff, the colours of George Washington's army, and openly taunted the government about its handling of the crisis.

In the event, the issue was decided militarily, not in the House of Commons. George III himself never quite recovered from the loss of a land he cherished but had never visited. It's not altogether fair that he has become known as 'King Who Lost America', yet the fact remains that it was a government whose ministers he appointed that increased transatlantic tensions to the point where a fissure was inevitable.

prime minister again tenders his resignation, which George III now accepts. A new administration is formed under **Charles Watson-Wentworth, 2nd Marquess of**

Rockingham. George III insists on the inclusion of the Chathamite **Lord Shelburne**. When Rockingham dies in July, the King appoints Shelburne prime minister, prompting Fox and the **duke of Portland** to resign in protest.

Although **Admiral Rodney** reasserts British dominance in the Caribbean by defeating a **French** navy at the **Battle of the Saints** in July, **Spanish** forces recapture **Florida**, and also the island of **Minorca** in the Mediterranean.

British forces abandon **Savannah** in the same month, and in December the surrender of **Charleston** marks the effective end of the British campaign in America.

1783 The **American War of Independence** ends in comprehensive victory for the colonials, sealed by a multinational **Treaty of Versailles** signed on 3 September, but not before further political turmoil in England. Earlier in the year, as preliminary talks are held with **France** and **Spain**, **Charles James Fox** and **Lord North** form an opportunistic alliance against prime minister **Shelburne** that stuns their friends, foes and society alike. Yet the alliance holds together, Shelburne is forced to resign, and a **'Fox–North'** ministry under the nominal leadership of the **duke of Portland** takes office in April. **George III**, determined to remove a government imposed upon him through Parliament, at once seeks to undermine it. The ministry comes under immediate fire from the king and his supporters when it attempts to secure funds to pay off the debts of the king's heir, **George, Prince of Wales**. Fox, a close associate of the Prince, is held responsible for his predicament.

In November the government introduces a bill to further regulate and provide subsidies for the **East India Company**, now in serious debt as a result of its administrative costs in India. The bill aims to establish a Commission to oversee the Company, but fears that it will be filled with Fox's own appointees lead to concerns that the bill will concentrate too much power in his hands, and so it is roundly defeated. George demands Fox's, North's and Portland's resignations. In their place he appoints as prime minister the precocious but untried 24-year-old son of Chatham, **William Pitt the Younger**.

1784 The Rockingham Whigs, now called **Foxites**, are annihilated in a **general election**. Fox himself comes under pressure in his Westminster seat, where the returns are submitted for scrutiny by a parliamentary committee. The **duchess of Devonshire** and other society ladies campaigning for Fox are lampooned in the press for attempting to woo the Westminster electorate by offering kisses for votes.

Pitt the Younger's substantial parliamentary majority enables him to introduce a series of **economic reforms** not dissimilar to those earlier proposed by Edmund Burke. In August, he introduces an **India Act** that adopts many of the measures proposed by Fox and North the previous year: in return for government subsidies to repay its debts, the **East India Company** is made answerable to a government-appointed **Board of Control**, effectively making India a British colony in all but name.

1785 Pitt introduces a bill proposing to **reform Parliament**, but its defeat permanently dissuades him from any further work in that direction, leading some to question his commitment to political innovation.

The Times newspaper is founded.

1786 Pitt continues his economic reforms by introducing the **Sinking Fund**; revenue placed in the Fund is earmarked to pay off the **national debt**.

A **commercial treaty** with **France** creates the most open trading relationship between the two countries in more than fifty years as tariffs are lowered on both sides of the Channel; but while French wine becomes cheaper in England, the export of inexpensive British manufactured goods quickly leads to protests in Paris.

1787 The **Foxites** attempt to damage Pitt's ministry by impeaching **Warren Hastings** for corruption and embezzlement during his time as **governor of Bengal**. But the (finally unsuccessful) eight-year hearings merely distract opposition energies, allowing Pitt to concentrate on his own agenda.

George, Prince of Wales begins building the **Brighton Pavilion**, an oriental pleasure dome that will become a centre for political dissent and dissolute elements in high society.

The **East India Company** establish a trading post on the island of **Penang**, the beginning of Britain's colonization of **Malaya**.

1788 Britain's diplomatic isolation in the wake of the American War of Independence is ended when the government concludes an alliance with the **Dutch** in April, joined by **Prussia** in August.

George III slides into a second episode of insanity.

1789 By the time the opposition is able to introduce a **Bill of Regency** into the Commons, the king exhibits signs of recovery.

From the spring onwards, England and the rest of Europe are increasingly preoccupied with the events unfolding in **France**. The storming of the **Bastille** on 14 July heralds the beginnings of the **French Revolution**, which will eventually lead to the overthrow of the monarchy. In London, responses are sharply divided. **Charles James Fox** salutes the revolution as a re-enactment by French Whigs of the **'Glorious Revolution'** of 1689. **Edmund Burke**

Charles James Fox (1749–1806)

The darling of the Rockingham Whigs, and for many the finest prime minister England never had, Charles James Fox was an unmistakable and glamorous figure in Georgian society. An eager follower of every passing fashion, in the 1770s he was among the most prominent of the 'Macaronis', so called because of their Italianate style, perched on high heels and sporting a tall blue-powdered periwig. In the 1780s he adopted a fashionable undress, abandoning wig and closely tailored outfits for blue and buff (the colours of the American rebels) and a healthy growth of stubble. And Fox was certainly well-connected: in appearance he was remarkably like his great-grandfather Charles II – his mother was a daughter of the duke of Richmond.

In politics he was an inveterate foe of George III, coming to see in the king all the woes that befell his own party, particularly the period in the 1760s when Whig ministries were destabilized in George III's quest for his 'non-party' patriot government. And it was to combat what he regarded as autocracy that he sided with the Americans in the War of Independence, using his formidable powers of oratory on their behalf. He rallied to the cause of the French Revolution, at least in its initial phases, for similar reasons, but was devastated by the terrors into which France was plunged and was disappointed to find so little to admire in Napoleon Bonaparte.

But Fox's career, so much a part of the Whig cult, is a story of unfulfilled potential. Despite becoming foreign secretary twice, he was never prime minister. Partly this was down to personal weakness: although he could be brilliant at times, he was also cripplingly lazy and was frequently absent from Parliament. His gambling was legendary, and to the end he was unable to manage his own finances. He also caused widespread consternation by following an epic series of love affairs by settling down with his mistress Elizabeth Armistead. But when he died at the age of 57, he was widely mourned.

divides from his Foxite companions, and in his *Reflections on the Revolution in France* (1790), paints a disturbing picture of events across the Channel – which he fears will soon replicate themselves in England.

In the south Pacific, the crew of **HMS Bounty** mutinies against the harsh regimen of its captain, **William Bligh**.

1790 Charles James Fox weeps in the House of Commons as it becomes apparent that his differences with his old ally **Burke** concerning the French Revolution are irreconcilable.

A **general election** in October–November confirms Pitt's political dominance, returning him with an overwhelming majority over the Foxites and other parties.

The Spanish agree to pay **compensation** to Britain following a series of attacks on British fishing boats at **Nootka Sound**, off the northwest coast of Canada.

1791 Although **Pitt** suffers a foreign policy reverse when **Russia** seizes the Turkish port of **Ochakov**, he successfully prevents England's immediate entanglement in the hostilities that threaten Europe in the wake of the French Revolution.

Responding to Burke's *Reflections*, **Thomas Paine** publishes the first part of his *The Rights of Man*, destined after its completion in 1792 to become a mainstay of Western radical liberalism.

The **Canada Act** creates a partition between English-speaking **Upper Canada** and mainly French-speaking **Lower Canada**, each awarded a representative assembly.

James Boswell publishes *The Life of Samuel Johnson*, an unprecedentedly intimate literary biography that establishes Johnson's reputation as his generation's leading man of letters.

The Observer newspaper is founded.

William Pitt the Younger (1759–1806)

The younger son of the 'Great Commoner', Pitt the Elder, **William Pitt the Younger** is often described as a Tory prime minister. But he always described himself as an Independent Whig, and it was as such, at the head of a small association of MPs, that he was chosen by George III to form a government after the fall of the Fox–North administration in 1782. Mockingly described by the Foxites as a 'mince-pie administration' it was not expected to last beyond Christmas, but in fact survived eighteen years.

Pitt had entered the Commons as an avowed supporter of reform, but it was only in the financial sphere that he was able to muster sufficient support to make real changes. His plans for electoral reform – based on a widening of the franchise by abolishing rotten boroughs and redistributing seats to more populous areas – were shelved within two years of taking office, and Pitt dedicated his first decade in power to balancing the books. Like others, he initially welcomed the **French Revolution**, not least because he thought it would weaken France to England's benefit. But the Terror – and with it a French declaration of war – forced his hand, and the remainder of the 1790s found him grappling with the prohibitive costs of a conflict that undermined many of his earlier fiscal achievements. He believed deeply that the Irish should be given a better deal if their loyalty was to be assured, and it was over his plans for **Catholic Emancipation** that he clashed with George III – and then resigned in 1801.

Recalled as prime minister in 1804, he presided over England's great victory at **Trafalgar** in 1805. Worn out though by years of unrelenting hard work (not to mention unrelenting hard drinking), he died the following January, to be remembered, in George Canning's phrase of 1802, as 'the Pilot that weathered the Storm'.

1792 Pressure for radical political reform in England grows with the founding of the **London Corresponding Society** and the **Whig Friends of the People**.

Mary Wollstonecraft, cattily (and unfairly) described by Horace Walpole as a 'hyena in petticoats', publishes *A Vindication of the Rights of Women*, widely regarded as the first attempt in English to establish feminist principles and an immensely influential work.

Disillusionment with the French Revolution sets in toward the end of the year as the full horror of the **September Massacres** becomes known.

1793 The executions of **Louis XVI** and **Marie Antoinette** add to the English establishment's nervousness over the course of events in France. In February Britain enters the European war against the revolutionaries, but some English radicals persist in defending the Revolution's values, among them **William Godwin**, author of *Enquiry Concerning Human Justice* (and husband of Mary Wollstonecraft).

A trade and diplomatic mission to **China**, led by **Lord Macartney**, funded by the **East India Company** and directly supported by **George III**, is snubbed by the **Emperor Qianlong**. As a result the East India Company increases its supplies of opium to the Chinese market, and increasingly contemplates the use of force to overcome Chinese isolationism.

1794 Amid growing fears of a threat to national security, Pitt lays aside his own inclinations toward reform and suspends **Habeas Corpus**. In his defence of the English constitution, Pitt is supported by a majority of Whigs, leaving Fox and his reduced following politically isolated.

On 1 June, **Admiral Richard Howe** defeats a French fleet outside **Ushant**.

A diplomatic breakthrough is achieved when differences with England's former American colonies, now called the **United States of America**, are resolved by the **Jay Treaty** on 19 November.

1795 Though bankrupted by his legal costs, **Warren Hastings** is finally acquitted of wrongdoing by the House of Lords.

Pitt strengthens his increasingly authoritarian regime by securing a **Treasonable Practices and Seditious Meetings Act**, banning unlicensed public gatherings and fringe political parties.

Cape Colony (South Africa) and the Malayan port of **Melaka** (Malacca), both seized from the Dutch, are added to England's rapidly expanding portmanteau of overseas possessions.

Food shortages and high prices, induced by failing harvests and wartime expenditure, provoke widespread disturbance.

A new system of part-means-tested **poor relief** is introduced by magistrates in the Berkshire town of **Speenhamland**.

1796 Bourbon **Spain** joins **France** in the war against Britain after peace negotiations between London and Paris fail. **Ceylon** (Sri Lanka) is seized from the Dutch and becomes a British colony.

Edward Jenner invents and disseminates a vaccine against **smallpox**.

1797 The war against **France**, until now broadly confined to naval operations, is placed under severe strain by naval mutinies at **Spithead** (May) and the **Nore** (June), eventually suppressed by force.

A small French force lands at **Fishguard** in **Wales**, but fails to establish a beachhead for an invasion of Britain.

Economic crisis induces the **Bank of England** to suspend cash payments temporarily.

1798 To the dismay of **William Cobbett** and other extra-parliamentary radicals, Pitt's government imposes a **stamp duty** on British newspapers.

As **Napoleon Bonaparte** campaigns in **Egypt**, a British fleet under the command of **Horatio Nelson** daringly destroys the French fleet anchored at **Aboukir** on 1 August – an engagement known as the **Battle of the Nile**.

The poets **William Wordsworth** and **Samuel Taylor Coleridge** publish their joint anthology *Lyrical Ballads*, widely regarded as a watershed in the emergence of English Romanticism.

Thomas Malthus publishes *An Essay on the Principle of Population*, which will influence **Charles Darwin**'s theory of natural selection (see p.382).

1799 Pitt's government introduces **Income Tax**, an entirely new revenue with variable rates affecting higher and lower earners. Intended as a stopgap to defray Britain's mounting war expenditure, Income Tax will eventually become the bedrock of the Treasury's fiscal policies.

While a number of radical organisations, among them the **London Corresponding Society**, are outlawed, the **Missionary Society** is founded with the specific purpose of spreading the gospel among Britain's 'heathen' colonies.

1800 The **Combination Act** proscribes trade unions.

The social idealist **Robert Owen** founds a 'model' factory at **New Lanark**, greatly improving the working and living conditions of his workforce.

Richard Trevithick designs a new **high-pressure steam engine**, used to power the first mechanical road vehicle.

Sir William Herschel discovers **infrared rays**, and the **Royal College of Surgeons** is founded.

The Industrial Revolution

Britain in the latter stages of the 18th century experienced an unprecedentedly rapid acceleration in the development of technology that eventually transformed the face of the land. The country could boast, particularly in areas such as **south Wales** and **Derbyshire**, essential resources like coal, iron and water, and it had an established tradition of capital investment. But there was also a revolution in transport. A new network of roads run by 'turnpike' trusts was followed by canals, and finally – in the 19th century – a sophisticated rail system, meaning that raw materials, finished goods and labour could be moved with increasing ease. At the same time a stream of new inventions came on line – not least steam power itself, enabling the mass production of textiles and other consumables.

In England alone the population shot from 7.1 to 13.1 million between 1780 and 1831, and many gravitated towards the newly productive towns and cities, which offered an alternative to agricultural labour or a life in service. Urban conglomerates such as **Liverpool** and **Manchester** mushroomed, bringing with them a renewed sense of civic pride – embodied in impressive city halls, monuments and bridges – but also unprecedented problems of overcrowding and disease. And working conditions inside the factories were frequently brutal: hours were long and wages were low. This too brought positive change, though. If the industrial townships provided a natural opportunity for the positive social involvement of the Methodists and for charities dedicated to ministering the needy, the organisation of trade unions contributed to the pressure for electoral reform and the institution of a fuller democracy.

Yet even so, until well into the 19th century the majority of English people still worked the land or served in the houses of the affluent. The Industrial Revolution altered England forever, but its progress was more gradual than some of its startling images suggest.

1801 On 1 January the **United Kingdom** comes into being as a further **Act of Union** fully incorporates **Ireland**

(subject to recent attempted French interference in its affairs). As Parliament is expanded to include Irish members, Ireland's own parliament is dissolved.

In March **William Pitt** dramatically resigns as prime minister after failing to win the king's support for Catholic Emancipation, and is replaced by **Henry Addington**.

On 2 April a Danish fleet is defeated at the **Battle of Copenhagen**, but only after **Vice Admiral Nelson** turns his blind eye on an order to retreat issued by **Admiral Sir Hyde Parker**. Faced with possibility of a court martial, Nelson is instead created a viscount and replaces Parker as **admiral of the fleet**.

The first **national census** confirms that **London**, with a population of just over a million, is Europe's largest city.

Legislation known as the **Horne Tooke Act** disqualifies Anglican clergymen from sitting in the House of Commons.

1802 In March the **Treaty of Amiens** buys Europe's warring nations temporary respite from the **Wars of the French Revolution**. Britain is ceded **Trinidad** by Spain.

Fox leads a delegation of Whigs to Paris to meet **Napoleon** himself, but is unimpressed both by the man and by conditions in France.

1803 The **Amiens** peace collapses and war with **France** resumes in May.

The Manchester scientist **John Dalton** devises a table of **atomic weights** and so founds the modern discipline of physical chemistry.

1804 **Addington**'s ministry collapses in May and **Pitt** returns as prime minister. In the same month **Napoleon** is proclaimed **emperor** in France.

An improved **steam engine** designed by **Trevithick** comes on line at the **Penydarran** ironworks in south Wales.

Around this time the artist, poet and engraver **William Blake** starts to compose a work later published as *Milton: A Poem in Two Books, To Justify the Ways of God to Men*, an epic visionary poem. Its preface ends with what will become some of the most famous lines in English poetry: 'And did those feet in ancient time / Walk upon England's mountains green?', and attacks the rapidly developing industries by describing their 'dark Satanic mills'.

1805 The French admiral **Pierre Villeneuve** takes a fleet intended to ferry an army of invasion assembled by **Napoleon** at **Boulogne** to **Cadiz**, where he is blockaded by **Admiral Lord Nelson**. Attempting to break the blockade, his own and Spanish men-of-war are crushed at **Trafalgar** on 21 October, a sea battle that confirms Britain's overwhelming naval supremacy. But Nelson is shot on board his flagship *HMS Victory* and dies in the heat of the action, whispering what might be either 'kismet' (fate) or 'kiss me' to his comrade **Captain Thomas Hardy**.

1806 **Pitt** dies in January, and is succeeded by a mainly Whig coalition 'Ministry of all the Talents' led by **Lord Grenville**. **Charles James Fox** is made foreign secretary, ending 25 years out of office, but dies in September.

1807 The **'Talents'** ministry falls in March, and is replaced by a mainly Tory government led by the **duke of Portland**.

George III continues to resist **Catholic Emancipation**.

During a year in which relations with the **USA** deteriorate, Britain is threatened with isolation when **Napoleon** concludes the **Treaty of Tilsit** with **Russia** following a series of brilliant land victories. But **Portugal** refuses to join Napoleon's **'Continental System'**.

A detail from James Gillray's *L'Assemblée Nationale* – a fictional gathering of political luminaries honouring Fox and Mrs Armistead.

1808 **Sir Arthur Wellesley,** having demonstrated his military acumen in **India**, is dispatched with an army to **Portugal** in August after **France** invades **Spain**. His campaign, known as the **Peninsular War**, marks the beginning of the end of Napoleon's ambition to rule all Europe. **Crabb Robinson** is sent by the *Times* to follow Wellesley and so becomes the world's first paid **war correspondent**.

1809 **Sir John Moore** is defeated and killed by French forces at **La Corunna** in January, but in July Wellesley defeats Napoleon's brother **Joseph Bonaparte** at **Talavera** – a victory that earns Wellesley the title of **viscount**.

At home, **Portland** resigns and **Spencer Perceval** becomes prime minister.

1810 **Trading relations** with the **USA** resume, but England is split by industrial unrest caused by the government's harsh policies, which are geared to furthering the war effort.

In September, the secretary of state **George Canning** retires in protest at the War Office's reluctance to give Wellesley (later made the **duke of Wellington**) the supplies he needs. The Secretary for War, **Viscount Castlereagh**, takes personal umbrage and wounds Canning in a duel.

George III, now blind, makes a final and permanent descent into insanity.

1811 In January **George, Prince of Wales** becomes **Regent**, taking over the throne from his incapacitated father.

Industrial unrest turns to violence as the machine-breaking **Luddites**, named after their mythical leader 'General Ludd', attack cotton factories in **Nottingham**, claiming that mechanization is causing unemployment.

British forces twice defeat French forces in the **Peninsula** in May, at **Fuentes de Onoro** and **Albuera**.

The architect **John Nash** begins work on London's **Regent Street**.

1812 As food prices rise, **Luddite** attacks against factories become widespread.

In June Britain finds itself at war with the **USA** following a trade dispute.

Spencer Perceval becomes the only British prime minister to date to be assassinated when he is shot by a merchant called **John Bellingham** in the lobby of the House of Commons, mistaken for someone else. He is succeeded by **Lord Liverpool**.

Wellington again defeats the **French**, at Salamanca on 22 July, and enters **Madrid** in August.

In the east, **Napoleon** faces further humiliation as his army is forced to retreat from **Moscow** in October.

Gas lighting is installed in some of **London**'s streets.

1813 Following a victory over **Marshal Jourdan** at **Vittoria** on 21 June, which secures the independence of **Spain** and **Portugal**, Wellington pushes French forces out of the Iberian peninsula and pursues **Marshal Soult** into **France** itself. Simultaneously **Napoleon**'s armies suffer a series of setbacks in central Europe.

The **East India Company** is stripped of its monopoly in Britain's Indian trade.

Jane Austen publishes *Pride and Prejudice*, the first of several witty satires of rural gentry life.

1814 Napoleon abdicates as emperor in April and 'retires' to the Mediterranean island of **Elba**.

In September the **Congress of Vienna** meets to restore order in Europe; Britain agrees to back the accession to the French throne of **Louis XVIII**.

The **'War of 1812'** between Britain and the USA is formally ended by the **Treaty of Ghent**, signed on 24 December.

The world's first **steam rail locomotive**, adapted from an earlier design by **Trevithick** by **George Stephenson**, is unveiled at **Killingworth Colliery**.

The **Marylebone Cricket Club** (MCC) adopts the **Lord's Ground** in North London as its permanent home.

1815 **Napoleon** escapes confinement on Elba, rallies his supporters in France and launches his **'Hundred Days'**. His forces defeat **Wellington** at **Quatre-Bras** and a Prussian army at nearby **Ligny**, both on 16 June, but on 18 June, close to the Belgian town of **Waterloo**, he is decisively defeated by Wellington and **Marshal von Blücher**, supported by Dutch and Belgian troops. The **Congress of Vienna** reconvenes, and Napoleon is exiled to the Atlantic island of **St Helena**.

The war's end – initiating the demobilizing of many regiments – induces **economic crisis** as prices tumble. Parliament enacts the first **Corn Law**, helping English farmers maintain their income by regulating the import of foreign grain. **Income tax**, however, is abolished, and will remain so until 1842.

1816 As England's economic depression deepens, **Luddism** is rekindled.

Demobbed soldiers, failing to find employment, are encouraged to join **'Hampden' clubs**, seeking political reform through a broadening of the franchise. A reform meeting held at **Spa Fields** in Bermondsey, London, erupts into violence, though, and is broken up by the authorities.

1817 As social unrest continues, **Lord Liverpool** reintroduces some of **Pitt the Younger's** repressive measures, including a revised **Seditious Meetings Act**.

In Ireland, where unrest is verging on rebellion, the English minister **Robert Peel** introduces a new **police force**, known as 'Peelers' and later transferred to the mainland, where they will also be known as 'Bobbies'.

1818 The Tories enjoy a comfortable majority in a **general election** and **Lord Liverpool** continues as prime minister.

The Battle of Waterloo

Waterloo was a watershed in European political history. It
inspired generations of historians, poets and novelists. It was also
the first battle to be commemorated with a medal for all those
who participated, irrespective of rank.

It was triggered by Napoleon's return from exile in March 1815.
Within a month of his arrival in France, the restored monarchy
collapsed, and Napoleon calculated that it would be in the allies'
best interests to leave him be. But he was wrong: a coordinated
assault was planned between an Anglo-Belgian-Dutch force
under Wellington, the Prussians under Marshal Gebhardt von
Blücher, and the Austrians and Russians. Unable to withstand
such a massive attack, Napoleon resolved to take on his nearest
enemies – the British and Prussians – in the hope that this would
deter the others. On 16 June he attacked the Prussians at Ligny,
defeating both them and the British at Quatre-Bras. Believing
Blücher to be finished, it only remained for Napoleon to defeat the
main British army to have achieved his goal.

On 18 June Napoleon caught up with Wellington's forces, who
were commanding a defensive position on high ground across the
Brussels road. Concerned that remaining Prussians might attempt
to link up with their allies, Napoleon opted for a risky frontal
attack, hoping that a diversionary assault on the British lines at
Hougumont would compel the enemy to spread its forces too
thinly. As the day wore on, though, the foot guards at Hougumont
held out, and the French were forced to pour in more troops.
Next, the French infantry mounted an attack on the British centre,
but although some defensive positions fell, a counter-attack under
General Thomas Picton recovered the ground, and a charge by
the heavy cavalry put the French to flight. The French then
responded with their own cavalry assault, but were met with well-
prepared troops, who withstood all that the French could throw at
them.

As the situation began to look increasingly desperate, news
began to filter through that the Prussians were appearing on the
eastern flank. Under extreme pressure, the French undertook

another huge infantry assault and managed to dislodge the soldiers of the King's German Legion from **La Haye Sainte**, but as the French mounted the ridge they were presented with Wellington's fresh reserve troops. With the Prussians now pressurizing him, Napoleon had no choice but to engage his elite reserve force, the **Imperial Guards**, but they too were forced back. As they retreated down the slope, Wellington at last – after withstanding eight hours of continual assault – ordered his men to advance.

French guns being captured by the British, after a painting by W.B Wollen.

The **Treaty of Aix-la-Chapelle** readmits France to the 'concert' of nations.

Mary Shelley, who married the poet **Percy Bysshe Shelley** two years earlier, creates a sensation with the publication of *Frankenstein: or, The Modern Prometheus*, in which Frankenstein, a student from Geneva, creates a monster and brings it to life.

The first successful **blood transfusion** is carried out at Guy's Hospital, London.

1819 An illegal gathering on 16 August at **St Peter's Fields, Manchester**, breaks up in violence after an attempt is made to arrest the main speaker, the radical **Henry 'Orator' Hunt**. In the ensuing **'Massacre of Peterloo'** eleven citizens are killed by a cavalry charge. In response, Liverpool's government pushes through the **Six Acts**, each designed to further suppress the expression and dissemination of radical ideas.

Stamford Raffles founds a colony on the Malayan island of **Singapore**.

The English engineer **Thomas Telford** begins construction of a suspension bridge across the **Menai Straits** between mainland Wales and Anglesey.

1820 George III dies aged 81 on 29 January.

9
The age of empire

1820–1914

The accession of **George IV** in 1820 was a disappointment to those who had once looked upon him as a figurehead for reform. Now aged sixty, the former Prince Regent was portly in stature, politically conservative and the constant butt of satirists. Almost immediately a crisis developed when he attempted to divorce his wife, **Caroline of Brunswick**. In the indecorous squabbling that ensued the monarchy itself came under serious threat. Actual government, however, continued in the hands of Lord Liverpool, and the 1820s proved a period of steady economic and social improvement. Although the throne still had an important part to play in English and British affairs, the political agenda was being increasingly determined by Parliament.

The point is made by the reign of **Queen Victoria** (1837–1901), the longest in English history. Her husband, **Prince Albert of Saxe-Coburg**, was publicly active, notably in promoting the **Great Exhibition** of 1851 and encouraging entrepreneurs and inventors. At his side Victoria willingly undertook the public duties expected of her. But after Albert's death in 1861 she retreated into a shell of grief, rarely appearing in public and playing little part in political developments. Only after cajoling from the Conservative prime minister **Benjamin Disraeli**, who was eager to improve his popularity ratings, did she emerge in the late 1870s.

But in a way Disraeli's manoeuvrings proved that the royal family were still an integral part of England's (and Britain's) make-up. While previous prime ministers had managed to survive despite the queen's absence, Disraeli saw that the nature of political life had yet again moved on. Even before Victoria's accession, the **Great Reform Act** of 1832 had taken a hesitant step toward greater democratization, widening the franchise to include a further 200,000 voters. A second reform act in 1867 tripled the number of men qualified to vote to around two million, and a third in 1884 extended the franchise still further, even though as late as 1911 no more than 60 percent of potential electors were registered – and of course women would be excluded until 1918. This new mass electorate meant that politicians had to take notice of middle- and working-class views, perhaps for the first time, spurring Disraeli to refashion the old Tory party into the modern Conservatives. By allying a new sense of patriotism with an idealized image of the monarchy (helped, of course, by the queen's re-emergence), he created a populist platform designed to appeal to a broad cross-section of the nation. Leadership styles also changed: both Disraeli and his Liberal adversary, **W.E. Gladstone**, developed the modern system of a prime minister backed by a cabinet and party machine – all aware that at regular intervals their policies must be vindicated at the polling booths.

But greater democratization was only one aspect of a wider programme of reform, sponsored mainly by the Whigs (called the **Liberals** after 1859 following the amalgamation of the old Whig party and liberal radicals), which sought to deliver a fairer society. Religious freedom, labour relations, education, health, and social benefits – including unemployment support and pensions at the beginning of the 20th century – were areas in which successive governments made lasting changes. These changes were spurred on by increasingly vocal popular movements. At its beginning Victoria's reign was marked by the **Chartist** protests, which sought to reverse the limitations of the 1832 Act. And the 19th century ended with the birth of the **Labour Party** – dedicated to defending and advancing the interests of those who had been ignored by previous administrations.

And then of course there was the Empire. Though **India** under the Raj was the jewel in the imperial crown, British colonies and dependencies stretched across **Asia**, **Australasia**, **Africa**, the **Caribbean** and **Canada**. It has been estimated that, by 1905, something in excess of 345 million people were ruled by a United Kingdom with just 40 million domestic inhabitants. And although the colonies were maintained with Britain's maritime strength, it was commercial industry that held the Empire together – it was a profitable source of labour, a captive market for British goods and a lucrative area for investment. For all the talk of 'free trade', a conspicuous theme in parliamentary debates, the Empire was run almost entirely as a closed shop.

British rulers, assured of their supremacy, saw themselves as exporting positive values – among them the efficacy of hard work, a strong sense of Christian endeavour and (far more nebulously) a sense of moral 'fair play'. That such ideas were frequently optimistic at best is evidenced by the genocidal outrages perpetrated by British colonists in the rush to acquire land, horrors which recent historians have painstakingly attempted to catalogue. In all corners of the empire, and throughout its history, various methods were used to remove indigenous peoples from their land. The native peoples of Tasmania were almost totally wiped out by colonizers in the first half of the 19th century; maize meal laced with arsenic was regularly used to decimate Australian aboriginal populations in the early 19th century; Canadian Indians, swamped by an immigrant population, saw their numbers halve between 1815 and 1911; when local communities in Rhodesia objected to their land being seized in 1896, dynamite was dropped into the caves in which they were hiding; even smallpox was pressed deliberately into service in the mid-18th century to reduce the population of Native Americans colonists had to deal with.

For all this, the British Empire was to prove short-lived. Within less than a century of its zenith it had all but disappeared – even if it left behind the widespread use of English as the language of business and a parliamentary model for democratic institutions in many former colonies. Partly it was facing mounting competition from other nations. By 1900 the American economy was stronger and more dynamic; in Central Asia, Russia was growing more powerful; in the East, Japan flexed new-found muscle; while in Europe, Germany, now unified under Prussian leadership and determined to enter the imperial game, expressly announced its intention to challenge Britain.

Rivalry between England and Germany led directly to the **Great War** of 1914–18, confirming an alliance between Britain and its traditional enemy, France. Yet before the onset of that cataclysm, England itself enjoyed a decade of curious tranquillity, the 'Edwardian Era', named after Victoria's son and immediate successor **Edward VII**. If you were rich enough, this was a time to look back on a century of rare cultural, technological and scientific achievement: to read through a library of gifted novelists and poets; to enjoy the prestige of swift travel by train, steamship and latterly the motorcar; to follow the fortunes of Scott and Shackleton in the Antarctic; to ponder the implications of Charles Darwin's new theory of evolution.

1820 The Prince of Wales succeeds his father as **George IV**. When his estranged wife, **Caroline of Brunswick**, presses to be acknowledged queen, the king reveals his plans for a divorce. When a **general election** affirms Lord Liverpool as prime minister, his Tory government introduces a bill of divorce into Parliament. During her trial Caroline – previously an unpopular figure – becomes a magnet for political opposition to both Liverpool and George IV.

In February, a plot to assassinate the cabinet known as the **Cato Street Conspiracy** is uncovered by an informer, Oliver 'the Spy', and its ringleaders executed.

1821 Parliament refuses to pass a **divorce bill** for George IV and Caroline, instead voting Caroline a personal annuity. The king's **coronation** descends into a farce when Caroline attempts to enter Westminster Abbey but is barred from entering its doors.

Following his discovery of **electromagnetic rotation**, **Michael Faraday** invents a simple electric motor.

John Constable paints *The Hay Wain*, which influences the modern school of landscape and Romantic painters.

Thomas de Quincey establishes his reputation by publishing *Confessions of an Opium Eater* in the *London Magazine* – a lurid account of his addiction to the drug.

The *Manchester Guardian* newspaper is founded.

The poet **John Keats** dies of tuberculosis in Rome, aged 25.

1822 **Lord Castlereagh**, embroiled in a scandal over a male prostitute he assumed was a woman and unable to face the onslaught of adverse publicity, commits suicide. He is succeeded as foreign secretary by his former rival **George Canning**. Against a background of economic revival, Liverpool uses Castlereagh's exit to promote younger ministers, among them **Robert Peel**.

The *Sunday Times* newspaper is founded.

Francis Place MP urges working-class men and women to adopt the **uterine sponge** as a form of contraception.

The poet **Percy Bysshe Shelley** drowns off Livorno, aged 29.

1823 As prosperity returns, the government abolishes the **death penalty** for over a hundred minor crimes, and Peel introduces the **Gaol Act**, alleviating conditions in England's crowded prisons. Some trade restrictions are also lifted,

The English Romantic Poets

There is no simple formula for literary Romanticism. It was more a pan-European cultural watershed than a movement, and is more easily defined by what it reacted against rather than what it embodied – many of its adherents detested Classicism, organized religion, sexual inhibition, authoritarian politics and Enlightenment rationality. The Romantic idiom caught on early in England, and although it produced no one of the poet **Johann Wolfgang von Goethe's** philosophical reach or the novelist **Walter Scott's** continental reputation, it did create a cluster of gifted poets who flourished in the last decades of the 18th century and during the first half of the 19th.

The thinking of the French philosopher **Jean-Jacques Rousseau**, with its emphasis on humanity and utopian ideals, was one starting point for English Romanticism. Another was the 1765 publication of **Thomas Percy's** *Reliques of Ancient English Poetry*, which included traditional ballads and other 'metrical romances'. Yet another was the work of the brilliantly idiosyncratic engraver and poet, **William Blake**, who rejected rationalism and authority in favour of imaginative freedom and mysticism – wonderfully exemplified in his long poem, *Jerusalem* (1804–20), which proclaims that 'Poetry Fettr'd Fetters the Human Race'.

But it was the 1798 publication of *Lyrical Ballads*, a joint anthology by **William Wordsworth** and **Samuel Taylor Coleridge**, that gave English Romanticism its first manifesto. Wordsworth added a preface calling for a poetry that operated although the **Corn Laws** remain on the statute books.

William Wilberforce establishes the **Anti-Slavery Society** in London.

Lord Byron publishes *Don Juan*.

William Webb Ellis, a student at **Rugby College**, unwittingly creates the game of rugby when he attempts to score a goal using his hands during a game of football.

with simple language and themes, placed emotive subjectivity at its core and tried to establish a dialogue between consciousness and memory (which he termed 'recollection in tranquillity') – ideas that he would exploit in various versions of his autobiographical *The Prelude*, which is subtitled 'Growth of a Poet's Mind' and addressed to Coleridge.

Later Romantic poets – sometimes called the 'second generation' Romantics by family-minded critics – included the sometime apothecary John Keats, the rebellious Percy Bysshe Shelley and the libertine and dashing George Gordon, Lord Byron. Keats's major works, including *The Fall of Hyperion*, 'The Eve of St Agnes', 'To Autumn' and six 'Odes', were squeezed into a brilliantly productive twelve-month period between 1818 and 1819, but two years later he was dead of tuberculosis. Shelley argued that poets were the 'unacknowledged legislators' of the world in his 1821 *Defence of Poetry*, and his great drama *Prometheus Unbound* (1820) is a bold exposition of the yearning for intellectual and physical liberty. Like Keats, though, his life was cut short by a boating accident. Byron's career was scarcely longer: he died of fever after rushing to fight for Greek independence, leaving behind a copious quantity of poems, drama, letters and journals – not to mention a fashionably amoral reputation only enhanced when his body was refused burial by both Westminster Abbey and St Paul's Cathedral.

1824 **Canning** begins to support selected independence movements against Spanish rule in South and Central America, including **Mexico** and **Colombia**.

The **National Gallery** and the **Royal Society for the Prevention of Cruelty to Animals** are both founded in London.

Lord Byron dies at **Missolonghi** aged 36, fighting for Greek independence from the Ottoman Empire.

The *Westminster Review*, a radical quarterly dedicated to opposing the Tory-leaning *Quarterly Review* and the Whig *Edinburgh Review*, is founded by **James Mill** and **Jeremy Bentham**. It will become one of the most influential journals of the 19th century and in its early years will publish work by **John Stuart Mill**, **Samuel Taylor Coleridge**, **Thomas Carlyle** and **Alfred Tennyson**, among others.

1825 A **Catholic emancipation bill** is defeated in Parliament, but laws against trade unions are partially relaxed, making it legal for workers to delegate representatives to discuss wages and other issues with employers.

The **Stockton and Darlington Railway Company** begins operating the world's first rail passenger service, its locomotive *Active* designed by **George Stephenson**.

John Nash begins rebuilding Buckingham House, known as **Buckingham Palace** from 1837 when it becomes the capital's principal royal residence.

1827 **Lord Liverpool**, incapacitated by a stroke, resigns as prime minister in February and is succeeded first by **George Canning** in April then, when Canning dies in August, by **Viscount Goderich**.

Peel continues his reforms of the **criminal code**.

1828 **Goderich** resigns in January when it becomes clear he lacks any following in Parliament. The **duke of**

Wellington is appointed prime minister. He introduces a new **Corn Law** to protect domestic grain production, but is forced by public pressure to repeal the **Test and Corporation Acts**.

London University is founded.

Dr Thomas Arnold becomes headmaster of **Rugby School**. The reforms he introduces form the blueprint for public school education in the 19th century and well into the 20th – a liberal curriculum based on the classics, a particular brand of 'muscular Christianity', harsh discipline and an emphasis on sporting prowess.

1829 **Wellington** effects the passage of the **Catholic Emancipation Act**, which allows Catholics the rights to vote, to stand for Parliament and to hold most public offices.

Peel creates a new **police force** for London, modelled on his previous experiments in Ireland.

Stephenson's *Rocket* wins the Liverpool and Manchester Railway Competition for the fastest locomotive.

The first **Boat Race** between **Oxford** and **Cambridge universities** is held.

> 66 The law does nothing for us. We must save ourselves. We have a little land which we need for ourselves and our families to live on, and they drove us out of it. To whom should we address ourselves? We ask for work at eightpence a day and we are refused. To whom should we address ourselves? Emancipation has done nothing for us. Mr O'Connell and the rich Catholics go to Parliament. We die of starvation just the same. 99
>
> Alexis de Tocqueville, *Journeys to England and Ireland* (1835)

1830 Britain joins with **France** and **Russia** in guaranteeing **Greece**'s freshly won independence.

George IV dies on 26 June aged 67 and is succeeded by his brother, the duke of Clarence, as **William IV** (aged 64).

Amidst growing agitation for political reform, a severely divided Tory party is badly beaten in an autumn **election**, and on 22 November the Whig **Earl Grey** replaces Wellington as prime minister.

The official opening of the **Manchester–Liverpool passenger railway line** in September is marred when a cabinet minister, **George Huskisson**, is killed after he falls in front of the train.

William Cobbett publishes *Rural Rides*, a documentary account of the Industrial Revolution's adverse impact on England's poorer classes.

1831 As clamour for reform mounts, the radical Whig politician **Lord John Russell** (later **Earl Russell**) introduces his first **Reform Bill** into Parliament. It is defeated, but a **general election** returns a Commons even more committed to electoral change. A **second bill** passes through the Commons, but is defeated in the Lords. As a result there are **mass protests**, aimed also at the bishops, who have opposed reform.

The naturalist **Charles Darwin** sets out on a voyage aboard *HMS Beagle* to the **Galapagos Islands**, where his observations of previously unknown species of finch and turtle encourage him to formulate a theory of **natural selection** (see p.382).

1832 A third **Reform Bill** passes in the Commons, but is again blocked in the Lords. **Earl Grey**, who supports the legislation, briefly resigns in May, but Wellington is unable to form a replacement administration. Grey resumes office, and the **First ('Great') Reform Act**, pertaining to English and Welsh constituencies, passes in the Lords on 4 June. Separate bills for **Scotland** and **Ireland** are steered through Parliament in July and August.

Jeremy Bentham, founder of **utilitarianism** – a social philosophy that promotes the 'greatest happiness of the greatest number' – dies aged 83.

The 'Great' Reform Act (1832)

The Great Reform Act was less an exercise in democracy than a last-ditch attempt by England's landowners to shore up their own interests. It admitted the principle of change while giving most people little experience of it.

Its rationale was essentially to increase democracy by bumping up the size of the electorate (the 'franchise') from 450,000 to 650,000 males – which of course left most of the adult population still without the vote. An arbitrary figure of £10 was set as the minimum amount of property one had to own in order to count, meaning that in some areas skilled craftsmen qualified, while in others clerks and other 'minor' professionals were cut out. And this democratizing impetus was really a defensive measure: after the upheavals in France and elsewhere, the elite were paranoid that the same thing might happen on home soil. When disturbing symptoms of social unrest emerged, especially in the new industrial towns, they were galvanized into action.

The changes had a mixed effect. Although the Act brought about the end of 'rotten boroughs', where MPs had been returned to Parliament on the basis of a handful of buyable votes, the bias was simply shifted, not removed – many newly organized constituencies were fixed by the Whig administration to the Tories' disadvantage. Yet for all its imperfections, the Act became an important milestone in that it created a precedent for further reform. Within a century full adult suffrage in England was a reality.

1833 Following persistent pressure from the Anti-Slavery Society, **slavery** is finally abolished in all British territories and colonies, including those administered by the East India Company.

A **Factory Act** alleviates some of the more shocking working conditions in the worst of England's factories, including the employment of very young children.

Britain occupies the **Falkland Islands**.

The **East India Company** loses its monopoly in the China tea trade.

John Keble publishes *National Apostasy Considered*, a defence of 'high church' values within the Anglican communion that inspires a group of like-minded clergymen and scholars to found the **Oxford Movement**.

1834 In the year of four prime ministers, **Lord Grey** resigns in July and is replaced by **Lord Melbourne**. In November Melbourne gives way to **Wellington**, and in December Wellington is superseded by **Sir Robert Peel**, who issues the **Tamworth Manifesto** to revive flagging Tory spirits. The rapid turnover of ministries points to the instability still rife in English politics following the Great Reform Act.

Parliament burns down on 16 October.

At the beginning of the year, a **Grand National Consolidated Trades Union** is formed under the leadership of **Robert Owen** and **John Doherty** to press for an eight-hour working day in Britain's factories, if necessary by means of a general strike. In March six of its members, known as the **Tolpuddle Martyrs**, are arrested outside **Dorchester** and deported to **Australia**. Sporadic strikes occur, but the immediate crisis passes.

1835 Following a general election, Whigs join forces with

Irish and radical politicians (known as the **Lichfield House Compact**).

Peel is removed from office, and **Melbourne** returns as Prime Minister.

The **Municipal Corporations Act** introduces long-over-due reforms in local government.

1836 The **Tithe Commutation Act** abolishes the practice – established in medieval times – of paying taxes in kind to the Church.

The **London Working Men's Association** is formed to promote further industrial and political reform.

1837 William IV dies and on 20 June his niece **Alexandrina Victoria**, daughter of Edward, Duke of Kent, becomes queen. In **Hanover**, where female succession is disallowed, the Crown passes to Victoria's uncle, the **duke of Cumberland**.

Lord Melbourne, an avuncular influence over the young monarch, remains in power, though a **general election** reduces the Whigs' parliamentary majority.

The **civil registration** of births, marriages and deaths begins.

The publication in book form of **Charles Dickens'** comic novel *Pickwick Papers* marks the arrival of an innovative writing talent.

Charles Wheatstone invents the **electric telegraph**, enabling the near-instant transmission of information over potentially unlimited distances.

1838 The politically radical **Chartist** movement, calling for far wider reforms than those enshrined in the 1832 Reform Act, is inaugurated with the publication in May of a **People's Charter** devised by **Richard Lovett**. The

Chartists launch their own increasingly influential newspaper, the *Northern Star*, edited by **Feargus O'Connor**. At the same time a mainly middle-class organization, the **Anti-Corn Law League**, calling for the abolition of protectionist grain tariffs, is founded in **Manchester** by **Richard Cobden**. While the Leaguers describe the landowners who benefit from the Corn Laws as a 'bread-taxing oligarchy', prime minister **Melbourne** vilifies the League as 'the wildest, maddest scheme that has ever entered into the imagination of man to conceive'.

A British army invades **Afghanistan** in an attempt to counter **Russian expansionism** in Central Asia.

The first **transatlantic crossings** achieved by steam power alone are made by two British vessels, the *Sirius* and **Isambard Kingdom Brunel**'s *Great Western*.

The **Public Record Office**, a government archive, is founded in Chancery Lane, London.

The **National Gallery** opens in London.

William Henry Fox Talbot, an inventor and scientist from Wiltshire, sets up an exhibition in London demonstrating his use of the negative – one of the defining moments in the development of **photography**.

1839 The first **Chartist National Convention** meets in February, but almost immediately descends into squabbling about aims and methods. In July Parliament rejects a **Chartist Petition**, prompting further infighting within the movement's leadership – some preferring persuasion as the proper means to success, others openly advocating violence.

In April the **Treaty of London** guarantees Belgian independence following the partition of the **Netherlands** in 1830 – a pledge that, 75 years later, takes Britain into World War I.

Chartism

Following widespread dismay at the limitations of the 1832 **Reform Act**, it was clear to many that the changes it brought were not going to be enough. A radical movement sprang up to campaign for further reform, named **'chartism'** after the demands set out in the **'Six Points'** of its **People's Charter** of 1838: universal male suffrage; a secret ballot; equal size of constituencies; the abolition of any property qualification for MPs; a salary for MPs; and annual parliaments. Individually there was nothing new in any of these – they had each been proposed by radicals back in the 18th century – but as a package they presented a manifesto to which the working and lower middle classes could alike subscribe.

Despite the fact that the Chartists' demands had all been met by the end of the century (with the exception of annual parliaments), no less an authority than **Karl Marx** regarded Chartism as a failure. He argued that, while its ends were transparent, its means were contradictory. Two of the movement's leading lights, **William Lovett** and **Francis Place**, favoured peaceable persuasion, but a third, the flamboyant Irishman **Feargus O'Connor**, advocated force in the last resort – and it was the eruption of sporadic and uncoordinated episodes of violence (such as the Newport uprising in November 1839) that discouraged a greater following. Also, Chartism has been viewed by some as being too dependent on 'bread-and-butter issues'. At times of hardship it attracted widespread support, but the majority of workers were unprepared to campaign actively when the price of bread was low and employment was plentiful.

In the end, perhaps it was what Chartism led to that made it truly significant. The Chartist Convention showed that working people could organize an assembly and co-ordinate their efforts. Although it was short-lived (it was effectively dead by 1848), it paved the way for other collectivist bodies, notably the **Trades Union Congress**, the assembly of all the major unions in Britain. More broadly and profoundly, the movement bequeathed a legacy of hope for the disenfranchised.

In the Far East the **Opium War** is triggered when the Chinese government attempts to prevent English and other foreign merchants importing opium into **China**. To protect British interests, the foreign secretary, **Lord Palmerston** – instituting the **'gunboat diplomacy'** for which he will later become famous – orders a fleet of twenty warships into the South China Sea.

J.M.W. Turner, one of the best-known English artists of the 19th century, paints *The Fighting Temeraire* – one of his most famous seascapes.

The first **Grand National steeplechase** is run at **Aintree**, Liverpool, and the **Henley Regatta** is founded.

1840 **Queen Victoria** marries **Prince Albert of Saxe-Coburg and Gotha**.

A British fleet commanded by **George Elliot** blockades the **Bai He** river in northern China, threatening the capital, **Beijing**.

Upper and Lower **Canada** are reunited, and Britain adds **New Zealand** to its Australian dominion.

Sir Rowland Hill introduces the **penny post** as the world's first adhesive postage stamp, the **Penny Black**, goes on sale.

The **Royal Botanical Gardens** at **Kew** are opened to the public.

The architect **Charles Barry**, assisted by the young **A.W. Pugin**, begins rebuilding the **Houses of Parliament** in the increasingly fashionable **Neo-Gothic** style.

1841 **Sir Robert Peel** displaces Melbourne as prime minister in August after Peel's Tory **'conservatives'** win a July General Election. Peel abolishes some **trade tariffs**, but is unable to gain enough support to repeal the **Corn Laws**. Nor is he able to avert a downturn in the economy, and **Chartist** activities revive.

In China, **George Elliot** comes to terms with the emperor's representatives. The opium trade is allowed to continue, and the island of **Hong Kong** is ceded to Britain. War resumes almost immediately, however, when **Palmerston** sacks Elliot for not having secured better terms. **Sir Henry Pottinger** again harasses China's coast with a British fleet.

The satirical magazine *Punch* is founded under the editorship of **Henry Mayhew** and **Mark Lemon**.

1842 Peel reintroduces **income tax**, abandoned in 1816. Parliament's rejection of a **Second Chartist Petition** sparks widespread riots and strikes, particularly in England's northern cities.

The war in **Afghanistan** ends when British troops concede defeat and withdraw from the territory.

In China, **Pottinger** secures the **Treaty of Nanjing**, ending the Opium War and securing unfettered trading rights for British merchants and the future opening-up of designated treaty ports.

Edwin Chadwick completes a government report on the **'sanitary conditions'** of the labouring classes, drawing attention to the much greater prevalence of disease among the poor.

An Act of Parliament prohibits **women and children** working underground in Britain's mines.

1843 The *Economist* magazine is founded to promote free trade.

Dickens writes *A Christmas Carol*, a novella described by fellow writer **William Makepeace Thackeray** as 'a national benefit, and to every man or woman who reads it a personal kindness'.

The coming of the railways

Nothing epitomizes the Industrial Revolution and the changing face of England so much as the spectacular growth of the railways. By the end of the century there were 9000 stations in all, servicing a network of lines that connected every city and town, every port and a great number of country villages, cutting journey times across Britain to seldom more than a few hours. Some stations, notably London's **St Pancras** – fronted by **George Gilbert Scott**'s fashionably Neo-Gothic Midland Grand Hotel – were nothing less than grandiose monuments to steam, whose splendour and scale were designed to rival England's ancient cathedrals.

The emphasis on speed and the need to create locomotives capable of pulling heavy payloads provided an enormous impetus to the engineering industry, and the export of engines and rolling stock to other countries became a significant money-spinner. Copious reserves of coal and iron ensured Britain's temporary pre-eminence in the new technology. And the domestic social consequences were equally far-reaching. Though the railways were initially developed as a means of transporting manufactured goods and raw materials, when fresh produce began to be carried by rail, the effects were revolutionary. Even remote fishing communities such as **Milford Haven** in west Wales found

1844 A **Railways Act** requires rail companies to run at least one train per weekday at a maximum fare of one penny for adults and a halfpenny for children.

The **YMCA** (Young Men's Christian Association) is founded, as is the first modern **co-operative society**, by a group of Rochdale weavers known as the **'Pioneers'**.

1845 Peel alienates the support of many followers by increasing government aid to a Catholic seminary at **Maynooth** in Ireland.

Throughout the British Isles – but particularly in **Ireland**, themselves rapidly connected to markets in London, Birmingham and elsewhere.

But it was passenger services that initiated the most telling social changes. Private companies such as the **GWR** (Great Western Railway) and the **LNER** (London North Eastern Railway) began offering third-class as well as first- and second-class carriages, putting rail travel within the reach of more people than ever before. Aristocratic watering holes like **Brighton** found themselves besieged by working-class day trippers, and brand-new seaside resorts like **Blackpool** catered specifically for budget holidaymakers. Nor was it just leisure activities that were transformed. The opening of London's **Victoria Station** in 1860 heralded commuterism, expanded further by the first **metropolitan underground line** between **Paddington** and **Farringdon Street**, which appeared three years later. The sheer growth in passenger numbers over the century demonstrates the scale of these changes: the number of journeys made by rail rose from 73 million in 1850 to a dizzying 2000 million by 1912. The railways were perceived as good for business, good for people and good for Britain.

where serious **famine** sets in – **potato crops** are blighted. Although many Irish people emigrate to the United States in the coming years, many also move to Liverpool, London and other English cities. As food shortages grow, the government comes under heavy pressure over the **Corn Laws**. Peel earnestly favours repeal, but is unable to persuade a majority in the Commons. He resigns, but **Lord John Russell** is unable to form a government and Peel continues in office.

Benjamin Disraeli (see p.388) publishes *Sybil*, a novel with Chartist sympathies that depicts England as being composed of 'two nations', the haves and the have-nots.

1846 Relying on Whig support in Parliament, Peel is able to effect the **repeal of the Corn Laws**. Tory opposition is led by Lord **George Bentinck** and **Benjamin Disraeli**. The Tory party splits, Peel resigns as prime minister, and **Lord John Russell** forms a Whig administration on 30 June. Although Peel is castigated for wrecking the Tory party, his followers, around a hundred in number and called the **'Peelites'**, continue as a separate parliamentary faction occupying the political ground between Tories and Whigs. Under Russell, the government expands its social role, creating a new teacher-training scheme.

Edward Lear publishes his first book of limericks, *A Book of Nonsense*.

1847 The reforming Lord John Russell continues in power after his Whig party, now known as the **Liberals**, win a **general election**. Responding to extra-parliamentary pressure, Russell's government passes the **Ten Hours Act**, restricting the working hours of women and children in textile factories.

The new **parliament buildings** are completed at last.

As the price of grain temporarily rises Britain experiences its last **food riots**.

Charlotte Brontë publishes *Jane Eyre* and her sister **Emily** publishes *Wuthering Heights*, both under male pseudonyms – but the identity of the authors is an open secret in London literary circles.

1848 While the rest of Europe is gripped by revolutionary fever (King Louis Philippe is displaced in France by Louis Napoleon, and other attempted uprisings spread across Germany and Italy), Britain escapes serious disruption.

The **Chartists** hold their last great meeting on **Kennington Common**, but a Chartist petition is exposed as a largely fictitious assemblage of names.

In **Ireland**, the continuing famine leads to widespread **rioting**.

A **Public Health Act** establishes a General Board of Health headed by **Edwin Chadwick** to monitor the outbreak and spread of epidemics.

Commissioned by London's **Communist League**, *The Communist Manifesto*, written by **Karl Marx** and **Friedrich Engels**, is published.

The **Pre-Raphaelite Brotherhood**, a school of artists and writers devoted to a highly mannered appreciation of late medieval values, is formed by **Holman Hunt**, **John Everett Millais** and **Dante Gabriel Rossetti**.

W.M. Thackeray publishes his masterpiece, *Vanity Fair*, a novel that caricatures the pretensions and hypocrisies of English society.

1849 **Charles Kingsley** and **Frederick Maurice** launch the **Christian Socialist** movement.

Women gain a foothold in higher education with the foundation of **Bedford College** in London.

The future department store **Harrods** begins as a grocery shop in Knightsbridge.

1850 Britain enters a period of sustained **prosperity**, during which wages rise but prices either fall or remain level.

Foreign secretary **Lord Palmerston** earns the distrust of the queen and many of his colleagues by resorting to gunboat diplomacy on behalf of **Don Pacifico**, a Portuguese Jew with a British passport mistreated by anti-Semites in Athens.

Sir Robert Peel dies after a riding accident in July.

The **Vatican** begins funding new **Catholic bishoprics** in England, the first since the Reformation.

The English novel

The name of **Samuel Richardson** is indelibly associated with the development of the novel in English. He perfected one of its earliest forms, that of the **epistolary novel** (in which characters communicate by letter), in *Pamela* (1740–41) and *Clarissa* (1747–48). The latter was lampooned by **Henry Fielding** in *An Apology for the Life of Mrs Shamela Andrews* (1741), the success of which encouraged Fielding to write his comic masterpiece of eight years later, *Tom Jones*. A more extraordinary book still was the Irish-born **Laurence Sterne's** *The Life and Opinions of Tristam Shandy, Gentleman* (1760–67), which has been called the first and greatest English experimental novel. Women writers also found themselves catering for large new audiences. **Ann Radcliffe** was a leading early exponent of the Gothic novel, and the hugely successful work of **Jane Austen** – including *Pride and Prejudice* (1813), *Mansfield Park* (1814) and *Emma* (1816) – fed an appetite among readers for her particular brand of social observation and subtle satire. Books like these established a new enthusiasm for English literature, and from the mid-18th century no educated household was without a few works of fiction.

Although novels in the next century engaged with a bewildering array of concerns and themes, practically all owed their popularity to the growth in middle-class book buying and reflected the preoccupations of that audience. **William Makepeace Thackeray** began his career as a journalist and ended it as one of the most popular novelists of his generation, drawing vivid tableaux of London society including *Vanity Fair* (1848) and *The History of Henry Esmond* (1852). **Anthony Trollope's** workmanlike 'Barsetshire' series, set in the fictional town of Barchester, was

Alfred Tennyson (later Lord Tennyson) publishes *In Memoriam A.H.H.*, an elegy for his dead friend Arthur Henry Hallam – one of his most celebrated works.

1851 An **Ecclesiastical Titles Act** prohibits Catholic bishops from adopting the same titles as their Anglican counterparts.

just one section of a prolific output that totalled some 47 novels. **Charles Dickens** was even more successful, using serial publication – in which novels were published in monthly magazines such as the author's own *Household Words* – so astutely that by the time of his death he was one of the best-loved writers in English and the first international literary celebrity. Novels such as *Oliver Twist* (1837–38), *David Copperfield* (1850), *Bleak House* (1853), *Little Dorrit* (1857) and *Great Expectations* (1861), despite their London backdrops, won Dickens plaudits the world over.

Perhaps it is the writing of 19th-century female novelists that has had the most impact on the course of English literature. The books of **Elizabeth Gaskell** – including *Ruth* (1853) and *Wives and Daughters* (1866) – articulated the author's concern with social issues and focus closely on female characters. The work of the three **Brontë** sisters, Anne, Emily and Charlotte, pushed the novel in new directions – most famously in Charlotte's *Jane Eyre* and Emily's *Wuthering Heights* (both 1847), which drew directly upon experience of life in Yorkshire and passionately assert their female characters' need for independence. But Marian Evans, published as **George Eliot**, was perhaps the most cosmopolitan (and learned) novelistic talent of her time, drawing on topics as diverse as German philosophy and first-hand observation of small-town English life in an extraordinary range of works – among them *Adam Bede* (1859), *The Mill on the Floss* (1860), *Middlemarch* (1871–72) and *Daniel Deronda* (1874–76) – which guaranteed her reputation as the foremost English novelist then alive.

The first religious census shows that support for the **Church of England** is in steep decline, fuelling arguments for its disestablishment.

Britain's worldwide commercial and colonial prestige is celebrated under the patronage of Albert, the prince consort, by the **Great Exhibition**. It is housed in the glass-walled **Crystal Palace** designed by **Joseph Paxton** and erected in London's **Hyde Park**. Opening in May, it attracts six million visitors over five months. When the exhibition closes, the Crystal Palace is removed to **Sydenham**, where it is destroyed by fire in 1936.

1852 Weakened by Palmerston's resignation the previous year, **Russell**'s Liberal government falls in February. **Lord Derby** forms a minority Tory government, with **Disraeli** as chancellor of the exchequer, but this too fails in

© BETTMANN/CORBIS

The Crystal Palace, built for the 1851 Great Exhibition.

December, after Derby's budget proposals are defeated in Parliament. **Lord Aberdeen** forms a new Whig administration with **W. E. Gladstone** as Chancellor.

1853 The **Northcote–Trevelyan Report** criticizes the way in which patronage rather than merit often determines promotion in the **Civil Service**.

John Ruskin publishes *The Stones of Venice*, an architectural study that measures aesthetic ideals against social and moral values.

1854 **Britain** and **France** form a military alliance against **Russia** as Russia seeks to take territorial advantage of the crumbling Islamic **Ottoman Empire**, popularly known as the 'Sick Man of Europe'. British involvement in the **Crimean War**, fought on the Crimean peninsula of the **Black Sea**, lasts two years. The allies gain victories at **Balaklava** in October and **Inkerman** in November, but neither proves decisive.

1855 **Lord Aberdeen** resigns at the beginning of February amidst mounting criticisms that the Crimean War is being unnecessarily prolonged. A new Liberal government is formed by 70-year-old **Lord Palmerston**, who will continue as prime minister until his death in 1865.

Sebastopol, the main Russian stronghold in the **Crimea**, besieged by the French and British, falls in September, while **Florence Nightingale** wins public acclaim for her reforms of military nursing conditions.

Stamp duty is abolished on British newspapers and the *Daily Telegraph* is founded.

In Africa, the Scottish evangelical explorer **David Livingstone** discovers what he christens the **Victoria Falls**. **Anthony Trollope** publishes *The Warden*, the first of his Barchester novels depicting English provincial life.

The Crimean War (1853–56)

As Russia sought to incorporate vast areas of central and western Asia into its expanding empire, it inevitably ran head-on into the Turkish Ottoman empire. The immediate pretext for war between the two countries was a Russian demand to be allowed to 'protect' Orthodox Christians living in Ottoman domains around the Black Sea, but the conflict also involved an obscure dispute between Russia and France about the rights of Russian Orthodox and Roman Catholic monks living in Palestine.

Hostilities began in 1853 when Turkey defensively occupied the eastern part of present-day Romania. Anxious to contain Russian aggrandizement, Britain joined France in sending a fleet to the Black Sea in January 1854, and war was formally declared in March. For much of the conflict fighting centred on Sebastopol – a Russian stronghold on the Crimean peninsula besieged by Turkish, French and British troops – but there were tactical engagements at the Alma River, Balaklava, Inkerman and elsewhere. The war effectively ended in September 1855 when Russia withdrew from Sebastopol.

While one key significance of Crimea was that the English and French willingly fought together against a common enemy, it also became the first media war. The *Times* journalist William Russell used the newly invented telegraph to file his reports, so that for the first time a distant conflict landed fresh on English breakfast tables. Great public excitement was also generated by the Charge of the Light Brigade, famously commemorated in a specially penned poem by Alfred Tennyson, who described how a detachment of British cavalry rode futilely into Russian guns at Balaklava, watched by civilian spectators who had travelled to the Crimea in holiday mood. The hapless earl of Cardigan was publicly ridiculed for his role in the debacle, but it also demonstrated the shortcomings of wider military planning. Total casualties climbed to 250,000, many dying not from wounds but from cholera and other contagions. While the originality and success of the medical improvements initiated by the 'Lady with the Lamp', Florence Nightingale, have been hotly debated since, no one could have made a better media icon.

> **"** At ten minutes past eleven our Light Cavalry advanced. The whole Brigade scarcely made one effective regiment, according to the numbers of continental armies, and yet it was more than we could spare. As they rushed toward the front, the Russians opened fire on them from the guns in the redoubt on the right, with volleys of musketry and rifles. They swept proudly past, glittering in the morning sun in all the pride and splendour of war. We could scarcely believe the evidence of our senses! Surely that handful of men were not going to charge an army in position? Alas, it was but too true – their desperate valour knew no bounds, and far indeed was it removed from its so-called better part – discretion. **"**
>
> W.H. Russell, *The British Expedition to the Crimea* (1858)

1856 Hostilities in the **Crimea** end in February.

In March a congress of European powers meets in **Paris** and resolves to uphold the independence of the **Ottoman Empire**.

Britain faces mounting tension in **India**, and in October a fresh **Anglo-Chinese war** breaks out.

Henry Bessemer discovers a new method of **processing steel** that is cheaper than any of its predecessors.

1857 In India, a major revolt erupts against East India Company rule, known in England as the **Indian Mutiny**. On 15 February, over 200 English women and children are massacred at **Cawnpore**, fuelling anti-Indian sentiment at home. Palmerston's popularity is undiminished, though, and his Liberals win a convincing **general election** victory.

The **Science Museum** opens in London.

Thomas Hughes publishes *Tom Brown's Schooldays*, a novel based on the author's experiences at Rugby School during the headmastership of Thomas Arnold.

1858 Discontented Liberals and Tories form an **alliance** against **Palmerston**, whose government falls in February. **Lord Derby** forms a minority Tory government.

Largely with the help of 'loyal' local troops, the revolt in **India** is finally crushed. The **East India Company** is sidelined, however, and in its place **direct colonial government** is imposed on the subcontinent.

Darwinism

Few books have had as profound an impact on modern culture as *On the Origin of Species*. By apparently establishing the principle of biological evolution, its author Charles Darwin (1809–82) not only provided a framework for work in the 'life' sciences worldwide, but challenged Christian and other scriptural accounts of creation.

That it did so was partly due to the thoroughness with which Darwin presented his thesis: namely, that all existing species in the plant and animal kingdoms are relatively complex adaptations of earlier, less complex life forms, and that those adaptations are brought about by mutation and inheritance. To prove his case Darwin left no stone unturned. The first-hand observations he made while voyaging on the *HMS Beagle* – including descriptions of new species of turtle and finch in the Galapagos Islands – were central to his research, but Darwin's argument was also sustained by findings from fields such as embryology and morphology. He cast his net outside biology, too: Thomas Malthus's *Essay on the Principle of Population* (1798) gave Darwin the idea of the 'struggle for existence', from which came the notion that adaptive advantage and evolutionary success are directly related; and Sir Charles Lyell's ground-breaking *Principles of Geology* (1830–32) described a huge swathe of prehistoric time in which the gradual

1859 A Tory attempt to introduce further **electoral reform** is heavily defeated in Parliament, and in June **Palmerston** returns to power as Liberal prime minister.

Charles Darwin publishes *On the Origin of Species by Means of Natural Selection*, which argues the principle of **evolution** – an uncomfortable and unwelcome theory for many (see p.382).

John Stuart Mill, a disciple of **Jeremy Bentham** and a keen advocate of Utilitarianism, publishes *On Liberty*, a seminal defence of England's emergent liberal democratic ideology.

processes of biological evolution were able to take place. Evolution was not exactly a new idea, though. The French biologist Jean-Baptiste Lamarck had proposed the inheritance of acquired characteristics as an evolutionary mechanism back in the 1790s, and Darwin himself was only persuaded to publish his findings because another Englishman, Alfred Wallace, had arrived at a similar theory independently.

Within hours of its publication the *Origin* had sold out, and it immediately created a furore – not least because Darwin's examination of the fossil record indicated evolutionary dead ends that undermined the idea of a divinely purposed creationist programme. Darwin was reluctant to engage in theological controversy, however, leaving it to his champion T.H. Huxley (1826–95) to publicly fight the evolutionist corner. It also befell an obscure Austrian monk, Gregor Mendel (1822–84), who studied pea plants at a monastery in Brno, to discover genetics – the 'chance' biological mechanism that has underpinned the scientific validity of Darwinian evolution in the 20th century and beyond. Ironically, a paper by Mendel found its way into Darwin's library at Down House in Kent, but at Darwin's death its pages remained uncut.

Samuel Smiles publishes *Self-help*, extolling the 'Victorian' values of thrift, moderation and hard work.

1860 Chancellor **W.E. Gladstone** continues to lower tariffs and so promote free trade in his annual budget.

T.H. Huxley, championing Darwin's theory of evolution, vehemently clashes with the creationist **Bishop Samuel Wilberforce**.

The right of **Jews** to claim **full citizenship** in England is finally acknowledged by parliamentary legislation.

The **Open Golf Championship** is founded.

1861 As the **American Civil War** erupts, Britain remains neutral, dependent upon both grain imports from the northern Union states and cotton imports from the slave-owning Confederacy of southern states.

The first entirely **iron warship**, *HMS Warrior*, is launched. **Prince Albert** contracts typhoid and dies in December. **Queen Victoria** will mourn the loss of her husband for the rest of her long life.

Mrs Isabella Beeton publishes her *Book of Household Management*, a comprehensive practical guide for middle-class housewives that quickly becomes a bestseller.

1862 Gladstone enhances his reputation as a popular reformer by undertaking the first of several tours of northern England.

As **cotton supplies** from the American slave states are interrupted, a British-built war vessel, the *Alabama*, inflicts damage on Union shipping.

Gilbert Scott designs the **Albert Memorial** for London's Hyde Park, the first of several projects to commemorate the prince. Others will include the nearby **Albert Hall** and the **Albert Bridge** crossing the Thames.

A second great **trade fair** in the capital creates a vogue for Japonaiserie.

Notts F.C. (later Notts County) becomes England's first professional **football club**.

For the first time an **English cricket team** tours **Australia**.

1863 Although the recent 'reunification' of Italy by its military leader **Giuseppe Garibaldi** has been warmly welcomed in England, the progressive unification of an industrialized **Germany** by the Prussian **Otto von Bismarck** is viewed with mounting apprehension because it threatens Britain's imperial and commercial interests.

The **London Metropolitan Railway** marks the beginning of the world's first underground railway system.

Charles Kingsley publishes *The Water Babies* – a children's book that practically caricatures the Victorian belief in the innocence of children.

1865 **Lord Palmerston**'s continuing popularity ensures a handsome Liberal victory in a July **general election**, but in October he dies. **Lord Russell** becomes prime minister, and agrees to consider further changes to the electoral system under pressure from **Gladstone** and the **Manchester Reform Union**. The **Reform League** is founded, a nationwide association of political radicals.

William Booth establishes his **Christian Mission** – later the **Salvation Army** – to alleviate the suffering of Britain's increasing number of urban destitutes.

The Reverend **Charles Dodgson**, an Oxford mathematician writing under the pseudonym **Lewis Carroll**, publishes *Alice's Adventures in Wonderland*, a children's fantasy constructed out of logical absurdities.

Lord Palmerston (1784–1865)

Henry John Temple, 3rd Viscount Palmerston, was a curiously modern politician, and one often accused of being of no fixed political abode. During a long career he served in Tory, Canningite, Whig and Liberal governments. He was war secretary once, foreign secretary three times, home secretary once and prime minister twice. Most innovatively, he actively wooed popular success, writing articles and leaking information to the *Morning Post*.

Palmerston ruthlessly promoted Britain's imperial ambitions, advocating and frequently employing his patented 'gunboat diplomacy' as a way of cajoling other nations to respect and abide by his concept of a 'Pax Britannica'. Both Queen Victoria and Prince Albert found his high-handedness in dealing with foreign monarchs (not to mention his reluctance to brief them properly) outrageous, and were always looking for excuses to fire him. In an earlier age enemies such as these would have ruined Palmerston, but in the circumstances of the mid-19th century he could demonstrate to the full his skills as a political survivor. When he died, the *Times* obituary column cattily remarked: 'constant only in the retention of office … his one principle was that of the Vicar of Bray', drawing a parallel between Palmerston's political principles and that of the famous 17th-century cleric who made self-preservation his sole policy.

1866 Following almost two decades of steady economic growth there is a sudden panic amongst Britain's financial institutions, leading to a run on the banks on 11 May, known as **'Black Friday'**. **Lord Russell**, already faced by a split among his ranks over the matter of reform, is unable to manage the crisis, and resigns in June. **Lord Derby** becomes prime minister for a third time at the head of a minority government.

Following decades of unrest in **Ireland**, the **Irish Republican Brotherhood** (also known as the **Fenians**), a new militant grouping seeking the end of English rule, begin to campaign.

Dr Thomas John Barnardo opens a home for orphans in **London**.

The **Amateur Athletics Association** is founded.

The **Marquis of Queensbury** sets out a code of rules for **boxing**.

1867 In February the **Fenians** begin campaigning on the mainland, attacking a police barracks in **Chester**, followed by an assault on **Clerkenwell Prison** in **London** during which twelve people are killed.

On 15 August Parliament passes the **Second Reform Act**, which extends the franchise to 36 percent of adult males aged 21 and over. A companion bill to give **women** the vote fails.

Joseph Lister pioneers the use of **antiseptics** in surgery.

1868 Amidst fierce political infighting, **Benjamin Disraeli** scrambles to the top of what he calls the 'greasy pole' and replaces Derby as prime minister on 27 February. But his minority Conservative government collapses after the Liberals convincingly win a November **election**, and on 3 December **W.E. Gladstone** becomes prime minister.

The first **Trades Union Congress** is held.

The **Royal Historical Society** is founded.

1869 The opening of the **Suez Canal**, linking the Mediterranean to the Red Sea, dramatically reduces the journey time of goods and people between Britain and its eastern possessions.

A **Contagious Diseases Act** gives police the power to arrest prostitutes but not their clients, and therefore does little to halt the spread of syphilis and other venereal infections in England.

1870 William Forster's **Elementary Education Act** provides for state-funded elementary schools to be established wherever church schools do not already furnish an equivalent facility.

Entry into the **British Civil Service** by competitive examination is introduced, based on an already successful similar system in India.

A **Married Women's Property Act** for the first time gives married women significant legal rights over their own possessions.

Benjamin Disraeli (1804–81)

Disraeli did more than any other 19th-century politician to adjust his party to the needs of an electorate that was larger than ever before, transforming the declining Tories to the rebranded 'Conservatives', who went on to dominate Britain well beyond his death. Put simply, he realized the way to win votes was to offer populist policies – or at least policies that could, with adequate spin, be made to look populist. Looked at one way, this was a triumph for democracy. Looked at another, it was blatant opportunism, a charge from which Disraeli has never been wholly exonerated.

Perhaps his background had something to do with this chameleonic instinct. His father, Isaac, was of Italian–Jewish descent and, but for an altercation with the local synagogue, Benjamin would never have been baptized a Christian – which would have automatically barred him from any kind of political career. Having tried and failed to become the Whig member for **Wycombe** in 1832, he drifted towards the Tories, and was elected MP for **Maidstone** in 1837. His maiden Commons speech was judged a failure, but he made his mark by demonstrating that he had a head for figures and adopting an independent line on specific issues. Marriage to the widowed **Anne Wyndham Lewis**

Disraeli sets out to rebuild the **Conservative Party**, which opens a **Central Office** to co-ordinate the party's activities across the country.

In July, the **Franco-Prussian War** erupts and a German army invades France, but Britain stands aloof.

The novelist **Charles Dickens** (see p.377) dies.

1871 **Gladstone**'s Liberal government passes the **Trade Union Act**, for the first time giving unions legal status.

1872 Swayed by a vociferous temperance movement, the

gave him status and financial security, though these were insufficient to obtain office in Peel's 1841 government – a setback Disraeli met by reviving an earlier interest in fiction, publishing a trilogy of books (*Coningsby*, *Sybil* and *Tancred*) between 1844 and 1847 that have sometimes been considered the first political novels in English.

Peel's death in 1850 revived Disraeli's parliamentary fortunes. Determined to reunite the Tories, he emerged as their natural leader in the Commons, and in 1852 briefly became chancellor under **Lord Derby**. Disraeli made his mark overseeing the **Second Reform Bill** in 1867, and a year later became prime minister for a few months. After six years in opposition, during which time he greatly strengthened the Conservatives' party organization, he returned to power in 1874, and remained there another six years – much to the satisfaction of Queen Victoria. Gladstone (see p.395), she found, always addressed her 'as though I were a public meeting', but 'Dizzie' knew how to lay on the charm. In 1876 he saw to it that she was proclaimed empress of India, and so the Tories became the party of Crown and Empire.

government passes a **Licensing Act** that regulates and restricts the sale and consumption of alcohol.

The **Ballot Act** introduces the secret ballot into British elections.

Marian (or Mary Anne) Evans, a well-known editor and translator, completes what many regard as her masterpiece, the novel *Middlemarch*, which she publishes under the pseudonym **George Eliot** (see p.377).

Thomas Hardy publishes *Under the Greenwood Tree*, the first of his 'Wessex' novels, exploring rural and town life in the West Country.

1873 A **'New Domesday'** survey of England reveals that 80 percent of the land is owned by only seven thousand people.

The first season of the cricket **County Championship** is dominated by the tall, heavily bearded figure of **Dr W.G. Grace**, unrivalled as both batsman and bowler.

1874 Disraeli becomes prime minister for a second time in February.

1875 On Disraeli's initiative Britain acquires a controlling interest in the **Suez Canal** from the Egyptian leader, thus guaranteeing passage of its vessels to eastern waters.

As trade union membership steadily increases, a new **Trades Union Act** legalises peaceful picketing.

Trial By Jury, the first of the **'Savoy' operettas** written by **W.S. Gilbert** and set to music by **Arthur Sullivan**, is produced by **Richard D'Oyly-Carte** at the Royalty Theatre, London.

1876 Queen Victoria is proclaimed **Empress of India** by Disraeli's Conservative government in April.

In India, **Viceroy Lord Lytton** attempts to establish a

protectorate in **Afghanistan** as **Russia** continues to exert pressure in Central Asia.

In August Disraeli is created **earl of Beaconsfield**. In September his political adversary **Gladstone** orchestrates an anti-Turkish campaign following a massacre of Christians by Turks in **Bulgaria**.

1877 The **Society for the Protection of Ancient Buildings** is founded by craftsman and artist **William Morris**, primarily in order to preserve medieval buildings from modern development.

1878 Following a Russo-Turkish war, Disraeli attends the **Congress of Berlin**. He returns to England proudly announcing 'peace ... with honour'. In return for providing limited military guarantees for a greatly diminished

Russian aggression as seen by Britain – a serio-comic war map from 1877.

Ottoman empire, Britain gains control of Cyprus. Anglo-Turkish relations are soon soured, though, when Turkey develops an alliance with **Austro-Germany**.

The **Bicycling Touring Club** is founded.

1879 In **southern Africa**, British forces set about subjugating the **Zulu** nation. Disaster threatens when 895 British troops are massacred at **Isandhlwana**, but 140 British troops resist an all-out assault by 4000 Zulu warriors at **Rorke's Drift** in March.

An uprising in **Afghanistan** in September leads to armed intervention by British Indian forces, but the results are inconclusive.

Campaigning in Scotland, **Gladstone** comes out strongly against the pursuit of imperial policies in **Africa** and **Afghanistan**.

The British government is dismayed by the formation of the **Irish Land League**, which openly calls for Irish independence.

The **telephone** is introduced into England from the USA.

John Henry Newman is made a cardinal by **Pope Leo XIII**.

> ❝ You have accused me of being a flatterer. It is true. I am a flatterer. I have found it useful. Everyone likes flattery; and when you come to Royalty you should lay it on with a trowel. ❞
>
> Benjamin Disraeli, speaking to Matthew Arnold c.1880,
> in G.W.E. Russell, *Collections and Recollections* (1898)

1880 Following a Conservative defeat in a March **general election**, **Lord Beaconsfield** (Disraeli) resigns in April and **Gladstone** becomes prime minister. Gladstone moves swiftly to pull British troops out of **Afghanistan**, but in December he is drawn into the **1st Boer War** in southern Africa when the Dutch Boers declare a **Boer Republic** independent of Britain's **Cape Colony**.

1881 Following a series of military defeats, Britain concedes Boer independence in the **Transvaal** and **Orange Free State** by the **Treaty of Pretoria** in April.

The arrest and imprisonment of the Irish patriot **Charles Stewart Parnell** creates a further surge of anti-English feeling in Ireland.

1882 In May **Parnell** is released from prison. Four days later the secretary of state for Ireland, **Lord Frederick Cavendish**, and his deputy are assassinated by Fenians in Dublin. As a result, the powers of the Irish constabulary are greatly extended, but 'terrorist' activities revive on the mainland.

In July, British troops are deployed to defend the **Suez Canal** from Egyptian nationalists – the first step in a strategy that leads to the annexation of many further African territories in the hope that this will curtail any further threats.

> ❝ I would not be too much impressed by what the soldiers tell you about the strategic importance of these places. If they were allowed full scope they would insist on the importance of garrisoning the moon in order to protect us from Mars. ❞
>
> Lord Salisbury commenting on the continuing acquisition of African colonies, in a letter to Sir Edward Baring, 5 February, 1892

1883 British forces begin a two-year campaign in **Burma** to suppress a 'native' uprising led by **Ba Thone**.

The recently restored peace in Egypt is threatened by the Islamic leader **Mohammed Ahmed ibn-Seyyid Abdullah** (known as the **Mahdi**), who raises revolt in the Egyptian-controlled territory of **Sudan**.

1884 **General Charles Gordon** campaigns against the Mahdi on behalf of the Egyptian government, but without support from London becomes trapped in the Sudanese city of **Khartoum** in March.

In November, Parliament passes a **Third Reform Act**, doubling the size of the (male) electorate.

In London, the socialist **Fabian Society** is founded. Its members include the social reformers **Sidney** and **Beatrice Webb**, the author **H.G. Wells**, the future prime minister **Ramsay MacDonald** and the Irish playwright **George Bernard Shaw**.

Partly in response to pressure created by **Josephine Butler** and her 'moral purity alliance', Gladstone's government passes a **Criminal Law Amendment Act** that raises the age of consent for girls to 16, outlaws brothels and introduces harsh penalties for homosexuals – though lesbianism remains legal as Queen Victoria supposedly refuses to acknowledge its existence when she comes to sign the Act.

The Mikado, the latest operetta by Gilbert and Sullivan, is premiered at the Savoy Theatre in London. Reflecting the fashionable vogue for all things Japanese, this astoundingly popular production will run for 672 performances in all.

1885 Because of the late arrival of a British relief force, **Khartoum** falls to the **Mahdi** on 26 January. Gordon and his soldiers are massacred – an event that evokes calls for greater strong-arm methods in Africa.

The war in **Burma** ends with British suzerainty now extending into the upper reaches of the country. As imperial sentiments stiffen, Gladstone's Liberals are defeated in a

W.E. Gladstone (1809–98)

Gladstone, one of the great reforming statesmen of the Victorian era, was prime minister four times between 1868 and 1894. Born into a wealthy Liverpool merchant family, he trod the conventional path of late Victorian statesmen – education at Eton and Oxford, marriage to the aristocracy – and first became an MP in 1833 via the duke of Newcastle's patronage, representing Newark. He made an immediate impression with impassioned speeches about slavery, religion and Ireland. Within a year he was given a ministerial appointment in Peel's government, and in 1835 was promoted to undersecretary for the colonies. He was again given office by Peel in 1841, but resigned in 1845 after objecting to an offer of public funds to the Roman Catholic college at Maynooth in Ireland. It wasn't long before he was back in office, however, this time as colonial secretary. Having lost Newcastle's confidence, he also lost his Newark seat, but in 1847 became the member for the University of Oxford. He remained a Peelite until 1859 when he astonished everyone by crossing the floor to serve in Palmerston's administration as chancellor of the exchequer. After Palmerston's death he remained with the Liberals, serving first under Lord Russell and then becoming party leader.

Although Gladstone never abandoned his commitment to the Church of England – the inspiration of his markedly moral character – he modified his early conservatism to a more equitable (and ultimately more radical) politics. But although his own first administration (1868–74) was able to introduce the disestablishment of the Church of Ireland and the Irish Land Act of 1870, he failed in what became his dominant long-term objective – Irish Home Rule. Because of the entrenched interests of the mainland British establishment, Anglo-Irish landowners and the large Protestant community in Ulster, the Irish question remained intractable. Even his great adversary, Benjamin Disraeli (see p.388), struggled to criticize the politician who did more than most to make Britain a fairer place – he said of Gladstone, only half tongue-in-cheek, that 'he has not a single redeeming defect'.

June general election, and a new Conservative government under **Lord Salisbury** takes power.

1886 Salisbury's government falls in January, and **Gladstone** becomes prime minister for a third time at the beginning of February. In April he attempts to introduce a **Home Rule** (self-rule) bill for **Ireland**, but this divides his Liberal Party. **Joseph Chamberlain** resigns from the cabinet, the bill is defeated in July, and the Conservatives win a snap **general election**. **Salisbury** returns as prime minister, at the head of a coalition government, appointing his nephew **Andrew Balfour** secretary of state for Ireland.

1888 Local government is reformed with the passing of the **County Councils Act**, providing for elected local authorities.

The *Financial Times* newspaper is founded.

The **English Football League** is established.

'Jack the Ripper', a murderer of unknown identity, terrorizes London's East End prostitutes.

1889 A month-long strike by **dockers** in London beginning in mid-August threatens to bring England's economy to a halt.

1890 The **National Telephone Company**, with near-monopolistic powers, is established under licence from the Post Office.

1891 The Anglo-Irish aesthete **Oscar Wilde** courts notoriety by the publication of his novel *The Picture of Dorian Gray*, condemned by many for its ambiguous celebration of moral decadence.

1892 An August **general election** returns the Liberal Party to power. **Gladstone** becomes prime minister for the fourth time.

Aubrey Beardsley's cover design for the prospectus of *The Yellow Book*.

Keir Hardie, a Scottish socialist, is returned as MP for London's West Ham constituency.

1893 Led by **Keir Hardie**, the **Independent Labour Party** is formed in Bradford specifically to represent and advance the interests of working-class people.

A second **Irish Home Rule Bill**, sponsored by Gladstone, is defeated in the House of Lords.

1894 **Gladstone**'s government falls in March following the prime minister's failure to promote Irish Home Rule, but the Liberals remain in power under the new prime minister, **Lord Rosebery**.

The first issue of *The Yellow Book*, a quarterly literary and art magazine, appears. Its notoriety as a 'decadent' publication derives largely from the flamboyant drawings of its art editor **Aubrey Beardsley**, who had achieved notoriety with his illustrations for Wilde's *Salomé* a year earlier.

1895 In a June **general election**, Rosebery's Liberals are defeated, and **Lord Salisbury** forms a Conservative administration. Also defeated are every one of the **Independent Labour Party**'s 28 candidates.

Frederick Lanchester manufactures England's first four-wheel motor car.

The **London School of Economics** is founded by members of the Fabian Society.

The **National Trust** is founded to protect Britain's natural and architectural heritages.

Oscar Wilde, now a successful playwright and one of London's best-known artistic figures, is sentenced to two years in prison for homosexual offences after bringing an unsuccessful libel case against the **Marquis of Queensberry**.

1896 An Anglo-Egyptian force under the command of **Horatio Herbert Kitchener** begins the pacification of **Sudan**.

War between Britain and Germany is narrowly averted after **Kaiser Wilhelm II** sends a telegram to the Boer leader **Paul Kruger** congratulating him on a successful raid against Britain's **Cape Colony** in South Africa.

Alfred Harmsworth (later Lord Northcliffe) founds the *Daily Mail* newspaper, promising his readers that in it 'four leading articles, a page of parliament, and columns of speeches will NOT be found.'

England's first **cinema** opens in London's **Leicester Square**.

The Italian inventor-entrepreneur **Guglielmo Marconi** creates the world's first **radio station** on the Isle of Wight.

1897 Celebrating her Diamond Jubilee, Queen Victoria makes use of the **electric telegraph** to send messages to her subjects worldwide.

The physicist **J.J. Thomson** advances atomic theory by postulating the existence of **electrons** and a **nucleus** within every atom.

1898 Despite French interference, Kitchener completes the pacification of **Sudan**, following a brutal victory over Sudanese forces at **Omdurman** on 2 September.

H.G. Wells publishes *The War of the Worlds*, a tale of alien invasion.

1899 Tensions between Britons and Dutch Boers in southern Africa escalate into all-out war in October – the beginning of the **2nd Boer War**. Ill-prepared British forces are besieged at **Mafeking**, **Kimberley** and **Ladysmith**. At home, such affronts to national imperial pride are greeted with near-hysteria in the press.

Queen Victoria's Diamond Jubilee, caught on film by the Lumière brothers.

The first performance of **Edward Elgar**'s *Enigma Variations* marks the emergence of the first internationally regarded English composer since Henry Purcell.

1900 Following the appointment of **General Frederick Roberts** as commander-in-chief against the Boers, **Kimberley** is relieved on 15 February, **Ladysmith** on 28 February and **Mafeking** on 17 May. Further British successes lead to the annexation of the **Transvaal** and **Orange Free State**. But the Boers prolong the war by adopting guerilla tactics. Roberts' replacement, **Lord Kitchener**, rounds up 120,000 Boer civilians in **concentration camps**, where one in six die of neglect and malnutrition.

In China, Britain leads its fellow European powers, Russia and the USA, in suppressing the 'anti-imperialist' **Boxer Rebellion**. Largely as a result of 'great power' reprisals, China's own imperial system will collapse at the end of 1911.

1901 On 1 January Britain's Australian colonies are formally amalgamated to form the **Commonwealth of Australia**.

On 22 January, after 64 years on the throne, **Queen Victoria** dies. She is succeeded by her son **Prince Albert**, crowned as **Edward VII**.

As Boer resistance continues, **Kitchener** orders the construction of **blockhouses** (fortifications built to house small groups of troops) to defeat their guerilla tactics.

Seebohm Rowntree publishes *Poverty: A Study of Town Life*, based on a survey of York. His conclusion – that poverty is a social rather than a legal phenomenon – will have far-reaching consequences for 20th-century social and political planning.

An inexperienced naval officer, **Robert Falcon Scott**, sets out aboard *HMS Discovery* to conduct scientific research in **Antarctica**.

The **population** of the United Kingdom (including Ireland) rises to forty million, with London accounting for over six million people.

1902 **Lord Salisbury** resigns as prime minister in July, and is replaced by his nephew **Arthur James Balfour**.

In May the Boer War ends with the **Treaty of Vereeniging**, the Boers conceding British sovereignty in South Africa.

The first of **Beatrix Potter**'s illustrated children's books, *The Tale of Peter Rabbit*, is published.

> **❝** Before the Boer war, we were spoiling for a fight ... Any government here, during the last ten years of the last century, could have had a war by lifting a finger. The people would have shouted for it. They had a craving for excitement, and a rush of blood to the head. Now, this generation has had enough of excitement, and has lost a little blood, and is sane and normal. **❞**
>
> Foreign Secretary Edward Grey, in a communication
> to President Theodore Roosevelt, 1906

1903 Allying herself with the Independent Labour Party, **Emmeline Pankhurst** founds the **Women's Social and Political Union** to lobby for the right of women to vote. Her followers swiftly become known as **suffragettes**.

Ramsay MacDonald, secretary of the newly formed **Labour Representation Committee**, concludes an anti-Conservative pact with the **Liberal Party**.

The **Conservative Party**, also known as the **Unionist Party** because of its opposition to Home Rule for Ireland, is damaged by the resignation of **Joseph Chamberlain**, after Chamberlain fails to persuade Balfour to safeguard the Empire by adopting protectionist **trade tariffs**. Balfour

The early Labour Party

Concerns within England's ruling elite that the electoral reforms of 1832, 1867 and 1884 would inevitably place government in the hands of the 'great unwashed' proved to have little substance. Partly this was because the existing Liberal and Tory parties had already grasped the importance of electioneering; partly because the British working class was more diverse in its loyalties and opinions than upper-crust alarmists imagined; and partly because working men were slow to organize themselves politically. The Liberals had always claimed to represent the interests of labour, and the Conservatives did their best to assert likewise .

But the creation of an **Independent Labour Party** by **Keir Hardie** in 1893 began a process in which the political realities began – slowly – to change. The ILP's big strategy was to woo voters away from other parties by forging an alliance with the trade unions. Initially this failed – the unions had their own agendas, and in any case their restrictive practices made them less than ideal in the eyes of some wage earners. As a result the ILP performed disastrously in the 1895 general election. But Hardie and his followers persisted, and an agreement with the unions in 1900 (coupled with the formation of a **Labour Representation Committee**) consolidated the ILP's impact. Almost as important was the fact that the Liberals had begun to buckle, agreeing with Labour not to contest certain parliamentary seats in the hope of keeping out the Unionist Conservatives. In the long term, though, it was the two world wars of the 20th century that cemented Labour's place in British politics. The men who had fought and died for 'King and Country' demanded a better deal when peace resumed.

finds sympathy among Liberals, however, who contest that protectionism will only raise domestic food prices.

1904 Britain and France enter into an **Entente Cordiale**, a mutual defence pact aimed principally against **German expansionism** but also against **Russia**.

Scott's Antarctic expedition returns home with a new 'furthest south' record, but having failed to reach the South Pole.

1905 Emmeline Pankhurst's suffragettes resort to hunger strikes, arson and other 'public outrages' to publicize their cause.

Balfour resigns as prime minister, replaced on 4 December by **Sir Henry Campbell Bannerman**, who is committed to free trade.

1906 In a January **general election** the **Labour Party** wins 29 seats in the Commons, but the **Liberals** are returned to power and **Campbell Bannerman** continues as prime minister.

Britain launches the first 'modern' **battleship**, *HMS Dreadnought*. Germany responds by ordering its own fleet of battleships.

© MUSEUM OF LONDON/HERITAGE-IMAGES

Christabel Pankhurst being modelled by Mr Tussaud.

In England, the **Rolls Royce Company** is founded, dedicated to manufacturing advanced luxurious automobiles.

1907 As perceptions of a 'German threat' grow, Britain and France admit **Russia** into the **Entente Cordiale**.

The government introduces **free school meals** as part of its social reform programme.

Ernest Shackleton sets out for the Antarctic in command of the **Nimrod Expedition**, aiming like Scott to reach the South Pole.

The first motorized **public omnibuses** begin operating in London.

1908 Herbert Henry Asquith succeeds Campbell Bannerman as Liberal prime minister in April and introduces a **national pension scheme** for the elderly.

The **4th Olympic Games** are held in London.

1909 To pay for the government's social spending, chancellor **David Lloyd George** introduces a **surtax** on higher incomes and increases **death duties**.

Shackleton returns to England having set a new 'furthest south' record in **Antarctica**. He is praised for not risking the lives of his men by pressing to reach the South Pole.

1910 Edward VII dies on 6 May, and is succeeded by his son **George V**.

Asquith continues as prime minister after the Liberals win a fresh **general election**.

Captain Scott sets out on a second South Pole expedition, competing against the veteran Norwegian explorer **Roald Amundsen**.

1911 After prolonged public debate, Asquith's government brings about a major constitutional change by introducing

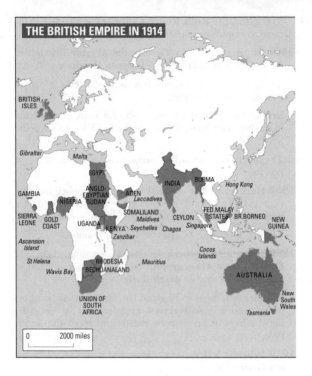

THE BRITISH EMPIRE IN 1914

BRITISH ISLES

Gibraltar Malta

EGYPT

GAMBIA
SIERRA LEONE
GOLD COAST
NIGERIA
ANGLO-EGYPTIAN SUDAN
UGANDA
KENYA
SOMALILAND
Zanzibar
Ascension Island
St Helena
Wavis Bay
RHODESIA
BECHUANALAND
UNION OF SOUTH AFRICA

ADEN
Laccadives
INDIA
BURMA
Hong Kong
CEYLON
Maldives
Seychelles Chagos
Mauritius
FED.MALAY STATES
Singapore
Cocos Islands
BR.BORNEO
NEW GUINEA

AUSTRALIA
New South Wales
Tasmania

0   2000 miles

a **Parliament Act** that curtails the powers of the **House of Lords** by abolishing its right of veto over legislation passed by the House of Commons, and by limiting its rights of amendment.

Lloyd George introduces a **National Insurance Bill**, affording selected workers state-funded benefits during sickness and unemployment.

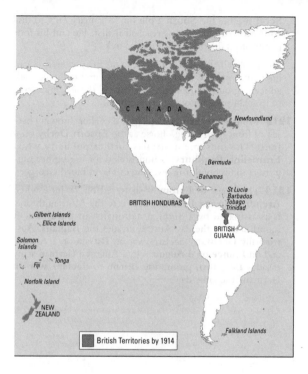

British Territories by 1914

During a year in which international tensions are heightened by German intervention in **Morocco**, traditionally a French sphere of influence, **George V** becomes the first British monarch to visit **India**.

1912 Attempts at an Anglo-German **arms limitation agreement** fail.

Scott reaches the **South Pole** on 18 January only to discover that Amundsen has reached it first. He and his four companions die on the homeward trek.

On 15 April the *RMS Titanic*, a steam-powered ocean liner run by the White Star Line, sinks after colliding with an iceberg on her maiden voyage across the Atlantic. 1513 of its 2224 passengers and crew drown.

1913 A suffragette, **Emily Davison**, dies after throwing herself in front of the king's horse at the **Epsom Derby** on 4 June. The movement attracts further publicity when **Emmeline Pankhurst** is imprisoned for urging her supporters to firebomb the dwelling of David Lloyd George.

1914 The peace of Europe is shattered on 28 June when **Archduke Franz Ferdinand**, heir to the Austrian throne, is assassinated by a Serbian nationalist in **Sarajevo**. A month later to the day Austria invades the **Balkans**. Austria's ally **Germany** declares war on **Russia** on 1 August, and on **France** on 3 August. On 4 August a German army invades **Belgium**, prompting Britain to **declare war** on Germany the same day.

10
England and the two World Wars

1914–45

Throughout the 19th century Britain pursued a dual policy: outside Europe, large-scale imperial expansion; nearer home, the preservation of a 'balance of powers'. In India, the Far East and Africa, Britain's armed forces were kept busy maintaining order in the colonies and protecting British trade monopolies – the closest heavy fighting was in the distant Crimea. Domestically, the same period was one of comparative tranquillity – the only major exception being in Ireland, where a vigorous independence movement began to take shape.

But in 1914, when Germany invaded Belgium, all that changed. The decline of the **Habsburg** and **Ottoman** empires and the emergence of a united Germany determined to rival England upset the European equilibrium in a way that Britain could no longer hope to deal with through diplomacy alone. The **Great War**, later called **World War I**, saw British troops committed directly across the English Channel for the first time since the fall of Napoleon in 1815. And a direct consequence of this conflict was that 25 years later Britain again found itself at loggerheads with Germany, now led by **Adolf Hitler** and the Nazi Party, in what would become known as **World War II**.

Though the second war was more wide-ranging than its predecessor – a truly global conflict – it directly confronted

England with the prospect of invasion. During the summer of 1940 the German Luftwaffe relentlessly bombed British ports and cities. And yet invasion was averted: partly because of the courage of British, Canadian and Polish fighter pilots who prevented German air superiority during the **Battle of Britain**; partly because Hitler turned his attentions instead to the Russian front. Yet until December 1941, when Germany's ally Japan attacked **Pearl Harbor** – and in doing so brought the United States into the war – Britain was largely isolated in its struggle against German and Italian fascism inside Europe itself.

In both World Wars American intervention proved decisive, which in turn brought about an alternative world order. In the years that followed 1945, Britain would find itself gradually displaced from the centre of global politics. And even at this early stage, behind the facade of British imperialism there were counter-currents. Because of reforms to the electoral franchise and the introduction of salaries for members of Parliament, the House of Commons began to reflect an increasingly broad spectrum of opinion – not least the socialist aspirations of British labour, which was now strongly organized and eager to agitate for reform. In fact both wars resulted in significant political rewards for more people than ever before. Perhaps the starkest example is that of women: having proved their wage-earning credentials in the munitions factories of World War I, they were finally given the vote in 1918.

But it wasn't just war that accelerated political change. In the 31 years that separated the beginning of World War I from the end of World War II, there were a bewildering variety of events – many of them closely attuned to developments elsewhere in Europe. The **Liberal Party** met its demise as a political force, displaced by Ramsay MacDonald's Labour Party; Stafford Cripps advocated a **Popular Front** in alliance with the USSR; Oswald Mosley launched the **British Union of Fascists** in 1932; the **'Cliveden Set'**, directed by Lord and Lady Astor, urged appeasement with Hitler after 1933; and when the **Spanish Civil War** broke out in 1936, hundreds of socialist-minded volunteers eagerly joined the International Brigade to resist General Franco's fascist Falange party.

True to form, however, Britain proved resistant to widespread reform. The dominant figure of the inter-war years was the unobtrusive Conservative prime minister **Stanley Baldwin**, who made a public virtue of his quietist instincts and middle-class moderation. The **Great Depression**, which followed the collapse of America's Wall Street stock market in 1929, brought down government after government abroad, but in Britain its effects were localized. Although unemployment reached a staggering 80 percent in some areas of the country (inciting the **Jarrow March** of 1936, when 200 unemployed workers walked from Tyneside to London to protest), little changed and Baldwin's government was never seriously threatened. Baldwin's hands were at any rate occupied later in the year by the **'constitutional crisis'** initiated by Edward VIII's eagerness to marry the American divorcée Wallis Simpson. The furore the abdication crisis caused (despite being officially held from the British press) demonstrates how little the political life of England had really changed in the opening half of the 20th century.

1914 On 4 August Britain enters **World War I** – known at the time as the **Great War** – by declaring war on Germany following that country's invasion of Belgium. At the end of the month Germany inflicts defeat on Russia at **Tannenburg**, shattering hopes of a swift conclusion to hostilities.

A **British Expeditionary Force** (**BEF**) is dispatched to the continent and only narrowly escapes encirclement after a breakdown in communications between British and French commands.

The German advance into France is halted at the **Battle of the Marne** in early September. As German forces withdraw beyond **Verdun**, both sides begin constructing networks of **fortified trenches** immediately opposite each other; by the

© UNDERWOOD&UNDERWOOD/CORBIS

The British tank *Winston's Folly* crosses a trench, c.1917.

end of the year these stretch from the English Channel to Switzerland. For four years the pattern of the war on this 'western front' will consist of heavy artillery exchanges interspersed with desperate attempts to overrun the enemy's lines. In the opening months of this **trench warfare** the English officer corps is devastated, six peers and 85 sons of peers among the fallen, while the BEF as a whole suffers the loss of some 300 troops a day throughout 1914 and 1915.

On the 'home front', war fever grips the nation as tens of thousands respond to a call to arms orchestrated by the charismatic secretary for war, **Lord Kitchener**. A minority protest against the growing carnage and, as the conflict develops, increasing numbers of **pacifists** are imprisoned.

Despite the carnage, the opening months of the war see some of the more bizarre camaraderie of warfare extended across the lines, as some of the English and German troops enjoy a **Christmas Day cease-fire** and an ad hoc game of soccer.

1915 In February German submarines armed with torpedoes, known as **U-boats**, begin a blockade of Britain, attacking merchant as well as naval shipping.

Following pressure put upon Prime Minister **Herbert Asquith**'s cabinet by the Admiralty later in February, Britain endeavours to relieve Russia and turn the German flank by opening a new front in the Turkish **Dardanelles**. The doomed campaign gets off to a disastrous start when four Royal Navy battleships and other vessels are lost to mines in the narrow straits.

Disaster continues in April, when an Allied landing force is held down by Turkish fire on the beaches of the **Gallipoli Peninsula**. Troops from Australia and New Zealand (known as the **ANZACs**) sustain particularly high casualties. The failure of the Gallipoli campaign leads to **Winston Churchill** being sacked as first lord of the admiralty in May. The senior naval officer, **Sir John Fisher**, resigns during the summer.

Poison gas (chlorine) is first used in trench warfare by the Germans. When the British and French protest that it is contrary to international military law, the Germans claim the Allies have already done so themselves. This is disproved, but by the end of the year both sides are using gas indiscriminately.

On 7 May the passenger liner *Lusitania*, rightly suspected of carrying military supplies, is torpedoed by German U-boats. Among the thousand or so dead are 128 American civilians, increasing pressure on the **United States** to enter the war.

On 23 May **Italy** joins the Allies by declaring war on **Austria**, raising (eventually unrealized) hopes for the creation of a fresh anti-German front.

Bombs are dropped on English cities from German airships, called **zeppelins**, named after their developer **Count Ferdinand von Zeppelin**.

In December the **Dardanelles** campaign is finally abandoned, Churchill being widely blamed for its failure. *The Rainbow*, a novel by **D.H. Lawrence**, is seized by police shortly after its publication on grounds of obscenity.

1916 Between February and July fighting along the Western Front is concentrated around **Verdun**, the defence of which costs the French army 350,000 lives.

On 24 April an insurrection against English rule in the Irish capital **Dublin**, known as the **Easter Uprising**, begins, but is swiftly crushed. Although some 250,000 Irish volunteers are fighting in the British army, the widespread resentment about British rule in Ireland is unmistakable, and the hanging of twenty ringleaders on 3 August only increases it.

On 21 May the two-day **Battle of Jutland** begins, the war's only major engagement between the British and German navies. The British lose more ships, but the German fleet returns to port and remains there for the duration of the war.

An Arab revolt against Turkish rule in **Arabia**, led by **Prince Faisal** with the assistance of the English army officer **T.E. Lawrence**, begins in June.

Under pressure from the French, the British commander-in-chief, **Sir Douglas Haig**, launches an all-out offensive known as the **Battle of the Somme**. On 1 July, Britain loses almost 20,000 men, and by the end of the 140-day battle – during which the British army introduces the **tank** – Allied casualties from many countries climb to over 800,000. To replenish its losses, the British government introduces **conscription**.

In July, **Lord Kitchener** drowns on his way to Russia after his ship, *HMS Hampshire*, is torpedoed.

David Lloyd George becomes secretary for war in July.

On 28 November German warplanes begin bombing **London**.

On 4 December Asquith resigns, and **Lloyd George** takes over as prime minister at the head of a coalition War Cabinet.

1917 On 3 February the **USA** severs relations with Germany after British intelligence intercepts the **'Zimmermann telegram'**, from the German government to its ambassador in Mexico, urging the latter to encourage Mexico to attack America. On 6 April the USA **declares war** on Germany, and begins transporting troops to Europe.

In May the **convoy system** for protecting merchant ships is set in place, and U-boats become gradually less effective.

World War I (1914–18)

The **Great War** put paid to any lingering notions of warfare as a chivalric pursuit. New developments in weaponry – machine guns, aeroplanes, tanks, gas shells, specially designed barbed wire – were not accompanied by a revolution in communications technology, so commanders on both sides possessed neither the tactics nor the physical means to develop or control the fighting they initiated. Unable to achieve breakthroughs, armies were left with little choice but to dig in and pound each other with shellfire. Waves of infantry periodically went 'over the top' to charge enemy positions or advance the front line, only to be mown down in no-man's-land. The sheer scale of this static conflict is apparent in the fact that by the end of 1914 the front lines extended from the Channel coast all the way to the Swiss border; in some places they were only thirty yards apart.

Nor did the rat-infested trenches themselves offer much in the way of comfort. They filled knee-high with rain, and attempts by the British army to limit lice, 'trench foot' and a panoply of other infections were ineffective. Some soldiers (many in 'Pals' Brigades', recruited from one town to improve morale) named their trenches after landmarks in an attempt to humanize this new kind of war. Others went mad, or braved the death penalty for desertion and tried to escape. Most hoped to get a 'Blighty' – an injury that would get them sent home. Huge numbers of survivors suffered for the rest of their lives from 'shell-shock': by 1928 there were 48 mental hospitals catering for 60,000 long-term victims.

All told Britain lost some 960,000 servicemen. Whole villages saw their menfolk disappear, and universities were depleted of students as conscription was introduced for the first time. The 'home front' also experienced a new threat, aerial bombardment – technology which had, ironically, been developed to control native populations elsewhere in the Empire. As more and more families lost relatives, the best hope was that this would indeed be 'the war to end all wars'. In reality it set the pattern for what was to come: the involvement of entire populations in a national war effort and their vulnerability to long-range assault.

On the **Western Front**, shortly after an unreported mutiny amongst British troops at Étaples, the **3rd Battle of Ypres**, also known as **Passchendaele**, begins on 31 July. Again British and Allied troops fail to break through German lines, and the loss of a further 400,000 men undermines the British army's morale.

In September, as British forces take control of **Palestine**, foreign secretary **Arthur Balfour** declares Britain's support for the creation of a **Jewish homeland** there.

On 20 November the first massed tank attack is made at **Cambrai**; but although the assault achieves instant results, the Germany army repossesses all of its lost ground by the year's end.

The prolific novelist **P.G. Wodehouse** publishes *The Man with Two Left Feet*, a collection of stories that introduces his readership to the monied Bertie Wooster and his redoubtable valet Jeeves.

1918 On 21 March, Germany launches the **Ludendorff Offensive**, a 'big push' against Allied Forces on the Western Front that lasts until early April. British, French and American forces resist, and begin preparing a **counter-offensive**.

On 1 April, Britain's Royal Flying Corps and the Royal Naval Air Service are amalgamated to form the **Royal Air Force**.

In the early summer Britain is swept by a peculiarly virulent **influenza epidemic** (the 'Spanish 'flu'), that kills twice as many people worldwide as die fighting in the Great War.

In August, as German defences begin to crumble, British tanks again demonstrate their usefulness at the **Battle of Amiens**.

In September, **General Edmund Allenby** masterminds the climactic **Battle of Megiddo**, finally breaking the power of the 450-year-old **Ottoman Empire** and ensuring Western access to Middle Eastern **oil reserves** for the rest of the century.

After further Allied successes, the German army in Europe falls back on the **Hindenburg Line**. In October a German **naval mutiny** suggests the war may be drawing to a close. On 7 November **Kaiser Wilhelm II** abdicates, and four days later Germany and the Allies sign an **armistice**.

Partly in recognition of **Emmeline Pankhurst**'s efforts to organize female labour during the war, a **Representation of the People Act** gives women aged 30 and over the vote.

The **Labour Party**, inspired by the 1917 Russian Revolution, calls for public ownership of 'the means of production' in **Clause Four** of its revised constitution.

The pacifist **Lytton Strachey** publishes *Eminent Victorians*, a book that debunks the reputations of Florence Nightingale, General Gordon and other Victorian worthies.

Edward Elgar publishes his *Cello Concerto*, an autumnal work that reflects the composer's feelings about the tremendous futility of war.

1919 On 28 June the **Treaty of Versailles** formally concludes the Great War. Germany and its allies are stripped of their weapons, colonies and even raw materials. Britain immediately gains by the acquisition of territories in German **Southwest Africa**, and a mandate to govern **Palestine**, formerly part of the Ottoman Empire. Britain also takes a prominent role in the **League of Nations**, founded as a consequence of Versailles to safeguard future international security. Reservations about the treaty are felt by many, and are best expressed in *The Economic Consequences of Peace* by **John Maynard Keynes**, who warns that economic penalties can only lead to a resumption of hostilities.

> **❝** What passing-bells for these who die as cattle?
> Only the monstrous anger of the guns.
> Only the stuttering rifles' rapid rattle
> Can patter out their hasty orisons.
> No mockeries now for them; no prayers nor bells,
> Nor any voice of mourning save the choirs, –
> The shrill, demented choirs of wailing shells;
> And bugles calling for them from sad shires. **❞**
>
> Wilfred Owen, 'Anthem for Doomed Youth' (1917)

> **❝** The Great War is God's vengeance on the people who held women in subjection. **❞**
>
> Dame Christabel Pankhurst

The American-born **Nancy, Lady Astor** becomes the first woman to sit in the House of Commons.

1920 Following a nationwide manhunt, one of the leaders of the 1917 Étaples mutiny, **Percy Toplis**, convicted in his absence of a murder committed after the war, is gunned down outside **Penrith** in Cumbria.

The **Cenotaph**, designed by the renowned architect **Sir Edwin Lutyens** as a tribute to Britain's fallen servicemen, is unveiled in Whitehall, and becomes the focus of an annual commemoration service.

1921 In the face of widespread disturbances in Ireland, Prime Minister **Lloyd George** concludes a pact with the Irish nationalist party **Sinn Féin**. As a result an **Irish Free State** is created, consisting of 26 southern 'Catholic' counties. Six predominantly Protestant northern counties remain a part of the United Kingdom, however, and are known as **Northern Ireland**.

1922 In October, Lloyd George's coalition government

disintegrates over fears that Britain may be dragged into a war between **Greece** and **Turkey**.

Following a general election in which the Labour Party gains an unprecedented 142 Commons seats under the leadership of **Ramsay MacDonald**, **Andrew Bonar Law** forms a Conservative government.

The **British Broadcasting Company** (later Corporation) begins making public service radio broadcasts.

The American-born poet **T.S. Eliot** publishes *The Waste Land*, a brilliant display of Modernist erudition that employs unsettling and self-consciously complex poetic techniques.

1923 **Bonar Law** resigns in May after being diagnosed with an incurable cancer of the throat. He is succeeded as Conservative prime minister by the eminently respectable **Stanley Baldwin**. In December Baldwin calls an election to secure his mandate, but the Conservatives suffer heavy losses and the result is a hung parliament. The Liberal and Labour parties decide to co-operate to oust the Tories.

1924 In January **Ramsay MacDonald** becomes Britain's first Labour prime minister, but his coalition government lasts only until November, when Baldwin resumes office.

E.M. Forster publishes *A Passage to India*, a novel that questions the cultural and social assumptions underpinning Britain's imperial ideology.

1925 Chancellor **Winston Churchill** announces that Britain will return to the **Gold Standard** at a fixed rate of $4.80 to the pound. The move is designed to restore confidence in British industry, but is later criticized for prolonging the economic slump.

The popular professional cricketer, **Jack Hobbs**, overtakes W.G. Grace's record of 125 centuries scored in first-class matches.

1926 After the government refuses to renew a subsidy to Britain's **coal miners**, they come out on strike. Coupled with the slow pace of postwar economic recovery, the spread of trade union membership and the recalcitrance of many British managers, this leads to a **General Strike** beginning on 3 May, which closes down many industries and virtually all public services. Amidst panic that the state might be overthrown, the **army** is drafted in to restore and maintain order on England's streets, and students and professionals are sworn in as **special constables**. Baldwin's cabinet holds its nerve, however, and the **TUC** (Trades Union Congress) capitulates on 12 May. Only the miners remain on strike.

An **Imperial Conference** agrees that neither Britain nor its dominions should be expected to become involved in their own private disputes without the compliance of their own national governments.

1927 The **British Broadcasting Corporation** (formerly the British Broadcasting Company) is re-established by government charter with a monopoly in radio broadcasting and funded by licence fees (see p.453).

Revisions to the **Anglican Prayer Book** revive debate and ill-feeling between the Church of England's two most vociferous factions, the Anglo-Catholics and the Evangelical Protestants.

Virginia Woolf publishes *To the Lighthouse*, a novel that attempts to catalogue the moment-by-moment feelings and impressions of its characters.

1928 New legislation gives women full **electoral equality** with men.

D.H. Lawrence completes his final novel, *Lady Chatterley's Lover*, in Florence, where it is privately printed to avoid prosecution under English obscenity laws. It will not be published in full in England until 1960.

The Bloomsbury Group

'Bloomsbury' became the shorthand for a group of writers and artists associated with the Bloomsbury area of London, close to the British Museum and London University, from 1907 onwards. Although the group was influenced by the philosopher **G.E. Moore** – who argued for philosophy to be anchored to direct experience – and shared pacifist beliefs, it never really amounted to a distinctive movement. Rather it was an informal society of gifted individuals who had little interest in espousing a common creed but who decisively influenced cultural life in the early decades of the century.

At Bloomsbury's hub were the Woolfs: **Virginia**, the novelist and essayist whose 'stream-of-consciousness' fiction explored new psychological ground; her husband **Leonard**, a left-wing commentator and novelist who set up the Hogarth Press (which printed many Bloomsbury publications); and Virginia's artist sister **Vanessa Bell** and her companion **Duncan Grant**. Orbiting closely round this inner core were the economist **John Maynard Keynes**, whose monetarist theories still influence economic policy; and the biographer–historian **Lytton Strachey**, who scandalized society with *Eminent Victorians*, a no-holds-barred exposé of various

1929 Following the Labour Party's best performance yet in a general election, **Ramsay MacDonald** becomes prime minister for a second time on 5 June.

The sudden collapse of the New York stock market, which becomes known as the **Wall Street Crash**, threatens to plunge the whole world into economic recession. In England unemployment soars, particularly in the steel and shipbuilding industries located in the north of the country.

1931 Stricken by financial crisis, Britain abandons the **gold standard** – the system for matching paper currency against actual reserves of gold. MacDonald resigns as prime minister, but returns immediately as head of a coalition

Victorian worthies. There were also a galaxy of other associates, among them the philosopher **Bertrand Russell**, the society hostess **Lady Ottoline Morrell**, the orientalist **Arthur Waley**, the novelist **E.M. Forster**, the playwright **Roger Fry**, and **Vita Sackville-West** – a writer better remembered for the gardens she created at Sissinghurst.

But perhaps it was the gossip about what the Bloomsbury group got up to that proved its most memorable legacy. Its associates developed a reputation for experimental 'free living' at Vanessa's farm at Charleston in Sussex, which she had taken partly to help Grant claim exemption from conscription by declaring himself a farm labourer. Strachey might turn up with his devoted companion Dora Carrington or one of a series of male lovers; Maynard Keynes could be accompanied by his Polish wife Lydia Lopokova or, more rarely, Clive Bell. This revolt against what the group saw as Victorian restrictions – whether artistic, sexual or social – reflected less extreme changes in English society, but the group's attitudes were beginning to seem outmoded in the political atmosphere of the early 1930s.

National Government, stunning his Labour supporters. In an October **general election** the Coalition takes 556 seats, while Labour wins only 51.

In the Far East, the Japanese invasion of **Manchuria** in northeastern China threatens not only Anglo-Chinese commercial relations but Britain's oriental colonies.

1932 Britain abandons the **free trade** principle with regard to imported foodstuffs, in existence since the repeal of the Corn Laws of 1847. In an agreement reached at the **Ottawa Convention**, Britain's colonies – including the 'commonwealths' of **Canada**, **Australia** and **New Zealand** – are exempted from newly imposed tariffs,

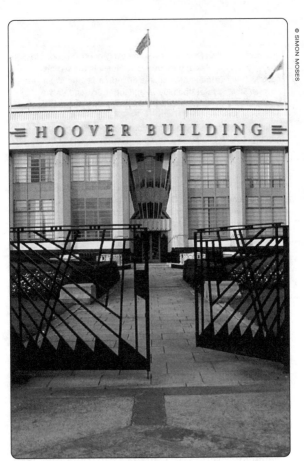

Art Deco manufacturing – the Hoover plant at Perivale, West London.

strengthening what is already an imperial trading bloc.

Imitating Benito Mussolini, the leader of the Italian fascist party, the sometime Labour MP **Sir Oswald Mosley** establishes the **British Union of Fascists**.

In Cambridge, **John Cockcroft** and **Ernest Walton**, working with the New Zealand-born atomic physicist **Ernest Rutherford**, split the atom – an important step towards the creation of **nuclear energy** and **nuclear weapons**.

1933 Sir Owen Williams' Art Deco **Daily Express** building on Fleet Street opens, the first true curtain-walled building to be constructed in London. Other Art Deco buildings of this period include the **Firestone Factory** (1929) and the **Hoover Building** (1935), both by Wallis, Gilbert and Partners.

1935 **George V** celebrates his **Silver Jubilee**. The coalition National Government, now almost wholly Conservative, wins a substantial majority in a June **general election**. **Stanley Baldwin** replaces Ramsay MacDonald as prime minister and promotes legislation that gives **India** limited powers of self-government.

The foreign secretary, **Sir Samuel Hoare**, is forced to resign after the secret **'Hoare–Laval' pact** signed with his French counterpart is leaked to the press. The pact itself undermines the League of Nations' demand that **Mussolini** withdraw troops from **Abyssinia** (Ethiopia), which he seeks to make an Italian colony.

1936 **George V** dies on 20 January, and is succeeded by his popular eldest son, David, who takes the name **Edward VIII**. The new king immediately creates a constitutional crisis by announcing his intention to marry an American divorcée, **Wallis Simpson**. The marriage is opposed by Baldwin, senior Church figures and other members of the establishment, and on 11 December Edward abdicates, his brother **George VI** becoming king.

In July **civil war** breaks out in **Spain**. Volunteers from all parts of Britain travel to the peninsula to join the International Brigade in its fight against the fascist leader **Francisco Franco**.

The financial crisis continues, and in October 200 unemployed workers from **Jarrow** in Tyneside – led by their local MP, **Ellen Wilkinson** – march over 300 miles to London to protest at their plight and those of the area.

The BBC launches the first high-definition **television broadcasting** service.

1937 In May, following Baldwin's resignation, **Neville Chamberlain** becomes prime minister.

In June, the ex-king **Edward** marries Wallis Simpson.

1938 In March the German chancellor **Adolph Hitler** seizes **Austria** and annexes it as German territory. He also makes it clear that he intends to incorporate the **Sudetenland**, comprising the German-speaking part of **Czechoslovakia**. During talks held in **Munich** in September Britain and France allow Hitler to have his way in Czechoslovakia on the understanding he will not attempt further invasions. **Neville Chamberlain**, returning to London, proclaims that he has secured 'peace in our time'.

Belfast-born **Louis MacNeice** writes *Autumn Journal*, a poem cycle that captures the confused mood of England's younger generation during 1938 as the country is felt to be heading inevitably back to war with Germany.

1939 As the international situation deteriorates both in Europe and the Far East – where **Japan** enlarges its colony in **China** – mainland Britain is subjected to a terrorist campaign of bombings perpetrated by the **IRA** (Irish

The General Strike

By 1925 the immediate economic problems thrown up by the war were beginning to abate. Unemployment was falling, and the prime minister, **Stanley Baldwin**, seemed in a good position to reap the political rewards. But all was not well. The coal industry, faced with competition from German and Polish markets, was struggling. Many thought it outmoded, and private mine owners showed little inclination to improve working conditions – indeed they even proposed lowering pay and increasing working hours so that they could keep up with the rest of Europe. It was in this climate that the mine workers walked out on strike in May 1926, joined shortly afterwards by the rest of the unions. In response to this **General Strike**, students and others rallied to make sure that essential services continued to operate, while in some areas strikers engaged in running battles with the police.

Despite expectations that this might prove the overture to the long-awaited 'British Revolution', for the most part the strike proved far from radical. The union leaders discouraged its activists from attempting to take over local government, and in most places picketing was good-humoured – strikers and police even taking part in games of football against each other. After little more than a week, the strike had collapsed and most returned to work, leaving the miners to continue their solitary protest.

This was to prove the pattern for industrial unrest in England before World War II. The **Jarrow Marches** of 1936 – in which some 200 unemployed workers traipsed down to London with their local MP – have remained ingrained in the public imagination, but little was actually achieved by their protest. England was never to experience the kind of industrial and political turmoil seen in the rest of Europe.

Republican Army), a group determined to join the 'Six Counties' of Northern Ireland to the Irish Republic.

In January **W.H. Auden**, one of the most successful English poets of the century and a committed pacifist, emigrates to America. He is joined by the brilliant young composer **Benjamin Britten** and his companion, the tenor **Peter Pears**.

In the House of Commons, **Chamberlain** is attacked for giving recognition to **General Franco**'s fascist government in Spain.

On 23 August **Hitler** and the Soviet leader **Josef Stalin** conclude a **non-aggression pact**.

On 1 September, reneging on its assurances given at Munich the previous year, Germany invades **Poland**. In response, on 3 September **Britain** and **France** jointly **declare war** on Germany, officially beginning **World War II**. On the same day **Winston Churchill**, who has consistently advocated re-armament against the German Nazi threat, returns as **first lord of the admiralty**.

In November, having agreed with Germany to partition **Poland**, the **Soviet Union** attacks **Finland**.

Despite long-overdue preparations for war in Britain, little seems to happen for the first few months of conflict, and this period quickly becomes known as the **'phoney war'**. Over 827,000 children are **evacuated** from major towns and cities to safety in rural areas, and **rationing** of essential foodstuffs and consumables begins.

In September a 150,000-strong British **expeditionary force** is dispatched to France, and in mid-December the German 'pocket battleship' *Graf Spee* (one of several small German ships) is scuttled by its captain in the estuary of the River Plate off **Montevideo** rather than surrender to the Royal Navy.

1940 In April German forces occupy **Denmark** and **Norway**. On 14 May **the Netherlands** falls, and German armies begin marching on **France** and **Belgium**.

On 7 May Chamberlain, widely condemned for his policy of appeasement toward Hitler, resigns and **Winston Churchill** becomes prime minister.

On 28 May **Belgium** falls to Germany, and a day later the **evacuation** of encircled British forces and the remains of the French army from the port of **Dunkirk** begins, to be completed on 4 June. In all 320,000 troops are ferried to safety across the Channel in a flotilla of boats (many of them civilian), but 30,000 men are killed and the French later accuse the British of leaving many of their own soldiers to their fate.

On 10 June Mussolini's Italy **declares war** on the Allies, but the USA remains neutral.

On 14 June German troops enter **Paris**, and eight days later France and Germany sign an **armistice**. To oppose the German occupation in France and other countries, **resistance movements** spring up, increasingly supported by Britain as the war continues.

In June, prior to a planned invasion of Britain itself, German **bombing raids** against England intensify. The raids initially focus on British airbases, but switch to major ports and cities in August. The attempt to defend Britain in the air becomes known, in Churchill's phrase, as the **'Battle of Britain'**, in which pilots from the RAF's **Fighter Command** combat the **Luftwaffe**'s bombers and fighters over British territory.

Hitler declares a **naval blockade** against Britain, German submarines once again causing havoc amongst merchant shipping.

On 23 August **nighttime bombing raids** are launched against **London** and, later, other major cities including **Manchester**, **Belfast**, **Sheffield**, **Liverpool**, **Glasgow**, **Hull**, **Plymouth**, **Coventry** and **Sunderland**. These become known colloquially as the **'Blitz'**, after the German word for 'lightning warfare', *blitzkrieg*. In all some 60,000 civilians die as a result. Hitler's tactics mean that invasion is postponed, however.

In September the **USA** provides Churchill with 50 badly needed **naval destroyers** in return for military rights in **Canada** and the **Caribbean**.

On 27 September Germany, Italy and Japan form the **Axis** coalition, the three states agreeing to assist each other.

In November British forces occupy **Crete** in an endeavour to provide support for **Greece**.

On 11 November the Royal Navy incapacitates the Italian fleet at **Taranto**.

In December **General Archibald Wavell** campaigns successfully against Italian forces in **Libya**.

The *Queen Elizabeth*, the world's largest passenger liner, is launched and immediately requisitioned by the War Office.

> **❝** We shall not flag or fail. We shall go on to the end, we shall fight in France, we shall fight in the seas and oceans, we shall fight with growing confidence and growing strength in the air, we shall defend our island, whatever the cost may be, we shall fight on the beaches, we shall fight on the landing grounds, we shall fight in the fields and in the streets, we shall fight in the hills; we shall never surrender. **❞**
>
> Winston Churchill, broadcast to the nation from the House of Commons, 4 June, 1940

1941 Germany invades **Greece** on 6 April, and on 22 May British forces evacuate **Crete**.

On 24 May the German battleship *Bismarck* sinks the British flagship *Hood* in the North Atlantic, but is itself sunk three days later.

In **Palestine** Jewish nationalists, led by the **Stern Gang**, begin a terrorist campaign against British administrators.

On 22 June German forces invade the **Soviet Union**, which consequently becomes a British ally.

On 7 December **Japan** launches a surprise attack against the American Pacific fleet at **Pearl Harbor**, Hawaii. On the same day Japan **declares war** on Britain, and the USA **declares war** on Japan as Japanese forces move into **British Malaya**. On 11 November Germany **declares war** on the USA.

On 25 December Japan seizes **Hong Kong**.

In North Africa, Wavell's campaign flounders as the German **Afrika Korps**, commanded by **Erwin Rommel**, begins assisting the Italians; British forces are pushed eastwards toward **Egypt**.

World War II (1939–45)

Nearly sixty million people died as a result of World War II. The majority of them were civilians (unlike during the Great War) and many of them lived in Russia and the Far East, where nuclear weapons were deployed for the first time by the USA against Japan. The war was really a conflation of two separate conflicts – one against Hitler's 'Third Reich', the other against an equally warlike Japanese Empire – but because Germany, Japan and Mussolini's Italy clubbed together to form the **Axis**, the war came to be seen (by the Allies at least) as a single struggle against a dark totalitarian menace.

In the long term there were two winners: the **Soviet Union** and its temporary ally, the **USA**. Only American intervention made victory possible, and this hard fact also confirmed that Britain's age of empire was drawing to a close. The **'cold war'** between the two superpowers dominated the world order after 1945, and America's huge investment in rebuilding Western Europe ensured that it would stay on the side of the USA. Many in Britain and America had regarded Stalin's totalitarian state as quite as much a threat as Nazi Germany, and the aftermath of the war saw their fears realized as Stalin extended his influence over a communist bloc covering most of Eastern Europe, while other communist

1942 On 15 February **Singapore**, home to Britain's Far Eastern fleet, falls to **Japan** – an event described by Churchill as 'the worst capitulation in British history' after 80,000 imperial troops are taken prisoner. As the Japanese Empire continues to expand, the British **Solomon Islands** are lost in March, and in May **Burma** is overrun. As Japanese forces threaten **India**, there is a resurgence of Indian nationalism, leading to the imprisonment of **Mahatma Gandhi** and other political leaders.

On 30 May British bombers bomb **Cologne**, the start of a continuing air campaign against German industrial centres regimes secured power in **China**, **North Korea** and **Vietnam**.

Yet Britain's involvement in the conflict – whatever its original reasons for joining – was far from insignificant. British forces reversed the German–Italian occupation of North Africa, fought side-by-side with American troops in Italy and were a main component in the D-Day landings. In the Far East, having lost Malaya, Singapore and Burma, Britain fought back against Japan, saving its interests in India in the process. In the Atlantic, the Royal Navy countered German U-boats intent on destroying life-supporting convoys from America; and the Royal Air Force defended Britain with its fighters, and later helped to bring about the end of the Third Reich by its devastating raids on German towns and cities.

On the home front, too, there was a massive mobilization of resources – assisted by the government's tight control of information and an effective propaganda apparatus. In the face of devastating air raids on Britain's cities, many people performed their civilian duties, putting in long hours in weapons and munitions factories, coping with rationing by whatever means and 'digging for victory' in an attempt to maximize agricultural production.

and civilian targets, masterminded by **Air Chief Marshal Arthur 'Bomber' Harris**.

Although Rommel takes **Tobruk** on 21 June, a British bastion in **Libya**, his advance upon Egypt is decisively rebuffed by the British 8th Army under the inspirational command of **General Bernard Montgomery** at **El Alamein** during October and November.

On the Eastern Front, the German assault on **Russia** becomes bogged down in the brutal siege of **Stalingrad**, which begins in August.

In November Allied forces in **North Africa** are placed under the overall command of the American general **Dwight Eisenhower**.

The Oxford academic **W.H. Beveridge** completes a report outlining a programme for far-reaching social reconstruction once the war is finished; in retrospect it will be regarded as the blueprint for the **'welfare state'**.

Gilbert Murray founds the **Oxford Committee for Famine Relief** (later **Oxfam**), a charitable organization

Bletchley Park

In 1923 two publications shocked the defeated German military into reappraising their communications strategy. One was Winston Churchill's *The World Crisis*; the other was the Royal Navy's official history of World War I. Both revealed that the British had succeeded in breaking the Germans' codes regularly throughout the war. The Germans' response was the Enigma machine: a complex encrypting device that even in its simplest form necessitated a code breaker working through a possible 10,000,000,000,000,000 permutations before the hidden message could be deciphered.

When World War II broke out, the Allies discovered that they were totally unprepared to deal with Germany's new secret weapon. Fortunately, others had not been so complacent. The Poles had invested considerable energy into cracking Enigma in the 1930s, and thanks to the inspirational breakthrough of one of their most talented code breakers, Marian Rejewski, had invented a 'bombe' – a mechanical apparatus – that enabled them to break the code. Shortly before the fall of Poland in 1939, the Poles shared their discovery with their British and French allies, and it was to Bletchley Park in Buckinghamshire, a rambling Victorian country house and home of the government's code and cipher school, that Rejewski's work (and one of the Polish replica Enigma machines) was sent.

that will become a leading relief agency in the postwar fight against famine in developing countries.

1943 In the Pacific, US forces recapture the **Solomon Islands** and other islands from the Japanese.

On 7 May the capture of **Tunis** by the British 8th Army effectively ends Germany's African campaign, enabling African ports and cities to be used as bases for an assault on **Sicily**, which falls into Allied hands in July.

Bletchley quickly developed into an important – if eccentric – military centre. The government recruited a bewildering array of 'boffins' to its service, among them university dons, chess masters, crossword experts and linguists. One of the most outstanding was **Alan Turing**, a Cambridge mathematician who was put on the Enigma project. The problem he faced was not breaking Enigma, but doing it rapidly enough to cope with the fact that the Germans changed the machine's settings every 24 hours – meaning that each day the cryptographers had to start again. Like Rejewski, Turing turned to a 'thinking machine' to save time, and invented his own 'bombe' or **'Turing Machine'**. Armed with this, the Allies were able to read the Germans' messages and anticipate their activities. Other brilliant machines followed, among them Max Newman and Tommy Flowers' **'Colossus'**, which unpicked the **Lorenz** cipher.

The success of the Bletchley staff, though, created its own problems. The British government had access to more information than it could use without revealing that German codes had been compromised, so some British missions were deliberately allowed to fail. Less easy to excuse was the government's readiness to allow its former colonies access to Enigma machines after the war, knowing that in doing so their secret despatches could continue to be monitored.

As British and American forces create bridgeheads in southern Italy, **Mussolini** resigns on 28 July. Earlier in July, the Soviet army inflicts a defeat on Germany at **Kursk**.

On 8 September the Italian government formally **surrenders**, but fierce fighting against German forces in Italy continues.

In late November, **Churchill**, **President Franklin Roosevelt** and **Stalin** meet in **Teheran** to co-ordinate strategy.

Barnes Wallis invents the **'bouncing bomb'**, used by RAF 'dambusters' to create floods in the **Ruhr Valley**, Germany's industrial heartland.

1944 On 4 June Allied forces enter **Rome**.

On 6 June – known as **'D-Day'** – the principal Allied counteroffensive against Germany (**Operation Overlord**) begins, under Eisenhower's overall command. An advance force of 175,000 troops, mainly British and American, are able to establish a chain of bridgeheads.

On 23 July Soviet forces, advancing westward, enter **Poland**. On 25 August Free French and American troops enter **Paris**, and on 5 September **Brussels** is liberated. As the Allies push eastwards toward the Rhine, however, German troops put up strong resistance during the **Battle of the Bulge**, and a British airborne division participating in Montgomery's **Operation Market Garden** is badly mauled at **Arnhem** in late September.

In September **long-range missiles** (V1s) are launched by Germany against Britain, causing civilian casualties in London and elsewhere.

An **Education Act**, introduced by the Conservative minister **Richard 'Rab' Butler**, makes secondary education compulsory for all British children, and provides for the necessary schools to be built.

A V-1 bomb about to land in a residential area of Southern England, c.1944.

Sir Winston Churchill (1874–1965)

It is a curious fact that the man described in a famous footnote by the historian A.J.P. Taylor as 'the saviour of his country' had, in 1939, a distinctly unconvincing track record both as a politician and as a military strategist.

The son of a cabinet minister, Lord Randolph Churchill, Winston was a descendant of John Churchill, the great 1st duke of Marlborough, victor of Blenheim and Ramillies, whose biography he wrote. Despite these starry connections, however, he never achieved much military success – having quit the army, the young Churchill managed to be taken prisoner in the Boer War despite his accreditation as a journalist. Elected a Conservative MP in 1900, he gained a reputation for deviousness, crossing the floor to join the Liberals in 1906. He became first lord of the admiralty during the Great War, but lost his job after the Gallipoli fiasco. Nor was his reputation enhanced when he rejoined the Conservatives after the war. He served without any great distinction as chancellor of the exchequer between 1924 and 1929 under Baldwin (his role in breaking the 1926 General Strike earned him the hatred of many), but after the Great Depression he spent the following ten years in the wilderness – a backbench MP going on 60 who irritated nearly everyone by his alarmist prophecies about the German menace. When war broke out, however, he was immediately reinstated as first sea lord, and in 1940 replaced Neville Chamberlain as prime minister.

Once in the job, he attempted to maximize Britain's chances of winning the war; during its course he would personally oversee every major campaign in which British servicemen were involved, sleeping in his underground bunker and once suffering an unreported heart attack. He was also active above ground, using radio broadcasts and his unmistakable oratorical gifts to chivvy and encourage the nation. After war was over he simply shifted his sights, warning of the new menace posed by Stalin's Soviet Union. Following the partition of Germany, he coined the phrase 'iron curtain' to describe the growing rift between West and East, but failed to persuade President Truman to sponsor a pre-emptive strike. In 1951 Churchill became prime minister for a second time, but retired after four years in office. It is a mark of the esteem in which he was held that on his death in 1965 he was given the honour of a state funeral.

© MARK THOMAS

Ivor Robert Jones's statue of Churchill in Parliament Square.

1945 The true extent of what becomes known as the **Holocaust** begins to become apparent when Russian forces arrive at **Auschwitz** in Poland on 28 January and discover that over a million people – the large majority of them Jews – have been exterminated at a single prison camp.

In February Churchill, Roosevelt and Stalin hold a further conference at **Yalta**.

On 13 February the RAF destroys the cathedral city of **Dresden**, creating a firestorm in which an estimated 135,000 civilians die.

> ❝ Bomber Command had to be left out of the Myth of the Blitz, or mythology would have ceased to be efficacious. The heroism of the British under bombardment was quasi-Christian – its great symbol, after all, was St Paul's dome flourishing above the flames. The Myth could not accommodate acts, even would-be acts, of killing of civilians and domestic destruction initiated by the British themselves, however they might be justified strategically. Its construction involved putting together facts known or believed to be true, overlaying these with inspirational rhetoric – and leaving out everything known or believed to be factual which didn't fit. ❞
>
> Angus Calder on the Allied bombing of Dresden, in *The Myth of the Blitz* (1992)

Allied forces cross the Rhine, occupying **Cologne** on 10 March.

On 21 April Soviet forces reach **Berlin**. On 29 April German forces in **Italy** surrender, and the following day Hitler **commits suicide**. As Germany capitulates, 8 May is declared **Victory in Europe Day** (VE Day). On 8 May Montgomery formally receives Germany's unconditional surrender at **Luneburg**. Fighting continues in the Far East.

On 17 July Churchill joins Stalin and the new US President **Harry Truman** at the **Potsdam Conference** to determine how the spoils of war will be divided between the Western Allies and the Communist Soviets. During the conference, the results of a **general election** at home become known, revealing that Churchill's Conservative party has been heavily defeated. The new Labour prime minister, **Clement Attlee**, replaces Churchill at the conference.

With Britain's approval, the US Air Force drops **nuclear bombs** on **Hiroshima** (6 August) and **Nagasaki** (9 August), inducing Japan's **surrender** on 10 August.

World War II finally ends on 12 September, with the formal surrender of Japanese forces in **Singapore**.

George Orwell publishes *Animal Farm*, an allegorical novel warning of dictatorship in supposedly democratic societies.

Evelyn Waugh publishes *Brideshead Revisited*, an elegiac novel that charts the declining fortunes of a wealthy Roman Catholic family.

11
Postwar England
1946–2002

I n the July 1945 general election the Labour Party gained 394 Commons seats to the Conservatives' 210 – a landslide victory that took even Labour's leaders by surprise. 'After this, what?' asked the minister James Griffiths. The answer would take time to emerge, but the results would be unmistakable. In the decades ahead England changed more rapidly, and more profoundly, than during any previous fifty- or sixty-year period of its history.

Much of the change followed global developments, particularly the growth of low-wage manufacturing economies in the Far East. From the 1960s onwards, Western markets began to be swamped with competitively priced electronic goods, automobiles, steel and other products that have steadily eroded Britain's once mighty industrial base. Nearer home, Britain also had to face challenges posed by the emerging **European Union** – originally a purely economic arrangement between six of Europe's war-ravaged nations but, from the late 1970s onwards, a pan-continental political grouping as well. In 1972 Britain joined an enlarging **Common Market**, as the Union was then called, but its membership has never been full-blooded, and scepticism revived sharply during the 1990s when the Union decided to introduce a **single European currency** in 2002. For many people, the prospect of replacing sterling pounds with euros meant (and means) nothing less than an abandonment of national sovereignty. Although the then prime minister **John**

Major achieved opt-outs on certain issues at the Maastricht Conference in 1992, the issue of Europe has proved consistently hard to resolve.

Outside Europe, all Britain's recent prime ministers have had to contend with Britain's diminished status as a world power, dramatically brought home by the **Suez Crisis** of 1956. But the influence of history has proved powerful. For a variety of reasons – its imperial past, perhaps, or what some like to consider its 'special relationship' with the United States – Britain has been reluctant to abandon its international profile. Through its leadership of a **Commonwealth** made up of its former colonies and its permanent seat on the **United Nations** Security Council, Britain has sought to exert an influence out of all proportion to its size and resources – a mindset that led to Britain playing significant roles in the **Korean War** of 1950–53, the **Gulf War** against Saddam Hussein's Iraq in 1992, in the **Bosnian** and **Kosovan** crises that followed and in the 'war against terrorism' launched by President George W. Bush after the terrorist attacks in the US on 11 September, 2001. From its voluntary participation in these conflicts the United Kingdom has emerged with some credit. Whether the same may be said of the **Falklands War** waged by Margaret Thatcher against Argentina in 1982 – which has been called Britain's last imperial adventure – is more open to question.

As Britain steadily relinquished its empire after 1945, the development of separatism within the constituent parts of the United Kingdom became a conspicuous feature of domestic politics. Conflict between majority Protestant **Unionists** and minority Catholic **Republicans** in Northern Ireland spilled over into civil war between rival terrorist groupings. The **Scottish National Party** (SNP) and the Welsh **Plaid Cymru**, both founded before 1939, campaigned hard for greater autonomy in their respective countries. And though the situation in Northern Ireland still remains uncertain, following referendums in 1997 Scotland gained a Parliament of its own and Wales a National Assembly. The legislative powers of both bodies are restricted as yet, but many have speculated that the future of the United Kingdom lies in the balance.

Devolution has been accompanied by growing republican sentiment in all parts of the United Kingdom. While **Elizabeth II** – monarch since 1952 – has proved to be a ruler of some tact and talent, in recent years the royal family has repeatedly experienced adverse publicity in the media. Some commentators have questioned the very survival of the monarchy. But no mainstream political party has taken a republican line, and no alternative to the existing system has gained popular credibility. Post-war, other British institutions began to show their age, not least a 'first-past-the-post' electoral system, superseded elsewhere by the adoption of more inclusive systems of **proportional representation** (**PR**). But despite an attempt to place PR at the top of the political agenda by the newly formed **Social Democrat Party** in the 1980s, both Britain's main parties, Labour and the Conservatives, have resisted change in that direction. Indeed, after 1945, political life in England settled back down once more into adversarial combat between two main parties within the framework of a constitutional monarchy. Sometimes both Labour and the Conservatives have laid claim to the 'middle ground', promoting a politics of consensus. At other times, far more radical programmes have been advanced – notably by **Clement Attlee** in 1945 and by **Margaret Thatcher** in 1979.

Attlee's and Thatcher's administrations, probably the two most influential governments since 1945, have been seen as representing opposite poles in their views of how Britain should function. Attlee's Labour government created a powerful state apparatus extending all the way from the 'cradle to grave' philosophy of state-funded health care and social security to nationalized industries such as coal, iron and the railways. Thatcher sought to reverse those policies one by one: **privatization** returned industries old and new to private ownership; the state provision of health care was steadily eroded and private insurance encouraged; financial stability, low taxation and low inflation were all-important. Whether Thatcher's reforms proved beneficial is still hotly debated: economically the results have been inconclusive, and it seems certain that her government renewed many of the inequalities between rich and poor that have dogged Britain in the 20th century. Especially hard hit were underprivileged immigrant communities, many of whose members had been encouraged to settle in Britain in the 1950s and 1960s.

Discontent with Thatcher's government (and that of her Tory successor, John Major) opened the door for **Tony Blair** and his 'New Labour' party. Blair achieved a huge electoral landslide in 1997, it has been argued, by speaking the language of socialism – improved public services, renewed social justice – while adhering to Thatcherite economic precepts, creating a so-called 'third way' centrist approach which won the endorsement of many. Though Blair's government is designed to appeal to as many voters as possible, it remains to be seen whether the bold changes it has promised to deliver will appear.

Perhaps the most profound change England has experienced in the years following World War II has been the growth of sizeable 'ethnic minority' communities. The arrival of the *SS Empire Windrush* in 1948, a cruiser carrying nearly 500 Jamaicans, was one turning point: in the decades to follow, large numbers of immigrants from former colonies were encouraged to settle in England to meet shortages in the labour force. Reactions to this influx were not generally positive, and tensions have escalated on numerous occasions – notably when **Enoch Powell** encouraged repatriation in 1968, more recently when the bungled investigation into the 1994 murder of the black teenager **Stephen Lawrence** exposed London's police force as institutionally racist. Despite these and other flash points, though, Britain has not witnessed the development of a coherent far-right political movement (unlike some of its European neighbours), and political milestones such as the **race relations acts** of 1965, 1968 and 1976 have made a significant contribution to shifting attitudes. The 21st-century debate about the effects of pluralism on the nature of British identity seems likely to rumble on for many years yet, but in the historical perspective there is nothing new about that.

1946 As **Clement Attlee**'s Labour government struggles with the problems caused by massive postwar demobilization, Welsh-born **Aneurin 'Nye' Bevan** creates the **National Health Service**, which aims to offer free health care to all. While Labour makes it clear that the NHS must be paid for by increased taxation, Bevan's revolutionary measures are broadly welcomed, although some doctors object to the idea of becoming state employees.

Britain becomes a founding member of the **United Nations**, an organisation designed to promote both peace and democratic rights worldwide.

In **Palestine**, the Jewish terrorist campaign against Britain intensifies after the government announces its plans to **partition** Palestine into Israeli and Arab Palestinian states.

1947 An extremely cold **winter** paralyses Britain: the army is mobilised to transport basic supplies and prisoners are used to clear snowdrifts.

Notwithstanding a strike by **road hauliers** at the very beginning of the year, Labour presses ahead with its

nationalization of key industries, including **coal**, **steel production** and the **railways**, in accordance with Clause 4 of the party constitution.

On 15 August Britain restores **independence** to **India**, the largest step in the break-up of the British Empire. In the years immediately ahead nearly all Britain's colonies are liberated, although many opt to join the **British Commonwealth** – an association of nations that acknowledges the British monarch as its titular head. India is partitioned, its northwestern and northeastern areas forming the new state of **Pakistan**, which is inhabited by Muslim majorities.

In November, **King George VI's** eldest daughter and heir to the throne, **Princess Elizabeth**, marries **Philip**, son of the exiled Prince Andrew of Greece and a nephew of the last viceroy of India, **Earl Mountbatten**. The day before their wedding Philip is created **duke of Edinburgh**.

1948 A **Representation of the People Act** abolishes the two university constituencies of Oxford and Cambridge, which have allowed some electors to vote twice.

A strike by dock workers forces the government to declare a **state of emergency** in order to maintain essential food supplies.

The **11th Olympic Games** are held in London.

The *SS Empire Windrush* docks in Tilbury on 22 June, carrying immigrants from Jamaica.

1949 In the face of severe economic pressures, the chancellor of the exchequer, **Sir Stafford Cripps**, devalues the pound, despite previous assurances that he wouldn't.

A **Housing Act** provides subsidies to landlords to improve rented accommodation where Labour's ambitious programme of **public housing** is insufficient to meet demand.

Britain becomes a founder member of the **North Atlantic**

One of many new immigrants, London, c.1950.

Treaty Organization (NATO), a mutual-defence pact between the USA and western European nations intended to counter Soviet expansionism.

Laurence Olivier's film of Shakespeare's *Hamlet* wins five American **Academy Awards** (Oscars), the first British film to win any.

A year before his death, **George Orwell** publishes *Nineteen Eighty-Four*, a chilling futuristic novel depicting the helplessness of the individual caught between warring totalitarian governments.

1950 Labour narrowly holds on to power following a **general election** during which the Conservatives stage a significant recovery.

British soldiers are dispatched to **Korea**, which was partitioned in 1948, to fight alongside Americans and other United Nations troops against an attempted takeover of the whole country by the Communist North, supported by the **People's Republic of China**. But although a **Cold War** between the West and the Soviet Union is already well-entrenched, mainly as a result of a gathering **nuclear arms race**, and although China and the Soviet Union

Persuading voters in the 1951 general election.

have a mutual defence pact, the military conflict fails to widen – averting fears of a third world war.

1951 The Labour government sponsors the **Festival of Britain** – an occasion for the nation to give itself 'a pat on the back', in the words of the minister in charge, **Herbert Morrison**. Exhibits on London's South Bank include a temporary **'Dome of Discovery'** and, more permanently, the **Royal Festival Hall**. The cost of the Festival is criticized by Conservative MPs.

In October Attlee is obliged to call a fresh **general election**. The Conservatives win, and **Winston Churchill** returns as prime minister. His government promises to build 300,000 new houses a year to resolve an increasingly acute **housing crisis** – a target never actually achieved, although the availability of public housing continues to expand.

Two British diplomats, **Guy Burgess** and **Donald Maclean**, disappear after the double agent **Harold 'Kim' Philby** warns them that their espionage activities on behalf of the Soviet Union have been detected. They subsequently resurface in **Moscow**.

1952 George VI dies of lung cancer on 6 February and is succeeded by his daughter **Elizabeth II**.

In October, following extensive tests with a British-made plutonium bomb developed mainly at **Aldermaston** in Berkshire, Britain becomes one of the few nations with access to **nuclear weapons**.

1953 In April the Cambridge scientists **Francis Crick** and **James Watson** announce their discovery of **DNA** (deoxyribose nucleic acid), the 'basic building block of life' and the key to further genetic research.

In May the **Queen's coronation** coincides with the conquest of **Mount Everest** in Nepal by the New Zealander **Edmund Hillary** and **Sherpa Tenzing Norgay**.

Although during World War II the government censored media in ways that would seem utterly alien in today's cultural environment, the war provided a great fillip to the English **film industry**. Familiar names turned patriotism to their advantage by making new films – **Noel Coward**'s *In Which We Serve* and **Leslie Howard**'s *The First of the Few* attracted audiences by the hundreds of thousands. A more remarkable offering still was **Laurence Olivier**'s film version of Shakespeare's *Henry V* – highly stylized, shot in Ireland at huge cost and, emphasizing the Battle of Agincourt (see p.161) with a score by **William Walton**, guaranteed to make collateral sense of the struggle against Germany. The film was a huge success and even pulled in England's first Oscars. Although seldom able to compete globally with the glamour and wealth of Hollywood, English cinema developed into an important industry during the 1950s and beyond, its products ranging from mannered 'Ealing' comedies through the popular 'Carry On' series to epics such as *Lawrence of Arabia* (1962) and *Doctor Zhivago* (1965), both directed by **David Lean**. From the 1960s it also supported an influential school of social realism from directors such as **Karel Reisz** (*Saturday Night and Sunday Morning*, 1960), **Lindsay Anderson**

An **armistice** signed on 25 July effectively ends the Korean War.

In London the recurrence of deadly **smogs**, caused by fossil fuel emissions and nicknamed 'peasoupers', leads doctors to issue masks to those most vulnerable.

1954 In May **Roger Bannister** becomes the first human on record to run a mile in under four minutes.

The government announces an end to **rationing**, introduced as a wartime measure in 1940.

An **Independent Television Authority** is established as

(*This Sporting Life*, 1963), **John Schlesinger** (*Billy Liar!*, 1963) and **Ken Loach** (*Kes*, 1969).

British **television** also took off in the 1950s, receiving significant boosts with the televised coronation in 1953 and the launch of commercial services in 1954. TV soon became an integral part of British life and, despite commercial competition, is still largely shaped by one of the most influential institutions of the 20th century – the **BBC**. First floated in 1922, then incorporated as a public body in 1927, the corporation soon developed into a powerful arbiter of national culture through both radio and TV, striving to justify its peculiar method of funding (in effect compulsory taxation) by maintaining a balance between mass entertainment and responsible output. It has also played cat-and-mouse with political authority and, after further deregulation, with a host of competitors ranging from satellite and digital channels to independent radio stations eager to steal market share. The international face of the BBC has long been the **World Service**, funded by the Foreign Office. During the Cold War it offered radio broadcasts in over a hundred languages, though today that number has been drastically cut as its rationale has become harder to justify in the face of powerful international competition.

the **BBC** (British Broadcasting Corporation) loses its monopoly of television broadcasting. It retains one in radio broadcasting for another twenty years, however.

J.R.R. Tolkien publishes the first two volumes of his trilogy, *The Lord of the Rings*, which is destined to become a cult novel among adults as well as children.

1955 Following Churchill's voluntary resignation in April **Anthony Eden** becomes prime minister and leads the Conservatives to victory in a May **general election**.

Hugh Gaitskell succeeds Clement Attlee as leader of the Labour Party.

The government announces plans to construct a network of **motorways**.

> ❝ There aren't any good, brave causes left. If the big bang does come, and we all get killed off, it won't be in aid of the old-fashioned, grand design. It'll just be for the Brave New-nothing-very-much-thank-you. About as pointless and inglorious as stepping in front of a bus. ❞
>
> John Osborne, from *Look Back in Anger* (1956)

1956 On 4 June Egypt's **President Nasser** announces that his government will not renew Britain's concession on the **Suez Canal** when it falls due for renewal in 1968. Three weeks later Nasser seizes and mines the Canal, sparking an international crisis during which the newly formed state of **Israel** launches an attack on the **Sinai Peninsula** at the end of October and the Soviet Union threatens to use missiles against an Anglo-French force dispatched to recapture the Canal. Spurning a UN resolution, British paratroopers land at **Port Said** on 5 November, but, after intense diplomatic activity that fatally damages Eden's reputation, withdraw on 22 December following the arrival of a UN peacekeeping force.

John Osborne's controversial play *Look Back in Anger*, which ridicules middle-class values, is first performed in August at the **Royal Court Theatre** in London.

1957 In January Eden resigns in the wake of the Suez Crisis, and is replaced as Conservative prime minister by **Harold Macmillan**.

1958 The **Campaign for Nuclear Disarmament** (CND) is formed and holds a mass rally in London's Trafalgar Square, then marches on a weapons research centre at **Aldermaston** in Berkshire.

The Suez Crisis (1956)

Built during the 19th century mainly by French engineers, the Suez Canal connected the eastern Mediterranean to the Red Sea and the Indian Ocean beyond, slashing journey times and therefore transportation costs. Such was its maritime and commercial importance that Britain acquired control of Suez under Disraeli (see p.388) when the British Empire was at its zenith.

It was in a very different political climate that the Egyptian leader, Colonel Abdel Nasser, announced his intention in 1956 to nationalize the canal. Already there were the beginnings of an Islamic resurgence seeking to limit Western influence in the Middle East, but more immediately Nasser was angered by an Anglo-American decision not to proceed with a project to build the hydroelectric Aswan Dam across the Nile. There was also considerable Islamic resentment at the West's intention to support the newly created Jewish state of Israel.

Rather than attempt a diplomatic solution, Prime Minister Anthony Eden opted for military action supported by France (perhaps mindful of Egypt's recent decision to purchase 200 million dollars' worth of Soviet weaponry). British troops were mobilized, and Israel was secretly persuaded to launch a simultaneous attack on Egypt across the Sinai desert. The campaign, however, ended in fiasco – the US rounded on Eden, as did the United Nations. Despite initial successes on the ground, Britain and France were forced to hand over captured territory to a UN peacekeeping force in November.

A new world order had been confirmed, in which the old imperial powers – most significantly, Britain – were demonstrated to be impotent without American backing. In some of its surviving colonies (notably Malaya, Aden and Kenya), Britain continued to apply force to get its way, and in 1982 Margaret Thatcher successfully countered Argentinian aggression in the Falkland Islands. But in the places that really mattered, Palmerstonian gunboat diplomacy (see p.386) was dead in the water.

Debutantes – 'eligible' young aristocratic ladies presented to the monarch – make their way to Buckingham Palace for the last time before the tradition is discontinued.

During a partial Cold War thaw, the actress **Coral Browne** meets the missing diplomat and spy **Guy Burgess** while performing *Hamlet* in Moscow.

The first section of British **motorway** – a small stretch of the M6 around **Preston** – is opened to motorists.

1959 Campaigning under Macmillan's slogan 'You've never had it so good' – supposedly reflecting a steady rise in national prosperity – and relying on 'Super Mac's' patrician unflappability, the Conservatives easily win a **general election**.

The British Motor Corporation unveils its new compact motorcar, the **Mini**, which becomes an immediate best-seller and something of a fashion accessory.

1960 Britain and France begin collaboration on **Concorde**, the world's first supersonic passenger airliner.

The queen's sister **Princess Margaret** marries a 'commoner', the photographer **Anthony Armstrong-Jones**, who is created earl of Snowdon.

The **Royal Shakespeare Company** (previously the Shakespeare Theatre Company) is refounded under the direction of **Peter Hall**, with theatres in both Stratford-on-Avon and London.

Penguin Books successfully defends its decision to mass-market D.H. Lawrence's novel *Lady Chatterley's Lover* against charges brought under the **Obscene Publications Act**. The publisher's victory is heralded as a landmark in the relaxation of censorship.

1961 The need to provide greater opportunities in higher education in Britain is reflected in the opening of the

University of Sussex in Brighton. Other new universities at **York**, **Canterbury**, **East Anglia**, **Warwick** and elsewhere soon follow.

The **birth control pill** goes on sale in Britain, but is only available for use by married women.

1962 James Watson, Maurice Wilkins and Francis Crick win a **Nobel Prize** for their discovery of the helical structure of DNA.

The BBC launches *That Was The Week That Was*, an irreverent weekly TV programme that satirizes politicians. The similarly irreverent and satirical weekly magazine *Private Eye* is also launched.

The consecration of a new cathedral in **Coventry** – designed by **Sir Basil Spence** and decorated with stained glass by **John Piper**, a tapestry by **Graham Sutherland** and a statue by **Jacob Epstein** – is marked by the first performance of **Benjamin Britten**'s *War Requiem*.

1963 Britain's application to join the **European Common Market** – formed by France, West Germany, Italy, Belgium, Holland and Luxembourg in 1957 to provide a tariff-free trading zone within Europe – is **vetoed** by France.

The **Profumo Affair** dominates domestic politics. It centres on the minister for war, **John Profumo**, and his involvement with the 'call girl' Christine Keeler and another of her lovers, the Soviet naval attaché **Evgeny Ivanov.** Profumo lies to the Commons before being forced to resign, and Macmillan himself is compromised, resigning in October. He is replaced as prime minister by the Scottish aristocrat **Alec Douglas-Home**.

Hugh Gaitskell dies, and **Harold Wilson** becomes leader of the Labour Party.

A CND demonstration in Trafalgar Square, Easter 1964.

The **Beatles** form in Liverpool. Along with the **Rolling Stones** and other English bands, they start a shockwave of youth culture characterized by throngs of screaming fans and the explosion of youth fashion.

1964 In an October **general election** the Labour Party narrowly defeats the Conservatives and **Harold Wilson** becomes prime minister. Wilson begins his premiership by introducing **comprehensive schools**, which are designed to replace what many see as the socially divisive system of fast-track grammar and slow-track secondary moderns.

The private school system is left undisturbed, however, as is the unelected House of Lords.

In May **Brighton seafront** becomes a battleground as groups of rival 'mods' and 'rockers' engage in violent clashes.

1965 In July, **Douglas-Home** retires as Conservative leader. As the Conservative Party adopts a more open leadership contest system, he is succeeded by **Edward Heath**.

Britain's long-term economic prospects are buoyed by the discovery of substantial deposits of **North Sea oil**.

Partly to offset the influence of the TUC (Trades Union Congress) under Labour rule, the **Confederation of British Industry** (CBI) is founded to provide employers with a forum of their own.

Mary Whitehouse, outspoken in her criticisms of 'permissive society', founds the **National Viewers' and Listeners' Association** – a watchdog body that campaigns for greater censorship.

A **Race Relations Act** is passed by Parliament, prohibiting discrimination in public places and the promotion of hatred on grounds of 'colour, race, or ethnic or national origins'.

1966 In a March **general election** the Labour Party increases its parliamentary majority.

In football, England hosts the **World Cup** and, to the delight of the nation, wins.

1967 Unable to reverse a steady decline in Britain's manufacturing industries and confronted by an increasingly adverse balance of payments, Wilson is forced to **devalue the pound**. Amongst other emergency measures tight restrictions are placed on the amounts of sterling holidaymakers can take abroad.

The Sixties

The 'Swinging Sixties' were part of a steady continuum of change in postwar Britain – less an era, perhaps, than a succession of small explosions that together shifted the basis of society. One revolution was the introduction in 1961 of the birth control pill: initially available only to married women, the pill was championed by campaigners for women's rights and by the end of the decade it had over a million UK users. It did more than perhaps anything else to alter attitudes to sex, and, with Britain's student population rocketing as the so-called 'baby boomers' came of age, sexual liberation and feminist politics began to shape the lives of an entire generation.

Many young people were hungry for American culture, which became more and more powerful throughout the decade as the effect of international idols such as Jim Morrison and Bob Dylan took hold. This in turn triggered home-grown musical talent, which rapidly became exportable. The story of the Beatles is in some ways a representative tale: they climbed from church-fête origins, via a stint in Hamburg strip-bars, to national success then global stardom. Equally successful – and certainly edgier – were the Rolling Stones, a band whose 1964 '(I Can't Get No)

Abortion is legalized.

Agriculture is hit by an epidemic of **foot-and-mouth** disease, which necessitates the slaughter of over 400,000 animals.

1968 An **'I'm Backing Britain'** campaign is launched by five Surrey workers who pledge to work an extra thirty minutes a day to help continuing economic difficulties.

In April the Conservative MP **Enoch Powell** heightens racial tensions (and gathers a great deal of popular support) by warning of 'rivers of blood' unless immigrant workers from the Caribbean, India, Pakistan and other former colonies are repatriated. In the same year **South Africa**

Satisfaction' guaranteed them a number-one position on both sides of the Atlantic.

The music industry's later engagement with political themes echoed and amplified that of its target audience, and the protests for which the British Sixties became infamous – the student revolts of 1968, the peace protests against the war in Vietnam, the civil rights movement in Northern Ireland – revealed that many were eager to overturn what they saw as 'establishment' values, whether that meant indulging in free love, plotting Marxist rebellion or experimenting with LSD (or just talking about all of those things).

But it was consumer culture that benefited most. English style – or a certain version of it – became marketable for the first time that century. James Bond movies starring the impossibly debonair (and certainly Scottish) Sean Connery were a worldwide hit; the designs of Mary Quant and Ossie Clark and London's fashionable Kings Road and Carnaby Street were making headlines; the sleek lines of Jaguar's E-type sports cars embodied English chic. In the end the 'Swinging Sixties' might make little overall sense, but that is somehow their point.

refuses to allow a touring English cricket team to enter the country if **Basil d'Oliviera**, the first black player to be considered for the English squad, is selected. The MCC later drops d'Oliviera.

Partly in imitation of militant student activities in **Paris** and other foreign capitals, Britain's students begin agitating on British university campuses. There are also demonstrations outside the **American embassy** in London's Grosvenor Square in protest at the USA's military involvement in **Vietnam**.

The growing civil rights movement in Northern Ireland erupts into violence when a march by the anti-Unionist **Northern Ireland Civil Rights Association** on 5

October in **Derry** is broken up by the Royal Ulster Constabulary. The RUC is widely criticized for its brutality in dealing with the marchers, further destabilizing the region.

1969 As student protests spread, the **London School of Economics** becomes a centre for militant students demanding the overthrow of the 'capitalist' state. Thirteen ringleaders are barred from the college after police are called in to end a mass sit-in.

In July **Prince Charles** is invested as **prince of Wales** by the Queen at Caernarvon Castle in Wales.

The first Anglo-French **Concorde** supersonic aircraft take to the skies.

A splinter group of the Irish Republican Army, the **Provisional IRA**, is formed towards the end of the year and initiates a high-profile bombing campaign in **Northern Ireland**.

The **Open University**, a distance-learning institution designed to provide tuition to students irrespective of their location or social background, is founded.

1970 Defying the predictions of most opinion polls, the Conservatives win a June **general election** and Edward Heath – who is committed to taking Britain into the **Common Market** – becomes prime minister.

Economic prospects improve as more and more **North Sea oil** comes on tap.

The **Gay Liberation Front** begins campaigning for an end to legal and other kinds of discrimination against gay men and women.

1971 Heath's government begins to be confronted by **industrial action**, often prompted by 'militant' trade unionists. For the first time mail workers strike, demanding a 20 percent pay increase.

Decimalization simplifies the structure of Britain's currency, changing it from pounds (twenty shillings), shillings (twelve pence) and pence to just pounds (100 pence) and pence.

The **Rolls-Royce** group goes into receivership, before being split into engineering and automobile production components after the government intervenes.

1972 Following intense negotiations, the European **Common Market** admits Britain into its community, which now comprises nine members. Britain's membership is confirmed by Parliament in July.

A six-week strike by coal miners leads to the **rationing of power**, and there are subsequent strikes by rail workers and dockers.

Sectarian violence in **Northern Ireland** continues to escalate. In what becomes known as **'Bloody Sunday'**, on 30 January members of the British Parachute Regiment open fire on a Catholic protest in **Derry**, killing thirteen people.

1973 The Northern Ireland Assembly at **Stormont** is suspended and the 'six provinces' are brought under **direct rule** from Westminster.

Strikes and industrial disputes continue throughout the year, and the economy is further bruised by a decision by **OPEC** (the Organization of Petroleum Exporting Countries, centred in the Middle East) to quadruple **oil prices** – even though the effect on Britain is mitigated by its own oil production in the North Sea.

Chancellor of the exchequer **Anthony Barber** announces a pre-Christmas **crisis budget** that includes swingeing cuts in public spending, instigating the closure of one in five of Britain's schools. Industry and commerce are limited to five days' electricity consumption per fortnight, and public services are put on a three-day working week.

1974 As Barber's budget bites, power cuts become routine, some foodstuffs become scarce, coal miners go back on strike and unemployment mounts. Determined to force a showdown with the trade unions, Heath calls a **general election** on 6 March and campaigns under the slogan 'Who Governs Britain?'. He loses, and Labour is returned to power by the narrowest of margins. **Harold Wilson** becomes prime minister once more at the head of a minority government, but is obliged to contemplate a **'Lib-Lab' pact** with the minority Liberal Party. He calls a second election on 11 October, and increases his Commons majority to 3.

As the **IRA** escalates its campaign of terror on the mainland, 21 people are killed in **Birmingham** by bombs that explode within minutes of each other. Six men – who become widely known as the **Birmingham Six** – are later convicted, but are freed on appeal 16 years later.

1975 A **national referendum** promised by Labour confirms Britain's membership of the European Common Market by a margin of two to one.

As trade unions press for wage rises of anything up to 30 percent, **inflation** worsens. In response Wilson attempts to negotiate a **'social contract'** with union leaders.

1976 Harold Wilson resigns, and **James Callaghan** becomes prime minister in April.

As Britain's underlying economic instability continues, the government is forced to turn to the **International Monetary Fund** for assistance.

An unusually hot summer leads to the first **drought** in living memory.

The **National Theatre** opens, housed in a complex designed by **Denys Lasdun** on London's South Bank.

A further amendment to the 1965 **Race Relations Act** is passed by Parliament, setting up a **Race Relations Commission** to promote 'equality of opportunity and good relations'.

1977 Queen Elizabeth II's **Silver Jubilee** is celebrated in June throughout England with street parties and other events.

The home secretary, **Roy Jenkins**, resigns his seat in Parliament to become Britain's first president of the **EEC Commission**.

1978 As Labour fails to resolve tensions with the unions and public sector strikes proliferate, Britain experiences a **'winter of discontent'**: power cuts and fuel shortages become commonplace, the Army has to assume the responsibilities

© JOHN STURROCK/NETWORK PHOTOGRAPHERS

Firefighters striking in Bridlington, 1977.

of the fire brigade, rubbish accumulates on city streets and even some dead are left unburied.

1979 At a **general election** held in May the Conservative Party gains a majority of Commons seats, and its leader **Margaret Thatcher** becomes prime minister, the first woman to hold the office. She will remain in power for thirteen years.

In January the country is troubled by a series of **strikes** by a number of public sector unions, but the following month the TUC and the government attempt to patch up a mutual co-operation agreement.

Margaret Thatcher (b.1925)

A genuinely radical Tory, the 'Iron Lady' took over leadership of the Conservative Party after widespread disappointment with Edward Heath's government of 1970–74. Elected prime minister in 1979, she retained power until 1992, when a party putsch brought about her downfall.

In power, she invited adoration and loathing in equal measure – largely because she had the strength of character to follow through her convictions. Abroad she was often better thought of than at home, forging a close personal bond with US President Ronald Reagan and impressing Mikhail Gorbachev of the Soviet Union. Both in the UK and internationally her policies were unashamedly capitalistic. An apostle of free enterprise, she curbed the powers of the trade unions, overhauled the civil service, and created tax breaks and other incentives for small and big businesses alike. Most famously, she carried through a wide-ranging programme of privatization, returning nationalized industries such as steel, electricity, gas, water and telecommunications to private ownership. Although this led many to criticize her for favouring City 'fat cats', her vision was wider than that. She was unashamedly populist in the Disraeli tradition – privatization went hand-in-hand with a well-advertised concept of

On 30 March the Irish MP **Airey Neave** is assassinated by the IRA, who plant an explosive device in his car parked underneath the houses of parliament.

Violent demonstrations break out at **Southall** in April against the far-right **British National Party**, in which one man is killed.

1980 Britain achieves **self-sufficiency in oil**, able to trade high-grade North Sea oil, of use particularly in producing aviation fuel, for lower-grade Middle Eastern oil, used for ordinary industrial and motoring purposes.

a 'share-owning democracy'. Everybody, her reasoning went, should have the opportunity to become a 'stakeholder' in their own society.

How successful such policies have been is bitterly contested, however. Her celebrated dictum that 'there is no such thing as society' has been taken by some to celebrate the spirit of free enterprise that saved Britain from its postwar decline; others blame it for creating an abrasive 'get-rich-quick' society which benefited the few, not the many. Her erosion of funding for public services was widely criticized, and many felt that her increasing extremism (particularly towards Europe) left the government increasingly isolated. And indeed Thatcher herself was capable of startling inflexibility. If her decisiveness over the Falklands crisis early in her premiership did wonders for her popularity ratings, her autocratic decision to introduce the unpopular Poll Tax – a system of taxation which many felt to be grossly unfair – was badly handled. In the end, though, it was her party, not Thatcher, who panicked. When a cyclical recession took hold at the end of the 1980s, an alliance of Tory grandees and ministers, fearing that Thatcher's reputation as an 'uncaring' leader would lose them the next election, decided to dump her.

Inflation reaches a high of 20 percent, and Thatcher faces critics inside her cabinet (collectively known as the 'wets') as she begins implementing a draconian programme to revive the economy.

In October, **Michael Foot** replaces James Callaghan as leader of the Labour Party.

1981 Thatcher reorganizes her cabinet to sideline the 'wets': **Lord Soames** is sacked as leader of the House of Lords and **James Prior** is moved to the Northern Ireland office. Among those promoted are **Nigel Lawson**, who becomes secretary of state for energy, and **Norman Tebbit**, who becomes secretary of state for employment.

The Labour Party, suffering weak leadership, continues to be divided between traditional and militant socialists, and those who wish to modernize the party. In an attempt to 'break the mould of British politics' the 'Gang of Four' – **Roy Jenkins**, **Shirley Williams**, **David Owen** and **William Rogers**, all former Labour cabinet members – split off to form the **Social Democrat Party**, dedicated to replacing Britain's 'first-past-the-post' voting system with **proportional representation**.

On 29 July the queen's eldest son and heir, **Prince Charles**, marries **Lady Diana Spencer**, daughter of Earl Spencer – the first time a Prince of Wales has married an Englishwoman since the Black Prince's marriage to Joan of Kent in the 14th century. The wedding ceremony, held in St Paul's Cathedral, is broadcast worldwide.

In the summer, there are **race riots** in **Brixton**, following tensions between the police and Brixton's large black community. Later in the year further riots and violence occur in Liverpool's **Toxteth** area and Manchester's **Moss Side**.

1982 In April **Argentina**, under the dictatorship of **General Leopoldo Galtieri**, launches an invasion of the **Falkland**

Islands in the South Atlantic, laying claim to an isolated sheep-farming territory under British control since 1833. Despite pressure from the international community to arrive at a diplomatic solution, Thatcher orders a combined-services **task force**, commanded by **Rear-Admiral Sandy Woodward**, to reclaim the colony. A swift campaign is ended on 14 June when British commandos enter the Falklands' capital, **Port Stanley**, but not without significant casualties on both sides. The frailty of Britain's warships is exposed when *HMS Sheffield* is sunk by missiles fired from an Argentinian aircraft, and British tactics are called seriously into question when Argentina's *General Belgrano* is sunk on 2 May sailing away from the Falklands, with the loss of 400 lives. Although the *Belgrano* incident eventually forces the resignation of defence secretary **John Nott**, Thatcher reaps the full benefit of Britain's military success, and her personal popularity soars to new heights.

At home **unemployment** rises, seen by some as a deliberate ploy on the government's part to restrict demands for higher wages.

> ❝ Walking into the hotel was the fulfilment of a dream, a fantasy that had filled all our thoughts for almost three months. 'We never doubted for a moment that the British would come,' said the proprietor Desmond King. 'We have just been waiting for the moment.' It was like liberating an English suburban golf club. ❞
>
> Max Hastings, syndicated press dispatch
> from Port Stanley in the Falklands, 14 June, 1982

1983 Buoyed by the Falklands campaign, Thatcher calls a **general election** in June and the Conservatives win a landslide victory. The **Social Democrats** gain a handful of seats, but fail to make a significant breakthrough despite opinion poll predictions. **Michael Foot** resigns as leader of the Labour Party. His successor, **Neil Kinnock**, immediately sets about rooting out Labour's militants.

1984 A strike by **coal-miners** for higher wages beginning in March enables Thatcher to stage a showdown with the trade unions. Refusing to give way to the miners' demands, the government demonizes the leader of the National Union of Mineworkers, **Arthur Scargill**, as a militant subversive. After numerous running battles with police, in November the strike begins to collapse and miners return to work. Although Thatcher seizes the opportunity to initiate a legislative programme curbing trade unions' powers and influence, the strikes highlight a wider industrial problem – that British industry is being priced out of the market.

In October the IRA executes one of its most high-profile attacks when it bombs the **Grand Hotel** in **Brighton** during a Conservative party conference. Five are killed and over 30 injured, but Thatcher herself narrowly escapes injury.

1985 Criticism of Mrs Thatcher resurfaces within the ranks of the Conservative Party. The former cabinet minister **Francis Pym** publishes *The Politics of Consent*, attacking the prime minister's lack of interest in views substantially different from her own. In the House of Lords, the former prime minister, **Harold Macmillan**, now earl of Stockton, rebukes Thatcher for her blind pursuit of monetarist policies. These rifts come to a head over the **Westland Affair**, which begins to make headlines in December. The proposed sale of Britain's only helicopter-manufacturing company to the American Sikorski corporation, backed by the Thatcherite trade and industry secretary **Leon Brittan**, is opposed by defence secretary **Michael Heseltine**, who favours the creation of a European consortium instead.

Thatcher in triumphant mood – just hours after the IRA bomb in Brighton.

1986 Amidst gathering acrimony as to how the Westland dispute has been leaked to the press, in January **Heseltine** resigns from government, to become a dangerously popular rival to Thatcher. Brittan is also forced to resign, and discontented Tories begin contemplating a replacement leader.

A **strike** by prison officers indicates that Thatcher's muzzling of the trade unions is less comprehensive than she would wish.

The government's programme of **privatization** – returning state-owned industries to the private sector – gets properly underway with the offer of shares in **British Gas** to the public.

In some opinion polls, the minority **Social Democrat** and **Liberal** parties, joining forces as the **Liberal–SDP Alliance**, attract up to 30 percent support, while in others Neil Kinnock's reformed **Labour Party** attracts 40 percent.

In the winter, newspaper headlines are dominated by the government's attempts to prevent a former intelligence agent, **Peter Wright**, from publishing his memoirs, *Spycatcher*. Since the book is easily obtainable abroad, the campaign proves futile.

The explosion of the **Chernobyl** nuclear power station in the Ukraine causes panic in Britain, and in some parts of the country lamb grazed in contaminated fields is banned from the shops.

1987 Ahead of a June **general election**, Thatcher travels to **Moscow** for talks with **Mikhail Gorbachev**, whose twin policies of *glasnost* (liberalization) and *perestroika* (economic and political restructuring) are already transforming the Soviet Union. Returning to Britain, Thatcher pronounces that Gorbachev is a man she can 'do business with', a critical step in the ending of the Cold War.

In the **election** itself the Conservatives are returned to power with a reduced majority, and Thatcher continues as prime minister.

A severe storm (rapidly nicknamed the '**Great Storm**' and the most destructive for many years) causes havoc, particularly across the south of the country, in October. It kills 18 people in all.

1989 Thatcher's decision to reform local government income by replacing rates, levied on the basis of property values, with a **Poll Tax**, levied on people, creates a furore inside the Conservative Party and in the country at large. Her proposals mean that a rich adult living alone in a very large house makes one-fifth the contribution to local services of five adults living in a very small house in the same local authority. Notwithstanding widespread objections, Thatcher proceeds with the legislation.

In April Neil Kinnock stages a 'Red Rose Rally' in **Birmingham**, correctly predicting that forthcoming local elections will deliver an adverse verdict on 'ten years of Thatcherism'. The Conservatives are trounced, and in July Thatcher reshuffles her cabinet.

Further political divisions, affecting all parties, are created over the issue of whether or not Britain should join the **EMS** (European Monetary System), a first step toward the creation of a common European currency. Chancellor **Nigel Lawson** cautiously supports entry, but Thatcher's 'special adviser' **Sir Alan Walters** dismisses the scheme as 'half-baked'. Lawson resigns, adding his weight to the Tories' backbench dissenters, and Thatcher again reshuffles her cabinet.

In November, a relatively obscure Conservative MP, **Sir Anthony Meyer**, challenges Thatcher for the party leadership. Although he is convincingly beaten, his ability to attract the votes of 33 fellow MPs, and the abstention of another 27, suggest that Thatcher's days may be numbered.

The Iranian leader **Ayatollah Khomeini** issues a *fatwah* against the Indian-born author Salman Rushdie after his Islamically 'sacrilegious' novel *Satanic Verses* is published in London.

1990 Despite the building of Japanese-owned **car plants** in England's northeast (and continued investment from overseas companies), an **economic recession** begun in 1988 continues in Britain.

As disquiet over the Poll Tax grows, there are clashes between protestors and police in **Manchester** in February. On 21 March a national **anti-Poll Tax demonstration** is held in London's **Trafalgar Square**. The meeting becomes violent, some shops are looted and in the 'Second Battle of Trafalgar' 450 are injured and 339 arrests are made.

Tension continues into the summer, when the Conservatives again lose seats in a second round of **local elections**.

In August, the invasion of **Kuwait** by **Iraq** under the leadership of **Saddam Hussein** creates an immediate international crisis.

In November the resignation of the Conservative deputy leader **Sir Geoffrey Howe**, accompanied by an uncharacteristically forthright speech in the House of Commons, heralds Thatcher's downfall. Forced to submit herself to a leadership contest, Thatcher runs against **Heseltine** in the first ballot. She wins, but fails to achieve an outright majority and is forced to step down. A second ballot contested by Heseltine, the foreign secretary **Douglas Hurd** and chancellor of the exchequer **John Major** sees Major win through; he becomes prime minister.

1991 On 16 January a military coalition – led by the USA, including British forces, approved by the UN and backed by an alliance of 28 Western and Arab states – begins operations **Desert Shield** and **Desert Storm**, designed to expel Saddam Hussein from **Kuwait**. The campaign, lasting 42 days, begins with a massive display of air power against Iraq, and ends with the humiliation of Iraqi forces.

At home, in February the IRA fires mortar shells into the **Cabinet Office** at Downing Street.

John Major scraps the Poll Tax, replacing it with a **Community Charge** – in effect a restitution of property rates.

1992 At a **European Union** (formerly EEC) conference in **Maastricht** in February, Major secures important concessions for Britain, including an 'opt-out' clause with regard to entry into the **single currency**.

Despite opinion poll predictions, the Conservatives narrowly win an April **general election**, and Major continues as prime minister. Neil Kinnock, accused of premature triumphalism at a rally held in **Sheffield** on 1 April, resigns as leader of the Labour Party, which elects Scottish-born **John Smith** in his stead.

As conflict between Serbs, Croatians and Bosnian Muslims develops in **Yugoslavia**, Britain agrees to deploy troops as part of a **UN peacekeeping force**.

Chris Patten, the architect of Major's surprise election victory, is rewarded by being appointed the last governor general of **Hong Kong** ahead of the colony's agreed handover to the People's Republic of China in July 1997.

On 16 September, known as **Black Wednesday**, Britain withdraws from the **ERM** (European Exchange Rate Mechanism) amidst turmoil in the financial markets. Overnight the chancellor, **Norman Lamont**, raises base lending rates (already running at 12 percent) to 15 percent, but Major intervenes the following day to reverse his policy. Although it is from about this time that the economy enters a decade of sustained growth, the episode tarnishes the reputation of Major's government and hardens anti-European feelings.

The general synod of the Church of England votes to permit the **ordination of women** into the Anglican priesthood, provoking some traditionalists to join the Roman Catholic Church.

In October fire destroys part of **Windsor Castle**. In the ensuing wrangle over who should pay for repairs, the queen agrees to begin paying **income tax**, from which she had been exempt.

1993 As parliamentary by-elections continue to erode the Conservatives' slender majority, the party exhibits signs of being torn apart on the **'European'** issue. Neither pro- nor anti-Europeans are satisfied by the prime minister's 'wait-and-see' policy over monetary union.

In April the black teenager **Stephen Lawrence** is killed in London in what appears to be a racially motivated attack; to date no one has been convicted of his murder. The 'institutionally racist' Metropolitan police are later heavily criticized for their handling of the investigation in a report by **Sir William Macpherson**.

In November Major opens talks with the **Irish government** in a bid to end the sectarian violence in Northern Ireland, the beginnings of a **'peace process'** that continues to the present.

1994 The massively expensive **Channel Tunnel** between England and France opens in May – seen by some as a symbol of future European integration, by others as the possible harbinger of a rabies epidemic.

Sir Michael Rose, commander of the UN peacekeeping force in Bosnia, brokers a fragile **cease-fire** between the contending sides.

In May, **John Smith** dies of a heart attack. After a brief hiatus **Tony Blair**, who has made clear his ambition to modernize the Labour Party still further, becomes its leader.

The IRA announces a **suspension of hostilities** against the British government – the first agreed cease-fire in 25 years. Major promises that if it holds he will open negotiations with the IRA's political wing, **Sinn Féin**.

1995 As talks between the British government and Sinn Féin commence, Major and the Irish Taoiseach **John Bruton** issue a joint declaration outlining a 'twin track' initiative to secure peace. The American senator **George Mitchell** is invited to oversee the **decommissioning of weapons** held by both Republican and Protestant militant groups in Northern Ireland.

As feuding within the Conservative Party escalates, in June Major **resigns** as leader and challenges his detractors to 'put up or shut up'. The secretary of state for Wales and hardline Eurosceptic **John Redwood** takes up the challenge, but Major is re-elected by his party.

The **National Lottery** is set up, the first time that a weekly competition on this scale has been seen in Britain. Controversy greets its arrival, not least because the profit-making operator with the contract to run it, **Camelot**, will only give a certain percentage of its proceeds to so-called 'good causes'.

1996 The **cease-fire** in Northern Ireland breaks down following disagreements with Sinn Féin about the timing of arms decommissioning and other aspects of the peace process. The IRA resumes its **terrorist campaign** in mainland Britain. Bomb attacks leave two dead and scores of civilians injured in **London** and **Manchester**.

An outbreak of **BSE** (Bovine Spongiform Encephalopathy) – the apparent cause of the deadly **Creutzfelt-Jakob disease** in humans – leads to a **mass cull** of British cattle and a prohibition of **beef exports** being imposed by the European Union.

1997 Damaged by a series of scandals involving senior Conservatives, Major loses a **general election** held on 1 May. With a Commons majority of 179 seats, **Tony Blair** becomes prime minister at the head of a 'New Labour' government. Major resigns as Conservative leader and is succeeded by former secretary of state for Wales, **William Hague**. The government immediately acts to relocate control of **base lending rates** from the Treasury to the Bank of England, removing at least one temptation to manipulate the economy for political ends. Aware that 'Europe' is potentially also a divisive issue for Labour, Blair announces that Britain will adopt the **single European currency** – scheduled to come into effect in the EU in 2002 – only if certain economic tests are met.

In July, following a renewal of the peace initiative by Blair, the IRA announces a further **cease-fire**.

In the early hours of 31 August, **Diana, Princess of Wales** (now divorced from her husband Prince Charles) is killed in an automobile accident in Paris along with her companion 'Dodi' Fayed, the son of the Egyptian-born owner of Harrods department store, Mohammed al-Fayed. Immediately eulogized as the 'People's Princess' by Prime Minister Blair, Diana's death leads to public mourning verging on mass hysteria.

In September, decades of lobbying by the **SNP** (Scottish National Party) and **Plaid Cymru** (Welsh Party) pays off when New Labour announces its intention to create **national assemblies** in Scotland and Wales. In referendums held in September, 74 percent of Scots vote for the creation of a Scottish Parliament, and just over 50 percent in Wales for a Welsh Assembly. While **'devolution'** is seen by some as a natural expansion of democracy within Britain, others foresee the eventual break-up of the United Kingdom itself.

1998 In April the British and Irish governments arrive at the **Good Friday Agreement**, calling for the restitution of a **Northern Irish Assembly** and provincial administration at **Stormont** in which the Catholic minority will be guaranteed participation.

At Westminster, in fulfilment of New Labour's election manifesto, Blair sets in motion legislation to curtail the voting rights of **hereditary peers** in the House of Lords. Critics on the left of the party, however, complain that such reform does not go far enough.

1999 British troops are sent as part of a UN peacekeeping force to **Kosovo**, a breakaway state of the 'former' Yugoslav republic, to contain violence between **Serbs** and ethnic **Albanians**.

Ahead of planned celebrations to mark the advent of the coming Millennium, controversy surrounds the central **Millennium Project**, part of which involves a vast dome situated on cleaned-up industrial land in the London borough of Greenwich (and originally commissioned by Major's Conservative government). What it will contain – and what it will eventually be used for – remain uncertain.

In October 31 people die and over four hundred are injured in a **train crash** near London's **Paddington** station. As with a similar crash near **Southall** in 1997, safety failings are blamed on private operators – the train companies involved and the firm responsible for the rail infrastructure since privatization, **Railtrack**.

2000 The **New Year** is greeted by celebrations across Britain. Inside the Greenwich **Dome**, Elizabeth II, Prime Minister Blair and other notables attend an entertainment which is widely derided for its amateurishness. Other millennium projects encounter difficulties: a **'river of fire'** intended to sweep majestically up the Thames passes by unnoticed; a new **footbridge** over the Thames sways so

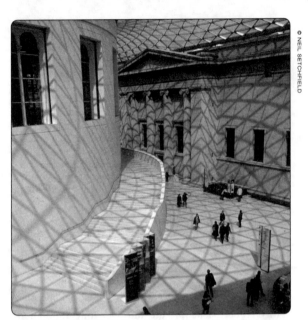

The Great Court of Smirke's British Museum, newly enclosed by Foster.

badly it has to be closed; an (eventually successful) **Millennium Wheel** opens late and refuses to turn. The Dome itself opens as an enclosed technological theme park, attracting far fewer than the twelve million visitors needed during the course of the year for it to break even financially. Some millennium projects – such as the new Great Court at the **British Museum** in London, covered with a new roof by architect **Norman Foster** – are more enthusiastically received, however.

The **BSE scandal** resurfaces once more with the publication of a report analyzing its handling. The government is heavily criticized for covering up scientific evidence that pointed to the threats of the disease and the way it was managed.

Following an October train crash at **Hatfield** in which four people die, **Railtrack** imposes widespread speed restrictions while it attempts to repair the rail infrastructure. Delays paralyse the network for months to come, and are a major factor in Railtrack's slide into government-managed **receivership** a year later.

2001 Just as the threat of BSE seems to have evaporated, England's countryside is hit by **foot-and-mouth disease**. The government's policy of slaughter (encouraged by the farmers' unions) is widely criticized, and TV pictures of burning carcasses cause a crisis in British **tourism**, both domestic and international.

On 1 May, worldwide **'anti-capitalist'** riots, orchestrated by increasingly well-organized international protest groups, dominate the news. As in previous years, protests in London turn violent, to widespread condemnation.

In a June **general election** Blair is re-elected with a parliamentary majority similar to his 1997 landslide (but turnout is significantly lower). William Hague resigns as Conservative leader, to be replaced by the little-known Eurosceptic **Iain Duncan-Smith**. In the same election, the centrist **Liberal Democrats** (the rebranded Liberal-SDP alliance) gain an unprecedented 52 seats, and, under their Scottish leader **Charles Kennedy**, begin claiming that they and not the Tories are the real Opposition. Public anxiety about the continuing poor performance of the National Health Service, the education system, an overstretched police force and Britain's privatized rail services (all areas New Labour has pledged to improve) continue to dominate headlines.

In June **riots** between different racial communities break out in several British cities, among them **Oldham** and **Bradford**.

Tony Blair and New Labour

By the mid-1980s several things had made the 'old' Labour Party of Wilson and Callaghan distinctly unappealing to the electorate. Many thought they embodied the worst of the 1970s – industrial unrest, political division, economic instability. More generally, though, there was a Europe-wide drift toward middle-ground, 'consensus' politics: the product of more diversified economies, greater individual wealth and growing disillusionment with outright socialist precepts. In Britain the process was accelerated by **Thatcherism**, for all that Thatcher's government was scarcely centrist. By undermining the trade unions (Labour's traditional bankrollers) and offering greater scope for individual investment, Thatcher pulled the rug from under the feet of her opponents.

Successive leaders – beginning with **Michael Foot** and continuing with **Neil Kinnock** and **John Smith** – attempted to remould the Labour party, aligning it more closely with its continental Christian Democrat counterparts. But it befell **Tony Blair** to reap the rewards. In 1997, after 18 years of Conservative rule, the country wanted a change, and Blair provided it. New Labour won a huge majority in the House of Commons. On the hustings he had promised a Britain that would be 'fair to all', and

On 11 September, however, domestic concerns are temporarily set aside when two hijacked aircraft are piloted into the **New York World Trade Centre**, whilst another hits the Pentagon in Washington. Among the estimated three thousand civilians killed are several hundred British people. Amidst condemnation of the atrocities in Britain (particularly by many Muslim organizations), it becomes apparent that they have been perpetrated by an Islamic fundamentalist network centred on the Afghanistan-based **al-Qaida** group, headed by **Osama Bin Laden**. The American president, **George W. Bush**, declares a **'War Against Terrorism'** which Prime Minister Blair pledges he started in dramatic style, exiling hereditary peers from the House of Lords and offering limited autonomy to Scotland and Wales. There was, however, no significant alteration to the tax regime – jealously guarded by Chancellor **Gordon Brown** – and in the key areas of public health, education and crime control beneficial changes were slow to appear.

Press attention soon focused on the character of Blair himself. What the media reported was a prime minister determined to institute a presidential style of leadership, constantly in front of the cameras and surrounded by media-manipulating 'spin doctors'. Since he seemed unwilling to abandon much of Thatcher's legislation (until recently), critics also began to ask whether Blair – for all his claims to follow a 'third way' politics – was in fact a neo-Conservative. Yet he has proved a complex figure to analyse. Some have picked up on his consciously Christian beliefs; others have inferred control-freakish tendencies; many have been bemused by his claims to be 'just an ordinary guy'. Perhaps the answer lies somewhere in the middle, like New Labour itself. Quite what 'Blairism' will finally stand for remains an open question.

to support. By November British special forces are participating in a **ground war** against al-Qaida and the **Taliban** Afghan government. Blair embarks on a series of alliance-building diplomatic missions to countries in the Middle East and elsewhere, while repeatedly assuring Britain's two million Muslims that a war on terrorism is not a war on Islam. But doubts are raised about the scope of hostilities, and Blair is criticized for ignoring his domestic responsibilities in order to cut a figure on the world stage.

2002 **Queen Elizabeth the Queen Mother** dies at Windsor on 30 March, and is widely mourned.

THE EUROPEAN UNION IN 2002

Joined 1957
Joined 1973
Joined 1981
Joined 1986
Joined 1995
Not in European Union

FINLAND

HELSINKI

St Petersburg

TALLINN
ESTONIA

RIGA
LATVIA

LITHUANIA
VILNIUS

MINSK
BELARUS

WARSAW

RUSSIA

MOSCOW

N

KIEV

UKRAINE

CHISINAU
MOLDOVA

ROMANIA

BELGRADE   BUCHAREST

BULGARIA
SOFIA

MACEDONIA

GREECE

Thessaloniki

Izmir

ATHENS

Crete

İstanbul

BLACK SEA

ANKARA

TURKEY

CYPRUS

GEORGIA
T'BILISI

AZABAIJAN

ARMENIA
YEREVAN

IRAN

SYRIA

IRAQ

BAGHDAD

In an April **budget**, the chancellor **Gordon Brown** announces that taxes will rise in order to fund increasing expenditure on the NHS – a decision cheered by many 'old Labour' supporters as a return to the party's socialist roots. In the same month the government announces plans for **regional assemblies** in some areas of England.

Millions turn out for events across the country in June, celebrating the Queen's **Golden Jubilee**.

Europe-wide controversy over **illegal immigration** continues. At an EU summit held in Seville in June, Britain agrees to tighter border controls and a common policy on refugees.

books

books

There is an embarrassment of riches in all areas of English history, making it an impossible task to present a comprehensive list of all that is worth reading in the space allowed. What follows, therefore, should be treated as a thumbnail sketch of some books that will carry the story onwards.

Many of the titles listed below are in paperback and in print. Those that aren't (marked 'o/p') should be available in secondhand bookshops, or via online retailers. Publishers are detailed with the UK publisher listed first, separated by an oblique slash from the US publisher where both exist. When a book is only available in one market, 'UK' or 'US' follows the publishing information; if the same publisher handles both, it is simply listed once.

General

John Cannon (ed.), *The Oxford Companion to British History* (Oxford University Press). This one-volume reference work is both handy and comprehensive, and is in general fairly reliable.

Margaret Drabble (ed.), *The Oxford Companion to English Literature* (Oxford University Press). Invaluable general reference guide to the essentials in English literature, recently updated.

J.R.H. Moorman, *A History of the Church in England* (Morehouse UK). A comprehensive survey of the development of Christianity in England, now in its third edition.

Kenneth O. Morgan (ed.), *The Oxford Illustrated History of Britain* (Oxford University Press). Don't be put off by the 'illustrated' tag. This is a scholarly but readable introduction to British history.

J.E. Morpurgo (gen. ed.), *The Pelican History of England* (Penguin). This nine-volume series provides a set of good, manageable guides to the key periods of English history from the Romans to the present day. It includes titles by S.T. Bindoff (Tudors), J.P. Kenyon (Stuarts) and J.H. Plumb (18th-century England).

Leslie Stephen and Sidney Lee (eds), *The Dictionary of National Biography* (Oxford University Press o/p). Although it's shortly to be superseded by the *New Dictionary of National Biography*, this 22-volume edition remains the first point of call for anyone looking for a concise life of any of the major figures of English history – more than that, it's a national institution.

Culture and Science

John Brewer, *The Pleasures of the Imagination: English culture in the 18th century* (HarperCollins; Chicago University Press). Delightful – if weighty – study of the finer things.

Asa Briggs, *A Social History of England* (Penguin). A thoroughly worthwhile book to thumb through.

Linda Colley, *Britons: Forging the nation* (Penguin; Yale University Press). Controversial but rewarding assessment of what it means to be British.

Adrian Desmond and James Moore, *Darwin* (Penguin). A textbook example of science-as-autobiography, this study attempts to read Darwin's achievements through the prism of his frequently troubled life.

Maureen Duffy, *England: The making of the myth from Stonehenge to Albert Square* (Fourth Estate UK). Poet and dramatist Maureen Duffy's fascinating survey of the myths that have helped to create a sense of national identity in England.

Lisa Jardine, *Ingenious Pursuits: Building the scientific revolution* (Abacus; Anchor). Lisa Jardine is one of the most interesting literary and cultural critics around, and her books never fail to surprise nor intrigue. This study of early Enlightenment science in England is typically engaging.

Oliver MacDonagh, *Jane Austen: Real and imagined worlds* (Yale University Press). An imaginative analysis of Regency Society through the medium of Austen's books. Each chapter tackles a theme based on one or more of the novels: a marvellous way to become acquainted with Austen and the world in which she lived.

John Summerson, *Architecture in Britain 1530–1830* (Yale University Press). Seminal study of English architecture from the Tudors to the close of the Regency, now in its ninth edition.

Ian Watt, *The Rise of the Novel: Studies in Defoe, Richardson and Fielding* (Pimlico; University of California Press). Watt's study of the novel has become the standard point of departure for anyone wanting to know more about where this peculiar literary form came from. He examines a variety of causal factors – among them the rise of the middle class and the changing status of women.

Michael White, *Isaac Newton: The last sorcerer* (Fourth Estate; Helix Books). An engaging account of one of the founders of English science, which attempts to uncover the more mysterious (and far less 'scientific') sides of Newton's work – his interest in alchemy and numerology in particular.

Andrew Wilton, *Five Centuries of British Painting* (Thames & Hudson). Part of the enormously popular World of Art series, Wilton's book is a reliable and informative guide to the major themes in British painting and their involvement in social history.

Classic Texts

The Anglo-Saxon Chronicle, trans. G.N. Garmonsway (Everyman UK o/p). An absorbing edition of this unique source, providing side-by-side translations of the main manuscripts that make up the Chronicle.

Asser's Life of King Alfred and other contemporary sources, trans. S.

Keynes and M. Lapidge (Penguin). A fine volume of Alfredian sources. The principal one is a hagiography of Alfred written by the Welsh monk Asser, who later became bishop of Sherborne: a revealing piece about 'British' attitudes to the 'English' in the 9th century AD.

John Aubrey, *Brief Lives*, ed. J Buchanan-Brown (Penguin). Aubrey's character sketches were initially compiled as research material for Anthony Wood's histories of Oxford University, but they contain fascinating insights into Jacobean England in their own right.

Bede, *The Ecclesiastical History of the English People*, ed. J. McClure and R. Collins (Oxford University Press). Bede's most celebrated work, charting the history of the English and the spread of Christianity from the time of Julius Caesar to the beginning of the 8th century AD.

Thomas Babington Macaulay, *The History of England* (Penguin). Still the best general history of England from the reign of James II until the 19th century. Full of enjoyable anecdotes and wonderfully partial interpretation, and introduced in this edition by Hugh Trevor-Roper.

Thomas More, *The History of King Richard III*, ed. Richard Sylvester (Yale University Press; Vail-Ballou Press). One of the principal sources for Richard-as-monster. Brilliant – if factually skewed – character assassination of one of England's more unfortunate monarchs.

George Orwell, *The Road to Wigan Pier* (Penguin). Orwell's classic account of unemployment in the industrial north, commissioned by the Left Book Club and first published in 1937.

Samuel Pepys, *Diaries* (HarperCollins). The most famous of all English diaries, Pepys' candid account of a ten-year period at the end of the 17th century – detailing everything from the Great Fire to his numerous sexual adventures – makes for an involving and absorbing read, and it's an appealing insight into daily London life during an unusually hectic period. If you can't stomach the full eleven volumes, there is an abbreviated paperback version available.

Biographies

John Ehrman, *The Younger Pitt* (Constable UK). A life's work: John Ehrman's phenomenal study of Pitt may appear unwieldy at three volumes, but it's incisively written and a pleasure to dip into.

Amanda Foreman, *Georgiana, Duchess of Devonshire* (HarperCollins; Random House). Charming and provocative assessment of one of 18th-century England's most glamorous figures.

Martin Gilbert, *Churchill: A Life* (Park Lane; Henry Holt). Gilbert's book is detailed (perhaps overly so in parts) and does assume a certain amount of basic knowledge of the periods he covers, but this is nonetheless an engaging examination of Churchill, carefully researched.

John Grigg, *Lloyd George* (HarperCollins; Fontana). John Grigg's exhaustive three-volume study uncovers the mysteries of one of England's most enigmatic prime ministers, a man who attracted loathing and affection in equal measure.

Peter Gwyn, *Cardinal Wolsey* (Sussex; Barrie & Jenkins o/p). Gwyn's account is a welcome relief from the withering attacks Wolsey has suffered at the hands of some, though in attempting to right the balance this is perhaps too generous.

Roland Huntford, *The Last Place On Earth* (Abacus; Modern Library). Controversial dual biography of Captain Scott and the Norwegian who beat him to the South Pole, Roald Amundsen. Loathed by some for its uncompromisingly critical assessment of Scott, it is in places perhaps too quick to damn, but is nevertheless a scintillating examination not only of the rival explorers but of Edwardian society on the brink of World War I.

L.G. Mitchell, *Charles James Fox* (Penguin). The best account of this mercurial politician to date, and an engaging exposition of 18th-century Whig society.

J.J. Scarisbrick, *Henry VIII* (Yale University Press; University of California Press). Unsurpassed scholarly biography of one of England's most notorious rulers, revealing the extensive political and religious changes that his reign oversaw.

Hugo Young, *One of Us: a biography of Margaret Thatcher* (Macmillan). Exhaustive study of the transformation of Margaret Thatcher from research chemist to one of the most controversial of all British prime ministers.

Prehistory and Roman Britain

Nora Chadwick, *The Celts* (Penguin). Classic survey of this mysterious people, tracing the spread of the Celts through Europe until their transformation by the conquering Romans and Saxons.

H.H. Scullard, *Roman Britain: Outpost of the Empire* (Thames & Hudson/Norton). Accessible guide to the major themes in Roman Britain.

Peter Salway, *Roman Britain* (Oxford University Press). Hefty but readable study of Britain and the Roman empire, recently reissued.

Anglo-Saxon and Medieval England

James Campbell (ed.), *The Anglo-Saxons* (Penguin). Masterly thumbnail sketch of Anglo-Saxon England, lavishly illustrated.

Christine Carpenter, *The Wars of the Roses: Politics and the Constitution in England c.1437–1509* (Cambridge University Press). One of the best studies of the Wars of the Roses to have been published in the last few years.

M.T. Clanchy, *England and its Rulers 1066–1272*, (Blackwell UK). Valuable assessment of England from conquered nation beneath the Norman yoke to reinvigorated country with a renewed sense of identity, culminating in the accession of the warlike Edward I.

J.C. Holt, *Robin Hood* (Thames & Hudson). Enjoyable historical study of one of England's most famous myths.

G.L. Harriss (ed.), *Henry V: The practice of kingship* (Alan Sutton). A rewarding series of essays on – arguably – England's greatest king.

R. Horrox, *Richard III: A study in service* (Cambridge University Press). Scholarly reassessment of Richard III, for once placing the emphasis on his policies and followers rather than on speculation about his psychological motivation.

Michael Prestwich, *The Three Edwards: War and state in England 1272–1377* (Routledge). A fine study of three very different kings. Prestwich arranges his materially both thematically across the period, and by studying each individual – a satisfying combination.

Tudor and Stuart England

Geoffrey Elton, *England Under the Tudors* (Routledge). A classic assessment of the Tudor regime, now in its third edition.

Christopher Hibbert, *Cavaliers and Roundheads: The English at war 1642–49,* (HarperCollins; Scribner). A fascinating study of the English Civil Wars, including individual studies of some of the major players.

Christopher Hill, *The World Turned Upside Down: Radical ideas during the English Revolution* (Penguin). Hill's Marxist interpretation of the English Revolution. It's treated with a degree of scepticism now, but its thoroughly rewarding nevertheless.

Mark Kishlansky, *A Monarchy Transformed: Britain 1603–1714* (Penguin). Shrewd and lucid overview of this often turbulent and confusing period of English history.

D.M. Loades, *Politics and the Nation 1450–1660* (Blackwell). Part of the extremely valuable Blackwell 'classic history' series. Detailed yet readable.

W.A. Speck, *Reluctant Revolutionaries: Englishmen and the Revolution of 1688* (Oxford University Press). Refreshing reappraisal of the 'Glorious' Revolution.

David Starkey, *The Reign of Henry VIII: Personalities and politics* (Vintage; Trafalgar Square). Accessible and well-illustrated study of the court intrigue that surrounded Henry VIII.

The 18th century

J.C.D. Clark, *English Society 1688–1832* (Cambridge University Press). Controversial study of the 'long 18th century's propounding the view that England truly was an *ancien régime* society.

Douglas Hay, Peter Linebaugh, John Rule, E.P. Thompson and C. Winslow, *Albion's Fatal Tree: Crime and Society in 18th-century England* (Penguin). Important and eminently readable interpretation of the criminal underclass in 18th-century England. A classic Marxist appraisal of the 'Black Acts' – the criminal code that maintained the property-owning interests of society in a position of dominance over the rest.

Geoffrey Holmes and Daniel Szechi, *The Age of Oligarchy: Pre-industrial Britain 1722–83* (Longman). A fine overview of the 18th century, which emphasizes only too clearly the difficulties inherent in marking cut-off points in English history.

Paul Langford, *A Polite and Commercial People* (Oxford University Press). A real gem – scholarly yet accessible. This weighty book is one of the best things to come out on the 18th century in the last few years.

Frank O'Gorman, *Voters, Patrons and Parties: The unreformed electoral system of Hanoverian England 1734–1832* (Oxford University Press o/p). Detailed study of the political culture of England before the Reform Act. Required reading for anyone serious about the subject.

J.H. Plumb, *The First Four Georges* (Penguin). Elegant study of the first four Hanoverians.

Roy Porter, *English Society in the 18th Century* (Penguin). Porter, one of the most popular historians of the 'Enlightenment', here considers the full range of English culture and society. The result is a bold, comprehensive survey of England in one of its most controversial periods.

The 19th century

Paul Adelman, *Gladstone, Disraeli and Later Victorian Politics* (Longman). Part of the invaluable Longman Seminar Series. This provides a clear insight into the world of late 19th-century politics, and also includes a selection of interesting documents at the back.

Eric Evans, *The Forging of the Modern State: Early industrial Britain 1783–1870* (Longman). One of the most dependable surveys of this intricate period, which saw England recover from the loss of America and develop a powerful empire in the East and Africa.

Eric Hobsbawm, *The Age of Empire 1875–1914* (Vintage). Towering work by one of England's most influential historians, charting the downfall of the empires which dominated the world in the 19th century.

Lytton Strachey, *Eminent Victorians* (Penguin; Random House). Bitingly satirical reassessment of some of the great figures of Victorian England, written by one of Bloomsbury's leading lights.

The 20th century

Alan Clark, *Diaries* (Phoenix UK). These caused a minor sensation when they were published in 1994. Clarke's unashamedly un-PC and rude – but endearingly honest – reflections on political society in the 1980s have helped to shape the way we think of the Thatcher years.

Peter Hennessy, *The Prime Minister: The office and its holders since 1945* (Penguin). Hennessy's new study of central British political office charts its changing role in the years after World War II, and the pressures that have forced it to adapt.

Arthur Marwick, *British Society since 1945* (Penguin). Marwick's survey of the changing face of British society considers a variety of causes and trends (among them the 'permissive society'), and asks important questions about the nature of Britain's relationship with the European Union.

Norman Rose, *The Cliveden Set: Portrait of an exclusive fraternity* (Jonathan Cape). Engaging and thoroughly balanced study of the politicians, academics and aristocrats who were demonized for advocating a more sympathetic response to Hitler's Germany.

A.J.P. Taylor, *English History 1914–45* (Oxford University Press). A provocative study of England from the outbreak of the first world war to the end of the second. As ever, Taylor's work is entertaining but scholarly history at its best.

A.J.P. Taylor, *The Origins of the Second World War* (Penguin). Taylor's work upset many who had made it their life's work to assault the appeasers and put the whole blame on Hitler for the catastrophe that overtook Europe in the 1930s and 1940s. Willing to challenge the conventional view, Taylor's marvellously sceptical book dares to examine the events leading up to the outbreak of war objectively.

index

Entries in **colour** represent feature boxes

f

j

k

l

m

n

t

u

v

around the world

Alaska ★ Algarve ★ Amsterdam ★ Andalucía ★ Antigua & Barbuda ★ Argentina ★ Auckland Restaurants ★ Australia ★ Austria ★ Bahamas ★ Bali & Lombok ★ Bangkok ★ Barbados ★ Barcelona ★ Beijing ★ Belgium & Luxembourg ★ Belize ★ Berlin ★ Big Island of Hawaii ★ Bolivia ★ Boston ★ Brazil ★ Britain ★ Brittany & Normandy ★ Bruges & Ghent ★ Brussels ★ Budapest ★ Bulgaria ★ California ★ Cambodia ★ Canada ★ Cape Town ★ The Caribbean ★ Central America ★ Chile ★ China ★ Copenhagen ★ Corsica ★ Costa Brava ★ Costa Rica ★ Crete ★ Croatia ★ Cuba ★ Cyprus ★ Czech & Slovak Republics ★ Devon & Cornwall ★ Dodecanese & East Aegean ★ Dominican Republic ★ The Dordogne & the Lot ★ Dublin ★ Ecuador ★ Edinburgh ★ Egypt ★ England ★ Europe ★ First-time Asia ★ First-time Europe ★ Florence ★ Florida ★ France ★ French Hotels & Restaurants ★ Gay & Lesbian Australia ★ Germany ★ Goa ★ Greece ★ Greek Islands ★ Guatemala ★ Hawaii ★ Holland ★ Hong Kong & Macau ★ Honolulu ★ Hungary ★ Ibiza & Formentera ★ Iceland ★ India ★ Indonesia ★ Ionian Islands ★ Ireland ★ Israel & the Palestinian Territories ★ Italy ★ Jamaica ★ Japan ★ Jerusalem ★ Jordan ★ Kenya ★ The Lake District ★ Languedoc & Roussillon ★ Laos ★ Las Vegas ★ Lisbon ★ London ★

in twenty years

London Mini Guide ★ London Restaurants ★ Los Angeles ★ Madeira ★ Madrid ★ Malaysia, Singapore & Brunei ★ Mallorca ★ Malta & Gozo ★ Maui ★ Maya World ★ Melbourne ★ Menorca ★ Mexico ★ Miami & the Florida Keys ★ Montréal ★ Morocco ★ Moscow ★ Nepal ★ New England ★ New Orleans ★ New York City ★ New York Mini Guide ★ New York Restaurants ★ New Zealand ★ Norway ★ Pacific Northwest ★ Paris ★ Paris Mini Guide ★ Peru ★ Poland ★ Portugal ★ Prague ★ Provence & the Côte d'Azur ★ Pyrenees ★ The Rocky Mountains ★ Romania ★ Rome ★ San Francisco ★ San Francisco Restaurants ★ Sardinia ★ Scandinavia ★ Scotland ★ Scottish Highlands & Islands ★ Seattle ★ Sicily ★ Singapore ★ South Africa, Lesotho & Swaziland ★ South India ★ Southeast Asia ★ Southwest USA ★ Spain ★ St Lucia ★ St Petersburg ★ Sweden ★ Switzerland ★ Sydney ★ Syria ★ Tanzania ★ Tenerife and La Gomera ★ Thailand ★ Thailand's Beaches & Islands ★ Tokyo ★ Toronto ★ Travel Health ★ Trinidad & Tobago ★ Tunisia ★ Turkey ★ Tuscany & Umbria ★ USA ★ Vancouver ★ Venice & the Veneto ★ Vienna ★ Vietnam ★ Wales ★ Washington DC ★ West Africa ★ Women Travel ★ Yosemite ★ Zanzibar ★ Zimbabwe

also look out for our maps, phrasebooks, music guides and reference books

100

Essential

CDs

Ten titles,
one name

ROUGH GUIDES